Sears List of
Subject Headings

Sears List of Subject Headings

20th Edition

JOSEPH   MILLER

Editor

SUSAN McCARTHY

Associate Editor

New York   •   Dublin

The H. W. Wilson Company

2010

Abridged Dewey Decimal Classification and
Relative Index, Edition 14 is © 2004-2010
OCLC Online Computer Library Center, Inc.
Used with Permission. DDC, Dewey, Dewey
Decimal Classification, and WebDewey are
registered trademarks of OCLC.

Printed in the United States of America

ISBN 978-0-8242-1105-9

Library of Congress Cataloging-in-Publication Data

Sears list of subject headings. – 20th ed. / Joseph Miller, editor; Susan
McCarthy, associate editor.
    p. cm.
  Includes bibliographical references.
  ISBN 978-0-8242-1105-9 (alk. paper)
  1. Subject headings. I. Miller, Joseph, 1946- II. McCarthy, Susan, 1958-
III. Sears, Minnie Earl, 1873-1933. Sears list of subject headings.
  Z695.Z8S43 2010
  025.4'9–dc22

                                           2010005731

Contents

Principles of the Sears List—*Continued*

Preface

Since the first edition in 1923, the Sears List has served the unique needs of small and medium-sized libraries, suggesting headings appropriate for use in their catalogs and providing patterns and instructions for adding new headings as they are required. The successive editors of the List have faced the need to accommodate change while maintaining a sound continuity. The new and revised headings in each edition reflect developments in the material catalogued, in the use of the English language, and in cataloging theory and practice. The aim is always to make library collections as easily available as possible to library users.

The Principles of the Sears List, which follows this Preface, is intended both as a statement of the theoretical foundations of the Sears List and as a concise introduction to subject cataloging in general. The List of Commonly Used Subdivisions, which follows the Principles, lists, for the purpose of easy reference, every subdivision for which there is a provision in the List, no matter how specialized. For every subdivision there is also an entry in the alphabetical List with full instructions for the use of that particular subdivision. There are also many examples of the use of subdivisions, emphasizing that the use of subdivisions is an essential method of expanding and adapting the List to a library's particular needs.

What is new in this edition

The major feature of this new edition of the Sears List is the inclusion of more than three hundred new subject headings. New headings in this edition reflect the growing literature in the areas of ecology and environment, such as **Rainforest ecology**, **Grassland ecology**, **Climate change**, and **Sustainable agriculture**. Headings have been established for all the various kinds of dinosaurs, such as **Raptorex**, **Pteranodon**, and **Edmontosaurus**. The literature on dinosaurs continues to expand, both in adult materials and in titles for children and young adults. New trends in social networking are represented with new headings such as **Twitter (Web site)** and **Facebook (Web site)**. A number of new headings for arts and crafts have been established, such as **Acrylic painting** and **Wire craft**. In these and other areas many provisions have been added for creating more new headings as needed. Many of the headings new to this edition were suggested by librarians representing various sizes and types of libraries, by commercial vendors of bibliographic records, and by the catalogers, indexers, and subject specialists at the H.W. Wilson Company.

The most significant revision in this edition deals with subject headings relating to Russia and India. Where materials on Russia were formerly separated among three headings: **Russia**, **Soviet Union**, and **Russia (Federation)**, there is now a single heading, simply **Russia**. All the headings for the Soviet Union have been canceled in favor of period subdivisions under **Russia—History**. This revision is in keeping with the treatment of other countries that have undergone boundary and regime changes over time and still kept their national identity. Headings for the Baltic states and the other independent republics of the former Soviet Union have been established. The heading for the **Commonwealth of Independent States**, which no longer exists, has been canceled.

It was in the seventeenth edition of the Sears List (2000) that the headings **Indians**, **Indians of North America**, **Indians of Mexico**, etc., were canceled in favor or **Native Americans**, which may be subdivided geographically by continent, region, country, state, or city. Further headings were added as a pattern for headings relating to Native American, such as **Native American women**, **Native American music**, etc. In this edition the heading **Indians** has been re-established to denote the people of India, replacing **East Indians**, and a number of headings relating to the literature and culture of India have been similarly established, such as **Indian literature** and **Indian music**, replacing **Indic literature**, etc. New chronological subdivisions have been established for the history of India as well. This revision reflects the increasing globalization of our culture and the international use of the Sears List in library cataloging.

For the convenience of librarians maintaining their catalogs, these revisions and all other revisions are spelled out in the List of Canceled and Replacement Headings found on page xliv.

Another revision in this edition is the addition of more than 1,400 notes indicating that headings may be subdivided geographically. The rationale for subdividing or not subdividing a heading geographically has been expanded in the Principles of the Sears List under Geographic Subdivision.

Additional scope notes have also been added in this edition so that now every heading in the List that may be used for individual works and collections as well as for materials about a topic, such as **Picture dictionaries**, is so identified. This note indicates that in cataloging a heading can be coded as a form or genre heading rather than as a topical subject.

A History of the Sears List

Minnie Earl Sears prepared the first edition of this work in response to demands for a list of subject headings that was better suited to the needs of the small library than the existing American Library Association and Library of Congress lists. Published in 1923, the *List of Subject Headings for Small Libraries* was based on the headings used by nine small libraries that were known to be well cataloged. Minnie Sears used only *See* and "refer from" references in the first edition. In the second edition (1926) she added *See also* references at the request of teachers of cataloging who were using the List as a textbook. To make the List more useful for that purpose, she wrote a chapter on "Practical Suggestions for the Beginner in Subject Heading Work" for the third edition (1933).

Isabel Stevenson Monro edited the fourth (1939) and fifth (1944) editions. A new feature of the fourth edition was the inclusion of Dewey Decimal Classification numbers as applied in the *Standard Catalog for Public Libraries*. The new subjects added to the List were based on those used in the Standard Catalog Series and on the catalog cards issued by the H.W. Wilson Company. Consequently, the original subtitle "Compiled from Lists used in Nine Representative Small Libraries" was dropped.

The sixth (1950), seventh (1954), and eighth (1959) editions were prepared by Bertha M. Frick. In recognition of the pioneering and fundamental contribution made by Minnie Sears the title was changed to *Sears List of Subject Headings* with the sixth edition. Since the List was being used by medium-sized libraries as well as small ones, the phrase "for Small Libraries" was deleted from the title. The symbols x and xx were substituted for the "Refer from (see ref.)" and "Refer from (see also ref.)" phrases to conform to the format adopted by the Library of Congress.

The ninth edition (1965), the first of four to be prepared by Barbara M. Westby, continued the policies of the earlier editions. With the eleventh edition, the "Practical Suggestions for the Beginner in Subject Heading Work" was retitled "Principles of the Sears List of Subject Headings" to emphasize "principles," and a section dealing with nonbook materials was added.

The thirteenth edition (1986), prepared by Carmen Rovira and Caroline Reyes, was the first to take advantage of computer validation capabilities. It also responded to the changing theory in subject analysis occasioned by the development of online public access catalogs. This effort was taken further in the fourteenth edition (1991) under the editorship of Martha T. Mooney, who reduced the number of compound terms, simplified many subdivisions, and advanced the work of uninverting inverted headings.

In accord with a suggestion of the Cataloging of Children's Materials Committee of the American Library Association, many of the headings from *Subject Headings for Children's Literature* (Library of Congress) were incorporated into the Sears List with the thirteenth edition. Since the Sears List is intended for both adult and juvenile collections, wherever the Library of Congress has two different headings for adult and juvenile approaches to a single subject, a choice of a single term was made for Sears. In cases where the Sears List uses the adult form, the cataloger of children's materials may prefer to use the juvenile form found in *Subject Headings for Children's Literature.*

In the fifteenth edition (1994), the first edited by Joseph Miller, the interval between publication of editions was shortened to provide a more timely updating of subject headings. In keeping with prevailing thinking in the field of library and information science, all remaining inverted headings were canceled in favor of the uninverted form. Likewise, the display of the List on the page was changed to conform to the NISO standards for thesauri approved in 1993. While Sears remains a list of subject headings and not a true thesaurus, it uses the labels BT, NT, RT, SA, and UF for broader terms, narrower terms, related terms, See Also, and Used for. A List of Canceled and Replacement Headings was added to facilitate the updating of catalogs. Also in the fifteenth edition many headings were added to enhance access to individual works of fiction, poetry, drama, and other imaginative works, such as films and radio and television programs, based on the *Guidelines on Subject Access to Individual Works of Fiction, Drama, etc.* prepared by a subcommittee of the Subject Analysis Committee of the ALA. These headings have since been updated in accordance with the Second edition of the *Guidelines* (2000).

In the sixteenth edition (1997) further instructions were added for the application of subdivisions, and the headings in the field of religion were extensively revised to reduce their exclusively Christian application and make them more useful for cataloging materials on other religions.

The major feature of the seventeenth edition (2000) was the revision of the headings for the native peoples of the Western Hemisphere. The headings **Indians**, **Indians of North America**, **Indians of Mexico**, etc., were cancelled in favor of **Native Americans**, which may be subdivided geographically by continent, region, country, state, or city. In further revisions in the seventeenth edition, many headings that formerly incorporated the word "modern" were simplified and clarified, such as **Modern history** and **Modern art**, and headings for various kinds of government policy were revised and regularized.

The eighteenth edition of the Sears List (2004) and the nineteenth edition (2007) saw the inclusion of many hundreds of new subject headings. The eighteenth edition included significant addition to the Principles of the Sears List regarding the treatment of individual works of fiction, drama, and poetry. The nineteenth edition features a major development of new headings in the areas of Islam and Graphic novels

The Scope of the Sears List

No list can possibly provide a heading for every idea, object, process, or relationship, especially not within the scope of a single volume. What Sears hopes to offer instead is a basic list that includes many of the headings most likely to be needed in small libraries together with patterns and examples that will guide the cataloger in creating additional headings as needed. New topics appear every day, and books on those topics require new subject headings. Headings for new topics can be developed from the Sears List in two ways, by establishing new terms as needed and by subdividing the headings already in the List. Instructions for creating new headings based on the pattern in Sears and sources for establishing the wording of new headings are given in the Principles of the Sears List. The various kinds of subdivisions and the rules for their application are also discussed in the Principles of the Sears List.

It is only by being flexible and expandable that Sears has been able over the years to fill the needs of various kinds of libraries. The degree or level of specificity required for a collection depends entirely on the material being collected. While a small library is unlikely to need very narrow topics of a technical or scientific nature, it is not at all unlikely that it might have a gardening book on **Irises**. That term is not in the List, but it would be added as a narrower term under **Flowers**.

Form of Headings

It was the policy of Minnie Sears to use the Library of Congress form of subject headings with some modification, chiefly the simplification of phrasing. The Sears List still reflects the usage of the Library of Congress unless there is some compelling reason to vary, but those instances of variation have become numerous over the years. A major difference between the two lists is that in Sears the direct form of entry has replaced the inverted form, on the theory that most library users search for multiple-word terms in the order in which they occur naturally in the language. In most cases cross-references have been made from the inverted form and from the Library of Congress form where it otherwise varies.

Scope Notes

As in previous editions, all the new and revised headings in this edition have been provided with scope notes where such notes are required. Scope notes are intended to clarify the specialized use of a term or to distinguish between terms that might be confused. If there is any question of what a term means, the cataloger should simply consult a dictionary. There are times, however, when subject headings require a stricter limitation of a term than the common usage given in a dictionary would allow, as in the case of **Marketing**, a term in business and economics, not to be confused with **Grocery shopping**. Here a scope note is required. Some scope notes distinguish between topics and forms, such as **Encyclopedias and dictionaries** for critical and historical materials and the subdivisions *Encyclopedias* and *Dictionaries* under topics for items that are themselves encyclopedias or dictionaries. There are also scope notes in Sears that identify any headings in the area of literature that may be assigned to individual works of drama, fiction, poetry, etc.

PREFACE

Classification

The classification numbers in this edition of Sears are taken from the *Abridged WebDewey*, the continuously updated online version of the *Abridged Dewey Decimal Classification*. The numbers are intended only to direct the cataloger to a place in the DDC schedules where material on that subject is often found. They are not intended as a substitute for consulting the schedules, notes, and manual of the DDC itself when classifying a particular item. The relationship between subject headings and classification is further discussed in the Principles of the Sears List.

Usually only one number is assigned to a subject heading. In some cases, however, when a subject can be treated in more than one discipline, the subject is then given more than one number in the List. The heading **Chemical industry**, for example, is given two numbers, **338.4** and **660**, which represent possible classification numbers for materials dealing with the chemical industry from the viewpoints of economics and technology respectively. Classification numbers are not assigned to a few very general subject headings, such as **Charters**, **Exhibitions**, **Hallmarks**, and **Identification**, which cannot be classified unless a specific application is identified. The alphabetic notation of B for individual biographies is occasionally provided in addition to Dewey classification numbers for such materials. Numbers in the 810s and 840s prefixed by a C are given as optional numbers for topics in Canadian literature.

The Dewey numbers given in Sears are extended as far as is authorized by the *Abridged Dewey Decimal Classification*, which is seldom more than four places beyond the decimal point. When an item being classified has a particular form or geographic specificity, the number may be extended by adding form and geographic subdivisions from the Dewey tables. Only a few examples of built numbers are given in Sears, such as **940.53022** for **World War, 1939-1945—Pictorial works**. No library should feel the need to extend classification numbers beyond what is practical for the size of the library's collection. For a discussion of close and broad classification and for instructions on building numbers from the Dewey tables, the cataloger should consult the introduction to the most recent edition of the *Abridged Dewey Decimal Classification and Relative Index*.

Style, Filing, Etc.

For spelling and definitions the editor has relied upon *Webster's Third New International Dictionary of the English Language, Unabridged* (1961) and the *Random House Webster's Unabridged Dictionary*, 2nd ed., revised and updated (1997). Capitalization and the forms of corporate and geographic names used as examples are based on the *Anglo-American Cataloguing Rules*, 2nd ed., 2002 revision. The filing of entries follows the *ALA Filing Rules* (1980).

Every term in the List that may be used as a subject heading is printed in boldface type whether it is a main term; a term in a USE reference; a broader, narrower, or related term; or an example in a scope note or general reference. If a term is not printed in boldface type, it is not used as a heading.

Acknowledgments

The editors wish to acknowledge with gratitude the contributions to this edition of the individual catalogers, reference librarians, and vendors of cataloging services who have offered suggestions for headings to be added to the List. Of special note are the many headings suggested by Bryan Baldus, Cataloger, of Quality Books Inc.

The Cataloging of Children's Materials Committee of the American Library Association has been, as ever, an important source of advice in the editorial work on the Sears List. ALA's Subject Analysis Committee and its various subcommittees have also been a constant source of advice and guidance in the continuing development of the Sears List.

Thanks are extended to Tina Gross, Catalog Librarian, Learning Resources & Technology Services, St. Cloud State University, and her students in IM 624, "Organization of Information Resources" for their help in identifying form/genre headings in the List.

The bibliography at the end of the Principle of the Sears List in this edition was updated by Sara Rofofsky Marcus, Assistant Professor, Electronic Resource/Web Librarian, Queensborough Community College. To her we extend our gratitude.

The classification numbers given in this edition of Sears conform to the *Abridged WebDewey,* the continuously updated online version of the *Abridged Dewey Decimal Classification*, produced by OCLC. We extend special thanks to Joan S. Mitchell, editor in chief of the Dewey Decimal Classification (DDC), and to the assistant editors of the DDC for their generous help and advice.

Every edition of the Sears List represents the work of many hands, especially those of the previous editors over the years. The contributions of the users of the List have also been invaluable. Every comment, suggestion, question, or request from a user represents an opportunity for improvement and is greatly valued.

J. Miller
S. McCarthy

Principles of the Sears List of Subject Headings

Certain principles and practices of subject cataloging should be understood before an attempt is made to assign subject headings to library materials. The discussion that follows makes reference to the *Sears List of Subject Headings*, henceforth referred to as the Sears List or the List, but the principles are applicable to other lists of subject headings as well.

1. THE PURPOSE OF SUBJECT CATALOGING

All library work is a matter of the storage and retrieval of information, and cataloging is that aspect of library work devoted to storage. The best cataloging is simply that which facilitates the most accurate and complete retrieval. The two basic branches of cataloging are descriptive cataloging and subject cataloging. Descriptive cataloging makes possible the retrieval of materials in a library by title, author, date, etc.—in short all the searchable elements of a cataloging record except the subjects. Only by conforming to the standards for descriptive cataloging can a librarian assure the user accurate retrieval on the descriptive elements. Those standards are codified in *Resource Description and Access* (*RDA*), which is in the process of replacing the older *Anglo-American Cataloguing Rules*, second revised edition (*AACR2*).

Until the second half of the nineteenth century, descriptive cataloging was the only library cataloging that was found necessary. Libraries were much smaller than they are today, and scholarly librarians then were able, with the aid of printed bibliographies, to be familiar with everything available on a given subject and guide the users to it. With the rapid growth of knowledge in many fields in the course of the nineteenth century and the resulting increase in the volume of books and other library materials, it became desirable to do a preliminary subject analysis of such works and then to represent them in the catalog in such a way that they would be retrievable by subject.

Subject cataloging deals with what a book or other library item is about, and the purpose of subject cataloging is to list under one uniform word or phrase all the materials on a given topic that a library has in its collection. A subject heading is that uniform word or phrase used in the library catalog to express a topic. The use of authorized words or phrases only, with cross-references from unauthorized synonyms, is the essence of bibliographic control in subject cataloging. The purpose of a subject authority, such as the Sears List, is to provide a basic vocabulary of authorized terms together with suggestions for useful cross-references.

The two most common types of subject authorities are the thesaurus and the subject heading list. A true thesaurus, in the realm of information science, is a comprehensive controlled vocabulary of discrete unit terms, called descriptors, arranged is such a way as to display the hierarchical and associative relationships among terms. It is usually limited to a particular realm of knowledge, as in the case of the *Art and Architecture Thesaurus*. The American national standards for thesauri are spelled out in the NISO *Guidelines for the Construction, Format, and Management of Monolingual Thesauri*. A subject heading list, such as the Sears List or the

Library of Congress Subject Headings, is simply an alphabetical list of terms that have been established over time as warranted by the materials being cataloged. A subject heading list also indicates relationships among terms but does not attempt to establish any comprehensive hierarchies. In addition to simple descriptors, a subject heading list can include pre-coordinated strings composed of subject terms with subdivisions.

The *Library of Congress Subject Headings*, which in print now comprises five large volumes, is primarily a list of headings that have been used in the Library. Likewise *Medical Subject Headings* derives from the holdings of the National Library of Medicine. The Sears List is unique among subject heading lists in that it does not attempt to be a complete list of terms used in any single library but only a list of headings most likely to be needed in a typical small library and a skeleton or pattern for creating other headings as needed. By using the Sears List as a foundation, the cataloger in a small library can develop a local authority list that is consistent in form and comprehensive for that library. This has proven over the years to be a practical and economical solution to the cataloging needs of small libraries. In other ways, such as the use of uninverted headings only and of popular rather than technical vocabulary, the Sears List is specifically tailored to the needs of small libraries of any kind, including school libraries, small public libraries, church libraries, etc.

Because the Sears List is not a complete authority list, the cataloger using the Sears List must take an active part in developing a larger vocabulary of terms. As an aid in this process we offer the following discussion of the basic principles of subject analysis and the construction and control of subject headings.

2. DETERMINING THE SUBJECT OF THE WORK

The first and most important step in subject cataloging is to ascertain the true subject of the material being cataloged. This concept of "aboutness" should never be far from a subject cataloger's thoughts. It is a serious mistake to think of subject analysis as a matter of sorting through material and fitting it into the available categories, like sorting the mail, rather than focusing first on the material and determining what it is really about.

Many times the subject of a work is readily determined. **Hummingbirds** is obviously the subject of a book entitled *The Complete Book of Hummingbirds*. In other cases the subject is not so easy to discern, because it may be a complex one or the author may not express it in a manner clear to someone unfamiliar with the subject. The subject of a work cannot always be determined from the title alone, which is often uninformative or misleading, and undue dependence on it can result in error. A book entitled *Great Masters in Art* immediately suggests the subject **Artists**, but closer examination may reveal the book to be only about painters, not about artists in general. After reading the title page, the cataloger should examine the table of contents and skim the preface and introduction, and then, if the subject is still not clear, examine the text carefully and read parts of it, if necessary. In the case of nonbook materials, the cataloger should examine the container, the label, any accompanying guides, etc., and view or listen to the contents if possible. Only after this preliminary examination has been made is it possible to determine the subject of a work. If the meaning of technical terminology is not clearly understood, reference sources should be consulted.

Only when the cataloger has determined the subject content of a work and identified it with explicit words can the Sears List be used to advantage. The List is consulted to determine one of three possibilities. If the word the cataloger chose to describe the subject content of the work is an established heading in the List, then that heading should be assigned to the work.

If the word the cataloger chose is a synonym or alternate form of an established heading in the List, then the cataloger forgoes the word that first came to mind in favor of the term from the List. A third possibility is that there is no heading in the List for the subject of the work at hand, in which case the cataloger must formulate the appropriate heading, add it to the library's subject authority file with its attendant references, and then assign it to the work.

Many books are about more than one subject. In that case a second or third subject heading is necessary. Theoretically there is no limit to the number of subject entries that could be made for one work, but in practice an excess of entries is a disservice to the user of the catalog. More than three subject headings should be assigned to a single item only after careful consideration. The need for more than three may be due to the cataloger's inability to identify precisely the single broader heading that would cover all the topics in the work. Similarly, a subject heading should not be assigned for a topic that comprises less than one third of a work. The commonest practice, known as the Rule of Three, may be stated as follows: As many as three specific subject headings in a given area may be assigned to a work, but if the work treats of more than three subjects, then a broader heading is used instead and the specific headings are omitted. A work about snakes and lizards, for example, would be assigned the headings **Snakes** and **Lizards**. If the work also included material on turtles, a third heading **Turtles** would be added. But if the work discussed alligators and crocodiles as well, the only subject heading assigned would be **Reptiles**.

Subject headings are used for materials that have definite, definable subjects. There are always a few works so indefinite in their subject content that it is better not to assign a heading at all. Such a work might be a collection of materials produced by several individuals on a variety of topics or one person's random thoughts and ideas. If a cataloger cannot determine a definite subject, the reader is unlikely to find the item under a makeshift or general heading. The headings **Human behavior** and **Happiness**, for example, would be misleading when assigned to a book titled *Appreciation*, which is a personal account of the sources of the author's pleasure in life. The book has no specific subject and so it should be assigned no subject headings.

3. SPECIFIC AND DIRECT ENTRY

The principle of specific and direct entry is fundamental in modern subject cataloging. According to that rule a work is entered in the catalog directly under the most specific subject heading that accurately represents its content. This term should be neither broader nor narrower but co-extensive in scope with the subject of the work cataloged. The principle was definitively formulated by Charles A. Cutter (1837-1903) in his *Rules for a Dictionary Catalog*. Cutter wrote: "Enter a work under its subject-heading, not under the heading of a class which includes that subject." His example is: "Put Lady Cust's book on 'The Cat' under Cat, not under Zoology or Mammals, or Domestic animals; and put Garnier's 'Le Fer' under Iron, not under Metals or Metallurgy." The reason this principle has become sacred to modern cataloging is simply that there is no other way to insure uniformity. In subject cataloging uniformity means simply that all materials on a single topic are assigned the same subject heading. If the headings **Cats**, **Zoology**, **Mammals**, and **Domestic animals** were all equally correct for a book on cats, as they would be without Cutter's rule, there would be no single heading for that topic and consequently no assurance of uniformity. One cataloger could assign the heading **Cats** to Lady Cust's book, another cataloger could assign the heading **Mammals** to another book on cats, and a third cataloguer could assign the heading **Domestic animals** or **Pets** to yet another book on cats. There would then be no simple way to retrieve all the materials on cats in the library's collection.

The principle of specific entry holds that a work is always entered under a specific term rather than under a broader heading that includes the specific concept. This principle is of particular importance to the cataloguer using the Sears List, since the heading of appropriate specificity must be added if it is not already there. If, for example, a work being catalogued is about penguins, it should be entered only under the most specific term that is not narrower than the scope of the book itself, that is, **Penguins**. It should not be assigned the heading **Birds** or **Water birds**. This is true even though the heading **Penguins** does not appear in the List. When a specific subject is not found in the List, the heading for the larger group or category to which it belongs should be consulted, in this case **Birds**. There the cataloger finds a general reference that reads: "SA [See also] types of birds, e.g. **Birds of prey**; **Canaries**; etc. {to be added as needed}." The cataloger must establish the heading **Penguins** as a narrower term under the heading **Birds** and then assign it to the book on penguins. In many cases the most specific entry will be a general subject. A book entitled *Birds of the World* would have the subject heading **Birds**. Even though **Birds** is a very broad term, it is the narrowest term that comprehends the subject content of that work.

Having assigned a work the most specific subject heading that is applicable, the cataloger should not then make an additional entry under a broader heading. A work with the title *Birds of the Ocean* should not be entered under both **Birds** and **Water birds** but only under **Water birds**. To eliminate this duplication, the *See also* references in the public catalog direct the user from the broader subject headings to the more specific ones. At **Birds**, for example, the reference would read: "See also **Birds of prey; Canaries; Pelicans; Penguins; Water birds**," etc.

The principle of direct entry holds that a subject heading should stand as a separate term rather than as a subdivision under a broader heading. If the reader wants information about owls, the direct approach is to consult the catalog under the heading **Owls**, not under the broader subject **Birds** subdivided by the narrower topic **Owls**. In other words, the cataloger has entered the book directly under **Owls**, not indirectly under "Birds—Owls," or under "Birds—Birds of prey—Owls." The latter two subject strings are both specific, but they are not direct.

4. TYPES OF SUBJECT HEADINGS

There are four types of subject headings: topical headings, form headings, geographic headings, and proper names.

4. A. TOPICAL HEADINGS

Topical subject headings are simply the words or phrases for common things or concepts that represent the content of various works. In choosing the word or phrase that makes the best subject heading several things should be considered. The first and most obvious is the literary warrant, or the language of the material being cataloged. The word most commonly used in the literature is most likely the word that best represents the item cataloged. If nine out of ten books on the subject use the phrase "Gun control," there is no reason to use any word or phrase other than **Gun control** as a subject heading, so long as that phrase meets certain other criteria.

A second consideration, and one of the criteria that a subject heading should meet, is that of common usage. In so far as possible a subject heading should represent the common usage of the English language. In American libraries this means current American spelling and terminology: **Labor** not Labour; **Elevators** not Lifts. (In British libraries these choices would be reversed.) Foreign terms such as **Film noir** are not used unless they have been fully incorporated into the English language. By the same token contemporary usage gradually should replace antiquated words or phrases. The heading **Blacks**, for example, replaced **Negroes** as common usage changed. In time the heading **African Americans** was added to the Sears List for greater specificity, as the use of that term stabilized. What is common usage depends, in part, upon who the users of a library are. In most small libraries the popular or common word for a thing is to be preferred to the scientific or technical word, when the two are truly synonymous. For example, **Desert animals** is preferable in most small libraries to **Desert fauna**. In such a case the scientific term should be a *See* reference to the established term.

In order to maintain uniformity in a library catalog two things are necessary. The first is abiding by Cutter's rule of specificity, and the second is choosing a single word or phrase from among its synonyms or near-synonyms in establishing a subject heading. If **Desert animals** and Desert fauna were both allowed as established headings, the material on one subject would end up in two places. Sometimes a single word or phrase must be chosen from among several choices that do not mean exactly the same thing but are too close to be easily distinguished. In the Sears List, for example, **Regional planning** is an established heading with *See* references from County planning, Metropolitan planning, and State planning. The term chosen as the established heading is the one that is most inclusive.

Another important consideration in establishing topical subject headings is that they should be clear and unambiguous. Sometimes the most common term for a topic is not suitable as a subject heading because it is ambiguous. Civil War, for example, must be rejected in favor of **United States—History—1861-1865, Civil War**, since not all civil wars are the American Civil War. The term **Civil wars** could itself become a heading, if it were needed for general materials on rebellions or internal revolutions.

When a single word has several meanings, that word can be used as a subject heading only when it is somehow rendered unambiguous. The word Depression, for example, can mean either an economic or a mental state, but as subject headings one is formulated **Depressions** and the other **Depression (Psychology)**. Stress can mean either stress on materials or stress on the mind, and the two headings are **Strength of materials** and **Stress (Psychology)**. Notice that the ambiguous word is qualified even when the other meaning is expressed in other words. Furthermore, an ambiguous term such as Feedback should be qualified, **Feedback (Psychology)**, even when the other meaning, **Feedback (Electronics)**, does not yet exist in the catalog. Whenever identical words with different meanings are used in the catalog, both require a parenthetical qualifier, which is usually either a broader term or discipline of study, as in the case of **Seals (Animals)** and **Seals (Numismatics)**.

In choosing one term as a subject heading from among several possibilities the cataloger must also think of the spelling, number, and connotations of the various forms. When variant spellings are in use, one must be selected and uniformly applied, such as **Archeology** rather than Archaeology. A decision also must be made between the singular and plural form, which will be further discussed under Grammar of Subject Headings below. Sometimes variant forms of words can have different connotations, as with Arab, Arabian, and Arabic. It may seem inconsistent to use all three forms in subject headings, but, in fact, they are used consistently in the following ways: Arab relating to the people; Arabian referring to the geographical area and to horses; and Arabic for the language, script, or literature.

4. B. FORM HEADINGS

The second kind of heading that is found in a library catalog is the form heading, which describes not the subject content of a work but its form. In other words, a form heading tells us not what a work is about but what it is. Form in this context means the intellectual form of the materials rather than the physical form of the item, although the physical forms of some nonbook materials, such as puzzles, sound recordings, or comedy films are also identified by form headings.

Some form headings describe the general arrangement of the material and the purpose of the work, such as **Almanacs**, **Atlases**, **Directories**, and **Gazetteers**. These headings are customarily assigned to individual works as well as to materials about such forms. Theoretically, at least, any form can also be a topic, since it is possible for someone to write a book about almanacs or gazetteers.

Other form headings are the names of literary forms and genres. Headings for the major literary forms, **Fiction**, **Poetry**, **Drama**, and **Essays**, are usually used as topical subject headings. As form headings they are used for collections only rather than for individual literary works. Minor literary forms, also known as genres, such as **Science fiction**, **Epistolary poetry**, and **Children's plays**, are much more numerous and are often assigned to individual literary works. These headings will be discussed at greater length below under Literature. The distinction between form headings and topical headings in literature can sometimes be made by using the singular form for the topical heading and the plural for the form heading. **Short story**, for example, is topical, for materials about the short story as a literary form, while **Short stories** is a form. Likewise, **Essay** is topical, while **Essays** is a form. The peculiarities of language, however, do not always permit this distinction.

4. C. GEOGRAPHIC HEADINGS

Many works in a library's collection are about geographic areas, countries, cities, etc. The appropriate subject heading for such a work is the name of the place in question. Geographic headings are the established names of individual places, from places as large as **Africa** to places as small as **Walden Pond (Mass.)**. They signify not only physical places but also political jurisdictions. These headings differ from topical subject headings in that they refer to a unique entity rather than to an abstraction or category of things.

The Sears List does not attempt to provide geographic headings, which are numerous far beyond the scope of a single volume. The geographic headings that are found in Sears, such as **United States**, **Ohio**, and **Chicago (Ill.)**, are offered only as examples. The cataloger using the Sears List must establish geographic headings as needed with the aid of standard references sources. Some suggested sources are the most current editions of *The Columbia Gazetteer of the World*; *National Geographic Atlas of the World*; *Statesman's Year-book*; *Times Atlas of the World*; *Merriam-Webster's Geographical Dictionary*; and the Web site of the U.S. Board of Geographic Names. The geographic headings and geographic subdivisions found in Sears follow the form of abbreviation for qualifying states, provinces, etc., found in Appendix B (Abbreviations) of *AACR2*.

4. D. NAMES

Still other materials in a library's collection are about individual persons, families, corporate bodies, literary works, motion pictures, etc. The appropriate heading for such material is the unique name of the entity in question. The three major types of name headings are personal names, corporate names, and uniform titles. Individual or personal name headings are usually established in the inverted form, with dates if necessary, and with *See* references from alternate forms. The heading **Clinton, Bill**, for example, would require a *See* reference from "Clinton, William Jefferson," and if the library had material about any other person called Bill Clinton, the name heading for the president would need to take the form **Clinton, Bill, 1946-** . Corporate name headings are the commonly established names of corporate bodies, such as business firms, institutions, buildings, sports teams, performing groups, etc. Materials about a corporate body, such as **Rockefeller Center** or **Fort Lauderdale International Boat Show**, are entered directly under the corporate name heading as a subject. Uniform titles are the established names of sacred scriptures, anonymous literary works, periodicals, motion pictures, radio and television programs, etc. Materials about a particular motion picture or about an anonymous literary work, for example, are entered directly under the uniform title, such as **Gone with the wind (Motion picture)** or **Beowulf**, as a subject. Materials about a literary work with a known author are entered under a name-title heading consisting of the author's name followed by the title, such as **Shakespeare, William, 1564-1616. Hamlet** for a book about Shakespeare's play.

Like geographic headings, name headings are numerous beyond the scope of the Sears List and must be established by the cataloger as needed. Suggested sources for personal and corporate names are *Who's Who*; *Who's Who in America*; *Merriam-Webster's Biograph-ical Dictionary*; *The Dictionary of National Biography*; the *Encyclopedia of Associations*; and the Library of Congress Name Authories on the Web. General encyclopedias and standard reference works limited to specific fields are also useful sources for names.

5. THE GRAMMAR OF SUBJECT HEADINGS

While many subject headings are simple terms like **Reptiles** or **Electricity**, other subjects can be very complex, in some cases involving several levels of subdivision. In order to construct subject headings consistently the cataloger should understand the grammar of subject headings.

5. A. THE FORMS OF HEADINGS

5. A. i. Single Nouns

A single noun is the ideal type of subject heading when the language supplies it. Such terms are not only the simplest in form but often the easiest to comprehend. A choice must be made between the singular and plural forms of a noun. The plural is the more common, but in practice both are used. Abstract ideas and the names of disciplines of study are usually stated in the singular, such as **Biology** or **Existentialism**. An action, such as **Editing** or **Fraud**, is also expressed in the singular. Headings for concrete things are most commonly in the plural form, when those things can be counted, such as **Playgrounds** or **Children**. Concrete things that cannot be counted, such as **Steel** or **Milk**, obviously remain in the singular. In most cases common sense can be relied upon. In some instances both the singular and the plural of a word can be subject headings when they have two different meanings, such as **Theater** for the activity and **Theaters** for the buildings. In the case of **Arts** and **Art**, the one means the arts in general, while the other means the fine and decorative arts specifically.

5. A. ii. Compound Headings

Subject headings that consist of two nouns joined by "and" are of several types. Some headings link two things because together they form a single concept or topic, such as **Bow and arrow** or **Good and evil**; because they are so closely related they are rarely treated separately, such as **Forests and forestry** or **Publishers and publishing**; or because they are so closely synonymous they are seldom distinguished, such as **Cities and towns** or **Rugs and carpets**. Other headings that link two words with "and" stand for the relationship between the two things, such as

Church and state or **Television and children**. Compound headings of this type should not be made without careful consideration. Often there is a better way to formulate the heading. A heading like "Medicine and religion," for example, is less accurate than the form established in Sears, which is **Medicine—Religious aspects**. (There is not likely to be material on the medical aspects of religion.) One question that arises in forming compound headings is word order. The only rule is that common usage takes precedence (no one says "Arrow and bow"), and, where there is no established common usage, alphabetic order is preferred. Whatever the order, a *See* reference should be made from either the second term or from the pair of terms reversed, as in Forestry, *See* **Forests and forestry**, or Children and television, *See* **Television and children**.

5. A. iii. Adjectives with Nouns

Often a specific concept is best expressed by a noun with an adjective, such as **Unemployment insurance** or **Buddhist art**. In the past the expression was frequently inverted (Insurance, Unemployment; Art, Buddhist). There were two possible reasons for inversion: 1) an assumption was made that the searcher would think first of the noun; or 2) the noun was placed first in order to keep all aspects of a broad subject together in an alphabetical listing, as in a card catalog. In recent years these arguments have been abandoned in favor of the direct order because users have become more and more accustomed to searching in the order of natural language. The only headings that have been retained in Sears in the inverted form are proper names, including the names of battles and massacres.

5. A. iv. Phrase Headings

Some concepts that involve two or more elements can be expressed only by more or less complex phrases. These are the least satisfactory headings, as they offer the greatest variation in wording, are often the longest, and may not be thought of readily by either the maker or the user of the catalog, but for many topics the English language seems to offer no more compact terminology. Examples are **Insects as carriers of disease** and **Violence in popular culture**.

5. B. SUBDIVISIONS

Specific entry in subject headings is achieved in two basic ways. The first, as noted above, is the creation of narrower terms as needed. The second is the use of subdivisions under an established term to designate aspects of that term, such as **Birds—Eggs** or **Food—Analysis**, or the form of the item itself, such as **Agriculture—Bibliography**. The scope of the Sears List can be expanded far beyond the actual headings printed through the use of subdivisions. Some subdivisions are applicable to only a few subjects. *Eggs*, for example, is applicable only under headings for oviparous animals. Other subdivisions, such as *Analysis*, are applicable under many subjects. Still other subdivisions, such as *Bibliography*, are applicable under nearly any heading. The Sears List does not attempt to list all possible subdivisions, but all those that are most likely to be used in a small library are included. For every subdivision included there is an instruction in the List for the use of that subdivision. Some subdivisions are also headings, such as **Bibliography**, and in such cases the instruction is given in a general reference as part of the entry for that heading. Other subdivisions, such as *Economic aspects*, are not themselves headings, and in such cases the instruction for the use of the subdivision is a free-standing general reference in the alphabetical List.

5. B. i. Topical Subdivisions

Topical subdivisions are those subdivisions that bring out the aspect of a subject or point of view presented in a particular work. A work may be a history of the subject, as in **Clothing and**

dress—History; or it may deal with the philosophy of the subject, as in **Religion—Philosophy**; research in the field, as in **Oceanography—Research**; the laws about it, as in **Automobiles—Law and legislation**; or how to study or teach the subject, as in **Mathematics—Study and teaching**. The advantage of subdivisions over phrase headings for complex subjects is that uniformity can be more readily achieved with subdivisions. Once the subdivisions have been established, they can be appended to any applicable subject heading without guessing or straining the language for a suitable phrase. Subject strings with topical subdivisions can be read backwards: **Clothing and dress—History**, for example, means the history of clothing and dress, and **Oceanography—Research—Ethical aspects** means ethical aspects of research in the field of oceanography.

5. B. ii. Geographic Subdivisions

Another aspect of subjects that can be brought out in subdivisions is geographic specificity. The unit used as a subdivision may be the name of a country, state, city, or other geographic area. A topical heading with a geographic subdivision means simply that topic in a particular place. **Bridges—France**, for example, is the appropriate subject string for a work on bridges in France, and **Agriculture—Ohio** for a work on agriculture in Ohio.

There are only two types of topical subject headings that can never be subdivided geographically. The first are those headings, such as **Exploration** or **Church history,** that are used instead as subdivisions under geographic headings, as in **Arctic regions—Exploration** or **United States—Church history**.

The second are those subjects, mostly in the fields of literature and the arts, for which the geographic qualification is conveyed by a modifying adjective rather than by a subdivision. Many of these subjects have a general reference similar to this reference at the subject **Authors**: "SA [See also] authors of particular countries or regions, e.g. **American authors**."

Beyond these two types of headings that are never subdivided geographically there is a broad spectrum. Not all other topical headings lend themselves logically or practically to geographic subdivision. Some topics, such as **Fractions** or **Femininity of God**, are either non-physical or too abstract to have a geographic location. Others are physical but not easily located in a particular place, such as **Computer viruses** or **Space debris**. Still other headings, such as **Pet therapy** or **Lung cancer**, are unlikely to be dealt with geographically, at least in works that would be found in a small library.

Many subject headings in the Sears List are followed by the parenthetical phrase (May subdiv. geog.). In application this means that if the work in hand deals with that subject in general, only the heading itself is used; but if it deals with the subject in a particular place, the heading may be subdivided geographically. If, however, a library feels the need to subdivide any subject heading geographically that is not so indicated in the List, the library should do so without hesitating, provided, of course, that the heading does not fall into one of the two types of headings that can never be subdivided geographically.

Headings with a geographic adjective may sometimes be further subdivided geographically. The adjective then denotes the place of origin while the subdivision represents the location where the thing is found, as dealt with in the work being cataloged, such in **Italian art—Great Britain** or **American authors—Paris (France)**.

Geographic subdivisions can be either direct or indirect. The Sears List uses the direct form of subdivision, whereby topics are subdivided directly by cities, counties, metropolitan areas, etc., as in **Theater—Paris (France)** or **Hospitals—Chicago (Ill.)**. The indirect form of subdivision, used by the Library of Congress and certain other subject heading systems, interposes the name of the country or state (the larger geographic area) between the topical subject and the smaller area, as in "Theater—France—Paris" and "Hospitals—Illinois—Chicago."

5. B. iii. Chronological Subdivisions

In any catalog, large or small, there will be many works on American history. If these works are all entered under the general heading **United States—History**, the library user is required to look through many entries to find materials about any specific period of American history. Chronological subdivisions, which correspond to generally accepted periods of a country's history or to the spans of time most frequently treated in the literature, make such a search much simpler by bringing together all works on a single period of history, such as **United States—History—1945-1953**. If a chronological period has been given a name, this name is included in the heading following the dates, as in **United States—History—1600-1775, Colonial period**.

Historical periods vary from one country to another and usually correspond to major dynastic or governmental changes. The Sears List includes chronological subdivisions only for those countries about which a small library is likely to have much historical material, with the greatest number of period subdivisions under **United States**, **Canada**, **Great Britain**, **France**, **Germany**, and **Italy**, and a few subdivisions only under several other countries. Whenever there is only a small amount of material on the history of a country, it should simply be entered under the name of the country with the subdivision *History*, without a chronological subdivision. For most small libraries in North America the heading **Turkey—History** will suffice for all historical material about Turkey, even though Turkey has a very long history. If, however, a library should acquire a large amount of historical material about any such country or region, period subdivisions should be established beyond those spelled out in the Sears List. For these the cataloger may wish to consult *LC Period Subdivisions under Names of Places*.

The subdivision *Politics and government* under countries should be reserved for general and theoretical material. Historical material on the politics and government of a country are entered under the name of the country subdivided by *History* with or without a further chronological subdivision. Other kinds of subjects, especially those relating to literature and the arts, may also be subdivided chronologically as appropriate, usually by century.

5. B. iv. Form Subdivisions

The most common item found in a library is an expository prose treatise on a subject. Many works, however, present their material in other forms, such as lists, tables, maps, pictures, etc. Form subdivisions specify the form an item takes. Like form headings they tell what an item is rather than what it is about. Some of the most common form subdivisions are *Bibliography*; *Catalogs*; *Dictionaries*; *Directories*; *Gazetteers*; *Handbooks, manuals, etc.*; *Indexes*; *Maps*; *Pictorial works*; *Portraits*; *Registers*; and *Statistics*.

Topical headings with form subdivisions, such as **Children's literature—Bibliography** or **Geology—Maps**, render such works retrievable by form and separate them from expository treatises. Apart from a few examples, these combinations of subject heading with form subdivision are not given in the Sears List but are to be added by the cataloger as needed. Form subdivisions are particularly valuable under headings for the large fields of knowledge that are represented by many entries in a library's catalog. In applying form subdivisions the cataloger should be guided by the character of an item itself, not by the title.

Many works with titles beginning with Outline of, Handbook of, or Manual of, are in fact expository works. For example, H. G. Wells's *Outline of History* and H. J. Rose's *Handbook of Latin Literature* are lengthy, comprehensive treatises, and to use the form subdivisions that the titles suggest would be inaccurate. Other so-titled Outlines or Manuals or Handbooks may prove to be bibliographies, dictionaries, or statistics of the subject.

5. B. v. The Order of Subdivisions

At the Subject Subdivision Conference that took place at Airlie House, Virginia, in May 1991, organized by the Library of Congress, it was recommended that subdivisions follow the standard order of **[Topical]—[Geographic]—[Chronological]—[Form]**. Since that time the library community has endeavored to implement that recommendation. Only in a few subject areas, especially in the field of art, have exceptions been made. A cataloger using the Sears List can safely assume that subject strings made in the recommended order will provide the greatest uniformity. By following this standard the cataloger will know, for example, to prefer **Elderly—Housing—United States** to "Elderly—United States—Housing," and **Sports—United States—Statistics** to "Sports—Statistics—United States." (*Housing* is a topical subdivision, and *Statistics* is a form subdivision.)

The order of subdivisions also indicates against subdividing any subject heading in the List geographically that already incorporates a chronological or form subdivision. The heading **Physicians—Directories**, for example, would not be subdivided by **Ohio**, because the correct order of subdivisions would be **Physicians—Ohio—Directories**.

5. B. vi. Geographic Headings Subdivided by Topic

A longstanding exception to the practice of subdividing topics geographically, and one that remains apart from the Airlie House recommendation, is that of subdividing geographic headings by topics, when those topics pertain to the history, geography, or politics of a place. For works discussing the history of California, a census of Peru, the government of Italy, the boundaries of Bolivia, the population of Paris, or the climate of Alaska, the appropriate subject strings would be **California—History**; **Peru—Census**; **Italy—Politics and government**; **Bolivia—Boundaries**; **Paris (France)—Population**; and **Alaska—Climate**.

Many subdivisions, such as *Defenses* or *Description and travel*, are used only under geographic headings; many subdivisions are never used under geographic headings; and others, such as *History* or *Biography*, are used under geographic headings exactly as they are under topical subjects. Specific instructions for the application of subdivisions are given at the general reference for the subdivision in the List. For example, at **Census** in the List the general reference reads: "SA [See also] names of countries, cities, etc., with the subdivision *Census* {to be added as needed}." Similar instructions appear under **Boundaries**; **Climate**; **Population**; etc. Some topics that are used as subdivisions under geographic headings are applicable to countries only. The subdivision *Foreign relations*, for example, can be used only under countries, since only countries have foreign relations. The instructions for applications are explicit. At *Foreign relations* in the List, for example, the general reference reads: "USE names of countries with the subdivision *Foreign relations*, e.g. **United States—Foreign relations** {to be added as needed}."

A list of suggested topical subdivisions that may be used under the name of any city is given in the List under **Chicago (Ill.)**; those that may be used under the name of any state are listed under **Ohio**; and those that may be used under the name of any country or region, except for *History* further subdivided chronologically, are given under **United States**. Since each country's history is unique, the period subdivisions for its history are also unique.

6. SOME DIFFICULT AREAS OF APPLICATION

In many areas the application of subject headings and their appropriate subdivisions is a simple and straightforward matter. There are, however, areas in which either the complexity of the material or the vagaries of the English language create persistent problems. Even in these areas, by maintaining sound principles, following instructions carefully, and using common sense, it is possible to catalog library materials in such a way that users can find what they need. Some of these problem areas are dealt with here.

6. A. BIOGRAPHY

Discussions of biography as a form of writing are given the topical subject heading **Biography as a literary form**. Works that are themselves biographies are given either the form heading **Biography** or the form subdivision *Biography*. Such works are considered here in two groups, collective biographies and individual biographies.

6. A. i. Collective Biographies

Collective biographies are works containing biographies of more than three persons. Works consisting of biographies of three persons or fewer are treated as individual biographies and given headings for the names of the persons individually. Collective biographies not limited to any area or to any class of persons, such as *Lives of Famous Men and Women*, are simply assigned the heading **Biography**. Often collective biographies are devoted to persons of a single country or geographic area, such as *Leaders of the Arab World*, or *Dictionary of American Biography*; or to ethnic groups, such as *Who's Who among Hispanic Americans*. For such works the appropriate subject heading is the name of the geographic area or ethnic group with the subdivision *Biography*, in this case **Arab countries—Biography**; **United States—Biography**; and **Hispanic Americans—Biography**. If there are many entries under any such heading, the biographical dictionaries, which list a large number of names in alphabetical order, may be separated from the works with longer articles intended for continuous reading by adding the form subdivision *Dictionaries*. The heading for such a work as *Dictionary of American Biography* or *Who's Who in America* would then be **United States—Biography—Dictionaries**.

Some collective biographies are devoted to lives of a particular class of persons, such as women, or persons of a particular occupation or profession, such as librarians. These are entered under the heading for the class of persons or occupational group with the subdivision *Biography*, such as **Women—Biography** or **Librarians—Biography**. Still other collective biographies are devoted to any or all persons connected with a particular industry, institution, or field of endeavor. For these works the appropriate heading is the heading for that industry, institution, or field with the subdivision *Biography*, such as **Computer industry—Biography**; **Catholic Church—Biography**; or **Baseball—Biography**. A subject is usually broader in scope than a single category of persons associated with that subject, and likewise **Baseball—Biography** is broader than **Baseball players—Biography** and would be more suitable for a collective biography that includes managers, owners of teams, and other persons associated with the sport.

6. A. ii. Individual Biographies

Usually the only subject heading needed for the life of an individual is the name of the person, established in the same way as an author entry. The rules for establishing names are in *AACR2*. If a work is an autobiography, the author's name is entered in the bibliographic record twice, once as the author and again as the subject. There are a few individual persons about whom much has been written other than biographical material, such as works about their writings or other activities. In such cases, subdivisions are added to the person's name to specify the various aspects treated, among them *Biography*. As examples of such persons, the Sears List includes **Jesus Christ** and **Shakespeare, William, 1564-1616**, with subdivisions appropriate to material written about them. The subdivisions listed under Shakespeare may also be used, if needed, under the name of any voluminous author. The subdivisions provided under **Presidents— United States** may also be used under the name of any president or other ruler, if applicable. The subdivisions needed will vary from one individual to another. Different topics will be applicable, for example, to the material on Martin Luther, Napoleon, and Sigmund Freud. It should be noted that this use of subdivisions represents the exceptional, not the usual, treatment. For most individual biographies the name alone is sufficient.

Occasionally a biography will include enough material about the field in which the person worked that a second subject heading is required in addition to the personal name. A life of Mary Baker Eddy, for example, may include an account of the development of Christian Science substantial enough to warrant the subject heading **Christian Science—History**. The additional subject headings should be used only when the work contains a significant amount of material about the field of endeavor in addition to the subject's personal life, not simply because the subject was prominent in that field.

It is not customary practice to categorize the subjects of individual biographies by race, sex, occupation, etc. with the subdivision *Biography*. Headings such as **African American musicians—Biography** or **Women politicians—Biography** are appropriate only to collective biographies. Some catalogers are tempted to assign such headings to individual biographies as well, but there are several compelling reasons for not doing so. The first and most obvious is that in the case of a collective biography it is the author or compiler of the work who classifies or categorizes the persons included, not the cataloger. For a book such as *Black Women Scientists in the United States*, the subject heading **African American women scientists** is applicable because the author has selected the subjects of the biographies expressly for being African Americans, women, and scientists. For a collective biography entitled *Just as I Am: Famous Men and Women with Disabilities*, the subject string **Handicapped—Biography** would be appropriate because the author has written about several handicapped persons with their handicapped condition as the common feature. It would be impertinent labeling, however, for a cataloger to assign the subject string **Handicapped—Biography** to a biography of an individual person who happened to be handicapped, even if that condition were an important element of the person's story. In other words, three or more handicapped persons constitute the category Handicapped, but a single person can never constitute a category. Entering individual biographies under categories of persons violates the principle of specific entry. The only heading that is neither broader nor narrower but is co-extensive in scope with the subject content of the work is the personal name heading for the person written about. *See also* references can be made, if such references are deemed useful, from a category of persons to the names of individuals about whom the library has material. At the heading **African American women authors**, for example, one would then find any books that are really about African American women authors, followed by a reference: "See also **Angelou, Maya; McMillan, Terry; Morrison, Toni**," etc. Increasingly, in an online environment, tagging or bookmarking is used to identify examples of things. Tag are typically flexible and uncontrolled and serve local needs. As such they can be inconsistent without compromising the essential integrity of the catalog.

6. B. NATIONALITIES

An aspect of subject headings fraught with confusion is that of nationalities. Even though some headings are given national adjectives, the general rule is that the national aspects of subjects are expressed by geographic subdivisions under the topical subject headings. Headings for things that are always stationary are never given national adjectives but are instead subdivided geographically, such as **Architecture—France**. Things that are not stationary are also usually expressed as topical headings with a geographic subdivision, such as **Automobiles—Germany** or **Corporations—Japan**. When those things are replicated or transported to foreign countries, however, they are given national adjectives to express national style, ownership, or origin, and subdivided by the place where they are found, such as **German automobiles—United States** or **Japanese corporations—France**.

Headings for topics in literature and the arts are given national adjectives to express national character, such as **American literature**, **Spanish art**, etc. These headings may then be subdivided geographically by any place except for the country expressed in the national adjective. **American literature—Southern States** is therefore allowable, but not "Spanish art—Spain."

In the area of people, all headings for categories of persons are subdivided geographically in the Sears List with the exception of **Authors**, **Novelists**, **Dramatists**, and **Poets**, which are given national adjectives. All other categories of writers, such as **Biographers**, **Journalists**, etc., are subdivided geographically. A collective biography of American poets would be entered under **American poets—Biography**, but a collective biography of American composers or journalists would be given the heading **Composers—United States—Biography** or **Journalists—United States—Biography**. When a book deals with a category of persons from one country living or working in a foreign country, such as American composers in France, the book requires two subject strings rather than one, in this case **Composers—United States** and **Americans—France**.

6. C. LITERATURE

The field of literature presents special difficulties in cataloging because it includes two distinct types of material. The first consists of works about literature, and such works are assigned topical subject headings for whatever they are about. The second consists of literary works themselves, and those works are assigned form headings to describe what the item is rather than what it is about.

6. C. i. Works about Literature

The subject headings for works about the various literary forms are the headings for those forms, such as **Drama**, **Fiction**, and **Poetry**. A work about poetry is simply given the heading **Poetry**. Topical subdivisions are added to such headings as needed. A work about the history of poetry or about the criticism of poetry would be entered under **Poetry—History and criticism**. A work about the technique of writing plays would be entered under **Drama—Technique**. Form subdivisions may also be used under these headings to indicate the form the work takes, such as **Drama—Dictionaries** or **Poetry—Indexes**. In addition to the major forms of literature there are also lesser genres, which are subsets of the major literary forms, such as **Science fiction** or

Epic poetry. These headings are also applicable to works about literature, with topical and form subdivisions added as needed.

Literary works are commonly studied and written about according to categories characterized by nationality, language, religions, etc. The primary consideration in discussing literature is nationality, as in **American literature**, **Mexican literature**, and **Brazilian literature**. These topics are never dealt with as subsets of **English literature**, **Spanish literature**, or **Portuguese literature** simply because they are written in the English, Spanish, and Portuguese languages. Nationality takes precedence over language. Only a few national literatures are included in the List, and others are to be added as needed. Works about the major literary forms of national literatures are entered under the direct phrase, such as **Italian poetry** or **Russian fiction**, and again specific aspects or forms are expressed by subdivisions, as in **Italian poetry—History and criticism** or **Russian fiction—Dictionaries**. The subdivisions that appear under **English literature** may be used under any national literature, and headings for the major literary forms for any national literature may be formulated by substituting its national name for the word English.

Apart from national literatures there are also literatures characterized by areas larger than countries, such as **Latin American literature** or **African literature**; by languages not limited to or identified with a single country, such as **Latin literature** or **Arabic literature**; or by religions, such as **Catholic literature** or **Buddhist literature**. All these kinds of literature are treated in the same way as national literatures. Where a national literature is written in two or more prominent languages, the language is identified in parentheses after the name of the literature for material specifically limited to literature in that language, such as **Canadian literature (French)**. Materials about the literatures of minority groups within a country, written in the predominant language of that country's literature, are identified by subdivisions indicating the author group under the name of the literature, such as **American literature—African American authors**. Materials about the literatures of indigenous minority groups written in their own language are given the name of the language, such as **Navajo literature**.

6. C. ii. Literary Works

Items that are literary works themselves are of two types: collections of several authors, or anthologies, and works by a single author, or individual literary works. Literary anthologies are given a heading for the most specific literary form that includes every item in the anthology. Very general anthologies are given broad headings, such as **Literature—Collections**; **Poetry—Collections**; or **Drama—Collections**. Anthologies of national litera-tures and the forms of national literatures are given the headings for those literatures or forms with the subdivision *Collections*, such as **American literature—Collections** and **Italian poetry—Collections**. Headings for minor literary genres, such as **Science fiction** or **Pastoral poetry**, are usually assigned to anthologies without any subdivision.

Traditionally the literary works of individual authors receive no subject headings. Literary works are best known by author and title, and readers usually want a specific novel or play, or poetry by a specific poet—material that can be located in the catalog by the author and title entries. Headings describing the major literary forms (such as **Drama**, **Fiction**, and **Poetry**) and the headings for the major forms of a national literature (such as **Irish drama**, **Russian fiction**, and **Italian poetry**) are never assigned to an individual work or to a collection by a single author. It would be counterproductive, for example, to assign the heading **Fiction** to every novel in a library's collection, since the numbers of records with the same heading would be impracticably large. Furthermore, the form and national origin of a work are expressed in the classification.

In recent years, however, many libraries have felt the need for access by genre to individual works of imaginative literature. In the Sears List the headings for minor literary forms and genres—such as **Ballads**, **Fables**, **Fairy tales**, **Horror fiction**, **Science fiction**, etc.—are identified in the scope notes as applicable to individual works as well as to collections and materials about the topic. If there is no scope note indicating that a literature heading can be applied to an individual work, it can be assumed that it is not intended to be so applied. This policy is in accordance with the *Guidelines on Subject Access to Individual Works of Fiction, Drama, etc.* prepared by the Subcommittee on Subject Access to Individual Works of Fiction, Drama, etc., of the ALA Subject Analysis Committee (ALA, 1990; 2nd ed., 2000). It varies from the usage of the Library of Congress *Subject Cataloging Manual* in that it allows form and genre access to certain kinds of literary works that are often requested in libraries. Genre headings with national or linguistic adjectives, such as **Australian science fiction** or **Latin epic poetry**, are applicable to collections but are never assigned to individual works. If they were assigned to individual works, since all authors fall into the purview of one nationality or another, there would be nothing remaining under the heading **Science fiction** or **Epic poetry** but collections of international scope. Likewise, the cataloger is discouraged from adding the qualifier "juvenile" to the genre headings. The subdivision *Juvenile literature* may be added to genre headings in libraries where it is necessary to distinguish juvenile materials from adult materials, that is, in libraries not devoted exclusively or primarily to children's materials, or where juvenile material is not indicated in the shelf number. No other subdivision is ever applicable to genre headings, as applied to individual works.

The cataloger is also discouraged, except in the most unusual cases, from devising new genre terms. The *Guidelines on Subject Access* of the ALA aim to limit the number of genre terms in order to bring like material together, while the proliferation of genres and subgenres would only scatter like material and do the user a disservice. As stated on page 4 of the *Guidelines*, "Genre terms are determined by convention, as set by the bibliographic community of publishers, booksellers, librarians, and readers." It is only by conforming to these conventions that the application of genre headings to individual works is really useful.

In some libraries subject access is provided to works of literature by using any applicable subject heading from the List with the subdivision *Fiction*, *Drama*, or *Poetry*. Hence a collection of stories all set in Los Angeles could be assigned the heading **Los Angeles (Calif.)—Fiction**; a collections of plays in which the main characters are all nurses could be assigned the heading **Nurses—Drama**; and a volume of poems by several authors all on the theme of baseball could be assigned the heading **Baseball—Poetry**. Personal and corporate names can always be added to the List in order to be used with the subdivisions *Fiction*, *Drama*, and *Poetry* to provide subject access to literary collections that deal with real persons or corporate entities.

Providing the same kind of access by setting, character, or theme to individual works of fiction, drama, or poetry is more problematic. For the collection of stories set in Los Angeles, the appropriate level of specificity can be determined by finding what is common to all the stories. The plays about nurses may be about a variety of nurses, one elderly, one Hispanic American, one male, etc., but their being nurses is what they have in common. The topic **Nurses**, then, is of equal specificity with the collection itself. In individual stories or plays, however, the characters and settings are unique. All subject headings are all less specific than a unique character or a unique situation, and to assign any of them is to violate the principle of specificity and abandon uniformity in cataloging.

It is the case, nonetheless, that some libraries, for the purpose of readers' advisory or for curriculum enhancement, require the application of topical subjects and geographic headings to individual works of fiction, drama, and poetry. In this endeavor they leave behind the logic of subject analysis and embrace a kind of tagging or labeling that is approximate and pragmatic and not subject to hard rules. Even without the principles of specificity and uniformity, however, there are still some guidelines that may be useful in the application of topical subject and geographic headings to individual literary works:

1)   Use only terms that come readily to mind. Only if a novel is extensively set in the milieu of the motion picture industry, for example, would the heading **Motion picture industry—Fiction** be suitable.

2)   Use only terms that are specific enough to limit retrieval in a meaningful way. Headings such as **Family life—Fiction** or **Popular culture—Fiction** are dubiously useful, since they would apply equally to innumerable novels.

3)   Use only discrete terms, not terms that combine two or more concepts. Use two headings, such as **Hispanic Americans—Fiction** and **Nurses—Fiction** instead of **Hispanic American nurses—Fiction**.

4)   Apply headings for categories of persons only when the main character or several principal characters are representative of that category in a more than incidental way.

5)   Use geographic headings only when the setting of a novel is prominent and central to the work. All novels are set somewhere, but many novels have very little in the way of local color.

6)   In applying geographic headings, use only place names of intermediate specificity. Headings for countries are usually too broad for purposes of setting or local color. Only a few novels of epic scope ever deal with the history and geography of an entire country, and the concept of local color implies something more limited than a country. On the other hand the names of most towns and villages are unknown outside their own region. For most novels the most useful geographic headings will be the names of states or regions and certain large cities.

7)   If both a topical subject and a geographic location are central to a work, they should be expressed separately rather than as a subject string.

8)   Historical novels should be given headings only for the broadest historical periods under a place name, usually a century. The only exception to this rule would be for a few distinct periods or events that have stimulated a great number of literary works, such as **United States—History—1861-1865, Civil War—Fiction**.

9)   Do not hesitate to catalog an individual work of fiction, drama, or poetry without topical or geographic headings. Many literary works do not lend themselves to this kind of treatment, and to go beyond the obvious will only lead users to items that do not satisfy their needs.

In applying topical and geographic headings to individual works of fiction, drama, and poetry, the most important rule is to remember or imagine the needs of the users in a particular library setting, either readers who want novels, plays, etc., with a particular theme or setting, or teachers who need fictional materials on curriculum topics.

6. C. iii. Themes in Literature

Some libraries have a significant amount of material about topics, locales, or themes in imaginative literature. The appropriate headings for such material is simply "Topic in literature," according to the pattern found in the Sears List under **Literature—Themes**, such as **Dogs in literature**, **Ohio in literature**, etc. Headings of this type are for critical discussions only, not for literary works. Materials about the depiction of historical persons in drama, fiction, or poetry are entered under the person's name with the subdivision *In literature*, such as **Napoleon I, Emperor of the French, 1769-1821—In literature**. Materials about the depiction of a particular war in drama, fiction, or poetry are entered under the heading for the war with the subdivision *Literature and the war*, such as **World War, 1939-1945—Literature and the war**.

6. D. WARS AND EVENTS

Catalogers are often called upon to formulate headings as needed for wars and current events, when those wars or events generate books and other library materials. Wars fought between two or more nations are given a name, followed by a date or dates, as appropriate, such as **War of 1812**; **Israel-Arab War, 1967**; **World War, 1939-1945**; etc. Civil wars, insurrec-tions, and invasions are entered under the history of the country involved (following the dates, as with other historical periods), such as **United States—History—1861-1865, Civil War**; **Cuba—History—1961, Invasion**; etc.

Events of short duration, including battles, are dealt with as isolated topics rather than as periods in a country's history. Events that have names are given a heading for the name, followed by the place, and then by the date, such as **Tiananmen Square Incident, Beijing (China), 1989**. Battles are entered under the name of the battle, but in the inverted form, with the place of the battle qualified as needed, such as **Hastings (East Sussex, England), Battle of, 1066**. Recurring events, such as games, festivals, etc., are given the recurring name, followed by the date, with the place in parentheses, if the place changes, such as **Olympic Games, 1996 (Atlanta, Ga.)**. Unnamed events, such as individual tornadoes, are entered under the kind of event subdivided by the place of the event, such as **Tornadoes—Moore (Okla.)**.

6. E. NATIVE AMERICANS

The heading **Native Americans** may be subdivided geographically by continent, region, country, state, or city. Headings for individual nations or tribes of Native Americans may be established as needed according to the traditional formulation, such as **Aztecs** and **Navajo Indians**. Headings for classes of persons among the Native Americans, such as Women or Children, and for things distinctly ethnic, such as Medicine or Music, are expressed as phrase headings, such as **Native American women**, **Native American children**, **Native American medicine**, and **Native American music**. Topics not of an ethnic nature, such as Housing or Social conditions, are expressed as subdivisions under **Native Americans**, such as **Native Americans—Housing** and **Native Americans—Social conditions**.

6. F. GOVERNMENT POLICY

Following the principle that subject headings ought to reflect the common usage, subject headings relating to government policy are phrase headings when they apply to something general or when there is a common phrase available, such as **Fiscal policy** or **Social policy**. Where there is not a ready phrase available, the heading is formulated by the thing the policy applies to with the subdivision *Government policy*, such as **Genetic engineering—Government policy**.

6. G. MYTHOLOGY AND FOLKLORE

In general, deities that are still worshipped in the modern world are treated as religion rather than mythology. Ancient mythologies are expressed in phrase headings, such as **Celtic mythology** or **Roman mythology**. Materials on individual deities or legendary characters are given the name of the deity or character appropriately qualified, such as **Vesta (Roman deity)** or **Paris (Legendary character)**. Materials on a theme in mythology are assigned a heading for that theme, similar to a theme in literature, such as **Fire in mythology**. Unlike mythology, folklore pertains to modern peoples as well as ancient. The folklore of a people, that is, stories based on oral rather than written traditions, is expressed in subject headings by the name of the people subdivided by *Folklore*, such as **Inuit—Folklore**. Topics in folklore are expressed by the topic subdivided by *Folklore*, such as **Plants—Folklore**. Materials on the collective folklore of a place are assigned the heading **Folklore** subdivided by the continent, region, country, etc.

6. H. NONBOOK MATERIALS

The assignment of subject headings for electronic media and for audiovisual and special instructional materials should follow the same principles that are applied to books. The uniform application of the same headings to book and nonbook materials alike is especially important in an integrated catalog, which brings all materials on one subject together regardless of format. Because nonbook materials often concentrate on very small aspects of larger subjects, the cataloger may not find in the List the specific heading that should be used. In such instances the cataloger should be generous in adding new subjects as needed. There are many form and genre headings that apply equally to nonbook materials and to books about such materials, such as **Biographical films**; **Comedy television programs**; and **Science fiction comic books, strips, etc**.

Topical subject headings assigned to nonbook materials should not include form subdivisions to describe physical format, such as motion pictures, slides, sound recordings, etc. Information on format as an aspect of descriptive cataloging can be found in the most recent edition of the standard cataloging rules.

7. CLASSIFICATION AND SUBJECT HEADINGS

The cataloger should recognize a fundamental difference between classification and subject headings for the library catalog. In any system of classification that determines the arrangement of items on the shelves, a work can obviously have only one class number and stand in only one place, but in a catalog the same work can be entered, if necessary, under as many different points of entry as there are distinct subjects in the work (usually, however, not more than three). Classification is used to gather in one numerical place on the shelf works that give similar treatment to a subject. Subject headings gather in one alphabetical place in a catalog all treatments of a subject regardless of shelf location.

Another difference between classification and subject cataloging is that classification is frequently less precise than the subject entries for the catalog. Material on floriculture in general as well as on specific kinds of garden flowers are classed together in 635.9 in the Dewey Decimal Classification. A book on flower gardening, one on perennial gardening, and one on rose gardening will all three be classified in one number, while in the catalog each book will have its own specific subject heading: **Flower gardening**, **Perennials**, or **Roses**.

Library materials are classified by discipline, not by subject. A single subject may be dealt with in many disciplines. The Dewey classification numbers given with a heading in the Sears List are intended only to direct the cataloger to the disciplines where that subject is most likely to be treated. They are not meant to be absolute or cover all possibilities and should be used together with the Dewey Decimal Classification schedules. The cataloger must examine the work at hand and determine the discipline in which the author is writing. On the basis of that decision the cataloger classifies the work, not by the subject of the work alone.

8. MAINTAINING A CATALOG

The library catalog is a vital function at the very center of a library, and as such it is always growing and changing to reflect the growing collection and to meet the changing needs of the users. It is a challenge to the cataloger to add new records, revise existing records, and make all the appropriate references, and at the same time maintain the integrity of the catalog.

8. A. ADDING NEW HEADINGS

When a cataloger has determined what an item to be cataloged is about and formulated that concept into words, the next step is to find the subject heading that expresses that concept. The first thing to be determined is whether or not there is already an existing heading in the List for that concept. If, for example, there is a book on lawsuits, the cataloger may think of the terms Lawsuits, Suing, and Suits. Upon consulting the List it becomes clear that those words are not headings but references to the established heading **Litigation**. **Litigation** is slightly broader than Suing but is more suitable as a subject heading because it includes the matter of defending oneself against lawsuits. In this case the cataloger enters the book into the catalog under the heading **Litigation**. A new heading is not necessary.

At other times the appropriate heading for a book is not a new heading but a new combination of an established heading and a subdivision. If, for example, there is a book on the use and abuse of alcohol on college campuses, the cataloger may first think of the term Drunkenness. In the Sears List Drunkenness is an unpreferred term and a reference to two established headings: **Alcoholism** and **Temperance**. The scope note at **Temperance** reads: "Use for materials on the virtue of temperance or on the temperance movement." The book is not about drunkenness in relation to either vice and virtue or the temperance movement, so that heading can be eliminated. Neither is the book really about alcoholism, but at the heading **Alcoholism**, there is a general reference that reads: "SA [See also] classes of persons with the subdivision *Alcohol use*, e.g. **Employees—Alcohol use**; **Youth—Alcohol use**; etc., {to be added as needed}." At this point the cataloger realizes that the appropriate Sears subject heading for the book at hand would be **College students—Alcohol use**. **College students** is already an established heading in the List, but it could be added if it were not.

The cataloger should always keep in mind that it is not only appropriate but essential that types of things and examples of things not found in the List be established as headings and added to the List locally as needed. If there is a book on gloves, for example, and there is no heading in the Sears List for Gloves, the cataloger thinks of the concept or category of thing that would include gloves. Clothing comes to mind. At the heading **Clothing and dress** in the List there is a general reference: "SA [See also] types of clothing articles and accessories {to be added as needed}." The cataloger then establishes the heading **Gloves** and enters the book into the catalog under **Gloves**. It would be inappropriate to enter the book under the heading **Clothing and dress** simply because **Clothing and dress** is in the List and **Gloves** is not. It would mean that a user looking in the catalog under Gloves would find nothing. The general references in the List should reinforce the point that the List does not aim at completeness and must be expanded. Even where there is no general reference, narrower terms for types of things and examples and instances of things must be added as needed.

At times it is nearly impossible to determine what broader concept or category a new subject might be included under. This should not deter the cataloger from establishing any heading that is needed. Take, for example, the case of a book on thumb sucking, a common phenomenon among small children. The nearest terms in the List might be **Child psychology**, **Child rearing**, or **Human behavior**, but they are none too near. Nowhere is there a general reference instructing the cataloger to add headings for common childhood phenomena, and still the only appropriate heading for the book would be **Thumb sucking**. Here the intrepid cataloger, thinking how useless the headings **Child psychology**, **Child rearing**, or **Human behavior** would be on such a book, adds the heading **Thumb sucking** to the List and enters the book into the catalog under that heading.

There are resources that a cataloger can turn to for help in establishing subject headings that are not in the List. Other available databases and catalogs in which books are listed by subject can always be consulted, such as the Web site of any large library whose catalog is online. Periodical indexes, such as *Readers' Guide to Periodical Literature* or *Applied Science & Technology Index,* are especially helpful in establishing headings for current events and very new topics and trends and for technical headings. The index and the schedules of the *Dewey Decimal Classification* are a useful source of subject terminology as well as a way of seeing a topic in its relation to other topics. The Library of Congress issues lists of new subject headings in *Library of Congress Subject Headings Weekly Lists* on its Web site and includes new subject headings of current interest in its quarterly *Cataloging Service Bulletin*. Library of Congress cataloging information, including subject headings, emanating from its Cataloging in Publication (CIP) program, is available in various online databases and is also printed on the title page verso of many books.

8. B. REVISING SUBJECT HEADINGS

Because the English language does not stand still, neither do subject headings. It would be impossible today for a catalog to maintain the headings Negroes or Dinosauria, since common usage has relegated these terms to history. The prevailing thinking about the form of subject headings also changes, and as a result whole groups of headings need to be revised. All the inverted headings in the Sears List, for example, were eventually revised to the uninverted form, such as **Health insurance** for "Insurance, Health." With each new edition of the Sears List a library should consult the List of Canceled and Replacement Headings in the front of the volume and revise its catalog accordingly. Any headings created locally based on the pattern set by a Sears heading, and strings consisting of a Sears heading and a subdivision, must also be revised if that heading is revised in Sears. If, for example, a library had added the headings "Insurance, Title" and "Insurance, Health—Law and legislation," those headings would need to be revised to **Title insurance** and **Health insurance—Law and legislation**.

How a library revises its catalog depends upon the kind of catalog. In an online catalog the revision process depends upon the software employed in the catalog. If the software provides global update capability, the revision of many bibliographic records at once is simple. If they must be revised one by one, the process is still immensely easier than revising cards in a card catalog. In a card catalog the subjects are physically erased and retyped, either on all the cards on which they appear or on the subject entry cards alone. If in a card catalog replacement of a term is desirable but the number of bibliographic records to be revised is prohibitive, a history note can be used instead. A history note is simply a card at both the old and the new form indicating the change. When, for example, the heading "Insurance, Health" is changed in Sears to **Health insurance**, the two cards would read as follows:

> **Insurance, Health**. For materials issued after [date] consult the following heading: **Health insurance**

and

> **Health insurance**. For materials issued before [date] consult the following heading: **Insurance, Health**.

There is also the option, provided the software allows for it, of displaying a history note in an online catalog in lieu of revising the bibliographic records.

8. C. MAKING REFERENCES

Once an item has been assigned a subject heading, either a heading found in the List or one added as needed, attention must be directed to insuring that the reader who is searching for this material will not fail to find it because of insufficient references to the proper heading. References direct the user from terms not used as headings to the term that is used, and from broader and related terms to the term chosen to represent a given subject. The Sears List uses the symbols found in most thesauri to point out the relationships among the terms found in the List and to assist the cataloger in establishing appropriate references in the public catalog based upon these relationships. There are three types of references: *See* references, *See also* references, and general references.

8. C. i. *See* References

In the public catalog *See* references direct the user from unpreferred or unestablished terms and phrases to the preferred or established terms that are used as subject headings. Under most headings in the Sears List, following the UF [Used for] label, is one or more suggested terms for *See* references in the public catalog. A cataloger may want to use some or all of them as references, and many catalogers add other *See* references they deem useful. In theory there is no limit to the number of *See* references to a particular term, but in practice there may well be, especially in a card catalog. The references will be more useful if the cataloger considers materials from the reader's point of view. The reader's profile depends on age, background, education, occupation, and geographical location, and takes into account the type of library, such as school, public, university, or special.

The following are some types of unpreferred terms that might be used as *See* references in a catalog:

1) Synonyms or terms so nearly synonymous that they would cover the same material. For example, **Instructional materials centers** requires a reference from School media centers.

2) The second part of compound headings. For example, **Antique and vintage motorcycles** requires a reference from Vintage motorcycles.

3) The inverted form of a heading, either an adjective-noun combination or a phrase heading, especially if the word brought forward is not also the broader term.

For example, **Theory of knowledge** requires a reference from "Knowledge, Theory of," there being no heading Knowledge.

4)   Variant spellings. For example, **Archeology** requires a reference from Archaeology.

5)   The opposite of a term, when it is included in the meaning of a term without being specifically mentioned. For example, **School attendance** requires a reference from Absence from school and from Absenteeism (Schools), and **Equality** requires a reference from Inequality.

6)   The former forms of headings revised to reflect common usage, when the older term still has any currency. For example, Negroes remains as a reference to **Blacks** and to **African Americans**, but Dinosauria is no longer retained as a reference to **Dinosaurs**.

The first time a heading from the List is assigned to a work in the collection, the terms in the UF field in the List are entered, at the cataloger's discretion, as *See* references in the public catalog. When the same heading is subsequently assigned to other works, the references are already in place. When the cataloger adds a heading to the authority file as needed, all the appropriate *See* references are entered as well the first time the heading is used. For the heading **College students—Alcohol use**, for example, suitable *See* references might be Campus drinking, College drinking, and Drinking on campus.

8. C. ii. *See also* References

In the public catalog *See also* references direct the user from one established heading to another established heading. Under most headings in the Sears List, following the BT [Broader term] label, is a term that is broader in scope than the heading itself. As a rule, a term has only one broader term, unless it is an example or aspect of two or more things. The broader term serves two functions in the List. The first is to aid the cataloger in finding the best term to assign to a work. If the first term the cataloger thinks of to describe the contents of the work does not cover all aspects of work, the broader term may be the more appropriate heading for that work. The second function is to indicate where *See also* references should be made in the public catalog. A *See also* reference is made from a broader term to a narrower term, but not from a narrower term to a broader term. Take, for example, the broader term **Clothing and dress** on the heading **Gloves**. When the heading **Gloves** is assigned for the first time to a work in the collection, a reference is made at **Clothing and dress** "See also **Gloves**." If **Clothing and dress** has never been assigned to a work in the collection, it is entered in the catalog for the sake of the reference, and the reference "See also **Gloves**" is made. The point is that the user who is interested in works on clothing and dress in general may also be interested in works limited to gloves. The book on gloves need not be entered under both **Clothing and dress** and **Gloves**, but only under the appropriately specific heading, because the *See also* reference will direct the user from the broader to the narrower term. If the book on gloves were entered under both **Clothing and dress** and **Gloves**, the catalog would first list the book under the heading **Clothing and dress** and then direct the user to look as well under **Gloves** only to find the same book.

Under many headings in the Sears List, following the RT [Related term] label, one or more terms are listed that represent similar or associated subjects. These related terms are neither broader nor narrower than the main term but roughly equal in specificity. The term **Pardon**, for example, is related to **Amnesty**. The cataloger or the user may easily look first to one term only to realize that the other is the more precise term for the material being cataloged or being sought in the catalog. Related terms are reciprocal. When the term **Pardon** is assigned for the first time to a work in the collection, a reference is made in the catalog at **Amnesty** "See also **Pardon**." The reciprocal reference at **Pardon** "See also **Amnesty**" is also made, but only if **Amnesty** has also been assigned to a work in the collection. A reference is never made to a heading until there is a work entered under that heading in the collection, and if the only work entered under a heading is lost or discarded the references to that heading must be deleted. References to headings under which there is no material in the collection are called blind references and are to be avoided.

8. C. iii. General References

Under many headings in the Sears List, following the SA [See also] label, there is what is called a general reference, not to a specific heading but to a general group or category of things that may be established as headings as needed. In the example of **Clothing and dress** given above, the general reference is to "types of clothing articles and accessories, {to be added as needed}." This reference is addressed to the cataloger as a reminder not to be limited to the types of clothing and dress items given as examples in the List—**Hats**, **Hosiery**, **Shoes**, etc.—but to create a heading for any other clothing item, such as **Gloves**, when the need arises.

A second function of general references is to provide instruction in the application of subdivisions. Only a few subdivisions are universally applicable. All others apply only to certain types of headings. For every subdivision provided in the List, except those of unique application, there is a general reference spelling out the use of that subdivision. If the subdivision is also a heading, the general reference is given under the heading. **Folklore**, for example, is both a heading and a subdivision. Under the heading **Folklore** the general reference reads: "SA [See also] topics as themes in folklore with the subdivision *Folklore*, e.g. **Plants—Folklore**; names of ethnic or occupational groups with the subdivision *Folklore*, e.g. **Inuit—Folklore**; and names of individual legendary characters, e.g. **Bunyan, Paul (Legendary character)** {to be added as needed}." When the subdivision is not also a heading, there is a free-standing general reference in the alphabetical List with instructions on the use of that subdivision. For example, at *Industrial applications*, which is not a heading but only a subdivision, there is a general reference that reads: "USE types of scientific phenomena, chemicals, plants, and crops with the subdivision *Industrial applications*, e.g. **Ultrasonic waves—Industrial applications** {to be added as needed}."

Some libraries also display general references in the public catalog. Rather than make a specific *See also* reference from the broader term to every narrower term, they adapt the general reference in the List to address it to the user of the catalog. At **Flowers**, for example, rather than a specific *See also* reference to **Day lilies**, **Orchids**, **Peonies**, **Poppies**, **Roses**, **Tulips**, and **Violets**, there would be a general reference "See also types of flowers." The drawback of this procedure and the reason it is not recommended is that the user who wants to see all the books on specific flower types would have to think of every type of flower and look in dozens of places in the catalog. Many online catalogs are now able to provide the user with an expanded display of all the narrower terms under **Flowers** that have been used in the catalog.

8. D. RECORDING HEADINGS AND REFERENCES

The cataloger should keep a record of all the subject headings used in the catalog and all the references made to and from them. This local authority file may be kept on cards or on a computer. Some catalogers are tempted to forgo this process and merely consult the catalog whenever there is a question of previous practice. Without a local authority file, however, there can be no consistency in the cataloging. It is not possible to consult the catalog at the heading **Teachers—Ethics**, for example, and find what *See also* references were made to that term from any broader or related terms or what *See* references were made from unpreferred terms. Since **Teachers—Ethics** is not in the Sears List but was added as needed, consulting the List is not the answer. When a book appears on the ethics of psychologists, the cataloger will create **Psychologists—Ethics**, but without knowing what references were made to the heading **Teachers—Ethics**, there is no way the cataloger can create similar and consistent references for the new term. Likewise, if there is only one book entered under **Teachers—Ethics**, and if that book is lost or discarded, without a local authority file there would be no way of knowing what to delete in order to avoid blind references.

Many libraries today do little original cataloging but instead get their cataloging records from outside sources, either from computerized cooperative cataloging utilities or from vendors, often the same companies that sell them their books and other library materials. This procurement of cataloging from outside sources can save libraries a great deal of money, but it does not mean that there is no work for the cataloger in the library. Someone must order the cataloging, specifying to the vendor the particular needs of the library. If a library is devoted largely or entirely to children's materials, for example, a librarian will need to specify that the library does not want the subdivision *Juvenile literature* on every subject heading. A library using Sears subject headings will need to apprise the vendor of that fact. When the cataloging records arrive in the library, only a cataloger can check them to be sure they are what was ordered. And lastly, only a cataloger can make the appropriate references in the local catalog, tailored to that library's particular collection, which make the records useful to the users.

9. CATALOGING IN THE TWENTY-FIRST CENTURY

It is useful to view modern cataloging practice in an historical perspective. In the nineteenth century, as libraries grew and cataloging became more thorough, it was clear that some form of cooperation among libraries was desirable. For many years the distribution of printed library cards was the principal method of cooperative cataloging. Later computerized utilities replaced printed cards. From the beginning it was clear that without principles and standards guaranteeing uniformity, cooperative cataloging would be impossible. In the very first volume of the American Library Association's *Library Journal* (1876-77) there are several lengthy discussions of cooperative cataloging, including an article on the topic by Melvil Dewey. It was out of these discussions and the voluminous correspondence that ensued that the modern standards of cataloging developed, both the rules for descriptive cataloging and Cutter's *Rules for a Dictionary Catalog*. These rules are not arbitrary but are firmly grounded in logic. They have stood unchallenged for over a hundred years because they have served to facilitate accurate and comprehensive retrieval in the modern library.

The world of libraries in the twenty-first century is already quite different from what it was only recently. More information is available in machine-readable form, and ready access to the Internet has changed the way many users seek and find information. Traditional methods of storage and retrieval in libraries will increasingly be supplemented by new methods engendered by artificial intelligence. The challenge of catalogers in the future is to approach every new technology and theory knowledgeably and fearlessly, judge them against what we know are the soundest principles, and embrace the good and reject the spurious, always keeping in mind the ultimate goal of meeting, even anticipating, the changing needs of the library users.

10. BIBLIOGRAPHY

American Library Association. Filing Committee. *ALA Filing Rules*. Chicago: American Library Association, 1980.

American Library Association. Subject Analysis Committee. *Guidelines on Subject Access to Individual Works of Fiction, Drama, etc.* 2nd ed. Chicago: American Library Association, 2000.

Anglo-American Cataloguing Rules. 2nd ed., 2002 Revision, 2005 update. Chicago: American Library Association, 2005.

Chan, Lois Mai and Theodora Hodges. *Cataloging and Classification: an Introduction*. 3rd ed. New York: McGraw-Hill, 2007.

Chan, Lois Mai, Phyllis A. Richmond, and Elaine Svenonius, eds. *Theory of Subject Analysis: a Sourcebook*. Englewood, Colo.: Libraries Unlimited, 1985. [Contains excerpts from Charles A. Cutter's *Rules for a Dictionary Catalog*]

Dewey, Melvil. *Abridged Dewey Decimal Classification and Relative Index*. 14th ed. Edited by Joan S. Mitchell, et al. Dublin, Ohio: OCLC, 2004.

Gateley, Stephen. *Using Sears Subject Headings* [in church libraries]. Nahsville, Tenn.: Convention Press, 1994.

Hoffman, Herbert H. *Small Library Cataloging*. 3rd ed. Lanham, Md.: Scarecrow Press, 2002.

Intner, Sheila S., and Jean Riddle Weihs. *Standard Cataloging for School and Public Libraries*. 4th ed. Englewood, Colo.: Libraries Unlimited, 2007.

Intner, Sheila S. Joanna F. Fountain, and Jean Weihs, eds. *Cataloging Correctly for Kids: An Introduction to the Tools*. 5th ed. Chicago: American Library Association, 2010.

Library Literature & Information Science. New York: The H. W. Wilson Co., 1921-

Library of Congress. Cataloging Policy and Support Office. *Subject Headings Manual*. 5th ed. Washington, D.C.: Library of Congress, 2008-

Library of Congress. Office for Subject Cataloging Policy. *LC Period Subdivisions under Names of Places*. 5th ed. Washington, D.C.: Library of Congress, 1994.

Lighthall, Lynne, ed. *Sears List of Subject Headings: Canadian Companion*. 6th ed. New York: The H. W. Wilson Co., 2001.

Satija, M. P. "Sears List of Subject Headings: An Introduction to the Nineteenth Edition (2007)." *Pakistan Journal of Library & Information Science* no. 9 (July 2008): 31-48.

Satija, M. P., and Elizabeth Haynes. *User's Guide to Sears List of Subject Headings*. Lanham, MD: Scarecrow Press, 2008.

Sears Lista de Ecabezamientos de Materia: Nueva Traduccion y Adaptacion de la Lista Sears. Iván E. Calimano, editor ; Ageo García, editor asociado ; Judy Medina, Carmen Torres, traductores ; incorporando el trabajo de 1984 de Carmen Rovira. New York: The H.W. Wilson Co., 2008.

Taylor, Arlene G., and Daniel N. Joudrey. *The Organization of Information.* 3rd ed. Westport, Conn.: Libraries Unlimited, 2009.

Taylor, Arlene G. *Introduction to Cataloging and Classification.* 10th ed. Westport, Conn.: Libraries Unlimited, 2006.

Weihs, Jean. "Musings on an Unscientific Survey of Sears Use." *Technicalities* 24, no. 3 (May 2004): 5-7.

Headings to be Added by the Cataloger

Sears is not intended to be a complete list of subject headings but only a list of many of the most commonly used headings and a pattern for creating other headings as needed. Types of things and names of individual things must always be added when they are not already provided in the List. The general references in the List explicitly instruct the cataloger to create headings in areas where the need for such additions is most obvious (such as under **Flowers**, where the general reference reads "SA [See also] types of flowers, e.g. **Roses** {to be added as needed}"). Where there is no general reference the same instruction is implicit. A further discussion of adding headings can be found in the Principles of the Sears List. Some of the additional headings most likely to be needed are the following:

Topical Subjects
1. Types of common things—foods, tools, sports, musical instruments, etc.
2. Types of plants and animals—fruits, flowers, birds, fishes, etc.
3. Types of chemicals and minerals
4. Types of enterprises and industries
5. Types of diseases
6. Names of organs and regions of the body
7. Names of languages, language groups, and national literatures
8. Names of ethnic groups and nationalities
9. Names of wars, battles, treaties, etc.

Geographic Headings
1. Names of political jurisdictions—countries, states, cities, provinces, etc.
2. Groups of states, groups of countries, alliances, etc.
3. Names of geographic features—regions, mountain ranges, island groups, individual mountains, individual islands, rivers, river valleys, oceans, lakes, etc.

Names
1. Personal names—individual persons and families
2. Corporate names—associations, societies, government bodies, religious denominations, business firms, performing groups, colleges, libraries, hospitals, hotels, ships, etc.
3. Uniform titles—anonymous literary works, newspapers, periodicals, sacred scriptures, motion pictures, etc.

The Key Headings on the following page can be used as a guide in applying subdivisions to any similar headings. Subdivisions not provided for in the Sears List may also be established and used as needed.T

"Key" Headings

Certain headings in the Sears List have been chosen to serve as examples, at which the subdivisions particularly applicable to certain categories of headings are given. If a subdivision is provided under the "key" heading, it may also be used under any heading of that type.

Authors: **Shakespeare, William, 1564-1616** (to illustrate the subdivisions that may be used under any voluminous author, and in some cases other individual persons)

Ethnic groups: **Native Americans** (to illustrate the subdivisions that may be used under any ethnic group or native people)

Languages: **English language** (to illustrate the subdivisions that may be used under any language or group of languages)

Literature: **English literature** (to illustrate the subdivisions that may be used under any literature)

Places: **United States**
Ohio
Chicago (Ill.)
(to illustrate the subdivisions—except for historical periods—that may be used under any country, state, or city)

Public figures: **Presidents—United States** (to illustrate the subdivisions that may be used under the presidents, prime ministers, governors, and rulers of any country, state, etc., and in some cases under the names of individual presidents, prime ministers, etc.)

Wars: **World War, 1939-1945** (to illustrate the subdivisions that may be used under any war, and in some cases individual battles)

List of Canceled and Replacement Headings

CANCELED HEADINGS	REPLACEMENT HEADINGS
Charity organization	Charitable organizations
Commonwealth of Independent States	[no replacement]
Communism—Soviet Union	Communism—Russia
East Indians	Indians
Fans	Fans (Dress accessories)
Former Soviet republics	[no replacement]
Fringe benefits	Employee benefits
Greenhouse effect	Global warming
High fidelity sound systems	[no replacement]
Holocaust, 1933-1945	Holocaust, 1939-1945
Holocaust, 1933-1945—Personal narratives	Holocaust, 1939-1945—Personal narratives
Hypertext	Hyperlinks
Indic literature	Indian literature
In-line skating	Rollerblading
Interviews (Journalism)	Interviewing in journalism
Sex (Biology)	Sex—Physiological aspects
Sex (Psychology)	Sex—Psychological aspects
Russia (Federation)	Russia
Russia (Federation)—History—1991-	Russia—History—1991-
Soviet literature	Russian literature
Soviet Union	Russia—History—1917-1991, Soviet Union
Soviet Union—History	Russia—History—1917-1991, Soviet Union
Soviet Union—History—1917-1921, Revolution	Russia—History—1917-1921, Revolution
Soviet Union—History—1917-1925	Russia—History—1917-1925
Soviet Union—History—1925-1953	Russia—History—1925-1953
Soviet Union—History—1953-1991	Russia—History—1953-1991
Soviets (People)	[no replacement]
State rights	States' rights
Videodiscs	DVDs
United States—Armed forces—Recruiting, enlistment, etc.	United States—Armed forces—Recruiting and enlistment
United States. Army—Recruiting, enlistment, etc.	United States. Army—Recruiting and enlistment
United States. Navy—Recruiting, enlistment, etc.	United States. Navy—Recruiting and enlistment

The Use of Subdivisions in the Sears List

To allow for a standardized formulation of many complex subjects, there are a large number of topical and form subdivisions that may be used under a variety of subjects as needed. There are provisions and examples for more than five hundred subdivisions in the Sears List. The List of Subdivisions found on the following pages is meant for handy reference only. For each of the subdivisions provided for in Sears there is also a general reference in the alphabetical List with specific instructions as to what types of headings that subdivision can be used under.

SUBDIVISIONS OF BROAD APPLICATION

Some subdivisions are of very broad application and can be used under nearly any subject heading. The following are examples of two general references for such subdivisions—one for a topical subdivision, *Computer simulation*, which is also a heading, and one for a form subdivision, *Interactive multimedia*, which is only a subdivision:

> **Computer simulation**
> SA   subjects with the subdivision *Computer simulation*, e.g. **Psychology— Computer simulation** [to be added as needed]

> Interactive multimedia
> USE   subjects with the subdivision *Interactive multimedia*, e.g. **Geology— Interactive multimedia** [to be added as needed]

SUBDIVISIONS OF LIMITED APPLICATION

Some subdivisions are of limited application and can be used only under certain categories of subject heading. The following are examples of two general references for such subdivisions—one for a topical subdivision, *Satellites*, which is also a heading, and one for a form subdivision, *Facsimiles*, which is only a subdivision:

> **Satellites**
> SA   names of planets with the subdivision *Satellites*, e.g. **Mars (Planet)— Satellites** [to be added as needed]

> Facsimiles
> USE   types of printed or written materials, documents, etc., with the subdivision *Facsimiles*, e.g. **Autographs—Facsimiles** [to be added as needed]

List of Subdivisions Provided for in the Sears List

The following is a list of every subdivision for which there is a specific provision in the Sears List. This list is meant for handy reference only. For instructions on the use of a particular subdivision, see the entry for that subdivision in the main body of the alphabetical List. The following list is not exhaustive. It does not, for example, contain geographic or chronological subdivisions, which should be established by the cataloger as needed. Further topical and form subdivisions may also be required in libraries that contain specialized material, and they too should be established as needed and used consistently.

<table>
<tr><td>Accidents</td><td>Auditing</td></tr>
<tr><td>Accounting</td><td>Autographs</td></tr>
<tr><td>Accreditation</td><td>Authorship</td></tr>
<tr><td>Adaptations</td><td>Automation</td></tr>
<tr><td>Administration</td><td>Autonomy and independence</td></tr>
<tr><td>Aerial operations</td><td>   movements</td></tr>
<tr><td>African American authors</td><td>Awards</td></tr>
<tr><td>Age</td><td>Battlefields</td></tr>
<tr><td>Aging</td><td>Behavior</td></tr>
<tr><td>Agriculture</td><td>Biblical teaching</td></tr>
<tr><td>Air conditioning</td><td>Bibliography</td></tr>
<tr><td>Alcohol use</td><td>Bio-bibliography</td></tr>
<tr><td>Allusions</td><td>Biography</td></tr>
<tr><td>Alphabet</td><td>Bishops</td></tr>
<tr><td>Amphibious operations</td><td>Black authors</td></tr>
<tr><td>Analysis</td><td>Blockades</td></tr>
<tr><td>Anatomy</td><td>Book reviews</td></tr>
<tr><td>Anecdotes</td><td>Books and reading</td></tr>
<tr><td>Anniversaries</td><td>Boundaries</td></tr>
<tr><td>Antiquities</td><td>Brakes</td></tr>
<tr><td>Apologetic works</td><td>Breeding</td></tr>
<tr><td>Appointment</td><td>Buildings</td></tr>
<tr><td>Appointments and retirements</td><td>Calendars</td></tr>
<tr><td>Appropriations and expenditures</td><td>Campaigns</td></tr>
<tr><td>Archives</td><td>Captivities</td></tr>
<tr><td>Armed forces</td><td>Care</td></tr>
<tr><td>Armistices</td><td>Cartoons and caricatures</td></tr>
<tr><td>Army</td><td>Case studies</td></tr>
<tr><td>Art and the war</td><td>Casualties</td></tr>
<tr><td>Art collections</td><td>Catalogs</td></tr>
<tr><td>Assassination</td><td>Catechisms</td></tr>
<tr><td>Atlases</td><td>Catholic Church</td></tr>
<tr><td>Atrocities</td><td>Causes</td></tr>
<tr><td>Attitudes</td><td>Censorship</td></tr>
<tr><td>Audiences</td><td>Census</td></tr>
<tr><td>Audiovisual aids</td><td>Centennial celebrations, etc.</td></tr>
</table>

Chaplains
Characters
Charities
Charts, diagrams, etc.
Chemical warfare
Children
Christian missions
Chronology
Church history
Citizen participation
Civil rights
Civilian relief
Civilization
Claims
Classification
Cleaning
Clergy
Climate
Clothing
Coaching
Collaborationists
Collectibles
Collection and preservation
Collections
Collectors and collecting
Colonies
Color
Comic books, strips, etc.
Commentaries
Commerce
Communication systems
Comparative studies
Comparison
Competitions
Composition
Composition and exercises
Computer networks
Computer software
Computer simulation
Computer-assisted instruction
Concordances
Conduct of life
Conference proceedings
Conferences
Conscientious objectors
Conservation and restoration
Control
Controversial literature
Conversation and phrase books
Correspondence
Corrupt practices
Cost effectiveness

Costs
Counseling of
Courts and courtiers
Creeds
Cross-cultural studies
Curricula
Customs and practices
Data processing
Databases
Death
Death and burial
Defenses
Demobilization
Dental care
Deregulation
Description and travel
Desertions
Design
Design and construction
Designs and plans
Destruction and pillage
Dialects
Diaries
Dictionaries
Diet therapy
Diplomatic history
Directories
Discography
Diseases
Diseases and pests
Dissection
Doctrines
Documentation
Draft resisters
Drama
Dramatic production
Drug testing
Drug therapy
Drug use
Drying
Dwellings
Early works to 1800
Earthquake effects
Ecology
Economic aspects
Economic conditions
Economic policy
Editing
Education
Education and the war
Eggs
Election

Employees
Employment
Encyclopedias
Endowments
Engineering and construction
Entrance examinations
Entrance requirements
Environmental aspects
Equipment and supplies
Errors of usage
Estimates
Ethical aspects
Ethics
Ethnic identity
Ethnic relations
Ethnobiology
Ethnobotany
Ethnozoology
Etymology
Evacuation of civilians
Evaluation
Evidences, authority, etc.
Evolution
Examinations
Exhibitions
Experiments
Exploration
Exploring expeditions
Facsimiles
Faculty
Family
Fiction
Filmography
Finance
Finishing
Fires and fire prevention
First editions
Flight
Folklore
Food
Food supply
Forced repatriation
Forecasting
Foreign countries
Foreign economic relations
Foreign influences
Foreign opinion
Foreign relations
Foreign words and phrases
Forgeries
Friends and associates
Fuel consumption

Funeral customs and rites
Gazetteers
Genealogy
Genetic aspects
Geographical distribution
Geography
Geology
Gold discoveries
Government
Government ownership
Government policy
Government relations
Governments in exile
Grammar
Graphic novels
Grooming
Growth
Guidebooks
Habitations
Handbooks, manuals, etc.
Health and hygiene
Health aspects
Heating and ventilation
Hispanic American authors
Historical geography
Historiography
History
History and criticism
History of doctrines
Home care
Homes
Homonyms
Housing
Humor
Hunting
Identification
Identity
Idioms
Illustrations
Immigration and emigration
Impeachment
In art
Inaugural addresses
Inauguration
Indexes
Industrial applications
Industries
Infinitive
Influence
Information resources
Information services
In literature

In-service training
Insignia
Inspection
Institutional care
Intellectual life
Interactive multimedia
International cooperation
Internet resources
Interviews
Jargon
Journalists
Juvenile drama
Juvenile fiction
Juvenile literature
Juvenile poetry
Kings and rulers
Kinship
Knowledge
Labeling
Laboratory manuals
Labor productivity
Language
Languages
Law and legislation
Legal status, laws, etc.
Legends
Library resources
Licenses
Life cycles
Life skills guides
Lighting
Lists
Literary collections
Literature and the war
Liturgy
Local history
Localisms
Maintenance and repair
Malpractice
Management
Manpower
Manuscripts
Maps
Marketing
Marks
Material culture
Materials
Mathematical models
Mathematics
Measurement
Medals, badges, decorations, etc.
Medical care

Medical examinations
Meditations
Memorizing
Mental health
Mental health services
Mergers
Messages
Metamorphosis
Methodology
Mexican American authors
Microbiology
Migration
Military history
Military intelligence
Military life
Militia
Miscellanea
Missing in action
Missions
Models
Monuments
Moral conditions
Morphology
Mortality
Motion pictures and the war
Motors
Museums
Name
Names
Naval history
Naval operations
Navy
Nazi persecution
Nests
Noise
Nomenclature
Nomenclature (Popular)
Nomination
Nursing
Nutrition
Obituaries
Occupied territories
Ordnance
Officers
Officials and employees
Origin
Outlines, syllabi, etc.
Packaging
Painting
Parachute troops
Paralysis
Parasites

Parodies, imitations, etc.
Parts of speech
Patients
Patterns
Peace
Pensions
Periodicals
Persecutions
Personal finance
Personal narratives
Personnel management
Philosophy
Physical fitness
Physical therapy
Physiological aspects
Physiological effect
Physiology
Pictorial works
Piloting
Planning
Poetry
Political activity
Political aspects
Politics and government
Population
Portraits
Posters
Practice
Prayers
Preservation
Press coverage
Press relations
Prevention
Price guides
Prices
Prisoners and prisons
Problems, exercises, etc.
Production standards
Programmed instruction
Pronunciation
Propaganda
Prophecies
Protection
Protest movements
Provincialisms
Psychological aspects
Psychology
Public opinion
Publishing
Purchasing
Quality control
Queens

Quotations
Race identity
Race relations
Rates
Rating
Reading materials
Recruiting
Recruiting and enlistment
Recycling
Refugees
Regimental histories
Registers
Rehabilitation
Relations with Congress
Religion
Religious aspects
Religious life
Relocation
Remedial teaching
Remodeling
Repairing
Reparations
Research
Reservations
Resignation
Reviews
Rhyme
Riots
Rites and ceremonies
Romances
Rural conditions
Safety devices
Safety measures
Safety regulations
Salaries, wages, etc.
Sanitation
Satellites
Scholarships
Secret service
Security measures
Segregation
Sermons
Services for
Sexual behavior
Signaling
Slang
Social aspects
Social conditions
Social life and customs
Societies
Songs
Sound recordings

Sources
Specifications
Spelling
Staff
Stage history
Standards
Statistics
Storage
Stories
Stories, plots, etc.
Strategic aspects
Study and teaching
Study guides
Succession
Suffrage
Suicide
Supply and demand
Surgery
Surveys
Synonyms and antonyms
Tables
Tank warfare
Taxation
Technique
Technological innovations
Telephone directories
Terminology
Terms and phrases
Territorial expansion
Territorial questions
Territories and possessions
Testing

Textbooks
Texts
Theater and the war
Therapeutic use
Thermodynamics
Tombs
Tournaments
Toxicology
Trademarks
Training
Transplantation
Transportation
Travel
Treaties
Tropical conditions
Tropics
Tuning
Underground movements
Uniforms
Usage
Vaccination
Vital statistics
Vocational guidance
War use
War work
Wars
Waste disposal
Weight
Women authors
Wounds and injuries
Writing

Symbols Used

UF = Used for

SA = See also

BT = Broader term

NT = Narrower term

RT = Related term

[Former heading] = Term that was once used as a heading and is no longer

(May subdiv. geog.) = Heading that may be subdivided by name of place

Sears List of Subject Headings

3-D photography
    USE   **Three dimensional photography**

4-H clubs (May subdiv. geog.)   **630.6**
    UF   Four-H clubs
    BT   **Agriculture—Societies**
          Agriculture—Study and teaching
          Boys' clubs
          Girls' clubs

4th of July
    USE   **Fourth of July**

100 years' war
    USE   **Hundred Years' War, 1339-1453**

401(k) plans   **332.024**
    BT   **Individual retirement accounts**

1920s
    USE   **Nineteen twenties**

1930s
    USE   **Nineteen thirties**

1940s
    USE   **Nineteen forties**

1950s
    USE   **Nineteen fifties**

1960s
    USE   **Nineteen sixties**

1970s
    USE   **Nineteen seventies**

1980s
    USE   **Nineteen eighties**

1990s
    USE   **Nineteen nineties**

Abacus   **513.028**
    BT   **Calculators**

Abandoned children (May subdiv. geog.)
    362.73
    UF   Exposed children
    BT   **Child welfare**
          Children
    RT   **Orphans**

Abandoned towns
    USE   **Extinct cities**
           Ghost towns

Abandonment of family
    USE   **Desertion and nonsupport**

Abbeys (May subdiv. geog.)   **271; 726**
    SA   names of individual abbeys [to be added as needed]
    BT   **Church architecture**
          Monasteries
    NT   **Westminster Abbey**
    RT   **Cathedrals**

Abbreviations   **411**
    UF   Contractions
    BT   **Writing**
    NT   **Acronyms**
          Code names
    RT   **Ciphers**
          Shorthand
          Signs and symbols

ABCs
    USE   **Alphabet**

Abdominal exercises   **613.7**
    UF   Stomach exercises
    BT   **Exercise**

Abduction
    USE   **Kidnapping**

Abduction of humans by aliens
    USE   **Alien abduction**

Abilities
    USE   **Ability**

Ability   **153.9**
    UF   Abilities
          Aptitude
          Skill
          Skills
          Talent
          Talents
    SA   types of ability [to be added as needed]
    NT   **Creative ability**
          Executive ability
          Leadership
          Mathematical ability
          Musical ability
    RT   **Success**

Ability grouping in education (May
subdiv. geog.)   **371.2**
UF   Grouping by ability
BT   **Education**
Educational psychology
**Grading and marking (Educa-
tion)**
NT   **Nongraded schools**
Ability—Testing (May subdiv. geog.)
153.9; 371.26
UF   Aptitude testing
BT   **Educational tests and measure-
ments**
Intelligence tests
Psychological tests
ABMs
USE   **Antimissile missiles**
Abnormal children
USE   **Exceptional children**
Handicapped children
Abnormal growth
USE   **Growth disorders**
Abnormal psychology   **616.89**

Use for systematic descriptions of mental
disorders. Materials on clinical aspects of
mental disorders, including therapy, are entered under **Psychiatry**. Popular materials and
materials on regional or social aspects of
mental disorders are entered under **Mental illness**.

UF   Mental diseases
Pathological psychology
Psychology, Pathological
Psychopathology
Psychopathy
BT   **Mind and body**
Nervous system
NT   **Affective disorders**
Attention deficit disorder
Codependency
Compulsive behavior
Depression (Psychology)
Eating disorders
Hallucinations and illusions
Mental illness
Mental retardation
Multiple personality
Neuroses
Panic disorders
Personality disorders
Psychosomatic medicine
Self-mutilation

RT   **Criminal psychology**
Mental health
Psychiatry
Psychoanalysis
Abnormalities, Human
USE   **Birth defects**
Growth disorders
Abolition of capital punishment
USE   **Capital punishment**
Abolition of slavery
USE   **Abolitionists**
Slavery
Slaves—Emancipation
Abolitionists (May subdiv. geog.)   **326;
920**
UF   Abolition of slavery
Antislavery
BT   **Reformers**
RT   **Slavery**
Slaves—Emancipation
Abominable snowman
USE   **Yeti**
Aboriginal Australians (May subdiv.
geog.)   **305.89**
UF   Australian aborigines
BT   **Australians**
Indigenous peoples
Aborigines
USE   **Indigenous peoples**
Abortion (May subdiv. geog.)   **618.8**
UF   Induced abortion
Termination of pregnancy
Abortion—Ethical aspects   **179.7**
UF   Abortion—Moral and religious
aspects
BT   **Ethics**
RT   **Pro-choice movement**
Pro-life movement
Abortion—Law and legislation (May
subdiv. geog.)   **344; 363.46**
BT   **Law**
Legislation
Abortion—Moral and religious aspects
USE   **Abortion—Ethical aspects**
Abortion—Religious aspects
Abortion—Religious aspects   **205**
May be further subdivided by religion or
sect.
UF   Abortion—Moral and religious
aspects
RT   **Pro-choice movement**
Pro-life movement

Abortion—Religious aspects—Catholic
    Church   241
Abortion rights movement
    USE   **Pro-choice movement**
Abrasives   553.6
    BT   **Ceramics**
Absence from school
    USE   **School attendance**
Absenteeism (Labor)   331.25; 658.3
    UF   Employee absenteeism
          Labor absenteeism
    BT   **Hours of labor**
          Personnel management
    RT   **Employee morale**
Absenteeism (Schools)
    USE   **School attendance**
Abstinence
    USE   **Fasting**
          Temperance
Abstinence, Sexual
    USE   **Sexual abstinence**
Abstract art (May subdiv. geog.)
    709.04; 759.06
    UF   Abstract painting
          Geometric art
          Nonobjective art
    BT   **Art**
Abstract painting
    USE   **Abstract art**
Abuse of animals
    USE   **Animal welfare**
Abuse of children
    USE   **Child abuse**
Abuse of husbands
    USE   **Husband abuse**
Abuse of medications
    USE   **Medication abuse**
Abuse of medicines
    USE   **Medication abuse**
Abuse of persons
    USE   **Offenses against the person**
Abuse of substances
    USE   **Substance abuse**
Abuse of the elderly
    USE   **Elderly abuse**
Abuse of wives
    USE   **Wife abuse**
Abuse, Verbal
    USE   **Invective**
Abused aged
    USE   **Elderly abuse**

Abused children
    USE   **Child abuse**
Abused wives
    USE   **Abused women**
          Wife abuse
Abused women (May subdiv. geog.)
    362.82
    UF   Abused wives
          Battered wives
          Battered women
    BT   **Victims of crimes**
          Women
    RT   **Wife abuse**
Academic achievement (May subdiv.
    geog.)   **370.1; 371.2**
    UF   Academic failure
          Achievement, Academic
          Educational achievement
          Scholastic achievement
          Student achievement
    BT   **Success**
    NT   **Achievement tests**
Academic advising
    USE   **Educational counseling**
Academic degrees (May subdiv. geog.)
    378.2
    UF   College degrees
          Degrees, Academic
          Doctors' degrees
          Honorary degrees
          University degrees
    BT   **Colleges and universities**
Academic dishonesty
    USE   **Cheating (Education)**
Academic dissertations
    USE   **Dissertations**
Academic failure
    USE   **Academic achievement**
Academic freedom (May subdiv. geog.)
    371.1; 378.1
    Use for materials on the freedom of teach-
    ers and students to teach, discuss, or investi-
    gate controversial subjects without penalty or
    restraint from officials, governments, or orga-
    nized groups.
    UF   Educational freedom
          Freedom, Academic
          Freedom of teaching
          Teaching, Freedom of
    BT   **Intellectual freedom**
          Toleration
Academic libraries (May subdiv. geog.)
    027.7

Academic libraries—*Continued*
- UF   College and university libraries
      College libraries
      University libraries
- BT   **Libraries**

Academy Awards (Motion pictures)
791.43
- UF   Oscars (Motion pictures)
- BT   **Motion pictures**

Acadians—Louisiana
- USE   **Cajuns**

Accelerated reading
- USE   **Speed reading**

Access to health care (May subdiv. geog.)
362.1
- UF   Accessibility of health services
      Availability of health services
      Health services accessibility
      Medical care—Access
- BT   **Medical care**

Accessibility of health services
- USE   **Access to health care**

Accident insurance (May subdiv. geog.)
368.38
- UF   Insurance, Accident
- BT   **Casualty insurance**
- NT   **Workers' compensation**

Accidents (May subdiv. geog.)   **363.1**
- UF   Emergencies
      Injuries
      Wrecks
- SA   types of accidents, e.g. **Railroad**
accidents; subjects with the
subdivision *Accidents*, e.g.
Chemical industry—Acci-
dents; **Nuclear power**
plants—Accidents; etc.; and
groups and classes of persons,
animals, organs of the body,
and plants and crops with the
subdivision *Wounds and inju-*
ries, e.g. **Horses—Wounds**
and injuries; **Foot—Wounds**
and injuries [to be added as
needed]
- NT   **Aircraft accidents**
Explosions
Fires
Home accidents
Industrial accidents
Poisons and poisoning
Railroad accidents

Shipwrecks
Space vehicle accidents
Traffic accidents
Wounds and injuries
- RT   **Disasters**
First aid

Accidents—Prevention (May subdiv.
geog.)   **363.1; 658.3**
- UF   Prevention of accidents
      Safety measures
- SA   subjects with the subdivision
Safety devices or *Safety mea-*
sures, e.g. **Railroads—Safety**
devices; **Radiation—Safety**
measures; etc. [to be added
as needed]
- NT   **Aeronautics—Safety measures**
Radiation—Safety measures
Railroads—Safety devices
Safety education
Safety regulations
Water safety
- RT   **Safety devices**

Acclimatization
- USE   **Adaptation (Biology)**
Environmental influence on
humans

Accompaniment, Musical
- USE   **Musical accompaniment**

Accountability
- USE   **Liability (Law)**
Responsibility

Accountants (May subdiv. geog.)
657.092; 920
- UF   Bookkeepers
      Certified public accountants
- RT   **Accounting**

Accounting (May subdiv. geog.)   **657**
- UF   Financial accounting
- SA   types of industries, professions,
and organizations with the
subdivision *Accounting* [to be
added as needed]
- BT   **Business**
Business education
Business mathematics
- NT   **Corporations—Accounting**
Cost accounting
- RT   **Accountants**
Auditing
Bookkeeping

Accounting machines
USE **Calculators**
Accounts, Collecting of
USE **Collecting of accounts**
Accreditation
USE types of hospitals and service institutions, types of educational institutions, and names of individual institutions with the subdivision *Accreditation*, e.g. **Colleges and universities—Accreditation**; and subjects with the subdivision *Study and teaching*, for accreditation of programs of study in those subjects, e.g. **Mathematics—Study and teaching** [to be added as needed]
Accreditation (Education)
USE **Schools—Accreditation**
Acculturation (May subdiv. geog.) **303.48**
UF Culture contact
BT **Anthropology**
Civilization
Culture
Ethnology
NT **Ethnic relations**
Multicultural education
Race relations
Socialization
RT **East and West**
Achievement, Academic
USE **Academic achievement**
Achievement motivation 153.8
UF Performance motivation
BT **Educational psychology**
Motivation (Psychology)
Performance
Achievement tests (May subdiv. geog.) **371.26**
UF Scholastic achievement tests
School achievement tests
BT **Academic achievement**
Educational tests and measurements
Acid (Drug)
USE **LSD (Drug)**
Acid precipitation
USE **Acid rain**

Acid rain (May subdiv. geog.) **363.738; 628.5**
UF Acid precipitation
BT **Rain**
Water pollution
Acids 546; 661
SA types of acids [to be added as needed]
BT **Chemicals**
Chemistry
NT **Carbolic acid**
Acne 616.5
UF Blackheads (Acne)
Pimples (Acne)
BT **Skin—Diseases**
ACOAs
USE **Adult children of alcoholics**
Acoustics
USE **Architectural acoustics**
Hearing
Music—Acoustics and physics
Sound
Acquaintance rape
USE **Date rape**
Acquired immune deficiency syndrome
USE **AIDS (Disease)**
Acquisitions, Corporate
USE **Corporate mergers and acquisitions**
Acquisitions (Libraries)
USE **Libraries—Acquisitions**
Acrobats and acrobatics (May subdiv. geog.) **791.3; 796.47**
SA types of acrobatic activities, e.g. **Tumbling** [to be added as needed]
BT **Circus**
NT **Tumbling**
RT **Gymnastics**
Acronyms 411
UF English language—Acronyms
Initialisms
BT **Abbreviations**
Code names
Acrylic painting 751.4
BT **Painting**
Acting (May subdiv. geog.) **791.4; 792**
Use for materials on the art and technique of acting in any medium (stage, television, etc.) and on acting as a profession. Materials limited to the presentation of plays are entered under **Amateur theater** or **Theater—Production and direction**.

5

Acting—*Continued*
    UF   Dramatic art
            Stage
    BT   **Drama**
            Public speaking
    NT   **Commedia dell'arte**
            Mime
            Pageants
            Pantomimes
    RT   **Actors**
            Amateur theater
            Drama in education
            Theater
Acting—Costume
    USE   **Costume**
Actions and defenses
    USE   **Litigation**
Activities curriculum
    USE   **Creative activities**
Activity schools
    USE   **Education—Experimental
            methods**
Actors (May subdiv. geog.)   **791.4; 792;
    920**

    Use for materials on several persons of the acting profession, whether male or female. Materials on several female actors that emphasize their identity as women are entered under **Actresses**. Materials on several male actors that emphasize their identity as men are entered under **Male actors**.

    UF   Actors and actresses
            Motion picture actors and ac-
               tresses
            Television actors
    SA   names of individual actors [to
            be added as needed]
    BT   **Entertainers**
    NT   **Actors—United States**
            Actresses
            African American actors
            Black actors
            Child actors
            Comedians
            Male actors
            Stunt performers
    RT   **Acting**
Actors and actresses
    USE   **Actors**
Actors, Black
    USE   **Black actors**
Actors—United States   **791.4; 792; 920**

    UF   American actors
            American actors and actresses
    BT   **Actors**
Actresses (May subdiv. geog.)   **791.4;
    792; 920**

    Use for materials on several female actors that emphasize their identity as women. General materials on persons of the acting profession, whether male or female, are entered under **Actors**.

    UF   Female actors
            Women actors
    BT   **Actors**
Acupressure   **615.8**
    UF   Finger pressure therapy
            Myotherapy
    BT   **Alternative medicine**
            Massage
Acupuncture   **615.8**
    BT   **Alternative medicine**
Adages
    USE   **Proverbs**
Adaptability (Psychology)
    USE   **Adjustment (Psychology)**
Adaptation (Biology)   **578.4; 581.4;
    591.4**
    UF   Acclimatization
    BT   **Biology**
            Ecology
            Genetics
            Variation (Biology)
    NT   **Environmental influence on
            humans**
            Stress (Physiology)
Adaptation (Psychology)
    USE   **Adjustment (Psychology)**
Adaptations
    USE   **Film adaptations
            Television adaptations**
            and names of authors, titles of
            anonymous literary works,
            types of literature, and types
            of musical compositions with
            the subdivision *Adaptations*,
            for individual works, collec-
            tions, or criticism and inter-
            pretation of literary, cinemat-
            ic, video, or television adapta-
            tions, e.g., **Shakespeare, Wil-
            liam, 1564-1616—Adapta-
            tions; Beowulf—Adaptations;
            Arthurian romances—Adap-**

Adaptations—*Continued*
   tations; etc. [to be added as needed]
ADD (Child behavior disorder)
 USE **Attention deficit disorder**
Addiction
 USE types of addiction, e.g. **Alcoholism**; **Drug abuse**; **Exercise addiction**; etc. [to be added as needed]
Addiction to alcohol
 USE **Alcoholism**
Addiction to drugs
 USE **Drug abuse**
Addiction to exercise
 USE **Exercise addiction**
Addiction to gambling
 USE **Compulsive gambling**
Addiction to nicotine
 USE **Tobacco habit**
Addiction to tobacco
 USE **Tobacco habit**
Addiction to work
 USE **Workaholism**
Addictive behavior
 USE **Compulsive behavior**
Addicts
 USE **Drug addicts**
Adding machines
 USE **Calculators**
Addition **513.2**
 BT **Arithmetic**
Additives, Food
 USE **Food additives**
Addresses
 USE **Lectures and lecturing**
   Speeches
Adhesives **620.1; 668; 691**
 SA types of adhesives [to be added as needed]
 BT **Materials**
 NT **Cement**
   Glue
   Mortar
Adjustment (Psychology) **155.2**
 UF Adaptability (Psychology)
   Adaptation (Psychology)
   Coping behavior
   Maladjustment (Psychology)
 BT **Psychology**
Adjustment, Social
 USE **Social adjustment**

Administration
 USE **Civil service**
   Management
   Public administration
   and types of institutions in the sphere of health, education, and social services, and names of individual institutions with the subdivision *Administration,* e.g. **Libraries—Administration; Schools—Administration;** etc.; types of management, e.g. **Office management;** types of industries, types of industrial plants and processes, and names of individual corporate bodies, with the subdivision *Management,* e.g. **Information systems—Management;** and names of countries, cities, etc., with the subdivision *Politics and government,* e.g. **United States—Politics and government** [to be added as needed]
Administration of criminal justice (May subdiv. geog.) **353.4**
 UF Criminal justice, Administration of
 BT **Administration of justice**
   Criminal law
 NT **Amnesty**
   Clemency
   Corrections
   Crime
   Law enforcement
   Pardon
   Parole
   Police
   Prisons
   Punishment
Administration of justice (May subdiv. geog.) **347; 353.4**
 UF Justice, Administration of
 BT **Law**
 NT **Administration of criminal justice**
   Due process of law
   Governmental investigations
   Impeachments
 RT **Courts**

Administrative ability
  USE **Executive ability**
Administrative agencies (May subdiv.
  geog.) **351**
  Use for materials on governmental bodies,
  such as boards, commissions, departments,
  etc., responsible for implementing and admin-
  istering legislation.
  UF Administrative agencies—Law
       and legislation
     Executive agencies
     Government agencies
     Regulatory agencies
  SA names of administrative agencies
       [to be added as needed]
  BT **Administrative law**
     Public administration
  NT **Executive departments**
Administrative agencies—Law and legisla-
  tion
  USE **Administrative agencies**
Administrative agencies—Reorganization
  (May subdiv. geog.) **351**
  UF Executive departments—Reorga-
       nization
     Executive reorganization
     Government reorganization
     Reorganization of administrative
       agencies
**Administrative agencies—Reorganiza-
  tion—Ohio 352.2**
  UF Ohio—Executive departments—
       Reorganization
**Administrative agencies—Reorganiza-
  tion—United States 352.2**
  UF United States—Executive depart-
       ments—Reorganization
Administrative law (May subdiv. geog.)
  342
  BT **Law**
  NT **Administrative agencies**
     Civil service
     Local government
     Ombudsman
  RT **Constitutional law**
     Public administration
Administrators and executors
  USE **Executors and administrators**
Admirals (May subdiv. geog.) **359.0092;
  920**
  BT **Military personnel**
     Navies

Admissions applications
  USE **College applications**
Admissions essays
  USE **College applications**
Adolescence 155.5; 305.235
  Use for materials on the process or the state
  of growing to maturity. Materials on the time
  of life between thirteen and twenty-five years,
  and on people in this general age range, are
  entered under **Youth**. Materials limited to teen
  youth are entered under **Teenagers**. Materials
  limited to people in the general age range of
  eighteen through twenty-five years are entered
  under **Young men** or **Young women**.
  UF Teen age
     Teenagers—Development
  BT **Age**
  RT **Puberty**
     Youth
Adolescence—Psychology
  USE **Adolescent psychology**
Adolescent fathers
  USE **Teenage fathers**
Adolescent mothers
  USE **Teenage mothers**
Adolescent pregnancy
  USE **Teenage pregnancy**
Adolescent prostitution
  USE **Juvenile prostitution**
Adolescent psychiatry 616.89
  UF Teenagers—Psychiatry
  BT **Psychiatry**
Adolescent psychology 155.5
  UF Adolescence—Psychology
     Behavior of teenagers
     Teenage behavior
     Teenagers—Psychology
  BT **Psychology**
Adolescents
  USE **Teenagers**
Adopted children (May subdiv. geog.)
  306.87; 362.82
  BT **Adoptees**
     Children
  RT **Adoption**
     Orphans
Adoptees 346.01; 362.73
  Use for materials on anyone formally adopt-
  ed as a dependent.
  UF Adult adoptees
  NT **Adopted children**
  RT **Adoption**
     Birthparents

Adoption (May subdiv. geog.) **346.01; 362.734**
    UF   Child placing
          Children—Adoption
          Children—Placing out
    BT   **Parent-child relationship**
    NT   **International adoption**
          Interracial adoption
    RT   **Adopted children**
          Adoptees
          Foster home care
Adoption—Corrupt practices **364.1**
    UF   Black market children
          Sale of infants
          Selling of infants
    BT   **Criminal law**
Adult adoptees
    USE **Adoptees**
Adult child abuse victims **362.76**
    UF   Adult survivors of child abuse
          Adults abused as children
          Child abuse survivors
          Grown-up abused children
    BT   **Victims of crimes**
    NT   **Adult child sexual abuse victims**
    RT   **Child abuse**
Adult child sexual abuse victims **362.76**
    UF   Adult survivors of child sexual abuse
          Adults sexually abused as children
    BT   **Adult child abuse victims**
    RT   **Child sexual abuse**
Adult children of alcoholics **362.292**
    UF   ACOAs
          Alcoholic parents
    BT   **Children of alcoholics**
    RT   **Alcoholics**
Adult education (May subdiv. geog.) **374**
    UF   Education of adults
          Lifelong education
    BT   **Education**
          Higher education
          Secondary education
          University extension
    NT   **Agricultural extension work**
          Prisoners—Education

    RT   **Continuing education**
          Evening and continuation schools
Adult fiction
    USE **Erotic fiction**
Adult films
    USE **Erotic films**
Adult survivors of child abuse
    USE **Adult child abuse victims**
Adult survivors of child sexual abuse
    USE **Adult child sexual abuse victims**
Adulteration of food
    USE **Food adulteration and inspection**
Adultery **176; 306.73; 363.4**
    UF   Extramarital relationships
          Marital infidelity
    BT   **Sexual ethics**
Adults (May subdiv. geog.) **305.26**
    UF   Grown-ups
          Grownups
    BT   **Age**
Adults abused as children
    USE **Adult child abuse victims**
Adults and children
    USE **Child-adult relationship**
Adults sexually abused as children
    USE **Adult child sexual abuse victims**
Advent **263**
    BT   **Church year**
          Religious holidays
Adventure and adventurers (May subdiv. geog.) **904; 904.092; 910.4; 920**
    NT   **Escapes**
          Exploration
          Explorers
          Frontier and pioneer life
          Heroes and heroines
          Safaris
          Sea stories
          Seafaring life
          Shipwrecks
    RT   **Voyages and travels**
Adventure and adventurers—Fiction
    USE **Adventure fiction**
Adventure fiction **808.3; 808.83**
    Use for individual works, collections, or materials about adventure fiction.
    UF   Adventure and adventurers—Fiction

Adventure fiction—*Continued*
>> Adventure stories
>> Suspense novels
>> Swashbucklers
>> Thrillers
> BT **Fiction**
> NT **Robinsonades**
>> **Romantic suspense novels**
>> **Science fiction**
>> **Sea stories**
>> **Spy stories**
>> **Western stories**

Adventure films   791.43
> Use for individual works, collections, or materials about adventure films.
> UF   Suspense films
>> Swashbucklers
>> Thrillers
> BT   **Motion pictures**
> NT   **Superhero films**
>> **Western films**
> RT   **Adventure television programs**

Adventure graphic novels   741.5
> Use for individual works, collections, or materials about adventure graphic novels.
> BT   **Graphic novels**

Adventure radio programs   791.44
> Use for individual works, collections, or materials about adventure radio programs.
> BT   **Radio programs**
> NT   **Superhero radio programs**

Adventure stories
> USE   **Adventure fiction**

Adventure television programs   791.45
> Use for individual works, collections, or materials about adventure television programs.
> BT   **Television programs**
> NT   **Superhero television programs**
> RT   **Adventure films**

Adventure travel (May subdiv. geog.)
904
> Use for materials on travel to remote and sometimes dangerous places without normal tourist amenities.
> BT   **Travel**
>> **Voyages and travels**

Advertisement writing
> USE   **Advertising copy**

Advertising (May subdiv. geog.)   **659.1**
> May be subdivided by topic, e.g. **Advertising—Cosmetics**; to specify the thing advertised.
> BT   **Business**
>> **Retail trade**

> NT   **Advertising and children**
>> **Advertising copy**
>> **Advertising layout and typography**
>> **Commercial art**
>> **Commercial catalogs**
>> **Coupons (Retail trade)**
>> **Deceptive advertising**
>> **Electric signs**
>> **Fashion models**
>> **Market surveys**
>> **Newspaper advertising**
>> **Packaging**
>> **Posters**
>> **Printing—Specimens**
>> **Radio advertising**
>> **Show windows**
>> **Sign painting**
>> **Signs and signboards**
>> **Television advertising**
> RT   **Marketing**
>> **Propaganda**
>> **Public relations**
>> **Publicity**
>> **Selling**

Advertising and children (May subdiv. geog.)   **659.1**
> UF   Children and advertising
> BT   **Advertising**
>> **Children**

Advertising art
> USE   **Commercial art**

Advertising copy   659.13
> UF   Advertisement writing
>> Copy writing
> BT   **Advertising**
>> **Authorship**

Advertising—Cosmetics   659.1
> UF   Cosmetics—Advertising

Advertising layout and typography
659.13
> BT   **Advertising**
>> **Printing**
>> **Typography**

Advertising, Newspaper
> USE   **Newspaper advertising**

Advertising—Newspapers (May subdiv. geog.)   **659.1**
> Use for materials on the advertising of newspapers. Materials on advertising in newspapers are entered under **Newspaper advertising**.

Advertising—Newspapers—*Continued*
    UF   Newspapers—Advertising
Advice columns (May subdiv. geog.)
    070.4
    BT   **Counseling**
         **Newspapers—Sections, col-
           umns, etc.**
Advisors
    USE **Consultants**
Aerial bombs
    USE **Bombs**
Aerial navigation
    USE **Navigation (Aeronautics)**
Aerial operations
    USE names of wars with the subdivi-
          sion *Aerial operations,* e.g.
          **World War, 1939-1945—Ae-
          rial operations** [to be added
          as needed]
Aerial photography   778.3
    BT   **Photography**
    NT   **Remote sensing**
Aerial propellers   629.134
    UF   Airplanes—Propellers
         Propellers, Aerial
    BT   **Airplanes**
Aerial reconnaissance (May subdiv. geog.)
    355.4; 358.4
    UF   Reconnaissance, Aerial
    BT   **Military aeronautics**
         Remote sensing
Aerial rockets
    USE **Rockets (Aeronautics)**
Aerial spraying and dusting
    USE **Aeronautics in agriculture**
Aerobatics
    USE **Stunt flying**
Aerobic dancing
    USE **Aerobics**
Aerobic exercises
    USE **Aerobics**
Aerobics   613.7
    UF   Aerobic dancing
         Aerobic exercises
    BT   **Exercise**
    NT   **Walking**
    RT   **Dance**
Aerobiology
    USE **Air—Microbiology**
Aerodromes
    USE **Airports**
Aerodynamics   533; 629.132

    UF   Streamlining
    BT   **Air**
         Dynamics
         Pneumatics
    NT   **Supersonic aerodynamics**
    RT   **Aeronautics**
Aerodynamics, Supersonic
    USE **Supersonic aerodynamics**
Aeronautical instruments   629.135
    UF   Airplanes—Instruments
         Instruments, Aeronautical
    SA   types of instruments, e.g. **Gyro-
         scope** [to be added as need-
         ed]
    BT   **Scientific apparatus and in-
         struments**
    NT   **Airplanes—Electric equipment**
         Gyroscope
         Instrument flying
Aeronautical sports (May subdiv. geog.)
    797.5
    SA   types of aeronautical sports [to
         be added as needed]
    BT   **Aeronautics**
         Sports
    NT   **Airplane racing**
         Skydiving
Aeronautics (May subdiv. geog.)   **629.13**
    Use for materials dealing collectively with
various types of aircraft and for materials on
the scientific or technical aspects of aircraft
and their construction and operation. Materials
on companies engaged in commercial aviation
are entered under **Airlines.**
    UF   Air routes
         Airways
         Aviation
    SA   aeronautics in particular indus-
         tries or fields of endeavor,
           e.g. **Aeronautics in agricul-
           ture** [to be added as needed]
    BT   **Engineering**
         Locomotion
    NT   **Aeronautical sports**
         Aeronautics and civilization
         Aeronautics in agriculture
         Aerospace engineering
         Air pilots
         Airplanes
         Airports
         Airships
         Astronautics
         Balloons

Aeronautics—*Continued*

      Gliders (Aeronautics)
      Gliding and soaring
      Helicopters
      High speed aeronautics
      Kites
      Lasers in aeronautics
      Meteorology in aeronautics
      Military aeronautics
      Navigation (Aeronautics)
      Parachutes
      Radio in aeronautics
      Rocketry
      Rockets (Aeronautics)
      Unidentified flying objects
 RT Aerodynamics
      Flight

Aeronautics—Accidents
 USE Aircraft accidents

Aeronautics and civilization (May subdiv. geog.) **306**
 UF Civilization and aeronautics
 BT Aeronautics
      Civilization
 NT Astronautics and civilization

Aeronautics, Commercial
 USE Commercial aeronautics

Aeronautics—Flights (May subdiv. geog.) **387.7; 629.13**
 UF Aeronautics—Voyages
      Flights around the world
      Transatlantic flights
 BT Voyages and travels
 NT Space flight

Aeronautics in agriculture (May subdiv. geog.) **631.3**
 UF Aerial spraying and dusting
      Airplanes in agriculture
      Crop dusting
      Crop spraying
 BT Aeronautics
      Agriculture
      Spraying and dusting
 RT Agricultural pests

Aeronautics—Medical aspects
 USE Aviation medicine

Aeronautics, Military
 USE Military aeronautics

Aeronautics—Navigation
 USE Navigation (Aeronautics)

Aeronautics—Piloting
 USE Airplanes—Piloting

Aeronautics—Safety measures (May subdiv. geog.) **387.7; 629.134**
 BT Accidents—Prevention
 NT Air traffic control

Aeronautics—Study and teaching
      629.1307
 UF Flight training
 NT Airplanes—Piloting

Aeronautics—Voyages
 USE Aeronautics—Flights

Aeroplanes
 USE Airplanes

Aerosol sniffing
 USE Solvent abuse

Aerosols **541; 551.51; 660**
 BT Air pollution

Aerospace engineering **629.1**
 BT Aeronautics
      Astronautics
      Engineering

Aerospace industries
 USE Aerospace industry

Aerospace industry (May subdiv. geog.)
      338.4
 UF Aerospace industries
      Aircraft production
 BT Industries
 NT Airplane industry

Aerospace law
 USE Space law

Aerospace medicine
 USE Aviation medicine
      Space medicine

Aerothermodynamics **629.132; 629.4**
 UF Thermoaerodynamics
 BT Astronautics
      High speed aeronautics
      Supersonic aerodynamics
      Thermodynamics

Aesthetics **111; 701; 801**
 UF Beauty
      Esthetics
      Taste (Aesthetics)
 SA styles and movements in the arts, e.g. **Classicism**; **Postmodernism**; etc., and aesthetics of particular countries, e.g. **Japanese aesthetics** [to be added as needed]
 BT Philosophy

Aesthetics—*Continued*
  NT **Art appreciation**
      Avant-garde (Aesthetics)
      Classicism
      Color
      Criticism
      Japanese aesthetics
      Kitsch
      Modernism (Aesthetics)
      Postmodernism
      Rhythm
      Romanticism
      Values
  RT **Arts**
Aesthetics, Japanese
  USE **Japanese aesthetics**
Affection
  USE **Friendship**
       Love
Affective disorders   616.85
  UF Mood disorders
  BT **Abnormal psychology**
  NT **Depression (Psychology)**
      Manic-depressive illness
Affirmations   158.1
  BT **Self-help techniques**
Affirmative action programs (May
      subdiv. geog.)   **331.13; 658.3**
  UF Equal employment opportunity
      Equal opportunity in employ-
        ment
  BT **Discrimination in employment**
      Personnel management
Affliction
  USE **Joy and sorrow**
       Suffering
Affluent people
  USE **Rich**
Affordable housing
  USE **Housing**
Afghanistan   958.1
    May be subdivided like United States ex-
  cept for History.
Africa   960
  NT **Central Africa**
      East Africa
      North Africa
      Northeast Africa
      Northwest Africa
      South Africa
      Southern Africa
      Sub-Saharan Africa

      West Africa
  RT **Africans**
Africa, Central
  USE **Central Africa**
Africa—Civilization   306.096; 960
  UF African civilization
  BT **Civilization**
Africa, East
  USE **East Africa**
Africa, Eastern
  USE **East Africa**
Africa, French-speaking Equatorial
  USE **French-speaking Equatorial Af-
         rica**
Africa, French-speaking West
  USE **French-speaking West Africa**
Africa—History   960
Africa—History—1960-   960.3
Africa, North
  USE **North Africa**
Africa, Northeast
  USE **Northeast Africa**
Africa, Northwest
  USE **Northwest Africa**
Africa—Politics and government   320.96
  NT **Pan-Africanism**
Africa, Southern
  USE **Southern Africa**
Africa—Study and teaching   960.07
  UF African studies
  BT **Area studies**
Africa, Sub-Saharan
  USE **Sub-Saharan Africa**
Africa, West
  USE **West Africa**
African American actors (May subdiv.
      geog.)   **791.4; 792; 920**
  UF African American actors and ac-
        tresses
      Afro-American actors
  BT **Actors**
      Black actors
African American actors and actresses
  USE **African American actors**
African American art (May subdiv.
      geog.)   **704**
    Use for materials on works of art by several
  African American artists. Materials on African
  Americans depicted in works of art are en-
  tered under **African Americans in art**.
  UF Afro-American art

African American art—*Continued*
  BT   **Art**
       Black art
  NT   **Harlem Renaissance**
  RT   **African American artists**
African American artists (May subdiv.
    geog.)   **709.2; 920**
    Use for materials on several African Americans artists.
  UF   Afro-American artists
  BT   **Artists**
       Black artists
  RT   **African American art**
African American athletes (May subdiv.
    geog.)   **796.092; 920**
  UF   Afro-American athletes
  BT   **Athletes**
       Black athletes
African American authors **810.9; 920**
    Use for materials on several African American authors.
  UF   Afro-American authors
  SA   genres of American literature
       with the subdivision *African*
       American authors, e.g. **Amer-**
       ican poetry—African Ameri-
       can authors; etc. [to be add-
       ed as needed]
  BT   **American authors**
       Black authors
African American baseball players (May
    subdiv. geog.)   **796.357; 920**
  UF   Afro-American baseball players
  BT   **Baseball players**
African American business people
  USE **African American**
        businesspeople
African American businesspeople (May
    subdiv. geog.)   **338.092; 658.0092;**
    920
  UF   African American business peo-
       ple
       Afro-American businesspeople
  BT   **Black businesspeople**
       Businesspeople
African American children (May subdiv.
    geog.)   **305.23**
  UF   Afro-American children
  BT   **Black children**
       Children
African American dancers (May subdiv.
    geog.)   **792.8092; 793.3092; 920**

  BT   **African Americans**
       Dancers
African American educators (May subdiv.
    geog.)   **370.92; 920**
  BT   **African Americans**
       Educators
African American elderly (May subdiv.
    geog.)   **305.26**
  BT   **Elderly**
African American folklore
  USE **African Americans—Folklore**
African American History Month
  USE **Black History Month**
African American inventors (May subdiv.
    geog.)   **609.2; 920**
  BT   **African Americans**
       Inventors
African American librarians (May
    subdiv. geog.)   **020.92; 920**
  UF   Afro-American librarians
  BT   **Black librarians**
       Librarians
African American literature
  USE **American literature—African**
        American authors
African American men (May subdiv.
    geog.)   **305.38**
  UF   Afro-American men
  BT   **Men**
African American music (May subdiv.
    geog.)   **780.089**
    Use for materials on the music of African Americans. Materials on the music of Blacks not limited to the United States are entered under **Black music**.
  UF   African American songs
       Afro-Americans—Music
       Songs, African American
  BT   **Black music**
       Music
  NT   **Blues music**
       Gospel music
       Harlem Renaissance
       Rap music
  RT   **African American musicians**
       Spirituals (Songs)
African American musicians (May
    subdiv. geog.)   **780.92; 920**
  UF   Afro-American musicians
  BT   **Black musicians**
       Musicians
  RT   **African American music**

African American poetry
> USE **American poetry—African American authors**

African American singers (May subdiv. geog.) **782.0092; 920**
> BT **African Americans**
> **Singers**

African American songs
> USE **African American music**

African American suffrage
> USE **African Americans—Suffrage**

African American women (May subdiv. geog.) **305.48**
> UF Afro-American women
> BT **Black women**
> **Women**

African American youth (May subdiv. geog.) **305.235**
> BT **Youth**

African Americans (May subdiv. geog. by cities, states, or regions of the U.S.) **305.896; 973**

Use for materials dealing collectively with Blacks in the United States. General materials and materials on Blacks in places other than the United States are entered under **Blacks**.

> UF Afro-Americans
> Black Americans
> Blacks—United States
> Negroes
> SA African Americans in various occupations and professions, e.g. **African American artists**; **African American librarians**; etc. [to be added as needed]
> BT **Blacks**
> NT **African American dancers**
> **African American educators**
> **African American inventors**
> **African American singers**
> **Libraries and African Americans**
> **World War, 1939-1945—African Americans**

African Americans and libraries
> USE **Libraries and African Americans**

African Americans—Biography **920**
> BT **Blacks—Biography**

African Americans—Chicago (Ill.)
> **305.896; 977.3**

African Americans—Civil rights (May subdiv. geog.) **323.1196; 342**
> BT **Blacks—Civil rights**
> **Civil rights**
> NT **African Americans—Suffrage**

African Americans—Economic conditions (May subdiv. geog.) **330.973**
> BT **Blacks—Economic conditions**
> **Economic conditions**

African Americans—Education (May subdiv. geog.) **370.89; 371.829**
> BT **Blacks—Education**
> **Education**

African Americans—Employment (May subdiv. geog.) **331.6**
> BT **Blacks—Employment**
> **Employment**

African Americans—Folklore (May subdiv. geog.) **398**
> UF African American folklore
> BT **Blacks—Folklore**
> **Folklore**

African Americans—Housing (May subdiv. geog.) **307.3; 363.5**
> BT **Blacks—Housing**
> **Housing**

African Americans in art **704.9**

Use for materials on African Americans depicted in works of art. Materials on the attainments of several African Americans in the area of art are entered under **African American artists**. Materials on works of art by several African American artists are entered under **African American art**.

> UF Afro-Americans in art
> BT **Art—Themes**

African Americans in literature **809**

Use for materials on the theme of African Americans in works of literature. Materials on several African American authors are entered under **African American authors**. Materials on works of literature by several African American authors are entered under **American literature—African American authors** and the various forms of American literature with the subdivision *African American authors*, e.g. **American poetry—African American authors**.

> UF Afro-Americans in literature
> BT **Literature—Themes**

African Americans in motion pictures **791.43**

Use for materials on the depiction of African Americans in motion pictures. Materials on several African American actors are entered under African American actors. Materi-

African Americans in motion pictures— *Continued*

als discussing all aspects of African Americans' involvement in motion pictures are entered under African Americans in the motion picture industry.

BT **Blacks in motion pictures**
Minorities in motion pictures
Motion pictures

African Americans in television

USE **African Americans on television**

African Americans in television broadcasting (May subdiv. geog.)
791.45; 384.55

Use for materials on all aspects of African Americans' involvement in the television industry. Materials on the portrayal of African Americans in television programs are entered under **African Americans on television**.

UF African Americans in the television industry

Afro-Americans in television broadcasting

BT **Television broadcasting**

African Americans in the motion picture industry (May subdiv. geog.)
791.43092

Use for materials on all aspects of African Americans' involvement in motion pictures. Materials on the depiction of African Americans in motion pictures are entered under African Americans in motion pictures.

BT **Blacks in the motion picture industry**
Minorities in the motion picture industry
Motion picture industry

African Americans in the television industry

USE **African Americans in television broadcasting**

African Americans—Intellectual life (May subdiv. geog.) **305.896**

BT **Blacks—Intellectual life**
Intellectual life

African Americans—Ohio **305.896; 977.1**

African Americans on television **791.45**

Use for materials on the portrayal of African Americans in television programs. Materials on all aspects of African Americans' involvement in the television industry are entered under **African Americans in television broadcasting**.

UF African Americans in television
Afro-Americans on television

BT **Television**

African Americans—Political activity (May subdiv. geog.) **322.4; 324**

BT **Blacks—Political activity**
Political participation

NT **Black nationalism**
Black power

African Americans—Race identity
305.896

BT **Blacks—Race identity**
Race awareness

NT **Black nationalism**

African Americans—Religion **270.089; 299.6**

BT **Blacks—Religion**
Religion

NT **Black Muslims**

African Americans—Segregation (May subdiv. geog.) **305.896**

BT **Blacks—Segregation**
Segregation

African Americans—Social conditions (May subdiv. geog.) **305.896**

BT **Blacks—Social conditions**
Social conditions

African Americans—Social life and customs (May subdiv. geog.)
305.896

BT **Blacks—Social life and customs**
Manners and customs

African Americans—Southern States
305.896; 975

UF Southern States—African Americans

African Americans—Suffrage (May subdiv. geog.) **324.6**

UF African American suffrage

BT **African Americans—Civil rights**
Blacks—Suffrage
Suffrage

African art (May subdiv. geog.) **709.6**

BT **Art**

African civilization

USE **Africa—Civilization**

African diaspora **304.8096**

UF Black diaspora
Diaspora, African

BT **Human geography**

African literature **896**

African literature—*Continued*
  BT **Literature**
African literature (English) 820
  BT **Literature**
African music 780.96
  BT **Music**
African mythology 398.2096
  BT **Mythology**
African peoples
  USE **Africans**
African relations
  USE **Pan-Africanism**
African songs 782.42096
  UF Songs, African
  BT **Songs**
African studies
  USE **Africa—Study and teaching**
Africans (May subdiv. geog.) **305.896;
    960**
  UF African peoples
  SA names of African peoples, e.g.
      Yoruba (African people) [to
      be added as needed]
  NT **Ashanti (African people)**
      Blacks—Africa
      Masai (African people)
      Tutsi (African people)
      Yoruba (African people)
      Zulu (African people)
  RT **Africa**
Afrikaaners
  USE **Afrikaners**
Afrikaners (May subdiv. geog.) **305.83;
    968**
  UF Afrikaaners
      Boers
      South African Dutch
      South Africans, Afrikaans-
        speaking
Afro-American actors
  USE **African American actors**
Afro-American art
  USE **African American art**
Afro-American artists
  USE **African American artists**
Afro-American athletes
  USE **African American athletes**
Afro-American authors
  USE **African American authors**
Afro-American baseball players
  USE **African American baseball
      players**

Afro-American businesspeople
  USE **African American
      businesspeople**
Afro-American children
  USE **African American children**
Afro-American librarians
  USE **African American librarians**
Afro-American men
  USE **African American men**
Afro-American musicians
  USE **African American musicians**
Afro-American women
  USE **African American women**
Afro-Americans
  USE **African Americans**
Afro-Americans and libraries
  USE **Libraries and African Ameri-
      cans**
Afro-Americans in art
  USE **African Americans in art**
Afro-Americans in literature
  USE **African Americans in litera-
      ture**
Afro-Americans in television broadcasting
  USE **African Americans in television
      broadcasting**
Afro-Americans—Music
  USE **African American music**
Afro-Americans on television
  USE **African Americans on televi-
      sion**
After dinner speeches 808.5; 808.85
  BT **Speeches**
  RT **Toasts**
After school day care
  USE **After school programs**
After school programs 362.71; 372.12
  UF After school day care
  BT **Student activities**
Afterlife
  USE **Future life**
Afternoon teas 641.5
  UF Teas
  BT **Cooking**
  RT **Entertaining
      Tea**
Age 305.2
  UF Age groups
  SA types of animals, plants, and
      crops with the subdivision
      Age [to be added as needed]

Age—*Continued*
    NT   **Adolescence**
          Adults
          Age and employment
          Aging
          Children
          Drinking age
          Elderly
          Life expectancy
          Longevity
          Middle age
          Middle aged persons
          Old age
          Teenagers
          Youth

Age and employment (May subdiv. geog.)
        331.3
    UF   Employment and age
    BT   **Age**
          Employment
    NT   **Career changes**
          Child labor
          Teenagers—Employment
          Youth—Employment

Age discrimination (May subdiv. geog.)
        305.2
    BT   **Discrimination**

Age groups
    USE   **Age**

Age—Physiological effect
    USE   **Aging**

Aged
    USE   **Elderly**

Aged men
    USE   **Elderly men**

Aged parents
    USE   **Aging parents**

Aged—Pensions
    USE   **Old age pensions**

Aged women
    USE   **Elderly women**

Ageing
    USE   **Aging**

Agent Orange (May subdiv. geog.)
        363.17; 615.9
    BT   **Herbicides**

Aggregates
    USE   **Set theory**

Aggressive behavior
    USE   **Aggressiveness (Psychology)**

Aggressiveness (Psychology)   **152.4;**
        155.2

    UF   Aggressive behavior
    BT   **Human behavior**
          Psychology
    NT   **Assertiveness (Psychology)**
          Bullies
          Teasing
          Violence

Aging   **571.8; 612.6**
    UF   Age—Physiological effect
          Ageing
          Senescence
    SA   types of animals, organs of the
          body, plants, and crops with
          the subdivision *Aging* [to be
          added as needed]
    BT   **Age**
          Elderly
          Gerontology
          Longevity
          Middle age
          Old age
    NT   **Male climacteric**
          Menopause

Aging parents (May subdiv. geog.)
        306.874
    UF   Aged parents
          Elderly parents
    BT   **Elderly**
          Parents

Aging persons
    USE   **Elderly**

Agnosticism   **149; 211**
    BT   **Free thought**
          Religion
    RT   **Atheism**
          Belief and doubt
          Positivism
          Rationalism
          Skepticism

Agoraphobia   **616.85**
    UF   Fear of open spaces
    BT   **Phobias**

Agrarian question
    USE   **Agriculture—Economic aspects**
          Agriculture—Government poli-
          cy
          Land tenure

Agrarian reform
    USE   **Land reform**

Agreements
  USE **Contracts**
       Covenants
Agribusiness
  USE **Agricultural industry**
Agricultural bacteriology 630.2
  UF Bacteriology, Agricultural
      Diseases and pests
  SA types of crops, plants, trees, etc.,
      with the subdivision *Diseases*
      and pests, e.g. **Fruit—Diseas-**
      es and pests [to be added as
      needed]
  BT **Bacteriology**
  RT **Soil microbiology**
Agricultural botany
  USE **Economic botany**
Agricultural chemicals 631.8; 668
  SA types of agricultural chemicals
      and names of individual
      chemicals [to be added as
      needed]
  BT **Agricultural chemistry**
      Chemicals
  NT **Fertilizers**
      Herbicides
      Insecticides
      Pesticides
Agricultural chemistry 630.2
  BT **Chemistry**
  NT **Agricultural chemicals**
  RT **Soils**
Agricultural clubs
  USE **Agriculture—Societies**
Agricultural cooperation
  USE **Cooperative agriculture**
Agricultural credit (May subdiv. geog.)
    332.7
  UF Farm credit
      Farm loans
      Rural credit
  BT **Agriculture—Economic aspects**
      Banks and banking
      Credit
Agricultural economics
  USE **Agriculture—Economic aspects**
Agricultural education
  USE **Agriculture—Study and teach-**
      ing
Agricultural engineering (May subdiv.
    geog.) **630**

  UF Agricultural mechanics
      Farm mechanics
  BT **Engineering**
  NT **Drainage**
      Electricity in agriculture
      Irrigation
  RT **Agricultural machinery**
Agricultural experiment stations (May
    subdiv. geog.) **630.7**
  UF Experimental farms
  BT **Agriculture—Government poli-**
      cy
      Agriculture—Research
      Agriculture—Study and teach-
      ing
  RT **Agricultural extension work**
Agricultural extension work (May subdiv.
    geog.) **630.7**
  BT **Adult education**
      Agriculture—Government poli-
      cy
  NT **County agricultural agents**
  RT **Agricultural experiment sta-**
      tions
      Agriculture—Study and teach-
      ing
      Community development
Agricultural industries
  USE **Agricultural industry**
Agricultural industry (May subdiv. geog.)
    338.1
  UF Agribusiness
      Agricultural industries
  BT **Agriculture—Economic aspects**
      Industries
  NT **Food industry**
Agricultural innovations (May subdiv.
    geog.) **631**
  UF Agriculture—Innovations
  BT **Technological innovations**
Agricultural laborers (May subdiv. geog.)
    331.7
  UF Farm laborers
  BT **Labor**
  RT **Migrant labor**
      Peasantry
Agricultural machinery (May subdiv.
    geog.) **631.3**
  UF Agricultural tools
      Farm engines
      Farm equipment

Agricultural machinery—*Continued*
  Farm implements
  Farm machinery
  Farm mechanics
 SA types of farm machinery [to be
   added as needed]
 BT **Machinery**
   Tools
 NT **Electricity in agriculture**
   Harvesting machinery
   Plows
   Tractors
 RT **Agricultural engineering**
Agricultural mechanics
 USE **Agricultural engineering**
Agricultural pests (May subdiv. geog.)
  632
 UF Diseases and pests
   Garden pests
 SA types of crops, plants, trees, etc.,
   with the subdivision *Diseases*
   and pests, e.g. **Fruit—Diseas-**
   es and pests [to be added as
   needed]
 BT **Economic zoology**
   Pests
 NT **Fruit—Diseases and pests**
   Fungi
   Pest control
   Plant diseases
   Spraying and dusting
   Weeds
 RT **Aeronautics in agriculture**
   Insect pests
Agricultural policy
 USE **Agriculture—Government poli-**
   cy
Agricultural products
 USE **Farm produce**
Agricultural research
 USE **Agriculture—Research**
Agricultural societies
 USE **Agriculture—Societies**
Agricultural subsidies (May subdiv.
  geog.) **338.9**
 UF Farm subsidies
 BT **Subsidies**
 RT **Agriculture—Government poli-**
   cy
Agricultural tools
 USE **Agricultural machinery**

Agriculture (May subdiv. geog.) **338.1;**
  630
 UF Agronomy
   Farming
   Planting
 SA types of agriculture, e.g. **Truck**
   farming; types of agricultural
   products, e.g. **Corn**; and eth-
   nic groups with the subdivi-
   sion *Agriculture*, e.g. **Native**
   Americans—Agriculture [to
   be added as needed]
 BT **Life sciences**
 NT **Aeronautics in agriculture**
   Aquaculture
   Beekeeping
   Cooperative agriculture
   Crop rotation
   Cultivated plants
   Dairying
   Dry farming
   Economic botany
   Farmers
   Forests and forestry
   Fruit culture
   Gardening
   Horticulture
   Livestock industry
   Native Americans—Agriculture
   Organic farming
   Pastures
   Plant breeding
   Reclamation of land
   Soils
   Sustainable agriculture
   Truck farming
   Urban agriculture
 RT **Farms**
   Food supply
Agriculture and state
 USE **Agriculture—Government poli-**
   cy
Agriculture—Bibliography **016.63**
Agriculture, Cooperative
 USE **Cooperative agriculture**
Agriculture—Documentation **025**
 BT **Documentation**
Agriculture—Economic aspects (May
  subdiv. geog.) **338.1**
 UF Agrarian question
   Agricultural economics

Agriculture—Economic aspects—*Continued*
- BT **Economics**
- NT **Agricultural credit**
  Agricultural industry
  Land tenure
- RT **Farm management**
  Farm produce—Marketing

Agriculture—Government policy (May subdiv. geog.)   **338.9**
- UF Agrarian question
  Agricultural policy
  Agriculture and state
  State and agriculture
- BT **Industrial policy**
- NT **Agricultural experiment stations**
  Agricultural extension work
  Rural development
- RT **Agricultural subsidies**
  Land reform

Agriculture—Innovations
- USE **Agricultural innovations**

Agriculture—Research (May subdiv. geog.)   **630.7**
- UF Agricultural research
- BT **Research**
- NT **Agricultural experiment stations**

Agriculture—Societies (May subdiv. geog.)   **630.6**
- UF Agricultural clubs
  Agricultural societies
- SA names of agricultural societies [to be added as needed]
- BT **Associations**
  Country life
  Societies
- NT **4-H clubs**
  Grange

Agriculture—Statistics   **338.1; 630.2**
- UF Crop reports
- BT **Statistics**

Agriculture—Study and teaching (May subdiv. geog.)   **630.7**
- UF Agricultural education
- BT **Vocational education**
- NT **4-H clubs**
  Agricultural experiment stations
  County agricultural agents
- RT **Agricultural extension work**

Agriculture—Tenant farming
- USE **Farm tenancy**

Agriculture—Tropics   **630.913**
- BT **Tropics**

Agriculture—United States   **630.973**

Agronomy
- USE **Agriculture**

AI (Artificial intelligence)
- USE **Artificial intelligence**

Aid to dependent children
- USE **Child welfare**

Aid to developing areas
- USE **Foreign aid**
  Technical assistance

AIDS (Disease) (May subdiv. geog.)   **616.97**
- UF Acquired immune deficiency syndrome
  HIV disease
- BT **Communicable diseases**
  Diseases

AIDS (Disease)—Prevention (May subdiv. geog.)   **616.97**

Use for materials on AIDS prevention in general not limited to safe sexual practices. Materials limited to safe sexual practices in the prevention of AIDS are entered under **Safe sex in AIDS prevention**.
- NT **Safe sex in AIDS prevention**

AIDS (Disease)—Treatment (May subdiv. geog.)   **615.5**
- BT **Therapeutics**

Air   **533; 546**

Use for materials dealing with air in general and with its chemical and physical properties. Materials on the body of air surrounding the earth are entered under **Atmosphere**.
- BT **Meteorology**
- NT **Aerodynamics**
  Atmosphere
  Bubbles
  Ventilation
- RT **Atmosphere**

Air bases (May subdiv. geog.)   **358.4**
- UF Military air bases
  Naval air bases
- BT **Airports**
  Military aeronautics

Air cargo
- USE **Commercial aeronautics**

Air carriers
- USE **Airlines**

Air charters
- USE **Airlines—Chartering**

Air conditioning (May subdiv. geog.)
    644; 697.9
    SA   subjects with the subdivision *Air conditioning* [to be added as needed]
    NT   **Automobiles—Air conditioning**
    RT   **Refrigeration**
          Ventilation
Air crashes
    USE **Aircraft accidents**
Air-cushion vehicles (May subdiv. geog.)
    629.3
    UF   Ground effect machines
          Hovercraft
    BT   **Vehicles**
Air defenses (May subdiv. geog.)   **363.3**
    Use for materials on military defense against air attack. Materials on the protection of civilians from enemy attack are entered under **Civil defense**.
    UF   Air raid defensive measures
    BT   **Military aeronautics**
    NT   **Radar defense networks**
Air freight
    USE **Commercial aeronautics**
Air guitar   **787.87**
    BT   **Guitars**
Air lines
    USE **Airlines**
Air mail service (May subdiv. geog.)
    383
    BT   **Commercial aeronautics**
          Postal service
Air—Microbiology   **579**
    UF   Aerobiology
    BT   **Microbiology**
Air, Moisture of
    USE **Humidity**
Air navigation
    USE **Navigation (Aeronautics)**
Air pilots (May subdiv. geog.)
    629.13092; 920
    UF   Airplane pilots
          Aviators
          Pilots
          Test pilots
    BT   **Aeronautics**
    NT   **Astronauts**
          Women air pilots
Air piracy
    USE **Hijacking of airplanes**

Air pollution (May subdiv. geog.)
    363.739; 628.5
    UF   Atmosphere—Pollution
          Pollution of air
    BT   **Environmental health**
          Pollution
    NT   **Aerosols**
          Dust
          Indoor air pollution
Air pollution—Measurement (May subdiv. geog.)   **363.739; 628.5**
    BT   **Measurement**
Air pollution—United States   **363.739; 628.5**
Air power (May subdiv. geog.)   **358.4**
    BT   **Military aeronautics**
Air raid defensive measures
    USE **Air defenses**
Air raid shelters (May subdiv. geog.)
    363.3
    UF   Blast shelters
          Bomb shelters
          Fallout shelters
          Nuclear bomb shelters
          Public shelters
          Shelters, Air raid
    BT   **Civil defense**
Air rights law
    USE **Airspace law**
Air routes
    USE **Aeronautics**
Air-ships
    USE **Airships**
Air space law
    USE **Airspace law**
Air surfing
    USE **Gliding and soaring**
Air terminals
    USE **Airports**
Air traffic control (May subdiv. geog.)
    387.7
    UF   Airports—Traffic control
    BT   **Aeronautics—Safety measures**
Air transport
    USE **Commercial aeronautics**
Air travel (May subdiv. geog.)   **387.7**
    BT   **Transportation**
          Travel
          Voyages and travels

Air warfare
USE **Military aeronautics**
Military airplanes
Aircraft
USE **Airplanes**
Airships
Balloons
Gliders (Aeronautics)
Helicopters
Aircraft accidents (May subdiv. geog.)
363.12; 629.13
UF Aeronautics—Accidents
Air crashes
Airplane accidents
Airplane crashes
Airplanes—Accidents
Aviation accidents
Plane crashes
BT **Accidents**
RT **Survival after airplane acci-**
dents, shipwrecks, etc.
Aircraft carriers (May subdiv. geog.)
359.3; 623
UF Airplane carriers
BT **Military aeronautics**
Warships
Aircraft industry
USE **Airplane industry**
Aircraft production
USE **Aerospace industry**
Airplane industry
Airdromes
USE **Airports**
Airline hostesses
USE **Flight attendants**
Airline stewardesses
USE **Flight attendants**
Airline stewards
USE **Flight attendants**
Airlines (May subdiv. geog.) **387.7**
Use for materials on companies engaged in
commercial aviation. Materials on various
types of aircraft and on the scientific or tech-
nical aspects of aircraft and their construction
and operation are entered under **Aeronautics**.
UF Air carriers
Air lines
BT **Commercial aeronautics**
NT **Flight attendants**
Airlines—Chartering (May subdiv. geog.)
387.7
UF Air charters
Airplanes—Chartering

Charter flights
Airlines—Hijacking
USE **Hijacking of airplanes**
Airplane accidents
USE **Aircraft accidents**
Airplane carriers
USE **Aircraft carriers**
Airplane crashes
USE **Aircraft accidents**
Airplane engines **629.134**
UF Airplane motors
Airplanes—Engines
Airplanes—Motors
BT **Engines**
NT **Jet propulsion**
Airplane hijacking
USE **Hijacking of airplanes**
Airplane industry (May subdiv. geog.)
338.4; 387.7
UF Aircraft industry
Aircraft production
BT **Aerospace industry**
Airplane motors
USE **Airplane engines**
Airplane pilots
USE **Air pilots**
Airplane racing (May subdiv. geog.)
797.5
UF Airplanes—Racing
BT **Aeronautical sports**
Racing
Airplane spotting
USE **Airplanes—Identification**
Airplanes (May subdiv. geog.) **387.7;**
629.133
UF Aeroplanes
Aircraft
SA types of airplanes and specific
makes of airplanes [to be
added as needed]
BT **Aeronautics**
NT **Aerial propellers**
Bombers
Gliders (Aeronautics)
Helicopters
Jet planes
Military airplanes
Airplanes—Accidents
USE **Aircraft accidents**
Airplanes—Chartering
USE **Airlines—Chartering**

Airplanes—Design and construction
629.134

Airplanes—Electric equipment   629.135
UF   Airplanes—Instruments
BT   **Aeronautical instruments**
Airplanes—Engines
USE   **Airplane engines**
Airplanes—Flight testing
USE   **Airplanes—Testing**
Airplanes—Hijacking
USE   **Hijacking of airplanes**
Airplanes—Identification   623.74;
629.133
UF   Airplane spotting
Airplanes—Recognition
BT   **Identification**
Airplanes in agriculture
USE   **Aeronautics in agriculture**
Airplanes—Inspection (May subdiv.
geog.)   **387.7; 629.134**
Airplanes—Instruments
USE   **Aeronautical instruments**
Airplanes—Electric equipment
Airplanes—Maintenance and repair
629.134
UF   Airplanes—Repair
Airplanes—Materials   629.134
BT   **Materials**
Airplanes, Military
USE   **Military airplanes**
Airplanes—Models   629.133
UF   Model airplanes
Paper airplanes
BT   **Models and modelmaking**
Airplanes—Motors
USE   **Airplane engines**
Airplanes—Noise (May subdiv. geog.)
629.132
BT   **Noise**
Noise pollution
Airplanes—Operation
USE   **Airplanes—Piloting**
Airplanes—Piloting   629.132
UF   Aeronautics—Piloting
Airplanes—Operation
Flight training
SA   types and names of airplanes
with the subdivision *Piloting*
[to be added as needed]
BT   **Aeronautics—Study and teach-
ing**

Navigation (Aeronautics)
NT   **Helicopters—Piloting**
Instrument flying
Stunt flying
Airplanes—Propellers
USE   **Aerial propellers**
Airplanes—Racing
USE   **Airplane racing**
Airplanes—Recognition
USE   **Airplanes—Identification**
Airplanes—Repair
USE   **Airplanes—Maintenance and
repair**
Airplanes, Rocket propelled
USE   **Rocket planes**
Airplanes—Testing (May subdiv. geog.)
629.134
UF   Airplanes—Flight testing
Test pilots
Airports (May subdiv. geog.)   387.7;
629.136
UF   Aerodromes
Air terminals
Airdromes
SA   names of individual airports [to
be added as needed]
BT   **Aeronautics**
NT   **Air bases**
Heliports
Airports—Security measures (May
subdiv. geog.)   363.28
Airports—Traffic control
USE   **Air traffic control**
Airships (May subdiv. geog.)   629.133
Use for materials on self-propelled aircraft
that are lighter than air and steerable. Materi-
als on aircraft held aloft by hot air or light
gases that are nondirigible and propelled only
by the wind are entered under **Balloons**.
UF   Air-ships
Aircraft
Balloons, Dirigible
Blimps
Dirigible balloons
Zeppelins
BT   **Aeronautics**
RT   **Balloons**
Airspace law (May subdiv. geog.)   341.4
UF   Air rights law
Air space law
BT   **Property**
Airways
USE   **Aeronautics**

24

Alaska Highway (Alaska and Canada)
    388.1; 979.8
  BT   **Roads**
Alchemy (May subdiv. geog.)   **540.1**
  Use for materials on medieval attempts to
  change base metals into gold. Materials on the
  transmutation of metals in nuclear physics are
  entered under **Transmutation (Chemistry)**.
  UF   Hermetic art and philosophy
         Philosophers' stone
         Transmutation of metals
  BT   **Chemistry**
         Occultism
  RT   **Transmutation (Chemistry)**
Alcohol   **547; 661**
  UF   Alcohol use
         Intoxicants
  SA   classes of persons with the sub-
         division *Alcohol use*, e.g. **Em-**
         ployees—Alcohol use;
         Youth—Alcohol use; etc. [to
         be added as needed]
  BT   **Chemicals**
  NT   **Alcohol fuels**
         Alcoholic beverages
         Denatured alcohol
  RT   **Alcoholism**
         Distillation
Alcohol and employees
  USE   **Employees— Alcohol use**
Alcohol and teenagers
  USE   **Teenagers—Alcohol use**
Alcohol and youth
  USE   **Youth—Alcohol use**
Alcohol as fuel
  USE   **Alcohol fuels**
Alcohol consumption
  USE   **Drinking of alcoholic beverages**
Alcohol, Denatured
  USE   **Denatured alcohol**
Alcohol fuels   **662**
  UF   Alcohol as fuel
         Ethyl alcohol fuel
  BT   **Alcohol**
         Fuel
Alcohol in the workplace
  USE   **Employees—Alcohol use**
Alcohol—Physiological effect   **615**
Alcohol use
  USE   **Alcohol**
         Alcoholism
         Drinking of alcoholic beverages

and classes of persons with the
  subdivision *Alcohol use,* e.g.
  Employees—Alcohol use;
  Youth—Alcohol use; etc. [to
  be added as needed]
Alcoholic beverage consumption
  USE   **Drinking of alcoholic beverages**
Alcoholic beverages (May subdiv. geog.)
    641.2
  UF   Drinks
         Intoxicants
  BT   **Alcohol**
         Beverages
  NT   **Beer**
         Liquors
         Wine and wine making
  RT   **Drinking of alcoholic beverages**
Alcoholic parents
  USE   **Adult children of alcoholics**
         Children of alcoholics
Alcoholics (May subdiv. geog.)   **362.292;**
    616.86
  UF   Drunkards
  NT   **Recovering alcoholics**
  RT   **Adult children of alcoholics**
         Alcoholism
         Children of alcoholics
Alcoholism (May subdiv. geog.)
    362.292; 616.86
  UF   Addiction to alcohol
         Alcohol use
         Drinking problem
         Drunkenness
         Intemperance
         Intoxication
         Liquor problem
         Problem drinking
  SA   classes of persons with the sub-
         division *Alcohol use*, e.g. **Em-**
         ployees—Alcohol use;
         Youth—Alcohol use; etc. [to
         be added as needed]
  BT   **Social problems**
  RT   **Alcohol**
         Alcoholics
         Drinking of alcoholic beverages
         Temperance
         Twelve-step programs
Alfalfa   **583; 633.3**
  BT   **Forage plants**
Algae   **579.8**

Algae—*Continued*
  UF   Sea mosses
       Seaweeds
  BT   **Marine plants**
Algebra   512
  BT   **Mathematical analysis**
       Mathematics
  NT   **Graph theory**
       Group theory
       Linear algebra
       Logarithms
       Number theory
       Probabilities
       Sequences (Mathematics)
Algebra, Boolean
  USE   **Boolean algebra**
Algeria   965
       May be subdivided like United States except for History.
Alien abduction (May subdiv. geog.)
       001.942
  UF   Abduction of humans by aliens
       Extraterrestrial abduction
       UFO abduction
  BT   **Human-alien encounters**
Alien encounters with humans
  USE   **Human-alien encounters**
Alien labor (May subdiv. geog.)   331.6
  BT   **Labor**
  RT   **Migrant labor**
Alienation (Social psychology)   302.5
  UF   Estrangement (Social psychology)
       Rebels (Social psychology)
       Social alienation
  BT   **Social psychology**
Aliens (May subdiv. geog.)   323.6
  UF   Foreign population
       Foreigners
       Noncitizens
       Nonnationals
  SA   national groups subdivided by
       the place of their residence,
       e.g. **Mexicans—United States**
       [to be added as needed]
  BT   **Minorities**
  NT   **Illegal aliens**
       Refugees
  RT   **Citizenship**
       Immigrants
       Immigration and emigration
       Naturalization

Aliens from outer space
  USE   **Extraterrestrial beings**
Aliens—United States   325.73
  UF   United States—Foreign population
  NT   **Mexicans—United States**
  RT   **United States—Immigration
        and emigration**
Alimony (May subdiv. geog.)   346.01
  BT   **Divorce**
All Fools' Day
  USE   **April Fools' Day**
All Hallows' Eve
  USE   **Halloween**
All terrain bicycles
  USE   **Mountain bikes**
All terrain cycling
  USE   **Mountain biking**
All terrain vehicles (May subdiv. geog.)
       629.22
  UF   ATVs
  SA   types of vehicles, e.g. **Snowmobiles** [to be added as needed]
  BT   **Vehicles**
  NT   **Mountain bikes**
       Snowmobiles
Allegories   808.88
       Use for individual works or for collections of allegories. Materials on allegory as a literary form or on allegory in the fine and decorative arts are entered under **Allegory**.
  BT   **Fiction**
  RT   **Fables**
       Parables
Allegory   704.9; 808
       Use for materials on allegory as a literary form as well as for allegory in the fine and decorative arts. Individual allegories and collections of allegories are entered under **Allegories**.
  BT   **Arts**
       Fiction
  RT   **Symbolism in literature**
Allergies
  USE   **Allergy**
Allergies, Food
  USE   **Food allergy**
Allergy   616.97
  UF   Allergies
  SA   types of allergies [to be added as needed]
  BT   **Immunity**
  NT   **Asthma**
       Food allergy

Allergy—*Continued*
>> **Hay fever**

Allergy, Food
> USE **Food allergy**

Alleys
> USE **Streets**

Allied health personnel (May subdiv. geog.) **610.69**
> UF Paramedical personnel
> SA types of allied health personnel [to be added as needed]
> NT **Emergency medical technicians**
>> **Medical technologists**
>> **Nurse practitioners**

Alligators (May subdiv. geog.) **597.98**
> BT **Reptiles**
> RT **Crocodiles**

Allocation of time
> USE **Time management**

Allosaurus **567.912**
> BT **Dinosaurs**

Allowances, Children's
> USE **Children's allowances**

Alloys **669**
> SA types of alloys [to be added as needed]
> BT **Industrial chemistry**
>> **Metals**
> NT **Aluminum alloys**
>> **Brass**
>> **Pewter**
> RT **Metallurgy**

Allusions **031.02; 803**
> SA names of individual persons with the subdivision *Allusions*, for materials on allusions to that person, e.g. **Shakespeare, William, 1564-1616—Allusions** [to be added as needed]
> RT **Terms and phrases**

Almanacs **030**
> UF Annuals
> BT **Serial publications**
> NT **Nautical almanacs**
> RT **Calendars**
>> **Chronology**
>> **Yearbooks**

Alphabet **411**
>> Use for materials on the series of characters that form the elements of a written language and for materials to be used in teaching children the ABCs. Materials on the styles of alphabets used by artists, etc., are entered under **Alphabets**.
> UF ABCs
>> Alphabet books
>> Letters of the alphabet
> SA names of languages with the subdivision *Alphabet*, e.g. **English language—Alphabet** [to be added as needed]
> BT **Writing**
> NT **Alphabets**

Alphabet books
> USE **Alphabet**

Alphabetizing
> USE **Files and filing**

Alphabets **745.6**
>> Use for materials on the styles of alphabets used by artists, etc. Materials on the series of characters that form the elements of a written language and for materials to be used in teaching children the ABCs are entered under **Alphabet**.
> UF Ornamental alphabets
> BT **Alphabet**
>> **Sign painting**
> NT **Monograms**
> RT **Illumination of books and manuscripts**
>> **Initials**
>> **Lettering**

Alpine animals
> USE **Mountain animals**

Alpine fauna
> USE **Mountain animals**

Alpine flora
> USE **Mountain plants**

Alpine plants
> USE **Mountain plants**

Alternate energy resources
> USE **Renewable energy resources**

Alternate work sites
> USE **Telecommuting**

Alternating current machinery
> USE **Electric machinery—Alternating current**

Alternating currents
> USE **Alternating electric currents**

Alternating electric currents **621.31**
> UF Alternating currents
>> Electric currents, Alternating
> BT **Electric currents**

Alternative education (May subdiv. geog.) **371.04**

Alternative education—*Continued*
  BT   **Education**
  RT   **Education—Experimental**
          methods
        Experimental schools
Alternative energy resources
  USE   **Renewable energy resources**
Alternative fuel vehicles (May subdiv.
    geog.) **388.3**
  BT   **Motor vehicles**
Alternative histories   **808.3; 808.83**
    Use for individual works, collections, or
    materials about imaginative works featuring
    key changes in historical facts.
  BT   **Fantasy fiction**
Alternative lifestyles (May subdiv. geog.)
    306
    Use for materials on ways of living regard-
    ed as unacceptable by conventional standards,
    especially those that reject consumerism, the
    work ethic, etc.
  BT   **Lifestyles**
  RT   **Counter culture**
Alternative medicine (May subdiv. geog.)
    610; 613; 615.5
  UF   Therapeutic systems
  SA   types of alternative medicine [to
          be added as needed]
  BT   **Medicine**
  NT   **Acupressure**
        Acupuncture
        Chiropractic
        Health self-care
        Holistic medicine
        Homeopathy
        Mental healing
        Naturopathy
        Reflexology
Alternative military service
  USE   **National service**
Alternative press (May subdiv. geog.)
    070.4
    Use for materials about publications issued
    clandestinely and contrary to government reg-
    ulation and for materials about publications is-
    sued legally (and usually serially) and pro-
    duced by radical, anti-establishment, or count-
    er-culture groups.
  UF   Underground literature
        Underground press
  BT   **Press**
Alternative schools
  USE   **Experimental schools**
Alternative universities
  USE   **Free universities**

Alternative work schedules
  USE   **Flexible hours of labor**
        Part-time employment
Altitude, Influence of
  USE   **Environmental influence on**
          humans
Altruism   **171**
  UF   Altruistic behavior
        Unselfishness
  BT   **Conduct of life**
  RT   **Charity**
        Helping behavior
Altruistic behavior
  USE   **Altruism**
Altruists
  USE   **Philanthropists**
Aluminum   **669; 673**
  BT   **Metals**
  NT   **Aluminum foil**
Aluminum alloys   **669; 673**
  BT   **Alloys**
Aluminum foil   **673**
  BT   **Aluminum**
        Packaging
Aluminum—Recycling (May subdiv.
    geog.) **628.4; 673**
  BT   **Recycling**
Alzheimer's disease   **616.8**
  BT   **Brain—Diseases**
Amateur films (May subdiv. geog.)
    778.5; 791.43
    Use for individual works, collections, or
    materials about amateur films.
  UF   Amateur motion pictures
        Home movies
        Home video movies
        Personal films
  BT   **Motion pictures**
  RT   **Camcorders**
        Motion picture cameras
Amateur motion pictures
  USE   **Amateur films**
Amateur radio stations (May subdiv.
    geog.) **384.54; 621.3841**
  UF   Ham radio stations
  BT   **Radio stations**
        Shortwave radio
Amateur theater (May subdiv. geog.)
    792
  UF   Non-professional theater
        Play production
        Private theater

28

Amateur theater—*Continued*
- BT Amusements
-      Theater
- NT Charades
-      Children's plays
-      College and school drama
-      One act plays
-      Pantomimes
-      Shadow pantomimes and plays
- RT Acting
-      Drama in education
-      Little theater movement

Ambassadors (May subdiv. geog.)
  327.2092
- BT Diplomats

Ambition   302.5
- BT Social psychology

Amendments, Equal rights
- USE Equal rights amendments

America   970

Use for general materials on the Western Hemisphere.
- UF Western Hemisphere
- SA names of individual countries of the Western Hemisphere [to be added as needed]
- NT Caribbean Region
-      Latin America
-      North America
-      South America

America—Antiquities   970.01
- BT Antiquities

America—Civilization   970; 980

Use for general materials on the civilization of the Western Hemisphere in modern times. Materials on ancient civilizations in America are entered under **America—Antiquities**; under a region, country, city, etc., with the subdivision *Antiquities*; or under the name of an ancient people. Materials limited to the civilization of the United States are entered under **United States—Civilization**.
- UF American civilization
- BT Civilization

America—Discovery and exploration
- USE America—Exploration

America—Exploration   970.01
- UF America—Discovery and exploration
- BT Exploration
- NT Northwest Passage
-      United States—Exploration

America—History   970
- UF American history

America—Politics and government   970
- NT Pan-Americanism

American actors
- USE Actors—United States

American actors and actresses
- USE Actors—United States

American architecture
- USE Architecture—United States

American art   709.73
- UF Art, American
- BT Art
- NT American folk art

American artificial satellites   629.43; 629.46
- UF Artificial satellites, American
- BT Artificial satellites

American artists
- USE Artists—United States

American arts
- USE Arts—United States

American authors (May subdiv. geog.)
  810.9; 920
- UF Authors, American
- BT Authors
- NT African American authors
-      American dramatists
-      American novelists
-      American poets
-      Hispanic American authors

American ballads   811
- BT American poetry

American Bicentennial
- USE American Revolution Bicentennial, 1776-1976

American Bill of rights
- USE United States. Constitution. 1st-10th amendments

American bison
- USE Bison

American characteristics
- USE American national characteristics

American Civil War
- USE United States—History—1861-1865, Civil War

American civilization
- USE America—Civilization

American colonial style in architecture   724
- UF Colonial architecture
- BT Architecture

American colonies
USE **United States—History—1600-1775, Colonial period**

American color prints 769.973
UF Color prints, American
BT **Color prints**

American composers
USE **Composers—United States**

American constitution
USE **United States. Constitution**

American cooking 641.5973

Use for materials on cooking limited to American national and regional styles.

UF Cookery, American
SA styles of regional American cooking, e.g. **Southern cooking** [to be added as needed]
BT **Cooking**

American decoration and ornament
USE **Decoration and ornament—United States**

American diaries 809; 920

Use for collections of American diaries and for materials about American diaries.

BT **American literature**
Diaries

American diplomatic and consular service (May subdiv. geog.) 327.73; 353.1
UF Diplomatic and consular service, American
United States—Diplomatic and consular service
BT **Diplomatic and consular service**

American drama 812

Use for general materials about American drama, not for individual works.

BT **American literature**
Drama
NT **American folk drama**

American drama—Collections 812.008

American drama—History and criticism 812.009

American dramatists (May subdiv. geog.) 812.009; 920
UF Dramatists, American
BT **American authors**
Dramatists

American drawing 741.973
UF Drawing, American
BT **Drawing**

American economic assistance
USE **American foreign aid**

American engraving 760; 769
UF Engraving, American
BT **Engraving**

American espionage (May subdiv. geog.) 327.127; 355.3
UF Espionage, American
BT **Espionage**

American essays 814; 814.008
BT **American literature**
Essays

American ethics
USE **Ethics—United States**

American exploring expeditions
USE **United States—Exploring expeditions**

American fables 813
BT **Fables**

American fiction 813

Use for collections or materials about American fiction, not for individual works.

BT **American literature**
Fiction

American films
USE **Motion pictures—United States**

American flag
USE **Flags—United States**

American folk art 745.0973
UF Folk art, American
BT **American art**
Folk art

American folk dancing
USE **Folk dancing—United States**

American folk drama 812
BT **American drama**
Folk drama

American folk music
USE **Folk music—United States**

American folk songs
USE **Folk songs—United States**

American foreign aid (May subdiv. geog.) 338.91; 361.6
UF American economic assistance
Economic assistance, American
BT **Foreign aid**

American furniture 684.100973; 749.09073
UF Furniture, American
SA styles of American furniture o be added as needed]
BT **Furniture**

American government
USE **United States—Politics and government**

American graphic arts
USE **Graphic arts—United States**

American historians
USE **Historians—United States**

American history
USE **America—History**
United States—History

American hostages (May subdiv. geog. except U.S.) **920**
BT **Hostages**

American hostages—Iran 920
NT **Iran hostage crisis, 1979-1981**

American illustrators
USE **Illustrators—United States**

American Indian authors
USE **Native American authors**

American Indians
USE **Native Americans**

American letters 816; 816.008
BT **American literature**
Letters

American literature (May subdiv. geog. by state or region) **810**

May be subdivided by the topical subdivisions and literary forms used under **English literature**; or geographically by states or regions of the United States for works by or about several authors from a state or region or writing about a state or region, e.g. **American literature—Massachusetts; American literature—Southern States**; etc.

SA various forms of American literature, e.g. **American poetry**; **American satire**; etc. [to be added as needed]
BT **Literature**
NT **American diaries**
American drama
American essays
American fiction
American letters
American literature (Spanish)
American poetry
American prose literature
American satire
American sermons
American speeches
American wit and humor
Beat generation

American literature—17th and 18th centuries 810
UF American literature—Colonial period

American literature—19th century 810
American literature—20th century 810
American literature—21st century 810
American literature—African American authors 810.8; 810.9

Use for collections or materials about American literature by several African American authors, not for individual works. Use same pattern for literatures and literary forms written by other ethnic groups or classes of authors.

UF African American literature
American literature—Afro-American authors
American literature—Black authors
Black literature (American)
SA particular forms of American literature with the subdivision *African American authors*; e.g., **American poetry—African American authors** [to be added as needed]
NT **Harlem Renaissance**

American literature—Afro-American authors
USE **American literature—African American authors**

American literature—American Indian authors
USE **American literature—Native American authors**

American literature—Black authors
USE **American literature—African American authors**

American literature—Collections 810.8

Use for collections of both poetry and prose by several American authors. Collections consisting of prose only are entered under **American prose literature**; collections of poetry are entered under **American poetry—Collections**.

American literature—Colonial period
USE **American literature—17th and 18th centuries**

American literature—Hispanic American authors 810

Use for materials on American literature in English written by American authors of Spanish or Latin American origins. Materials on American literature written in Spanish are entered under **American literature (Spanish)**.

American literature—Hispanic American authors—*Continued*

UF   American literature—Latin American authors

Hispanic American literature (English)

SA   genres of American literature with the subdivision *Hispanic American authors*; and **American literature** and genres of American literature with subdivisions for specific groups of Hispanic American authors, e.g. **American literature—Mexican American authors** [to be added as needed]

NT   **American literature—Mexican American authors**

American literature—Latin American authors

USE   **American literature—Hispanic American authors**

American literature—Massachusetts 810

American literature—Mexican American authors   810

Use for materials on American literature written in English by American authors of Mexican origins.

UF   Chicano literature (English)

Mexican American literature (English)

SA   genres of American literature with the subdivision *Mexican American authors* [to be added as needed]

BT   **American literature—Hispanic American authors**

American literature—Native American authors   810.8; 810.9

Use for collections or materials about American literature written in English by several Native American authors, not for individual works. Collections or materials about literature written in Native American languages by several Native American authors are entered under **Native American literature**.

UF   American literature—American Indian authors

American literature—Southern States 810

UF   Southern literature

American literature (Spanish)   860

Use for materials on American literature written in Spanish. Materials on American literature in English written by American authors of Spanish or Latin American origins are entered under **American literature—Hispanic American authors**.

UF   Hispanic American literature (Spanish)

Spanish American literature

SA   genres of American literature with the qualifier (Spanish) [to be added as needed]

BT   **American literature**

American literature—Women authors 810.8; 810.9

Use for collections or for materials about several American women authors.

American Loyalists (May subdiv. geog.) **973.3**

UF   Loyalists, American

Tories, American

BT   **United States—History—1775-1783, Revolution**

American military assistance (May subdiv. geog.)   **355**

UF   Military assistance, American

BT   **Military assistance**

American motion pictures

USE   **Motion pictures—United States**

American music   780.973

UF   Music, American

BT   **Music**

American musicians

USE   **Musicians—United States**

American national characteristics 306.0973; 973

UF   American characteristics

National characteristics, American

United States—National characteristics

BT   **National characteristics**

American national songs

USE   **National songs—United States**

American newspapers

USE   **Newspapers—United States**

American novelists (May subdiv. geog.) **813.009; 920**

UF   Novelists, American

BT   **American authors**

Novelists

American orations
   USE   **American speeches**
American painters
   USE   **Painters—United States**
American painting   759.13
   UF   Painting, American
   BT   **Painting**
American periodicals
   USE   **Periodicals—United States**
American personal names
   USE   **Personal names—United States**
American philosophers
   USE   **Philosophers—United States**
American philosophy   191
   UF   Philosophy, American
   BT   **Philosophy**
American poetry   811
   Use for general materials about American
   poetry, not for individual works.
   BT   **American literature**
         Poetry
   NT   **American ballads**
**American poetry—African American au-
   thors   811**
   Use for collections or materials about
   American poetry by several African American
   authors, not for individual works.
   UF   African American poetry
         American poetry—Afro-American
         authors
         American poetry—Black authors
         Black poetry (American)
American poetry—Afro-American authors
   USE   **American poetry—African
         American authors**
American poetry—Black authors
   USE   **American poetry—African
         American authors**
American poetry—Collections   811.008
**American poetry—History and criticism
   811.009**
American poets   811.009; 920
   UF   Poets, American
   BT   **American authors**
         Poets
American politicians
   USE   **Politicians—United States**
American politics
   USE   **United States—Politics and
         government**
American pottery   738.0973
   UF   Pottery, American

   BT   **Pottery**
American prints   769.973
   UF   Prints, American
   BT   **Prints**
American propaganda   303.3; 327.1
   UF   Propaganda, American
   BT   **Propaganda**
American prose literature   818
   Use for collections of prose writings by
   several American authors that may include a
   variety of literary forms, such as essays, fic-
   tion, orations, etc. May also be used for gen-
   eral materials about such prose writings.
   UF   Prose literature, American
   BT   **American literature**
American Revolution
   USE   **United States—History—1775-
         1783, Revolution**
**American Revolution Bicentennial, 1776-
   1976   973.3**
   UF   American Bicentennial
         Bicentennial celebrations—United
         States—1976
         United States—Bicentennial cele-
         brations
         United States—History—1775-
         1783, Revolution—Centennial
         celebrations, etc.
   BT   **United States—Centennial cele-
         brations, etc.**
**American Revolution Bicentennial, 1776-
   1976—Collectibles   973.3075**
   BT   **Collectors and collecting**
American satire   817; 817.008
   UF   Satire, American
   BT   **American literature**
         Satire
American schools
   USE   **Schools—United States**
American sculptors
   USE   **Sculptors—United States**
American sculpture   730.973
   BT   **Sculpture**
American sermons   204; 252
   BT   **American literature**
         Sermons
American songs   782.420973
   BT   **Songs**
   NT   **Folk songs—United States**
         National songs—United States
American-Spanish War, 1898
   USE   **Spanish-American War, 1898**
American speeches   815; 815.008

American speeches—*Continued*
    UF   American orations
          Speeches, addresses, etc., American
    BT   **American literature**
          Speeches
American technical assistance (May subdiv. geog.) **338.91; 361.6**
    UF   Technical assistance, American
    BT   **Technical assistance**
American teenagers
    USE **Teenagers—United States**
American tourists
    USE **American travelers**
American travelers (May subdiv. geog.) **910.92; 920**
    UF   American tourists
    BT   **Travelers**
American wit and humor **817; 817.008; 817.009**
    Use for collections by several authors or for materials about American wit and humor. Individual works by American humorists are entered under **Wit and humor**.
    BT   **American literature**
          Wit and humor
American youth
    USE **Youth—United States**
Americana **069; 973**
    Use for materials about American objects of interest to collectors for their historical value, such as documents, relics, etc., including items of little intrinsic value. Materials about old American objects that have aesthetic as well as financial value, usually furniture or decorative arts, are entered under **Antiques—United States**.
    BT   **Collectors and collecting**
          Popular culture—United States
          United States—Civilization
          United States—History
    RT   **Antiques—United States**
Americanisms **427**
    Use for materials on words and expressions peculiar to the United States.
    UF   English language—Americanisms
    BT   **English language—Dialects**
Americanization (May subdiv. geog.) **305.813; 306.0973**
    BT   **Socialization**
    NT   **United States—Immigration and emigration**
    RT   **Immigration and emigration**
          Naturalization

Americans (May subdiv. geog. except U.S.) **305.813; 920; 973**
    Use for materials on citizens of the United States.
    NT   **Japanese Americans**
    RT   **United States**
Americans—Foreign countries **305.813; 920; 973**
Americans—Greece **305.813**
Amish (May subdiv. geog.) **289.7**
    BT   **Christian sects**
          Mennonites
Ammunition **623.4**
    SA   types of ammunition, e.g. **Bombs** [to be added as needed]
    BT   **Explosives**
          Ordnance
          Projectiles
    NT   **Bombs**
    RT   **Firearms**
          Gunpowder
Amnesia **616.85**
    BT   **Memory**
Amnesty (May subdiv. geog.) **364.6**
    BT   **Administration of criminal justice**
          Executive power
    RT   **Clemency**
          Forgiveness
          Pardon
Amniocentesis **618.3**
    BT   **Prenatal diagnosis**
Amphetamines **615**
    UF   Pep pills
    SA   types of amphetamines, e.g. **Methamphetamine** [to be added as needed]
    BT   **Stimulants**
    NT   **Methamphetamine**
Amphibians (May subdiv. geog.) **567; 597.8**
    SA   types of amphibians [to be added as needed]
    BT   **Animals**
    NT   **Frogs**
          Salamanders
Amphibious operations
    USE names of wars with the subdivision *Amphibious operations,* e.g. **World War, 1939-**

Amphibious operations—*Continued*
>> **1945—Amphibious opera-**
>> **tions** [to be added as needed]

Amplifiers (Electronics)   621.3815
> SA   types of amplifiers [to be added
>> as needed]
> BT   **Electronics**
> NT   **Masers**
>> **Transistor amplifiers**

Amplifiers, Transistor
> USE   **Transistor amplifiers**

Amusement parks (May subdiv. geog.)
>> **791.06**
> UF   Theme parks
> SA   names of specific parks [to bc
>> added as needed]
> BT   **Parks**
> NT   **Walt Disney World (Fla.)**
> RT   **Carnivals**

Amusements (May subdiv. geog.)   **790**
> UF   Entertainments
>> Pastimes
> SA   types of amusements, e.g. **Car-**
>> **nivals** [to be added as need-
>> ed]
> NT   **Amateur theater**
>> **Carnivals**
>> **Charades**
>> **Children's parties**
>> **Christmas entertainments**
>> **Church entertainments**
>> **Circus**
>> **Concerts**
>> **Creative activities**
>> **Dance**
>> **Fireworks**
>> **Fortune telling**
>> **Hobbies**
>> **Juggling**
>> **Literary recreations**
>> **Magic tricks**
>> **Mathematical recreations**
>> **Puzzles**
>> **Riddles**
>> **Roller coasters**
>> **Scientific recreations**
>> **Shadow pictures**
>> **Skits**
>> **String figures**
>> **Theater**
>> **Toys**
>> **Tricks**

>> **Vaudeville**
>> **Ventriloquism**
> RT   **Entertaining**
>> **Games**
>> **Indoor games**
>> **Play**
>> **Recreation**
>> **Sports**

Anabolic steroids
> USE   **Steroids**

Anaesthetics
> USE   **Anesthetics**

Analysis
> USE   types of chemicals and sub-
>> stances with the subdivision
>> *Analysis,* e.g. **Water—Analy-**
>> **sis; Milk—Analysis;** etc., for
>> materials on methods of ana-
>> lyzing those items [to be add-
>> ed as needed]

Analysis (Chemistry)
> USE   **Analytical chemistry**

Analysis (Mathematics)
> USE   **Calculus**
>> **Functions**
>> **Mathematical analysis**

Analysis of food
> USE   **Food adulteration and inspec-**
>> **tion**
>> **Food—Analysis**

Analytic geometry   516.3
> UF   Geometry, Analytic
> BT   **Geometry**

Analytical chemistry   543
> UF   Analysis (Chemistry)
>> Chemical analysis
>> Chemistry, Analytic
>> Qualitative analysis
>> Quantitative analysis
> SA   types of substances with the
>> subdivision *Analysis*, e.g. **Wa-**
>> **ter—Analysis** [to be added as
>> needed]
> BT   **Chemistry**
> NT   **Distillation**
>> **Food—Analysis**
>> **Water—Analysis**

Anansi (Legendary character)   398.22
> BT   **Legendary characters**

Anarchism and anarchists (May subdiv.
>> geog.)   **320.5; 335**

Anarchism and anarchists—*Continued*
- BT **Freedom**
  Political crimes and offenses
  Political science
- RT **Terrorism**

Anatomy   571.3; 611
- SA names of organs and regions of the body and subjects with the subdivision *Anatomy*, e.g. **Heart—Anatomy**; **Birds—Anatomy**; etc. [to be added as needed]
- BT **Biology**
  Medicine
- NT **Animals—Anatomy**
  Artistic anatomy
  Birds—Anatomy
  Cardiovascular system
  Comparative anatomy
  Digestive system
  Foot
  Glands
  Head
  Heart—Anatomy
  Human anatomy
  Immune system
  Musculoskeletal system
  Nervous system
  Plants—Anatomy
  Reproductive system
  Respiratory system
  Skin
  Stomach
  Throat
- RT **Physiology**

Anatomy, Artistic
- USE **Artistic anatomy**

Anatomy, Comparative
- USE **Comparative anatomy**

Anatomy of animals
- USE **Animals—Anatomy**

Anatomy of plants
- USE **Plants—Anatomy**

Ancestor worship (May subdiv. geog.)   202
- UF Worship of the dead
- BT **Religion**

Ancestry
- USE **Genealogy**
  Heredity

Ancient architecture (May subdiv. geog.)   722
- UF Architecture, Ancient
- BT **Archeology**
  Architecture
- NT **Byzantine architecture**
  Greek architecture
  Pyramids
  Roman architecture
  Seven Wonders of the World

Ancient art (May subdiv. geog.)   709.01
- UF Art, Ancient
- BT **Art**
- NT **Byzantine art**
  Greek art
  Roman art
  Seven Wonders of the World

Ancient civilization   306.093; 930
- UF Civilization, Ancient
- BT **Ancient history**
  Civilization
- NT **Classical civilization**

Ancient geography   913

Use for materials on the geography of the ancient world in general. Materials on the ancient geography of one country or region still existing in modern times are entered under the name of the place with the subdivision *Historical geography*. Materials on the geography of regions or countries of antiquity that no longer exist as such in modern times are entered under the name of the place with the subdivision *Geography*.

- UF Classical geography
  Geography, Ancient
- SA names of modern countries with the subdivision *Historical geography*, e.g. **Greece—Historical geography**; and names of places of antiquity with the subdivision *Geography*, e.g. **Gaul—Geography** [to be added as needed]
- BT **Ancient history**
  Historical geography
- NT **Gaul—Geography**
  Greece—Historical geography
  Rome—Geography

Ancient Greece
- USE **Greece—History—0-323**

Ancient Greece—Description
- USE **Greece—Description and travel—0-323**

Ancient history   930

Use for materials on the history of the ancient world up to the fall of Rome not limited to a single country or region.

Ancient history—*Continued*
UF History, Ancient
SA names of ancient peoples, e.g.
Hittites; and names of countries of antiquity, with the subdivision *History* [to be added as needed]
BT **World history**
NT **Ancient civilization**
Ancient geography
Bible
Classical dictionaries
Hittites
Inscriptions
Numismatics
Phoenicians
Ancient philosophy 180
UF Greek philosophy
Philosophy, Ancient
Roman philosophy
BT **Philosophy**
NT **Stoics**
Androgyny 155.3; 305.3
BT **Sex differences (Psychology)**
Sex role
Anecdotes 808.88
Use for collections of anecdotes and for materials about anecdotes.
UF Facetiae
Stories
SA subjects with the subdivision *Anecdotes* [to be added as needed]
NT **Music—Anecdotes**
RT **Wit and humor**
Anesthetics 615; 617.9
UF Anaesthetics
BT **Materia medica**
RT **Pain**
Surgery
Angels 235
BT **Heaven**
Spirits
Anger 152.4
UF Rage
Wrath
BT **Emotions**
Angina pectoris 616.1
BT **Heart diseases**
Anglican Church
USE **Church of England**

Angling
USE **Fishing**
Anglo-American law
USE **Common law**
Anglo-French intervention in Egypt, 1956
USE **Sinai Campaign, 1956**
Anglo-Saxon language
USE **English language—Old English period**
Anglo-Saxon literature
USE **English literature—Old English period**
Anglo-Saxons (May subdiv. geog.)
305.82; 941.01
BT **Great Britain—History—0-1066**
Teutonic peoples
Animal abuse
USE **Animal welfare**
Animal attacks (May subdiv. geog.)
591.6
UF Attacks by animals
RT **Dangerous animals**
Animal babies 591.3
Use for materials on baby animals of several species. Baby animals of a particular species are entered under the name of the species.
UF Animals—Infancy
Baby animals
BT **Animals**
Animal behavior 591.5
UF Animals—Behavior
Behavior
Habits of animals
SA types of specific behavior, e.g.
Animals—Migration; Hibernation; Sexual behavior in animals; etc.; and types of animals with the subdivision *Behavior*, e.g. **Birds—Behavior** [to be added as needed]
BT **Animals**
Zoology
NT **Animal communication**
Animal courtship
Animal defenses
Animal sounds
Animals—Food
Animals—Migration
Birds—Behavior
Hibernation
Instinct

Animal behavior—*Continued*
       Monkeys—Behavior
       Nest building
       Primates—Behavior
       Sexual behavior in animals
  RT Animal intelligence
       Tracking and trailing
Animal camouflage
  USE **Camouflage (Biology)**
Animal communication 591.59
  UF Animal language
       Animals—Language
       Communication among animals
  BT **Animal behavior**
  RT **Animal sounds**
Animal courtship 591.56
  UF Animals—Courtship
       Courtship (Animal behavior)
       Courtship of animals
       Mate selection in animals
       Mating behavior
  BT **Animal behavior**
       Sexual behavior in animals
Animal defenses 591.47
  UF Defense mechanisms of animals
       Self-defense in animals
       Self-protection in animals
  BT **Animal behavior**
  NT **Camouflage (Biology)**
Animal drawing
  USE **Animal painting and illustration**
Animal embryos, Frozen
  USE **Frozen embryos**
Animal experimentation (May subdiv. geog.) **616**
  UF Experimentation on animals
       Laboratory animal experimentation
  BT **Research**
  NT **Vivisection**
  RT **Animal welfare**
Animal exploitation
  USE **Animal welfare**
Animal-facilitated therapy
  USE **Pet therapy**
Animal flight 573.7
  UF Animals—Flight
  SA types of animals with the subdivision *Flight*, e.g. **Birds—Flight** [to be added as needed]

  BT **Animal locomotion**
       Flight
  NT **Birds—Flight**
Animal food
  USE **Animals—Food**
       Food of animal origin
Animal habitations
  USE **Animals—Habitations**
Animal homes
  USE **Animals—Habitations**
Animal housing 636.08
    Use for materials on houses or habitations provided by humans for either wild or domestic animals. Materials on the natural shelters and homes animals build for themselves, such as burrows, dens, lairs, etc., are entered under **Animals—Habitations**.
  UF Animals—Housing
       Domestic animal dwellings
       Domestic animals—Housing
       Habitations of domestic animals
  SA types of animals with the subdivision *Housing*, e.g. **Pets—Housing** [to be added as needed]
  BT **Animals**
  NT **Beehives**
       Birdhouses
       Pets—Housing
  RT **Animals—Habitations**
Animal husbandry
  USE **Livestock industry**
Animal industry
  USE **Livestock industry**
Animal instinct
  USE **Instinct**
Animal intelligence 591.5
  UF Animal psychology
       Intelligence of animals
  SA types of animals with the subdivision *Psychology* [to be added as needed]
  BT **Animals**
  NT **Dogs—Psychology**
       Psychology of learning
  RT **Animal behavior**
       Comparative psychology
       Instinct
Animal kingdom
  USE **Zoology**
Animal language
  USE **Animal communication**
       Animal sounds

Animal light
USE **Bioluminescence**
Animal locomotion   573.7; 591.57
UF   Animals—Movements
Movements of animals
BT   **Animals**
Locomotion
NT   **Animal flight**
Animal lore
USE   **Animals—Folklore**
Animals in literature
Mythical animals
Natural history
Animal luminescence
USE   **Bioluminescence**
Animal magnetism
USE   **Hypnotism**
Animal migration
USE   **Animals—Migration**
Animal oils
USE   **Oils and fats**
Animal painting and illustration   704.9;
743.6; 758
Use for materials on the art of painting or
drawing animals. Materials on the depiction of
animals in works of art are entered under **An-**
imals in art. Popular materials consisting
chiefly of photographs or illustrations of ani-
mals are entered under **Animals—Pictorial**
works.
UF   Animal drawing
BT   **Painting**
RT   **Animals in art**
Animals—Pictorial works
Photography of animals
Animal parasites
USE   **Parasites**
Animal photography
USE   **Photography of animals**
Animal physiology
USE   **Zoology**
Animal pictures
USE   **Animals—Pictorial works**
Animal pounds
USE   **Animal shelters**
Animal products   338.1; 338.4
UF   Products, Animal
SA   types of animal products [to be
added as needed]
BT   **Commercial products**
NT   **Dairy products**
Hides and skins
Ivory

Leather
Wool
Animal psychology
USE   **Animal intelligence**
Comparative psychology
Animal reproduction   571.8
UF   Animals—Birth
Animals—Reproduction
BT   **Animals**
Reproduction
Animal rights (May subdiv. geog.)   **179**
Use for materials on the inherent rights at-
tributed to animals. Materials on the protec-
tion and treatment of animals are entered un-
der **Animal welfare**. Materials on the political
movement to promote the idea of animal
rights are entered under **Animal rights move-**
ment.
UF   Animals' rights
Rights of animals
RT   **Animal rights movement**
Animal welfare
Animal rights movement (May subdiv.
geog.)   **179**
UF   Animal rights movements
Animal welfare movement
Antivivisection movement
BT   **Social movements**
RT   **Animal rights**
Animal welfare
Animal rights movements
USE   **Animal rights movement**
Animal senses
USE   **Senses and sensation in ani-**
mals
Animal sexual behavior
USE   **Sexual behavior in animals**
Animal shelters (May subdiv. geog.)
179; 636.08
UF   Animal pounds
BT   **Animal welfare**
Animal signs
USE   **Animal tracks**
Animal sounds   573.9; 591.59
UF   Animal language
Animals—Sounds
BT   **Animal behavior**
NT   **Birdsongs**
RT   **Animal communication**
Animal stories
USE   **Animals—Fiction**
Animal tracks   590

Animal tracks—*Continued*
  UF Animal signs
      Tracks of animals
  BT **Tracking and trailing**
Animal training
  USE **Animals—Training**
Animal welfare (May subdiv. geog.)
      179
  Use for materials on the protection and
  treatment of animals. Materials on the inher-
  ent rights attributed to animals are entered un-
  der **Animal rights**. Materials on the political
  movement to promote the idea of animal
  rights are entered under **Animal rights move-
  ment**.
  UF Abuse of animals
      Animal abuse
      Animal exploitation
      Animals—Mistreatment
      Animals—Protection
      Animals—Treatment
      Cruelty to animals
      Humane treatment of animals
      Laboratory animal welfare
      Prevention of cruelty to animals
      Protection of animals
  NT **Animal shelters**
  RT **Animal experimentation**
      Animal rights
      Animal rights movement
Animal welfare movement
  USE **Animal rights movement**
Animals (May subdiv. geog.) **590**
  Use for nonscientific materials. Materials on
  the science of animals are entered under **Zool-
  ogy**. Subdivisions used under this heading
  may be used under the names of orders, class-
  es, or individual species of animals.
  UF Beasts
      Fauna
      Wild animals
  SA names of orders and classes of
      the animal kingdom; kinds of
      animals characterized by their
      environments; names of indi-
      vidual species; and names of
      individual animals [to be add-
      ed as needed]
  NT **Amphibians**
      Animal babies
      Animal behavior
      Animal housing
      Animal intelligence
      Animal locomotion
      Animal reproduction
      Aquatic animals
      Arachnids
      Birds
      Carnivorous animals
      Dangerous animals
      Desert animals
      Domestic animals
      Extinct animals
      Forest animals
      Furbearing animals
      Game and game birds
      Herbivores
      Insects
      Invertebrates
      Jungle animals
      Mammals
      Mountain animals
      Pets
      Poisonous animals
      Predatory animals
      Prehistoric animals
      Rare animals
      Reptiles
      Stream animals
      Swamp animals
      Vertebrates
      Wildlife
      Wildlife attracting
      Working animals
      Worms
  RT **Zoology**
      Zoos
Animals—Anatomy **571.3**
  UF Anatomy of animals
      Structural zoology
      Zoology—Anatomy
  BT **Anatomy**
      Zoology
  NT **Fur**
Animals and the handicapped **636.088**
  UF Handicapped and animals
      Pets and the handicapped
  BT **Animals—Training**
  NT **Guide dogs**
      Hearing ear dogs
      Pet therapy
Animals as food
  USE **Food of animal origin**
Animals—Behavior
  USE **Animal behavior**

Animals—Birth
USE **Animal reproduction**
Animals—Camouflage
USE **Camouflage (Biology)**
Animals—Color   573.5; 591.47
BT **Color**
Animals—Courtship
USE **Animal courtship**
Animals—Diseases   571.9; 636.089
UF   Diseases of animals
        Domestic animals—Diseases
SA   types of animals with the subdi-
        vision *Diseases* [to be added
        as needed]
BT **Diseases**
NT **Horses—Diseases**
RT **Veterinary medicine**
Animals, Edible
USE **Food of animal origin**
Animals—Fiction   808.83
Use for collections of stories about animals.
Materials about the portrayal of animals in lit-
erature are entered under **Animals in litera-
ture**.
UF   Animal stories
SA   types of animals with the subdi-
        vision *Fiction*, e.g. **Dogs—
        Fiction** [to be added as need
        cd]
RT **Animals in literature
        Fables**
Animals—Filmography   016.591
Animals—Flight
USE **Animal flight**
Animals—Folklore (May subdiv. geog.)
        398.24
UF   Animal lore
BT **Folklore**
NT **Dragons
        Ethnozoology
        Monsters**
RT **Mythical animals**
Animals—Food (May subdiv. geog.)
        591.5
Use for materials on the food and food hab-
its of animals. Materials on human food of
animal origin are entered under **Food of ani-
mal origin**.
UF   Animal food
        Feeding behavior in animals
SA   types of animals and species of
        animals with the subdivision
        Food [to be added as needed]

BT **Animal behavior
        Food**
NT **Feeds
        Food chains (Ecology)**
Animals—Habitations   591.56
Use for materials on the natural shelters and
homes animals build for themselves, such as
burrows, dens, lairs, etc. Materials on houses
or habitations provided by humans for either
wild or domestic animals are entered under
Animal housing.
UF   Animal habitations
        Animal homes
        Habitations of wild animals
        Wild animal dwellings
SA   types of animals and individual
        species of animals with the
        subdivision *Habitations*, or
        Nests, e.g. **Beavers—Habita-
        tions**; **Birds—Nests**; etc. [to
        be added as needed]
NT **Nest building**
RT **Animal housing**
Animals—Hearing
USE **Hearing in animals**
Animals—Hibernation
USE **Hibernation**
Animals—Housing
USE **Animal housing**
Animals in art   704.9
Use for materials on the depiction of ani-
mals in works of art. Materials on the art of
painting or drawing animals are entered under
Animal painting and illustration. Materials
consisting chiefly of photographs or illustra-
tions of animals are entered under **Animals—
Pictorial works**.
BT **Art—Themes**
RT **Animal painting and illustra-
        tion
        Animals—Pictorial works**
Animals in literature   809
Use for materials on the theme of animals
in literature. Collections of poems or stories
about animals are entered under **Animals—
Poetry** or **Animals—Fiction**.
UF   Animal lore
SA   phrase headings for specific ani-
        mals in literature, e.g. **Dogs
        in literature** [to be added as
        needed]
BT **Literature—Themes**
RT **Animals—Fiction
        Animals—Poetry**
Animals in motion pictures   791.43
BT **Motion pictures**

Animals in police work (May subdiv.
  geog.) **363.2; 636.088**
  BT **Police**
      Working animals
Animals—Infancy
  USE **Animal babies**
Animals—Language
  USE **Animal communication**
Animals—Migration (May subdiv. geog.)
  591.56
  UF Animal migration
      Migration
  SA types of animals with the subdi-
      vision *Migration*, e.g. **Birds—
      Migration** [to be added as
      needed]
  BT **Animal behavior**
Animals—Mistreatment
  USE **Animal welfare**
Animals—Movements
  USE **Animal locomotion**
Animals, Mythical
  USE **Mythical animals**
Animals—Photography
  USE **Photography of animals**
Animals—Pictorial works 590.22
  Use for popular materials consisting chiefly
  of photographs or illustrations of animals. Ma-
  terials on the art of painting or drawing ani-
  mals are entered under **Animal painting and
  illustration**. Materials on the depiction of ani-
  mals in works of art are entered under **Ani-
  mals in art**.
  UF Animal pictures
  RT **Animal painting and illustra-
      tion**
      Animals in art
      Photography of animals
Animals—Poetry 808.81
  Use for collections of poetry about animals.
  Materials on the theme of animals in literature
  are entered under **Animals in literature**.
  RT **Animals in literature**
Animals, Prehistoric
  USE **Prehistoric animals**
Animals—Protection
  USE **Animal welfare**
Animals—Reproduction
  USE **Animal reproduction**
Animals' rights
  USE **Animal rights**
Animals—Senses and sensation
  USE **Senses and sensation in ani-
      mals**

Animals—Sexual behavior
  USE **Sexual behavior in animals**
Animals—Sounds
  USE **Animal sounds**
Animals—Temperature
  USE **Body temperature**
Animals—Training (May subdiv. geog.)
  636.088
  UF Animal training
      Training of animals
  SA types of animals with the subdi-
      vision *Training*, e.g. **Horses—
      Training** [to be added as
      needed]
  NT **Animals and the handicapped**
      Dogs—Training
Animals—Treatment
  USE **Animal welfare**
Animals—United States 591.973
  UF Zoology—United States
Animals, Useful and harmful
  USE **Economic zoology**
Animals—Vision
  USE **Vision in animals**
Animals—War use (May subdiv. geog.)
  355.4
  UF War use of animals
  BT **Working animals**
  NT **Dogs—War use**
Animated cartoons
  USE **Animated films**
Animated films (May subdiv. geog.)
  741.5; 791.43
  Use for individual works, collections, or
  materials about animated films.
  UF Animated cartoons
      Cartoons, Animated
      Motion picture cartoons
  BT **Cartoons and caricatures**
      Motion pictures
  NT **Anime**
  RT **Animation (Cinematography)**
Animated television programs 791.45
  Use for individual works, collections, or
  materials about animated television programs.
  UF Cartoons, Television
      Television cartoons
  BT **Television programs**
  NT **Anime**
**Animation (Cinematography) 741.5;
  778.5**
  BT **Cinematography**

Animation (Cinematography)—*Continued*
  NT **Computer animation**
  RT **Animated films**
Anime 791.4
  BT **Animated films**
      Animated television programs
Animism (May subdiv. geog.) **147; 299**
  BT **Religion**
Anniversaries 394.2
  UF Celebrations, anniversaries, etc.
      Commemorations
  SA ethnic groups, classes of per-
      sons, individuals, corporate
      bodies, places, religious de-
      nominations, historic or social
      movements, and historic
      events with the subdivision
      Anniversaries, for materials
      about anniversary celebrations,
      e.g. **Shakespeare, William,
      1564-1616—Anniversaries**,
      and names of places, corpo-
      rate bodies, and historical
      events with the subdivision
      Centennial celebrations, etc.,
      e.g. **United States—History—
      1861-1865, Civil War—Cen-
      tennial celebrations, etc.** [to
      be added as needed]
  BT **Manners and customs**
  NT **Birthdays**
  RT **Days**
      Festivals
      Holidays
Annual income guarantee
  USE **Guaranteed annual income**
Annuals
  USE **Almanacs**
       Calendars
       Periodicals
       School yearbooks
       Yearbooks
       and subjects and names of
       countries, cities, etc., individu-
       al persons, families, and cor-
       porate bodies with the subdi-
       vision *Periodicals,* e.g. **Engi-
       neering—Periodicals** [to be
       added as needed]
Annuals (Plants) 582.1; 635.9
  BT **Cultivated plants**
      Flower gardening

Flowers
Annuities (May subdiv. geog.) **368.3**
  BT **Investments**
      Retirement income
  NT **Pensions**
  RT **Life insurance**
Annulment of marriage
  USE **Marriage—Annulment**
Anointing of the sick 265
  UF Extreme unction
      Last rites (Sacraments)
      Last sacraments
  BT **Sacraments**
Anonyms
  USE **Pseudonyms**
Anorexia nervosa 616.85
  BT **Eating disorders**
Answers to questions
  USE **Questions and answers**
Antarctic expeditions
  USE **Antarctica—Exploration**
Antarctic regions
  USE **Antarctica**
Antarctica 998
    Use for materials on the continent of Ant-
    arctica and the regions adjacent to it.
  UF Antarctic regions
  BT **Earth**
      Polar regions
  RT **South Pole**
Antarctica—Exploration 919.8
  UF Antarctic expeditions
      Polar expeditions
  SA names of expeditions, e.g. **Byrd
      Antarctic Expedition** [to be
      added as needed]
  BT **Exploration**
      Scientific expeditions
  NT **Byrd Antarctic Expedition**
Antenuptial contracts
  USE **Marriage contracts**
Anthologies 080; 808.8
    Use for collections of general interest by
    several authors not limited to works of litera-
    ture or focused on a single subject.
  UF Collected papers (Anthologies)
      Collected works
      Collections (Anthologies)
      Collections of literature
      Literary collections
      Readings (Anthologies)

Anthologies—*Continued*
    SA   form headings for minor literary forms that represent collections of works of several authors, e.g. **Essays**; **American essays**; **Parodies**; **Short stories**; etc.; major literary forms and national literatures with the subdivision *Collections*, e.g. **Poetry—Collections**; **English literature—Collections**; etc.; and subjects with the subdivision *Literary collections*, for collections focused on a single subject by two or more authors involving two or more literary forms, e.g. **Cats—Literary collections** [to be added as needed]
    BT   **Books**
Anthropogeography
    USE **Human geography**
Anthropology (May subdiv. geog.)   **301; 599.9**
    UF   Human race
    SA   names of races and peoples, e.g. **Navajo Indians** [to be added as needed]
    BT   **Social sciences**
    NT   **Acculturation**
          Anthropometry
          Ethnopsychology
          Forensic anthropology
          Human geography
          Language and languages
          National characteristics
          Physical anthropology
          Social change
    RT   **Civilization**
          Culture
          Ethnology
          Human beings
Anthropometry   **599.9**
    UF   Skeletal remains
    BT   **Anthropology**
          Ethnology
          Human beings
    NT   **Fingerprints**
Anti-abortion movement
    USE **Pro-life movement**
Anti-Americanism
    USE **United States—Foreign opinion**

Anti-apartheid movement (May subdiv. geog.)   **172; 320.5; 323.1**
    BT   **Civil rights**
          Social movements
          South Africa—Race relations
    RT   **Apartheid**
Anti-fascist movements
    USE **World War, 1939-1945—Underground movements**
Anti-Nazi movement
    USE **World War, 1939-1945—Underground movements**
Anti-poverty programs
    USE **Domestic economic assistance**
Anti-Reformation
    USE **Counter-Reformation**
Anti-terrorism
    USE **Terrorism—Prevention**
Anti-utopias
    USE **Dystopias**
Anti-war films
    USE **War films**
Anti-war poetry
    USE **War poetry**
Anti-war stories
    USE **War stories**
Antiabortion movement
    USE **Pro-life movement**
Antiamericanism
    USE **United States—Foreign opinion**
Antiballistic missiles
    USE **Antimissile missiles**
Antibiotic resistance in microorganisms
    USE **Drug resistance in microorganisms**
Antibiotics   **615**
    SA   names of specific antibiotics [to be added as needed]
    BT   **Drug therapy**
    NT   **Penicillin**
Antibusing
    USE **Busing (School integration)**
Anticommunist movements (May subdiv. geog.)   **322.4**
    BT   **Communism**
Anticorrosive paint
    USE **Corrosion and anticorrosives**
Antidepressants   **615**
    BT   **Psychotropic drugs**
Antietam (Md.), Battle of, 1862   **973.7**

Antietam (Md.), Battle of, 1862—*Continued*

   BT **Battles**

       United States—History—1861-1865, Civil War—Campaigns

Antimissile missiles (May subdiv. geog.) **358.1; 623.4**

   UF ABMs

       Antiballistic missiles

   BT **Guided missiles**

Antinuclear movement (May subdiv. geog.) **303.48; 327.1; 363.17**

   UF Nuclear freeze movement

   BT **Arms control**

       Nuclear weapons

       Social movements

   RT **Nuclear power plants—Environmental aspects**

Antipoverty programs

   USE **Domestic economic assistance**

Antiquarian books

   USE **Rare books**

Antique and classic cars (May subdiv. geog.) **629.222**

   UF Antique automobiles

       Antique cars

       Classic automobiles

       Classic cars

       Vintage automobiles

       Vintage cars

   BT **Automobiles**

Antique and vintage motorcycles (May subdiv. geog.) **629.227**

   UF Antique motorcycles

       Classic motorcycles

       Vintage motorcycles

   BT **Motorcycles**

Antique automobiles

   USE **Antique and classic cars**

Antique cars

   USE **Antique and classic cars**

Antique motorcycles

   USE **Antique and vintage motorcycles**

Antiques (May subdiv. geog.) **745.1**

   Use for materials on old decorative or utilitarian objects that have aesthetic or historical importance and financial value. Materials on any objects of interest to collectors, including mass produced items of little intrinsic value, are entered under **Collectibles**.

   SA subjects and names with the subdivision *Collectibles*, e.g. **American Revolution Bicentennial, 1776-1976—Collectibles**; and types of objects collected, excluding antiquities and natural objects, with the subdivision *Collectors and collecting*, e.g. **Boxes—Collectors and collecting** [to be added as needed]

   BT **Antiquities**

       Collectors and collecting

       Decoration and ornament

       Decorative arts

   NT **Art objects**

       Collectors and collecting

       Victoriana

Antiques—Price guides **745.075**

Antiques—United States **745.10973**

   Use for materials about old American objects that have aesthetic as well as financial value, usually furniture or decorative arts. Materials about American objects of interest to collectors for their historical value, such as documents, relics, etc., including items of little intrinsic value, are entered under **Americana**.

   RT **Americana**

Antiquities **930.1**

   Use for general materials on the relics or monuments of ancient times. Materials on the relics or monuments of an extinct city or town are entered under the name of the city or town.

   UF Archeological specimens

       Ruins

   SA names of extinct cities, e.g. **Delphi (Extinct city)**; and names of groups of people extant in modern times and names of cities (except extinct cities), countries, regions, etc., with the subdivision *Antiquities*, e.g. **Native Americans—Antiquities**; **United States—Antiquities**; etc. [to be added as needed]

   NT **America—Antiquities**

       Antiques

       Bible—Antiquities

       Chicago (Ill.)—Antiquities

       Christian antiquities

       Classical antiquities

       Egypt—Antiquities

Antiquities—*Continued*
  Italy—Antiquities
  Jews—Antiquities
  Megalithic monuments
  Native Americans—Antiquities
  Ohio—Antiquities
  Prehistoric peoples
  Turkey—Antiquities
  United States—Antiquities
 RT **Archeology**
Antiquities—Collection and preservation
 (May subdiv. geog.) **069**
 UF Preservation of antiquities
 BT **Collectors and collecting**
Antiquity of man
 USE **Human origins**
Antisemitism (May subdiv. geog.)
  305.892
 BT **Prejudices**
 NT **Holocaust, 1939-1945**
  Jews—Persecutions
Antiseptics **614.4; 617.9**
 BT **Therapeutics**
 RT **Disinfection and disinfectants**
  Surgery
Antislavery
 USE **Abolitionists**
  Slavery
  Slaves—Emancipation
Antistalking laws
 USE **Stalking**
Antitank warfare
 USE **Tank warfare**
Antitrust law (May subdiv. geog.)
  343.07
 UF Industrial trusts—Law and legis-
   lation
 BT **Commercial law**
 RT **Industrial trusts**
Antivivisection movement
 USE **Animal rights movement**
Antiwar movements
 USE **Peace movements**
Antonyms
 USE **Opposites**
  and names of languages with
   the subdivision *Synonyms and*
   antonyms, e.g. **English lan-**
   guage—Synonyms and ant-
   onyms [to be added as need-
   ed]
Ants **595.79**

 BT **Insects**
Anxieties
 USE **Anxiety**
Anxiety **152.4**
 UF Anxieties
  Anxiousness
 BT **Emotions**
  Neuroses
  Stress (Psychology)
 NT **Post-traumatic stress disorder**
  Separation anxiety in children
 RT **Fear**
  Worry
Anxiousness
 USE **Anxiety**
Apartheid (May subdiv. geog.) **320.5**
 Use for materials on the economic, political,
 and social policies of the government of
 South Africa designed to segregate racial
 groups in South Africa and Namibia.
 UF Separate development (Race re-
   lations)
 BT **Segregation**
  South Africa—Race relations
 RT **Anti-apartheid movement**
Apartment houses (May subdiv. geog.)
  647; 728
 BT **Buildings**
  Domestic architecture
  Houses
  Housing
 NT **Apartments**
  Condominiums
  Tenement houses
Apartments (May subdiv. geog.) **643**
 UF Flats
 BT **Apartment houses**
Apes (May subdiv. geog.) **599.88**
 BT **Primates**
 NT **Baboons**
  Chimpanzees
  Gorillas
Aphasia **371.91; 616.85**
 Use for materials that discuss language in-
 abilities.
 UF Speech problems
 BT **Brain—Diseases**
  Language disorders
  Speech disorders
Aphrodite (Greek deity) **202**
 BT **Gods and goddesses**
Apiculture
 USE **Beekeeping**

Apocalyptic fiction 808.3; 808.83

Use for individual works, collections, or materials about apocalyptic fiction

UF End-of-the-world fiction

BT **Fiction**

Apocalyptic films 791.43

Use for individual works, collections, or materials about apocalyptic films.

UF End-of-the-world films

BT **Motion pictures**

Apollo (Greek deity) 202

BT **Gods and goddesses**

Apollo project 629.45

UF Project Apollo

BT **Life support systems (Space environment)**

Orbital rendezvous (Space flight)

Space flight to the moon

Apologetic works

USE **Apologetics**

and religions and denominations with the subdivision *Apologetic works,* for materials defending those religions or denominations, e.g. **Christianity—Apologetic works** for materials defending Christianity; and religions, denominations, religious orders, and sacred works with the subdivision *Controversial literature,* for materials that argue against or express opposition to those groups or works, e.g. **Christianity—Controversial literature** for materials attacking Christianity [to be added as needed]

Apologetics 202; 239

UF Apologetic works

SA religions and denominations with the subdivision *Apologetic works*, for materials defending those religions or denominations, e.g. **Christianity—Apologetic works** for materials defending Christianity; and religions, denominations, religious orders, and sacred works with the subdivision

Controversial literature, for materials that argue against or express opposition to those groups or works, e.g. **Christianity—Controversial literature** for materials attacking Christianity [to be added as needed]

BT **Theology**

NT **Christianity—Apologetic works**

Natural theology

Apoplexy

USE **Stroke**

Apostles 225.92

UF Disciples, Twelve

BT **Christian saints**

Church history—30-600, Early church

Apostles' Creed 238

BT **Creeds**

Apostolic Church

USE **Church history—30-600, Early church**

Appalachia

USE **Appalachian Region**

Appalachian Mountains Region

USE **Appalachian Region**

Appalachian Region 974

UF Appalachia

Appalachian Mountains Region

BT **United States**

Appalachian Trail 973

BT **Trails**

Apparatus, Chemical

USE **Chemical apparatus**

Apparatus, Electric

USE **Electric apparatus and appliances**

Apparatus, Electronic

USE **Electronic apparatus and appliances**

Apparatus, Scientific

USE **Scientific apparatus and instruments**

Apparitions (May subdiv. geog.) 133.1

UF Phantoms

Specters

BT **Parapsychology**

Spirits

NT **Ghosts**

Apparitions—*Continued*
   RT   **Hallucinations and illusions**
         Spiritualism
         Visions
Appearance, Personal
   USE **Personal appearance**
Apperception   153.7
   BT   **Educational psychology**
         Psychology
   NT   **Attention**
         Consciousness
         Number concept
   RT   **Perception**
         Theory of knowledge
Appetizers   641.812
   UF   Canapés
         Hors d'oeuvres
   BT   **Cooking**
Apple
   USE **Apples**
Apple Macintosh (Computer)
   USE **Macintosh (Computer)**
Apples (May subdiv. geog.)   **641.3**
   UF   Apple
   BT   **Fruit**
Appliances, Electric
   USE **Electric apparatus and appliances**
         Electric household appliances
Appliances, Electronic
   USE **Electronic apparatus and appliances**
Applications for college
   USE **College applications**
Applications for positions   331.12; 650.14
   UF   Employment applications
         Employment references
         Job applications
         Letters of recommendation
         Recommendations for positions
   BT   **Job hunting**
         Personnel management
   NT   **Job interviews**
         Résumés (Employment)
Applied arts
   USE **Decorative arts**
Applied mechanics   620.1
   Use for materials on the application of the principles of mechanics to engineering structures other than machinery. Materials on the application of the principles of mechanics to the design, construction, and operation of machinery are entered under **Mechanical engineering**.
   UF   Mechanics, Applied
   BT   **Mechanics**
Applied psychology   158
   UF   Industrial psychology
         Practical psychology
         Psychology, Applied
   SA   subjects with the subdivision *Psychological aspects*, e.g. **Drugs—Psychological aspects** [to be added as needed]
   BT   **Psychology**
   NT   **Behavior modification**
         Counseling
         Drugs—Psychological aspects
         Employee morale
         Human engineering
         Negotiation
         Organizational behavior
         Pastoral psychology
         Psychological warfare
         Self-help techniques
   RT   **Educational psychology**
         Interviewing
         Social psychology
Applied science
   USE **Technology**
Appliqué   746.44
   BT   **Needlework**
Appointment
   USE types of public officials and names of individual public officials with the subdivision *Appointment,* e.g. **Presidents—United States—Appointment** [to be added as needed]
Appointments and retirements
   USE names of armed forces with the subdivision *Appointments and retirements,* e.g. **United States. Army—Appointments and retirements** [to be added as needed]
Appomattox Campaign, 1865   973.7
   BT   **United States—History—1861-1865, Civil War—Campaigns**
Apportionment (Election law) (May subdiv. geog.)   **324; 328.3; 342**

Apportionment (Election law)—*Continued*
- UF   Legislative reapportionment
-       Reapportionment (Election law)
- BT   **Representative government and representation**

Appraisal
- USE   **Tax assessment**
-       **Valuation**

Appraisal of books
- USE   **Book reviewing**
-       **Books and reading**
-       **Criticism**
-       **Literature—History and criticism**

Appreciation of art
- USE   **Art appreciation**

Appreciation of music
- USE   **Music appreciation**

Apprentices   **331.5**
- BT   **Labor**
-       **Technical education**
- RT   **Employees—Training**

Apprenticeship novels
- USE   **Bildungsromans**

Appropriations and expenditures
- USE   names of countries and names of individual government departments, agencies, etc., with the subdivision *Appropriations and expenditures,* e.g. **United States—Appropriations and expenditures** [to be added as needed]

Approximate computation   **372.7; 511**
- UF   Arithmetic—Estimation
-       Computation, Approximate
-       Estimation (Mathematics)
- BT   **Numerical analysis**

April First
- USE   **April Fools' Day**

April Fools' Day   **394.262**
- UF   All Fools' Day
-       April First
- BT   **Holidays**

Aptitude
- USE   **Ability**

Aptitude testing
- USE   **Ability—Testing**

Aquaculture (May subdiv. geog.)   **639**
- UF   Aquiculture
-       Freshwater aquaculture
-       Mariculture
-       Marine aquaculture
-       Ocean farming
-       Sea farming
- BT   **Agriculture**
-       **Marine resources**
- NT   **Fish culture**

Aquarian Age movement
- USE   **New Age movement**

Aquariums (May subdiv. geog.)   **597.073; 639.34**
- SA   names of specific aquariums [to be added as needed]
- BT   **Freshwater biology**
-       **Natural history**
- NT   **Marine aquariums**
- RT   **Fish culture**
-       **Fishes**

Aquatic animals (May subdiv. geog.)   **591.76**
- UF   Aquatic fauna
-       Water animals
- BT   **Animals**
- NT   **Fishes**
-       **Freshwater animals**
-       **Marine animals**
-       **Shellfish**
-       **Sponges**

Aquatic birds
- USE   **Water birds**

Aquatic exercises   **613.7**
- UF   Underwater exercises
-       Water exercises
- BT   **Exercise**

Aquatic fauna
- USE   **Aquatic animals**

Aquatic gardens
- USE   **Water gardens**

Aquatic plants
- USE   **Freshwater plants**
-       **Marine plants**

Aquatic sports
- USE   **Water sports**

Aquatic sports—Safety measures
- USE   **Water safety**

Aqueducts (May subdiv. geog.)   **628.1**
- UF   Water conduits
- BT   **Civil engineering**
-       **Hydraulic structures**
-       **Water supply**

Aquiculture
- USE   **Aquaculture**

Arab countries   956

Use for materials on several Arabic-speaking countries. Materials on the region consisting of northeastern Africa and Asia west of Afghanistan are entered under **Middle East**.

    BT   **Islamic countries**
           Middle East

Arab countries—Foreign relations—Israel 956

    UF   Arab-Israel relations
           Arab-Israeli relations
           Israel-Arab relations
           Israeli-Arab relations
    NT   **Israel-Arab conflicts**
    RT   **Israel—Foreign relations— Arab countries**
           Jewish-Arab relations

Arab countries—Politics and government 956

    BT   **Politics**
    NT   **Pan-Arabism**

Arab-Israel conflicts
    USE **Israel-Arab conflicts**

Arab-Israel relations
    USE **Arab countries—Foreign relations—Israel**
           Israel—Foreign relations— Arab countries

Arab-Israel War, 1948-1949
    USE **Israel-Arab War, 1948-1949**

Arab-Israel War, 1956
    USE **Sinai Campaign, 1956**

Arab-Israel War, 1967
    USE **Israel-Arab War, 1967**

Arab-Israel War, 1973
    USE **Israel-Arab War, 1973**

Arab-Israeli conflict, 1987-1992
    USE **Intifada, 1987-1992**

Arab-Israeli conflict, 2000-
    USE **Intifada, 2000-**

Arab-Israeli conflicts
    USE **Israel-Arab conflicts**

Arab-Israeli relations
    USE **Arab countries—Foreign relations—Israel**
           Israel—Foreign relations— Arab countries

Arab-Jewish relations
    USE **Jewish-Arab relations**

Arab refugees (May subdiv. geog.) **305.9**

    UF   Refugees, Arab

    BT   **Refugees**

Arab science
    USE **Science—Islamic countries**

Arabia
    USE **Arabian Peninsula**

Arabian Peninsula   953

    UF   Arabia
    BT   **Peninsulas**

Arabic civilization   306.0917; 909

    UF   Civilization, Arab
    BT   **Civilization**

Arabic language   492.7

    BT   **Language and languages**

Arabic literature   892.7

    BT   **Literature**

Arabs (May subdiv. geog.)   **305.892; 909**

    SA   names of specific Arab peoples [to be added as needed]
    NT   **Bedouins**
           Jewish-Arab relations
           Palestinian Arabs

Arabs—Palestine
    USE **Palestinian Arabs**

Arachnida
    USE **Arachnids**

Arachnids (May subdiv. geog.)   **595.4**

    UF   Arachnida
    BT   **Animals**
    NT   **Spiders**
           Ticks

Arbitration and award (May subdiv. geog.)   **347**

Use for materials on the settlement of civil disputes by arbitration instead of a court trial.

    UF   Awards (Law)
           Mediation
    BT   **Commercial law**
           Courts
    RT   **Litigation**

Arbitration, Industrial
    USE **Industrial arbitration**

Arbitration, International
    USE **International arbitration**

Arboriculture
    USE **Forests and forestry**
           Fruit culture
           Trees

Arc light
    USE **Electric lighting**

Arc welding
    USE **Electric welding**

Archaeology
USE **Archeology**
Archaeopteryx 568
BT **Dinosaurs**
Archbishops
USE **Bishops**
Archeological specimens
USE **Antiquities**
Archeologists (May subdiv. geog.) **920;
930.1092**
BT **Historians**
Archeology (May subdiv. geog.) **930.1**
> Use for materials on the discipline of arche-ology. General materials on the relics or mon-uments of ancient times are entered under **An-tiquities**. Materials on the relics or monu-ments of an extinct city or town are entered under the name of the city or town.

UF Archaeology
Prehistory
SA names of extinct cities, e.g. **Del-phi (Extinct city)**; and names
of groups of people and of
cities (except extinct cities),
countries, regions, etc., with
the subdivision *Antiquities*,
e.g. **Native Americans—An-tiquities; United States—An-tiquities**; etc. [to be added as
needed]
BT **History**
NT **Ancient architecture
Bible—Antiquities
Bronzes
Burial
Buried treasure
Cliff dwellers and cliff dwell-ings
Excavations (Archeology)
Extinct cities
Fossil hominids
Gems
Heraldry
Historic sites
Industrial archeology
Inscriptions
Megalithic monuments
Mounds and mound builders
Mummies
Numismatics
Obelisks
Prehistoric peoples
Pyramids**

**Radiocarbon dating
Rock drawings, paintings, and
engravings
Tombs**
RT **Antiquities**
Archery (May subdiv. geog.) **799.3**
BT **Martial arts
Shooting**
RT **Bow and arrow**
Architects (May subdiv. geog.) **720.92;
920**
BT **Artists**
Architectural acoustics 729; 690
UF Acoustics
BT **Sound**
NT **Soundproofing**
Architectural decoration and ornament
(May subdiv. geog.) **729**
UF Architecture—Decoration and or-nament
Decoration and ornament, Archi-tectural
BT **Architecture
Decoration and ornament**
NT **Gargoyles**
Architectural design 720
> Use for materials on the process and meth-odology of designing buildings.

BT **Architecture
Design**
Architectural designs
USE **Architecture—Designs and
plans**
Architectural details
USE **Architecture—Details**
Architectural drawing 720.28
BT **Drawing**
Architectural engineering
USE **Building
Structural analysis (Engineer-ing)
Structural engineering**
Architectural features
USE **Architecture—Details**
Architectural metalwork (May subdiv.
geog.) **721**
BT **Metalwork**
Architectural perspective
USE **Perspective**
Architecture (May subdiv. geog.) **720**
> Use for materials on the design and style of
structures. Materials on the process of con-

Architecture—*Continued*
struction are entered under **Building**. General materials on buildings are entered under **Buildings**.

- UF   Building design
  Construction
- SA   styles of architecture, e.g. **Byzantine architecture**; and types of buildings, e.g. **Farm buildings** [to be added as needed]
- BT   **Art**
- NT   **American colonial style in architecture**
  Ancient architecture
  Architectural decoration and ornament
  Architectural design
  Asian architecture
  Baroque architecture
  Byzantine architecture
  Church architecture
  Classicism in architecture
  Domestic architecture
  Gothic revival (Architecture)
  Greek architecture
  Industrial buildings—Design and construction
  Islamic architecture
  Landscape architecture
  Library architecture
  Lost architecture
  Medieval architecture
  Modernism in architecture
  Monuments
  Native American architecture
  Naval architecture
  Obelisks
  Roman architecture
  Romanesque architecture
  Spires
  Sustainable architecture
  Tombs
  Underground architecture
- RT   **Building**
  Buildings

Architecture—15th and 16th centuries **724**
- UF   Architecture, Renaissance
  Renaissance architecture

Architecture—17th and 18th centuries **724**
- UF   Architecture, Modern—17th-18th centuries
  Modern architecture—1600-1799 (17th and 18th centuries)

Architecture—19th century **724**
- UF   Architecture, Modern—19th century
  Modern architecture—1800-1899 (19th century)
- NT   **Victorian architecture**

Architecture—20th century **724**
- UF   Architecture, Modern—20th century
  Modern architecture—1900-1999 (20th century)

Architecture—21st century **724**
- UF   Architecture, Modern—21st century
  Modern architecture—2000-2099 (21st century)

Architecture, American
- USE   **Architecture—United States**

Architecture, Ancient
- USE   **Ancient architecture**

Architecture and the handicapped (May subdiv. geog.) **720**
- UF   Barrier free design
  Handicapped and architecture
- BT   **Handicapped**

Architecture—Awards (May subdiv. geog.) **720.79**

Architecture, Baroque
- USE   **Baroque architecture**

Architecture, Byzantine
- USE   **Byzantine architecture**

Architecture—Composition, proportion, etc. **720; 729**
- UF   Architecture—Proportion
  Proportion (Architecture)
- BT   **Composition (Art)**

Architecture—Conservation and restoration (May subdiv. geog.) **690; 720.28**
- UF   Architecture—Restoration
  Buildings, Restoration of
  Conservation of buildings
  Preservation of buildings
  Restoration of buildings
- RT   **Buildings—Maintenance and repair**

Architecture—Decoration and ornament
    USE   **Architectural decoration and ornament**

Architecture—Designs and plans
    720.28; 729
    UF   Architectural designs
          Architecture—Plans
          Designs, Architectural
    NT   **Domestic architecture—Designs and plans**

Architecture—Details (May subdiv. geog.)
    721; 729
    UF   Architectural details
          Architectural features
    SA   types of architectural features,
          e.g. **Windows**; **Fireplaces**;
          etc. [to be added as needed]
    NT   **Chimneys**
          Doors
          Fireplaces
          Floors
          Foundations
          Gargoyles
          Roofs
          Windows
          Woodwork

Architecture, Domestic
    USE   **Domestic architecture**

Architecture, Gothic
    USE   **Gothic architecture**

Architecture, Greek
    USE   **Greek architecture**

Architecture—India   **720.954**
    UF   Indian architecture
          Indic architecture

Architecture, Islamic
    USE   **Islamic architecture**

Architecture, Medieval
    USE   **Medieval architecture**

Architecture, Modern
    USE   **Modernism in architecture**

Architecture, Modern—17th-18th centuries
    USE   **Architecture—17th and 18th centuries**

Architecture, Modern—19th century
    USE   **Architecture—19th century**

Architecture, Modern—20th century
    USE   **Architecture—20th century**

Architecture, Modern—21st century
    USE   **Architecture—21st century**

Architecture—Plans
    USE   **Architecture—Designs and plans**

Architecture—Proportion
    USE   **Architecture—Composition, proportion, etc.**

Architecture, Renaissance
    USE   **Architecture—15th and 16th centuries**

Architecture—Restoration
    USE   **Architecture—Conservation and restoration**

Architecture, Roman
    USE   **Roman architecture**

Architecture, Romanesque
    USE   **Romanesque architecture**

Architecture, Rural
    USE   **Farm buildings**

Architecture—United States   **720.973**
    UF   American architecture
          Architecture, American

Architecture—United States—1600-1775, Colonial period   **720.973**
    UF   Colonial architecture

Archives (May subdiv. geog.)   **026; 027**
    UF   Documents
          Government records—Preservation
          Historical records—Preservation
          Preservation of historical records
          Public records—Preservation
          Records—Preservation
    SA   subjects, ethnic groups, classes
          of persons, individuals, fami-
          lies, schools, and military ser-
          vices with the subdivision *Ar-*
          chives [to be added as need-
          ed]
    BT   **Bibliography**
          Documentation
          History—Sources
          Information services
    NT   **Manuscripts**
          Presidents—United States—Archives
    RT   **Charters**
          Libraries

Archives—United States   **027.0973; 353.0071**
    UF   United States—Archives

Arctic expeditions
USE **Arctic regions—Exploration**
Arctic regions   919.8; 998
UF   Far north
BT   **Earth**
     Polar regions
NT   **Northeast Passage**
     Northwest Passage
RT   **North Pole**
Arctic regions—Exploration   919.8
UF   Arctic expeditions
     Polar expeditions
SA   names of expeditions [to be add-
     ed as needed]
BT   **Exploration**
     Scientific expeditions
**Ardennes (France), Battle of the, 1944-
     1945   940.54**
UF   Bastogne, Battle of
     Battle of the Bulge
     Bulge, Battle of the
BT   **Battles**
     **World War, 1939-1945—Cam-
     paigns**
Area studies   940-999
     Use for general materials on area studies.
UF   Foreign area studies
SA   continents, countries, and geo-
     graphic regions with the sub-
     division *Study and teaching*
     [to be added as needed]
BT   **Education**
NT   **Africa—Study and teaching**
Arena theater (May subdiv. geog.)   **725;
     792**
UF   Round stage
     Theater-in-the-round
BT   **Theater**
Argentina   982
     May be subdivided like United States ex-
     cept for History.
Argentine rummy
USE   **Canasta (Game)**
**Argonauts (Legendary characters)
     398.22**
BT   **Legendary characters**
Argumentation
USE   **Debates and debating**
     Logic
Arid regions (May subdiv. geog.)
     551.41

UF   Arid zones
     Semiarid regions
BT   **Earth**
Arid zones
USE   **Arid regions**
Aristocracy (May subdiv. geog.)   **305.5**
BT   **Political science**
     Upper class
RT   **Nobility**
Arithmetic   513
UF   Computation (Mathematics)
SA   types of arithmetic operations [to
     be added as needed]
BT   **Mathematics**
     Set theory
NT   **Addition**
     Average
     Cube root
     Division
     Fractions
     Mental arithmetic
     Metric system
     Multiplication
     Percentage
     Ratio and proportion
     Square root
     Subtraction
RT   **Numbers**
Arithmetic, Commercial
USE   **Business mathematics**
Arithmetic—Estimation
USE   **Approximate computation**
Arithmetic—Study and teaching (May
     subdiv. geog.)   **372.7; 513.07**
NT   **Counting**
     Mathematical readiness
     Number games
Arithmetic—Textbooks   513
Arithmetical ability
USE   **Mathematical ability**
Arithmetical readiness
USE   **Mathematical readiness**
Armada, 1588
USE   **Spanish Armada, 1588**
Armaments
USE   **Military readiness**
     Military weapons
Armaments industries
USE   **Defense industry**
Armed forces   343; 355

Armed forces—*Continued*
- UF   Armed services
  - Military forces
- SA   specific branches of the armed forces under names of countries, e.g. **United States. Army**; and names of countries, regions, and international organizations with the subdivision *Armed forces*, e.g. **United States—Armed forces; United Nations—Armed forces**; etc. [to be added as needed]
- BT   **Military art and science**
- NT   **Armies**
  - **Military personnel**
  - **Navies**
  - **Ohio—Militia**
  - **Recruiting and enlistment**
  - **United Nations—Armed forces**
  - **United States—Armed forces**
  - **United States—Militia**
  - **Voluntary military service**
- RT   **Military readiness**
  - **War**

Armed forces—Recruiting, enlistment, etc.
- USE   **Recruiting and enlistment**

Armed forces—Women
- USE   **Women in the military**

Armed services
- USE   **Armed forces**

Armenia (Republic)   947.56

Armies   355.3
- UF   Army
  - Military power
- SA   names of countries with the subhead *Army*, e.g. **United States. Army** [to be added as needed]
- BT   **Armed forces**
  - **Military personnel**
- NT   **Draft**
  - **Soldiers**
  - **United States. Army**
- RT   **Military art and science**

Armies—Medical care   355.3
- SA   names of wars with the subdivision *Health aspects* or *Medical care*, e.g. **World War, 1939-1945—Health aspects**;

World War, 1939-1945—Medical care; etc. [to be added as needed]
- BT   **Medical care**
  - **Military medicine**
- RT   **Military personnel—Health and hygiene**

Armistice Day
- USE   **Veterans Day**

Armistices
- USE   names of wars with the subdivision *Armistices,* e.g. **World War, 1939-1945—Armistices** [to be added as needed]

Armor (May subdiv. geog.)   **355.8; 623.4; 739.7**

Use for materials on protective covering worn as a defense against weapons.
- UF   Arms and armor
  - Suits of armor
- BT   **Art metalwork**
  - **Costume**
  - **Military art and science**
- RT   **Weapons**

Armored cars (Tanks)
- USE   **Military tanks**

Arms and armor
- USE   **Armor**
  - **Weapons**

Arms control (May subdiv. geog.)   **327.1; 341.7**
- UF   Disarmament
  - Limitation of armament
  - Non-proliferation of nuclear weapons
  - Nuclear non-proliferation
  - Nuclear test ban
- BT   **International relations**
  - **International security**
  - **War**
- NT   **Antinuclear movement**
  - **Arms race**
- RT   **International arbitration**
  - **Military readiness**
  - **Peace**

Arms proliferation
- USE   **Arms race**

Arms race (May subdiv. geog.)   **327.1; 355**

Use for materials on the competitive increase in the military power of two or more nations or blocs.

Arms race—*Continued*
    UF   Arms proliferation
          Proliferation of arms
    BT   **Arms control**
          International security
    RT   **Arms transfers**
          Military readiness
          Military weapons
Arms sales
    USE **Arms transfers**
          Defense industry
          Military assistance
          Military weapons
Arms traffic
    USE **Arms transfers**
Arms transfers (May subdiv. geog.)
          327.1; 382
    UF   Arms sales
          Arms traffic
          Foreign military sales
          Military sales
    BT   **International trade**
    RT   **Arms race**
          Defense industry
          Military assistance
Army
    USE **Armies**
          Military art and science
          and names of countries with the
             subhead *Army*, e.g. **United**
             States. Army [to be added as
             needed]
Army bases
    USE **Military bases**
Army desertion
    USE **Military desertion**
Army life
    USE **Soldiers**
          and names of armies with the
             subdivision *Military life*, e.g.
             United States. Army—Military life [to be added as
             needed]
Army posts
    USE **Military bases**
Army schools
    USE **Military education**
Army tests
    USE **United States. Army—Examinations**
Army vehicles
    USE **Military vehicles**

Aromatherapy   **615**
    BT   **Therapeutics**
Aromatic plant products
    USE **Essences and essential oils**
Aromatic plants (May subdiv. geog.)
          582; 635.9
    BT   **Plants**
    RT   **Essences and essential oils**
          Fragrant gardens
Arrow
    USE **Bow and arrow**
Arson (May subdiv. geog.)   **364.16**
    BT   **Offenses against property**
Art   **700**
    Use for materials on the visual arts only (architecture, painting, etc.). Materials on the arts in general, including the visual arts, literature, and the performing arts, are entered under **Arts**.
    SA   types of art, e.g. **Commercial art**; art of particular religions, e.g. **Christian art**; movements in art, e.g. **Romanticism in art**; art and other subjects, e.g. **Art and mythology**; subjects and themes in art, e.g. **Animals in art**; and art of particular countries, regions, or ethnic groups, e.g. **American art**; **Greek art**; **Native American art**; etc. [to be added as needed]
    BT   **Arts**
    NT   **Abstract art**
          African American art
          African art
          American art
          Ancient art
          Architecture
          Art and mythology
          Art and religion
          Art and society
          Art objects
          Artistic anatomy
          Artistic photography
          Artists' models
          Arts and crafts movement
          Asian art
          Baroque art
          Black art
          Botanical illustration
          Bronzes
          Buddhist art

Byzantine art
Celtic art
Children's art
Christian art
Collage
Collectors and collecting
Commercial art
Composition (Art)
Computer art
Copy art
Cubism
Decoration and ornament
Drawing
Earthworks (Art)
Engraving
Erotic art
Etching
Ethnic art
Etruscan art
Expressionism (Art)
Folk art
Futurism (Art)
Gems
Gothic revival (Art)
Graphic arts
Greek art
Illumination of books and
   manuscripts
Illustration of books
Impressionism (Art)
Indian art
Interior design
Islamic art
Kinetic art
Medieval art
Modernism in art
Municipal art
Native American art
Outsider art
Painting
Performance art
Pictures
Pop art
Portraits
Postimpressionism (Art)
Prehistoric art
Realism in art
Religious art
Roman art
Romanticism in art
Sculpture

Symbolism
Video art
World War, 1939-1945—Art
   and the war
RT   Artists
Art—15th and 16th centuries   709.02;
      709.03
   UF   Art, Renaissance
         Renaissance art
Art—17th and 18th centuries   709.03
   UF   Art, Modern—17th-18th centu-
         ries
Art—19th century   709.03
   UF   Art, Modern—19th century
         Modern art—1800-1899 (19th
         century)
   NT   **Art nouveau**
Art—20th century   709.04
   UF   Art, Modern—20th century
         Modern art—1900-1999 (20th
         century)
   SA   types of twentieth-century art,
         e.g. **Cubism** [to be added as
         needed]
   NT   **Art deco**
Art—21st century   709.05
   UF   Art, Modern—21st century
         Modern art—2000-2099 (21st
         century)
Art, American
   USE   **American art**
Art—Analysis, interpretation, appreciation
   USE   **Art appreciation**
         Art criticism
         Art—Study and teaching
Art, Ancient
   USE   **Ancient art**
Art and mythology   704.9
   UF   Mythology in art
   BT   **Art**
         Mythology
   RT   **Art and religion**
Art and religion   201; 246; 701
   UF   Arts in the church
         Religion and art
   BT   **Art**
         Religion
   RT   **Art and mythology**
         Religious art
Art and society (May subdiv. geog.)
      701

Art and society—*Continued*
   UF   Art and sociology
         Society and art
         Sociology and art
   BT   **Art**
   NT   **Art patronage**
         Art—Political aspects
         Folk art
Art and sociology
   USE   **Art and society**
Art and the war
   USE   names of wars with the subdivision *Art and the war,* e.g. **World War, 1939-1945—Art and the war** [to be added as needed]

Art appreciation   701
   UF   Appreciation of art
         Art—Analysis, interpretation, appreciation
   BT   **Aesthetics**
         Art criticism
Art, Asian
   USE   **Asian art**
Art, Baroque
   USE   **Baroque art**
Art, Black
   USE   **Black art**
Art, Buddhist
   USE   **Buddhist art**
Art, Byzantine
   USE   **Byzantine art**

Art collections (May subdiv. geog.)   **708**
   UF   Art—Collections
         Art—Private collections
         Collections of art, painting, etc.
         Private art collections
   SA   names of collectors or of the original owners of private art collections with the subdivision *Art collections* [to be added as needed]
   RT   **Art museums**
         Collectors and collecting
Art—Collections
   USE   **Art collections**
Art—Composition
   USE   **Composition (Art)**

Art criticism   701; 709
   UF   Art—Analysis, interpretation, appreciation
   BT   **Criticism**

   NT   **Art appreciation**
Art deco (May subdiv. geog.)   **709.04**
   BT   **Art—20th century**
Art education
   USE   **Art—Study and teaching**
Art—Exhibitions (May subdiv. geog.)   **707.4**
   BT   **Exhibitions**
Art—Federal aid
   USE   **Federal aid to the arts**
Art—Forgeries (May subdiv. geog.)   **702.8; 751.5**
   UF   Art forgeries
         Forgery of works of art
   BT   **Counterfeits and counterfeiting**
         Forgery
Art forgeries
   USE   **Art—Forgeries**
Art galleries
   USE   **Art museums**
         Commercial art galleries
Art, Gothic
   USE   **Gothic art**
Art, Greek
   USE   **Greek art**
Art—History   709
   BT   **History**
Art in advertising
   USE   **Commercial art**
Art in motion
   USE   **Kinetic art**
Art industries and trade
   USE   **Decorative arts**
Art, Islamic
   USE   **Islamic art**
Art, Kinetic
   USE   **Kinetic art**
Art, Medieval
   USE   **Medieval art**
Art metalwork (May subdiv. geog.)   **739; 745.56**
   UF   Decorative metalwork
   SA   types of art metalwork [to be added as needed]
   BT   **Decorative arts**
         Metalwork
   NT   **Armor**
         Brasses
         Bronzes
         Goldwork
         Pewter

Art metalwork—*Continued*
>   **Silverwork**

Art, Modern—17th-18th centuries
>   USE   **Art—17th and 18th centuries**

Art, Modern—19th century
>   USE   **Art—19th century**

Art, Modern—20th century
>   USE   **Art—20th century**

Art, Modern—21st century
>   USE   **Art—21st century**

Art, Municipal
>   USE   **Municipal art**

Art museums (May subdiv. geog.)   **708**
>   UF   Art galleries
>
>   Art—Museums
>
>   Collections of art, painting, etc.
>
>   Picture galleries
>
>   SA   names of individual art museums
>
>   [to be added as needed]
>
>   BT   **Museums**
>
>   RT   **Art collections**

Art—Museums
>   USE   **Art museums**

Art nouveau (May subdiv. geog.)
>   **709.03**
>
>   UF   Jugendstil
>
>   BT   **Art—19th century**

Art objects   700; 745
>   Use for general materials about decorative articles of artistic merit such as snuff boxes, brasses, pottery, needlework, glassware, etc. Materials on old decorative objects having historical or financial value are entered under **Antiques**.
>
>   UF   Objets d'art
>
>   SA   types of art objects, e.g. **Furniture**; **Pottery**; etc. [to be added as needed]
>
>   BT   **Antiques**
>
>   **Art**
>
>   **Decoration and ornament**
>
>   **Decorative arts**
>
>   NT   **Miniature objects**

Art, Oriental
>   USE   **Asian art**

Art patronage (May subdiv. geog.)   **700**
>   Use for materials on patronage of the arts by individuals or corporations. Materials on government support of the arts are entered under **Arts—Government policy** or **Federal aid to the arts**.
>
>   UF   Art patrons
>
>   Business patronage of the arts
>
>   Corporate patronage of the arts

>   Corporations—Art patronage
>
>   Funding for the arts
>
>   Patronage of the arts
>
>   Private funding of the arts
>
>   BT   **Art and society**
>
>   RT   **Arts—Government policy**
>
>   **Federal aid to the arts**

Art patrons
>   USE   **Art patronage**

Art—Political aspects (May subdiv. geog.)
>   **701**
>
>   BT   **Art and society**

Art pottery (May subdiv. geog.)   **738**
>   UF   Studio pottery
>
>   SA   types of art pottery, e.g.
>
>   **Rookwood pottery** [to be added as needed]
>
>   BT   **Pottery**
>
>   NT   **Rookwood pottery**

Art, Prehistoric
>   USE   **Prehistoric art**

Art—Prices (May subdiv. geog.)   **707.5**
>   BT   **Prices**

Art—Private collections
>   USE   **Art collections**

Art, Renaissance
>   USE   **Art— 15th and 16th centuries**

Art robberies
>   USE   **Art thefts**

Art, Roman
>   USE   **Roman art**

Art, Romanesque
>   USE   **Romanesque art**

Art schools
>   USE   **Art—Study and teaching**

Art—Study and teaching   707
>   UF   Art—Analysis, interpretation, appreciation
>
>   Art education
>
>   Art schools

Art—Technique   702.8

Art thefts (May subdiv. geog.)   **364.16**
>   UF   Art robberies
>
>   BT   **Theft**

Art—Themes   704.9
>   UF   Iconography
>
>   Themes in art
>
>   SA   topics in art, e.g. **Dogs in art**; and names of persons, families, and corporate bodies with the subdivision *In art*,

Art—Themes—*Continued*
  e.g. **Napoleon I, Emperor of the French, 1769-1821—In art** [to be added as needed]
 NT **African Americans in art**
   Animals in art
   Blacks in art
   Children in art
   Dogs in art
   Flowers in art
   Napoleon I, 1769-1821—In art
   Nude in art
   Plants in art
   Women in art
Art—Therapeutic use
 USE **Art therapy**
Art therapy 615.8; 616.89
 UF Art—Therapeutic use
 BT **Therapeutics**
Arthritis 616.7
 BT **Diseases**
 NT **Gout**
Arthritis—Physical therapy 616.7
Arthurian romances 398.22; 808.8; 809
 Use for individual works, collections, or materials about Arthurian romances.
 UF Knights of the Round Table
 BT **Romances**
 RT **Grail—Legends**
Arthurian romances—Adaptations 808.8
Articles of war
 USE **Military law**
Articulation (Education) 371.2
 Use for materials that discuss the integration of various elements of the school system, between levels, between schools, between subjects, or between the school's programs and outside activities, aimed at promoting a continuous advancement by the student.
 BT **Education—Curricula**
   Schools—Administration
Artificial flies 688.7; 799.1
 UF Fishing flies
   Flies, Artificial
 BT **Fishing—Equipment and supplies**
   Fly casting
Artificial flowers 745.594
 UF Flowers, Artificial
 BT **Decoration and ornament**
Artificial foods (May subdiv. geog.)
   641.3; 664
 UF Synthetic foods
 BT **Food**
   Synthetic products
Artificial fuels
 USE **Synthetic fuels**
Artificial heart 617.4
 BT **Artificial organs**
   Heart
Artificial insemination 636.08
 Use for general materials on artificial insemination and materials specifically on the artificial insemination of livestock and other animals. Materials limited to artificial insemination in humans are entered under **Human artificial insemination**.
 BT **Reproduction**
 NT **Human artificial insemination**
Artificial insemination, Human
 USE **Human artificial insemination**
Artificial intelligence 006.3
 UF AI (Artificial intelligence)
   Machine intelligence
 BT **Computer science**
 NT **Expert systems (Computer science)**
Artificial limbs 617.5
 UF Limbs, Artificial
   Prosthesis
 BT **Orthopedics**
Artificial organs 617.9
 UF Organs, Artificial
   Prosthesis
 SA names of artificial organs, e.g. **Artificial heart** [to be added as needed]
 BT **Surgery**
 NT **Artificial heart**
Artificial reality
 USE **Virtual reality**
Artificial respiration 617.1
 UF Pulmonary resuscitation
   Respiration, Artificial
   Resuscitation, Pulmonary
 BT **First aid**
Artificial satellites 629.43; 629.46
 UF Orbiting vehicles
   Satellites, Artificial
 SA satellites of particular countries, e.g. **American artificial satellites**; types of satellites; and names of specific satellites [to be added as needed]
 BT **Astronautics**

Artificial satellites—*Continued*
  NT **American artificial satellites**
      Explorer (Artificial satellite)
      Meteorological satellites
      Space stations
  RT **Space vehicles**
Artificial satellites, American
  USE **American artificial satellites**
Artificial satellites—Control systems
    629.46
Artificial satellites in telecommunication
    384.5; 621.382
  UF Communication satellites
      Communications relay satellites
      Global satellite communications
        systems
      Satellite communication systems
  SA names of specific satellites or
      projects [to be added as need-
      ed]
  BT **Telecommunication**
  NT **Telstar project**
Artificial satellites—Launching   629.43
  UF Launching of satellites
  BT **Rockets (Aeronautics)**
Artificial satellites—Law and legislation
  USE **Space law**
Artificial satellites—Orbits   629.4
  BT **Astrodynamics**
Artificial satellites—Tracking   629.43
  UF Tracking of satellites
Artificial selection
  USE **Breeding**
Artificial sweeteners
  USE **Sugar substitutes**
Artificial weather control
  USE **Weather control**
Artillery (May subdiv. geog.)   **355.8;**
    623.4
  BT **Military art and science**
  RT **Ordnance**
Artistic anatomy   704.9; 743.4
  UF Anatomy, Artistic
      Human anatomy in art
      Human figure in art
  BT **Anatomy**
      Art
      Drawing
      Nude in art
  NT **Figure drawing**
      Figure painting
Artistic photography   770; 779

  UF Photography—Aesthetics
      Photography, Artistic
  BT **Art**
      Photography
Artists (May subdiv. geog.)   **709.2; 920**
  SA types of artists and names of in-
      dividual artists [to be added
      as needed]
  NT **African American artists**
      Architects
      Black artists
      Child artists
      Designers
      Engravers
      Etchers
      Illustrators
      Lithographers
      Painters
      Photographers
      Potters
      Sculptors
      Women artists
  RT **Art**
      Arts
Artists, American
  USE **Artists—United States**
Artists, Black
  USE **Black artists**
Artists' materials   741.2; 751.2
  UF Drawing materials
      Painters' materials
  SA types of artists' materials [to be
      added as needed]
  BT **Materials**
Artists' models (May subdiv. geog.)
    702.8
  UF Models
      Models, Artists'
      Models (Persons)
  BT **Art**
Artists—United States   709.2; 920
  UF American artists
      Artists, American
Arts (May subdiv. geog.)   **700**
    Use for materials on the arts in general, in-
    cluding the visual arts, literature, and the per-
    forming arts. Materials on the visual arts only
    (architecture, painting, etc.) are entered under
    Art.
  BT **Humanities**
  NT **Allegory**
      Art
      Decorative arts

Arts—*Continued*
    Handicraft
    Performing arts
    Surrealism
    Visual literacy
  RT   **Aesthetics**
    Artists
Arts, American
  USE   **Arts—United States**
Arts and crafts movement (May subdiv.
    geog.)   **745**
    Use for materials on the movement originating in England in the nineteenth century that promoted a return to craftsmanship in the applied and decorative arts.
  UF   Crafts (Arts)
  BT   **Art**
    Decoration and ornament
    Decorative arts
    Industrial arts
  RT   **Folk art**
    Handicraft
Arts and state
  USE   **Arts—Government policy**
    Federal aid to the arts
Arts—Federal aid
  USE   **Federal aid to the arts**
Arts—Government policy (May subdiv.
    geog.)   **353.7; 700**
  UF   Arts and state
    Funding for the arts
    State encouragement of the arts
  BT   **Social policy**
  RT   **Art patronage**
    Federal aid to the arts
Arts, Graphic
  USE   **Graphic arts**
Arts in the church
  USE   **Art and religion**
Arts—United States   **700.973**
  UF   American arts
    Arts, American
Aryans
  USE   **Indo-Europeans**
Asbestos   **553.6; 620.1; 666; 691**
  BT   **Minerals**
Asceticism (May subdiv. geog.)   **204;
    248.4**
    May be subdivided by religion or sect.
  BT   **Ethics**
    Religious life
  NT   **Fasting**
    Sexual abstinence

Asceticism—Catholic Church (May
    subdiv. geog.)   **248.4**
Ashanti (African people) (May subdiv.
    geog.)   **305.896**
  BT   **Africans**
    Indigenous peoples
Asia   **950**
  UF   East
    Orient
  SA   areas of Asia [to be added as
      needed]
  NT   **Central Asia**
    East Asia
    Middle East
    Southeast Asia
Asia, Central
  USE   **Central Asia**
Asia—Civilization   **306.095; 950**
  UF   Asian civilization
    Civilization, Oriental
    Oriental civilization
  BT   **Civilization**
    East and West
Asia—Politics and government   **950**
  BT   **Politics**
Asia, Southeastern
  USE   **Southeast Asia**
Asian Americans   **305.895**
  BT   **Ethnic groups**
Asian architecture   **720.95**
  UF   Oriental architecture
  BT   **Architecture**
Asian art   **709.5**
  UF   Art, Asian
    Art, Oriental
    Oriental art
  BT   **Art**
Asian civilization
  USE   **Asia—Civilization**
Asperger's syndrome   **616.85; 618.92**
  BT   **Autism**
Asphyxiating gases
  USE   **Poisonous gases**
Assassination   **364.15**
  SA   classes of persons and names of
      individuals with the subdivision *Assassination* [to be added as needed]
  BT   **Crime**
    Homicide
    Political crimes and offenses

Assassination—*Continued*
    NT   **Presidents—United States—Assassination**
Assault, Criminal
    USE   **Offenses against the person**
Assault, Sexual
    USE   **Rape**
Assembly programs, School
    USE   **School assembly programs**
Assembly, Right of
    USE   **Freedom of assembly**
Assertive behavior
    USE   **Assertiveness (Psychology)**
Assertiveness (Psychology)   **155.2; 158.2**
    UF   Assertive behavior
    BT   **Aggressiveness (Psychology)**
           Psychology
    RT   **Self-confidence**
Assessment
    USE   **Tax assessment**
Assessment, Tax
    USE   **Tax assessment**
Assistance in emergencies
    USE   **Helping behavior**
Assistance to developing areas
    USE   **Foreign aid**
           Technical assistance
Assisted independent residential living
    USE   **Assisted living**
Assisted living (May subdiv. geog.)
           362.6; 363.5
    UF   Assisted independent residential living
           Congregate housing
    BT   **Housing**
    RT   **Elderly—Housing**
Assisted reproduction
    USE   **Reproductive technology**
Association, Freedom of
    USE   **Freedom of association**
Associations (May subdiv. geog.)   **060;**
           302.3; 366
    UF   Associations, institutions, etc.
           Networks (Associations, institutions, etc.)
           Organizations
           Voluntary associations
           Voluntary organizations
    SA   types of associations; subjects, classes of persons, ethnic groups, and names of individ-

ual persons, families, and corporate bodies, with the subdivision *Societies*; and names of specific associations [to be added as needed]
    NT   **Agriculture—Societies**
           Charitable organizations
           Clubs
           Community life
           Cooperation
           Financial institutions
           Nonprofit organizations
           Religious institutions
           Societies
           Trade and professional associations
Associations, institutions, etc.
    USE   **Associations**
Associations, International
    USE   **International agencies**
Asteroids   **523.44**
    UF   Minor planets
           Planetoids
    BT   **Astronomy**
           Solar system
    RT   **Planets**
Asthma (May subdiv. geog.)   **616.2**
    UF   Bronchial asthma
    BT   **Allergy**
           Lungs—Diseases
Astral projection   **133.9**
    UF   Astral travel
           Out-of-body experiences
    BT   **Parapsychology**
Astral travel
    USE   **Astral projection**
Astrobiology
    USE   **Life on other planets**
           Space biology
Astrochemistry
    USE   **Space chemistry**
Astrodynamics   **521; 629.4**
    BT   **Dynamics**
    NT   **Artificial satellites—Orbits**
           Navigation (Astronautics)
    RT   **Astronautics**
           Space flight
Astrogeology   **559.9**
    SA   names of planets with the subdivision *Geology* [to be added as needed]

Astrogeology—*Continued*
- BT Geology
- NT Lunar geology
  - Mars (Planet)—Geology

Astrology (May subdiv. geog.) **133.5**
- UF Hermetic art and philosophy
- BT Astronomy
  - Divination
  - Occultism
- NT Horoscopes
  - Zodiac
- RT Constellations

Astronautical accidents
- USE Space vehicle accidents

Astronautical communication systems
- USE Astronautics—Communication systems

Astronautical instruments (May subdiv. geog.) **629.4**
- UF Instruments, Astronautical
  - Space vehicles—Instruments
- BT Navigation (Astronautics)
  - Space optics
- RT Astronautics—Communication systems

Astronautics (May subdiv. geog.) **629.4**
- BT Aeronautics
- NT Aerospace engineering
  - Aerothermodynamics
  - Artificial satellites
  - Astronautics and civilization
  - Interplanetary voyages
  - Navigation (Astronautics)
  - Outer space
  - Rocketry
  - Space flight
  - Space flight to the moon
  - Space stations
  - Unidentified flying objects
- RT Astrodynamics
  - Space sciences
  - Space vehicles

Astronautics—Accidents
- USE Space vehicle accidents

Astronautics and civilization (May subdiv. geog.) **306.4**
- UF Civilization and astronautics
  - Outer space and civilization
  - Space age
  - Space power
- BT Aeronautics and civilization
  - Astronautics

  - Civilization
- NT Space colonies
  - Space law

Astronautics—Communication systems **629.47**
- UF Astronautical communication systems
  - Space communication
- BT Interstellar communication
  - Telecommunication
- NT Radio in astronautics
- RT Astronautical instruments

Astronautics—International cooperation **629.4**
- UF International space cooperation
- BT International cooperation

Astronautics—Law and legislation
- USE Space law

Astronautics—United States **629.40973**
- NT Project Voyager

Astronauts (May subdiv. geog.) **629.450092; 920**
- UF Cosmonauts
- BT Air pilots
  - Space flight
- NT Space vehicles—Piloting
  - Women astronauts

Astronauts—Clothing
- USE Space suits

Astronauts—Nutrition **629.47**
- UF Space nutrition
- BT Nutrition

Astronavigation
- USE Navigation (Astronautics)

Astronomers (May subdiv. geog.) **520.92; 920**
- BT Scientists

Astronomical instruments **522**
- UF Instruments, Astronomical
- SA types of instruments, e.g. **Telescopes** [to be added as needed]
- BT Scientific apparatus and instruments
  - Space optics
- NT Astronomical photography
  - Telescopes

Astronomical observatories (May subdiv. geog.) **522**
- UF Observatories, Astronomical
- RT Astronomy

Astronomical photography   522
  UF   Astrophotography
  BT   **Astronomical instruments**
       Photography
Astronomical physics
  USE   **Astrophysics**
Astronomy   520
  BT   **Physical sciences**
       Science
       Universe
  NT   **Asteroids**
       Astrology
       Astrophysics
       Bible—Astronomy
       Black holes (Astronomy)
       Chronology
       Comets
       Galaxies
       Life on other planets
       Lunar eclipses
       Meteorites
       Meteors
       Moon
       Nautical astronomy
       Outer space
       Planetariums
       Planets
       Pulsars
       Quasars
       Radio astronomy
       Seasons
       Sky
       Solar eclipses
       Solar system
       Space environment
       Spectrum analysis
       Sun
       Zodiac
  RT   **Astronomical observatories**
       Constellations
       Space sciences
       Stars
Astronomy—Atlases
  USE   **Stars—Atlases**
Astronomy—Mathematics   520.1
  BT   **Mathematics**
Astrophotography
  USE   **Astronomical photography**
Astrophysics   523.01
  UF   Astronomical physics

  BT   **Astronomy**
       Physics
  NT   **Black holes (Astronomy)**
       Spectrum analysis
Astros (Baseball team)
  USE   **Houston Astros (Baseball
         team)**
Asylum   323.6; 342.08
  UF   Asylum, Right of
       Political asylum
       Right of asylum
       Sanctuary (Law)
  BT   **International law**
  NT   **Political refugees**
       Sanctuary movement
Asylum, Right of
  USE   **Asylum**
Asylums
  USE   **Institutional care**
At-home employment
  USE   **Home-based business**
At risk students   371.93
    Use for materials on students considered
  prone to academic failure or other problems.
  UF   Disadvantaged students
       High risk students
       Students with problems
       Underprivileged students
  BT   **Students**
  RT   **Dropouts**
       Socially handicapped children
Atheism   211
  BT   **Religion**
       Secularism
       Theology
  RT   **Agnosticism**
       Deism
       Rationalism
       Theism
Athena (Greek deity)   202
  BT   **Gods and goddesses**
Athletes (May subdiv. geog.)   **796.092;
       920**
  SA   types of athletes, e.g. **Baseball
       players** [to be added as need-
       ed]
  NT   **African American athletes**
       Baseball players
       Black athletes
       Women athletes
  RT   **Sports**

Athletes, Black
    USE   **Black athletes**
Athletes—Drug use (May subdiv. geog.)
        362.29; 796
    UF   Drugs and sports
           Sports and drugs
    RT   **Steroids**
Athletic coaching
    USE   **Coaching (Athletics)**
Athletic medicine
    USE   **Sports medicine**
Athletics (May subdiv. geog.)   **796**
    SA   types of athletic activities [to be
           added as needed]
    NT   **Boxing**
           Coaching (Athletics)
           Gymnastics
           Martial arts
           Olympic games
           Rowing
           Track athletics
           Walking
           Weight lifting
           Wrestling
    RT   **Physical education**
           Sports
Atlantic Ocean   **910.9163**
    BT   **Ocean**
    NT   **Bermuda Triangle**
Atlantic States   **974; 975**
    UF   Eastern Seaboard
           Middle Atlantic States
           South Atlantic States
    BT   **United States**
Atlantis (Legendary place)   **001.94;
        398.23**
    BT   **Geographical myths**
           Lost continents
Atlas (Missile)   **623.4; 629.47**
    BT   **Ballistic missiles**
           **Intercontinental ballistic mis-
             siles**
Atlases   **912**
    Use as a form heading for geographical at-
    lases of world coverage. General materials
    about maps and their history are entered under
    Maps.
    UF   Geographical atlases
    SA   scientific and technical subjects
           with the subdivision *Atlases*,
           for materials consisting of

comprehensive, often systematically arranged, collections
of illustrative plates, charts,
etc., usually with explanatory
captions, e.g. **Human anatomy—Atlases**; and names of
countries, cities, etc., with the
subdivision *Maps*, e.g. **United
States—Maps** [to be added
as needed]
    BT   **Geography**
           Maps
    NT   **Bible—Geography**
           Historical atlases
           Human anatomy—Atlases
           Stars—Atlases
           United States—Maps
Atlases, Astronomical
    USE   **Stars—Atlases**
Atmosphere   **551.5**
    Use for materials on the body of air sur-
    rounding the earth. Materials on the chemical
    and physical properties of air are entered un-
    der **Air**.
    BT   **Air**
           Earth
    NT   **Clouds**
           Fog
           Sky
           Upper atmosphere
    RT   **Biosphere**
           Meteorology
Atmosphere—Pollution
    USE   **Air pollution**
Atmosphere, Upper
    USE   **Upper atmosphere**
Atmospheric chemistry   **551.51**
    BT   **Physical chemistry**
Atmospheric dust
    USE   **Dust**
Atmospheric greenhouse effect
    USE   **Global warming**
Atmospheric humidity
    USE   **Humidity**
Atolls
    USE   **Coral reefs and islands**
Atom smashing
    USE   **Cyclotrons**
Atomic bomb   **355.8; 623.4**
    BT   **Bombs**
           Nuclear weapons
    NT   **Radioactive fallout**

Atomic bomb—*Continued*
    RT   **Hydrogen bomb**
Atomic bomb—Physiological effect (May subdiv. geog.) **616.9**
    RT   **Radiation—Physiological effect**
Atomic bomb—Testing (May subdiv. geog.) **623.4**
Atomic bomb victims (May subdiv. geog.) **940.54**
    UF   Victims of atomic bombings
Atomic energy
    USE **Nuclear energy**
Atomic industry
    USE **Nuclear industry**
Atomic medicine
    USE **Nuclear medicine**
Atomic nuclei
    USE **Nuclear physics**
Atomic power
    USE **Nuclear energy**
Atomic power plants
    USE **Nuclear power plants**
Atomic-powered vehicles
    USE **Nuclear propulsion**
Atomic submarines
    USE **Nuclear submarines**
Atomic theory **539.7; 541**
    BT   **Physical chemistry**
    RT   **Quantum theory**
Atomic warfare
    USE **Nuclear warfare**
Atomic weapons
    USE **Nuclear weapons**
Atoms **539.7; 541**
    BT   **Physical chemistry**
    NT   **Cyclotrons**
          Electrons
          Isotopes
          Neutrons
          Protons
          Transmutation (Chemistry)
Atonement—Christianity **232; 234**
    UF   Vicarious atonement
    BT   **Christianity**
          Sacrifice
          Salvation
Atonement, Day of
    USE **Yom Kippur**
Atonement—Judaism **296.3**
    UF   Atonement (Judaism)
    BT   **Judaism**

Atonement (Judaism)
    USE **Atonement—Judaism**
Atrocities (May subdiv. geog.) **909**
    UF   Military atrocities
    SA   names of wars with the subdivision *Atrocities*, e.g. **World War, 1939-1945—Atrocities**; and names of specific atrocities [to be added as needed]
    BT   **Crime**
          Cruelty
    NT   **Massacres**
          Persecution
          World War, 1939-1945—Atrocities
Attacks by animals
    USE **Animal attacks**
Attempted suicide
    USE **Suicide**
Attendance, School
    USE **School attendance**
Attention **153.1; 153.7**
    UF   Concentration
    BT   **Apperception**
          Educational psychology
          Memory
          Psychology
          Thought and thinking
    NT   **Listening**
Attention deficit disorder **616.85**
    UF   ADD (Child behavior disorder)
          Attention deficit disorder in adolescence
          Attention deficit disorder in adults
          Attention-deficit hyperactivity disorder
          Hyperactivity disorder
          Hyperkinesia
    BT   **Abnormal psychology**
Attention deficit disorder in adolescence
    USE **Attention deficit disorder**
Attention deficit disorder in adults
    USE **Attention deficit disorder**
Attention-deficit hyperactivity disorder
    USE **Attention deficit disorder**
Attention-seeking
    USE **Showing off**
Attitude (Psychology) **152.4**
    UF   Attitudes

Attitude (Psychology)—*Continued*

SA   ethnic groups and classes of persons with the subdivision *Attitudes*, e.g. **Teenagers—Attitudes** [to be added as needed]

BT   **Emotions**
      Psychology

NT   **Conformity**
      Empathy
      Frustration
      Job satisfaction
      Prejudices
      Racism
      Sexism
      Stereotype (Social psychology)
      Teenagers—Attitudes
      Trust

RT   **Public opinion**

Attitudes

USE   **Attitude (Psychology)**
      and ethnic groups and classes of persons with the subdivision *Attitudes,* e.g.
      Teenagers—Attitudes [to be added as needed]

Attorneys

USE   **Lawyers**

Attracting birds

USE   **Bird attracting**

Attracting wildlife

USE   **Wildlife attracting**

ATVs

USE   **All terrain vehicles**

Auction bridge

USE   **Bridge (Game)**

Auctions (May subdiv. geog.)   **658.8**

UF   Sales, Auction

BT   **Selling**

NT   **Internet auctions**

Audiences (May subdiv. geog.)   **302.3**

SA   types of performances or events with the subdivision *Audiences*, e.g. **Performing arts—Audiences** [to be added as needed]

BT   **Communication**
      Social psychology

NT   **Performing arts—Audiences**
      Sports spectators
      Television viewers

Audio amplifiers, Transistor

USE   **Transistor amplifiers**

Audio cassettes

USE   **Sound recordings**

Audiobooks   **028**

Use for materials on sound recordings of books, including but not limited to materials recorded specifically for the blind.

UF   Books on cassette
      Books on tape
      Cassette books
      Recorded books
      Talking books

BT   **Sound recordings**

RT   **Blind—Books and reading**

Audiodisc players

USE   **Compact disc players**

Audiotapes

USE   **Sound recordings**

Audiovisual aids

USE   subjects with the subdivision *Audiovisual aids,* e.g. **Library education—Audiovisual aids;** and subjects with the subdivisions *Study and teaching—Audiovisual aids,* for the use of audiovisual aids in the teaching of those subjects, e.g. **Science—Study and teaching—Audiovisual aids** [to be added as needed]

Audiovisual education   **371.33**

UF   Visual instruction

SA   subjects with the subdivision *Audiovisual aids* to be added as needed]

BT   **Education**

NT   **Audiovisual materials**
      Library education—Audiovisual aids
      Motion pictures in education
      Radio in education
      Television in education

Audiovisual equipment   **621.389**

NT   **Audiovisual materials**

RT   **Audiovisual materials**

Audiovisual materials   **025.17; 371.33**

UF   Multimedia materials
      Nonbook materials
      Nonprint materials

SA   subjects with the subdivision *Audiovisual aids*; and names of specific audiovisual materials [to be added as needed]

Audiovisual materials—*Continued*
    BT   **Audiovisual education**
          Audiovisual equipment
          Teaching—Aids and devices
    NT   **Filmstrips**
          Library education—Audiovisual aids
          Manipulatives
          Motion pictures
          Sound recordings
          Video recordings
          Videotapes
Audiovisual materials centers
    USE **Instructional materials centers**
Auditing (May subdiv. geog.)   **657**
    SA   topics and names of corporate bodies with the subdivision *Auditing* [to be added as needed]
    BT   **Bookkeeping**
    RT   **Accounting**
Auditoriums (May subdiv. geog.)   **725**
    BT   **Buildings**
          Centers for the performing arts
    NT   **Concert halls**
Aunts (May subdiv. geog.)   **306.87**
    BT   **Family**
Auricular confession
    USE **Confession**
Aurora australis
    USE **Auroras**
Aurora borealis
    USE **Auroras**
Auroras   **538**
    UF   Aurora australis
          Aurora borealis
          Northern lights
          Polar lights
          Southern lights
    BT   **Geophysics**
          Meteorology
Auschwitz (Poland: Concentration camp)   **365; 943.8**
    BT   **Concentration camps**
Australia   **994**
    May be subdivided like United States except for History.
    NT   **Australians**
Australian aborigines
    USE **Aboriginal Australians**

Australians (May subdiv. geog.)   **305.82; 994**
    BT   **Australia**
    NT   **Aboriginal Australians**
Austria   **943.6**
    May be subdivided like United States except for History.
Author and publisher
    USE **Authors and publishers**
Authoring programs for computer-assisted instruction
    USE **Computer-assisted instruction—Authoring programs**
Authoritarianism
    USE **Fascism**
          Totalitarianism
Authority   **303.3**
    BT   **Political science**
Authors   **809; 920**
    UF   Writers
    SA   authors of particular countries, e.g. **American authors**; types of writers, e.g. **Poets**; names of national literatures with the subdivision for a particular kind of author, e.g. **American literature—Women authors**; **American literature—African American authors**; etc.; subjects and names of countries, cities, etc. with the subdivision *Bio-bibliography*; and names of individual authors [to be added as needed]
    NT   **American authors**
          Black authors
          Child authors
          Dramatists
          English authors
          Historians
          Journalists
          Native American authors
          Novelists
          Poets
          Women authors
    RT   **Books**
          Literature—Bio-bibliography
Authors, American
    USE **American authors**

Authors and publishers (May subdiv. geog.) **070.5**

Use for materials on the relations between author and publisher.

UF Author and publisher

Publishers and authors

BT **Authorship**

Contracts

Publishers and publishing

RT **Copyright**

Authors, Black

USE **Black authors**

Authors—Correspondence 808.6; 808.86

BT **Letters**

Authors, English

USE **English authors**

Authors—Homes and haunts

USE **Literary landmarks**

Authors—Interviews 808

BT **Interviews**

Authorship 808

Use for general materials on being or becoming an author. Materials concerning the composition of special types of literature are entered under more specific headings such as **Fiction—Technique**; **Biography as a literary form**; **Short story**; etc.

UF Writing (Authorship)

SA individual writers, titles of literary works, and sacred works with the subdivision *Authorship*; e.g. **Shakespeare, William, 1564-1616—Authorship** [to be added as needed]

BT **Literature**

NT **Advertising copy**

Authors and publishers

Biography as a literary form

Creative writing

Drama—Technique

Editing

Fiction—Technique

Historiography

Journaling

Journalism

Love stories—Technique

Plagiarism

Radio authorship

Report writing

Short story

Technical writing

Television authorship

Travel writing

Versification

Authorship—Handbooks, manuals, etc. 808

RT **Printing—Style manuals**

Autism 616.85; 618.92

UF Autism spectrum disorders

Autistic spectrum disorders

BT **Child psychiatry**

NT **Asperger's syndrome**

Autism spectrum disorders

USE **Autism**

Autistic spectrum disorders

USE **Autism**

Autobiographical fiction 808.3; 808.83

Use for individual works, collections, or materials about autobiographical fiction.

UF Autobiographical novels

BT **Biographical fiction**

Autobiographical graphic novels 741.5

Use for individual works, collections, or materials about autobiographical graphic novels.

BT **Graphic novels**

Autobiographical novels

USE **Autobiographical fiction**

Autobiographies 920

Use for collections of autobiographies. Materials about autobiography as a literary form are entered under **Autobiography**.

UF Memoirs

Personal narratives

SA ethnic groups, classes of persons, and subjects with the subdivision *Biography* or *Correspondence*, e.g. **Women—Biography**; **Authors—Correspondence**; etc.; and names of diseases, events, and wars with the subdivision *Personal narratives* [to be added as needed]

BT **Biography**

NT **Holocaust, 1939-1945—Personal narratives**

United States—History—1861-1865, Civil War—Personal narratives

World War, 1939-1945—Personal narratives

RT **Diaries**

Autobiography   809

Use for materials on autobiography as a literary form. Collections of autobiographies are entered under **Autobiographies**.

UF   Autobiography as a literary form
Autobiography—History and criticism
Autobiography—Technique
Memoirs

BT   **Biography as a literary form**

NT   **Slave narratives**

Autobiography as a literary form
USE   **Autobiography**

Autobiography—History and criticism
USE   **Autobiography**

Autobiography—Technique
USE   **Autobiography**

Autographed copies
USE   **Autographed editions**

Autographed editions   016

UF   Autographed copies
Signed editions

BT   **Autographs**
Editions

Autographs   929.8

SA   classes of persons, ethnic groups, wars, and names of individual persons with the subdivision *Autographs*, or *Autographs—Facsimiles* [to be added as needed]

BT   **Biography**
Writing

NT   **Autographed editions**

RT   **Manuscripts**

Autographs—Facsimiles   929.8

SA   classes of persons, ethnic groups, wars, and names of individual persons with the subdivisions *Autographs—Facsimiles* [to be added as needed]

Autoimmune diseases   616.97

BT   **Diseases**

NT   **Lupus erythematosus**

Automata
USE   **Robots**

Automated cataloging   025.3

UF   Cataloging—Data processing

BT   **Cataloging**

Automatic bread machines
USE   **Bread machines**

Automatic control
USE   **Cybernetics**
Electric controllers
Servomechanisms

Automatic data processing
USE   **Data processing**

Automatic drafting
USE   **Computer graphics**

Automatic drawing
USE   **Computer graphics**

Automatic machinery
USE   **Automation**

Automatic speech recognition   006.4

UF   Mechanical speech recognition
Speech recognition, Automatic

BT   **Speech processing systems**
Voice

Automation   629.8; 670.42

UF   Automatic machinery
Computer control

SA   subjects with the subdivision *Automation*, e.g. **Libraries—Automation** [to be added as needed]

BT   **Industrial equipment**
Machinery in the workplace

NT   **Feedback control systems**
Industrial robots
Libraries—Automation
Servomechanisms
Systems engineering
Telecommuting

Automatons
USE   **Robots**

Automobile accidents
USE   **Traffic accidents**

Automobile design
USE   **Automobiles—Design and construction**

Automobile driver education (May subdiv. geog.)   **629.28**

UF   Automobile drivers—Education
Car driver education
Driver education

BT   **Education**

Automobile drivers (May subdiv. geog.)   **629.28**

UF   Automobile driving
Automobiles—Driving
Car drivers
Drivers, Automobile

Automobile drivers—Education
   USE **Automobile driver education**
Automobile drivers' licenses
   USE **Drivers' licenses**
Automobile driving
   USE **Automobile drivers**
Automobile engines
   USE **Automobiles—Motors**
Automobile guides
   USE **Automobile travel—Guidebooks**
Automobile industry (May subdiv. geog.)
   338.4; 388.3
   UF Automotive industry
       Car industry
       Motor vehicle industry
   BT **Industries**
   NT **Service stations**
Automobile industry—Production stan-
   dards (May subdiv. geog.) **658.5**
   BT **Production standards**
Automobile insurance (May subdiv.
   geog.) **368**
   UF Car insurance
       Insurance, Automobile
   BT **Insurance**
Automobile motors
   USE **Automobiles—Motors**
Automobile parts **629.28**
   UF Automobiles—Parts
       Car parts
   BT **Automobiles**
Automobile pools
   USE **Car pools**
Automobile racing (May subdiv. geog.)
   796.72
   UF Automobiles—Racing
       Car racing
   SA types of automobile racing and
       names of specific races, e.g.
       Indianapolis 500 (Race) [to
       be added as needed]
   BT **Racing**
   NT **Karts and karting**
       Stock car racing
Automobile repairs
   USE **Automobiles—Maintenance and**
       repair
Automobile touring
   USE **Automobile travel**

Automobile transmission
   USE **Automobiles—Transmission de-**
       vices
Automobile travel (May subdiv. geog.)
   796.7
   UF Automobile touring
       Automobiles—Touring
       Car travel
       Motoring
   BT **Transportation**
       Travel
       Voyages and travels
Automobile travel—Guidebooks **912**
   UF Automobile guides
       Automobiles—Road guides
       Travel guides
   BT **Maps**
   RT **Road maps**
Automobiles (May subdiv. geog.) **388.3;**
   629.222
   UF Cars (Automobiles)
       Motor cars
   SA names of specific makes and
       models of automobiles, e.g.
       Ford automobile [to be add-
       ed as needed]
   BT **Highway transportation**
       Motor vehicles
       Vehicles
   NT **Antique and classic cars**
       Automobile parts
       Buses
       Compact cars
       Diesel automobiles
       Electric automobiles
       Ford automobile
       Foreign automobiles
       Sports cars
       Trucks
Automobiles—Accidents
   USE **Traffic accidents**
Automobiles—Air conditioning **629.2**
   BT **Air conditioning**
Automobiles—Brakes **629.2**
   BT **Brakes**
Automobiles—Conservation and restora-
   tion (May subdiv. geog.) **629.28**
   UF Automobiles—Restoration
       Restoration of automobiles

Automobiles—Construction
  USE **Automobiles—Design and construction**
Automobiles—Design
  USE **Automobiles—Design and construction**
Automobiles—Design and construction
  (May subdiv. geog.) **629.222**
  UF Automobile design
      Automobiles—Construction
      Automobiles—Design
      Automotive engineering
      Car design
  BT **Industrial design**
Automobiles—Drivers' licenses
  USE **Drivers' licenses**
Automobiles—Driving
  USE **Automobile drivers**
Automobiles, Electric
  USE **Electric automobiles**
Automobiles—Electric equipment
  629.25
  UF Electric equipment of automobiles
Automobiles—Engines
  USE **Automobiles—Motors**
Automobiles, Foreign
  USE **Foreign automobiles**
Automobiles—Fuel consumption   629.28
  BT **Energy consumption**
      Fuel
Automobiles—Gearing
  USE **Automobiles—Transmission devices**
Automobiles—Inspection (May subdiv.
  geog.) **353.9**
Automobiles—Law and legislation (May
  subdiv. geog.) **343.09**
  BT **Law**
      Legislation
  RT **Traffic regulations**
Automobiles—Maintenance and repair
  629.28
  UF Automobile repairs
      Automobiles—Repairing
      Car maintenance
      Car repair
Automobiles—Models   629.22
  UF Model cars
  BT **Models and modelmaking**
Automobiles—Motors   629.25

  UF Automobile engines
      Automobile motors
      Automobiles—Engines
      Car engines
  SA types of automobiles and makes
      and models of automobiles
      with the subdivision *Motors*
      [to be added as needed]
  BT **Engines**
Automobiles—Painting   667
  UF Car painting
  BT **Industrial painting**
Automobiles—Parts
  USE **Automobile parts**
Automobiles—Pollution control devices
  629.25
  UF Pollution control devices (Motor
      vehicles)
  BT **Pollution control industry**
Automobiles—Purchasing (May subdiv.
  geog.) **381**
Automobiles—Racing
  USE **Automobile racing**
Automobiles—Repairing
  USE **Automobiles—Maintenance and repair**
Automobiles—Restoration
  USE **Automobiles—Conservation and restoration**
Automobiles—Road guides
  USE **Automobile travel—Guidebooks**
Automobiles—Technological innovations
  629.22
  BT **Technological innovations**
Automobiles—Touring
  USE **Automobile travel**
Automobiles—Trailers
  USE **Travel trailers and campers**
Automobiles—Transmission devices
  629.2
  UF Automobile transmission
      Automobiles—Gearing
      Car transmissions
      Transmissions, Automobile
  BT **Gearing**
Automotive engineering
  USE **Automobiles—Design and construction**
Automotive industry
  USE **Automobile industry**
Autonomy (Psychology)   153.8

Autonomy (Psychology)—*Continued*
UF   Freedom (Psychology)
        Independence (Psychology)
        Self-determination (Psychology)
        Self-direction (Psychology)
BT   **Psychology**
Autosuggestion
USE   **Hypnotism**
        Mental suggestion
Autumn   508; 525
UF   Fall
BT   **Seasons**
Availability of health services
USE   **Access to health care**
Avalanches (May subdiv. geog.)   **553.1**
BT   **Snow**
Avant-garde (Aesthetics) (May subdiv.
    geog.)   **700.1**
BT   **Aesthetics**
        Modernism (Aesthetics)
Avant-garde churches
USE   **Non-institutional churches**
Avant-garde films
USE   **Experimental films**
Avant-garde theater
USE   **Experimental theater**
Avarice   178; 205
    Use for materials on an inordinate desire
    for wealth. Materials on any excessive desire
    for food, personal possessions, etc. are entered
    under **Greed**.
UF   Covetousness
BT   **Sin**
RT   **Greed**
Avenues
USE   **Streets**
Average   519.5
BT   **Arithmetic**
        Probabilities
        Statistics
Aviation
USE   **Aeronautics**
Aviation accidents
USE   **Aircraft accidents**
Aviation medicine   616.9
UF   Aeronautics—Medical aspects
        Aerospace medicine
BT   **Medicine**
NT   **Jet lag**
RT   **Space medicine**
Aviators
USE   **Air pilots**

Avocations
USE   **Hobbies**
Awakening, Religious
USE   **Religious awakening**
Awards   001.4
UF   Competitions
        Prizes (Rewards)
        Rewards (Prizes, etc.)
SA   types of awards and prizes; sub-
        jects, corporate entities, per-
        sons, and military services
        with the subdivision *Awards*,
        e.g. **Architecture—Awards**;
        and names of specific awards
        and prizes, e.g. **Nobel Prizes**
        [to be added as needed]
NT   **Literary prizes**
        Nobel Prizes
RT   **Contests**
Awards (Law)
USE   **Arbitration and award**
Axiology
USE   **Values**
Azerbaijan   947.54
Aztecs   972.004
BT   **Native Americans—Mexico**
B-52 bomber   623.74
BT   **Bombers**
B and B accommodations
USE   **Bed and breakfast accommo-
        dations**
Babies
USE   **Infants**
Baboons (May subdiv. geog.)   **599.8**
BT   **Apes**
Baby animals
USE   **Animal babies**
Baby boom generation (May subdiv.
    geog.)   **305.2**
UF   Baby boomers
BT   **Population**
Baby boomers
USE   **Baby boom generation**
Baby care
USE   **Infants—Care**
Baby clothes
USE   **Infants' clothing**
Baby names
USE   **Personal names**
Baby showers
USE   **Showers (Parties)**

Baby sitters
USE **Babysitters**
Baby sitting
USE **Babysitting**
Babysitters   649
UF   Baby sitters
Sitters (Babysitters)
RT   **Babysitting**
Babysitting   649
UF   Baby sitting
BT   **Child care**
Infants—Care
RT   **Babysitters**
Bachelors
USE   **Single men**
Back packing
USE   **Backpacking**
Backpack cycling
USE   **Bicycle touring**
Backpacking (May subdiv. geog.)
796.51
UF   Back packing
Pack transportation
BT   **Camping**
Hiking
Bacon-Shakespeare controversy
USE   **Shakespeare, William, 1564-
1616—Authorship**
Bacon's Rebellion, 1676   973.2
BT   **United States—History—1600-
1775, Colonial period**
Bacteria   579.3
Use for general materials on bacteria. Materials on the science of studying bacteria are entered under **Bacteriology**.
UF   Disease germs
Germs
Microbes
BT   **Microorganisms**
Parasites
RT   **Bacteriology**
Bacterial resistance to antibiotics
USE   **Drug resistance in microorganisms**
Bacterial warfare
USE   **Biological warfare**
Bacteriology   579.3
Use for materials on the science of studying bacteria. General materials on bacteria are entered under **Bacteria**.
SA   types of bacteriology, e.g. **Agricultural bacteriology**; types of microbiology, e.g. **Soil mi-**

crobiology; and subjects with the subdivision *Microbiology*, e.g. **Cheese—Microbiology**
[to be added as needed]
BT   **Microbiology**
NT   **Agricultural bacteriology**
RT   **Bacteria**
Bacteriology, Agricultural
USE   **Agricultural bacteriology**
Bad behavior   179; 302.3; 395
UF   Meanness
Rudeness
BT   **Human behavior**
Bad breath   616.3
UF   Halitosis
BT   **Mouth—Diseases**
Bad sportsmanship
USE   **Sportsmanship**
Badgers (May subdiv. geog.)   **599.76**
BT   **Mammals**
Badges   355.1; 737; 929.9
BT   **Heraldry**
Insignia
Badges of honor
USE   **Decorations of honor**
Insignia
Medals
Baggage
USE   **Luggage**
Bahai Faith (May subdiv. geog.)   **297.9**
UF   Bahaism
BT   **Religions**
Bahaism
USE   **Bahai Faith**
Baking   641.7
SA   types of baked products [to be added as needed]
BT   **Cooking**
NT   **Bread**
Cake
Cookies
Pastry
Pies
RT   **Bread machines**
Balance of nature
USE   **Ecology**
Balance of payments (May subdiv. geog.)
382
BT   **International economic relations**
RT   **Balance of trade**

Balance of power   327.1
UF   Power politics
BT   International relations
Balance of trade (May subdiv. geog.)
       382
UF   Trade, Balance of
       Trade deficits
       Trade surpluses
BT   International trade
RT   Balance of payments
Ball bearings
USE   Bearings (Machinery)
Ball games (May subdiv. geog.)   796.3
SA   types of games, e.g. Baseball;
       and names of competitions [to
       be added as needed]
BT   Games
NT   Baseball
       Basketball
       Billiards
       Bowling
       Football
       Lacrosse
       Racquetball
       Soccer
       Softball
       Table tennis
       Volleyball
Ball room dancing
USE   Ballroom dancing
Ballads   808.1; 808.81
Use for individual works, collections, or
materials about ballads. Materials on the folk
tunes associated with these ballads and collec-
tions that include both words and music are
entered under Folk songs.
BT   Literature
       Poetry
       Songs
RT   Folk songs
Ballet (May subdiv. geog.)   792.8
Use for musical works composed for the
ballet and for materials about the ballet. Indi-
vidual ballet plots or collections of ballet plots
are entered under Ballet—Stories, plots, etc.
UF   Ballets
BT   Dance
       Drama
       Performing arts
       Theater
RT   Pantomimes
Ballet dancers (May subdiv. geog.)
       792.8092; 920
BT   Dancers

Ballet plots
USE   Ballet—Stories, plots, etc.
Ballet—Stories, plots, etc.   792.8
UF   Ballet plots
Ballets
USE   Ballet
Ballistic missiles (May subdiv. geog.)
       358.1; 623.4
Use for materials on high-altitude, high-
speed missiles that are self-propelled and
guided in the first stage of flight only and lat-
er have a natural and uncontrolled trajectory.
UF   Missiles, Ballistic
SA   types of ballistic missiles and
       names of specific missiles [to
       be added as needed]
BT   Guided missiles
       Nuclear weapons
       Rockets (Aeronautics)
NT   Atlas (Missile)
       Intercontinental ballistic mis-
       siles
Balloons (May subdiv. geog.)   629.133
Use for materials on aircraft held aloft by
hot air or light gases that are nondirigible and
propelled only by the wind. Materials on self-
propelled aircraft that are lighter than air and
steerable are entered under Airships.
UF   Aircraft
BT   Aeronautics
RT   Airships
Balloons, Dirigible
USE   Airships
Ballot
USE   Elections
Ballparks
USE   Stadiums
Ballroom dancing (May subdiv. geog.)
       793.3
UF   Ball room dancing
BT   Dance
Band music (May subdiv. geog.)   784
BT   Instrumental music
       Military music
Bandages   616.02
UF   Bandages and bandaging
BT   First aid
Bandages and bandaging
USE   Bandages
Bandits
USE   Thieves
Bandmasters
USE   Conductors (Music)
Bands (Music) (May subdiv. geog.)   784

Bands (Music)—*Continued*

SA   types of bands and names of individual bands [to be added as needed]

NT   **Drum majoring**

       Instrumentation and orchestration

RT   **Conducting**

       Orchestra

Bangladesh   954.92

     May be subdivided like United States except for History.

Bank credit cards

USE   **Credit cards**

Bank debit cards

USE   **Debit cards**

Bank failures (May subdiv. geog.)   **332.1**

UF   Failure of banks

BT   **Bankruptcy**

       Banks and banking

       Business failures

Bank robberies (May subdiv. geog.)   **364.15**

BT   **Theft**

Banking

USE   **Banks and banking**

Bankruptcy (May subdiv. geog.)   **332.7; 336.3; 346.07**

UF   Business mortality

       Failure in business

       Insolvency

BT   **Business failures**

       Commercial law

       Debtor and creditor

       Finance

NT   **Bank failures**

Banks and banking (May subdiv. geog.)   **332.1**

UF   Banking

       Savings banks

SA   names of individual banks [to be added as needed]

BT   **Business**

       Capital

       Commerce

       Finance

NT   **Agricultural credit**

       Bank failures

       Consumer credit

       Cooperative banks

       Debit cards

       Federal Reserve banks

       Foreign exchange

       Interest (Economics)

       Investments

       Negotiable instruments

       Savings and loan associations

RT   **Credit**

       Money

       Trust companies

Banks and banking, Cooperative

USE   **Cooperative banks**

Banks and banking—Credit cards

USE   **Credit cards**

Banks and banking—Data processing   332.10285

BT   **Data processing**

Banks and banking—United States   332.10973

Banned books

USE   **Books—Censorship**

Banners

USE   **Flags**

Banquets

USE   **Dining**

       Dinners

Baptism   234; 265

UF   Christening

RT   **Sacraments**

Baptists (May subdiv. geog.)   **286**

BT   **Christian sects**

Bar

USE   **Lawyers**

Bar coding   006.4; 658.7

BT   **Identification**

Bar mitzvah (May subdiv. geog.)   **296.4**

BT   **Judaism—Customs and practices**

Barbary States

USE   **North Africa**

Barbecue cookery

USE   **Barbecue cooking**

Barbecue cooking   641.7

UF   Barbecue cookery

       Grill cooking

       Grilling

BT   **Outdoor cooking**

Barbering

USE   **Hair**

Barbie dolls   688.7

BT   **Dolls**

Bargaining

USE   **Negotiation**

Barns (May subdiv. geog.)   **631.2; 728**
   BT   **Farm buildings**
Barometers   **551.5; 681**
   BT   **Meteorological instruments**
Baroque architecture (May subdiv. geog.)
      724
   UF   Architecture, Baroque
   BT   **Architecture**
Baroque art (May subdiv. geog.)   **709.03**
   UF   Art, Baroque
   BT   **Art**
Barrier free design
   USE   **Architecture and the handi-**
        capped
Barristers
   USE   **Lawyers**
Barrooms
   USE   **Bars**
Barrows
   USE   **Mounds and mound builders**
Bars (May subdiv. geog.)   **647.95**
   Use for materials on public drinking establishments.
   UF   Barrooms
        Pubs
        Restaurants, bars, etc.
        Saloons
        Taverns
   BT   **Liquor industry**
   RT   **Restaurants**
Bartending   **641.8**
   UF   Mixology
   BT   **Food service**
Barter (May subdiv. geog.)   **332**
   UF   Exchange, Barter
   BT   **Commerce**
        Economics
        Money
        Subsistence economy
        Underground economy
Basal readers   **372.41; 418**
   Use for readers providing controlled vocabulary in a series of books intended to be read sequentially and for materials about such readers.
   UF   English language—Basal readers
   BT   **Reading materials**
Baseball (May subdiv. geog.)   **796.357**
   BT   **Ball games**
        Sports
   NT   **Baseball teams**
        Little League baseball
        Negro leagues

        Softball
   RT   **Baseball players**
Baseball cards (May subdiv. geog.)   **769**
   BT   **Sports cards**
Baseball clubs
   USE   **Baseball teams**
Baseball—Fiction   **808.83**
   Use for collections of baseball stories.
   UF   Baseball stories
Baseball players (May subdiv. geog.)
      796.357; 920
   BT   **Athletes**
   NT   **African American baseball**
        players
   RT   **Baseball**
Baseball stories
   USE   **Baseball—Fiction**
Baseball teams (May subdiv. geog.)
      796.35706
   UF   Baseball clubs
   SA   names of individual baseball
        teams, e.g. **Houston Astros**
        (Baseball team) [to be added
        as needed]
   BT   **Baseball**
        Sports teams
   NT   **Houston Astros (Baseball**
        team)
Basements   **721**
   UF   Cellars
   BT   **Foundations**
        Underground architecture
Bases (Chemistry)   **546; 661**
   BT   **Chemistry**
Bashfulness
   USE   **Shyness**
Basic education (May subdiv. geog.)
      370.11
   UF   Basic skills education
        Fundamental education
   BT   **Education**
Basic life skills
   USE   **Life skills**
Basic needs (May subdiv. geog.)   **306**
   Use for materials on human needs such as food, shelter, education, health, water, employment, etc., that provide a minimum quality of life.
   RT   **Poverty**
        Quality of life

Basic rights
USE **Civil rights**
    Human rights
Basic skills education
USE **Basic education**
Basket making (May subdiv. geog.)
    746.41
UF Basketry
BT **Weaving**
Basketball (May subdiv. geog.) **796.323**
BT **Ball games**
    Sports
NT **Basketball teams**
    Wheelchair basketball
Basketball for women (May subdiv.
    geog.) **796.323**
BT **Sports for women**
Basketball teams (May subdiv. geog.)
    796.323
SA names of individual basketball
    teams, e.g. **New York Knicks
    (Basketball team)** [to be add-
    ed as needed]
BT **Basketball**
    Sports teams
NT **New York Knicks (Basketball
    team)**
Basketry
USE **Basket making**
Baskets (May subdiv. geog.) **746.41**
BT **Containers**
Bastogne, Battle of
USE **Ardennes (France), Battle of
    the, 1944-1945**
Bat mitzvah (May subdiv. geog.) **296.4**
BT **Judaism—Customs and prac-
    tices**
Bathrooms (May subdiv. geog.) **643**
BT **Rooms**
Baths (May subdiv. geog.) **613; 615.8**
BT **Cleanliness**
    Hygiene
    Physical therapy
RT **Hydrotherapy**
Bathyscaphe **387.2; 623.8**
BT **Oceanography—Research**
    Submersibles
Batik (May subdiv. geog.) **746.6**
BT **Dyes and dyeing**
Baton twirling **791.6**
RT **Drum majoring**

Bats (May subdiv. geog.) **599.4**
BT **Mammals**
Battered elderly
USE **Elderly abuse**
Battered wives
USE **Abused women**
Battered women
USE **Abused women**
Batteries, Electric
USE **Electric batteries**
    Storage batteries
Batteries, Solar
USE **Solar batteries**
Battering of husbands
USE **Husband abuse**
Battering of wives
USE **Wife abuse**
Battle of the Bulge
USE **Ardennes (France), Battle of
    the, 1944-1945**
Battle ships
USE **Warships**
Battle songs
USE **War songs**
Battlefields (May subdiv. geog.) **904**
UF Battlegrounds
SA names of wars with the subdivi-
    sion *Battlefields*, e.g. **World
    War, 1939-1945—Battle-
    fields**; and names of individu-
    al battlefields [to be added as
    needed]
BT **Battles**
Battlegrounds
USE **Battlefields**
Battles (May subdiv. geog.) **355.4; 904;
    909**
UF Fighting
    Sieges
SA names of wars with the subdivi-
    sion *Campaigns*, e.g. **United
    States—History—1861-1865,
    Civil War—Campaigns**; and
    names of individual battles,
    e.g. **Ardennes (France), Bat-
    tle of the, 1944-1945** [to be
    added as needed]
BT **Military art and science**
    Military history
    War

Battles—*Continued*
 NT Antietam (Md.), Battle of, 1862
 Ardennes (France), Battle of
 the, 1944-1945
 Battlefields
 Britain, Battle of, 1940
 Bunker Hill (Boston, Mass.),
 Battle of, 1775
 Concord (Mass.), Battle of,
 1775
 Gettysburg (Pa.), Battle of,
 1863
 Hastings (East Sussex, En-
 gland), Battle of, 1066
 Lexington (Mass.), Battle of,
 1775
 Naval battles
Battleships
 USE Warships
Bay of Pigs invasion
 USE Cuba—History—1961, Invasion
Bazaars
 USE Fairs
BBBs (Better business bureaus)
 USE Better business bureaus
Beaches (May subdiv. geog.) 551.45
 BT Seashore
Beads (May subdiv. geog.) 745.58
 BT Decoration and ornament
 RT Jewelry
Beadwork (May subdiv. geog.) 746.5
 BT Handicraft
Bearings (Machinery) 621.8
 UF Ball bearings
 BT Machinery
 RT Lubrication and lubricants
Bears (May subdiv. geog.) 599.78
 BT Mammals
Beasts
 USE Animals
Beat generation 810.9
 UF Beatniks
 Beats
 BT American literature
 Bohemianism
Beatniks
 USE Beat generation
Beats
 USE Beat generation
Beautification of landscape
 USE Landscape protection

Beauty
 USE Aesthetics
Beauty contests (May subdiv. geog.)
 791.6
 UF Beauty pageants
 BT Contests
Beauty pageants
 USE Beauty contests
Beauty parlors
 USE Beauty shops
Beauty, Personal
 USE Personal appearance
 Personal grooming
Beauty salons
 USE Beauty shops
Beauty shops (May subdiv. geog.) 646.7
 UF Beauty parlors
 Beauty salons
 BT Business enterprises
Beavers (May subdiv. geog.) 599.37
 BT Furbearing animals
 Mammals
Beavers—Habitations 599.37
Bed and breakfast accommodations (May
 subdiv. geog.) 910.46
 UF B and B accommodations
 BT Hotels and motels
Bedouins (May subdiv. geog.) 305.892;
 909
 BT Arabs
Bedspreads (May subdiv. geog.) 643;
 746.9
 UF Coverlets
 BT Interior design
Bedtime 306.4; 392.3
 UF Getting ready for bed
 BT Night
 Sleep
 NT Lullabies
Bee culture
 USE Beekeeping
Bee hives
 USE Beehives
Bee houses
 USE Beehives
Beef 641.3; 664
 BT Meat
Beef cattle (May subdiv. geog.) 636.2
 UF Steers
 SA names of breeds of beef cattle
 [to be added as needed]

Beef cattle—*Continued*
    BT   **Cattle**
    NT   **Hereford cattle**
Beehives (May subdiv. geog.)   **638**
    UF   Bee hives
          Bee houses
          Bees—Housing
    BT   **Animal housing**
    RT   **Beekeeping**
Beekeeping (May subdiv. geog.)   **638**
    UF   Apiculture
          Bee culture
          Honeybee culture
    BT   **Agriculture**
    RT   **Beehives**
          Bees
Beer (May subdiv. geog.)   **641.2**
    BT   **Alcoholic beverages**
    RT   **Brewing**
Beer making
    USE **Brewing**
Bees (May subdiv. geog.)   **595.79; 638**
    BT   **Insects**
    RT   **Beekeeping**
          Honey
Bees—Housing
    USE **Beehives**
Beetles (May subdiv. geog.)   **595.76**
    BT   **Insects**
Begging (May subdiv. geog.)   **362.5**
    UF   Mendicancy
          Panhandling
    BT   **Poor**
    RT   **Tramps**
Beginning reading materials
    USE **Easy reading materials**
Behavior
    USE **Animal behavior**
          Human behavior
          and types of specific behavior,
          e.g. **Sexual behavior;** and
          types of animals with the
          subdivision *Behavior,* e.g.
          Birds—Behavior [to be add-
          ed as needed]
Behavior genetics   **155.7**
    UF   Psychogenetics
    BT   **Genetics**
          Psychology
Behavior, Helping
    USE **Helping behavior**

Behavior in organizations
    USE **Organizational behavior**
Behavior modification   **153.8**
    BT   **Applied psychology**
          Human behavior
          Psychology of learning
    NT   **Brainwashing**
          Twelve-step programs
Behavior of children
    USE **Child psychology**
          Children—Conduct of life
          Etiquette for children and
             teenagers
Behavior of teenagers
    USE **Adolescent psychology**
          Etiquette for children and
             teenagers
          Teenagers—Conduct of life
Behavior problems (Children)
    USE **Emotionally disturbed children**
Behavioral psychology
    USE **Psychophysiology**
Behaviorism   **150.19**
    Use for materials on empirical psychology
    dealing with the observable actions of organ-
    isms rather than with mental phenomena.
    UF   Behavioristic psychology
          Interbehavioral psychology
    BT   **Human behavior**
          Psychology
          Psychophysiology
Behavioristic psychology
    USE **Behaviorism**
Beijing Massacre, 1989
    USE **Tiananmen Square Incident,**
          Beijing (China), 1989
Belarus   **947.8**
Belgium   **949.3**
    May be subdivided like United States ex-
    cept for History.
Belief and doubt   **121**
    Use for materials on belief and doubt from
    the philosophical standpoint. Materials on reli-
    gious belief and doubt are entered under
    Faith.
    UF   Doubt
    BT   **Philosophy**
          Theory of knowledge
    NT   **Truth**
    RT   **Agnosticism**
          Faith
          Rationalism
          Skepticism

Bell System Telstar satellite
USE **Telstar project**
Belles lettres
USE **Literature**
Bells (May subdiv. geog.) **786.8**
UF Carillons
Chimes
Church bells
BT **Musical instruments**
Belly dancing (May subdiv. geog.) **793.3**
BT **Dance**
Belts and belting 621.8
UF Chain belting
BT **Machinery**
RT **Power transmission**
Beneficial insects (May subdiv. geog.)
591.6
UF Helpful insects
Useful insects
SA types of beneficial insects, e.g.
Silkworms [to be added as
needed]
BT **Economic zoology**
Insects
NT **Silkworms**
Benefit cost analysis
USE **Cost effectiveness**
Benefits, Employee
USE **Employee benefits**
Benefits, Fringe
USE **Employee benefits**
Benevolent institutions
USE **Institutional care**
Bengali language 491.4
BT **Indian languages**
Language and languages
Beowulf—Adaptations 829
Bequests
USE **Gifts**
Inheritance and succession
Wills
Bereavement 155.9; 248.8
Use for materials on the suffering of those
who have lost a loved one. Materials on men-
tal suffering or sorrow from other causes, es-
pecially loss or remorse, are entered under
Grief.
UF Mourning
Sorrow
BT **Emotions**
RT **Consolation**
Grief

**Bergen-Belsen (Germany: Concentration
camp) 365; 943**
BT **Concentration camps**
Bermuda Triangle 001.9
UF Devil's Triangle
BT **Atlantic Ocean**
Berries 634
SA types of berries, e.g. **Strawber-
ries** [to be added as needed],
in the plural form
BT **Fruit**
Fruit culture
NT **Strawberries**
Best-book lists
USE **Best books**
Best books 011
Use for lists of recommended books and
materials about recommended books. Materi-
als on the principles of book selection for li-
braries are entered under **Book selection**.
UF Best-book lists
Bibliography—Best books
Book lists
Books and reading—Best books
Choice of books
Evaluation of literature
Literature—Evaluation
BT **Books**
RT **Book selection**
Best sellers (Books) (May subdiv. geog.)
028; 070.5
UF Books—Best sellers
BT **Books and reading**
Bestiaries 002
BT **Books**
Betrothal (May subdiv. geog.) **392.4**
UF Engagement
BT **Courtship**
Marriage
Better business bureaus (May subdiv.
geog.) **381.3**
UF BBBs (Better business bureaus)
BT **Consumer protection**
Betting
USE **Gambling**
Bevel gearing
USE **Gearing**
Beverage industry (May subdiv. geog.)
338.4
SA types of beverage industries, e.g.
Coffee industry [to be added
as needed]

Beverage industry—*Continued*

BT **Food industry**

NT **Coffee industry**

Liquor industry

Tea industry

Beverages 613; 641.2; 641.8; 663

UF Drinks

SA types of beverages and names of specific beverages [to be added as needed]

BT **Diet**

Food

NT **Alcoholic beverages**

Cocoa

Coffee

Liquors

Tea

Bi-racial people

USE **Racially mixed people**

Bias attacks

USE **Hate crimes**

Bias crimes

USE **Hate crimes**

Bias in testing

USE **Test bias**

Bias (Psychology)

USE **Prejudices**

Bible 220

The subdivisions provided under Bible may also be used with any part of the Bible, with single books of the Bible, and with groups of books, e.g. **Bible. O.T.—Biography**; **Bible. O.T. Pentateuch—Commentaries**; **Bible. O.T. Psalms—History**; **Bible. N.T. Gospels—Inspiration**; etc.

UF Holy Scriptures

Scriptures, Holy

BT **Ancient history**

Hebrew literature

Jewish literature

Sacred books

Bible. N.T. 225

Use same subdivisions as those given under **Bible**. They may also be used for groups of books, e.g. **Bible. N.T. Gospels—Inspiration**; and for single books, e.g. **Bible. N.T. Matthew—Commentaries**.

UF New Testament

Bible. O.T. 221

Use same subdivisions as those given under **Bible**. They may also be used for groups of books, e.g. **Bible. O.T. Pentateuch—Commentaries**; and for single books, e.g. **Bible. O.T. Psalms—History**.

UF Old Testament

Bible and science 220.8

UF Science and the Bible

BT **Religion and science**

Science

RT **Creationism**

Bible—Animals

USE **Bible—Natural history**

Bible—Antiquities 220.9

UF Biblical archeology

BT **Antiquities**

Archeology

Bible as literature 809

UF Bible—Language, style, etc.

Bible—Literary character

NT **Bible—Criticism**

Bible—Parables

RT **Religious literature**

Bible—Astronomy 220.8

BT **Astronomy**

Bible—Biography 220.92

UF Biblical characters

BT **Biography**

Bible—Birds

USE **Bible—Natural history**

Bible—Botany

USE **Bible—Natural history**

Bible—Catechism, question books

USE **Bible—Catechisms**

Bible—Catechisms 220

UF Bible—Catechism, question books

Bible—Question books

BT **Catechisms**

Bible—Chronology 220.9

Use for materials on the dates of events related in the Bible and their correlation with the dates of general history.

UF Bible—History of biblical events—Chronology

Biblical chronology

BT **Chronology**

Bible classes

USE **Bible—Study and teaching**

Religious summer schools

Sunday schools

Bible—Commentaries 220.7

UF Bible—Interpretation

Commentaries, Biblical

Bible—Concordances 220.3

Use for works that list the words of the Bible and give the passages where each word occurs. Works that list topics or names found in the Bible and give the passages where those topics or names rather than exact words are found are entered under **Bible—Indexes**.

Bible—Cosmology
USE **Biblical cosmology**
Bible—Criticism   220.6
UF   Bible—Criticism, interpretation,
etc.
Bible—Exegesis
Bible—Hermeneutics
Bible—Interpretation
Exegesis, Biblical
Hermeneutics, Biblical
Higher criticism
BT   **Bible as literature**
Bible—Criticism, interpretation, etc.
USE   **Bible—Criticism**
Bible—Dictionaries   220.3
BT   **Encyclopedias and dictionaries**
Bible—Drama
USE   **Bible plays**
Bible—Evidences, authority, etc.   220.1
Use for materials that attempt to establish
the truth of statements in the Bible or the au-
thority of its precepts. Materials on the divine
inspiration of the Bible are entered under **Bi-
ble—Inspiration**.
UF   Evidences of the Bible
Bible—Exegesis
USE   **Bible—Criticism**
Bible fiction   808.3; 808.83
Use for individual works, collections, or
materials about imaginative fiction in which
characters and settings are taken from the Bi-
ble. Stories that are retold or adapted from the
Bible while remaining faithful to the original
are entered under **Bible stories**.
SA   names of biblical characters with
the subdivision *Fiction* [to be
added as needed]
BT   **Fiction**
RT   **Bible stories**
Bible films   791.43
Use for individual works, collections, or
materials about bible films.
UF   Biblical films
BT   **Motion pictures**
Bible—Flowers
USE   **Bible—Natural history**
**Bible games and puzzles   220.07;
793.73**
UF   Bible puzzles
BT   **Games**
Puzzles
Bible—Gardens
USE   **Bible—Natural history**
Bible—Geography   220.91

UF   Bible—Maps
Biblical geography
BT   **Atlases**
Geography
Bible—Hermeneutics
USE   **Bible—Criticism**
Bible—History   220.9
Use for materials on the origin, authorship,
and composition of the Bible as a book. Ma-
terials on historical events as described in the
Bible are entered under **Bible—History of
biblical events**.
Bible—History of biblical events   220.9
Use for materials on historical events as de-
scribed in the Bible. Materials on the origin,
authorship, and composition of the Bible as a
book are entered under **Bible—History**.
UF   History, Biblical
Bible—History of biblical events—Chronol-
ogy
USE   **Bible—Chronology**
Bible—Illustrations
USE   **Bible—Pictorial works**
Bible in literature   809
Use for materials that discuss the Bible as
a theme in literature.
BT   **Literature**
RT   **Religion in literature**
Bible in the schools
USE   **Religion in the public schools**
Bible—Indexes   220.3
Use for works that list topics or names
found in the Bible and give the passages
where those topics or names rather than exact
words are found. Works that list the words of
the Bible and give the passages where the ex-
act word occurs are entered under **Bible—
Concordances**.
Bible—Inspiration   220.1
Use for materials on the divine inspiration
of the Bible. Materials that attempt to estab-
lish the truth of statements in the Bible or the
authority of its precepts are entered under **Bi-
ble—Evidence, authority, etc.**
UF   Inspiration, Biblical
Bible—Interpretation
USE   **Bible—Commentaries**
Bible—Criticism
Bible—Introductions
USE   **Bible—Study and teaching**
Bible—Language, style, etc.
USE   **Bible as literature**
Bible—Literary character
USE   **Bible as literature**
Bible—Maps
USE   **Bible—Geography**
Bible—Natural history   220.8

Bible—Natural history—*Continued*
> UF Bible—Animals
> > Bible—Birds
> > Bible—Botany
> > Bible—Flowers
> > Bible—Gardens
> > Bible—Plants
> > Bible—Zoology
> > Botany of the Bible
> > Nature in the bible
> > Zoology of the Bible
>
> BT **Natural history**

Bible—Parables 226.8
> BT **Bible as literature**
> > **Parables**

Bible—Pictorial works 220.022
> UF Bible—Illustrations

Bible—Plants
> USE **Bible—Natural history**

Bible plays 808.82
> Use for individual plays, collections, or materials about dramatizations of biblical events.
>
> UF Bible—Drama
> > Biblical plays
>
> SA names of biblical characters with the subdivision *Drama* [to be added as needed]
>
> BT **Religious drama**
> NT **Mysteries and miracle plays**
> > **Passion plays**

Bible—Prophecies 220.1
> UF Prophecies (Bible)

Bible—Psychology 220.8
> UF Biblical psychology
> BT **Psychology**

Bible puzzles
> USE **Bible games and puzzles**

Bible—Question books
> USE **Bible—Catechisms**

Bible—Reading 220.5
> BT **Books and reading**

Bible stories 220.9
> Use for individual works, collections, or materials about stories that are retold or adapted from the Bible while remaining faithful to the original. Imaginative fiction in which characters and settings are taken from the Bible is entered under **Bible fiction**.
>
> UF Stories
> RT **Bible fiction**

Bible—Study
> USE **Bible—Study and teaching**

Bible—Study and teaching 220.07

> UF Bible classes
> > Bible—Introductions
> > Bible—Study
>
> BT **Sunday schools**

Bible—Use 220.6
> Use for materials that show how the Bible is used as a guide to living, to cultivation of a spiritual life, and to problems of doctrine.

Bible—Versions 220.4; 220.5
> Use for materials on the various versions and translations of the Bible.

Bible—Women
> USE **Women in the Bible**

Bible—Zoology
> USE **Bible—Natural history**

Biblical archeology
> USE **Bible—Antiquities**

Biblical characters
> USE **Bible—Biography**

Biblical chronology
> USE **Bible—Chronology**

Biblical cosmology 202; 231.7; 296.3
> UF Bible—Cosmology
> BT **Cosmology**
> RT **Creation**

Biblical films
> USE **Bible films**

Biblical geography
> USE **Bible—Geography**

Biblical plays
> USE **Bible plays**

Biblical psychology
> USE **Bible—Psychology**

Biblical teaching
> USE religious or secular topics with the subdivision *Biblical teaching,* e.g. **Salvation—Biblical teaching; Family—Biblical teaching;** etc. [to be added as needed]

Bibliographic control (May subdiv. geog.) 025.3
> UF Universal bibliographic control
> BT **Documentation**
> NT **Cataloging**
> > **Indexing**
> > **Information systems**
> > **MARC formats**

Bibliographic data in machine readable form
> USE **Machine readable bibliographic data**

Bibliographic instruction   025.5

Use for materials on the instruction of readers in library use. Materials on the education of librarians are entered under **Library education**.

UF   Library instruction

Library orientation

Library skills

Library user orientation

BT   **Library services**

Bibliography   010

SA   subjects and names of persons and places with the subdivision *Bibliography*, e.g. **Agriculture—Bibliography; Shakespeare, William, 1564-1616—Bibliography; United States—Bibliography**; etc. [to be added as needed]

BT   **Documentation**

NT   **Archives**

Editions

Indexes

Indexing

Manuscripts

Printing

Reference books

Serial publications

RT   **Books**

Cataloging

Library science

Bibliography—Best books

USE   **Best books**

Bibliography—Bilingual books

USE   **Bilingual books**

Bibliography—Editions

USE   **Editions**

Bibliography—First editions

USE   **First editions**

Bibliography—Rare books

USE   **Rare books**

Bibliography—Reprint editions

USE   **Reprints (Publications)**

Bibliomania

USE   **Book collecting**

Bibliophily

USE   **Book collecting**

Bicentennial celebrations—United States—1976

USE   **American Revolution Bicentennial, 1776-1976**

Biculturalism (May subdiv. geog.)   **305.8; 306.44**

Use for materials on the presence of two distinct cultures within a single country or region. Materials on the coexistence of several distinct ethnic, religious, or cultural groups within one society are entered under **Pluralism (Social sciences)**. Materials on policies or programs that foster the preservation of various cultures or cultural identities within a unified society are entered under **Multiculturalism**.

BT   **Pluralism (Social sciences)**

RT   **Multiculturalism**

Biculturalism—United States   305.8; 306.44

Bicycle camping

USE   **Bicycle touring**

Bicycle racing (May subdiv. geog.)   **796.6**

BT   **Cycling**

Racing

RT   **Bicycle touring**

Bicycles

Bicycle touring (May subdiv. geog.)   **796.6**

UF   Backpack cycling

Bicycle camping

Touring, Bicycle

BT   **Camping**

Cycling

Travel

RT   **Bicycle racing**

Bicycles

Bicycles (May subdiv. geog.)   **629.227**

UF   Bicycles and bicycling

Bikes

BT   **Vehicles**

NT   **Minibikes**

Motorcycles

Mountain bikes

RT   **Bicycle racing**

Bicycle touring

Cycling

Bicycles and bicycling

USE   **Bicycles**

Cycling

Bicycling

USE   **Cycling**

Big bang cosmology

USE   **Big bang theory**

Big bang theory   523.1

UF   Big bang cosmology

BT   **Cosmology**

Big books   372.41

Use for books produced in an oversize format and intended for use in shared-reading learning experiences or for materials about such books.

UF   Enlarged texts for shared reading

Oversize books

Oversized books for shared reading

Shared reading books

BT   **Children's literature**

Reading materials

RT   **Large print books**

Big foot

USE   **Sasquatch**

Big game hunting (May subdiv. geog.)

799.2

BT   **Hunting**

Bigfoot

USE   **Sasquatch**

Bigotry

USE   **Prejudices**

Toleration

Bigotry-motivated crimes

USE   **Hate crimes**

Bikes

USE   **Bicycles**

Biking

USE   **Cycling**

Bildungsromans   808.3

Use for individual works, collections, or materials about fiction in which the theme is the development of a character from youth to adulthood.

UF   Apprenticeship novels

Coming of age stories

BT   **Fiction**

Bilingual books   002; 011

Use for materials about bilingual books. As a form heading for the bilingual materials themselves, use this heading subdivided by the languages, e.g. **Bilingual books—English-Spanish**.

UF   Bibliography—Bilingual books

Books—Bilingual editions

BT   **Books**

Editions

Bilingual books—English-Spanish

Use as a form heading for bilingual materials in English and Spanish.

UF   Bilingual books—Spanish-English

Bilingual books—Spanish-English

USE   **Bilingual books—English-Spanish**

Bilingual education (May subdiv. geog.)

370.117

UF   Education, Bilingual

BT   **Bilingualism**

Multicultural education

Bilingualism (May subdiv. geog.)

306.44; 400

BT   **Language and languages**

NT   **Bilingual education**

Bilingualism—United States   306.44; 420

Bill collecting

USE   **Collecting of accounts**

Bill of rights (U.S.)

USE   **United States. Constitution. 1st-10th amendments**

Billboards

USE   **Signs and signboards**

Billiards   794.92

BT   **Ball games**

NT   **Pool (Game)**

Bills and notes

USE   **Negotiable instruments**

Bills of credit

USE   **Credit**

Negotiable instruments

Bills of fare

USE   **Menus**

Binary system (Mathematics)   513.5

UF   Pair system

BT   **Mathematics**

Numbers

Binding of books

USE   **Bookbinding**

Binge eating behavior

USE   **Bulimia**

Binge-purge behavior

USE   **Bulimia**

Bio-bibliography

USE   subjects, groups and classes of persons, names of places, and names of individual persons with the subdivision *Bio-bibliography,* e.g. **English literature—Bio-bibliography; United States—Bio-bibliography;** etc. [to be added as needed]

Bioastronautics

USE   **Space medicine**

Biochemistry   572

Biochemistry—*Continued*
- UF   Biological chemistry
  - Physiological chemistry
- BT   **Biology**
  - **Chemistry**
  - **Medicine**
- NT   **Carbohydrates**
  - **Clinical chemistry**
  - **Metabolism**
  - **Molecular biology**
  - **Nucleic acids**
  - **Proteins**
  - **Steroids**

Bioconversion
- USE   **Biomass energy**

Biodiversity (May subdiv. geog.)   **333.95**

Use for materials on the variety and variability among living organisms and the ecological complexes in which they occur, including ecosystem diversity, species diversity, and genetic diversity.
- UF   Biological diversification
  - Biological diversity
  - Diversity, Biological
- BT   **Biology**
- RT   **Ecology**

Biodiversity conservation (May subdiv. geog.)   **333.95**
- UF   Biological diversity conservation
  - Conservation of biodiversity
  - Maintenance of biodiversity
  - Preservation of biodiversity
- BT   **Conservation of natural resources**

Bioethics   **174**
- UF   Biological ethics
  - Biology—Ethical aspects
  - Biomedical ethics
  - Life sciences ethics
- BT   **Ethics**
- NT   **Medical ethics**
  - **Transplantation of organs, tissues, etc.—Ethical aspects**

Biofeedback training   **152.1**
- UF   Visceral learning
- BT   **Feedback (Psychology)**
  - **Mind and body**
  - **Psychology of learning**
  - **Psychotherapy**

Biogeography (May subdiv. geog.)   **578.09**

Use for materials on the geographical distribution of animals and plants collectively or of animals only. Materials on the geographical distribution of plants are entered under **Plants—Geographical distribution**.
- UF   Distribution of animals and plants
  - Geographical distribution of animals and plants
- SA   types of plants and animals with the subdivision *Geographical distribution*, e.g. **Fishes—Geographical distribution** [to be added as needed]
- BT   **Ecology**
  - **Geography**
- NT   **Fishes—Geographical distribution**
  - **Plants—Geographical distribution**
- RT   **Natural history**

Biographical dictionaries
- USE   **Biography—Dictionaries**

Biographical fiction   **808.3; 808.83**

Use for individual works, collections, or materials about fictionalized accounts of the lives of real persons.
- UF   Biographical novels
- SA   names of real persons with the subdivision *Fiction*, e.g. **Napoleon I, Emperor of the French, 1769-1821—Fiction**; or *In literature*, e.g. **Napoleon I, Emperor of the French, 1769-1821—In literature**; [to be added as needed]
- BT   **Fiction**
- NT   **Autobiographical fiction**
- RT   **Historical fiction**

Biographical films   **791.43**

Use for individual works, collections, or materials about films depicting the lives of real persons.
- BT   **Motion pictures**

Biographical graphic novels   **741.5**

Use for individual works, collections, or materials about biographical graphic novels.
- BT   **Graphic novels**

Biographical novels
- USE   **Biographical fiction**

Biographical radio programs   **791.44**

Use for individual works, collections, or materials about radio programs recounting the lives of real persons.
- BT   **Radio programs**

Biographical television programs
791.45

Use for individual works, collections, or materials about television programs depicting the lives of real persons.

BT **Television programs**

Biography   920

Use for collections of biographies not limited to one country or to one group or class of persons. Materials on the writing of biography are entered under **Biography as a literary form**.

UF   Life histories

Memoirs

Personal narratives

SA   subjects and names of places and corporate bodies with the subdivision *Biography*; ethnic groups and classes of persons with the subdivision *Biography* or *Correspondence*; and names of diseases, events, and wars with the subdivision *Personal narratives* [to be added as needed]

BT   **History**

NT   **Autobiographies**

Autographs

Bible—Biography

Blacks—Biography

Chicago (Ill.)—Biography

Christian biography

Epitaphs

Greece—Biography

Medicine—Biography

Men—Biography

Motion pictures—Biography

Musicians—Biography

Obituaries

Ohio—Biography

Portraits

Religious biography

Rome—Biography

United States. Army—Biography

United States. Navy—Biography

United States. Supreme Court—Biography

United States—Biography

United States—History—1861-1865, Civil War—Biography

United States—History—1861-1865, Civil War—Personal narratives

Women—Biography

World War, 1939-1945—Biography

World War, 1939-1945—Personal narratives

RT   **Genealogy**

Biography (as a literary form)

USE   **Biography as a literary form**

Biography as a literary form   809

Use for materials on the writing of biography.

UF   Biography (as a literary form)

Biography—History and criticism

Biography—Technique

BT   **Authorship**

Literature

NT   **Autobiography**

Biography—Dictionaries   920.02

Use for collections of biographies in dictionary form not limited to one group or class of persons.

UF   Biographical dictionaries

Dictionaries, Biographical

SA   subjects, groups or classes of persons, and names of places with the subdivisions *Biography—Dictionaries*, e.g. **Women—Biography—Dictionaries**; **United States—Biography—Dictionaries**; etc. [to be added as needed]

BT   **Encyclopedias and dictionaries**

Biography—History and criticism

USE   **Biography as a literary form**

Biography—Technique

USE   **Biography as a literary form**

Biological anthropology

USE   **Physical anthropology**

Biological chemistry

USE   **Biochemistry**

Biological clocks

USE   **Biological rhythms**

Biological diversification

USE   **Biodiversity**

Biological diversity

USE   **Biodiversity**

Biological diversity conservation

USE   **Biodiversity conservation**

Biological ethics
    USE **Bioethics**

Biological form
    USE **Morphology**

Biological parents
    USE **Birthparents**

Biological physics
    USE **Biophysics**

Biological rhythms   571.7
    UF Biological clocks
         Biology—Periodicity
         Biorhythms
    BT **Cycles**
    NT **Jet lag**

Biological structure
    USE **Morphology**

Biological terrorism
    USE **Bioterrorism**

Biological warfare (May subdiv. geog.)
        358; 623.4
    UF Bacterial warfare
         Germ warfare
    BT **Military art and science**
         Tactics

Biologists (May subdiv. geog.)   **570.92;**
    920
    BT **Naturalists**
         Scientists

Biology   **570**
    BT **Life sciences**
         Science
    NT **Adaptation (Biology)**
         Anatomy
         Biochemistry
         Biodiversity
         Biomathematics
         Biophysics
         Botany
         Cells
         Cryobiology
         Death
         Ecology
         Embryology
         Ethnobiology
         Fossils
         Freshwater biology
         Gaia hypothesis
         Genetics
         Heredity
         Life (Biology)
         Life cycles (Biology)

         Marine biology
         Microbiology
         Physiology
         Protoplasm
         Radiobiology
         Reproduction
         Sex—Physiological aspects
         Space biology
         Symbiosis
         Variation (Biology)
         Zoology
    RT **Evolution**

Biology—Ecology
    USE **Ecology**

Biology—Ethical aspects
    USE **Bioethics**

Biology, Molecular
    USE **Molecular biology**

Biology—Periodicity
    USE **Biological rhythms**

Biology—Social aspects
    USE **Sociobiology**

Bioluminescence   **572**
    UF Animal light
         Animal luminescence
         Light production in animals
    BT **Luminescence**

Biomass energy (May subdiv. geog.)
        333.95

      Use for materials on organic matter that can
    be converted to fuel and is therefore regarded
    as a potential energy source.

    UF Bioconversion
         Energy, Biomass
         Energy conversion, Microbial
         Microbial energy conversion
    SA types of matter as fuels, e.g.
         Waste products as fuel [to
           be added as needed]
    BT **Energy resources**
         Fuel
    RT **Waste products as fuel**

Biomathematics   **570.1**
    BT **Biology**
         Mathematics

Biomechanics
    USE **Human engineering**
         Human locomotion

Biomedical ethics
    USE **Bioethics**

Bionics   003
> Use for materials on the science of techno-
> logical systems that function in the manner of
> living systems.

    BT   **Biophysics**
          Cybernetics
          Systems engineering

Biophysics   571.4
    UF   Biological physics
    BT   **Biology**
          Physics
    NT   **Bionics**
          Molecular biology
          Radiobiology

Biorhythms
    USE **Biological rhythms**

Biosciences
    USE **Life sciences**

Biosphere   333.95
    BT   **Life (Biology)**
    RT   **Atmosphere**
          Earth
          Gaia hypothesis

Biotechnology (May subdiv. geog.)
        620.8; 660.6
> Use for materials on the application of liv-
> ing organisms or their biological systems or
> processes to the manufacture of products.

    BT   **Chemical engineering**
          Microbiology
    NT   **Reproductive technology**
    RT   **Genetic engineering**

Bioterrorism (May subdiv. geog.)   **303.6**
    UF   Biological terrorism
    BT   **Terrorism**

Bipolar depression
    USE **Manic-depressive illness**

Bipolar disorder
    USE **Manic-depressive illness**

Bird attracting   639.9
    UF   Attracting birds
    BT   **Wildlife attracting**

Bird decoys (Hunting)
    USE **Decoys (Hunting)**

Bird eggs
    USE **Birds—Eggs**

Bird houses
    USE **Birdhouses**

Bird photography
    USE **Photography of birds**

Bird song
    USE **Birdsongs**

Bird watching (May subdiv. geog.)
        598.07
    UF   Birding
    BT   **Natural history**

Birdbanding   598.07
    UF   Birds—Banding
          Birds—Marking
    BT   **Wildlife conservation**

Birdhouses (May subdiv. geog.)   **690**
    UF   Bird houses
    BT   **Animal housing**

Birding
    USE **Bird watching**

Birds (May subdiv. geog.)   **598**
    SA   types of birds, e.g. **Birds of**
          prey; **Canaries**; etc. [to be
          added as needed]
    BT   **Animals**
    NT   **Birds of prey**
          Cage birds
          Canaries
          Ducks
          Eagles
          Game and game birds
          Geese
          Peacocks
          Penguins
          Pheasants
          Poultry
          Puffins
          Robins
          State birds
          Terns
          Turkeys
          Water birds

Birds—Anatomy   598
    BT   **Anatomy**

Birds—Banding
    USE **Birdbanding**

Birds—Behavior   598.15
    UF   Birds—Habits and behavior
    BT   **Animal behavior**

Birds—Collection and preservation (May
        subdiv. geog.)   **598.075**
    BT   **Zoological specimens—Collec-
          tion and preservation**

Birds—Color   598.147
    BT   **Color**

Birds—Eggs   598.14
    UF   Bird eggs
          Birds' eggs

Birds—Eggs—*Continued*
   Birds—Eggs and nests
 BT **Eggs**
Birds' eggs
 USE **Birds—Eggs**
Birds—Eggs and nests
 USE **Birds—Eggs**
   Birds—Nests
Birds—Flight 591.5; 598.15
 BT **Animal flight**
Birds—Habits and behavior
 USE **Birds—Behavior**
Birds—Marking
 USE **Birdbanding**
Birds—Migration (May subdiv. geog.)
  598.156
 UF Migration of birds
Birds—Nests 598.156
 UF Birds—Eggs and nests
   Birds' nests
Birds' nests
 USE **Birds—Nests**
Birds of prey (May subdiv. geog.) **598.9**
 SA names of specific birds of prey
   [to be added as needed]
 BT **Birds**
   Predatory animals
 NT **Eagles**
Birds—Photography
 USE **Photography of birds**
Birds—Protection (May subdiv. geog.)
  333.95; 639.9
 UF Protection of birds
 BT **Wildlife conservation**
 RT **Game protection**
Birds—Song
 USE **Birdsongs**
Birds—United States 598.0973
Birdsongs 598.159
 UF Bird song
   Birds—Song
 BT **Animal sounds**
Birth
 USE **Childbirth**
Birth attendants
 USE **Midwives**
Birth control (May subdiv. geog.)
  353.5; 363.9; 613.9
 UF Conception—Prevention
   Contraception
   Family planning
   Fertility control

   Planned parenthood
 BT **Population**
   Sexual hygiene
 NT **Sterilization (Birth control)**
 RT **Birth rate**
   Childlessness
   Family size
   Human fertility
   Infertility
Birth control—Ethical aspects 176
 UF Birth control—Moral and reli-
   gious aspects
 BT **Ethics**
Birth control—Moral and religious aspects
 USE **Birth control—Ethical aspects**
   Birth control—Religious as-
   pects
Birth control—Religious aspects 205;
  248.4
 UF Birth control—Moral and reli-
   gious aspects
Birth customs
 USE **Childbirth**
Birth defects (May subdiv. geog.) 616
 UF Abnormalities, Human
   Birth injuries
   Deformities
   Human abnormalities
   Infants—Birth defects
   Malformations, Congenital
 BT **Medical genetics**
   Pathology
 RT **Fetal alcohol syndrome**
   Growth disorders
Birth injuries
 USE **Birth defects**
Birth, Multiple
 USE **Multiple birth**
Birth order 306.87
 UF Firstborn child
   Middle child
   Oldest child
   Sibling sequence
   Youngest child
 BT **Children**
   Family
Birth rate (May subdiv. geog.) 304.6
 UF Birthrate
 BT **Vital statistics**
 NT **Human fertility**

Birth rate—*Continued*
RT **Birth control**
Population
Birth records
USE **Registers of births, etc.**
Birthday books 394.2
Use for books with birthdays of famous persons for every day or month of the year and for similar books with space for recording birthdays of acquaintances.
BT **Birthdays**
Calendars
Birthdays 394.2
BT **Anniversaries**
Days
NT **Birthday books**
Birthparents 306.874
Use for materials on natural, i.e. biological, parents who relinquished their children for adoption.
UF Biological parents
Natural parents
Parents, Biological
BT **Parents**
RT **Adoptees**
Birthrate
USE **Birth rate**
Births, Registers of
USE **Registers of births, etc.**
Bisexuality 306.76
BT **Sex**
Bishops (May subdiv. geog.) 270.092
UF Archbishops
SA church denominations with the subdivision *Bishops*, e.g. **Catholic Church—Bishops** [to be added as needed]
BT **Clergy**
NT **Catholic Church—Bishops**
Bison (May subdiv. geog.) 599.64; 636.2
UF American bison
Buffalo, American
BT **Mammals**
Black actors (May subdiv. geog.) 791.4; 792; 920
UF Actors, Black
Black actors and actresses
BT **Actors**
NT **African American actors**
Black actors and actresses
USE **Black actors**
Black Africa
USE **Sub-Saharan Africa**

Black Americans
USE **African Americans**
Black art (May subdiv. geog.) 704.03
Use for materials on works of art by several Black artists. Materials on Blacks depicted in works of art are entered under **Blacks in art**.
UF Art, Black
Blacks—Art
BT **Art**
NT **African American art**
RT **Black artists**
Black art (Magic)
USE **Magic**
Witchcraft
Black artists (May subdiv. geog.) 709.2; 920
Use for materials on several Black artists.
UF Artists, Black
BT **Artists**
NT **African American artists**
RT **Black art**
Black athletes (May subdiv. geog.) 796.092; 920
UF Athletes, Black
BT **Athletes**
NT **African American athletes**
Black authors (May subdiv. geog.) 809; 920
Use for collections and for materials on several Black authors not limited to a single national literature or literary form.
UF Authors, Black
SA names of national literatures other than American literature and forms of literature with the subdivision *Black authors*, e.g. **French literature—Black authors; French poetry—Black authors**; etc. [to be added as needed]
BT **Authors**
NT **African American authors**
Black business people
USE **Black businesspeople**
Black businesspeople (May subdiv. geog.) 338.092; 658.0092; 920
UF Black business people
BT **Businesspeople**
NT **African American businesspeople**
Black children (May subdiv. geog.) 305.23

Black children—*Continued*
  UF Blacks—Children
      Children, Black
  BT **Children**
  NT **African American children**
Black comedy (Literature)
  USE **Black humor (Literature)**
Black death
  USE **Plague**
Black diaspora
  USE **African diaspora**
Black folk songs
  USE **Black music**
Black folklore
  USE **Blacks—Folklore**
Black Hawk War, 1832 973.5
  BT **Native Americans—Wars**
      United States—History—1815-
      1861
Black History Month 394.261
  UF African American History Month
  BT **Special months**
Black holes (Astronomy) 523.8
  UF Frozen stars
  BT **Astronomy**
      Astrophysics
      Stars
Black humor (Literature) 808.7; 808.87
   Use for individual works, collections, or materials about literary works characterized by a desperate, sardonic humor intended to induce laughter as the appropriate response to the apparent meaninglessness and absurdity of existence.
  UF Black comedy (Literature)
      Dark humor (Literature)
  BT **Fiction**
      Literature
      Wit and humor
Black lead
  USE **Graphite**
Black librarians (May subdiv. geog.)
      020.92; 920
  BT **Librarians**
  NT **African American librarians**
Black literature (American)
  USE **American literature—African**
      American authors
Black literature (French)
  USE **French literature—Black au-**
      thors

Black magic (Witchcraft)
  USE **Magic**
      Witchcraft
Black market (May subdiv. geog.) 381
   Use for materials on illegal trade aimed at avoiding government regulations, such as fixed prices or rationing. Materials on goods and services that are produced and sold legally but not reported or taxed are entered under **Underground economy**.
  UF Grey market
  BT **Commerce**
  RT **Underground economy**
Black market children
  USE **Adoption—Corrupt practices**
Black music (May subdiv. geog.)
      780.089
   Use for general materials and for materials on the music of Blacks not in the United States. Materials on the music of African Americans are entered under **African American music**.
  UF Black folk songs
      Black songs
      Blacks—Music
      Blacks—Songs and music
  BT **Music**
  NT **African American music**
  RT **Black musicians**
Black musicians (May subdiv. geog.)
      780.92; 920
  UF Musicians, Black
  BT **Musicians**
  NT **African American musicians**
  RT **Black music**
Black Muslims (May subdiv. geog.)
      297.8
  UF Nation of Islam
  BT **African Americans—Religion**
      Black nationalism
      Muslims—United States
Black nationalism (May subdiv. geog.)
      320.54
  UF Black separatism
      Nationalism, Black
      Separatism, Black
  BT **African Americans—Political**
      activity
      African Americans—Race iden-
      tity
      Blacks—Political activity
      Blacks—Race identity
  NT **Black Muslims**
  RT **Black power**

Black poetry (American)
  USE **American poetry—African
       American authors**
Black poetry (French)
  USE **French poetry—Black authors**
Black power (May subdiv. geog.)   **322.4**
  BT **African Americans—Political
       activity
       Blacks—Political activity**
  RT **Black nationalism**
Black separatism
  USE **Black nationalism**
Black songs
  USE **Black music**
Black suffrage
  USE **Blacks—Suffrage**
Black women (May subdiv. geog.)
       305.48
  UF Women, Black
  BT **Women**
  NT **African American women**
Blackboard drawing
  USE **Chalk talks
       Crayon drawing**
Blackheads (Acne)
  USE **Acne**
Blackmail
  USE **Extortion**
Blackouts, Electric power
  USE **Electric power failures**
Blacks (May subdiv. geog. except U.S.)
       305.896
  Use for materials on the Black race in gen-
  eral or for materials on Blacks as an element
  in the population, especially in countries
  where they are a minority. Works on Black
  people in countries with a population predom-
  inantly Black are assigned headings appropri-
  ate for the country without the use of the
  heading Blacks, except when the works dis-
  cuss Blacks as distinct from other groups in
  the country. Materials on Blacks in the United
  States are entered under **African Americans**.
  UF Negroes
  SA Blacks in various occupations
       and professions, e.g. **Black
       artists**; **Black librarians**; etc.
       [to be added as needed]
  NT **African Americans**
Blacks—Africa   305.896; 960
  BT **Africans**
Blacks—Art
  USE **Black art**
Blacks—Biography   920

  BT **Biography**
  NT **African Americans—Biography**
Blacks—Children
  USE **Black children**
Blacks—Civil rights (May subdiv. geog.)
       323.1196; 342
  BT **Blacks—Political activity
       Civil rights**
  NT **African Americans—Civil
       rights**
Blacks—Economic conditions (May
       subdiv. geog.)   **330.9**
  BT **Economic conditions**
  NT **African Americans—Economic
       conditions**
Blacks—Education (May subdiv. geog.)
       370.89; 371.829
  BT **Education**
  NT **African Americans—Education**
Blacks—Employment (May subdiv. geog.)
       331.6
  BT **Employment**
  NT **African Americans—Employ-
       ment**
Blacks—Folklore (May subdiv. geog.)
       398
  UF Black folklore
  BT **Folklore**
  NT **African Americans—Folklore**
Blacks—France   305.896; 944
  UF France—Blacks
Blacks—Housing (May subdiv. geog.)
       307.3; 363.5
  BT **Housing**
  NT **African Americans—Housing**
Blacks in art   704.9
  Use for materials on Blacks depicted in
  works of art. Materials on African Americans
  depicted in works of art are entered under **Af-
  rican Americans in art**. Materials on the at-
  tainments of several Blacks in the area of art
  are entered under **Black artists**. Materials on
  the attainments of several African Americans
  in the area of art are entered under **African
  American artists**. Materials on works of art
  by several Black artists are entered under
  Black art. Materials on works of art by several African American artists are entered under
  African American art.
  BT **Art—Themes**
Blacks in literature   809
  Use for materials on the theme of Blacks in
  works of literature. Materials on the attainments of several Blacks in the area of literature are entered under **Black authors**. Materi-

Blacks in literature—*Continued*

als on works of literature by several Black authors are entered under individual literatures and forms of literature with the subdivision *Black authors*, e.g. **French literature—Black authors**; **French poetry—Black authors**; etc. Materials on the theme of African Americans in works of literature are entered under **African Americans in literature**. Materials on the attainments of several African Americans in the area of literature are entered under **African American authors**. Materials on works of literature by several African American authors are entered under **American literature—African American authors** and the various forms of American literature with the subdivision *African American authors*, e.g. **American poetry—African American authors**.

   BT   **Literature—Themes**

Blacks in motion pictures (May subdiv. geog.)   **791.43**

Use for materials on the depiction of Blacks in motion pictures. Materials on several Black actors are entered under Black actors. Materials discussing all aspects of Blacks' involvement in motion pictures are entered under Blacks in the motion picture industry.

   BT   **Minorities in motion pictures**
           Motion pictures
   NT   **African Americans in motion pictures**

Blacks in the motion picture industry (May subdiv. geog.)   **791.43092**

Use for materials on all aspects of Blacks' involvement in motion pictures. Materials on the depiction of Blacks in motion pictures are entered under Blacks in motion pictures.

   BT   **Minorities in the motion picture industry**
           Motion picture industry
   NT   **African Americans in the motion picture industry**

Blacks—Intellectual life (May subdiv. geog.)   **305.896**

   BT   **Intellectual life**
   NT   **African Americans—Intellectual life**

Blacks—Music

   USE   **Black music**

Blacks—Political activity (May subdiv. geog.)   **322.4; 324**

   BT   **Political participation**
   NT   **African Americans—Political activity**
           Black nationalism
           Black power
           Blacks—Civil rights

Blacks—Race identity (May subdiv. geog.)   **305.896**

   UF   Negritude
   BT   **Race awareness**
   NT   **African Americans—Race identity**
           Black nationalism

Blacks—Religion (May subdiv. geog.)   **270.089; 299.6**

   BT   **Religion**
   NT   **African Americans—Religion**

Blacks—Segregation (May subdiv. geog.)   **305.896**

   BT   **Segregation**
   NT   **African Americans—Segregation**

Blacks—Social conditions (May subdiv. geog.)   **305.896**

   BT   **Social conditions**
   NT   **African Americans—Social conditions**

Blacks—Social life and customs (May subdiv. geog.)   **305.896**

   BT   **Manners and customs**
   NT   **African Americans—Social life and customs**

Blacks—Songs and music

   USE   **Black music**

Blacks—Suffrage (May subdiv. geog.)   **324.6**

   UF   Black suffrage
   BT   **Suffrage**
   NT   **African Americans—Suffrage**

Blacks—United States

   USE   **African Americans**

Blacksmithing (May subdiv. geog.)   **682**

   BT   **Ironwork**
   NT   **Welding**
   RT   **Forging**

Blast furnaces (May subdiv. geog.)   **669**

   BT   **Furnaces**
           Smelting

Blast shelters

   USE   **Air raid shelters**

Bleaching   **667**

   BT   **Cleaning**
           Industrial chemistry
           Textile industry
   RT   **Dyes and dyeing**

Blessed Virgin Mary

   USE   **Mary**

Blimps
USE **Airships**
Blind (May subdiv. geog.)   **362.4**
  BT **Physically handicapped**
  RT **Blindness**
Blind—Books and reading   011.63;
  027.6; 028
  UF Books for the blind
  BT **Books and reading**
  NT **Large print books**
  RT **Audiobooks**
    Braille books
Blind—Education (May subdiv. geog.)
  371.91
  UF Education of the blind
  BT **Education**
Blind—Institutional care (May subdiv.
  geog.)   **362.4**
  BT **Institutional care**
Blindness   617.7
  BT **Vision disorders**
  RT **Blind**
    Vision
Blizzards (May subdiv. geog.)   **551.55**
  BT **Storms**
  RT **Snow**
Block printing
  USE **Color prints**
    Linoleum block printing
    Textile printing
    Wood engraving
    Woodcuts
Block signal systems
  USE **Railroads—Signaling**
Blockades
  USE names of wars with the subdivi-
    sion *Blockades,* e.g. **World**
    War, 1939-1945—Blockades
    [to be added as needed]
Blogs
  USE **Weblogs**
Blood   573.1; 612.1
  BT **Physiology**
  NT **Blood groups**
    Blood pressure
Blood—Circulation   573.1; 612.1
  UF Circulation of the blood
  RT **Blood pressure**
    Cardiovascular system
Blood—Diseases   616.1
  UF Diseases of the blood

  SA types of blood diseases, e.g.
    Leukemia [to be added as
    needed]
  BT **Diseases**
  NT **Hemophilia**
    Leukemia
Blood feuds
  USE **Vendetta**
Blood groups   612.1
  UF Rh factor
  BT **Blood**
  RT **Blood—Transfusion**
Blood pressure   612.1
  BT **Blood**
  NT **Hypertension**
  RT **Blood—Circulation**
Blood—Transfusion   615
  RT **Blood groups**
Blowing the whistle
  USE **Whistle blowing**
Blowouts, Oil well
  USE **Oil wells—Blowouts**
Blue collar workers
  USE **Labor**
    Working class
Blue prints
  USE **Blueprints**
Bluegrass music (May subdiv. geog.)
  781.642
  BT **Music**
Blueprints   604.2; 692
  UF Blue prints
  BT **Mechanical drawing**
Blues music (May subdiv. geog.)
  781.643; 782.421643
  UF Blues songs
  BT **African American music**
    Folk music—United States
    Popular music
  RT **Jazz music**
Blues songs
  USE **Blues music**
Board books for children
  Use for individual works, collections, or
  materials about board books for children.
  BT **Picture books for children**
Board games   794
  BT **Games**
  NT **Checkers**
    Chess
Board sailing
  USE **Windsurfing**

Boarding houses
 USE **Hotels and motels**
Boarding schools
 USE **Private schools**
Boards of education
 USE **School boards**
Boards of health
 USE **Health boards**
Boards of trade
 USE **Chambers of commerce**
Boards of trustees
 USE **Trusts and trustees**
Boat building
 USE **Boatbuilding**
Boat racing (May subdiv. geog.) **797.1**
 UF Regattas
 SA types of boat racing and names
  of specific races [to be added
  as needed]
 BT **Boats and boating**
  Racing
Boatbuilding (May subdiv. geog.) **623.8**
 UF Boat building
  Boats—Construction
 BT **Naval architecture**
 NT **Yachts and yachting**
 RT **Boats and boating**
  Shipbuilding
Boating
 USE **Boats and boating**
Boats and boating (May subdiv. geog.)
  797.1
 UF Boating
 BT **Water sports**
 NT **Boat racing**
  Canoes and canoeing
  Catamarans
  Houseboats
  Hydrofoil boats
  Iceboats
  Marinas
  Motorboats
  Rowing
  Steamboats
  Tugboats
  Yachts and yachting
 RT **Boatbuilding**
  Sailing
  Ships
Boats—Construction
 USE **Boatbuilding**

Body
 USE **Human body**
Body and mind
 USE **Mind and body**
Body building
 USE **Bodybuilding**
Body care
 USE **Hygiene**
Body heat
 USE **Body temperature**
Body image **128; 155.2**
 Use for materials on the visual, mental, or
 memory image of one's own body or anoth-
 er's body, and one's attitude towards that im-
 age.
 BT **Human body**
  Mind and body
  Personality
  Self-perception
Body language **153.6; 302.2**
 BT **Nonverbal communication**
Body piercing (May subdiv. geog.)
  391.6
 BT **Personal appearance**
Body surfing
 USE **Surfing**
Body temperature **571.7; 612**
 UF Animals—Temperature
  Body heat
  Temperature, Animal and human
  Temperature, Body
 BT **Diagnosis**
  Physiology
 RT **Fever**
Body weight **613**
 BT **Human body**
  Weight
 NT **Obesity**
  Weight gain
  Weight loss
Bodybuilding (May subdiv. geog.) **646.7**
 UF Body building
  Physique
 BT **Exercise**
  Physical fitness
 RT **Weight lifting**
Boers
 USE **Afrikaners**
Bogs (May subdiv. geog.) **551.41**
 BT **Wetlands**
Bohemianism (May subdiv. geog.) **306**

Bohemianism—*Continued*
  BT **Counter culture**
      Manners and customs
  NT **Beat generation**
      Hippies
Bolshevism
  USE **Communism**
Bomb attacks
  USE **Bombings**
Bomb shelters
  USE **Air raid shelters**
Bombers (May subdiv. geog.) **358.4;**
      623.74
  SA types of bombers, e.g. **B-52**
      bomber [to be added as
      needed]
  BT **Airplanes**
      Military airplanes
  NT **B-52 bomber**
Bombings (May subdiv. geog.) **364.1**
    Use for materials on the use of explosive
  devices for the purposes of political terrorism
  or protest. Materials on bombs in general and
  on bombs launched from aircraft are entered
  under **Bombs**.
  UF Bomb attacks
      Terrorist bombings
  SA names of individual bombings
      incidents [to be added as
      needed]
  BT **Offenses against public safety**
      Political crimes and offenses
      Terrorism
Bombs (May subdiv. geog.) **355.8; 623.4**
    Use for materials on bombs in general and
  and on bombs launched from aircraft. Materi-
  als on the use of explosive devices for the
  purposes of political terrorism or protest are
  entered under **Bombings**.
  UF Aerial bombs
  SA types of bombs, e.g. **Atomic**
      bomb [to be added as need-
      ed]
  BT **Ammunition**
      Explosives
      Ordnance
      Projectiles
  NT **Atomic bomb**
      Guided missiles
      Hydrogen bomb
      Incendiary bombs
      Neutron bomb
Bonds (May subdiv. geog.) **332.63**

  BT **Finance**
      Investments
      Negotiable instruments
      Securities
      Stock exchanges
  NT **Junk bonds**
  RT **Public debts**
      Stocks
Bonds—Rating (May subdiv. geog.)
      332.63
Bones **573.7; 611; 612.7**
    Use for comprehensive and systematic ma-
  terials on the anatomy of bones. Materials
  limited to the morphology or mechanics of the
  skeleton, human or animal, are entered under
  Skeleton.
  BT **Musculoskeletal system**
  NT **Fractures**
  RT **Skeleton**
Bones—Diseases **616.7**
  BT **Diseases**
  NT **Osteoporosis**
Bonsai **635.9**
  BT **Dwarf trees**
Book arts—Exhibitions
  USE **Books—Exhibitions**
Book awards
  USE **Literary prizes**
        and names of awards, e.g.
        *Caldecott Medal; Newbery
        Medal;* etc. [to be added as
        needed]
Book buying (Libraries)
  USE **Libraries—Acquisitions**
Book clubs (Discussion groups) (May
      subdiv. geog.) **028**
  UF Book discussion groups
  BT **Clubs**
Book collecting (May subdiv. geog.)
      002.075
  UF Bibliomania
      Bibliophily
      Books—Collectors and collecting
  BT **Book selection**
      Collectors and collecting
  RT **Bookplates**
      Books
Book discussion groups
  USE **Book clubs (Discussion groups)**
Book fairs
  USE **Books—Exhibitions**
Book illustration
  USE **Illustration of books**

Book industries
    USE **Book industry**
Book industries and trade
    USE **Book industry**
Book industries—Exhibitions
    USE **Books—Exhibitions**
Book industry (May subdiv. geog.)   **686**
    UF   Book industries
         Book industries and trade
         Book trade
    BT   **Industries**
    NT   **Bookbinding**
         Booksellers and bookselling
         Printing
    RT   **Publishers and publishing**
Book lending
    USE **Library circulation**
Book lists
    USE **Best books**
Book numbers, Publishers' standard
    USE **Publishers' standard book
         numbers**
Book plates
    USE **Bookplates**
Book prices
    USE **Books—Prices**
Book prizes
    USE **Literary prizes**
         and names of prizes, e.g.
         *Caldecott Medal; Newbery
         Medal;* etc. [to be added as
         needed]
Book rarities
    USE **Rare books**
Book reviewing (May subdiv. geog.)
         028.1; 808
    Use for materials on the technique of re-
viewing books. Collections of miscellaneous
book reviews are entered under **Book re-
views**.
    UF   Appraisal of books
         Books—Appraisal
         Evaluation of books
         Literature—Evaluation
         Reviewing (Books)
    SA   types of books with the subdivi-
         sion *Reviews*, and topics,
         types of literature, ethnic
         groups, classes of persons,
         and names of places with the
         subdivision *Book reviews*; for

collections of book reviews
devoted to a particular type
of book or subject, e.g. **Reference books—Reviews; So-
ciology—Book reviews; Children's literature—Book reviews**; etc. [to be added as
needed]
    BT   **Books and reading**
         Criticism
    RT   **Book reviews**
Book reviews   028.1; 808.8
    Use for collections of book reviews. Materi-
als on the technique of reviewing books are
entered under **Book reviewing**.
    UF   Books—Reviews
    SA   types of books with the subdivi-
         sion *Reviews*, and topics,
         types of literature, ethnic
         groups, classes of persons,
         and names of places with the
         subdivision *Book reviews*; for
         collections of book reviews
         devoted to a particular type
         of book or subject, e.g. **Ref-
         erence books—Reviews; So-
         ciology—Book reviews; Chil-
         dren's literature—Book re-
         views**; etc. [to be added as
         needed]
    NT   **Book talks**
    RT   **Book reviewing**
Book sales
    USE **Books—Prices**
Book selection   025.2
    Use for materials on the principles of book
selection for libraries. Lists of recommended
books and materials about recommended
books are entered under **Best books**.
    UF   Books—Selection
         Choice of books
    BT   **Libraries—Acquisitions**
         **Libraries—Collection develop-
         ment**
    NT   **Book collecting**
    RT   **Best books**
Book talks   021.7; 028.1
    UF   Booktalking
         Booktalks
    BT   **Book reviews**
         Libraries—Public relations
         Public speaking

Book trade
    USE **Book industry**
           Booksellers and bookselling
           Publishers and publishing
Book trade—Exhibitions
    USE **Books—Exhibitions**
Book Week, National
    USE **National Book Week**
Bookbinding (May subdiv. geog.)   **025.7;**
    095; 686.3
    UF Binding of books
    BT **Book industry**
          Books
Bookkeepers
    USE **Accountants**
Bookkeeping   **657**
    SA types of industries, professions,
         and organizations with the
         subdivision *Accounting* [to be
         added as needed]
    BT **Business**
          Business education
          Business mathematics
    NT **Auditing**
          Corporations—Accounting
          Cost accounting
          Office equipment and supplies
    RT **Accounting**
Bookmaking (Betting)
    USE **Gambling**
Bookmobiles (May subdiv. geog.)   **027.4**
    BT **Library extension**
Bookplates (May subdiv. geog.)   **025.7;**
    769.5
    UF Book plates
         Ex libris
    BT **Prints**
    RT **Book collecting**
Books (May subdiv. geog.)   **002**
    NT **Anthologies**
         Best books
         Bestiaries
         Bilingual books
         Bookbinding
         Books of hours
         Braille books
         Chapbooks
         Cookbooks
         Early printed books
         Electronic books

         **Illumination of books and
           manuscripts**
         Illustration of books
         Incunabula
         Librettos
         Manuscripts
         Paperback books
         Rare books
         Reference books
         Reprints (Publications)
         Textbooks
    RT **Authors**
         Bibliography
         Book collecting
         Literature
         Printing
         Publishers and publishing
Books and reading (May subdiv. geog.)
    028
    Use for general materials on reading for in-
    formation and culture, advice to readers, and
    surveys of reading habits.
    UF Appraisal of books
         Books—Appraisal
         Choice of books
         Evaluation of literature
         Literature—Evaluation
         Reading interests
    SA names of individuals and classes
         of persons with the subdivi-
         sion *Books and reading*, e.g.
         Blind—Books and reading
         [to be added as needed]
    BT **Communication**
         Education
         Reading
    NT **Best sellers (Books)**
         Bible—Reading
         Blind—Books and reading
         Book reviewing
         Children—Books and reading
         National Book Week
         Reference books
         Teenagers—Books and reading
    RT **Reading materials**
Books and reading—Best books
    USE **Best books**
Books and reading for children
    USE **Children—Books and reading**
Books and reading for teenagers
    USE **Teenagers—Books and reading**

Books and reading for young adults
USE **Teenagers—Books and reading**
Books—Appraisal
USE **Book reviewing**
Books and reading
Criticism
Literature—History and criticism
Books—Best sellers
USE **Best sellers (Books)**
Books—Bilingual editions
USE **Bilingual books**
Books—Catalogs
USE **Booksellers' catalogs**
Publishers' catalogs
Books—Censorship (May subdiv. geog.)
025.2; 323.44
UF Banned books
Index librorum prohibitorum
Prohibited books
BT **Censorship**
Books—Classification
USE **Library classification**
Books—Collectors and collecting
USE **Book collecting**
Books—Exhibitions (May subdiv. geog.)
070.5074; 686.074
UF Book arts—Exhibitions
Book fairs
Book industries—Exhibitions
Book trade—Exhibitions
Library book fairs
Publishers and publishing—Exhibitions
BT **Exhibitions**
Books—First editions
USE **First editions**
Books for children
USE **Children's literature**
Books for sight saving
USE **Large print books**
Books for teenagers
USE **Young adult literature**
Books for the blind
USE **Blind—Books and reading**
Braille books
Books in machine-readable form
USE **Electronic books**
Books—Large print
USE **Large print books**

Books of hours (May subdiv. geog.)
242; 745.6
BT **Books**
RT **Illumination of books and manuscripts**
Books of lists   030
Use as a form heading for books consisting of miscellaneous lists of facts, names, etc.
UF Facts, Miscellaneous
List books
Lists
Miscellanea
Miscellaneous facts
SA topics with the subdivision *Lists*, e.g. **Sports—Lists** [to be added as needed]
Books on cassette
USE **Audiobooks**
Books on tape
USE **Audiobooks**
Books—Preservation
USE **Library resources—Conservation and restoration**
Books—Prices (May subdiv. geog.)
002.075
UF Book prices
Book sales
BT **Booksellers and bookselling**
Prices
Books—Reviews
USE **Book reviews**
Books—Selection
USE **Book selection**
Booksellers and bookselling (May subdiv. geog.)   **070.5; 381; 658.8**
UF Book trade
BT **Book industry**
NT **Books—Prices**
Booksellers' catalogs
RT **Publishers and publishing**
Booksellers' catalogs   017
Use for retail book catalogs and book auction catalogs and materials about such catalogs. Materials on library catalogs in book form are entered under **Book catalogs**. Publishers' book catalogs and materials about such catalogs are entered under **Publishers' catalogs**.
UF Books—Catalogs
Catalogs
Catalogs, Booksellers'
BT **Booksellers and bookselling**
Booktalking
USE **Book talks**

Booktalks
USE **Book talks**
Boolean algebra   511.3
UF   Algebra, Boolean
BT   **Group theory**
Set theory
Symbolic logic
Boots
USE   **Shoes**
Border life
USE   **Frontier and pioneer life**
Border patrols (May subdiv. geog.)
363.28
BT   **Police**
Borders (Geography)
USE   **Boundaries**
Boring
USE   **Drilling and boring (Earth and rocks)**
Drilling and boring (Metal, wood, etc.)
Born again Christianity
USE   **Regeneration (Christianity)**
Borrowing
USE   **Loans**
Boss rule
USE   **Political corruption**
Bossiness   155.2
BT   **Personality**
Boston Tea Party, 1773   973.3
BT   **United States—History—1775-1783, Revolution**
Botanic gardens
USE   **Botanical gardens**
Botanical chemistry   572
UF   Plant chemistry
BT   **Chemistry**
NT   **Plants—Analysis**
Botanical classification
USE   **Botany—Classification**
Botanical gardens (May subdiv. geog.)
580.73
UF   Botanic gardens
SA   names of individual botanical gardens [to be added as needed]
BT   **Gardens**
Parks
Botanical illustration (May subdiv. geog.)
758
UF   Flower painting and illustration
Fruit painting and illustration
BT   **Art**
Illustration of books
RT   **Botany**
Plants in art
Botanical specimens—Collection and preservation
USE   **Plants—Collection and preservation**
Botanists (May subdiv. geog.)   **580.92; 920**
BT   **Naturalists**
Botany   580
Use for materials on the science of plants. Nonscientific materials on plants are entered under **Plants**.
UF   Flora
Vegetable kingdom
BT   **Biology**
Science
NT   **Economic botany**
Medical botany
Photosynthesis
Plant physiology
Plants—Anatomy
RT   **Botanical illustration**
Natural history
Plants
Botany—Anatomy
USE   **Plants—Anatomy**
Botany—Classification   580.1
UF   Botanical classification
Botany—Taxonomy
Classification—Botany
Classification—Plants
Plant classification
Plant taxonomy
Plants—Classification
Systematic botany
Taxonomy (Botany)
BT   **Classification**
Botany—Ecology
USE   **Plant ecology**
Botany, Economic
USE   **Economic botany**
Botany, Medical
USE   **Medical botany**
Botany—Nomenclature   580.1
Use for systematically derived lists of names or designations of plants and for materials about such names. Materials on the com-

Botany—Nomenclature—_Continued_
mon or vernacular names of plants are entered
under **Popular plant names**.

UF   Plants—Names

       Plants—Nomenclature

       Scientific names of plants

       Scientific plant names

RT   **Botany—Terminology**

       Popular plant names

Botany of the Bible

USE   **Bible—Natural history**

Botany—Pathology

USE   **Plant diseases**

Botany—Physiology

USE   **Plant physiology**

Botany—Structure

USE   **Plants—Anatomy**

Botany—Taxonomy

USE   **Botany—Classification**

Botany—Terminology   580.1

Use for lists or discussions of words and
expressions in the field of botany. Systematically derived lists of names or designations of
plants and materials about such names are entered under **Botany—Nomenclature**. Materials on the common or vernacular names of
plants are entered under **Popular plant
names**.

RT   **Botany—Nomenclature**

       Popular plant names

Botany—United States

USE   **Plants—United States**

Boulder Dam (Ariz. and Nev.)

USE   **Hoover Dam (Ariz. and Nev.)**

Boulevards

USE   **Streets**

Boundaries   320.1; 341.4

UF   Borders (Geography)

       Frontiers

       Political boundaries

       Political geography

SA   names of wars with the subdivision _Territorial questions_, and
countries, cities, etc., with the
subdivision _Boundaries_ [to be
added as needed]

BT   **Geography**

       International law

       International relations

NT   **Chicago (Ill.)—Boundaries**

       Ohio—Boundaries

       United States—Boundaries

       World War, 1914-1918—Territorial questions

World War, 1939-1945—Territorial questions

RT   **Geopolitics**

Bourgeoisie

USE   **Middle class**

Boutique breweries

USE   **Microbreweries**

Bow and arrow   799.2028

UF   Arrow

BT   **Weapons**

RT   **Archery**

Bow and arrow hunting

USE   **Bowhunting**

Bowed instruments

USE   **Stringed instruments**

Bowhunting (May subdiv. geog.)
   799.2028

UF   Bow and arrow hunting

BT   **Hunting**

Bowling (May subdiv. geog.)   **794.6;
796.31**

UF   Tenpins

BT   **Ball games**

Boxes   688.8; 745.593

UF   Crates

BT   **Containers**

Boxes—Collectors and collecting (May
subdiv. geog.)   **745.593**

BT   **Collectors and collecting**

Boxing (May subdiv. geog.)   **796.83**

UF   Fighting

       Prize fighting

       Pugilism

       Sparring

BT   **Athletics**

       Self-defense

Boy-love manga

USE   **Shonen-ai**

Boy Scouts (May subdiv. geog.)   **369.43**

UF   Cub Scouts

BT   **Boys' clubs**

       Scouts and scouting

Boycott

USE   **Boycotts**

Boycotts (May subdiv. geog.)   **331.89;
338.6; 341.5; 327.1**

UF   Boycott

       Consumer boycotts

BT   **Commerce**

       Consumers

       Passive resistance

Boycotts—*Continued*
  RT   **Restraint of trade**
Boys (May subdiv. geog.)   **155.43;**
      305.23081
  BT   **Children**
  RT   **Teenagers**
       Young men
Boys' clubs (May subdiv. geog.)   **369.42**
  UF   Boys—Societies
  BT   **Clubs**
       Societies
  NT   **4-H clubs**
       Boy Scouts
Boys—Education (May subdiv. geog.)
      371.823
  BT   **Education**
  RT   **Coeducation**
Boys—Employment
  USE   **Youth—Employment**
Boys—Societies
  USE   **Boys' clubs**
Boys' towns
  USE   **Children—Institutional care**
Brachiosaurus   567.913
  BT   **Dinosaurs**
Brahmanism (May subdiv. geog.)   **294.5**
  BT   **Religions**
  RT   **Hinduism**
Braids (Hairstyling)   646.7
  BT   **Hair**
Braille   411
  BT   **Writing**
Braille books (May subdiv. geog.)
      011.63; 411
  UF   Books for the blind
  BT   **Books**
  RT   **Blind—Books and reading**
Brain   573.8; 611; 612.8
  BT   **Head**
       Nervous system
  NT   **Memory**
       Mind and body
       Phrenology
       Psychology
Brain damaged children   618.92
  BT   **Exceptional children**
       Handicapped children
Brain death   616.07
  UF   Irreversible coma
  BT   **Death**
Brain—Diseases   616.8
  BT   **Diseases**

  NT   **Alzheimer's disease**
       Aphasia
       Cerebral palsy
       Dementia
       Parkinson's disease
       Stroke
Brain storming
  USE   **Group problem solving**
Brainwashing (May subdiv. geog.)   **153.8**
      Use for materials on the forcible indoctrina-
      tion of an individual or group in order to alter
      basic political, social, religious, or moral be-
      liefs.
  UF   Deprogramming
       Forced indoctrination
       Indoctrination, Forced
       Mind control
       Thought control
       Will
  BT   **Behavior modification**
       Mental suggestion
       Psychological warfare
       Psychology of learning
Brakes   625.2; 629.2
  SA   types of vehicles with the subdi-
       vision *Brakes*, e.g. **Automo-
       biles—Brakes** [to be added
       as needed]
  NT   **Automobiles—Brakes**
Branch stores
  USE   **Chain stores**
Brand name products (May subdiv.
      geog.)   **381; 658.8**
  UF   Branded merchandise
  BT   **Commercial products**
       Manufactures
  RT   **Trademarks**
Branded merchandise
  USE   **Brand name products**
Brass   669; 673
  BT   **Alloys**
       Metals
  NT   **Brasses**
Brass instruments (May subdiv. geog.)
      788.9
  BT   **Wind instruments**
Brasses (May subdiv. geog.)   **739.5**
  UF   Monumental brasses
       Sepulchral brasses
  BT   **Art metalwork**
       Brass
       Inscriptions

Brasses—*Continued*
>> **Sculpture**
>> **Tombs**

Bravery
>> USE **Courage**

Brazil   981
> May be subdivided like United States except for History.

Brazilian literature   869
> May use same subdivisions and names of literary forms as for **English literature**.
>> BT **Latin American literature**
>> **Literature**

Bread (May subdiv. geog.)   **641.8; 664**
>> BT **Baking**
>> **Cooking**
>> **Food**
>> RT **Bread machines**

Bread machines   641.7
>> UF Automatic bread machines
>> BT **Kitchen utensils**
>> RT **Baking**
>> **Bread**

Break dancing   793.3
>> BT **Dance**

Breakers
>> USE **Ocean waves**

Breakfast cereals
>> USE **Prepared cereals**

Breakfasts (May subdiv. geog.)   **642**
>> BT **Cooking**
>> **Menus**
>> NT **Prepared cereals**

Breakthroughs, Scientific
>> USE **Discoveries in science**

Breast—Cancer
>> USE **Breast cancer**

Breast cancer   616.99
>> UF Breast—Cancer
>> BT **Cancer**
>> **Women—Diseases**

Breast feeding   649
>> UF Nursing (Infant feeding)
>> BT **Infants—Nutrition**

Breathing
>> USE **Respiration**

Breeding (May subdiv. geog.)   **631.5; 636.08**
> Use for materials on the controlled propagation of plants and animals with the purpose of producing or maintaining desired characteristics.

>> UF Artificial selection
>> Selection, Artificial
>> SA types of animals with the subdivision *Breeding* [to be added as needed]
>> BT **Reproduction**
>> NT **Dogs—Breeding**
>> **Heredity**
>> **Horses—Breeding**
>> **Livestock breeding**
>> **Mendel's law**
>> **Plant breeding**
>> RT **Genetics**

Breeding behavior
>> USE **Sexual behavior in animals**

Breweries (May subdiv. geog.)   **663**
>> BT **Factories**
>> NT **Microbreweries**
>> RT **Brewing**

Brewing (May subdiv. geog.)   **641.8; 663**
>> UF Beer making
>> RT **Beer**
>> **Breweries**
>> **Liquors**

Bricklaying (May subdiv. geog.)   **693**
>> BT **Building**
>> RT **Bricks**
>> **Masonry**

Bricks   666; 691
>> BT **Building materials**
>> RT **Bricklaying**

Bridal customs
>> USE **Marriage customs and rites**

Bridal showers
>> USE **Showers (Parties)**

Bridge (Game)   795.41
>> UF Auction bridge
>> Contract bridge
>> Duplicate bridge
>> BT **Card games**

Bridges (May subdiv. geog.)   **624.2; 725**
> This heading may be subdivided by the names of rivers, lakes, canals, etc. as well as by countries, states, cities, etc.

>> UF Viaducts
>> SA types of bridges and names of individual bridges, e.g. **Golden Gate Bridge (San Francisco, Calif.)** [to be added as needed]
>> BT **Civil engineering**
>> **Transportation**

Bridges—*Continued*
 NT   Golden Gate Bridge (San
        Francisco, Calif.)
Bridges—Chicago (Ill.)   624.209773
 UF   Chicago (Ill.)—Bridges
Bridges—Hudson River (N.Y. and N.J.)
        624.20973
 UF   Hudson River (N.Y. and N.J.)—
        Bridges
Brigands
 USE   Thieves
Bright children
 USE   Gifted children
Britain, Battle of, 1940   940.54
 BT   Battles
        World War, 1939-1945—Cam-
          paigns
British Commonwealth countries
 USE   Commonwealth countries
British Commonwealth of Nations
 USE   Commonwealth countries
British Dominions
 USE   Commonwealth countries
British Empire
 USE   Great Britain—Colonies
Broadcast journalism (May subdiv. geog.)
        070.4
 UF   Radio journalism
        Television journalism
 BT   Broadcasting
        Journalism
        Press
 NT   Radio broadcasting of sports
        Television broadcasting of
          news
        Television broadcasting of
          sports
Broadcasting (May subdiv. geog.)
        384.54
 BT   Telecommunication
 NT   Broadcast journalism
        Equal time rule (Broadcasting)
        Fairness doctrine (Broadcast-
          ing)
        Minorities in broadcasting
        Radio broadcasting
        Television broadcasting
Brokers (May subdiv. geog.)
 NT   Stockbrokers
Brokers (Stocks)
 USE   Stockbrokers

Bronchial asthma
 USE   Asthma
Bronze Age (May subdiv. geog.)   930.1
 BT   Civilization
Bronzes (May subdiv. geog.)   739.5
 BT   Archeology
        Art
        Art metalwork
        Decoration and ornament
        Metalwork
        Sculpture
Brothers   306.875
 BT   Men
        Siblings
Brothers and sisters
 USE   Siblings
Brownies (Girl Scouts)
 USE   Girl Scouts
Brownouts
 USE   Electric power failures
Brutality
 USE   Cruelty
Bubbles   530.4
 BT   Air
        Gases
Bubonic plague
 USE   Plague
Buccaneers
 USE   Pirates
Buchenwald (Germany: Concentration
        camp)   365; 943
 BT   Concentration camps
Bucolic poetry
 USE   Pastoral poetry
Buddhism (May subdiv. geog.)   294.3
 BT   Religions
 NT   Zen Buddhism
Buddhism—Prayers   294.3
 UF   Buddhist prayers
 BT   Prayers
Buddhist art (May subdiv. geog.)   294.3;
        704.9
 UF   Art, Buddhist
 BT   Art
Buddhist prayers
 USE   Buddhism—Prayers
Budget (May subdiv. geog.)   352.4
    Use for materials on government budgets or
 reports on governmental appropriations and
 expenditures. Materials on business budgets
 are entered under **Business budgets**. Materials
 on household budgets are entered under

Budget—*Continued*
Household budgets. Materials on personal budgets are entered under **Personal finance**.
UF Government budgets
SA names of countries and names of individual government departments, agencies, etc., with the subdivision *Appropriations and expenditures*, e.g. **United States—Appropriations and expenditures** [to be added as needed]
BT **Public finance**
Budget—United States 352.4
UF Federal budget
    United States—Budget
NT **United States—Appropriations and expenditures**
Budgets, Business
USE **Business budgets**
Budgets, Household
USE **Household budgets**
Budgets, Personal
USE **Personal finance**
Buffalo, American
USE **Bison**
Buffing
USE **Grinding and polishing**
Bugging, Electronic
USE **Eavesdropping**
Building (May subdiv. geog.) 690
Use for materials on the process of constructing buildings and other structures. Materials on the design and style of structures are entered under **Architecture**. General materials on buildings and materials on buildings in a particular place are entered under **Buildings**.
UF Architectural engineering
    Construction
SA types of buildings with the subdivision *Design and construction*, e.g. **Industrial buildings—Design and construction** [to be added as needed]
BT **Structural engineering**
NT **Bricklaying**
    Carpentry
    Concrete construction
    Construction industry
    House construction
    Industrial buildings—Design and construction
    Masonry
    Plumbing

Steel construction
RT **Architecture**
    Building materials
Building and earthquakes
USE **Buildings—Earthquake effects**
Building and loan associations
USE **Savings and loan associations**
Building contracts
USE **Construction contracts**
Building—Contracts and specifications
USE **Construction contracts**
Building design
USE **Architecture**
Building—Estimates 692
Building failures (May subdiv. geog.) 690
BT **Structural failures**
Building industry
USE **Construction industry**
Building, Iron and steel
USE **Steel construction**
Building machinery
USE **Construction equipment**
Building materials (May subdiv. geog.) 691
UF Structural materials
SA types of building materials, e.g. **Bricks** [to be added as needed]
BT **Materials**
NT **Bricks**
    Cement
    Concrete
    Glass
    Glass construction
    Reinforced concrete
    Stone
    Structural steel
    Stucco
    Terra cotta
    Tiles
    Wood
RT **Building**
    Strength of materials
Building nests
USE **Nest building**
Building repair
USE **Buildings—Maintenance and repair**

Building—Repair and reconstruction
  USE **Buildings—Maintenance and**
        repair
Building security
  USE **Burglary protection**
Building—Tropical conditions (May
        subdiv. geog.) **690**
Buildings (May subdiv. geog.) **690; 720**
  Use for general materials on buildings and,
  with geographic subdivisions, for materials on
  buildings in a particular place. Materials on
  the design and style of structures are entered
  under **Architecture**. Materials on the process
  of constructing buildings and other structures
  are entered under **Building**.
  UF   Edifices
        Structures
  SA   types of building features, e.g.
        Doors; **Windows**; etc.; types
        of buildings and construction,
        e.g. **Farm buildings**; types of
        institutions and names of indi-
        vidual institutions and corpo-
        rate bodies with the subdivi-
        sion *Buildings*, e.g. **Colleges**
        and universities—Buildings;
        and names of specific build-
        ings [to be added as needed]
  NT   **Apartment houses**
        Auditoriums
        Castles
        Children's playhouses
        Chimneys
        Church buildings
        Colleges and universities—
          Buildings
        Commercial buildings
        Doors
        Farm buildings
        Fireplaces
        Floors
        Foundations
        Garden structures
        Historic buildings
        Houses
        Industrial buildings
        Office buildings
        Palaces
        Prefabricated buildings
        Public buildings
        Roofs
        Rooms
        School buildings

        Skyscrapers
        Synagogues
        Temples
        Theaters
        Tree houses
        Walls
        Windows
  RT   **Architecture**
Buildings—Earthquake effects (May
        subdiv. geog.) **693.8**
  Use for materials on the design and con-
  struction of buildings to withstand earth-
  quakes.
  UF   Building and earthquakes
        Earthquakes and building
  BT   **Earthquakes**
  NT   **Skyscrapers—Earthquake ef-**
          fects
Buildings, Industrial
  USE **Industrial buildings**
Buildings—Maintenance and repair (May
        subdiv. geog.) **690**
  UF   Building repair
        Building—Repair and reconstruc-
          tion
        Buildings—Remodeling
  SA   types of buildings with the sub-
        division *Maintenance and re-*
        pair, e.g. **Houses—Mainte-**
        nance and repair; and types
        of buildings and parts of
        buildings with the subdivision
        Remodeling, e.g. **Houses—Re-**
        modeling; **Kitchens—Remod-**
        eling; etc. [to be added as
        needed]
  RT   **Architecture—Conservation**
          and restoration
Buildings, Office
  USE **Office buildings**
Buildings, Prefabricated
  USE **Prefabricated buildings**
Buildings—Remodeling
  USE **Buildings—Maintenance and**
        repair
Buildings, Restoration of
  USE **Architecture—Conservation**
        and restoration
Buildings, School
  USE **School buildings**
Buildings—Security
  USE **Burglary protection**

Built-in furniture   645; 684.1; 749
  BT   **Furniture**
Bulbs   584; 635.9
  BT   **Flower gardening**
       Plants
Bulge, Battle of the
  USE   **Ardennes (France), Battle of**
         the, 1944-1945
Bulimia   616.85
  UF   Binge eating behavior
       Binge-purge behavior
       Gorge-purge syndrome
  BT   **Eating disorders**
Bulletin boards   371.33
  BT   **Teaching—Aids and devices**
  NT   **Computer bulletin boards**
Bullfights (May subdiv. geog.)   791.8
  UF   Fighting
  BT   **Sports**
Bullies   155.4; 302.3
  UF   Bullying
       Bullyism
  BT   **Aggressiveness (Psychology)**
  NT   **Cyberbullying**
Bullion
  USE   **Precious metals**
Bullying
  USE   **Bullies**
Bullyism
  USE   **Bullies**
Bunker Hill (Boston, Mass.), Battle of,
  1775   973.3
  BT   **Battles**
       United States—History—1775-
       1783, Revolution—Cam-
       paigns
Bunnies
  USE   **Rabbits**
Bunny rabbits
  USE   **Rabbits**
Bunyan, Paul (Legendary character)
  398.22
  UF   Paul Bunyan
  BT   **Folklore—United States**
Bureaucracy (May subdiv. geog.)   302.3
  BT   **Political science**
       Public administration
  RT   **Civil service**
       Organizational sociology
Burglar alarms   621.389

  BT   **Burglary protection**
       Electric apparatus and appli-
       ances
Burglars
  USE   **Thieves**
Burglary protection   621.389; 643
  UF   Building security
       Buildings—Security
       Protection against burglary
       Residential security
  SA   types of protective devices, e.g.
       Burglar alarms; and types of
       buildings with the subdivision
       Security measures, e.g. **Nucle-**
       ar power plants—Security
       measures [to be added as
       needed]
  BT   **Crime prevention**
  NT   **Burglar alarms**
       Locks and keys
Burial (May subdiv. geog.)   363.7; 393
  UF   Burial customs
       Burying grounds
       Graves
       Interment
  SA   names of individual persons and
       groups of notable persons
       with the subdivision *Death*
       and burial, e.g. **Presidents—**
       United States—Death and
       burial [to be added as need-
       ed]
  BT   **Archeology**
       Public health
  NT   **Catacombs**
       Cemeteries
       Cryonics
       Dead
       Mounds and mound builders
       Mummies
       Premature burial
       Tombs
  RT   **Cremation**
       Death
       Funeral rites and ceremonies
Burial customs
  USE   **Burial**
Burial, Premature
  USE   **Premature burial**

Burial statistics
 USE **Mortality**
   Registers of births, etc.
   Vital statistics
Buried cities
 USE **Extinct cities**
Buried treasure (May subdiv. geog.)
   622; 910.4
 UF Hidden treasure
   Sunken treasure
   Treasure trove
 BT **Archeology**
   Underwater exploration
Burlesque (Literature)   808.7

Use for materials on burlesque as a literary composition. Materials on burlesque as a theatrical entertainment are entered under **Burlesque (Theater)**.

 UF Comic literature
 BT **Comedy**
   Parody
   Satire
Burlesque (Theater) (May subdiv. geog.)
   792.7

Use for materials on burlesque as a theatrical entertainment. Materials on burlesque as a literary composition are entered under **Burlesque (Literature)**.

 UF Travesty
 BT **Theater**
Burma
 USE **Myanmar**
Burn out (Psychology)   158.7
 UF Burnout syndrome
 BT **Job satisfaction**
   Job stress
   Mental health
   Motivation (Psychology)
   Occupational health and safety
   Stress (Psychology)
Burnout syndrome
 USE **Burn out (Psychology)**
Burnt offering
 USE **Sacrifice**
Bursaries
 USE **Scholarships**
Burying grounds
 USE **Burial**
   Cemeteries
Buses (May subdiv. geog.)   **388.4;**
   629.222
 UF Motor buses

 BT **Automobiles**
   Highway transportation
   Local transit
   Motor vehicles
Bush survival
 USE **Wilderness survival**
Business (May subdiv. geog.)   **650**
 UF Trade
 BT **Commerce**
   Economics
 NT **Accounting**
   Advertising
   Banks and banking
   Bookkeeping
   Business budgets
   Business enterprises
   Business failures
   Businesspeople
   Competition
   Customer relations
   Department stores
   Economic conditions
   Entrepreneurship
   Home-based business
   Installment plan
   Mail-order business
   Management
   Marketing
   Markets
   Office management
   Profit
   Real estate business
   Selling
   Small business
   Social responsibility of business
   Trust companies
Business administration
 USE **Management**
Business and government
 USE **Economic policy**
Business and politics (May subdiv. geog.)
   322
 UF Business—Political activity
   Politics and business
 BT **Politics**
Business arithmetic
 USE **Business mathematics**
Business budgets (May subdiv. geog.)
   658.15
 UF Budgets, Business
 BT **Business**

Business colleges
USE **Business schools**
Business consultants (May subdiv. geog.)
658.4
UF Management consultants
BT **Consultants**
Business correspondence
USE **Business letters**
Business cycles (May subdiv. geog.)
338.5
UF Economic cycles
Stabilization in industry
SA types of business cycles, e.g.
Depressions [to be added as
needed]
BT **Cycles**
Economic conditions
NT **Depressions**
Economic forecasting
Recessions
RT **Financial crises**
Business—Databases **650**
BT **Databases**
Business depression, 1929-1939
USE **Great Depression, 1929-1939**
Business depressions
USE **Depressions**
Business education (May subdiv. geog.)
650.07
UF Business—Study and teaching
Clerical work—Training
Commercial education
Office work—Training
BT **Education**
NT **Accounting**
Bookkeeping
Keyboarding (Electronics)
Shorthand
Typewriting
Business English
USE **English language—Business
English**
Business enterprises (May subdiv. geog.)
338.7
Use for materials on business concerns as
legal entities, regardless of the form of organi-
zation.
UF Business organizations
Businesses
Companies
Enterprises
Firms

SA types of businesses [to be added
as needed]
BT **Business**
NT **Beauty shops**
**Christian-owned business en-
terprises**
Commercial art galleries
Corporations
**Government business enter-
prises**
Joint ventures
Minority business enterprises
**Money-making projects for
children**
Multinational corporations
New business enterprises
Partnership
**Business enterprises—Computer net-
works** **004.6; 658**
BT **Computer networks**
NT **Intranets**
Business entertaining **395.3; 658**
BT **Entertaining**
Public relations
Business ethics (May subdiv. geog.) **174**
BT **Ethics**
Professional ethics
NT **Competition**
Deceptive advertising
Social responsibility of business
Success
Business etiquette (May subdiv. geog.)
395.5
UF Office etiquette
BT **Etiquette**
Business failures (May subdiv. geog.)
338; 658
UF Business mortality
Failure in business
BT **Business**
NT **Bank failures**
Bankruptcy
Business forecasting (May subdiv. geog.)
338.5
BT **Economic forecasting**
Forecasting
Business—Government policy
USE **Economic policy**
Business—Information resources **650**
BT **Information resources**

Business—Information services (May subdiv. geog.) **658.4**
    BT **Information services**
Business—International aspects
    USE **Multinational corporations**
Business—Internet resources **650**
    BT **Internet resources**
Business—Internet resources—Directories
    650.025
Business Japanese
    USE **Japanese language—Business**
          Japanese
Business language
    USE names of languages with unique
          language subdivisions, e.g.
          English language—Business
          English; Japanese lan-
          guage—Business Japanese;
          etc. [to be added as needed]
Business law
    USE **Commercial law**
Business—Law and legislation
    USE **Commercial law**
Business letters **651.7**
    UF Business correspondence
          Commercial correspondence
          Correspondence
    BT **Letter writing**
Business libraries (May subdiv. geog.)
    026
    Use for materials on libraries with a subject
    focus on business. Materials on libraries locat-
    ed within companies, firms, or private busi-
    nesses, covering any subject area, are entered
    under **Corporate libraries**.
    UF Libraries, Business
    BT **Special libraries**
Business machines
    USE **Office equipment and supplies**
Business management
    USE **Management**
Business math
    USE **Business mathematics**
Business mathematics **650.01**
    UF Arithmetic, Commercial
          Business arithmetic
          Business math
          Commercial arithmetic
          Commercial mathematics
          Finance—Mathematics
    BT **Mathematics**
    NT **Accounting**
          Bookkeeping

          Interest (Economics)
Business mortality
    USE **Bankruptcy**
          Business failures
Business organizations
    USE **Business enterprises**
Business patronage of the arts
    USE **Art patronage**
Business people
    USE **Businesspeople**
Business—Political activity
    USE **Business and politics**
Business recessions
    USE **Recessions**
Business schools (May subdiv. geog.)
    650.071
    UF Business colleges
    BT **Schools**
Business secrets
    USE **Trade secrets**
Business—Social responsibility
    USE **Social responsibility of business**
Business—Study and teaching
    USE **Business education**
Businesses
    USE **Business enterprises**
Businessmen (May subdiv. geog.)
    338.092; 658.0092; 920
    UF Men in business
    BT **Businesspeople**
Businesspeople (May subdiv. geog.)
    338.092; 658.0092; 920
    UF Business people
    BT **Business**
    NT **African American**
          businesspeople
          Black businesspeople
          Businessmen
          Businesswomen
          Capitalists and financiers
          Entrepreneurs
          Merchants
          Self-employed
Businesswomen (May subdiv. geog.)
    338.092; 658.0092; 920
    UF Women in business
    BT **Businesspeople**
          Women
Busing (School integration) (May subdiv.
    geog.) **379.2**

Busing (School integration)—*Continued*
    UF   Antibusing
            School busing
            Student busing
    BT   **School children—Transportation**
            School integration

Butter   637; 641.3
    BT   **Dairy products**

Butterflies (May subdiv. geog.)   595.78
    UF   Cocoons
            Lepidoptera
    BT   **Insects**
    NT   **Caterpillars**
    RT   **Moths**

Buttons (May subdiv. geog.)   646; 687
    BT   **Clothing and dress**

Buy American policy
    USE   **Buy national policy—United States**

Buy national policy (May subdiv. geog.)   352.5

    Use for materials on the requirement that a national government procure goods produced domestically.

    UF   Government policy
    BT   **Commercial policy**
            Government purchasing

Buy national policy—United States   352.5
    UF   Buy American policy

Buyers' guides
    USE   **Consumer education**
            Shopping

Buying
    USE   **Purchasing**

Buyouts, Corporate
    USE   **Corporate mergers and acquisitions**

Buyouts, Leveraged
    USE   **Leveraged buyouts**

By-products
    USE   **Waste products**

Byrd Antarctic Expedition   919.8
    BT   **Antarctica—Exploration**

Byzantine architecture (May subdiv. geog.)   723
    UF   Architecture, Byzantine
    BT   **Ancient architecture**
            Architecture
            Medieval architecture

Byzantine art   709.02
    UF   Art, Byzantine
    BT   **Ancient art**
            Art
            Medieval art

Byzantine Empire   949.5
    UF   Eastern Empire

Cabala   135; 296.1
    UF   Cabbala
            Kabbala
    BT   **Hebrew literature**
            Jewish literature
            Judaism
            Mysticism
            Occultism
    RT   **Symbolism of numbers**

Cabarets
    USE   **Night clubs, cabarets, etc.**

Cabbala
    USE   **Cabala**

Cabinet officers (May subdiv. geog.)   352.24; 920
    UF   Ministers of state
    NT   **Prime ministers**

Cabinet work
    USE   **Cabinetwork**

Cabinetwork (May subdiv. geog.)   684.1

    Use for materials on the making and finishing of fine woodwork, such as furniture or interior details. Materials on the construction of a wooden building or the wooden portion of any building are entered under **Carpentry**.

    UF   Cabinet work
    BT   **Carpentry**
    NT   **Veneers and veneering**
    RT   **Furniture**
            Woodwork

Cabins
    USE   **Log cabins and houses**

Cable railroads (May subdiv. geog.)   385; 625.5
    UF   Funicular railroads
            Railroads, Cable
    BT   **Railroads**
    RT   **Street railroads**

Cable television (May subdiv. geog.)   384.55
    BT   **Television broadcasting**

Cables (May subdiv. geog.)   384.6; 621.319; 624.1
    BT   **Power transmission**
            Rope

Cables, Submarine
    USE   **Submarine cables**

Cabs
USE **Taxicabs**
Cactus (May subdiv. geog.)   **583; 635.9**
BT **Desert plants**
CAD
USE **Computer-aided design**
CAD/CAM software
USE **Computer-aided design software**
CAD software
USE **Computer-aided design software**
Cadavers
USE **Dead**
Cafes
USE **Coffeehouses**
Restaurants
Caffeine   613.2
Cage birds   636.6
SA types of cage birds [to be added as needed]
BT **Birds**
NT **Canaries**
CAI
USE **Computer-assisted instruction**
Cajun music (May subdiv. geog.)
781.62
BT **Music**
Cajuns (May subdiv. geog.)   **976.3**
UF Acadians—Louisiana
BT **Ethnic groups**
Cake (May subdiv. geog.)   **641.8; 664**
BT **Baking**
Confectionery
Cooking
Desserts
NT **Cheesecake (Cooking)**
RT **Pastry**
Cake decorating (May subdiv. geog.)
641.8
BT **Confectionery**
Calculating machines
USE **Calculators**
Calculators   510.28; 651.8; 681
Use for materials on present-day calculators or on calculators and mechanical computers made before 1945. Materials on modern electronic computers developed after 1945 are entered under **Computers**.
UF Accounting machines
Adding machines
Calculating machines
Pocket calculators

BT **Office equipment and supplies**
NT **Abacus**
Slide rule
RT **Computers**
Calculus   515
UF Analysis (Mathematics)
BT **Mathematical analysis**
Mathematics
NT **Differential equations**
RT **Functions**
Caldecott Awards
USE **Caldecott Medal**
Caldecott Medal   028.5
UF Caldecott Awards
Caldecott Medal books
BT **Children's literature**
Illustration of books
Literary prizes
Caldecott Medal books
USE **Caldecott Medal**
Calendars (May subdiv. geog.)   **529**
UF Annuals
SA subjects, corporate bodies, and names of countries, cities, etc., with the subdivision *Calendars*, for works that list recurring, coming, or past events in those places or related to those topics or organizations [to be added as needed]
BT **Time**
NT **Birthday books**
Church year
Days
Devotional calendars
Months
Week
RT **Almanacs**
California—Gold discoveries   979.4
UF California gold rush
California gold rush
USE **California—Gold discoveries**
Calisthenics
USE **Gymnastics**
Physical education
Calligraphy (May subdiv. geog.)   **745.6**
BT **Decorative arts**
Handwriting
Writing

Caloric content of foods
    USE **Food—Caloric content**
Calories (Food)
    USE **Food—Caloric content**
Calvinism (May subdiv. geog.)   284
    BT **Reformation**
    RT **Congregationalism**
        Puritans
Cambodia   959.6
    May be subdivided like United States except for History.
    UF Kampuchea
Camcorders   621.388; 778.59
    UF Home video cameras
        Video cameras, Home
    BT **Cameras**
        Home video systems
        Video recording
    RT **Amateur films**
Camels (May subdiv. geog.)   599.63; 636.2
    UF Dromedaries
    BT **Desert animals**
        Mammals
Cameras (May subdiv. geog.)   681; 771.3
    SA types of cameras and names of individual makes of cameras [to be added as needed]
    BT **Photography**
        Photography—Equipment and supplies
    NT **Camcorders**
        Digital cameras
        Kodak camera
        Motion picture cameras
Camouflage (Biology)   591.47
    UF Animal camouflage
        Animals—Camouflage
    BT **Animal defenses**
Camouflage (Military science)   355.4; 623
    BT **Military art and science**
        Naval art and science
Camp cooking
    USE **Outdoor cooking**
Camp Fire Girls   369.47
    BT **Girls' clubs**
Camp sites
    USE **Campgrounds**
Campaign funds (May subdiv. geog.) 324.7

    UF Elections—Finance
        Political parties—Finance
    BT **Elections**
        Politics
Campaign funds—United States   324.7
    UF Elections—United States—Finance
        United States—Campaign funds
Campaign literature (May subdiv. geog.) 324.2
    UF Political campaign literature
    BT **Literature**
        Politics
Campaigns
    USE names of wars with the subdivision *Campaigns,* e.g. **World War, 1939-1945—Campaigns;** which may be further subdivided geographically [to be added as needed]
Campaigns, Political
    USE **Politics**
Campaigns, Presidential—United States
    USE **Presidents—United States—Election**
Campers and trailers
    USE **Travel trailers and campers**
Campgrounds (May subdiv. geog.) 796.54
    UF Camp sites
    NT **Trailer parks**
    RT **Camping**
Camping (May subdiv. geog.)   796.54
    Use for materials on the technique of camping. Materials on camps with a definite program of activities are entered under **Camps**.
    BT **Outdoor recreation**
    NT **Backpacking**
        Bicycle touring
        Outdoor cooking
        Tents
        Travel trailers and campers
        Wilderness survival
    RT **Campgrounds**
        Outdoor life
Camps (May subdiv. geog.)   796.54
    Use for materials on camps with a definite program of activities. Materials on the technique of camping are entered under **Camping**.
    UF Summer camps
    BT **Recreation**
Camps (Military)
    USE **Military camps**

Campus disorders
  USE College students—Political ac-
        tivity
Canada 971
    May be subdivided like United States ex-
    cept for *History.*
  SA names of individual provinces,
       territories, or regions [to be
       added as needed]
Canada—English-French relations
        305.811; 306.44
  UF Canada—French-English relations
Canada—French-English relations
  USE Canada—English-French rela-
        tions
Canada—History—0-1763 (New France)
        971.01
  UF New France—History
Canada—History—1755-1763   971.01
Canada—History—1763-1791   971.02
Canada—History—1763-1867   971.02
Canada—History—1775-1783   971.02
Canada—History—1791-1841   971.03
Canada—History—19th century   971.03
Canada—History—1841-1867   971.04
Canada—History—1867-   971.05
Canada—History—1867-1914   971.05
Canada—History—20th century   971.06
Canada—History—1914-1945   971.06
Canada—History—1945-   971.06
Canada—History—21st century   971.07
Canadian Indians
  USE Native Americans—Canada
Canadian Invasion, 1775-1776   973.3
  BT United States—History—1775-
        1783, Revolution
Canadian literature (May subdiv. geog.)
        810; C810
    Use for general materials not limited to lit-
    erature in a particular language or form. May
    use same subdivision and names of literary
    forms as for English literature; e.g. Canadi-
    an poetry; etc.
  BT Literature
  NT Canadian literature (English)
       Canadian literature (French)
       Canadian poetry
Canadian literature (English) (May
       subdiv. geog.)   810; C810
    May use same subdivisions and names of
    literary forms as for English literature; e.g.
    Canadian poetry (English); etc.
  UF English Canadian literature
  BT Canadian literature

  NT Canadian poetry (English)
Canadian literature (French) (May
       subdiv. geog.)   C840; 840
    May use same subdivisions and names of
    literary forms as for English literature; e.g.
    Canadian poetry (French); etc.
  UF French Canadian literature
       French literature—Canada
  BT Canadian literature
  NT Canadian poetry (French)
Canadian poetry (May subdiv. geog.)
        811; C811
    Use for general materials about Canadian
    poetry not limited to a particular language, not
    for individual works.
  BT Canadian literature
  NT Canadian poetry (English)
       Canadian poetry (French)
Canadian poetry (English) (May subdiv.
       geog.)   811; C811
    Use for general materials about Canadian
    poetry in English, not for individual works.
  UF English Canadian poetry
  BT Canadian literature (English)
       Canadian poetry
Canadian poetry (French) (May subdiv.
       geog.)   841; C841
    Use for general materials about Canadian
    poetry in French, not for individual works.
  UF French Canadian poetry
  BT Canadian literature (French)
       Canadian poetry
Canadians (May subdiv. geog.)   305.811;
        971
  NT French Canadians
Canals (May subdiv. geog.)   386; 627
  SA names of individual canals [to
       be added as needed]
  BT Civil engineering
       Hydraulic structures
       Transportation
       Waterways
  NT Panama Canal
  RT Inland navigation
Canapés
  USE Appetizers
Canaries (May subdiv. geog.)   598.8;
        636.6
  BT Birds
       Cage birds
Canasta (Game)   795.41
  UF Argentine rummy
  BT Card games

Cancer (May subdiv. geog.)   **616.99**
  UF   Carcinoma
        Malignant tumors
  SA   types of cancer [to be added as
        needed]
  BT   **Diseases**
        Tumors
  NT   **Breast cancer**
        Leukemia
        Lung cancer
Cancer—Chemotherapy   616.99
  UF   Chemotherapy
  BT   **Drug therapy**
Cancer—Diet therapy   616.99
  BT   **Diet therapy**
Cancer—Environmental aspects (May
    subdiv. geog.)   **616.07**
  BT   **Environmentally induced dis-
        eases**
Cancer—Genetic aspects   616.99
  BT   **Medical genetics**
Cancer—Nursing   616.99
  BT   **Nursing**
Cancer patients
  USE   **Cancer—Patients**
Cancer—Patients (May subdiv. geog.)
    616.99
  UF   Cancer patients
  BT   **Patients**
Cancer—Surgery   616.99
  BT   **Surgery**
Candies
  USE   **Candy**
Candles   621.32; 745.593
  BT   **Lighting**
Candy   641.8
  UF   Candies
        Sweets
  BT   **Confectionery**
Caning of chairs
  USE   **Chair caning**
Cannabis
  USE   **Marijuana**
Canned goods
  USE   **Canning and preserving**
Cannibalism (May subdiv. geog.)   **394**
  BT   **Ethnology**
        Human behavior
Canning and preserving   641.4; 664
  UF   Canned goods
        Food, Canned

Pickling
Preserving
  SA   types of foods with the subdivi-
        sion *Preservation* [to be add-
        ed as needed]
  BT   **Cooking**
        Food—Preservation
        Industrial chemistry
  NT   **Fruit—Preservation**
        Vegetables—Preservation
Cannon
  USE   **Ordnance**
Canoes and canoeing (May subdiv. geog.)
    797.122
  BT   **Boats and boating**
        Water sports
  NT   **Kayaking**
Canon law
  USE   **Ecclesiastical law**
Canonization (May subdiv. geog.)   **235**
  BT   **Christian saints**
        Rites and ceremonies
Canons, fugues, etc.
  USE   **Fugue**
Cantatas   782.2
    Use for musical scores and for materials on
  the cantata as a musical form.
  BT   **Choral music**
        Vocal music
Canvas embroidery
  USE   **Needlepoint**
Capital (May subdiv. geog.)   **332**
  BT   **Economics**
        Finance
  NT   **Banks and banking**
        Human capital
        Industrial trusts
        Interest (Economics)
        Investments
        Profit
        Saving and investment
        Venture capital
  RT   **Capitalism**
        Wealth
Capital accumulation
  USE   **Saving and investment**
Capital and labor
  USE   **Industrial relations**
Capital equipment
  USE   **Industrial equipment**
Capital formation
  USE   **Saving and investment**

Capital goods
USE **Industrial equipment**
Capital market (May subdiv. geog.) **332**
BT **Finance**
Financial institutions
Loans
Securities
NT **Euro**
Capital punishment (May subdiv. geog.)
179.7; 364.6
UF Abolition of capital punishment
Death penalty
Hanging
BT **Criminal law**
Punishment
RT **Executions and executioners**
Capital punishment—United States
364.6
Capitalism (May subdiv. geog.) **330.12**
BT **Economics**
Labor
Profit
NT **Entrepreneurship**
RT **Capital**
Capitalists and financiers
Free enterprise
Capitalists and financiers (May subdiv.
geog.) **332.092; 920**
UF Financiers
BT **Businesspeople**
RT **Capitalism**
Capitalization (Finance)
USE **Corporations—Finance**
Securities
Valuation
Capitals (Cities) **307.76**
Use for materials on the capital cities of
several countries or states.
BT **Cities and towns**
NT **Capitols**
Capitols **725**
BT **Capitals (Cities)**
Public buildings
Captivities
USE ethnic groups with the subdivi-
sion *Captivities*, e.g. **Native
Americans—Captivities** [to
be added as needed]
Car accidents
USE **Traffic accidents**

Car design
USE **Automobiles—Design and con-
struction**
Car driver education
USE **Automobile driver education**
Car drivers
USE **Automobile drivers**
Car engines
USE **Automobiles—Motors**
Car industry
USE **Automobile industry**
Car insurance
USE **Automobile insurance**
Car maintenance
USE **Automobiles—Maintenance and
repair**
Car painting
USE **Automobiles—Painting**
Car parts
USE **Automobile parts**
Car pools (May subdiv. geog.) **388.4**
UF Automobile pools
Carpools
Ride sharing
Van pools
BT **Traffic engineering**
Transportation
Car racing
USE **Automobile racing**
Car repair
USE **Automobiles—Maintenance and
repair**
Car transmissions
USE **Automobiles—Transmission de-
vices**
Car travel
USE **Automobile travel**
Car wheels
USE **Wheels**
Car wrecks
USE **Traffic accidents**
Carbines
USE **Rifles**
Carbohydrates **613.2**
BT **Biochemistry**
Nutrition
RT **High-carbohydrate diet**
Low-carbohydrate diet
Carbolic acid **547; 661**
BT **Acids**
Chemicals

Carbon   540; 660
  BT   **Chemical elements**
  NT   **Diamonds**
        Graphite
Carbon 14 dating
  USE   **Radiocarbon dating**
Carbon dioxide greenhouse effect
  USE   **Global warming**
Carburetors   621.43
  BT   **Internal combustion engines**
Carcinoma
  USE   **Cancer**
Card catalogs   025.3
  UF   Catalogs, Card
  BT   **Library catalogs**
Card games (May subdiv. geog.)   **795.4**
  SA   types of card games [to be add-
        ed as needed]
  BT   **Games**
  NT   **Bridge (Game)**
        Canasta (Game)
        Card tricks
        Collectible card games
        Poker
        Solitaire (Game)
        Tarot
  RT   **Playing cards**
Card tricks   795.4
  BT   **Card games**
        Magic tricks
        Tricks
Cardiac diseases
  USE   **Heart diseases**
Cardiac resuscitation   616.1
  UF   Heart resuscitation
        Resuscitation, Heart
  BT   **Emergency medicine**
  RT   **CPR (First aid)**
Cardinals (May subdiv. geog.)   **262**
  BT   **Catholic Church—Clergy**
Cardiopulmonary resuscitation
  USE   **CPR (First aid)**
Cardiovascular system   612.1
  UF   Circulatory system
        Vascular system
  BT   **Anatomy**
        Physiology
  NT   **Heart**
  RT   **Blood—Circulation**
Cards, Debit
  USE   **Debit cards**

Cards, Greeting
  USE   **Greeting cards**
Cards, Playing
  USE   **Playing cards**
Cards, Sports
  USE   **Sports cards**
Care
  USE   parts of the body, classes of
        persons, and types of animals
        with the subdivision *Care,*
        e.g. **Foot—Care; Infants—
        Care; Dogs—Care;** etc.;
        classes of persons with the
        subdivisions *Medical care, In-
        stitutional care,* and *Home
        care,* e.g. **Elderly—Medical
        care; Elderly—Institutional
        care; Elderly—Home care;**
        etc.; ethnic groups and classes
        of persons with the subdivi-
        sion *Health and hygiene,* e.g.
        **Infants—Health and hy-
        giene;** and inanimate things
        with the subdivision *Mainte-
        nance and repair,* e.g. **Auto-
        mobiles—Maintenance and
        repair** [to be added as need-
        ed]
Care givers
  USE   **Caregivers**
Care of children
  USE   **Child care**
Care of the dying
  USE   **Terminal care**
Career changes   650.14; 658.4
  UF   Changing careers
        Mid-career changes
  SA   fields of knowledge, professions,
        industries, and trades with the
        subdivision *Vocational guid-
        ance* [to be added as needed]
  BT   **Age and employment**
        Vocational guidance
Career counseling
  USE   **Vocational guidance**
Career development
  USE   **Personnel management**
        Vocational guidance
Career education
  USE   **Vocational education**

Career guidance
　　USE　**Vocational guidance**
Careers
　　USE　**Occupations**
　　　　　Professions
　　　　　Vocational guidance
Caregivers (May subdiv. geog.)　**362;**
　　649.8
　　Use for materials on family and friends
　who on a voluntary basis provide personal
　home care for the elderly, ill, or handicapped.
　　UF　Care givers
　　　　　Family caregivers
　　BT　**Volunteer work**
　　RT　**Home care services**
Caribbean Area
　　USE　**Caribbean Region**
Caribbean Region　**972.9**
　　UF　Caribbean Area
　　　　　Caribbean Sea Region
　　　　　West Indies Region
　　BT　**America**
Caribbean Sea Region
　　USE　**Caribbean Region**
Caricatures and cartoons
　　USE　**Cartoons and caricatures**
Carillons
　　USE　**Bells**
Carnival (May subdiv. geog.)　**394.25**
　　Use for materials on festivals, merrymaking,
　and revelry before Lent. Materials on travel-
　ing amusement enterprises, consisting of side-
　shows, games of chance, etc., are entered un-
　der **Carnivals**.
　　UF　Mardi Gras
　　　　　Pre-Lenten festivities
　　BT　**Festivals**
Carnivals (May subdiv. geog.)　**394.26;**
　　791
　　Use for materials on traveling amusement
　enterprises, consisting of sideshows, games of
　chance, merry-go-rounds, etc. Materials on
　festivals, merrymaking, and revelry before
　Lent are entered under **Carnival**.
　　BT　**Amusements**
　　　　　Festivals
　　RT　**Amusement parks**
　　　　　Circus
　　　　　Fairs
Carnivora
　　USE　**Carnivorous animals**
Carnivores
　　USE　**Carnivorous animals**

Carnivorous animals (May subdiv. geog.)
　　599.7
　　UF　Carnivora
　　　　　Carnivores
　　　　　Meat-eating animals
　　SA　types of carnivorous animals [to
　　　　　be added as needed]
　　BT　**Animals**
Carnivorous plants (May subdiv. geog.)
　　583; 635.9
　　UF　Insect-eating plants
　　　　　Insectivorous plants
　　BT　**Plants**
Carols　**782.28**
　　UF　Christmas carols
　　　　　Easter carols
　　BT　**Church music**
　　　　　Folk songs
　　　　　Hymns
　　　　　Songs
　　　　　Vocal music
Carpentry (May subdiv. geog.)　**694**
　　Use for materials on the construction of a
　wooden building or the wooden portion of
　any building. Materials on the making and
　finishing of fine woodwork, such as furniture
　or interior details, are entered under **Cabinet-
　work**.
　　BT　**Building**
　　NT　**Cabinetwork**
　　　　　Turning
　　RT　**Woodwork**
Carpentry—Tools
　　USE　**Carpentry tools**
Carpentry tools　**694**
　　UF　Carpentry—Tools
　　SA　types of carpentry tools [to be
　　　　　added as needed]
　　BT　**Tools**
　　NT　**Saws**
Carpet cleaning
　　USE　**Rugs and carpets—Cleaning**
Carpetbag rule
　　USE　**Reconstruction (1865-1876)**
Carpets
　　USE　**Rugs and carpets**
Carpools
　　USE　**Car pools**
Carriages and carts (May subdiv. geog.)
　　388.3; 688.6
　　UF　Carts
　　　　　Stagecoaches
　　　　　Wagons

Carriages and carts—*Continued*
   BT   **Vehicles**
Cars (Automobiles)
   USE   **Automobiles**
Cartels
   USE   **Industrial trusts**
Carthage (Extinct city)   **939**
   BT   **Extinct cities**
Cartography
   USE   **Map drawing**
          Maps
Cartooning (May subdiv. geog.)   **741.5**
   BT   **Cartoons and caricatures**
          Wit and humor
Cartoons and caricatures (May subdiv.
   geog.)   **741.5**
   Use for collections of pictorial humor and
   for materials about cartoons and caricatures.
   UF   Caricatures and cartoons
   SA   subjects, classes of persons,
          names of individuals, and
          names of wars with the sub-
          division *Cartoons and carica-*
          tures [to be added as needed]
   BT   **Pictures**
          Portraits
   NT   **Animated films**
          Cartooning
          Computers—Cartoons and car-
          icatures
          World War, 1939-1945—Car-
          toons and caricatures
   RT   **Comic books, strips, etc.**
Cartoons, Animated
   USE   **Animated films**
Cartoons, Television
   USE   **Animated television programs**
Carts
   USE   **Carriages and carts**
Carts (Midget cars)
   USE   **Karts and karting**
Carving (Arts)
   USE   **Carving (Decorative arts)**
Carving (Decorative arts) (May subdiv.
   geog.)   **731.4; 736**
   UF   Carving (Arts)
   SA   types of carving, e.g. **Wood**
          carving [to be added as need-
          ed]
   BT   **Decorative arts**
   NT   **Wood carving**
   RT   **Sculpture**

Carving (Meat, etc.)   **642**
   BT   **Dining**
          Entertaining
          Meat
Carving, Wood
   USE   **Wood carving**
Case studies
   USE   subjects with the subdivision
          Case studies, e.g. **Juvenile**
          delinquency—Case studies
          [to be added as needed]
Case work, Social
   USE   **Social case work**
Cassandra (Legendary character)
   398.22
   BT   **Legendary characters**
Cassette books
   USE   **Audiobooks**
Cassette recorders and recording
   USE   **Magnetic recorders and re-**
          cording
Cassette tapes, Audio
   USE   **Sound recordings**
Castaways
   USE   **Survival after airplane acci-**
          dents, shipwrecks, etc.
Caste (May subdiv. geog.)   **305.5**
   BT   **Manners and customs**
   NT   **Social classes**
Casting
   USE   **Founding**
          Plaster casts
Castles (May subdiv. geog.)   **728.8**
   UF   Chateaux
   BT   **Buildings**
   RT   **Medieval architecture**
Casts, Plaster
   USE   **Plaster casts**
Casualty insurance (May subdiv. geog.)
   368.5
   UF   Insurance, Casualty
   BT   **Insurance**
   NT   **Accident insurance**
CAT scan
   USE   **Tomography**
Catacombs (May subdiv. geog.)   **393;**
   726
   BT   **Burial**
          Cemeteries
          Christian antiquities
          Tombs

Catacombs—*Continued*
    RT   **Church history—30-600, Early church**
Cataloging   **025.3**
    UF   Cataloguing
          Libraries—Cataloging
          Library cataloging
    SA   cataloging of particular subjects, e.g., **Cataloging of music** [to be added as needed]
    BT   **Bibliographic control**
          Documentation
          Library science
          Library technical processes
    NT   **Automated cataloging**
          Cataloging of music
          International Standard Bibliographic Description
          Library classification
          Machine readable bibliographic data
          Subject headings
    RT   **Bibliography**
          Indexing
          Library catalogs
Cataloging data in machine readable form
    USE   **Machine readable bibliographic data**
Cataloging—Data processing
    USE   **Automated cataloging**
Cataloging—Music
    USE   **Cataloging of music**
Cataloging of music   **025.3**
    UF   Cataloging—Music
          Music—Cataloging
    BT   **Cataloging**
Catalogs
    USE   **Booksellers' catalogs**
          Commercial catalogs
          Library catalogs
          Publishers' catalogs
          and subjects and names of museums with the subdivision *Catalogs*, e.g. **Motion pictures—Catalogs** [to be added as needed]
Catalogs, Booksellers'
    USE   **Booksellers' catalogs**
Catalogs, Card
    USE   **Card catalogs**
Catalogs, Classified
    USE   **Classified catalogs**

Catalogs, Film
    USE   **Motion pictures—Catalogs**
Catalogs, Library
    USE   **Library catalogs**
Catalogs, Online
    USE   **Online catalogs**
Catalogs, Publishers'
    USE   **Publishers' catalogs**
Catalogs, Subject
    USE   **Subject catalogs**
Cataloguing
    USE   **Cataloging**
Catalysis   **541**
    BT   **Physical chemistry**
    RT   **Catalytic RNA**
Catalytic RNA   **572.8**
    UF   Ribozymes
    BT   **Enzymes**
          RNA
    RT   **Catalysis**
Catamarans (May subdiv. geog.)   **797.1**
    BT   **Boats and boating**
Catastrophes
    USE   **Disasters**
Catechisms   **202; 238**
    SA   names of religions and sects and titles of sacred works with the subdivision *Catechisms* [to be added as needed]
    BT   **Theology—Study and teaching**
    NT   **Bible—Catechisms**
    RT   **Creeds**
Categories of persons
    USE   **Persons**
          and classes of persons, e.g. **Elderly**; **Handicapped**; **Explorers**; **Drug addicts**; etc. [to be added as needed]
Caterers and catering
    USE   **Catering**
Catering (May subdiv. geog.)   **642**
    UF   Caterers and catering
    BT   **Cooking**
          Food service
    RT   **Menus**
Caterpillars   **595.78**
    UF   Cocoons
    BT   **Butterflies**
          Moths
Cathedrals (May subdiv. geog.)   **726.6**

Cathedrals—*Continued*

    SA   names of individual cathedrals
            [to be added as needed]

    BT   **Church buildings**

    RT   **Abbeys**
          Church architecture
          Gothic architecture
          Medieval architecture

Cathedrals—United States   **726.60973**

Cathode ray tubes   **537.5; 621.3815**

    UF   CRTs

    BT   **Vacuum tubes**

Catholic charismatic movement (May
    subdiv. geog.)   **282**

    UF   Charismatic movement
          Charismatic renewal movement

    BT   **Catholic Church**
          Episcopal Church

    RT   **Pentecostalism**
          Spiritual gifts

Catholic Church (May subdiv. geog.)
    282

    UF   Catholic faith
          Catholicism
          Roman Catholic Church

    SA   religious subjects with the subdi-
          vision *Catholic Church*, e.g.
          Asceticism—Catholic
          Church; **Laity—Catholic**
          Church; etc., and other sub-
          jects with the subdivisions
          Religious aspects—Catholic
          Church; e.g. **Abortion—Reli-**
          gious aspects—Catholic
          Church [to be added as
          needed]

    BT   **Christian sects**
          Christianity

    NT   **Catholic charismatic movement**
          Inquisition
          Laity—Catholic Church
          Papacy

    RT   **Catholics**

Catholic Church—Bishops (May subdiv.
    geog.)   **280**

    BT   **Bishops**

Catholic Church—Charities (May subdiv.
    geog.)   **361.7**

    BT   **Charities**

Catholic Church—Clergy (May subdiv.
    geog.)   **253**

    BT   **Clergy**
          Priests

    NT   **Cardinals**
          Ex-priests

Catholic Church—Converts

    USE   **Converts to Catholicism**

Catholic Church—Creeds   **238**

    Use for materials about the concise, formal,
    authorized statements of Catholic doctrine and
    for the texts of such statements.

    UF   Catholic creeds

    BT   **Creeds**

Catholic Church—Foreign relations (May
    subdiv. geog.)   **282; 327.456**

    Use for materials on diplomatic relations
    between the Catholic Church and various gov-
    ernments or political bodies. When this head-
    ing is subdivided geographically, an additional
    entry is provided with the Catholic Church
    and the place in reversed positions. Materials
    on the relations between the Catholic Church
    and other churches or religions are entered
    under **Catholic Church—Relations**.

    UF   Catholic Church—Relations
          (Diplomatic)
          Vatican City—Foreign relations

    BT   **International relations**

Catholic Church—Liturgy   **264**

    Use for materials on the forms of prayers,
    rituals, and ceremonies used in the official
    public worship of the Catholic Church. Texts
    of Catholic liturgies are entered under **Catho-
    lic Church—Liturgy—Texts**.

    UF   Catholic liturgies

    BT   **Liturgies**
          Rites and ceremonies

Catholic Church—Liturgy—Texts   **264**

Catholic Church—Missions (May subdiv.
    geog.)   **266**

    BT   **Christian missions**

Catholic Church—Relations   **282**

    Use for materials on relations between the
    Catholic Church and other churches or reli-
    gions. This heading may be further subdivided
    by church or religion, in which case an addi-
    tional entry is provided with the two churches
    or religions in reversed positions. Materials on
    diplomatic relations between the Catholic
    Church and various governments or political
    bodies are entered under **Catholic Church—
    Foreign relations**.

Catholic Church—Relations (Diplomatic)

    USE   **Catholic Church—Foreign rela-
          tions**

Catholic Church—United States   **282**

Catholic colleges and universities (May
    subdiv. geog.)   **378**

    UF   Catholic universities and colleges

Catholic colleges and universities—*Continued*

    BT   **Colleges and universities**

Catholic converts
    USE   **Converts to Catholicism**

Catholic creeds
    USE   **Catholic Church—Creeds**

Catholic ex-nuns
    USE   **Ex-nuns**

Catholic ex-priests
    USE   **Ex-priests**

Catholic faith
    USE   **Catholic Church**

Catholic laity
    USE   **Laity—Catholic Church**

Catholic literature (May subdiv. geog.)
    282; 808; 809
    BT   **Christian literature**
           Literature

Catholic liturgies
    USE   **Catholic Church—Liturgy**

Catholic universities and colleges
    USE   **Catholic colleges and universities**

Catholicism
    USE   **Catholic Church**

Catholics (May subdiv. geog.)   **282.092; 305.6**
    NT   **Converts to Catholicism**
    RT   **Catholic Church**

Catholics—United States   282.092; 305.6

Cats (May subdiv. geog.)   **599.75; 636.8**
    UF   Felines
           Kittens
    SA   names of specific breeds of cat
           [to be added as needed]
    BT   **Domestic animals**
           Mammals
    RT   **Wild cats**

Cat's cradle
    USE   **String figures**

Cats—Literary collections   808.8

Cattle (May subdiv. geog.)   **599.64; 636.2**
    UF   Cows
    BT   **Domestic animals**
           Mammals
    NT   **Beef cattle**
           Dairy cattle

Cattle brands (May subdiv. geog.)
    636.2

Cattle—Vaccination   636.089

    BT   **Vaccination**

Causality
    USE   **Causation**

Causation   **122**
    UF   Causality
           Cause and effect
    BT   **Metaphysics**
           Philosophy

Cause and effect
    USE   **Causation**

Causes
    USE   names of wars with the subdivision *Causes,* e.g. **World War, 1939-1945—Causes** [to be added as needed]

Causes of diseases
    USE   **Diseases—Causes**

Cautionary tales and verses
    USE   **Didactic fiction**
           Didactic poetry
           Fables
           Parables

Cave drawings
    USE   **Cave drawings and paintings**

Cave drawings and paintings (May subdiv. geog.)   **743; 759.01**
    UF   Cave drawings
           Cave paintings
    BT   **Rock drawings, paintings, and engravings**

Cave dwellers (May subdiv. geog.)
    569.9; 930.1
    BT   **Prehistoric peoples**

Cave ecology (May subdiv. geog.)   **577.5**
    BT   **Ecology**

Cave paintings
    USE   **Cave drawings and paintings**

Caves (May subdiv. geog.)   **551.44**
    UF   Grottoes
           Speleology

CB radio
    USE   **Citizens band radio**

CD-I technology   **006.7**
    UF   CDI technology
           Compact disc interactive technology
           Interactive CD technology
    BT   **Compact discs**
           Optical storage devices

CD players
    USE   **Compact disc players**

CD-ROM
USE **CD-ROMs**
CD-ROMs **004.5**
UF CD-ROM
CDROM
CDROMs
Compact disc read-only memory
BT **Compact discs**
Optical storage devices
CDI technology
USE **CD-I technology**
CDROM
USE **CD-ROMs**
CDROMs
USE **CD-ROMs**
CDs (Compact discs)
USE **Compact discs**
Celebrations, anniversaries, etc.
USE **Anniversaries**
Celebrities (May subdiv. geog.) **920**
UF Famous people
Public figures
SA types of celebrities, e.g. **Actors**;
Television personalities; and
names of individual celebrities
[to be added as needed]
BT **Persons**
NT **Television personalities**
RT **Fame**
Celebrity
USE **Fame**
Celery **635; 641.3**
BT **Vegetables**
Celibacy **204; 248.4**
Use for materials on the renunciation of
marriage for religious reasons. Materials on
the virtue that moderates and regulates the
sexual appetite in human beings are entered
under **Chastity**. Materials on abstinence from
sexual activity are entered under **Sexual absti-
nence**.
UF Clerical celibacy
BT **Clergy**
Religious life
RT **Chastity**
Sexual abstinence
Cell phones
USE **Cellular telephones**
Cellars
USE **Basements**
Cellists
USE **Violoncellists**

Cello
USE **Violoncellos**
Cello players
USE **Violoncellists**
Cells **571.6**
UF Cytology
BT **Biology**
Physiology
Reproduction
NT **DNA**
RT **Embryology**
Protoplasm
Cells, Electric
USE **Electric batteries**
Cellular phones
USE **Cellular telephones**
Cellular telephones **384.5**
UF Cell phones
Cellular phones
BT **Telephone**
Celtic art (May subdiv. geog.) **709.01**
BT **Art**
Celtic civilization **936.4**
BT **Civilization**
Celtic legends **398.208991**
BT **Legends**
Celtic mythology **299; 936.4**
UF Mythology, Celtic
BT **Mythology**
Celts (May subdiv. geog.) **305.891;
936.4**
UF Gaels
BT **France—History—0-1328**
Great Britain—History—0-1066
NT **Druids and Druidism**
Cement **691; 620.1; 666**
UF Hydraulic cement
BT **Adhesives**
Building materials
Ceramics
Masonry
Plaster and plastering
RT **Concrete**
Cemeteries (May subdiv. geog.) **393;
718**
UF Burying grounds
Churchyards
Graves
Graveyards

Cemeteries—*Continued*

    SA   types of cemeteries and names
           of individual cemeteries [to
           be added as needed]

    BT   **Burial**

         Public health

         Sanitation

    NT   **Catacombs**

         Epitaphs

    RT   **Tombs**

Censorship (May subdiv. geog.)   **303.3;
363.31**

Use for general materials on the limitation of freedom of expression in various fields.

    SA   subjects and names of wars with
           the subdivision *Censorship*,
           e.g. **Books—Censorship** [to
           be added as needed]

    BT   **Intellectual freedom**

    NT   **Books—Censorship**

         Freedom of speech

         Libraries—Censorship

         Motion pictures—Censorship

         Television—Censorship

         World War, 1939-1945—Censorship

    RT   **Freedom of information**

         Freedom of the press

Census   **304.6; 310; 352.7**

    SA   names of countries, cities, etc.,
           with the subdivision *Census*
           [to be added as needed]

    BT   **Population**

         Statistics

         Vital statistics

    NT   **Chicago (Ill.)—Census**

         Ohio—Census

         United States—Census

Centennial celebrations, etc.

    USE names of places, wars, and historical events with the subdivision *Centennial celebrations, etc.,* e.g. **United States—History—1861-1865, Civil War—Centennial celebrations, etc.**; and ethnic groups, classes of persons, individuals, corporate bodies, places, religious denominations, historic or social movements, and historic events with the subdivi-

sion *Anniversaries,* for materials about anniversary celebrations, e.g. **Shakespeare, William, 1564-1616—Anniversaries** [to be added as needed]

Centers for older people

    USE **Senior centers**

Centers for the elderly

    USE **Senior centers**

Centers for the performing arts (May subdiv. geog.) **725; 790.2**

    SA   names of individual centers [to
           be added as needed]

    BT   **Performing arts**

    NT   **Auditoriums**

         Theaters

Central Africa   **967**

Use for materials dealing collectively with the region of Africa that includes the Central African Republic, Equatorial Guinea, Gabon, Congo (Republic), and Congo (Democratic Republic).

    UF   Africa, Central

    BT   **Africa**

    NT   **French-speaking Equatorial Africa**

Central America   **972.8**

    BT   **North America**

Central Asia   **958**

    UF   Asia, Central

    BT   **Asia**

Central Asia—History   **958**

Central Asia—History—1991-   **958**

Central Europe   **943**

Use for materials on the area included in the basins of the Danube, Elbe and Rhine rivers.

    UF   Europe, Central

Central planning

    USE **Economic policy**

Central States

    USE **Middle West**

Centralization of schools

    USE **Schools—Centralization**

Centralized processing (Libraries)

    USE **Library technical processes**

Ceramic industries

    USE **Ceramic industry**

Ceramic industry (May subdiv. geog.)   **338.4**

    UF   Ceramic industries

Ceramic industry—*Continued*

    SA   types of ceramic industries, e.g.

            Glass manufacture [to be added as needed]

    BT   **Industries**

    NT   **Clay industry**

          Glass manufacture

    RT   **Ceramics**

Ceramic materials

    USE   **Ceramics**

Ceramic tiles

    USE   **Tiles**

Ceramics (May subdiv. geog.)   **666**

    Use for materials on the technology of fired earth products or on ceramic products intended for industrial use. Materials on ceramic products intended for the table or decorative use are entered under **Pottery** or **Porcelain**.

    UF   Ceramic materials

    BT   **Industrial chemistry**

          Materials

    NT   **Abrasives**

          Cement

          Clay

          Glass

          Glazes

          Pottery

          Tiles

    RT   **Ceramic industry**

Cereals

    USE   **Grain**

Cereals, Prepared

    USE   **Prepared cereals**

Cerebral palsy   **616.8**

    UF   Paralysis, Cerebral

    BT   **Brain—Diseases**

Cerebrovascular disease

    USE   **Stroke**

Ceremonies

    USE   **Etiquette**

          Manners and customs

          Rites and ceremonies

Certainty   **121**

    BT   **Logic**

          Theory of knowledge

    RT   **Truth**

Certified public accountants

    USE   **Accountants**

Ceylon

    USE   **Sri Lanka**

CGI (Cinematography)

    USE   **Computer animation**

Chain belting

    USE   **Belts and belting**

Chain stores (May subdiv. geog.)   **658.8**

    UF   Branch stores

    BT   **Retail trade**

          Stores

Chair caning   **684.1**

    UF   Caning of chairs

    BT   **Handicraft**

Chairs   **645; 684.1; 749**

    BT   **Furniture**

    NT   **Wheelchairs**

Chakras   **131; 181**

    BT   **Yoga**

Chalk talks   **741.2**

    UF   Blackboard drawing

    BT   **Public speaking**

Chamber music   **785**

    BT   **Instrumental music**

          Music

    NT   **Quintets**

Chambers of commerce (May subdiv. geog.)   **380.106; 381.06**

    UF   Boards of trade

          Trade, Boards of

    BT   **Commerce**

Change   **116**

    BT   **Metaphysics**

    NT   **Metamorphosis**

Change of life in men

    USE   **Male climacteric**

Change of life in women

    USE   **Menopause**

Change of sex

    USE   **Transsexualism**

Change, Organizational

    USE   **Organizational change**

Change (Psychology)   **153; 155.2**

    BT   **Psychology**

Change, Social

    USE   **Social change**

Changing careers

    USE   **Career changes**

Chanties

    USE   **Sea songs**

Chants (Plain, Gregorian, etc.)   **782.32**

    Use for books of chants and for materials about chants.

    UF   Gregorian chant

          Plain chant

          Plainsong

    BT   **Church music**

Chanukah
USE **Hanukkah**
Chaos (Science)   003
UF   Chaotic behavior in systems
BT   **Dynamics**
Science
System theory
Chaotic behavior in systems
USE   **Chaos (Science)**
Chap-books
USE   **Chapbooks**
Chapbooks   398
Use for individual works, collections, or materials about chapbooks.
UF   Chap-books
Jestbooks
BT   **Books**
Folklore
Literature
Pamphlets
Periodicals
Wit and humor
NT   **Tracts**
RT   **Comic books, strips, etc.**
Chaplains (May subdiv. geog.)   **253**
SA   corporate bodies and institutions with the subdivision *Chaplains*, e.g. **United States. Army—Chaplains** [to be added as needed]
BT   **Clergy**
NT   **United States. Army—Chaplains**
Character   155.2
BT   **Ethics**
Personality
NT   **Human behavior**
RT   **Temperament**
Character assassination
USE   **Libel and slander**
Character education
USE   **Moral education**
Characters
USE   **Characters and characteristics in literature**
and   names of authors with the subdivision *Characters;* e.g. **Shakespeare, William, 1564-1616—Characters** [to be added as needed]
Characters and characteristics in literature   809

UF   Characters
Literary characters
SA   names of authors with the subdivision *Characters*; e.g. **Shakespeare, William, 1564-1616—Characters**; racial and ethnic groups and classes of persons in literature, e.g. **African Americans in literature**; **Children in literature**; etc.; names of persons, families, and corporate bodies with the subdivision *In literature*, e.g. **Napoleon I, Emperor of the French, 1769-1821—In literature** [to be added as needed]
BT   **Literature**
NT   **Fictional characters**
RT   **Literature—Themes**
Charades   793.2
BT   **Amateur theater**
Amusements
Literary recreations
Riddles
Charcoal   662
BT   **Fuel**
Charcoal drawing   741
BT   **Drawing**
Charismata
USE   **Spiritual gifts**
Charismatic movement
USE   **Catholic charismatic movement**
Pentecostalism
Charismatic renewal movement
USE   **Catholic charismatic movement**
Pentecostalism
Charitable institutions
USE   **Charities**
Institutional care
Orphanages
Charitable organizations   361
BT   **Associations**
RT   **Charities**
Philanthropy
Charities (May subdiv. geog.)   **361.7**
Use for materials on privately supported welfare activities. Materials on tax supported welfare activities are entered under **Public welfare**. Materials on the methods employed in welfare work, public or private, are entered under **Social work**. General materials on the various policies, programs, services, and facilities to meet basic human needs, such as

Charities—*Continued*
health, education, and welfare, are entered under **Human services**.

    UF   Charitable institutions
           Endowed charities
           Homes (Institutions)
           Institutions, Charitable and phil-
             anthropic
           Poor relief
           Social welfare
           Welfare agencies
           Welfare work
    SA   names of appropriate corporate
           bodies with the subdivision
           Charities, e.g. **Catholic**
           Church—Charities; and
           names of wars with the sub-
           division *Civilian relief*, e.g.
           World War, 1939-1945—Ci-
           vilian relief [to be added as
           needed]
    BT   **Human services**
           Social work
    NT   **Catholic Church—Charities**
           Child welfare
           Disaster relief
           Food relief
           Institutional care
           Medical charities
           Orphanages
           Social settlements
           World War, 1939-1945—Civil-
           ian relief
    RT   **Charitable organizations**
           Endowments
           Philanthropy
           Public welfare
           Volunteer work

Charities, Medical
    USE **Medical charities**

Charity   **177**
    BT   **Ethics**
           Virtue
    RT   **Altruism**
           Love—Religious aspects

Charity shops
    USE **Thrift shops**

Charlatans
    USE **Impostors and imposture**

Charms   **133.4**
    UF   Spells
           Talismans

    BT   **Folklore**
           Superstition

Charter flights
    USE **Airlines—Chartering**

Charter schools (May subdiv. geog.)
    371.01
    Use for materials on legislatively autho-
    rized, independent, and innovative public
    schools that operate under the authority of a
    charter.
    BT   **Schools**

Charters (May subdiv. geog.)
    UF   Documents
    BT   **History—Sources**
    NT   **Magna Carta**
    RT   **Archives**
           Manuscripts

Chartography
    USE **Maps**

Charts
    USE **Charts, diagrams, etc.**

Charts, diagrams, etc.   **912**
    UF   Charts
    SA   topics with the subdivision
           Charts, diagrams, etc., for
           works consisting of charts or
           diagrams illustrating those
           topics, e.g. **Electric wiring—**
           Charts, diagrams, etc. [to be
           added as needed]
    RT   **Maps**

Charts, Nautical
    USE **Nautical charts**

Chasidism
    USE **Hasidism**

Chastity   **176**
    Use for materials on the virtue that moder-
    ates and regulates the sexual appetite in hu-
    man beings. Materials on the renunciation of
    marriage for religious reasons are entered un-
    der **Celibacy**. Materials on abstinence from
    sexual activity are entered under **Sexual absti-**
    nence.
    BT   **Sexual ethics**
           Virtue
    RT   **Celibacy**
           Sexual abstinence

Chat groups, Online
    USE **Online chat groups**

Chat rooms, Online
    USE **Online chat groups**

Chateaux
    USE **Castles**

Cheating (Education) (May subdiv. geog.)
    371.26; 371.5
    UF Academic dishonesty
        Student cheating
        Student dishonesty
    BT Honesty
Cheating in sports
    USE Sports—Corrupt practices
Checkers 794.2
    UF Draughts
    BT Board games
Cheerleaders
    USE Cheerleading
Cheerleading 371.8; 791.6
    UF Cheerleaders
        Cheers and cheerleading
    BT Student activities
Cheers and cheerleading
    USE Cheerleading
Cheese (May subdiv. geog.) 637; 641.3
    BT Dairy products
Cheese—Bacteriology
    USE Cheese—Microbiology
Cheese—Microbiology 637
    UF Cheese—Bacteriology
    BT Microbiology
Cheesecake (Cooking) 641.8653
    BT Cake
Chemical analysis
    USE Analytical chemistry
Chemical apparatus 542
    UF Apparatus, Chemical
        Chemistry—Apparatus
    BT Scientific apparatus and in-
        struments
Chemical dependency
    USE Substance abuse
Chemical elements 546
    UF Elements, Chemical
    SA names of chemical elements [to
        be added as needed]
    BT Chemistry
    NT Carbon
        Gold
        Helium
        Hydrogen
        Iron
        Mercury
        Oxygen
        Radium
        Silver

Sulphur
Tin
Uranium
Zinc
    RT Periodic law
Chemical engineering (May subdiv. geog.)
    660
    UF Chemistry, Industrial
        Chemistry, Technical
    BT Engineering
    NT Biotechnology
        Fermentation
    RT Industrial chemistry
        Metallurgy
Chemical equations 540
    UF Equations, Chemical
    BT Chemical reactions
Chemical geology
    USE Geochemistry
Chemical industries
    USE Chemical industry
Chemical industry (May subdiv. geog.)
    338.4; 660
    Use for materials about industries that pro-
    duce chemicals or are based on chemical pro-
    cesses. General materials on chemicals, in-
    cluding their manufacture, are entered under
    Chemicals.
    UF Chemical industries
        Chemistry, Industrial
        Chemistry, Technical
    SA types of industries, e.g. Plastics
        industry [to be added as
        needed]
    BT Industries
    NT Plastics industry
    RT Chemicals
        Industrial chemistry
Chemical industry—Accidents (May
    subdiv. geog.) 363.11
    BT Industrial accidents
Chemical industry—Employees (May
    subdiv. geog.) 331.11
    UF Chemical workers
    BT Employees
Chemical industry—Employees—Diseases
    (May subdiv. geog.) 616.9
    UF Chemical workers' diseases
    BT Occupational diseases
Chemical industry—Employees—Pensions
    (May subdiv. geog.) 331.25

Chemical industry—Employees—Salaries, wages, etc. (May subdiv. geog.) **331.2**
   BT **Salaries, wages, etc.**
Chemical industry—Employees—Supply and demand **331.12**
   BT **Supply and demand**
Chemical industry—Law and legislation (May subdiv. geog.) **343**
   BT **Law**
      Legislation
Chemical industry—Waste disposal (May subdiv. geog.) **363.72; 628.4**
   BT **Refuse and refuse disposal**
Chemical landfills
   USE **Hazardous waste sites**
Chemical pollution
   USE **Pollution**
Chemical reactions **541**
   UF Reactions, Chemical
   BT **Chemistry**
   NT **Chemical equations**
Chemical societies
   USE **Chemistry—Societies**
Chemical technology
   USE **Industrial chemistry**
Chemical warfare (May subdiv. geog.) **358; 623.4**
   UF Gas warfare
      Poisonous gases—War use
   SA names of wars with the subdivision *Chemical warfare* [to be added as needed]
   BT **Military art and science**
      War
   NT **Incendiary weapons**
      World War, 1914-1918—Chemical warfare
      World War, 1939-1945—Chemical warfare
Chemical workers
   USE **Chemical industry—Employees**
Chemical workers' diseases
   USE **Chemical industry—Employees—Diseases**
Chemicals **540; 661**
   Use for general materials on chemicals, including their manufacture. Materials about industries that produce chemicals or are based on chemical processes are entered under **Chemical industry**.

   SA types of chemicals, e.g. **Acids**; **Agricultural chemicals**; etc.; and names of individual chemicals [to be added as needed]
   NT **Acids**
      Agricultural chemicals
      Alcohol
      Carbolic acid
      Deuterium oxide
      Nitrates
      Organic compounds
      Petrochemicals
   RT **Chemical industry**
      Industrial chemistry
Chemicals—Toxicology
   USE **Toxicology**
Chemistry **540**
   BT **Physical sciences**
      Science
   NT **Acids**
      Agricultural chemistry
      Alchemy
      Analytical chemistry
      Bases (Chemistry)
      Biochemistry
      Botanical chemistry
      Chemical elements
      Chemical reactions
      Color
      Combustion
      Explosives
      Fermentation
      Fire
      Geochemistry
      Industrial chemistry
      Inorganic chemistry
      Microchemistry
      Organic chemistry
      Pharmaceutical chemistry
      Pharmacy
      Photographic chemistry
      Physical chemistry
      Space chemistry
      Spectrum analysis
Chemistry, Analytic
   USE **Analytical chemistry**
Chemistry—Apparatus
   USE **Chemical apparatus**
Chemistry, Diagnostic
   USE **Clinical chemistry**

Chemistry—Dictionaries   540.3
　　BT   Encyclopedias and dictionaries
Chemistry—Experiments   540; 542
Chemistry, Industrial
　　USE   Chemical engineering
　　　　　Chemical industry
Chemistry, Inorganic
　　USE   Inorganic chemistry
Chemistry—Laboratory manuals
　　　　　540.78
Chemistry, Medical
　　USE   Clinical chemistry
Chemistry of food
　　USE   Food—Analysis
　　　　　Food—Composition
Chemistry, Organic
　　USE   Organic chemistry
Chemistry, Physical and theoretical
　　USE   Physical chemistry
Chemistry—Problems, exercises, etc.
　　　　　540.76
Chemistry—Societies (May subdiv. geog.)
　　　　　540.6
　　UF   Chemical societies
　　BT   Societies
Chemistry, Synthetic
　　USE   Organic compounds—Synthesis
Chemistry, Technical
　　USE   Chemical engineering
　　　　　Chemical industry
　　　　　Industrial chemistry
Chemistry, Textile
　　USE   Textile chemistry
Chemists (May subdiv. geog.)   540.92;
　　　　　920
　　BT   Scientists
Chemists' shops
　　USE   Drugstores
Chemotherapy
　　USE   Cancer—Chemotherapy
　　　　　Drug therapy
Chess (May subdiv. geog.)   794.1
　　BT   Board games
Chests (May subdiv. geog.)   749
　　BT   Furniture
Chicago (Ill.)   917.73; 977.3
　　The subdivisions under Chicago (Ill.) may
　be used under the name of any city. The sub-
　divisions under United States may be further
　consulted as a guide for formulating other
　headings as needed.
Chicago (Ill.)—Antiquities   977.3
　　BT   Antiquities

Chicago (Ill.)—Bibliography   015.773;
　　　　　016.9773
Chicago (Ill.)—Bio-bibliography   012
Chicago (Ill.)—Biography   920.0773
　　BT   Biography
Chicago (Ill.)—Biography—Portraits
　　　　　920.0773
Chicago (Ill.)—Boundaries   977.3
　　BT   Boundaries
Chicago (Ill.)—Bridges
　　USE   Bridges—Chicago (Ill.)
Chicago (Ill.)—Census   317.73
　　BT   Census
Chicago (Ill.)—City planning
　　USE   City planning—Chicago (Ill.)
Chicago (Ill.)—Civil defense
　　USE   Civil defense—Chicago (Ill.)
Chicago (Ill.)—Climate   551.69773
　　BT   Climate
Chicago (Ill.)—Commerce   381
　　BT   Commerce
Chicago (Ill.)—Description
　　USE   Chicago (Ill.)—Description and
　　　　　travel
Chicago (Ill.)—Description and travel
　　　　　917.73
　　UF   Chicago (Ill.)—Description
Chicago (Ill.)—Description and travel—
　　　　　Guidebooks
　　USE   Chicago (Ill.)—Guidebooks
Chicago (Ill.)—Description and travel—
　　　　　Views
　　USE   Chicago (Ill.)—Pictorial works
Chicago (Ill.)—Directories   917.73
　　Use for lists of names and addresses. Lists
　of names without addresses are entered under
　Chicago (Ill.)—Registers.
　　BT   Directories
　　NT   Chicago (Ill.)—Telephone di-
　　　　　rectories
　　RT   Chicago (Ill.)—Registers
Chicago (Ill.)—Directories—Telephone
　　USE   Chicago (Ill.)—Telephone di-
　　　　　rectories
Chicago (Ill.)—Economic conditions
　　　　　330.9773
　　BT   Economic conditions
Chicago (Ill.)—Employees
　　USE   Chicago (Ill.)—Officials and
　　　　　employees

Chicago (Ill.)—Government
USE **Chicago (Ill.)—Politics and government**
Chicago (Ill.)—Government employees
USE **Chicago (Ill.)—Officials and employees**
Chicago (Ill.)—Government publications
USE **Government publications—Chicago (Ill.)**
Chicago (Ill.)—Guidebooks   917.73
UF Chicago (Ill.)—Description and travel—Guidebooks
Chicago (Ill.)—Historic buildings
USE **Historic buildings—Chicago (Ill.)**
Chicago (Ill.)—History   977.3
Chicago (Ill.)—History—Societies 977.3006
BT **History—Societies**
Chicago (Ill.)—Industries
USE **Industries—Chicago (Ill.)**
Chicago (Ill.)—Intellectual life   977.3
BT **Intellectual life**
Chicago (Ill.)—Manufactures
USE **Manufactures—Chicago (Ill.)**
Chicago (Ill.)—Maps   912.773
BT **Maps**
Chicago (Ill.)—Moral conditions   977.3
BT **Moral conditions**
Chicago (Ill.)—Occupations
USE **Occupations—Chicago (Ill.)**
Chicago (Ill.)—Officials and employees 352.1773
UF Chicago (Ill.)—Employees
Chicago (Ill.)—Government employees
Chicago (Ill.)—Pictorial works   917.73
UF Chicago (Ill.)—Description and travel—Views
Chicago (Ill.)—Politics and government 977.3
UF Chicago (Ill.)—Government
BT **Municipal government Politics**
Chicago (Ill.)—Popular culture
USE **Popular culture—Chicago (Ill.)**
Chicago (Ill.)—Population   304.609773
BT **Population**
Chicago (Ill.)—Public buildings
USE **Public buildings—Chicago (Ill.)**

Chicago (Ill.)—Public works
USE **Public works—Chicago (Ill.)**
Chicago (Ill.)—Race relations 305.8009773
BT **Race relations**
Chicago (Ill.)—Registers   917.73
Use for lists of names without addresses. Lists of names that include addresses are entered under **Chicago (Ill.)—Directories.**
RT **Chicago (Ill.)—Directories**
Chicago (Ill.)—Social conditions   977.3
BT **Social conditions**
Chicago (Ill.)—Social life and customs 977.3
BT **Manners and customs**
Chicago (Ill.)—Social policy
USE **Social policy—Chicago (Ill.)**
Chicago (Ill.)—Statistics   317.73
BT **Statistics**
Chicago (Ill.)—Streets
USE **Streets—Chicago (Ill.)**
Chicago (Ill.)—Suburbs and environs
USE **Chicago Suburban Area (Ill.)**
Chicago (Ill.)—Telephone directories 917.73
UF Chicago (Ill.)—Directories—Telephone
BT **Chicago (Ill.)—Directories**
Chicago (Ill.)—Urban renewal
USE **Urban renewal—Chicago (Ill.)**
Chicago Metropolitan Area (Ill.)   977.3
RT **Chicago Suburban Area (Ill.)**
Chicago Metropolitan Area (Ill.)—Politics and government   977.3
BT **Metropolitan government**
Chicago Suburban Area (Ill.)   977.3
UF Chicago (Ill.)—Suburbs and environs
RT **Chicago Metropolitan Area (Ill.)**
Chicanas
USE **Mexican American women**
Chicanery
USE **Deception**
Chicano literature (English)
USE **American literature—Mexican American authors**
Chicanos
USE **Mexican Americans**
Chicken pox
USE **Chickenpox**
Chickenpox   616.9

Chickenpox—*Continued*
- UF   Chicken pox
- BT   **Diseases**
        Viruses

Chickens (May subdiv. geog.)   **598.6; 636.5**
- BT   **Poultry**

Chief justices
- USE   **Judges**

Child abuse (May subdiv. geog.)   **305.23086; 362.76; 364.15**
- UF   Abuse of children
        Abused children
        Child neglect
        Children—Abuse
        Cruelty to children
- BT   **Child welfare**
        Domestic violence
        Parent-child relationship
- NT   **Child sexual abuse**
- RT   **Adult child abuse victims**

Child abuse survivors
- USE   **Adult child abuse victims**

Child actors (May subdiv. geog.)   **792.02; 791.4302**
- BT   **Actors**

Child-adult relationship   **305.23; 362.7; 649**
- UF   Adults and children
        Children and adults
- BT   **Children**
- NT   **Child rearing**
        Children and strangers
        Conflict of generations
        Parent-child relationship
        Teacher-student relationship

Child and father
- USE   **Father-child relationship**

Child and mother
- USE   **Mother-child relationship**

Child and parent
- USE   **Parent-child relationship**

Child artists (May subdiv. geog.)   **704; 709.2; 920**

Use for materials on children as artists and on works of art by children.
- UF   Children as artists
- BT   **Artists**
        Gifted children
- NT   **Finger painting**

Child authors   **809; 920**

Use for materials on children as authors and discussions of literary works written by children. Individual literary works and collections of literary works written by children are entered under the form heading **Children's writings**.
- UF   Children as authors
- BT   **Authors**
        Gifted children
- RT   **Children's writings**

Child behavior
- USE   **Child psychology**
        Children—Conduct of life
        Etiquette for children and teenagers

Child birth
- USE   **Childbirth**

Child care (May subdiv. geog.)   **649**
- UF   Care of children
        Children—Care
- NT   **Babysitting**
        Child rearing
        Day care centers
        Infants—Care
        Nannies

Child care centers
- USE   **Day care centers**

Child care services (May subdiv. geog.)   **362.7**
- BT   **Public welfare**
        Social work

Child custody (May subdiv. geog.)   **306.89; 346.01; 362.7**
- UF   Children—Custody
        Custody of children
        Joint custody of children
        Parental custody
        Shared custody
- BT   **Divorce mediation**
        Parent-child relationship
- NT   **Parental kidnapping**
- RT   **Visitation rights (Domestic relations)**

Child death
- USE   **Children—Death**

Child development   **155.4; 305.231; 612.6**
- UF   Child study
        Children—Development
- BT   **Children**
- NT   **Children—Growth**

Child development—*Continued*
    RT   **Child psychology**
           Child rearing
Child labor (May subdiv. geog.)   **331.3**
    UF   Children—Employment
           Employment of children
           Working children
    BT   **Age and employment**
           Child welfare
           Labor
           Social problems
Child labor—United States   **331.3**
Child molesting
    USE **Child sexual abuse**
Child mortality
    USE **Children—Mortality**
Child neglect
    USE **Child abuse**
Child placing
    USE **Adoption**
          Foster home care
Child pornography (May subdiv. geog.)
        363.4
    BT   **Pornography**
Child prostitution
    USE **Juvenile prostitution**
Child psychiatry   **616.89; 618.92**
    Use for materials on the clinical and therapeutic aspects of mental disorders in children. Materials on children suffering from mental or emotional illnesses are entered under **Emotionally distrubed children**.
    UF   Children—Mental health
           Pediatric psychiatry
    BT   **Psychiatry**
    NT   **Autism**
           Mentally handicapped children
    RT   **Child psychology**
           Emotionally disturbed children
Child psychology   **155.4**
    UF   Behavior of children
           Child behavior
           Child study
           Children—Psychology
    BT   **Psychology**
    NT   **Cognitive styles in children**
           Emotions in children
           Fear in children
           Imaginary playmates
           Intelligence tests
           Moral development
           Psychology of learning
           Separation anxiety in children

           Sibling rivalry
    RT   **Child development**
           Child psychiatry
           Child rearing
           Educational psychology
Child raising
    USE **Child rearing**
Child rearing (May subdiv. geog.)
        392.1; 649
    Use for materials on the principles and techniques of rearing children. Materials on the psychological and social interaction between parents and their minor children are entered under **Parent-child relationship**. Materials on the skills, attributes, and attitudes needed for parenthood are entered under **Parenting**.
    UF   Child raising
           Children—Management
           Children—Training
           Discipline of children
           Training of children
    BT   **Child-adult relationship**
           Child care
           Parent-child relationship
    NT   **Children's allowances**
           Socialization
           Toilet training
    RT   **Child development**
           Child psychology
           Parenting
Child sex abuse
    USE **Child sexual abuse**
Child sexual abuse (May subdiv. geog.)
        362.76; 364.15
    UF   Child molesting
           Child sex abuse
           Children—Molesting
           Molesting of children
           Sexual abuse
           Sexually abused children
    BT   **Child abuse**
           Incest
           Sex crimes
    RT   **Adult child sexual abuse victims**
Child snatching by parents
    USE **Parental kidnapping**
Child study
    USE **Child development**
          Child psychology
Child support (May subdiv. geog.)
        346.01

Child support—*Continued*
  UF Support of children
  BT **Child welfare**
     Desertion and nonsupport
     Divorce mediation
Child welfare (May subdiv. geog.) **362.7**
  Use for materials on the aid, support, and protection of children, by the state or by private welfare organizations.
  UF Aid to dependent children
     Children—Charities, protection, etc.
     Mothers' pensions
     Protection of children
  BT **Charities**
     Public welfare
     Social work
  NT **Abandoned children**
     Child abuse
     Child labor
     Child support
     Children—Institutional care
     Day care centers
     Foster home care
  RT **Children's hospitals**
     Juvenile delinquency
     Orphanages
Childbirth (May subdiv. geog.) **612.6;**
     618.2
  UF Birth
     Birth customs
     Child birth
     Labor (Childbirth)
     Obstetrics
  NT **Midwives**
     Multiple birth
     Natural childbirth
  RT **Pregnancy**
Childhood diseases
  USE **Children—Diseases**
Childlessness 306.85
  BT **Children**
     Family size
  RT **Birth control**
     Human fertility
     Infertility
Children (May subdiv. geog.) **305.23**
  Use for materials on people from birth through age twelve. Materials limited to the first two years of a child's life are entered under **Infants**.
  UF Preschool children

  SA children of particular racial or ethnic groups, e.g. **African American children**; children and other subjects, e.g. **Children and war**; and names of wars with the subdivision *Children*, e.g. **World War, 1939-1945—Children** [to be added as needed]
  BT **Age**
     Family
  NT **Abandoned children**
     Adopted children
     Advertising and children
     African American children
     Birth order
     Black children
     Boys
     Child-adult relationship
     Child development
     Childlessness
     Children and war
     Children of alcoholics
     Children of divorced parents
     Children of drug addicts
     Children of gay parents
     Children of immigrants
     Children of single parents
     Children of working parents
     Computers and children
     Exceptional children
     Father-child relationship
     Foster children
     Girls
     Handicapped children
     Infants
     Internet and children
     Missing children
     Mother-child relationship
     Motion pictures and children
     Native American children
     Only child
     Orphans
     Parent-child relationship
     Runaway children
     School children
     Stepchildren
     Television and children
Children, Abnormal
  USE **Handicapped children**

Children—Abuse
USE **Child abuse**

Children—Adoption
USE **Adoption**

Children and adults
USE **Child-adult relationship**

Children and advertising
USE **Advertising and children**

Children and death   155.9

Use for materials on children's experiences with, conceptions of, and reactions to death. Materials on the death of children are entered under **Children—Death**. Materials on children's death rates and causes are entered under **Children—Mortality**.

UF   Death and children

BT   **Death**

Children and motion pictures
USE **Motion pictures and children**

Children and strangers   362.7

UF   Infants and strangers
        Strangers and children

BT   **Child-adult relationship**

Children and television
USE **Television and children**

Children and the Internet
USE **Internet and children**

Children and war (May subdiv. geog.)   305.23

UF   War and children

SA   names of particular wars with the subdivision *Children*, e.g. **World War, 1939-1945—Children** [to be added as needed]

BT   **Children**
        War

NT   **World War, 1939-1945—Children**

Children as artists
USE **Child artists**

Children as authors
USE **Child authors**

Children as consumers
USE **Young consumers**

Children, Black
USE **Black children**

Children—Books and reading (May subdiv. geog.)   011.62; 028.5

Use for materials on the reading interests of children and lists of books for children. Collections or materials about literature published for children are entered under **Children's lit-**

erature. Individual literary works and collections of literary works written by children are entered under **Children's writings**. Materials about works written by children and materials about children as authors are entered under **Child authors**.

UF   Books and reading for children
        Children's reading
        Reading interests of children

BT   **Books and reading**

Children—Care
USE **Child care**

Children—Charities, protection, etc.
USE **Child welfare**

Children—Civil rights (May subdiv. geog.)   323.3; 342

BT   **Civil rights**

Children—Clothing
USE **Children's clothing**

Children—Conduct of life   173

UF   Behavior of children
        Child behavior

BT   **Conduct of life**

NT   **Etiquette for children and teenagers**

Children—Costume
USE **Children's costumes**

Children, Crippled
USE **Physically handicapped children**

Children—Custody
USE **Child custody**

Children—Day care
USE **Day care centers**

Children—Death   306.9

Use for materials on the death of children. Materials on children's experiences with, conceptions of, and reactions to death are entered under **Children and death**. Materials on children's death rates and causes are entered under **Children—Mortality**.

UF   Child death

BT   **Death**

RT   **Terminally ill children**

Children—Death—Causes
USE **Children—Mortality**

Children—Death rate
USE **Children—Mortality**

Children—Defense
USE **Self-defense for children**

Children—Dental care (May subdiv. geog.)   617.6

Children—Development
USE **Child development**

Children—Diseases (May subdiv. geog.)
618.92
- UF Childhood diseases
  Children's diseases
  Diseases of children
  Medicine, Pediatric
  Pediatrics
- SA types of diseases, e.g.
  Chickenpox [to be added as needed]
- BT **Diseases**
- RT **Children—Health and hygiene**

Children—Education
- USE **Elementary education**
  Preschool education

Children—Employment
- USE **Child labor**

Children—Etiquette
- USE **Etiquette for children and teenagers**

Children—Food
- USE **Children—Nutrition**

Children, Gifted
- USE **Gifted children**

Children—Growth   155.4; 612.6
- RT **Child development**

Children—Health and hygiene (May subdiv. geog.)   **613**
- UF Children—Hygiene
  Pediatrics
- BT **Health**
  Hygiene
- NT **Children—Nutrition**
  Children—Physical fitness
  School hygiene
- RT **Children—Diseases**
  Children's hospitals
  Health education

Children—Hospitals
- USE **Children's hospitals**

Children—Hygiene
- USE **Children—Health and hygiene**

Children, Hyperactive
- USE **Hyperactive children**

Children in art   704.9

Use for materials on children depicted in works of art. Materials on children as artists are entered under **Child artists**.
- BT **Art—Themes**

Children in literature   809

Use for materials on the theme of children in works of literature. Individual literary works or collections of literary works written by children are entered under the form heading **Children's writings**. Materials about children as authors and about works written by children are entered under **Child authors**.
- BT **Literature—Themes**

Children—Institutional care (May subdiv. geog.)   **362.73**
- UF Boys' towns
  Children's homes
- BT **Child welfare**
  Institutional care
- NT **Day care centers**
  Orphanages
  Reformatories
- RT **Foster home care**

Children—Language   155.4
- BT **Language and languages**

Children—Management
- USE **Child rearing**

Children—Medical examinations (May subdiv. geog.)   **616.07**
- UF Medical inspection in schools
  School children—Medical examinations

Children—Mental health
- USE **Child psychiatry**

Children—Molesting
- USE **Child sexual abuse**

Children—Mortality (May subdiv. geog.)
304.6

Use for material on children's death rates and causes. Material on children's experiences with, conceptions of, and reactions to death are entered under **Children and death**. Materials on the death of children are entered under **Children—Death**.
- UF Child mortality
  Children—Death—Causes
  Children—Death rate
- BT **Mortality**

Children—Nutrition (May subdiv. geog.)
613.2083; 641.1083; 649
- UF Children—Food
  Children's food
- BT **Children—Health and hygiene**
  Nutrition
- NT **School children—Food**

Children of alcoholics   362.292
- UF Alcoholic parents
  COAs
- BT **Children**
- NT **Adult children of alcoholics**
- RT **Alcoholics**

Children of divorced parents   306.874;
        646.7
   BT   **Children**
        Divorce
        Parent-child relationship
   RT   **Part-time parenting**
Children of drug addicts   362.29
   UF   Children of narcotic addicts
        Cocaine babies
        Crack babies
   BT   **Children**
        Drug addicts
Children of gay parents (May subdiv.
        geog.)   **306.874**
   BT   **Children**
   RT   **Gay parents**
Children of immigrants (May subdiv.
        geog.)   **305.23**
   UF   First generation children
   BT   **Children**
        Immigration and emigration
Children of narcotic addicts
   USE   **Children of drug addicts**
Children of single fathers
   USE   **Children of single parents**
Children of single mothers
   USE   **Children of single parents**
Children of single parents   306.874
   UF   Children of single fathers
        Children of single mothers
        Single parents' children
   BT   **Children**
        Single parents
Children of working parents   306.874;
        362.7
   UF   Working parents' children
   BT   **Children**
        Parent-child relationship
   NT   **Latchkey children**
Children—Physical fitness (May subdiv.
        geog.)   **613.7**
   BT   **Children—Health and hygiene**
        Physical fitness
Children—Placing out
   USE   **Adoption**
        Foster home care
Children—Psychology
   USE   **Child psychology**
Children, Retarded
   USE   **Mentally handicapped children**

Children—Self-defense
   USE   **Self-defense for children**
Children—Socialization
   USE   **Socialization**
Children—Surgery   617
   UF   Pediatric surgery
   BT   **Surgery**
Children—Training
   USE   **Child rearing**
Children—United States   305.230973
Children's allowances   332.024; 649
   UF   Allowances, Children's
   BT   **Child rearing**
        Money
        Personal finance
   RT   **Money-making projects for
        children**
Children's art (May subdiv. geog.)
        704.083
   BT   **Art**
Children's books
   USE   **Children's literature**
Children's clothing (May subdiv. geog.)
        391; 646.4
     Use for materials on children's clothing that
is worn from day to day, including historical
materials. Works on children's costumes for
fancy dress or theatricals are entered under
Children's costumes.
   UF   Children—Clothing
   BT   **Clothing and dress**
   NT   **Infants' clothing**
   RT   **Children's costumes**
Children's costumes (May subdiv. geog.)
        646.4; 792
     Use for materials on children's costumes for
fancy dress or theatricals. Materials on chil-
dren's clothing that is worn from day to day
are entered under **Children's clothing**.
   UF   Children—Costume
   BT   **Costume**
   RT   **Children's clothing**
Children's courts
   USE   **Juvenile courts**
Children's day care centers
   USE   **Day care centers**
Children's diseases
   USE   **Children—Diseases**
Children's food
   USE   **Children—Nutrition**
Children's homes
   USE   **Children—Institutional care**
Children's hospitals (May subdiv. geog.)
        362.11

Children's hospitals—*Continued*
  UF   Children—Hospitals
  BT   **Hospitals**
  RT   **Child welfare**
       Children—Health and hygiene
Children's libraries (May subdiv. geog.)
    027.62
  UF   Libraries and children
       Library services to children
  BT   **Libraries**
  RT   **Libraries and schools**
Children's literature 808.8

    Use for collections or materials about literature published for children. Materials on the reading interests of children and lists of books for children are entered under **Children—Books and reading**. Individual literary works and collections of literary works written by children are entered under **Children's writings**. Materials about works written by children and materials about children as authors are entered under **Child authors**.

  UF   Books for children
       Children's books
       Juvenile literature
  SA   subjects and personal, corporate, and place names with the subdivision *Juvenile literature*, for non-fiction materials e.g. **Computers—Juvenile literature**; and with the subdivisions *Juvenile fiction*; *Juvenile poetry*; and *Juvenile drama*; for materials in those forms, e.g. **Christmas—Juvenile fiction**; **Christmas—Juvenile poetry**; **Christmas—Juvenile drama**; etc. [to be added as needed]
  BT   **Literature**
  NT   **Big books**
       Caldecott Medal
       Children's plays
       Children's poetry
       Children's stories
       Coretta Scott King Award
       Easy reading materials
       Fairy tales
       Newbery Medal
       Picture books for children
       Plot-your-own stories
       Reading materials
       Storytelling

Children's literature—Book reviews
    808.8
Children's literature—History and criticism 809
Children's moneymaking projects
  USE **Money-making projects for children**
Children's parties 395.3; 793.2
  BT   **Amusements**
       Entertaining
       Parties
Children's playhouses 690
  BT   **Buildings**
Children's plays 808.82

    Use for individual works, collections, or materials about plays for children. Materials about plays for production in colleges and schools are entered under **College and school drama**. Individual works and collections of plays written by children are entered under **Children's writings**. Materials about plays written by children are entered under **Child authors**.

  UF   Plays for children
       School plays
  SA   subjects and personal, corporate, and place names with the subdivision *Juvenile drama*, e.g. **Christmas—Juvenile drama** [to be added as needed]
  BT   **Amateur theater**
       Children's literature
       Drama
       Theater
Children's poetry 808.81

    Use for individual poems, collections, or materials about poetry written for children. Individual works and collections of poetry written by children are entered under **Children's writings**. Materials about poetry written by children are entered under **Child authors**.

  UF   Poetry for children
  SA   subjects and personal, corporate, and place names with the subdivision *Juvenile poetry*; e.g. **Christmas—Juvenile poetry** [to be added as needed]
  BT   **Children's literature**
       Poetry
  NT   **Children's songs**
       Lullabies
       Nonsense verses
       Nursery rhymes
       Tongue twisters

Children's reading
USE **Children—Books and reading**
Reading
Children's secrets   155.4
BT **Secrecy**
Children's songs (May subdiv. geog.)
782.42
Use for collections of songs that contain both words and music, and for materials about songs for children. Collections of songs without the music are entered under **Children's poetry**.
UF Songs for children
BT **Children's poetry**
School songbooks
Songs
NT **Lullabies**
Nursery rhymes
Children's stories   808.3; 808.83
Use for individual stories and collections of stories written for children. Individual works and collections of stories written by children are entered under **Children's writings**. Materials about stories written by children are entered under **Child authors**.
UF Fiction for children
Stories for children
SA subjects and personal, corporate, and place names with the subdivision *Juvenile fiction*, e.g. **Christmas—Juvenile fiction** [to be added as needed]
BT **Children's literature**
Fiction
Children's writings   808.8
Use for individual literary works or collections of literary works written by children. Materials on children as authors and discussions of literary works written by children are entered under **Child authors**. Collections of works published for children are entered under **Children's literature**.
UF School prose
School verse
RT **Child authors**
College and school journalism
Chile   983
May be subdivided like **United States** except for *History*.
Chimes
USE **Bells**
Chimneys (May subdiv. geog.)   697; 721
UF Smoke stacks
BT **Architecture—Details**
Buildings
RT **Fireplaces**

Chimpanzees (May subdiv. geog.)
599.85
UF Chimps
BT **Apes**
Chimps
USE **Chimpanzees**
China   951
May be subdivided like **United States** except for *History*. Use for materials dealing with mainland China, regardless of time period, or with the People's Republic of China, or for comprehensive materials on China including Taiwan. Materials dealing with the island of Taiwan, regardless of time period, or with the post-1948 Republic of China are entered under **Taiwan**.
UF China (People's Republic of China)
People's Republic of China
China—History   951
China—History—1912-1949   951.04
China—History—1949-   951.05
China—History—1949-1976   951.05
China—History—1976-   951.05
China—History—1989, Tiananmen Square Incident
USE **Tiananmen Square Incident, Beijing (China), 1989**
China painting   738.1
UF Porcelain painting
BT **Decoration and ornament**
Painting
Porcelain
China (People's Republic of China)
USE **China**
China (Porcelain)
USE **Porcelain**
China (Republic)
USE **Taiwan**
Chinaware
USE **Porcelain**
Chinese Americans (May subdiv. geog.)
305.895; 973
BT **Ethnic groups**
Chinese cooking   641.5953
BT **Cooking**
Chinese language   495.1
BT **Language and languages**
Chinese literature   895.1
BT **Literature**
NT **Chinese poetry**
Chinese medicine   610
BT **Medicine**
Chinese mythology   299.5

Chinese mythology—*Continued*
    BT   Mythology
Chinese New Year (May subdiv. geog.)
    394.261
    BT   **Holidays**
Chinese poetry   895.1
    BT   **Chinese literature**
          Poetry
Chipmunks   599.36
    BT   **Mammals**
          Squirrels
Chiropody
    USE **Podiatry**
Chiropractic   615.5
    BT   **Alternative medicine**
          Massage
    RT   **Naturopathy**
          Osteopathic medicine
Chivalry (May subdiv. geog.)   **394**
    BT   **Manners and customs**
    NT   **Medieval tournaments**
    RT   **Crusades**
          Feudalism
          Heraldry
          Knights and knighthood
          Medieval civilization
          Romances
Chivalry—Romances
    USE **Romances**
Chocolate   641.3
    BT   **Food**
    RT   **Cocoa**
          Desserts
Choice, Freedom of
    USE **Free will and determinism**
Choice of books
    USE **Best books**
          Book selection
          Books and reading
Choice of college
    USE **College choice**
Choice of profession, occupation, vocation,
    etc.
    USE **Vocational guidance**
Choice of school
    USE **School choice**
Choice of sex of offspring
    USE **Sex preselection**
Choice (Psychology)   153.8
    BT   **Psychology**
    NT   **Commitment (Psychology)**
    RT   **Decision making**

Choirs (Music) (May subdiv. geog.)
    782.5
    BT   **Church music**
    RT   **Choral conducting**
          Choral music
          Choral societies
          Singing
Cholesterol   572
    RT   **Low-cholesterol diet**
Cholesterol content of food
    USE **Food—Cholesterol content**
Choose-your-own story plots
    USE **Plot-your-own stories**
Choral conducting (May subdiv. geog.)
    782.5
    UF   Conducting, Choral
    BT   **Conducting**
    RT   **Choirs (Music)**
          Choral music
          Conductors (Music)
Choral music   782.5
    UF   Music, Choral
    BT   **Church music**
          Vocal music
    NT   **Cantatas**
    RT   **Choirs (Music)**
          Choral conducting
          Choral societies
Choral societies (May subdiv. geog.)
    782.506
    UF   Singing societies
    BT   **Societies**
    RT   **Choirs (Music)**
          Choral music
Choral speaking   808.5
    UF   Speaking choirs
          Unison speaking
    BT   **Drama**
          Recitations
Christ
    USE **Jesus Christ**
Christening
    USE **Baptism**
Christian antiquities (May subdiv. geog.)
    225.9; 270; 930.1
    UF   Christian archeology
          Church antiquities
          Ecclesiastical antiquities
    BT   **Antiquities**
    NT   **Catacombs**
    RT   **Christian art**

Christian archeology
  USE **Christian antiquities**
Christian art (May subdiv. geog.) **246;
  704.9**
  UF Christian art and symbolism
      Ecclesiastical art
  BT **Art**
      Religious art
  NT **Icons (Religion)**
      Jesus Christ—Art
      Mary—Art
  RT **Christian antiquities**
      Christian symbolism
      Gothic art
Christian art and symbolism
  USE **Christian art**
       Christian symbolism
Christian biography **270.092; 920**
  UF Christianity—Biography
      Christians—Biography
      Ecclesiastical biography
  BT **Biography**
      Religious biography
  NT **Fathers of the church**
Christian civilization **270; 909**
  UF Civilization, Christian
  BT **Christianity**
      Civilization
Christian denominations
  USE **Christian sects**
Christian devotional calendars
  USE **Devotional calendars**
Christian doctrinal theology
  USE **Christianity—Doctrines**
Christian doctrine
  USE **Christianity—Doctrines**
Christian education (May subdiv. geog.)
  268
  Use for materials on the instruction of
  Christian religion in schools and private life.
  General materials on the instruction of reli-
  gion in schools and private life are entered
  under **Religious education**. Materials on the
  relation of the church to education and materi-
  als on the history of the part that the church
  has taken in secular education are entered un-
  der **Church and education**. Materials on
  church supported and controlled elementary
  and secondary schools are entered under
  Church schools.
  UF Education, Christian
  BT **Religious education**
  RT **Church and education**
Christian ethics **241**

  UF Christian moral theology
      Moral theology, Christian
  BT **Ethics**
  NT **Conscience**
  RT **Christian life**
Christian fasts and feasts
  USE **Christian holidays**
Christian fiction **808.83**
  Use for individual works, collections, or
  materials about fiction that promotes Christian
  teachings or exemplifies a Christian way of
  life.
  BT **Fiction**
      Religious fiction
Christian fundamentalism (May subdiv.
  geog.) **230; 270.8**
  Use for materials on the modern conserva-
  tive movement in Protestantism emphasizing
  literal interpretation of the Bible, as opposed
  to religious liberalism, modernism, or evolu-
  tionism.
  UF Fundamentalism
      Modernist-fundamentalist contro-
        versy
  BT **Christianity—Doctrines**
      Religious fundamentalism
  RT **Modernism (Theology)**
Christian heresies (May subdiv. geog.)
  273
  UF Heresies, Christian
  BT **Doctrinal theology**
      Heresy
Christian holidays **263; 394.266**
  UF Christian fasts and feasts
      Christian holy days
      Fasts and feasts—Christianity
  SA names of Christian holidays, e.g.
      Christmas [to be added as
        needed]
  BT **Church year**
      Religious holidays
  NT **Christmas**
      Easter
      Epiphany
      Good Friday
Christian holy days
  USE **Christian holidays**
Christian-Jewish relations
  USE **Christianity—Relations—Juda-
        ism**
       **Judaism—Relations—Christian-
        ity**
Christian legends (May subdiv. geog.)
  270.9; 398.2

Christian legends—*Continued*
   BT   **Legends**
Christian life   **248.4**
   UF   Religious life (Christian)
   BT   **Religious life**
   RT   **Christian ethics**
Christian life—Sermons   **252**
   BT   **Sermons**
Christian literature   **230**
   BT   **Religious literature**
   NT   **Catholic literature**
          Early Christian literature
          Papal encyclicals
          Sermons
Christian literature—30-600, Early
   USE   **Early Christian literature**
Christian literature, Early
   USE   **Early Christian literature**
Christian ministry (May subdiv. geog.)
   253
   BT   **Ministry**
Christian missionaries (May subdiv.
   geog.)   **266.0092; 920**
   UF   Missionaries, Christian
   RT   **Christian missions**
Christian missions (May subdiv. geog.)
   266
   UF   Foreign missions, Christian
          Home missions, Christian
          Missions, Christian
   SA   names of Christian churches, de-
          nominations, religious orders,
          etc., with the subdivision *Mis-*
          sions, e.g. **Catholic Church—**
          Missions; and names of peo-
          ples evangelized with the sub-
          division *Christian missions,*
          e.g. **Native Americans—**
          Christian missions [to be
          added as needed]
   BT   **Christianity**
          Church history
          Church work
   NT   **Catholic Church—Missions**
          Native Americans—Christian
          missions
          Salvation Army
   RT   **Christian missionaries**
          Evangelistic work
Christian moral theology
   USE   **Christian ethics**

Christian names
   USE   **Personal names**
Christian-owned business enterprises
   (May subdiv. geog.)   **338.7**
   BT   **Business enterprises**
Christian philosophy   **190; 230.01**
      Use for materials on philosophy as prac-
      ticed by Christian philosophers or on the na-
      ture, origins, or validity of Christian beliefs
      from a philosophical point of view.
   UF   Christianity—Philosophy
   BT   **Philosophy**
Christian saints (May subdiv. geog.)
   270.092; 920
   BT   **Saints**
   NT   **Apostles**
          Canonization
Christian Science (May subdiv. geog.)
   289.5
   UF   Church of Christ, Scientist
   BT   **Christian sects**
   RT   **Spiritual healing**
Christian sects (May subdiv. geog.)   **280**
   UF   Christian denominations
          Church denominations
          Denominations, Christian
   SA   names of Christian sects, e.g.
          Presbyterian Church [to be
          added as needed]
   BT   **Christianity**
          Church history
          Sects
   NT   **Amish**
          Baptists
          Catholic Church
          Christian Science
          Christian union
          Church of England
          Church of Jesus Christ of Lat-
          ter-day Saints
          Community churches
          Congregationalism
          Eastern churches
          Ecumenical movement
          Episcopal Church
          Greek Orthodox Church
          Huguenots
          Interdenominational coopera-
          tion
          Mennonites
          Moravians
          Non-institutional churches

Christian sects—*Continued*
>Orthodox Eastern Church
>Pentecostal churches
>Presbyterian Church
>Protestant churches
>Puritans
>Russian Orthodox Church
>Salvation Army
>Shakers
>Society of Friends
>Unitarianism

Christian sects—Government
>USE **Church polity**

Christian sociology (May subdiv. geog.)
>**261**

Use for materials on social theory from a Christian point of view. Materials on religious sociology in general are entered under **Religion and sociology**. Materials on the practical treatment of social problems from the point of view of the church are entered under **Church and social problems**.

>UF Sociology, Christian
>BT **Religion and sociology**
>>**Sociology**
>RT **Christianity and economics**
>>**Church and social problems**

Christian symbolism (May subdiv. geog.)
>**246; 704.9**
>UF Christian art and symbolism
>BT **Symbolism**
>RT **Christian art**

Christian union (May subdiv. geog.)
>**280**

Use for materials on prospective and actual mergers within and across denominational lines. Materials on unity as one of the marks of the church are entered under **Church—Unity**. Materials on a movement originating in the twentieth century aimed at promoting church cooperation and unity are entered under **Ecumenical movement**. Materials on religious activities planned and conducted cooperatively by two or more Christian sects are entered under **Interdenominational cooperation**.

>UF Christian unity
>>Christianity—Union between churches
>>Ecumenism
>BT **Christian sects**
>>**Church**
>RT **Ecumenical movement**

Christian unity
>USE **Christian union**
>>**Church—Unity**

>Ecumenical movement
>Interdenominational cooperation

Christian year
>USE **Church year**

Christianity (May subdiv. geog.) **230**
>SA names of Christian churches and sects, e.g. **Catholic Church**; **Huguenots**; etc.; and Christianity and other subjects, e.g. **Christianity and economics** [to be added as needed]
>BT **Religions**
>NT **Atonement—Christianity**
>>**Catholic Church**
>>**Christian civilization**
>>**Christian missions**
>>**Christian sects**
>>**Christianity and economics**
>>**Councils and synods**
>>**Counter-Reformation**
>>**Eastern churches**
>>**Pentecostalism**
>>**Protestantism**
>>**Reformation**
>RT **Christians**
>>**Church**

Christianity and economics (May subdiv. geog.) **261.8**
>UF Economics and Christianity
>BT **Christianity**
>>**Economics**
>RT **Christian sociology**
>>**Church and labor**

Christianity and evolution
>USE **Creationism**

Christianity and other religions **261.2**

Use for materials on the relations between Christianity and several other religions. Materials on the relations between Christianity and one other religion are entered under **Christianity** subdivided by *Relations* further subdivided by the other religion, and also under the other religion subdivided by *Relations—Christianity*, e.g. **Christianity—Relations—Judaism** and **Judaism—Relations—Christianity**. The same pattern is followed for sects and denominations.

>UF Comparative religion
>BT **Religions**
>NT **Christianity—Relations—Judaism**
>>**Judaism—Relations—Christianity**

Christianity and other religions—*Continued*

    Paganism

Christianity and other religions—Judaism
    USE   **Christianity—Relations—Judaism**
        Judaism—Relations—Christianity

Christianity and politics (May subdiv. geog.) **261.7; 322**
    UF   Christianity—Political aspects
        Politics and Christianity
    BT   **Church and state**
        Religion and politics

Christianity—Apologetic works **239**

    Use for materials defending Christianity. Materials attacking Christianity are entered under **Christianity—Controversial literature**.

    BT   **Apologetics**

Christianity—Biography
    USE   **Christian biography**

Christianity—Controversial literature **239**

    Use for materials attacking Christianity. Materials defending Christianity are entered under **Christianity—Apologetic works**.

Christianity—Doctrines **230**
    UF   Christian doctrinal theology
        Christian doctrine
    BT   **Doctrinal theology**
    NT   **Christian fundamentalism**
        Creationism
        God—Christianity
        Liberation theology
        Modernism (Theology)
        Regeneration (Christianity)
        Trinity

Christianity—Government
    USE   **Church polity**

Christianity—History
    USE   **Church history**

Christianity—Origin
    USE   **Church history—30-600, Early church**

Christianity—Philosophy
    USE   **Christian philosophy**

Christianity—Political aspects
    USE   **Christianity and politics**

Christianity—Polity
    USE   **Church polity**

Christianity—Psychology **230.01; 253.5**
    BT   **Psychology of religion**

Christianity—Relations—Judaism
    261.2; 296.3

    Use for materials on the relations between Christianity and Judaism. When assigning this heading, provide an additional subject entry under **Judaism—Relations—Christianity**.

    UF   Christian-Jewish relations
        Christianity and other religions—Judaism
        Jewish-Christian relations
    BT   **Christianity and other religions**
        Judaism

Christianity—Union between churches
    USE   **Christian union**

Christians (May subdiv. geog.) **270.092**
    RT   **Christianity**

Christians—Biography
    USE   **Christian biography**

Christians—Persecutions (May subdiv. geog.) **272**
    BT   **Church history**
        Persecution

Christmas (May subdiv. geog.) **263; 394.2663**
    BT   **Christian holidays**
        Holidays
    NT   **Christmas entertainments**
        Santa Claus

Christmas cards (May subdiv. geog.) **741.6; 745.594**
    BT   **Greeting cards**

Christmas carols
    USE   **Carols**

Christmas cooking (May subdiv. geog.) **641.5**
    BT   **Cooking**

Christmas decorations (May subdiv. geog.) **394.2663; 745.594**
    UF   Christmas ornaments
    BT   **Decoration and ornament**
    NT   **Christmas trees**

Christmas—Drama **394.2663; 792; 808.82**

    Use for collections of plays about Christmas.

    UF   Christmas plays

Christmas entertainments (May subdiv. geog.) **394.2663; 791**
    BT   **Amusements**
        Christmas

Christmas—Fiction **808.83**

    Use for collections of stories about Christmas.

Christmas—Fiction—*Continued*
UF Christmas stories

Christmas—Juvenile drama   808.82
Use for collections of plays about Christmas written for children.

Christmas—Juvenile fiction   808.83
Use for collections of stories about Christmas written for children.

Christmas—Juvenile poetry   808.81
Use for collections of poems about Christmas written for children.

Christmas ornaments
USE **Christmas decorations**

Christmas plays
USE **Christmas—Drama**

Christmas poetry
USE **Christmas—Poetry**

Christmas—Poetry   808.81
Use for collections of poems about Christmas.
UF Christmas poetry

Christmas stories
USE **Christmas—Fiction**

Christmas tree growing (May subdiv. geog.)   **635.9**
UF Growing of Christmas trees
BT **Forests and forestry**
RT **Christmas trees**

Christmas trees (May subdiv. geog.)
394.2663; 745.594
BT **Christmas decorations**
Trees
RT **Christmas tree growing**

Christmas—United States   394.2663

Christology
USE **Jesus Christ**

Chromosome mapping
USE **Gene mapping**

Chromosomes   572.8
BT **Genetics**
Heredity
NT **Genetic recombination**

Chronic diseases (May subdiv. geog.)
616
UF Diseases, Chronic
BT **Diseases**
NT **Chronic pain**

Chronic fatigue syndrome   616
BT **Diseases**

Chronic pain   616
UF Persistent pain
BT **Chronic diseases**
Pain

Chronicle history (Drama)
USE **Historical drama**

Chronicle plays
USE **Historical drama**

Chronology   529
Use for materials on the science that deals with measuring time by regular divisions and that assigns proper dates to events.
SA individual persons, wars, sacred works, topics that are inherently historical, and topics not subdivided by *History*, such as art, music, literature, etc., with the subdivision *Chronology*, e.g. **Bible—Chronology**; and ethnic groups, corporate bodies, military services, topics not inherently historical, and names of places with the subdivision *History—Chronology*, e.g. **Native Americans—History—Chronology** [to be added as needed]
BT **Astronomy**
History
Time
NT **Bible—Chronology**
Day
Historical chronology
Months
Night
Week
RT **Almanacs**

Chronology, Historical
USE **Historical chronology**

Church   260
Use for materials on the concept and function of the Christian Church as a whole.
SA church and other subjects, e.g. **Church and education** [to be added as needed]
BT **Theology**
NT **Christian union**
Church and education
Church and social problems
Church and state
Church polity
Church work
Clergy
Ecclesiastical law
Ecumenical movement
Laity

Church—*Continued*
>
> **Sacraments**
>
> RT **Christianity**

Church and education (May subdiv.
>
> geog.) **261**

Use for materials on the relation of the
church to education in general, and for materials on the history of the part that the church
has taken in secular education. Materials on
church supported and controlled elementary
and secondary schools are entered under
Church schools. Materials on the instruction
of religion in schools and private life are entered under Religious education, and of Christian religion under **Christian education**.

> UF Education and church
>
> Education and religion
>
> Fundamentalism and education
>
> Religion and education
>
> BT **Church**
>
> **Education**
>
> NT **Religion in the public schools**
>
> RT **Christian education**

Church and labor (May subdiv. geog.)
>
> **261.8**

> UF Labor and the church
>
> BT **Labor**
>
> RT **Christianity and economics**

Church and race relations (May subdiv.
>
> geog.) **261.8**

> UF Integrated churches
>
> Race relations and the church
>
> BT **Church work**

Church and social problems (May
>
> subdiv. geog.) **261.8**

Use for materials on the practical treatment
of social problems from the point of view of
the church. Materials on social theory from a
Christian point of view are entered under
Christian sociology. Materials on religious
sociology in general are entered under **Religion and sociology**.

> UF Religion and social problems
>
> Social problems and the church
>
> BT **Church**
>
> **Social problems**
>
> NT **Liberation theology**
>
> **Sanctuary movement**
>
> RT **Christian sociology**
>
> **Church work**

Church and state (May subdiv. geog.)
>
> **201; 261.7; 322**

> UF Church—Government policy
>
> Religion and state
>
> Religion—Government policy
>
> Separation of church and state

> BT **Church**
>
> **State, The**
>
> NT **Christianity and politics**
>
> **Religion in the public schools**
>
> **Theocracy**

Church and state—United States **322**

> UF United States—Church and state

Church antiquities

> USE **Christian antiquities**

Church architecture (May subdiv. geog.)
>
> **726.5**

> UF Ecclesiastical architecture
>
> BT **Architecture**
>
> NT **Abbeys**
>
> **Monasteries**
>
> **Spires**
>
> RT **Cathedrals**
>
> **Church buildings**
>
> **Gothic architecture**

Church attendance

> USE **Public worship**

Church bells

> USE **Bells**

Church buildings (May subdiv. geog.)
>
> **726.5**

Use for general descriptive and historical
materials on church buildings that cannot be
entered under **Church architecture**.

> UF Churches
>
> SA names of individual churches,
>
> e.g. **Westminster Abbey** [to
>
> be added as needed]
>
> BT **Buildings**
>
> NT **Cathedrals**
>
> **Westminster Abbey**
>
> RT **Church architecture**

Church buildings—United States
>
> **726.50973**

Church councils

> USE **Councils and synods**

Church denominations

> USE **Christian sects**
>
> **Sects**

Church entertainments (May subdiv.
>
> geog.) **253.7**

> UF Church sociables
>
> Socials
>
> BT **Amusements**
>
> **Church work**

Church fathers

> USE **Fathers of the church**

Church festivals
  USE **Religious holidays**
Church finance (May subdiv. geog.)
      254; 262.0068
  BT **Finance**
  NT **Tithes**
Church furniture (May subdiv. geog.)
      247
  UF Ecclesiastical furniture
  BT **Furniture**
Church government
  USE **Church polity**
Church—Government policy
  USE **Church and state**
Church history   270
   Use for materials dealing with the develop-
   ment of Christianity and church organization.
  UF Christianity—History
      Ecclesiastical history
      Religious history
  SA names of countries, states, etc.
      with the subdivision *Church
      history*, e.g. **United States—
      Church history**; and names
      of individual denominations,
      sects, churches, etc. [to be
      added as needed]
  BT **History**
  NT **Christian missions**
      Christian sects
      Christians—Persecutions
      Councils and synods
      Martyrs
      Monasteries
      Ohio—Church history
      Papacy
      Popes
      Popes—Temporal power
      Protestant churches
      Protestantism
      Sects
      United States—Church history
Church history—30-600, Early church
      270.1
  UF Apostolic Church
      Christianity—Origin
      Early church history
      Primitive Christianity
  NT **Apostles**
      Gnosticism
  RT **Catacombs**
      Early Christian literature

Church history—600-1500, Middle Ages
      270.3
  UF Medieval church history
  BT **Middle Ages**
  NT **Crusades**
Church history—1500-, Modern period
      270.6
  UF Modern church history
  NT **Counter-Reformation**
      Reformation
Church history—Ohio
  USE **Ohio—Church history**
Church history—United States
  USE **United States—Church history**
Church law
  USE **Ecclesiastical law**
Church libraries (May subdiv. geog.)
      027.6
  UF Parish libraries
  BT **Libraries**
Church music (May subdiv. geog.)
      781.71
   This heading may be subdivided by religion
   or denomination as needed.
  UF Religious music
      Sacred music
  SA types of church music, e.g.
      Hymns [to be added as need-
      ed]
  BT **Music**
  NT **Carols**
      Chants (Plain, Gregorian, etc.)
      Choirs (Music)
      Choral music
      Gospel music
      Hymnals
      Hymns
      Oratorio
      Organ music
  RT **Liturgies**
Church of Christ, Scientist
  USE **Christian Science**
Church of England (May subdiv. geog.)
      283
  UF Anglican Church
      England, Church of
  BT **Christian sects**
Church of England—Government   283
Church of England—United States   283
   Use for materials on the Episcopal Church
   in the United States prior to 1789. Materials

Church of England—United States—_Continued_

on the Episcopal Church in the United States after 1789 are entered under **Episcopal Church**.

　RT　**Episcopal Church**
　　　　Puritans

Church of Jesus Christ of Latter-day Saints (May subdiv. geog.)　**289.3**

　UF　Latter-day Saints
　　　　Mormon Church

　BT　**Christian sects**

　RT　**Mormons**

Church polity　262

　UF　Christian sects—Government
　　　　Christianity—Government
　　　　Christianity—Polity
　　　　Church government
　　　　Ecclesiastical polity
　　　　Polity, Ecclesiastical

　SA　names of church denominations with the subdivision _Government_, e.g. **Church of England—Government** [to be added as needed]

　BT　**Church**

Church schools (May subdiv. geog.)　**371.07**

Use for materials on church supported and controlled elementary and secondary schools. Materials on the relation of the church to education and on the history of the part that the church has taken in secular education are entered under **Church and education**. Materials on the instruction of religion in schools and private life are entered under **Religious education**, and of Christian religion under **Christian education**.

　UF　Denominational schools
　　　　Nonpublic schools
　　　　Parochial schools

　BT　**Private schools**
　　　　Schools

Church service books

　USE　**Liturgies**

Church settlements

　USE　**Social settlements**

Church sociables

　USE　**Church entertainments**

Church—Unity　262

Use for materials on unity as one of the marks of the church. Materials on prospective and actual mergers within and across denominational lines are entered under **Christian union**. Materials on a movement originating in the twentieth century aimed at promoting church cooperation and unity are entered under **Ecumenical movement**. Materials on religious activities planned and conducted cooperatively by two or more Christian sects are entered under **Interdenominational cooperation**.

　UF　Christian unity

Church work (May subdiv. geog.)　**200; 253**

　SA　church work with particular groups of persons, e.g. **Church work with the sick** [to be added as needed]

　BT　**Church**

　NT　**Christian missions**
　　　　Church and race relations
　　　　Church entertainments
　　　　Church work with the sick
　　　　Church work with youth
　　　　Evangelistic work
　　　　Interdenominational cooperation
　　　　Lay ministry
　　　　Ministry
　　　　Pastoral psychology
　　　　Rural churches
　　　　Sunday schools

　RT　**Church and social problems**
　　　　Pastoral theology

Church work with the sick (May subdiv. geog.)　**259; 362.1023**

　BT　**Church work**
　　　　Sick

Church work with youth (May subdiv. geog.)　**259**

　BT　**Church work**
　　　　Youth

Church year　263

Use for materials on the seasons of observance and Christian festivals with their cycles, as making up the Christian or church year. Works on the origins of Christian festivals and fasts are entered under **Christian holidays**.

　UF　Christian year
　　　　Ecclesiastical year
　　　　Liturgical year

　SA　festival seasons and seasons of the church year, e.g. **Lent** [to be added as needed]

　BT　**Calendars**
　　　　Religious holidays
　　　　Worship

　NT　**Advent**
　　　　Christian holidays

Church year—*Continued*
>> Holy Week
>> Lent
Churches
>> USE **Church buildings**
>> **Religious institutions**
Churches, Community
>> USE **Community churches**
Churches, Country
>> USE **Rural churches**
Churches, Non-institutional
>> USE **Non-institutional churches**
Churches, Rural
>> USE **Rural churches**
Churches, Undenominational
>> USE **Community churches**
Churchyards
>> USE **Cemeteries**
Cigarettes (May subdiv. geog.) **679**
>> BT **Smoking**
>> **Tobacco**
Cigars (May subdiv. geog.) **679**
>> BT **Smoking**
>> **Tobacco**
Cinco de Mayo (Holiday) (May subdiv. geog.) **391.262**
>> UF Fifth of May (Holiday)
>> BT **Holidays**
Cinema
>> USE **Motion pictures**
Cinemas
>> USE **Motion picture theaters**
Cinematography (May subdiv. geog.) **778.5**

> Use for materials on the technical aspects of making motion pictures and their projection onto a screen. General materials on motion pictures, including motion pictures as an art form, are entered under **Motion pictures**.

>> UF Motion picture photography
>> Photography—Motion pictures
>> BT **Photography**
>> NT **Animation (Cinematography)**
>> **Motion picture cameras**
Cinesiology
>> USE **Kinesiology**
Cipher and telegraph codes (May subdiv. geog.) **384.1**
>> UF Codes, Telegraph
>> Morse code
>> Telegraph codes
>> BT **Ciphers**
>> **Telegraph**

Ciphers **652**
>> UF Codes
>> Contractions
>> BT **Signs and symbols**
>> NT **Cipher and telegraph codes**
>> RT **Abbreviations**
>> **Cryptography**
>> **Writing**
Ciphers (Lettering)
>> USE **Monograms**
Circle **516**
>> BT **Geometry**
>> **Shape**
Circuits, Electric
>> USE **Electric circuits**
Circulation of library materials
>> USE **Library circulation**
Circulation of the blood
>> USE **Blood—Circulation**
Circulatory system
>> USE **Cardiovascular system**
Circumcision (May subdiv. geog.) **392.1**
>> UF Male circumcision
>> BT **Initiation rites**
Circumcision, Female
>> USE **Female circumcision**
Circumnavigation
>> USE **Voyages around the world**
Circus (May subdiv. geog.) **791.3**
>> BT **Amusements**
>> NT **Acrobats and acrobatics**
>> **Clowns**
>> RT **Carnivals**
Cities and towns (May subdiv. geog.) **307.76**

> Use for general materials on cities and towns. For materials on large cities and their surrounding areas use **Metropolitan areas**. General materials on the government of cities are entered under **Municipal government**. General materials on local government other than that of cities are entered under **Local government**.

>> UF Municipalities
>> Towns
>> Urban areas
>> SA names of individual cities and towns [to be added as needed]
>> BT **Sociology**
>> NT **Capitals (Cities)**
>> **City and town life**
>> **Extinct cities**

Cities and towns—*Continued*
> Inner cities
> **Markets**
> **Municipal art**
> **Parks**
> **Streets**
> **Urban ecology**
> **Urbanization**
> **Villages**
> RT **Urban sociology**

Cities and towns—Civic improvement
> (May subdiv. geog.) **307.3; 354.3**
> UF Civic improvement
> Municipal improvements
> NT **City planning**
> **Community centers**

Cities and towns—Finance
> USE **Municipal finance**

Cities and towns—Government
> USE **Municipal government**

Cities and towns—Growth (May subdiv.
> geog.) **307.76**
> UF Cities and towns, Movement to
> Urban development
> BT **Internal migration**
> **Population**
> NT **Metropolitan areas**
> **Suburbs**
> RT **Urbanization**

Cities and towns—Lighting
> USE **Streets—Lighting**

Cities and towns, Movement to
> USE **Cities and towns—Growth**
> **Urbanization**

Cities and towns—Planning
> USE **City planning**

Cities and towns—United States
> **307.760973; 973**
> UF United States—Cities and towns

Cities, Imaginary
> USE **Geographical myths**

Citizen participation
> USE **Political participation**
> and subjects designating govern-
> ment activity with the subdi-
> vision *Citizen participation,*
> e.g. **City planning—Citizen**
> **participation** [to be added as
> needed]

Citizens band radio **384.5; 621.3845**
> UF CB radio
> Citizens radio service

> BT **Shortwave radio**

Citizen's defender
> USE **Ombudsman**

Citizens radio service
> USE **Citizens band radio**

Citizenship (May subdiv. geog.) **172;**
> **323.6**
> UF Civics
> Franchise
> Nationality (Citizenship)
> BT **Constitutional law**
> **Political ethics**
> **Political science**
> NT **Patriotism**
> **Suffrage**
> RT **Aliens**
> **Naturalization**

Citrus
> USE **Citrus fruits**

Citrus fruit
> USE **Citrus fruits**

Citrus fruits (May subdiv. geog.) **634**
> Names of particular fruits may be used for
> either the fruit or the tree.
> UF Citrus
> Citrus fruit
> SA types of citrus fruits, e.g. **Lem-**
> **ons** [to be added as needed]
> BT **Fruit**
> NT **Lemons**
> **Limes**
> **Oranges**

City and town life (May subdiv. geog.)
> **307.76**
> UF City life
> Town life
> Urban life
> BT **Cities and towns**
> **Urban sociology**
> NT **Street life**
> **Urban policy**

City-federal relations
> USE **Federal-city relations**

City forestry
> USE **Urban forestry**

City government
> USE **Municipal government**

City life
> USE **City and town life**

City manager
> USE **Municipal government by city**
> **manager**

City planning (May subdiv. geog.)
    307.1; 354.3; 711

Use for materials on the architectural and engineering aspects of urban redevelopment. Materials on the economic, sociological, and political aspects are entered under **Urban renewal**.

    UF   Cities and towns—Planning
           Municipal planning
           Town planning
           Urban development
           Urban planning
    BT   **Cities and towns—Civic improvement**
           Planning
    NT   **Planned communities**
           Suburbs
           Zoning
    RT   **Community development**
           Housing
           Municipal art
           Public works
           Regional planning
           Urban policy
           Urban renewal

City planning—Chicago (Ill.)   307.1;
    354.3; 711
    UF   Chicago (Ill.)—City planning
City planning—Citizen participation
    (May subdiv. geog.)   307.1
    BT   **Political participation**
           Social action
City planning—United States   307.1;
    354.3; 711
City planning—Zone system
    USE **Zoning**
City schools
    USE **Urban schools**
City-state relations
    USE **State-local relations**
City traffic (May subdiv. geog.)   388.4
    UF   Local traffic
           Street traffic
           Traffic, City
           Urban traffic
    BT   **Streets**
           Traffic engineering
City transit
    USE **Local transit**
Civic art
    USE **Municipal art**

Civic improvement
    USE **Cities and towns—Civic improvement**
Civic involvement
    USE **Political participation**
          and subjects with the subdivision *Citizen participation,* e.g.
          City planning—United States—Citizen participation
          [to be added as needed]
Civics
    USE **Citizenship**
           Political science
Civil defense (May subdiv. geog.)
    363.35

Use for materials on the protection of civilians from enemy attack. Materials on military defenses against air attack are entered under **Air defenses**.

    UF   Civilian defense
    SA   names of wars with the subdivision *Evacuation of civilians*
          [to be added as needed]
    BT   **Military art and science**
    NT   **Air raid shelters**
           Evacuation of civilians
           Rescue work
           Survival skills
           World War, 1939-1945—Evacuation of civilians
Civil defense—Chicago (Ill.)   363.35
    UF   Chicago (Ill.)—Civil defense
Civil defense—United States   363.35
    UF   United States—Civil defense
Civil disobedience (May subdiv. geog.)
    303.6; 322.4
    BT   **Resistance to government**
Civil disorders
    USE **Riots**
Civil engineering (May subdiv. geog.)
    624
    BT   **Engineering**
    NT   **Aqueducts**
           Bridges
           Canals
           Dams
           Drainage
           Dredging
           Excavation
           Extraterrestrial bases
           Harbors
           Highway engineering

Civil engineering—*Continued*
        Hydraulic engineering
        Lunar bases
        Marine engineering
        Mechanical engineering
        Military engineering
        Mining engineering
        Public works
        Railroad engineering
        Reclamation of land
        Roads
        Streets
        Structural engineering
        Structural steel
        Surveying
        Tunnels
        Walls
        Water supply engineering
Civil government
  USE **Political science**
Civil law suits
  USE **Litigation**
Civil liberty
  USE **Freedom**
Civil procedure (May subdiv. geog.)
    347
  BT **Courts**
  NT **Probate law and practice**
        Small claims courts
  RT **Litigation**
Civil rights (May subdiv. geog.) **323;**
    342.08

    Use for materials on citizens' rights as established by law or protected by a constitution. Materials on the rights of persons regardless of their legal, socioeconomic, or cultural status and as recognized by the international community are entered under **Human rights**.

  UF Basic rights
        Constitutional rights
        Fundamental rights
  SA ethnic groups and classes of persons with the subdivision *Civil rights* [to be added as needed]
  BT **Constitutional law**
        Human rights
        Political science
  NT **African Americans—Civil rights**
        Anti-apartheid movement
        Blacks—Civil rights
        Children—Civil rights

        Due process of law
        Employee rights
        Fair trial
        Freedom of assembly
        Freedom of association
        Freedom of information
        Freedom of movement
        Freedom of religion
        Freedom of speech
        Freedom of the press
        Gay rights
        Habeas corpus
        Right of privacy
        Right of property
        Right to counsel
        Women's rights
  RT **Civil rights demonstrations**
        Discrimination
        Freedom
Civil rights demonstrations (May subdiv. geog.) **322.4**
  UF Demonstrations for civil rights
        Freedom marches for civil rights
        Marches for civil rights
        Sit-ins for civil rights
  BT **Demonstrations**
  RT **Civil rights**
Civil rights (International law)
  USE **Human rights**
Civil servants
  USE **Civil service**
Civil service (May subdiv. geog.) **351;**
    352.6; 342

    Use for general materials on career government service and the laws governing it. Materials on civil service employees are entered under the name of the country, state, city, corporate body, or government agency with the subdivision *Officials and employees*.

  UF Administration
        Civil servants
        Employees and officials
        Government employees
        Government service
        Officials and employees
        Tenure of office
  SA names of countries, states, cities, etc., and corporate bodies with the subdivision *Officials and employees*, e.g. **United States—Officials and employees; Ohio—Officials and**

Civil service—*Continued*
    employees; Chicago (Ill.)—
    Officials and employees;
    United Nations—Officials
    and employees; etc. [to be
    added as needed]
  BT Administrative law
      Political science
      Public administration
  NT Municipal officials and em-
      ployees
  RT Bureaucracy
      Public officers
Civil service—Examinations (May subdiv.
  geog.) **351.076**
  BT Examinations
Civil service—United States 351.73
  UF United States—Civil service
  RT United States—Officials and
      employees
Civil War—England
  USE Great Britain—History—1642-
      1660, Civil War and Com-
      monwealth
Civil War—United States
  USE United States—History—1861-
      1865, Civil War
Civilian defense
  USE Civil defense
Civilian evacuation
  USE Evacuation of civilians
      World War, 1939-1945—Evac-
      uation of civilians
Civilian relief
  USE names of wars with the subdivi-
      sion *Civilian relief,* e.g.
      World War, 1939-1945—Ci-
      vilian relief [to be added as
      needed]
Civilization 306; 909
  Use for materials on civilization in general
and on the development of social customs, art,
industry, religion, etc., of several countries or
peoples.
  SA names of continents, regions,
      countries, states, etc., with the
      subdivision *Civilization,* e.g.
      United States—Civilization;
      and the civilizations of peo-
      ples not confined to a single
      place, e.g. **Arab civilization**;

      Western civilization; etc. [to
      be added as needed]
  NT Acculturation
      Aeronautics and civilization
      Africa—Civilization
      America—Civilization
      Ancient civilization
      Arabic civilization
      Asia—Civilization
      Astronautics and civilization
      Bronze Age
      Celtic civilization
      Christian civilization
      Computers and civilization
      Education
      Iron Age
      Islamic civilization
      Jewish civilization
      Learning and scholarship
      Manners and customs
      Medieval civilization
      Modern civilization
      Ohio—Civilization
      Primitive societies
      Progress
      Religions
      Renaissance
      Science and civilization
      Social sciences
      Stone Age
      Technology and civilization
      United States—Civilization
      War and civilization
      Western civilization
  RT Anthropology
      Culture
      Ethnology
      History
      Sociology
Civilization, Ancient
  USE Ancient civilization
Civilization and aeronautics
  USE Aeronautics and civilization
Civilization and astronautics
  USE Astronautics and civilization
Civilization and computers
  USE Computers and civilization
Civilization and science
  USE Science and civilization
Civilization and technology
  USE Technology and civilization

Civilization and war
  USE **War and civilization**
Civilization, Arab
  USE **Arabic civilization**
Civilization, Christian
  USE **Christian civilization**
Civilization, Classical
  USE **Classical civilization**
Civilization, Greek
  USE **Greece—Civilization**
Civilization, Medieval
  USE **Medieval civilization**
Civilization, Modern
  USE **Modern civilization**
Civilization, Oriental
  USE **Asia—Civilization**
Civilization, Western
  USE **Western civilization**
Claims
  USE ethnic groups, places, and wars
        with the subdivision *Claims,*
        e.g. **Native Americans—**
        Claims [to be added as need-
        ed]
Clairvoyance · **133.8**
  BT **Extrasensory perception**
        Occultism
  RT **Telepathy**
Clairvoyants
  USE **Psychics**
Clans (May subdiv. geog.) **306.85; 941.1**
  SA names of clans or of families
        [to be added as needed]
  BT **Family**
  NT **Tribes**
  RT **Kinship**
Clans—Scotland 941.1
  UF Highland clans
        Scottish clans
  NT **Tartans**
Class action lawsuits
  USE **Class actions (Civil procedure)**
Class actions (Civil procedure) (May
    subdiv. geog.) **347**
  UF Class action lawsuits
  BT **Litigation**
Class conflict
  USE **Social conflict**
Class consciousness (May subdiv. geog.)
    305.5

  BT **Social classes**
        Social psychology
  RT **Marxism**
Class distinction
  USE **Social classes**
Class struggle
  USE **Social conflict**
Classed catalogs
  USE **Classified catalogs**
Classes (Mathematics)
  USE **Set theory**
Classes of persons
  USE **Persons**
        and classes of persons, e.g. **El-**
        derly; Handicapped; Explor-
        ers; Drug addicts; etc. [to be
        added as needed]
Classic automobiles
  USE **Antique and classic cars**
Classic cars
  USE **Antique and classic cars**
Classic motorcycles
  USE **Antique and vintage motorcy-**
        cles
Classical antiquities 937; 938
  UF Classical archeology
        Greek antiquities
        Roman antiquities
  SA names of extinct cities of Greek
        and Roman antiquity e.g. **Del-**
        phi (Extinct city); and names
        of groups of people extant in
        modern times and names of
        cities (except extinct cities),
        countries, regions, etc., with
        the subdivision *Antiquities* [to
        be added as needed]
  BT **Antiquities**
  NT **Greece—Antiquities**
        Greek art
        Roman art
        Rome—Antiquities
        Rome (Italy)—Antiquities
Classical antiquities—Dictionaries
  USE **Classical dictionaries**
Classical archeology
  USE **Classical antiquities**
Classical art
  USE **Greek art**
        Roman art

Classical biography
  USE **Greece—Biography**
       Rome—Biography
Classical civilization (May subdiv. geog.)
       937

  Use for materials on both ancient Greek
  and Roman civilizations. Materials on the
  spread of Greek civilization throughout the
  ancient world following the conquests of Alexander the Great are entered under **Hellenism**.

  UF   Civilization, Classical
  BT   **Ancient civilization**
  NT   **Greece—Civilization**
       Rome—Civilization
  RT   **Classicism**
Classical dictionaries   937.003; 938.003
  UF   Classical antiquities—Dictionaries
       Dictionaries, Classical
  BT   **Ancient history**
       Encyclopedias and dictionaries
Classical drama   882
  UF   Greek and Latin drama
  BT   **Classical literature**
       Drama
Classical education (May subdiv. geog.)
       370.11
  BT   **Education**
  RT   **Humanism**
       Humanities
Classical geography
  USE **Ancient geography**
       Greece—Historical geography
       Rome—Geography
Classical languages
  USE **Greek language**
       Latin language
Classical literature   870; 880
  BT   **Literature**
  NT   **Classical drama**
  RT   **Greek literature**
       Latin literature
Classical music
  USE **Music**
Classical mythology   292.1
  UF   Mythology, Classical
  BT   **Mythology**
  NT   **Greek mythology**
       Roman mythology
Classicism   709; 809
  BT   **Aesthetics**
       Literature
  NT   **Classicism in architecture**

  RT   **Classical civilization**
Classicism in architecture (May subdiv.
       geog.)   **723; 724**
  BT   **Architecture**
       Classicism
Classification   001

  Use for materials on the organization of
  knowledge into a systematic arrangement of
  topics or categories. Materials on the classification of library materials are entered under
  Library classification, which may be subdivided by the type of literature or the subject
  of the materials classified.

  UF   Classification of knowledge
  SA   subjects with the subdivision
         Classification, e.g. **Botany—
         Classification** [to be added as
         needed]
  NT   **Botany—Classification**
       Library classification
Classification—Books
  USE **Library classification**
Classification—Botany
  USE **Botany—Classification**
Classification, Dewey Decimal
  USE **Dewey Decimal Classification**
Classification of knowledge
  USE **Classification**
Classification—Plants
  USE **Botany—Classification**
Classified catalogs   017; 025.3
  UF   Catalogs, Classified
       Classed catalogs
  BT   **Library catalogs**
  RT   **Library classification**
Classroom management   371.102
  BT   **School discipline**
       Teaching
Clay   553.6; 666; 738.1
  BT   **Ceramics**
       Soils
  NT   **Modeling**
Clay industries
  USE **Clay industry**
Clay industry (May subdiv. geog.)
       338.4; 666
  UF   Clay industries
  BT   **Ceramic industry**
  NT   **Pottery**
Clay modeling
  USE **Modeling**
Cleaning   648; 667

Cleaning—*Continued*
- SA topics with the subdivision *Cleaning*, e.g. **Rugs and carpets—Cleaning** [to be added as needed]
- BT **Sanitation**
- NT **Bleaching**
  Cleaning compounds
  Dry cleaning
  House cleaning
  Laundry
  Street cleaning

Cleaning compounds   648; 667
- BT **Cleaning**
- NT **Detergents**
  Soap

Cleanliness   391.6; 613
- UF Neatness
- BT **Hygiene**
  Sanitation
- NT **Baths**

Clearing of land
- USE **Reclamation of land**

Clemency (May subdiv. geog.)   **364.6**
- BT **Administration of criminal justice**
  Executive power
- RT **Amnesty**
  Forgiveness
  Pardon

Clergy (May subdiv. geog.)   **200.92; 270.092**
- UF Curates
  Ministers of the gospel
  Pastors
  Preachers
  Rectors
- SA church denominations with the subdivision *Clergy*, e.g. **Catholic Church—Clergy** [to be added as needed]
- BT **Church**
- NT **Bishops**
  Catholic Church—Clergy
  Celibacy
  Chaplains
  Priests
  Rabbis
  Televangelists
  Women clergy
- RT **Ministry**
  Ordination

Pastoral theology

Clergy—Office
- USE **Ministry**

Clergy—Political activity (May subdiv. geog.)   **201; 261.7**
- BT **Political participation**

Clerical celibacy
- USE **Celibacy**

Clerical employees
- USE **Office workers**

Clerical personnel
- USE **Office workers**

Clerical psychology
- USE **Pastoral psychology**

Clerical work—Training
- USE **Business education**

Clerks
- USE **Office workers**

Clerks (Retail trade)
- USE **Sales personnel**

Cliff dwellers and cliff dwellings (May subdiv. geog.)   **979**
- BT **Archeology**
  Native Americans—Southwestern States

Climacteric, Female
- USE **Menopause**

Climacteric, Male
- USE **Male climacteric**

Climate   551.6

Use for materials on climate as it relates to humans and to plant and animal life, including the effects of changes of climate. Materials limited to the climate of a particular region are entered under the name of the place with the subdivision **Climate**. Materials on the state of the atmosphere at a given time and place with respect to heat or cold, wetness or dryness, calm or storm, are entered under **Weather**. Scientific materials on the atmosphere, especially weather factors, are entered under **Meteorology**.

- UF Climatology
- SA names of countries, cities, etc., with the subdivision *Climate* [to be added as needed]
- BT **Earth sciences**
- NT **Chicago (Ill.)—Climate**
  Climate change
  Desertification
  Forest influences
  Global warming
  Ohio—Climate
  Seasons
  United States—Climate

Climate—*Continued*

    RT   **Meteorology**

          Weather

Climate and forests

    USE   **Forest influences**

Climate change (May subdiv. geog.)

         551.5

    BT   **Climate**

    RT   **Global warming**

Climatology

    USE   **Climate**

Climbing plants   **582.1; 635.9**

    UF   Vines

    BT   **Gardening**

          Plants

Clinical chemistry   **616.07**

    Use for materials on the chemical diagnosis of disease and health monitoring.

    UF   Chemistry, Diagnostic

          Chemistry, Medical

          Diagnostic chemistry

          Medical chemistry

    BT   **Biochemistry**

          Diagnosis

Clinical drug trials

    USE   **Drugs—Testing**

Clinical genetics

    USE   **Medical genetics**

Clinical imaging

    USE   **Diagnostic imaging**

Clinical records

    USE   **Medical records**

Clinical trials of drugs

    USE   **Drugs—Testing**

Clinics

    USE   **Health facilities**

          Medical practice

Clip art   **741.6**

    Use for materials on clipping art work from published sources to use in creating documents, posters, newsletters, etc. Materials on the use of photocopying machines to create original works of art are entered under **Copy art**.

    BT   **Graphic arts**

Clipper ships   **387.2; 623.82**

    BT   **Ships**

Clippings (Books, newspapers, etc.)

         025.17

    UF   Newspaper clippings

          Press clippings

    BT   **Newspapers**

Clitoridotomy

    USE   **Female circumcision**

Clocks and watches (May subdiv. geog.)

         681.1; 739.3

    UF   Horology

          Watches

    BT   **Time**

    NT   **Sundials**

Clog dancing (May subdiv. geog.)   **793.3**

    UF   Clog-dancing

          Clogging (Dance)

    BT   **Dance**

Clog-dancing

    USE   **Clog dancing**

Clogging (Dance)

    USE   **Clog dancing**

Cloisters

    USE   **Convents**

          Monasteries

Clones and cloning

    USE   **Cloning**

Cloning   **571.8; 660.6**

    UF   Clones and cloning

    BT   **Genetic engineering**

    NT   **Human cloning**

          Molecular cloning

Cloning—Ethical aspects   **174**

    BT   **Ethics**

Closed caption television   **384.55**

    BT   **Deaf**

          Television

Closed caption video recordings   **384.55**

    Use for individual works, collections, or materials about closed caption video recordings.

    UF   Video recordings, Closed caption

          Video recordings for the hearing impaired

    BT   **Deaf**

          Video recordings

Closed-circuit television   **384.55**

    UF   Television, Closed-circuit

    BT   **Intercommunication systems**

          Microwave communication systems

          Television

Closed shop

    USE   **Open and closed shop**

Closing of factories

    USE   **Plant shutdowns**

Cloth

    USE   **Fabrics**

Clothes
USE   **Clothing and dress**
Clothiers
USE   **Clothing industry**
Clothing
USE   types of clothing articles and ac-
cessories; costume of particu-
lar ethnic groups, e.g. **Native
American costume;** and pro-
fessions and classes of per-
sons with the subdivision
Clothing, e.g. **Handicapped—
Clothing** [to be added as
needed]
Clothing and dress (May subdiv. geog.)
    391; 646.4
  Use for materials on clothing and the art of
dress from day to day in practical situations,
including historical dress and the clothing of
various professions or classes of persons. Ma-
terials on the characteristic costume of ethnic
groups and on fancy dress and theatrical cos-
tumes are entered under **Costume**. Materials
on the prevailing mode or style of dress are
entered under **Fashion**.
   UF   Clothes
         Dress
         Garments
         Style in dress
   SA   types of clothing articles and ac-
cessories; costume of particu-
lar ethnic groups, e.g. **Native
American costume;** and pro-
fessions and classes of per-
sons with the subdivision
Clothing, e.g. **Handicapped—
Clothing** [to be added as
needed]
   BT   **Manners and customs**
   NT   **Buttons**
         Children's clothing
         Dress accessories
         Dressmaking
         Fans (Dress accessories)
         Fashion
         Handicapped—Clothing
         Hats
         Hosiery
         Infants' clothing
         Jewelry
         Leather garments
         Men's clothing
         Shoes
         T-shirts

         Tailoring
         Umbrellas and parasols
         Uniforms
         Wigs
         Women's clothing
   RT   **Clothing industry**
         Costume
         Personal appearance
         Personal grooming
Clothing and dress—Dry cleaning
   USE   **Dry cleaning**
Clothing and dress—France   **391**
  Use for materials on day to day dress in
France.
Clothing and dress—France—History
    391
  Use for materials on day to day dress in
France in the past.
Clothing and dress—History   **391**
  Use for materials on day to day dress in the
past.
Clothing and dress—Repairing   **646.2**
   UF   Mending
Clothing and dress—Social aspects (May
    subdiv. geog.)   **391**
   NT   **Dress codes**
Clothing designers
   USE   **Fashion designers**
Clothing industry (May subdiv. geog.)
    338.4; 687
   UF   Clothiers
         Clothing trade
         Fashion industry
         Garment industry
   BT   **Industries**
   NT   **Dressmaking**
         Fashion design
         Shoe industry
         Tailoring
   RT   **Clothing and dress**
Clothing trade
   USE   **Clothing industry**
Cloud seeding
   USE   **Weather control**
Clouds   **551.57**
   BT   **Atmosphere**
         Meteorology
Clowns (May subdiv. geog.)   **791.3;**
    791.3092; 920
   BT   **Circus**
         Entertainers
Clubs (May subdiv. geog.)   **367**

Clubs—*Continued*
    BT   **Associations**
    NT   **Book clubs (Discussion groups)**
          Boys' clubs
          Girls' clubs
          Men—Societies
          Scouts and scouting
          Women—Societies
    RT   **Societies**
Co-dependence
    USE   **Codependency**
Co-dependency
    USE   **Codependency**
Co-ops
    USE   **Cooperative societies**
Co-ops (Housing)
    USE   **Cooperative housing**
Co-parenting
    USE   **Part-time parenting**
Coaching
    USE   **Coaching (Athletics)**
          Horsemanship
          and types of sports with the
            subdivision *Coaching* [to be
            added as needed]
Coaching (Athletics)   796.07
    UF   Athletic coaching
          Coaching
          Sports coaching
    SA   types of sports with the subdivi-
          sion *Coaching* [to be added
          as needed]
    BT   **Athletics**
          Physical education
          Sports
    NT   **Football—Coaching**
Coal (May subdiv. geog.)   **553.2**
    BT   **Fuel**
    NT   **Coal gasification**
          Coal liquefaction
          Coal mines and mining
Coal gas
    USE   **Gas**
Coal gasification (May subdiv. geog.)
       665.7
    UF   Gasification of coal
    BT   **Coal**
Coal liquefaction (May subdiv. geog.)
       622
    UF   Liquefaction of coal
    BT   **Coal**

Coal miners (May subdiv. geog.)   **622;
       920**
    BT   **Miners**
Coal mines and mining (May subdiv.
       geog.)   **622**
    BT   **Coal**
          Mines and mineral resources
    NT   **Mining engineering**
Coal oil
    USE   **Petroleum**
Coal tar products (May subdiv. geog.)
       547; 661
    BT   **Petroleum**
    RT   **Gas**
COAs
    USE   **Children of alcoholics**
Coast ecology
    USE   **Coastal ecology**
Coast pilot guides
    USE   **Pilot guides**
Coastal ecology (May subdiv. geog.)
       577.5
    UF   Coast ecology
          Coastal zone ecology
    BT   **Ecology**
Coastal landforms
    USE   **Coasts**
Coastal signals
    USE   **Signals and signaling**
Coastal zone ecology
    USE   **Coastal ecology**
Coastal zone management (May subdiv.
       geog.)   **333.91**
    BT   **Coasts**
          Regional planning
Coasts (May subdiv. geog.)   **551.45**
    UF   Coastal landforms
    BT   **Landforms**
    NT   **Coastal zone management**
    RT   **Seashore**
Coats of arms
    USE   **Heraldry**
Cocaine (May subdiv. geog.)   **362.29;
       615**
    BT   **Narcotics**
    NT   **Crack (Drug)**
Cocaine babies
    USE   **Children of drug addicts**
Cockroaches (May subdiv. geog.)   **595.7**
    UF   Roaches (Insects)
    BT   **Insects**

Cocoa   633.7; 641.3
    BT   **Beverages**
    RT   **Chocolate**
Cocoons
    USE **Butterflies**
           Caterpillars
           Moths
           Silkworms
Code deciphering
    USE **Cryptography**
Code enciphering
    USE **Cryptography**
Code names   423
    BT   **Abbreviations**
           Names
    NT   **Acronyms**
Codependency   616.86
    UF   Co-dependence
           Co-dependency
           Codependent behavior
    BT   **Abnormal psychology**
Codependent behavior
    USE **Codependency**
Codes
    USE **Ciphers**
Codes, Penal
    USE **Criminal law**
Codes, Telegraph
    USE **Cipher and telegraph codes**
Coeducation (May subdiv. geog.)
           371.822
    BT   **Education**
    RT   **Boys—Education**
           Girls—Education
           Men—Education
           Women—Education
Coffee (May subdiv. geog.)   **633.7; 641.8**
    BT   **Beverages**
    RT   **Coffee industry**
Coffee bars
    USE **Coffeehouses**
Coffee houses
    USE **Coffeehouses**
Coffee industry (May subdiv. geog.)
           338.1; 338.4
    UF   Coffee trade
    BT   **Beverage industry**
    NT   **Coffeehouses**
    RT   **Coffee**
Coffee shops
    USE **Restaurants**

Coffee trade
    USE **Coffee industry**
Coffeehouses (May subdiv. geog.)
           647.95
       Use for materials on public establishments devoted primarily to serving coffee. Materials on coffee shops and cafes as small inexpensive restaurants are entered under **Restaurants**.
    UF   Cafes
           Coffee bars
           Coffee houses
    BT   **Coffee industry**
           Restaurants
Cog wheels
    USE **Gearing**
Cognition
    USE **Theory of knowledge**
Cognitive styles   153; 370.15
    BT   **Intellect**
           Theory of knowledge
Cognitive styles in children   155.4;
           370.15
    BT   **Child psychology**
Cohabitation
    USE **Unmarried couples**
Cohousing
    USE **Cooperative housing**
Coiffure
    USE **Hair**
Coin collecting
    USE **Coins—Collectors and collect-**
           ing
Coinage (May subdiv. geog.)   **332.4**
       Use for materials on the processing and history of metal money. Lists of coins and general materials about coins are entered under **Coins**.
    BT   **Money**
    NT   **Counterfeits and counterfeiting**
    RT   **Gold**
           Mints
           Silver
Coinage of words
    USE **New words**
Coins (May subdiv. geog.)   **737.4**
       Use for lists of coins and general materials about coins. Materials on coins from the point of view of art and archeology are entered under **Numismatics**. Materials on the processing of metal money are entered under **Coinage**.
    UF   Specie
    BT   **Money**
Coins—Collectors and collecting (May subdiv. geog.)   **737.4**

Coins—Collectors and collecting—*Continued*

    UF   Coin collecting

    RT   **Numismatics**

Cold   536; 551.5

    NT   **Cryobiology**

           Ice

    RT   **Low temperatures**

           Temperature

Cold (Disease)   616.2

    UF   Common cold

    BT   **Communicable diseases**

           Diseases

Cold—Physiological effect   613

    BT   **Cryobiology**

Cold storage   641.4; 664

    BT   **Food—Preservation**

    NT   **Compressed air**

    RT   **Refrigeration**

Cold—Therapeutic use   615.8

    UF   Cryotherapy

    BT   **Therapeutics**

    NT   **Cryosurgery**

Cold war   909.82

    UF   Power politics

    BT   **World politics—1945-1991**

Collaborationists (May subdiv. geog.)
    364.1

    UF   Collaborators (Traitors)

    SA   names of wars with the subdivi-
           sion *Collaborationists*, e.g.
           World War, 1939-1945—
           Collaborationists [to be add-
           ed as needed]

    BT   **Traitors**

    NT   **World War, 1939-1945—Col-**
           laborationists

Collaborators (Traitors)

    USE **Collaborationists**

Collage   702.8; 751.4

    BT   **Art**

           Handicraft

Collapse of structures

    USE **Structural failures**

Collectables

    USE **Collectibles**

Collected papers (Anthologies)

    USE **Anthologies**

Collected works

    USE **Anthologies**

           Literature—Collections

           Storytelling—Collections

and form headings for minor literary forms that represent collections of works of several authors, e.g. **Essays**; **American essays**; **Parodies**; **Short stories**; etc.; major literary forms and national literatures with the subdivision *Collections*, e.g. **Poetry—Collections**; **English literature—Collections**; etc.; and subjects with the subdivision *Literary collections*, for collections focused on a single subject by two or more authors involving two or more literary forms, e.g. **Cats—Literary collections** [to be added as needed]

Collectible card games   795.4

    UF   Trading card games

    BT   **Card games**

Collectibles (May subdiv. geog.)   **745.1**

    Use for materials on any objects of interest to collectors, including mass produced items of little intrinsic value. Materials on old decorative or utilitarian objects that have aesthetic or historical importance and financial value are entered under **Antiques**.

    UF   Collectables

           Memorabilia

    SA   subjects and names with the
           subdivision *Collectibles*, e.g.
           American Revolution Bicen-
           tennial, 1776-1976—Collect-
           ibles; and types of objects
           collected, excluding antiquities
           and natural objects, with the
           subdivision *Collectors and*
           collecting, e.g. **Boxes—Col-**
           lectors and collecting [to be
           added as needed]

    BT   **Collectors and collecting**

    NT   **Trading cards**

           Victoriana

Collecting

    USE **Collectors and collecting**

Collecting of accounts   658.8

    UF   Accounts, Collecting of

           Bill collecting

           Collection of accounts

    BT   **Commercial law**

           Credit

           Debt

Collecting of accounts—*Continued*
    Debtor and creditor
Collection and preservation
    USE   types of antiquities and types of
            natural objects, including ani-
            mal specimens and plant
            specimens, with the subdivi-
            sion *Collection and preserva-*
            tion, e.g. **Birds—Collection**
            and preservation; for materi-
            als on methods of collecting
            and preserving those objects
            [to be added as needed]
Collection development (Libraries)
    USE   **Libraries—Collection develop-**
            ment
Collection of accounts
    USE   **Collecting of accounts**
Collections
    USE   form headings for minor literary
            forms that represent collec-
            tions of works of several au-
            thors, e.g. **Essays; American**
            essays; Parodies; Short sto-
            ries; etc.; major literary forms
            and national literatures with
            the subdivision *Collections,*
            e.g. **Poetry—Collections; En-**
            glish literature—Collections;
            etc.; and subjects with the
            subdivision *Literary collec-*
            tions, for collections focused
            on a single subject by two or
            more authors involving two or
            more literary forms, e.g.
            Cats—Literary collections [to
            be added as needed]
Collections (Anthologies)
    USE   **Anthologies**
Collections of art, painting, etc.
    USE   **Art collections**
            Art museums
Collections of literature
    USE   **Anthologies**
            Literature—Collections
            Storytelling—Collections
            and form headings for minor
            literary forms that represent
            collections of works of sever-
            al authors, e.g. **Essays;**
            American essays; Parodies;

Short stories; etc.; major literary forms and national literatures with the subdivision
Collections, e.g. **Poetry—Col-**
lections; English literature—
Collections; etc.; and subjects
with the subdivision *Literary*
collections, for collections focused on a single subject by
two or more authors involving
two or more literary forms,
e.g. **Cats—Literary collec-**
tions [to be added as needed]
Collections of natural specimens
    USE   **Plants—Collection and preser-**
            vation
            Zoological specimens—Collec-
            tion and preservation
            and types of natural specimens
            with the subdivision *Collec-*
            tion and preservation, e.g.
            Birds—Collection and pres-
            ervation [to be added as
            needed]
Collections of objects
    USE   **Collectors and collecting**
            and subjects and names with
            the subdivision *Collectibles,*
            e.g. **American Revolution Bi-**
            centennial, 1776-1976—Col-
            lectibles; and types of objects
            collected, excluding antiquities
            and natural objects, with the
            subdivision *Collectors and*
            collecting, e.g. **Boxes—Col-**
            lectors and collecting [to be
            added as needed]
Collective bargaining (May subdiv. geog.)
    331.89; 658.3
    May be subdivided by groups of profession-
al or nonprofessional workers, e.g. **Collective**
bargaining—Librarians.
    UF   Labor negotiations
    BT   **Industrial relations**
            Labor
            Labor disputes
            Negotiation
    RT   **Industrial arbitration**
            Labor contract
            Labor unions
            Participative management
            Strikes

Collective bargaining—Librarians (May subdiv. geog.)   **331.89**
    UF   Librarians—Collective bargaining
         Libraries—Collective bargaining
Collective farms
    USE **Collective settlements**
         Cooperative agriculture
Collective identity
    USE **Group identity**
Collective labor agreements
    USE **Labor contract**
Collective security
    USE **International security**
Collective settlements (May subdiv. geog.)
    307.77; 335
    Use for materials on traditional, formally organized communal ventures, usually based on ideological, political, or religious affiliation. Materials on arrangements in voluntary cooperative living, usually informal, are entered under **Communal living**.
    UF   Collective farms
         Communal settlements
         Communes
         Cooperative living
    SA   names of individual collective settlements [to be added as needed]
    BT   **Communism**
         Cooperation
         Socialism
    RT   **Communal living**
         Cooperative agriculture
         Counter culture
         Utopias
Collective settlements—Israel   **307.77**
    UF   Israel—Collective settlements
         Kibbutz
Collective settlements—United States
    307.77
Collectivism (May subdiv. geog.)
    320.53; 335
    BT   **Economics**
         Political science
    NT   **Communism**
         Socialism
Collectors and collecting (May subdiv. geog.)   **790.1**
    UF   Collecting
         Collections of objects
    SA   types of collecting, e.g. **Book collecting**; types of objects collected, excluding antiquities

and natural objects, with the subdivision *Collectors and collecting*, e.g. **Postcards—Collectors and collecting**; names of original owners of private art collections with the subdivision *Art collections*; subjects and names with the subdivision *Collectibles*, e.g. **American Revolution Bicentennial, 1776-1976—Collectibles**; and antiquities and types of natural objects with the subdivision *Collection and preservation*, e.g. **Birds—Collection and preservation** [to be added as needed]
    BT   **Antiques**
         Art
         Hobbies
    NT   **American Revolution Bicentennial, 1776-1976—Collectibles**
         Americana
         Antiques
         Antiquities—Collection and preservation
         Book collecting
         Boxes—Collectors and collecting
         Collectibles
         Plants—Collection and preservation
         Stamp collecting
         Zoological specimens—Collection and preservation
    RT   **Art collections**
Collects
    USE **Prayers**
College admissions essays
    USE **College applications**
College and school drama   **371.8; 792**
    Use for materials about college and school drama. Individual works, collections, and materials about plays for children are entered under **Children's plays**. Plays for children on a particular theme are entered under subjects and personal, corporate, and place names with the subdivision *Juvenile drama*.
    UF   College drama
         School plays
    BT   **Amateur theater**
         Drama
         Student activities

College and school drama—*Continued*
  RT **Drama in education**
College and school journalism (May
      subdiv. geog.) **371.8**
  UF College journalism
       College periodicals
       School journalism
       School newspapers
  BT **Journalism**
       Student activities
  RT **Children's writings**
College and university libraries
  USE **Academic libraries**
College applications **378.1**
  UF Admissions applications
       Admissions essays
       Applications for college
       College admissions essays
       Colleges and universities—Appli-
         cations
  RT **Colleges and universities—En-
       trance requirements**
College athletics
  USE **College sports**
College choice **378**
  UF Choice of college
       Colleges and universities—Selec
         tion
  BT **Colleges and universities**
       School choice
College costs (May subdiv. geog.) **378.3**
  UF Tuition
  BT **Colleges and universities—Fi-
       nance**
  NT **Student aid**
       Student loan funds
College degrees
  USE **Academic degrees**
College drama
  USE **College and school drama**
College dropouts
  USE **Dropouts**
College entrance examinations
  USE **Colleges and universities—En-
       trance examinations**
College entrance requirements
  USE **Colleges and universities—En-
       trance requirements**
College fraternities
  USE **Fraternities and sororities**
College graduates (May subdiv. geog.)
      305.5; 378

  UF Graduates, College
       University graduates
  BT **Professions**
  RT **College students**
College journalism
  USE **College and school journalism**
College libraries
  USE **Academic libraries**
College life
  USE **College students**
College periodicals
  USE **College and school journalism**
College songs
  USE **Students' songs**
College sororities
  USE **Fraternities and sororities**
College sports (May subdiv. geog.)
      371.8; 796
  UF College athletics
       Intercollegiate athletics
       Varsity sports
  SA types of sports [to be added as
       needed]
  BT **Sports**
       Student activities
  RT **School sports**
College students (May subdiv. geog.)
      371.8; 378
  UF College life
       Colleges and universities—Stu-
        dents
       Student life
       Undergraduates
       University students
  BT **Students**
  RT **College graduates**
College students, Foreign
  USE **Foreign students**
College students—Political activity (May
      subdiv. geog.) **371.8; 378**
  UF Campus disorders
  BT **Political participation**
College students—Sexual behavior (May
      subdiv. geog.) **371.8; 378**
  BT **Sex**
College teachers
  USE **Colleges and universities—Fac-
       ulty**
       Educators
       Teachers

College yearbooks
    USE **School yearbooks**
Colleges and universities (May subdiv.
        geog.) **378**
    UF Universities
        Universities and colleges
    SA types of colleges and universi-
        ties, e.g. **Catholic colleges
        and universities**; and names
        of individual colleges and
        universities [to be added as
        needed]
    BT **Education**
        Higher education
        Professional education
        Schools
    NT **Academic degrees**
        **Catholic colleges and universi-
        ties**
        College choice
        Commencements
        Fraternities and sororities
        Free universities
        Junior colleges
        Law schools
        Medical colleges
        Teachers colleges
        **United States Military Acade-
        my**
        University extension
**Colleges and universities—Accreditation
    378; 379.1**
Colleges and universities—Applications
    USE **College applications**
Colleges and universities—Buildings
    (May subdiv. geog.) **727**
    BT **Buildings**
**Colleges and universities—Curricula
    378.1**
    UF Core curriculum
    SA types of education and schools
        with the subdivision *Curricu-
        la*, e.g. **Library education—
        Curricula** [to be added as
        needed]
    BT **Education—Curricula**
Colleges and universities—Employees
    (May subdiv. geog.) **378.1**
    BT **Employees**

**Colleges and universities—Employees—
    Salaries, wages, etc.** (May subdiv.
    geog.) **331.2**
    BT **Salaries, wages, etc.**
**Colleges and universities—Endowments
    378**
    BT **Endowments**
**Colleges and universities—Entrance ex-
    aminations 378.1**
    UF College entrance examinations
        Entrance examinations for col-
        leges
    BT **Educational tests and measure-
        ments**
        Examinations
    NT **Graduate Record Examination**
        Scholastic Assessment Test
**Colleges and universities—Entrance re-
    quirements 378.1**
    UF College entrance requirements
        Entrance requirements for col-
        leges and universities
    SA names of individual colleges and
        universities with the subdivi-
        sion *Entrance requirements*
        [to be added as needed]
    BT **Examinations**
    RT **College applications**
Colleges and universities—Faculty (May
        subdiv. geog.) **378.1**
    UF College teachers
        Faculty (Education)
    BT **Teachers**
**Colleges and universities—Faculty—Pen-
    sions** (May subdiv. geog.) **331.25**
Colleges and universities—Finance (May
        subdiv. geog.) **378.1**
    UF Tuition
    BT **Finance**
    NT **College costs**
    RT **Federal aid to education**
Colleges and universities—Insignia (May
        subdiv. geog.) **378.2**
    BT **Insignia**
Colleges and universities—Selection
    USE **College choice**
Colleges and universities—Students
    USE **College students**
**Colleges and universities—United States
    378.73**
Collies (May subdiv. geog.) **636.737**

Collies—*Continued*
    BT **Dogs**
Collisions, Railroad
    USE **Railroad accidents**
Colloids   541
    BT **Physical chemistry**
Colombia   986.1
    May be subdivided like United States except for History.
Colonial architecture
    USE **American colonial style in architecture**
         Architecture—United States—1600-1775, Colonial period
Colonial history (U.S.)
    USE **United States—History—1600-1775, Colonial period**
Colonialism
    USE **Colonies**
         Imperialism
Colonies   321; 325
    Use for materials on general colonial policy. Materials on the policy of settling immigrants or nationals abroad are entered under **Colonization**. Materials on migration from one country to another are entered under **Immigration and emigration**. Materials on the movement of population within a country for permanent settlement are entered under **Internal migration**.
    UF Colonialism
        Dependencies
    SA names of countries with the subdivision *Colonies*, or *Territories and possessions*, e.g.
        Great Britain—Colonies;
        United States—Territories and possessions; etc. [to be added as needed]
    BT **Imperialism**
    NT **Great Britain—Colonies**
        Land settlement
        Penal colonies
    RT **Colonization**
Colonies, Space
    USE **Space colonies**
Colonization   325
    Use for materials on the policy of settling immigrants or nationals abroad. Materials on general colonial policy are entered under **Colonies**. Materials on migration from one country to another are entered under **Immigration and emigration**. Materials on the movement of population within a country for permanent settlement are entered under **Internal migration**.

    SA names of countries with the subdivision *Immigration and emigration*, e.g. **United States—Immigration and emigration** [to be added as needed]
    BT **Imperialism**
        Land settlement
    NT **Internal migration**
        Land grants
        Public lands
    RT **Colonies**
        Immigration and emigration
Color   752; 535.6; 701
    UF Colour
    SA subjects with the subdivision *Color*, and names of specific colors [to be added as needed]
    BT **Aesthetics**
        Chemistry
        Light
        Optics
        Painting
        Photometry
    NT **Animals—Color**
        Birds—Color
        Dyes and dyeing
        Red
    RT **Pigments**
Color blindness   617.7
    BT **Color sense**
        Vision disorders
Color etchings
    USE **Color prints**
Color photography   778.6
    UF Color slides
        Photography, Color
    BT **Photography**
Color printing   686.2
    Use for materials on practical printing in color. Materials on hand-colored prints or on pictures printed in color are entered under **Color prints**.
    SA types of color printing processes [to be added as needed]
    BT **Printing**
    NT **Illustration of books**
        Lithography
        Silk screen printing
    RT **Color prints**

Color prints   769

Use for materials on hand-colored prints or on pictures printed in color. Materials on practical printing in color are entered under **Color printing**.

UF   Block printing

Color etchings

Painting—Color reproductions

SA   color prints of particular countries, e.g. **American color prints** [to be added as needed]

BT   **Prints**

NT   **American color prints**

Japanese color prints

RT   **Color printing**

Color prints, American

USE   **American color prints**

Color prints, Japanese

USE   **Japanese color prints**

Color—Psychological aspects   152.14

UF   Psychology of color

BT   **Color sense**

Psychology

Color sense   152.14

BT   **Psychophysiology**

Senses and sensation

Vision

NT   **Color blindness**

Color—Psychological aspects

Color slides

USE   **Color photography**

Slides (Photography)

Color television   621.388

BT   **Television**

Colorado River—Hoover Dam

USE   **Hoover Dam (Ariz. and Nev.)**

Coloring books   372.5

Use for individual works, collections, or materials about coloring books.

UF   Painting books

BT   **Picture books for children**

Colour

USE   **Color**

Columbus Day   394.264

BT   **Holidays**

Columnists

USE   **Journalists**

Combat photography

USE   **War photography**

Combustion   541; 621.402

BT   **Chemistry**

NT   **Fuel**

RT   **Fire**

Heat

Comedians (May subdiv. geog.)   **791; 792.2; 920**

BT   **Actors**

Entertainers

NT   **Fools and jesters**

Comedies   808.82

Use for individual works or for collections. Materials about comedy as a literary form are entered under **Comedy**.

UF   Comic drama

Comic plays

Humorous plays

Slapstick comedies

BT   **Drama**

Wit and humor

NT   **Comedy films**

Comedy television programs

Farces

Comedy   792.2; 809.2

Use for materials on comedy as a literary form. Individual works and collections of comedies are entered under **Comedies**.

UF   Comic drama

Comic literature

BT   **Drama**

Wit and humor

NT   **Burlesque (Literature)**

Commedia dell'arte

RT   **Tragicomedy**

Comedy films (May subdiv. geog.)   **791.43**

Use for individual works, collections, or materials about comedy films.

UF   Comic films

Humorous films

Slapstick comedies

SA   types of comedy films, e.g. **Three Stooges films** [to be added as needed]

BT   **Comedies**

Motion pictures

NT   **Three Stooges films**

RT   **Comedy television programs**

Comedy radio programs   791.44

Use for individual works, collections, or materials about comedy radio programs.

UF   Radio comedies

Radio comedy programs

BT   **Radio programs**

Comedy television programs   791.45

Use for individual works, collections, or materials about television comedies.

Comedy television programs—*Continued*
  UF Comic television programs
      Sitcoms
      Situation comedies
      Slapstick comedies
      Television comedies
      Television comedy programs
  BT **Comedies**
      Television programs
  RT **Comedy films**
Comets 523.6
  BT **Astronomy**
      Solar system
  NT **Halley's comet**
Comic book novels
  USE **Graphic novels**
Comic books, strips, etc. (May subdiv.
    geog.) **741.5**
  Use for individual works, collections, or
  materials about printed comic strips, i.e.
  groups of cartoons in narrative sequence, and
  books and magazines consisting of comic
  strips, etc.
  UF Comic strips
      Funnies
      Humorous pictures
  SA ethnic groups, classes of per-
      sons, corporate bodies, indi-
      vidual persons, literary au-
      thors, or sacred works with
      the subdivision *Comic books,
      strips, etc.*; and names of
      comic books, comic strips,
      and comic strip characters [to
      be added as needed]
  BT **Wit and humor**
  NT **Graphic novels**
      **Mystery comic books, strips,
      etc.**
      **Science fiction comic books,
      strips, etc.**
      **Superhero comic books, strips,
      etc.**
      **Western comic books, strips,
      etc.**
  RT **Cartoons and caricatures**
      Chapbooks
Comic drama
  USE **Comedies**
       Comedy
Comic epic literature
  USE **Mock-heroic literature**

Comic films
  USE **Comedy films**
Comic literature
  USE **Burlesque (Literature)**
       Comedy
       Parody
       Satire
Comic novels
  USE **Humorous fiction**
Comic opera
  USE **Opera**
       Operetta
Comic plays
  USE **Comedies**
Comic strips
  USE **Comic books, strips, etc.**
Comic television programs
  USE **Comedy television programs**
Comic verse
  USE **Humorous poetry**
Coming of age stories
  USE **Bildungsromans**
Commedia dell'arte (May subdiv. geog.)
    792.2
  BT **Acting**
      Comedy
      Farces
Commemorations
  USE **Anniversaries**
Commencements (May subdiv. geog.)
    394.2
  UF Graduation
  BT **Colleges and universities**
      High schools
      School assembly programs
Commentaries
  USE names of sacred works, includ-
       ing named parts of sacred
       works, with the subdivision
       Commentaries, e.g. **Bible—
       Commentaries** [to be added
       as needed]
Commentaries, Biblical
  USE **Bible—Commentaries**
Commerce 381
  Use for general materials on foreign and
  domestic commerce. Materials limited to com-
  merce between states are entered under **Inter-
  state commerce.**
  UF Distribution (Economics)
      Trade

Commerce—*Continued*

SA names of countries, cities, etc., with the subdivision *Commerce*, e.g. **United States—Commerce**; and names of articles of commerce, e.g. **Cotton** [to be added as needed]

BT **Economics**
Finance

NT **Banks and banking**
Barter
Black market
Boycotts
Business
Chambers of commerce
Chicago (Ill.)—Commerce
Commercial geography
Commercial products
Competition
Contracts
Cooperation
Developing countries—Commerce
Electronic commerce
Exchange
Industrial trusts
International trade
Interstate commerce
Marine insurance
Markets
Monopolies
Multinational corporations
Ohio—Commerce
Prices
Profit sharing
Restraint of trade
Retail trade
Stocks
Tourist trade
Trade routes
Trademarks
United States—Commerce

RT **Transportation**

Commerce—Law and legislation
USE **Commercial law**

Commercial aeronautics (May subdiv. geog.) **387.7**

UF Aeronautics, Commercial
Air cargo
Air freight
Air transport
Commercial aviation

BT **Freight**
Transportation

NT **Air mail service**
Airlines

Commercial arithmetic
USE **Business mathematics**

Commercial art (May subdiv. geog.) **741.6**

UF Advertising art
Art in advertising

BT **Advertising**
Art
Drawing

NT **Fashion design**
Posters
Textile design

Commercial art galleries (May subdiv. geog.) **338.7; 708**

UF Art galleries
Picture galleries

BT **Business enterprises**

Commercial aviation
USE **Commercial aeronautics**

Commercial buildings (May subdiv. geog.) **333.33; 725**

UF Mercantile buildings
Store buildings

BT **Buildings**

NT **Shopping centers and malls**
Stores

Commercial catalogs **380.1029; 659.13**

UF Catalogs
Commercial products—Catalogs
Mail order catalogs
Trade catalogs

SA types of merchandise, objects, products, etc., and names of individual companies with the subdivision *Catalogs* [to be added as needed]

BT **Advertising**

Commercial correspondence
USE **Business letters**

Commercial education
USE **Business education**

Commercial employees
USE **Office workers**

Commercial endeavors in space
USE **Space industrialization**

Commercial fishing (May subdiv. geog.)
338.3; 639.2

Use for materials on the fishing industry. Materials on the cultivation of fish in captivity are entered under **Fish culture**. Materials on fishing as a sport are entered under **Fishing**.

UF   Fisheries

      Fishing, Commercial

      Fishing industry

      Sea fisheries

BT   **Industries**

NT   **Pearl fisheries**

      Whaling

Commercial fishing—United States
338.3; 639.2

Commercial geography (May subdiv. geog.)   **330.9**

UF   Economic geography

      World economics

BT   **Commerce**

      Geography

NT   **Trade routes**

RT   **Economic conditions**

Commercial law (May subdiv. geog.)
346.07

UF   Business law

      Business—Law and legislation

      Commerce—Law and legislation

      Mercantile law

BT   **Law**

NT   **Antitrust law**

      Arbitration and award

      Bankruptcy

      Collecting of accounts

      Contracts

      Corporation law

      Debtor and creditor

      Fraud

      Insider trading

      Landlord and tenant

      Licenses

      Negotiable instruments

      Restraint of trade

      Unfair competition

RT   **Maritime law**

Commercial mathematics

USE   **Business mathematics**

Commercial paper

USE   **Negotiable instruments**

Commercial photography (May subdiv. geog.)   **778**

BT   **Photography**

NT   **Photojournalism**

Commercial policy (May subdiv. geog.)
381.3; 382

Use for general materials on the various regulations by which governments seek to protect and increase the commerce of a country, such as subsidies, tariffs, free ports, etc.

UF   Government policy

      Government regulation of commerce

      Reciprocity

      Trade barriers

      World economics

BT   **Economic policy**

      International economic relations

NT   **Buy national policy**

      Free trade

      Protectionism

      Tariff

Commercial policy—United States
381.3; 382

UF   United States—Commercial policy

Commercial products (May subdiv. geog.)
338; 381

UF   Merchandise

      Products, Commercial

SA   types of products and names of specific products [to be added as needed]

BT   **Commerce**

NT   **Animal products**

      Brand name products

      Consumer goods

      Forest products

      Generic products

      Manufactures

      Marine resources

      New products

      Raw materials

      Substitute products

Commercial products—Catalogs

USE   **Commercial catalogs**

Commercial products recall

USE   **Product recall**

Commercial secrets

USE   **Trade secrets**

Commercials, Radio

USE   **Radio advertising**

Commercials, Television

USE   **Television advertising**

Commission government
USE **Municipal government by commission**

Commission government with city manager
USE **Municipal government by city manager**

Commitment (Psychology) 153.8
BT **Choice (Psychology)**

Common cold
USE **Cold (Disease)**

Common currencies
USE **Monetary unions**

Common law (May subdiv. geog.) 340.5
UF Anglo-American law
BT **Law**

Common law marriage
USE **Unmarried couples**

Common market
USE **European Union**

Commonplaces
USE **Terms and phrases**

Commonwealth countries 909

Use for materials dealing collectively with the member countries of the international organization that was founded in 1931 as the British Commonwealth of Nations, changed its name to the Commonwealth of Nations in 1950, and became known as the Commonwealth in 1969.
UF British Commonwealth countries
British Commonwealth of Nations
British Dominions
Commonwealth of Nations
Dominions, British
RT **Great Britain—Colonies**

Commonwealth of England
USE **Great Britain—History—1642-1660, Civil War and Commonwealth**

Commonwealth of Nations
USE **Commonwealth countries**

Commonwealth, The
USE **Political science**
Republics
State, The

Communal living (May subdiv. geog.) 307.77

Use for materials on arrangements in voluntary cooperative living, usually informal. Materials on traditional, formally organized communal ventures, usually based on ideological, political, or religious affiliation are entered under **Collective settlements**.

UF Communal settlements
Communes
Cooperative living
Group living
BT **Cooperation**
RT **Collective settlements**
Cooperative housing
Counter culture

Communal settlements
USE **Collective settlements**
Communal living

Communes
USE **Collective settlements**
Communal living

Communicable diseases (May subdiv. geog.) 614.4; 616.9
UF Contagion and contagious diseases
Contagious diseases
Infection and infectious diseases
Quarantine
SA names of communicable diseases [to be added as needed]
BT **Diseases**
Public health
NT **AIDS (Disease)**
Cold (Disease)
Fumigation
Germ theory of disease
Influenza
Plague
Rabies
Sexually transmitted diseases
RT **Epidemics**
Immunity
Insects as carriers of disease

Communicable diseases—Prevention (May subdiv. geog.) 614.4
BT **Preventive medicine**

Communication 302.2

Use for general materials on communication in its broadest sense, including the use of the spoken and written word, signs, symbols, or behavior.
UF Mass communication
BT **Sociology**
NT **Audiences**
Books and reading
Conversation
Cybernetics
Deaf—Means of communication

Communication—*Continued*
>> Information science
>> Language and languages
>> Language arts
>> Mass media
>> Nonverbal communication
>> Persuasion (Psychology)
>> Popular culture
>> Postal service
>> Public speaking
>> Signals and signaling
>> Signs and symbols
>> Social networking
>> Telecommunication
>> Writing

Communication among animals
> USE **Animal communication**

Communication arts
> USE **Language arts**

Communication disorders (Medicine)
> USE **Communicative disorders**

Communication in marriage **646.7**
> UF Marital communication
> BT **Marriage**

Communication satellites
> USE **Artificial satellites in telecommunication**

Communication systems
> USE subjects with the subdivision
> *Communication systems*, e.g.
> **Astronautics—Communication systems** [to be added as needed]

Communication systems, Wireless
> USE **Wireless communication systems**

Communications relay satellites
> USE **Artificial satellites in telecommunication**

Communicative disorders **616.85**
> UF Communication disorders (Medicine)
> Disorders of communication
> BT **Nervous system—Diseases**
> NT **Language disorders**
> **Speech disorders**

Communion
> USE **Eucharist**

Communism (May subdiv. geog.) **320.5;**
321.9; 324.1; 335.43
> UF Bolshevism

> SA communism and other subjects,
> e.g. **Communism and literature** [to be added as needed]
> BT **Collectivism**
> **Political science**
> **Totalitarianism**
> NT **Anticommunist movements**
> **Collective settlements**
> **Communism and literature**
> **Communism and religion**
> **Dialectical materialism**
> RT **Communist countries**
> **Marxism**
> **Socialism**

Communism and literature (May subdiv. geog.) **335.4; 809**
> UF Literature and communism
> BT **Communism**
> **Literature**

Communism and religion (May subdiv. geog.) **261.7; 335.4**
> UF Communism—Religious aspects
> Religion and communism
> BT **Communism**
> **Religion**

Communism—Religious aspects
> USE **Communism and religion**

Communism—Russia **320.5;**
335.430947; 947.084
> UF Communism—Soviet Union
> [*Former heading*]
> Russia—Communism
> Russian communism
> Soviet communism
> Soviet Union—Communism

Communism—Soviet Union
> USE **Communism—Russia**

Communism—United States **320.5;**
335.43; 973

Communist countries **909**
> RT **Communism**

Communities, Space
> USE **Space colonies**

Community action
> USE **Political participation**

Community and libraries
> USE **Libraries and community**

Community and school (May subdiv. geog.) **371.19**
> UF School and community
> BT **Community life**

Community and school—*Continued*
  NT   **Parent-teacher associations**
Community based residences
  USE   **Group homes**
Community centers (May subdiv. geog.)
      374; 790.06
  UF   Neighborhood centers
       Play centers
       Recreation centers
  BT   **Cities and towns—Civic im-
         provement**
       Community life
       Community organization
       Recreation
       Social settlements
  NT   **Senior centers**
       Youth hostels
  RT   **Playgrounds**
Community chests
  USE   **Fund raising**
Community churches (May subdiv. geog.)
      254
    Use for materials on local churches that
  have no denominational affiliations.
  UF   Churches, Community
       Churches, Undenominational
       Nondenominational churches
       Undenominational churches
       Union churches
  BT   **Christian sects**
Community colleges
  USE   **Junior colleges**
Community councils
  USE   **Community organization**
Community development (May subdiv.
      geog.)   **307.1; 361.6**
  UF   Neighborhood development
       Regional development
  BT   **Domestic economic assistance**
       Social change
       Urban renewal
  NT   **Rural development**
  RT   **Agricultural extension work**
       City planning
       Technical assistance
Community gardens (May subdiv. geog.)
      635
  UF   Neighborhood gardens
  BT   **Gardens**
Community health services (May subdiv.
      geog.)   **362.12**

  BT   **Community services**
       Public health
Community history
  USE   **Local history**
Community identity
  USE   **Group identity**
Community life (May subdiv. geog.)
      307
  BT   **Associations**
  NT   **Community and school**
       Community centers
       Community organization
       Neighborhood
       Scouts and scouting
Community organization (May subdiv.
      geog.)   **307**
  UF   Community councils
  BT   **Community life**
       Social work
  NT   **Community centers**
       Local government
  RT   **Urban renewal**
Community services (May subdiv. geog.)
      361.7; 361.8
  SA   types of services, e.g. **Commu-
         nity health services** [to be
         added as needed]
  BT   **Social work**
  NT   **Community health services**
Community surveys
  USE   **Social surveys**
Community theater
  USE   **Little theater movement**
Compact automobiles
  USE   **Compact cars**
Compact cars (May subdiv. geog.)
      629.222
  UF   Compact automobiles
       Compacts (Automobiles)
       Economy cars
       Small cars
  SA   names of specific makes and
         models of compact cars [to
         be added as needed]
  BT   **Automobiles**
Compact disc interactive technology
  USE   **CD-I technology**
Compact disc players   **621.389**
  UF   Audiodisc players
       CD players
       Digital audio disc players

Compact disc players—*Continued*
- BT **Phonograph**
  Sound—Recording and reproducing

Compact disc read-only memory
- USE **CD-ROMs**

Compact discs   621.389; 780.26
Use for materials on small optical discs in general and on the compact disc format for sound recordings. Materials about sound recordings that emphasize the content of the recording rather than the format are entered under **Sound recordings**.
- UF   CDs (Compact discs)
  Compact disks
  Digital compact discs
- BT **Optical storage devices**
  Sound recordings
- NT **CD-I technology**
  CD-ROMs

Compact disks
- USE **Compact discs**

Compacts (Automobiles)
- USE **Compact cars**

Companies
- USE **Business enterprises**
  Corporations
  Partnership

Companion-animal partnership
- USE **Pet therapy**

Company libraries
- USE **Corporate libraries**

Company symbols
- USE **Trademarks**

Comparative anatomy   571.3
- UF   Anatomy, Comparative
- BT **Anatomy**
  Zoology
- NT **Morphology**

Comparative government   320.3
- UF   Government, Comparative
- SA   names of countries, cities, etc., with the subdivision *Politics and government*, e.g. **United States—Politics and government** [to be added as needed]
- BT **Political science**

Comparative linguistics
- USE **Linguistics**

Comparative literature   809
This heading may be subdivided by the nationalities of literatures compared, with duplicate entry, e.g. **Comparative literature—En-** glish **and German** and **Comparative literature—German and English**.
- UF   Literature, Comparative
- BT **Literature**

Comparative literature—English and German   809

Comparative literature—German and English   809

Comparative morphology
- USE **Morphology**

Comparative philology
- USE **Linguistics**

Comparative philosophy   100
- BT **Philosophy**

Comparative physiology   571.1
- UF   Physiology, Comparative
- BT **Physiology**

Comparative psychology   156
- UF   Animal psychology
  Psychology, Comparative
- SA   types of animals with the subdivision *Psychology*, e.g. **Dogs—Psychology** [to be added as needed]
- BT **Zoology**
- NT **Dogs—Psychology**
  Sociobiology
- RT **Animal intelligence**
  Instinct

Comparative religion
- USE **Christianity and other religions**
  Religions

Comparative studies
- USE   religious topics and names of sacred works and individual Christian denominations with the subdivision *Comparative studies,* e.g. **Mysticism—Comparative studies** [to be added as needed]

Comparison
- USE   names of languages with the subdivision *Comparison,* e.g. **English language—Comparison** [to be added as needed]

Comparison (English grammar)
- USE **English language—Comparison**

Comparison of cultures
- USE **Cross-cultural studies**

Compass   538; 623.8
- UF   Magnetic needle
  Mariner's compass

177

Compass—*Continued*
 BT **Magnetism**
   Navigation
Compassion **177**
 BT **Emotions**
Compensation
 USE **Pensions**
   Salaries, wages, etc.
   Workers' compensation
Compensatory spending
 USE **Deficit financing**
Competence
 USE **Performance**
Competition (May subdiv. geog.) **338.6**
 BT **Business**
   Business ethics
   Commerce
 RT **Industrial trusts**
   Monopolies
   Supply and demand
Competition, International
 USE **International competition**
Competition (Psychology) **158.2**
 UF Competitive behavior
   Competitiveness (Psychology)
 BT **Interpersonal relations**
   Motivation (Psychology)
   Psychology
Competition, Unfair
 USE **Unfair competition**
Competitions
 USE **Awards**
   Contests
   and subjects with the subdivi-
    sion *Competitions,* e.g. **Liter-**
    ature—Competitions [to be
    added as needed]
Competitive behavior
 USE **Competition (Psychology)**
Competitiveness (Psychology)
 USE **Competition (Psychology)**
Composers (May subdiv. geog.) **780.92;
920**
 UF Songwriters
 BT **Musicians**
Composers, American
 USE **Composers—United States**
Composers—United States **780.92; 920**
 UF American composers
   Composers, American

Composition
 USE types of natural substances of
   unfixed composition, including
   soils, plants and crops, animals, farm products, etc., with
   the subdivision *Composition,*
   for the results of analyses of
   those substances, e.g. **Food—
   Composition** [to be added as
   needed]
Composition and exercises
 USE names of languages with the
   subdivision *Composition and
   exercises,* e.g. **English lan-
   guage—Composition and ex-
   ercises** [to be added as need-
   ed]
Composition (Art) **701**
 UF Art—Composition
 BT **Art**
 NT **Architecture—Composition,
   proportion, etc.**
 RT **Painting**
Composition (Music) **781.3**
 UF Music—Composition
   Musical composition
   Song writing
   Songwriting
 BT **Music**
   Music—Theory
 NT **Counterpoint**
   Harmony
   **Instrumentation and orchestra-
   tion**
   Musical accompaniment
   Musical form
   **Popular music—Writing and
   publishing**
Composition of natural substances
 USE types of natural substances of
   unfixed composition, including
   soils, plants and crops, ani-
   mals, farm products, etc., with
   the subdivision *Composition*
   for the results of analyses of
   those substances, e.g. **Food—
   Composition** [to be added as
   needed]
Composition (Printing)
 USE **Typesetting**

Composition (Rhetoric)
    USE **Rhetoric**
        and names of languages with
        the subdivision *Composition*
        and exercises, e.g. **English**
        language—Composition and
        exercises [to be added as
        needed]
Compost   631.8
    BT **Fertilizers**
        Soils
    RT **Organic gardening**
Comprehensive health care organizations
    USE **Health maintenance organiza-**
         tions
Compressed air   621.5
    UF Pneumatic transmission
    BT **Cold storage**
        Pneumatics
        Power (Mechanics)
Compulsion (Psychology)
    USE **Compulsive behavior**
Compulsive behavior   616.85
    UF Addictive behavior
        Compulsion (Psychology)
    SA types of compulsive behavior [to
        be added as needed]
    BT **Abnormal psychology**
        Human behavior
    NT **Compulsive gambling**
        Exercise addiction
        Workaholism
    RT **Obsessive-compulsive disorder**
        Twelve-step programs
Compulsive exercising
    USE **Exercise addiction**
Compulsive gambling   616.85
    UF Addiction to gambling
    BT **Compulsive behavior**
        Gambling
Compulsive working
    USE **Workaholism**
Compulsory education (May subdiv.
    geog.)   **379.2**
    UF Compulsory school attendance
        Education, Compulsory
    BT **Education—Government policy**
    NT **Evening and continuation**
        schools
    RT **School attendance**

Compulsory labor
    USE **Forced labor**
Compulsory military service
    USE **Draft**
Compulsory school attendance
    USE **Compulsory education**
        School attendance
Computation, Approximate
    USE **Approximate computation**
Computation (Mathematics)
    USE **Arithmetic**
Computer-aided design   620
    Use for materials on the use of computer
    graphics to design tools, vehicles, buildings,
    etc.
    UF CAD
        Computer aided design
        Computer-assisted design
        Electronic design
    BT **Computer graphics**
        Design
    RT **Computer-aided design soft-**
         ware
Computer aided design
    USE **Computer-aided design**
Computer-aided design software   006.6
    UF CAD/CAM software
        CAD software
    BT **Computer software**
    RT **Computer-aided design**
Computer animation   741.5
    UF CGI (Cinematography)
        Computer-generated animation
    BT **Animation (Cinematography)**
Computer art (May subdiv. geog.)   **776;**
    700; 760
    Use for materials on the use of computer
    graphics to create artistic designs, drawings,
    or other works of art.
    BT **Art**
        Computer graphics
Computer-assisted design
    USE **Computer-aided design**
Computer-assisted instruction   371.33
    Use for materials on automated instruction
    in which a student interacts directly with a
    computer.
    UF CAI
        Computer assisted instruction
        Computers—Educational use
        Education—Automation
        Education—Data processing
        Teaching—Data processing

Computer-assisted instruction—*Continued*

    SA   subjects with the subdivision
             Computer-assisted instruction
             [to be added as needed]

    BT   **Programmed instruction**

    NT   **Mathematics—Computer-**
           assisted instruction

Computer assisted instruction

    USE **Computer-assisted instruction**

Computer-assisted instruction—Authoring
    programs   005.5; 371.33

    Use for materials on computer programs that allow the user with comparatively little expertise to design customized computer programs for educational purposes.

    UF   Authoring programs for comput-
           er-assisted instruction

    BT   **Computer software**

Computer awareness

    USE **Computer literacy**

Computer-based information systems

    USE **Information systems**
          Management information sys-
            tems

Computer-based multimedia information
    systems

    USE **Multimedia**

Computer bulletin boards   004.693;
    384.3

    Use for materials on services that allow users to post messages and retrieve messages from others who have some common interest. Materials on services that allow users to engage in conversations in real time are entered under **Online chat groups**. Materials on services, commonly called electronic mailing lists, that allow subscribers to post messages that are then distributed to other subscribers are entered under **Electronic discussion groups**.

    UF   Electronic bulletin boards

    BT   **Bulletin boards**

    RT   **Electronic discussion groups**
          Online chat groups

Computer control

    USE **Automation**

Computer crimes (May subdiv. geog.)
    364.16

    UF   Computer fraud

    BT   **Crime**

    NT   **Computer hackers**
          Computer viruses
          Cyberbullying

    RT   **Computer security**

Computer drafting

    USE **Computer graphics**

Computer drawing

    USE **Computer graphics**

Computer fonts   686.2

    BT   **Type and type-founding**

Computer fraud

    USE **Computer crimes**

Computer games   794.8

    BT   **Computer software**
          Games

Computer-generated animation

    USE **Computer animation**

Computer graphics   006.6

    Use for materials on the production of drawings, pictures, or diagrams, as distinct from letters and numbers, on a computer screen or hard-copy output devices. Materials on the use of computer graphics to create artistic designs, drawings, or other works of art are entered under **Computer art**. Materials on the use of computer graphics to design tools, vehicles, buildings, etc., are entered under **Computer-aided design**.

    UF   Automatic drafting
          Automatic drawing
          Computer drafting
          Computer drawing
          Electronic drafting
          Electronic drawing
          Graphics, Computer

    BT   **Data processing**

    NT   **Computer-aided design**
          Computer art
          Icons (Computer graphics)

Computer hackers (May subdiv. geog.)
    005.8092

    BT   **Computer crimes**
          Criminals

Computer hardware

    USE **Computers**

Computer icons

    USE **Icons (Computer graphics)**

Computer industry (May subdiv. geog.)
    338.7

    BT   **Industries**

    RT   **Computers**

Computer input-output equipment

    USE **Computer peripherals**

Computer interfaces   004.6; 621.39

    Use for materials on equipment and techniques linking computers to peripheral devices or to other computers.

    UF   Interfaces, Computer

    BT   **Computer peripherals**

Computer keyboarding
USE **Keyboarding (Electronics)**
Computer keyboards
USE **Keyboards (Electronics)**
Computer languages
USE **Programming languages**
Computer literacy (May subdiv. geog.)
004

Use for materials on the basic knowledge of computers a person needs in order to function in a computer-based society.

UF Computer awareness
BT **Computers and civilization**
Literacy
Computer memory systems
USE **Computer storage devices**
Computer modeling
USE **Computer simulation**
Computer models
USE **Computer simulation**
Computer monitors   004.7

Use for materials on video display devices connected to a personal computer.

UF CRT display terminals
Video display terminals
BT **Computer peripherals**
Computer music (May subdiv. geog.)
786.7
BT **Music**
RT **Computer sound processing**
Electronic music
Computer network resources
USE **Internet resources**
Computer networks   004.6; 384.3

Use for materials on systems consisting of two or more interconnected computers.

UF Information superhighway
Networks, Computer
SA types of computer networks, names of specific computer networks, and subjects with the subdivision *Computer networks*, e.g. **Business enterprises—Computer networks** [to be added as needed]
BT **Data transmission systems**
Telecommunication
NT **Business enterprises—Computer networks**
Cyberspace
Internet
Local area networks
RT **Information networks**

Computer operating systems   005.4
UF Computers—Operating systems
Operating systems (Computers)
BT **Computer software**
Computer peripherals   004.7; 621.39
UF Computer input-output equipment
Input equipment (Computers)
Output equipment (Computers)
SA types of computer peripherals [to be added as needed]
BT **Computers**
NT **Computer interfaces**
Computer monitors
Computer storage devices
Computer terminals
Keyboards (Electronics)
Optical scanners
Computer program languages
USE **Programming languages**
Computer programming   005.1
UF Computers—Programming
Programming (Computers)
SA subjects with the subdivision *Computer software*, e.g. **Database management—Computer software** [to be added as needed]
BT **Computer science**
Data processing
RT **Computer software**
Programming languages
Computer programs
USE **Computer software**
Computer science   004

Use for materials discussing collectively the disciplines that deal with the general theory and application of computers.

BT **Science**
NT **Artificial intelligence**
Computer programming
Database management
RT **Computers**
Computer science—Dictionaries   004.03
UF Computer terms
Computers—Dictionaries
BT **Encyclopedias and dictionaries**
Computer security (May subdiv. geog.)
005.8

Use for materials on protecting computer hardware and software from accidental or malicious access, use, modification, disclosure, or destruction.

Computer security—*Continued*
  UF   Computers—Access control
       Computers—Security measures
  BT   **Computers**
  RT   **Computer crimes**
       Computer viruses
Computer sex   306.7
  UF   Cybersex
       Online sex
  BT   **Sex**
Computer simulation   003
  UF   Computer modeling
       Computer models
       Simulation, Computer
  SA   subjects with the subdivision
       Computer simulation, e.g.
       **Psychology—Computer simu-
       lation** [to be added as need-
       ed]
  BT   **Mathematical models**
  NT   **Psychology—Computer simula-
       tion**
       Virtual reality
Computer software   005.3
  UF   Computer programs
       Programs, Computer
       Software, Computer
  SA   types of computer software, e.g.
       **Computer games;
       Spreadsheet software**; etc.;
       subjects with the subdivision
       Computer software, e.g.
       **Oceanography—Computer
       software**; and names of indi-
       vidual computer programs
       qualified by *(Computer soft-
       ware)*, e.g. **Microsoft Word
       (Computer software)** [to be
       added as needed]
  NT   **Computer-aided design soft-
       ware**
       **Computer-assisted instruction—
       Authoring programs**
       Computer games
       Computer operating systems
       Computer viruses
       **Database management—Com-
       puter software**
       Educational software
       Free computer software
       Image processing software
       Internet software

       **Microsoft Word (Computer
       software)**
       Multimedia
       **Oceanography—Computer soft-
       ware**
       Open source software
       Programming languages
       **Shareware (Computer soft-
       ware)**
       Spreadsheet software
       Utilities (Computer software)
       Word processing software
  RT   **Computer programming**
       Computer software industry
       Computers
Computer software industry (May subdiv.
  geog.)   **338.4**
  BT   **Industries**
  RT   **Computer software**
Computer sound processing (May subdiv.
  geog.)   **006.5**
  UF   Sound processing, Computer
  BT   **Computers**
       Sound
  NT   **MP3 players**
  RT   **Computer music**
       Speech processing systems
Computer speech processing systems
  USE   **Speech processing systems**
Computer storage devices   004.5;
  621.39
  UF   Computer memory systems
       Computers—Memory systems
       Computers—Storage devices
       Memory devices (Computers)
       Storage devices, Computer
  BT   **Computer peripherals**
  NT   **Optical storage devices**
Computer terminals   004.7; 621.39
       Use for materials on video display devices
       connected to a mainframe computer.
  UF   Terminals, Computer
  BT   **Computer peripherals**
Computer terms
  USE   **Computer science—Dictionaries**
Computer utility programs
  USE   **Utilities (Computer software)**
Computer viruses   005.8
  UF   Software viruses
       Viruses, Computer
  BT   **Computer crimes**
       Computer software

Computer viruses—*Continued*

  RT **Computer security**

Computerized tomography

  USE **Tomography**

Computers (May subdiv. geog.)   **004; 621.39**

    Use for materials on modern electronic computers developed after 1945. Materials on present-day calculators and on calculating machines and mechanical computers made before 1945 are entered under **Calculators**.

  UF Computer hardware

  SA types of computers, e.g. **Personal computers**; and names of specific computers [to be added as needed]

  BT **Electronic apparatus and appliances**

  NT **Computer peripherals**
      Computer security
      Computer sound processing
      Computers and children
      Computers and civilization
      Computers and the handicapped
      Data processing
      Information systems
      Macintosh (Computer)
      Microprocessors
      Personal computers
      Portable computers
      Supercomputers

  RT **Calculators**
      Computer industry
      Computer science
      Computer software

Computers—Access control

  USE **Computer security**

Computers and children (May subdiv. geog.)   **004.083**

  BT **Children**
      Computers

Computers and civilization (May subdiv. geog.)   **004; 303.48**

  UF Civilization and computers

  BT **Civilization**
      Computers
      Technology and civilization

  NT **Computer literacy**

Computers and the handicapped (May subdiv. geog.)   **004.6; 362.4**

  BT **Computers**
      Handicapped

Computers—Cartoons and caricatures
      621.39; 741.5

  BT **Cartoons and caricatures**

Computers—Dictionaries

  USE **Computer science—Dictionaries**

Computers—Educational use

  USE **Computer-assisted instruction**

Computers—Juvenile literature   **004**

Computers—Memory systems

  USE **Computer storage devices**

Computers—Operating systems

  USE **Computer operating systems**

Computers—Programming

  USE **Computer programming**

Computers—Security measures

  USE **Computer security**

Computers—Storage devices

  USE **Computer storage devices**

Computers—Utility programs

  USE **Utilities (Computer software)**

Con artists

  USE **Swindlers and swindling**

Con game

  USE **Swindlers and swindling**

Concealment

  USE **Secrecy**

Concentration

  USE **Attention**

Concentration camps (May subdiv. geog.)   **365**

  UF Internment camps

  SA names of wars with the subdivision *Prisoners and prisons*; and names of individual camps, e.g. **Auschwitz (Poland: Concentration camp)** [to be added as needed]

  BT **Military camps**
      Political crimes and offenses

  NT **Auschwitz (Poland: Concentration camp)**
      Bergen-Belsen (Germany: Concentration camp)
      Buchenwald (Germany: Concentration camp)
      Terezin (Czechoslovakia: Concentration camp)
      World War, 1939-1945—Prisoners and prisons

  RT **Prisoners of war**

Concept formation
USE **Concept learning**

Concept learning   153.2; 370.15

Use for materials on the process of discovering the distinguishing features of particular concepts and the ensuing ability to use the concepts appropriately.

UF   Concept formation

BT   **Concepts**

Psychology of learning

Conception—Prevention
USE   **Birth control**

Concepts   153.2

SA   types of concepts and images, e.g. **Size**; **Shape**; etc. [to be added as needed]

BT   **Perception**

NT   **Concept learning**

Opposites

Shape

Size

Concert halls (May subdiv. geog.)   **725**

UF   Music-halls

BT   **Auditoriums**

Concerto   784.18

Use for musical scores and for materials on the concerto as a musical form.

UF   Concertos

BT   **Musical form**

Orchestral music

Concertos
USE   **Concerto**

Concerts (May subdiv. geog.)   **780.78**

BT   **Amusements**

Music

RT   **Music festivals**

Concord (Mass.), Battle of, 1775   973.3

BT   **Battles**

United States—History—1775-1783, Revolution—Campaigns

Concordances   010

Use for works that list words with references to passages in a text where the exact word occurs. Works that list topics or names with references to books, articles, or passages where those topics or name are to be found are entered under **Indexes**.

SA   names of individual authors, literary works, sacred works, literatures, and literary forms, with the subdivision *Concordances*, e.g. **Shakespeare,**

William, 1564-1616—Concordances; **Bible—Concordances**; etc. [to be added as needed]

BT   **Indexes**

Concrete (May subdiv. geog.)   **691; 693**

BT   **Building materials**

Foundations

Masonry

Plaster and plastering

NT   **Reinforced concrete**

RT   **Cement**

Concrete construction

Concrete building
USE   **Concrete construction**

Concrete construction (May subdiv. geog.)   **693**

UF   Concrete building

Construction, Concrete

BT   **Building**

RT   **Concrete**

Concrete—Testing (May subdiv. geog.)   **620.1**

BT   **Strength of materials**

Condemnation of land
USE   **Eminent domain**

Condensers (Electricity)   621.31

UF   Electric condensers

BT   **Induction coils**

Condensers (Steam)   621.1

BT   **Steam engines**

Condominium timesharing
USE   **Timesharing (Real estate)**

Condominiums (May subdiv. geog.)   **346.04; 643**

BT   **Apartment houses**

NT   **Timesharing (Real estate)**

Conduct of life   170

Use for materials on standards of behavior and materials containing moral guidance and advice to the individual.

UF   Morals

Personal conduct

SA   classes of persons with the subdivision *Conduct of life*, e.g. **Children—Conduct of life**; and names of vices and virtues [to be added as needed]

BT   **Ethics**

Human behavior

Life skills

Conduct of life—*Continued*
   NT   **Altruism**
        Children—Conduct of life
        Fairness
        Honor
        Pride and vanity
        Simplicity
        Sympathy
        Teenagers—Conduct of life
        Vice
        Virtue
Conducting   781.45
   Use for materials on orchestral conducting
   or a combination of orchestral and choral con-
   ducting. Materials limited to choral conduct-
   ing are entered under **Choral conducting**.
   BT   **Music**
   NT   **Choral conducting**
   RT   **Bands (Music)**
        Conductors (Music)
        Orchestra
Conducting, Choral
   USE   **Choral conducting**
Conductors, Electric
   USE   **Electric conductors**
Conductors (Music) (May subdiv. geog.)
        784.2092, 920
   UF   Bandmasters
        Music conductors
   BT   **Musicians**
        Orchestra
   RT   **Choral conducting**
        Conducting
Confectionary
   USE   **Confectionery**
Confectionery (May subdiv. geog.)
        641.8; 664
   UF   Confectionary
        Sweets
   BT   **Cooking**
   NT   **Cake**
        Cake decorating
        Candy
Confederacies
   USE   **Federal government**
Confederate States of America   973.7
   BT   **United States—History—1861-
        1865, Civil War**
Confederation of American colonies
   USE   **United States—History—1783-
        1815**

Conference calls (Teleconferencing)
   USE   **Teleconferencing**
Conference papers
   USE   **Conference proceedings**
Conference proceedings (May subdiv.
        geog.)   **060**
   Use for materials about the papers and oth-
   er documents stemming from a conference
   and for collections of various conference pro-
   ceedings. Materials about conferences apart
   from the proceedings are entered under **Con-
   ferences**.
   UF   Conference papers
   SA   topics and names of corporate
        bodies with the subdivision
        Conference proceedings [to be
        added as needed]
   BT   **Documentation**
   RT   **Conferences**
Conferences (May subdiv. geog.)   **060**
   Use for materials about conferences, congresses, or conventions. Materials about the
   papers and other documents stemming from a
   conference and collections of various confer-
   ence proceedings are entered under **Confer-
   ence proceedings**.
   UF   Congresses
        Congresses and conventions
        Conventions
        International conferences
   SA   subjects and names of corporate
        bodies with the subdivision
        Conferences, e.g. **World
        War, 1939-1945—Confer-
        ences**; **Physics—Conferences**;
        names of specific conferences,
        congresses, or conventions;
        and subjects and names of
        corporate bodies with the sub-
        division *Conference proceed-
        ings* [to be added as needed]
   BT   **Intellectual cooperation**
        International cooperation
   NT   **Constitutional conventions**
        Political conventions
        **World War, 1939-1945—Con-
        ferences**
   RT   **Conference proceedings**
Conferences, Parent-teacher
   USE   **Parent-teacher conferences**
Confession   265
   UF   Auricular confession
   RT   **Forgiveness of sin**
        Penance

Confessions of faith
　USE　**Creeds**
Confidence game
　USE　**Swindlers and swindling**
Configuration (Psychology)
　USE　**Gestalt psychology**
Confirmation　265
　BT　**Sacraments**
Conflict management (May subdiv. geog.)
　　303.6
　UF　Conflict resolution
　　　Dispute settlement
　　　Management of conflict
　BT　**Management**
　　　Negotiation
　　　Problem solving
　　　Social conflict
　RT　**Crisis management**
Conflict of cultures
　USE　**Culture conflict**
Conflict of generations (May subdiv.
　　geog.)　**306.874**
　UF　Generation gap
　BT　**Child-adult relationship**
　　　Interpersonal relations
　　　Parent-child relationship
　　　Social conflict
Conflict of interests (May subdiv. geog.)
　　172; 353.4
　BT　**Political ethics**
　NT　**Misconduct in office**
　　　Political corruption
Conflict resolution
　USE　**Conflict management**
Conflict, Social
　USE　**Social conflict**
Conformity　153.8; 302.5; 303.3
　UF　Nonconformity
　　　Social conformity
　BT　**Attitude (Psychology)**
　　　Freedom
　NT　**Persuasion (Psychology)**
　RT　**Deviant behavior**
　　　Dissent
　　　Individuality
Confucianism (May subdiv. geog.)　**181;**
　　299.5
　BT　**Religions**
Congenital diseases
　USE　**Medical genetics**

Conglomerate corporations (May subdiv.
　　geog.)　**338.8**
　UF　Diversified corporations
　BT　**Corporations**
　RT　**Corporate mergers and acqui-
　　　sitions**
Congo (Democratic Republic)　**967.5**
　　May be subdivided like United States ex-
　　cept for History.
　UF　Democratic Republic of the
　　　Congo
　　　Zaire
Congo (Republic)　**967.2**
　　May be subdivided like United States ex-
　　cept for History.
　UF　Republic of the Congo
Congregate housing
　USE　**Assisted living**
Congregationalism (May subdiv. geog.)
　　285.8
　BT　**Christian sects**
　NT　**Unitarianism**
　RT　**Calvinism**
　　　Puritans
Congregations
　USE　**Religious institutions**
Congress (U.S.)
　USE　**United States. Congress**
Congresses
　USE　**Conferences**
　　　and subjects with the subdivi-
　　　sion *Conferences,* e.g. **World
　　　War, 1939-1945—Confer-
　　　ences; Physics—Conferences;**
　　　and names of specific confer-
　　　ences, congresses, or conven-
　　　tions [to be added as needed]
Congresses and conventions
　USE　**Conferences**
Congressional investigations
　USE　**Governmental investigations**
Conjuring
　USE　**Magic tricks**
Conscience　170; 241
　BT　**Christian ethics**
　　　Duty
　　　Ethics
　NT　**Freedom of conscience**
　　　Guilt
Conscientious objectors (May subdiv.
　　geog.)　**343; 355.2**

Conscientious objectors—*Continued*
>   SA   names of wars with the subdivision *Conscientious objectors* [to be added as needed]
>   BT   **Freedom of conscience**
>   **War—Religious aspects**
>   NT   **World War, 1939-1945—Conscientious objectors**
>   RT   **Draft resisters**
>   **Pacifism**

Consciousness   126; 153
>   BT   **Apperception**
>   **Mind and body**
>   **Perception**
>   **Psychology**
>   NT   **Gestalt psychology**
>   **Individuality**
>   **Personality**
>   **Self**
>   **Theory of knowledge**
>   RT   **Subconsciousness**

Consciousness expanding drugs
>   USE   **Hallucinogens**

Conscript labor
>   USE   **Forced labor**

Conscription, Military
>   USE   **Draft**

Conservation and restoration
>   USE   types of art objects, library materials, architecture, and land vehicles with the subdivision *Conservation and restoration,* c.g. **Automobiles—Conservation and restoration** [to be added as needed]

Conservation movement
>   USE   **Environmental movement**

Conservation of biodiversity
>   USE   **Biodiversity conservation**

Conservation of buildings
>   USE   **Architecture—Conservation and restoration**

Conservation of energy
>   USE   **Energy conservation**
>   **Force and energy**

Conservation of forests
>   USE   **Forest conservation**

Conservation of natural resources (May subdiv. geog.)   **333.72; 639.9**
>   UF   Preservation of natural resources
>   Resource management
>   SA   types of conservation, e.g. **Soil conservation** [to be added as needed]
>   BT   **Environmental protection**
>   **Natural resources**
>   NT   **Biodiversity conservation**
>   **Energy conservation**
>   **Forest conservation**
>   **Nature conservation**
>   **Plant conservation**
>   **Soil conservation**
>   **Water conservation**
>   **Wildlife conservation**
>   RT   **Environmental policy**
>   **National parks and reserves**
>   **Wilderness areas**

Conservation of nature
>   USE   **Nature conservation**

Conservation of photographs
>   USE   **Photographs—Conservation and restoration**

Conservation of plants
>   USE   **Plant conservation**

Conservation of power resources
>   USE   **Energy conservation**

Conservation of the soil
>   USE   **Soil conservation**

Conservation of water
>   USE   **Water conservation**

Conservation of wildlife
>   USE   **Wildlife conservation**

Conservation of works of art, books, etc.
>   USE   subjects with the subdivision *Conservation and restoration,* e.g. **Library resources—Conservation and restoration; Painting—Conservation and restoration;** etc. [to be added as needed]

Conservatism (May subdiv. geog.)   **320.5**
>   UF   Reaction (Political science)
>   Right (Political science)
>   BT   **Political science**
>   **Social sciences**
>   RT   **Right and left (Political science)**

Conservatories, Home
>   USE   **Garden rooms**

Consolation   **152.4; 155.9**
>   UF   Solace

Consolation—*Continued*
    BT   **Emotions**
          Human behavior
    RT   **Bereavement**
          Grief
Consolidation and merger of corporations
    USE **Corporate mergers and acqui-
           sitions**
Consolidation of schools
    USE **Schools—Centralization**
Consortia, Library
    USE **Library cooperation**
Conspiracies (May subdiv. geog.)   **364.1**
    BT   **Crime**
          Political crimes and offenses
Constellations   **523.8**
    SA   names of constellations [to be
          added as needed]
    BT   **Sky**
    RT   **Astrology**
          Astronomy
          Stars
Constitution (U.S.)
    USE **United States. Constitution**
Constitutional amendments (May subdiv.
    geog.)   **342**
    Use for texts of constitutional amendments
    and materials about constitutional amendments
    and the amending process.
    SA   subjects dealt with in constitu-
          tional amendments with the
          subdivision *Law and legisla-
          tion*, or *Legal status, laws,
          etc.* [to be added as needed]
    BT   **Constitutional law**
          Constitutions
Constitutional conventions (May subdiv.
    geog.)   **342**
    UF   Conventions, Constitutional
    BT   **Conferences**
Constitutional history (May subdiv. geog.)
    342
    Use for materials on the history of constitu-
    tions. Texts of constitutions are entered under
    Constitutions.
    UF   Constitutional law—History
    BT   **History**
    NT   **Democracy**
          Monarchy
          **Representative government and
          representation**
          Republics
    RT   **Constitutions**

Constitutional history—Ohio   **342.771;
    977.1**
    UF   Ohio—Constitutional history
    BT   **Ohio—History**
**Constitutional history—United States
    342.73; 973**
    UF   United States—Constitutional
          history
    BT   **United States—History**
Constitutional law (May subdiv. geog.)
    342
    Use for materials on constitutions or consti-
    tutional law. Texts of constitutions are entered
    under **Constitutions**.
    BT   **Law**
    NT   **Citizenship**
          Civil rights
          Constitutional amendments
          Democracy
          Election law
          Eminent domain
          Executive power
          Federal government
          Habeas corpus
          Injunctions
          Legislative bodies
          Monarchy
          Proportional representation
          Referendum
          **Representative government and
          representation**
          Republics
          Separation of powers
          Suffrage
          War and emergency powers
    RT   **Administrative law**
          Constitutions
Constitutional law—History
    USE **Constitutional history**
Constitutional law—Ohio   **342.771**
    UF   Ohio—Constitutional law
**Constitutional law—United States
    342.73**
    UF   United States—Constitutional
          law
Constitutional rights
    USE **Civil rights**
Constitutions (May subdiv. geog.)   **342**
    Use for texts of constitutions. Materials
    about constitutions are entered under either
    Constitutional law or **Constitutional history**.
    UF   State constitutions
    BT   **Law**

Constitutions—*Continued*
- NT **Constitutional amendments**
  Equal rights amendments
- RT **Constitutional history**
  Constitutional law

Constitutions—Ohio 342.771
- UF Ohio—Constitution

Constitutions—United States 342.73; 973

Use for collections of texts of several state or federal constitutions. Materials about constitutions are entered under either **Constitutional history** or **Constitutional law**. Materials on the United States Constitution alone are entered under **United States—Constitution**.

- UF State constitutions
  United States—Constitutions

Construction
- USE **Architecture**
  Building
  Engineering

Construction, Concrete
- USE **Concrete construction**

Construction contracts (May subdiv. geog.) 692
- UF Building contracts
  Building—Contracts and specifications
- BT **Contracts**

Construction equipment (May subdiv. geog.) 621.8
- UF Building machinery
- BT **Machinery**
- NT **Road machinery**

Construction, House
- USE **House construction**

Construction industry (May subdiv. geog.) 690
- UF Building industry
  Home building industry
- BT **Building**
  Industries

Construction of roads
- USE **Roads**

Consular service
- USE **Diplomatic and consular service**

Consulates
- USE **Diplomatic and consular service**

Consuls (May subdiv. geog.) 327.2092
- BT **Diplomats**

Consultants 001

- UF Advisors
- SA types of consultants [to be added as needed]
- BT **Counseling**
- NT **Business consultants**
  Educational consultants

Consultative management
- USE **Participative management**

Consumer behavior
- USE **Consumers**

Consumer boycotts
- USE **Boycotts**

Consumer credit (May subdiv. geog.) 332.7
- BT **Banks and banking**
  Credit
  Personal finance
- NT **Credit cards**
  Installment plan
  Personal loans

Consumer demand
- USE **Consumption (Economics)**

Consumer education (May subdiv. geog.) 640.73

Use for materials on the selection and efficient use of consumer goods and services and on methods of educating consumers. Materials on the decision-making processes, external factors, and individual characteristics of consumers that determine their purchasing behavior are entered under **Consumers**. Materials on the economic theory of consumption and on consumerism or consumer demand are entered under **Consumption (Economics)**.

- UF Buyers' guides
  Consumers' guides
  Shoppers' guides
- BT **Education**
  Home economics
- RT **Consumers**
  Shopping

Consumer goods (May subdiv. geog.) 338.4

Use for materials on products that are purchased for personal or household purposes.

- UF Consumer products
  Merchandise
- BT **Commercial products**
  Manufactures
- RT **Consumption (Economics)**

Consumer loans
- USE **Personal loans**

Consumer organizations
- USE **Cooperative societies**

Consumer price indexes (May subdiv. geog.) **338.5**

UF Cost of living indexes
Price indexes, Consumer

BT **Cost and standard of living**
Prices

Consumer products

USE **Consumer goods**

Consumer protection (May subdiv. geog.) **343.07; 381.3**

Use for materials on governmental and private activities that guard consumers against dangers to their health, safety, or economic well-being.

UF Consumerism

BT **Industrial policy**

NT **Better business bureaus**
Drugs—Testing
Food adulteration and inspection
Product recall
Product safety

Consumer spending

USE **Consumption (Economics)**

Consumerism

USE **Consumer protection**
Consumption (Economics)

Consumers (May subdiv. geog.) **640.73; 658.8**

Use for materials on the decision-making processes, external factors, and individual characteristics of consumers that determine their purchasing behavior. Materials on the selection and efficient use of consumer goods and services and on methods of educating consumers are entered under **Consumer education**. Materials on the economic theory of consumption and on consumerism or consumer demand are entered under **Consumption (Economics)**.

UF Consumer behavior

NT **Boycotts**
Young consumers

RT **Consumer education**
Consumption (Economics)
Shopping

Consumers' cooperative societies

USE **Cooperative societies**

Consumers' guides

USE **Consumer education**

Consumers—Information services (May subdiv. geog.) **658.8**

BT **Information services**

Consumption (Economics) (May subdiv. geog.) **339.4**

Use for materials on the economic theory of consumption and on consumerism or consumer demand. Materials on the decision-making processes, external factors, and individual characteristics of consumers that determine their purchasing behavior are entered under **Consumers**. Materials on the selection and efficient use of consumer goods and services and on methods of educating consumers are entered under **Consumer education**.

UF Consumer demand
Consumer spending
Consumerism

BT **Economics**

NT **Prices**

RT **Consumer goods**
Consumers

Consumption of alcoholic beverages

USE **Drinking of alcoholic beverages**

Consumption of energy

USE **Energy consumption**

Contact lenses 617.7

BT **Eyeglasses**
Lenses

Contagion and contagious diseases

USE **Communicable diseases**

Contagious diseases

USE **Communicable diseases**

Container gardening (May subdiv. geog.) **635.9**

BT **Gardening**

RT **Flower gardening**
House plants
Indoor gardening
Miniature gardens
Window gardening

Containers 688.8

BT **Implements, utensils, etc.**

NT **Baskets**
Boxes
Luggage

RT **Packaging**

Contaminated food

USE **Food contamination**

Contamination of environment

USE **Pollution**

Contests (May subdiv. geog.) **001.4; 790.1**

UF Competitions

SA types of contests and names of specific contests, e.g. **Olympic games**; and subjects with

Contests—*Continued*
the subdivision *Competitions* or *Tournaments*, e.g. **Literature—Competitions**; **Tennis—Tournaments** [to be added as needed]
- NT **Beauty contests**
  Literature—Competitions
  Olympic games
  Sports tournaments
- RT **Awards**

Continental drift   **551.1**
- UF Drifting of continents
- BT **Continents**
  Geology
- RT **Plate tectonics**

Continental shelf   **551.41**
- BT **Geology**
- RT **Territorial waters**

Continents   **551.41**
- BT **Earth**
- NT **Continental drift**
  Lost continents

Continuation schools
- USE **Evening and continuation schools**

Continuing care communities
- USE **Life care communities**

Continuing care retirement communities
- USE **Life care communities**

Continuing education (May subdiv. geog.)   **374**
- UF Lifelong education
  Permanent education
  Recurrent education
- BT **Education**
- NT **Elderhostels**
  Evening and continuation schools
- RT **Adult education**

Contraband trade
- USE **Smuggling**

Contraception
- USE **Birth control**

Contract bridge
- USE **Bridge (Game)**

Contract labor (May subdiv. geog.)   **331.5**
- UF Indentured servants
- BT **Labor**
- RT **Peonage**

Contracting for services
- USE **Outsourcing**

Contracting out
- USE **Outsourcing**

Contractions
- USE **Abbreviations**
  Ciphers

Contracts (May subdiv. geog.)   **346.02**
- UF Agreements
- SA types of contracts, e.g. **Construction contracts** [to be added as needed]
- BT **Commerce**
  Commercial law
- NT **Authors and publishers**
  Construction contracts
  Covenants
  Labor contract
  Liability (Law)
  Marriage contracts
  Negotiable instruments
  Outsourcing
  Trusts and trustees

Contrition
- USE **Penance**
  Repentance

Control
- USE types of control, e.g. **Flood control; Weather control;** etc., and animals, plants, or processes with the subdivision *Control*, e.g. **Mosquitoes—Control** [to be added as needed]

Control of guns
- USE **Gun control**

Controversial literature
- USE types of religions, denominations, religious orders, and sacred works with the subdivision *Controversial literature,* for materials that argue against or express opposition to those groups or works, e.g. **Christianity—Controversial literature** for materials attacking Christianity; and religions and denominations with the subdivision *Apologetic works,* for materials defending those religions or denominations,

Controversial literature—*Continued*
e.g. **Christianity—Apologetic works** for materials defending Christianity [to be added as needed]

Conundrums
USE **Riddles**

Convenience cooking
USE **Quick and easy cooking**

Convenience foods (May subdiv. geog.)
641.3; 664
Use for materials on prepackaged foods that are easy to prepare for eating.
UF Fast foods
BT **Food**
NT **Fast food restaurants**

Conventions
USE **Conferences**
and subjects with the subdivision *Conferences,* e.g. **World War, 1939-1945—Conferences; Physics—Conferences;** and names of specific conferences, congresses, or conventions [to be added as needed]

Conventions, Constitutional
USE **Constitutional conventions**

Conventions, Political
USE **Political conventions**

Convents (May subdiv. geog.) **271; 726**
UF Cloisters
Nunneries
BT **Monasteries**
NT **Monasticism and religious orders for women**

Conversation (May subdiv. geog.)
808.56
UF Discussion
Table talk
Talking
BT **Communication**
Language and languages
NT **Discussion groups**
Interviews
Online chat groups

Conversation and phrase books
USE **Modern languages—Conversation and phrase books**
and names of languages and groups of languages with the subdivision *Conversation and phrase books,* e.g. **English language—Conversation and phrase books** [to be added as needed]

Conversation in foreign languages
USE **Modern languages—Conversation and phrase books**

Conversations and phrases
USE **Modern languages—Conversation and phrase books**

Conversion   **204; 248.2**
BT **Evangelistic work**
Salvation
Spiritual life
NT **Converts**
RT **Regeneration (Christianity)**

Conversion of saline water
USE **Sea water conversion**

Conversion of waste products
USE **Recycling**

Converts   **204; 248.2**
Use for materials on converts from one religion or denomination to another.
SA converts to a particular religion or denomination, e.g. **Converts to Catholicism** [to be added as needed]
BT **Conversion**
NT **Converts to Catholicism**

Converts to Catholicism (May subdiv. geog.)   **282**
UF Catholic Church—Converts
Catholic converts
BT **Catholics**
Converts

Conveying machinery   **621.8**
UF Conveyors
BT **Machinery**
Materials handling
RT **Hoisting machinery**

Conveyors
USE **Conveying machinery**

Convict labor (May subdiv. geog.)
331.5; 365
UF Prison labor
BT **Forced labor**
Prisoners

Convicts
USE **Criminals**
Prisoners

Cookbooks   **641.5**
BT **Books**

Cookbooks—*Continued*
  RT **Cooking**
Cookery
  USE **Cooking**
Cookery, American
  USE **American cooking**
Cookery for the sick
  USE **Cooking for the sick**
Cookery, French
  USE **French cooking**
Cookies 641.8654
  BT **Baking**
      Cooking
Cooking (May subdiv. geog.) **641.5**

  Use a phrase heading, e.g. **French cooking**; **Southern cooking**; etc., for distinctive national or regional styles of cooking. For cooking as it is practiced in a particular city, state, province, etc., subdivide **Cooking** geographically.

  UF Cookery
      Food preparation
      Recipes
  SA types of cooking, e.g. **Micro-wave cooking**; cooking of particular countries or regions, e.g. **French cooking**; **American cooking**; **Southern cooking**; etc.; and, for materials on the cooking of specific foods or kinds of food, **Cooking** with a subdivision for the food, e.g. **Cooking—Vegetables**; **Cooking—Natural foods**; etc. [to be added as needed]
  BT **Home economics**
  NT **Afternoon teas**
      American cooking
      Appetizers
      Baking
      Bread
      Breakfasts
      Cake
      Canning and preserving
      Catering
      Chinese cooking
      Christmas cooking
      Confectionery
      Cookies
      Cooking for one
      Cooking for the sick
      Cooking for two

      Dairy-free cooking
      Desserts
      Dinners
      Fish as food
      Flavoring essences
      French cooking
      Holiday cooking
      Indian cooking
      Luncheons
      Menus
      Microwave cooking
      Outdoor cooking
      Pastry
      Pies
      Quantity cooking
      Quick and easy cooking
      Salads
      Salt-free diet
      Sandwiches
      Sauces
      Soups
      Southern cooking
      Vegetarian cooking
      Wok cooking
  RT **Diet**
      Food
      Gastronomy
Cooking—Fish 641.692
  BT **Cooking—Seafood**
  RT **Fish as food**
Cooking for institutions
  USE **Food service**
Cooking for large numbers
  USE **Quantity cooking**
Cooking for one 641.561
  BT **Cooking**
Cooking for the sick 641.5
  UF Cookery for the sick
      Food for invalids
      Invalid cooking
  SA types of diets, e.g. **Salt-free diet** [to be added as needed]
  BT **Cooking**
      Diet in disease
      Nursing
      Sick
  NT **Diet therapy**
Cooking for two 641.561
  BT **Cooking**
Cooking—Meat 641.66
  BT **Meat**

Cooking—Natural foods 641.5
  UF   Natural food cooking
  RT   **Natural foods**
Cooking—Poultry 641.665
  BT   **Poultry**
Cooking—Seafood 641.692
  BT   **Seafood**
  NT   **Cooking—Fish**
Cooking utensils
  USE **Kitchen utensils**
Cooking—Vegetables 641.6
  BT   **Vegetables**
  RT   **Salads**
       Vegetarian cooking
Cooling appliances
  USE **Refrigeration**
Cooperation (May subdiv. geog.) **334**
    Use for general materials on the theory and history of cooperation and the cooperative movement. Materials dealing specifically with cooperative enterprises are entered under **Cooperative societies**.
  UF   Cooperative distribution
       Distribution, Cooperative
  BT   **Associations**
       Commerce
       Economics
  NT   **Collective settlements**
       Communal living
       Cooperative agriculture
       Cooperative banks
       Cooperative housing
       Cooperative societies
       International cooperation
       Savings and loan associations
  RT   **Profit sharing**
Cooperation, Intellectual
  USE **Intellectual cooperation**
Cooperation, Interchurch
  USE **Interdenominational cooperation**
Cooperation, Interdenominational
  USE **Interdenominational cooperation**
Cooperation (Psychology)
  USE **Cooperativeness**
Cooperative agriculture (May subdiv. geog.) **334**
    Use for materials on cooperation in the production and disposal of agricultural products.
  UF   Agricultural cooperation
       Agriculture, Cooperative
       Collective farms

       Farmers' cooperatives
  BT   **Agriculture**
       Cooperation
  RT   **Collective settlements**
Cooperative banks (May subdiv. geog.) **334**
  UF   Banks and banking, Cooperative
       People's banks
  BT   **Banks and banking**
       Cooperation
       Cooperative societies
       Personal loans
  NT   **Credit unions**
  RT   **Savings and loan associations**
Cooperative distribution
  USE **Cooperation**
       Cooperative societies
Cooperative education (May subdiv. geog.) **371.2**
  UF   Education, Cooperative
       Study-work plan
       Work-based learning
  BT   **Vocational education**
Cooperative housing (May subdiv. geog.) **334**
  UF   Co-ops (Housing)
       Cohousing
       Housing, Cooperative
  BT   **Cooperation**
       Housing
  RT   **Communal living**
Cooperative learning (May subdiv. geog.) **371.3**
    Use for materials on the method of education that involves having students work together on projects in a structured manner.
  UF   Group method in teaching
       Group teaching
       Group work in education
  BT   **Education**
       Teaching
Cooperative living
  USE **Collective settlements**
       Communal living
Cooperative societies (May subdiv. geog.) **334; 658.8**
    Use for materials dealing specifically with cooperative enterprises. General materials on the theory and history of cooperation and the cooperative movement are entered under **Cooperation**.
  UF   Co-ops
       Consumer organizations

Cooperative societies—*Continued*
        Consumers' cooperative societies
        Cooperative distribution
        Cooperative stores
        Cooperatives
  SA   types of cooperative societies,
        e.g. **Credit unions** [to be
        added as needed]
  BT **Cooperation**
       Corporations
       Societies
  NT **Cooperative banks**
       Savings and loan associations
Cooperative stores
  USE **Cooperative societies**
Cooperativeness **158**
  UF Cooperation (Psychology)
  BT **Social psychology**
Cooperatives
  USE **Cooperative societies**
Copiers
  USE **Copying machines**
Coping behavior
  USE **Adjustment (Psychology)**
Coping skills
  USE **Life skills**
Copper engraving
  USE **Engraving**
Copperwork (May subdiv. geog.) **673;
739.5**
  BT **Metalwork**
Copy art (May subdiv. geog.) **760**
    Use for materials on the use of photocopying machines to create original works of art. Materials on clipping art work from published sources to use in creating documents, posters, newsletters, etc., are entered under **Clip art**.
  UF Copying machine art
       Reprographic art
       Xerographic art
  BT **Art**
  RT **Photocopying**
Copy writing
  USE **Advertising copy**
Copying machine art
  USE **Copy art**
Copying machines **681**
  UF Copiers
       Copying processes and machines
       Duplicating machines
       Photocopying machines
  BT **Office equipment and supplies**
  RT **Copying processes**

Copying processes **686**
  UF Copying processes and machines
       Duplicating processes
       Reproduction processes
       Reprography
  SA   names of specific processes [to
        be added as needed]
  BT **Documentation**
  NT **Photocopying**
  RT **Copying machines**
Copying processes and machines
  USE **Copying machines**
       Copying processes
Copyright (May subdiv. geog.)   **346.04;
352.7**
    May be subdivided by topic, e.g. **Copyright—Sound recordings**.
  UF International copyright
       Literary property
  NT **Fair use (Copyright)**
  RT **Authors and publishers**
       Intellectual property
Copyright—Sound recordings (May
    subdiv. geog.) **346.04**
  UF Sound recordings—Copyright
Coral reef ecology (May subdiv. geog.)
    577.7
  BT **Ecology**
Coral reefs and islands (May subdiv.
    geog.) **551.42**
  UF Atolls
  BT **Geology**
       Islands
Corals **563; 593.6**
  BT **Marine animals**
Cordials (Liquor)
  USE **Liquors**
Core curriculum
  USE **Colleges and universities—Cur
        ricula**
       Education—Curricula
Coretta Scott King Award **028.5**
  UF King Award
  BT **Children's literature**
       Literary prizes
Corn (May subdiv. geog.) **633.1; 633.2**
  UF Maize
  BT **Forage plants**
       Grain
Coronary diseases
  USE **Heart diseases**

Corporate accountability
USE **Social responsibility of business**
Corporate acquisitions
USE **Corporate mergers and acqui-**
sitions
Corporate culture (May subdiv. geog.)
302.3
UF Culture, Corporate
Organizational culture
BT **Corporations**
Corporate downsizing
USE **Downsizing of organizations**
Corporate libraries (May subdiv. geog.)
027.6
Use for materials on libraries located within
companies, firms, or private businesses, cover-
ing any subject areas. Materials on libraries
with a subject focus on business are entered
under **Business libraries**.
UF Company libraries
Industrial libraries
Libraries, Corporate
BT **Special libraries**
Corporate mergers and acquisitions
(May subdiv. geog.)   **338.8; 658.1**
UF Acquisitions, Corporate
Buyouts, Corporate
Consolidation and merger of
corporations
Corporate acquisitions
Corporate takeovers
Industrial mergers
Mergers
Takeovers, Corporate
SA types of institutions and types of
industries and businesses with
the subdivision *Mergers*, e.g.
Railroads—Mergers to be
added as needed]
NT **Leveraged buyouts**
Railroads—Mergers
RT **Conglomerate corporations**
Industrial trusts
Corporate patronage of the arts
USE **Art patronage**
Corporate responsibility
USE **Social responsibility of business**
Corporate symbols
USE **Trademarks**
Corporate takeovers
USE **Corporate mergers and acqui-**
sitions

Corporate welfare
USE **Subsidies**
Corporation law (May subdiv. geog.)
346
BT **Commercial law**
Corporations
Law
NT **Limited liability companies**
Public service commissions
RT **Industrial trusts**
Monopolies
Restraint of trade
Corporations (May subdiv. geog.)
338.7; 658.1
UF Companies
BT **Business enterprises**
NT **Conglomerate corporations**
Cooperative societies
Corporate culture
Corporation law
Limited liability companies
Multinational corporations
Municipal ownership
Public service commissions
Trust companies
RT **Industrial trusts**
Stocks
Corporations—Accounting (May subdiv.
geog.)   **657; 658.15**
BT **Accounting**
Bookkeeping
Corporations—Art patronage
USE **Art patronage**
Corporations—Finance (May subdiv.
geog.)   **658.15**
UF Capitalization (Finance)
BT **Finance**
Corporations, Multinational
USE **Multinational corporations**
Corporations, Nonprofit
USE **Nonprofit organizations**
Corporations—Social responsibility
USE **Social responsibility of business**
Corpses
USE **Dead**
Corpulence
USE **Obesity**
Correctional institutions (May subdiv.
geog.)   **365**
UF Penal institutions

Correctional institutions—*Continued*
    SA   types of correctional institutions
           [to be added as needed]
    BT   **Punishment**
    NT   **Halfway houses**
           Penal colonies
           Prisons
           Reformatories

Correctional services
    USE   **Corrections**

Corrections (May subdiv. geog.)   **364.6**
    Use for materials on the rehabilitation and treatment of offenders through parole, penal custody, and probation programs, and on the administration of such programs.
    UF   Correctional services
           Criminals—Rehabilitation programs
           Penology
           Reform of criminals
    BT   **Administration of criminal justice**
    NT   **Parole**
           Probation
           Punishment

Correspondence
    USE   **Business letters**
           Letter writing
           Letters
           and ethnic groups, classes of persons, and names of individual persons and families with the subdivision *Correspondence,* e.g. **Authors—Correspondence** [to be added as needed]

Correspondence schools and courses
    (May subdiv. geog.)   **374.35**
    UF   Home education
           Home study courses
    BT   **Distance education**
           Schools
           Technical education
           University extension
    RT   **Self-instruction**

Corrosion and anticorrosives   **620.1**
    UF   Anticorrosive paint
           Rust
           Rustless coatings
    BT   **Industrial chemistry**
    RT   **Paint**

Corrupt practices
    USE   subjects with the subdivision *Corrupt practices,* e.g. **Adoption—Corrupt practices; Sports—Corrupt practices;** etc. [to be added as needed]

Corruption in politics
    USE   **Political corruption**

Corruption in sports
    USE   **Sports—Corrupt practices**

Corruption, Police
    USE   **Police corruption**

Corsairs
    USE   **Pirates**

Cosmetic surgery
    USE   **Plastic surgery**

Cosmetics (May subdiv. geog.)   **646.7**
    UF   Makeup (Cosmetics)
    SA   types of cosmetics [to be added as needed]
    BT   **Personal grooming**
    NT   **Perfumes**
           Theatrical makeup
    RT   **Toiletries**

Cosmetics—Advertising
    USE   **Advertising—Cosmetics**

Cosmic rays   **539.7**
    UF   Millikan rays
    BT   **Nuclear physics**
           Radiation
           Radioactivity
           Space environment

Cosmobiology
    USE   **Space biology**

Cosmochemistry
    USE   **Space chemistry**

Cosmogony
    USE   **Cosmology**
           Universe

Cosmography
    USE   **Cosmology**
           Universe

Cosmology   **113; 523.1**
    Use for general or theoretical materials on the science or philosophy of the universe. Materials limited to the physical description of the universe are entered under **Universe**.
    UF   Cosmogony
           Cosmography
    BT   **Universe**
    NT   **Biblical cosmology**
           Big bang theory

Cosmonauts
  USE **Astronauts**
Cost accounting (May subdiv. geog.)
  657
  BT **Accounting**
      Bookkeeping
Cost and standard of living (May subdiv.
  geog.) **339.4**
  UF Cost of living
      Food, Cost of
      Household finances
      Standard of living
  BT **Economics**
      Home economics
      Quality of life
      Social conditions
      Wealth
  NT **Consumer price indexes**
      Household budgets
      Subsistence economy
  RT **Prices**
      Salaries, wages, etc.
Cost benefit analysis
  USE **Cost effectiveness**
Cost effectiveness **658.15**
  UF Benefit cost analysis
      Cost benefit analysis
  SA topics with the subdivision *Cost
      effectiveness*, e.g. **Electric au-
      tomobiles—Cost effectiveness**
      [to be added as needed]
  BT **Economics**
  NT **Electric automobiles—Cost ef-
      fectiveness**
Cost of living
  USE **Cost and standard of living**
Cost of living indexes
  USE **Consumer price indexes**
Cost of medical care
  USE **Medical care—Costs**
Costs
  USE subjects with the subdivision
      Costs, e.g. **Medical care—
      Costs** [to be added as need-
      ed]
Costume (May subdiv. geog.) **391; 792**
  Use for materials on the characteristic cos-
  tume of ethnic or national groups and for ma-
  terials on fancy dress and theatrical costumes.
  For the traditional national costume of a par-
  ticular country subdivide geographically. Materials on clothing and the art of dress from
day to day in practical situations, including
historical dress and the clothing of various
professions or classes of persons, are entered
under **Clothing and dress**. Materials on the
prevailing mode or style of dress are entered
under **Fashion**.
  UF Acting—Costume
      Fancy dress
      Style in dress
      Theatrical costume
  SA costume of particular ethnic
      groups, e.g. **Native American
      costume**; and professions and
      classes of persons with the
      subdivision *Clothing*, e.g.
      Handicapped—Clothing [to
      be added as needed]
  BT **Decorative arts**
      Ethnology
      Manners and customs
  NT **Armor**
      Children's costumes
      Disguise
      Fans (Dress accessories)
      Hats
      Jewelry
      Masks (Facial)
      Native American costume
      Theatrical makeup
      Uniforms
      Wigs
  RT **Clothing and dress**
Cot death
  USE **Sudden infant death syndrome**
Côte d'Ivoire **966.6**
  May be subdivided like United States ex-
  cept for History.
  UF Ivory Coast
Cottage industry
  USE **Home-based business**
Cotton (May subdiv. geog.) **633.5; 677**
  BT **Economic botany**
      Fabrics
      Fibers
Cotton manufacture (May subdiv. geog.)
  677
  BT **Textile industry**
Councils and synods **262**
  UF Church councils
      Ecumenical councils
      Synods

Councils and synods—*Continued*
- SA names of specific councils and synods, e.g. **Vatican Council (2nd: 1962-1965)** [to be added as needed]
- BT **Christianity**
  Church history
- NT **Vatican Council (2nd: 1962-1965)**

Counseling   361; 371.4
- UF Guidance
- SA types of counseling; and ethnic groups and classes of persons with the subdivision *Counseling of*, e.g. **Employees—Counseling of** [to be added as needed]
- BT **Applied psychology**
  Helping behavior
  Personnel management
- NT **Advice columns**
  Consultants
  Crisis centers
  Drug abuse counseling
  Educational counseling
  Elderly—Counseling of
  Employees—Counseling of
  Family therapy
  Health counseling
  Hotlines (Telephone counseling)
  Marriage counseling
  Mentoring
  Peer counseling
  School counseling
  Self-help groups
  Social group work
  Vocational guidance
- RT **Interviewing**
  Social case work

Counseling of
- USE classes of persons and ethnic groups with the subdivision *Counseling of,* e.g. **Elderly—Counseling of** [to be added as needed]

Counseling of the elderly
- USE **Elderly—Counseling of**

Counseling with the aged
- USE **Elderly—Counseling of**

Count Dracula (Fictional character)
- USE **Dracula, Count (Fictional character)**

Counted thread embroidery   746.44
- BT **Embroidery**

Counter culture (May subdiv. geog.) **306**
- UF Counterculture
  Nonconformity
  Subculture
- BT **Lifestyles**
  Social conditions
- NT **Bohemianism**
- RT **Alternative lifestyles**
  Collective settlements
  Communal living
  Radicalism

Counter-Reformation (May subdiv. geog.) **270.6**
- UF Anti-Reformation
- BT **Christianity**
  Church history—1500-, Modern period
- RT **Reformation**

Counter-terrorism
- USE **Terrorism—Prevention**

Counterculture
- USE **Counter culture**

Counterespionage
- USE **Intelligence service**

Counterfeits and counterfeiting (May subdiv. geog.) **332; 364.1**
- BT **Coinage**
  Crime
  Forgery
  Impostors and imposture
  Money
  Swindlers and swindling
- NT **Art—Forgeries**
  Literary forgeries

Counterinsurgency (May subdiv. geog.) **355.02**
- BT **Guerrilla warfare**
  Insurgency

Counterintelligence
- USE **Intelligence service**

Counterpoint   781.2
- BT **Composition (Music)**
  Music—Theory
- NT **Fugue**

Counting   513.2

Use for materials on counting, including counting books. Materials on numbers, numbering, and systems of numeration are entered

Counting—*Continued*

under **Numbers**. Materials on the conceptualization of numbers are entered under **Number
concept**.

UF Counting books

BT **Arithmetic—Study and teaching**

NT **Number games**

RT **Numbers**

Counting books

USE **Counting**

Countries

USE **Nations**

Country and western music

USE **Country music**

Country churches

USE **Rural churches**

Country life (May subdiv. geog.)
307.72; 630

Use for descriptive, popular, and literary
materials on living in the country. Materials
on social organization and conditions in rural
communities are entered under **Rural sociology**.

UF Rural life

BT **Manners and customs**

NT **Agriculture—Societies**
Farm life
Mountain life
Plantation life

RT **Outdoor life**
Rural sociology

**Country life—United States   307.72;
630**

Country music (May subdiv. geog.)
781.642

UF Country and western music
Hillbilly music

BT **Folk music—United States**
Popular music

Country schools

USE **Rural schools**

Country stores

USE **General stores**

County agricultural agents (May subdiv.
geog.)   **630.7**

BT **Agricultural extension work**
**Agriculture—Study and teach-
ing**

County government (May subdiv. geog.)
320.8; 352.15

UF County officers

BT **Local government**

County libraries

USE **Public libraries**
Regional libraries

County officers

USE **County government**

County planning

USE **Regional planning**

Coupons (Retail trade)   659

BT **Advertising**

Coups d'état

USE **Revolutions**

Courage   179

UF Bravery
Heroism

BT **Virtue**

NT **Encouragement**
Morale

RT **Heroes and heroines**

Courses of study

USE **Education—Curricula**

Court fools

USE **Fools and jesters**

Court life

USE **Courts and courtiers**

Court martial

USE **Courts martial and courts of
inquiry**

Courtesy (May subdiv. geog.)   **177; 395**

UF Manners
Politeness

BT **Etiquette**
Virtue

Courtiers

USE **Courts and courtiers**

Courting

USE **Courtship**

Courtroom drama

USE **Legal drama (Films)**
Legal drama (Radio programs)
**Legal drama (Television pro-
grams)**

Courts (May subdiv. geog.)   **347**

UF Judiciary

BT **Law**

NT **Arbitration and award**
Civil procedure
**Courts martial and courts of
inquiry**
Criminal procedure
Jury
Juvenile courts

Courts—*Continued*
    Small claims courts
    United States. Supreme Court
  RT **Administration of justice**
      Judges
Courts and courtiers   394; 929.7
  UF Court life
      Courtiers
  SA names of countries, cities, etc.,
      with the subdivision *Courts*
      and courtiers [to be added as
      needed]
  BT **Manners and customs**
  NT **Fools and jesters**
      Princes
      Princesses
  RT **Kings and rulers**
      Queens
Courts martial and courts of inquiry
  (May subdiv. geog.) **343**
  UF Court martial
      Military courts
  BT **Courts**
      Trials
  RT **Military law**
Courts—United States   347.73
  UF Federal courts
      United States—Courts
Courtship (May subdiv. geog.) **306.73;
  392.4**
  UF Courting
  BT **Love**
  NT **Betrothal**
      Dating (Social customs)
  RT **Marriage**
Courtship (Animal behavior)
  USE **Animal courtship**
Courtship of animals
  USE **Animal courtship**
Cousins   306.87
  BT **Family**
Couturiers
  USE **Fashion designers**
Covenants   202; 231.7
  Use for materials on religious covenants.
  May be subdivided by religion as needed. Ma-
  terials on non-religious covenants are entered
  under **Contracts**.
  UF Agreements
      Religious covenants
  BT **Contracts**
      Theology

Covens
  USE **Witches**
Coverlets
  USE **Bedspreads**
      Quilts
Covetousness
  USE **Avarice**
Cowboys
  USE **Cowhands**
Cowgirls
  USE **Cowhands**
Cowhands (May subdiv. geog.) **636.2;
  978**
  UF Cowboys
      Cowgirls
      Gauchos
  BT **Frontier and pioneer life**
      Ranch life
  RT **Rodeos**
Cowhands—Songs   782.42
  UF Cowhands—Songs and music
  BT **Music**
      Songs
Cowhands—Songs and music
  USE **Cowhands—Songs**
Cows
  USE **Cattle**
CPR (First aid)   616.1
  UF Cardiopulmonary resuscitation
  BT **First aid**
  RT **Cardiac resuscitation**
Crabs   565; 595.3
  BT **Crustacea**
      Shellfish
Crack babies
  USE **Children of drug addicts**
Crack cocaine
  USE **Crack (Drug)**
Crack (Drug) (May subdiv. geog.)
      362.29; 615
  UF Crack cocaine
  BT **Cocaine**
Cradle songs
  USE **Lullabies**
Craft festivals
  USE **Craft shows**
Craft shows (May subdiv. geog.) **745**
  UF Craft festivals
  BT **Exhibitions**
      Festivals
      Handicraft

Crafts (Arts)
USE **Arts and crafts movement**
Handicraft
Cranes, derricks, etc. (May subdiv. geog.)
621.8
UF Derricks
BT **Hoisting machinery**
Crank (Drug)
USE **Crystal meth (Drug)**
Cranks
USE **Eccentrics and eccentricities**
Crashes (Finance)
USE **Financial crises**
Crates
USE **Boxes**
Crayon drawing 741.2
UF Blackboard drawing
BT **Drawing**
RT **Pastel drawing**
Crazes
USE **Fads**
Creation 231.7; 213
BT **Natural theology**
RT **Biblical cosmology**
Creationism
Evolution
Universe
Creation (Literary, artistic, etc.) 153.3
UF Inspiration
BT **Genius**
Imagination
Intellect
Inventions
NT **Creative writing**
Planning
RT **Creative ability**
Creation—Study and teaching
USE **Creationism**
Evolution—Study and teaching
Creationism 231.7
Use for materials on the doctrine that the universe was created by God out of nothing in the initial seven days of time and that all biological species were created rather than evolving from pre-existing types through modifications in successive generations.
UF Christianity and evolution
Creation—Study and teaching
Evolution and Christianity
Fundamentalism and education
Fundamentalism and evolution
Scientific creationism
BT **Christianity—Doctrines**

RT **Bible and science**
Creation
Evolution
Evolution—Study and teaching
Religion and science
Creative ability 153.3; 701; 801
UF Creativity
BT **Ability**
NT **Creative thinking**
RT **Creation (Literary, artistic, etc.)**
Creative activities 372.5
Use for materials on activities for children that result in some form of personal expression such as painting, cooking, drama, etc.
UF Activities curriculum
BT **Amusements**
Elementary education
Kindergarten
RT **Handicraft**
Creative movement
USE **Movement education**
Creative thinking 153.4
BT **Creative ability**
Creative writing 808
UF Writing (Authorship)
BT **Authorship**
Creation (Literary, artistic, etc.)
Language arts
Creativity
USE **Creative ability**
Creature films
USE **Horror films**
Credibility
USE **Truthfulness and falsehood**
Credit (May subdiv. geog.) **332.7**
UF Bills of credit
Letters of credit
BT **Finance**
Money
NT **Agricultural credit**
Collecting of accounts
Consumer credit
Installment plan
Negotiable instruments
RT **Banks and banking**
Debtor and creditor
Loans
Credit card crimes
USE **Credit card fraud**

Credit card fraud (May subdiv. geog.)
   364.16
   UF   Credit card crimes
   BT   **Fraud**
         Swindlers and swindling
Credit cards (May subdiv. geog.)   **332.7**
   UF   Bank credit cards
         Banks and banking—Credit
            cards
   BT   **Consumer credit**
Credit unions (May subdiv. geog.)   **334**
      Use for materials on cooperative associa-
   tions that make small loans to its members at
   low interest rates.
   BT   **Cooperative banks**
Creditor
   USE   **Debtor and creditor**
Creeds (May subdiv. geog.)   **202; 238**
      Use for materials about the concise, formal,
   and authorized statements of doctrines and for
   the texts of those statements.
   UF   Confessions of faith
   SA   names of religions and individu-
         al denominations with the
         subdivision *Creeds*, e.g. **Cath-
         olic Church—Creeds** [to be
         added as needed]
   BT   **Doctrinal theology**
   NT   **Apostles' Creed**
         Catholic Church—Creeds
         Nicene Creed
   RT   **Catechisms**
Cremation (May subdiv. geog.)   **363.7;
         393; 614**
   UF   Incineration
         Mortuary customs
   BT   **Public health**
         Sanitation
   NT   **Dead**
   RT   **Burial**
         Funeral rites and ceremonies
Creole folk songs   **782.42162**
   UF   Folk songs, Creole
   BT   **Folk songs**
Creoles (May subdiv. geog.)   **305.84;
         972.9; 976**
   BT   **Ethnic groups**
Crests
   USE   **Heraldry**
Crew (Rowing)
   USE   **Rowing**
Crewelwork   **746.44**
   BT   **Embroidery**

Crib death
   USE   **Sudden infant death syndrome**
Crickets (May subdiv. geog.)   **595.7**
   BT   **Insects**
Crime (May subdiv. geog.)   **364**
   UF   Crimes
         Criminology
         Felony
   SA   types of crimes, e.g. **Computer
         crimes** [to be added as need-
         ed]
   BT   **Administration of criminal jus-
         tice**
         Social problems
   NT   **Assassination**
         Atrocities
         Computer crimes
         Conspiracies
         Counterfeits and counterfeiting
         Crime prevention
         Crimes against humanity
         Crimes without victims
         Criminals
         Drugs and crime
         Drunk driving
         Forgery
         Fraud
         Hate crimes
         Homicide
         Impostors and imposture
         Juvenile delinquency
         Lynching
         Offenses against property
         Offenses against public safety
         Offenses against the person
         Organized crime
         Racketeering
         Riots
         School shootings
         Sex crimes
         Smuggling
         Swindlers and swindling
         Theft
         Treason
         Victims of crimes
         Vigilantes
         White collar crimes
   RT   **Criminal law**
         Police
         Punishment
         Trials

Crime—*Continued*
    Vice
Crime and drugs
    USE **Drugs and crime**
Crime and narcotics
    USE **Drugs and crime**
Crime comics
    USE **Mystery comic books, strips, etc.**
Crime films
    USE **Film noir**
              Gangster films
              Mystery films
Crime plays
    USE **Mystery and detective plays**
Crime prevention (May subdiv. geog.)
    364.4
    UF Prevention of crime
    BT **Crime**
    NT **Burglary protection**
Crime prevention—Citizen participation
    (May subdiv. geog.) **364.4**
    BT **Political participation**
Crime programs
    USE **Mystery radio programs**
              Mystery television programs
Crime stories
    USE **Mystery fiction**
Crime syndicates
    USE **Organized crime**
              Racketeering
Crime—United States **364.973**
Crime victims
    USE **Victims of crimes**
Crimean War, 1853-1856 **947**
    UF Great Britain—History—1853-1856, Crimean War
          Russo-Turkish War, 1853-1856
Crimes
    USE **Crime**
Crimes against humanity (May subdiv. geog.) **364.1**
    BT **Crime**
    NT **Forced labor**
          Genocide
          Slavery
          War crimes
Crimes against property
    USE **Offenses against property**
Crimes against public safety
    USE **Offenses against public safety**

Crimes against the person
    USE **Offenses against the person**
Crimes, Military
    USE **Military offenses**
Crimes of hate
    USE **Hate crimes**
Crimes, Political
    USE **Political crimes and offenses**
Crimes without victims (May subdiv. geog.) **364.1**
    UF Non-victim crimes
          Nonvictim crimes
          Victimless crimes
    BT **Crime**
          Criminal law
Criminal assault
    USE **Offenses against the person**
Criminal behavior
    USE **Criminal psychology**
Criminal investigation (May subdiv. geog.) **363.25**
    BT **Law enforcement**
    NT **Criminals—Identification**
          Eavesdropping
          Fingerprints
          Lie detectors and detection
          Missing persons
          Wiretapping
    RT **Detectives**
          Forensic sciences
          Police
Criminal justice, Administration of
    USE **Administration of criminal justice**
Criminal law (May subdiv. geog.) **345**
    UF Codes, Penal
          Misdemeanors (Law)
          Penal codes
          Penal law
    SA types of crimes, e.g. **Homicide**
          [to be added as needed]
    BT **Law**
    NT **Administration of criminal justice**
          Adoption—Corrupt practices
          Capital punishment
          Crimes without victims
          Executions and executioners
          Homicide
          Insanity defense
          Jury

Criminal law—*Continued*
>Kidnapping
>Military offenses
>Misconduct in office
>Obscenity (Law)
>Offenses against property
>Offenses against public safety
>Offenses against the person
>Political crimes and offenses
>Probation
>Prohibition
>Sports—Corrupt practices
>Tax evasion
>Trials
>Vigilantes
>>RT   Crime
>>>Criminal procedure
>>>Punishment

Criminal procedure (May subdiv. geog.) 345
>BT   Courts
>NT   Executions and executioners
>>Habeas corpus
>>Torture
>RT   Criminal law

Criminal psychiatry
>USE   Criminal psychology

Criminal psychology   364.3
>UF   Criminal behavior
>>Criminal psychiatry
>BT   Psychology
>RT   Abnormal psychology

Criminalistics
>USE   Forensic sciences

Criminals (May subdiv. geog.)   364.3; 364.6
>UF   Convicts
>>Delinquents
>>Outlaws
>BT   Crime
>NT   Computer hackers
>>Gangs
>>Impostors and imposture
>>Pirates
>>Prisoners
>>Serial killers
>>Swindlers and swindling
>>Thieves

Criminals and drugs
>USE   Criminals—Drug use

Criminals and narcotics
>USE   Criminals—Drug use

Criminals—Drug use (May subdiv. geog.) 362.29; 364.3
>UF   Criminals and drugs
>>Criminals and narcotics
>>Drugs and criminals
>>Narcotics and criminals
>RT   Drugs and crime

Criminals—Identification (May subdiv. geog.)   363.25
>BT   Criminal investigation
>>Identification
>NT   Fingerprints

Criminals—Rehabilitation programs
>USE   Corrections

Criminology
>USE   Crime

Crippled children
>USE   Physically handicapped children

Crippled people
>USE   Physically handicapped

Crisis centers (May subdiv. geog.) 361.3; 362
>UF   Crisis intervention centers
>SA   types of crisis centers, e.g.
>>Hotlines (Telephone counseling) [to be added as needed]
>BT   Counseling
>>Social work
>RT   Hotlines (Telephone counseling)

Crisis counseling
>USE   Hotlines (Telephone counseling)

Crisis intervention centers
>USE   Crisis centers

Crisis intervention (Mental health services) (May subdiv. geog.)   362.2; 616.89
>UF   Crisis intervention (Psychiatry)
>>Emergency mental health services
>BT   Mental health services

Crisis intervention (Psychiatry)
>USE   Crisis intervention (Mental health services)

Crisis intervention telephone service
>USE   Hotlines (Telephone counseling)

Crisis management   658.4
>BT   Management
>>Problem solving
>RT   Conflict management

Critical thinking   153.4; 160

Use for materials on thinking that is based on sound logic and the careful evaluation of all pertinent evidence.

BT   **Decision making**

Logic

Problem solving

Reasoning

Thought and thinking

Criticism   801

Use for materials on the history, principles, methods, etc., of criticism in general and of literary criticism in particular. Materials that are themselves histories or criticisms of literature are entered under **Literature—History and criticism**. Criticism of the work of an individual author, artist, composer, etc., is entered under that person's name as a subject; only in the case of voluminous authors is it necessary to add the subdivision *Criticism*. Criticism of a single work is entered under the name of the author, artist, or composer, followed by the title of the work.

UF   Appraisal of books

Books—Appraisal

Criticism and interpretation

Criticism, interpretation, etc.

Evaluation of literature

Literary criticism

Literature—Evaluation

SA   literature, film, and music subjects with the subdivision *History and criticism*, e.g. **English poetry—History and criticism**; and names of voluminous authors and of sacred works with the subdivision *Criticism*, e.g. **Shakespeare, William, 1564-1616—Criticism**; **Bible—Criticism**; etc. [to be added as needed]

BT   **Aesthetics**

Literature

Rhetoric

NT   **Art criticism**

Book reviewing

Dramatic criticism

Feminist criticism

RT   **Literary style**

Criticism and interpretation

USE   **Criticism**

and literature, film, and music subjects with the subdivision *History and criticism,* e.g. **English poetry—History and**
criticism; and names of voluminous authors and of sacred works with the subdivision *Criticism*, e.g. **Shakespeare, William, 1564-1616—Criticism; Bible—Criticism**; etc. [to be added as needed]

Criticism, Feminist

USE   **Feminist criticism**

Criticism, interpretation, etc.

USE   **Criticism**

and literature, film, and music subjects with the subdivision *History and criticism,* e.g. **English poetry—History and criticism**; and names of voluminous authors and of sacred works with the subdivision *Criticism,* e.g. **Shakespeare, William, 1564-1616—Criticism; Bible—Criticism**; etc. [to be added as needed]

Cro-Magnons (May subdiv. geog.)   **569.9; 930.1**

UF   Cromagnons

BT   **Prehistoric peoples**

Crocheting   746.43

BT   **Needlework**

NT   **Lace and lace making**

Crockery

USE   **Pottery**

Crocodiles (May subdiv. geog.)   **597.98**

BT   **Reptiles**

RT   **Alligators**

Cromagnons

USE   **Cro-Magnons**

Crop dusting

USE   **Aeronautics in agriculture**

Crop reports

USE   **Agriculture—Statistics**

Crop rotation (May subdiv. geog.)   **631.5**

UF   Rotation of crops

BT   **Agriculture**

Crop spraying

USE   **Aeronautics in agriculture**

Crops

USE   **Farm produce**

Cross cultural conflict

USE   **Culture conflict**

Cross-cultural psychology
USE **Ethnopsychology**
Cross-cultural studies (May subdiv. geog.)
306

    Use for materials on the systematic comparison of two or more cultural groups, either within the same country or in separate countries.

UF   Comparison of cultures
       Cross cultural studies
       Intercultural studies
       Transcultural studies
SA   topics with the subdivision
       Cross-cultural studies, e.g.
       Marriage—Cross-cultural studies [to be added as needed]
BT   **Culture**
       Social sciences
Cross cultural studies
USE **Cross-cultural studies**
Cross-examination
USE **Witnesses**
Cross-stitch **746.44**
BT   **Embroidery**
Crossdressers
USE **Transvestites**
Crossword puzzles **793.73**
BT   **Puzzles**
       Word games
Crowds (May subdiv. geog.) **302.3**
UF   Mobs
NT   **Demonstrations**
       Riot control
RT   **Riots**
       Social psychology
Crown lands
USE **Public lands**
CRT display terminals
USE **Computer monitors**
CRTs
USE **Cathode ray tubes**
Crucifixion of Jesus Christ
USE **Jesus Christ—Crucifixion**
Crude oil
USE **Petroleum**
Cruelty **179**
UF   Brutality
BT   **Ethics**
NT   **Atrocities**
       Torture

Cruelty to animals
USE **Animal welfare**
Cruelty to children
USE **Child abuse**
Cruises
USE **Ocean travel**
Crusades (May subdiv. geog.) **909.07**
BT   **Church history—600-1500, Middle Ages**
RT   **Chivalry**
Crushes **152.4; 177**
UF   Romantic crushes
BT   **Friendship**
       Love
Crustacea **565; 595.3**
SA   names of specific crustaceans, e.g. **Lobsters** [to be added as needed]
BT   **Shellfish**
NT   **Crabs**
       Lobsters
Cryobiology **571.4**
UF   Freezing
       Low temperature biology
BT   **Biology**
       Cold
       Low temperatures
NT   **Cold—Physiological effect**
       Frozen embryos
Cryogenic interment
USE **Cryonics**
Cryogenic surgery
USE **Cryosurgery**
Cryogenics
USE **Low temperatures**
Cryonics **621.5**
UF   Cryogenic interment
       Freezing of human bodies
       Human cold storage
BT   **Burial**
Cryosurgery **617**
UF   Cryogenic surgery
BT   **Cold—Therapeutic use**
       Surgery
Cryotherapy
USE **Cold—Therapeutic use**
Cryptography **652**
UF   Code deciphering
       Code enciphering
       Secret writing

Cryptography—*Continued*
- BT **Signs and symbols**
  Writing
- RT **Ciphers**

Crystal gazing
- USE **Divination**

Crystal meth (Drug) 362.29; 615
- UF Crank (Drug)
  Ice (Drug)
- BT **Designer drugs**
  Methamphetamine

Crystallization
- USE **Crystals**

Crystallography
- USE **Crystals**

Crystals 548
- UF Crystallization
  Crystallography
- SA types of crystals, e.g. **Quartz** [to be added as needed]
- BT **Physical chemistry**
  Solids
- NT **Quartz**
- RT **Minerals**

Cub Scouts
- USE **Boy Scouts**

Cuba 972.91

> May be subdivided like United States except for History.

- BT **Islands**

Cuba—History 972.91

Cuba—History—1958-1959, Revolution
972.9106

Cuba—History—1959- 972.9106

Cuba—History—1961, Invasion
972.9106
- UF Bay of Pigs invasion
  Cuban invasion, 1961
  Invasion of Cuba, 1961

Cuban invasion, 1961
- USE **Cuba—History—1961, Invasion**

Cube root 513.2
- BT **Arithmetic**

Cubic measurement
- USE **Volume (Cubic content)**

Cubism (May subdiv. geog.) 709.04;
759.06
- BT **Art**

Cuchulain (Legendary character)
398.22
- BT **Legendary characters**

Cultivated plants (May subdiv. geog.)
581.6; 631.5
- UF Plants, Cultivated
- BT **Agriculture**
  Gardening
  Plants
- NT **Annuals (Plants)**
  House plants
  Ornamental plants
  Perennials

Cultivated plants—United States 581.6;
631.5

Cults (May subdiv. geog.) 209; 306.6

> Use for materials on groups or movements whose beliefs or practices differ significantly from the traditional religions and are often focused upon a charismatic leader. Materials on the major world religions are entered under **Religions**. Materials on independent religious groups whose teachings or practices fall within the normative bounds of the major world religions are entered under **Sects**.

- UF Religious cults
- BT **Religions**
- NT **New Age movement**
- RT **Sects**

Cultural anthropology
- USE **Ethnology**

Cultural change
- USE **Social change**

Cultural diversity in the workplace
- USE **Diversity in the workplace**

Cultural exchange programs
- USE **Exchange of persons programs**

Cultural heritage
- USE **Cultural property**

Cultural life
- USE **Intellectual life**

Cultural patrimony
- USE **Cultural property**

Cultural policy (May subdiv. geog.) 306

> Use for materials on official government policy toward educational, artistic, intellectual, or other cultural activities and organizations in general.

- UF Government policy
  Intellectual life—Government policy
  State encouragement of science, literature, and art
- SA types of artistic or intellectual activities with the subdivision *Government policy* [to be added as needed]

Cultural policy—*Continued*

   BT   **Culture**

         Intellectual life

   NT   **Cultural property—Protection**

Cultural policy—United States   **306**

   UF   United States—Cultural policy

Cultural property (May subdiv. geog.)
    344

   Use for materials on property that is considered essential to a nation's cultural heritage.

   UF   Cultural heritage

         Cultural patrimony

         Heritage property

         National heritage

         National patrimony

         National treasure

   BT   **Property**

Cultural property—Protection (May
    subdiv. geog.)   **344**

   Use for materials on protecting cultural heritage property from theft, misappropriation, or exportation. Materials on identifying and preserving historically important towns, buildings, sites, etc., are entered under **Historic preservation**.

   UF   Cultural property—Protection—
         Government policy

         Cultural resources management

   BT   **Cultural policy**

   RT   **Historic preservation**

Cultural property—Protection—Government
   policy

   USE   **Cultural property—Protection**

Cultural relations (May subdiv. geog.)
    303.48; 306; 344

   UF   Intercultural relations

   BT   **Intellectual cooperation**

         International cooperation

         International relations

   NT   **Exchange of persons programs**

         Interfaith relations

Cultural resources management

   USE   **Cultural property—Protection**

Cultural tourism (May subdiv. geog.)
    910

   UF   Heritage tourism

         Historical tourism

         History tourism

   BT   **Tourist trade**

Culturally deprived

   USE   **Socially handicapped**

Culturally deprived children

   USE   **Socially handicapped children**

Culturally handicapped

   USE   **Socially handicapped**

Culturally handicapped children

   USE   **Socially handicapped children**

Culture   **306; 909**

   Use for materials on the sum total of ways of living or thinking established by a group of human beings and transmitted from one generation to the next, including a concern for what is regarded as excellent in the arts, manners, scholarship, etc.

   SA   regions, countries, states, etc.,
         with the subdivisions *Intellectual life*; *Civilization*; or *Social life and customs*, e.g.
         United States—Intellectual life; **United States—Civilization**; **United States—Social life and customs**; etc. [to be added as needed]

   NT   **Acculturation**

         Cross-cultural studies

         Cultural policy

         Humanism

         Intellectual life

         Language and culture

         Material culture

         Multiculturalism

         Pluralism (Social sciences)

         Popular culture

   RT   **Anthropology**

         Civilization

         Education

         Learning and scholarship

         Sociology

Culture conflict (May subdiv. geog.)
    155.8; 306; 155.8

   UF   Conflict of cultures

         Cross cultural conflict

         Culture shock

         Future shock

   BT   **Ethnic relations**

         Ethnopsychology

         Race relations

Culture contact

   USE   **Acculturation**

Culture, Corporate

   USE   **Corporate culture**

Culture shock

   USE   **Culture conflict**

Cuneiform inscriptions (May subdiv.
    geog.)   **411**

   UF   Inscriptions, Cuneiform

Cuneiform inscriptions—*Continued*
   BT   **Inscriptions**
         Writing
Curates
   USE   **Clergy**
Curiosities and wonders (May subdiv.
      geog.)   **030**
   UF   Enigmas
         Facts, Miscellaneous
         Miscellanea
         Miscellaneous facts
         Oddities
         Trivia
         Wonders
   SA   subjects with the subdivision
         Miscellanea, e.g. **Medicine—**
         Miscellanea [to be added as
         needed]
   NT   **Eccentrics and eccentricities**
         Medicine—Miscellanea
         Monsters
         World records
Curiosity   155.2
   UF   Exploratory behavior
         Inquisitiveness
   BT   **Human behavior**
Currency
   USE   **Money**
Currency devaluation
   USE   **Monetary policy**
Current events   909.82
   Use for materials on the study and teaching
of current events. Accounts or discussions of
the events themselves are entered under the
appropriate heading for historical period or
history of a place. Periodicals and yearbooks
devoted to current events are entered under
History—Periodicals.
   BT   **Modern history—Study and**
         teaching
Currents, Electric
   USE   **Electric currents**
Currents, Ocean
   USE   **Ocean currents**
Curricula
   USE   **Education—Curricula**
         and types of education and
         schools with the subdivision
         Curricula, e.g. **Library edu-**
         cation—Curricula [to be
         added as needed]
Curriculum development
   USE   **Curriculum planning**

Curriculum materials centers
   USE   **Instructional materials centers**
Curriculum planning (May subdiv. geog.)
      375
   UF   Curriculum development
   BT   **Education—Curricula**
         Planning
   NT   **Interdisciplinary approach in**
         education
Curtains
   USE   **Draperies**
Custody kidnapping
   USE   **Parental kidnapping**
Custody of children
   USE   **Child custody**
Custom duties
   USE   **Tariff**
Customer relations   658.8
   BT   **Business**
         Public relations
   NT   **Customer services**
Customer service
   USE   **Customer services**
Customer services   658.8
   UF   Customer service
         Service, Customer
         Service (in industry)
         Services, Customer
         Technical service
   BT   **Customer relations**
Customs and practices
   USE   religions, denominations, reli-
         gious orders, and religious
         holidays with the subdivision
         Customs and practices, e.g.
         Judaism—Customs and
         practices [to be added as
         needed]
Customs, Social
   USE   **Manners and customs**
Customs (Tariff)
   USE   **Tariff**
Cyberbullying   302.3
   BT   **Bullies**
         Computer crimes
Cybercommerce
   USE   **Electronic commerce**
Cybernetics   003
   UF   Automatic control
         Mechanical brains

Cybernetics—*Continued*
- BT **Communication**
  Electronics
  System theory
- NT **Bionics**
  System analysis
  Systems engineering

Cybersex
- USE **Computer sex**

Cybershopping
- USE **Internet shopping**

Cyberspace 006

Use for materials on the non-physical environment created by the Internet or other computer networks.
- BT **Computer networks**
  Space and time

Cycles 115
- UF Cyclic theory
  Natural cycles
  Periodicity
- NT **Biological rhythms**
  Business cycles
  Life cycles (Biology)
- RT **Rhythm**
  Time

Cyclic theory
- USE **Cycles**

Cycling (May subdiv. geog.) **796.6**
- UF Bicycles and bicycling
  Bicycling
  Biking
- BT **Exercise**
  Outdoor recreation
  Sports
- NT **Bicycle racing**
  Bicycle touring
  Motorcycling
  Mountain biking
- RT **Bicycles**
  Tricycles

Cyclones (May subdiv. geog.) **551.55**

Use for materials on large-scale storms that involve high winds rotating around a center of low atmospheric pressure. Materials on the cyclones of the West Indies are entered under **Hurricanes**. Materials on the cyclones of the China Seas and the Philippines are entered under **Typhoons**.
- BT **Meteorology**
  Storms
  Winds
- NT **Hurricanes**
  Typhoons

Cyclopedias
- USE **Encyclopedias and dictionaries**

Cyclotron
- USE **Cyclotrons**

Cyclotrons 539.7
- UF Atom smashing
  Cyclotron
  Magnetic resonance accelerator
- BT **Atoms**
  Nuclear physics
  Transmutation (Chemistry)

Cytology
- USE **Cells**

Czech Republic 943.71

Use for materials on this part of the former country of Czechoslovakia since its becoming independent on January 1, 1993. May be subdivided like United States except for History.
- RT **Czechoslovakia**

Czechoslovakia 943.703

Use for materials on the former country of Czechoslovakia through December 31, 1992. Materials on the two parts of the former country of Czechoslovakia, which became independent on January 1, 1993, are entered under **Czech Republic** and **Slovakia**.
- RT **Czech Republic**
  Slovakia

Czechoslovakia—History—1918-1968 943.703

Czechoslovakia—History—1945-1992 943.704
- UF Czechoslovakia—History—1989-1992

Czechoslovakia—History—1968-1989 943.704

Czechoslovakia—History—1989-1992
- USE **Czechoslovakia—History—1945-1992**

D Day
- USE **Normandy (France), Attack on, 1944**

Daily readings (Spiritual exercises)
- USE **Devotional calendars**

Dairies
- USE **Dairying**

Dairy cattle (May subdiv. geog.) **636.2**
- SA names of breeds of dairy cattle [to be added as needed]
- BT **Cattle**
  Dairying
- NT **Holstein-Friesian cattle**

Dairy farming
- USE **Dairying**

Dairy-free cooking 641.8

Dairy-free cooking—*Continued*
  UF   Lactose intolerance—Diet thera-
          py—Recipes
  BT   **Cooking**
  RT   **Lactose intolerance**
Dairy industry
  USE   **Dairying**
Dairy products (May subdiv. geog.)
          637; 641.3
  UF   Products, Dairy
  SA   types of dairy products [to be
          added as needed]
  BT   **Animal products**
  NT   **Butter**
        Cheese
        Milk
Dairying (May subdiv. geog.)   **636.2;
          637**
    Use for materials on the production and
  marketing of milk and milk products and for
  general materials on dairy farming.
  UF   Dairies
        Dairy farming
        Dairy industry
  BT   **Agriculture**
        Livestock industry
  NT   **Dairy cattle**
        Milk
Dams (May subdiv. geog.)   **627**
  SA   names of dams, e.g. **Hoover
          Dam (Ariz. and Nev.)** [to be
          added as needed]
  BT   **Civil engineering**
        Hydraulic structures
        Water supply
  NT   **Hoover Dam (Ariz. and Nev.)**
Dance (May subdiv. geog.)   **792.8; 793.3**
    Use for materials on recreational dancing as
  well as performance dance.
  UF   Dances
        Dancing
  SA   types of dances and dancing [to
          be added as needed]
  BT   **Amusements**
        Performing arts
  NT   **Ballet**
        Ballroom dancing
        Belly dancing
        Break dancing
        Clog dancing
        Folk dancing
        Modern dance
        Step dancing

  Tap dancing
  RT   **Aerobics**
        Dance music
Dance music (May subdiv. geog.)   **781.5;
          784.18**
  BT   **Music**
  RT   **Dance**
Dance—United States   **792.80973;
          793.30973**
Dancers (May subdiv. geog.)   **792.8092;
          793.3092; 920**
  SA   types of dancers, e.g. **Ballet
          dancers** [to be added as
          needed]
  BT   **Entertainers**
  NT   **African American dancers**
        Ballet dancers
Dances
  USE   **Dance**
Dancing
  USE   **Dance**
Dangerous animals (May subdiv. geog.)
          591.6
  BT   **Animals**
  NT   **Poisonous animals**
  RT   **Animal attacks**
Dangerous materials
  USE   **Hazardous substances**
Dangerous occupations
  USE   **Hazardous occupations**
Danish language   **439.8**
    May be subdivided like **English language**.
  BT   **Language and languages**
        Norwegian language
        Scandinavian languages
Danish literature   **839.81**
    May use same subdivisions and names of
  literary forms as for **English literature**.
  BT   **Literature**
        Scandinavian literature
Dao
  USE   **Tao**
Dark Ages
  USE   **Middle Ages**
Dark humor (Literature)
  USE   **Black humor (Literature)**
Dark matter (Astronomy)   **523.1**
  BT   **Matter**
Dark night of the soul
  USE   **Mysticism**
Darkroom technique in photography
  USE   **Photography—Processing**

Darwinism
USE **Evolution**
Data banks
USE **Databases**
Data base design
USE **Database design**
Data bases
USE **Databases**
Data processing (May subdiv. geog.)
004
UF Automatic data processing
Electronic data processing
SA subjects with the subdivision
Data processing, e.g. **Banks
and banking—Data process-
ing** [to be added as needed]
BT **Computers**
Information systems
NT **Banks and banking—Data pro-
cessing**
Computer graphics
Computer programming
Database management
**Expert systems (Computer sci-
ence)**
Optical data processing
RT **Computer science**
Data processing—Keyboarding
USE **Keyboarding (Electronics)**
Data retrieval
USE **Information retrieval**
Data storage and retrieval systems
USE **Information systems**
**Data transmission systems   004.6;
621.38; 621.39**
UF Transmission of data
BT **Telecommunication**
NT **Computer networks**
Electronic mail systems
Fax transmission
Instant messaging
Video telephone
Databanks
USE **Databases**
Database design   005.74
UF Data base design
BT **System design**
Database management (May subdiv.
geog.)   **005.74**
UF Systems, Database management

BT **Computer science**
Data processing
Information systems
Database management—Computer programs
USE **Database management—Com-
puter software**
**Database management—Computer soft-
ware   005.74**
UF Database management—Comput-
er programs
BT **Computer software**
Databases   025.04
Use for materials on any type of organized
body of information, including written, numerical, and visual information, not limited to a
particular subject.
UF Data banks
Data bases
Databanks
SA subjects with the subdivision
Databases, for materials about
data files on a subject regardless of the medium of distribution, e.g. **Business—
Databases**; subjects with the
subdivision *Information resources*, for general materials
about information on a subject, e.g. **Business—Information resources**; subjects with
the subdivision *Internet resources*, for materials about
information available on the
Internet on a subject, e.g.
Business—Internet resources;
and headings for the providers
or the users of information
with the subdivision *Information services*, for materials
about organizations that provide information services, e.g.
**United Nations—Information
services**; **Consumers—Information services**; etc. [to be
added as needed]
BT **Information resources**
NT **Business—Databases**
Web databases
Date etiquette
USE **Dating (Social customs)**
Date rape (May subdiv. geog.)   **362.883;
364.15**

Date rape—*Continued*
    UF   Acquaintance rape
            Dating violence
    BT   **Dating (Social customs)**
            Rape
Dates, Historical
    USE   **Historical chronology**
Dating etiquette
    USE   **Dating (Social customs)**
Dating, Radiocarbon
    USE   **Radiocarbon dating**
Dating (Social customs) (May subdiv.
    geog.)   **306.73; 392.4; 646.7**
    UF   Date etiquette
            Dating etiquette
    BT   **Courtship**
            Etiquette
            Manners and customs
    NT   **Date rape**
    RT   **Man-woman relationship**
Dating violence
    USE   **Date rape**
Daughters   **306.874**
    BT   **Family**
            Women
    NT   **Father-daughter relationship**
            Mother-daughter relationship
Daughters and fathers
    USE   **Father-daughter relationship**
Daughters and mothers
    USE   **Mother-daughter relationship**
Day   **529**
    BT   **Chronology**
            Time
    RT   **Night**
Day care centers (May subdiv. geog.)
    362.71
    UF   Child care centers
            Children—Day care
            Children's day care centers
            Day nurseries
            Nurseries, Day
    BT   **Child care**
            Child welfare
            Children—Institutional care
    RT   **Nursery schools**
Day dreams
    USE   **Fantasy**
Day nurseries
    USE   **Day care centers**
Day of Atonement
    USE   **Yom Kippur**

Day trading (Securities)   **332.64**
    BT   **Securities**
Days   **394.2**
    UF   Days of the week
    SA   types of days and names of par-
            ticular days [to be added as
            needed]
    BT   **Calendars**
    NT   **Birthdays**
            Holidays
    RT   **Anniversaries**
            Festivals
            Week
Days of the week
    USE   **Days**
D.D.T. (Insecticide)
    USE   **DDT (Insecticide)**
DDT (Insecticide)   **668**
    UF   D.D.T. (Insecticide)
            Dichloro-diphenyl-trichloroethane
    BT   **Insecticides**
Dead (May subdiv. geog.)   **306.9; 571.9**
    UF   Cadavers
            Corpses
            Deceased
    BT   **Burial**
            Cremation
            Death
            Funeral rites and ceremonies
            Obituaries
    NT   **Zombies**
Dead Sea scrolls   **221.4; 229; 296.1**
    UF   Qumran texts
    RT   **Essenes**
Deaf (May subdiv. geog.)   **362.4**
    BT   **Hearing impaired**
            Physically handicapped
    NT   **Closed caption television**
            Closed caption video record-
            ings
    RT   **Deafness**
Deaf—Education (May subdiv. geog.)
    371.91
    UF   Education of the deaf
    BT   **Education**
Deaf—Institutional care (May subdiv.
    geog.)   **362.4**
    BT   **Institutional care**
Deaf—Means of communication   **362.4;**
    419
    Use for general materials on communication
in the broadest sense by people who are deaf.

Deaf—Means of communication—*Continued*

Materials on language systems based on hand gestures are entered under **Sign language**.

BT   **Communication**

NT   **Hearing ear dogs**

      Lipreading

RT   **Nonverbal communication**

      Sign language

Deaf—Sign language

USE   **Sign language**

Deafness   **362.4; 617.8**

NT   **Hearing aids**

RT   **Deaf**

      Hearing

Death (May subdiv. geog.)   **128; 236; 306.9; 571.9**

SA   ethnic groups and classes of persons with the subdivision *Death*, e.g. **Infants—Death**; and names of individual persons and groups of notable persons with the subdivision *Death and burial*, e.g. **Presidents—United States—Death and burial** [to be added as needed]

BT   **Biology**

      Eschatology

      Life

NT   **Brain death**

      Children and death

      Children—Death

      Dead

      Future life

      Infants—Death

      Near-death experiences

      Right to die

RT   **Burial**

      Mortality

      Terminal care

      Terminally ill

Death and burial

USE   names of individual persons and groups of notable persons with the subdivision *Death and burial*, e.g. **Presidents—United States—Death and burial** [to be added as needed]

Death and children

USE   **Children and death**

Death masks

USE   **Masks (Sculpture)**

Death notices

USE   **Obituaries**

Death penalty

USE   **Capital punishment**

Death rate

USE   **Mortality**

      Vital statistics

Deaths, Registers of

USE   **Registers of births, etc.**

Debates and debating (May subdiv. geog.)   **808.53**

UF   Argumentation

      Discussion

      Speaking

BT   **Public speaking**

      Rhetoric

NT   **Parliamentary practice**

      Radio addresses, debates, etc.

RT   **Discussion groups**

Debit cards   **332.1**

UF   Bank debit cards

      Cards, Debit

BT   **Banks and banking**

Debris in space

USE   **Space debris**

Debt (May subdiv. geog.)   **332.7**

Use for economic and statistical materials on debt. Legal materials regarding debtor and creditor are entered under **Debtor and creditor**.

UF   Indebtedness

BT   **Finance**

NT   **Collecting of accounts**

      Public debts

RT   **Debtor and creditor**

Debtor

USE   **Debtor and creditor**

Debtor and creditor (May subdiv. geog.)   **346.07**

Use for legal materials regarding debtor and creditor. Economic and statistical materials on debt are entered under **Debt**.

UF   Creditor

      Debtor

BT   **Commercial law**

NT   **Bankruptcy**

      Collecting of accounts

RT   **Credit**

      Debt

Debts, Public

USE   **Public debts**

Decalogue
USE **Ten commandments**
Deceased
USE **Dead**
Deceit
USE **Deception**
Fraud
Decentralization of schools
USE **Schools—Decentralization**
Deception 001.9; 177
UF Chicanery
Deceit
Subterfuge
BT **Truthfulness and falsehood**
NT **Disguise**
Deceptive advertising (May subdiv. geog.)
343.07
UF False advertising
Fraudulent advertising
Misleading advertising
Misrepresentation in advertising
Truth in advertising
BT **Advertising**
Business ethics
Decimal system 513.5
BT **Numbers**
RT **Metric system**
Decision making (May subdiv. geog.)
153.8; 302.3; 658.4
NT **Critical thinking**
Group decision making
RT **Choice (Psychology)**
Problem solving
Decks (Domestic architecture)
USE **Patios**
Declamations
USE **Monologues**
Recitations
Declaration of independence (U.S.)
USE **United States—Declaration of independence**
Decoration and ornament (May subdiv. geog.) **745.4**

Use for general materials on the forms and styles of decoration in various fields of fine arts or applied art and on the history of various styles of ornament. In addition to geographic subdivision, this heading may be subdivided by date or by style of ornament, e.g. **Decoration and ornament—15th and 16th centuries**; **Decoration and ornament—Gothic style**; etc. Materials limited to the decoration of houses are entered under **Interior design**.

UF Decorative art
Decorative design
Decorative painting
Ornament
Painting, Decorative
BT **Art**
Decorative arts
NT **Antiques**
Architectural decoration and ornament
Art objects
Artificial flowers
Arts and crafts movement
Beads
Bronzes
China painting
Christmas decorations
Decoupage
Design
Egg decoration
Embroidery
Enamel and enameling
Flower arrangement
Furniture
Garden ornaments and furniture
Gems
Glass painting and staining
Holiday decorations
Illumination of books and manuscripts
Illustration of books
Interior design
Ironwork
Leather work
Lettering
Metalwork
Monograms
Mosaics
Mural painting and decoration
Needlework
Picture frames and framing
Pottery
Sculpture
Show windows
Stencil work
Stucco
Table setting and decoration
Tapestry
Terra cotta
Textile design

Decoration and ornament—*Continued*
Wood carving
RT **Handicraft**
Painting
Decoration and ornament—15th and 16th centuries (May subdiv. geog.) **745.4**
UF Decoration and ornament, Renaissance
Renaissance decoration and ornament
Decoration and ornament, American
USE **Decoration and ornament— United States**
Decoration and ornament, Architectural
USE **Architectural decoration and ornament**
Decoration and ornament, Gothic
USE **Decoration and ornament— Gothic style**
Decoration and ornament—Gothic style (May subdiv. geog.) **745.4**
UF Decoration and ornament, Gothic
Gothic decoration and ornament
Decoration and ornament, Renaissance
USE **Decoration and ornament— 15th and 16th centuries**
Decoration and ornament—United States **745.4**
UF American decoration and ornament
Decoration and ornament, American
Decoration Day
USE **Memorial Day**
Decorations, Holiday
USE **Holiday decorations**
Decorations of honor (May subdiv. geog.) **355.1; 929.8**
UF Badges of honor
Emblems
SA names of medals [to be added as needed]
RT **Heraldry**
Insignia
Medals
Decorative art
USE **Decoration and ornament**
Decorative arts
Decorative arts (May subdiv. geog.) **745**
Use for general materials on the various applied art forms having some utilitarian as well

as decorative purpose, including furniture, silverware, the decoration of buildings, etc.
UF Applied arts
Art industries and trade
Decorative art
Minor arts
SA types of decorative arts [to be added as needed]
BT **Arts**
NT **Antiques**
Art metalwork
Art objects
Arts and crafts movement
Calligraphy
Carving (Decorative arts)
Costume
Decoration and ornament
Decoupage
Enamel and enameling
Fabrics
Furniture
Glassware
Jewelry
Lacquer and lacquering
Leather work
Mosaics
Needlework
Porcelain
Pottery
Rugs and carpets
Silverware
Tapestry
Woodwork
RT **Folk art**
Handicraft
Decorative arts—United States **745.0973**
Decorative design
USE **Decoration and ornament**
Decorative metalwork
USE **Art metalwork**
Decorative painting
USE **Decoration and ornament**
Decoupage **745.54**
BT **Decoration and ornament**
Decorative arts
Paper crafts
Decoys (Hunting) (May subdiv. geog.) **745.593; 799.2**
UF Bird decoys (Hunting)
BT **Hunting**
Shooting

Deduction (Logic)
USE **Logic**
Deejays
USE **Disc jockeys**
Deep diving (May subdiv. geog.)   **627**

Use for materials on underwater diving with equipment. Materials on diving from a board or platform are entered under **Diving**. Materials on free diving with mask, fins, and snorkel are entered under **Skin diving**. Materials on free diving with the aid of a self-contained underwater breathing apparatus are entered under **Scuba diving**.

  UF   Deep sea diving
         Submarine diving
         Underwater diving
  BT   **Underwater exploration**
         Water sports
  NT   **Scuba diving**
         Skin diving
  RT   **Diving**

Deep sea diving
USE **Deep diving**
Deep sea drilling (Petroleum)
USE **Offshore oil well drilling**
Deep sea engineering
USE **Ocean engineering**
Deep sea mining
USE **Ocean mining**
Deep-sea photography
USE **Underwater photography**
Deer (May subdiv. geog.)   **599.65**
  UF   Fawns
  BT   **Game and game birds**
         Mammals
  NT   **Reindeer**
Defamation
USE **Libel and slander**
Defective speech
USE **Speech disorders**
Defective vision
USE **Vision disorders**
Defectors (May subdiv. geog.)   **325; 327.12**
  UF   Political defectors
         Turncoats
  BT   **Political refugees**
Defense industries
USE **Defense industry**
Defense industry (May subdiv. geog.)   **338.4**

Use for materials on the industries producing the implements of war. Materials on the implements of war themselves are entered under **Ordnance** or under **Military weapons**.

  UF   Armaments industries
         Arms sales
         Defense industries
         Military sales
         Military supplies industry
         Munitions
         Weapons industry
  BT   **Industries**
  RT   **Arms transfers**
         Military readiness
         Military weapons
         Ordnance
Defense (Law)
USE **Litigation**
Defense mechanisms of animals
USE **Animal defenses**
Defense mechanisms of plants
USE **Plant defenses**
Defense policy
USE **Military policy**
Defense readiness
USE **Military readiness**
Defense research
USE **Military research**
Defenses
  USE types of defenses, e.g. **Air defenses;** and names of continents, regions, countries, and individual colonies with the subdivision *Defenses,* e.g. **United States—Defenses** [to be added as needed]
Defenses, Radar
USE **Radar defense networks**
Deficit financing (May subdiv. geog.)   **336.3**
  UF   Compensatory spending
         Deficit spending
  BT   **Public finance**
  RT   **Public debts**
Deficit spending
USE **Deficit financing**
Defoliants
USE **Herbicides**
Deforestation (May subdiv. geog.)   **634.9**
  UF   Forest depletion
  BT   **Forests and forestry**
Deformities
USE **Birth defects**

Degrees, Academic
 USE **Academic degrees**
Degrees of latitude and longitude
 USE **Geodesy**
   Latitude
   Longitude
Dehydrated foods
 USE **Dried foods**
Dehydrated milk
 USE **Dried milk**
Deism (May subdiv. geog.) **211**
 BT **Religion**
   Theology
 RT **Atheism**
   Free thought
   Positivism
   Rationalism
   Theism
Deities
 USE **Gods and goddesses**
Dejection
 USE **Depression (Psychology)**
Delayed memory
 USE **Recovered memory**
Delinquency, Juvenile
 USE **Juvenile delinquency**
Delinquents
 USE **Criminals**
Delivery of health care
 USE **Medical care**
Delivery of medical care
 USE **Medical care**
Delphi (Ancient city)
 USE **Delphi (Extinct city)**
Delphi (Extinct city) **938**
 UF Delphi (Ancient city)
 BT **Extinct cities—Greece**
   Greece—Antiquities
Delusions
 USE **Hallucinations and illusions**
Dementia **616.8**
 BT **Brain—Diseases**
Demobilization
 USE names of armed forces with the
   subdivision *Demobilization,*
   e.g. **United States. Army—**
   Demobilization [to be added
   as needed]
Democracy (May subdiv. geog.) **321.8**
 UF Popular government
   Self-government

 BT **Constitutional history**
   Constitutional law
   Political science
 NT **Freedom**
   Referendum
   Suffrage
 RT **Equality**
   Representative government and
    representation
   Republics
Democratic Party (U.S.) **324.2736**
 BT **Political parties**
Democratic Republic of the Congo
 USE **Congo (Democratic Republic)**
Demography
 USE **Population**
Demoniac possession **133.4**
 BT **Demonology**
 RT **Devil**
   Exorcism
Demonology (May subdiv. geog.) **133.4**
 UF Evil spirits
 BT **Occultism**
 NT **Demoniac possession**
 RT **Devil**
   Exorcism
   Spirits
Demonstrations (May subdiv. geog.)
   322.4; 361.2
 Use for materials on public gatherings,
 marches, etc., organized for nonviolent protest
 even though incidental disturbances or rioting
 may occur.
 UF Marches (Demonstrations)
   Protest marches and rallies
   Protests, demonstrations, etc.
   Public demonstrations
   Rallies (Protest)
 SA names of specific wars or other
   objects of protest with the
   subdivision *Protest move-*
   ments, e.g. **World War,**
   1939-1945—Protest move-
   ments [to be added as need-
   ed]
 BT **Crowds**
   Public meetings
 NT **Civil rights demonstrations**
   Hunger strikes
 RT **Peace movements**
   Protest movements
   Riots

Demonstrations—Chicago (Ill.)
322.409773
Demonstrations for civil rights
USE **Civil rights demonstrations**
Demonstrations—United States
322.40973; 361.2
Denationalization
USE **Privatization**
Denatured alcohol   661
UF   Alcohol, Denatured
Industrial alcohol
BT   **Alcohol**
Denmark   948.9
May be subdivided like United States except for History.
Denominational schools
USE **Church schools**
Denominations, Christian
USE **Christian sects**
Denominations, Protestant
USE **Protestant churches**
Denominations, Religious
USE **Sects**
Dental care (May subdiv. geog.)   **617.6**
Use for materials on the organization of services and facilities for dental care. Materials on the technical and medical aspects of dental care are entered under **Dentistry**.
SA   ethnic groups, classes of persons, and military services with the subdivision *Dental care*, e.g. **Children—Dental care** [to be added as needed]
BT   **Medical care**
RT   **Dentistry**
Dentistry (May subdiv. geog.)   **617.6**
Use for materials on the technical and medical aspects of dental care. Materials on the organization of services and facilities for dental care are entered under **Dental care**.
SA   ethnic groups, classes of persons, and military services with the subdivision *Dental care*, e.g. **Children—Dental care** [to be added as needed]
BT   **Medicine**
RT   **Dental care**
Teeth
Deoxyribonucleic acid
USE **DNA**
Department stores (May subdiv. geog.)
658.8
BT   **Business**
Retail trade

Stores
Dependencies
USE **Colonies**
Depression, Mental
USE **Depression (Psychology)**
Depression (Psychology)   616.85
UF   Dejection
Depression, Mental
Depressive psychoses
Melancholia
Mental depression
Mentally depressed
BT   **Abnormal psychology**
Affective disorders
Neuroses
NT   **Postpartum depression**
RT   **Manic-depressive illness**
Depressions (May subdiv. geog.)   **338.5**
UF   Business depressions
Economic depressions
SA   names of countries, states, cities, etc., with the subdivision *Economic conditions* [to be added as needed]
BT   **Business cycles**
NT   **Great Depression, 1929-1939**
Depressive psychoses
USE **Depression (Psychology)**
Deprogramming
USE **Brainwashing**
Derailments
USE **Railroad accidents**
Deregulation (May subdiv. geog.)   **338.9;**
352.8
UF   Industries—Deregulation
SA   types of industry with the subdivision *Deregulation*, e.g. **Petroleum industry—Deregulation** to be added as needed]
BT   **Industrial policy**
Dermatitis
USE **Skin—Diseases**
Derricks
USE **Cranes, derricks, etc.**
Dervishes (May subdiv. geog.)   **297.4**
RT   **Sufism**
Desalination of water
USE **Sea water conversion**
Desalting of water
USE **Sea water conversion**

Descent
USE **Genealogy**
Heredity
Description
USE names of cities (except extinct cities), countries, states, and regions with the subdivision *Description and travel,* e.g. **Chicago (Ill.)—Description and travel; United States—Description and travel;** etc., for descriptive materials and accounts of travel, including the history of travel, in those places; names of places with the subdivision *Geography* for broad geographical materials about a specific place, e.g. **United States—Geography;** and names of extinct cities or towns, without further subdivision, for general descriptive materials on those places, e.g. **Delphi (Extinct city)** [to be added as needed]
Description and travel
USE names of cities (except extinct cities), countries, states, etc., with the subdivision *Description and travel,* e.g. **Chicago (Ill.)—Description and travel; United States—Description and travel;** etc., for descriptive materials and accounts of travel, including the history of travel, in those places; names of places with the subdivision *Geography* for broad geographical materials about a specific place, e.g. **United States—Geography;** names of extinct cities or towns, without further subdivision, for general descriptive materials on those places, e.g. **Delphi (Extinct city);** and ethnic groups, classes of persons, and names of individuals with the subdivision *Travel,* e.g. **Handicapped—Travel** [to be added as needed]

Descriptive geometry   516
UF Geometry, Descriptive
BT **Geometrical drawing**
Geometry
NT **Perspective**
Desegregated schools
USE **School integration**
Desegregation
USE **Segregation**
Desegregation in education
USE **School integration**
Desert animals (May subdiv. geog.) **578.754**
UF Desert fauna
SA types of desert animals, e.g. **Camels** [to be added as needed]
BT **Animals**
Deserts
NT **Camels**
Desert ecology (May subdiv. geog.) **577.54**
BT **Ecology**
Desert fauna
USE **Desert animals**
Desert plants (May subdiv. geog.)   **581.7**
SA types of desert plants, e.g. **Cactus** [to be added as needed]
BT **Deserts**
Plant ecology
Plants
NT **Cactus**
Desertification (May subdiv. geog.) **333.73**
BT **Climate**
Deserts
Desertion
USE **Desertion and nonsupport**
Military desertion
Desertion and nonsupport (May subdiv. geog.) **306.88; 346.01**
UF Abandonment of family
Desertion
Nonsupport
BT **Divorce**
Domestic relations
NT **Child support**
Runaway adults
Desertion, Military
USE **Military desertion**

Desertions
    USE   names of wars with the subdivision *Desertions,* e.g. **World War, 1939-1945—Desertions** [to be added as needed]

Deserts (May subdiv. geog.)   **551.41**
    BT   **Physical geography**
    NT   **Desert animals**
        Desert plants
        Desertification

Design (May subdiv. geog.)   **745.4**
    SA   types of design, e.g. **Industrial design**; **Fashion design**; etc.; types of objects, structures, machines, equipment, etc., and types of educational tests and examinations with the subdivision *Design and construction,* e.g. **Automobiles—Design and construction**; topical headings with which the subdivision *Design and construction* would be inappropriate with the subdivision *Design,* e.g. **Quilts—Design**; **Pamphlets—Design**; etc.; and types of architecture and landscape with the form subdivision *Designs and plans,* for materials containing designs and drawings, e.g. **Domestic architecture—Designs and plans** [to be added as needed]
    BT   **Decoration and ornament**
    NT   **Architectural design**
        Computer-aided design
        Fashion design
        Garden design
        Industrial design
        Interior design
        Machine design
        Pamphlets—Design
        Quilts—Design
        Textile design
        Web sites—Design
    RT   **Designers**
        Patternmaking

Design and construction
    USE   types of objects, structures, machines, equipment, etc., and types of educational tests and examinations with the subdivision *Design and construction,* e.g. **Airplanes—Design and construction** [to be added as needed]

Design, Industrial
    USE   **Industrial design**

Design perception
    USE   **Pattern perception**

Designed genetic change
    USE   **Genetic engineering**

Designer drugs   **362.29; 615**
    Use for materials on illicit drugs manufactured by altering the molecular structure of existing drugs to mimic the effects of standard narcotics, stimulants, or hallucinogens.
    UF   Synthetic drugs of abuse
    SA   types of designer drugs, e.g. **Crystal meth (Drug)** [to be added as needed]
    BT   **Drugs**
    NT   **Crystal meth (Drug)**

Designers (May subdiv. geog.)   **709.2**
    BT   **Artists**
    NT   **Fashion designers**
    RT   **Design**

Designs and plans
    USE   types of architecture and landscape with the form subdivision *Designs and plans,* for materials containing designs and drawings, e.g. **Domestic architecture—Designs and plans** [to be added as needed]

Designs, Architectural
    USE   **Architecture—Designs and plans**

Designs, Floral
    USE   **Flower arrangement**

Desktop computers
    USE   **Personal computers**

Desktop icons (Computer graphics)
    USE   **Icons (Computer graphics)**

Desktop publishing (May subdiv. geog.)   **070.5; 686.2**
    Use for materials on the use of a personal computer with writing, graphics, and page layout software to produce printed material for publication. Materials on the process of publishing by which books and articles or any kind of data are made available as an electronic product are entered under **Electronic publishing**.

Desktop publishing—*Continued*
   RT   **Electronic publishing**
         Word processing
Desserts (May subdiv. geog.)   **641.8**
   SA   types of desserts and names of
         specific desserts [to be added
         as needed]
   BT   **Cooking**
   NT   **Cake**
         Ice cream, ices, etc.
   RT   **Chocolate**
Destiny
   USE   **Fate and fatalism**
Destitution
   USE   **Poverty**
Destruction and pillage
   USE   names of wars with the subdivi-
         sion *Destruction and pillage,*
         e.g. **World War, 1939-
         1945—Destruction and pil-
         lage** [to be added as needed]
Destruction of property
   USE   **Vandalism**
Destructive insects
   USE   **Insect pests**
Detective and mystery comic books, strips,
   etc.
   USE   **Mystery comic books, strips,
         etc.**
Detective and mystery films
   USE   **Mystery films**
Detective and mystery plays
   USE   **Mystery and detective plays**
Detective and mystery radio programs
   USE   **Mystery radio programs**
Detective and mystery stories
   USE   **Mystery fiction**
Detective and mystery television programs
   USE   **Mystery television programs**
Detective comics
   USE   **Mystery comic books, strips,
         etc.**
Detective fiction
   USE   **Mystery fiction**
Detective stories
   USE   **Mystery fiction**
Detectives (May subdiv. geog.)   **363.25;
   920**
   BT   **Police**
   RT   **Criminal investigation**
         Secret service

Detergent pollution of rivers, lakes, etc.
   USE   **Water pollution**
Detergents   668
   UF   Synthetic detergents
   BT   **Cleaning compounds**
   RT   **Soap**
Determinism and indeterminism
   USE   **Free will and determinism**
Deuterium oxide   546
   UF   Heavy water
   BT   **Chemicals**
Devaluation of currency
   USE   **Monetary policy**
Developing countries   330.9
   Use for comprehensive materials on coun-
   tries that are not fully modernized or industri-
   alized. This heading may be subdivided by the
   topical subdivisions used under countries, re-
   gions, etc., and may also be used as a geo-
   graphic subdivision e.g. **Education—Develop-
   ing countries**.
   UF   Less developed countries
         Third World
         Underdeveloped areas
   BT   **Economic conditions**
         Industrialization
   NT   **New states**
**Developing countries—Commerce
   338.91; 382**
   BT   **Commerce**
Developing countries—Education
   USE   **Education—Developing coun-
         tries**
Development
   USE   **Embryology**
         Evolution
         Growth disorders
         Modernization (Sociology)
Development, Economic
   USE   **Economic development**
Developmental psychology   155
   BT   **Psychology**
Deviancy
   USE   **Deviant behavior**
Deviant behavior   155.2; 302.5
   UF   Deviancy
         Social deviance
   BT   **Human behavior**
   RT   **Conformity**
         Social adjustment
Deviation, Sexual
   USE   **Sexual deviation**

Devices (Heraldry)
    USE   **Heraldry**
             Insignia
Devil   235
    UF   Satan
    RT   **Demoniac possession**
            Demonology
Devil's Triangle
    USE   **Bermuda Triangle**
Devotion
    USE   **Prayer**
            Worship
Devotional calendars   242
    UF   Christian devotional calendars
            Daily readings (Spiritual exercises)
            Devotional exercises (Daily readings)
    BT   **Calendars**
            Devotional literature
Devotional exercises   242; 248.3
    Use for general materials on acts of private prayer and private worship and for materials on religious practices other than the corporate worship of a congregation. Materials on the religious literature used as aids in devotional exercises are entered under **Devotional literature**.
    UF   Devotional theology
            Devotions
            Family devotions
            Family prayers
    BT   **Worship**
    NT   **Meditation**
    RT   **Prayer**
Devotional exercises (Daily readings)
    USE   **Devotional calendars**
Devotional literature   242
    Use for materials on the religious literature used as aids in devotional exercises. General materials on acts of private prayer and private worship and materials on religious practices other than the corporate worship of a congregation are entered under **Devotional exercises**.
    BT   **Religious literature**
    NT   **Devotional calendars**
            Devotional literature for children
            Meditations
            Prayers
Devotional literature for children   242
    BT   **Devotional literature**

Devotional theology
    USE   **Devotional exercises**
            Prayer
Devotions
    USE   **Devotional exercises**
Dewey Decimal Classification   025.4
    UF   Classification, Dewey Decimal
    BT   **Library classification**
Diabetes   616.4
    BT   **Diseases**
Diagnosis   616.07
    UF   Medical diagnosis
            Symptoms
    BT   **Medicine**
    NT   **Body temperature**
            Clinical chemistry
            Electrocardiogram
            Magnetic resonance imaging
            Pain
            Prenatal diagnosis
    RT   **Pathology**
Diagnostic chemistry
    USE   **Clinical chemistry**
Diagnostic imaging   616.07
    UF   Clinical imaging
            Medical diagnostic imaging
    BT   **Pathology**
Dialectical materialism   335.4
    UF   Historical materialism
    BT   **Communism**
            Socialism
    RT   **Marxism**
Dialectics
    USE   **Logic**
Dialects
    USE   names of languages with the subdivision *Dialects,* e.g. **English language—Dialects** [to be added as needed]
Diamonds (May subdiv. geog.)   553.8
    BT   **Carbon**
            Precious stones
Diaries   808; 920
    Use for collections of diaries from various countries and for materials about diaries in general.
    UF   Journals (Diaries)
    SA   diaries of particular countries, e.g. **American diaries**; and classes of persons, ethnic groups, and names of individ-

Diaries—*Continued*

    ual persons and families with the subdivision *Diaries* [to be added as needed]

  BT **Literature**

  NT **American diaries**

       Journaling

       Weblogs

  RT **Autobiographies**

Diaspora, African

  USE **African diaspora**

Diaspora, Jewish

  USE **Jewish diaspora**

Dichloro-diphenyl-trichloroethane

  USE **DDT (Insecticide)**

Dictators (May subdiv. geog.)   **321.909; 920**

  BT **Heads of state**

       Totalitarianism

Dictionaries

  USE **Encyclopedias and dictionaries** and subjects, names of languages, and names of voluminous authors with the subdivision *Dictionaries,* e.g. **English language—Dictionaries; Biography—Dictionaries; Shakespeare, William, 1564-1616—Dictionaries** etc. [to be added as needed]

Dictionaries, Biographical

  USE **Biography—Dictionaries**

Dictionaries, Classical

  USE **Classical dictionaries**

Dictionaries, Machine readable

  USE **Machine readable dictionaries**

Dictionaries, Multilingual

  USE **Polyglot dictionaries**

Dictionaries, Picture

  USE **Picture dictionaries**

Dictionaries, Polyglot

  USE **Polyglot dictionaries**

Didactic drama   **808.82**

  Use for individual works, collections, or materials about didactic drama.

  BT **Drama**

Didactic fiction   **808.3; 808.83**

  Use for individual works, collections, or materials about didactic fiction.

  UF Cautionary tales and verses

       Moral and philosophic stories

       Morality stories

  BT **Fiction**

  RT **Fables**

       Parables

Didactic poetry   **808.1; 808.81**

  Use for individual works, collections, or materials about didactic poetry.

  UF Cautionary tales and verses

  BT **Poetry**

  RT **Fables**

       Parables

Dies (Metalworking)   **621.9; 671.2**

  BT **Metalwork**

Diesel automobiles (May subdiv. geog.)   **629.222**

  UF Diesel cars

  BT **Automobiles**

Diesel cars

  USE **Diesel automobiles**

Diesel engines   **621.43**

  BT **Engines**

       Internal combustion engines

Diet (May subdiv. geog.)   **613.2**

  UF Dietetics

  SA types of diets, e.g. **Salt-free diet** [to be added as needed]

  BT **Health**

       Hygiene

  NT **Beverages**

       Dietetic foods

       Eating customs

       Fasting

       Gastronomy

       High-carbohydrate diet

       High-fiber diet

       Low-calorie diet

       Low-carbohydrate diet

       Low-cholesterol diet

       Low-fat diet

       Menus

       Salt-free diet

       School children—Food

       Vegetarianism

  RT **Cooking**

       Digestion

       Food

       Nutrition

       Weight gain

       Weight loss

Diet in disease   **613.2; 616.3**

  SA types of diets [to be added as needed]

  BT **Therapeutics**

Diet in disease—*Continued*
    NT   **Cooking for the sick**
          Diet therapy
Diet supplements
    USE   **Dietary supplements**
Diet—Therapeutic use
    USE   **Diet therapy**
Diet therapy   615.8
    UF   Diet—Therapeutic use
          Invalid cooking
    SA   names of diseases with the sub-
          division *Diet therapy*, e.g.
          Cancer—Diet therapy; and
          types of food with the subdi-
          vision *Therapeutic use*, e.g.
          Herbs—Therapeutic use [to
          be added as needed]
    BT   **Cooking for the sick**
          Diet in disease
          Therapeutics
    NT   **Cancer—Diet therapy**
Dietary fiber
    USE   **Food—Fiber content**
Dietary supplements   613.2; 615.1
    UF   Diet supplements
          Food supplements
          Nutritional supplements
    BT   **Nutrition**
          Vitamins
    NT   **Probiotics**
    RT   **Food additives**
Dietetic foods (May subdiv. geog.)
    641.3; 664
    BT   **Diet**
          Food
Dietetics
    USE   **Diet**
Dieting
    USE   **Weight loss**
Diets, Reducing
    USE   **Weight loss**
Differential equations   515
    BT   **Calculus**
    NT   **Functions**
Digestion   573.3; 612.3
    BT   **Physiology**
    NT   **Indigestion**
    RT   **Diet**
          Nutrition
          Stomach
Digestive system   573.3; 612.3; 616.3
    BT   **Anatomy**

Digital audio disc players
    USE   **Compact disc players**
Digital cameras   771.3
    BT   **Cameras**
Digital circuits
    USE   **Digital electronics**
Digital compact discs
    USE   **Compact discs**
Digital electronics   621.381
    UF   Digital circuits
    BT   **Electronics**
    NT   **Digital photography**
Digital libraries (May subdiv. geog.)
    025.00285
    UF   Electronic libraries
          Virtual libraries
    BT   **Information systems**
          Libraries
Digital photography   775
    UF   Photography—Digital techniques
    BT   **Digital electronics**
          Photography
Digital reference services (Libraries)
    USE   **Electronic reference services**
          (Libraries)
Dimension, Fourth
    USE   **Fourth dimension**
Dining (May subdiv. geog.)   641.01
    Use for materials on dining customs and gastronomic travel. Materials on menus and recipes for dinners are entered under **Dinners**.
    UF   Banquets
          Dinners and dining
          Eating
    BT   **Food**
    NT   **Carving (Meat, etc.)**
    RT   **Dinners**
          Eating customs
          Entertaining
          Gastronomy
          Table etiquette
Dinners   642
    Use for materials on menus and recipes for dinners. Materials on dining customs and gastronomic travel are entered under **Dining**.
    UF   Banquets
          Dinners and dining
    BT   **Cooking**
          Menus
    RT   **Dining**
Dinners and dining
    USE   **Dining**
          Dinners

Dinosaur eggs
  USE **Dinosaurs—Eggs**
Dinosaurs (May subdiv. geog.) **567.9**
  SA types of dinosaurs and names of
       specific dinosaurs [to be add-
       ed as needed]
  BT **Fossil reptiles**
       Prehistoric animals
  NT **Allosaurus**
       Archaeopteryx
       Brachiosaurus
       Diplodocus
       Edmontosaurus
       Ichthyosaurus
       Iguanodon
       Maiasaura
       Pachycephalosaurus
       Parasaurolophus
       Pteranodon
       Pterodactyls
       Pterosaurs
       Raptorex
       Sarcosuchus imperator
       Scipionyx
       Spinosaurus
       Stegosaurus
       Triceratops
       Troodon
       Tyrannosaurus Rex
       Velociraptors
Dinosaurs—Eggs **567.9**
  UF Dinosaur eggs
  BT **Eggs**
Dionysus (Greek deity) **202**
  BT **Gods and goddesses**
Dioptrics
  USE **Refraction**
Diphtheria **616.9**
  BT **Diseases**
Diplodocus **567.913**
  BT **Dinosaurs**
Diplomacy **327.2; 341.3**
  SA names of countries with the sub-
       division *Foreign relations* [to
       be added as needed]
  BT **International relations**
  NT **Diplomats**
       Treaties
       **United States—Foreign rela-
       tions**

  RT **Diplomatic and consular ser-
       vice**
Diplomatic and consular service (May
       subdiv. geog.) **327.2**
  Use for materials on diplomatic and consular service in general or on the diplomatic and
  consular officials of various countries stationed abroad in various countries. Materials
  on the diplomatic and consular officials of
  various countries stationed in a specific country are entered under **Diplomatic and consular service** subdivided by the country where
  they are stationed. Materials on the diplomatic
  and consular officials of a specific country,
  regardless of where they are stationed, are entered under the appropriately modified heading, e.g. **American diplomatic and consular
  service**. Materials on the diplomatic and consular officials of a specific country stationed
  in a specific country are entered under the appropriately modified heading subdivided by
  the place where they are stationed.
  UF Consular service
       Consulates
       Embassies
       Foreign service
       Legations
  SA diplomatic and consular services
       of particular countries, e.g.
       **American diplomatic and
       consular service** [to be added
       as needed]
  BT **International relations**
  NT **American diplomatic and con-
       sular service**
  RT **Diplomacy**
       Diplomats
Diplomatic and consular service, American
  USE **American diplomatic and con-
       sular service**
Diplomatic history
  USE names of wars with the subdivi-
       sion *Diplomatic history,* e.g.
       **World War, 1939-1945—
       Diplomatic history** [to be
       added as needed]
Diplomats (May subdiv. geog.)
       327.2092; 920
  UF Ministers (Diplomatic agents)
  BT **Diplomacy**
       International relations
       Statesmen
  NT **Ambassadors**
       Consuls
  RT **Diplomatic and consular ser-
       vice**

Direct current machinery
USE **Electric machinery—Direct current**
Direct legislation
USE **Referendum**
Direct mail campaigns
USE **Direct marketing**
Direct marketing (May subdiv. geog.)
381; 658.8
UF Direct mail campaigns
BT **Mail-order business**
Marketing
RT **Direct selling**
Direct primaries
USE **Primaries**
Direct selling (May subdiv. geog.) **658.8**
BT **Marketing**
Retail trade
Selling
NT **Mail-order business**
Peddlers and peddling
Telemarketing
RT **Direct marketing**
Direct taxation
USE **Taxation**
Direction sense **152.1; 912**
UF Orientation
Sense of direction
NT **Left and right (Direction)**
RT **Navigation**
Orienteering
Direction (Theater)
USE **Theater—Production and direction**
Directories **910.25**
Use for materials about directories and for bibliographies of directories.
SA subjects and names of countries, cities, etc., with the subdivision *Directories*, for lists of persons, organizations, objects, etc., together with addresses or other identifying data [to be added as needed]
NT **Chicago (Ill.)—Directories**
Junior colleges—Directories
Ohio—Directories
Physicians—Directories
United States—Directories

Directories—Telephone
USE names of cities with the subdivision *Telephone directories,* e.g. **Chicago (Ill.)—Telephone directories** [to be added as needed]
Directors
USE types of producers and directors in specific media, e.g. **Motion picture producers and directors**; **Theatrical producers and directors**; etc. [to be added as needed]
Directory, French, 1795-1799
USE **France—History—1789-1799, Revolution**
Dirigible balloons
USE **Airships**
Disabilities **362.1**
UF Disabling conditions
Handicaps
Impairment
Physical disabilities
BT **Diseases**
Wounds and injuries
NT **Movement disorders**
Disability income insurance
USE **Disability insurance**
Disability insurance (May subdiv. geog.)
368.38
UF Disability income insurance
Insurance, Disability
BT **Insurance**
Disability law
USE **Handicapped—Legal status, laws, etc.**
Disabled
USE **Handicapped**
Disabling conditions
USE **Disabilities**
Disadvantaged
USE **Socially handicapped**
Disadvantaged children
USE **Socially handicapped children**
Disadvantaged students
USE **At risk students**
Disappointment **152.4**
BT **Emotions**
Disarmament
USE **Arms control**

Disaster preparedness
    USE **Disaster relief**
Disaster relief (May subdiv. geog.)
    363.34
    UF Disaster preparedness
          Emergency preparedness
          Emergency relief
    BT **Charities**
          Humanitarian intervention
          Public welfare
    NT **Evacuation of civilians**
          Food relief
Disasters (May subdiv. geog.)   **904**
    UF Catastrophes
          Emergencies
    SA types of disasters [to be added
          as needed]
    NT **Fires**
          Natural disasters
          Railroad accidents
          Shipwrecks
    RT **Accidents**
Disc jockeys (May subdiv. geog.)
    791.44092; 780.92
    UF Deejays
          Disk jockeys
          DJs (Disc jockeys)
    BT **Musicians**
          Radio and music
Disciples, Twelve
    USE **Apostles**
Discipline
    USE **Punishment**
Discipline of children
    USE **Child rearing**
          School discipline
Discography
    USE **Sound recordings**
          and subjects and names of per-
          sons with the subdivision *Dis-*
          cography, e.g. **Music—Dis-**
          cography; Shakespeare, Wil-
          liam, 1564-1616—Discogra-
          phy; etc., for lists or catalogs
          of sound recordings [to be
          added as needed]
Discount stores (May subdiv. geog.)
    381; 658.8
    BT **Retail trade**
          Stores

Discoverers
    USE **Explorers**
Discoveries and exploration
    USE **Exploration**
Discoveries in geography
    USE **Exploration**
Discoveries in science (May subdiv. geog.)
    500
    UF Breakthroughs, Scientific
          Discoveries, Scientific
          Scientific breakthroughs
          Scientific discoveries
    BT **Research**
          Science
Discoveries, Scientific
    USE **Discoveries in science**
Discrimination (May subdiv. geog.)   **177;**
    305
    Use for general materials on discrimination
    by race, religion, sex, age, social status, or
    other factors, including reverse discrimination.
    SA phrase headings for discrimina-
          tion in particular realms of
          activity, e.g. **Discrimination**
          in employment; or discrimi-
          nation against particular ethnic
          groups or classes of persons,
          e.g. **Discrimination against**
          the handicapped; and ethnic
          groups and classes of persons
          with the subdivision *Civil*
          rights, or *Legal status, laws,*
          etc., e.g. **African Ameri-**
          cans—Civil rights; Handi-
          capped—Legal status, laws,
          etc. [to be added as needed]
    BT **Ethnic relations**
          Interpersonal relations
          Prejudices
          Race relations
          Social problems
          Social psychology
    NT **Age discrimination**
          Discrimination against the
          handicapped
          Discrimination in education
          Discrimination in employment
          Discrimination in housing
          Discrimination in public ac-
          commodations
          Hate crimes
          Race discrimination

Discrimination—*Continued*
> **Sex discrimination**
> RT **Civil rights**
> **Minorities**
> **Segregation**
> **Toleration**

Discrimination against disabled persons
> USE **Discrimination against the handicapped**

Discrimination against handicapped persons
> USE **Discrimination against the handicapped**

Discrimination against the disabled
> USE **Discrimination against the handicapped**

Discrimination against the handicapped
> (May subdiv. geog.) **305.9; 362.4**
> UF Discrimination against disabled persons
> Discrimination against handicapped persons
> Discrimination against the disabled
> BT **Discrimination**
> **Handicapped**

Discrimination in education (May subdiv. geog.) **379.2**
> BT **Discrimination**
> NT **Test bias**
> RT **Segregation in education**

Discrimination in employment (May subdiv. geog.) **331.13**
> UF Employment discrimination
> Equal employment opportunity
> Equal opportunity in employment
> Fair employment practice
> Job discrimination
> SA ethnic groups and classes of persons with the subdivision *Employment*, e.g. **African Americans—Employment** [to be added as needed]
> BT **Discrimination**
> NT **Affirmative action programs**
> **Equal pay for equal work**

Discrimination in housing (May subdiv. geog.) **363.5**
> UF Fair housing
> Open housing
> Segregation in housing

> BT **Discrimination**
> **Housing**

Discrimination in public accommodations (May subdiv. geog.) **305**
> UF Public accommodations, Discrimination in
> Segregation in public accommodations
> BT **Discrimination**

Discussion
> USE **Conversation**
> **Debates and debating**
> **Negotiation**

Discussion groups **374**
> UF Forums (Discussions)
> Great books program
> Group discussion
> Panel discussions
> BT **Conversation**
> NT **Electronic discussion groups**
> RT **Debates and debating**

Disease germs
> USE **Bacteria**
> **Germ theory of disease**

Disease (Pathology)
> USE **Pathology**

Diseases (May subdiv. geog.) **616**
> UF Illness
> Sickness
> SA types of diseases, e.g. **Communicable diseases**; names of specific diseases, e.g. **Influenza**; and types of animals, classes of persons, and parts of the body with the subdivision *Diseases*, e.g. **Nervous system—Diseases** [to be added as needed]
> NT **AIDS (Disease)**
> **Animals—Diseases**
> **Arthritis**
> **Autoimmune diseases**
> **Blood—Diseases**
> **Bones—Diseases**
> **Brain—Diseases**
> **Cancer**
> **Chickenpox**
> **Children—Diseases**
> **Chronic diseases**
> **Chronic fatigue syndrome**
> **Cold (Disease)**

Diseases—*Continued*
    Communicable diseases
    Diabetes
    Diphtheria
    Disabilities
    Elderly—Diseases
    Epidemics
    Heart diseases
    Hyperactivity
    Impotence
    Infants—Diseases
    Influenza
    Leprosy
    Lungs—Diseases
    Lyme disease
    Malaria
    Men—Diseases
    Mental illness
    Mouth—Diseases
    Nervous system—Diseases
    Occupational diseases
    Plant diseases
    Poliomyelitis
    Rheumatism
    Skin—Diseases
    Teeth—Diseases
    Typhoid fever
    Women—Diseases
  RT **Health**
    Medicine
    Pathology
    Sick
Diseases and pests
  USE **Agricultural bacteriology**
    Agricultural pests
    Fungi
    Household pests
    Insect pests
    Parasites
    Plant diseases
    and names of individual pests, e.g. **Locusts;** and types of crops, plants, trees, etc., with the subdivision *Diseases and pests,* e.g. **Fruit—Diseases and pests** [to be added as needed]
Diseases—Causes 616.07
  UF Causes of diseases
  NT **Environmentally induced diseases**

Diseases, Chronic
  USE **Chronic diseases**
Diseases—Environmental aspects
  USE **Environmentally induced diseases**
Diseases of animals
  USE **Animals—Diseases**
Diseases of children
  USE **Children—Diseases**
Diseases of plants
  USE **Plant diseases**
Diseases of the blood
  USE **Blood—Diseases**
Diseases of women
  USE **Women—Diseases**
Diseases—Prevention
  USE **Preventive medicine**
Diseases—Treatment
  USE **Therapeutics**
Diseases, Tropical
  USE **Tropical medicine**
Disguise 306.4
  BT **Costume**
    Deception
Dishes
  USE **Porcelain**
    Pottery
    Tableware
Dishonesty
  USE **Honesty**
Disinfection and disinfectants 614.4
  UF Germicides
  BT **Hygiene**
    Pharmaceutical chemistry
    Public health
    Sanitation
  RT **Antiseptics**
    Fumigation
Disk jockeys
  USE **Disc jockeys**
Diskinesia
  USE **Movement disorders**
Disney World (Fla.)
  USE **Walt Disney World (Fla.)**
Disobedience
  USE **Obedience**
Disorderliness
  USE **Messiness**
Disorders of communication
  USE **Communicative disorders**

Displaced persons
   USE   **Political refugees**
          Refugees
Disposal of medical waste
   USE   **Medical wastes**
Disposal of refuse
   USE   **Refuse and refuse disposal**
Dispute settlement
   USE   **Conflict management**
Dissection   **570.2**
   SA   types of animals, groups of ani-
          mals, and organs and regions
          of the body with the subdivi-
          sion *Dissection*, e.g., **Frogs—**
          Dissection [to be added as
          needed]
   NT   **Frogs—Dissection**
Dissent (May subdiv. geog.)   **303.48;**
     361.2
   UF   Nonconformity
          Protest
   BT   **Freedom of conscience**
          Freedom of religion
   RT   **Conformity**
Dissertations   **378.2; 808**
   Use for materials about academic theses and
   dissertations.
   UF   Academic dissertations
          Dissertations, Academic
          Doctoral theses
          Theses
   BT   **Research**
Dissertations, Academic
   USE   **Dissertations**
Distance education (May subdiv. geog.)
   371.35
   Use for materials on the various forms of
   long-distance instruction, usually in the field
   of adult education, made possible by written,
   audiovisual, or electronic communication be-
   tween a student and a teacher.
   UF   Distance learning
   BT   **Education**
   NT   **Correspondence schools and**
          courses
          University extension
Distance learning
   USE   **Distance education**
Distillation   **641.2; 663**
   UF   Stills
   BT   **Analytical chemistry**
          Industrial chemistry
          Technology

   NT   **Essences and essential oils**
   RT   **Alcohol**
          Liquors
Distribution, Cooperative
   USE   **Cooperation**
Distribution (Economics)
   USE   **Commerce**
          Marketing
Distribution of animals and plants
   USE   **Biogeography**
Distribution of wealth
   USE   **Economics**
          Wealth
District libraries
   USE   **Regional libraries**
District schools
   USE   **Rural schools**
Districting (in city planning)
   USE   **Zoning**
Diversified corporations
   USE   **Conglomerate corporations**
Diversity, Biological
   USE   **Biodiversity**
Diversity in the workplace (May subdiv.
   geog.)   **331.11; 658.3**
   UF   Cultural diversity in the
          workplace
          Multicultural diversity in the
          workplace
          Workforce diversity
   BT   **Multiculturalism**
          Personnel management
Diversity movement
   USE   **Multiculturalism**
Dividends
   USE   **Securities**
          Stocks
Divination (May subdiv. geog.)   **133.3**
   UF   Crystal gazing
          Necromancy
          Soothsaying
   BT   **Occultism**
   NT   **Astrology**
          Feng shui
          Fortune telling
          Palmistry
   RT   **Oracles**
          Prophecies
Divine healing
   USE   **Spiritual healing**

Diving   797.2

Use for materials on diving from a board or platform. Materials on free diving with the aid of a self-contained underwater breathing apparatus are entered under **Scuba diving**. Materials on free diving with mask, fins, and snorkel are entered under **Skin diving**. Materials on underwater diving with equipment are entered under **Deep diving**.

BT   **Swimming**

Water sports

RT   **Deep diving**

Divinity of Jesus Christ

USE   **Jesus Christ—Divinity**

Division   513.2

BT   **Arithmetic**

Division of powers

USE   **Separation of powers**

Divorce (May subdiv. geog.)   **173;**

306.89; 346.01

BT   **Family**

NT   **Alimony**

Children of divorced parents

Desertion and nonsupport

Divorce mediation

Separation (Law)

RT   **Divorced people**

Domestic relations

Divorce counseling

USE   **Divorce mediation**

Divorce mediation   362.82

UF   Divorce counseling

Mediation, Divorce

BT   **Divorce**

NT   **Child custody**

Child support

RT   **Marriage counseling**

Divorced fathers   306.874

BT   **Divorced parents**

Divorced people

Fathers

Divorced men (May subdiv. geog.)

306.892

BT   **Divorced people**

Single men

Divorced mothers   306.874

BT   **Divorced parents**

Divorced people

Mothers

Divorced parents   306.874

BT   **Divorced people**

Parents

NT   **Divorced fathers**

Divorced mothers

Divorced people (May subdiv. geog.)

306.89

UF   Divorced persons

BT   **Single people**

NT   **Divorced fathers**

Divorced men

Divorced mothers

Divorced parents

Divorced women

RT   **Divorce**

Divorced persons

USE   **Divorced people**

Divorced women (May subdiv. geog.)

306.893

BT   **Divorced people**

Single women

DJs (Disc jockeys)

USE   **Disc jockeys**

DNA   572.8

UF   Deoxyribonucleic acid

BT   **Cells**

Heredity

Nucleic acids

NT   **Recombinant DNA**

DNA cloning

USE   **Molecular cloning**

DNA fingerprinting   614

UF   DNA fingerprints

DNA identification

DNA profiling

Genetic fingerprinting

Genetic fingerprints

Genetic profiling

BT   **Identification**

Medical jurisprudence

DNA fingerprints

USE   **DNA fingerprinting**

DNA identification

USE   **DNA fingerprinting**

DNA profiling

USE   **DNA fingerprinting**

Docks (May subdiv. geog.)   **386; 387.1;**

627

BT   **Hydraulic structures**

Marinas

RT   **Harbors**

Doctor films

USE   **Medical drama (Films)**

Doctor novels
USE **Medical novels**
Doctor radio programs
USE **Medical drama (Radio programs)**
Doctor television programs
USE **Medical drama (Television programs)**
Doctoral theses
USE **Dissertations**
Doctors
USE **Physicians**
Doctors' degrees
USE **Academic degrees**
Doctrinal theology (May subdiv. geog.)
202; 230
UF Dogmatic theology
Dogmatics
Systematic theology
Theology, Doctrinal
SA names of religions or individual
denominations with the subdivision *Doctrines*, e.g. **Christianity—Doctrines**; **Judaism—Doctrines**; etc., and religious topics with the subdivision *History of doctrines*, e.g. **Salvation—History of doctrines** [to be added as needed]
BT **Theology**
NT **Christian heresies**
Christianity—Doctrines
Creeds
Grace (Theology)
Human beings (Theology)
Judaism—Doctrines
Salvation
Salvation—History of doctrines
Doctrine of fairness (Broadcasting)
USE **Fairness doctrine (Broadcasting)**
Doctrines
USE names of religions or individual
denominations with the subdivision *Doctrines,* e.g. **Christianity—Doctrines; Judaism—Doctrines;** etc. [to be added as needed]
Documentaries (Motion pictures)
USE **Documentary films**

Documentary films (May subdiv. geog.)
070.1
Use for individual works, collections, or materials about documentary films.
UF Documentaries (Motion pictures)
Nonfiction films
BT **Motion pictures**
Documentary television programs
791.45
Use for individual works, collections, or materials about documentary television programs.
BT **Television programs**
Documentation 025
SA subjects with the subdivision
Documentation, e.g. **Agriculture—Documentation** [to be added as needed]
BT **Information science**
NT **Agriculture—Documentation**
Archives
Bibliographic control
Bibliography
Cataloging
Conference proceedings
Copying processes
Information retrieval
Libraries
Library science
RT **Information services**
Documents
USE **Archives**
Charters
Government publications
Dog
USE **Dogs**
Dog breeding
USE **Dogs—Breeding**
Dog care
USE **Dogs—Care**
Dog guides
USE **Guide dogs**
Dog shows (May subdiv. geog.) **636.7**
UF Dogs—Exhibitions
BT **Dogs**
Dog sled racing
USE **Sled dog racing**
Dogmatic theology
USE **Doctrinal theology**
Dogmatics
USE **Doctrinal theology**
Dogs (May subdiv. geog.) **599.77; 636.7**

Dogs—*Continued*
UF   Dog
       Puppies
SA   types of dogs, e.g. **Guide dogs**;
       and names of specific breeds
       of dogs [to be added as need-
       ed]
BT   **Domestic animals**
       Mammals
NT   **Collies**
       Dog shows
       Working dogs

Dogs—Breeding (May subdiv. geog.)
       636.7
UF   Dog breeding
BT   **Breeding**

Dogs—Care   636.7
UF   Dog care

Dogs—Exhibitions
USE   **Dog shows**

Dogs—Fiction   808.83
Use for collections of stories about dogs. Materials about dog stories are entered under **Dogs in literature**.

Dogs for the blind
USE   **Guide dogs**

Dogs for the deaf
USE   **Hearing ear dogs**

Dogs in art   704.9
BT   **Art—Themes**

Dogs in literature   809
Use for materials about the depiction of dogs in literary works. Collections of dog stories are entered under **Dogs—Fiction**.
BT   **Literature—Themes**

Dogs—Psychology   636.7
BT   **Animal intelligence**
       Comparative psychology
       Psychology

Dogs—Training   636.7
BT   **Animals—Training**

Dogs—War use (May subdiv. geog.)
       355.4
UF   War use of dogs
BT   **Animals—War use**

Doll
USE   **Dolls**

Doll furniture (May subdiv. geog.)
       688.7; 745.592
BT   **Miniature objects**
       Toys

Dollhouses (May subdiv. geog.)   **688.7**

BT   **Miniature objects**
       Toys

Dollmaking (May subdiv. geog.)   **745.592**
BT   **Dolls**

Dolls (May subdiv. geog.)   **688.7**
UF   Doll
BT   **Toys**
NT   **Barbie dolls**
       Dollmaking

Dolphins (May subdiv. geog.)   **599.53**
BT   **Marine mammals**

Domesday book   942.02
UF   Doomsday book
BT   **Great Britain—History—1066-
       1154, Norman period**

Domestic animal dwellings
USE   **Animal housing**

Domestic animals (May subdiv. geog.)
       636
Use for general materials on farm animals. Materials limited to animals as pets are entered under **Pets**. Materials on stock raising as an industry are entered under **Livestock industry**.
UF   Domestication
       Farm animals
       Livestock
SA   types of domestic animals, e.g.
       Cattle [to be added as need-
       ed]
BT   **Animals**
NT   **Cats**
       Cattle
       Dogs
       Pigs
       Poultry
       Reindeer
       Sheep
       Working animals
RT   **Livestock industry**
       Pets

Domestic animals—Diseases
USE   **Animals—Diseases**

Domestic animals—Housing
USE   **Animal housing**

Domestic appliances
USE   **Electric household appliances**
       **Household equipment and sup-
       plies**

Domestic architecture (May subdiv.
      geog.)   **728**
Use for materials on residential buildings from the standpoint of style and design. Gen-

Domestic architecture—*Continued*
eral materials on buildings in which people live are entered under **Houses**.

UF   Architecture, Domestic
        Dwellings
        Residences

SA   types of residential buildings,
        e.g. **Apartment houses** [to be
        added as needed]

BT   **Architecture**

NT   **Apartment houses**
        House construction
        Prefabricated houses
        Solar homes

RT   **Houses**

Domestic architecture—Designs and plans   **728**

UF   Home designs
        House plans

BT   **Architecture—Designs and plans**

Domestic economic assistance (May subdiv. geog.)   **338.9**

UF   Anti-poverty programs
        Antipoverty programs
        Economic assistance
        Economic assistance, Domestic
        Poor relief

BT   **Economic policy**

NT   **Community development**
        Government lending
        Public works
        Subsidies
        Transfer payments

RT   **Grants-in-aid**
        Poverty
        Unemployed

Domestic finance

USE   **Household budgets**
        Personal finance

Domestic relations (May subdiv. geog.)   **346.01**

UF   Family relations

BT   **Interpersonal relations**

NT   **Desertion and nonsupport**
        Visitation rights (Domestic relations)

RT   **Divorce**
        Family
        Family life education
        Marriage

Domestic terrorism (May subdiv. geog.)   **363.325**

BT   **Terrorism**

Domestic violence (May subdiv. geog.)   **362.82**

UF   Family violence
        Household violence

BT   **Violence**

NT   **Child abuse**
        Elderly abuse
        Husband abuse
        Wife abuse

Domestic workers

USE   **Household employees**

Domestication

USE   **Domestic animals**

Dominion of the sea

USE   **Sea power**

Dominions, British

USE   **Commonwealth countries**

Donation of organs, tissues, etc.   **362.1**

UF   Organ donation
        Tissue donation

BT   **Gifts**

RT   **Transplantation of organs, tissues, etc.**

Donations

USE   **Gifts**

Doomsday

USE   **Judgment Day**

Doomsday book

USE   **Domesday book**

Door to door selling

USE   **Peddlers and peddling**

Doors (May subdiv. geog.)   **721**

BT   **Architecture—Details**
        Buildings

Double consciousness

USE   **Multiple personality**

Doubt

USE   **Belief and doubt**

Down syndrome   **616.85**

UF   Down's syndrome

BT   **Mental retardation**

Down's syndrome

USE   **Down syndrome**

Downsizing of organizations (May subdiv. geog.)   **658.1**

UF   Corporate downsizing
        Organizational downsizing
        Organizational retrenchment

Downsizing of organizations—*Continued*
    Retrenchment of organizations
BT **Organizational change**
RT **Employees—Dismissal**
Dracula, Count (Fictional character)
    823
UF Count Dracula (Fictional character)
BT **Fictional characters**
Draft (May subdiv. geog.)   **355.2**
UF Compulsory military service
    Conscription, Military
    Military conscription
    Military draft
    Military service, Compulsory
    Military training, Universal
    Selective service
    Universal military training
BT **Armies**
    Military law
    Recruiting and enlistment
RT **Draft resisters**
Draft dodgers
USE **Draft resisters**
Draft evaders
USE **Draft resisters**
Draft resisters (May subdiv. geog.)
    355.2
UF Draft dodgers
    Draft evaders
SA names of wars with the subdivision *Draft resisters* [to be added as needed]
NT **World War, 1939-1945—Draft resisters**
RT **Conscientious objectors**
    Draft
    Military desertion
Drafting, Mechanical
USE **Mechanical drawing**
Dragons **398.24**
BT **Animals—Folklore**
    Folklore
    Monsters
    Mythical animals
Drainage (May subdiv. geog.)   **631.6**
    Use for materials on land drainage. Materials on house drainage are entered under **House drainage**.
UF Land drainage
BT **Agricultural engineering**
    Civil engineering

    Hydraulic engineering
    Municipal engineering
    Reclamation of land
    Sanitary engineering
RT **Sewerage**
Drainage, House
USE **House drainage**
Drama **808.2; 808.82**
    Use for general materials on drama, not for individual works. Materials on the history and criticism of drama as literature are entered under **Drama—History and criticism**. Materials on criticism of drama as presented on the stage are entered under **Dramatic criticism**. Materials on the presentation of plays are entered under **Acting**; **Amateur theater**; or **Theater—Production and direction**. Collections of plays are entered under **Drama—Collections**; **American drama—Collections**; **English drama—Collections**; etc.
UF Stage
SA subjects, historical events, names of countries, cities, etc., ethnic groups, classes of persons, and names of individual persons with the subdivision *Drama*, to express the theme or subject content of collections of plays, e.g. **Easter—Drama**; **United States—History—1861-1865, Civil War—Drama**; **Napoleon I, Emperor of the French, 1769-1821—Drama**; etc. [to be added as needed]
BT **Literature**
NT **Acting**
    American drama
    Ballet
    Children's plays
    Choral speaking
    Classical drama
    College and school drama
    Comedies
    Comedy
    Didactic drama
    Drama in education
    Dramatists
    English drama
    Folk drama
    Greek drama
    Historical drama
    Horror plays
    Indian drama
    Indian drama (English)

Drama—*Continued*

      Masks (Plays)

      Melodrama

      Morality plays

      Mystery and detective plays

      One act plays

      Opera

      Pantomimes

      Pastoral drama

      Puppets and puppet plays

      Radio plays

      Religious drama

      Science fiction plays

      Screenplays

      Television plays

      Tragedies

      Tragedy

      Tragicomedy

  RT   Dramatic criticism

      Theater

Drama—Collections   808.82

    Use for collections of plays by several authors.

  UF   Plays

Drama—History and criticism   809.2

    Use for materials on criticism of drama as a literary form. Materials on criticism of drama as presented on the stage are entered under **Dramatic criticism.**

  NT   **English drama—History and criticism**

  RT   **Dramatic criticism**

Drama in education (May subdiv. geog.)   372.66

  BT   **Drama**

  RT   **Acting**

      Amateur theater

      College and school drama

      School assembly programs

Drama—Technique   808.2

  UF   Play writing

      Playwriting

  BT   **Authorship**

  NT   **Motion picture plays—Technique**

      Radio plays—Technique

      Television plays—Technique

Dramatic art

  USE   **Acting**

Dramatic criticism (May subdiv. geog.)   792.9

    Use for materials on criticism of drama as presented on the stage. Materials on criticism

of drama as a literary form are entered under **Drama—History and criticism; American drama—History and criticism**; etc.

  UF   Theater criticism

  BT   **Criticism**

  RT   **Drama**

      Drama—History and criticism

      Theater

Dramatic music

  USE   **Musicals**

      Opera

      Operetta

Dramatic plots

  USE   **Stories, plots, etc.**

Dramatic production

  USE   names of dramatists with the subdivision *Dramatic production,* e.g. **Shakespeare, William, 1564-1616—Dramatic production** [to be added as needed]

Dramatists   809.2; 920

    Use for materials on the personal lives of several playwrights, not limited to a single national literature. Materials dealing with their literary work are entered under **Drama—History and criticism; English drama—History and criticism**; etc.

  UF   Playwrights

  SA   dramatists of particular countries, e.g. **American dramatists** [to be added as needed]

  BT   **Authors**

      Drama

  NT   **American dramatists**

Dramatists, American

  USE   **American dramatists**

Draperies (May subdiv. geog.)   645; 684

  UF   Curtains

      Drapery

  BT   **Interior design**

      Upholstery

Drapery

  USE   **Draperies**

Draughts

  USE   **Checkers**

Drawing   741; 743

  UF   Drawings

      Sketching

  SA   drawing of particular countries, e.g. **American drawing** [to be added as needed]

  BT   **Art**

      Graphic arts

Drawing—*Continued*
- NT **American drawing**
  - **Architectural drawing**
  - **Artistic anatomy**
  - **Charcoal drawing**
  - **Commercial art**
  - **Crayon drawing**
  - **Figure drawing**
  - **Geometrical drawing**
  - **Graphic methods**
  - **Landscape drawing**
  - **Map drawing**
  - **Mechanical drawing**
  - **Pastel drawing**
  - **Pen drawing**
  - **Pencil drawing**
  - **Shades and shadows**
  - **Topographical drawing**
- RT **Illustration of books**
  - **Painting**
  - **Perspective**

Drawing, American
- USE **American drawing**

Drawing materials
- USE **Artists' materials**

Drawings
- USE **Drawing**

Drawn work   746.44
- BT **Embroidery**
  - **Needlework**
- NT **Hardanger needlework**

Dream interpretation
- USE **Dreams**

Dreaming
- USE **Dreams**

Dreams   154.6
- UF Dream interpretation
  - Dreaming
- BT **Visions**
- NT **Fantasy**
- RT **Sleep**
  - **Subconsciousness**

Dredging (May subdiv. geog.)   627
- BT **Civil engineering**
  - **Hydraulic engineering**

Dress
- USE **Clothing and dress**

Dress accessories (May subdiv. geog.)   391.4; 646
- BT **Clothing and dress**
- NT **Fans (Dress accessories)**

Dress codes (May subdiv. geog.)   391
- BT **Clothing and dress—Social aspects**

Dressage
- USE **Horsemanship**

Dressing of ores
- USE **Ore dressing**

Dressmaking (May subdiv. geog.)   646.4; 687
- UF Garment making
- BT **Clothing and dress**
  - **Clothing industry**
- RT **Needlework**
  - **Sewing**
  - **Tailoring**

Dressmaking—Patterns   646.4; 687

Dried flowers
- USE **Flowers—Drying**

Dried foods (May subdiv. geog.)   641.4; 664
- UF Dehydrated foods
- BT **Food**
- NT **Dried milk**
  - **Freeze-dried foods**
- RT **Food—Preservation**

Dried milk   637
- UF Dehydrated milk
  - Powdered milk
- BT **Dried foods**
  - **Milk**

Drifting of continents
- USE **Continental drift**

Drill and minor tactics   355.5
- UF Military drill
  - Minor tactics
- BT **Tactics**
- RT **Military art and science**

Drill (Nonmilitary)
- USE **Marching drills**

Drilling and boring
- USE **Drilling and boring (Earth and rocks)**
  - **Drilling and boring (Metal, wood, etc.)**

Drilling and boring (Earth and rocks) (May subdiv. geog.)   622

Use for materials on the operation of cutting holes in earth or rock. Materials on workshop operations in metal, wood, etc., are entered under **Drilling and boring (Metal, wood, etc.)**.

- UF Boring
  - Drilling and boring
  - Shaft sinking

Drilling and boring (Earth and rocks)—
Continued
        Well boring
   BT **Hydraulic engineering**
        Mining engineering
        Water supply engineering
   NT **Oil well drilling**
   RT **Tunnels**
        Wells

Drilling and boring (Metal, wood, etc.)
       621.9

Use for materials on workshop operations in metal, wood, etc. Materials on the operation of cutting holes in earth or rock are entered under **Drilling and boring (Earth and rocks)**.

   UF Boring
        Drilling and boring
   BT **Machine shop practice**
   RT **Machine tools**

Drilling, Oil well
   USE **Oil well drilling**

Drilling platforms 627
   UF Marine drilling platforms
        Ocean drilling platforms
        Oil drilling platforms
        Platforms, Drilling
   BT **Ocean engineering**
        Offshore oil well drilling

Drills, Marching
   USE **Marching drills**

Drinking age (May subdiv. geog.) **344;**
       363.4
   UF Minimum drinking age
   BT **Age**
        Teenagers—Alcohol use
        Youth—Alcohol use

Drinking and employees
   USE **Employees—Alcohol use**

Drinking and teenagers
   USE **Teenagers—Alcohol use**

Drinking and youth
   USE **Youth—Alcohol use**

Drinking in the workplace
   USE **Employees—Alcohol use**

Drinking of alcoholic beverages (May
     subdiv. geog.) **178; 363.4; 394.1;**
     613.81

Use for materials on drinking in its social aspects and as a social problem.

   UF Alcohol consumption
        Alcohol use
        Alcoholic beverage consumption

        Consumption of alcoholic bever-
          ages
        Drinking problem
        Liquor problem
        Social drinking
   SA classes of persons and ethnic
        groups with the subdivision
        Alcohol use, e.g. **Employ-**
        ees—Alcohol use; **Youth—**
        Alcohol use; etc. [to be add-
        ed as needed]
   NT **Drunk driving**
   RT **Alcoholic beverages**
        Alcoholism
        Temperance

Drinking problem
   USE **Alcoholism**
        Drinking of alcoholic beverages

Drinking water (May subdiv. geog.)
       363.6; 628.1
   UF Potable water
        Tap water
   BT **Water**
        Water supply

Drinks
   USE **Alcoholic beverages**
        Beverages
        Liquors

Driver education
   USE **Automobile driver education**

Drivers, Automobile
   USE **Automobile drivers**

Drivers' licenses (May subdiv. geog.)
       353.9; 629.28
   UF Automobile drivers' licenses
        Automobiles—Drivers' licenses
        Motor vehicles—Drivers' li-
          censes
   BT **Safety regulations**

Driving under the influence of alcohol
   USE **Drunk driving**

Driving while intoxicated
   USE **Drunk driving**

Dromedaries
   USE **Camels**

Drop forging
   USE **Forging**

Dropouts (May subdiv. geog.) **371.2**
   UF College dropouts
        Elementary school dropouts
        High school dropouts

Dropouts—*Continued*

  School dropouts
  Student dropouts
  Teenage dropouts
 BT **Students**
   Youth
 RT **At risk students**
   Educational counseling
   School attendance
Droughts (May subdiv. geog.) **551.57;
  632**
 BT **Meteorology**
 NT **Dust storms**
 RT **Rain**
Drowning prevention
 USE **Water safety**
Drug abuse (May subdiv. geog.) **362.29;
  613.8; 616.86**

Use for general materials on the misuse or abuse of drugs. Materials on the abuse of a particular drug or kind of drugs are entered under this heading and also under the drug or kind of drugs, e.g. **Cocaine**; **Hallucinogens**; etc.

 UF Addiction to drugs
   Drug addiction
   Drug habit
   Drug misuse
   Drug use
   Drugs—Abuse
   Drugs—Misuse
   Narcotic abuse
   Narcotic addiction
   Narcotic habit
 SA classes of persons with the sub-
    division *Drug use*, e.g. **Crim-
    inals—Drug use**; and types
    of drug abuse, e.g. **Medica-
    tion abuse** [to be added as
    needed]
 BT **Social problems**
   Substance abuse
 NT **Medication abuse**
 RT **Drug addicts**
   Drugs
   Solvent abuse
   Twelve-step programs
Drug abuse counseling (May subdiv.
  geog.) **362.29; 613.8**
 UF Drug addiction counseling
   Drug counseling
   Narcotic addiction counseling
 BT **Counseling**

 NT **Drug addicts—Rehabilitation**
Drug abuse education
 USE **Drug education**
Drug abuse—Physiological effect
 USE **Drugs—Physiological effect**
Drug abuse screening
 USE **Drug testing**
Drug abuse—Study and teaching
 USE **Drug education**
Drug abuse—Testing
 USE **Drug testing**
Drug abuse—Treatment **362.29**
 BT **Therapeutics**
Drug abusing physicians
 USE **Physicians—Drug use**
Drug addicted physicians
 USE **Physicians—Drug use**
Drug addiction
 USE **Drug abuse**
Drug addiction counseling
 USE **Drug abuse counseling**
Drug addiction education
 USE **Drug education**
Drug addicts (May subdiv. geog.)
    362.29; 616.86
 UF Addicts
   Narcotic addicts
 SA classes of persons with the sub-
    division *Drug use*, e.g. **Crim-
    inals—Drug use** [to be added
    as needed]
 NT **Children of drug addicts**
   Recovering addicts
 RT **Drug abuse**
Drug addicts—Rehabilitation (May
  subdiv. geog.) **362.29; 613.8;
  616.86**
 BT **Drug abuse counseling**
Drug counseling
 USE **Drug abuse counseling**
Drug dealing
 USE **Drug traffic**
Drug education (May subdiv. geog.)
    362.29; 371.7; 613.8

Use for materials on the study of drugs, in-cluding their source, abuse, chemical composi-tion, and social, physical, and personal effects.

 UF Drug abuse education
   Drug abuse—Study and teaching
   Drug addiction education
 BT **Health education**

Drug habit
USE **Drug abuse**
Drug misuse
USE **Drug abuse**
Drug plants
USE **Medical botany**
Drug pushers
USE **Drug traffic**
Drug resistance in microorganisms
616.01
UF Antibiotic resistance in microor-
ganisms
Bacterial resistance to antibiotics
Microbial drug resistance
Resistance to drugs in microor-
ganisms
BT **Microorganisms**
Drug stores
USE **Drugstores**
Drug testing (May subdiv. geog.) **344;**
658.3
Use for materials on testing to identify per-
sonal use or misuse of drugs. Materials on the
testing of drugs for safety or effectiveness are
entered under **Drugs—Testing**.
UF Drug abuse screening
Drug abuse—Testing
Screening for drug abuse
Testing for drug abuse
SA classes of persons with the sub-
division *Drug testing*, e.g.
Employees—Drug testing [to
be added as needed]
NT **Employees—Drug testing**
Drug testing in the workplace
USE **Employees—Drug testing**
Drug therapy (May subdiv. geog.) **615.5**
UF Chemotherapy
Pharmacotherapy
SA names of diseases other than
cancer with the subdivision
Drug therapy, e.g. **Mental ill-
ness—Drug therapy** [to be
added as needed]
BT **Therapeutics**
NT **Antibiotics**
Cancer—Chemotherapy
Mental illness—Drug therapy
RT **Drugs**
Pharmacology
Drug trade, Illicit
USE **Drug traffic**

Drug traffic (May subdiv. geog.)
363.45; 364.1
UF Drug dealing
Drug pushers
Drug trade, Illicit
Narcotic traffic
Smuggling of drugs
Trafficking in drugs
Trafficking in narcotics
BT **Drugs and crime**
Drug use
USE **Drug abuse**
Drugs
and classes of persons with the
subdivision *Drug use*, e.g.
**Criminals—Drug use; Em-
ployees—Drug use;
Teenagers—Drug use;
Youth—Drug use;** etc. [to be
added as needed]
Drugs 615
UF Drug use
Pharmaceuticals
SA classes of persons with the sub-
division *Drug use*, e.g. **Crim-
inals—Drug use;** types of
drugs, e.g. **Amphetamines;
Hallucinogens; Narcotics;
Stimulants;** etc.; and names
of individual drugs, e.g.
Crack (Drug); Marijuana;
etc. [to be added as needed]
BT **Pharmacy**
Therapeutics
NT **Designer drugs**
Drugs and crime
Generic drugs
Hallucinogens
Narcotics
Nonprescription drugs
Orphan drugs
Psychotropic drugs
Steroids
Stimulants
Sulfonamides
RT **Drug abuse**
Drug therapy
Materia medica
Pharmacology
Drugs—Abuse
USE **Drug abuse**

242

Drugs—Adulteration and analysis
USE **Pharmacology**
Drugs and crime (May subdiv. geog.)
364.1

Use for general materials on the relationship of drugs and crime. Materials on the illicit drug trade are entered under **Drug traffic**. Materials on the use of drugs by criminals are entered under **Criminals—Drug use**.

UF Crime and drugs
Crime and narcotics
Narcotics and crime
BT **Crime**
Drugs
NT **Drug traffic**
RT **Criminals—Drug use**
Drugs and criminals
USE **Criminals—Drug use**
Drugs and employees
USE **Employees—Drug use**
Drugs and sports
USE **Athletes—Drug use**
Drugs and teenagers
USE **Teenagers—Drug use**
Drugs and youth
USE **Youth—Drug use**
Drugs—Chemistry
USE **Pharmaceutical chemistry**
Drugs—Generic substitution
USE **Generic drugs**
Drugs in the workplace
USE **Employees—Drug use**
Drugs—Misuse
USE **Drug abuse**
Drugs, Nonprescription
USE **Nonprescription drugs**
Drugs—Physiological effect   615; 616.86

Use for materials limited to the effect of drugs on the functions of living organisms.

UF Drug abuse—Physiological effect
SA names of drugs with the subdivision *Physiological effect* [to be added as needed]
BT **Pharmacology**
NT **Opium—Physiological effect**
Drugs—Psychological aspects   615;
616.86
BT **Applied psychology**
Drugs—Testing (May subdiv. geog.)
363.19

Use for materials on the testing of drugs for safety or effectiveness. Materials on testing to identify the personal use or misuse or drugs are entered under **Drug testing**.

UF Clinical drug trials
Clinical trials of drugs
BT **Consumer protection**
Pharmacology
Drugstores (May subdiv. geog.)   **381**

Use for materials on business establishments that sell drugs. Materials on the art or practice of preparing, preserving, and dispensing drugs are entered under **Pharmacy**.

UF Chemists' shops
Drug stores
Pharmacies
BT **Retail trade**
Stores
Druids and Druidism (May subdiv. geog.)
299
BT **Celts**
Religions
Drum
USE **Drums**
Drum majoring   784.9; 791.6
BT **Bands (Music)**
RT **Baton twirling**
Drums   786.9
UF Drum
BT **Musical instruments**
Percussion instruments
Drunk driving   363.12; 364.1
UF Driving under the influence of alcohol
Driving while intoxicated
BT **Crime**
Drinking of alcoholic beverages
Drunkards
USE **Alcoholics**
Drunkenness
USE **Alcoholism**
Temperance
Dry cleaning   667
UF Clothing and dress—Dry cleaning
BT **Cleaning**
Dry farming (May subdiv. geog.)   **631.5**
UF Farming, Dry
BT **Agriculture**
Dry goods
USE **Fabrics**
Drying   660
SA materials, products, or objects dried with the subdivision *Drying*, e.g. **Flowers—Drying** [to be added as needed]

Drying—*Continued*

   BT   **Industrial chemistry**

Dual-career couples

   USE   **Dual-career families**

Dual-career families (May subdiv. geog.)
     306.85; 646.7

    Use for materials on families in which both the husband and wife are pursuing careers.

   UF   Dual-career couples

        Dual career family

        Dual-career marriage

        Dual-income couples

        Two-career couples

        Two-career families

        Two-career family

        Two-income families

        Working couples

   BT   **Family**

   RT   **Work and family**

Dual career family

   USE   **Dual-career families**

Dual-career marriage

   USE   **Dual-career families**

Dual-income couples

   USE   **Dual-career families**

Ducks   **598.4; 636.5**

   BT   **Birds**

        Poultry

Ductless glands

   USE   **Endocrine glands**

Due process of law (May subdiv. geog.)
     347

    Use for materials on the regular administration of the law, according to which citizens may not be denied their legal rights and all laws must conform to fundamental and accepted legal principles. Materials on legal hearings before an impartial and disinterested tribunal are entered under **Fair trial**.

   UF   Procedural due process

        Substantive due process

   BT   **Administration of justice**

        Civil rights

   NT   **Fair trial**

Dueling (May subdiv. geog.)   **179.7; 394**

   UF   Fighting

   BT   **Manners and customs**

        Martial arts

   NT   **Fencing**

Dumps, Toxic

   USE   **Hazardous waste sites**

Dunes

   USE   **Sand dunes**

Duplicate bridge

   USE   **Bridge (Game)**

Duplicating machines

   USE   **Copying machines**

Duplicating processes

   USE   **Copying processes**

Durable power of attorney

   USE   **Power of attorney**

Dust   **551.51**

   UF   Atmospheric dust

        Dust particles

   BT   **Air pollution**

Dust particles

   USE   **Dust**

Dust, Radioactive

   USE   **Radioactive fallout**

Dust storms (May subdiv. geog.)   **551.55**

   BT   **Droughts**

        Erosion

        Storms

Dusting and spraying

   USE   **Spraying and dusting**

Duties

   USE   **Tariff**

        Taxation

Duty   **170**

   BT   **Ethics**

        Human behavior

   NT   **Conscience**

        Vocation

DVDs   **004.5**

   UF   Videodiscs [*Former heading*]

   BT   **Optical storage devices**

Dwarf trees   **582.16; 635.9**

   SA   types of dwarf trees, e.g. **Bonsai**
        [to be added as needed]

   BT   **Trees**

   NT   **Bonsai**

Dwarfism   **616.4**

   UF   Growth retardation

   BT   **Growth disorders**

Dwellings

   USE   **Domestic architecture**

        Houses

        Housing

        and ethnic groups and classes of persons with the subdivision *Dwellings,* for materials on the residential buildings of a group from the standpoint of architecture, construction,

Dwellings—*Continued*

or ethnology, e.g. **Native Americans—Dwellings;** and ethnic groups and classes of persons with the subdivision *Housing,* for materials on the social and economic aspects of providing housing for the group, e.g. **Physically handicapped—Housing** [to be added as needed]

Dyes and dyeing (May subdiv. geog.) **646.6; 667; 746.6**
- SA types of dyes and types of dyeing [to be added as needed]
- BT **Color**
  Pigments
  Textile chemistry
  Textile industry
- NT **Batik**
  Tie dyeing
- RT **Bleaching**

Dying children
- USE **Terminally ill children**

Dying patients
- USE **Terminally ill**

Dynamics 531
- UF Kinetics
- BT **Mathematics**
  Mechanics
- NT **Aerodynamics**
  Astrodynamics
  Chaos (Science)
  Hydrodynamics
  Kinematics
  Matter
  Motion
  Quantum theory
  Thermodynamics
- RT **Force and energy**
  Physics
  Statics

Dynamite 662
- BT **Explosives**

Dynamos
- USE **Electric generators**

Dyslexia 371.91; 616.85
- BT **Reading disability**

Dyspepsia
- USE **Indigestion**

Dysphasia
- USE **Language disorders**

Dystopias 808.3
Use for individual works, collections, or materials about dystopias.
- UF Anti-utopias
- BT **Fantasy fiction**
  Science fiction
- RT **Utopian fiction**

E-mail
- USE **Electronic mail systems**

E-mail discussion groups
- USE **Electronic discussion groups**

E-mail reference services (Libraries)
- USE **Electronic reference services (Libraries)**

Eagles (May subdiv. geog.) **598.9**
- BT **Birds**
  Birds of prey

Ear 611; 612.8
- BT **Head**
- RT **Hearing**

Early childhood education (May subdiv. geog.) **372.21**
Use for materials on formal or informal education of children up to grade three.
- BT **Education**

Early Christian literature 270.1
Use for individual works or collections of the writings of early Christian authors. Materials on the lives and thought of the leaders of the Christian church up to the time of Gregory the Great in the West and John of Damascus in the East are entered under **Fathers of the church**.
- UF Christian literature—30-600, Early
  Christian literature, Early
- BT **Christian literature**
  Literature
  Medieval literature
- RT **Church history—30-600, Early church**
  Fathers of the church
  Latin literature

Early church history
- USE **Church history—30-600, Early church**

Early printed books (May subdiv. geog.) **094**
- SA subjects with the subdivision *Early works to 1800,* for materials on those subjects written before 1800, e.g. **Political science—Early works to 1800** [to be added as needed]

245

Early printed books—*Continued*
    BT   **Books**
Early printed books—15th century
    USE   **Incunabula**
Early works to 1800
    USE   subjects with the subdivision
            Early works to 1800, for ma-
            terials on those subjects writ-
            ten before 1800, e.g. **Political**
            science—Early works to
            1800 [to be added as needed]
Earth   **525; 550**

    Use for general materials on the whole
planet. Materials limited to the structure and
composition of the earth and the physical
changes it has undergone and is still undergoing are entered under **Geology.**
    UF   World
    BT   **Planets**
          Solar system
    NT   **Antarctica**
          Arctic regions
          Arid regions
          Atmosphere
          Continents
          Earthquakes
          Gaia hypothesis
          Geodesy
          Geography
          Ice age
          Latitude
          Longitude
          Ocean
          Seas
          Tropics
    RT   **Biosphere**
          Earth sciences
          Geology
          Physical geography
Earth—Age   **551.7**
Earth—Chemical composition
    USE   **Geochemistry**
Earth—Crust   **551.1**
    BT   **Earth—Internal structure**
    NT   **Plate tectonics**
    RT   **Earth—Surface**
Earth, Effect of man on
    USE   **Human influence on nature**
Earth fills
    USE   **Landfills**
Earth-friendly technology
    USE   **Green technology**

Earth—Gravity
    USE   **Gravity**
Earth—Internal structure   **551.1**
    NT   **Earth—Crust**
Earth magnetic field
    USE   **Geomagnetism**
Earth—Magnetism
    USE   **Geomagnetism**
Earth sciences   **550**
    UF   Geoscience
    BT   **Physical sciences**
          Science
    NT   **Climate**
          Geochemistry
          Geography
          Geology
          Geophysics
          Meteorology
          Oceanography
          Water
    RT   **Earth**
Earth sheltered houses   **690; 728**
    UF   Underground houses
    BT   **House construction**
          Houses
          Underground architecture
Earth—Surface   **551.1**
    UF   Surface of the earth
    NT   **Landforms**
    RT   **Earth—Crust**
Earthenware
    USE   **Pottery**
Earthly paradise
    USE   **Paradise**
Earthquake effects
    USE   types of structures with the sub-
            division *Earthquake effects,*
            e.g. **Skyscrapers—Earth-**
            quake effects [to be added as
            needed]
Earthquake sea waves
    USE   **Tsunamis**
Earthquakes (May subdiv. geog.)   **551.22**
    UF   Seismography
          Seismology
    SA   types of structures subject to
          earthquake forces with the
          subdivision *Earthquake effects,*
          e.g. **Skyscrapers—Earth-**
          quake effects [to be added as
          needed]

Earthquakes—*Continued*
  BT **Earth**
      Geology
      Natural disasters
      Physical geography
  NT **Buildings—Earthquake effects**
      Skyscrapers—Earthquake effects
Earthquakes and building
  USE **Buildings—Earthquake effects**
Earthquakes—California   551.2209794
Earthquakes—United States   551.220973
Earthworks (Archeology)
  USE **Excavations (Archeology)**
Earthworks (Art) (May subdiv. geog.)
      709.04
  UF Landscape sculpture
      Site oriented art
  BT **Art**
East
  USE **Asia**
East Africa   967.6
  Use for materials dealing collectively with the eastern regions of Africa. The term usually includes the areas now occupied by Burundi, Kenya, Rwanda, Tanzania, Uganda, and Somalia, and sometimes Malawi and Mozambique as well.
  UF Africa, East
      Africa, Eastern
      Eastern Africa
  BT **Africa**
East and West   306; 909
  Use for materials on both acculturation and cultural conflict between Asian and Occidental civilizations.
  BT **International relations**
  NT **Asia—Civilization**
      Orientalism
      Western civilization
  RT **Acculturation**
East Asia   950
  Use for materials that deal collectively with the eastern regions of Asia including China, Japan, Korea, and Taiwan.
  UF East (Far East)
      Far East
      Orient
  BT **Asia**
  RT **Pacific rim**
East (Far East)
  USE **East Asia**
East Germany
  USE **Germany (East)**

East Goths
  USE **Goths**
East Indian art
  USE **Indian art**
East Indian cooking
  USE **Indian cooking**
East Indian drama
  USE **Indian drama**
East Indian drama (English)
  USE **Indian drama (English)**
East Indian epic poetry
  USE **Indian epic poetry**
East Indian fiction
  USE **Indian fiction**
East Indian fiction (English)
  USE **Indian fiction (English)**
East Indian languages
  USE **Indian languages**
East Indian literature
  USE **Indian literature**
East Indian literature (English)
  USE **Indian literature (English)**
East Indian painting
  USE **Indian painting**
East Indian philosophy
  USE **Indian philosophy**
East Indian poetry
  USE **Indian poetry**
East Indian poetry (English)
  USE **Indian poetry (English)**
East Indian sculpture
  USE **Indian sculpture**
East Indians
  USE **Indians**
East Timor   959.87
  May be subdivided like United States except for History.
Easter (May subdiv. geog.)   **263;**
      394.2667
  BT **Christian holidays**
      Holy Week
  RT **Lent**
Easter carols
  USE **Carols**
Easter—Drama   808.82
  Use for collections of plays about Easter.
  BT **Religious drama**
Easter egg decoration
  USE **Egg decoration**
Easter Island   961
Eastern Africa
  USE **East Africa**

Eastern churches (May subdiv. geog.)
  281
  BT **Christian sects**
      Christianity
  NT **Orthodox Eastern Church**
Eastern Empire
  USE **Byzantine Empire**
Eastern Europe   947
  UF Europe, Eastern
Eastern Europe—History   947
Eastern Europe—History—1989-
  947.085; 947.086
Eastern Seaboard
  USE **Atlantic States**
Easy and quick cooking
  USE **Quick and easy cooking**
Easy reading materials   372.41
    Use for individual works, collections, or
    materials about easy reading materials.
  UF Beginning reading materials
      Preprimers
      Preschool reading materials
      Primers
  BT **Children's literature**
      Reading materials
Eating
  USE **Dining**
       Gastronomy
Eating customs (May subdiv. geog.)
  394.1
  UF Food customs
      Food habits
  BT **Diet**
      Human behavior
      Nutrition
  NT **Table etiquette**
  RT **Dining**
Eating disorders (May subdiv. geog.)
  616.85
  SA types of eating disorders [to be
      added as needed]
  BT **Abnormal psychology**
  NT **Anorexia nervosa**
      Bulimia
Eavesdropping   363.25
  UF Bugging, Electronic
      Electronic bugging
      Electronic eavesdropping
      Electronic listening devices
      Listening devices
  BT **Criminal investigation**
      Right of privacy

  RT **Wiretapping**
Eccentrics and eccentricities (May subdiv.
  geog.)   **920**
  UF Cranks
  BT **Curiosities and wonders**
      Personality
  NT **Hermits**
Ecclesiastical antiquities
  USE **Christian antiquities**
Ecclesiastical architecture
  USE **Church architecture**
Ecclesiastical art
  USE **Christian art**
Ecclesiastical biography
  USE **Christian biography**
Ecclesiastical fasts and feasts
  USE **Religious holidays**
Ecclesiastical furniture
  USE **Church furniture**
Ecclesiastical history
  USE **Church history**
Ecclesiastical institutions
  USE **Religious institutions**
Ecclesiastical law   262.9
  UF Canon law
      Church law
  BT **Church**
      Law
  NT **Tithes**
Ecclesiastical polity
  USE **Church polity**
Ecclesiastical rites and ceremonies
  USE **Rites and ceremonies**
Ecclesiastical year
  USE **Church year**
Eclipses, Lunar
  USE **Lunar eclipses**
Eclipses, Solar
  USE **Solar eclipses**
Eclogues
  USE **Pastoral poetry**
Eco-development
  USE **Economic development—Envi-
        ronmental aspects**
Ecodevelopment
  USE **Economic development—Envi-
        ronmental aspects**
Ecological movement
  USE **Environmental movement**
Ecological tourism
  USE **Ecotourism**

Ecology (May subdiv. geog.)   **577**
>   UF   Balance of nature
>   Biology—Ecology
>   Ecosystems
>   SA   types of ecology, e.g. **Marine**
>   **ecology**; and types of animals,
>   plants, and crops with the
>   subdivision *Ecology* [to be
>   added as needed]
>   BT   **Biology**
>   **Environment**
>   NT   **Adaptation (Biology)**
>   **Biogeography**
>   **Cave ecology**
>   **Coastal ecology**
>   **Coral reef ecology**
>   **Desert ecology**
>   **Environmental protection**
>   **Fire ecology**
>   **Fishes—Ecology**
>   **Food chains (Ecology)**
>   **Forest ecology**
>   **Freshwater ecology**
>   **Gaia hypothesis**
>   **Garden ecology**
>   **Grassland ecology**
>   **Habitat (Ecology)**
>   **Island ecology**
>   **Jungle ecology**
>   **Lake ecology**
>   **Marine ecology**
>   **Marsh ecology**
>   **Mountain ecology**
>   **Plant ecology**
>   **Pond ecology**
>   **Prairie ecology**
>   **Rain forest ecology**
>   **Reef ecology**
>   **River ecology**
>   **Seashore ecology**
>   **Soil ecology**
>   **Stream ecology**
>   **Swamp ecology**
>   **Symbiosis**
>   **Tide pool ecology**
>   **Tundra ecology**
>   **Urban ecology**
>   **Wetland ecology**
>   RT   **Biodiversity**
>   **Environmental sciences**

Ecology, Human
>   USE   **Human ecology**

Ecology, Social
>   USE   **Human ecology**

Economic aid
>   USE   **Foreign aid**

Economic aspects
>   USE   subjects with the subdivision
>   *Economic aspects,* e.g. **Agri-**
>   **culture—Economic aspects**
>   [to be added as needed]

Economic assistance
>   USE   **Domestic economic assistance**
>   **Foreign aid**

Economic assistance, American
>   USE   **American foreign aid**

Economic assistance, Domestic
>   USE   **Domestic economic assistance**

Economic biology
>   USE   **Economic botany**
>   **Economic zoology**

Economic botany   **581.6**
>   UF   Agricultural botany
>   Botany, Economic
>   Economic biology
>   BT   **Agriculture**
>   **Botany**
>   NT   **Cotton**
>   **Edible plants**
>   **Forage plants**
>   **Forest products**
>   **Plant conservation**
>   **Plant introduction**
>   **Poisonous plants**
>   **Weeds**

Economic conditions   **330.9**
>   Use for general materials on some or all of
>   the following: natural resources, business,
>   commerce, industry, labor, manufactures, fi-
>   nancial conditions. Materials on the history of
>   the economic development of several coun-
>   tries are entered under **Economic develop-**
>   **ment**.
>   UF   Economic history
>   National resources
>   World economics
>   SA   racial and ethnic groups, classes
>   of persons, and names of
>   countries, cities, areas, etc.,
>   with the subdivision *Economic*
>   *conditions,* e.g. **African**
>   **Americans—Economic condi-**

Economic conditions—*Continued*

> tions; **United States—Economic conditions**; etc. [to be added as needed]

BT **Business**
Economics
Social conditions
Wealth

NT **African Americans—Economic conditions**
Blacks—Economic conditions
Business cycles
Chicago (Ill.)—Economic conditions
Developing countries
Great Depression, 1929-1939
Industrial revolution
Jews—Economic conditions
Labor supply
Native Americans—Economic conditions
Natural resources
Ohio—Economic conditions
Poverty
Quality of life
United States—Economic conditions

RT **Commercial geography**
Economic development

Economic cycles
USE **Business cycles**

Economic depressions
USE **Depressions**

Economic development 338.9

Use for materials on the theory and policy of economic development. Materials restricted to a particular place are entered under the name of the country, city, or area with the subdivisions *Economic conditions*; *Economic policy*; or *Industries*.

UF Development, Economic
Economic growth

BT **Economic policy**
Economics

NT **Infrastructure (Economics)**
Rural development
Sustainable development

RT **Economic conditions**

Economic development—Environmental aspects (May subdiv. geog.)
333.71; 338.9

Use for general materials on the environmental impact of economic development. Ma-

terials on economic development that satisfies the needs of the present generation without depleting natural resources for the future or having adverse environmental effects are entered under **Sustainable development**.

UF Eco-development
Ecodevelopment

Economic equilibrium
USE **Equilibrium (Economics)**

Economic forecasting (May subdiv. geog.)
338.5

BT **Business cycles**
Economics
Forecasting

NT **Business forecasting**
Employment forecasting

Economic geography
USE **Commercial geography**

Economic geology 553

UF Geology, Economic

SA types of geological products, e.g. **Asbestos**; **Gypsum**; etc. [to be added as needed]

BT **Geology**

NT **Mines and mineral resources**
Petroleum geology
Quarries and quarrying
Soils
Stone

Economic growth
USE **Economic development**

Economic history
USE **Economic conditions**

Economic mobilization
USE **Industrial mobilization**

Economic planning
USE **Economic policy**

Economic policy (May subdiv. geog.)
338.9

Use for materials on the policy of government in economic affairs.

UF Business and government
Business—Government policy
Central planning
Economic planning
Government and business
Government policy
National planning
State planning

SA subjects with the subdivision *Government policy*, e.g. **Agriculture—Government policy**;

Economic policy—*Continued*

and types of activities, facilities, industries, services, and undertakings with the subdivision *Planning*, e.g. **Transportation—Planning** [to be added as needed]

BT **Economics**

Planning

NT **Commercial policy**

Domestic economic assistance

Economic development

Fiscal policy

Foreign aid

Free enterprise

Government lending

Government ownership

Industrial mobilization

Industrial policy

Industrialization

International economic relations

Labor policy

Land reform

Monetary policy

Municipal ownership

Privatization

Sanctions (International law)

Subsidies

Tariff

Transfer payments

Urban policy

Welfare state

RT **National security**

Social policy

Economic policy—Ohio   338.9771

UF Ohio—Economic policy

Economic policy—United States 338.973

UF United States—Economic policy

Economic recessions

USE **Recessions**

Economic relations, Foreign

USE **International economic relations**

Economic sanctions

USE **Sanctions (International law)**

Economic sustainability

USE **Sustainable development**

Economic zones (Maritime law)

USE **Territorial waters**

Economic zoology (May subdiv. geog.)
591.6

Use for general materials on animals injurious or beneficial to agriculture, and for materials on the extermination of wild animals, venomous snakes, etc.

UF Animals, Useful and harmful

Economic biology

Zoology, Economic

BT **Zoology**

NT **Agricultural pests**

Beneficial insects

Furbearing animals

Insect pests

Livestock industry

Pest control

Pests

Poisonous animals

Wildlife conservation

Working animals

Economics (May subdiv. geog.)   **330**

Use for materials on the science of economics. This heading may be subdivided geographically for materials on this branch of learning in a particular place. Materials on the economic conditions of a particular place are entered under the name of the place with the subdivision *Economic conditions*.

UF Distribution of wealth

Political economy

Production

SA subjects with the subdivision *Economic aspects*, e.g. **Agriculture—Economic aspects**; and countries, states, cities, regions, etc., with the subdivision *Economic conditions*, e.g. **United States—Economic conditions** [to be added as needed]

BT **Social sciences**

NT **Agriculture—Economic aspects**

Barter

Business

Capital

Capitalism

Christianity and economics

Collectivism

Commerce

Consumption (Economics)

Cooperation

Cost and standard of living

Cost effectiveness

Economic conditions

Economics—*Continued*
    Economic development
    Economic forecasting
    Economic policy
    Employment
    Equilibrium (Economics)
    Finance
    Gross national product
    Income
    Individualism
    Industrial trusts
    Industries
    Labor
    Labor economics
    Land use
    Macroeconomics
    Marxism
    Medical economics
    Microeconomics
    Money
    Monopolies
    Population
    Prices
    Profit
    Property
    Risk
    Saving and investment
    Socialism
    Statistics
    Supply and demand
    Underground economy
    Waste (Economics)
    Wealth
Economics and Christianity
  USE **Christianity and economics**
Economics—History   330.09; 330.1
   Use for materials describing the development of economic theories. Materials on the economic conditions and development of countries are entered under **Economic conditions**.
Economics of war
  USE **War—Economic aspects**
Economy
  USE **Saving and investment**
Economy cars
  USE **Compact cars**
Economy, Underground
  USE **Underground economy**
Ecosystems
  USE **Ecology**
Ecoterrorism (May subdiv. geog.)   303.6

  BT **Environmental movement**
       Terrorism
Ecotourism (May subdiv. geog.)   **338.4**
  UF Ecological tourism
       Environmental tourism
       Green tourism
       Nature tourism
  BT **Tourist trade**
Ecumenical councils
  USE **Councils and synods**
Ecumenical movement (May subdiv. geog.)   **280**
   Use for materials on a movement originating in the twentieth century aimed at promoting church cooperation and unity. Materials on unity as one of the marks of the church are entered under **Church—Unity**. Materials on prospective and actual mergers within and across denominational lines are entered under **Christian union**. Materials on religious activities planned and conducted cooperatively by two or more Christian sects are entered under **Interdenominational cooperation**.
  UF Christian unity
       Ecumenism
  BT **Christian sects**
       Church
  RT **Christian union**
Ecumenism
  USE **Christian union**
       Ecumenical movement
Edaphology
  USE **Soil ecology**
Eddas   839
   Use for individual works, collections, or materials about eddas.
  BT **Old Norse literature**
       Poetry
       Scandinavian literature
Eden
  USE **Paradise**
Edgar Allan Poe Awards   808.3
  UF Edgars
  BT **Literary prizes**
       Mystery fiction
Edgars
  USE **Edgar Allan Poe Awards**
Edible plants (May subdiv. geog.)   581.6
  UF Food plants
       Plants, Edible
  BT **Economic botany**
       Food
       Plants
Edifices
  USE **Buildings**

Editing   070.5; 808

Use for materials on the editing of books and texts. Materials on the editing of newspapers and periodicals are entered under **Journalism—Editing**.

SA   subjects and types of literature with the subdivision *Editing*, e.g. **Poetry—Editing**; etc. [to be added as needed]

BT   **Authorship**
  Publishers and publishing

NT   **Journalism—Editing**
  Poetry—Editing

Editions (May subdiv. geog.)   **016**

UF   Bibliography—Editions

BT   **Bibliography**

NT   **Autographed editions**
  Bilingual books
  First editions
  Paperback books
  Reprints (Publications)

Edmontosaurus   567.914

BT   **Dinosaurs**

Education (May subdiv. geog.)   **370**

Subdivisions listed under this heading may be used under other education headings where applicable.

UF   Instruction
  Pedagogy
  Study and teaching

SA   types of education, e.g. **Vocational education**; classes of persons and social and ethnic groups with the subdivision *Education*, e.g. **Deaf—Education**; **African Americans—Education**; etc.; and subjects with the subdivision *Study and teaching*, e.g. **Science—Study and teaching** [to be added as needed]

BT   **Civilization**

NT   **Ability grouping in education**
  Adult education
  African Americans—Education
  Alternative education
  Area studies
  Audiovisual education
  Automobile driver education
  Basic education
  Blacks—Education
  Blind—Education
  Books and reading
  Boys—Education
  Business education
  Church and education
  Classical education
  Coeducation
  Colleges and universities
  Consumer education
  Continuing education
  Cooperative learning
  Deaf—Education
  Distance education
  Early childhood education
  Educational evaluation
  Educational games
  Educational technology
  Educational tests and measurements
  Educators
  Elderly—Education
  Elementary education
  Evening and continuation schools
  Family life education
  Foreign study
  Girls—Education
  Health education
  Higher education
  Home and school
  Home schooling
  International education
  Internet in education
  Labor—Education
  Library education
  Literacy
  Mainstreaming in education
  Men—Education
  Mentally handicapped children—Education
  Military education
  Moral education
  Multicultural education
  Native Americans—Education
  Nature study
  Naval education
  Outdoor education
  Physical education
  Preschool education
  Professional education
  Psychology of learning
  Religious education
  Scholarships

Education—*Continued*

> School choice
> Secondary education
> Self-instruction
> Simulation games in education
> Socialization
> Special education
> Study skills
> Teaching
> Technical education
> Veterans—Education
> Vocational education
> Women—Education
> World War, 1939-1945—Education and the war

> RT   **Culture**
> **Learning and scholarship**
> **Schools**

Education—Aims and objectives   370.11

Education and church
> USE   **Church and education**

Education and radio
> USE   **Radio in education**

Education and religion
> USE   **Church and education**

Education and state
> USE   **Education—Government policy**

Education and television
> USE   **Television in education**

Education and the war
> USE   names of wars with the subdivision *Education and the war,* e.g. **World War, 1939-1945—Education and the war** [to be added as needed]

Education associations
> USE   **Education—Societies**

Education—Automation
> USE   **Computer-assisted instruction**

Education, Bilingual
> USE   **Bilingual education**

Education, Christian
> USE   **Christian education**

Education, Compulsory
> USE   **Compulsory education**

Education—Computer software
> USE   **Educational software**

Education, Cooperative
> USE   **Cooperative education**

Education—Curricula (May subdiv. geog.)   **375**

> UF   Core curriculum
> Courses of study
> Curricula
> Schools—Curricula

> SA   types of education and schools with the subdivision *Curricula*, e.g. **Library education—Curricula** [to be added as needed]

> NT   **Articulation (Education)**
> **Colleges and universities—Curricula**
> **Curriculum planning**
> **Library education—Curricula**

Education—Data processing
> USE   **Computer-assisted instruction**

Education—Developing countries   370.9172

> UF   Developing countries—Education

Education, Elementary
> USE   **Elementary education**

Education—Experimental methods   371.3

> UF   Activity schools
> Experimental methods in education
> Progressive education
> Teaching—Experimental methods

> SA   types of experimental methods, e.g. **Nongraded schools**; **Open plan schools**; etc. [to be added as needed]

> NT   **Experimental schools**
> **Nongraded schools**
> **Open plan schools**
> **Whole language**

> RT   **Alternative education**

Education—Federal aid
> USE   **Federal aid to education**

Education—Finance (May subdiv. geog.)   **371.2; 379.1**

> UF   School finance
> School taxes
> Tuition

> BT   **Finance**

> NT   **Educational vouchers**
> **Government aid to education**

> RT   **Federal aid to education**

Education for librarianship
> USE   **Library education**

Education—Government aid
  USE **Government aid to education**
Education—Government policy (May
      subdiv. geog.) **379**
  UF Education and state
      Educational policy
  BT **Social policy**
  NT **Compulsory education**
      Federal aid to education
      Government aid to education
Education, Higher
  USE **Higher education**
Education, Industrial
  USE **Industrial arts education**
Education—Integration
  USE **School integration**
       Segregation in education
Education of adults
  USE **Adult education**
Education of children
  USE **Elementary education**
Education of criminals
  USE **Prisoners—Education**
Education of men
  USE **Men—Education**
Education of prisoners
  USE **Prisoners—Education**
Education of the blind
  USE **Blind—Education**
Education of the deaf
  USE **Deaf—Education**
Education of veterans
  USE **Veterans—Education**
Education of women
  USE **Women—Education**
Education of workers
  USE **Labor—Education**
Education—Parent participation (May
      subdiv. geog.) **371.19**
  UF Parent participation in children's
      education
      Parental involvement in chil-
      dren's education
  RT **Home schooling**
Education—Personnel service
  USE **Educational counseling**
Education, Preschool
  USE **Preschool education**
Education, Primary
  USE **Elementary education**

Education, Secondary
  USE **Secondary education**
Education—Segregation
  USE **Segregation in education**
Education—Societies (May subdiv. geog.)
      370.6
  UF Education associations
      Educational associations
  BT **Societies**
  NT **Parent-teacher associations**
Education—State aid
  USE **Government aid to education**
Education—Statistics (May subdiv. geog.)
      370
  BT **Statistics**
Education—Study and teaching **370.7**
      Use for materials on the study of education
      as a discipline. Materials on the history and
      methods of training teachers, including the ed-
      ucational functions of teachers colleges, are
      entered under **Teachers—Training**. Materials
      on the art of teaching and methods of teach-
      ing are entered under **Teaching**.
  UF Pedagogy
  NT **Teachers colleges**
      Teachers—Training
Education, Theological
  USE **Theology—Study and teaching**
Education—United States **370.973**
Educational accreditation
  USE **Schools—Accreditation**
Educational achievement
  USE **Academic achievement**
Educational administration
  USE **Schools—Administration**
Educational assessment
  USE **Educational evaluation**
Educational associations
  USE **Education—Societies**
Educational consultants (May subdiv.
      geog.) **370.7**
  BT **Consultants**
Educational counseling (May subdiv.
      geog.) **371.4**
      Use for materials on the assistance given to
      students by schools, colleges, or universities
      in the selection of a program of studies suited
      to their abilities, interests, future plans, and
      general circumstances. Materials on the assis-
      tance given to students in understanding and
      coping with adjustment problems are entered
      under **School counseling**. Materials on the ac-
      tivities and programs designed to help people
      plan, choose, and succeed in their careers are
      entered under **Vocational guidance**.

Educational counseling—*Continued*

    UF   Academic advising
           Education—Personnel service
           Educational guidance
           Guidance counseling, Educational
           Personnel service in education
           Student guidance
           Students—Counseling
    BT   **Counseling**
    RT   **Dropouts**
           School counseling
           Vocational guidance

Educational evaluation (May subdiv. geog.) **370.7; 379.1**

    UF   Educational assessment
           Educational program evaluation
           Evaluation research in education
           Instructional systems analysis
           Program evaluation in education
           Self-evaluation in education
    SA   topics in education with the subdivision *Evaluation*, e.g. **Science—Study and teaching—Evaluation** [to be added as needed]
    BT   **Education**

Educational films
    USE **Motion pictures in education**
Educational freedom
    USE **Academic freedom**
Educational games **371.33**

    UF   Instructional games
           Instructive games
    BT   **Education**
           Games
    NT   **Simulation games in education**

Educational gaming
    USE **Simulation games in education**
Educational guidance
    USE **Educational counseling**
Educational measurements
    USE **Educational tests and measurements**
Educational media
    USE **Teaching—Aids and devices**
Educational media centers
    USE **Instructional materials centers**
Educational policy
    USE **Education—Government policy**
Educational program evaluation
    USE **Educational evaluation**
Educational psychology **370.15**

    BT   **Psychology**
           Teaching
    NT   **Ability grouping in education**
           Achievement motivation
           Apperception
           Attention
           Imagination
           Intelligence tests
           Listening
           Memory
           Psychology of learning
           Thought and thinking
    RT   **Applied psychology**
           Child psychology

Educational reports
    USE **School reports**
Educational simulation games
    USE **Simulation games in education**
Educational sociology (May subdiv. geog.) **306.43**

    UF   Social problems in education
    BT   **Sociology**
Educational software **005.3**

    UF   Education—Computer software
    BT   **Computer software**
Educational surveys (May subdiv. geog.) **370**

    UF   School surveys
    BT   **Surveys**
Educational technology (May subdiv. geog.) **371.33**

    UF   Instructional technology
    BT   **Education**
    RT   **Teaching—Aids and devices**
Educational television
    USE **Public television**
           Television in education
Educational tests and measurements (May subdiv. geog.) **371.26**

    UF   Educational measurements
           Tests
    BT   **Education**
    NT   **Ability—Testing**
           Achievement tests
           Colleges and universities—Entrance examinations
           Grading and marking (Education)
           Test bias
    RT   **Examinations**
           Intelligence tests

Educational tests and measurements— *Continued*

> **Psychological tests**

Educational vouchers (May subdiv. geog.) **379.1**

> UF School vouchers
> Vouchers, Educational
> BT **Education—Finance**

Educators (May subdiv. geog.) **370.92; 920**

> Use for materials on people engaged professionally in the field of education in general. Materials on educators engaged in classroom or other instruction are entered under **Teachers**.

> UF College teachers
> Faculty (Education)
> Professors
> BT **Education**
> NT **African American educators**
> **Teachers**

EEC

> USE **European Union**

Efficiency, Industrial

> USE **Industrial efficiency**

Egg decoration (May subdiv. geog.) **745.59**

> UF Easter egg decoration
> BT **Decoration and ornament**
> **Handicraft**

Eggs **636.5; 641**

> Use for materials on chicken eggs or on animal eggs in general.

> SA types of animals other than chickens with the subdivision *Eggs*, e.g. **Dinosaurs—Eggs** [to be added as needed]
> BT **Food**
> NT **Birds—Eggs**
> **Dinosaurs—Eggs**

Ego (Psychology) **154.2**

> BT **Personality**
> **Psychoanalysis**
> **Psychology**
> **Self**
> RT **Identity (Psychology)**

Egypt **962**

> May be subdivided like United States except for History.

> NT **Nile River valley**

Egypt—Antiquities **932**

> UF Egyptology
> BT **Antiquities**

Egypt—History **932; 962**

> NT **Sinai Campaign, 1956**

Egypt—History—1970- **962.05**

Egyptian mythology **398.20962**

> BT **Mythology**

Egyptology

> USE **Egypt—Antiquities**

Eight-hour day

> USE **Hours of labor**

Eighteenth century

> USE **World history—18th century**

EKG (Medicine)

> USE **Electrocardiogram**

El Niño Current **551.46**

> BT **Ocean currents**

Elder abuse

> USE **Elderly abuse**

Elder care

> USE **Elderly—Care**

Elderhostels (May subdiv. geog.) **647.94**

> UF Hostels, Elder
> BT **Continuing education**
> **Elderly—Education**

Elderly (May subdiv. geog.) **155.67; 305.26**

> UF Aged
> Aging persons
> Elderly persons
> Older persons
> Senior citizens
> SA elderly of particular racial or ethnic groups [to be added as needed]
> BT **Age**
> **Gerontology**
> NT **African American elderly**
> **Aging**
> **Aging parents**
> **Elderly—Library services**
> **Elderly men**
> **Elderly women**
> **Social work with the elderly**
> RT **Old age**
> **Retirees**

Elderly abuse (May subdiv. geog.) **362.6**

> UF Abuse of the elderly
> Abused aged
> Battered elderly
> Elder abuse
> Elderly—Mistreatment
> Elderly neglect

Elderly abuse—*Continued*
    Parent abuse
  BT **Domestic violence**
Elderly and libraries
  USE **Elderly—Library services**
Elderly—Care (May subdiv. geog.)
    362.6
    Use for general materials on the care of the dependent elderly.
  UF Elder care
  NT **Elderly—Home care**
      Elderly—Institutional care
      Elderly—Medical care
Elderly centers
  USE **Senior centers**
Elderly—Counseling of (May subdiv.
    geog.) **362.6**
  UF Counseling of the elderly
      Counseling with the aged
  BT **Counseling**
Elderly—Diseases (May subdiv. geog.)
    618.97
  UF Geriatrics
  BT **Diseases**
  RT **Elderly—Health and hygiene**
Elderly—Education (May subdiv. geog.)
    371.824
  BT **Education**
  NT **Elderhostels**
Elderly—Health and hygiene (May
    subdiv. geog.) **618.97**
  UF Geriatrics
  BT **Health**
      Hygiene
  RT **Elderly—Diseases**
Elderly—Home care (May subdiv. geog.)
    362.14; 362.6; 649.8
  BT **Elderly—Care**
      Home care services
Elderly—Housing (May subdiv. geog.)
    362.6
  UF Housing for the elderly
  BT **Housing**
  NT **Retirement communities**
  RT **Assisted living**
Elderly—Institutional care (May subdiv.
    geog.) **362.61**
  UF Homes for the elderly
      Old age homes
  BT **Elderly—Care**
      Institutional care

Elderly—Library services (May subdiv.
    geog.) **027.6**
  UF Elderly and libraries
      Libraries and the elderly
      Library services to the elderly
  BT **Elderly**
      Library services
Elderly—Life skills guides **362.6; 646.7**
  BT **Life skills**
  RT **Retirement**
Elderly—Medical care (May subdiv.
    geog.) **362.1; 618.97**
  UF Medical care for the elderly
  BT **Elderly—Care**
      Medical care
  NT **Medicare**
Elderly men (May subdiv. geog.) **305.26**
  UF Aged men
  BT **Elderly**
Elderly—Mistreatment
  USE **Elderly abuse**
Elderly neglect
  USE **Elderly abuse**
Elderly parents
  USE **Aging parents**
Elderly persons
  USE **Elderly**
Elderly—Recreation (May subdiv. geog.)
    790.084
  BT **Recreation**
Elderly—Societies (May subdiv. geog.)
    367
  BT **Societies**
Elderly—United States **305.260973**
Elderly women (May subdiv. geog.)
    305.26
  UF Aged women
  BT **Elderly**
Elected officials
  USE **Public officers**
Election
  USE **Elections**
      and types of public officials
      and names of individual pub-
      lic officials with the subdivi-
      sion *Election,* e.g. **Presi-
      dents—United States—Elec-
      tion** [to be added as needed]
Election law (May subdiv. geog.) **342**
  UF Law, Election
  BT **Constitutional law**

Election (Theology)
USE **Predestination**
Electioneering
USE **Politics**
Elections (May subdiv. geog.)   **324**
UF Ballot
Election
Franchise
Polls
Voting
SA types of public officials and
names of individual public of-
ficials with the subdivision
Election, e.g. **Presidents—
United States—Election** [to
be added as needed]
BT **Politics**
NT **Campaign funds
Presidents—United States—
Election
Primaries
Referendum
Suffrage
Voter registration**
RT **Proportional representation
Representative government and
representation**
Elections—Finance
USE **Campaign funds**
Elections—United States   324.973
UF United States—Elections
Elections—United States—Finance
USE **Campaign funds—United
States**
Electoral college
USE **Presidents—United States—
Election**
**Electric apparatus and appliances
621.3028; 643**

Use for materials on small electrical machines and appliances. Materials on large machines powered by electricity are entered under **Electric machinery.**

UF Apparatus, Electric
Appliances, Electric
Electric appliances
SA types of electric apparatus and
appliances, e.g. **Burglar
alarms** [to be added as need-
ed]
BT **Scientific apparatus and instruments**

NT **Burglar alarms
Electric batteries
Electric generators
Electric household appliances
Electric lamps
Induction coils
Storage batteries**
Electric appliances
USE **Electric apparatus and appli-
ances
Electric household appliances**
Electric automobiles (May subdiv. geog.)
629.222
UF Automobiles, Electric
Electric cars
BT **Automobiles**
**Electric automobiles—Cost effectiveness
388.3**
BT **Cost effectiveness**
Electric batteries   621.31
UF Batteries, Electric
Cells, Electric
BT **Electric apparatus and appli-
ances
Electrochemistry**
NT **Fuel cells
Solar batteries**
RT **Storage batteries**
Electric cars
USE **Electric automobiles**
Electric circuits   621.319
UF Circuits, Electric
BT **Electric lines
Electricity**
NT **Electronic circuits**
Electric companies
USE **Electric utilities**
Electric condensers
USE **Condensers (Electricity)**
Electric conductors   621.319
UF Conductors, Electric
BT **Electronics**
NT **Semiconductors
Superconductors**
Electric controllers   629.8
UF Automatic control
BT **Electric machinery**
Electric currents   537.6; 621.31
UF Currents, Electric
BT **Electricity**

259

Electric currents—*Continued*
 NT   **Alternating electric currents**
       Electric measurements
       Electric transformers
Electric currents, Alternating
 USE   **Alternating electric currents**
Electric distribution
 USE   **Electric lines**
       Electric power distribution
Electric engineering
 USE   **Electrical engineering**
Electric equipment of automobiles
 USE   **Automobiles—Electric equip-**
            ment
Electric eye
 USE   **Photoelectric cells**
Electric generators   621.31
 UF   Dynamos
       Generators, Electric
 BT   **Electric apparatus and appli-**
          ances
       Electric machinery
Electric guitar (May subdiv. geog.)
       787.87
 BT   **Electronic musical instruments**
       Guitars
Electric heating (May subdiv. geog.)
       621.402; 644; 697
 UF   Electricity in the home
 BT   **Heating**
Electric household appliances   643
 UF   Appliances, Electric
       Domestic appliances
       Electric appliances
       Electricity in the home
       Household appliances, Electric
       Labor saving devices, Household
 SA   types of specific appliances [to
          be added as needed]
 BT   **Electric apparatus and appli-**
          ances
       Household equipment and sup-
          plies
Electric industries
 USE   **Electric products industry**
Electric lamps   621.32; 645
 UF   Incandescent lamps
 BT   **Electric apparatus and appli-**
          ances
       Lamps
 RT   **Electric lighting**

Electric light
 USE   **Electric lighting**
       Photometry
       Phototherapy
Electric light and power industry
 USE   **Electric utilities**
Electric lighting (May subdiv. geog.)
       621.32
 UF   Arc light
       Electric light
       Electricity in the home
       Light, Electric
 BT   **Lighting**
 NT   **Fluorescent lighting**
 RT   **Electric lamps**
Electric lighting, Fluorescent
 USE   **Fluorescent lighting**
Electric lines (May subdiv. geog.)
       621.319
     Use for materials on power transmission
   lines, their construction and properties.
 UF   Electric distribution
       Electric power transmission
       Electric transmission
       Electricity—Distribution
       Power transmission, Electric
       Transmission of power
 BT   **Electric power distribution**
 NT   **Electric circuits**
       Electric wiring
Electric machinery (May subdiv. geog.)
       621.31
     Use for materials on large machines pow-
   ered by electricity. Materials on smaller ma-
   chines and appliances are entered under **Elec-**
   tric apparatus and appliances.
 BT   **Machinery**
 NT   **Electric controllers**
       Electric generators
       Electric motors
       Electric transformers
Electric machinery—Alternating current
       621.319
 UF   Alternating current machinery
Electric machinery—Direct current
       621.319
 UF   Direct current machinery
Electric measurements   621.37
 UF   Measurements, Electric
 BT   **Electric currents**
       Weights and measures
 NT   **Electric meters**
 RT   **Electric testing**

Electric meters (May subdiv. geog.)
    621.37
  UF   Meters, Electric
  BT   **Electric measurements**
Electric motors (May subdiv. geog.)
    621.46
  UF   Induction motors
       Motors
  BT   **Electric machinery**
  NT   **Electric transformers**
Electric power (May subdiv. geog.)
    621.31
  BT   **Electricity**
       Energy resources
       Power (Mechanics)
Electric power development
  USE **Electrification**
Electric power distribution (May subdiv.
    geog.) **621.319**
  UF   Electric distribution
       Electric power transmission
       Electric transmission
       Electricity—Distribution
       Power transmission, Electric
       Transmission of power
  BT   **Electrical engineering**
       Power transmission
  NT   **Electric lines**
       Electric utilities
       Electric wiring
Electric power failures (May subdiv.
    geog.) **621.319**
  UF   Blackouts, Electric power
       Brownouts
       Electric power interruptions
       Power blackouts
       Power failures
Electric power in mining
  USE **Electricity in mining**
Electric power industry
  USE **Electric utilities**
Electric power interruptions
  USE **Electric power failures**
Electric power plants (May subdiv. geog.)
    621.31
  UF   Power plants
       Power stations
  SA   types of electric power plants,
       e.g. **Nuclear power plants**
       [to be added as needed]

  NT   **Hydroelectric power plants**
       Nuclear power plants
       Steam power plants
Electric power transmission
  USE **Electric lines**
       Electric power distribution
Electric products industry (May subdiv.
    geog.) **338.4**
    Use for materials on industries producing
  products that contain electrical motors or oth-
  erwise employ electricity.
  UF   Electric industries
  BT   **Industries**
Electric railroads (May subdiv. geog.)
    621.33; 625.1; 385
  UF   Interurban railroads
  BT   **Railroads**
  RT   **Street railroads**
Electric signs (May subdiv. geog.)
    621.32; 659.13
  BT   **Advertising**
       Signs and signboards
  NT   **Neon tubes**
Electric smelting
  USE **Electrometallurgy**
Electric testing (May subdiv. geog.)
    621.37
  BT   **Testing**
  RT   **Electric measurements**
Electric toys (May subdiv. geog.) **688.7**
  BT   **Toys**
Electric transformers **621.31**
  UF   Transformers, Electric
  BT   **Electric currents**
       Electric machinery
       Electric motors
Electric transmission
  USE **Electric lines**
       Electric power distribution
Electric utilities (May subdiv. geog.)
    333.793
    Use for materials on businesses that sell
  and distribute electricity to customers.
  UF   Electric companies
       Electric light and power industry
       Electric power industry
  BT   **Electric power distribution**
       Public utilities
  NT   **Electrification**
Electric utilities—Government ownership
    (May subdiv. geog.) **333.793**
Electric waves **537; 621.381**

Electric waves—*Continued*
>UF Hertzian waves
>>Radio waves
>BT **Electricity**
>>**Waves**
>NT **Electromagnetic waves**
>>**Microwaves**

Electric welding (May subdiv. geog.)
>**671.5**
>UF Arc welding
>>Resistance welding
>>Spot welding
>>Welding, Electric
>BT **Welding**

Electric wiring (May subdiv. geog.)
>**621.319**
>UF Wiring, Electric
>BT **Electric lines**
>>**Electric power distribution**

Electric wiring—Charts, diagrams, etc.
>**621.319**

Electrical engineering (May subdiv. geog.)
>**621.3**
>UF Electric engineering
>BT **Engineering**
>>**Mechanical engineering**
>NT **Electric power distribution**
>>**Electricity in mining**
>>**Electrification**

Electricity (May subdiv. geog.)   **537;**
>**621.3**
>SA electricity in various endeavors,
>>e.g. **Electricity in agriculture**
>>[to be added as needed]
>BT **Physics**
>NT **Electric circuits**
>>**Electric currents**
>>**Electric power**
>>**Electric waves**
>>**Electricity in agriculture**
>>**Electricity in mining**
>>**Lightning**
>RT **Magnetism**

Electricity—Distribution
>USE **Electric lines**
>>**Electric power distribution**

Electricity in agriculture (May subdiv.
>geog.)   **333.79; 631.3**
>UF Electricity on the farm
>BT **Agricultural engineering**
>>**Agricultural machinery**
>>**Electricity**

>RT **Rural electrification**

Electricity in medicine
>USE **Electrotherapeutics**

Electricity in mining (May subdiv. geog.)
>**622**
>UF Electric power in mining
>>Mining, Electric
>BT **Electrical engineering**
>>**Electricity**
>RT **Mining engineering**

Electricity in the home
>USE **Electric heating**
>>**Electric household appliances**
>>**Electric lighting**

Electricity on the farm
>USE **Electricity in agriculture**

Electrification (May subdiv. geog.)
>**621.319**
>UF Electric power development
>BT **Electric utilities**
>>**Electrical engineering**
>NT **Rural electrification**

Electrocardiogram   **616.1**
>UF EKG (Medicine)
>>Electrocardiography
>BT **Diagnosis**

Electrocardiography
>USE **Electrocardiogram**

Electrochemistry   **541; 660**
>BT **Industrial chemistry**
>>**Physical chemistry**
>NT **Electric batteries**
>>**Electrometallurgy**
>>**Electroplating**
>>**Electrotyping**
>>**Fuel cells**

Electromagnetic waves   **539.2**
>UF Waves, Electromagnetic
>BT **Electric waves**
>>**Radiation**
>NT **Gamma rays**
>>**Heat**
>>**Infrared radiation**
>>**Light**
>>**Microwaves**
>>**Ultraviolet rays**
>>**X-rays**

Electromagnetism   **621.34**
>BT **Magnetism**
>NT **Masers**

Electromagnets   **621.34**

Electromagnets—*Continued*

    UF   Magnet winding

    BT   **Magnetism**

          Magnets

Electrometallurgy   669.028

    UF   Electric smelting

    BT   **Electrochemistry**

          Metallurgy

          Smelting

    RT   **Electroplating**

          Electrotyping

Electron microscope and microscopy

    USE **Electron microscopes**

Electron microscopes (May subdiv. geog.)
    502.8

    UF   Electron microscope and micros-
           copy

    BT   **Microscopes**

Electron tubes

    USE **Vacuum tubes**

Electronic apparatus and appliances
    621.381

    UF   Apparatus, Electronic

          Appliances, Electronic

    SA   types of electronic apparatus and
          appliances, e.g. **Computers**
          [to be added as needed]

    BT   **Electronics**

          **Scientific apparatus and in-
            struments**

    NT   **Computers**

          Electronic toys

          Intercommunication systems

          **Magnetic recorders and re-
            cording**

          Vacuum tubes

Electronic art

    USE **Video art**

Electronic books   070.5

    UF   Books in machine-readable form

          Online books

    BT   **Books**

Electronic bugging

    USE **Eavesdropping**

Electronic bulletin boards

    USE **Computer bulletin boards**

Electronic circuits   621.319; 621.3815

    BT   **Electric circuits**

          Electronics

Electronic commerce (May subdiv. geog.)
    381; 658

    Use for materials on the exchange of goods
and services and the transfer of funds through
electronic communications.

    UF   Cybercommerce

          Internet commerce

          Online commerce

    BT   **Commerce**

    NT   **Internet auctions**

          Internet marketing

          Internet shopping

Electronic data processing

    USE **Data processing**

Electronic design

    USE **Computer-aided design**

Electronic discussion groups   004.692

    Use for materials on services, commonly
called electronic mailing lists, that allow subscribers to post messages that are then distributed to other subscribers. Materials on services that allow users to engage in conversations in real time are entered under **Online
chat groups**. Materials on services that allow
users to post messages and retrieve messages
from others who have some common interest
are entered under **Computer bulletin boards**.

    UF   E-mail discussion groups

          Online discussion groups

    BT   **Discussion groups**

    RT   **Computer bulletin boards**

          Online chat groups

Electronic drafting

    USE **Computer graphics**

Electronic drawing

    USE **Computer graphics**

Electronic eavesdropping

    USE **Eavesdropping**

Electronic games

    USE **Video games**

Electronic journalism

    USE **Online journalism**

Electronic libraries

    USE **Digital libraries**

Electronic listening devices

    USE **Eavesdropping**

Electronic mail reference services (Li-
    braries)

    USE **Electronic reference services
            (Libraries)**

Electronic mail systems (May subdiv.
    geog.)   **004.692; 384.3**

    Use for materials on the electronic transmis-
sion of letters, messages, etc., primarily
through the use of computers.

Electronic mail systems—*Continued*
   UF   E-mail
         Email
   BT   **Data transmission systems**
         Telecommunication
Electronic marketing
   USE **Telemarketing**
Electronic music (May subdiv. geog.)
      786.7
   UF   Synthesizer music
   BT   **Music**
   RT   **Computer music**
Electronic musical instruments (May
      subdiv. geog.) **786.7**
   UF   Musical instruments, Electronic
   SA   types of instruments, e.g. **Syn-**
         thesizer (Musical instrument)
         [to be added as needed]
   BT   **Musical instruments**
   NT   **Electric guitar**
         Synthesizers (Musical instru-
         ments)
Electronic publishing (May subdiv. geog.)
      070.5; 686.2
     Use for materials on the process of publishing by which books and articles or any kind of data are made available as an electronic product. Materials on the use of a personal computer with writing, graphics, and page layout software to produce printed material for publication are entered under **Desktop publishing**.
   UF   Online publishing
         Web publishing
   BT   **Information services**
         Publishers and publishing
   NT   **Open access publishing**
   RT   **Desktop publishing**
Electronic reference services (Libraries)
      (May subdiv. geog.) **025.5**
   UF   Digital reference services (Libraries)
         E-mail reference services (Libraries)
         Electronic mail reference services (Libraries)
         Online reference services
   BT   **Reference services (Libraries)**
Electronic speech processing systems
   USE **Speech processing systems**
Electronic spreadsheets
   USE **Spreadsheet software**
Electronic surveillance (May subdiv. geog.) **621.389**

   UF   Surveillance, Electronic
   BT   **Remote sensing**
Electronic toys (May subdiv. geog.)
      688.7
   BT   **Electronic apparatus and appliances**
         Toys
   NT   **Video games**
Electronics   **537.5; 621.381**
   BT   **Engineering**
         Physics
         Technology
   NT   **Amplifiers (Electronics)**
         Cybernetics
         Digital electronics
         Electric conductors
         Electronic apparatus and appliances
         Electronic circuits
         Microelectronics
         Semiconductors
         Superconductors
         Transistors
Electrons   **539.7**
   BT   **Atoms**
         Particles (Nuclear physics)
Electroplating (May subdiv. geog.)
      671.7
   BT   **Electrochemistry**
         Metalwork
   RT   **Electrometallurgy**
Electrotherapeutics (May subdiv. geog.)
      615.8
   UF   Electricity in medicine
         Medical electricity
   BT   **Massage**
         Physical therapy
         Therapeutics
   NT   **Radiotherapy**
Electrotyping   **686.2**
   BT   **Electrochemistry**
         Printing
   RT   **Electrometallurgy**
Elegiac poetry   **808.1; 808.81**
     Use for individual works, collections, or materials about elegiac poetry.
   UF   Elegies
         Lamentations
   BT   **Poetry**
Elegies
   USE **Elegiac poetry**

Elementary education (May subdiv. geog.) **372**
- UF Children—Education
  Education, Elementary
  Education of children
  Education, Primary
  Grammar schools
  Primary education
- BT **Education**
- NT **Creative activities**
  Exceptional children
  Kindergarten
  Montessori method of education
  Nursery schools
  Readiness for school

Elementary particles (Physics)
- USE **Particles (Nuclear physics)**

Elementary school dropouts
- USE **Dropouts**

Elementary school libraries (May subdiv. geog.) **027.8**
- BT **School libraries**

Elementary schools (May subdiv. geog.) **373.236**
- UF Grade schools
- BT **Schools**
- RT **Middle schools**

Elements, Chemical
- USE **Chemical elements**

Elephants (May subdiv. geog.) **599.67**
- BT **Mammals**

Elevators (May subdiv. geog.) **621.8**
- UF Lifts
- BT **Hoisting machinery**

Elite (Social sciences) (May subdiv. geog.) **305.5**
- BT **Leadership**
  Power (Social sciences)
  Social classes
  Social groups

Elizabeth II, 1926- 92; B
- BT **Queens**

Elocution
- USE **Public speaking**

Elves 398.21
- BT **Folklore**

Email
- USE **Electronic mail systems**

Emancipation
- USE **Freedom**

Emancipation of slaves
- USE **Slaves—Emancipation**

Emancipation of women
- USE **Women's rights**

Embarrassment
- USE **Self-consciousness**

Embassies
- USE **Diplomatic and consular service**

Emblems
- USE **Decorations of honor**
  Heraldry
  Insignia
  Mottoes
  National emblems
  Seals (Numismatics)
  Signs and symbols

Emblems, State
- USE **State emblems**

Embracing
- USE **Hugging**

Embroidery (May subdiv. geog.) **746.44**
- SA types of embroidery [to be added as needed]
- BT **Decoration and ornament**
  Needlework
  Sewing
- NT **Counted thread embroidery**
  Crewelwork
  Cross-stitch
  Drawn work
  Hardanger needlework
  Needlepoint
  Samplers

Embryology 571.8; 612.6
- UF Development
- BT **Biology**
  Zoology
- NT **Fetus**
  Frozen embryos
  Genetics
- RT **Cells**
  Protoplasm
  Reproduction

Embryos, Frozen
- USE **Frozen embryos**

Emergencies
- USE **Accidents**
  Disasters
  First aid

Emergency assistance
    USE   **Helping behavior**
Emergency medical technicians (May
       subdiv. geog.)   **610.69; 616.02**
    UF   Emergency paramedics
         EMTs (Medicine)
         Paramedical personnel
         Paramedics, Emergency
    BT   **Allied health personnel**
Emergency medicine   **616.02**
    BT   **Medicine**
    NT   **Cardiac resuscitation**
Emergency mental health services
    USE   **Crisis intervention (Mental**
          health services)
Emergency paramedics
    USE   **Emergency medical technicians**
Emergency powers
    USE   **War and emergency powers**
Emergency preparedness
    USE   **Disaster relief**
Emergency relief
    USE   **Disaster relief**
Emergency survival
    USE   **Survival skills**
Emigrants
    USE   **Immigrants**
Emigration
    USE   **Immigration and emigration**
Eminent domain (May subdiv. geog.)
       333.1; 343
    UF   Condemnation of land
         Expropriation
    BT   **Constitutional law**
        Land use
        Property
Emmy Awards   **791.45**
    BT   **Television broadcasting**
Emotional stress
    USE   **Stress (Psychology)**
Emotionally disturbed children (May
       subdiv. geog.)   **155.4; 362.2;**
       371.94; 618.92

Use for general materials on children suffering from mental or emotional illnesses. Materials on the clinical and therapeutic aspects of
mental disorders in children are entered under
Child psychiatry.

    UF   Behavior problems (Children)
         Maladjusted children
         Mentally ill children
         Neurotic children
         Problem children

         Psychotic children
    BT   **Exceptional children**
        Mentally ill
    RT   **Child psychiatry**
        Juvenile delinquency
Emotions   **152.4**
    UF   Feelings
         Passions
    SA   types of emotions [to be added
         as needed]
    BT   **Psychology**
        Psychophysiology
    NT   **Anger**
        Anxiety
        Attitude (Psychology)
        Bereavement
        Compassion
        Consolation
        Disappointment
        Emotions in children
        Empathy
        Fanaticism
        Fear
        Frustration
        Gratitude
        Grief
        Guilt
        Happiness
        Hate
        Helplessness (Psychology)
        Hope
        Horror
        Intimacy (Psychology)
        Jealousy
        Joy and sorrow
        Laughter
        Loneliness
        Love
        Melancholy
        Pain
        Pleasure
        Prejudices
        Security (Psychology)
        Self-confidence
        Shame
        Shyness
        Sympathy
        Temper tantrums
        Trust
        Worry
Emotions in children   **155.4**

Emotions in children—*Continued*
   BT **Child psychology**
        Emotions
Empathy   152.4
   BT **Attitude (Psychology)**
        Emotions
        Social psychology
Emperors (May subdiv. geog.)   **920;
   929.7**
   UF Rulers
        Sovereigns
   SA names of emperors, e.g. **Nero,
        Emperor of Rome, 37-68** [to
        be added as needed]
   BT **Kings and rulers**
Emperors—Rome   **920; 937**
   UF Roman emperors
   SA names of Roman emperors, e.g.
        **Nero, Emperor of Rome, 37-
        68** [to be added as needed]
   NT **Nero, 37-68**
Empiricism   146
   UF Experience
   BT **Philosophy**
        Rationalism
        Theory of knowledge
   RT **Pragmatism**
Employee absenteeism
   USE **Absenteeism (Labor)**
Employee assistance programs   658.3
   BT **Personnel management**
Employee benefits   331.25
   UF Benefits, Employee
        Benefits, Fringe
        Employee fringe benefits
        Non-wage payments
        Nonwage payments
   BT **Salaries, wages, etc.**
Employee counseling
   USE **Employees—Counseling of**
Employee drinking
   USE **Employees—Alcohol use**
Employee drug testing
   USE **Employees—Drug testing**
Employee fringe benefits
   USE **Employee benefits**
Employee health services
   USE **Occupational health services**
Employee morale (May subdiv. geog.)
   158.7; 658.3
   BT **Applied psychology**
        Morale

        Personnel management
   NT **Job satisfaction**
   RT **Absenteeism (Labor)**
Employee rights (May subdiv. geog.)
   331.01
   UF Employees—Civil rights
        Labor rights
        Rights of employees
   BT **Civil rights**
        Labor laws and legislation
Employees (May subdiv. geog.)   **331.11;
   920**
   UF Workers
   SA types of employees, e.g. **Office
        workers**; types of industries,
        services, establishments, or in-
        stitutions, with the subdivision
        Employees; e.g. **Chemical in-
        dustry—Employees; Rail-
        roads—Employees**; etc.; and
        names of countries, states, cit-
        ies, etc., and corporate bodies
        with the subdivision *Officials
        and employees*, e.g. **United
        States—Officials and em-
        ployees; Ohio—Officials and
        employees; Chicago (Ill.)—
        Officials and employees;
        United Nations—Officials
        and employees**; etc. [to be
        added as needed]
   BT **Labor**
   NT **Chemical industry—Employees**
        **Colleges and universities—Em-
        ployees**
        Medical personnel
        Migrant labor
        Office workers
        Railroads—Employees
   RT **Personnel management**
Employees—Accidents
   USE **Industrial accidents**
Employees—Alcohol use (May subdiv.
   geog.)   **331.25; 658.3**
   UF Alcohol and employees
        Alcohol in the workplace
        Drinking and employees
        Drinking in the workplace
        Employee drinking
        Employees and alcohol

Employees and alcohol
    USE   **Employees—Alcohol use**
Employees and drugs
    USE   **Employees—Drug use**
Employees and narcotics
    USE   **Employees—Drug use**
Employees and officials
    USE   **Civil service**
Employees—Civil rights
    USE   **Employee rights**
Employees—Counseling of   658.3
    UF   Employee counseling
            Industrial counseling
    BT   **Counseling**
Employees—Dismissal (May subdiv.
        geog.)   **331.25; 658.3**
    BT   **Job security**
            Personnel management
‛   RT   **Downsizing of organizations**
Employees—Drug testing (May subdiv.
        geog.)   **331.25; 658.3**
    UF   Drug testing in the workplace
            Employee drug testing
    BT   **Drug testing**
Employees—Drug use (May subdiv.
        geog.)   **331.25; 658.3**
    UF   Drugs and employees
            Drugs in the workplace
            Employees and drugs
            Employees and narcotics
Employees—Pensions
    USE   **Old age pensions**
Employees—Rating   331.25; 658.3
Employees' representation in management
    USE   **Participative management**
Employees—Salaries, wages, etc.
    USE   **Salaries, wages, etc.**
Employees—Training (May subdiv. geog.)
        331.25; 658.3
    Use for materials discussing on-the-job
    training. Materials on teaching people a skill
    during the educational process are entered un-
    der **Vocational education**. Materials on teach-
    ing people a skill after formal education are
    entered under **Occupational training**. Materi-
    als on retraining are entered under **Occupa-
    tional retraining**.
    UF   In-service training
            Inservice training
            Training of employees
    SA   types of employees or personnel
            with the subdivision *Training*,
            e.g. **Teachers—Training**; or

with the subdivision *In-service
    training*, e.g. **Librarians—In-
    service training** [to be added
    as needed]
    BT   **Occupational training**
            Personnel management
            Vocational education
    NT   **Internship programs**
            Occupational retraining
    RT   **Apprentices**
            Technical education
Employer-employee relations
    USE   **Industrial relations**
Employers' liability
    USE   **Workers' compensation**
Employment (May subdiv. geog.)   **331.1**
    Use for materials on the economic theory of
    employment.
    SA   racial and ethnic groups and
            classes of persons with the
            subdivision *Employment*, e.g.
            **African Americans—Employ-
            ment; Veterans—Employ-
            ment**; etc. [to be added as
            needed]
    BT   **Economics**
            Labor
    NT   **African Americans—Employ-
            ment**
            Age and employment
            Blacks—Employment
            Labor supply
            Men—Employment
            Part-time employment
            Summer employment
            Teenagers—Employment
            Temporary employment
            Unemployment
            Veterans—Employment
            Women—Employment
            Youth—Employment
    RT   **Occupations**
            Vocational guidance
Employment agencies (May subdiv. geog.)
        331.12
    BT   **Labor**
            Labor turnover
            Personnel management
            Recruiting of employees
            Unemployment
    NT   **Job hunting**
    RT   **Labor supply**

Employment and age
USE **Age and employment**
Employment applications
USE **Applications for positions**
Employment discrimination
USE **Discrimination in employment**
Employment forecasting (May subdiv.
geog.) **331.1**
UF Occupational forecasting
BT **Economic forecasting**
RT **Labor supply**
Employment guidance
USE **Vocational guidance**
Employment interviewing
USE **Job interviews**
Employment management
USE **Personnel management**
Employment of children
USE **Child labor**
Employment references
USE **Applications for positions**
Employment security
USE **Job security**
Employment, Supplementary
USE **Supplementary employment**
Employment, Temporary
USE **Temporary employment**
Empresses (May subdiv. geog.) **920**
SA names of empresses; and coun-
tries, cities, etc., with the sub-
division *Kings and rulers* [to
be added as needed]
BT **Monarchy**
RT **Queens**
EMTs (Medicine)
USE **Emergency medical technicians**
Enamel and enameling 738.4
UF Porcelain enamels
BT **Decoration and ornament**
Decorative arts
Encounter groups
USE **Group relations training**
Encouragement 158
BT **Courage**
Helping behavior
Encyclicals, Papal
USE **Papal encyclicals**
Encyclopedias
USE **Encyclopedias and dictionaries**
and subjects, groups or classes
of persons, and names of

places with the subdivision
Encyclopedias, e.g. **Philoso-**
phy—Encyclopedias; Jews—
Encyclopedias; etc., for materials that provide topical information usually in alphabetical order [to be added as
needed]
Encyclopedias and dictionaries 030;
403
Use for general materials about encyclopedias and dictionaries.
UF Cyclopedias
Dictionaries
Encyclopedias
Glossaries
Subject dictionaries
SA subjects and names of languages
with the subdivision *Dictio-*
naries, for materials in alphabetical order that define terms
or identify things, e.g. **Chem-**
istry—Dictionaries; English
language—Dictionaries; etc.;
subjects, groups or classes of
persons, and names of places
with the subdivision *Biogra-*
phy—Dictionaries, for biographical dictionaries, e.g.
Women—Biography—Dictio-
naries; Ohio—Biography—
Dictionaries; etc.; and subjects, groups or classes of
persons, and names of places
with the subdivision *Encyclo-*
pedias, e.g. **Philosophy—En-**
cyclopedias; Jews—Encyclo-
pedias; etc., for materials that
provide topical information
usually in alphabetical order
[to be added as needed]
BT **Reference books**
NT **Bible—Dictionaries**
Biography—Dictionaries
Chemistry—Dictionaries
Classical dictionaries
Computer science—Dictionaries
English language—Dictionaries
English language—Dictionar-
ies—French
French language—Dictionar-
ies—English

Encyclopedias and dictionaries—*Continued*

> Geography—Dictionaries
> History—Dictionaries
> Jews—Encyclopedias
> Literature—Dictionaries
> Machine readable dictionaries
> Philosophy—Encyclopedias
> Picture dictionaries
> Polyglot dictionaries
> Shakespeare, William, 1564-1616—Dictionaries
> Technology—Dictionaries

End of the earth
 USE **End of the world**

End of the world   001.9; 202; 236; 523.1

Use for materials on the end of the world from an eschatological point of view (including Judgment Day, signs, fulfillments of prophecies, etc.) or from a scientific point of view.

 UF End of the earth
   End of the world (Astronomy)
 BT **Eschatology**
 NT **Judgment Day**

End of the world (Astronomy)
 USE **End of the world**

End-of-the-world fiction
 USE **Apocalyptic fiction**

End-of-the-world films
 USE **Apocalyptic films**

Endangered species (May subdiv. geog.) 333.95; 578.68
 UF Threatened species
   Vanishing species
 BT **Environmental protection**
   Nature conservation
 NT **Plant conservation**
   Wildlife conservation
 RT **Rare animals**
   Rare plants

Endocrine glands   616.4
 UF Ductless glands
   Glands, Ductless
 BT **Endocrinology**
 RT **Hormones**

Endocrinology   616.4
 BT **Medicine**
 NT **Endocrine glands**
   Hormones

Endorphins   612.8; 615

Endowed charities
 USE **Charities**
   Endowments

Endowments (May subdiv. geog.)   001.4; 361.6; 361.7
 UF Endowed charities
   Foundations (Endowments)
 SA disciplines, types of corporate bodies, and names of individual corporate bodies with the subdivision *Endowments*, e.g. **Colleges and universities—Endowments** [to be added as needed]
 BT **Finance**
 NT **Colleges and universities—Endowments**
   Scholarships
 RT **Charities**
   Philanthropy

Endurance, Physical
 USE **Physical fitness**

Energy
 USE **Energy resources**
   Force and energy

Energy and state
 USE **Energy policy**

Energy, Biomass
 USE **Biomass energy**

Energy conservation (May subdiv. geog.) 333.791
 UF Conservation of energy
   Conservation of power resources
   Power resources conservation
 SA types of energy conservation, e.g. **Recycling** [to be added as needed]
 BT **Conservation of natural resources**
   Energy resources
 NT **Recycling**
 RT **Energy consumption**
   Energy policy

Energy consumption (May subdiv. geog.) 333.79
 UF Consumption of energy
 SA subjects with the subdivision *Fuel consumption*, e.g. **Automobiles—Fuel consumption** [to be added as needed]
 BT **Energy resources**

Energy consumption—*Continued*
> NT **Automobiles—Fuel consumption**
>
> RT **Energy conservation**

Energy consumption—Forecasting (May subdiv. geog.) **333.79**

Energy conversion from waste
> USE **Waste products as fuel**

Energy conversion, Microbial
> USE **Biomass energy**

Energy development (May subdiv. geog.) **333.79**
> UF Energy resources development
>
> Power resources development
>
> BT **Energy resources**
>
> NT **Water resources development**

Energy policy (May subdiv. geog.) **333.79; 354.3**
> UF Energy and state
>
> Energy resources—Government policy
>
> Government policy
>
> BT **Energy resources**
>
> **Industrial policy**
>
> RT **Energy conservation**

Energy resources (May subdiv. geog.) **333.79**

Use for materials on the available sources of mechanical power in general. Materials on the physics and engineering aspects of power are entered under **Power (Mechanics)**.
> UF Energy
>
> Power resources
>
> Power supply
>
> BT **Natural resources**
>
> **Power (Mechanics)**
>
> NT **Biomass energy**
>
> **Electric power**
>
> **Energy conservation**
>
> **Energy consumption**
>
> **Energy development**
>
> **Energy policy**
>
> **Fuel**
>
> **Ocean energy resources**
>
> **Renewable energy resources**
>
> **Solar energy**
>
> **Water power**
>
> **Wind power**

Energy resources development
> USE **Energy development**

Energy resources—Government policy
> USE **Energy policy**

Energy technology
> USE **Power (Mechanics)**

Engagement
> USE **Betrothal**

Engineering (May subdiv. geog.) **620**
> UF Construction
>
> SA types of engineering, e.g. **Chemical engineering** [to be added as needed]
>
> BT **Industrial arts**
>
> **Technology**
>
> NT **Aeronautics**
>
> **Aerospace engineering**
>
> **Agricultural engineering**
>
> **Chemical engineering**
>
> **Civil engineering**
>
> **Electrical engineering**
>
> **Electronics**
>
> **Genetic engineering**
>
> **Highway engineering**
>
> **Human engineering**
>
> **Hydraulic engineering**
>
> **Marine engineering**
>
> **Mechanical drawing**
>
> **Military engineering**
>
> **Mining engineering**
>
> **Minorities in engineering**
>
> **Municipal engineering**
>
> **Nuclear engineering**
>
> **Ocean engineering**
>
> **Railroad engineering**
>
> **Reliability (Engineering)**
>
> **Sanitary engineering**
>
> **Steam engineering**
>
> **Structural engineering**
>
> **Systems engineering**
>
> **Traffic engineering**
>
> **Water supply engineering**
>
> RT **Engineers**
>
> **Materials**

Engineering and construction
> USE names of wars with the subdivision *Engineering and construction,* e.g. **World War, 1939-1945—Engineering and construction** [to be added as needed]

Engineering drawing
> USE **Mechanical drawing**

Engineering, Genetic
> USE **Genetic engineering**

Engineering instruments (May subdiv. geog.) **620.0028**
UF Instruments, Engineering
BT **Scientific apparatus and instruments**
Engineering materials
USE **Materials**
Engineering—Periodicals 620.005
Engineering—Study and teaching (May subdiv. geog.) **620.007**
BT **Technical education**
Engineers (May subdiv. geog.) **620.0092; 920**
RT **Engineering**
Inventors
Engines 621.4
UF Motors
SA types of engines and motors, e.g. **Steam engines**; **Electric motors**; etc., and types of vehicles and makes and models of vehicles with the subdivision *Motors*, e.g. **Automobiles—Motors** [to be added as needed]
BT **Machinery**
NT **Airplane engines**
Automobiles—Motors
Diesel engines
Fire engines
Fuel
Heat engines
Internal combustion engines
Marine engines
Pumping machinery
Solar engines
Steam engines
Turbines
England 942
May be subdivided like **United States** except for *History*, and *Politics and government*, or any subdivisions relating to history or politics and government. Such materials are entered instead under **Great Britain**.
BT **Great Britain**
England, Church of
USE **Church of England**
England—History
USE **Great Britain—History**
English as a foreign language
USE **English as a second language**
English as a second language (May subdiv. geog.) **420.7; 428**

UF English as a foreign language
English for foreigners
English language as a second language
English language—Study and teaching, Foreign
English language—Texts for foreigners
BT **English language—Study and teaching**
NT **English language—Conversation and phrase books**
English authors (May subdiv. geog.) **820.9; 920**
UF Authors, English
BT **Authors**
English authors—First editions
USE **English literature—First editions**
English authors—Homes (May subdiv. geog.) **820.9; 920**
BT **Literary landmarks**
English Canadian literature
USE **Canadian literature (English)**
English Canadian poetry
USE **Canadian poetry (English)**
English Channel 910.9163
English composition
USE **English language—Composition and exercises**
English drama 822
Use for general materials about English drama, not for individual works.
BT **Drama**
English literature
NT **Morality plays**
Mysteries and miracle plays
English drama—Collections 822.008
English drama—History and criticism 822.009
BT **Drama—History and criticism**
English essays 824; 824.008
Use for collections of literary essays by several authors.
BT **English literature**
Essays
English fiction 823
Use for collections or materials about English fiction, not for individual works.
BT **English literature**
Fiction

English fiction—History and criticism
   823.009

English for foreigners
   USE   **English as a second language**
          English language—Conversa-
             tion and phrase books

English grammar
   USE   **English language—Grammar**

English history
   USE   **Great Britain—History**

English language (May subdiv. geog.)
   420

   Subdivisions used under this heading may
   be used under other languages unless otherwise specified.

   BT   **Language and languages**

English language—0-1100
   USE   **English language—Old English**
             period

English language—Acronyms
   USE   **Acronyms**

English language—Alphabet   421

English language—Americanisms
   USE   **Americanisms**

English language—Antonyms
   USE   **English language—Synonyms**
             and antonyms

English language as a second language
   USE   **English as a second language**

English language—Basal readers
   USE   **Basal readers**

English language—Business English
   428

   Business English is a unique subdivision for
   English language. Use same pattern with
   unique subdivisions for other languages, e.g.
   Japanese language—Business Japanese; etc.

   UF   Business English

English language—Comparison   425

   UF   Comparison (English grammar)

English language—Composition and ex-
   ercises   428

   UF   English composition

   RT   **Rhetoric**

English language—Conversation and
   phrase books   428

   UF   English for foreigners
          English language—Conversations
             and phrases

   BT   **English as a second language**

English language—Conversations and
   phrases
   USE   **English language—Conversa-**
             tion and phrase books

English language—Dialects   427
   NT   **Americanisms**

English language—Dictionaries   423

   Use for English language dictionaries. Dictionaries from English to another language are
   entered under this heading further subdivided
   by the other language, e.g. **English lan-**
   guage—Dictionaries—French.   French-
   English dictionaries are entered under **French**
   language—Dictionaries—English. Combined
   English-French and French-English dictionaries are entered under both headings.

   BT   **Encyclopedias and dictionaries**

   RT   **English language—Terms and**
             phrases

English language—Dictionaries—French
   443

   Use for English-French dictionaries. French-
   English dictionaries are entered under **French**
   language—Dictionaries—English. Combined
   English-French and French-English dictionaries are entered under both headings.

   UF   Foreign language dictionaries

   BT   **Encyclopedias and dictionaries**

   RT   **French language—Dictionar-**
             ies—English

English language—Errors
   USE   **English language—Errors of**
             usage

English language—Errors of usage   428

   UF   English language—Errors

English language—Etymology   422

   BT   **English language—History**

English language—Examinations   420.76

   BT   **Examinations**

English language—Examinations—Study
   guides   420.76

English language—Figures of speech
   USE   **Figures of speech**

English language—Foreign words and
   phrases   422

   Use for materials on foreign words and
   phrases incorporated into the English language.

   UF   Foreign language phrases

English language—Grammar   425

   UF   English grammar

   SA   **English language** subdivided by
             topics in the study of gram-
             mar, e.g. **English language—**
             Parts of speech; English lan-

English language—Grammar—*Continued*
    guage—**Infinitive**; etc. [to be
    added as needed]
  BT **Grammar**
  NT **English language—Usage**
English language—**History** 420.9
  NT **English language—Etymology**
English language—**Homonyms** 423
English language—**Idioms** 428
  RT **English language—Provincial-
    isms**
English language—**Infinitive** 425
English language—**Jargon** 427
English language—**Middle English period**
    420
  UF Middle English language
English language—**Old English period**
    429
  UF Anglo-Saxon language
    English language—0-1100
    Old English language
English language—Orthography
  USE **English language—Spelling**
English language—**Parts of speech** 425
English language—Phonetics
  USE **English language—Pronuncia-
    tion**
English language—Phrases and terms
  USE **English language—Terms and
    phrases**
English language—**Programmed instruc-
    tion** 420.7
  BT **Programmed instruction**
English language—**Pronunciation** 421
  UF English language—Phonetics
  BT **Phonetics**
  NT **Reading—Phonetic method**
English language—**Provincialisms** 427
  RT **English language—Idioms**
English language—Punctuation
  USE **Punctuation**
English language—Reading materials
  USE **Reading materials**
English language—Rhetoric
  USE **Rhetoric**
English language—**Rhyme** 428.1
  BT **Rhyme**
English language—**Slang** 427
English language—**Social aspects** 420
English language—**Spelling** 421
  UF English language—Orthography
  BT **Spelling**

  NT **Spellers**
  RT **Word skills**
English language—Spelling reform
  USE **Spelling reform**
English language—**Study and teaching**
    420.7
  NT **English as a second language**
English language—Study and teaching,
    Foreign
  USE **English as a second language**
English language—**Synonyms and ant-
    onyms** 423
  UF English language—Antonyms
  RT **Opposites**
English language—**Terms and phrases**
    420
    Use for general lists of words and phrases
    and for lists that are applicable to certain situ-
    ations (collective nouns, curious expressions,
    etc.) rather than to specific subjects. Lists of
    words and phrases limited to specific subjects
    are entered under the subject with the subdivi-
    sion *Dictionaries*, e.g. **Chemistry—Dictionar-
    ies**.
  UF English language—Phrases and
    terms
  RT **English language—Dictionaries**
English language—Texts for foreigners
  USE **English as a second language**
English language—**Usage** 428
  BT **English language—Grammar**
English language—Versification
  USE **Versification**
English language—Vocabulary
  USE **Vocabulary**
English letters 826; 826.008
  BT **English literature**
    Letters
English literature 820
    Subdivisions used under this heading may
  be used under other literatures.
  BT **Literature**
  NT **English drama**
    English essays
    English fiction
    English letters
    English poetry
    English prose literature
    English satire
    English sermons
    English speeches
    English wit and humor

English literature—0 1100
USE **English literature—Old English period**
English literature—16th and 17th centuries 820
UF English literature—Early modern, 1500-1700
Renaissance English literature
English literature—18th century 820
English literature—19th century 820
UF Victorian literature
English literature—20th century 820
English literature—21st century 820
English literature—Bibliography 016.82
English literature—Bio-bibliography 820.9
English literature—Collections 820.8

Use for collections of English literature by several authors in more than one genre. Collections of prose are entered under **English prose literature**. Collections of poetry are entered under **English poetry—Collections**. Collections of drama are entered under **English drama—Collections**.

English literature—Criticism
USE **English literature—History and criticism**
English literature—Dictionaries 820.3
BT **Literature—Dictionaries**
English literature—Early modern, 1500-1700
USE **English literature—16th and 17th centuries**
English literature—Examinations 820.76
BT **English literature—Study and teaching**
English literature—First editions 820
UF English authors—First editions
English literature—History and criticism 820.9
UF English literature—Criticism
English literature—Indexes 016.82
English literature—Middle English period 820
UF Middle English literature
English literature—Old English period 829
UF Anglo-Saxon literature
English literature—0-1100
Old English literature
English literature—Outlines, syllabi, etc. 820.2

BT **Literature—Outlines, syllabi, etc.**
RT **English literature—Study and teaching**
English literature—Study and teaching 820.7
NT **English literature—Examinations**
RT **English literature—Outlines, syllabi, etc.**
English newspapers
USE **Newspapers—Great Britain**
English novelists 823; 920
BT **Novelists**
English orations
USE **English speeches**
English periodicals 052
BT **Periodicals**
English poetry 821

Use for general materials about English poetry, not for individual works.

BT **English literature**
Poetry
English poetry—Collections 821.008
English poetry—History and criticism 821.009
English poets 821; 920
BT **Poets**
English prose literature 828

Use for collections of prose writings that may include several literary forms, such as essays, fiction, orations, etc.

UF Prose literature, English
BT **English literature**
English public schools 373.2

Use for materials on British endowed secondary schools that are open to public admission but are not financed or administered by any government body.

UF Public schools, Endowed (Great Britain)
Public schools, English
BT **Private schools**
English satire 827; 827.008
UF Satire, English
BT **English literature**
Satire
English sermons 252
BT **English literature**
Sermons
English speeches 825; 825.008

English speeches—*Continued*
  UF English orations
      Speeches, addresses, etc., English
  BT **English literature**
      Speeches
**English wit and humor   827; 827.008;
    827.009**
  Use for collections by several authors or for materials about English wit and humor. Individual works by English humorists are entered under **Wit and humor**.
  BT **English literature**
      Wit and humor
Engravers (May subdiv. geog.)   760.92;
    920
  BT **Artists**
  NT **Etchers**
Engraving (May subdiv. geog.)   760;
    765
  UF Copper engraving
      Engravings
      Line engraving
      Steel engraving
  SA engraving of particular countries,
        e.g. **American engraving** [to
        be added as needed]
  BT **Art**
      Graphic arts
      Illustration of books
      Pictures
  NT **American engraving**
      Gems
      Mezzotint engraving
      Photoengraving
      Wood engraving
  RT **Etching**
Engraving, American
  USE **American engraving**
Engravings
  USE **Engraving**
Enhanced radiation weapons
  USE **Neutron weapons**
Enigmas
  USE **Curiosities and wonders**
       Riddles
Enlarged texts for shared reading
  USE **Big books**
Enlarging (Photography)
  USE **Photography—Enlarging**

Enlightenment (May subdiv. geog.)   190;
    909.7; 940.2
  Use for materials on the philosophic movement of the 18th century marked by the questioning of traditional doctrines and values, naturalistic and individualistic tendencies, and an emphasis on the empirical method in science and the free use of reason.
  BT **Modern civilization**
      Modern philosophy
      Rationalism
Enlistment
  USE **Recruiting and enlistment**
Enneagram   155.2
  BT **Typology (Psychology)**
Ensemble playing
  USE **Ensembles (Music)**
Ensembles (Mathematics)
  USE **Set theory**
Ensembles (Music) (May subdiv. geog.)
    782; 784
  Use for materials on small instrumental or vocal groups and for the music written for such groups.
  UF Ensemble playing
      Instrumental ensembles
      Musical ensembles
      Vocal ensembles
  SA types of vocal or instrumental
        ensembles, e.g. **Jazz ensembles** [to be added as needed]
  BT **Music**
      Musical form
      Musicians
  NT **Jazz ensembles**
  RT **Orchestra**
Ensigns
  USE **Flags**
Enteric fever
  USE **Typhoid fever**
Enterprises
  USE **Business enterprises**
Entertainers (May subdiv. geog.)
    791.092; 920
  SA types of entertainers and names
        of individual entertainers [to
        be added as needed]
  NT **Actors**
      Clowns
      Comedians
      Dancers
      Fools and jesters
      Geishas

Entertaining (May subdiv. geog.) **395.3;
642**

Use for materials on hospitality and the art of entertaining guests.

UF   Guests

      Hospitality

BT   **Etiquette**

      Home economics

NT   **Business entertaining**

      Carving (Meat, etc.)

      Children's parties

      Games

      Parties

RT   **Afternoon teas**

      Amusements

      Dining

      Luncheons

Entertainments

USE   **Amusements**

Entozoa

USE   **Parasites**

Entrance examinations

USE   types of educational institutions and names of individual institutions with the subdivision *Entrance examinations,* e.g. **Colleges and universities—Entrance examinations** [to be added as needed]

Entrance examinations for colleges

USE   **Colleges and universities—Entrance examinations**

Entrance requirements

USE   types of educational institutions and names of individual institutions with the subdivision *Entrance requirements,* e.g **Colleges and universities—Entrance requirements** [to be added as needed]

Entrance requirements for colleges and universities

USE   **Colleges and universities—Entrance requirements**

Entrepreneurs (May subdiv. geog.) **338;
920**

BT   **Businesspeople**

      Self-employed

Entrepreneurship (May subdiv. geog.) **338; 658.4**

BT   **Business**

      Capitalism

      Small business

Entropy   **536**

BT   **Thermodynamics**

Environment (May subdiv. geog.) **304.2;
333.7; 363.7**

Use for materials on the habitat or surroundings of a population or on all factors external to the individual.

SA   subjects with the subdivision *Environmental aspects,* e.g. **Nuclear power plants—Environmental aspects** [to be added as needed]

NT   **Ecology**

      Environmental degradation

      Environmental movement

      Environmental policy

      Environmental protection

      Nuclear power plants—Environmental aspects

      Pesticides—Environmental aspects

      Work environment

RT   **Environmental sciences**

Environment and pesticides

USE   **Pesticides—Environmental aspects**

Environment and state

USE   **Environmental policy**

Environment—Government policy

USE   **Environmental policy**

Environment, Space

USE   **Space environment**

Environmental aspects

USE   subjects with the subdivision *Environmental aspects,* e.g. **Nuclear power plants—Environmental aspects; Economic development—Environmental aspects** [to be added as needed]

Environmental control

USE   **Environmental law**

Environmental damages, Liability for

USE   **Liability for environmental damages**

Environmental degradation (May subdiv. geog.) **333.7; 363.7**

UF   Environmental destruction

      Environmental deterioration

BT   **Environment**

      Natural disasters

Environmental destruction
    USE **Environmental degradation**
Environmental deterioration
    USE **Environmental degradation**
Environmental ethics   179
    UF Environmental quality—Ethical
        aspects
        Human ecology—Ethical aspects
    BT **Ethics**
Environmental health (May subdiv. geog.)
    616.9
    UF Health—Environmental aspects
    SA subjects with the subdivision *En-*
        vironmental aspects, e.g. **Nu-**
        clear power plants—Envi-
        ronmental aspects [to be
        added as needed]
    BT **Environmental influence on**
        humans
        Public health
    NT **Air pollution**
        Environmentally induced dis-
        eases
        Nuclear power plants—Envi-
        ronmental aspects
        Occupational health and safety
        Pollution
        Water pollution
Environmental health engineering
    USE **Sanitary engineering**
Environmental illness
    USE **Environmentally induced dis-**
        eases
Environmental influence on humans
    (May subdiv. geog.)   **304.2; 599.9**
    UF Acclimatization
        Altitude, Influence of
        Man—Influence of environment
    BT **Adaptation (Biology)**
        Human ecology
        Human geography
    NT **Environmental health**
        Survival skills
        Weightlessness
Environmental law (May subdiv. geog.)
    344
    UF Environmental control
        Environmental protection—Law
        and legislation
    BT **Environmental policy**
        Environmental protection

    Law
    NT **Liability for environmental**
        damages
Environmental lobby
    USE **Environmental movement**
Environmental movement (May subdiv.
    geog.)   **320.5; 322.4; 363.7**
    UF Conservation movement
        Ecological movement
        Environmental lobby
        Environmentalism
        Green movement
    BT **Environment**
        Social movements
    NT **Ecoterrorism**
Environmental policy (May subdiv. geog.)
    344; 354.3; 363.7
    UF Environment and state
        Environment—Government poli-
        cy
        Environmental quality—Govern-
        ment policy
        Government policy
        State and environment
    BT **Environment**
    NT **Environmental law**
    RT **Conservation of natural re-**
        sources
Environmental policy—United States
    344; 354.30973; 363.7
    UF United States—Environmental
        policy
Environmental pollution
    USE **Pollution**
Environmental protection (May subdiv.
    geog.)   **344; 363.7**
    UF Environmentalism
        Protection of environment
    BT **Ecology**
        Environment
    NT **Conservation of natural re-**
        sources
        Endangered species
        Environmental law
        Landscape protection
        Soil conservation
        Wildlife conservation
    RT **Pollution**
Environmental protection—Law and legisla-
    tion
    USE **Environmental law**

Environmental protection—Standards
(May subdiv. geog.)   **354.3**

Environmental quality—Ethical aspects
USE   **Environmental ethics**

Environmental quality—Government policy
USE   **Environmental policy**

Environmental radioactivity
USE   **Radioactive pollution**

**Environmental sciences   304.2; 333.7;
363.7**
BT   **Science**
RT   **Ecology**
Environment

Environmental technology
USE   **Green technology**

Environmental tourism
USE   **Ecotourism**

Environmentalism
USE   **Environmental movement**
Environmental protection

Environmentally friendly architecture
USE   **Sustainable architecture**

Environmentally induced diseases (May
subdiv. geog.)   **616.07**
UF   Diseases—Environmental aspects
Environmental illness
SA   names of individual diseases
with the subdivision *Environ-
mental aspects*, e.g. **Can-
cer/Environmental aspects**
[to be added as needed]
BT   **Diseases—Causes**
Environmental health
NT   **Cancer—Environmental aspects**

Enzymes   547; 572
BT   **Proteins**
NT   **Catalytic RNA**

Eolithic period
USE   **Stone Age**

Epic films   791.43
Use for individual works, collections, or
materials about epic films.
UF   Film epics
BT   **Motion pictures**

Epic literature   800
Use for individual works, collections, or
materials about epic literature.
BT   **Literature**
NT   **Epic poetry**
RT   **Mock-heroic literature**

Epic poetry   808.81; 808.1
Use for individual works, collections, or
materials about epic poetry.
BT   **Epic literature**
Narrative poetry
NT   **Indian epic poetry**
RT   **Romances**

Epidemics (May subdiv. geog.)   **614.4**
UF   Pestilences
SA   names of contagious diseases,
e.g. **AIDS (Disease)** [to be
added as needed]
BT   **Diseases**
Public health
NT   **Plague**
RT   **Communicable diseases**

Epigrams   808.88
Use for collections of epigrams and for ma-
terials about epigrams.
UF   Sayings
BT   **Wit and humor**
NT   **Quotations**
Toasts
RT   **Proverbs**

Epigraphy
USE   **Inscriptions**

Epilepsy   616.8
BT   **Nervous system—Diseases**

Epiphany   394.2663
BT   **Christian holidays**

Episcopal Church (May subdiv. geog.)
283
Use for materials on the Episcopal Church
in the United States after 1789. Materials on
the Episcopal Church in the United States pri-
or to 1789 are entered under **Church of England—United States**.
UF   Protestant Episcopal Church in
the U.S.A.
BT   **Christian sects**
NT   **Catholic charismatic movement**
RT   **Church of England—United
States**

Epistemology
USE   **Theory of knowledge**

Epistolary fiction   808.3
Use for individual works, collections, or
materials about novels written in the form of
a series of letters.
UF   Epistolary novels
Novels in letters
BT   **Fiction**

Epistolary novels
USE   **Epistolary fiction**

Epistolary poetry   808.1; 808.81

  Use for individual works, collections, or materials about epistolary verse.

  UF   Verse epistles

  BT   **Poetry**

Epitaphs   929

  UF   Graves

  BT   **Biography**

     Cemeteries

     Inscriptions

     Tombs

Epithets

  USE   **Names**

      Nicknames

Epizoa

  USE   **Parasites**

Equal employment opportunity

  USE   **Affirmative action programs**

      Discrimination in employment

Equal opportunity in employment

  USE   **Affirmative action programs**

      Discrimination in employment

Equal pay for equal work (May subdiv. geog.)   331.2; 658.3

  UF   Pay equity

  BT   **Discrimination in employment**

     Salaries, wages, etc.

     Women—Employment

Equal rights amendments (May subdiv. geog.)   305.42; 323.4; 342

  UF   Amendments, Equal rights

     ERAs

  BT   **Constitutions**

     Sex discrimination

Equal time rule (Broadcasting)   324

  Use for materials on the requirement that all qualified candidates for public office be granted equal broadcast time if one of one such candidates is permitted to broadcast. Materials on the requirement that, if one side of a controversial issue of public importance is aired, the same opportunity must be given for the presentation of contrasting views are entered under **Fairness doctrine (Broadcasting)**.

  UF   Rule of equal time (Broadcasting)

  BT   **Broadcasting**

     Television and politics

  RT   **Fairness doctrine (Broadcasting)**

Equality (May subdiv. geog.)   323.42

  UF   Inequality

     Social equality

  BT   **Political science**

     Sociology

  NT   **Individualism**

     Social justice

  RT   **Democracy**

     Freedom

Equations, Chemical

  USE   **Chemical equations**

Equestrianism

  USE   **Horsemanship**

Equilibrium (Economics)   339.5

  UF   Economic equilibrium

  BT   **Economics**

Equipment and supplies

  USE   subjects and names of wars with the subdivision *Equipment and supplies,* e.g. **Television—Equipment and supplies; World War, 1939-1945—Equipment and supplies** [to be added as needed]

ERAs

  USE   **Equal rights amendments**

Ergonomics

  USE   **Human engineering**

Eritrea   963.5

  May be subdivided like United States except for History.

Erosion (May subdiv. geog.)   551.3

  SA   types of erosion, e.g. **Soil erosion** [to be added as needed]

  BT   **Geology**

  NT   **Dust storms**

     Soil erosion

  RT   **Soil conservation**

Erotic art (May subdiv. geog.)   704.9

  UF   Sex in art

  BT   **Art**

     Erotica

Erotic fiction   808.3; 808.83

  Use for individual works, collections, or materials about erotic fiction.

  UF   Adult fiction

     Erotic novels

     Erotic stories

  BT   **Erotic literature**

     Fiction

Erotic films (May subdiv. geog.)   791.43

  Use for individual works, collections, or materials about erotic films.

  UF   Adult films

  BT   **Motion pictures**

Erotic literature   808.8; 809
  UF   Literature, Erotic
  BT   **Erotica**
        Literature
  NT   **Erotic fiction**
        Erotic poetry
Erotic novels
  USE   **Erotic fiction**
Erotic poetry   808.1; 808.81
  Use for individual works, collections, or materials about erotic poetry.
  BT   **Erotic literature**
        Poetry
  RT   **Love poetry**
Erotic stories
  USE   **Erotic fiction**
Erotica   704.9; 809
  SA   types of erotica, e.g. **Erotic art**; **Erotic literature**; etc. [to be added as needed]
  NT   **Erotic art**
        Erotic literature
  RT   **Obscenity (Law)**
        Pornography
Errors   001.9; 153.7; 165
  Use for materials on errors of judgment, errors of observation, scientific errors, popular misconceptions, etc. Errors in language are entered under names of languages with the subdivision *Errors of usage*, e.g. **English language—Errors of usage**.
  UF   Fallacies
        Medical errors
        Mistakes
        Scientific errors
  RT   **Superstition**
Errors of usage
  USE   names of languages with the subdivision *Errors of usage,* e.g. **English language—Errors of usage** [to be added as needed]
Erudition
  USE   **Learning and scholarship**
Eruptions
  USE   **Geysers**
Escapes (May subdiv. geog.)   **365; 904**
  UF   Hostage escapes
        Prison escapes
  BT   **Adventure and adventurers**
        Prisons
Eschatology   202; 236

  UF   Intermediate state
        Last things (Theology)
  BT   **Theology**
  NT   **Death**
        End of the world
        Future life
        Heaven
        Hell
        Immortality
        Millennium
        Purgatory
        Second Advent
Eskimos
  USE   **Inuit**
ESP
  USE   **Extrasensory perception**
Esperanto   499
  BT   **Universal language**
Espionage (May subdiv. geog.)   **327.12**
  UF   Spying
  SA   espionage practiced by particular countries, e.g. **American espionage** [to be added as needed]
  BT   **Intelligence service**
        Secret service
        Subversive activities
  NT   **American espionage**
        Spies
Espionage, American
  USE   **American espionage**
Espionage films
  USE   **Spy films**
Espionage stories
  USE   **Spy stories**
Espionage television programs
  USE   **Spy television programs**
Esquimaux
  USE   **Inuit**
Essay   808.4
  Use for materials on the appreciation of the essay and on the technique of writing essays. Collections of essays are entered under **Essays; American essays**; etc.
  BT   **Literature**
Essays   808.4; 808.84
  Use for collections of literary essays by authors of several nationalities. Collections of literary essays by American authors are entered under **American essays**; by English authors, under **English essays**; etc. Essays limited to a particular subject, by one or more authors, are entered under that subject. Materials on the appreciation of the essay and on the

Essays—*Continued*
technique of writing essays are entered under
Essay.
  NT **American essays**
      English essays
Essences and essential oils **664; 668**
  UF Aromatic plant products
      Essential oils
      Vegetable oils
      Volatile oils
  BT **Distillation**
      Oils and fats
  NT **Flavoring essences**
      Perfumes
  RT **Aromatic plants**
Essenes **296.8**
  BT **Jews**
Essential oils
  USE **Essences and essential oils**
Estate planning (May subdiv. geog.)
      332.024; 343.05; 346.05
  BT **Personal finance**
      Planning
  NT **Inheritance and transfer tax**
      Insurance
  RT **Investments**
      Tax planning
      Trusts and trustees
Estate tax
  USE **Inheritance and transfer tax**
Esthetics
  USE **Aesthetics**
Estimates
  USE types of engineering, technical
      processes, industries, etc.,
      with the subdivision *Esti-*
      mates, e.g. **Building—Esti-**
      mates [to be added as need-
      ed]
Estimation (Mathematics)
  USE **Approximate computation**
Estonia **947.98**
Estrangement (Social psychology)
  USE **Alienation (Social psychology)**
Etchers (May subdiv. geog.) **769.92;**
      920
  BT **Artists**
      Engravers
Etching **767**
  UF Etchings
  BT **Art**
      Pictures

  NT **Pyrography**
  RT **Engraving**
Etchings
  USE **Etching**
Eternal life
  USE **Eternity**
      Future life
      Immortality
Eternal punishment
  USE **Hell**
Eternity **115**
    Use for materials on the philosophical con-
    cept of eternity. Materials on the character
    and form of a future life are entered under
    Future life. Materials on the question of the
    endless existence of the soul are entered under
    Immortality.
  UF Eternal life
  RT **Future life**
Ethical aspects
  USE subjects with the subdivision
      Ethical aspects, e.g. **Birth**
      control—Ethical aspects [to
      be added as needed]
Ethical development
  USE **Moral development**
Ethical education
  USE **Moral education**
Ethics (May subdiv. geog.) **170**
  UF Moral philosophy
      Morality
      Morals
  SA types of ethics, e.g. **Business**
      ethics; ethics of particular re-
      ligions, e.g. **Christian ethics**;
      names of individual persons,
      classes of persons, types of
      professions, and types of pro-
      fessional personnel with the
      subdivision *Ethics,* e.g. **Li-**
      brarians—Ethics; **Shake-**
      speare, William, 1564-1616—
      Ethics; etc., and subjects with
      the subdivision *Ethical as-*
      pects, e.g. **Birth control—**
      Ethical aspects [to be added
      as needed]
  BT **Philosophy**
  NT **Abortion—Ethical aspects**
      Asceticism
      Bioethics
      Birth control—Ethical aspects
      Business ethics

Ethics—*Continued*
>> Character
>> Charity
>> Christian ethics
>> Cloning—Ethical aspects
>> Conduct of life
>> Conscience
>> Cruelty
>> Duty
>> Environmental ethics
>> Feminist ethics
>> Golden rule
>> Good and evil
>> Guilt
>> Honesty
>> Human cloning—Ethical aspects
>> Jewish ethics
>> Justice
>> Legal ethics
>> Loyalty
>> Medical ethics
>> Moral education
>> Motion pictures—Ethical aspects
>> Natural law
>> Perseverance
>> Political ethics
>> Professional ethics
>> Promises
>> Responsibility
>> Secularism
>> Sexual ethics
>> Sin
>> Social ethics
>> Stoics
>> Utilitarianism
>> Values
>> Vice
>> Virtue
>> Vocation
>> Work ethic
>> World War, 1939-1945—Ethical aspects
> RT   Human behavior

Ethics—United States   170.973
> UF   American ethics

Ethiopia   963
> May be subdivided like United States except for History.

Ethiopian-Italian War, 1935-1936
> USE   **Italo-Ethiopian War, 1935-1936**

Ethnic art (May subdiv. geog.)   709
> BT   **Art**
>> **Ethnic groups**

Ethnic cleansing
> USE   **Genocide**

Ethnic conflict
> USE   **Ethnic relations**

Ethnic diversity
> USE   **Pluralism (Social sciences)**

Ethnic groups (May subdiv. geog.)
> **305.8**
>
> Use for materials on groups of people bound together by common ancestry and culture. Materials on indigenous minorities are entered under **Indigenous peoples**. Materials on the subjective sense of belonging to a particular ethnic group are entered under **Ethnicity**. Materials on several ethnic groups in a particular region or country are entered under **Ethnology** subdivided geographically. Materials on individual ethnic groups are entered under the name of the group, e.g. **Mexican Americans**.
>
> UF   People
> SA   names of individual ethnic groups [to be added as needed]
> BT   **Ethnology**
> NT   **Asian Americans**
>> **Cajuns**
>> **Chinese Americans**
>> **Creoles**
>> **Ethnic art**
>> **Hispanic Americans**
>> **Mexican Americans**
>> **Racially mixed people**
> RT   **Ethnic relations**
>> **Ethnicity**

Ethnic identity
> USE   **Ethnicity**
>> and ethnic groups with the subdivision *Ethnic identity*, e.g. **Mexican Americans—Ethnic identity** [to be added as needed]

Ethnic psychology
> USE   **Ethnopsychology**

Ethnic relations   305.8
> UF   Ethnic conflict
>> Relations among ethnic groups
> SA   names of regions, countries, cities, etc., with the subdivision *Ethnic relations*; e.g. **United States—Ethnic relations** [to be added as needed]

Ethnic relations—*Continued*
- BT **Acculturation**
  Ethnology
  Sociology
- NT **Culture conflict**
  Discrimination
- RT **Ethnic groups**
  Minorities
  Multiculturalism
  Pluralism (Social sciences)
  Race relations

Ethnic relations—Political aspects
  305.8

Ethnic relations—Religious aspects (May subdiv. geog.) 305.8

Ethnicity (May subdiv. geog.) 305.8

  Use for materials on the subjective sense of belonging to a particular ethnic group. Materials on groups of people bound together by a common ancestry or culture are entered under **Ethnic groups**. Materials on several ethnic groups in a particular region or country are entered under **Ethnology**.

- UF Ethnic identity
- SA ethnic groups with the subdivision *Ethnic identity*, e.g. **Mexican Americans—Ethnic identity**; and racial groups with the subdivision *Race identity*, e.g. **African Americans—Race identity** [to be added as needed]
- BT **Identity (Psychology)**
- RT **Ethnic groups**
  Multiculturalism
  Pluralism (Social sciences)

Ethnobiology (May subdiv. geog.)
  306.4; 578.6
- UF Folk biology
- SA names of ethnic groups with the subdivision *Ethnobiology*, e.g. **Native Americans—Ethnobiology** [to be added as needed]
- BT **Biology**
  Ethnology
- NT **Ethnobotany**
  Ethnozoology
  Native Americans—Ethnobiology

Ethnobotany (May subdiv. geog.) 581.6

- SA names of ethnic groups with the subdivision *Ethnobotany*, e.g. **Native Americans—Ethnobotany** [to be added as needed]
- BT **Ethnobiology**
  Ethnology
  Plants—Folklore
- NT **Native Americans—Ethnobotany**

Ethnocentrism (May subdiv. geog.)
  305.8
- BT **Ethnopsychology**
  Nationalism
  Prejudices
  Race

Ethnocide
- USE **Genocide**

Ethnography
- USE **Ethnology**

Ethnology (May subdiv. geog.) 305.8;
  306; 599.97

  Use for materials on the disciplines of ethnology and cultural anthropology, and, with appropriate geographic subdivisions, for materials on the origin, distribution, and characteristics of the elements of the population of a particular region or country. General materials on groups of people who are bound together by common ties of ancestry and culture are entered under **Ethnic groups**. Materials on individual racial or ethnic groups are entered under the name of the group, e.g. **Aboriginal Australians**.

- UF Cultural anthropology
  Ethnography
  Races of people
  Social anthropology
- SA names of countries with the subdivision *Social life and customs*, e.g. **United States—Social life and customs**; and names of individual ethnic groups [to be added as needed]
- BT **Human beings**
- NT **Acculturation**
  Anthropometry
  Cannibalism
  Costume
  Ethnic groups
  Ethnic relations
  Ethnobiology
  Ethnobotany
  Ethnopsychology

Ethnology—*Continued*
    Ethnozoology
    Folklore
    Human geography
    Indigenous peoples
    Kinship
    Language and languages
    Manners and customs
    Mountain people
    Physical anthropology
    Primitive societies
    Race
    Race relations
    Semitic peoples
    Totems and totemism
  RT Anthropology
    Archeology
    Civilization

Ethnology—United States   305.813
  UF United States—Ethnology
    United States—Peoples
  SA names of individual ethnic
      groups [to be added as need-
      ed]

Ethnopsychology (May subdiv. geog.)
  155.8
  UF Cross-cultural psychology
    Ethnic psychology
    Folk psychology
    National psychology
    Race psychology
  SA names of racial or ethnic groups
      with the subdivision *Psycholo-*
      gy [to be added as needed]
  BT **Anthropology**
    Ethnology
    Psychology
    Sociology
  NT **Culture conflict**
    Ethnocentrism
    Native Americans—Psychology
  RT **National characteristics**
    Social psychology

Ethnozoology (May subdiv. geog.)   **591.6**
  UF Folk zoology
  SA names of ethnic groups with the
      subdivision *Ethnozoology*, e.g.
      Native Americans—
      Ethnozoology [to be added as
      needed]
  BT **Animals—Folklore**
    Ethnobiology

    Ethnology
  NT **Native Americans—**
      Ethnozoology
Ethyl alcohol fuel
  USE **Alcohol fuels**
Etiquette (May subdiv. geog.)   **395**
  UF Ceremonies
    Manners
    Politeness
    Salutations
  SA types of etiquette, e.g. **Table et-**
      iquette; and names of coun-
      tries with the subdivision *So-*
      cial life and customs, e.g.
      United States—Social life
      and customs [to be added as
      needed]
  BT **Human behavior**
  NT **Business etiquette**
    Courtesy
    Dating (Social customs)
    Entertaining
    Excuses
    Letter writing
    Table etiquette
  RT **Manners and customs**
Etiquette for children and teenagers
  177.1; 395.1
  UF Behavior of children
    Behavior of teenagers
    Child behavior
    Children—Etiquette
    Etiquette for teenagers
    Teenage behavior
    Teenagers—Etiquette
  BT **Children—Conduct of life**
    Teenagers—Conduct of life
Etiquette for teenagers
  USE **Etiquette for children and**
      teenagers
Etruscan art   **709.01**
  BT **Art**
Etymology
  USE **Language and languages—Ety-**
      mology
      and names of languages with
      the subdivision *Etymology,*
      e.g. **English language—Ety-**
      mology [to be added as need-
      ed]

Eucharist   234; 264

May be subdivided by Christian sect or denomination.

UF   Communion

Holy communion

Lord's Supper

BT   **Liturgies**

Sacraments

RT   **Mass (Liturgy)**

Eugenics (May subdiv. geog.)   **363.9**

BT   **Genetics**

Population

RT   **Heredity**

Euro   332.4

BT   **Capital market**

Money

Europe   940

UF   Europe, Western

Western Europe

Europe, Central

USE   **Central Europe**

Europe, Eastern

USE   **Eastern Europe**

Europe—History   940

NT   **Holy Roman Empire**

Europe—History—0-476   936; 937

Europe—History—476-1492   940.1;
940.2

NT   **Hundred Years' War, 1339-**
1453

RT   **Middle Ages**

Europe—History—1492-1789   940.2

NT   **Seven Years' War, 1756-1763**

Thirty Years' War, 1618-1648

Europe—History—18th century   940.2

Europe—History—1789-1815   940.2

NT   **Napoleonic Wars, 1800-1815**

Europe—History—1789-1900   940.2

UF   Europe—History—19th century

Europe—History—19th century

USE   **Europe—History—1789-1900**

Europe—History—1815-1848   940.2

Europe—History—1848-1871   940.2

Europe—History—1871-1918   940.2

NT   **World War, 1914-1918**

Europe—History—20th century   940.5

Europe—History—1918-1945   940.5

NT   **Russo-Finnish War, 1939-1940**

World War, 1939-1945

Europe—History—1945-   940.55

Europe—History—21st century   940.56

Europe—Politics and government   940

May be subdivided by period using the
same subdivisions as are listed under **Europe—History**.

NT   **European federation**

Europe, Western

USE   **Europe**

European Common Market

USE   **European Union**

European Community

USE   **European Union**

European Economic Community

USE   **European Union**

European federation   321; 940

Use for general materials on the political or
economic union of European countries. Materials on the corporate body formerly known as
the European Economic Community and the
European Community, which became known
as the European Union upon ratification of the
Treaty of European Union on October 29,
1993, are entered under **European Union**.

UF   Federation of Europe

BT   **Europe—Politics and govern-**
ment

Federal government

International organization

NT   **European Union**

European Union   341.242; 382

Use for materials on the corporate body formerly known as the European Economic
Community and the European Community,
which became known as the European Union
upon ratification of the Treaty on European
Union on October 29, 1993. General materials
on the political or economic union of European countries are entered under **European federation**.

UF   Common market

EEC

European Common Market

European Community

European Economic Community

BT   **European federation**

Euthanasia (May subdiv. geog.)   **179.7**

UF   Mercy killing

BT   **Homicide**

Medical ethics

RT   **Right to die**

Evacuation and relocation of Japanese
Americans, 1942-1945

USE   **Japanese Americans—Evacua-**
tion and relocation, 1942-
1945

Evacuation of civilians (May subdiv.
geog.)   **363.3**

Evacuation of civilians—*Continued*
- UF Civilian evacuation
- SA names of wars with the subdivision *Evacuation of civilians*, e.g. **World War, 1939-1945—Evacuation of civilians** [to be added as needed]
- BT **Civil defense**
  Disaster relief

Evaluation
- USE types of evaluation, e.g. **Educational evaluation**; and names of corporate bodies and types of institutions, products, services, equipment, activities, projects, and programs with the subdivision *Evaluation*, e.g. **Public health—Evaluation**; **Science—Study and teaching—Evaluation**; etc. [to be added as needed]

Evaluation of books
- USE **Book reviewing**

Evaluation of literature
- USE **Best books**
  Books and reading
  Criticism
  Literature—History and criticism

Evaluation research in education
- USE **Educational evaluation**

Evangelical Protestantism
- USE **Evangelicalism**

Evangelicalism (May subdiv. geog.) **280**
- UF Evangelical Protestantism
- BT **Protestantism**

Evangelism
- USE **Evangelistic work**

Evangelistic healing
- USE **Spiritual healing**

Evangelistic work (May subdiv. geog.) **253; 269**
- UF Evangelism
  Revival (Religion)
- BT **Church work**
- NT **Conversion**
  Revivals
- RT **Christian missions**

Evening and continuation schools (May subdiv. geog.) **374**
- UF Continuation schools
  Evening schools
  Night schools
- BT **Compulsory education**
  Continuing education
  Education
  Public schools
  Schools
  Secondary education
  Technical education
- RT **Adult education**

Evening schools
- USE **Evening and continuation schools**

Everest, Mount (China and Nepal) 954.96
- UF Mount Everest (China and Nepal)
- BT **Mountains**

Evergreens (May subdiv. geog.) **582.1; 635.9**
- BT **Landscape gardening**
  Shrubs
  Trees

Evidences of the Bible
- USE **Bible—Evidences, authority, etc.**

Evil
- USE **Good and evil**

Evil spirits
- USE **Demonology**

Evolution 576.8
- UF Darwinism
  Development
  Mutation (Biology)
  Origin of species
- SA types of animals, plants, crops, chemicals, and organs of the body with the subdivision *Evolution* [to be added as needed]
- BT **Philosophy**
- NT **Life—Origin**
- RT **Biology**
  Creation
  Creationism
  Human origins
  Natural selection
  Religion and science
  Variation (Biology)

Evolution and Christianity
- USE **Creationism**

Evolution—Study and teaching (May subdiv. geog.) **576.807**
  UF Creation—Study and teaching
  RT **Creationism**
Ex libris
  USE **Bookplates**
Ex-nuns (May subdiv. geog.) **305.48**
  UF Catholic ex-nuns
      Former nuns
  BT **Nuns**
Ex-priests (May subdiv. geog.) **305.33; 920**
  UF Catholic ex-priests
      Former priests
  BT **Catholic Church—Clergy**
      Priests
Examinations (May subdiv. geog.) **371.26**
  Use for general materials on examinations. Materials discussing the requirements for examinations in particular branches of study, or compilations of questions and answers for such examinations, are entered under the subject with the subdivision *Examinations*.
  UF Tests
  SA branches of study with the subdivision *Examinations*, e.g. **English language—Examinations**; and names of individual examinations [to be added as needed]
  BT **Questions and answers**
      Teaching
  NT **Civil service—Examinations**
      Colleges and universities—Entrance examinations
      Colleges and universities—Entrance requirements
      English language—Examinations
      Graduate Record Examination
      Music—Examinations
      Scholastic Assessment Test
      United States. Army—Examinations
  RT **Educational tests and measurements**
Examinations—Design and construction 371.26
Examinations—Study guides 371.26
  Use for materials that provide directions on how to prepare for and pass examinations, usually with practice questions and answers included.

  UF Preparation guides for examinations
      Study guides for examinations
      Test preparation guides
  SA subjects, educational levels, and names of educational institutions with the subdivisions *Examinations—Study guides*, e.g. **English language—Examinations—Study guides**; and named examinations with the subdivision *Study guides*, e.g. **Graduate Record Examination—Study guides** [to be added as needed]
  BT **Study skills**
Excavation (May subdiv. geog.) **624.1**
  BT **Civil engineering**
      Tunnels
Excavations (Archeology) (May subdiv. geog.) **930.1**
  UF Earthworks (Archeology)
      Ruins
  BT **Archeology**
  RT **Extinct cities**
      Mounds and mound builders
Excavations (Archeology)—United States 973
Exceptional children (May subdiv. geog.) **155.45**
  UF Abnormal children
  BT **Children**
      Elementary education
  NT **Brain damaged children**
      Emotionally disturbed children
      Gifted children
      Handicapped children
      Mainstreaming in education
      Slow learning children
      Wild children
Excess government property
  USE **Surplus government property**
Exchange 332.4; 332.64
  BT **Commerce**
  NT **Foreign exchange**
      Money
  RT **Supply and demand**
Exchange, Barter
  USE **Barter**
Exchange of persons programs (May subdiv. geog.) **327.1; 370.116**

Exchange of persons programs—*Continued*

    UF   Cultural exchange programs

           Interchange of visitors

           Specialists exchange programs

           Visitors' exchange programs

    SA   types of exchange programs for particular classes of persons, e.g. **Teacher exchange** [to be added as needed]

    BT   **Cultural relations**

           International cooperation

    NT   **Student exchange programs**

           Teacher exchange programs

Exchange of prisoners of war

    USE   **Prisoners of war**

Exchange of students

    USE   **Student exchange programs**

Exchange of teachers

    USE   **Teacher exchange programs**

Exchange programs, Student

    USE   **Student exchange programs**

Exchange rates

    USE   **Foreign exchange**

Excuses   **395**

    BT   **Etiquette**

           Manners and customs

Executions and executioners (May subdiv. geog.)   **364.66**

    BT   **Criminal law**

           Criminal procedure

    RT   **Capital punishment**

Executive ability   **658.4**

    UF   Administrative ability

    BT   **Ability**

    NT   **Leadership**

           Planning

Executive agencies

    USE   **Administrative agencies**

Executive departments (May subdiv. geog.)   **351**

Use for materials on major administrative divisions of the executive branch of government, usually headed by an officer of cabinet rank.

    UF   Government departments

           Government ministries

           State ministries

    SA   names of executive departments [to be added as needed]

    BT   **Administrative agencies**

Executive departments—Ohio   **352.2**

    UF   Ohio—Executive departments

    SA   names of executive departments [to be added as needed]

Executive departments—Reorganization

    USE   **Administrative agencies—Reorganization**

Executive departments—United States   **352.2**

    UF   United States—Executive departments

    SA   names of executive departments [to be added as needed]

    NT   **Presidents—United States—Staff**

Executive investigations

    USE   **Governmental investigations**

Executive power (May subdiv. geog.)   **351**

Use for materials on the powers of the executive or administrative branch of government.

    UF   Presidents—Powers

    BT   **Constitutional law**

           Political science

    NT   **Amnesty**

           Clemency

           Heads of state

           Monarchy

           Pardon

           Prime ministers

           Separation of powers

           War and emergency powers

    RT   **Presidents**

Executive power—United States   **352.230973**

    UF   Presidents—United States—Power

           United States—Executive power

Executive reorganization

    USE   **Administrative agencies—Reorganization**

Executors and administrators (May subdiv. geog.)   **346.05**

    UF   Administrators and executors

    BT   **Inheritance and succession**

    RT   **Trusts and trustees**

           Wills

Exegesis, Biblical

    USE   **Bible—Criticism**

Exemption from taxation

    USE   **Tax exemption**

Exercise (May subdiv. geog.)   **613.7**

Exercise—*Continued*

SA types of exercises and physical activities [to be added as needed]

BT **Health**
Hygiene

NT **Abdominal exercises**
Aerobics
Aquatic exercises
Bodybuilding
Cycling
Gymnastics
Hatha yoga
Physical fitness
Pilates method
Rowing
Stretching exercises
Tai chi
Weight lifting

RT **Physical education**
Weight loss

Exercise addiction 616.85

UF Addiction to exercise
Compulsive exercising

BT **Compulsive behavior**

Exercises, problems, etc.

USE subjects with the subdivision *Problems, exercises, etc.,* for compilations of practice problems or exercises for use in the study of a topic, e.g. **Chemistry—Problems, exercises, etc.** [to be added as needed]

Exhaustion

USE **Fatigue**

Exhibitions (May subdiv. geog.)

UF Exhibits
Expositions
International exhibitions
World's fairs

SA types of exhibitions, e.g. **Flower shows**; subjects and names of individual persons with the subdivision *Exhibitions*, e.g. **Printing—Exhibitions**; and names of particular exhibitions, e.g. **Expo 92 (Seville, Spain)** [to be added as needed]

NT **Art—Exhibitions**
Books—Exhibitions
Craft shows
Expo 92 (Seville, Spain)
Fashion shows
Flower shows
Printing—Exhibitions
Science—Exhibitions
Trade shows

RT **Fairs**

Exhibits

USE **Exhibitions**

Exiles (May subdiv. geog.) **305.9**

Use for materials on persons banished from their native countries or homes as a punitive measure. This heading may be subdivided geographically to indicate the country of origin or the destination of the exiles.

BT **Persons**
Political refugees

Existentialism 142

BT **Metaphysics**
Modern philosophy
Phenomenology

Exorcism 133.4; 203

BT **Supernatural**

RT **Demoniac possession**
Demonology

Expansion (United States politics)

USE **United States—Territorial expansion**

Expectancy of life

USE **Life expectancy**

Expectation of life

USE **Life expectancy**

Expeditions, Scientific

USE **Scientific expeditions**

Experience

USE **Empiricism**

Experimental farms

USE **Agricultural experiment stations**

Experimental films (May subdiv. geog.) **791.43**

Use for individual works, collections, or materials about experimental films.

UF Avant-garde films
Personal films
Underground films

BT **Motion pictures**

Experimental medicine (May subdiv. geog.) **619**

BT **Medicine—Research**

Experimental methods in education
USE **Education—Experimental methods**

Experimental schools (May subdiv. geog.) **371.04**

Use for materials on schools in which new teaching methods, organizations of subject matter, educational theories, personnel practices, etc., are tested.

UF Alternative schools
Free schools
Nonformal schools
Project schools
Schools, Nonformal
BT **Education—Experimental methods**
Schools
RT **Alternative education**
Open plan schools

Experimental theater (May subdiv. geog.) **792**

UF Avant-garde theater
BT **Theater**

Experimental universities
USE **Free universities**

Experimentation on animals
USE **Animal experimentation**

Experimentation on humans, Medical
USE **Human experimentation in medicine**

Experiments
USE scientific subjects with the subdivision *Experiments,* e.g.
Chemistry—Experiments [to be added as needed]

Experiments, Scientific
USE **Science—Experiments**

Expert systems (Computer science) 006.3

UF Knowledge-based systems (Computer science)
BT **Artificial intelligence**
Data processing
Information systems

Exploration 910.9

Use for materials on voyages and explorations that have advanced geographic knowledge.

UF Discoveries and exploration
Discoveries in geography
Explorations
Maritime discoveries

SA names of celestial bodies, continents, regions, countries, states, etc., with the subdivision *Exploration* for materials on the exploration of those areas when they were unsettled or sparsely settled and largely unknown to the world at large, e.g. **America—Exploration**; or with the subdivision *Description and travel* for materials on later and recent travels in those areas, e.g. **United States—Description and travel**; and names of countries, states, etc., with the subdivision *Exploring expeditions* for materials on explorations sponsored by those governments, e.g. **United States—Exploring expeditions** [to be added as needed]

BT **Adventure and adventurers**
Geography
History
NT **America—Exploration**
Antarctica—Exploration
Arctic regions—Exploration
Northeast Passage
Outer space—Exploration
Underwater exploration
United States—Exploration
RT **Explorers**
Scientific expeditions
Voyages and travels

Exploration of space
USE **Outer space—Exploration**

Exploration—United States
USE **United States—Exploration**

Explorations
USE **Exploration**

Exploratory behavior
USE **Curiosity**

Explorer (Artificial satellite) 629.46

BT **Artificial satellites**

Explorers (May subdiv. geog.) **910.92; 920**

UF Discoverers
Navigators
Voyagers

Explorers—*Continued*
   SA   names of places explored with
         the subdivision *Exploration*,
         e.g. **America—Exploration**;
         names of countries with the
         subdivisions *Description* and
         Exploring expeditions; and
         names of individual explorers
         [to be added as needed]
   BT   **Adventure and adventurers**
         Heroes and heroines
   NT   **United States—Exploring expe-**
         ditions
   RT   **Exploration**
         Travelers
         Voyages and travels
Exploring expeditions
   USE   names of countries sponsoring
          exploring expeditions with the
          subdivision *Exploring expedi-*
          tions, e.g. **United States—Ex-**
          ploring expeditions; etc.; and
          names of expeditions, e.g.
          Lewis and Clark Expedition
          (1804-1806) [to be added as
          needed]
Explosions (May subdiv. geog.)   **904**
   BT   **Accidents**
Explosives (May subdiv. geog.)   **363.17;**
         363.33; 623.4; 662
   SA   types of explosives and explo-
         sive devices [to be added as
         needed]
   BT   **Chemistry**
   NT   **Ammunition**
         Bombs
         Dynamite
         Gunpowder
         Land mines
         Torpedoes
Expo 92 (Seville, Spain)   **909.82**
   UF   Seville (Spain). World's Fair,
         1992
         World's Fair (1992: Seville,
         Spain)
   BT   **Exhibitions**
         Fairs
Exports (May subdiv. geog.)   **382**
   BT   **International trade**
Exposed children
   USE   **Abandoned children**

Expositions
   USE   **Exhibitions**
Express highways (May subdiv. geog.)
         388.1; 625.7
   UF   Freeways
         Interstate highways
         Limited access highways
         Motorways
         Parkways
         Superhighways
         Toll roads
         Turnpikes (Modern)
   BT   **Roads**
         Traffic engineering
Express service (May subdiv. geog.)
         388
   BT   **Railroads**
         Transportation
   NT   **Pony express**
Expressionism (Art) (May subdiv. geog.)
         709.04; 759.06
   BT   **Art**
Expropriation
   USE   **Eminent domain**
Expulsion
   USE   **Penal colonies**
Extended care facilities
   USE   **Long-term care facilities**
Extermination of pests
   USE   **Pest control**
Extinct animals (May subdiv. geog.)
         560
   SA   types of extinct animals [to be
         added as needed]
   BT   **Animals**
   NT   **Mastodon**
   RT   **Fossils**
         Prehistoric animals
         Rare animals
Extinct cities (May subdiv. geog.)   **930**
   UF   Abandoned towns
         Buried cities
         Ruins
         Sunken cities
   SA   names of extinct cities and
         towns, e.g. **Delphi (Extinct**
         city) [to be added as needed]
   BT   **Archeology**
         Cities and towns
   NT   **Carthage (Extinct city)**
         Ghost towns

Extinct cities—*Continued*
    RT   **Excavations (Archeology)**
Extinct cities—Greece   938
    NT   **Delphi (Extinct city)**
           Mycenae (Extinct city)
Extinct cities—Italy   937
    NT   **Herculaneum (Extinct city)**
           Pompeii (Extinct city)
Extinct cities—Turkey   939
    NT   **Troy (Extinct city)**
Extinct plants
    USE   **Fossil plants**
Extortion (May subdiv. geog.)   **364.16**
    UF   Blackmail
    BT   **Offenses against property**
           Racketeering
Extracurricular activities
    USE   **Student activities**
Extragalactic nebulae
    USE   **Galaxies**
Extramarital relationships
    USE   **Adultery**
Extrasensory perception   133.8
    UF   ESP
    BT   **Parapsychology**
    NT   **Clairvoyance**
           Telepathy
Extrasolar planetary systems
    USE   **Extrasolar planets**
Extrasolar planets   523.2
    UF   Extrasolar planetary systems
    BT   **Planets**
Extraterrestrial abduction
    USE   **Alien abduction**
Extraterrestrial bases   629.44
    Use for materials on bases established on natural extraterrestrial bodies for specific functions other than colonization. Materials on communities established in space or on natural extraterrestrial bodies are entered under **Space colonies**. Materials on manned installations orbiting in space for specific functions, such as servicing space ships, are entered under **Space stations**.
    BT   **Civil engineering**
    RT   **Space colonies**
Extraterrestrial beings   576.8
    UF   Aliens from outer space
           Interplanetary visitors
    BT   **Life on other planets**
    RT   **Human-alien encounters**
Extraterrestrial communication
    USE   **Interstellar communication**

Extraterrestrial encounters with humans
    USE   **Human-alien encounters**
Extraterrestrial environment
    USE   **Space environment**
Extraterrestrial life
    USE   **Life on other planets**
Extravehicular activity (Space flight)
**   629.45**
    UF   Space vehicles—Extravehicular
           activity
           Space walk
           Walking in space
    BT   **Space flight**
Extreme sports (May subdiv. geog.)
**   796.04**
    BT   **Sports**
Extreme unction
    USE   **Anointing of the sick**
Extremism (Political science)
    USE   **Radicalism**
Eye   611; 612.8
    BT   **Face**
           Head
    RT   **Optometry**
           Vision
Eyeglasses   617.7; 681
    UF   Glasses
           Spectacles
    SA   types of eyeglasses, e.g. **Contact**
           lenses [to be added as need-
           ed]
    NT   **Contact lenses**
Fables   398.24; 808.8
    Use for individual works, collections, or materials about short tales intended to teach moral lessons, often with animals or inanimate objects speaking and acting like human beings, and usually with the lesson stated briefly at the end.
    UF   Cautionary tales and verses
           Moral and philosophic stories
           Tales
    SA   fables of particular countries,
           e.g. **American fables** [to be
           added as needed]
    BT   **Fiction**
           Literature
    NT   **American fables**
    RT   **Allegories**
           Animals—Fiction
           Didactic fiction
           Didactic poetry
           Folklore

Fables—*Continued*
>> Legends
>> Parables
>> Romances

Fabric design
> USE **Textile design**

Fabrics (May subdiv. geog.)   677
> UF   Cloth
>> Dry goods
>> Textiles
> SA   types of fabrics [to be added as needed]
> BT   **Decorative arts**
> NT   **Cotton**
>> **Linen**
>> **Silk**
>> **Synthetic fabrics**
>> **Wool**
> RT   **Weaving**

Face   611; 612
> BT   **Head**
> NT   **Eye**
>> **Mouth**
>> **Nose**
> RT   **Physiognomy**

Facebook (Web site)   004.69; 384.3
> BT   **Social networking**
>> **Web sites**

Facetiae
> USE   **Anecdotes**
>> **Wit and humor**

Facsimile transmission
> USE   **Fax transmission**

Facsimiles
> USE   types of printed or written materials, documents, etc., with the subdivision *Facsimiles,* e.g. **Autographs—Facsimiles** [to be added as needed]

Factories (May subdiv. geog.)   338.6; 670; 725
> UF   Industrial plants
>> Mill and factory buildings
>> Plants, Industrial
> SA   types of factories [to be added as needed]
> BT   **Industrial buildings**
> NT   **Breweries**
>> **Plant shutdowns**
> RT   **Factory management**
>> **Mills**

Factories—Management
> USE   **Factory management**

Factory and trade waste
> USE   **Industrial waste**

Factory management (May subdiv. geog.)   658.5

> Use for materials on the technical aspects of manufacturing processes. Materials on general principles of management of industries are entered under **Management**.

> UF   Factories—Management
>> Production engineering
>> Shop management
> BT   **Management**
> NT   **Job analysis**
>> **Motion study**
>> **Office management**
>> **Participative management**
>> **Supervisors**
>> **Time study**
> RT   **Factories**
>> **Personnel management**

Factory waste
> USE   **Industrial waste**

Factory workers
> USE   **Labor**
>> **Working class**

Facts, Miscellaneous
> USE   **Books of lists**
>> **Curiosities and wonders**

Faculty
> USE   types of educational institutions and names of individual educational institutions with the subdivision *Faculty,* e.g. **Colleges and universities—Faculty** [to be added as needed]

Faculty (Education)
> USE   **Colleges and universities—Faculty**
>> **Educators**
>> **Teachers**

Fads (May subdiv. geog.)   306
> UF   Crazes
> BT   **Manners and customs**
>> **Popular culture**

Faience
> USE   **Pottery**

Failure in business
> USE   **Bankruptcy**
>> **Business failures**

Failure of banks
USE **Bank failures**
Failure to thrive syndrome
USE **Growth disorders**
Failures, Structural
USE **Structural failures**
Fair employment practice
USE **Discrimination in employment**
Fair housing
USE **Discrimination in housing**
Fair trade
USE **Unfair competition**
Fair trade (Tariff)
USE **Free trade**
Fair trial (May subdiv. geog.) **345**

Use for materials on legal hearings before an impartial and disinterested tribunal. Materials on the regular administration of the law, according to which citizens may not be denied their legal rights and all laws must conform to fundamental and accepted legal principles, are entered under **Due process of law**.

UF Right to a fair trial
BT **Civil rights**
      Due process of law
NT **Freedom of the press and fair trial**
Fair trial and free press
USE **Freedom of the press and fair trial**
Fair use (Copyright) (May subdiv. geog.)
    346.04
BT **Copyright**
Fairies **398.21**
BT **Folklore**
Fairness **179**
UF Impartiality
BT **Conduct of life**
RT **Justice**
Fairness doctrine (Broadcasting) **343.09**

Use for materials on the requirement that, if one side of a controversial issue of public importance is aired, the same opportunity must be given for the presentation of contrasting views. Materials on the requirement that all qualified candidates for public office be granted equal broadcast time if any one such candidate is permitted to broadcast are entered under **Equal time rule (Broadcasting)**.

UF Doctrine of fairness (Broadcasting)
BT **Broadcasting**
      Television and politics
RT **Equal time rule (Broadcasting)**

Fairs (May subdiv. geog.) **381; 394; 607; 907.4**

Use for general materials on public showings that suggest a variety of kinds of display and entertainment, usually in an outdoor setting, sometimes for the promotion of sales and sometimes in competition for prizes of excellence.

UF Bazaars
     World's fairs
SA names of fairs, e.g. **Expo 92 (Seville, Spain)** [to be added as needed]
NT **Expo 92 (Seville, Spain)**
     Trade shows
RT **Carnivals**
     Exhibitions
     Markets
Fairy tales (May subdiv. geog.) **398.2; 808.83**

Use for individual works, collections, or materials about short, simple narratives, often of folk origin and usually intended for children, involving fantastic forces and magical beings such as dragons, elves, fairies, goblins, witches, and wizards.

UF Stories
     Tales
BT **Children's literature**
     Fiction
NT **Fractured fairy tales**
RT **Folklore**
Fairy tales—Parodies, imitations, etc.
USE **Fractured fairy tales**
Faith **121; 201; 234**

Use for materials on religious belief and doubt. Materials on belief and doubt from the philosophical standpoint are entered under **Belief and doubt**.

UF Religious belief
BT **Religion**
     Salvation
     Spiritual life
     Theology
     Virtue
RT **Belief and doubt**
Faith cure
USE **Spiritual healing**
Faith healing
USE **Spiritual healing**
Faith—Psychology **200.1; 248; 253.5**
BT **Psychology of religion**
Faithfulness
USE **Loyalty**
Falconry **799.2**

Falconry—*Continued*
UF Hawking
BT **Game and game birds**
Hunting
Fall
USE **Autumn**
Fallacies
USE **Errors**
Logic
Falling stars
USE **Meteors**
Fallout, Radioactive
USE **Radioactive fallout**
Fallout shelters
USE **Air raid shelters**
False advertising
USE **Deceptive advertising**
False memories
USE **False memory syndrome**
False memory syndrome   616.85
UF False memories
BT **Memory**
RT **Recovered memory**
Falsehood
USE **Truthfulness and falsehood**
Fame   306.4
UF Celebrity
Renown
RT **Celebrities**
Family (May subdiv. geog.)   **306.85**
Use for materials stressing the sociological
concept and structure of the family. Materials
stressing the everyday life, interaction, and re-
lationships of family members are entered un-
der **Family life**.
SA types of family members, e.g.
Children; **Fathers**; **Mothers**;
etc., types of family relation-
ships, e.g. **Mother-son rela-
tionship**; and names of indi-
vidual persons with the subdi-
vision *Family* [to be added as
needed]
BT **Interpersonal relations**
Sociology
NT **Aunts**
Birth order
Children
Clans
Cousins
Daughters
Divorce
Dual-career families

Family life
Family size
Farm family
Fathers
**Grandparent-grandchild rela-
tionship**
Grandparents
Husbands
Kinship
Marriage
Married people
Mothers
Parent-child relationship
Parenthood
Parents
Siblings
Single-parent families
Sons
Stepfamilies
Tribes
Uncles
Wives
Work and family
RT **Domestic relations**
Family reunions
Home
Family and work
USE **Work and family**
Family—Biblical teaching   248.4; 261.8
Family budget
USE **Household budgets**
Family caregivers
USE **Caregivers**
Family counseling
USE **Family therapy**
Family devotions
USE **Devotional exercises**
Family—Religious life
Family farms (May subdiv. geog.)
338.1; 630
BT **Farms**
RT **Farm family**
Farm life
Family finance
USE **Personal finance**
Family group therapy
USE **Family therapy**
Family histories
USE **Genealogy**
Family leave
USE **Parental leave**

Family life (May subdiv. geog.) **306.85;**
392.3; 646.7

Use for materials stressing the everyday life, interaction, and relationships of family members. Materials on the sociological concept and structure of the family are entered under **Family**.

UF Family relations
    Home life
BT **Family**
NT **Family traditions**

Family life education (May subdiv. geog.)
306.85; 362.82; 372.82

BT **Education**
NT **Home economics**
    Marriage counseling
    Sex education
RT **Domestic relations**

Family medicine (May subdiv. geog.)
610

UF Family practice (Medicine)
    General practice (Medicine)
BT **Medicine**

Family names
USE **Personal names**
Family planning
USE **Birth control**
Family practice (Medicine)
USE **Family medicine**
Family prayers
USE **Devotional exercises**
    Family—Religious life
Family psychotherapy
USE **Family therapy**
Family relations
USE **Domestic relations**
    Family life

Family—Religious life **204; 248.4; 249**

UF Family devotions
    Family prayers
    Family worship
BT **Religious life**

Family reunions **394.2**

UF Reunions, Family
RT **Family**

Family size (May subdiv. geog.) **304.6**

BT **Family**
NT **Childlessness**
    Only child
RT **Birth control**

Family social work
USE **Social case work**

Family therapy **616.89**

UF Family counseling
    Family group therapy
    Family psychotherapy
    Problem families—Counseling of
BT **Counseling**
    Psychotherapy

Family traditions (May subdiv. geog.)
306.85; 392.3

BT **Family life**
    Manners and customs

Family trees
USE **Genealogy**

Family—United States **306.850973**

Family violence
USE **Domestic violence**
Family worship
USE **Family—Religious life**

Famines (May subdiv. geog.) **904**

BT **Food supply**
    Starvation

Famines—United States **363.80973; 973**

Famous people
USE **Celebrities**
Fan fic
USE **Fan fiction**

Fan fiction **808.83**

Use for collections of fiction written by fans of specific authors, books, films, television series, etc., and for materials about such fiction.

UF Fan fic
    Fanfic
BT **Fiction**

Fan magazines
USE **Fanzines**

Fanaticism **152.4; 200.1; 303**

UF Intolerance
BT **Emotions**

Fancy dress
USE **Costume**
Fanfic
USE **Fan fiction**

Fans (Dress accessories) **391.4**

BT **Clothing and dress**
    Costume
    Dress accessories

Fantastic fiction
USE **Fantasy fiction**
Fantastic films
USE **Fantasy films**
Fantastic poetry
USE **Fantasy poetry**

Fantastic radio programs
USE **Fantasy radio programs**

Fantastic television programs
USE **Fantasy television programs**

Fantasy 154.3

Use for materials on fantasy as an aspect of psychology. Literary fantasies are entered under **Fantasy fiction**.

UF Day dreams

BT **Dreams**

Imagination

RT **Hallucinations and illusions**

Fantasy fiction 808.3; 808.83

Use for individual works, collections, or materials about imaginative fiction with strange settings, grotesque or fanciful characters, and supernatural or impossible events or forces.

UF Fantastic fiction

BT **Fiction**

NT **Alternative histories**

Dystopias

Ghost stories

Imaginary voyages

Utopian fiction

RT **Horror fiction**

Occult fiction

Science fiction

Fantasy films 791.43

Use for individual works, collections, or materials about fantasy films.

UF Fantastic films

BT **Motion pictures**

RT **Horror films**

Science fiction films

Fantasy games 793.93

UF Fantasy role playing games

Role playing games

BT **Games**

Role playing

Fantasy graphic novels 741.5

Use for individual works, collections, or materials about fantasy graphic novels.

BT **Graphic novels**

Fantasy poetry 808.1; 808.81

Use for individual works, collections, or materials about fantasy poetry.

UF Fantastic poetry

BT **Poetry**

Fantasy radio programs 791.44

Use for individual works, collections, or materials about fantasy radio programs.

UF Fantastic radio programs

BT **Radio programs**

Fantasy role playing games
USE **Fantasy games**

Fantasy television programs 791.45

Use for individual works, collections, or materials about fantasy television programs.

UF Fantastic television programs

BT **Television programs**

RT **Horror television programs**

Science fiction television programs

Fanzines (May subdiv. geog.) 070.4

UF Fan magazines

Zines

BT **Periodicals**

Far East
USE **East Asia**

Far north
USE **Arctic regions**

Farces 808.2; 808.82

Use for individual works, collections, or materials about farces.

BT **Comedies**

NT **Commedia dell'arte**

Farm animals
USE **Domestic animals**

Farm buildings (May subdiv. geog.)
631.2; 728

UF Architecture, Rural

Rural architecture

SA types of farm buildings [to be added as needed]

BT **Buildings**

NT **Barns**

Farm credit
USE **Agricultural credit**

Farm crops
USE **Farm produce**

Farm engines
USE **Agricultural machinery**

Farm equipment
USE **Agricultural machinery**

Farm family (May subdiv. geog.)
306.85

UF Rural families

BT **Family**

RT **Family farms**

Farm life

Rural sociology

Farm implements
USE **Agricultural machinery**

Farm laborers
USE **Agricultural laborers**

Farm life (May subdiv. geog.) **306.3; 630**
- UF   Rural life
- BT   **Country life**
-       **Farmers**
- NT   **Ranch life**
- RT   **Family farms**
-       **Farm family**
-       **Rural sociology**

Farm life—United States   **306.3; 630**

Farm loans
- USE   **Agricultural credit**

Farm machinery
- USE   **Agricultural machinery**

Farm management (May subdiv. geog.) **630**
- BT   **Farms**
-       **Management**
- RT   **Agriculture—Economic aspects**

Farm mechanics
- USE   **Agricultural engineering**
-       **Agricultural machinery**

Farm produce (May subdiv. geog.) **338.1; 630; 631.5**
- UF   Agricultural products
-       Crops
-       Farm crops
-       Products, Agricultural
- SA   types of farm products [to be added as needed]
- BT   **Food**
-       **Raw materials**
- NT   **Hay**

Farm produce—Marketing   **338.1**
- UF   Marketing of farm produce
- BT   **Marketing**
-       **Prices**
- RT   **Agriculture—Economic aspects**

Farm subsidies
- USE   **Agricultural subsidies**

Farm tenancy (May subdiv. geog.) **333.5**

Use for materials on the economic and social aspects of farm tenancy. Materials on the legal aspects are entered under **Landlord and tenant**.
- UF   Agriculture—Tenant farming
-       Tenant farming
- BT   **Farms**
-       **Land tenure**
- NT   **Sharecropping**
- RT   **Landlord and tenant**

Farmers (May subdiv. geog.) **305.9; 630.92; 920**
- BT   **Agriculture**
- NT   **Farm life**

Farmers' cooperatives
- USE   **Cooperative agriculture**

Farming
- USE   **Agriculture**

Farming, Dry
- USE   **Dry farming**

Farming, Organic
- USE   **Organic farming**

Farms (May subdiv. geog.) **333.76; 630; 636**
- BT   **Land use**
-       **Real estate**
- NT   **Family farms**
-       **Farm management**
-       **Farm tenancy**
-       **Plantations**
-       **Vineyards**
- RT   **Agriculture**

Fascism (May subdiv. geog.) **320.53; 321.9; 335.6**

Use for materials on the political philosophy, movements, or regimes that advocate a centralized autocratic government, severe economic and social regimentation, and the exaltation of nation and race over the individual. Materials on fascism in Germany during the Nazi regime are entered under **National socialism**.
- UF   Authoritarianism
-       Neo-fascism
- BT   **Totalitarianism**
- NT   **National socialism**
-       **Neo-Nazis**

Fascism—United States (May subdiv. geog.) **320.5; 973.9**

Fashion (May subdiv. geog.) **391**

Use for materials on the prevailing mode or style of dress. Materials on the characteristic costume of ethnic or national groups and for materials on fancy dress and theatrical costumes are entered under **Costume**. Materials on clothing and the art of dress from day to day in practical situations, including historical dress and the clothing of various professions or classes of persons, are entered under **Clothing and dress**.
- UF   Style in dress
- BT   **Clothing and dress**
- RT   **Fashion design**

Fashion design (May subdiv. geog.) **746.9**

Fashion design—*Continued*
  BT **Clothing industry**
      Commercial art
      Design
  RT **Fashion**
Fashion designers (May subdiv. geog.)
  746.9
  UF Clothing designers
      Couturiers
  BT **Designers**
Fashion industry
  USE **Clothing industry**
Fashion models (May subdiv. geog.)
  659.1; 746.9
  UF Manikins (Fashion models)
      Mannequins (Fashion models)
      Models
      Models (Persons)
      Style manikins
  BT **Advertising**
Fashion shows (May subdiv. geog.) **391;**
  659.1
  BT **Exhibitions**
Fashionable society
  USE **Upper class**
Fast food restaurants (May subdiv. geog.)
  647.95
  BT **Convenience foods**
      Restaurants
Fast foods
  USE **Convenience foods**
Faster reading
  USE **Speed reading**
Fasting **178; 204; 248.4; 296.7; 613.2**
  UF Abstinence
  BT **Asceticism**
      Diet
  NT **Hunger strikes**
  RT **Hunger**
      Religious holidays
      Starvation
Fasts and feasts
  USE **Religious holidays**
Fasts and feasts—Christianity
  USE **Christian holidays**
Fasts and feasts—Islam
  USE **Islamic holidays**
Fasts and feasts—Judaism
  USE **Jewish holidays**
Fatally ill children
  USE **Terminally ill children**

Fatally ill patients
  USE **Terminally ill**
Fate and fatalism **149**
  UF Destiny
      Fortune
  BT **Philosophy**
  RT **Free will and determinism**
      Predestination
Father and child
  USE **Father-child relationship**
Father-child relationship **306.874**
  UF Child and father
      Father and child
  BT **Children**
      Fathers
      Parent-child relationship
  NT **Father-daughter relationship**
      Father-son relationship
Father-daughter relationship **306.874**
  UF Daughters and fathers
      Fathers and daughters
  BT **Daughters**
      Father-child relationship
      Fathers
Father-son relationship **306.874**
  UF Fathers and sons
      Sons and fathers
  BT **Father-child relationship**
      Fathers
      Sons
Fatherhood **306.874**
  BT **Parenthood**
  RT **Fathers**
Fathers (May subdiv. geog.) **306.874**
  BT **Family**
      Men
  NT **Divorced fathers**
      Father-child relationship
      Father-daughter relationship
      Father-son relationship
      Stepfathers
      Teenage fathers
      Unmarried fathers
  RT **Fatherhood**
Fathers and daughters
  USE **Father-daughter relationship**
Fathers and sons
  USE **Father-son relationship**
Father's Day **394.263**
  BT **Holidays**

Fathers of the church   270.1; 920

Use for materials on the lives and thought of the leaders of the Christian church up to the time of Gregory the Great in the West and John of Damascus in the East. Individual works or collections of the writings of early Christian authors are entered under **Early Christian literature.**

UF   Church fathers

Patristic philosophy

Patristics

BT   **Christian biography**

RT   **Early Christian literature**

Fatigue   613.7; 152.1; 612

UF   Exhaustion

Weariness

BT   **Physiology**

NT   **Jet lag**

RT   **Rest**

Fatness

USE   **Obesity**

Fats

USE   **Oils and fats**

Faults (Geology) (May subdiv. geog.) **551.8**

BT   **Geology**

Fauna

USE   **Animals**

Zoology

Fawns

USE   **Deer**

Fax machines

USE   **Fax transmission**

Fax transmission   384.1; 621.382

Use for the machines, the processes, and the products of facsimile transmission.

UF   Facsimile transmission

Fax machines

BT   **Data transmission systems**

Telecommunication

Fear   152.4

BT   **Emotions**

NT   **Fear in children**

Fear of the dark

Horror

Phobias

RT   **Anxiety**

Fear in children   155.41246

BT   **Child psychology**

Fear

NT   **Fear of the dark**

Fear of open spaces

USE   **Agoraphobia**

Fear of the dark   152.4

BT   **Fear**

Fear in children

Feast days

USE   **Religious holidays**

Feast of Dedication

USE   **Hanukkah**

Feast of Lights

USE   **Hanukkah**

Fecundity

USE   **Fertility**

Federal aid (May subdiv. geog.)   **336**

Use for materials on central government aid in federal systems. Materials on aid from governments at any level in non-federal systems and on aid from states, provinces, or local governments in federal systems are entered under **Government aid.**

SA   federal aid to specific endeavors, e.g. **Federal aid to the arts** [to be added as needed]

BT   **Public finance**

NT   **Federal aid to education**

Federal aid to libraries

Federal aid to minority business enterprises

Federal aid to the arts

RT   **Government aid**

Federal aid to education (May subdiv. geog.)   **379.1**

UF   Education—Federal aid

BT   **Education—Government policy**

Federal aid

RT   **Colleges and universities—Finance**

Education—Finance

Federal aid to libraries (May subdiv. geog.)   **021.8**

UF   Libraries—Federal aid

BT   **Federal aid**

Libraries—Government policy

RT   **Library finance**

Federal aid to minority business enterprises (May subdiv. geog.)   **338.6**

UF   Minority business enterprises—Federal aid

BT   **Federal aid**

Subsidies

Federal aid to the arts (May subdiv. geog.)   **353.7; 700**

UF   Art—Federal aid

Arts and state

Arts—Federal aid

Funding for the arts

Federal aid to the arts—*Continued*
    State and the arts
    State encouragement of the arts
  BT **Federal aid**
  RT **Art patronage**
      Arts—Government policy
Federal budget
  USE **Budget—United States**
Federal-city relations (May subdiv. geog.)
    351.09
  UF City-federal relations
      Federal-municipal relations
      Municipal-federal relations
      Urban-federal relations
  BT **Federal government**
      Municipal government
Federal courts
  USE **Courts—United States**
Federal debt
  USE **Public debts**
Federal government (May subdiv. geog.)
    321.02; 351
  UF Confederacies
      Federalism
  BT **Constitutional law**
      Political science
      Republics
  NT **European federation**
      Federal-city relations
      Federal-state relations
  RT **State governments**
Federal-Indian relations
  USE **Native Americans—Govern-
      ment relations**
Federal libraries
  USE **Government libraries**
Federal-municipal relations
  USE **Federal-city relations**
Federal Republic of Germany
  USE **Germany**
      Germany (West)
Federal Reserve banks (May subdiv.
    geog.) **332.1**
  BT **Banks and banking**
Federal revenue sharing
  USE **Revenue sharing**
Federal spending policy
  USE **United States—Appropriations
      and expenditures**
Federal-state relations (May subdiv.
    geog.) **321.02**
  UF State-federal relations

  BT **Federal government**
      State governments
Federal-state tax relations
  USE **Intergovernmental tax relations**
Federalism
  USE **Federal government**
Federation of Europe
  USE **European federation**
Feedback control systems **629.8**
  BT **Automation**
  NT **Servomechanisms**
Feedback (Psychology) **153.1**
  BT **Psychology of learning**
  NT **Biofeedback training**
Feeding behavior in animals
  USE **Animals—Food**
Feeds **633.2; 633.3**
  UF Fodder
  SA types of feeds, e.g. **Oats** [to be
      added as needed]
  BT **Animals—Food**
  NT **Forage plants**
      Oats
      Silage and silos
  RT **Grasses**
      Hay
      Root crops
Feeling
  USE **Perception**
      Touch
Feelings
  USE **Emotions**
Fees
  USE **Salaries, wages, etc.**
Feet
  USE **Foot**
Felidae
  USE **Wild cats**
Felines
  USE **Cats**
Fellowships
  USE **Scholarships**
Felony
  USE **Crime**
Female actors
  USE **Actresses**
Female circumcision (May subdiv. geog.)
    392.1
  UF Circumcision, Female
      Clitoridotomy
      Female genital mutilation

Female circumcision—*Continued*
>> Genital mutilation, Female
>> Mutilation, Female genital
> BT **Initiation rites**

Female climacteric
> USE **Menopause**

Female friendship 302.4
> UF Friendship between women
> Friendship in women
> Women's friendship
> BT **Friendship**

Female genital mutilation
> USE **Female circumcision**

Female identity
> USE **Women—Identity**

Female impersonators (May subdiv. geog.) **791.4**

> Use for materials on men who impersonate women for purposes of entertainment or comic effect. Materials on persons, especially men, who assume the dress of the opposite sex for psychological gratification are entered under **Transvestites**.

> BT **Impostors and imposture**

Female-male relationship
> USE **Man-woman relationship**

Female role
> USE **Sex role**

Female superhero graphic novels 741.5

> Use for individual works, collections, or materials about female superhero graphic novels.

> BT **Female superhero graphic novels**
> **Graphic novels**
> NT **Female superhero graphic novels**

Feminine identity
> USE **Women—Identity**

Feminine psychology
> USE **Women—Psychology**

Femininity (May subdiv. geog.) **155.3**
> UF Femininity (Psychology)
> BT **Sex—Psychological aspects**
> RT **Women**

Femininity of God 212; 231
> UF God—Femininity
> BT **God**

Femininity (Psychology)
> USE **Femininity**

Feminism (May subdiv. geog.) **305.42; 323.3**

> Use for materials on the theory of the political and social equality of the sexes and wom-en's perspectives on various subjects. Materials on activities aimed at obtaining equal rights and opportunities for women are entered under **Women's movement**.

> UF Feminist theory
> SA types of feminist endeavors, e.g. **Feminist criticism**; **Feminist theology**; etc. [to be added as needed]
> NT **Feminist ethics**
> **Women—History**
> RT **Suffragists**
> **Women's movement**
> **Women's rights**

Feminist criticism 801
> UF Criticism, Feminist
> BT **Criticism**

Feminist ethics (May subdiv. geog.) **170**
> BT **Ethics**
> **Feminism**

Feminist fiction 808.3; 808.83

> Use for individual works, collections, or materials about feminist fiction.

> BT **Fiction**

Feminist theology (May subdiv. geog.) **230**

> Use for materials on the feminist critique of traditional theology and on alternative theology from a feminist perspective.

> BT **Theology**

Feminist theory
> USE **Feminism**

Fencing (May subdiv. geog.) **796.86**
> UF Fighting
> BT **Dueling**

Feng shui (May subdiv. geog.) **133.3**
> BT **Divination**

Feral animals
> USE **Wildlife**

Feral cats
> USE **Wild cats**

Feral children
> USE **Wild children**

Fermentation 547; 660; 663
> UF Ferments
> BT **Chemical engineering**
> **Chemistry**
> **Microbiology**

Ferments
> USE **Fermentation**

Ferns (May subdiv. geog.) **587; 635.9**
> BT **Plants**

Fertility   573.6; 591.1

Use for general materials on fertility in animals, including humans. Materials limited to fertility in humans are entered under **Human fertility**.

UF   Fecundity

BT   **Reproduction**

NT   **Human fertility**

RT   **Infertility**

Fertility control

USE   **Birth control**

Fertility, Human

USE   **Human fertility**

Fertilization in vitro   176; 618.1; 636.089

UF   Fertilization in vitro, Human

Fertilization, Test tube

In vitro fertilization

Laboratory fertilization

Test tube babies

Test tube fertilization

BT   **Genetic engineering**

Reproduction

Fertilization in vitro, Human

USE   **Fertilization in vitro**

Fertilization of plants   575.6

UF   Plants—Fertilization

Pollination

BT   **Plant physiology**

Plants

Fertilization, Test tube

USE   **Fertilization in vitro**

Fertilizers   631.8; 668

UF   Fertilizers and manures

Manures

BT   **Agricultural chemicals**

Soils

NT   **Compost**

Lime

Nitrates

Phosphates

Potash

Fertilizers and manures

USE   **Fertilizers**

Festivals (May subdiv. geog.)   394.26

Use for materials on occasions other than holidays devoted to festive community observances or to programs of cultural events. Materials on days of general exemption from work or days publicly dedicated to the commemoration of some person, event, or principle are entered under **Holidays**. Materials on religious fasts and feasts are entered under **Religious holidays**.

UF   Fiestas

SA   types of festivals and names of specific festivals, e.g. **Carnival** [to be added as needed]

BT   **Manners and customs**

NT   **Carnival**

Carnivals

Craft shows

Film festivals

Music festivals

Parades

Powwows

RT   **Anniversaries**

Days

Holidays

Pageants

Religious holidays

Festivals—United States   394.260973

Fetal alcohol syndrome   618.3

BT   **Social problems**

RT   **Birth defects**

Growth disorders

Fetal death

USE   **Miscarriage**

Fetus   571.8; 612.6

UF   Unborn child

BT   **Embryology**

Reproduction

Feudalism (May subdiv. geog.)   321

UF   Fiefs

Vassals

BT   **Land tenure**

Medieval civilization

NT   **Peasantry**

RT   **Chivalry**

Feuds

USE   **Vendetta**

Fever   616

BT   **Pathology**

RT   **Body temperature**

Fiber content of food

USE   **Food—Fiber content**

Fiber glass

USE   **Glass fibers**

Fiber optics   621.36

BT   **Optics**

Fiberglass

USE   **Glass fibers**

Fibers   677

UF   Textile fibers

NT   **Cotton**

Flax

Fibers—*Continued*
>Glass fibers
>Hemp
>Linen
>Paper
>Silk
>Wool

Fibers, Glass
>USE **Glass fibers**

Fiction   808.3

>Use for collections and materials about fiction from several countries and for materials on fiction as a literary form, not for individual works.

>UF   Novels
>>Stories

>SA   fiction of particular national literatures, e.g. **American fiction**; genres of fiction, e.g. **Fantasy fiction**; and subjects, names of places, and personal and corporate names with the subdivision *Fiction*, to express the theme or subject content of collections of fiction, e.g. **Slavery—United States—Fiction; United States—History—1861-1865, Civil War—Fiction; Ohio—Fiction; Napoleon I, Emperor of the French, 1769-1821—Fiction;** etc. [to be added as needed]

>BT   **Literature**
>NT   **Adventure fiction**
>>**Allegories**
>>**Allegory**
>>**American fiction**
>>**Apocalyptic fiction**
>>**Bible fiction**
>>**Bildungsromans**
>>**Biographical fiction**
>>**Black humor (Literature)**
>>**Children's stories**
>>**Christian fiction**
>>**Didactic fiction**
>>**English fiction**
>>**Epistolary fiction**
>>**Erotic fiction**
>>**Fables**
>>**Fairy tales**
>>**Fan fiction**
>>**Fantasy fiction**

>>**Feminist fiction**
>>**Folklore**
>>**Graphic novels**
>>**Historical fiction**
>>**Horror fiction**
>>**Humorous fiction**
>>**Indian fiction**
>>**Indian fiction (English)**
>>**Interplanetary voyages**
>>**Jewish religious fiction**
>>**Legal stories**
>>**Legends**
>>**Love stories**
>>**Medical novels**
>>**Movie novels**
>>**Mystery fiction**
>>**Occult fiction**
>>**Pastoral fiction**
>>**Picaresque literature**
>>**Plot-your-own stories**
>>**Radio and television novels**
>>**Religious fiction**
>>**Romances**
>>**Romans à clef**
>>**School stories**
>>**Science fiction**
>>**Sea stories**
>>**Short stories**
>>**Short story**
>>**Urban fiction**
>>**War stories**
>>**Western stories**

Fiction for children
>USE   **Children's stories**

Fiction—History and criticism   809.3

Fiction—Technique   808.3
>BT   **Authorship**

Fictional characters   808.3
>UF   Fictitious characters
>SA   names of individual literary characters established in the inverted form with the qualifier (Fictional character), e.g. **Holmes, Sherlock (Fictional character)** [to be added as needed]
>BT   **Characters and characteristics in literature**
>NT   **Dracula, Count (Fictional character)**
>>**Fictional robots**

Fictional characters—*Continued*

> **Frankenstein (Fictional character)**
> **Gundam (Fictional character)**
> **Holmes, Sherlock (Fictional character)**
> **Justice League (Fictional characters)**
> **Potter, Harry (Fictional character)**
> **Shadowpact (Fictional characters)**
> **Spider-Man (Fictional character)**
> **Superman (Fictional character)**
> **Wonder Woman (Fictional character)**

Fictional places
  USE **Imaginary places**
Fictional plots
  USE **Stories, plots, etc.**
Fictional robots   741.5
  SA names of individual fictional robots, e.g. **Neon Genesis Evangelion (Fictional robot)** [to be added as needed]
  BT **Fictional characters**
    Mecha
  NT **Gundam (Fictional character)**
    Neon Genesis Evangelion (Fictional robot)
Fictitious characters
  USE **Fictional characters**
Fictitious names
  USE **Pseudonyms**
Fictitious places
  USE **Imaginary places**
Fiddle
  USE **Violins**
Fiduciaries
  USE **Trusts and trustees**
Fiefs
  USE **Feudalism**
    Land tenure
Field athletics
  USE **Track athletics**
Field hockey (May subdiv. geog.) **796.35**
  BT **Sports**
Field hospitals
  USE **Military hospitals**
    Military medicine

Field photography
  USE **Outdoor photography**
Field trips (May subdiv. geog.)   **069; 371.3**
  UF School excursions
    School trips
  BT **Student activities**
Fiestas
  USE **Festivals**
Fifteenth century
  USE **World history—15th century**
Fifth column
  USE **Subversive activities**
    World War, 1939-1945—Collaborationists
Fifth of May (Holiday)
  USE **Cinco de Mayo (Holiday)**
Fighting
  USE **Battles**
    Boxing
    Bullfights
    Dueling
    Fencing
    Gladiators
    Military art and science
    Naval art and science
    Self-defense
    Self-defense for women
    War
Figure drawing   743.4
  UF Human figure in art
  BT **Artistic anatomy**
    Drawing
  RT **Figure painting**
Figure painting   757
  UF Human figure in art
  BT **Artistic anatomy**
    Painting
  RT **Figure drawing**
    Portrait painting
Figure skating
  USE **Ice skating**
Figures of speech   808
  UF English language—Figures of speech
    Imagery
    Tropes
  BT **Rhetoric**
    Symbolism
Files and filing   005.74; 025.3; 651.5

Files and filing—*Continued*
  UF Alphabetizing
      Filing systems
  BT **Office management**
  RT **Indexing**
Filing systems
  USE **Files and filing**
Filling stations
  USE **Service stations**
Fills (Earthwork)
  USE **Landfills**
Film adaptations 791.43
  Use for individual works, collections, or materials about film adaptations of material from other media.
  UF Adaptations
      Filmed books
      Films from books
      Literature—Film and video adaptations
      Motion picture adaptations
  SA names of authors, titles of anonymous literary works, types of literature, and types of musical compositions with the subdivision *Adaptations*, for individual works, collections, or criticism and interpretation of literary, cinematic, video, or television adaptations, e.g., **Shakespeare, William, 1564-1616—Adaptations; Beowulf—Adaptations; Arthurian romances—Adaptations**; etc. [to be added as needed]
  BT **Motion pictures**
Film catalogs
  USE **Motion pictures—Catalogs**
Film direction
  USE **Motion pictures—Production and direction**
Film directors
  USE **Motion picture producers and directors**
Film epics
  USE **Epic films**
Film festivals (May subdiv. geog.)
      791.43
  UF Motion picture festivals
      Movie festivals
  BT **Festivals**

Film industry (Motion pictures)
  USE **Motion picture industry**
Film noir 791.43
  Use for individual works, collections, or materials about film noir.
  UF Crime films
      Films noirs
  BT **Motion pictures**
  RT **Mystery films**
Film posters (May subdiv. geog.) **741.6; 791.43**
  UF Motion picture posters
      Motion pictures—Posters
      Movie posters
      Playbills
  BT **Posters**
Film producers
  USE **Motion picture producers and directors**
Film production
  USE **Motion pictures—Production and direction**
Film projectors
  USE **Projectors**
Film scripts
  USE **Screenplays**
Filmed books
  USE **Film adaptations**
Filmmaking
  USE **Motion pictures—Production and direction**
Filmography
  USE **Motion pictures—Catalogs**
      and types of motion pictures with the subdivision *Catalogs*, e.g. **Science fiction films—Catalogs;** and subjects, classes of persons, corporate entities, and names of individual persons with the subdivision *Filmography*, e.g. **Animals—Filmography; Shakespeare, William, 1564-1616—Filmography;** etc. [to be added as needed]
Films
  USE **Filmstrips**
      Motion pictures
Films from books
  USE **Film adaptations**
Films noirs
  USE **Film noir**

Filmstrips   371.33; 778.2
>   UF   Films
>   BT   **Audiovisual materials**
>   **Photography**
>   RT   **Slides (Photography)**

Finance (May subdiv. geog.)   **332**
>   Use for general materials on the manage-
>   ment of money and credit. Materials on the
>   raising and expenditure of funds in the public
>   sector are entered under **Public finance.**
>   UF   Funding
>   Funds
>   SA   subjects, ethnic groups, names of
>   wars, and names of corporate
>   bodies with the subdivision
>   *Finance,* e.g. **Education—Fi-**
>   **nance** [to be added as need-
>   ed]
>   BT   **Economics**
>   NT   **Bankruptcy**
>   **Banks and banking**
>   **Bonds**
>   **Capital**
>   **Capital market**
>   **Church finance**
>   **Colleges and universities—Fi-**
>   **nance**
>   **Commerce**
>   **Corporations—Finance**
>   **Credit**
>   **Debt**
>   **Education—Finance**
>   **Endowments**
>   **Financial crises**
>   **Foreign exchange**
>   **Fund raising**
>   **Income**
>   **Inflation (Finance)**
>   **Insurance**
>   **Interest (Economics)**
>   **Investments**
>   **Library finance**
>   **Loans**
>   **Money**
>   **Personal finance**
>   **Prices**
>   **Public finance**
>   **Railroads—Finance**
>   **Securities**
>   **Speculation**
>   **Stock exchanges**
>   **United Nations—Finance**

>   **Wealth**
>   RT   **Monetary policy**

Finance, Household
>   USE   **Household budgets**

Finance—Mathematics
>   USE   **Business mathematics**

Finance, Municipal
>   USE   **Municipal finance**

Finance, Personal
>   USE   **Personal finance**

Finance, Public
>   USE   **Public finance**

Finance—United States   332.0973;
>   **336.73**

Financial accounting
>   USE   **Accounting**

Financial aid to students
>   USE   **Student aid**

Financial crashes
>   USE   **Financial crises**

Financial crises (May subdiv. geog.)
>   **338 5**
>   UF   Crashes (Finance)
>   Financial crashes
>   Financial panics
>   Panics (Finance)
>   Stock exchange crashes
>   Stock market panics
>   BT   **Finance**
>   RT   **Business cycles**

Financial institutions (May subdiv. geog.)
>   **332.1**
>   UF   Lending institutions
>   BT   **Associations**
>   NT   **Capital market**

Financial panics
>   USE   **Financial crises**

Financial planning, Personal
>   USE   **Personal finance**

Financial services industry (May subdiv.
>   geog.)   **332.1**
>   BT   **Industries**

Financiers
>   USE   **Capitalists and financiers**

Finding things
>   USE   **Lost and found possessions**

Finger games
>   USE   **Finger play**

Finger marks
>   USE   **Fingerprints**

Finger painting   751.4

Finger painting—*Continued*
  UF Painting, Finger
  BT **Child artists**
      Painting
Finger play   793.4
  UF Finger games
  BT **Play**
Finger pressure therapy
  USE **Acupressure**
Finger prints
  USE **Fingerprints**
Fingerprints 363.25
  UF Finger marks
      Finger prints
  BT **Anthropometry**
      Criminal investigation
      Criminals—Identification
      Identification
Finishes and finishing   667; 684.1; 698;
      745.7
  UF Finishing
      Finishing materials
  SA topics with the subdivision *Fin-*
      ishing, e.g. **Metals—Finish-**
      ing; or with the subdivision
      Painting, e.g. **Automobiles—**
      Painting [to be added as
      needed]
  BT **Materials**
  NT **Industrial painting**
      Lacquer and lacquering
      Metals—Finishing
      Paint
      Varnish and varnishing
      Wood finishing
Finishing
  USE **Finishes and finishing**
      and topics with the subdivision
      Finishing, e.g. **Metals—Fin-**
      ishing [to be added as need-
      ed]
Finishing materials
  USE **Finishes and finishing**
Finno-Russian War, 1939-1940
  USE **Russo-Finnish War, 1939-1940**
Fire (May subdiv. geog.)   536; 541
  BT **Chemistry**
  NT **Fires**
      Fuel
  RT **Combustion**
      Heat

Fire bombs
  USE **Incendiary bombs**
Fire departments (May subdiv. geog.)
      628.9
  UF Fire stations
  RT **Fire fighters**
Fire ecology (May subdiv. geog.)   577.2
  BT **Ecology**
Fire engines (May subdiv. geog.)   628.9
  BT **Engines**
      Fire fighting
Fire etching
  USE **Pyrography**
Fire fighters (May subdiv. geog.)
      363.37092; 920
  UF Firemen and firewomen
  RT **Fire departments**
Fire fighting (May subdiv. geog.)   628.9
  BT **Fire prevention**
      Fires
  NT **Fire engines**
Fire in mythology   398.2
  BT **Mythology**
Fire insurance (May subdiv. geog.)
      368.1
  UF Insurance, Fire
  BT **Insurance**
  NT **Fireproofing**
Fire prevention (May subdiv. geog.)
      363.37; 628.9
  UF Prevention of fire
  SA types of institutions, buildings,
      industries, and vehicles with
      the subdivision *Fires and fire*
      prevention, e.g. **Nuclear pow-**
      er plants—Fires and fire
      prevention [to be added as
      needed]
  BT **Fires**
  NT **Fire fighting**
      Fireproofing
      Nuclear power plants—Fires
        and fire prevention
Fire stations
  USE **Fire departments**
Firearms (May subdiv. geog.)   **623.4;**
      739.7
  UF Guns
      Small arms
  SA types of firearms [to be added
      as needed]

Firearms—*Continued*
  BT Weapons
  NT Gunpowder
      Handguns
      Rifles
      Shotguns
  RT Ammunition
      Shooting
Firearms control
  USE Gun control
Firearms industry (May subdiv. geog.)
      338.4; 683.4
    Use for materials on the small arms indus-
    try. Materials on the production of military
    weapons are entered under **Defense industry**.
  UF Firearms industry and trade
      Firearms trade
      Gunsmithing
      Weapons industry
  BT Industries
Firearms industry and trade
  USE Firearms industry
Firearms—Law and legislation
  USE Gun control
Firearms trade
  USE Firearms industry
Firemen and firewomen
  USE Fire fighters
Fireplaces (May subdiv. geog.) 697; 749
  BT Architecture—Details
      Buildings
      Heating
      Space heaters
  RT Chimneys
Fireproofing 628.9; 693.8
  BT Fire insurance
      Fire prevention
Fires (May subdiv. geog.) 363.37; 904
  SA types of institutions, buildings,
      industries, and vehicles with
      the subdivision *Fires and fire
      prevention*, e.g. **Nuclear pow-
      er plants—Fires and fire
      prevention** [to be added as
      needed]
  BT Accidents
      Disasters
      Fire
  NT Fire fighting
      Fire prevention
      Forest fires

Nuclear power plants—Fires
  and fire prevention
      Wildfires
Fires and fire prevention
  USE types of institutions, buildings,
      industries, and vehicles with
      the subdivision *Fires and fire
      prevention*, e.g. **Nuclear pow-
      er plants—Fires and fire
      prevention** [to be added as
      needed]
Fireworks (May subdiv. geog.) 662
  BT Amusements
Firms
  USE Business enterprises
First aid 362.18; 616.02
  UF Emergencies
      Injuries
      Wounded, First aid to
  BT Health self-care
      Home accidents
      Medicine
      Nursing
      Rescue work
      Sick
  NT Artificial respiration
      Bandages
      CPR (First aid)
  RT Accidents
      Lifesaving
First editions (May subdiv. geog.) 094
  UF Bibliography—First editions
      Books—First editions
  SA types of publications, types of
      literature, and names of au-
      thors and composers with the
      subdivision *First editions*, e.g.
      **English literature—First edi-
      tions** [to be added as needed]
  BT Editions
First generation children
  USE Children of immigrants
First ladies—United States
  USE Presidents' spouses—United
      States
First names
  USE Personal names
First nations
  USE Native Americans—Canada
First World War
  USE World War, 1914-1918

Firstborn child
    USE   **Birth order**

Fiscal policy (May subdiv. geog.)   **336.3**
    UF   Government policy
    BT   **Economic policy**
          Public finance
    RT   **Monetary policy**

Fiscal policy—United States   **336.73**
    UF   United States—Fiscal policy

Fish
    USE   **Fish as food**
            Fishes

Fish as food   **641.3**
    UF   Fish
    BT   **Cooking**
          Fishes
          Food
    RT   **Cooking—Fish**
          Seafood

Fish culture (May subdiv. geog.)   **639.3**
    Use for materials on the cultivation of fish in captivity. Materials on fishing as an industry are entered under **Commercial fishing**.
    UF   Fish farming
          Fish hatcheries
    BT   **Aquaculture**
    RT   **Aquariums**

Fish farming
    USE   **Fish culture**

Fish hatcheries
    USE   **Fish culture**

Fisheries
    USE   **Commercial fishing**

Fishes (May subdiv. geog.)   **597**
    UF   Fish
          Ichthyology
    SA   types of fishes, e.g. **Salmon** [to be added as needed]
    BT   **Aquatic animals**
    NT   **Fish as food**
          Goldfish
          Salmon
          Tropical fish
    RT   **Aquariums**

Fishes—Ecology (May subdiv. geog.)   **597**
    BT   **Ecology**

Fishes—Geographical distribution   **597.09**
    BT   **Biogeography**

Fishes—Photography
    USE   **Photography of fishes**

Fishes—United States   **597.0973**

Fishing (May subdiv. geog.)   **799.1**
    Use for materials on fishing as a sport. Materials on fishing as an industry are entered under **Commercial fishing**.
    UF   Angling
    SA   types of fishing [to be added as needed]
    BT   **Sports**
    NT   **Fly casting**
          Ice fishing
          Saltwater fishing
          Spear fishing
          Trout fishing

Fishing, Commercial
    USE   **Commercial fishing**

Fishing—Equipment and supplies   **799.1**
    UF   Fishing tackle
    NT   **Artificial flies**

Fishing flies
    USE   **Artificial flies**

Fishing industry
    USE   **Commercial fishing**

Fishing tackle
    USE   **Fishing—Equipment and supplies**

Fishing—United States   **799.10973**

Fitness
    USE   **Physical fitness**

Five-day work week
    USE   **Hours of labor**

Fixed ideas
    USE   **Obsessive-compulsive disorder**

Fixing
    USE   **Repairing**

Flags (May subdiv. geog.)   **929.9**
    UF   Banners
          Ensigns
    BT   **Heraldry**
    RT   **National emblems**
          Signals and signaling

Flags—United States   **929.9**
    UF   American flag
          United States—Flags

Flannel boards   **371.33**
    BT   **Teaching—Aids and devices**

Flats
    USE   **Apartments**

Flatware, Silver
    USE   **Silverware**

Flavoring essences   **664**

Flavoring essences—*Continued*
    BT   **Cooking**
          Essences and essential oils
          Food
Flax (May subdiv. geog.)   **633.5; 677**
    BT   **Fibers**
    RT   **Linen**
Flea markets (May subdiv. geog.)   **658.8**
    BT   **Markets**
          Secondhand trade
Flexible hours of labor   **331.25**
    UF   Alternative work schedules
          Flexible work hours
          Flextime
          Four-day week
          Hours of labor, Flexible
    BT   **Hours of labor**
Flexible work hours
    USE   **Flexible hours of labor**
Flextime
    USE   **Flexible hours of labor**
Flies   **595.77**
    UF   Fly
          House flies
    SA   types of flies [to be added as
          needed]
    BT   **Household pests**
          Insects
          Pests
    NT   **Fruit flies**
Flies, Artificial
    USE   **Artificial flies**
Flight   **629.13**
    UF   Flying
    SA   types of animals with the subdi-
          vision *Flight*, e.g. **Birds—**
          Flight [to be added as need-
          ed]
    BT   **Locomotion**
    NT   **Animal flight**
    RT   **Aeronautics**
Flight attendants   **387.7**
    UF   Airline hostesses
          Airline stewardesses
          Airline stewards
          Stewardesses, Airline
          Stewards, Airline
    BT   **Airlines**
Flight to the moon
    USE   **Space flight to the moon**

Flight training
    USE   **Aeronautics—Study and teach-
          ing**
          Airplanes—Piloting
Flights around the world
    USE   **Aeronautics—Flights**
Flint implements
    USE   **Stone implements**
Floating hospitals
    USE   **Hospital ships**
Floats (Parades)
    USE   **Parades**
Flood control (May subdiv. geog.)   **627**
    UF   Flood prevention
    BT   **Hydraulic engineering**
    RT   **Forest influences**
Flood prevention
    USE   **Flood control**
Floods (May subdiv. geog.)   **363.34;
          551.48; 904**
    May also be subdivided by names of rivers
    or river valleys, e.g. **Floods—Mississippi
    River**.
    BT   **Meteorology**
          Natural disasters
          Rain
          Water
    RT   **Rivers**
Floods and forests
    USE   **Forest influences**
Floods—Mississippi River   **363.34**
Floors   **690; 721**
    BT   **Architecture—Details**
          Buildings
Flora
    USE   **Botany**
          Plants
Floral decoration
    USE   **Flower arrangement**
Floriculture
    USE   **Flower gardening**
Florists' designs
    USE   **Flower arrangement**
Flour   **641.3; 664**
    RT   **Grain**
Flour mills   **664**
    UF   Grist mills
          Milling (Flour)
    BT   **Mills**
Flow charts
    USE   **Graphic methods**
          System analysis

Flowcharting
  USE **Graphic methods**
       System analysis
Flower arrangement **745.92**
   Use for materials on the artistic arrange-
   ment of flowers, including decoration of hous-
   es, churches, etc., with flowers.
  UF Designs, Floral
      Floral decoration
      Florists' designs
      Flowers—Arrangement
  BT **Decoration and ornament**
      Flowers
      Table setting and decoration
Flower drying
  USE **Flowers—Drying**
Flower gardening (May subdiv. geog.)
       635.9
   Use for practical materials on the cultiva-
   tion of flowering plants for either commercial
   or private purposes.
  UF Floriculture
  SA types of flowers, e.g. **Roses** [to
      be added as needed]
  BT **Gardening**
      Horticulture
  NT **Annuals (Plants)**
      Bulbs
      Greenhouses
      House plants
      Ornamental plants
      Perennials
  RT **Container gardening**
      Flowers
      Window gardening
Flower language
  USE **Language of flowers**
Flower painting and illustration
  USE **Botanical illustration**
       Flowers in art
Flower prints
  USE **Flowers in art**
Flower shows (May subdiv. geog.)
       635.9074
  UF Flowers—Exhibitions
  BT **Exhibitions**
Flowers (May subdiv. geog.) **575.6;**
       582.13
   Use for general materials on flowers. Mate-
   rials limited to the cultivation of flowers are
   entered under **Flower gardening**.
  SA types of flowers, e.g. **Roses** [to
      be added as needed]

  BT **Plants**
  NT **Annuals (Plants)**
      Flower arrangement
      Perennials
      Roses
      State flowers
      Wild flowers
  RT **Flower gardening**
Flowers—Arrangement
  USE **Flower arrangement**
Flowers, Artificial
  USE **Artificial flowers**
Flowers, Drying
  USE **Flowers—Drying**
Flowers—Drying **745.92**
  UF Dried flowers
      Flower drying
      Flowers, Drying
  BT **Plants—Collection and preser-**
      vation
Flowers—Exhibitions
  USE **Flower shows**
Flowers in art **758**
  UF Flower painting and illustration
      Flower prints
  BT **Art—Themes**
Flowers—United States **582.130973**
Flu
  USE **Influenza**
Fluid mechanics **532; 620.1**
   Use for materials on the branch of mechan-
   ics dealing with the properties of liquids or
   gases, either at rest or in motion.
  UF Hydromechanics
  BT **Mechanics**
  NT **Gases**
      Hydraulic engineering
      Hydraulics
      Hydrodynamics
      Hydrostatics
      Liquids
Fluorescent lighting **621.32**
  UF Electric lighting, Fluorescent
  BT **Electric lighting**
Fluoridation of water
  USE **Water fluoridation**
Flute
  USE **Flutes**
Flutes **788.3**
  UF Flute
  BT **Wind instruments**

Fly
   USE   **Flies**
Fly casting   **799.12**
   UF   Fly fishing
   BT   **Fishing**
   NT   **Artificial flies**
Fly fishing
   USE   **Fly casting**
Flying
   USE   **Flight**
Flying saucers
   USE   **Unidentified flying objects**
FM radio
   USE   **Radio frequency modulation**
Foals
   USE   **Horses**
           Ponies
Fodder
   USE   **Feeds**
Fog   **551.57**
   BT   **Atmosphere**
           Meteorology
Fog signals
   USE   **Signals and signaling**
Folding of napkins
   USE   **Napkin folding**
Foliage
   USE   **Leaves**
Folk art   **745**
   Use for materials on objects of fine or decorative art produced in a peasant, popular, or naive style, often in cultural isolation and by unschooled artists or artisans.
   UF   Peasant art
   SA   folk art of particular countries or ethnic groups, e.g. **American folk art** [to be added as needed]
   BT   **Art**
           Art and society
   NT   **American folk art**
   RT   **Arts and crafts movement**
           Decorative arts
           Handicraft
Folk art, American
   USE   **American folk art**
Folk beliefs
   USE   **Folklore**
           Superstition
Folk biology
   USE   **Ethnobiology**

Folk dances
   USE   **Folk dancing**
Folk dancing (May subdiv. geog.)   **793.3**
   UF   Folk dances
           National dances
   SA   dance of particular ethnic groups, e.g. **Native American dance** [to be added as needed]
   BT   **Dance**
   NT   **Native American dance**
           Square dancing
Folk dancing—United States   **793.3**
   UF   American folk dancing
Folk drama   **808.2; 808.82**
   Use for collections or materials about folk drama, not for individual works.
   UF   Folk plays
   SA   folk drama of particular countries or ethnic groups, e.g. **American folk drama** [to be added as needed]
   BT   **Drama**
           Folk drama
   NT   **American folk drama**
           Folk drama
           Puppets and puppet plays
Folk literature   **398.2**
   SA   types of folk literature, e.g. **Jewish folk literature** [to be added as needed]
   BT   **Folklore**
           Literature
   NT   **Jewish folk literature**
Folk lore
   USE   **Folklore**
Folk medicine
   USE   **Traditional medicine**
Folk music (May subdiv. geog.)   **781.62**
   BT   **Music**
   NT   **World music**
Folk music—United States   **781.6200973**
   UF   American folk music
   NT   **Blues music**
           Country music
Folk plays
   USE   **Folk drama**
Folk psychology
   USE   **Ethnopsychology**

Folk songs (May subdiv. geog.)
    782.42162
    Use for materials about folk songs and col-
lections of folk songs that include both words
and music. Materials about ballads and collections of ballads without music are entered under **Ballads.**
    SA   folk songs of particular ethnic
            groups, e.g. **Creole folk
            songs** [to be added as need-
            ed]
    BT   **Folklore**
            Songs
            Vocal music
    NT   **Carols**
            Creole folk songs
    RT   **Ballads**
            National songs
Folk songs, Creole
    USE   **Creole folk songs**
Folk songs—France   782.4216200944
    UF   Folk songs, French
            France—Folk songs
            French folk songs
Folk songs, French
    USE   **Folk songs—France**
Folk songs—Ohio   782.42162009771
Folk songs—United States
            782.4216200973
    UF   American folk songs
    BT   **American songs**
    NT   **Spirituals (Songs)**
Folk tales
    USE   **Folklore**
            Legends
Folk zoology
    USE   **Ethnozoology**
Folklore (May subdiv. geog.)   **398**
    Use for general materials on folklore. May
also be used for individual works, collections,
or materials about stories based on spoken
rather than written traditions.
    UF   Folk beliefs
            Folk lore
            Folk tales
            Tales
            Traditions
    SA   topics as themes in folklore with
            the subdivision Folklore, e.g.
            Plants—Folklore; names of
            ethnic or occupational groups
            with the subdivision *Folklore*,
            e.g. **Inuit—Folklore**; types of

folkloric creatures, e.g. **Elves**;
and names of individual legendary characters, e.g. **Bunyan, Paul (Legendary character)** [to be added as need-
ed]
    BT   **Ethnology**
            Fiction
            Manners and customs
    NT   **African Americans—Folklore**
            Animals—Folklore
            Blacks—Folklore
            Chapbooks
            Charms
            Dragons
            Elves
            Fairies
            Folk literature
            Folk songs
            Ghosts
            Giants
            Gnomes
            Goblins
            Grail
            Inuit—Folklore
            Jews—Folklore
            Monsters
            Native Americans—Folklore
            Nursery rhymes
            Plants—Folklore
            Proverbs
            Roland (Legendary character)
            Sagas
            Superstition
            Tall tales
            Tongue twisters
            Urban folklore
            Vampires
            Weather—Folklore
            Werewolves
            Witchcraft
            Zombies
    RT   **Fables**
            Fairy tales
            Legends
            Material culture
            Mythology
            Storytelling
Folklore, Medical
    USE   **Traditional medicine**
Folklore—United States   398.0973

315

Folklore—United States—*Continued*
  NT **Bunyan, Paul (Legendary character)**
Folkways
  USE **Manners and customs**
Food (May subdiv. geog.) **641; 641.3; 664**
  SA types of foods, names of specific foods, and subjects with the subdivision *Food* [to be added as needed]
  BT **Home economics**
  NT **Animals—Food**
      Artificial foods
      Beverages
      Bread
      Chocolate
      Convenience foods
      Dietetic foods
      Dining
      Dried foods
      Edible plants
      Eggs
      Farm produce
      Fish as food
      Flavoring essences
      Food of animal origin
      Frozen foods
      Fruit
      Honey
      Meat
      Milk
      Minerals in human nutrition
      Natural foods
      Nuts
      Pollen as food
      Prepared cereals
      School children—Food
      Seafood
      Snack foods
      Spices
      Sugar
      Vegetables
      Vitamins
  RT **Cooking**
      Diet
      Food industry
      Gastronomy
      Grocery trade
      Nutrition
Food additives **641.3; 664**
  UF Additives, Food

  BT **Food—Analysis**
      Food—Preservation
  RT **Dietary supplements**
Food adulteration and inspection (May subdiv. geog.) **363.19**
  UF Adulteration of food
      Analysis of food
      Food inspection
      Inspection of food
      Pure food
  BT **Consumer protection**
      Public health
  NT **Food contamination**
      Meat inspection
      Milk supply
  RT **Food—Law and legislation**
Food allergies
  USE **Food allergy**
Food allergy **616.97**
  UF Allergies, Food
      Allergy, Food
      Food allergies
  SA types of food allergies [to be added as needed]
  BT **Allergy**
Food—Analysis **664**
    Use for materials on methods of analyzing foods. Materials presenting the results of the analysis of foods are entered under **Food—Composition**.
  UF Analysis of food
      Chemistry of food
      Food chemistry
  SA types of foods with the subdivision *Analysis*, e.g. **Milk—Analysis** [to be added as needed]
  BT **Analytical chemistry**
      Industrial chemistry
  NT **Food additives**
  RT **Food—Composition**
Food assistance programs
  USE **Food relief**
Food—Bacteriology
  USE **Food—Microbiology**
Food banks (May subdiv. geog.) **363.8**
  BT **Food relief**
Food buying
  USE **Grocery shopping**
Food—Caloric content **613.2**
  UF Caloric content of foods
      Calories (Food)

Food—Caloric content—*Continued*
  Food calories
  BT **Food—Composition**
Food calories
  USE **Food—Caloric content**
Food, Canned
  USE **Canning and preserving**
Food chains (Ecology) (May subdiv. geog.) **577**
  BT **Animals—Food**
      Ecology
Food chemistry
  USE **Food—Analysis**
      Food—Composition
Food—Cholesterol content **613.2**
  UF Cholesterol content of food
  BT **Food—Composition**
Food—Composition **641; 664**
  Use for materials presenting the results of the analysis of foods. Materials on methods of analyzing foods are entered under **Food—Analysis**.
  UF Chemistry of food
      Food chemistry
  SA food and types of food with subdivisions to indicate the particular content being analyzed, e.g. **Food—Cholesterol content** [to be added as needed]
  NT **Food—Caloric content**
      Food—Cholesterol content
      Food—Fiber content
      Food—Sodium content
  RT **Food—Analysis**
Food contamination (May subdiv. geog.) **363.19**
  UF Contaminated food
  BT **Food adulteration and inspection**
Food contamination—Press coverage (May subdiv. geog.) **070.4**
Food control
  USE **Food supply**
Food, Cost of
  USE **Cost and standard of living**
Food coupons
  USE **Food stamps**
Food customs
  USE **Eating customs**
Food—Fiber content **613.2**

  UF Dietary fiber
      Fiber content of food
      Roughage
  BT **Food—Composition**
Food for invalids
  USE **Cooking for the sick**
Food for school children
  USE **School children—Food**
Food, Freeze-dried
  USE **Freeze-dried foods**
Food habits
  USE **Eating customs**
Food industry (May subdiv. geog.) **338.1**
  Use for materials on the processing and marketing of food.
  UF Food preparation
      Food preparation industry
      Food processing
      Food processing industry
      Food trade
  SA type of food industries, e.g. **Beverage industry** [to be added as needed]
  BT **Agricultural industry**
  NT **Beverage industry**
      Food service
      Grocery trade
      Meat industry
  RT **Food**
Food inspection
  USE **Food adulteration and inspection**
Food—Labeling **363.19; 641**
  UF Food labels
Food labels
  USE **Food—Labeling**
Food—Law and legislation (May subdiv. geog.) **344**
  UF Food laws
  BT **Law**
      Legislation
  RT **Food adulteration and inspection**
Food laws
  USE **Food—Law and legislation**
Food—Microbiology **664**
  UF Food—Bacteriology
  BT **Microbiology**

Food of animal origin   641.3

Use for materials on human food of animal origin. Materials on the food and food habits of animals are entered under **Animals—Food**.

UF   Animal food

Animals as food

Animals, Edible

BT   **Food**

Food—Packaging (May subdiv. geog.) **664**

UF   Groceries—Packaging

BT   **Packaging**

Food plants

USE   **Edible plants**

Food poisoning (May subdiv. geog.) **615.9**

BT   **Poisons and poisoning**

Food preparation

USE   **Cooking**

Food industry

Food preparation industry

USE   **Food industry**

Food—Preservation   641.4; 664

UF   Preservation of food

SA   types of foods with the subdivision *Preservation* [to be added as needed]

NT   **Canning and preserving**

Cold storage

Food additives

Fruit—Preservation

RT   **Dried foods**

Frozen foods

Food processing

USE   **Food industry**

Food processing industry

USE   **Food industry**

Food—Purchasing

USE   **Grocery shopping**

Food relief (May subdiv. geog.) **363.8**

UF   Food assistance programs

SA   types of food relief, e.g. **Meals on wheels programs**; and names of wars with the subdivision *Civilian relief* or *Food supply* [to be added as needed]

BT   **Charities**

Disaster relief

Public welfare

Unemployed

NT   **Food banks**

Food stamps

Meals on wheels programs

World War, 1939-1945—Civilian relief

World War, 1939-1945—Food supply

Food service (May subdiv. geog.) **642; 647.95**

Use for materials on the preparation, delivery, and serving of ready-to-eat foods in large quantities outside of the home. Materials solely on the preparation of food in large quantities are entered under **Quantity cooking**.

UF   Cooking for institutions

Mass feeding

Volume feeding

BT   **Food industry**

Service industries

NT   **Bartending**

Catering

Restaurants

Waiters and waitresses

RT   **Quantity cooking**

Food—Sodium content   613.2

UF   Sodium content of food

BT   **Food—Composition**

Food stamp program

USE   **Food stamps**

Food stamps (May subdiv. geog.) **363.8**

UF   Food coupons

Food stamp program

BT   **Food relief**

Food supplements

USE   **Dietary supplements**

Food supply (May subdiv. geog.) **363.8**

Use for economic materials on the availability of food in general and on the conservation of food in wartime.

UF   Food control

SA   names of wars with the subdivision *Food supply*, e.g. **World War, 1939-1945—Food supply** [to be added as needed]

NT   **Famines**

RT   **Agriculture**

Food trade

USE   **Food industry**

Fools and jesters (May subdiv. geog.) **791.092; 920**

UF   Court fools

Jesters

Fools and jesters—*Continued*
    BT   **Comedians**
          Courts and courtiers
          Entertainers
Foot   611; 612
    UF   Feet
    BT   **Anatomy**
Foot—Care   617.5
    UF   Foot—Care and hygiene
    BT   **Podiatry**
Foot—Care and hygiene
    USE   **Foot—Care**
Foot injuries
    USE   **Foot—Wounds and injuries**
Foot—Paralysis   616.8
    BT   **Paralysis**
Foot—Wounds and injuries   617.5
    UF   Foot injuries
    RT   **Podiatry**
Football (May subdiv. geog.)   796.332
    BT   **Ball games**
          Sports
    NT   **Soccer**
          Super Bowl (Game)
Football—Coaching   796.33207
    BT   **Coaching (Athletics)**
Footwear
    USE   **Shoes**
Forage plants (May subdiv. geog.)
    633.2
    SA   names of forage plants [to be
          added as needed]
    BT   **Economic botany**
          Feeds
          Plants
    NT   **Alfalfa**
          Corn
          Hay
          Silage and silos
          Soybean
    RT   **Grasses**
Force and energy   531
    UF   Conservation of energy
          Energy
    BT   **Power (Mechanics)**
    RT   **Dynamics**
          Mechanics
          Motion
          Quantum theory
Forced indoctrination
    USE   **Brainwashing**

Forced labor (May subdiv. geog.)
    331.11
    UF   Compulsory labor
          Conscript labor
    BT   **Crimes against humanity**
          Labor
    NT   **Convict labor**
          Peonage
    RT   **Slavery**
Forced migration (May subdiv. geog.)
    325
    BT   **Internal migration**
Forced removal of Indians
    USE   **Native Americans—Relocation**
Forced repatriation
    USE   names of wars with the subdivi-
          sion *Forced repatriation,* e.g.
          World War, 1939-1945—
          Forced repatriation [to be
          added as needed]
Ford automobile   629.222
    BT   **Automobiles**
Forecasting   003
    UF   Forecasts
          Futurology
          Predictions
    SA   types of forecasting, e.g. **Weath-**
          er forecasting; and subjects
          and names of countries, cities,
          etc., with the subdivision
          Forecasting, e.g. **Energy con-**
          sumption—Forecasting [to be
          added as needed]
    NT   **Business forecasting**
          Economic forecasting
          Weather forecasting
Forecasts
    USE   **Forecasting**
Foreign affairs
    USE   **International relations**
Foreign aid (May subdiv. geog.)   338.91
    Use for general materials on international
    economic aid given in the form of gifts, loans,
    relief grants, etc. Materials limited to foreign
    aid in the form of technical expertise are en-
    tered under **Technical assistance**.
    UF   Aid to developing areas
          Assistance to developing areas
          Economic aid
          Economic assistance
          Foreign aid program
          Foreign assistance

Foreign aid—*Continued*

  SA   foreign aid from particular coun-
        tries, e.g. **American foreign**
        aid [to be added as needed]

  BT   **Economic policy**
        International cooperation
        International economic rela-
        tions

  NT   **American foreign aid**
        Technical assistance
        World War, 1939-1945—Civil-
        ian relief

  RT   **Reconstruction (1914-1939)**
        Reconstruction (1939-1951)

Foreign aid program
  USE **Foreign aid**
        Military assistance
        Technical assistance

Foreign area studies
  USE **Area studies**

Foreign assistance
  USE **Foreign aid**

Foreign automobiles (May subdiv. geog.)
      629.222

  UF   Automobiles, Foreign
        Foreign cars

  SA   names of specific makes and
        models [to be added as need-
        ed]

  BT   **Automobiles**

Foreign cars
  USE **Foreign automobiles**

Foreign commerce
  USE **International trade**

Foreign countries
  USE ethnic and national groups, indi-
        vidual languages and litera-
        tures, military services, and
        types of publications qualified
        by language or nationality
        with the subdivision *Foreign*
        countries, e.g. **Americans—**
        Foreign countries [to be add-
        ed as needed]

Foreign economic relations
  USE **International economic rela-**
        tions
      and names of countries with the
        subdivision *Foreign economic*
        relations, e.g. **United**
        States—Foreign economic re-

lations [to be added as need-
ed]

Foreign economic relations—United States
  USE **United States—Foreign eco-**
        nomic relations

Foreign exchange (May subdiv. geog.)
      332.4

  UF   Exchange rates
        International exchange

  BT   **Banks and banking**
        Exchange
        Finance
        Money

Foreign influences
  USE subjects, ethnic groups, and liter-
        atures with the subdivision
        Foreign influences, e.g. **Unit-**
        ed States—Civilization—For-
        eign influences [to be added
        as needed]

Foreign investments (May subdiv. geog.)
      332.6

  UF   International investment
        Investments, Foreign

  BT   **Investments**
        Multinational corporations

Foreign language dictionaries
  USE **English language—Dictionar-**
        ies—French
        French language—Dictionar-
        ies—English

Foreign language laboratories
  USE **Language laboratories**

Foreign language phrases
  USE **English language—Foreign**
        words and phrases
        Modern languages—Conversa-
        tion and phrase books

Foreign military sales
  USE **Arms transfers**

Foreign missions, Christian
  USE **Christian missions**

Foreign opinion
  USE names of countries with the sub-
        division *Foreign opinion,*
        which may be further subdi-
        vided by the country holding
        the opinion, e.g. **United**
        States—Foreign opinion;
        United States—Foreign opin-

Foreign opinion—*Continued*
ion—**France;** etc. [to be added as needed]
Foreign policy
USE **International relations**
Foreign population
USE **Aliens**
Immigrants
Immigration and emigration
Minorities
Population
and names of countries with the subdivision *Population,* e.g. **United States—Population;** or with the subdivision *Immigration and emigration,* e.g. **United States—Immigration and emigration** [to be added as needed]
Foreign public opinion
USE names of countries with the subdivision *Foreign opinion,* which may be further subdivided by the country holding the opinion, e.g. **United States—Foreign opinion; United States—Foreign opinion—France;** etc. [to be added as needed]
Foreign relations
USE **International relations**
and names of countries with the subdivision *Foreign relations,* e.g. **United States—Foreign relations** [to be added as needed]
Foreign service
USE **Diplomatic and consular service**
Foreign students (May subdiv. geog.)
370.116
UF College students, Foreign
Students, Foreign
BT **Students**
Foreign study (May subdiv. geog.)
370.116
UF Overseas study
Study abroad
Study, Foreign
Study overseas
BT **Education**

Foreign trade
USE **International trade**
Foreign words and phrases
USE names of languages with the subdivision *Foreign words and phrases,* e.g. **English language—Foreign words and phrases** [to be added as needed]
Foreigners
USE **Aliens**
Immigrants
Foremen
USE **Supervisors**
Forensic anthropology 301; 363.25
BT **Anthropology**
Forensic sciences
Forensic medicine
USE **Medical jurisprudence**
Forensic science
USE **Forensic sciences**
Forensic sciences (May subdiv. geog.)
363.25
Use for materials on science as applied in courts of law or in criminal investigations.
UF Criminalistics
Forensic science
BT **Science**
NT **Forensic anthropology**
Medical jurisprudence
RT **Criminal investigation**
Foreordination
USE **Predestination**
Forest animals (May subdiv. geog.)
578.73
UF Forest fauna
BT **Animals**
NT **Jungle animals**
Forest conservation (May subdiv. geog.)
333.75
UF Conservation of forests
Forest preservation
Preservation of forests
BT **Conservation of natural resources**
RT **Forest reserves**
Forests and forestry
Forest depletion
USE **Deforestation**
Forest ecology (May subdiv. geog.)
577.3
BT **Ecology**

Forest ecology—*Continued*
   NT   **Jungle ecology**
Forest fauna
   USE   **Forest animals**
Forest fires (May subdiv. geog.)   **634.9**
   BT   **Fires**
Forest influences (May subdiv. geog.)
         577.3
   UF   Climate and forests
         Floods and forests
         Forests and climate
         Forests and floods
         Forests and rainfall
         Forests and water supply
         Rainfall and forests
   BT   **Climate**
         Water supply
   RT   **Flood control**
         Forests and forestry
         Plant ecology
         Rain
Forest plants (May subdiv. geog.)   **581.7**
   BT   **Forests and forestry**
         Plant ecology
         Plants
Forest preservation
   USE   **Forest conservation**
Forest products (May subdiv. geog.)
         634.9; 674
   BT   **Commercial products**
         Economic botany
         Raw materials
   NT   **Gums and resins**
         Lumber and lumbering
         Rubber
         Wood
Forest reserves (May subdiv. geog.)
         333.75; 719
   UF   National forests
   BT   **Public lands**
   NT   **Wilderness areas**
   RT   **Forest conservation**
         Forests and forestry
         National parks and reserves
Forestry
   USE   **Forests and forestry**
Forests and climate
   USE   **Forest influences**
Forests and floods
   USE   **Forest influences**
Forests and forestry (May subdiv. geog.)
         577.3; 634.9

   UF   Arboriculture
         Forestry
         Timber
         Woods
   BT   **Agriculture**
         Natural resources
   NT   **Christmas tree growing**
         Deforestation
         Forest plants
         Jungles
         Logging
         Lumber and lumbering
         Pruning
         Rain forests
         Reforestation
         Tree planting
         Urban forestry
   RT   **Forest conservation**
         Forest influences
         Forest reserves
         Trees
         Wood
Forests and forestry—United States
         577.30973; 634.90973
Forests and rainfall
   USE   **Forest influences**
Forests and water supply
   USE   **Forest influences**
Forgeries
   USE   names of individual persons and
         types of art objects, docu-
         ments, etc., with the subdivi-
         sion *Forgeries,* e.g. **Art—
         Forgeries** [to be added as
         needed]
Forgery (May subdiv. geog.)   **332;
         364.16**
   SA   names of individual persons and
         types of art objects, docu-
         ments, etc., with the subdivi-
         sion *Forgeries,* e.g. **Art—
         Forgeries** [to be added as
         needed]
   BT   **Crime**
         Fraud
         Impostors and imposture
   NT   **Art—Forgeries**
         Counterfeits and counterfeiting
         Literary forgeries
         Piltdown forgery

Forgery of works of art
    USE   **Art—Forgeries**
Forgetfulness   153.1
    BT   **Memory**
         Personality
Forging (May subdiv. geog.)   **671.3; 682**
    UF   Drop forging
    BT   **Manufacturing processes**
         Metalwork
    NT   **Welding**
    RT   **Blacksmithing**
         Ironwork
Forgiveness   179
    BT   **Virtue**
    RT   **Amnesty**
         Clemency
         Pardon
Forgiveness of sin   234
    UF   Sin, Forgiveness of
    RT   **Penance**
         Sin
Form in biology
    USE   **Morphology**
Formal gardens
    USE   **Gardens**
Former nuns
    USE   **Ex-nuns**
Former priests
    USE   **Ex-priests**
Formosa
    USE   **Taiwan**
Formula translation (Computer language)
    USE   **FORTRAN (Computer language)**
Fortification (May subdiv. geog.)   **623**
    UF   Forts
    SA   names of countries with the sub-
         division *Defenses* [to be add-
         ed as needed]
    BT   **Military art and science**
    RT   **Military engineering**
FORTRAN (Computer language)
    005.13
    UF   Formula translation (Computer
         language)
         FORTRAN (Computer program
         language)
    BT   **Programming languages**
FORTRAN (Computer program language)
    USE   **FORTRAN (Computer lan-
         guage)**

Forts
    USE   **Fortification**
Fortune
    USE   **Fate and fatalism**
         Probabilities
         Success
Fortune telling (May subdiv. geog.)
    133.3
    BT   **Amusements**
         Divination
    NT   **Palmistry**
         Tarot
Fortunes
    USE   **Income**
         Wealth
Forums (Discussions)
    USE   **Discussion groups**
Fossil botany
    USE   **Fossil plants**
Fossil hominids (May subdiv. geog.)
    569.9
    UF   Hominids, Fossil
         Human fossils
         Human paleontology
         Man, Prehistoric
         Prehistoric man
         Prehistory
    BT   **Archeology**
         Fossils
    NT   **Neanderthals**
         Piltdown forgery
    RT   **Human origins**
Fossil mammals (May subdiv. geog.)
    569
    UF   Mammals, Fossil
    SA   types of extinct mammals [to be
         added as needed]
    BT   **Fossils**
         Mammals
    NT   **Mammoths**
         Mastodon
Fossil plants (May subdiv. geog.)   **561**
    UF   Extinct plants
         Fossil botany
         Paleobotany
         Plants, Extinct
         Plants, Fossil
    BT   **Fossils**
         Plants
Fossil reptiles (May subdiv. geog.)
    567.9

Fossil reptiles—*Continued*
UF   Reptiles, Fossil
SA   types of fossil reptiles, e.g. **Dinosaurs** [to be added as needed]
BT   **Fossils**
      Reptiles
NT   **Dinosaurs**

Fossils (May subdiv. geog.)   **560**
BT   **Biology**
      Natural history
      Science
      Stratigraphic geology
NT   **Fossil hominids**
      Fossil mammals
      Fossil plants
      Fossil reptiles
      Prehistoric animals
RT   **Extinct animals**
      Paleontology

Foster children (May subdiv. geog.)   **306.874**
BT   **Children**
RT   **Foster home care**

Foster grandparents   **362.73**
BT   **Grandparents**
      Volunteer work

Foster home care (May subdiv. geog.)   **362.73**
UF   Child placing
      Children—Placing out
BT   **Child welfare**
RT   **Adoption**
      Children—Institutional care
      Foster children
      Group homes

Foundations (May subdiv. geog.)   **624.1; 721**
BT   **Architecture—Details**
      Buildings
      Structural engineering
NT   **Basements**
      Concrete
RT   **Soil mechanics**

Foundations (Endowments)
USE   **Endowments**

Founding (May subdiv. geog.)   **671.2**
Use for materials on the melting and casting of metals.
UF   Casting
      Foundry practice
      Molding (Metal)
      Moulding (Metal)
BT   **Manufacturing processes**
      Metalwork
NT   **Type and type-founding**
RT   **Patternmaking**

Founding Fathers of the United States   **973.4**
BT   **Statesmen—United States**

Foundlings
USE   **Orphans**

Foundry practice
USE   **Founding**

Four-day week
USE   **Flexible hours of labor**

Four-H clubs
USE   **4-H clubs**

Fourteenth century
USE   **World history—14th century**

Fourth dimension   **530.11**
UF   Dimension, Fourth
      Hyperspace
BT   **Mathematics**
NT   **Space and time**
      Time travel

Fourth of July   **394.2634**
UF   4th of July
      Independence Day (United States)
      July Fourth
BT   **Holidays**
      United States—History—1775-1783, Revolution

Fractal geometry
USE   **Fractals**

Fractals   **514**
UF   Fractal geometry
      Sets, Fractal
      Sets of fractional dimension
BT   **Geometry**
      Mathematical models
      Set theory
      Topology

Fractions   **513.2**
BT   **Arithmetic**
      Mathematics

Fractured fairy tales   **398.2; 808.83**
UF   Fairy tales—Parodies, imitations, etc.
BT   **Fairy tales**
      Parodies

Fractures   **617.1**

Fractures—*Continued*
    BT **Bones**
         Wounds and injuries
Fragrant gardens (May subdiv. geog.)
    635.9
    UF Gardening for fragrance
         Scented gardens
    BT **Gardens**
    RT **Aromatic plants**
Framing of pictures
    USE **Picture frames and framing**
France **944**
    May be subdivided like United States except for History.
France—Blacks
    USE **Blacks—France**
France—Folk songs
    USE **Folk songs—France**
France—History **944**
France—History—0-1328 **944**
    NT **Celts**
France—History—1328-1589, House of Valois **944**
    NT **Hundred Years' War, 1339-1453**
         Saint Bartholomew's Day, Massacre of, 1572
France—History—1589-1789, Bourbons **944**
France—History—1789-1799, Revolution **944.04**
    UF Directory, French, 1795-1799
         French Revolution
         Reign of Terror
         Revolution, French
         Terror, Reign of
    BT **Revolutions**
France—History—1799-1815 **944.05**
    NT **Napoleonic Wars, 1800-1815**
France—History—1815-1914 **944.06**
France—History—20th century **944.081**
France—History—1914-1940 **944.081**
France—History—1940-1945, German occupation **944.081**
    UF German occupation of France, 1940-1945
France—History—1945- **944.082**
France—History—1945-1958 **944.082**
France—History—1958- **944.083**
    UF France—History—1958-1969
         France—History—1969-

France—History—1958-1969
    USE **France—History—1958-**
France—History—1969-
    USE **France—History—1958-**
France—History—21st century **944.084**
Franchise
    USE **Citizenship**
         Elections
         Suffrage
Franchises (Retail trade) (May subdiv. geog.) **658.8**
    UF Franchising
         Retail franchises
    BT **Retail trade**
Franchising
    USE **Franchises (Retail trade)**
Franciscans **271**
    UF Friars Minor
         Gray Friars
         Grey Friars
         Mendicant orders
         Minorites
         Saint Francis, Order of
         St. Francis, Order of
    BT **Monasticism and religious orders**
Frankenstein (Fictional character) **823**
    BT **Fictional characters**
Fraternities and sororities (May subdiv. geog.) **371.8**
    UF College fraternities
         College sororities
         Greek letter societies
         Sororities
    BT **Colleges and universities**
         Students—Societies
    RT **Secret societies**
Fraud (May subdiv. geog.) **364.16**
    UF Deceit
         Ripoffs
    BT **Commercial law**
         Crime
         Offenses against property
         White collar crimes
    NT **Credit card fraud**
         Forgery
         Securities fraud
    RT **Impostors and imposture**
         Swindlers and swindling
Fraud in science (May subdiv. geog.) **501**

Fraud in science—*Continued*
    UF   Scientific fraud
    BT   **Science**
Frauds, Literary
    USE **Literary forgeries**
Fraudulent advertising
    USE **Deceptive advertising**
Free agency
    USE **Free will and determinism**
Free coinage
    USE **Monetary policy**
Free computer software   **005.3**
    UF   Free software
          Freeware
          Public domain software
    BT   **Computer software**
          Free material
Free diving
    USE **Scuba diving**
          Skin diving
Free enterprise (May subdiv. geog.)
    330.12
    UF   Free markets
          Laissez-faire
          Private enterprise
    BT   **Economic policy**
    RT   **Capitalism**
Free fall
    USE **Weightlessness**
Free love (May subdiv. geog.)   **176;**
    306.7
    BT   **Sexual ethics**
Free markets
    USE **Free enterprise**
Free material (May subdiv. geog.)
    UF   Freebies
          Giveaways
    BT   **Gifts**
    NT   **Free computer software**
Free press
    USE **Freedom of the press**
Free press and fair trial
    USE **Freedom of the press and fair
           trial**
Free schools
    USE **Experimental schools**
Free software
    USE **Free computer software**
Free speech
    USE **Freedom of speech**
Free thought (May subdiv. geog.)   **211**
    BT   **Freedom of conscience**

    NT   **Agnosticism**
          Skepticism
    RT   **Deism**
          Rationalism
Free time (Leisure)
    USE **Leisure**
Free trade (May subdiv. geog.)   **382**
    UF   Fair trade (Tariff)
          Free trade and protection
    BT   **Commercial policy**
          International trade
    RT   **Protectionism**
          Tariff
Free trade and protection
    USE **Free trade**
          Protectionism
Free universities (May subdiv. geog.)
    378
    UF   Alternative universities
          Experimental universities
          Open universities
    BT   **Colleges and universities**
Free verse   **808.1; 808.81**
    Use for collections or materials about free
    verse, not for individual works.
    UF   Vers libre
    BT   **Poetry**
Free will and determinism   **123**
    UF   Choice, Freedom of
          Determinism and indeterminism
          Free agency
          Freedom of choice
          Freedom of the will
          Indeterminism
          Liberty of the will
          Will
    BT   **Philosophy**
    RT   **Fate and fatalism**
          Predestination
Freebies
    USE **Free material**
Freedom (May subdiv. geog.)   **323.4**
    UF   Civil liberty
          Emancipation
          Liberty
          Personal freedom
    BT   **Democracy**
          Political science
    NT   **Anarchism and anarchists**
          Conformity
          Freedom of assembly
          Freedom of association

Freedom—*Continued*
        Freedom of conscience
        Freedom of movement
        Freedom of religion
        Freedom of speech
        Freedom of the press
        Intellectual freedom
        Slaves—Emancipation
  RT **Civil rights**
      Equality
Freedom, Academic
  USE **Academic freedom**
Freedom marches for civil rights
  USE **Civil rights demonstrations**
Freedom of assembly (May subdiv. geog.)
      323.4
  UF Assembly, Right of
      Right of assembly
  BT **Civil rights**
      Freedom
  NT **Public meetings**
      Riots
  RT **Freedom of association**
      Freedom of speech
Freedom of association (May subdiv. gcog.) **323.4**
  UF Association, Freedom of
      Right of association
  BT **Civil rights**
      Freedom
  RT **Freedom of assembly**
Freedom of choice
  USE **Free will and determinism**
Freedom of choice movement
  USE **Pro-choice movement**
Freedom of conscience (May subdiv. geog.) **323.44**
  UF Liberty of conscience
  BT **Conscience**
      Freedom
      Toleration
  NT **Conscientious objectors**
      Dissent
      Free thought
      Public opinion
  RT **Freedom of religion**
Freedom of information (May subdiv. geog.) **323.44**
  UF Information, Freedom of
      Right to know
  BT **Civil rights**
      Intellectual freedom

  NT **Press—Government policy**
  RT **Censorship**
      Freedom of speech
      Freedom of the press
Freedom of movement (May subdiv. geog.) **323.4**
  UF Movement, Freedom of
  BT **Civil rights**
      Freedom
Freedom of religion (May subdiv. geog.) **201; 261.7; 323.44**
  UF Freedom of worship
      Religious freedom
      Religious liberty
  BT **Civil rights**
      Freedom
      Toleration
  NT **Dissent**
  RT **Freedom of conscience**
      Persecution
Freedom of speech (May subdiv. geog.) **323.44**
  UF Free speech
      Liberty of speech
      Speech, Freedom of
  BT **Censorship**
      Civil rights
      Freedom
      Intellectual freedom
  RT **Freedom of assembly**
      Freedom of information
      Libel and slander
Freedom of teaching
  USE **Academic freedom**
Freedom of the press (May subdiv. geog.) **323.44**
  UF Free press
      Liberty of the press
      Press censorship
  BT **Civil rights**
      Freedom
      Intellectual freedom
      Press
  NT **Freedom of the press and fair trial**
  RT **Censorship**
      Freedom of information
      Libel and slander
Freedom of the press and fair trial **323.42; 323.44; 342**

Freedom of the press and fair trial—*Continued*

    UF   Fair trial and free press

          Free press and fair trial

          Prejudicial publicity

          Trial by publicity

    BT   **Fair trial**

          Freedom of the press

          Press

Freedom of the will

    USE   **Free will and determinism**

Freedom of worship

    USE   **Freedom of religion**

Freedom (Psychology)

    USE   **Autonomy (Psychology)**

Freelancers

    USE   **Self-employed**

Freemasons   366

    UF   Masonic orders

          Masons (Secret order)

    BT   **Secret societies**

Freeware

    USE   **Free computer software**

Freeways

    USE   **Express highways**

Freeze-dried foods   641.4; 664

    UF   Food, Freeze-dried

    BT   **Dried foods**

Freezing

    USE   **Cryobiology**

          Frost

          Ice

          Refrigeration

Freezing of human bodies

    USE   **Cryonics**

Freight (May subdiv. geog.)   388

    UF   Freight and freightage

    BT   **Maritime law**

          Materials handling

          Railroads

          Transportation

    NT   **Commercial aeronautics**

          Trucking

    RT   **Railroads—Rates**

Freight and freightage

    USE   **Freight**

French and Indian War

    USE   **United States—History—1755-1763, French and Indian War**

French Canadian literature

    USE   **Canadian literature (French)**

French Canadian poetry

    USE   **Canadian poetry (French)**

French Canadians (May subdiv. geog.)   305.811; 971

    BT   **Canadians**

French cookery

    USE   **French cooking**

French cooking   641.5944

    UF   Cookery, French

          French cookery

    BT   **Cooking**

French Equatorial Africa

    USE   **French-speaking Equatorial Africa**

French folk songs

    USE   **Folk songs—France**

French language   440

    May be subdivided like **English language**.

    BT   **Language and languages**

          Romance languages

French language—Conversation and phrase books   448

    UF   French language—Conversations and phrases

French language—Conversations and phrases

    USE   **French language—Conversation and phrase books**

French language—Dictionaries—English   443

    Use for French-English dictionaries. English-French dictionaries are entered under **English language—Dictionaries—French**. Combined French-English and English-French dictionaries are entered under both headings.

    UF   Foreign language dictionaries

    BT   **Encyclopedias and dictionaries**

    RT   **English language—Dictionaries—French**

French language—Reading materials   448.6

French literature   840

    May use same subdivisions and names of literary forms as for **English literature**.

    BT   **Literature**

          Romance literature

    NT   **French poetry**

French literature—Black authors   840.8; 840.9

    Use for collections or materials about French literature by several Black authors, not for individual works.

    UF   Black literature (French)

French literature—Canada
  USE **Canadian literature (French)**
French poetry   841
  BT   **French literature**
       Poetry
  NT   **Troubadours**
French poetry—Black authors   841
  Use for collections or materials about French poetry by several Black authors, not for individual works.
  UF   Black poetry (French)
French Revolution
  USE **France—History—1789-1799,**
       Revolution
French-speaking Equatorial Africa   967
  Use for materials dealing collectively with the region of Africa that includes Central African Republic, Chad, Congo (Republic), and Gabon. The former name for the region was French Equatorial Africa.
  UF   Africa, French-speaking Equatorial
       French Equatorial Africa
  BT   **Central Africa**
French-speaking West Africa   966
  Use for materials dealing collectively with the region of Africa that includes Benin, Burkina Faso, Guinea, Ivory Coast, Mali, Mauritania, Niger, Senegal, and Togo.
  UF   Africa, French-speaking West
       French West Africa
  BT   **West Africa**
French West Africa
  USE **French-speaking West Africa**
Frequency modulation, Radio
  USE **Radio frequency modulation**
Fresco painting
  USE **Mural painting and decoration**
Freshwater animals (May subdiv. geog.)
       591.76
  UF   Freshwater fauna
  SA   types of freshwater animals [to be added as needed]
  BT   **Aquatic animals**
  RT   **Freshwater biology**
Freshwater aquaculture
  USE **Aquaculture**
Freshwater biology   578.76
  BT   **Biology**
  NT   **Aquariums**
       Freshwater plants
  RT   **Freshwater animals**
Freshwater ecology (May subdiv. geog.)
       577.6

  BT   **Ecology**
  NT   **Stream ecology**
Freshwater fauna
  USE **Freshwater animals**
Freshwater plants (May subdiv. geog.)
       581.7
  UF   Aquatic plants
       Water plants
  BT   **Freshwater biology**
       Plants
  RT   **Marine plants**
Friars Minor
  USE **Franciscans**
Friendly fire (Military science) (May subdiv. geog.)   **355.4**
  BT   **Military art and science**
Friends
  USE **Friendship**
Friends and associates
  USE names of individuals with the subdivision *Friends and associates* [to be added as needed]
Friends, Society of
  USE **Society of Friends**
Friendship   177
  UF   Affection
       Friends
  BT   **Human behavior**
  NT   **Crushes**
       Female friendship
  RT   **Love**
Friendship between women
  USE **Female friendship**
Friendship in women
  USE **Female friendship**
Friesian cattle
  USE **Holstein-Friesian cattle**
Frogs (May subdiv. geog.)   **597.8**
  UF   Tadpoles
  BT   **Amphibians**
Frogs—Dissection   597.8
  BT   **Dissection**
Frontier and pioneer life (May subdiv. geog.)   **978**
  UF   Border life
       Pioneer life
  BT   **Adventure and adventurers**
  NT   **Cowhands**
       Native Americans—Captivities

Frontier and pioneer life—*Continued*
       Overland journeys to the Pacific
       Ranch life
Frontiers
   USE **Boundaries**
Frost   551.57
   UF Freezing
   BT **Meteorology**
       Water
   NT **Ice**
       Refrigeration
Frozen animal embryos
   USE **Frozen embryos**
Frozen embryos   176; 571.8; 612.6
   UF Animal embryos, Frozen
       Embryos, Frozen
       Frozen animal embryos
       Frozen human embryos
       Human embryos, Frozen
   BT **Cryobiology**
       Embryology
Frozen foods   641.4; 664
   BT **Food**
   NT **Ice cream, ices, etc.**
   RT **Food—Preservation**
Frozen human embryos
   USE **Frozen embryos**
Frozen stars
   USE **Black holes (Astronomy)**
Fruit (May subdiv. geog.)   **634; 641.3**
   Names of tree fruits may be used for either the fruit or the tree.
   SA types of fruits, e.g. **Berries**; **Apples**; **Citrus fruits**; etc. [to be added as needed]
   BT **Food**
       Plants
   NT **Apples**
       Berries
       Citrus fruits
       Fruit culture
       Grapes
Fruit—Canning
   USE **Fruit—Preservation**
Fruit culture (May subdiv. geog.)   **634**
   Names of tree fruits may be used for either the fruit or the tree.
   UF Arboriculture
       Orchards
   BT **Agriculture**
       Fruit

       Gardening
       Horticulture
       Trees
   NT **Berries**
       Nurseries (Horticulture)
       Plant propagation
       Pruning
Fruit—Diseases and pests (May subdiv. geog.)   **634**
   BT **Agricultural pests**
       Insect pests
       Pests
       Plant diseases
   NT **Spraying and dusting**
Fruit flies (May subdiv. geog.)   **595.77**
   BT **Flies**
Fruit painting and illustration
   USE **Botanical illustration**
Fruit—Preservation (May subdiv. geog.)   **641.4; 664**
   UF Fruit—Canning
   BT **Canning and preserving**
       Food—Preservation
Frustration   152.4
   UF Futility
   BT **Attitude (Psychology)**
       Emotions
Fuel (May subdiv. geog.)   **333.8; 662**
   SA types of fuel; and subjects with the subdivision *Fuel consumption* [to be added as needed]
   BT **Combustion**
       Energy resources
       Engines
       Fire
       Home economics
   NT **Alcohol fuels**
       Automobiles—Fuel consumption
       Biomass energy
       Charcoal
       Coal
       Gas
       Gasoline
       Natural gas
       Petroleum as fuel
       Synthetic fuels
       Wood
   RT **Heating**
Fuel cells   621.31

Fuel cells—*Continued*
    BT   **Electric batteries**
           Electrochemistry
Fuel consumption
    USE   subjects with the subdivision
           Fuel consumption, e.g. **Auto-**
           mobiles—Fuel consumption
           [to be added as needed]
Fuel oil
    USE   **Petroleum as fuel**
Fugitive slaves (May subdiv. geog.)
    306.3
    UF   Runaway slaves
    BT   **Slaves**
Fugue   784.18
    Use for musical scores and for materials on
    the fugue as a musical form.
    UF   Canons, fugues, etc.
           Fugues
           Prelude and fugue
           Preludes and fugues
    BT   **Counterpoint**
           Musical form
Fugues
    USE   **Fugue**
Fulfillment, Self
    USE   **Self-realization**
Fumigation   614.4; 648
    BT   **Communicable diseases**
           Insecticides
    RT   **Disinfection and disinfectants**
Functional competencies
    USE   **Life skills**
Functional literacy (May subdiv. geog.)
    302.2; 374
    UF   Occupational literacy
    BT   **Literacy**
Functions   511.3
    UF   Analysis (Mathematics)
    BT   **Differential equations**
           Mathematical analysis
           Mathematics
           Set theory
    RT   **Calculus**
Fund raising (May subdiv. geog.)
    361.7068; 658.15
    UF   Community chests
           Money raising
    BT   **Finance**
    RT   **Gifts**
Fundamental education
    USE   **Basic education**

Fundamental life skills
    USE   **Life skills**
Fundamental rights
    USE   **Civil rights**
           Human rights
Fundamentalism
    USE   **Christian fundamentalism**
           Islamic fundamentalism
           Religious fundamentalism
Fundamentalism and education
    USE   **Church and education**
           Creationism
           Religion in the public schools
Fundamentalism and evolution
    USE   **Creationism**
Fundamentalist movements
    USE   **Religious fundamentalism**
Funding
    USE   **Finance**
Funding for the arts
    USE   **Art patronage**
           Arts—Government policy
           Federal aid to the arts
Funds
    USE   **Finance**
Funeral customs and rites
    USE   **Funeral rites and ceremonies**
           and ethnic groups and native
           peoples with the subdivision
           Funeral customs and rites [to
           be added as needed]
Funeral directors
    USE   **Undertakers and undertaking**
Funeral rites and ceremonies (May
    subdiv. geog.)   **393**
    UF   Funeral customs and rites
           Graves
           Mortuary customs
           Mourning customs
    SA   ethnic groups and native peoples
           with the subdivision *Funeral*
           customs and rites [to be add-
           ed as needed]
    BT   **Manners and customs**
           Rites and ceremonies
    NT   **Dead**
    RT   **Burial**
           Cremation
Fungi   579.5
    UF   Diseases and pests
           Mycology

Fungi—*Continued*
- BT **Agricultural pests**
  - **Pests**
  - **Plants**
- NT **Molds (Fungi)**
  - **Plant diseases**
  - **Yeast**
- RT **Mushrooms**

Fungicides   632; 668
- UF Germicides
- BT **Pesticides**
- RT **Spraying and dusting**

Funicular railroads
- USE **Cable railroads**

Funnies
- USE **Comic books, strips, etc.**

Fur   675; 685
- BT **Animals—Anatomy**
- RT **Hides and skins**

Fur-bearing animals
- USE **Furbearing animals**

Fur trade (May subdiv. geog.)   **338.3**
- BT **Trapping**

Furbearing animals (May subdiv. geog.) **599.7; 636.97**
- UF Fur-bearing animals
- SA types of furbearing animals, e.g. **Beavers** [to be added as needed]
- BT **Animals**
  - **Economic zoology**
- NT **Beavers**

Furnaces (May subdiv. geog.)   **697**
- BT **Heating**
- NT **Blast furnaces**
  - **Smelting**

Furniture   645; 749
- SA furniture of particular countries, e.g. **American furniture**; types of furniture, and names of specific articles of furniture, e.g. **Tables**; **Chairs**; etc. [to be added as needed]
- BT **Decoration and ornament**
  - **Decorative arts**
  - **Interior design**
- NT **American furniture**
  - **Built-in furniture**
  - **Chairs**
  - **Chests**
  - **Church furniture**
  - **Furniture making**

- **Garden ornaments and furniture**
- **Libraries—Equipment and supplies**
- **Mirrors**
- **Schools—Equipment and supplies**
- **Tables**
- **Veneers and veneering**
- RT **Cabinetwork**
  - **Upholstery**

Furniture, American
- USE **American furniture**

Furniture building
- USE **Furniture making**

Furniture—Conservation and restoration
- USE **Furniture finishing**
  - **Furniture—Repairing**

Furniture finishing   684.1; 749
- UF Furniture—Conservation and restoration
  - Furniture—Refinishing
  - Furniture—Restoration
  - Refinishing furniture
  - Restoration of furniture
- BT **Furniture making**
  - **Handicraft**
  - **Wood finishing**
- RT **Furniture—Repairing**

Furniture making (May subdiv. geog.) **684.1; 749**
- UF Furniture building
- BT **Furniture**
  - **Woodwork**
- NT **Furniture finishing**
  - **Furniture—Repairing**

Furniture—Refinishing
- USE **Furniture finishing**

Furniture—Repairing   684.1; 749
- UF Furniture—Conservation and restoration
  - Furniture—Restoration
  - Restoration of furniture
- BT **Furniture making**
- RT **Furniture finishing**

Furniture—Restoration
- USE **Furniture finishing**
  - **Furniture—Repairing**

Futility
- USE **Frustration**

Future life   129; 236

Use for materials on the character and form of a future existence. Materials on the question of the endless existence of the soul are entered under **Immortality**. Materials on the philosophical concept of eternity are entered under **Eternity**.

UF   Afterlife
       Eternal life
       Intermediate state
       Life after death
       Life, Future
       Resurrection
BT   **Death**
       Eschatology
NT   **Heaven**
       Hell
       Paradise
       Soul
RT   **Eternity**
       Immortality

Future shock
   USE   **Culture conflict**

Futures (May subdiv. geog.)   **332.64**

UF   Futures contracts
       Futures trading
BT   **Investments**
       Securities

Futures contracts
   USE   **Futures**

Futures trading
   USE   **Futures**

Futurism (Art) (May subdiv. geog.)
       709.04; 759.06

BT   **Art**

Futurology
   USE   **Forecasting**

Fuzzy logic
   USE   **Fuzzy systems**

Fuzzy systems   629.8

UF   Fuzzy logic
       Systems, Fuzzy
BT   **System analysis**

Gadgets
   USE   **Implements, utensils, etc.**

Gaels
   USE   **Celts**

Gaia concept
   USE   **Gaia hypothesis**

Gaia hypothesis   550.1; 570.1

UF   Gaia concept
       Gaia principle
       Gaia theory

       Living earth theory
BT   **Biology**
       Earth
       Ecology
       Life (Biology)
RT   **Biosphere**

Gaia principle
   USE   **Gaia hypothesis**

Gaia theory
   USE   **Gaia hypothesis**

Gaining weight
   USE   **Weight gain**

Galaxies   523.1

UF   Extragalactic nebulae
       Nebulae, Extragalactic
BT   **Astronomy**
       Stars
NT   **Milky Way**

Gales
   USE   **Winds**

Gambling (May subdiv. geog.)   **306.4;**
       795

UF   Betting
       Bookmaking (Betting)
       Gaming
SA   types of gambling, e.g. **Lotteries**
       [to be added as needed]
BT   **Games**
NT   **Compulsive gambling**
       Internet gambling
       Lotteries
       Sports betting

Game and game birds (May subdiv.
   geog.)   **636.6**

UF   Wild fowl
SA   types of animals and birds, e.g.
       Deer; **Pheasants**; etc. [to be
       added as needed]
BT   **Animals**
       Birds
       Wildlife
NT   **Deer**
       Falconry
       Game protection
       Pheasants
RT   **Hunting**
       Trapping

Game preserves
   USE   **Game reserves**

Game protection (May subdiv. geog.)
       333.95; 636.9

Game protection—*Continued*
  UF Game wardens
      Protection of game
  BT **Game and game birds**
      Hunting
      Wildlife conservation
  RT **Birds—Protection**
Game reserves (May subdiv. geog.)
      333.95
  UF Game preserves
  BT **Hunting**
      Wildlife conservation
Game theory 519.3
  UF Games, Theory of
      Theory of games
  BT **Mathematical models**
      Mathematics
      Probabilities
  NT **Simulation games**
      Simulation games in education
Game wardens
  USE **Game protection**
Games (May subdiv. geog.) **790**
  UF Pastimes
  SA types of games and names of
      individual games [to be added
      as needed]
  BT **Entertaining**
      Physical education
      Recreation
  NT **Ball games**
      Bible games and puzzles
      Board games
      Card games
      Computer games
      Educational games
      Fantasy games
      Gambling
      Indoor games
      Native American games
      Olympic games
      Singing games
      Video games
      Word games
  RT **Amusements**
      Play
      Sports
Games, Theory of
  USE **Game theory**
Gaming
  USE **Gambling**

Gaming, Educational
  USE **Simulation games in education**
Gaming simulations
  USE **Simulation games**
Gamma rays 537.5; 539.7
  BT **Electromagnetic waves**
      Radiation
      X-rays
Gangs (May subdiv. geog.) **302.3;**
      364.106
  UF Gangsters
      Street gangs
      Teenage gangs
  BT **Criminals**
      Juvenile delinquency
      Organized crime
Gangster films 791.43
      Use for individual works, collections, or
      materials about gangster films.
  UF Crime films
  BT **Motion pictures**
  RT **Mystery films**
Gangsters
  USE **Gangs**
Garage sales 381
  UF Yard sales
  BT **Secondhand trade**
Garbage
  USE **Refuse and refuse disposal**
Garbage disposal
  USE **Refuse and refuse disposal**
Garden architecture
  USE **Garden structures**
Garden design (May subdiv. geog.) **712**
  UF Gardens—Design
  BT **Design**
      Gardening
  RT **Landscape gardening**
Garden ecology (May subdiv. geog.)
      577.5
  BT **Ecology**
Garden farming
  USE **Truck farming**
Garden furniture
  USE **Garden ornaments and furni-
      ture**
Garden of Eden
  USE **Paradise**
Garden ornaments and furniture 717
  UF Garden furniture
  BT **Decoration and ornament**
      Furniture

Garden ornaments and furniture—*Continued*

> **Gardens**
> **Landscape architecture**
> NT   **Sundials**

Garden pests
> USE **Agricultural pests**
> **Insect pests**
> **Plant diseases**

Garden ponds
> USE **Water gardens**

Garden pools
> USE **Water gardens**

Garden rooms (May subdiv. geog.)   **643**
> UF   Conservatories, Home
> Home conservatories
> BT   **Houses**
> **Rooms**
> RT   **Greenhouses**

Garden structures (May subdiv. geog.)   **690**
> UF   Garden architecture
> Structures, Garden
> BT   **Buildings**
> **Landscape architecture**

Gardening (May subdiv. geog.)   **635**
> Use for materials on the practical aspects of creating gardens and cultivating flowers, fruits, vegetables, etc. Materials on the design or rearrangement of extensive gardens or estates are entered under **Landscape gardening**. Materials on the scientific and economic aspects of the cultivation of plants are entered under **Horticulture**. General materials about gardens, the history of gardens, various types of gardens, etc., are entered under **Gardens**.
> UF   Planting
> BT   **Agriculture**
> NT   **Climbing plants**
> **Container gardening**
> **Cultivated plants**
> **Flower gardening**
> **Fruit culture**
> **Garden design**
> **Gardening in the shade**
> **Greenhouses**
> **Grounds maintenance**
> **Herb gardening**
> **Indoor gardening**
> **Landscape gardening**
> **Nurseries (Horticulture)**
> **Organic gardening**
> **Plant propagation**
> **Pruning**

> Truck farming
> **Vegetable gardening**
> **Weeds**
> **Window gardening**
> **Winter gardening**
> RT   **Gardens**
> **Horticulture**
> **Plants**

Gardening for fragrance
> USE **Fragrant gardens**

Gardening in the shade   **635**
> UF   Gardens, Shade
> Shade gardens
> Shady gardens
> BT   **Gardening**

Gardens (May subdiv. geog.)   **635; 712**
> Use for general materials about gardens, the history of gardens, various types of gardens, etc. Materials on the design or rearrangement of extensive gardens or estates are entered under **Landscape gardening**. Materials on the practical aspects of creating gardens and cultivating flowers, fruits, vegetables, etc., are entered under **Gardening**.
> UF   Formal gardens
> SA   types of gardens, e.g. **Botanical gardens**; **Islamic gardens** etc., and names of individual gardens [to be added as needed]
> NT   **Botanical gardens**
> **Community gardens**
> **Fragrant gardens**
> **Garden ornaments and furniture**
> **Islamic gardens**
> **Maze gardens**
> **Miniature gardens**
> **Rock gardens**
> **Water gardens**
> RT   **Gardening**

Gardens—Design
> USE **Garden design**

Gardens, Miniature
> USE **Miniature gardens**

Gardens, Shade
> USE **Gardening in the shade**

Gargoyles (May subdiv. geog.)   **729**
> BT   **Architectural decoration and ornament**
> **Architecture—Details**

Garment industry
> USE **Clothing industry**

Garment making
    USE   **Dressmaking**
           Tailoring
Garments
    USE   **Clothing and dress**
Gas   **665.7**
    UF   Coal gas
    BT   **Fuel**
    RT   **Coal tar products**
Gas and oil engines
    USE   **Internal combustion engines**
Gas companies (May subdiv. geog.)
           363.6
       Use for materials on the sale and distribution of gas to consumers.
    UF   Natural gas companies
           Natural gas utilities
    BT   **Public utilities**
Gas engines
    USE   **Internal combustion engines**
Gas stations
    USE   **Service stations**
Gas turbines   **621.43**
    BT   **Turbines**
Gas warfare
    USE   **Chemical warfare**
Gases   **530.4; 533**
    SA   types of gases, e.g. **Nitrogen** [to be added as needed]
    BT   **Fluid mechanics**
           Hydrostatics
           Physics
    NT   **Bubbles**
           Helium
           Natural gas
           Nitrogen
           Oxygen
           Poisonous gases
    RT   **Pneumatics**
Gases, Asphyxiating and poisonous
    USE   **Poisonous gases**
Gasification of coal
    USE   **Coal gasification**
Gasoline   **665.5**
    BT   **Fuel**
           Petroleum
Gasoline engines
    USE   **Internal combustion engines**
Gastronomy   **641.01**
    UF   Eating
    BT   **Diet**
    NT   **Slow food movement**

    RT   **Cooking**
           Dining
           Food
Gauchos
    USE   **Cowhands**
Gaul—Geography   **914.4**
    BT   **Ancient geography**
           Historical geography
Gay and lesbian rights
    USE   **Gay rights**
Gay liberation movement (May subdiv. geog.)   **306.76**
    BT   **Homosexuality**
    RT   **Gay rights**
Gay lifestyle
    USE   **Homosexuality**
Gay marriage
    USE   **Same-sex marriage**
Gay men (May subdiv. geog.)   **306.76**
    UF   Gays, Male
           Homosexuals, Male
    BT   **Men**
    NT   **Gay parents**
           Gays and lesbians in the military
    RT   **Gay men's writings**
           Homosexuality
Gay men—Civil rights
    USE   **Gay rights**
Gay men—Ordination
    USE   **Ordination of gays and lesbians**
Gay men's writings   **808.8**
       Use for collections of gay men's writings by more than one author and for materials about such writings.
    UF   Writings of gay men
    BT   **Literature**
    RT   **Gay men**
Gay parents (May subdiv. geog.)
           306.85; 649
    UF   Homosexual parents
    BT   **Gay men**
           Lesbians
           Parents
    RT   **Children of gay parents**
Gay rights (May subdiv. geog.)
           323.3264
    UF   Gay and lesbian rights
           Gay men—Civil rights
           Lesbian rights
           Lesbians—Civil rights

Gay rights—*Continued*
    Rights of gays
    Rights of lesbians
  BT **Civil rights**
  RT **Gay liberation movement**
Gay teenagers (May subdiv. geog.)
    305.235; 306.76
  BT **Gay youth**
    Teenagers
Gay women
  USE **Lesbians**
Gay women's writings
  USE **Lesbians' writings**
Gay youth (May subdiv. geog.) **305.235;**
    306.76
  BT **Youth**
  NT **Gay teenagers**
Gays and lesbians in the military (May
    subdiv. geog.) **355.008**
  UF Gays in the military
    Lesbians and gays in the mili-
    tary
    Lesbians in the military
    United States—Armed forces—
    Gays
  BT **Gay men**
    Lesbians
    Military personnel
Gays, Female
  USE **Lesbians**
Gays in the military
  USE **Gays and lesbians in the mili-**
    tary
Gays, Male
  USE **Gay men**
Gazetteers **910.3**
  SA names of countries, states, etc.,
    with the subdivision *Gazet-*
    teers, e.g. **United States—**
    Gazetteers [to be added as
    needed]
  BT **Geography**
  NT **Ohio—Gazetteers**
    United States—Gazetteers
  RT **Geographic names**
Gearing **621.8**
  UF Bevel gearing
    Cog wheels
    Gears
    Spiral gearing
  BT **Machinery**
    Power transmission

    Wheels
  NT **Automobiles—Transmission de-**
    vices
  RT **Mechanical movements**
Gears
  USE **Gearing**
Geese (May subdiv. geog.) **598.4; 636.5**
  UF Goose
  BT **Birds**
    Poultry
Geishas **792.7**
  BT **Entertainers**
Gemini project **629.45**
  UF Project Gemini
  BT **Orbital rendezvous (Space**
    flight)
    Space flight
Gems (May subdiv. geog.) **736**
    Use for materials on cut and polished pre-
    cious stones treated from the point of view of
    art or antiquity. Materials on gem stones treat-
    ed from a mineralogical or technological point
    of view are entered under **Precious stones**.
    Materials on gems in which the emphasis is
    on the setting are entered under **Jewelry**.
  UF Jewels
  BT **Archeology**
    Art
    Decoration and ornament
    Engraving
    Minerals
  RT **Jewelry**
    Precious stones
Gemstones
  USE **Precious stones**
Gender identity
  USE **Sex role**
Gene mapping **572.8**
  UF Chromosome mapping
    Genetic mapping
    Genome mapping
  BT **Genetics**
Gene splicing
  USE **Genetic engineering**
Gene therapy **616**
    Use for materials on therapeutic efforts in-
    volving the replacement or supplementation of
    genes in order to cure diseases caused by ge-
    netic defects.
  UF Therapy, Gene
  BT **Genetic engineering**
    Therapeutics
Gene transfer
  USE **Genetic engineering**

Genealogy 929
  UF Ancestry
      Descent
      Family histories
      Family trees
      Pedigrees
  SA countries, cities, etc., corporate
      bodies, ethnic groups, and
      classes of persons with the
      subdivision *Genealogy*; names
      of individual persons with the
      subdivision *Family*; and
      names of families, e.g. **Lincoln family** [to be added as
      needed]
  BT **History**
  NT **Registers of births, etc.**
      Wills
  RT **Biography**
      Heraldry
General practice (Medicine)
  USE **Family medicine**
General stores (May subdiv. geog.)
      381.1
  UF Country stores
  BT **Retail trade**
      Stores
Generals (May subdiv. geog.)   **355.0092;**
      920
  BT **Military personnel**
Generation gap
  USE **Conflict of generations**
Generative organs
  USE **Reproductive system**
Generators, Electric
  USE **Electric generators**
Generic drugs   615
  UF Drugs—Generic substitution
  BT **Drugs**
      Generic products
Generic products   658.8
  UF Products, Generic
  BT **Commercial products**
      Manufactures
  NT **Generic drugs**
Generosity   179
  UF Giving
Genes
  USE **Heredity**

Genetic aspects
  USE types of diseases with the subdivision *Genetic aspects,* e.g.
      Cancer—Genetic aspects [to
      be added as needed]
Genetic code   572.8
  BT **Molecular biology**
Genetic counseling   616; 618
  BT **Medical genetics**
      Prenatal diagnosis
Genetic engineering (May subdiv. geog.)
      660.6
  UF Designed genetic change
      Engineering, Genetic
      Gene splicing
      Gene transfer
      Genetic intervention
      Genetic surgery
      Splicing of genes
      Transgenics
  BT **Engineering**
      Genetic recombination
  NT **Cloning**
      Fertilization in vitro
      Gene therapy
      Molecular cloning
      Recombinant DNA
  RT **Biotechnology**
Genetic engineering—Government policy
      (May subdiv. geog.)   **353.7; 660.6**
Genetic engineering—Social aspects
      306.4
Genetic fingerprinting
  USE **DNA fingerprinting**
Genetic fingerprints
  USE **DNA fingerprinting**
Genetic intervention
  USE **Genetic engineering**
Genetic mapping
  USE **Gene mapping**
Genetic profiling
  USE **DNA fingerprinting**
Genetic recombination   572.8
  UF Recombination, Genetic
  BT **Chromosomes**
  NT **Genetic engineering**
      Genetic transformation
      Recombinant DNA
Genetic surgery
  USE **Genetic engineering**
Genetic transformation   576.5

Genetic transformation—*Continued*
  UF Transformation (Genetics)
  BT **Genetic recombination**
Genetics **576.5**
  SA types of diseases with the subdi-
      vision *Genetic aspects*, e.g.
      Cancer—Genetic aspects [to
      be added as needed]
  BT **Biology**
      Embryology
      Life (Biology)
      Mendel's law
      Reproduction
  NT **Adaptation (Biology)**
      Behavior genetics
      Chromosomes
      Eugenics
      Gene mapping
      Genomes
      Human genome
      Medical genetics
      Natural selection
      Nature and nurture
      Variation (Biology)
  RT **Breeding**
      Heredity
Genetics and environment
  USE **Nature and nurture**
Genital mutilation, Female
  USE **Female circumcision**
Genitalia
  USE **Reproductive system**
Genius **153.9**
  UF Talent
  BT **Psychology**
  NT **Creation (Literary, artistic,**
      etc.)
Genocide (May subdiv. geog.) **179.7;**
      364.1
  UF Ethnic cleansing
      Ethnocide
  BT **Crimes against humanity**
Genome
  USE **Genomes**
Genome mapping
  USE **Gene mapping**
Genomes **572.8**
  UF Genome
  BT **Genetics**
Genre painting **754**
  BT **Painting**
Geochemistry **551.9**

  UF Chemical geology
      Earth—Chemical composition
      Geological chemistry
  BT **Chemistry**
      Earth sciences
      Petrology
  NT **Geothermal resources**
Geodesy **526**
  UF Degrees of latitude and longi-
      tude
  BT **Earth**
      Measurement
  NT **Latitude**
      Longitude
  RT **Surveying**
Geographic names (May subdiv. geog.)
      910
  UF Names, Geographical
      Place names
  BT **Names**
  RT **Gazetteers**
Geographic names—United States
      917.3
  UF United States—Geographic
      names
Geographical atlases
  USE **Atlases**
Geographical distribution
  USE types of plants and animals with
      the subdivision *Geographical*
      distribution, e.g. **Fishes—Geo-**
      graphical distribution [to be
      added as needed]
Geographical distribution of animals and
      plants
  USE **Biogeography**
Geographical distribution of people
  USE **Human geography**
Geographical distribution of plants
  USE **Plants—Geographical distribu-**
      tion
Geographical myths **398.23**

  Use for materials on legendary or mythical
  places. Materials on imaginary places created
  for literary or artistic purposes are entered under **Imaginary places**.

  UF Cities, Imaginary
  BT **Mythology**
  NT **Atlantis (Legendary place)**
      Lost continents

Geography   910

Use for general materials, frequently school materials, that describe the surface of the earth and its interrelationship with various peoples, animals, natural products, and industries. Materials limited to a particular place are entered under the name of the place with the subdivision *Geography*. General descriptive materials and travel materials limited to a particular place are entered under the name of the place (except extinct cities) with the subdivision *Description and travel*. Materials on the physical features of the earth's surface and its atmosphere are entered under **Physical geography**.

UF   Social studies
SA   names of countries, states, etc., with the subdivisions *Description and travel* and *Geography*; and sacred works with the subdivision *Geography*, e.g. **Bible—Geography** [to be added as needed]
BT   **Earth**
        Earth sciences
        World history
NT   **Atlases**
        Bible—Geography
        Biogeography
        Boundaries
        Commercial geography
        Exploration
        Gazetteers
        Greece—Geography
        Historical geography
        Human geography
        Maps
        Military geography
        Physical geography
        Regionalism
        Surveying
        United States—Description and travel
        United States—Geography
        Voyages and travels

Geography, Ancient
USE   **Ancient geography**

Geography—Dictionaries   910.3

Use for dictionaries of geographic terms. Materials listing names and descriptions of places are entered under **Gazetteers**.

BT   **Encyclopedias and dictionaries**

Geography, Historical
USE   **Historical geography**

Geography, Political
USE   **Geopolitics**

Geological chemistry
USE   **Geochemistry**
Geological physics
USE   **Geophysics**
Geologists (May subdiv. geog.)   551.092; 920
BT   **Scientists**
Geology (May subdiv. geog.)   550

Use for materials limited to the structure and composition of the earth and the physical changes it has undergone and is still undergoing. General materials on the whole planet are entered under **Earth**.

UF   Geoscience
SA   names of planets and types of ore with the subdivision *Geology* [to be added as needed]
BT   **Earth sciences**
        Science
NT   **Astrogeology**
        Continental drift
        Continental shelf
        Coral reefs and islands
        Earthquakes
        Economic geology
        Erosion
        Faults (Geology)
        Geysers
        Glaciers
        Historical geology
        Landforms
        Minerals
        Ore deposits
        Physical geography
        Stratigraphic geology
        Submarine geology
        Volcanoes
RT   **Earth**
        Petrology
        Rocks

Geology, Dynamic
USE   **Geophysics**
Geology, Economic
USE   **Economic geology**
Geology—Interactive multimedia   551
Geology, Lunar
USE   **Lunar geology**
Geology—Maps   550.22
BT   **Maps**
Geology—Moon
USE   **Lunar geology**
Geology, Petroleum
USE   **Petroleum geology**

Geology, Stratigraphic
   USE **Stratigraphic geology**
Geology—United States   557.3
Geomagnetic field
   USE **Geomagnetism**
Geomagnetism (May subdiv. geog.)   **538**
   UF Earth magnetic field
        Earth—Magnetism
        Geomagnetic field
   BT **Geophysics**
        Magnetism
Geometric art
   USE **Abstract art**
Geometric patterns
   USE **Patterns (Mathematics)**
Geometrical drawing   516; 604.2
   UF Mathematical drawing
        Plans
   BT **Drawing**
        Geometry
   NT **Descriptive geometry**
        Graphic methods
        Perspective
   RT **Mechanical drawing**
Geometry   516
   BT **Mathematics**
   NT **Analytic geometry**
        Circle
        Descriptive geometry
        Fractals
        Geometrical drawing
        Plane geometry
        Projective geometry
        Ratio and proportion
        Shape
        Solid geometry
        Square
        Topology
        Triangle
        Trigonometry
        Volume (Cubic content)
Geometry, Analytic
   USE **Analytic geometry**
Geometry, Descriptive
   USE **Descriptive geometry**
Geometry, Plane
   USE **Plane geometry**
Geometry, Projective
   USE **Projective geometry**
Geometry, Solid
   USE **Solid geometry**

Geophysics (May subdiv. geog.)   **550**
   UF Geological physics
        Geology, Dynamic
        Physics, Terrestrial
        Terrestrial physics
   BT **Earth sciences**
        Physics
   NT **Auroras**
        Geomagnetism
        Plate tectonics
Geopolitics   320.1; 327.101
   UF Geography, Political
        Political geography
   BT **International relations**
        Political science
   RT **Boundaries**
        Human geography
        World politics
Georgia (Republic)   947.58
Geoscience
   USE **Earth sciences**
        Geology
Geothermal resources (May subdiv.
   geog.)   **333.8**
   UF Natural steam energy
        Thermal waters
   SA types of geothermal resources,
        e.g. **Geysers** [to be added as
        needed]
   BT **Geochemistry**
        Ocean energy resources
        Renewable energy resources
   NT **Geysers**
Geriatrics
   USE **Elderly—Diseases**
        Elderly—Health and hygiene
Germ theory
   USE **Life—Origin**
Germ theory of disease   616
   UF Disease germs
        Germs
        Microbes
   BT **Communicable diseases**
Germ warfare
   USE **Biological warfare**
German Democratic Republic
   USE **Germany (East)**
German Federal Republic
   USE **Germany (West)**
German language   430
   May be subdivided like **English language**.

German language—*Continued*

BT **Language and languages**

German literature   830

May use same subdivisions and names of literary forms as for **English literature**.

BT **Literature**

German occupation of France, 1940-1945

USE **France—History—1940-1945, German occupation**

German occupation of Netherlands, 1940-1945

USE **Netherlands—History—1940-1945, German occupation**

Germany   943

Use for materials on Germany before or after the division of the country following World War II and for materials on East and West Germany discussed collectively as occupied zones or countries. Materials limited to the eastern part of Germany from 1945 to 1990, the Russian occupation zone, or the German Democratic Republic, are entered under **Germany (East)**. Materials limited to the western part of Germany from 1945 to 1990, the American, British, and French occupation zones, or the German Federal Republic, are entered under **Germany (West)**. May be subdivided like **United States** except for *History*.

UF   Federal Republic of Germany

NT   **Germany (East)**

Germany (West)

Germany (Democratic Republic)

USE   **Germany (East)**

Germany (East)   943

Use for materials limited to the eastern part of Germany from 1945 to 1990, the Russian occupation zone, or the German Democratic Republic. Materials on Germany before or after the division of the country following World War II and materials on East and West Germany discussed collectively as occupied zones or countries are entered under **Germany**.

UF   East Germany

German Democratic Republic

Germany (Democratic Republic)

BT   **Germany**

Germany (Federal Republic)

USE   **Germany (West)**

Germany—History   943

Germany—History—0-1517   943

Germany—History—1517-1740   943

NT   **Thirty Years' War, 1618-1648**

Germany—History—1740-1815   943

Germany—History—1815-1866   943

Germany—History—1848-1849, Revolution   943

Germany—History—1866-1918   943.08

Germany—History—1918-1933   943.085

Germany—History—1933-1945   943.086

NT   **Holocaust, 1939-1945**

Kristallnacht, 1938

Germany—History—1945-1990   943.087

Germany—History—1990-   943.088

UF   Germany—History—Unification, 1990

Germany—History—Unification, 1990

USE   **Germany—History—1990-**

Germany (West)   943.087

Use for materials limited to the western part of Germany from 1945 to 1990, the American, British, and French occupation zones, or the German Federal Republic. Materials on Germany before or after the division of the country following World War II and materials on East and West Germany discussed collectively as occupied zones or countries are entered under **Germany**.

UF   Federal Republic of Germany

German Federal Republic

Germany (Federal Republic)

West Germany

BT   **Germany**

Germicides

USE   **Disinfection and disinfectants**

Fungicides

Germination   571.8

UF   Seeds—Germination

BT   **Plant physiology**

Germs

USE   **Bacteria**

Germ theory of disease

Microorganisms

Gerontology   305.26; 362.6; 612.6

BT   **Social sciences**

NT   **Aging**

Elderly

RT   **Old age**

Gestalt psychology   150.19

UF   Configuration (Psychology)

Psychology, Structural

Structural psychology

BT   **Consciousness**

Perception

Psychology

Senses and sensation

Theory of knowledge

Getting ready for bed

USE   **Bedtime**

Gettysburg (Pa.), Battle of, 1863   973.7

Gettysburg (Pa.), Battle of, 1863—*Continued*

    BT   **Battles**

         United States—History—1861-
             1865, Civil War—Campaigns

Geysers (May subdiv. geog.)   **551.2**

    UF   Eruptions

         Thermal waters

    BT   **Geology**

         Geothermal resources

         Physical geography

         Water

Ghettos, Inner city

    USE **Inner cities**

Ghost stories   **808.3; 808.83**

    Use for individual works, collections, or materials about ghost stories.

    UF   Ghosts—Fiction

         Terror tales

    BT   **Fantasy fiction**

         Horror fiction

         Occult fiction

    RT   **Gothic novels**

         Mystery fiction

Ghost towns (May subdiv. geog.)   **307.76**

    UF   Abandoned towns

         Towns, Abandoned

    BT   **Extinct cities**

Ghosts (May subdiv. geog.)   **133.1**

    UF   Phantoms

         Poltergeists

         Specters

    BT   **Apparitions**

         Folklore

         Spirits

    RT   **Haunted houses**

         Parapsychology

Ghosts—Fiction

    USE **Ghost stories**

Giantism   **616.4**

    Use for materials on excessive growth in humans. Materials on beings with a human form but with superhuman size or strength in folklore or imaginative literature are entered under **Giants**.

    UF   Gigantism

    BT   **Growth disorders**

Giants   **398.21**

    Use for materials on beings with a human form but with superhuman size or strength in folklore or imaginative literature. Materials on excessive growth in humans are entered under **Giantism**.

    BT   **Folklore**

         Monsters

Gift of tongues

    USE **Glossolalia**

Gift wrapping   **745.54**

    UF   Wrapping of gifts

    BT   **Packaging**

         Paper crafts

Gifted children (May subdiv. geog.)   **155.45**

    UF   Bright children

         Children, Gifted

         Precocious children

    BT   **Exceptional children**

    NT   **Child artists**

         Child authors

Gifts   **306.4; 361.7**

    UF   Bequests

         Donations

         Presents

    BT   **Manners and customs**

    NT   **Donation of organs, tissues, etc.**

         Free material

    RT   **Fund raising**

Gifts of grace

    USE **Spiritual gifts**

Gifts of the Holy Spirit

    USE **Spiritual gifts**

Gifts, Spiritual

    USE **Spiritual gifts**

Gigantism

    USE **Giantism**

Gipsies

    USE **Gypsies**

Girl-love manga

    USE **Shojo-ai**

Girl Scouts (May subdiv. geog.)   **369.463**

    UF   Brownies (Girl Scouts)

    BT   **Girls' clubs**

         Scouts and scouting

Girls (May subdiv. geog.)   **155.43; 305.23082**

    BT   **Children**

    RT   **Teenagers**

         Young women

Girls' clubs (May subdiv. geog.)   **369.46**

    UF   Girls—Societies and clubs

    BT   **Clubs**

         Societies

Girls' clubs—*Continued*
  NT   **4-H clubs**
       Camp Fire Girls
       Girl Scouts
Girls—Education (May subdiv. geog.)
       371.822
  BT   **Education**
  RT   **Coeducation**
Girls—Employment
  USE   **Women—Employment**
        Youth—Employment
Girls—Societies and clubs
  USE   **Girls' clubs**
GIs
  USE   **Soldiers—United States**
Giveaways
  USE   **Free material**
Giving
  USE   **Generosity**
Glacial epoch
  USE   **Ice age**
Glaciers (May subdiv. geog.)   **551.3**
  BT   **Geology**
       Ice
       Physical geography
Gladiators   **796.8092; 920**
  UF   **Fighting**
Gladness
  USE   **Happiness**
Glands   **571.7; 573.4; 611; 612.4**
  BT   **Anatomy**
       Physiology
Glands, Ductless
  USE   **Endocrine glands**
Glass (May subdiv. geog.)   **666**
  BT   **Building materials**
       Ceramics
  NT   **Glass fibers**
Glass construction (May subdiv. geog.)
       693
  BT   **Building materials**
Glass fibers   **666**
  UF   Fiber glass
       Fiberglass
       Fibers, Glass
       Glass, Spun
       Spun glass
  BT   **Fibers**
       Glass
Glass industry
  USE   **Glass manufacture**

Glass manufacture (May subdiv. geog.)
       666
  UF   Glass industry
  BT   **Ceramic industry**
Glass painting and staining (May subdiv.
       geog.)   **748.5**
  UF   Glass, Stained
       Painted glass
       Stained glass
       Windows, Stained glass
  BT   **Decoration and ornament**
       Painting
Glass, Spun
  USE   **Glass fibers**
Glass, Stained
  USE   **Glass painting and staining**
Glasses
  USE   **Eyeglasses**
Glassware (May subdiv. geog.)   **642;**
       748.2
  BT   **Decorative arts**
       Tableware
  RT   **Vases**
Glassware—Trademarks   **748.2**
  BT   **Trademarks**
Glazes   **666; 738.1**
  BT   **Ceramics**
       Pottery
Gliders (Aeronautics)   **629.133**
  UF   Aircraft
       Sailplanes (Aeronautics)
  BT   **Aeronautics**
       Airplanes
Gliding and soaring (May subdiv. geog.)
       797.5
  UF   Air surfing
       Hang gliding
       Soaring flight
  BT   **Aeronautics**
Global Positioning System   **526; 623.89**
  UF   GPS (Navigation system)
  BT   **Navigation**
Global satellite communications systems
  USE   **Artificial satellites in telecom-**
        munication
Global warming (May subdiv. geog.)
       363.738; 551.5; 551.6
  UF   Atmospheric greenhouse effect
       Carbon dioxide greenhouse ef-
       fect

Global warming—*Continued*
  Greenhouse effect [*Former heading*]
  BT **Climate**
      Solar radiation
  RT **Climate change**
Globalization 303.48; 337
  UF Internationalization
  BT **International relations**
Globes 912
  BT **Maps**
Glossaries
  USE **Encyclopedias and dictionaries**
Glossolalia 234
  UF Gift of tongues
      Speaking in tongues
      Speaking with tongues
  BT **Spiritual gifts**
  RT **Pentecostalism**
Glow-in-the-dark books
    Use for individual works, collections, or materials about glow-in-the-dark books.
  UF Luminescent books
      Luminous books
  BT **Picture books for children**
      Toy and movable books
Gluc 668
  BT **Adhesives**
Glue sniffing
  USE **Solvent abuse**
Gnomes 398.21
  BT **Folklore**
Gnosticism (May subdiv. geog.) **273; 299**
  BT **Church history—30-600, Early church**
      Philosophy
      Religions
GNP
  USE **Gross national product**
Go-karts
  USE **Karts and karting**
Goblins 398.21
  BT **Folklore**
God 211; 212; 231
    May subdivide by religion as needed, e.g. **God—Christianity**.
  NT **Femininity of God**
      Providence and government of God
      Revelation

  RT **Metaphysics**
      Monotheism
      Religion
      Theism
      Theology
God—Christianity 231
  BT **Christianity—Doctrines**
  NT **Holy Spirit**
      Jesus Christ
      Trinity
God—Femininity
  USE **Femininity of God**
God—Praise
  USE **Praise of God**
God—Providence and government
  USE **Providence and government of God**
God—Sovereignty
  USE **Providence and government of God**
Goddess movement
  USE **Goddess religion**
Goddess religion (May subdiv. geog.) **201**
  UF Goddess movement
      Mother Goddess religion
  BT **Paganism**
  RT **Gods and goddesses**
      Wicca
Goddesses
  USE **Gods and goddesses**
Gods
  USE **Gods and goddesses**
Gods and goddesses 202
  UF Deities
      Goddesses
      Gods
  SA names of gods and goddesses, e.g. Zeus (Greek deity); Vesta (Roman deity); etc. [to be added as needed]
  NT **Aphrodite (Greek deity)**
      Apollo (Greek deity)
      Athena (Greek deity)
      Dionysus (Greek deity)
      Hera (Greek deity)
      Persephone (Greek deity)
      Psyche (Greek deity)
      Thor (Norse deity)
      Vesta (Roman deity)
      Zeus (Greek deity)

Gods and goddesses—*Continued*
    RT   **Goddess religion**
          Mythology
          Polytheism
          Religions
Gold (May subdiv. geog.)   **332.4; 553.4;**
    669
    BT   **Chemical elements**
          Precious metals
    NT   **Goldwork**
    RT   **Coinage**
          Gold mines and mining
          Money
Gold articles
    USE   **Goldwork**
Gold discoveries
    USE   names of places with the subdivision *Gold discoveries,* e.g.
          California—Gold discoveries
          [to be added as needed]
Gold fish
    USE   **Goldfish**
Gold mines and mining (May subdiv.
    geog.)   **622**
    UF   Gold rush
          Gold rushes
    SA   names of places with the subdivision *Gold discoveries*, e.g.
          California—Gold discoveries
          [to be added as needed]
    BT   **Mines and mineral resources**
    NT   **Prospecting**
    RT   **Gold**
Gold plate
    USE   **Plate**
Gold rush
    USE   **Gold mines and mining**
Gold rushes
    USE   **Gold mines and mining**
Gold work
    USE   **Goldwork**
Golden Gate Bridge (San Francisco,
    Calif.)   **624.209794; 979.4**
    BT   **Bridges**
Golden rule   **170**
    UF   Rule, Golden
    BT   **Ethics**
Goldfish   **597.5**
    UF   Gold fish
    BT   **Fishes**
Goldsmithing
    USE   **Goldwork**

Goldwork (May subdiv. geog.)   **739.2**
    UF   Gold articles
          Gold work
          Goldsmithing
    BT   **Art metalwork**
          Gold
          Metalwork
    NT   **Plate**
Golf (May subdiv. geog.)   **796.352**
    BT   **Sports**
Golf courses (May subdiv. geog.)
    796.352
    BT   **Sports facilities**
Good and evil   **170; 214; 241**
    UF   Evil
          Wickedness
    BT   **Ethics**
          Philosophy
          Theology
    NT   **Guilt**
          Sin
Good Friday   **263**
    BT   **Christian holidays**
          Holy Week
          Lent
Good grooming
    USE   **Personal grooming**
Google   **004.67; 384.3**
    BT   **Web search engines**
          Web sites
Goose
    USE   **Geese**
Gorge-purge syndrome
    USE   **Bulimia**
Gorillas (May subdiv. geog.)   **599.884**
    BT   **Apes**
Gospel music (May subdiv. geog.)
    781.71; 782.25
    UF   Music, Gospel
          Revivals—Music
    BT   **African American music**
          Church music
          Popular music
    RT   **Spirituals (Songs)**
Gossip   **070.4; 177; 302.2**
    BT   **Journalism**
          Libel and slander
    NT   **Tattling**
Gothic architecture (May subdiv. geog.)
    723
    UF   Architecture, Gothic

Gothic architecture—*Continued*
    BT   **Medieval architecture**
    RT   **Cathedrals**
           Church architecture
           Gothic art
Gothic art (May subdiv. geog.)   **709.02**
    UF   Art, Gothic
    BT   **Medieval art**
    RT   **Christian art**
           Gothic architecture
Gothic decoration and ornament
    USE   **Decoration and ornament—**
             Gothic style
Gothic fiction
    USE   **Gothic novels**
Gothic novels   **808.3**

Use for individual works, collections, or materials about contemporary novels that have a medieval setting and usually include castles and ghosts. For materials on literature of the eighteenth and nineteenth centuries featuring medieval settings and romantic gloom, use **Gothic revival (Literature)**.

    UF   Gothic fiction
    BT   **Historical fiction**
           Horror fiction
           Occult fiction
    RT   **Ghost stories**
           Love stories
           Romantic suspense novels
Gothic revival (Architecture) (May subdiv. geog.)   **724.3**
    BT   **Architecture**
    NT   **Victorian architecture**
    RT   **Victorian architecture**
Gothic revival (Art) (May subdiv. geog.)   **700.41**
    BT   **Art**
Gothic revival (Literature) (May subdiv. geog.)   **808.83; 823.08**

Use for materials on literature of the eighteenth and nineteenth centuries featuring medieval settings and romantic gloom. For contemporary novels that have a medieval setting and usually include castles and ghosts use **Gothic novels**.

    BT   **Literature**
Goths (May subdiv. geog.)   **305.83**
    UF   East Goths
           Ostrogoths
    BT   **Teutonic peoples**
Gout   **616.3**
    BT   **Arthritis**
           Rheumatism

Government
    USE   **Political science**
           and names of countries, cities, etc., with the subdivision *Politics and government,* e.g. **United States—Politics and government** and names of Christian denominations with the subdivision *Government,* e.g. **Church of England—Government** [to be added as needed]
Government agencies
    USE   **Administrative agencies**
Government aid (May subdiv. geog.)   **336**

Use for materials on aid from governments at any level in non-federal systems and on aid from state, provincial, or local governments in federal systems. Materials on central government aid in federal systems are entered under **Federal aid**.

    SA   government aid to specific endeavors, e.g. **Government aid to libraries** [to be added as needed]
    BT   **Government aid**
           Public finance
    NT   **Government aid**
           Government aid to education
           Government aid to libraries
    RT   **Federal aid**
Government aid to education (May subdiv. geog.)   **379.1**
    UF   Education—Government aid
           Education—State aid
           State aid to education
    BT   **Education—Finance**
           Education—Government policy
           Government aid
Government aid to libraries (May subdiv. geog.)   **021.8**
    UF   Libraries—Government aid
           Libraries—State aid
           State aid to libraries
    BT   **Government aid**
           Libraries—Government policy
           Library finance
Government and business
    USE   **Economic policy**
Government and the press
    USE   **Press—Government policy**

Government budgets
    USE **Budget**
Government buildings
    USE **Public buildings**
Government business enterprises (May
    subdiv. geog.) **338.7**
    UF Government companies
        Nationalized companies
        Public enterprises
    SA types of industries with the sub-
        division *Government owner-
        ship*, e.g. **Electric utilities—
        Government ownership**;
        which may be further subdi-
        vided geographically [to be
        added as needed]
    BT **Business enterprises**
Government by commission
    USE **Municipal government by com-
        mission**
Government companies
    USE **Government business enter-
        prises**
Government, Comparative
    USE **Comparative government**
Government debts
    USE **Public debts**
Government departments
    USE **Executive departments**
Government documents
    USE **Government publications**
Government employees
    USE **Civil service**
Government health insurance
    USE **National health insurance**
Government housing
    USE **Public housing**
Government investigations
    USE **Governmental investigations**
Government lending (May subdiv. geog.)
        332.7; 354.8
    BT **Domestic economic assistance
        Economic policy
        Loans
        Public finance**
Government libraries (May subdiv. geog.)
        027.5
    Use for materials on special libraries main-
    tained by government funds.
    UF Federal libraries
        Libraries, Governmental
    BT **Special libraries**

    NT **National libraries
        State libraries**
Government, Local
    USE **Local government**
Government, Military
    USE **Military government**
Government ministries
    USE **Executive departments**
Government, Municipal
    USE **Municipal government**
Government officials
    USE **Public officers**
Government ownership (May subdiv.
        geog.) **333.1; 338.9**
    UF Nationalization
        Public ownership
        Socialization of industry
        State ownership
    SA types of industries with the sub-
        division *Government owner-
        ship*, e.g. **Electric utilities—
        Government ownership**;
        which may be further subdi-
        vided geographically [to be
        added as needed]
    BT **Economic policy
        Industrial policy
        Socialism**
    NT **Municipal ownership
        Railroads—Government policy**
    RT **Privatization**
Government ownership of railroads
    USE **Railroads—Government policy**
Government policy
    USE **Buy national policy
        Commercial policy
        Cultural policy
        Economic policy
        Energy policy
        Environmental policy
        Fiscal policy
        Industrial policy
        Labor policy
        Medical policy
        Military policy
        Monetary policy
        Social policy
        Wage-price policy**
        and subjects, ethnic groups, and
        classes of persons with the
        subdivision *Government poli-*

Government policy—*Continued*

cy, e.g. **Genetic engineering—Government policy; Homeless persons—Government policy;** etc., which may be further subdivided geographically [to be added as needed]

Government procurement

USE **Government purchasing**

Government property, Surplus

USE **Surplus government property**

Government publications (May subdiv. geog.) **011; 015; 025.17**

UF Documents

Government documents

Official publications

Public documents

BT **Library resources**

Government publications—Chicago (Ill.) 015.773

UF Chicago (Ill.)—Government publications

Government publications—Ohio 015.771

UF Ohio—Government publications

Government publications—United States 015.73; 025.17

UF United States—Government publications

Government purchasing (May subdiv. geog.) **352.5**

UF Government procurement

Procurement, Government

Public procurement

Public purchasing

BT **Purchasing**

NT **Buy national policy**

Government records—Preservation

USE **Archives**

Government regulation of commerce

USE **Commercial policy**

Industrial laws and legislation

Interstate commerce

Government regulation of industry

USE **Industrial policy**

Government regulation of railroads

USE **Railroads—Government policy**

Government relations

USE ethnic groups with the subdivision *Government relations,* e.g. **Native Americans—Gov-**

ernment relations [to be added as needed]

Government reorganization

USE **Administrative agencies—Reorganization**

Government, Resistance to

USE **Resistance to government**

Government service

USE **Civil service**

Government spending policy

USE **United States—Appropriations and expenditures**

Government subsidies

USE **Subsidies**

Government surveys

USE **Surveys**

Government transfer payments

USE **Transfer payments**

Governmental investigations (May subdiv. geog.) **328.3; 353.4**

Use for materials on investigations initiated by the legislative, executive, or judicial branches of the government, usually of some particular problem of public interest.

UF Congressional investigations

Executive investigations

Government investigations

Judicial investigations

Legislative investigations

BT **Administration of justice**

Governmental investigations—United States 328.3; 353.4

UF United States—Governmental investigations

Governments in exile

USE names of wars with the subdivision *Governments in exile,* e.g. **World War, 1939-1945—Governments in exile** [to be added as needed]

Governors (May subdiv. geog.) **352.23; 920**

BT **State governments**

GPS (Navigation system)

USE **Global Positioning System**

Grace (Theology) 202; 234

BT **Doctrinal theology**

Salvation

NT **Sacraments**

Spiritual gifts

Grade repetition

USE **Promotion (School)**

Grade retention
USE **Promotion (School)**
Grade schools
USE **Elementary schools**
Grading and marking (Education)
371.27
UF Grading and marking (Students)
Marking and grading (Education)
Students—Grading and marking
BT **Educational tests and measurements**
NT **Ability grouping in education**
Promotion (School)
RT **School reports**
Grading and marking (Students)
USE **Grading and marking (Education)**
Graduate Record Examination 378.1
UF GRE
BT **Colleges and universities—Entrance examinations**
Examinations
Graduate Record Examination—Study
guides 378.1
Graduates, College
USE **College graduates**
Graduation
USE **Commencements**
Graffiti (May subdiv. geog.) **080;**
808.88
BT **Inscriptions**
Vandalism
Graft in politics
USE **Political corruption**
Grafting 631.5
BT **Plant propagation**
Grail 398
UF Holy Grail
BT **Folklore**
Grail—Legends 398; 809
RT **Arthurian romances**
Grain (May subdiv. geog.) **633.1**
UF Cereals
SA types of cereal plants, e.g.
Corn; **Wheat**; etc. [to be
added as needed]
NT **Corn**
Wheat
RT **Flour**
Grain—Storage (May subdiv. geog.)
633.1

Grammar 415
SA names of languages with the
subdivision *Grammar* [to be
added as needed]
BT **Language and languages**
Linguistics
NT **English language—Grammar**
Grammar schools
USE **Elementary education**
Grammy Awards 780.26
BT **Sound recordings**
Gramophone
USE **Phonograph**
Grandfathers (May subdiv. geog.)
306.874
BT **Grandparents**
Grandmothers (May subdiv. geog.)
306.874
BT **Grandparents**
Grandparent and child
USE **Grandparent-grandchild relationship**
Grandparent-grandchild relationship
306.874

Use for materials on the interaction between
grandparents and their grandchildren. Materials restricted to the legal right of grandparents
to visit their grandchildren are entered under
Visitation rights (Domestic relations). Materials on the skills, etc., needed for being an
effective grandparent are entered under
Grandparenting.

UF Grandparent and child
BT **Family**
Grandparents
Grandparenting 306.874

Use for materials on the skills, etc., needed
for being an effective grandparent. Materials
on the interaction between grandparents and
their grandchildren are entered under **Grandparent-grandchild relationship**.

BT **Grandparents**
Parenting
Grandparents 306.874
BT **Family**
NT **Foster grandparents**
Grandfathers
Grandmothers
Grandparent-grandchild relationship
Grandparenting
Grandparents as parents
Grandparents as parents 306.874
UF Parenting by grandparents

Grandparents as parents—*Continued*
  BT **Grandparents**
     Parenting
Grange 334
  BT **Agriculture—Societies**
Granite (May subdiv. geog.) **552; 553.5**
  BT **Rocks**
     Stone
Grants
  USE **Grants-in-aid**
     Subsidies
Grants-in-aid (May subdiv. geog.)
     336.1; 352.73
  Use for materials on grants of money made
  from a central government to a local govern-
  ment.
  UF Grants
  SA federal aid to particular endeav-
     ors, e.g. **Federal aid to edu-
     cation** [to be added as need-
     ed]
  BT **Public finance**
  RT **Domestic economic assistance**
Grapes 634.8; 641.3
  UF Viticulture
  BT **Fruit**
  RT **Vineyards**
     Wine and wine making
Graph theory 511
  UF Graphs, Theory of
     Theory of graphs
  BT **Algebra**
     Mathematical analysis
     Topology
Graphic arts (May subdiv. geog.) **760**
  UF Arts, Graphic
  SA types of graphic arts [to be add-
     ed as needed]
  BT **Art**
  NT **Clip art**
     Drawing
     Engraving
     Painting
     Photography
     Printing
     Prints
     Typography
Graphic arts—United States 760.097
  UF American graphic arts
Graphic fiction
  USE **Graphic novels**
Graphic methods 001.4; 511

  UF Flow charts
     Flowcharting
     Graphs
  BT **Drawing**
     Geometrical drawing
     Mechanical drawing
  NT **Statistics—Graphic methods**
Graphic novels 741.5
  Use for individual works, collections, or
  materials about graphic novels.
  UF Comic book novels
     Graphic fiction
  SA topics with the subdivision
     Graphic novels, e.g. **Sports—
     Graphic novels** [to be added
     as needed]
  BT **Comic books, strips, etc.**
     Fiction
  NT **Adventure graphic novels**
     **Autobiographical graphic nov-
     els**
     Biographical graphic novels
     Fantasy graphic novels
     **Female superhero graphic nov-
     els**
     Horror graphic novels
     Humorous graphic novels
     Manga
     Mystery graphic novels
     Religious graphic novels
     Romance graphic novels
     Science fiction graphic novels
     Sports—Graphic novels
     Superhero graphic novels
     Supernatural graphic novels
Graphics, Computer
  USE **Computer graphics**
Graphite 553.2
  UF Black lead
  BT **Carbon**
Graphology 137; 155.2
  Use for materials on handwriting as an ex-
  pression of the writer's character. General ma-
  terials on the history and art of writing are en-
  tered under **Writing**. Materials on writing
  with a pen or pencil and practical or prescrip-
  tive guides to penmanship are entered under
  Handwriting.
  BT **Handwriting**
     Writing
Graphs
  USE **Graphic methods**
Graphs, Theory of
  USE **Graph theory**

Grass (Drug)
   USE **Marijuana**
Grasses (May subdiv. geog.)   **584; 633.2**
   BT   **Plants**
   RT   **Feeds**
        Forage plants
        Hay
        Lawns
Grassland ecology (May subdiv. geog.)
        577.4
   BT   **Ecology**
   NT   **Prairie ecology**
Grasslands (May subdiv. geog.)   **577.4;**
        578.74
   BT   **Land use**
   NT   **Prairies**
Gratefulness
   USE   **Gratitude**
Gratitude   179
   UF   Gratefulness
        Thankfulness
   BT   **Emotions**
        Virtue
Graves
   USE   **Burial**
         Cemeteries
         Epitaphs
         Funeral rites and ceremonies
         Mounds and mound builders
         Tombs
Graveyards
   USE   **Cemeteries**
Gravitation   521; 531
   Use for materials on the phenomenon in
   physics of attraction between masses. Materi-
   als on the gravitational pull of the earth or
   other planets or celestial bodies on objects at
   or near their surface are entered under **Gravi-
   ty.**
   BT   **Physics**
   NT   **Gravity**
   RT   **Relativity (Physics)**
Gravity   531
   Use for materials on the gravitational pull
   of the earth or other planets or celestial bodies
   on objects at or near their surface. Materials
   on the phenomenon in physics of attraction
   between masses are entered under **Gravitation.**
   UF   Earth—Gravity
   BT   **Gravitation**
Gravity free state
   USE   **Weightlessness**

Gray Friars
   USE   **Franciscans**
GRE
   USE   **Graduate Record Examination**
Grease
   USE   **Lubrication and lubricants**
         Oils and fats
Great books program
   USE   **Discussion groups**
Great Britain   941
   Use for materials on the United Kingdom
   of Great Britain and Northern Ireland, which
   comprises England, Scotland, Wales, and
   Northern Ireland, as well as for materials on
   the island of Great Britain. May be subdivided
   like **United States** except for *History*. Materi-
   als limited to one of the constituent parts of
   the United Kingdom, apart from materials re-
   lating to history or politics and government,
   are entered under that part, e.g. **England.**
   NT   **England**
Great Britain—Antiquities   942.01
   NT   **Stonehenge (England)**
Great Britain—Colonies   325
   UF   British Empire
   BT   **Colonies**
   RT   **Commonwealth countries**
Great Britain—History   941
   UF   England—History
        English history
Great Britain—History—0-1066   941.01
   NT   **Anglo-Saxons**
        Celts
**Great Britain—History—1066-1154, Nor-
   man period   941.02**
   NT   **Domesday book**
        **Hastings (East Sussex, En-
           gland), Battle of, 1066**
        Normans
**Great Britain—History—1066-1485, Me-
   dieval period   941.03**
   NT   **Hundred Years' War, 1339-
           1453**
**Great Britain—History—1154-1399, Plan-
   tagenets   941.03**
   NT   **Magna Carta**
**Great Britain—History—1399-1485, Lan-
   caster and York   941.04**
**Great Britain—History—1455-1485,
   Wars of the Roses   941.04**
   UF   Wars of the Roses, 1455-1485
**Great Britain—History—1485-1603, Tu-
   dors   941.05**
   NT   **Spanish Armada, 1588**

Great Britain—History—1603-1714, Stu-
arts   941.06
Great Britain—History—1642-1660, Civil
War and Commonwealth   941.06
   UF   Civil War—England
        Commonwealth of England
Great Britain—History—1714-1837
941.07
   NT   War of 1812
Great Britain—History—19th century
941.081
   RT   Industrial revolution
Great Britain—History—1853-1856, Crime-
an War
   USE   Crimean War, 1853-1856
Great Britain—History—20th century
941.082
Great Britain—History—1945-1952
941.085
Great Britain—History—1952-   941.085
Great Britain—History—21st century
941.086
Great Britain—Kings and rulers   920;
941.092
   UF   Great Britain—Kings, queens,
        rulers, etc.
   BT   Kings and rulers
Great Britain—Kings, queens, rulers, etc.
   USE   Great Britain—Kings and rul-
         ers
Great Britain—Prime ministers
   USE   Prime ministers—Great Britain
Great Britain—Queens
   USE   Queens—Great Britain
Great Depression, 1929-1939 (May
subdiv. geog.)   338.5; 909.82
   UF   Business depression, 1929-1939
   BT   Depressions
        Economic conditions
Great Wall of China   951
Greece   938; 949.5
   May be subdivided like United States ex-
   cept for History.
Greece, Ancient
   USE   Greece—History—0-323
Greece—Antiquities   938
   BT   Classical antiquities
   NT   Delphi (Extinct city)
Greece—Biography   920.038; 920.0495
   UF   Classical biography
   BT   Biography

Greece—Civilization   938
   Use for materials on the civilization of
   Greece, ancient and modern. Materials on the
   spread of Greek civilization throughout the
   ancient world following the conquests of Al-
   exander the Great are entered under Helle-
   nism. Materials on both ancient Greek and
   Roman civilizations are entered under Classi-
   cal civilization.
   UF   Civilization, Greek
        Greek civilization
   BT   Classical civilization
   NT   Hellenism
Greece—Description
   USE   Greece—Description and travel
Greece—Description—0-323
   USE   Greece—Description and trav-
         el—0-323
Greece—Description and travel   914.95
   Use for descriptive materials on modern
   Greece, including materials for travelers. De-
   scriptive materials on ancient Greece, includ-
   ing accounts by travelers in ancient times, are
   entered under Greece—Description and trav-
   el—0-323.
   UF   Greece—Description
Greece—Description and travel—0-323
913.8
   Use for descriptive materials on ancient
   Greece including accounts by travelers of an-
   cient times.
   UF   Ancient Greece—Description
        Greece—Description—0-323
Greece—Geography   914.95
   Use for materials on the geography of mod-
   ern Greece. Materials on the geography of an-
   cient Greece are entered under Greece—His-
   torical geography.
   BT   Geography
   NT   Greece—Historical geography
Greece—Historical geography   911;
913.8
   UF   Classical geography
   BT   Ancient geography
        Greece—Geography
        Historical geography
Greece—History   938; 949.5
Greece—History—0-323   938
   UF   Ancient Greece
        Greece, Ancient
Greece—History—323-1453   949.5
   UF   Medieval Greece
Greece—History—1453-   949.5
   UF   Greece, Modern
Greece—History—20th century   949.507
Greece—History—1967-1974   949.507

Greece—History—1974- 949.507

Greece, Modern

    USE **Greece—History—1453-**

Greed 178

    Use for materials on any excessive desire for food, personal possessions, etc. Materials on an inordinate desire for wealth are entered under **Avarice**.

    BT **Human behavior**

    RT **Avarice**

Greek and Latin drama

    USE **Classical drama**

Greek antiquities

    USE **Classical antiquities**

Greek architecture (May subdiv. geog.) 722

    UF Architecture, Greek

    BT **Ancient architecture**

        Architecture

Greek art (May subdiv. geog.) 709.38; 709.495

    UF Art, Greek

        Classical art

    BT **Ancient art**

        Art

        Classical antiquities

Greek Church

    USE **Greek Orthodox Church**

Greek civilization

    USE **Greece—Civilization**

Greek drama 882

    BT **Drama**

        Greek literature

Greek language 480

    Use for classical Greek. Modern Greek is entered under **Modern Greek language**. May be subdivided like **English language**.

    UF Classical languages

    BT **Language and languages**

    RT **Modern Greek language**

Greek language, Modern

    USE **Modern Greek language**

Greek letter societies

    USE **Fraternities and sororities**

Greek literature 880

    May use same subdivisions and names of literary forms as for **English literature**.

    BT **Literature**

    NT **Greek drama**

    RT **Classical literature**

Greek literature, Modern

    USE **Modern Greek literature**

Greek mythology 292.1

    UF Mythology, Greek

    BT **Classical mythology**

    NT **Trojan War**

Greek Orthodox Church (May subdiv. geog.) 281.9

    UF Greek Church

    BT **Christian sects**

        Orthodox Eastern Church

Greek philosophy

    USE **Ancient philosophy**

Greek sculpture 730.938; 730.9495

    UF Sculpture, Greek

    BT **Sculpture**

Green movement

    USE **Environmental movement**

Green technology (May subdiv. geog.) 363.7

    UF Earth-friendly technology

        Environmental technology

    BT **Technology**

Green tourism

    USE **Ecotourism**

Greenhouse effect

    USE **Global warming**

Greenhouses (May subdiv. geog.) 631.5

    UF Hothouses

    BT **Flower gardening**

        Gardening

        Horticulture

    RT **Garden rooms**

Greeting cards (May subdiv. geog.) 741.6; 745.594

    UF Cards, Greeting

    SA types of greeting cards [to be added as needed]

    NT **Christmas cards**

Gregorian chant

    USE **Chants (Plain, Gregorian, etc.)**

Grey Friars

    USE **Franciscans**

Grey market

    USE **Black market**

Grief 152.4; 155.9

    Use for materials on mental suffering or sorrow from causes such as loss or remorse other than the loss of a loved one. Materials on the suffering of those who have lost a loved one are entered under **Bereavement**.

    UF Sorrow

    BT **Emotions**

    RT **Bereavement**

        Consolation

        Joy and sorrow

Grievance procedures (Public administration)
    USE **Ombudsman**
Griffins 398.2454
    UF Gryphons
    BT **Mythical animals**
Grill cooking
    USE **Barbecue cooking**
Grilling
    USE **Barbecue cooking**
Grinding and polishing 621.9
    UF Buffing
        Polishing
    BT **Machine shop practice**
    RT **Machine tools**
Grist mills
    USE **Flour mills**
Groceries—Packaging
    USE **Food—Packaging**
Groceries—Purchasing
    USE **Grocery shopping**
Grocery shopping 641.3
    Use for materials on food buying. Materials on the principles and methods involved in the transfer of merchandise from producer to consumer are entered under **Marketing**.
    UF Food buying
        Food—Purchasing
        Groceries—Purchasing
        Marketing (Home economics)
        Supermarket shopping
    BT **Home economics**
        Shopping
Grocery trade (May subdiv. geog.)
    338.4
    BT **Food industry**
    NT **Supermarkets**
    RT **Food**
Grooming
    USE types of animals with the subdivision *Grooming* [to be added as needed]
Grooming, Personal
    USE **Personal grooming**
Gross national product (May subdiv. geog.) **339.3**
    UF GNP
        National product, Gross
    BT **Economics**
        Statistics
        Wealth
    RT **Income**

Grottoes
    USE **Caves**
Ground effect machines
    USE **Air-cushion vehicles**
Ground water
    USE **Groundwater**
Grounds maintenance (May subdiv. geog.) **712**
    Use for materials on maintenance of public, industrial, and institutional grounds and large estates.
    BT **Gardening**
    NT **Roadside improvement**
Groundwater (May subdiv. geog.)
    551.49; 553.7
    UF Ground water
        Subterranean water
        Underground water
    BT **Water**
Group decision making 302.3; 658.4
    BT **Decision making**
Group discussion
    USE **Discussion groups**
Group dynamics
    USE **Social groups**
Group homes (May subdiv. geog.) **362; 363.5**
    Use for materials on planned housing for groups of unrelated people needing supervision.
    UF Community based residences
        Group residences
        Residential treatment centers
    BT **Institutional care**
        Social work
    NT **Halfway houses**
    RT **Foster home care**
Group hospitalization
    USE **Hospitalization insurance**
Group identity 302.4
    UF Collective identity
        Community identity
        Social identity
    BT **Identity (Psychology)**
Group insurance (May subdiv. geog.) **368.3**
    Use for materials on group life insurance. Materials on group insurance in other fields are entered under the specific kind of insurance, e.g. **Health insurance**.
    UF Insurance, Group
    BT **Life insurance**
Group living
    USE **Communal living**

Group medical practice
    USE   **Medical practice**
Group medical practice, Prepaid
    USE   **Health maintenance organiza-
          tions**
Group medical service
    USE   **Health insurance**
Group method in teaching
    USE   **Cooperative learning**
Group problem solving   153.4
    UF   Brain storming
          Team problem solving
          Think tanks
    BT   **Problem solving**
Group relations training   302
    UF   Encounter groups
          Sensitivity training
          T groups
    BT   **Interpersonal relations**
Group residences
    USE   **Group homes**
Group social work
    USE   **Social group work**
Group teaching
    USE   **Cooperative learning**
Group theory   512
    UF   Groups, Theory of
    BT   **Algebra**
          Mathematics
          Number theory
    NT   **Boolean algebra**
Group travel
    USE   **Travel**
Group values
    USE   **Social values**
Group work in education
    USE   **Cooperative learning**
Group work, Social
    USE   **Social group work**
Grouping by ability
    USE   **Ability grouping in education**
Groups of persons
    USE   **Persons**
Groups, Social
    USE   **Social groups**
Groups, Theory of
    USE   **Group theory**
Growing of Christmas trees
    USE   **Christmas tree growing**
Grown-up abused children
    USE   **Adult child abuse victims**

Grown-ups
    USE   **Adults**
Grownups
    USE   **Adults**
Growth   155; 571.8; 612.6
    SA   subjects with the subdivision
          Growth, e.g. **Children—
          Growth; Cities and towns—
          Growth; Plants—Growth;**
          etc. [to be added as needed]
    BT   **Physiology**
Growth disorders   616.4
    UF   Abnormal growth
          Abnormalities, Human
          Development
          Failure to thrive syndrome
          Human abnormalities
    BT   **Metabolism**
    NT   **Dwarfism**
          Giantism
    RT   **Birth defects**
          Fetal alcohol syndrome
Growth retardation
    USE   **Dwarfism**
Gryphons
    USE   **Griffins**
Guaranteed annual income (May subdiv.
          geog.)   **362.5**
    Use for materials on compensation provided
    by a government to anyone whose annual in-
    come falls below a specified level.
    UF   Annual income guarantee
          Guaranteed income
    BT   **Income**
Guaranteed income
    USE   **Guaranteed annual income**
Guerillas
    USE   **Guerrillas**
Guerrilla warfare (May subdiv. geog.)
          355.02; 355.4
    Use for materials on the military aspects of
    irregular warfare. General and historical mate-
    rials are entered under **Guerrillas**.
    UF   Unconventional warfare
    BT   **Insurgency**
          Military art and science
          Tactics
          War
    NT   **Counterinsurgency**
Guerrillas (May subdiv. geog.)   **356**
    Use for general and historical materials.
    Materials on the military aspects of irregular
    warfare are entered under **Guerrilla warfare**.

Guerrillas—*Continued*
UF Guerillas
Partisans
SA names of wars with the subdivision *Underground movements*, e.g. **World War, 1939-1945—Underground movements** [to be added as needed]
BT **National liberation movements**
Guests
USE **Entertaining**
Guidance
USE **Counseling**
Guidance counseling, Educational
USE **Educational counseling**
Guidance counseling, School
USE **School counseling**
Guidance, Vocational
USE **Vocational guidance**
Guide dogs (May subdiv. geog.) **636.7**
UF Dog guides
Dogs for the blind
Seeing eye dogs
BT **Animals and the handicapped**
Working dogs
Guidebooks
USE names of cities (except ancient cities), countries, states, etc., with the subdivision *Guidebooks,* e.g. **Chicago (Ill.)—Guidebooks; United States—Guidebooks;** etc. [to be added as needed]
Guided missiles (May subdiv. geog.) **358.1; 623.4**
UF Missiles, Guided
SA types of missiles and names of specific missiles [to be added as needed]
BT **Bombs**
Projectiles
Rocketry
Rockets (Aeronautics)
NT **Antimissile missiles**
Ballistic missiles
Nike rocket
Guilt **152.4**
BT **Conscience**
Emotions
Ethics
Good and evil

Sin
RT **Shame**
Guinevere (Legendary character) **398.22**
BT **Legendary characters**
Guitar
USE **Guitars**
Guitar music **787.87**
BT **Instrumental music**
Guitars (May subdiv. geog.) **787.87**
UF Guitar
BT **Stringed instruments**
NT **Air guitar**
Electric guitar
Gulf States (U.S.) **976**
BT **United States**
Gulf War, 1991
USE **Persian Gulf War, 1991**
Gums and resins **547; 668**
UF Resins
Rosin
BT **Forest products**
Industrial chemistry
Plastics
Gun control (May subdiv. geog.) **323.4; 344.05; 363.33**
Use for materials about existing laws governing the purchase and use of firearms and for materials about the political controversy over limiting legal access to firearms and stopping the traffic in illegal firearms.
UF Control of guns
Firearms control
Firearms—Law and legislation
Guns—Control
Handgun control
Right to bear arms
BT **Law**
Legislation
Gundam (Fictional character) **741.5**
BT **Fictional characters**
Fictional robots
Manga
Mecha
Gunpowder (May subdiv. geog.) **623.4**
UF Powder, Smokeless
Smokeless powder
BT **Explosives**
Firearms
RT **Ammunition**
Guns
USE **Firearms**
Ordnance

Guns—*Continued*
  Rifles
  Shotguns
Guns—Control
 USE **Gun control**
Gunsmithing
 USE **Firearms industry**
Gymnastics (May subdiv. geog.) **613.7;**
  796.44
 UF Calisthenics
 BT **Athletics**
  Exercise
  Sports
 RT **Acrobats and acrobatics**
  Physical education
Gynecology
 USE **Women—Diseases**
  Women—Health and hygiene
Gypsies (May subdiv. geog.) **305.891**
 UF Gipsies
  Romanies
Gypsum 553.6
 BT **Minerals**
Gyroscope 629.135; 681
 BT **Aeronautical instruments**
Habeas corpus 345
 BT **Civil rights**
  Constitutional law
  Criminal procedure
  Martial law
Habit 152.3
 BT **Human behavior**
  Psychology
 NT **Tobacco habit**
 RT **Instinct**
Habitat (Ecology) (May subdiv. geog.)
  577; 591.7
 SA types of ecology, e.g. **Marine**
  ecology; and types of animals,
  plants, and crops with the
  subdivision *Ecology,* e.g.
  Fishes—Ecology [to be added
  as needed]
 BT **Ecology**
Habitations
 USE types of animals with the subdi-
  vision *Habitations,* for materi-
  als on the natural shelters and
  homes animals build for
  themselves, such as burrows,
  dens, lairs, etc., e.g. **Bea-**

vers—Habitations [to be add-
 ed as needed]
Habitations, Human
 USE **Housing**
Habitations of domestic animals
 USE **Animal housing**
Habitations of wild animals
 USE **Animals—Habitations**
Habits of animals
 USE **Animal behavior**
Hades
 USE **Hell**
Haiku 808.1; 808.81
 Use for collections of haiku by one or sev-
 eral authors or for materials about haiku.
 BT **Poetry**
Hair (May subdiv. geog.) **612.7; 646.7**
 Use for general materials on hair as well
 for as materials on hairdressing and haircut-
 ting.
 UF Barbering
  Coiffure
  Haircutting
  Hairdressing
  Hairstyles
  Hairstyling
 BT **Head**
  Personal grooming
 NT **Braids (Hairstyling)**
  Wigs
Haircutting
 USE **Hair**
Hairdressing
 USE **Hair**
Hairstyles
 USE **Hair**
Hairstyling
 USE **Hair**
Haiti 972.94
Halftone process
 USE **Photoengraving**
Halfway houses (May subdiv. geog.)
  362; 365
 Use for materials on centers for formerly
 institutionalized individuals, such as mental
 patients or drug addicts, that are designed to
 facilitate their readjustment to private life.
 BT **Correctional institutions**
  Group homes
Halitosis
 USE **Bad breath**
Halley's comet 523.6
 BT **Comets**

Hallmarks
    UF   Marks
          Marks on plate
    SA   types of things with identifying
          marks, other than plate, with
          the subdivision *Marks*, e.g.
          Pottery—Marks [to be added
          as needed]
    BT   **Plate**
Halloween   **394.2646**
    UF   All Hallows' Eve
    BT   **Holidays**
Hallucinations and illusions   **616.85;**
    616.89
    UF   Delusions
          Illusions
    BT   **Abnormal psychology**
          Parapsychology
          Subconsciousness
          Visions
    NT   **Optical illusions**
    RT   **Apparitions**
          Fantasy
          Magic
          Magic tricks
          Personality disorders
Hallucinogenic drugs
    USE **Hallucinogens**
Hallucinogenic plants
    USE **Hallucinogens**
Hallucinogens   **615**
    UF   Consciousness expanding drugs
          Hallucinogenic drugs
          Hallucinogenic plants
    SA   types of hallucinogens [to be
          added as needed]
    BT   **Drugs**
          Psychotropic drugs
          Stimulants
    NT   **LSD (Drug)**
Ham radio stations
    USE **Amateur radio stations**
Hand shadows
    USE **Shadow pictures**
Hand weaving
    USE **Weaving**
Handbooks, manuals, etc.
    USE subjects, classes of persons, and
          names of places, corporate
          bodies, individual literary au-
          thors, and sacred works with

          the subdivision *Handbooks,*
          manuals, etc., e.g. **Photogra-**
          phy—Handbooks, manuals,
          etc.; United States. Army—
          Handbooks, manuals, etc. [to
          be added as needed]
Handedness
    USE **Left- and right-handedness**
Handgun control
    USE **Gun control**
Handguns (May subdiv. geog.)   **683.4**
    UF   Pistols
          Revolvers
    BT   **Firearms**
Handheld computers
    USE **Portable computers**
Handicapped (May subdiv. geog.)
    305.9; 362.4
    UF   Disabled
    NT   **Architecture and the handi-**
          capped
          Computers and the handi-
          capped
          Discrimination against the
          handicapped
          Handicapped children
          Mentally handicapped
          Physically handicapped
          Sick
          Socially handicapped
          Sports for the handicapped
          Vocational guidance for the
          handicapped
Handicapped and animals
    USE **Animals and the handicapped**
Handicapped and architecture
    USE **Architecture and the handi-**
          capped
Handicapped children (May subdiv.
    geog.)   **362.7**
    UF   Abnormal children
          Children, Abnormal
    BT   **Children**
          Exceptional children
          Handicapped
    NT   **Brain damaged children**
          Hyperactive children
          Mainstreaming in education
          Mentally handicapped children
          Parents of handicapped chil-
          dren

Handicapped children—*Continued*
      Physically handicapped children
      Socially handicapped children
Handicapped—Clothing   **646.4**
  BT **Clothing and dress**
Handicapped—Legal status, laws, etc.
    (May subdiv. geog.)   **346.01**
  UF Disability law
  BT **Law**
Handicapped—Nazi persecution (May
    subdiv. geog.)   **940.53**
  UF Nazi persecution of the handi-
      capped
  BT **Persecution**
      **World War, 1939-1945—Atroc-
      ities**
Handicapped—Salaries, wages, etc. (May
    subdiv. geog.)   **331.2**
  BT **Salaries, wages, etc.**
Handicapped—Services for (May subdiv.
    geog.)   **362.4**
  UF Services for the handicapped
  BT **Human services**
      Social work
Handicapped—Travel (May subdiv. geog.)
    910.2
  BT **Travel**
Handicaps
  USE **Disabilities**
Handicraft (May subdiv. geog.)   **745.5;
    746**
    Use for materials on creative work done by
  hand, sometimes with the aid of simple tools
  or machines.
  UF Crafts (Arts)
  SA types of handicrafts [to be added
      as needed]
  BT **Arts**
  NT **Beadwork**
      Chair caning
      Collage
      Craft shows
      Egg decoration
      Furniture finishing
      Hooked rugs
      Industrial arts
      Leather work
      Models and modelmaking
      Nature craft
      Paper crafts
      Picture frames and framing

      Plastics craft
      Polymer clay craft
      Ribbon work
      Scrapbooking
      Toy making
      Weaving
      Wire craft
  RT **Arts and crafts movement**
      Creative activities
      Decoration and ornament
      Decorative arts
      Folk art
      Hobbies
      Occupational therapy
Handling of materials
  USE **Materials handling**
Handwriting   **652**
    Use for materials on writing with a pen or
  pencil and for practical or prescriptive guides
  to penmanship. General materials on the histo-
  ry and art of writing are entered under **Writ-
  ing**. Materials on handwriting as an expres-
  sion of the writer's character are entered un-
  der **Graphology**.
  UF Legibility of handwriting
      Penmanship
      Writing—Study and teaching
  BT **Writing**
  NT **Calligraphy**
      Graphology
      Writing of numerals
Hang gliding
  USE **Gliding and soaring**
Hanging
  USE **Capital punishment**
Hansen's disease
  USE **Leprosy**
Hanukkah (May subdiv. geog.)   **296.4;
    394.267**
  UF Chanukah
      Feast of Dedication
      Feast of Lights
  BT **Jewish holidays**
Happening (Art)
  USE **Performance art**
Happiness   **158**
  UF Gladness
  BT **Emotions**
  NT **Mental health**
  RT **Joy and sorrow**
      Pleasure
Harassment, Sexual
  USE **Sexual harassment**

Harbors (May subdiv. geog.) **386; 387.1; 627**

   UF   Ports

   BT   **Civil engineering**

         Hydraulic structures

         Merchant marine

         Navigation

         Shipping

         Transportation

   NT   **Marinas**

   RT   **Docks**

Hard-of-hearing

   USE   **Hearing impaired**

Hardanger needlework **746.44**

   UF   Norwegian drawn work

   BT   **Drawn work**

         Embroidery

         Needlework

Hardware **683**

   BT   **Iron industry**

   NT   **Knives**

Hares

   USE   **Rabbits**

Harlem Renaissance **810.9; 974.7**

   UF   New Negro Movement

   BT   **African American art**

         African American music

         American literature—African American authors

Harmful insects

   USE   **Insect pests**

Harmony **781.2**

   BT   **Composition (Music)**

         Music

         Music—Theory

Harry Potter (Fictional character)

   USE   **Potter, Harry (Fictional character)**

Harry S. Truman Library (Independence, Mo.) **026**

   BT   **Presidents—United States—Archives**

Harvesting machinery (May subdiv. geog.) **631.3**

   UF   Reapers

   BT   **Agricultural machinery**

Hashish

   USE   **Marijuana**

Hasidism (May subdiv. geog.) **296.8**

   UF   Chasidism

         Hassidism

   BT   **Judaism**

Hassidism

   USE   **Hasidism**

Hastings (East Sussex, England), Battle of, 1066 **941.02**

   BT   **Battles**

         Great Britain—History—1066-1154, Norman period

Hate **152.4**

   BT   **Emotions**

Hate crimes (May subdiv. geog.) **364**

   UF   Bias attacks

         Bias crimes

         Bigotry-motivated crimes

         Crimes of hate

         Prejudice-motivated crimes

   BT   **Crime**

         Discrimination

         Violence

Hatha yoga **613.7**

   UF   Yoga exercises

         Yoga, Hatha

   BT   **Exercise**

         Yoga

Hats (May subdiv. geog.) **391.4; 646.5; 687**

   UF   Millinery

   BT   **Clothing and dress**

         Costume

Haunted houses (May subdiv. geog.) **133.1**

   BT   **Houses**

   RT   **Ghosts**

Hawking

   USE   **Falconry**

Hay **633.2**

   SA   types of hay crops, e.g. **Alfalfa** [to be added as needed]

   BT   **Farm produce**

         Forage plants

   RT   **Feeds**

         Grasses

Hay fever **616.2**

   BT   **Allergy**

Hazardous materials

   USE   **Hazardous substances**

Hazardous occupations **331.702**

   UF   Dangerous occupations

   BT   **Occupations**

   RT   **Industrial accidents**

         Occupational diseases

Hazardous occupations—*Continued*
> **Occupational health and safety**

Hazardous substances (May subdiv.
>   geog.)   **363.17; 604.7**
>   UF   Dangerous materials
>   Hazardous materials
>   Inflammable substances
>   Toxic substances
>   BT   **Materials**
>   NT   **Hazardous wastes**
>   **Poisons and poisoning**

Hazardous substances—Transportation
>   (May subdiv. geog.)   **363.17;**
>   **604.7**
>   BT   **Transportation**

Hazardous waste disposal
>   USE   **Hazardous wastes**

Hazardous waste sites (May subdiv.
>   geog.)   **363.72; 628.4**
>   UF   Chemical landfills
>   Dumps, Toxic
>   Toxic dumps
>   BT   **Landfills**
>   NT   **Love Canal Chemical Waste**
>   **Landfill (Niagara Falls,**
>   **N.Y.)**

Hazardous wastes (May subdiv. geog.)
>   **363.72**
>   UF   Hazardous waste disposal
>   Toxic wastes
>   Wastes, Hazardous
>   BT   **Hazardous substances**
>   **Industrial waste**
>   **Refuse and refuse disposal**
>   RT   **Medical wastes**
>   **Pollution**

HDTV (Television)
>   USE   **High definition television**

Head   611; 612
>   BT   **Anatomy**
>   NT   **Brain**
>   **Ear**
>   **Eye**
>   **Face**
>   **Hair**
>   **Mouth**
>   **Nose**
>   **Phrenology**
>   **Teeth**

Head pain
>   USE   **Headache**

Headache   616.8

>   UF   Head pain
>   BT   **Pain**
>   NT   **Migraine**

Heads of state (May subdiv. geog.)
>   **352.23; 920**
>   UF   Rulers
>   State, Heads of
>   SA   names of individual heads of
>   state [to be added as needed]
>   BT   **Executive power**
>   **Statesmen**
>   NT   **Dictators**
>   **Kings and rulers**
>   **Presidents**

Healing (May subdiv. geog.)   **615.5**
>   BT   **Therapeutics**

Healing, Mental
>   USE   **Mental healing**

Healing, Spiritual
>   USE   **Spiritual healing**

Health   613
>   Use for materials on physical, mental, and
> social well-being. Materials on personal body
> care are entered under **Hygiene**.
>   UF   Personal health
>   SA   parts of the body with the sub-
>   division *Care*, e.g. **Foot—**
>   **Care**; classes of persons and
>   ethnic groups with the subdi-
>   vision *Health and hygiene*,
>   e.g. **Women—Health and**
>   **hygiene**; and subjects and
>   names of wars with the sub-
>   division *Health aspects*, e.g.
>   **World War, 1939-1945—**
>   **Health aspects** [to be added
>   as needed]
>   BT   **Medicine**
>   **Physiology**
>   **Preventive medicine**
>   NT   **Children—Health and hygiene**
>   **Diet**
>   **Elderly—Health and hygiene**
>   **Exercise**
>   **Health education**
>   **Health self-care**
>   **Infants—Health and hygiene**
>   **Mental health**
>   **Nutrition**
>   **Physical fitness**
>   **Public health**
>   **Rest**

Health—*Continued*
     Sleep
     Stress management
     Women—Health and hygiene
  RT **Diseases**
     Holistic medicine
     Hygiene
Health and hygiene
  USE classes of persons and ethnic
      groups with the subdivision
      Health and hygiene, e.g.
      Women—Health and hy-
      giene; and parts of the body
      with the subdivision *Care,*
      e.g. **Foot—Care; Skin—**
      Care; etc. [to be added as
      needed]
Health aspects
  USE subjects, industries, and wars
      with the subdivision *Health*
      aspects, e.g. **World War,**
      1939-1945—Health aspects
      [to be added as needed]
Health boards (May subdiv. geog.)
     614.06
  UF Boards of health
     Public health boards
  BT **Public health**
Health care
  USE **Medical care**
Health care delivery
  USE **Medical care**
Health care facilities
  USE **Health facilities**
Health care personnel
  USE **Medical personnel**
Health care policy
  USE **Medical policy**
Health care reform (May subdiv. geog.)
     362.1
  UF Health reform
     Health system reform
     Medical care reform
     Reform of health care delivery
     Reform of medical care delivery
  RT **Health insurance**
     Medical care
Health care, Right to
  USE **Right to health care**
Health care, Self
  USE **Health self-care**

Health clubs
  USE **Physical fitness centers**
Health counseling (May subdiv. geog.)
     362.1; 613
  BT **Counseling**
     Health education
Health education (May subdiv. geog.)
     372.37; 613.07
  UF Health—Study and teaching
     Hygiene—Study and teaching
  BT **Education**
     Health
  NT **Drug education**
     Health counseling
     School hygiene
  RT **Children—Health and hygiene**
     School nurses
Health—Environmental aspects
  USE **Environmental health**
Health examinations
  USE **Periodic health examinations**
Health facilities (May subdiv. geog.)
     362.11
  UF Clinics
     Health care facilities
     Medical care facilities
  BT **Medical care**
     Public health
Health foods
  USE **Natural foods**
Health, Industrial
  USE **Occupational health and safety**
Health insurance (May subdiv. geog.)
     368.38
  UF Group medical service
     Insurance, Health
     Medical insurance
  BT **Insurance**
  NT **Health maintenance organiza-**
      tions
     Hospitalization insurance
     National health insurance
     Workers' compensation
  RT **Health care reform**
Health maintenance organizations (May
     subdiv. geog.) **362.1; 368.38;**
     610.6
  UF Comprehensive health care orga-
      nizations
     Group medical practice, Prepaid
     HMOs

Health maintenance organizations—*Continued*

        Prepaid group medical practice

  BT   **Health insurance**

       Medical practice

Health personnel

  USE **Medical personnel**

Health policy

  USE **Medical policy**

Health professions

  USE **Medical personnel**

Health program evaluation

  USE **Public health—Evaluation**

Health records

  USE **Medical records**

Health reform

  USE **Health care reform**

Health resorts (May subdiv. geog.)   613

  UF   Health resorts, spas, etc.

       Health spas

       Spas

       Watering places

  BT   **Resorts**

  RT   **Hydrotherapy**

Health resorts, spas, etc.

  USE **Health resorts**

Health sciences personnel

  USE **Medical personnel**

Health self-care   613; 616

  UF   Health care, Self

       Medical self-care

       Self-care, Health

       Self-care, Medical

       Self-examination, Medical

       Self health care

       Self-help medical care

       Self-medication

  BT   **Alternative medicine**

       Health

       Medical care

  NT   **First aid**

       Physical fitness

  RT   **Holistic medicine**

       Popular medicine

Health services accessibility

  USE **Access to health care**

Health services personnel

  USE **Medical personnel**

Health spas

  USE **Health resorts**

       Physical fitness centers

Health—Study and teaching

  USE **Health education**

Health system reform

  USE **Health care reform**

Healths, Drinking of

  USE **Toasts**

Hearing   152.1; 612.8

  UF   Acoustics

  BT   **Senses and sensation**

       Sound

  NT   **Hearing in animals**

  RT   **Deafness**

       Ear

       Listening

Hearing aids   617.8

  BT   **Deafness**

Hearing ear dogs (May subdiv. geog.)   636.7

  UF   Dogs for the deaf

  BT   **Animals and the handicapped**

       Deaf—Means of communication

       Working dogs

Hearing impaired   362.4; 617.8

  UF   Hard-of-hearing

       Partial hearing

       Partially hearing

  BT   **Physically handicapped**

  NT   **Deaf**

Hearing in animals   573.8

  UF   Animals—Hearing

  BT   **Hearing**

       Senses and sensation in animals

Heart   573.1; 611; 612.1

  BT   **Cardiovascular system**

  NT   **Artificial heart**

Heart—Anatomy   573.1; 611

  BT   **Anatomy**

Heart attack   616.1

  UF   Heart—Infarction

       Myocardial infarction

  BT   **Heart diseases**

Heart disease

  USE **Heart diseases**

Heart—Diseases

  USE **Heart diseases**

Heart diseases   616.1

  UF   Cardiac diseases

       Coronary diseases

       Heart disease

Heart diseases—*Continued*
        Heart—Diseases
    BT **Diseases**
    NT **Angina pectoris**
          Heart attack
Heart diseases—Prevention (May subdiv.
    geog.) **616.1**
    BT **Preventive medicine**
Heart—Infarction
    USE **Heart attack**
Heart—Physiology 612.1
    BT **Physiology**
Heart resuscitation
    USE **Cardiac resuscitation**
Heart—Surgery 617.4
    UF Open heart surgery
    BT **Surgery**
Heart—Surgery—Nursing 617.4
    BT **Nursing**
Heart—Transplantation (May subdiv.
    geog.) **617.4**
    BT **Transplantation of organs, tissues, etc.**
Heat 536
    BT **Electromagnetic waves**
    NT **Steam**
          Thermometers
    RT **Combustion**
          Fire
          Temperature
          Thermodynamics
Heat—Conduction 536
Heat engines 621.4
    UF Hot air engines
    BT **Engines**
          Thermodynamics
Heat insulating materials
    USE **Insulation (Heat)**
Heat pumps 621.4
    BT **Pumping machinery**
          Thermodynamics
Heat—Transmission 536
Heating (May subdiv. geog.) **644; 697**
    SA subjects with the subdivision
        Heating and ventilation, e.g.
        Houses—Heating and ventilation [to be added as needed]
    BT **Home economics**
    NT **Electric heating**
          Fireplaces
          Furnaces

          Hot air heating
          Hot water heating
          Houses—Heating and ventilation
          Insulation (Heat)
          Oil burners
          Radiant heating
          Solar heating
          Space heaters
          Steam heating
          Stoves
    RT **Fuel**
          Ventilation
Heating and ventilation
    USE types of buildings with the subdivision *Heating and ventilation,* e.g. **Houses—Heating and ventilation** [to be added as needed]
Heaven 202; 236
    BT **Eschatology**
          Future life
    NT **Angels**
    RT **Paradise**
Heavy water
    USE **Deuterium oxide**
Hebrew language 492.4
    May be subdivided like **English language**.
    UF Jewish language
          Jews—Language
    BT **Language and languages**
Hebrew literature 892.4
    May use same subdivisions and names of literary forms as for **English literature**.
    UF Jews—Literature
    BT **Literature**
    NT **Bible**
          Cabala
          Talmud
    RT **Jewish literature**
Hebrews
    USE **Jews**
Heirs
    USE **Inheritance and succession**
Helen of Troy (Legendary character) 398.22
    BT **Legendary characters**
Helicopters (May subdiv. geog.) **387.7; 629.133**
    UF Aircraft
    BT **Aeronautics**
          Airplanes

Helicopters—Piloting   629.132
   BT   Airplanes—Piloting
Heliports (May subdiv. geog.)   387.7
   BT   Airports
Helium   546
   BT   Chemical elements
       Gases
Hell   202; 236
   UF   Eternal punishment
       Hades
   BT   Eschatology
       Future life
Hellenism (May subdiv. geog.)   938
   Use for materials on the spread of Greek civilization throughout the ancient world following the conquests of Alexander the Great. Materials limited to the civilization of Greece, ancient and modern, are entered under **Greece—Civilization**. Materials on both ancient Greek and Roman civilizations are entered under **Classical civilization**.
   BT   Greece—Civilization
Helpful insects
   USE   Beneficial insects
Helpfulness
   USE   Helping behavior
Helping behavior   158
   UF   Assistance in emergencies
       Behavior, Helping
       Emergency assistance
       Helpfulness
   BT   Human behavior
       Interpersonal relations
   NT   Counseling
       Encouragement
   RT   Altruism
Helplessness (Psychology)   155.2
   BT   Emotions
Hemophilia   616.1
   BT   Blood—Diseases
Hemp   633.5; 677
   BT   Fibers
   RT   Rope
Hera (Greek deity)   202
   BT   Gods and goddesses
Heraldry (May subdiv. geog.)   929.6
   UF   Coats of arms
       Crests
       Devices (Heraldry)
       Emblems
       Pedigrees
   BT   Archeology
       Signs and symbols

       Symbolism
   NT   Badges
       Flags
       Insignia
       Mottoes
       Seals (Numismatics)
   RT   Chivalry
       Decorations of honor
       Genealogy
       Knights and knighthood
       National emblems
       Nobility
Herb gardening (May subdiv. geog.)   635
   BT   Gardening
   RT   Herb gardens
Herb gardens (May subdiv. geog.)   635
   RT   Herb gardening
Herb remedies
   USE   Herbs—Therapeutic use
Herbal medicine
   USE   Herbs—Therapeutic use
       Medical botany
Herbals
   USE   Herbs
       Materia medica
Herbaria
   USE   Plants—Collection and preservation
Herbicides   632; 668
   UF   Defoliants
       Weed killers
   SA   types of herbicides, e.g. **Agent Orange** [to be added as needed]
   BT   Agricultural chemicals
       Pesticides
   NT   Agent Orange
   RT   Plants
       Spraying and dusting
Herbivores   591.5
   UF   Plant-eating animals
   BT   Animals
Herbs   581.6; 635
   UF   Herbals
   BT   Plants
   NT   Potpourri
Herbs—Therapeutic use   615
   UF   Herb remedies
       Herbal medicine
       Medicinal herbs

Herbs—Therapeutic use—*Continued*
    BT   **Therapeutics**
Herculaneum (Extinct city)   937
    BT   **Extinct cities—Italy**
         Italy—Antiquities
Hercules (Legendary character)   398.22
    BT   **Legendary characters**
Hereditary diseases
    USE   **Medical genetics**
Hereditary succession
    USE   **Inheritance and succession**
Heredity   576.5
    UF   Ancestry
         Descent
         Genes
         Inheritance (Biology)
    BT   **Biology**
         Breeding
    NT   **Chromosomes**
         DNA
         Nature and nurture
         Variation (Biology)
    RT   **Eugenics**
         Genetics
         Mendel's law
         Natural selection
Heredity and environment
    USE   **Nature and nurture**
Heredity of diseases
    USE   **Medical genetics**
Hereford cattle (May subdiv. geog.)
    636.2
    BT   **Beef cattle**
Heresies
    USE   **Heresy**
Heresies, Christian
    USE   **Christian heresies**
Heresy (May subdiv. geog.)   202
    UF   Heresies
    BT   **Religion**
    NT   **Christian heresies**
Heritage property
    USE   **Cultural property**
Heritage tourism
    USE   **Cultural tourism**
Hermeneutics, Biblical
    USE   **Bible—Criticism**
Hermetic art and philosophy
    USE   **Alchemy**
         Astrology
         Occultism
Hermits (May subdiv. geog.)   920

    UF   Recluses
    BT   **Eccentrics and eccentricities**
    RT   **Monasticism and religious or-
         ders**
Heroes and heroines (May subdiv. geog.)
    920
    UF   Heroines
         Heroism
    BT   **Adventure and adventurers**
    NT   **Explorers**
         Martyrs
    RT   **Courage**
         Mythology
Heroin (May subdiv. geog.)   362.29; 615
    BT   **Morphine**
         Narcotics
Heroines
    USE   **Heroes and heroines**
Heroism
    USE   **Courage**
         Heroes and heroines
Hertzian waves
    USE   **Electric waves**
Hibernation   591.56
    UF   Animals—Hibernation
    BT   **Animal behavior**
Hidden children (Holocaust) (May subdiv.
    geog.)   940.53
    BT   **Jewish children in the Holo-
         caust**
Hidden economy
    USE   **Underground economy**
Hidden treasure
    USE   **Buried treasure**
Hides and skins   636.088; 675
    UF   Pelts
         Skins
    BT   **Animal products**
    RT   **Fur**
         Leather
         Tanning
Hieroglyphics (May subdiv. geog.)   411
    BT   **Inscriptions**
         Writing
    NT   **Rosetta stone**
    RT   **Picture writing**
High blood pressure
    USE   **Hypertension**
High-carbohydrate diet   613.2
    BT   **Diet**
    RT   **Carbohydrates**

High definition television (May subdiv. geog.) **621.388**
   UF   HDTV (Television)
   BT   **Television**
High-fiber diet   **613.2**
   BT   **Diet**
High-fidelity sound systems
   USE   **Sound—Recording and repro-**
          ducing
High-frequency radio
   USE   **Shortwave radio**
High income people
   USE   **Rich**
High rise buildings
   USE   **Skyscrapers**
High risk students
   USE   **At risk students**
High school dropouts
   USE   **Dropouts**
High school education
   USE   **Secondary education**
High school libraries (May subdiv. geog.) **027.8**
   UF   Junior high school libraries
          Secondary school libraries
   BT   **School libraries**
High school life
   USE   **High school students**
High school students (May subdiv. geog.) **373**
   UF   High school life
          High schools—Students
   BT   **Students**
High school yearbooks
   USE   **School yearbooks**
High schools (May subdiv. geog.)   **373**
   UF   Secondary schools
   BT   **Public schools**
          Schools
   NT   **Commencements**
          Junior high schools
   RT   **Secondary education**
High schools, Rural
   USE   **Rural schools**
High schools—Students
   USE   **High school students**
High society
   USE   **Upper class**
High speed aerodynamics
   USE   **Supersonic aerodynamics**

High speed aeronautics (May subdiv. geog.) **629.132**
   BT   **Aeronautics**
   NT   **Aerothermodynamics**
          Rocket planes
          Rockets (Aeronautics)
          Supersonic aerodynamics
High tech
   USE   **Technology**
High technology
   USE   **Technology**
High technology industry (May subdiv. geog.) **338.4**
   BT   **Industries**
High treason
   USE   **Treason**
High-yield junk bonds
   USE   **Junk bonds**
Higher criticism
   USE   **Bible—Criticism**
Higher education (May subdiv. geog.) **378**
   UF   Education, Higher
   BT   **Education**
   NT   **Adult education**
          Colleges and universities
          Junior colleges
          Professional education
          Technical education
          University extension
Highland clans
   USE   **Clans—Scotland**
Highland costume
   USE   **Tartans**
Highway accidents
   USE   **Traffic accidents**
Highway beautification
   USE   **Roadside improvement**
Highway construction
   USE   **Roads**
Highway engineering (May subdiv. geog.) **625.7**
   UF   Road engineering
   BT   **Civil engineering**
          Engineering
   NT   **Traffic engineering**
   RT   **Roads**
Highway safety
   USE   **Traffic safety**
Highway transportation (May subdiv. geog.) **388.3**

Highway transportation—*Continued*
  UF Transportation, Highway
  BT **Transportation**
  NT **Automobiles**
      Buses
      Traffic safety
      Trucks
Highwaymen
  USE **Thieves**
Highways
  USE **Roads**
Hijacking of aircraft
  USE **Hijacking of airplanes**
Hijacking of airplanes (May subdiv. geog.) **364.15**
  Use same form for the hijacking of other modes of transportation.
  UF Air piracy
      Airlines—Hijacking
      Airplane hijacking
      Airplanes—Hijacking
      Hijacking of aircraft
  BT **Offenses against public safety**
Hiking (May subdiv. geog.) **796.51**
  SA types of hiking, e.g.
      Backpacking [to be added as needed]
  RT **Outdoor life**
  NT **Backpacking**
      Orienteering
  RT **Trails**
      Walking
Hillbilly music
  USE **Country music**
Hindi drama **891.4**
  BT **Hindi literature**
      Indian drama
Hindi fiction **891.4**
  BT **Hindi literature**
      Indian fiction
Hindi language **491.4**
  BT **Indian languages**
      Language and languages
Hindi literature **891.4**
  BT **Indian epic poetry**
  NT **Hindi drama**
      Hindi fiction
      Hindi poetry
Hindi poetry **891.4**
  BT **Hindi literature**
      Indian poetry
Hindu philosophy **181**

  UF Philosophy, Hindu
  BT **Philosophy**
  NT **Yoga**
Hinduism (May subdiv. geog.) **294.5**
  BT **Religions**
  NT **Vedanta**
      Vedas
      Yoga
  RT **Brahmanism**
      Hindus
Hindus (May subdiv. geog.) **294.5092**
  RT **Hinduism**
Hip-hop culture (May subdiv. geog.) **306.4**
  BT **Popular culture—United States**
Hip-hop fiction
  USE **Urban fiction**
Hippies (May subdiv. geog.) **306**
  BT **Bohemianism**
Hippies—United States **306**
Hispanic American authors **810.9; 920**
  SA genres of American literature with the subdivision *Hispanic American authors* [to be added as needed]
  BT **American authors**
  NT **Mexican American authors**
Hispanic American literature (English)
  USE **American literature—Hispanic American authors**
Hispanic American literature (Spanish)
  USE **American literature (Spanish)**
Hispanic Americans (May subdiv. geog.) **305.868; 973**
  Use for materials on United States citizens of Latin American descent. Materials on citizens of Latin American countries are entered under **Latin Americans**.
  UF Latinos (U.S.)
  SA names of groups of United States citizens from specific countries, e.g. **Mexican Americans** [to be added as needed]
  BT **Ethnic groups**
  NT **Mexican Americans**
Historians (May subdiv. geog.) **907; 920**
  UF Historiographers
  BT **Authors**
  NT **Archeologists**
  RT **Historiography**
      History

Historians, American
USE **Historians—United States**
Historians—United States 907; 920
UF American historians
Historians, American
Historic buildings (May subdiv. geog.)
363.6; 720.9
Use for materials on buildings that are asso-
ciated with notable persons or events in histo-
ry. Materials on buildings that are merely old
are entered under **Buildings**; or under various
types of buildings, e.g. **Castles**; **Church
buildings**; **Theaters**; etc.
UF Historic houses
BT **Buildings**
Historic sites
Monuments
NT **Literary landmarks**
Historic buildings—Chicago (Ill.) 977.3
UF Chicago (Ill.)—Historic buildings
Historic buildings—Ohio 977.1
UF Ohio—Historic buildings
Historic buildings—United States 973
UF United States—Historic buildings
Historic houses
USE **Historic buildings**
Historic preservation (May subdiv. geog.)
363.6
Use for materials on identifying and pre-
serving historically important towns, build-
ings, sites, etc. Materials on protecting cultur-
al heritage property from theft, misappropria-
tion, or exportation are entered under **Cultur-
al property—Protection**.
UF Preservationism (Historic preser-
vation)
SA types of objects, architecture,
etc., with the subdivision
Conservation and restoration,
e.g. **Theaters—Conservation
and restoration** [to be added
as needed]
NT **Theaters—Conservation and
restoration**
RT **Cultural property—Protection**
Historic sites (May subdiv. geog.) **363.6**
UF Historical sites
BT **Archeology**
History
NT **Historic buildings**
RT **National monuments**
Historical atlases 911
UF Historical geography—Maps
History—Atlases

Maps, Historical
BT **Atlases**
RT **Historical geography**
Historical chronology 902
Use for materials in which historical events
are arranged by date.
UF Chronology, Historical
Dates, Historical
History—Chronology
SA ethnic groups, corporate bodies,
military services, topics not
inherently historical, and
names of places with the sub-
division *History—Chronology*,
e.g. **Native Americans—History—Chronology**; **United
States—History—Chronolo-
gy**; and names of individual
persons, wars, sacred works,
topics that are inherently his-
torical, and topics not subdi-
vided by *History*, such as art,
music, literture, etc., with the
subdivision *Chronology*, e.g.
Bible—Chronology [to be
added as needed]
BT **Chronology**
History
Historical dictionaries
USE **History—Dictionaries**
Historical drama 808.2; 808.82
Use for individual works, collections, or
materials about historical drama.
UF Chronicle history (Drama)
Chronicle plays
History plays
SA historical topics, events, or per-
sonages with the subdivision
Drama, e.g. **United States—
History—1861-1865, Civil
War—Drama**; **Napoleon I,
Emperor of the French,
1769-1821—Drama** [to be
added as needed]
BT **Drama**
NT **United States—History—1861-
1865, Civil War—Drama**
United States—History—Drama
War films
Western films

Historical fiction   808.3; 808.83

Use for individual works, collections, or materials about fiction set during a time significantly prior to the time in which it was written.

UF   Historical novels

Historical romances

SA   historical topics, events, or personages with the subdivision *Fiction*, e.g. **Slavery—United States—Fiction**; **United States—History—1861-1865, Civil War—Fiction**; **Napoleon I, Emperor of the French, 1769-1821—Fiction**; etc. [to be added as needed]

BT   **Fiction**

NT   **Gothic novels**

Regency novels

War stories

Western stories

RT   **Biographical fiction**

History

Historical geography   911

Use for materials that discuss the extent of territory held by the states or nations at a given period of history. Materials limited to one country or region still existing in modern times are entered under the name of the place with the subdivision *Historical geography*. Materials on the geography of regions or countries of antiquity that no longer exist as such in modern times are entered under the name of the place with the subdivision *Geography*.

UF   Geography, Historical

SA   names of modern countries or regions with the subdivision *Historical geography*, e.g. **Greece—Historical geography**; **United States—Historical geography**; etc.; and names of places of antiquity with the subdivision *Geography*, e.g. **Gaul—Geography** [to be added as needed]

BT   **Geography**

History

NT   **Ancient geography**

Gaul—Geography

Greece—Historical geography

Rome—Geography

United States—Historical geography

RT   **Historical atlases**

Historical geography—Maps

USE   **Historical atlases**

Historical geology (May subdiv. geog.) **551.7**

BT   **Geology**

NT   **Paleontology**

Historical materialism

USE   **Dialectical materialism**

Historical novels

USE   **Historical fiction**

Historical poetry   808.1; 808.81

Use for individual works, collections, or materials about historical poetry.

UF   Poetry, Historical

BT   **Narrative poetry**

NT   **United States—History—Poetry**

World War, 1939-1945—Poetry

Historical records—Preservation

USE   **Archives**

Historical reenactments (May subdiv. geog.) **900**

UF   History—Reenactments

Reenactment of historical events

BT   **History**

Historical romances

USE   **Historical fiction**

Historical sites

USE   **Historic sites**

Historical societies

USE   **History—Societies**

Historical tourism

USE   **Cultural tourism**

Historiographers

USE   **Historians**

Historiography   907

Use for materials limited to the study and criticism of sources of history, methods of historical research, and the writing of history. General materials on history as a science, including the principles of history, the influence of various factors on history, and the relation of the science of history to other subjects, are entered under **History**. Materials on the interpretation and meaning of history and on the course of events and their resulting consequences are entered under **History—Philosophy**.

UF   History—Criticism

History—Historiography

SA   subjects, wars, historical events, and names of countries, cities, etc., with the subdivision *Historiography* [to be added as needed]

Historiography—*Continued*
   BT   **Authorship**
         History
   NT   **History—Sources**
         Local history
         Philosophy—Historiography
         United States—Historiography
         United States—History—1861-1865, Civil War—Historiography
   RT   **Historians**

History   900

Use for general materials on history as a science, including the principles of history, the influence of various factors on history, and the relation of the science of history to other subjects. Materials on the interpretation and meaning of history and on the course of events and their resulting consequences are entered under **History—Philosophy**. Materials limited to the study and criticism of sources of history, methods of historical research, and the writing of history are entered under **Historiography**. Materials on past events themselves are entered under **World history**; or under the names of regions, countries, cities, etc., with the subdivision *History*.

   UF   Social studies
   SA   countries, states, etc., with the subdivisions *Antiquities*; *Foreign relations*; *History*; or *Politics and government*; and subjects with the subdivision *History*, or, for literature, film, and music headings, *History and criticism*, e.g. **Art—History**; **English literature—History and criticism** [to be added as needed]
   BT   **Humanities**
         Social sciences
   NT   **Archeology**
         Art—History
         Biography
         Chronology
         Church history
         Constitutional history
         Exploration
         Genealogy
         Historic sites
         Historical chronology
         Historical geography
         Historical reenactments
         Historiography
         Local history
         Massacres

         Military history
         Naval history
         Numismatics
         Oral history
         Scandals
         Seals (Numismatics)
         Women—History
         World history
   RT   **Civilization**
         Historians
         Historical fiction

History, Ancient
   USE   **Ancient history**
History and criticism
   USE   types of literature, music, and other arts with the subdivision *History and criticism,* e.g. **English literature—History and criticism** [to be added as needed]
History—Atlases
   USE   **Historical atlases**
History, Biblical
   USE   **Bible—History of biblical events**
History—Chronology
   USE   **Historical chronology**
History—Criticism
   USE   **Historiography**
History—Dictionaries   903
   UF   Historical dictionaries
   BT   **Encyclopedias and dictionaries**
   NT   **United States—History—Dictionaries**
History—Historiography
   USE   **Historiography**
History, Military
   USE   **Military history**
History, Modern
   USE   **Modern history**
History, Modern—16th century
   USE   **World history—16th century**
History, Modern—17th century
   USE   **World history—17th century**
History, Modern—18th century
   USE   **World history—18th century**
History, Modern—19th century
   USE   **World history—19th century**
History, Modern—20th century
   USE   **World history—20th century**

History, Modern—1945-
    USE **World history—1945-**
History, Modern—21st century
    USE **World history—21st century**
History of doctrines
    USE religious topics with the subdivision *History of doctrines,* e.g.
            Salvation—History of doctrines [to be added as needed]
History—Periodicals   905
History—Philosophy   901

Use for materials on the interpretation and meaning of history and on the course of events and their resulting consequences. General materials on history as a science, including the principles of history, the influences of various factors on history, and the relation of the science of history to other subjects, are entered under **History**. Materials limited to the study and criticism of the sources of history, methods of historical research, and the writing of history are entered under **Historiography**.

    UF Philosophy of history
    BT **Philosophy**
History plays
    USE **Historical drama**
History—Reenactments
    USE **Historical reenactments**
History—Societies (May subdiv. geog.)
            906
    UF Historical societies
    BT **Societies**
    NT **Chicago (Ill.)—History—
            Societies
            Ohio—History—Societies
            United States—History—
            Societies**
History—Sources   900

Use for collections of documents, records, and other source materials upon which narrative history is based and for materials about such sources.

    SA historical subjects, periods of history, individual literary and sacred works, and names of wars with the subdivision *Sources*, e.g. **World War, 1939-1945—Sources**; and subjects, ethnic groups, classes of persons, coporate bodies, and names of countries, states, etc., with the subdivision *History—Sources*; e.g. **United**

States—History—Sources [to be added as needed]
    BT **Historiography**
    NT **Archives
            Charters**
History tourism
    USE **Cultural tourism**
Hittites (May subdiv. geog.)   **939**
    BT **Ancient history**
HIV disease
    USE **AIDS (Disease)**
Hmong (Asian people) (May subdiv. geog.)   **305.895**
    BT **Indigenous peoples**
HMOs
    USE **Health maintenance organizations**
Hoaxes
    USE **Impostors and imposture**
Hobbies (May subdiv. geog.)   **790.1**
    UF Avocations
    SA types of hobbies [to be added as needed]
    BT **Amusements
            Leisure
            Recreation**
    NT **Collectors and collecting**
    RT **Handicraft**
Hoboes
    USE **Tramps**
Hockey (May subdiv. geog.)   **796.962**
    UF Ice hockey
    BT **Winter sports**
Hogs
    USE **Pigs**
Hoisting machinery   621.8
    UF Lifts
    SA types of hoisting machinery [to be added as needed]
    BT **Machinery**
    NT **Cranes, derricks, etc.
            Elevators**
    RT **Conveying machinery**
Holiday cooking (May subdiv. geog.)
            641.5
    SA cooking for particular holidays, e.g. **Christmas cooking** [to be added as needed]
    BT **Cooking**
Holiday decorations (May subdiv. geog.)
            394.26; 745.5

Holiday decorations—*Continued*
    UF   Decorations, Holiday
    BT   **Decoration and ornament**
Holidays (May subdiv. geog.)   **394.26**
    Use for materials on days of general exemption from work or days publicly dedicated to the commemoration of some person, event, or principle. Materials on occasions other than holidays devoted to festive community observances or to programs of cultural events are entered under **Festivals**.
    UF   Legal holidays
          National holidays
    SA   names of holidays [to be added as needed]
    BT   **Days**
          Manners and customs
    NT   **April Fools' Day**
          Chinese New Year
          Christmas
          Cinco de Mayo (Holiday)
          Columbus Day
          Father's Day
          Fourth of July
          Halloween
          Kwanzaa
          Lincoln's Birthday
          Martin Luther King Day
          Memorial Day
          Mother's Day
          New Year
          Religious holidays
          Thanksgiving Day
          Valentine's Day
          Veterans Day
    RT   **Anniversaries**
          Festivals
          Vacations
Holidays, Jewish
    USE   **Jewish holidays**
Holistic health
    USE   **Holistic medicine**
Holistic medicine (May subdiv. geog.)
    610; 615.5
    UF   Holistic health
          Wholistic medicine
    BT   **Alternative medicine**
          Medicine
    RT   **Health**
          Health self-care
          Mind and body
Holland
    USE   **Netherlands**

Holmes, Sherlock (Fictional character)
    823
    UF   Sherlock Holmes (Fictitious character)
    BT   **Fictional characters**
Holocaust, 1933-1945
    USE   **Holocaust, 1939-1945**
Holocaust, 1939-1945   **940.53**
    Use for materials on the killing of approximately six million Jews during World War II by the National Socialist regime in Germany.
    UF   Holocaust, 1933-1945 [*Former heading*]
          Holocaust, Jewish (1939-1945)
          Jewish Holocaust (1933-1945)
    SA   religious groups and classes of persons with the subdivision *Nazi persecution*, e.g. **Handicapped—Nazi persecution**, and names of concentration camps [to be added as needed]
    BT   **Antisemitism**
          Germany—History—1933-1945
          Jews—Persecutions
    NT   **Holocaust denial**
          Holocaust survivors
          Jewish children in the Holocaust
          Righteous Gentiles in the Holocaust
    RT   **World War, 1939-1945—Jews**
Holocaust, 1939-1945—Personal narratives   **920**
    BT   **Autobiographies**
Holocaust denial   **940.53**
    BT   **Holocaust, 1939-1945**
Holocaust, Jewish (1939-1945)
    USE   **Holocaust, 1939-1945**
Holocaust survivors (May subdiv. geog.)
    940.53
    Use for materials on Jews who survived persecution or imprisonment under the Nazis. Accounts by Holocaust survivors are entered under **Holocaust, 1939-1945—Personal narratives**.
    BT   **Holocaust, 1939-1945**
Holography   **774**
    UF   Laser photography
          Lensless photography
    BT   **Laser recording**
          Photography

Holography—*Continued*
RT **Three dimensional photography**

Holstein-Friesian cattle (May subdiv. geog.) **636.2**
UF Friesian cattle
BT **Dairy cattle**

Holy communion
USE **Eucharist**

Holy days
USE **Religious holidays**

Holy Ghost
USE **Holy Spirit**

Holy Grail
USE **Grail**

Holy Land
USE **Palestine**

Holy Office
USE **Inquisition**

Holy Roman Empire   943
BT **Europe—History**

Holy Scriptures
USE **Bible**

Holy See
USE **Papacy**
Popes

Holy Shroud   232.96
UF Shroud, Holy
Shroud of Turin
Turin Shroud

Holy Spirit   231
UF Holy Ghost
BT **God—Christianity**
Trinity
RT **Spiritual gifts**

Holy war (Islam)
USE **Jihad**

Holy Week   263
BT **Church year**
Lent
Special weeks
NT **Easter**
Good Friday

Home   306.8; 640
RT **Family**
Home economics

Home accidents   363.13
BT **Accidents**
NT **First aid**

Home and school (May subdiv. geog.) **371.19**
UF School and home

BT **Education**
RT **Parent-teacher associations**
Parent-teacher relationship

Home-based business (May subdiv. geog.) **338.6; 658**
UF At-home employment
Cottage industry
Home business
Home labor
Work at home
Working at home
BT **Business**
Self-employed
Small business

Home-based education
USE **Home schooling**

Home building industry
USE **Construction industry**

Home business
USE **Home-based business**

Home buying
USE **Houses—Buying and selling**

Home care
USE **Home care services**
and classes of persons with the subdivision *Home care,* e.g. **Elderly—Home care** [to be added as needed]

Home care services (May subdiv. geog.) **362.14; 649.8**
UF Home care
Home health care
Home medical care
Respite care
SA classes of persons with the subdivision *Home care*, e.g. **Elderly—Home care** [to be added as needed]
BT **Medical care**
NT **Elderly—Home care**
Home nursing

Home computers
USE **Personal computers**

Home conservatories
USE **Garden rooms**

Home construction
USE **House construction**

Home decoration
USE **Interior design**

Home delivered meals programs
USE **Meals on wheels programs**

Home designs
 USE **Domestic architecture—Designs and plans**
Home economics (May subdiv. geog.)
  640
 UF Homemaking
   Household management
   Housekeeping
 BT **Family life education**
 NT **Consumer education**
   Cooking
   Cost and standard of living
   Entertaining
   Food
   Fuel
   Grocery shopping
   Heating
   House cleaning
   Household employees
   Household equipment and supplies
   Household pests
   Interior design
   Laundry
   Mobile home living
   Moving
   Sewing
   Shopping
   Storage in the home
   Ventilation
 RT **Home**
   Homemakers
Home economics—Accounting
 USE **Household budgets**
Home education
 USE **Correspondence schools and courses**
   Home schooling
   Self-instruction
Home equity loans (May subdiv. geog.)
  332.7
 BT **Loans**
Home health care
 USE **Home care services**
Home instruction
 USE **Home schooling**
Home labor
 USE **Home-based business**
Home life
 USE **Family life**

Home loans
 USE **Mortgages**
Home medical care
 USE **Home care services**
Home missions, Christian
 USE **Christian missions**
Home movies
 USE **Amateur films**
Home nursing (May subdiv. geog.)
  649.8
 BT **Home care services**
   Nursing
 RT **Sick**
Home purchase
 USE **Houses—Buying and selling**
Home remodeling
 USE **Houses—Remodeling**
Home repairing
 USE **Houses—Maintenance and repair**
Home repairs
 USE **Houses—Maintenance and repair**
Home schooling (May subdiv. geog.)
  371.04
  Use for materials on the provision of compulsory education in the home as an alternative to traditional public or private schooling. General materials on the instruction of children in the home are entered under **Child rearing**.
 UF Home-based education
   Home education
   Home instruction
   Home teaching by parents
   Homeschooling
 BT **Education**
 RT **Education—Parent participation**
Home sharing
 USE **Shared housing**
Home storage
 USE **Storage in the home**
Home study courses
 USE **Correspondence schools and courses**
   Self-instruction
Home teaching by parents
 USE **Home schooling**
Home video cameras
 USE **Camcorders**
Home video movies
 USE **Amateur films**

Home video systems   384.55; 621.388;
    778.59
  BT   **Television**
  NT   **Camcorders**
       Videotapes
  RT   **Video recording**
Homeless
  USE   **Homeless persons**
        Homelessness
Homeless people
  USE   **Homeless persons**
Homeless persons (May subdiv. geog.)
    305.5; 362.5
  UF   Homeless
       Homeless people
       Street people
  BT   **Poor**
  NT   **Refugees**
       Runaway children
       Runaway teenagers
       Tramps
  RT   **Homelessness**
Homeless persons—Government policy
    (May subdiv. geog.)   362.5
  BT   **Social policy**
Homelessness (May subdiv. geog.)
    305.5; 362.5
  UF   Homeless
  BT   **Housing**
       Poverty
       Social problems
  RT   **Homeless persons**
Homemakers (May subdiv. geog.)
    306.85; 640
  UF   Househusbands
       Housewives
  RT   **Home economics**
Homemaking
  USE   **Home economics**
Homeopathy (May subdiv. geog.)   615.5
  BT   **Alternative medicine**
       Pharmacy
Homes
  USE   **Houses**
        and ethnic groups, classes of
        persons, and names of corpo-
        rate bodies, families, and indi-
        vidual persons with the subdi-
        vision *Homes,* e.g. **English
        authors—Homes;** which may
        be further subdivided geo-

        graphically [to be added as
        needed]
Homes for the elderly
  USE   **Elderly—Institutional care**
Homes (Institutions)
  USE   **Charities**
        Institutional care
        Orphanages
Homeschooling
  USE   **Home schooling**
Homework   371.3028
  BT   **Study skills**
Homicide (May subdiv. geog.)   364.152
  UF   Manslaughter
       Murder
  BT   **Crime**
       Criminal law
       Offenses against the person
  NT   **Assassination**
       Euthanasia
       Poisons and poisoning
       Serial killers
       Trials (Homicide)
  RT   **Suicide**
Homicide trials
  USE   **Trials (Homicide)**
Hominids
  USE   **Human origins**
Hominids, Fossil
  USE   **Fossil hominids**
Homo sapiens
  USE   **Human beings**
Homonyms
  USE   names of languages with the
        subdivision *Homonyms,* e.g.
        **English language—Hom-
        onyms** [to be added as need-
        ed]
Homosexual marriage
  USE   **Same-sex marriage**
Homosexual parents
  USE   **Gay parents**
Homosexuality (May subdiv. geog.)
    306.76
  UF   Gay lifestyle
  BT   **Sex**
  NT   **Gay liberation movement**
       Lesbianism
  RT   **Gay men**
       Lesbians

Homosexuals, Female
USE **Lesbians**
Homosexuals, Male
USE **Gay men**
Honesty 179
UF Dishonesty
BT **Ethics**
   Human behavior
NT **Cheating (Education)**
RT **Truthfulness and falsehood**
Honey 638; 641.3
BT **Food**
RT **Bees**
Honeybee culture
USE **Beekeeping**
Honor (May subdiv. geog.) **179**
UF Honour
BT **Conduct of life**
Honorary degrees
USE **Academic degrees**
Honour
USE **Honor**
Hooked rugs (May subdiv. geog.) **746.7**
BT **Handicraft**
   Rugs and carpets
Hoover Dam (Ariz. and Nev.) 627
UF Boulder Dam (Ariz. and Nev.)
   Colorado River—Hoover Dam
BT **Dams**
Hope 152.4; 179; 234
BT **Emotions**
   Spiritual life
   Virtue
Hormones 571.7; 573.4; 612.4
BT **Endocrinology**
RT **Endocrine glands**
   Steroids
Hornbooks (May subdiv. geog.) **028.5;
096; 372.41**
BT **Reading materials**
Horology
USE **Clocks and watches**
   Sundials
   Time
Horoscopes 133.5
BT **Astrology**
Horror 152.4
BT **Emotions**
   Fear
Horror—Fiction
USE **Horror fiction**

Horror fiction 808.3; 808.83
Use for individual works, collections, or materials about horror fiction.
UF Horror—Fiction
   Horror novels
   Horror stories
   Horror tales
   Terror tales
BT **Fiction**
NT **Ghost stories**
   Gothic novels
RT **Fantasy fiction**
   Occult fiction
Horror films 791.43
Use for individual works, collections, or materials about horror films.
UF Creature films
   Horror movies
   Monster films
SA types of horror films, e.g. **Vampire films** [to be added as needed]
BT **Motion pictures**
NT **Vampire films**
RT **Fantasy films**
Horror graphic novels 741.5
Use for individual works, collections, or materials about horror graphic novels.
BT **Graphic novels**
Horror movies
USE **Horror films**
Horror novels
USE **Horror fiction**
Horror plays 808.82
Use for individual works, collections, or materials about horror plays.
BT **Drama**
Horror radio programs 791.44
Use for individual works, collections, or materials about horror radio programs.
BT **Radio programs**
Horror stories
USE **Horror fiction**
Horror tales
USE **Horror fiction**
Horror television programs 791.45
Use for individual works, collections, or materials about horror television programs.
BT **Television programs**
RT **Fantasy television programs**
Hors d'oeuvres
USE **Appetizers**

Horse breeding
USE **Horses—Breeding**
Horse racing (May subdiv. geog.) **798.4**
BT **Racing**
RT **Horsemanship**
Horse riding
USE **Horsemanship**
Horseback riding
USE **Horsemanship**
Horsebreaking
USE **Horses—Training**
Horsemanship (May subdiv. geog.)
798.2
UF Coaching
Dressage
Equestrianism
Horse riding
Horseback riding
Riding
BT **Locomotion**
NT **Horses—Training**
Trail riding
RT **Horse racing**
Rodeos
Horses (May subdiv. geog.) **599.665;**
636.1
UF Foals
BT **Mammals**
NT **Ponies**
Horses—Breeding (May subdiv. geog.)
636.1
UF Horse breeding
BT **Breeding**
Horses—Diseases (May subdiv. geog.)
636.089
BT **Animals—Diseases**
Horses—Training (May subdiv. geog.)
636.1
UF Horsebreaking
BT **Horsemanship**
Horses—Wounds and injuries **636.1**
Horticulture (May subdiv. geog.) **635**

Use for materials on the scientific and economic aspects of the cultivation of flowers,
fruits, vegetables, etc. Materials on the practical aspects of creating gardens and cultivating
plants are entered under **Gardening**. General
materials about gardens, the history of gardens, various types of gardens, etc., are entered under **Gardens**.

BT **Agriculture**
Plants

NT **Flower gardening**
Fruit culture
Greenhouses
Hydroponics
Landscape gardening
Organic gardening
Plant breeding
Truck farming
Vegetable gardening
RT **Gardening**
Hosiery **391.4; 687**
UF Stockings
BT **Clothing and dress**
Textile industry
Hospices (May subdiv. geog.) **362.17**
BT **Hospitals**
Social medicine
Terminal care
Hospital care records
USE **Medical records**
Hospital libraries (May subdiv. geog.)
027.6
UF Libraries, Hospital
BT **Libraries**
Hospital personnel administration
USE **Hospitals—Personnel manage-
ment**
Hospital ships (May subdiv. geog.)
362.1; 623.826
UF Floating hospitals
BT **Hospitals**
Ships
Hospital wastes
USE **Medical wastes**
Hospitality
USE **Entertaining**
Hospitality industry (May subdiv. geog.)
910.46
BT **Service industries**
Hospitalization insurance (May subdiv.
geog.) **368.38**
UF Group hospitalization
Insurance, Hospitalization
BT **Health insurance**
Hospitals (May subdiv. geog.) **362.11**
UF Infirmaries
SA types of hospitals and names of
individual hospitals [to be
added as needed]
BT **Institutional care**
Public health

Hospitals—*Continued*
- NT **Children's hospitals**
  Hospices
  Hospital ships
  Life support systems (Medical environment)
  Long-term care facilities
  Military hospitals
  Nursing homes
  Psychiatric hospitals
- RT **Medical centers**
  Medical charities
  Sanatoriums

Hospitals—Personnel management (May subdiv. geog.) **362.11**
- UF Hospital personnel administration
- BT **Personnel management**

Hospitals—Sanitation (May subdiv. geog.) **614.4**
- BT **Sanitation**

Hospitals—United States 362.110973

Hostage escapes
- USE **Escapes**

Hostage negotiation (May subdiv. geog.) **363.3**
- BT **Hostages**
  Negotiation

Hostages (May subdiv. geog.) **920**
- SA hostages from a particular country, e.g. **American hostages** [to be added as needed]
- BT **Terrorism**
- NT **American hostages**
  Hostage negotiation

Hostels, Elder
- USE **Elderhostels**

Hostels, Youth
- USE **Youth hostels**

Hot air engines
- USE **Heat engines**

Hot air heating (May subdiv. geog.) **697**
- UF Warm air heating
- BT **Heating**

Hot links
- USE **Hyperlinks**

Hot water heating (May subdiv. geog.) **697**
- BT **Heating**

Hotels and motels (May subdiv. geog.) **728; 910.46**
  Use for materials on public accommodations, including inns and guest houses.
- UF Boarding houses
  Inns
  Motels
  Rooming houses
  Tourist accommodations
- BT **Service industries**
- NT **Bed and breakfast accommodations**
  Youth hostels

Hotels and motels—United States 728; 910.460973

Hothouses
- USE **Greenhouses**

Hotlines (Telephone counseling) 361; 362.2
- UF Crisis counseling
  Crisis intervention telephone service
  Switchboard hotlines
  Telephone counseling
- BT **Counseling**
  Information services
  Social work
- RT **Crisis centers**

Hours of labor 331.25
- UF Eight-hour day
  Five-day work week
  Overtime
  Working day
  Working hours
- BT **Labor**
- NT **Absenteeism (Labor)**
  Flexible hours of labor
  Leave of absence
  Part-time employment

Hours of labor, Flexible
- USE **Flexible hours of labor**

House boats
- USE **Houseboats**

House buying
- USE **Houses—Buying and selling**

House cleaning 648
- BT **Cleaning**
  Home economics
  Household sanitation

House construction (May subdiv. geog.) **690**

House construction—*Continued*
  UF Construction, House
      Home construction
  SA types of house construction and
      special kinds of houses [to be
      added as needed]
  BT **Building**
      Domestic architecture
  NT **Earth sheltered houses**
      House painting
      Houses—Remodeling
      Log cabins and houses
      Prefabricated houses
  RT **Houses**
House decoration
  USE **Interior design**
House drainage   690

   Use for materials on house drainage. Materials on land drainage are entered under
Drainage.

  UF Drainage, House
  BT **Household sanitation**
  NT **Sewerage**
  RT **Plumbing**
House flies
  USE **Flies**
House furnishing
  USE **Interior design**
House of Representatives (U.S.)
  USE **United States. Congress. House**
House painting   698
  BT **House construction**
  RT **Industrial painting**
House plans
  USE **Domestic architecture—Designs
      and plans**
House plants   635.9
  BT **Cultivated plants**
      Flower gardening
      Plants
      Window gardening
  RT **Container gardening**
      Indoor gardening
House purchase
  USE **Houses—Buying and selling**
House repairing
  USE **Houses—Maintenance and re-
      pair**
House repairs
  USE **Houses—Maintenance and re-
      pair**

House sanitation
  USE **Household sanitation**
House selling
  USE **Houses—Buying and selling**
House sharing
  USE **Shared housing**
House trailers
  USE **Mobile homes**
      Travel trailers and campers
Houseboats (May subdiv. geog.)   **728.7**
  UF House boats
  BT **Boats and boating**
Household appliances
  USE **Household equipment and sup-
      plies**
Household appliances, Electric
  USE **Electric household appliances**
Household budgets (May subdiv. geog.)
      640
  UF Budgets, Household
      Domestic finance
      Family budget
      Finance, Household
      Home economics—Accounting
      Household finances
  BT **Cost and standard of living**
      Personal finance
Household employees (May subdiv. geog.)
      640
  UF Domestic workers
      Housemaids
      Servants
  BT **Home economics**
      Labor
Household equipment and supplies
      643; 683
  UF Domestic appliances
      Household appliances
      Labor saving devices, Household
  BT **Home economics**
      Implements, utensils, etc.
  NT **Electric household appliances**
      Kitchen utensils
Household finances
  USE **Cost and standard of living**
      Household budgets
Household management
  USE **Home economics**
Household moving
  USE **Moving**

Household pests (May subdiv. geog.)
648
    UF   Diseases and pests
           Vermin
    SA   types of pests, e.g. **Flies** [to be
           added as needed]
    BT   **Home economics**
           Household sanitation
           Pests
    NT   **Flies**
    RT   **Insect pests**
Household repairs
    USE **Houses—Maintenance and repair**
Household sanitation   **648**
    UF   House sanitation
           Sanitation, Household
    BT   **Sanitation**
    NT   **House cleaning**
           House drainage
           Household pests
           Laundry
           Ventilation
    RT   **Plumbing**
Household utensils
    USE **Kitchen utensils**
Household violence
    USE **Domestic violence**
Househusbands
    USE **Homemakers**
Housekeeping
    USE **Home economics**
Housemaids
    USE **Household employees**
Houses (May subdiv. geog.)   **643; 728**
    Use for general materials on buildings in which people live. Materials on residential buildings from the standpoint of style and design are entered under **Domestic architecture**.
    UF   Dwellings
           Homes
           Residences
    SA   types of houses, e.g. **Earth sheltered houses**; types of architectural features, e.g. **Windows**; **Fireplaces**; etc.; and rooms and parts of the house, e.g. **Kitchens** [to be added as needed]
    BT   **Buildings**
    NT   **Apartment houses**
           Earth sheltered houses

           Garden rooms
           Haunted houses
           Housing
           Igloos
           Kitchens
           Log cabins and houses
           Prefabricated houses
           Rooms
           Solar homes
           Vacation homes
    RT   **Domestic architecture**
           House construction
Houses—Buying and selling (May subdiv. geog.)   **333.33**
    UF   Home buying
           Home purchase
           House buying
           House purchase
           House selling
    BT   **Real estate business**
    NT   **Urban homesteading**
Houses—Heating and ventilation   **644; 697**
    BT   **Heating**
Houses—Maintenance and repair   **643**
    UF   Home repairing
           Home repairs
           House repairing
           House repairs
           Household repairs
Houses—Remodeling   **643**
    UF   Home remodeling
           Remodeling (Architecture)
           Remodeling of houses
    SA   types of houses and parts of houses with the subdivision *Remodeling*, e.g. **Kitchens—Remodeling** [to be added as needed]
    BT   **House construction**
Housewives
    USE **Homemakers**
Housing (May subdiv. geog.)   **307.3; 363.5**
    Use for materials on the social and economic aspects of housing. Materials on the social and economic aspects of housing as it pertains to specific ethnic groups or classes of persons are entered under that group or class of persons with the subdivision *Housing*. Materials on the residential buildings of ethnic groups or classes of persons from the standpoint of architecture, construction, or ethnology are en-

Housing—*Continued*
tered under the name of the ethnic group or class of persons with the subdivision *Dwell-ings.*

UF   Affordable housing
      Dwellings
      Habitations, Human
      Housing needs
      Urban housing
SA   ethnic groups, classes of persons, and domestic animals with the subdivision *Housing*; e.g. **Native Americans—Housing; Physically handicapped—Housing**; etc. [to be added as needed]
BT   **Houses**
      Landlord and tenant
NT   **African Americans—Housing**
      Apartment houses
      Assisted living
      Blacks—Housing
      Cooperative housing
      Discrimination in housing
      Elderly—Housing
      Homelessness
      Labor—Housing
      Mobile homes
      Native Americans—Housing
      Physically handicapped—Housing
      Public housing
      Shared housing
      Timesharing (Real estate)
      Urban homesteading
RT   **City planning**

Housing, Cooperative
USE   **Cooperative housing**
Housing estates
USE   **Planned communities**
Housing for the elderly
USE   **Elderly—Housing**
Housing for the physically handicapped
USE   **Physically handicapped—Housing**
Housing needs
USE   **Housing**
Housing projects, Government
USE   **Public housing**
Houston Astros (Baseball team)   **796.357**

UF   Astros (Baseball team)
      Houston (Tex.). Baseball Club (National League)
BT   **Baseball teams**
Houston (Tex.). Baseball Club (National League)
USE   **Houston Astros (Baseball team)**
Hovercraft
USE   **Air-cushion vehicles**
How to start a business
USE   **New business enterprises**
How-to-stop-smoking programs
USE   **Smoking cessation programs**
How to study
USE   **Study skills**
HTML (Document markup language)   **006.7**
UF   HyperText Markup Language (Document markup language)
BT   **Programming languages**
Hubble Space Telescope   **522**
BT   **Telescopes**
Hudson River (N.Y. and N.J.)—Bridges
USE   **Bridges—Hudson River (N.Y. and N.J.)**
Hugging   **158; 302.2; 395**
UF   Embracing
      Hugs
BT   **Manners and customs**
      Nonverbal communication
      Touch
Hugo Award   **808.3**
BT   **Literary prizes**
      Science fiction
Hugs
USE   **Hugging**
Huguenots (May subdiv. geog.)   **284**
BT   **Christian sects**
      Reformation
NT   **Saint Bartholomew's Day, Massacre of, 1572**
Hull House
USE   **Hull House (Chicago, Ill.)**
Hull House (Chicago, Ill.)   **361.4**
UF   Hull House
BT   **Social settlements**
Human abnormalities
USE   **Birth defects**
      Growth disorders

Human-alien encounters (May subdiv. geog.) **001.942**
  UF Alien encounters with humans
      Extraterrestrial encounters with humans
      Human encounters with aliens
  NT **Alien abduction**
  RT **Extraterrestrial beings**
      Life on other planets
      Unidentified flying objects
Human anatomy **611**
  SA parts of the body, e.g. **Foot**; and names of organs and regions of the body with the subdivision *Anatomy*, e.g. **Heart—Anatomy** [to be added as needed]
  BT **Anatomy**
  RT **Human body**
Human anatomy—Atlases **611**
  BT **Atlases**
Human anatomy in art
  USE **Artistic anatomy**
       Nude in art
Human artificial insemination **346.01; 618.1**
  UF Artificial insemination, Human
  BT **Artificial insemination**
      Reproduction
Human assets
  USE **Human capital**
Human behavior **150; 302**
  UF Behavior
      Morals
      Social behavior
  BT **Character**
      Psychology
      Social sciences
  NT **Aggressiveness (Psychology)**
      Bad behavior
      Behavior modification
      Behaviorism
      Cannibalism
      Compulsive behavior
      Conduct of life
      Consolation
      Curiosity
      Deviant behavior
      Duty
      Eating customs
      Etiquette

Friendship
Greed
Habit
Helping behavior
Honesty
Lifestyles
Love
Messiness
Patience
Patriotism
Sex
Showing off
Social adjustment
Sportsmanship
Suicide—Psychological aspects
Temper tantrums
Truthfulness and falsehood
Vice
Virtue
  RT **Ethics**
      Interpersonal relations
      Life skills
Human beings (May subdiv. geog.) **128; 599.9**
  Use for materials on the human species from the point of view of biology or anthropology. Materials on human beings as individuals are entered under **Persons**.
  UF Homo sapiens
      Human race
      Man
  BT **Primates**
  NT **Anthropometry**
      Ethnology
      Human body
      Persons
      Prehistoric peoples
  RT **Anthropology**
Human beings—Sexual behavior
  USE **Sex**
Human beings (Theology) **202; 218; 233**
  UF Man (Theology)
  BT **Doctrinal theology**
  NT **Soul**
Human body **612**
  Use for materials on the human body not limited to anatomy or physiology.
  UF Body
  SA parts of the body, e.g. **Foot** [to be added as needed]
  BT **Human beings**
      Self

Human body—*Continued*
  NT   **Body image**
          Body weight
  RT   **Human anatomy**
          Mind and body
          Physiology
Human capital (May subdiv. geog.)
    658.3

Use for materials on investments of capital in training and educating employees to improve their productivity. Materials on the strength of a country in terms of available personnel, both military and industrial, are entered under **Manpower**.

  UF   Human assets
          Human resources
  BT   **Capital**
  RT   **Labor supply**
Human cloning (May subdiv. geog.)
    571.8; 660.6
  BT   **Cloning**
Human cloning—Ethical aspects   **174**
  BT   **Ethics**
Human cold storage
  USE   **Cryonics**
Human ecology (May subdiv. geog.)
    304.2
  UF   Ecology, Human
          Ecology, Social
          Social ecology
  BT   **Sociology**
  NT   **Environmental influence on**
          humans
          Human geography
          Human influence on nature
          Human settlements
          Population
          Social psychology
          Survival skills
Human ecology—Ethical aspects
  USE   **Environmental ethics**
Human embryos, Frozen
  USE   **Frozen embryos**
Human encounters with aliens
  USE   **Human-alien encounters**
Human engineering (May subdiv. geog.)
    620.8

Use for materials on engineering design as related to human anatomical, physiological, and psychological capabilities and limitations.

  UF   Biomechanics
          Ergonomics
  BT   **Applied psychology**
          Engineering

          Industrial design
          Psychophysiology
  NT   **Life support systems (Space**
          environment)
          Life support systems (Submarine environment)
  RT   **Machine design**
Human experimentation in medicine
    (May subdiv. geog.)   **174.2**
  UF   Experimentation on humans,
          Medical
          Medical experimentation on humans
  BT   **Medical ethics**
          Medicine—Research
Human fertility (May subdiv. geog.)
    304.6; 612.6; 616.6
  UF   Fertility, Human
  BT   **Birth rate**
          Fertility
          Population
  RT   **Birth control**
          Childlessness
Human figure in art
  USE   **Artistic anatomy**
          Figure drawing
          Figure painting
          Nude in art
Human fossils
  USE   **Fossil hominids**
Human genome   **611**
  BT   **Genetics**
Human geography (May subdiv. geog.)
    304.2
  UF   Anthropogeography
          Geographical distribution of people
          Social geography
  BT   **Anthropology**
          Ethnology
          Geography
          Human ecology
          Immigration and emigration
  NT   **African diaspora**
          Environmental influence on
          humans
          Human settlements
          Jewish diaspora
  RT   **Geopolitics**
Human habitat
  USE   **Human settlements**

Human influence on nature (May subdiv. geog.) **304.2; 363.7**

UF   Earth, Effect of man on

       Man—Influence on nature

       Nature—Effect of human beings on

BT   **Human ecology**

NT   **Pollution**

Human locomotion   **152.3; 612.7**

UF   Biomechanics

       Human mechanics

       Human movement

BT   **Locomotion**

       Physiology

NT   **Kinesiology**

       Walking

RT   **Musculoskeletal system**

Human mechanics

USE   **Human locomotion**

Human movement

USE   **Human locomotion**

Human origins   **599.9**

UF   Antiquity of man

       Hominids

       Man—Antiquity

       Man—Origin

       Origin of man

BT   **Physical anthropology**

RT   **Evolution**

       Fossil hominids

       Prehistoric peoples

Human paleontology

USE   **Fossil hominids**

Human physiology

USE   **Physiology**

Human race

USE   **Anthropology**

       Human beings

Human records

USE   **World records**

Human relations

USE   **Interpersonal relations**

Human resource management

USE   **Personnel management**

Human resources

USE   **Human capital**

       Manpower

Human rights (May subdiv. geog.)   **323; 341.4**

Use for materials on the rights of persons regardless of their legal, socioeconomic, or cultural status, as recognized by the international community. Materials on citizens' rights as established by law or protected by a constitution are entered under **Civil rights**.

UF   Basic rights

       Civil rights (International law)

       Fundamental rights

       Rights, Human

       Rights of man

NT   **Civil rights**

       Right to health care

Human services (May subdiv. geog.) **361**

Use for general materials on the various policies, programs, services, and facilities to meet basic human needs, such as health, education, and welfare. Materials on the methods employed in social work, public or private, are entered under **Social work**. Materials on privately supported welfare activities are entered under **Charities**. Materials on tax-supported welfare activities are entered under **Public welfare**.

SA   ethnic groups and classes of persons with the subdivision *Services for*, e.g. **Handicapped— Services for** [to be added as needed]

NT   **Charities**

       Handicapped—Services for

       Public health

       Public welfare

       Social work

Human settlements (May subdiv. geog.) **307**

UF   Human habitat

BT   **Human ecology**

       Human geography

       Population

       Sociology

RT   **Land settlement**

Human sexuality

USE   **Sex**

Human survival skills

USE   **Survival skills**

Human values

USE   **Values**

Humane treatment of animals

USE   **Animal welfare**

Humanism (May subdiv. geog.)   **001.2; 880**

Use for materials on culture founded on the study of the classics, or more narrowly on Greek and Roman scholarship. Materials on any intellectual or philosophical movement or set of beliefs that promotes human values as

Humanism—*Continued*
separate and distinct from religious doctrines are entered under **Secularism**.
- BT **Culture**
  Literature
  Philosophy
- NT **Humanities**
- RT **Classical education**
  Learning and scholarship
  Renaissance
  Secularism

Humanism, Secular
- USE **Secularism**

Humanitarian assistance
- USE **Humanitarian intervention**

Humanitarian intervention (May subdiv. geog.)   **361.2**
- UF Humanitarian assistance
- BT **Social action**
- NT **Disaster relief**

Humanitarians
- USE **Philanthropists**

Humanities (May subdiv. geog.)   **001.3**
- BT **Humanism**
  Learning and scholarship
- NT **Arts**
  History
  Literature
  Music
  Philosophy
  Science and the humanities
- RT **Classical education**

Humanities and science
- USE **Science and the humanities**

Humans in space
- USE **Space flight**

Humidity   **551.57**
- UF Air, Moisture of
  Atmospheric humidity
  Relative humidity
- BT **Meteorology**
  Weather

Humor
- USE **Wit and humor**
  and subjects with the subdivision *Humor*, e.g. **World War, 1939-1945—Humor** [to be added as needed]

Humorists (May subdiv. geog.)   **809.7; 920**
- BT **Wit and humor**

Humorous fiction   **808.3; 808.83**
Use for individual works, collections, or materials about humorous fiction.
- UF Comic novels
  Humorous stories
- BT **Fiction**
  Wit and humor
- RT **Mock-heroic literature**

Humorous films
- USE **Comedy films**

Humorous graphic novels   **741.5**
Use for individual works, collections, or materials about humorous graphic novels.
- BT **Graphic novels**

Humorous pictures
- USE **Comic books, strips, etc.**

Humorous plays
- USE **Comedies**

Humorous poetry   **808.1; 808.81**
Use for individual works, collections, or materials about humorous poetry.
- UF Comic verse
  Humorous verse
  Light verse
- BT **Poetry**
  Wit and humor
- NT **Limericks**
  Nonsense verses

Humorous stories
- USE **Humorous fiction**

Humorous verse
- USE **Humorous poetry**

Hundred Years' War, 1339-1453 (May subdiv. geog.)   **944**
- UF 100 years' war
- BT **Europe—History—476-1492**
  France—History—1328-1589, House of Valois
  Great Britain—History—1066-1485, Medieval period

Hungary—History   **943.9**

Hungary—History—1956, Revolution   **943.905**
- BT **Revolutions**

Hunger (May subdiv. geog.)   **363.8**
- RT **Fasting**
  Starvation

Hunger strikes (May subdiv. geog.)   **303.6**
- BT **Demonstrations**
  Fasting
  Nonviolence

Hunger strikes—*Continued*
  Passive resistance
  Resistance to government
Hunting (May subdiv. geog.)   **799.2**
  SA   types of hunting, e.g. **Whaling**;
     and ethnic groups with the
     subdivision *Hunting*, e.g. **Na-**
     tive Americans—Hunting [to
     be added as needed]
  NT   **Big game hunting**
     Bowhunting
     Decoys (Hunting)
     Falconry
     Game protection
     Game reserves
     Native Americans—Hunting
     Tracking and trailing
     Whaling
  RT   **Game and game birds**
     Safaris
     Shooting
     Trapping
Hunting—United States   **799.2973**
Hurricane Katrina, 2005   **551.55**
  UF   Katrina, Hurricane, 2005
  BT   **Hurricanes**
Hurricanes (May subdiv. geog.)   **551.55**
  Use for cyclonic storms originating in the
  region of the West Indies.
  SA   names of specific hurricanes [to
     be added as needed]
  BT   **Cyclones**
     Storms
     Winds
  NT   **Hurricane Katrina, 2005**
  RT   **Typhoons**
Husband abuse (May subdiv. geog.)
  362.82
  UF   Abuse of husbands
     Battering of husbands
     Husband battering
     Husband beating
  BT   **Domestic violence**
Husband battering
  USE   **Husband abuse**
Husband beating
  USE   **Husband abuse**
Husbands   **306.872**
  UF   Married men
     Spouses
  BT   **Family**
     Marriage

  Married people
  Men
  NT   **Military spouses**
Husbands, Runaway
  USE   **Runaway adults**
Hybridization
  USE   **Plant breeding**
Hydraulic cement
  USE   **Cement**
Hydraulic engineering (May subdiv.
  geog.)   **627**
  BT   **Civil engineering**
     Engineering
     Fluid mechanics
     Water power
  NT   **Drainage**
     Dredging
     Drilling and boring (Earth and
       rocks)
     Flood control
     Hydraulic structures
     Hydrodynamics
     Hydrostatics
     Irrigation
     Pumping machinery
     Reclamation of land
     Wells
  RT   **Hydraulics**
     Rivers
     Water
     Water supply engineering
Hydraulic machinery   **621.2**
  BT   **Machinery**
     Water power
  NT   **Turbines**
Hydraulic structures (May subdiv. geog.)
  627
  SA   types of hydraulic structures [to
       be added as needed]
  BT   **Hydraulic engineering**
     Structural engineering
  NT   **Aqueducts**
     Canals
     Dams
     Docks
     Harbors
     Pipelines
     Reservoirs
Hydraulics   **621.2; 627**
  Use for materials on technical applications
  of the theory of hydrodynamics.
  UF   Water flow

Hydraulics—*Continued*
  BT **Fluid mechanics**
      Liquids
      Mechanics
      Physics
  NT **Hydrodynamics**
      Hydrostatics
      Water
      Water power
  RT **Hydraulic engineering**
Hydrodynamics   532
  Use for materials on the theory of the motion and action of fluids. Materials on the experimental investigation and technical application of this theory are entered under **Hydraulics**.
  BT **Dynamics**
      Fluid mechanics
      Hydraulic engineering
      Hydraulics
      Liquids
      Mechanics
  NT **Hydrostatics**
      Viscosity
      Waves
Hydroelectric power
  USE **Water power**
Hydroelectric power plants (May subdiv. geog.)   **621.31**
  UF Power plants, Hydroelectric
  BT **Electric power plants**
      Water power
Hydrofoil boats   623.82
  BT **Boats and boating**
Hydrogen   546
  BT **Chemical elements**
Hydrogen bomb   623.4
  BT **Bombs**
      Nuclear weapons
  NT **Radioactive fallout**
  RT **Atomic bomb**
Hydrogen nucleus
  USE **Protons**
Hydrology
  USE **Water**
Hydromechanics
  USE **Fluid mechanics**
Hydropathy
  USE **Hydrotherapy**
Hydrophobia
  USE **Rabies**
Hydroponics (May subdiv. geog.)   **631.5;
      635**

  UF Plants—Soilless culture
      Soilless agriculture
      Water farming
  BT **Horticulture**
Hydrostatics   532
  BT **Fluid mechanics**
      Hydraulic engineering
      Hydraulics
      Hydrodynamics
      Liquids
      Mechanics
      Physics
      Statics
  NT **Gases**
Hydrotherapy   615.8
  UF Hydropathy
      Water cure
  BT **Physical therapy**
      Therapeutics
      Water
  RT **Baths**
      Health resorts
Hygiene   613
  UF Body care
      Personal cleanliness
      Personal hygiene
  SA parts of the body with the subdivision *Care*, e.g. **Foot—Care**; and classes of persons and ethnic groups with the subdivision *Health and hygiene*, e.g. **Women—Health and hygiene** [to be added as needed]
  BT **Medicine**
      Preventive medicine
  NT **Baths**
      Children—Health and hygiene
      Cleanliness
      Diet
      Disinfection and disinfectants
      Elderly—Health and hygiene
      Exercise
      Infants—Health and hygiene
      Military personnel—Health and hygiene
      Personal grooming
      Rest
      School hygiene
      Sexual hygiene
      Sleep

Hygiene—*Continued*
    Ventilation
    Women—Health and hygiene
  RT **Health**
    Sanitation
Hygiene, Military
  USE **Military personnel—Health and hygiene**
Hygiene, Sexual
  USE **Sexual hygiene**
Hygiene, Social
  USE **Public health**
Hygiene—Study and teaching
  USE **Health education**
Hymn books
  USE **Hymnals**
Hymnals 782.27
    Use for collections of sacred songs that contain both words and music. Materials about hymns are entered under **Hymns**.
  UF Hymn books
    Hymnbooks
  BT **Church music**
    Hymns
    Songbooks
Hymnbooks
  USE **Hymnals**
Hymnology
  USE **Hymns**
Hymns 264; 782.27
    Use for materials about hymns. Collections of hymns that contain both words and music are entered under **Hymnals**.
  UF Hymnology
  BT **Church music**
    Liturgies
    Songs
    Vocal music
  NT **Carols**
    Hymnals
    Spirituals (Songs)
  RT **Religious poetry**
Hyperactive children 155.4; 618.92
  UF Children, Hyperactive
    Hyperkinetic children
  BT **Handicapped children**
  RT **Hyperactivity**
Hyperactivity 616.85; 616.92
  UF Hyperkinesia
  BT **Diseases**
  RT **Hyperactive children**
Hyperactivity disorder
  USE **Attention deficit disorder**

Hyperkinesia
  USE **Attention deficit disorder**
    Hyperactivity
Hyperkinetic children
  USE **Hyperactive children**
Hyperlinks 005.75
  UF Hot links
  BT **Multimedia**
Hyperspace
  USE **Fourth dimension**
Hypertension 616.1
  UF High blood pressure
  BT **Blood pressure**
HyperText Markup Language (Document markup language)
  USE **HTML (Document markup language)**
Hypnosis
  USE **Hypnotism**
Hypnotism 154.7
  UF Animal magnetism
    Autosuggestion
    Hypnosis
    Mesmerism
  BT **Mental healing**
    Psychophysiology
  RT **Mental suggestion**
    Mind and body
    Psychoanalysis
    Subconsciousness
    Suggestive therapeutics
ICBM
  USE **Intercontinental ballistic missiles**
Ice (May subdiv. geog.) 551.3
  UF Freezing
  BT **Cold**
    Frost
    Physical geography
    Water
  NT **Glaciers**
    Icebergs
Ice age 551.7
  UF Glacial epoch
  BT **Earth**
Ice boats
  USE **Iceboats**
Ice cream, ices, etc. 637; 641.8
  UF Ices
  BT **Desserts**
    Frozen foods

Ice (Drug)
USE **Crystal meth (Drug)**
Ice fishing (May subdiv. geog.)   **799.1**
BT **Fishing**
Winter sports
Ice hockey
USE **Hockey**
Ice skating (May subdiv. geog.)   **796.91**
UF Figure skating
Skating
BT **Winter sports**
Ice sports
USE **Winter sports**
Icebergs   551.3
BT **Ice**
Ocean
Physical geography
Iceboats (May subdiv. geog.)   **623.82**
UF Ice boats
BT **Boats and boating**
Icelandic language   439
BT **Language and languages**
Scandinavian languages
Icelandic language—0-1500
USE **Old Norse language**
Icelandic literature   839
UF Icelandic literature, Modern
BT **Literature**
Scandinavian literature
RT **Old Norse literature**
Icelandic literature, Modern
USE **Icelandic literature**
Ices
USE **Ice cream, ices, etc.**
Ichthyology
USE **Fishes**
Ichthyosaurus   567.91
BT **Dinosaurs**
Iconography
USE **Art—Themes**
Icons (Computer graphics)   005.3; 005.4
UF Computer icons
Desktop icons (Computer graph-
ics)
BT **Computer graphics**
Icons (Religion)   704.9
BT **Christian art**
Ideal states
USE **Utopian fiction**
Utopias
Idealism   141

BT **Philosophy**
RT **Materialism**
Realism
Transcendentalism
Identification
SA subjects with the subdivision
Identification [to be added as
needed]
NT **Airplanes—Identification**
Bar coding
Criminals—Identification
DNA fingerprinting
Fingerprints
Identity
USE **Identity (Psychology)**
Individuality
Personality
and classes of persons with the
subdivision *Identity,* e.g.
Women—Identity; ethnic
groups with the subdivision
Ethnic identity, e.g. **Mexican**
Americans—Ethnic identity;
and racial groups with the
subdivision *Race identity,* e.g.
African Americans—Race
identity [to be added as
needed]
Identity (Psychology)   126
UF Identity
SA classes of persons with the sub-
division *Identity,* e.g. **Wom-**
en—Identity; ethnic groups
with the subdivision *Ethnic*
identity, e.g. **Mexican Ameri-**
cans—Ethnic identity; and
racial groups with the subdi-
vision *Race identity,* e.g. **Af-**
rican Americans—Race iden-
tity [to be added as needed]
BT **Personality**
Psychology
Self
NT **Ethnicity**
Group identity
Women—Identity
RT **Ego (Psychology)**
Identity theft (May subdiv. geog.)
364.15
BT **Offenses against the person**
Theft

Ideology (May subdiv. geog.)   **140**
    BT   **Philosophy**
           Political science
           Psychology
           Theory of knowledge
           Thought and thinking
    NT   **Political correctness**
Idioms
    USE   names of languages with the
            subdivision *Idioms,* e.g. **English language—Idioms** [to
            be added as needed]
Idyllic poetry
    USE   **Pastoral poetry**
Igloos (May subdiv. geog.)   **643.2**
    BT   **Houses**
           Inuit
Iguanodon   **567.914**
    BT   **Dinosaurs**
Ilium (Extinct city)
    USE   **Troy (Extinct city)**
Illegal aliens (May subdiv. geog.)   **323.6;
    325; 342**
    UF   Undocumented aliens
    BT   **Aliens**
           Immigration and emigration
           Underground economy
    RT   **Sanctuary movement**
Illegitimacy (May subdiv. geog.)
    306.874; 346.01
    UF   Illegitimate children
           Legitimacy (Law)
    RT   **Unmarried fathers**
           Unmarried mothers
Illegitimate children
    USE   **Illegitimacy**
Illiteracy
    USE   **Literacy**
Illness
    USE   **Diseases**
Illuminated manuscripts
    USE   **Illumination of books and
           manuscripts**
Illumination
    USE   **Lighting**
Illumination of books and manuscripts
    (May subdiv. geog.)   **096; 745.6**
    UF   Illuminated manuscripts
           Manuscripts, Illuminated
           Miniatures (Illumination of
           books and manuscripts)

           Ornamental alphabets
    BT   **Art**
           Books
           Decoration and ornament
           Illustration of books
           Manuscripts
           Medieval art
    RT   **Alphabets**
           Books of hours
           Initials
Illusions
    USE   **Hallucinations and illusions**
           Optical illusions
Illustration of books (May subdiv. geog.)
    741.6
    UF   Book illustration
    SA   types of illustration, e.g. **Botanical illustration** [to be added
           as needed]
    BT   **Art**
           Books
           Color printing
           Decoration and ornament
    NT   **Botanical illustration**
           Caldecott Medal
           Engraving
           **Illumination of books and
           manuscripts**
           Photomechanical processes
    RT   **Drawing**
           Picture books for children
Illustrations
    USE   subjects, names, and uniform titles with the subdivision *Pictorial works,* e.g. **Animals—
           Pictorial works; United
           States—History—1861-1865,
           Civil War—Pictorial works;**
           etc. [to be added as needed]
Illustrators (May subdiv. geog.)
    741.6092; 920
    BT   **Artists**
Illustrators, American
    USE   **Illustrators—United States**
Illustrators—United States   **741.6092;
    920**
    UF   American illustrators
           Illustrators, American
Image processing software   **006.6**
    BT   **Computer software**

Imagery
    USE **Figures of speech**
Imaginary animals
    USE **Mythical animals**
Imaginary companions
    USE **Imaginary playmates**
Imaginary creatures
    USE **Mythical animals**
Imaginary friends
    USE **Imaginary playmates**
Imaginary places   809

    Use for materials on imaginary places created for literary or artistic purposes. Materials on legendary or mythical places are entered under **Geographical myths**.

    UF   Fictional places
          Fictitious places
    NT   **Narnia (Imaginary place)**
Imaginary playmates   155.4
    UF   Imaginary companions
          Imaginary friends
          Make-believe playmates
    BT   **Child psychology**
          Imagination
          Play
Imaginary voyages   808.3; 808.83
    Use for individual works, collections, or materials about imaginary voyages.
    UF   Space flight (Fiction)
          Voyages to the moon
    BT   **Fantasy fiction**
          Science fiction
    NT   **Robinsonades**
    RT   **Interplanetary voyages**
Imagination   153.3
    BT   **Educational psychology**
          Intellect
          Psychology
    NT   **Creation (Literary, artistic, etc.)**
          Fantasy
          Imaginary playmates
Imaging, Magnetic resonance
    USE **Magnetic resonance imaging**
Imitations
    USE   types of literature and names of prominent authors with the subdivision *Parodies, imitations, etc.,* e.g. **Shakespeare, William, 1564-1616—Parodies, imitations, etc.** [to be added as needed]

Immigrants (May subdiv. geog.)   304.8

    Use for materials on foreign-born persons who enter a country intending to become permanent residents or citizens. This heading may be locally subdivided by the names of places where immigrants have settled.

    UF   Emigrants
          Foreign population
          Foreigners
    SA   names of immigrant ethnic groups, e.g. **Mexican Americans**; and, for immigrants who are not citizens, the names of national groups with the appropriate subdivision for the country of their residence, e.g. **Mexicans—United States** [to be added as needed]
    BT   **Minorities**
    RT   **Aliens**
          Immigration and emigration
Immigrants—United States   325.73
    UF   United States—Foreign population
    NT   **Mexican Americans**
    RT   **United States—Immigration and emigration**
Immigration and emigration   304.8; 325

    Use for materials on migration from one country to another. Materials on the movement of population within a country for permanent settlement are entered under **Internal migration**.

    UF   Emigration
          Foreign population
          Migration
    SA   names of countries with the subdivision *Immigration and emigration*, e.g. **United States—Immigration and emigration**; and names of immigrant minorities and national groups, e.g. **Mexican Americans**; **Mexicans—United States**; etc. [to be added as needed]
    BT   **Population**
    NT   **Children of immigrants**
          Human geography
          Illegal aliens
          Naturalization
          Refugees
          Return migration
          United States—Immigration and emigration

Immigration and emigration—*Continued*
- RT   **Aliens**
  - **Americanization**
  - **Colonization**
  - **Immigrants**
  - **Internal migration**

Immortality   129

Use for materials on the question of the endless existence of the soul. Materials on the character and form of a future existence are entered under **Future life**. Materials on the philosophical concept of eternity are entered under **Eternity**.
- UF   Eternal life
  - Life after death
- BT   **Eschatology**
  - **Soul**
  - **Theology**
- RT   **Future life**

Immune system   616.07
- UF   Immunological system
- BT   **Anatomy**
  - **Physiology**
- RT   **Immunity**

Immunity   571.9; 616.07
- NT   **Allergy**
  - **Immunization**
- RT   **Immune system**

Immunization (May subdiv. geog.)   **614.4**

Use for materials on any process, active or passive, that leads to increased immunity. Materials on active immunization with a vaccine are entered under **Vaccination**.
- BT   **Immunity**
  - **Public health**
- NT   **Vaccination**

Immunological system
- USE   **Immune system**

Immunology   571.9; 616.07
- BT   **Medicine**

Impaired vision
- USE   **Vision disorders**

Impairment
- USE   **Disabilities**

Impartiality
- USE   **Fairness**

Impeachment
- USE   types of public officials and names of individual public officials with the subdivision *Impeachment,* e.g. **Presidents—United States—Im-**

peachment [to be added as needed]

Impeachments (May subdiv. geog.)   **342**
- SA   types of public officials and names of individual officials with the subdivision *Impeachment* [to be added as needed]
- BT   **Administration of justice**
- NT   **Recall (Political science)**

Imperialism   325
- UF   Colonialism
- SA   names of countries with the subdivision *Foreign relations* or *Colonies* [to be added as needed]
- BT   **Political science**
- NT   **Colonies**
  - **Colonization**

Implements, utensils, etc. (May subdiv. geog.)   **683**
- UF   Gadgets
  - Utensils
- NT   **Containers**
  - **Household equipment and supplies**
  - **Stone implements**
  - **Tools**

Imports (May subdiv. geog.)   **382**
- BT   **International trade**

Impostors and imposture (May subdiv. geog.)   **364.1**
- UF   Charlatans
  - Hoaxes
  - Pretenders
- BT   **Crime**
  - **Criminals**
- NT   **Counterfeits and counterfeiting**
  - **Female impersonators**
  - **Forgery**
  - **Male impersonators**
  - **Quacks and quackery**
- RT   **Fraud**
  - **Swindlers and swindling**

Impotence   616.6
- BT   **Diseases**

Impressionism (Art) (May subdiv. geog.)   **709.03; 759.05**
- UF   Neo-impressionism (Art)
- BT   **Art**

Imprisonment
- USE   **Prisons**

In art
USE names of persons, families, and
corporate bodies with the subdivision *In art,* for materials
about the depiction of those
persons or bodies in works of
art, e.g. **Napoleon I, Emper-
or of the French, 1769-
1821—In art;** and phrase
headings denoting particular
themes in art for materials
about those themes, e.g. **Dogs
in art** [to be added as need-
ed]

In-line skating
USE **Rollerblading**

In literature
USE names of persons, families, and
corporate bodies with the subdivision *In literature,* for materials about the depiction of
those persons or bodies in literary works, e.g. **Napoleon I,
Emperor of the French,
1769-1821—In literature;** and
phrase headings denoting particular themes in literature for
materials about those themes,
e.g. **Dogs in literature** [to be
added as needed]

In-service training
USE types of employees or personnel
with the subdivision *In-service
training,* e.g. **Librarians—In-
service training** [to be added
as needed]

In-service training
USE **Employees—Training**

In vitro fertilization
USE **Fertilization in vitro**

Inaudible sound
USE **Ultrasonics**

Inaugural addresses
USE types of public officials and
names of individual public of-
ficials with the subdivision
Inaugural addresses, e.g.
**Presidents—United States—
Inaugural addresses** [to be
added as needed]

Inauguration
USE types of public officials and
names of individual public officials with the subdivision
Inauguration, e.g. **Presidents—United States—Inau-
guration** [to be added as
needed]

Incandescent lamps
USE **Electric lamps**

Incas 985
BT **Native Americans—South
America**

Incendiary bombs (May subdiv. geog.)
623.4
UF Fire bombs
BT **Bombs**
Incendiary weapons

Incendiary weapons (May subdiv. geog.)
623.4
BT **Chemical warfare**
NT **Incendiary bombs**

Incentive (Psychology)
USE **Motivation (Psychology)**

Incest (May subdiv. geog.) **306.877;
616.85**
BT **Sex crimes**
NT **Child sexual abuse**

Incineration
USE **Cremation**
Refuse and refuse disposal

Inclined planes 621.8
BT **Simple machines**

Income (May subdiv. geog.) **331.2;
339.3**
UF Fortunes
BT **Economics**
Finance
Property
Wealth
NT **Guaranteed annual income**
Retirement income
Salaries, wages, etc.
RT **Gross national product**
Profit

Income tax (May subdiv. geog.) **336.24**
UF Personal income tax
BT **Internal revenue**
Taxation
NT **Tax credits**

Incunabula (May subdiv. geog.)　**093**

    Use for materials on books printed before the year 1501.

    UF   Early printed books—15th century

    SA   subjects with the subdivision *Early works to 1800*, for materials on those subjects written before 1800, e.g. **Political science—Early works to 1800** [to be added as needed]

    BT   **Books**

Indebtedness

    USE **Debt**

Indentured servants

    USE **Contract labor**

Independence Day (United States)

    USE **Fourth of July**

Independence (Psychology)

    USE **Autonomy (Psychology)**

Independent films (May subdiv. geog.)　**791.43**

    UF   Indie films

    BT   **Motion pictures**

Independent schools

    USE **Private schools**

Independent study　**371.39**

    Use for materials on individual study that may be directed or assisted by instructional staff through periodic consultations.

    BT   **Study skills**

         Tutors and tutoring

Indeterminism

    USE **Free will and determinism**

Index librorum prohibitorum

    USE **Books—Censorship**

Indexes　**016**

    Use for works that list topics or names with references to books, articles, or passages where those topics or names are to be found. Works that list words with references to passages in a text where the exact word occurs are entered under **Concordances**.

    SA   subjects with the subdivision *Indexes*, e.g. **Newspapers—Indexes**; **Short stories—Indexes**; **English literature—Indexes**; etc. [to be added as needed]

    BT   **Bibliography**

    NT   **Concordances**

         Subject headings

Indexing　**025.3**

    BT   **Bibliographic control**

         Bibliography

    RT   **Cataloging**

         Files and filing

India　**954**

    May be subdivided like United States except for History.

India—History　**954**

India—History—324 B.C.-1000 A.D.　**954**

India—History—1000-1765　**954.02**

India—History—18th century　**954.02**

India—History—1765-1947, British occupation　**954.03**

India—History—19th century　**954.03**

India—History—20th century　**954.03; 954.04; 954.05**

India—History—1947-　**954.04; 954.05**

India—History—21st century　**954.05**

Indian architecture

    USE **Architecture—India**

Indian art　**709.54**

    UF   East Indian art

         Indic art

    BT   **Art**

    NT   **Indian painting**

         Indian sculpture

Indian cooking　**641.5954**

    UF   East Indian cooking

         Indic cooking

    BT   **Cooking**

Indian drama　**891.4**

    UF   East Indian drama

         Indic drama

    BT   **Drama**

         Indian literature

    NT   **Hindi drama**

Indian drama (English)　**822**

    UF   East Indian drama (English)

         Indic drama (English)

    BT   **Drama**

         Indian literature (English)

Indian epic poetry　**891.4**

    UF   East Indian epic poetry

         Indic epic poetry

    BT   **Epic poetry**

         Indian poetry

    NT   **Hindi literature**

         Indian fiction

         Indian literature (English)

         Indian poetry

         Mahābhārata

Indian epic poetry—*Continued*
    Rāmāyaṇa
Indian fiction   **891.4**
  UF East Indian fiction
       Indic fiction
  BT **Fiction**
       Indian epic poetry
  NT **Hindi fiction**
Indian fiction (English)   **823**
  UF East Indian fiction (English)
       Indic fiction (English)
  BT **Fiction**
       Indian literature (English)
Indian languages   **941.4**
  UF East Indian languages
       Indic languages
  BT **Language and languages**
  NT **Bengali language**
       Hindi language
       Sanskrit language
Indian languages (North American)
  USE **Native American languages**
Indian literature   **891.4**
  UF East Indian literature
       Indic literature [*Former heading*]
  BT **Literature**
  NT **Indian drama**
Indian literature (English)   **820**
  UF East Indian literature (English)
       Indic literature (English)
  BT **Indian epic poetry**
       Literature
  NT **Indian drama (English)**
       Indian fiction (English)
       Indian poetry (English)
Indian missions
  USE **Native Americans—Christian missions**
Indian Ocean   **551.4615**
  BT **Ocean**
Indian painting   **709.54**
  UF East Indian painting
       Indic painting
  BT **Indian art**
       Painting
Indian philosophy   **181**
  UF East Indian philosophy
       Indic philosophy
  BT **Philosophy**
Indian poetry   **891.4**
  UF East Indian poetry
       Indic poetry

  BT **Indian epic poetry**
       Poetry
  NT **Hindi poetry**
       Indian epic poetry
Indian poetry (English)   **821**
  UF East Indian poetry (English)
       Indic poetry (English)
  BT **Indian literature (English)**
       Poetry
Indian removal
  USE **Native Americans—Relocation**
Indian reservations
  USE **Native Americans—Reservations**
      and names of native peoples,
      tribes, etc., with the subdivision *Reservations* [to be added as needed]
Indian sculpture   **730.954**
  UF East Indian sculpture
       Indic sculpture
  BT **Indian art**
       Sculpture
Indians (May subdiv. geog.)   **305.891; 920; 954**
  UF East Indians [*Former heading*]
       Indians (of India)
Indians of Canada
  USE **Native Americans—Canada**
Indians of Central America
  USE **Native Americans—Central America**
Indians of Central America—Guatemala
  USE **Native Americans—Guatemala**
Indians (of India)
  USE **Indians**
Indians of Mexico
  USE **Native Americans—Mexico**
Indians of North America
  USE **Native Americans**
      Native Americans—North America
      Native Americans—United States
Indians of North America—Agriculture
  USE **Native Americans—Agriculture**
Indians of North America—Antiquities
  USE **Native Americans—Antiquities**
Indians of North America—Architecture
  USE **Native American architecture**

Indians of North America—Art
   USE **Native American art**
Indians of North America—Canada
   USE **Native Americans—Canada**
Indians of North America—Captivities
   USE **Native Americans—Captivities**
Indians of North America—Children
   USE **Native American children**
Indians of North America—Christian missions
   USE **Native Americans—Christian missions**
Indians of North America—Claims
   USE **Native Americans—Claims**
Indians of North America—Costume
   USE **Native American costume**
Indians of North America—Dances
   USE **Native American dance**
Indians of North America—Dwellings
   USE **Native Americans—Dwellings**
Indians of North America—Economic conditions
   USE **Native Americans—Economic conditions**
Indians of North America—Education
   USE **Native Americans—Education**
Indians of North America—First contact with Europeans
   USE **Native Americans—First contact with Europeans**
Indians of North America—Folklore
   USE **Native Americans—Folklore**
Indians of North America—Games
   USE **Native American games**
Indians of North America—Government relations
   USE **Native Americans—Government relations**
Indians of North America—History
   USE **Native Americans—History**
Indians of North America—History—Chronology
   USE **Native Americans—History—Chronology**
Indians of North America—Industries
   USE **Native Americans—Industries**
Indians of North America—Languages
   USE **Native American languages**
Indians of North America—Literature
   USE **Native American literature**

Indians of North America—Medicine
   USE **Native American medicine**
Indians of North America—Music
   USE **Native American music**
Indians of North America—Names
   USE **Native American names**
Indians of North America—Origin
   USE **Native Americans—Origin**
Indians of North America—Politics and government
   USE **Native Americans—Politics and government**
Indians of North America—Psychology
   USE **Native Americans—Psychology**
Indians of North America—Relations with early settlers
   USE **Native Americans—Relations with early settlers**
Indians of North America—Religion
   USE **Native Americans—Religion**
Indians of North America—Reservations
   USE **Native Americans—Reservations**
Indians of North America—Rites and ceremonies
   USE **Native Americans—Rites and ceremonies**
Indians of North America—Schools
   USE **Native Americans—Education**
Indians of North America—Sign language
   USE **Native American sign language**
Indians of North America—Silverwork
   USE **Native American silverwork**
Indians of North America—Social conditions
   USE **Native Americans—Social conditions**
Indians of North America—Social life and customs
   USE **Native Americans—Social life and customs**
Indians of North America—Wars
   USE **Native Americans—Wars**
Indians of North America—Women
   USE **Native American women**
Indians of South America
   USE **Native Americans—South America**
Indians of South America—Peru
   USE **Native Americans—Peru**

Indians of the West Indies
USE **Native Americans—West Indies**
Indians—West Indies 305.891; 920
Indic architecture
USE **Architecture—India**
Indic art
USE **Indian art**
Indic cooking
USE **Indian cooking**
Indic drama
USE **Indian drama**
Indic drama (English)
USE **Indian drama (English)**
Indic epic poetry
USE **Indian epic poetry**
Indic fiction
USE **Indian fiction**
Indic fiction (English)
USE **Indian fiction (English)**
Indic languages
USE **Indian languages**
Indic literature
USE **Indian literature**
Indic literature (English)
USE **Indian literature (English)**
Indic painting
USE **Indian painting**
Indic philosophy
USE **Indian philosophy**
Indic poetry
USE **Indian poetry**
Indic poetry (English)
USE **Indian poetry (English)**
Indic sculpture
USE **Indian sculpture**
Indie films
USE **Independent films**
Indigenous peoples (May subdiv. geog.)
305.8

Use for materials on indigenous groups
within a colonial area or modern state where
the group does not control the government.
General materials on people bound together
by common ancestry and culture are entered
under **Ethnic groups**. Materials on the various ethnic groups or native peoples in a particular region or country are entered under
Ethnology subdivided geographically.

UF   Aborigines
Native peoples
Natives
People

SA   names of individual indigenous
peoples e.g. **Yoruba (African
people)** [to be added as need-
ed]
BT   **Ethnology**
NT   **Aboriginal Australians**
Ashanti (African people)
Hmong (Asian people)
Inuit
Maoris
Masai (African people)
Native Americans
Tutsi (African people)
Yoruba (African people)
Zulu (African people)
Indigenous peoples—America
USE   **Native Americans**
Indigenous plants
USE   **Native plants**
Indigestion 616.3
UF   Dyspepsia
BT   **Digestion**
Individual retirement accounts (May
subdiv. geog.) **332.024**
UF   IRAs (Pensions)
BT   **Pensions**
Retirement income
NT   **401(k) plans**
Individualism (May subdiv. geog.) **141;
302.5; 330.1**
BT   **Economics**
Equality
Political science
Sociology
RT   **Persons**
Individuality 155.2
UF   Identity
BT   **Consciousness**
Psychology
NT   **Self**
RT   **Conformity**
Personality
Individualized instruction 371.39

Use for materials on the adaptation of instruction to meet individual needs within a
group. General materials on one-on-one instruction are entered under **Tutors and tutoring**.

BT   **Tutors and tutoring**
RT   **Open plan schools**
Indo-European civilization
USE   **Indo-Europeans**

Indo-Europeans (May subdiv. geog.)
    305-809
    UF   Aryans
            Indo-European civilization
Indochina   959
        Use for the area comprising Laos, Cambodia, and Vietnam.
    BT   **Southeast Asia**
Indoctrination, Forced
    USE   **Brainwashing**
Indolence
    USE   **Laziness**
Indonesia   959.8
        May be subdivided like United States except for History.
Indoor air pollution (May subdiv. geog.)
    363.739; 628.5
    BT   **Air pollution**
Indoor games (May subdiv. geog.)   **793**
    BT   **Games**
    RT   **Amusements**
Indoor gardening (May subdiv. geog.)
    635.9
    BT   **Gardening**
    NT   **Terrariums**
            Window gardening
    RT   **Container gardening**
            House plants
            Miniature gardens
Induced abortion
    USE   **Abortion**
Induction coils   537.6; 621.319
    BT   **Electric apparatus and appliances**
    NT   **Condensers (Electricity)**
Induction (Logic)
    USE   **Logic**
Induction motors
    USE   **Electric motors**
Industrial accidents (May subdiv. geog.)
    363.11; 658.3
    UF   Employees—Accidents
            Industrial disasters
            Industrial injuries
            Labor—Accidents
            Occupational accidents
            Occupational injuries
    SA   industries with the subdivision
            Accidents, e.g. **Chemical industry—Accidents** [to be added as needed]
    BT   **Accidents**

    NT   **Chemical industry—Accidents**
    RT   **Hazardous occupations**
Industrial alcohol
    USE   **Denatured alcohol**
Industrial antiquities
    USE   **Industrial archeology**
Industrial applications
    USE   types of scientific phenomena, chemicals, plants, and crops with the subdivision *Industrial applications,* e.g. **Ultrasonic waves—Industrial applications** [to be added as needed]
Industrial arbitration (May subdiv. geog.)
    331.89
    UF   Arbitration, Industrial
            Industrial conciliation
            Labor arbitration
            Labor courts
            Labor negotiations
            Mediation, Industrial
            Trade agreements (Labor)
    BT   **Industrial relations**
            Labor
            Labor disputes
            Labor unions
            Negotiation
    RT   **Collective bargaining**
            Strikes
Industrial archaeology
    USE   **Industrial archeology**
Industrial archeology (May subdiv. geog.)
    609
        Use for materials on the study of the physical remains of industries from the eighteenth and nineteenth centuries, including buildings, machinery, and tools.
    UF   Industrial antiquities
            Industrial archaeology
    BT   **Archeology**
            Industries—History
Industrial arts (May subdiv. geog.)   **600**
    UF   Mechanic arts
            Trades
    SA   types of industries, arts, and trades; and names of countries, cities, etc., with the subdivision *Industries* [to be added as needed]
    BT   **Handicraft**
    NT   **Arts and crafts movement**
            Engineering

Industrial arts—*Continued*
    Industrial arts education
    Manufacturing processes
    Printing
RT **Technology**
Industrial arts education (May subdiv. geog.) **607**
  UF Education, Industrial
      Industrial education
      Industrial schools
      Manual training
  BT **Industrial arts**
      Vocational education
  RT **Technical education**
Industrial arts shops
  USE **School shops**
Industrial buildings (May subdiv. geog.) **725**
  UF Buildings, Industrial
  BT **Buildings**
  NT **Factories**
Industrial buildings—Design and construction **690**
  BT **Architecture**
      Building
Industrial chemistry (May subdiv. geog.) **660**
  UF Chemical technology
      Chemistry, Technical
      Technical chemistry
  SA types of industries and products, e.g. **Clay industry**; **Dyes and dyeing**; etc. [to be added as needed]
  BT **Chemistry**
      Technology
  NT **Alloys**
      Bleaching
      Canning and preserving
      Ceramics
      Corrosion and anticorrosives
      Distillation
      Drying
      Electrochemistry
      Food—Analysis
      Gums and resins
      Synthetic products
      Tanning
      Textile chemistry
      Waste products
  RT **Chemical engineering**
      Chemical industry

      Chemicals
      Metallurgy
Industrial conciliation
  USE **Industrial arbitration**
Industrial councils
  USE **Participative management**
Industrial counseling
  USE **Employees—Counseling of**
Industrial design (May subdiv. geog.) **745.2**
  UF Design, Industrial
  BT **Design**
  NT **Automobiles—Design and construction**
      Human engineering
      Systems engineering
Industrial disasters
  USE **Industrial accidents**
Industrial diseases
  USE **Occupational diseases**
Industrial disputes
  USE **Labor disputes**
Industrial drawing
  USE **Mechanical drawing**
Industrial education
  USE **Industrial arts education**
      Technical education
Industrial efficiency (May subdiv. geog.) **658**
  Use for materials on the various means of increasing efficiency and output in business and industries, including time and motion studies and materials on the application of psychological principles to industrial production.
  UF Efficiency, Industrial
  BT **Management**
  NT **Job analysis**
      Labor productivity
      Motion study
      Office management
      Time study
Industrial equipment (May subdiv. geog.) **621.8**
  UF Capital equipment
      Capital goods
      Industries—Equipment and supplies
      Machinery in industry
  SA types of industries with the subdivision *Equipment and supplies* [to be added as needed]
  BT **Machinery**

Industrial equipment—*Continued*
  NT   **Automation**
        Industrial robots
Industrial exhibitions
  USE **Trade shows**
Industrial health
  USE **Occupational health and safety**
Industrial injuries
  USE **Industrial accidents**
Industrial laws and legislation (May
     subdiv. geog.) **343**
  UF Government regulation of com-
        merce
        Industries—Law and legislation
  SA types of industries with the sub-
        division *Law and legislation*,
        e.g. **Chemical industry—Law**
        and legislation [to be added
        as needed]
  BT **Law**
        Legislation
  NT **Labor laws and legislation**
Industrial libraries
  USE **Corporate libraries**
Industrial management
  USE **Management**
Industrial materials
  USE **Materials**
Industrial mergers
  USE **Corporate mergers and acqui-**
        sitions
Industrial mobilization (May subdiv.
     geog.) **355.2**
    Use for materials on industrial and labor
  policies and programs for defense mobiliza-
  tion.
  UF Economic mobilization
        Industry and war
        Mobilization, Industrial
        National defenses
  BT **Economic policy**
        Military art and science
        War—Economic aspects
  RT **Military readiness**
Industrial organization
  USE **Management**
Industrial painting (May subdiv. geog.)
     698
  SA topics with the subdivision
        Painting; e.g. **Automobiles—**
        Painting [to be added as
        needed]

  BT **Finishes and finishing**
  NT **Automobiles—Painting**
        Lettering
        Sign painting
  RT **House painting**
Industrial plants
  USE **Factories**
Industrial policy (May subdiv. geog.)
     338.9; 354
  UF Government policy
        Government regulation of indus-
        try
        Industries—Government policy
        Industries—Organization, control,
        etc.
        Industry and state
        State regulation of industry
  BT **Economic policy**
  NT **Agriculture—Government poli-**
        cy
        Consumer protection
        Deregulation
        Energy policy
        Government ownership
        Privatization
        Public service commissions
        Railroads—Government policy
Industrial policy—United States
     338.973; 354
  UF Industries—Government policy—
        United States
        United States—Industrial policy
Industrial processing
  USE **Manufacturing processes**
Industrial psychology
  USE **Applied psychology**
Industrial relations (May subdiv. geog.)
     331
    Use for general materials on employer-
  employee relations. Materials on problems of
  personnel and relations from the employer's
  point of view are entered under **Personnel**
  management.
  UF Capital and labor
        Employer-employee relations
        Labor and capital
        Labor-management relations
        Labor relations
  BT **Labor**
        Management
  NT **Collective bargaining**
        Industrial arbitration
        Labor contract

Industrial relations—*Continued*
    Labor disputes
    Labor unions
    Participative management
    Personnel management
    Strikes
Industrial research (May subdiv. geog.)
    607; 658.5
  BT **Research**
  NT **New products**
  RT **Inventions**
      Technological innovations
Industrial revolution (May subdiv. geog.)
    330.9; 909.81

Use for materials on the historical shift from home-based industries to large-scale factory production. Materials on the development of organized productions as industries, especially factory-based industries, are entered under **Industrialization**.

  SA names of countries with the sub-
       division *Economic conditions*
       [to be added as needed]
  BT **Economic conditions**
      Industries—History
  RT **Great Britain—History—19th**
      century
      Industrialization
      Technology and civilization
Industrial robots (May subdiv. geog.)
    629.8
  UF Robots, Industrial
      Working robots
  BT **Automation**
      Industrial equipment
      Robots
Industrial safety
  USE **Occupational health and safety**
Industrial schools
  USE **Industrial arts education**
       Technical education
Industrial secrets
  USE **Trade secrets**
Industrial trusts (May subdiv. geog.)
    338.8; 658

Use for materials on combinations in restraint of trade in which stock ownership is transferred to trustees, who in turn issue trust certificates and dividends and who attempt to achieve monopolistic control over output, prices, or markets.

  UF Cartels
      Trusts, Industrial

  BT **Capital**
      Commerce
      Economics
  RT **Antitrust law**
      Competition
      Corporate mergers and acqui-
        sitions
      Corporation law
      Corporations
      Monopolies
      Restraint of trade
Industrial trusts—Law and legislation
  USE **Antitrust law**
Industrial uses of space
  USE **Space industrialization**
Industrial waste (May subdiv. geog.)
    363.72; 628.4
  UF Factory and trade waste
      Factory waste
      Industrial wastes
      Trade waste
  BT **Refuse and refuse disposal**
      Waste products
  NT **Hazardous wastes**
  RT **Pollution**
      Water pollution
Industrial wastes
  USE **Industrial waste**
Industrial welfare (May subdiv. geog.)
    658.3
  UF Welfare work in industry
  BT **Labor**
      Management
      Social work
  NT **Social settlements**
Industrial workers
  USE **Labor**
      Working class
Industrialization (May subdiv. geog.)
    338

Use for materials on the development of organized productions as industries, especially factory-based industries. Materials on the historical shift from home-based industries to large-scale factory production are entered under **Industrial revolution**.

  BT **Economic policy**
      Industries
  NT **Developing countries**
      Space industrialization
  RT **Industrial revolution**
      Modernization (Sociology)

Industries (May subdiv. geog.)   **338**

Apart from **Manufacturing industries** and **Service industries**, all headings for types of industries are formulated in the singular.

UF   Industry
      Production
SA   types of industries, e.g. **Steel industry**; and ethnic groups with the subdivision *Industries*, e.g. **Native Americans—Industries** [to be added as needed]
BT   **Economics**
NT   **Aerospace industry**
      Agricultural industry
      Automobile industry
      Book industry
      Ceramic industry
      Chemical industry
      Clothing industry
      Commercial fishing
      Computer industry
      Computer software industry
      Construction industry
      Defense industry
      Electric products industry
      Financial services industry
      Firearms industry
      High technology industry
      Industrialization
      Internet industry
      Iron industry
      Leather industry
      Management
      Manufactures
      Manufacturing industries
      Motion picture industry
      Native Americans—Industries
      Nuclear industry
      Paper industry
      Petroleum industry
      Pollution control industry
      Radio supplies industry
      Service industries
      Steel industry
      Textile industry
      Tobacco industry

Industries—Chicago (Ill.)   **338.09773**

UF   Chicago (Ill.)—Industries

Industries—Deregulation
USE   **Deregulation**

Industries—Equipment and supplies
USE   **Industrial equipment**

Industries—Government policy
USE   **Industrial policy**

Industries—Government policy—United States
USE   **Industrial policy—United States**

Industries—History (May subdiv. geog.)   **338.09**
NT   **Industrial archeology**
      Industrial revolution

Industries—Law and legislation
USE   **Industrial laws and legislation**

Industries—Ohio   **338.09771**
UF   Ohio—Industries

Industries—Organization, control, etc.
USE   **Industrial policy**

Industries—Social responsibility
USE   **Social responsibility of business**

Industries—United States   **338.0973**
UF   United States—Industries

Industry
USE   **Industries**

Industry and state
USE   **Industrial policy**

Industry and war
USE   **Industrial mobilization**
      War—Economic aspects

Inequality
USE   **Equality**

Infallibility of the Pope
USE   **Popes—Infallibility**

Infant care
USE   **Infants—Care**

Infant care leave
USE   **Parental leave**

Infant mortality
USE   **Infants—Mortality**

Infant sudden death
USE   **Sudden infant death syndrome**

Infantile paralysis
USE   **Poliomyelitis**

Infants (May subdiv. geog.)   **155.42; 305.232; 362.7; 618.92**

Use for materials about children in the earliest period of life, usually the first two years only.

UF   Babies
BT   **Children**

Infants and strangers
USE   **Children and strangers**

Infants—Birth defects
USE **Birth defects**
Infants—Care (May subdiv. geog.)   **649**
UF Baby care
Infant care
BT **Child care**
NT **Babysitting**
Infants—Clothing
USE **Infants' clothing**
Infants' clothing (May subdiv. geog.)
646.4
UF Baby clothes
Infants—Clothing
BT **Children's clothing**
Clothing and dress
Infants—Death   **306.9; 618.92**
Use for general materials on the death of infants. Materials on infant death rates and causes are entered under **Infants—Mortality**.
BT **Death**
NT **Sudden infant death syndrome**
Infants—Diseases (May subdiv. geog.)
618.92
UF Pediatrics
BT **Diseases**
RT **Infants—Health and hygiene**
Infants—Education
USE **Preschool education**
Infants—Health and hygiene (May subdiv. geog.)   **613; 618.92**
UF Infants—Hygiene
Pediatrics
BT **Health**
Hygiene
RT **Infants—Diseases**
Infants—Hygiene
USE **Infants—Health and hygiene**
Infants—Mortality (May subdiv. geog.)
304.6
Use for materials on infant death rates and causes. General materials on the death of infants are entered under **Infants—Death**.
UF Infant mortality
BT **Mortality**
Infants—Nutrition (May subdiv. geog.)
613.2; 649
BT **Nutrition**
NT **Breast feeding**
Infection and infectious diseases
USE **Communicable diseases**
Infectious wastes
USE **Medical wastes**

Infertility   **616.6**
Use for materials on infertility in humans and in animals.
UF Sterility in animals
Sterility in humans
BT **Reproduction**
RT **Birth control**
Childlessness
Fertility
Human fertility
Infinitive
USE names of languages with the subdivision *Infinitive,* e.g. **English language—Infinitive** [to be added as needed]
Infirmaries
USE **Hospitals**
Inflammable substances
USE **Hazardous substances**
Inflation (Finance) (May subdiv. geog.)
332.4
BT **Finance**
NT **Wage-price policy**
RT **Monetary policy**
Paper money
Influence
USE subjects, corporate bodies, individual persons, literary authors, religions, denominations, sacred works, and wars with the subdivision *Influence,* e.g. **World War, 1939-1945—Influence; Shakespeare, William, 1564-1616—Influence** [to be added as needed]
Influenza (May subdiv. geog.)   **616.2**
UF Flu
BT **Communicable diseases**
Diseases
Informal sector (Economics)
USE **Underground economy**
Information centers
USE **Information services**
Information clearinghouses
USE **Information services**
Information, Freedom of
USE **Freedom of information**
Information literacy (May subdiv. geog.)
302.2
BT **Literacy**

Information networks (May subdiv. geog.) **004.6**

Use for materials on the interconnection through telecommunications of a geographically dispersed group of libraries or information centers for the purpose of sharing their total information resources.

UF Information superhighway
    Networks, Information
SA types of information networks and names of specific networks [to be added as needed]
BT **Information systems**
NT **Internet**
    Library information networks
RT **Computer networks**

Information resources (May subdiv. geog.) **025.04**

Use for materials on sources of information in general, not limited to a specific topic or format. Materials on organizations that provide information services are entered under **Information services**.

UF Information sources
SA subjects with the subdivision *Information resources*, for general materials about information on a subject, e.g. **Business—Information resources**; subjects with the subdivision *Internet resources*, for materials about information available on the Internet on a subject, e.g. **Business—Internet resources**; subjects with the subdivision *Databases*, for materials about data files on a subject regardless of the medium of distribution, e.g. **Business—Databases**; and headings for the providers or the users of information with the subdivision *Information services*, for materials about organizations that provide information services, e.g. **United Nations—Information services**; **Consumers—Information services**; etc. [to be added as needed]
BT **Information science**
NT **Business—Information resources**

Databases
Information services
Internet resources

Information retrieval **025.5**

UF Data retrieval
    Information storage and retrieval
    Retrieval of information
BT **Documentation**
    Information science
NT **Internet searching**
RT **Information systems**

Information science (May subdiv. geog.) **020**

BT **Communication**
NT **Documentation**
    Information resources
    Information retrieval
    Information systems
    Library science

Information services (May subdiv. geog.) **025.5**

Use for materials on organizations that provide information services. Materials on sources of information, not limited to a specific topic or format, are entered under **Information resources**.

UF Information centers
    Information clearinghouses
SA headings for the providers or the users of information with the subdivision *Information services*, for materials about organizatons that provide information services, e.g. **United Nations—Information services**; **Consumers—Information services**; etc.; subjects with the subdivision *Information resources*, for general materials about information on a subject, e.g. **Business—Information resources**; subjects with the subdivision *Internet resources*, for materials about information available on the Internet on a subject, e.g. **Business—Internet resources**; and subjects with the subdivision *Databases*, for materials about data files on a subject regardless of the medium of distribution, e.g. **Business—**

Information services—*Continued*
>   Databases [to be added as
>   needed]
>   BT **Information resources**
>   NT **Archives**
>   **Business—Information services**
>   **Consumers—Information ser-
>   vices**
>   **Electronic publishing**
>   **Hotlines (Telephone counseling)**
>   **Machine readable bibliographic
>   data**
>   **Reference services (Libraries)**
>   **United Nations—Information
>   services**
>   RT **Documentation**
>   **Information systems**
>   **Libraries**
>   **Research**

Information society (May subdiv. geog.)
303.48

Use for materials on a society whose primary activity is the production and communication of information by means of computer networks and other advanced technology.

>   BT **Sociology**

Information sources
>   USE **Information resources**

Information storage and retrieval
>   USE **Information retrieval**

Information storage and retrieval systems
>   USE **Information systems**

Information superhighway
>   USE **Computer networks**
>   **Information networks**
>   **Internet**

Information systems   025.04
>   UF Computer-based information sys-
>   tems
>   Data storage and retrieval sys-
>   tems
>   Information storage and retrieval
>   systems
>   BT **Bibliographic control**
>   **Computers**
>   **Information science**
>   NT **Data processing**
>   **Database management**
>   **Digital libraries**
>   **Expert systems (Computer sci-
>   ence)**
>   **Information networks**

>   Machine readable bibliographic
>   data
>   Management information sys-
>   tems
>   Multimedia
>   RT **Information retrieval**
>   **Information services**
>   **Libraries—Automation**

Information systems—Management (May
subdiv. geog.)   **025.04**

Use for materials on the management of information systems.

>   BT **Management**

Information technology (May subdiv.
geog.)   **004; 303.48**

Use for materials on the acquisition, processing, storage, and dissemination of any
type of information by microelectronics, computers, and telecommunication.

>   BT **Technology**
>   RT **Knowledge management**

Infrared radiation   535.01; 621.36
>   BT **Electromagnetic waves**
>   **Radiation**

Infrastructure (Economics) (May subdiv.
geog.)   **363**
>   BT **Economic development**
>   **Public works**

Inhalant abuse
>   USE **Solvent abuse**

Inhalation abuse of solvents
>   USE **Solvent abuse**

Inheritance and succession (May subdiv.
geog.)   **346.05**
>   UF Bequests
>   Heirs
>   Hereditary succession
>   Intestacy
>   Legacies
>   BT **Wealth**
>   NT **Executors and administrators**
>   **Inheritance and transfer tax**
>   **Probate law and practice**
>   RT **Trusts and trustees**
>   **Wills**

Inheritance and transfer tax (May
subdiv. geog.)   **343.05**
>   UF Estate tax
>   Taxation of legacies
>   Transfer tax
>   BT **Estate planning**
>   **Inheritance and succession**
>   **Internal revenue**

Inheritance and transfer tax—*Continued*
  Taxation
Inheritance (Biology)
  USE **Heredity**
Initialisms
  USE **Acronyms**
Initials (May subdiv. geog.) 745.6
  NT **Printing—Specimens**
  RT **Alphabets**
    Illumination of books and
      manuscripts
    Lettering
    Monograms
    Type and type-founding
Initiation ceremonies
  USE **Initiation rites**
Initiation rites (May subdiv. geog.) 203;
  392.1
  UF Initiation ceremonies
    Initiations
  BT **Rites and ceremonies**
  NT **Circumcision**
    Female circumcision
Initiations
  USE **Initiation rites**
Initiative and referendum
  USE **Referendum**
Injunctions (May subdiv. geog.) 331.89
  BT **Constitutional law**
    Labor unions
  RT **Strikes**
Injuries
  USE **Accidents**
    First aid
    Wounds and injuries
Injurious insects
  USE **Insect pests**
Ink drawing
  USE **Pen drawing**
Inland navigation (May subdiv. geog.)
  386
  May be subdivided by the names of rivers,
  lakes, canals, etc., as well as by countries,
  states, cities, etc.
  BT **Navigation**
    Shipping
    Transportation
  RT **Canals**
    Lakes
    Rivers
    Waterways

Inner cities (May subdiv. geog.) 307.76
  Use for materials on the densely populated,
  economically depressed, central areas of large
  cities.
  UF Ghettos, Inner city
    Inner city ghettos
    Inner city problems
  BT **Cities and towns**
Inner city ghettos
  USE **Inner cities**
Inner city problems
  USE **Inner cities**
Inner city schools
  USE **Urban schools**
Innovations, Technological
  USE **Technological innovations**
Inns
  USE **Hotels and motels**
Innuit
  USE **Inuit**
Inoculation
  USE **Vaccination**
Inorganic chemistry 546
  UF Chemistry, Inorganic
  BT **Chemistry**
  NT **Metals**
Input equipment (Computers)
  USE **Computer peripherals**
Inquisition (May subdiv. geog.) 272
  UF Holy Office
  BT **Catholic Church**
Inquisitiveness
  USE **Curiosity**
Insane
  USE **Mentally ill**
Insanity defense (May subdiv. geog.)
  345
  UF Insanity—Jurisprudence
    Insanity plea
    Mental illness—Jurisprudence
  BT **Criminal law**
Insanity—Jurisprudence
  USE **Insanity defense**
Insanity plea
  USE **Insanity defense**
Inscriptions (May subdiv. geog.) 411
  UF Epigraphy
  BT **Ancient history**
    Archeology
  NT **Brasses**
    Cuneiform inscriptions
    Epitaphs

Inscriptions—*Continued*
> **Graffiti**
> **Hieroglyphics**
> **Seals (Numismatics)**

Inscriptions, Cuneiform
> USE **Cuneiform inscriptions**

Insect-eating plants
> USE **Carnivorous plants**

Insect pests (May subdiv. geog.)   **632**
> UF Destructive insects
> Diseases and pests
> Garden pests
> Harmful insects
> Injurious insects
> SA types of insect pests, e.g. **Lo-custs**; etc.; and types of crops, plants, trees, etc., with the subdivision *Diseases and pests*, e.g. **Fruit—Diseases and pests** [to be added as needed]
> BT **Economic zoology**
> **Insects**
> **Pests**
> NT **Fruit—Diseases and pests**
> **Insects as carriers of disease**
> **Locusts**
> RT **Agricultural pests**
> **Household pests**
> **Parasites**

Insecticides   632; 668
> SA types of insecticides [to be added as needed]
> BT **Agricultural chemicals**
> **Pesticides**
> NT **DDT (Insecticide)**
> **Fumigation**
> RT **Spraying and dusting**

Insecticides—Toxicology   615.9
> BT **Poisons and poisoning**

Insectivorous plants
> USE **Carnivorous plants**

Insects (May subdiv. geog.)   **595.7**
> SA types of insects [to be added as needed]
> BT **Animals**
> NT **Ants**
> **Bees**
> **Beetles**
> **Beneficial insects**
> **Butterflies**
> **Cockroaches**
> **Crickets**
> **Flies**
> **Insect pests**
> **Locusts**
> **Mosquitoes**
> **Moths**
> **Silkworms**
> **Wasps**

Insects as carriers of disease   614.4
> BT **Insect pests**
> RT **Communicable diseases**

Insects—Metamorphosis   592.7

Inservice training
> USE **Employees—Training**

Insider trading (May subdiv. geog.)   **346.07; 364.16**
> UF Securities trading, Insider
> Stocks—Insider trading
> BT **Commercial law**
> **Securities**
> **Stock exchanges**

Insignia   929.9
> UF Badges of honor
> Devices (Heraldry)
> Emblems
> SA armies, navies, and other appropriate subjects with the subdivision *Insignia* or *Medals, badges, decorations, etc.* [to be added as needed]
> BT **Heraldry**
> NT **Badges**
> **Colleges and universities—Insignia**
> **United States. Army—Insignia**
> **United States. Army—Medals, badges, decorations, etc.**
> **United States. Navy—Insignia**
> **United States. Navy—Medals, badges, decorations, etc.**
> RT **Decorations of honor**
> **Medals**
> **National emblems**

Insolvency
> USE **Bankruptcy**

Insomnia   616.8
> UF Sleeplessness
> Wakefulness
> BT **Sleep**

Inspection
    USE   topics with the subdivision *In-spection,* e.g. **Automobiles—Inspection** [to be added as needed]
Inspection of food
    USE   **Food adulteration and inspection**
Inspection of meat
    USE   **Meat inspection**
Inspection of schools
    USE   **School supervision**
            Schools—Administration
Inspiration
    USE   **Creation (Literary, artistic, etc.)**
Inspiration, Biblical
    USE   **Bible—Inspiration**
Installment plan   658.8
    UF   Instalment plan
    BT   **Business**
            Consumer credit
            Credit
            Purchasing
Instalment plan
    USE   **Installment plan**
Instant messaging   004.69; 384.3
    BT   **Data transmission systems**
Instinct   152.3; 156
    UF   Animal instinct
    BT   **Animal behavior**
            Psychology
    RT   **Animal intelligence**
            Comparative psychology
            Habit
Institutional care (May subdiv. geog.)   **361**
    UF   Asylums
            Benevolent institutions
            Charitable institutions
            Homes (Institutions)
    SA   classes of persons with the subdivision *Institutional care* [to be added as needed]
    BT   **Charities**
            Medical charities
            Public welfare
    NT   **Blind—Institutional care**
            Children—Institutional care
            Deaf—Institutional care
            Elderly—Institutional care

            Group homes
            Hospitals
            Mentally ill—Institutional care
            Nursing homes
Institutions, Charitable and philanthropic
    USE   **Charities**
Institutions, Ecclesiastical
    USE   **Religious institutions**
Institutions, Religious
    USE   **Religious institutions**
Instruction
    USE   **Education**
            Teaching
Instructional games
    USE   **Educational games**
Instructional materials
    USE   **Teaching—Aids and devices**
Instructional materials centers (May subdiv. geog.)   **027.7**
    UF   Audiovisual materials centers
            Curriculum materials centers
            Educational media centers
            Learning resource centers
            Media centers (Education)
            Multimedia centers
            School media centers
    BT   **Libraries**
    NT   **School libraries**
Instructional supervision
    USE   **School supervision**
Instructional systems analysis
    USE   **Educational evaluation**
Instructional technology
    USE   **Educational technology**
Instructive games
    USE   **Educational games**
Instrument flying   629.132
    BT   **Aeronautical instruments**
            Airplanes—Piloting
Instrumental ensembles
    USE   **Ensembles (Music)**
Instrumental music (May subdiv. geog.)   **784**
    SA   types of instrumental music [to be added as needed]
    BT   **Music**
    NT   **Band music**
            Chamber music
            Guitar music
            Orchestral music
            Organ music

Instrumental music—*Continued*
  Piano music
  RT **Musical instruments**
Instrumentalists (May subdiv. geog.)
  784
  SA types of instrumentalists, e.g. **Violinists** [to be added as needed]
  BT **Musicians**
  NT **Organists**
    Pianists
    Violinists
    Violoncellists
Instrumentation and orchestration
  781.3; 784.13
  UF Orchestration
  BT **Bands (Music)**
    Composition (Music)
    Music
    Orchestra
  RT **Musical instruments**
Instruments, Aeronautical
  USE **Aeronautical instruments**
Instruments, Astronautical
  USE **Astronautical instruments**
Instruments, Astronomical
  USE **Astronomical instruments**
Instruments, Engineering
  USE **Engineering instruments**
Instruments, Measuring
  USE **Measuring instruments**
Instruments, Meteorological
  USE **Meteorological instruments**
Instruments, Musical
  USE **Musical instruments**
Instruments, Negotiable
  USE **Negotiable instruments**
Instruments, Optical
  USE **Optical instruments**
Instruments, Scientific
  USE **Scientific apparatus and instruments**
Insulation (Heat)   691; 693.8
  UF Heat insulating materials
    Thermal insulation
  BT **Heating**
Insulation (Sound)
  USE **Soundproofing**
Insults
  USE **Invective**
Insurance (May subdiv. geog.)   **368**

  SA types of insurance, e.g. **Automobile insurance** [to be added as needed]
  BT **Estate planning**
    Finance
    Personal finance
  NT **Automobile insurance**
    Casualty insurance
    Disability insurance
    Fire insurance
    Health insurance
    Life insurance
    Malpractice insurance
    Marine insurance
    Unemployment insurance
Insurance, Accident
  USE **Accident insurance**
Insurance, Automobile
  USE **Automobile insurance**
Insurance, Casualty
  USE **Casualty insurance**
Insurance, Disability
  USE **Disability insurance**
Insurance, Fire
  USE **Fire insurance**
Insurance, Group
  USE **Group insurance**
Insurance, Health
  USE **Health insurance**
Insurance, Hospitalization
  USE **Hospitalization insurance**
Insurance, Life
  USE **Life insurance**
Insurance, Malpractice
  USE **Malpractice insurance**
Insurance, Marine
  USE **Marine insurance**
Insurance, Professional liability
  USE **Malpractice insurance**
Insurance, Social
  USE **Social security**
Insurance, Unemployment
  USE **Unemployment insurance**
Insurance, Workers' compensation
  USE **Workers' compensation**
Insurgency (May subdiv. geog.)   **322.4; 355.02**
  UF Rebellions
  BT **Revolutions**
  NT **Counterinsurgency**
    Guerrilla warfare

Insurgency—*Continued*
> **Subversive activities**
> **Terrorism**
> RT **Internal security**
> **Resistance to government**

Integrated churches
> USE **Church and race relations**

Integrated curriculum
> USE **Interdisciplinary approach in education**

Integrated language arts (Holistic)
> USE **Whole language**

Integrated schools
> USE **School integration**

Integration in education
> USE **School integration**
> **Segregation in education**

Integration, Racial
> USE **Race relations**

Intellect   153.4
> UF Intelligence
> Mind
> Understanding
> BT **Psychology**
> NT **Cognitive styles**
> **Creation (Literary, artistic, etc.)**
> **Imagination**
> **Logic**
> **Memory**
> **Perception**
> **Reason**
> **Senses and sensation**
> RT **Reasoning**
> **Theory of knowledge**
> **Thought and thinking**

Intellectual cooperation (May subdiv. geog.)   **327.1; 370.116**
> UF Cooperation, Intellectual
> BT **International cooperation**
> NT **Conferences**
> **Cultural relations**
> RT **International education**

Intellectual freedom (May subdiv. geog.)   **323.44**
> BT **Freedom**
> NT **Academic freedom**
> **Censorship**
> **Freedom of information**
> **Freedom of speech**
> **Freedom of the press**

Intellectual life   001.1
> Use for general materials on learning and scholarship, literature, the arts, etc. Materials on literature, art, music, motion pictures, etc. produced for a mass audience are entered under **Popular culture**.
> UF Cultural life
> SA classes of persons, ethnic groups, and names of countries, cities, etc., with the subdivision *Intellectual life* [to be added as needed]
> BT **Culture**
> NT **African Americans—Intellectual life**
> **Blacks—Intellectual life**
> **Chicago (Ill.)—Intellectual life**
> **Cultural policy**
> **Learning and scholarship**
> **Ohio—Intellectual life**
> **Popular culture**
> **United States—Intellectual life**

Intellectual life—Government policy
> USE **Cultural policy**

Intellectual property (May subdiv. geog.)   **346.04**
> UF Literary property
> Proprietary rights
> Rights, Proprietary
> BT **Property**
> RT **Copyright**
> **Patents**

Intellectuals (May subdiv. geog.)   **305.5**
> UF Intelligentsia
> SA ethnic groups, classes of persons, and names of countries, cities, etc., with the subdivision *Intellectual life*, e.g. **African Americans—Intellectual life**; **United States—Intellectual life**; etc. [to be added as needed]
> BT **Persons**
> **Social classes**

Intelligence
> USE **Intellect**

Intelligence agents
> USE **Spies**

Intelligence of animals
> USE **Animal intelligence**

Intelligence service (May subdiv. geog.)
    327.12; 355.3

Use for materials on a government agency that is engaged in obtaining information, usually about an enemy but sometimes about an ally or a neutral country, and also in blocking the attempts by foreign agents to obtain information about one's own national secrets.

  UF Counterespionage
        Counterintelligence
  BT **Public administration**
        Research
  NT **Espionage**
        Military intelligence
  RT **Secret service**

Intelligence service—United States
    327.1273; 355.3

  UF United States—Intelligence service

Intelligence testing
  USE **Intelligence tests**

Intelligence tests (May subdiv. geog.)
    153.9

  UF Intelligence testing
        IQ tests
        Mental tests
  BT **Child psychology**
        Educational psychology
  NT **Ability—Testing**
  RT **Educational tests and measurements**

Intelligentsia
  USE **Intellectuals**

Intemperance
  USE **Alcoholism**
        Temperance

Inter-American relations
  USE **Pan-Americanism**

Interactive CD technology
  USE **CD-I technology**

Interactive media
  USE **Multimedia**

Interactive multimedia
  USE **Multimedia**
        and subjects with the subdivision *Interactive multimedia,* e.g. **Geology—Interactive multimedia** [to be added as needed]

Interbehaviorial psychology
  USE **Behaviorism**

Interchange of visitors
  USE **Exchange of persons programs**

Interchurch cooperation
  USE **Interdenominational cooperation**

Intercollegiate athletics
  USE **College sports**

Intercommunication systems   **621.38; 651.7**

  UF Interoffice communication systems
  BT **Electronic apparatus and appliances**
        Telecommunication
  NT **Closed-circuit television**
        Microwave communication systems

Intercontinental ballistic missiles (May subdiv. geog.) **623.4**

  UF ICBM
  SA names of specific ICBM missiles, e.g. **Atlas (Missile)** [to be added as needed]
  BT **Ballistic missiles**
  NT **Atlas (Missile)**

Intercountry adoption
  USE **International adoption**

Intercultural education
  USE **Multicultural education**

Intercultural relations
  USE **Cultural relations**

Intercultural studies
  USE **Cross-cultural studies**

Interdenominational cooperation (May subdiv. geog.) **280**

Use for materials on religious activities planned and conducted cooperatively by two or more Christian sects. Materials on unity as one of the marks of the church are entered under **Church—Unity**. Materials on prospective and actual mergers within and across denominational lines are entered under **Christian union**. Materials on a movement originating in the twentieth century aimed at promoting church cooperation and unity are entered under **Ecumenical movement**.

  UF Christian unity
        Cooperation, Interchurch
        Cooperation, Interdenominational
        Interchurch cooperation
  BT **Christian sects**
        Church work

Interdisciplinarity in education
  USE **Interdisciplinary approach in education**

Interdisciplinary approach in education
(May subdiv. geog.)   **375**
UF   Integrated curriculum
Interdisciplinarity in education
Interdisciplinary studies
BT   **Curriculum planning**
Interdisciplinary studies
USE   **Interdisciplinary approach in education**
Interest centers approach to teaching
USE   **Open plan schools**
Interest (Economics) (May subdiv. geog.)
332.8
BT   **Banks and banking**
Business mathematics
Capital
Finance
Loans
Interest groups
USE   **Lobbying**
Political action committees
Interfaces, Computer
USE   **Computer interfaces**
Interfaith marriage (May subdiv. geog.)
201; 261.8; 306.84
UF   Mixed marriage
BT   **Intermarriage**
Interfaith relations (May subdiv. geog.)
201; 261.2
BT   **Cultural relations**
Interfaith worship (May subdiv. geog.)
291.172
BT   **Worship**
Intergovernmental tax relations (May subdiv. geog.)   **336.2**
UF   Federal-state tax relations
State-local tax relations
Tax relations, Intergovernmental
Tax sharing
BT   **Taxation**
NT   **Revenue sharing**
Interior decoration
USE   **Interior design**
Interior design (May subdiv. geog.)
729; 747

Use for materials on the art and techniques of planning and supervising the design and execution of architectural interiors and their furnishings.

UF   Home decoration
House decoration
House furnishing

Interior decoration
BT   **Art**
Decoration and ornament
Design
Home economics
NT   **Bedspreads**
Draperies
Furniture
Lighting
Mural painting and decoration
Paperhanging
Quilts
Rugs and carpets
Tapestry
Upholstery
Wallpaper
RT   **Rooms**
Interlibrary loans (May subdiv. geog.)
025.6
BT   **Library circulation**
Library cooperation
Interlocking signals
USE   **Railroads—Signaling**
Intermarriage (May subdiv. geog.)
306.84

Use for materials that discuss collectively marriage between persons of different religions, religious denominations, races, or ethnic groups.

UF   Mixed marriage
BT   **Marriage**
NT   **Interfaith marriage**
Interracial marriage
Intermediate schools
USE   **Middle schools**
Intermediate state
USE   **Eschatology**
Future life
Interment
USE   **Burial**
Internal combustion engines   **621.43**
UF   Gas and oil engines
Gas engines
Gasoline engines
Oil engines
Petroleum engines
BT   **Engines**
NT   **Carburetors**
Diesel engines

Internal migration (May subdiv. geog.)
    304.8

Use for materials on the movement of population within a country for permanent settlement. Materials on casual or seasonal workers who move from place to place in search of employment are entered under **Migrant labor**. Materials on migration from one country to another are entered under **Immigration and emigration**.

    UF   Migration, Internal
          Rural-urban migration
          Urban-rural migration
    BT   **Colonization**
          Population
    NT   **Cities and towns—Growth**
          Forced migration
    RT   **Immigration and emigration**
          Land settlement
          Migrant labor

Internal revenue   **336.2**
    BT   **Taxation**
    NT   **Income tax**
          Inheritance and transfer tax

Internal revenue law (May subdiv. geog.)
    343.04
    BT   **Law**

Internal security (May subdiv. geog.)
    353.3; 363.2
    UF   Loyalty oaths
          Security, Internal
    RT   **Insurgency**
          Subversive activities

Internal security—United States   **353.3; 363.2**
    UF   United States—Internal security

International adoption (May subdiv. geog.)   **362.734**
    UF   Intercountry adoption
    BT   **Adoption**
    RT   **Interracial adoption**

International agencies (May subdiv. geog.)   **060**
    UF   Associations, International
          International associations
          International organizations
    SA   names of individual agencies [to be added as needed]
    BT   **International cooperation**

International arbitration (May subdiv. geog.)   **327.1**
    UF   Arbitration, International
          International mediation

          Mediation, International
    BT   **International cooperation**
          International law
          International relations
          International security
          Treaties
    NT   **League of Nations**
          United Nations
    RT   **Arms control**
          Peace

International associations
    USE   **International agencies**

International business enterprises
    USE   **Multinational corporations**

International competition   **337; 382; 658**
    UF   Competition, International
          World economics
    BT   **International relations**
          International trade
    RT   **War—Economic aspects**

International conferences
    USE   **Conferences**

International cooperation   **327.1; 341.7**

Use for general materials on international cooperative activities, with or without the participation of governments.

    SA   subjects with the subdivision *International cooperation*, e.g. **Astronautics—International cooperation** [to be added as needed]
    BT   **Cooperation**
          International law
          International relations
    NT   **Astronautics—International cooperation**
          Conferences
          Cultural relations
          Exchange of persons programs
          Foreign aid
          Intellectual cooperation
          International agencies
          International arbitration
          International police
          League of Nations
          Space sciences—International cooperation
          United Nations
    RT   **International education**
          International organization
          Reconstruction (1914-1939)

International cooperation—*Continued*
      Reconstruction (1939-1951)
      Technology transfer
International copyright
  USE **Copyright**
International economic relations   382
  UF Economic relations, Foreign
      Foreign economic relations
  BT **Economic policy**
      International relations
  NT **Balance of payments**
      Commercial policy
      Foreign aid
      International trade
      Multinational corporations
      Sanctions (International law)
      Technical assistance
      United States—Foreign economic relations
International education (May subdiv. geog.)   **370.116**
  Use for materials on education for international understanding, world citizenship, etc.
  BT **Education**
  NT **Student exchange programs**
      Teacher exchange programs
  RT **Intellectual cooperation**
      International cooperation
      Multicultural education
International exchange
  USE **Foreign exchange**
International exchange of students
  USE **Student exchange programs**
International exhibitions
  USE **Exhibitions**
International investment
  USE **Foreign investments**
International language
  USE **Universal language**
International law (May subdiv. geog.)   **341**
  UF Law of nations
  BT **Law**
  NT **Asylum**
      Boundaries
      International arbitration
      International cooperation
      Intervention (International law)
      Mandates
      Marine salvage
      Maritime law
      Military law

      Naturalization
      Neutrality
      Pirates
      Political refugees
      Privateering
      Sanctions (International law)
      Slave trade
      Sovereignty
      Space law
      Treaties
      War crimes
  RT **International organization**
      International relations
      Natural law
      War
International mediation
  USE **International arbitration**
International organization   341.2
  Use for materials on plans leading towards political organization of nations.
  UF World government
      World organization
  SA names of specific organizations, e.g. **United Nations** [to be added as needed]
  BT **International relations**
      International security
  NT **European federation**
      International police
      League of Nations
      Mandates
      North Atlantic Treaty Organization
      United Nations
  RT **International cooperation**
      International law
      World politics
International organizations
  USE **International agencies**
International police (May subdiv. geog.)   **341.7**
  UF Interpol
      Police, International
  BT **International cooperation**
      International organization
      International relations
      International security
International politics
  USE **World politics**
International relations   327; 341.3
  Use for materials on the theory of international relations. Historical accounts are en-

International relations—*Continued*
tered under **World politics**; **Europe—Politics and government**; etc. Materials on the foreign relations of an individual country are entered under the name of the country with the subdivison *Foreign relations*. Materials limited to diplomatic relations between two countries are entered under the name of each country with the subdivision *Foreign relations* further subdivided by the name of the other country, e.g. **United States—Foreign relations—Iran** and also **Iran—Foreign relations—United States**.

UF   Foreign affairs
       Foreign policy
       Foreign relations
       Peaceful coexistence
       World order

SA   names of countries with the subdivision *Foreign relations*, e.g. **United States—Foreign relations** [to be added as needed]

NT   **Arms control**
       Balance of power
       Boundaries
       Catholic Church—Foreign relations
       Cultural relations
       Diplomacy
       Diplomatic and consular service
       Diplomats
       East and West
       Geopolitics
       Globalization
       International arbitration
       International competition
       International cooperation
       International economic relations
       International organization
       International police
       International security
       Isolationism
       Jihad
       Mandates
       Monroe Doctrine
       Nationalism
       Neutrality
       Peace
       Political refugees
       Treaties
       United States—Foreign relations

RT   **International law**
       National security
       Technology transfer
       World politics

International security   327.1; 341.7
UF   Collective security
       Security, International
BT   **International relations**
NT   **Arms control**
       Arms race
       International arbitration
       International organization
       International police
       Neutrality
RT   **Peace**

International space cooperation
USE   **Astronautics—International cooperation**

International Standard Bibliographic Description   025.3
UF   ISBD
BT   **Cataloging**

International Standard Book Numbers   070.5
UF   ISBN
BT   **Publishers' standard book numbers**

International Standard Serial Numbers   070.5
UF   ISSN
RT   **Serial publications**

International trade (May subdiv. geog.)   382

Use for general materials about trade among nations. Materials on foreign trade of specific countries, cities, etc., are entered under the name of the place with the subdivision *Commerce*. Materials limited to trade between two countries are entered under the name of each country with the subdivision *Commerce* further subdivided by the name of the other country, i.e. **United States—Commerce—Japan** and also **Japan—Commerce—United States**.

UF   Foreign commerce
       Foreign trade
       Trade, International
BT   **Commerce**
       International economic relations
NT   **Arms transfers**
       Balance of trade
       Exports
       Free trade

International trade—*Continued*
    Imports
    International competition
Internationalization
  USE **Globalization**
Internet 004.67
  UF Information superhighway
      Internet (Computer network)
  BT **Computer networks**
     Information networks
  NT **Internet addresses**
     Internet resources
     World Wide Web
Internet access providers
  USE **Internet service providers**
Internet addresses 004.67
  BT **Internet**
Internet addresses—Directories 025.04
  SA topics, names of places, catego-
      ries of persons, ethnic groups,
      etc., with the subdivisions
      Internet resources—Directo-
      ries, e.g. **Business—Internet**
      resources—Directories [to be
      added as needed]
Internet and children 004.678083
  UF Children and the Internet
  BT **Children**
Internet auctions 381.177
  UF Online auctions
  BT **Auctions**
     Electronic commerce
Internet chat groups
  USE **Online chat groups**
Internet commerce
  USE **Electronic commerce**
Internet companies
  USE **Internet industry**
Internet (Computer network)
  USE **Internet**
Internet—Computer software
  USE **Internet software**
Internet gambling (May subdiv. geog.)
    795
  UF Online gambling
  BT **Gambling**
Internet—Home shopping services
  USE **Internet marketing**
     Internet shopping
Internet in education (May subdiv. geog.)
    004.678071
  BT **Education**

Internet industry (May subdiv. geog.)
    004.67; 338.7
  UF Internet companies
  BT **Industries**
  NT **Internet service providers**
Internet journalism
  USE **Online journalism**
Internet marketing (May subdiv. geog.)
    658.8
  UF Internet—Home shopping ser-
      vices
     Online marketing
     Online selling
  BT **Electronic commerce**
     Marketing
  RT **Internet shopping**
Internet resources 004.67
  UF Computer network resources
  SA subjects with the subdivision
      Internet resources, for materi-
      als about information avail-
      able on the Internet on a sub-
      ject, e.g. **Business—Internet**
      resources; subjects with the
      subdivision *Information re-*
      sources, for general materials
      about information on a sub-
      ject, e.g. **Business—Informa-**
      tion resources; subjects with
      the subdivision *Databases,* for
      materials about data files on a
      subject regardless of the me-
      dium of distribution, e.g.
      Business—Databases; and
      headings for the providers or
      the users of information with
      the subdivision *Information*
      services, for materials about
      organizations that provide in-
      formation services, e.g. **Unit-**
      ed Nations—Information ser-
      vices; **Consumers—Informa-**
      tion services; etc. [to be add-
      ed as needed]
  BT **Information resources**
     Internet
  NT **Business—Internet resources**
     Web sites
Internet searching 004.67; 025.5
  UF Searching the Internet
     Web searching

Internet searching—*Continued*
World Wide Web searching
BT **Information retrieval**
NT **Web search engines**
Internet service providers (May subdiv. geog.) **004.67**
UF Internet access providers
BT **Internet industry**
Internet shopping (May subdiv. geog.) **381; 640**
UF Cybershopping
Internet—Home shopping services
Online shopping
Shopping—Computer network resources
Shopping—Internet resources
BT **Electronic commerce**
Shopping
RT **Internet marketing**
Internet software   005.7
UF Internet—Computer software
BT **Computer software**
Internment camps
USE **Concentration camps**
Internment of Japanese Americans, 1942-1945
USE **Japanese Americans—Evacuation and relocation, 1942-1945**
Internship programs (May subdiv. geog.) **331.25**
UF Internships
BT **Employees—Training**
Internships
USE **Internship programs**
Interoffice communication systems
USE **Intercommunication systems**
Interpersonal competence
USE **Social skills**
Interpersonal relations (May subdiv. geog.) **158; 302**
Use for materials on group behavior, social relations between persons, and problems arising from organizational and interpersonal relations.
UF Human relations
SA relations between particular groups of persons or individuals, e.g. **Jewish-Arab relations; Parent-child relation-**

ship; etc. [to be added as needed]
BT **Social psychology**
NT **Competition (Psychology)**
Conflict of generations
Discrimination
Domestic relations
Family
Group relations training
Helping behavior
Intimacy (Psychology)
Life skills
Man-woman relationship
Personal space
Prejudices
Social adjustment
Social skills
Teacher-student relationship
Teasing
Toleration
RT **Human behavior**
Interplanetary communication
USE **Interstellar communication**
Interplanetary visitors
USE **Extraterrestrial beings**
Interplanetary voyages   808.3; 808.83; 919.904
Use for general materials about travel to other planets and for individual works, collections, or materials about imaginary accounts of such travels. Materials on the physics and technical details of flight beyond the earth's atmosphere are entered under **Space flight**.
UF Interstellar travel
Space travel
BT **Astronautics**
Fiction
NT **Outer space—Exploration**
RT **Imaginary voyages**
Rockets (Aeronautics)
Science fiction
Space flight
Interplanetary warfare
USE **Space warfare**
Interpol
USE **International police**
Interpreting and translating
USE **Translating and interpreting**
Interpretive dance
USE **Modern dance**
Interracial adoption (May subdiv. geog.) **362.73**

Interracial adoption—*Continued*
>   BT   **Adoption**
>   **Race relations**
>   RT   **International adoption**

Interracial marriage (May subdiv. geog.)
>   **306.84**
>   UF   Marriage, Interracial
>   Racial intermarriage
>   BT   **Intermarriage**

Interracial relations
>   USE   **Race relations**

Interscholastic sports
>   USE   **School sports**

Interstate commerce   381
>   Use for materials limited to commerce between states. General materials on foreign and domestic commerce are entered under **Commerce**.
>   UF   Government regulation of commerce
>   BT   **Commerce**

Interstate highways
>   USE   **Express highways**

Interstellar communication   621.382
>   UF   Extraterrestrial communication
>   Interplanetary communication
>   Outer space—Communication
>   Space communication
>   Space telecommunication
>   BT   **Life on other planets**
>   **Telecommunication**
>   NT   **Astronautics—Communication systems**
>   **Radio astronomy**

Interstellar travel
>   USE   **Interplanetary voyages**

Interstellar warfare
>   USE   **Space warfare**

Interurban railroads
>   USE   **Electric railroads**
>   **Street railroads**

Intervention (International law)   341.5
>   UF   Military intervention
>   BT   **International law**
>   **War**
>   NT   **Monroe Doctrine**
>   RT   **Neutrality**

Interviewing   158
>   BT   **Social psychology**
>   NT   **Interviewing in journalism**
>   **Job interviews**
>   **Talk shows**

>   RT   **Applied psychology**
>   **Counseling**
>   **Interviews**

Interviewing for employment
>   USE   **Job interviews**

Interviewing in journalism   070.4
>   UF   Interviews (Journalism) [*Former heading*]
>   BT   **Interviewing**
>   **Journalism**

Interviews   920; 808
>   Use for materials about interviews as a literary form and for collections of diverse interviews.
>   SA   subjects, ethnic groups, classes of persons, and names of corporate bodies and individual persons with the subdivision *Interviews*, e.g. **Authors—Interviews** [to be added as needed]
>   BT   **Conversation**
>   NT   **Authors—Interviews**
>   RT   **Interviewing**

Interviews (Journalism)
>   USE   **Interviewing in journalism**

Interviews, Parent-teacher
>   USE   **Parent-teacher conferences**

Intestacy
>   USE   **Inheritance and succession**

Intifada, 1987-1992   956.940
>   UF   Arab-Israeli conflict, 1987-1992
>   Israeli-Arab conflict, 1987-1992
>   Palestinian-Israeli conflict, 1987-1992
>   Palestinian uprising, 1987-1992
>   BT   **Israel-Arab conflicts**

Intifada, 2000-   956.940
>   UF   Arab-Israeli conflict, 2000-
>   Israeli-Arab conflict, 2000-
>   Palestinian-Israeli conflict, 2000-
>   Palestinian uprising, 2000-
>   BT   **Israel-Arab conflicts**

Intimacy (Psychology)   158.2
>   BT   **Emotions**
>   **Interpersonal relations**
>   **Love**
>   **Psychology**

Intolerance
>   USE   **Fanaticism**
>   **Toleration**

Intoxicants
    USE   **Alcohol**
           Alcoholic beverages
           Liquors
Intoxication
    USE   **Alcoholism**
           Temperance
Intranets   **004.6; 651.7**
    BT   **Business enterprises—Computer networks**
Intuition   **153.4**
    BT   **Philosophy**
           Psychology
           Rationalism
           Theory of knowledge
    RT   **Perception**
Inuit (May subdiv. geog.)   **970.004**
    Use for materials on the native peoples of the arctic regions of Alaska, Canada, and Greenland. If local usage dictates, libraries may establish Eskimos as a broader term than Inuit; and the names of other groups of Arctic peoples may be added as needed.
    UF   Eskimos
           Esquimaux
           Innuit
    BT   **Indigenous peoples**
    NT   **Igloos**
Inuit—Folklore (May subdiv. geog.)   **398**
    BT   **Folklore**
Invalid cooking
    USE   **Cooking for the sick**
           Diet therapy
Invalids (May subdiv. geog.)   **305.908**
    BT   **Sick**
Invasion of Cuba, 1961
    USE   **Cuba—History—1961, Invasion**
Invasion of privacy
    USE   **Right of privacy**
Invective   **808.88**
    UF   Abuse, Verbal
           Insults
           Verbal abuse
    BT   **Satire**
Inventions (May subdiv. geog.)   **608**
    Use for materials on original devices or processes. Materials on technological improvements in materials, production methods, processes, organization, or management are entered under **Technological innovations**.
    BT   **Technology**
    NT   **Creation (Literary, artistic, etc.)**
           Technological innovations

           Technology transfer
    RT   **Industrial research**
           Inventors
           Patents
Inventors (May subdiv. geog.)   **609.2; 920**
    NT   **African American inventors**
    RT   **Engineers**
           Inventions
Inventory control   **658.7**
    UF   Stock control
    BT   **Management**
           Retail trade
Invertebrates (May subdiv. geog.)   **592**
    BT   **Animals**
Investment and saving
    USE   **Saving and investment**
Investment brokers
    USE   **Stockbrokers**
Investment companies
    USE   **Mutual funds**
Investment in real estate
    USE   **Real estate investment**
Investment trusts
    USE   **Mutual funds**
Investments (May subdiv. geog.)   **332.6**
    BT   **Banks and banking**
           Capital
           Finance
    NT   **Annuities**
           Bonds
           Foreign investments
           Futures
           Mutual funds
           Real estate investment
           Savings and loan associations
           Securities
    RT   **Estate planning**
           Loans
           Saving and investment
           Speculation
           Stock exchanges
           Stocks
Investments, Foreign
    USE   **Foreign investments**
Invincible Armada
    USE   **Spanish Armada, 1588**
Invisible world
    USE   **Spirits**
IQ tests
    USE   **Intelligence tests**

Iran   935; 955

> May be subdivided like United States except for History.

UF   Persia

Iran—Foreign relations—United States   327.55073

NT   **Iran hostage crisis, 1979-1981**

Iran—History—1941-1979   955.05

Iran—History—1979-   955.05

Iran hostage crisis, 1979-1981   327.55073; 327.73055; 955

BT   **American hostages—Iran**
     Iran—Foreign relations—United States
     United States—Foreign relations—Iran

Iraq   956.7

> May be subdivided like United States except for History.

Iraq—History—2003-, Anglo-American invasion

USE   **Iraq War, 2003-**

Iraq War, 2003-   956.7044

UF   Iraq—History—2003-, Anglo-American invasion

IRAs (Pensions)

USE   **Individual retirement accounts**

Ireland   941.5

> May be subdivided like United States except for History.

Irish literature   820

BT   **Literature**

Iron   669; 672

BT   **Chemical elements**
     Metals

NT   **Iron in the body**
     Iron ores
     Ironwork
     Steel

Iron Age (May subdiv. geog.)   **930.1**

BT   **Civilization**

Iron and steel building

USE   **Steel construction**

Iron in the body   612.3; 613.2

BT   **Iron**
     Minerals in the body

Iron industry (May subdiv. geog.)   **338.2**

UF   Iron industry and trade

BT   **Industries**

NT   **Hardware**

RT   **Steel industry**

Iron industry and trade

USE   **Iron industry**

Iron ores (May subdiv. geog.)   **553.3**

BT   **Iron**
     Ores

Ironing

USE   **Laundry**

Ironwork (May subdiv. geog.)   **672; 682; 739.4**

UF   **Wrought iron work**

BT   **Decoration and ornament**
     Iron
     Metalwork

NT   **Blacksmithing**
     Welding

RT   **Forging**

Irreversible coma

USE   **Brain death**

Irrigation (May subdiv. geog.)   **333.91; 627; 631.5**

BT   **Agricultural engineering**
     Hydraulic engineering
     Water resources development
     Water supply

RT   **Reclamation of land**

Irrigation—United States   333.91; 627; 631.5

ISBD

USE   **International Standard Bibliographic Description**

ISBN

USE   **International Standard Book Numbers**

Islam (May subdiv. geog.)   **297**

> Use for materials on the religion. Materials on the believers in this religion are entered under **Muslims.**

BT   **Religions**

NT   **Islam—Relations—Judaism**
     Islamic fundamentalism
     Islamic sects
     Jihad
     Judaism—Relations—Islam
     Koran
     Mysticism—Islam

RT   **Islamic law**
     Muslims

Islam and politics (May subdiv. geog.)   **320.5**

UF   Islam—Political aspects
     Politics and Islam

BT   **Political science**

Islam—Poetry
USE **Islamic poetry**
Islam—Political aspects
USE **Islam and politics**
Islam—Relations—Judaism 297

Use for materials on the relations between Islam and Judaism. When assigning this heading, provide an additional subject entry under **Judaism—Relations—Islam**. Materials on the conflicts between the Arab countries and Israel are entered under **Israel-Arab conflicts**. Materials that discuss collectively the relations between Arabs and Jews, including religious, ethnic, and ideological relations, are entered under **Jewish-Arab relations**.

UF   Islamic-Jewish relations
Jewish-Islamic relations
BT   **Islam**
Judaism
RT   **Jewish-Arab relations**
Islam—Sermons
USE   **Islamic sermons**
Islamic architecture (May subdiv. geog.)
720.917
UF   Architecture, Islamic
Moorish architecture
Muslim architecture
BT   **Architecture**
NT   **Mosques**
Islamic art (May subdiv. geog.)   **709.1**
UF   Art, Islamic
Muslim art
BT   **Art**
Islamic civilization   909
UF   Muslim civilization
BT   **Civilization**
Islamic countries   956
UF   Muslim countries
NT   **Arab countries**
Islamic fundamentalism (May subdiv. geog.)   **297.09; 320.557; 322.1**
UF   Fundamentalism
BT   **Islam**
Religious fundamentalism
Islamic gardens (May subdiv. geog.)
635.9; 712
BT   **Gardens**
Islamic holidays (May subdiv. geog.)
297.3
UF   Fasts and feasts—Islam
BT   **Religious holidays**
NT   **Ramadan**
Islamic holy war
USE   **Jihad**

Islamic-Jewish relations
USE   **Islam—Relations—Judaism**
Judaism—Relations—Islam
Islamic law (May subdiv. geog.)   **340.5**
UF   Muslim law
BT   **Law**
RT   **Islam**
Islamic literature   297
UF   Muslim literature
BT   **Religious literature**
NT   **Islamic poetry**
Islamic sermons
Islamic music (May subdiv. geog.)
780.89
BT   **Music**
Islamic mysticism
USE   **Mysticism—Islam**
Islamic poetry   808.81
UF   Islam—Poetry
BT   **Islamic literature**
Poetry
Islamic science
USE   **Science—Islamic countries**
Islamic sects (May subdiv. geog.)   **297.8**
BT   **Islam**
Sects
NT   **Shiites**
Sunnis
Islamic sermons   297
UF   Islam—Sermons
Muslim sermons
SA   individual Islamic sects with the subdivision *Sermons* [to be added as needed]
BT   **Islamic literature**
Sermons
Islamic women
USE   **Muslim women**
Island ecology (May subdiv. geog.)
577.5
BT   **Ecology**
Islands (May subdiv. geog.)   **551.42**
SA   names of islands and groups of islands [to be added as needed]
NT   **Coral reefs and islands**
Cuba
Islands of the Pacific
Islands of the Pacific   990

Use for comprehensive materials on all the islands of the Pacific Ocean. Materials re-

Islands of the Pacific—*Continued*
stricted to comprehensive treatment of the island groups of Melanesia, Micronesia, and Polynesia are entered under **Oceania**.

UF   Pacific Islands
     Pacific Ocean Islands

BT   **Islands**

NT   **Oceania**

RT   **Pacific rim**

Isolationism (May subdiv. geog.)   **327.1**

BT   **International relations**

RT   **Neutrality**

Isotopes   **539.7; 541**

BT   **Atoms**

NT   **Radioisotopes**

Israel   **956.94**

May be subdivided like United States except for History.

BT   **Middle East**

Israel-Arab conflicts   **956.05; 965.04**

Use for materials on the conflicts between the Arab countries and Israel. Materials that discuss collectively the relations between Arabs and Jews, including religious, ethnic, and ideological relations, are entered under **Jewish-Arab relations**. Materials on relations between the religions of Judaism and Islam are entered under **Judaism—Relations—Islam** and under **Islam—Relations—Judaism**.

UF   Arab-Israel conflicts
     Arab-Israeli conflicts
     Israeli-Arab conflicts

BT   **Arab countries—Foreign relations—Israel**
     Israel—Foreign relations—Arab countries

NT   **Intifada, 1987-1992**
     Intifada, 2000-
     Israel-Arab War, 1948-1949
     Israel-Arab War, 1967
     Israel-Arab War, 1973
     Sinai Campaign, 1956

RT   **Jewish-Arab relations**

Israel-Arab relations
USE   **Arab countries—Foreign relations—Israel**
      Israel—Foreign relations—Arab countries

Israel-Arab War, 1948-1949   **956.04**

UF   Arab-Israel War, 1948-1949

BT   **Israel-Arab conflicts**

Israel-Arab War, 1956
USE   **Sinai Campaign, 1956**

Israel-Arab War, 1967   **956.04**

UF   Arab-Israel War, 1967
     Six Day War, 1967

BT   **Israel-Arab conflicts**

Israel-Arab War, 1973   **956.04**

UF   Arab-Israel War, 1973
     Yom Kippur War, 1973

BT   **Israel-Arab conflicts**

Israel—Collective settlements
USE   **Collective settlements—Israel**

Israel—Foreign relations—Arab countries   **956**

UF   Arab-Israel relations
     Arab-Israeli relations
     Israel-Arab relations
     Israeli-Arab relations

NT   **Israel-Arab conflicts**

RT   **Arab countries—Foreign relations—Israel**
     Jewish-Arab relations

Israel, Ten lost tribes of
USE   **Lost tribes of Israel**

Israeli-Arab conflict, 1987-1992
USE   **Intifada, 1987-1992**

Israeli-Arab conflict, 2000-
USE   **Intifada, 2000-**

Israeli-Arab conflicts
USE   **Israel-Arab conflicts**

Israeli-Arab relations
USE   **Arab countries—Foreign relations—Israel**
      Israel—Foreign relations—Arab countries

Israelis (May subdiv. geog.)   **305.892; 920; 956.94**

BT   **Jews**

Israelites
USE   **Jews**

ISSN
USE   **International Standard Serial Numbers**

Italo-Ethiopian War, 1935-1936   **963**

UF   Ethiopian-Italian War, 1935-1936

Italy   **945**

May be subdivided like United States except for History.

Italy—Antiquities   **937**

BT   **Antiquities**

NT   **Herculaneum (Extinct city)**
     Pompeii (Extinct city)

Italy—History   **945**

Italy—History—0-1559   **945**

Italy—History—1559-1789   **945**

Italy—History—1789-1815   945
Italy—History—1815-1914   945; 945.09
Italy—History—1914-1945   945.091
Italy—History—1945-1976   945.092
Italy—History—1976-   945.092
Ivory (May subdiv. geog.)   **679**
  BT   **Animal products**
Ivory Coast
  USE   **Côte d'Ivoire**
Jack the Ripper murders, London, England, 1888   362.152
  UF   Whitechapel murders, 1888
  BT   **Serial killers**
Jails
  USE   **Prisons**
Jainism (May subdiv. geog.)   **294.4**
  BT   **Religions**
Japan   952
  May be subdivided like United States except for History.
  RT   **Japanese**
Japan—Commerce—United States   382
Japan—History   952
Japan—History—0-1868   952
  NT   **Ninja**
    Samurai
Japan—History—1868-1945   952.03
Japan—History—1945-1952, Allied occupation   952.04
Japan—History—1952-   952.04
Japanese (May subdiv. geog.)   **952; 920**
  NT   **Japanese Americans**
  RT   **Japan**
Japanese aesthetics   111; 701; 801
  UF   Aesthetics, Japanese
  BT   **Aesthetics**
Japanese Americans (May subdiv. geog.)
    973.04956
  UF   Nisei
  BT   **Americans**
    Japanese
Japanese Americans—Evacuation and relocation, 1942-1945 (May subdiv. geog.)   **940.5317**
  UF   Evacuation and relocation of Japanese Americans, 1942-1945
    Internment of Japanese Americans, 1942-1945
    Relocation of Japanese Americans, 1942-1945

  BT   **World War, 1939-1945—Evacuation of civilians**
Japanese color prints   769.952
  UF   Color prints, Japanese
  BT   **Color prints**
Japanese language   495.6
  May be subdivided like **English language**.
  BT   **Language and languages**
Japanese language—Business Japanese   495.6
  Business Japanese is a unique subdivision for Japanese language.
  UF   Business Japanese
Japanese paper folding
  USE   **Origami**
Jargon
  USE   subjects and names of languages with the subdivision *Jargon*, e.g. **English language—Jargon** [to be added as needed]
Jason (Legendary character)   398.22
  BT   **Legendary characters**
Jazz ensembles (May subdiv. geog.)
    784.4
  BT   **Ensembles (Music)**
Jazz music (May subdiv. geog.)   **781.65; 782.42165**
  BT   **Music**
  RT   **Blues music**
Jealousy   152.4
  BT   **Emotions**
Jestbooks
  USE   **Chapbooks**
Jesters
  USE   **Fools and jesters**
Jesus Christ   232
  UF   Christ
    Christology
  BT   **God—Christianity**
  RT   **Christianity**
Jesus Christ—Art   704.9
  UF   Jesus Christ—Iconography
    Jesus Christ in art
  BT   **Christian art**
Jesus Christ—Birth
  USE   **Jesus Christ—Nativity**
Jesus Christ—Crucifixion   232.96
  UF   Crucifixion of Jesus Christ
  RT   **Good Friday**
Jesus Christ—Divinity   232
  UF   Divinity of Jesus Christ
  RT   **Trinity**

Jesus Christ—Drama   808.82

Use for collections of plays about Jesus Christ.

BT   **Religious drama**

Jesus Christ—Historicity   232.9

Jesus Christ—Iconography

USE   **Jesus Christ—Art**

Jesus Christ—Messiahship   232

Jesus Christ—Nativity   232.92

UF   Jesus Christ—Birth

Nativity of Jesus Christ

RT   **Christmas**

Jesus Christ—Parables   226.8; 232.9

BT   **Parables**

Jesus Christ—Passion   232.96

UF   Passion of Christ

Jesus Christ—Prayers   232.9

Jesus Christ—Prophecies   232

Jesus Christ—Resurrection   232.9

UF   Resurrection of Jesus Christ

Jesus Christ—Teachings   232.9

UF   Teachings of Jesus Christ

Jesus Christ in art

USE   **Jesus Christ—Art**

Jet airplanes

USE   **Jet planes**

Jet lag   616.9

BT   **Aviation medicine**

Biological rhythms

Fatigue

Jet planes (May subdiv. geog.)   629.133

UF   Jet airplanes

Jets (Airplanes)

BT   **Airplanes**

NT   **Supersonic transport planes**

Jet propulsion   621.43

BT   **Airplane engines**

RT   **Rockets (Aeronautics)**

Jets (Airplanes)

USE   **Jet planes**

Jewelry (May subdiv. geog.)   **391.7; 739.27**

Use for general materials on jewelry and for materials on gems in which the emphasis is on the setting. Materials on cut and polished precious stones treated from the point of view of art or antiquity are entered under **Gems**. Materials on gem stones treated from the mineralogical or technological point of view are entered under **Precious stones**.

UF   Jewels

SA   styles of jewelry and types of jewelry items [to be added as needed]

BT   **Clothing and dress**

Costume

Decorative arts

RT   **Beads**

Gems

Jewels

USE   **Gems**

Jewelry

Precious stones

Jewish-Arab relations   956

Use for materials that discuss collectively the relations between Arabs and Jews, including religious, ethnic, and ideological relations. Materials on the conflicts between the Arab countries and Israel are entered under **Israel-Arab conflicts**. Materials on relations between the religions of Judaism and Islam are entered under **Judaism—Relations—Islam**; and **Islam—Relations—Judaism**.

UF   Arab-Jewish relations

BT   **Arabs**

Jews

RT   **Arab countries—Foreign relations—Israel**

Islam—Relations—Judaism

Israel-Arab conflicts

Israel—Foreign relations—Arab countries

Judaism—Relations—Islam

Palestinian Arabs

Jewish children in the Holocaust (May subdiv. geog.)   **940.53**

BT   **Holocaust, 1939-1945**

NT   **Hidden children (Holocaust)**

Jewish-Christian relations

USE   **Christianity—Relations—Judaism**

Judaism—Relations—Christianity

Jewish civilization   909

UF   Jews—Civilization

BT   **Civilization**

Jewish customs

USE   **Jews—Social life and customs**

Judaism—Customs and practices

Jewish diaspora   909

UF   Diaspora, Jewish

Jews—Diaspora

SA   the heading **Jews** subdivided geographically, e.g. **Jews—France** [to be added as needed]

Jewish diaspora—*Continued*
   BT   **Human geography**
       Jews
Jewish doctrines
   USE   **Judaism—Doctrines**
Jewish ethics   **296.3**
   BT   **Ethics**
Jewish folk literature   **398.2**
   BT   **Folk literature**
       Jewish literature
Jewish folklore
   USE   **Jews—Folklore**
Jewish holidays (May subdiv. geog.)
       296.4; 394.267
   UF   Fasts and feasts—Judaism
       Holidays, Jewish
       Jews—Festivals
   SA   names of individual holidays,
       e.g. **Hanukkah** [to be added
       as needed]
   BT   **Judaism**
       Religious holidays
   NT   **Hanukkah**
       Passover
       Yom Kippur
Jewish Holocaust (1933-1945)
   USE   **Holocaust, 1939-1945**
Jewish Islamic relations
   USE   **Islam—Relations—Judaism**
       Judaism—Relations—Islam
Jewish language
   USE   **Hebrew language**
       Yiddish language
Jewish legends   **296.1; 398.2**
   Use for individual works, collections, or
   materials about Jewish legends.
   UF   Jews—Legends
       Legends, Jewish
   BT   **Legends**
Jewish life
   USE   **Jews—Social life and customs**
       Judaism—Customs and prac-
       tices
Jewish literature (May subdiv. geog.)
       296; 808.8
   UF   Jews—Literature
   BT   **Literature**
       Religious literature
   NT   **Bible**
       Cabala
       Jewish folk literature
       Jewish religious fiction

       Talmud
       Yiddish literature
   RT   **Hebrew literature**
Jewish liturgies
   USE   **Judaism—Liturgy**
Jewish men (May subdiv. geog.)   **305.38;**
       305.892
   BT   **Men**
Jewish religion
   USE   **Judaism**
Jewish religious fiction   **808.3; 808.83**
   Use for individual works, collections, or
   materials about fiction that promotes Jewish
   teachings or exemplifies a Jewish religious
   way of life.
   BT   **Fiction**
       Jewish literature
       Religious fiction
Jewish theology
   USE   **Judaism—Doctrines**
Jewish wit and humor   **808.87**
   BT   **Wit and humor**
Jewish women (May subdiv. geog.)
       305.48; 305.892
   BT   **Women**
Jews (May subdiv. geog.)   **305.892; 909;**
       296.092
   UF   Hebrews
       Israelites
   NT   **Essenes**
       Israelis
       Jewish-Arab relations
       Jewish diaspora
       Lost tribes of Israel
       World War, 1939-1945—Jews
   RT   **Judaism**
Jews—Antiquities   **933**
   BT   **Antiquities**
Jews—Civilization
   USE   **Jewish civilization**
Jews—Customs
   USE   **Jews—Social life and customs**
       Judaism—Customs and prac-
       tices
Jews—Diaspora
   USE   **Jewish diaspora**
Jews—Economic conditions (May subdiv.
   geog.)   **305.892; 330.9**
   BT   **Economic conditions**
Jews—Encyclopedias   **909**
   BT   **Encyclopedias and dictionaries**

Jews—Festivals
USE **Jewish holidays**
Jews—Folklore (May subdiv. geog.)   **398**
UF   Jewish folklore
BT   **Folklore**
Jews—France   305.892; 944
Jews—Language
USE   **Hebrew language**
Yiddish language
Jews—Legends
USE   **Jewish legends**
Jews—Literature
USE   **Hebrew literature**
Jewish literature
Jews—Lost tribes
USE   **Lost tribes of Israel**
Jews—Persecutions (May subdiv. geog.)
909; 933
BT   **Antisemitism**
Persecution
NT   **Holocaust, 1939-1945**
Kristallnacht, 1938
World War, 1939-1945—
Jews—Rescue
Jews—Political activity (May subdiv.
geog.)   **909; 956.94**
BT   **Political participation**
Jews—Religion
USE   **Judaism**
Jews—Restoration   956.94
Use for materials on the belief that the
Jews, in fulfillment of Biblical prophecy,
would some day return to Palestine.
RT   **Zionism**
Jews—Rites and ceremonies
USE   **Judaism—Customs and prac-**
tices
Jews—Ritual
USE   **Judaism—Customs and prac-**
tices
Judaism—Liturgy
Jews—Social conditions (May subdiv.
geog.)   **305.892; 909**
BT   **Social conditions**
Jews—Social life and customs (May
subdiv. geog.)   **305.892**
Use for materials on Jewish social customs.
General materials on Jewish religious prac-
tices are entered under **Judaism—Customs
and practices**. Materials on the forms of pub-
lic worship in Judaism are entered under **Ju-
daism—Liturgy**.
UF   Jewish customs
Jewish life

Jews—Customs
BT   **Manners and customs**
Jigsaw puzzles   793.73
BT   **Puzzles**
Jihad (May subdiv. geog.)   **297.7**
UF   Holy war (Islam)
Islamic holy war
Muslim holy war
BT   **International relations**
Islam
Jiu-jitsu (May subdiv. geog.)   **796.815**
UF   Jujitsu
BT   **Martial arts**
Self-defense
Job analysis (May subdiv. geog.)   **658.3**
UF   Personnel classification
BT   **Factory management**
Industrial efficiency
Management
Occupations
Personnel management
Salaries, wages, etc.
NT   **Motion study**
Time study
Job applications
USE   **Applications for positions**
Job discrimination
USE   **Discrimination in employment**
Job hunting   650.14
UF   Job searching
SA   fields of knowledge, professions,
industries, and trades with the
subdivision *Vocational guid-
ance* [to be added as needed]
BT   **Employment agencies**
Vocational guidance
NT   **Applications for positions**
Résumés (Employment)
Job interviews   650.14
UF   Employment interviewing
Interviewing for employment
BT   **Applications for positions**
Interviewing
Job performance standards
USE   **Performance standards**
Job placement guidance
USE   **Vocational guidance**
Job résumés
USE   **Résumés (Employment)**
Job retraining
USE   **Occupational retraining**

Job satisfaction (May subdiv. geog.)
  650.1; 658.3
  UF Work satisfaction
  BT **Attitude (Psychology)**
      Employee morale
      Personnel management
      Work
  NT **Burn out (Psychology)**
Job searching
  USE **Job hunting**
Job security **331.25; 650.1; 658.3**
  UF Employment security
  BT **Personnel management**
  NT **Employees—Dismissal**
Job sharing (May subdiv. geog.) **331.2;
  658.3**
  UF Sharing of jobs
  BT **Part-time employment**
Job stress (May subdiv. geog.) **158.7;
  658.3**
  UF Occupational stress
      Organizational stress
      Work stress
  BT **Stress (Physiology)**
      Stress (Psychology)
  NT **Burn out (Psychology)**
Job training
  USE **Occupational training**
Jobless people
  USE **Unemployed**
Joblessness
  USE **Unemployment**
Jobs
  USE **Occupations**
      Professions
Jogging (May subdiv. geog.) **613.7**
  BT **Running**
Joint custody of children
  USE **Child custody**
      Part-time parenting
Joint ventures (May subdiv. geog.)
  338.7
  BT **Business enterprises**
      Partnership
Joke books
  USE **Jokes**
Jokes **808.7; 808.88**
  Use for collections of jokes and for materials about jokes.
  UF Joke books
  BT **Wit and humor**
  NT **Practical jokes**

Jordan **956.95**
  May be subdivided like United States except for History.
Josei **741.5**
  Use for individual works, collections, or materials about manga for women ages 18-30.
  BT **Manga**
Journaling **808**
  BT **Authorship**
      Diaries
Journalism (May subdiv. geog.) **070.4**
  Use for materials on writing for the periodical press or on journalism as an occupation. Materials limited to the history, organization, and management of newspapers are entered under **Newspapers**.
  SA types of journalism, e.g. **Scientific journalism**; and topics with the subdivision *Press coverage*, e.g. **Food contamination—Press coverage** [to be added as needed]
  BT **Authorship**
      Literature
  NT **Broadcast journalism**
      College and school journalism
      Gossip
      Interviewing in journalism
      Libel and slander
      Newsletters
      Online journalism
      Photojournalism
      Press
      Reporters and reporting
      Scientific journalism
  RT **Journalists**
      Newspapers
      Periodicals
Journalism—Editing **070.4**
  UF Magazine editing
      News editing
      Newspapers—Editing
      Periodicals—Editing
  BT **Editing**
Journalism—Ethical aspects
  USE **Journalistic ethics**
Journalism—Objectivity **070.4**
  UF Slanted journalism
  BT **Journalistic ethics**
Journalism, Scientific
  USE **Scientific journalism**
Journalistic ethics (May subdiv. geog.)
  070.4; 174

Journalistic ethics—*Continued*

   UF   Journalism—Ethical aspects

   BT   **Professional ethics**

   NT   **Journalism—Objectivity**

Journalistic photography

   USE   **Photojournalism**

Journalists (May subdiv. geog.)   **070.92; 920**

   UF   Columnists

   SA   names of wars with the subdivision *Journalists*, e.g. **World War, 1939-1945—Journalists** [to be added as needed]

   BT   **Authors**

   NT   **World War, 1939-1945—Journalists**

   RT   **Journalism**

Journals

   USE   **Periodicals**

Journals (Diaries)

   USE   **Diaries**

Journeys

   USE   **Travel**

         Voyages and travels

Joy and sorrow   **152.4**

   UF   Affliction

         Sorrow

   BT   **Emotions**

   NT   **Pleasure**

   RT   **Grief**

         Happiness

         Suffering

Judaism (May subdiv. geog.)   **296**

   UF   Jewish religion

         Jews—Religion

   SA   names of Jewish sects, e.g. **Hasidism** [to be added as needed]

   BT   **Religions**

   NT   **Atonement—Judaism**

         Cabala

         Christianity—Relations—Judaism

         Hasidism

         Islam—Relations—Judaism

         Jewish holidays

         Judaism—Relations—Christianity

         Judaism—Relations—Islam

         Rabbis

         Sabbath

         Talmud

   RT   **Jews**

         Synagogues

Judaism—Customs and practices (May subdiv. geog.)   **296.4**

Use for materials on Jewish religious practices in general. Materials on the forms of public worship in Judaism are entered under **Judaism—Liturgy**. Materials on Jewish social customs are entered under **Jews—Social life and customs**.

   UF   Jewish customs

         Jewish life

         Jews—Customs

         Jews—Rites and ceremonies

         Jews—Ritual

   BT   **Rites and ceremonies**

   NT   **Bar mitzvah**

         Bat mitzvah

         Seder

   RT   **Judaism—Liturgy**

Judaism—Doctrines   **296.3**

   UF   Jewish doctrines

         Jewish theology

   BT   **Doctrinal theology**

Judaism—Liturgy   **296.4**

Use for materials on the forms of public worship in Judaism. Materials on Jewish religious practices in general are entered under **Judaism—Customs and practices**. Materials on Jewish social customs are entered under **Jews—Social life and customs**.

   UF   Jewish liturgies

         Jews—Ritual

   BT   **Liturgies**

   RT   **Judaism—Customs and practices**

Judaism—Relations—Christianity   **261.2; 296.3**

Use for materials on the relations between Judaism and Christianity. When assigning this heading, provide an additional subject entry under **Christianity—Relations—Judaism**.

   UF   Christian-Jewish relations

         Christianity and other religions—Judaism

         Jewish-Christian relations

   BT   **Christianity and other religions**

         Judaism

Judaism—Relations—Islam   **296.3**

Use for materials on the relations between Judaism and Islam. When assigning this heading, provide an additional subject entry under **Islam—Relations—Judaism**. Materials on the conflicts between the Arab countries and Israel are entered under **Israel-Arab conflicts**. Materials that discuss collectively the relations

Judaism—Relations—Islam—*Continued*
between Arabs and Jews, including religious, ethnic, and ideological relations, are entered under **Jewish-Arab relations**.

  UF Islamic-Jewish relations
      Jewish-Islamic relations
  BT **Islam**
      Judaism
  RT **Jewish-Arab relations**

Judea and Samaria
  USE **West Bank**

Judges (May subdiv. geog.) **347; 920**
  UF Chief justices
  BT **Lawyers**
  NT **Women judges**
  RT **Courts**

Judgment Day 202
  UF Doomsday
      Last judgment
  BT **End of the world**
      Second Advent

Judicial investigations
  USE **Governmental investigations**

Judiciary
  USE **Courts**

Judo (May subdiv. geog.) **796.815**
  BT **Martial arts**
      Self-defense
  NT **Karate**

Jugendstil
  USE **Art nouveau**

Juggling 793.8
  UF Legerdemain
      Sleight of hand
  BT **Amusements**
      Tricks

Jujitsu
  USE **Jiu-jitsu**

July Fourth
  USE **Fourth of July**

Jumble sales
  USE **Rummage sales**

Jungle animals (May subdiv. geog.)
      578.734
  UF Jungle fauna
  BT **Animals**
      Forest animals

Jungle ecology (May subdiv. geog.)
      577.34
  BT **Ecology**
      Forest ecology

Jungle fauna
  USE **Jungle animals**

Jungles (May subdiv. geog.) **634.9**
    Use for materials on impenetrable thickets of second-growth vegetation replacing tropical rain forests that have been disturbed or degraded. Materials on forests of broad-leaved, mainly evergreen trees found in moist climates in the tropics, subtropics, and some parts of the temperate zones, are entered under **Rain forests**.
  UF Tropical jungles
  BT **Forests and forestry**
  RT **Rain forests**

Junior colleges (May subdiv. geog.)
      378.1
  UF Community colleges
      Two-year colleges
  BT **Colleges and universities**
      Higher education

Junior colleges—Directories 378.1
  BT **Directories**

Junior high school libraries
  USE **High school libraries**

Junior high schools (May subdiv. geog.)
      373.236
  UF Secondary schools
  BT **High schools**
      Public schools
      Schools
  RT **Middle schools**
      Secondary education

Junk
  USE **Waste products**

Junk bonds 332.63
  UF High-yield junk bonds
  BT **Bonds**

Junk in space
  USE **Space debris**

Jupiter (Planet) 523.45
  BT **Planets**

Jurisprudence
  USE **Law**

Jurisprudence, Medical
  USE **Medical jurisprudence**

Jurists
  USE **Lawyers**

Jury (May subdiv. geog.) **345; 347**
  UF Trial by jury
  BT **Courts**
      Criminal law

Justice 340

Justice—*Continued*
  BT **Ethics**
      Law
      Virtue
  NT **Social justice**
  RT **Fairness**
Justice, Administration of
  USE **Administration of justice**
Justice League (Fictional characters)
  741.5
  BT **Fictional characters**
      Superheroes
Juvenile courts (May subdiv. geog.)   **345**
  UF Children's courts
  BT **Courts**
  RT **Juvenile delinquency**
      Probation
Juvenile delinquency (May subdiv. geog.)
  364.3
  UF Delinquency, Juvenile
      Juvenile delinquents
  BT **Crime**
      Social problems
  NT **Gangs**
      Juvenile prostitution
      School violence
  RT **Child welfare**
      Emotionally disturbed children
      Juvenile courts
      Reformatories
      Teenagers—Drug use
      Youth—Drug use
Juvenile delinquency—Case studies
  364.3
Juvenile delinquents
  USE **Juvenile delinquency**
Juvenile drama
  USE subjects and names with the
       subdivision *Juvenile drama,*
       e.g. **Christmas—Juvenile**
       drama [to be added as need-
       ed]
Juvenile fiction
  USE subjects and names with the
       subdivision *Juvenile fiction,*
       e.g. **Christmas—Juvenile fic-**
       tion [to be added as needed]
Juvenile literature
  USE **Children's literature**
       and subjects and names with
       the subdivision *Juvenile liter-*

ature, e.g. **Computers—Juve-**
nile literature [to be added
as needed]
Juvenile poetry
  USE subjects and names with the
       subdivision *Juvenile poetry,*
       e.g. **Christmas—Juvenile po-**
       etry [to be added as needed]
Juvenile prostitution (May subdiv. geog.)
  176; 306.74; 362.7; 363.4;
  364.1
  UF Adolescent prostitution
      Child prostitution
      Teenage prostitution
  BT **Juvenile delinquency**
      Prostitution
Kabbala
  USE **Cabala**
Kabuki   **792.0952**
  BT **Theater—Japan**
Kampuchea
  USE **Cambodia**
Karate (May subdiv. geog.)   **796.815**
  BT **Judo**
      Martial arts
      Self-defense
  NT **Tae kwon do**
Kart racing
  USE **Karts and karting**
Karting
  USE **Karts and karting**
Karts and karting (May subdiv. geog.)
  796.7
  UF Carts (Midget cars)
      Go-karts
      Kart racing
      Karting
      Karts (Midget cars)
      Midget cars
  BT **Automobile racing**
Karts (Midget cars)
  USE **Karts and karting**
Katrina, Hurricane, 2005
  USE **Hurricane Katrina, 2005**
Kayaking (May subdiv. geog.)   **797.122**
  BT **Canoes and canoeing**
Kazakhstan   **958.45**
Kempo
  USE **Kung fu**
KenKen   **793.73**
  BT **Puzzles**

Kennels (May subdiv. geog.)   **636**
  BT   **Pets—Housing**
Kenya   967.62
    May be subdivided like United States except for History.
Keyboarding (Electronics)   005.72
  UF   Computer keyboarding
        Data processing—Keyboarding
        Word processor keyboarding
  BT   **Business education**
        Office practice
  RT   **Typewriting**
Keyboards (Electronics)   004.7
  UF   Computer keyboards
  BT   **Computer peripherals**
        Office equipment and supplies
Keyboards (Musical instruments) (May subdiv. geog.)   **786**
  BT   **Organs (Musical instruments)**
        Pianos
Keys
  USE   **Locks and keys**
Kibbutz
  USE   **Collective settlements—Israel**
Kidnapping (May subdiv. geog.)   **364.15**
  UF   Abduction
  BT   **Criminal law**
        Offenses against the person
Kidnapping, Parental
  USE   **Parental kidnapping**
Kindergarten (May subdiv. geog.)   **372.21**
  BT   **Elementary education**
        Schools
  NT   **Creative activities**
        Montessori method of education
  RT   **Nursery schools**
        Preschool education
Kinematics   531
  BT   **Dynamics**
  NT   **Mechanical movements**
  RT   **Mechanics**
        Motion
Kinesiology   613.7
  UF   Cinesiology
  BT   **Human locomotion**
        Physical fitness
Kinetic art (May subdiv. geog.)   **709.04**
  UF   Art in motion
        Art, Kinetic
  BT   **Art**

  NT   **Kinetic sculpture**
Kinetic sculpture (May subdiv. geog.)   **731; 735**
  UF   Sculpture in motion
  BT   **Kinetic art**
        Sculpture
  NT   **Mobiles (Sculpture)**
Kinetics
  USE   **Dynamics**
        Motion
King Award
  USE   **Coretta Scott King Award**
King Philip's War, 1675-1676   973.2
  UF   United States—History—1675-1676, King Philip's War
  BT   **Native Americans—Wars**
        United States—History—1600-1775, Colonial period
King William's War, 1689-1697
  USE   **United States—History—1689-1697, King William's War**
Kings and rulers   352.23; 920; 929.7
    Use for materials on monarchs and other heads of state not democratically elected.
  UF   Kings, queens, rulers, etc.
        Monarchs
        Royal houses
        Royalty
        Rulers
        Sovereigns
  SA   names of places with the subdivision *Kings and rulers*, e.g. **Great Britain—Kings and rulers**; and names of individual monarchs or rulers [to be added as needed]
  BT   **Heads of state**
  NT   **Emperors**
        Great Britain—Kings and rulers
  RT   **Courts and courtiers**
        Monarchy
        Queens
Kings, queens, rulers, etc.
  USE   **Kings and rulers**
Kinship (May subdiv. geog.)   **306.83**
  SA   ethnic groups with the subdivision *Kinship* [to be added as needed]
  BT   **Ethnology**
        Family
  RT   **Clans**

Kitchen gardens
USE **Vegetable gardening**
Kitchen remodeling
USE **Kitchens—Remodeling**
Kitchen renovation
USE **Kitchens—Remodeling**
Kitchen utensils   643; 683
UF   Cooking utensils
Household utensils
Kitchenware
Utensils, Kitchen
SA   types of kitchen utensils, e.g.
Bread machines [to be added as needed]
BT   **Household equipment and supplies**
NT   **Bread machines**
Kitchens (May subdiv. geog.)   **643**
BT   **Houses**
Rooms
Kitchens—Remodeling   643
UF   Kitchen remodeling
Kitchen renovation
Remodeling of kitchens
Kitchenware
USE   **Kitchen utensils**
Kites (May subdiv. geog.)   **629.133; 796.1**
BT   **Aeronautics**
Kitsch   709.03
BT   **Aesthetics**
Kittens
USE   **Cats**
Knicks (Basketball team)
USE   **New York Knicks (Basketball team)**
Knighthood
USE   **Knights and knighthood**
Knights and knighthood (May subdiv. geog.)   **394; 940.1**
UF   Knighthood
BT   **Middle Ages**
Nobility
RT   **Chivalry**
Heraldry
Knights of the Round Table
USE   **Arthurian romances**
Knitting   677; 746.43
BT   **Needlework**
Knives   621.9; 623.4

BT   **Hardware**
Weapons
Knots and splices   623.88
UF   Splicing
BT   **Navigation**
Rope
Knowledge
USE   names of individual persons with the subdivision *Knowledge,* e.g. **Shakespeare, William, 1564-1616—Knowledge;** which may be further subdivided by the subject known, e.g. **Shakespeare, William, 1564-1616—Knowledge—Animals** [to be added as needed]
Knowledge-based systems (Computer science)
USE   **Expert systems (Computer science)**
Knowledge management (May subdiv. geog.)   **658.4**
UF   Management of knowledge assets
BT   **Management**
RT   **Information technology**
Knowledge, Theory of
USE   **Theory of knowledge**
Kodak camera   771.3
BT   **Cameras**
Kodomo   741.5
Use for individual works, collections, or materials about manga for children up to age 12.
BT   **Manga**
Koran   297.1
UF   Qur'an
BT   **Islam**
Sacred books
Koran—Recitation   297.1
UF   Recitation of the Koran
BT   **Recitations**
Korea   951.9
Use for comprehensive materials on all of Korea and for materials on Korea before it was divided in 1948 into two separate republics.
NT   **Korea (North)**
Korea (South)
Korea (Democratic People's Republic)
USE   **Korea (North)**

Korea (North)   951.93

Use for materials on the Democratic People's Republic of Korea, established in 1948. May be subdivided like United States except for History.

UF   Korea (Democratic People's Republic)

North Korea

BT   **Korea**

Korea (Republic)

USE   **Korea (South)**

Korea (South)   951.95

May be subdivided like United States except for History. Use for materials on the Republic of Korea, established in 1948.

UF   Korea (Republic)

South Korea

BT   **Korea**

Korean War, 1950-1953   951.904

Kristallnacht, 1938   943.086

BT   **Germany—History—1933-1945**

Jews—Persecutions

Ku Klux Klan   322.4

UF   Ku Klux Klan (1915-)

Ku Klux Klan (19th cent.)

BT   **Secret societies**

RT   **Reconstruction (1865-1876)**

Ku Klux Klan (1915-)

USE   **Ku Klux Klan**

Ku Klux Klan (19th cent.)

USE   **Ku Klux Klan**

Kung fu (May subdiv. geog.)   **796.815**

UF   Kempo

Wing chun

BT   **Martial arts**

Kwanzaa   394.2612

BT   **Holidays**

Kyrgyzstan   958.43

Labeling

USE   subjects with the subdivision *Labeling*, e.g. **Food—Labeling**
[to be added as needed]

Labor (May subdiv. geog.)   **331**

Use for materials on the collective human activities involved in the production and distribution of goods and services in an economy, especially activities performed by workers for wages as distinguished from those performed by entrepreneurs for profits. Also use for general materials on workers. Materials on laborers as a social class are entered under **Working class**. Materials on the physical or mental exertion of individuals to produce or accomplish something are entered under **Work**.

UF   Blue collar workers

Factory workers

Industrial workers

Labor and laboring classes

Laborers

Manual workers

Workers

SA   types of laborers, e.g. **Agricultural laborers**; **Miners**; etc.
[to be added as needed]

BT   **Economics**

Social conditions

Sociology

NT   **Agricultural laborers**

Alien labor

Apprentices

Capitalism

Child labor

Church and labor

Collective bargaining

Contract labor

Employees

Employment

Employment agencies

Forced labor

Hours of labor

Household employees

Industrial arbitration

Industrial relations

Industrial welfare

Labor supply

Labor unions

Migrant labor

Miners

Open and closed shop

Part-time employment

Peasantry

Proletariat

Skilled labor

Supplementary employment

Unskilled labor

RT   **Labor movement**

Work

Working class

Labor absenteeism

USE   **Absenteeism (Labor)**

Labor—Accidents

USE   **Industrial accidents**

Labor and capital

USE   **Industrial relations**

Labor and laboring classes
USE **Labor**
Labor movement
Working class
Labor and state
USE **Labor policy**
Labor and the church
USE **Church and labor**
Labor arbitration
USE **Industrial arbitration**
Labor (Childbirth)
USE **Childbirth**
Labor contract (May subdiv. geog.)
331.1; 331.89
Use for materials on agreements between employer and employee in which the latter agrees to perform work in return for compensation from the former.
UF Collective labor agreements
Trade agreements (Labor)
BT **Contracts**
Industrial relations
NT **Open and closed shop**
RT **Collective bargaining**
Labor courts
USE **Industrial arbitration**
Labor disputes (May subdiv. geog.)
331.89
UF Industrial disputes
BT **Industrial relations**
NT **Collective bargaining**
Industrial arbitration
Strikes
Labor economics (May subdiv. geog.)
331
BT **Economics**
Labor—Education (May subdiv. geog.)
331.25
UF Education of workers
BT **Education**
Labor force
USE **Labor supply**
Labor—Government policy
USE **Labor policy**
Labor—Housing (May subdiv. geog.)
363.5
BT **Housing**
Labor—Insurance
USE **Unemployment insurance**
Labor laws and legislation (May subdiv. geog.) **344.01**
UF Work—Law and legislation

BT **Industrial laws and legislation**
NT **Employee rights**
Labor-management relations
USE **Industrial relations**
Labor market
USE **Labor supply**
Labor movement (May subdiv. geog.)
331.8
Use for materials on the efforts of organizations and individuals to improve conditions for labor.
UF Labor and laboring classes
BT **Social movements**
RT **Labor**
Labor unions
Labor negotiations
USE **Collective bargaining**
Industrial arbitration
Labor organizations
USE **Labor unions**
Labor output
USE **Labor productivity**
Labor participation in management
USE **Participative management**
Labor policy (May subdiv. geog.) **331**
UF Government policy
Labor and state
Labor—Government policy
Manpower policy
BT **Economic policy**
Labor productivity (May subdiv. geog.)
331.11
UF Labor output
Productivity of labor
SA types of industries, occupations, and processes with the subdivision *Labor productivity*, e.g. **Steel industry—Labor productivity** [to be added as needed]
BT **Industrial efficiency**
NT **Production standards**
Steel industry—Labor productivity
Labor relations
USE **Industrial relations**
Labor rights
USE **Employee rights**
Labor saving devices, Household
USE **Electric household appliances**
Household equipment and supplies

Labor supply (May subdiv. geog.)
    331.11
  UF Labor force
      Labor market
  BT **Economic conditions**
      Employment
      Labor
  NT **Occupational retraining**
      Unemployed
      Unemployment
  RT **Employment agencies**
      Employment forecasting
      Human capital
      Manpower

Labor turnover (May subdiv. geog.)
    331.12
  BT **Personnel management**
  NT **Employment agencies**

Labor unions (May subdiv. geog.)
    331.88
  UF Labor organizations
      Organized labor
      Trade-unions
      Unions, Labor
  SA types of unions and names of
      individual labor unions [to be
      added as needed]
  BT **Industrial relations**
      Labor
      Societies
  NT **Industrial arbitration**
      Injunctions
      Librarians' unions
      Open and closed shop
      United Steelworkers of America
  RT **Collective bargaining**
      Labor movement
      Strikes

Labor unions—United States
    331.880973

Labor—United States **331.0973**

Laboratories (May subdiv. geog.) **001.4**
  UF Laboratory facilities
      Research buildings
      Science laboratories
      Scientific laboratories
  RT **Science**

Laboratory animal experimentation
  USE **Animal experimentation**

Laboratory animal welfare
  USE **Animal welfare**

Laboratory facilities
  USE **Laboratories**

Laboratory fertilization
  USE **Fertilization in vitro**

Laboratory manuals
  USE scientific and technical subjects
      with the subdivision *Labora-*
      tory manuals, e.g. **Chemis-**
      try—Laboratory manuals [to
      be added as needed]

Laborers
  USE **Labor**
      Working class
      and types of laborers, e.g. *Agri-*
      cultural laborers; Miners; etc.
      [to be added as needed]

Laboring class
  USE **Working class**

Laboring classes
  USE **Working class**

Labyrinth gardens
  USE **Maze gardens**

Labyrinths (May subdiv. geog.) **291.3; 302.2**

Lace and lace making (May subdiv. geog.) **677; 746.2**
  BT **Crocheting**
      Needlework
      Weaving
  NT **Tatting**

Lacquer and lacquering (May subdiv. geog.) **667; 745.7**
  BT **Decorative arts**
      Finishes and finishing

Lacrosse (May subdiv. geog.) **796.34**
  BT **Ball games**
      Sports

Lactose intolerance **616.3**
  RT **Dairy-free cooking**

Lactose intolerance—Diet therapy—Recipes
  USE **Dairy-free cooking**

Laissez-faire
  USE **Free enterprise**

Laity (May subdiv. geog.) **262**
    May be subdivided by religion or sect.
  UF Laymen
  BT **Church**
  RT **Lay ministry**

Laity—Catholic Church (May subdiv. geog.) **262**
    UF   Catholic laity
    BT   **Catholic Church**
Lake ecology (May subdiv. geog.)
    577.63
    BT   **Ecology**
Lakes (May subdiv. geog.) **551.48**
    SA   names of lakes [to be added as
         needed]
    BT   **Physical geography**
         Water
         Waterways
    RT   **Inland navigation**
Lakes—United States **551.48**
Lamaze method of childbirth
    USE **Natural childbirth**
Lambs
    USE **Sheep**
Lamentations
    USE **Elegiac poetry**
Lamps (May subdiv. geog.) **621.32; 749**
    BT   **Lighting**
    NT   **Electric lamps**
Lancelot (Legendary character) **398.22**
    BT   **Legendary characters**
Land
    USE **Land use**
         Landforms
Land drainage
    USE **Drainage**
Land forms
    USE **Landforms**
Land grants (May subdiv. geog.) **333.1**
    UF   Land patents
    BT   **Colonization**
         Public lands
Land mines (May subdiv. geog.) **355.8;**
    623.4
    BT   **Explosives**
         Ordnance
Land patents
    USE **Land grants**
Land question
    USE **Land tenure**
Land, Reclamation of
    USE **Reclamation of land**
Land reform (May subdiv. geog.) **333.3**
    UF   Agrarian reform
         Reform, Agrarian

    BT   **Economic policy**
         Land use
         Social policy
    NT   **Land tenure**
    RT   **Agriculture—Government poli-**
         cy
Land settlement (May subdiv. geog.)
    304.8; 325
    UF   Resettlement
         Settlement of land
    BT   **Colonies**
         Land use
    NT   **Colonization**
    RT   **Human settlements**
         Internal migration
Land settlement—United States **304.8;**
    325.73
    UF   United States—Land settlement
         Westward movement
Land slides
    USE **Landslides**
Land surveying
    USE **Surveying**
Land surveys
    USE **Surveying**
Land tenure (May subdiv. geog.) **333.3**
    Use for general and historical materials on
    systems of holding land. Materials on the le-
    gal relationships between landlord and tenant
    are entered under **Landlord and tenant**.
    UF   Agrarian question
         Fiefs
         Land question
         Tenure of land
    BT   **Agriculture—Economic aspects**
         Land reform
         Land use
    NT   **Farm tenancy**
         Feudalism
         Landlord and tenant
    RT   **Peasantry**
         Real estate
Land use (May subdiv. geog.) **333.73**
    Use for general materials that cover such
    topics as types of land; the utilization, distri-
    bution, and development of land; and the eco-
    nomic factors affecting the value of land. Ma-
    terials dealing only with ownership of land
    are entered under **Real estate**.
    UF   Land
    BT   **Economics**
    NT   **Eminent domain**
         Farms
         Grasslands

Land use—*Continued*

> Land reform
> Land settlement
> Land tenure
> Landfills
> Pastures
> Public lands
> Real estate
> Reclamation of land
> Regional planning

Landfills (May subdiv. geog.)   **363.72; 628.3; 628.4**

Use for materials on places for waste disposal in which waste is buried in layers of earth in low ground.

UF   Earth fills
       Fills (Earthwork)
       Sanitary landfills

SA   names of landfills [to be added as needed]

BT   **Land use**

NT   **Hazardous waste sites**
       Love Canal Chemical Waste Landfill (Niagara Falls, N.Y.)

Landforms (May subdiv. geog.)   **551.41**

UF   Land
       Land forms

SA   types of landforms, e.g. **Mountains**; **Coasts**; etc. [to be added as needed]

BT   **Earth—Surface**
       Geology

NT   **Coasts**
       Mountains
       Seashore
       Wetlands

Landlord and tenant (May subdiv. geog.)   **333.5; 346.04**

Use for materials on the legal relationships between landlord and tenant. General and historical materials on systems of holding land are entered under **Land tenure**.

UF   Tenant and landlord

BT   **Commercial law**
       Land tenure
       Real estate

NT   **Housing**

RT   **Farm tenancy**

Landmarks, Literary

USE   **Literary landmarks**

Landmarks, Preservation of

USE   **National monuments**
        Natural monuments

Landscape architecture (May subdiv. geog.)   **712**

Use for materials on modifying or arranging the features of a landscape, urban area, etc., for aesthetic or pragmatic purposes.

UF   Landscape design

BT   **Architecture**

NT   **Garden ornaments and furniture**
       Garden structures
       Parks
       Patios
       Roadside improvement
       Water gardens

RT   **Landscape gardening**
       Landscape protection

Landscape design

USE   **Landscape architecture**

Landscape drawing   **743**

BT   **Drawing**

RT   **Landscape painting**

Landscape gardening (May subdiv. geog.)   **712**

Use for materials on the design or rearrangement of extensive gardens or estates.

UF   Planting

BT   **Gardening**
       Horticulture

NT   **Evergreens**
       Lawns
       Ornamental plants
       Xeriscaping

RT   **Garden design**
       Landscape architecture
       Shrubs
       Trees

Landscape painting   **758**

BT   **Painting**

RT   **Landscape drawing**

Landscape protection (May subdiv. geog.)   **333.73**

UF   Beautification of landscape
       Natural beauty conservation
       Preservation of natural scenery
       Protection of natural scenery
       Scenery

BT   **Environmental protection**
       Nature conservation

NT   **Natural monuments**

Landscape protection—*Continued*
  RT **Landscape architecture**
      Regional planning
Landscape sculpture
  USE **Earthworks (Art)**
Landslides (May subdiv. geog.)   **551.3**
  UF Land slides
  BT **Natural disasters**
Language
  USE **Language and languages**
       and disciplines, classes of persons, types of newspapers, and names of individual persons, corporate bodies, and literary works entered under title with the subdivision *Language,* e.g. **Technology—Language; Children—Language;** etc. [to be added as needed]
Language and culture (May subdiv. geog.)   **306.44**
  BT **Culture**
      Language and languages
Language and languages   **400**
  Use for general materials on the history, philosophy, origin, etc., of language. Materials on the scientific study of speech and comparative studies of language are entered under **Linguistics**.
  UF Language
      Languages
      Philology
  SA names of languages or groups of languages, e.g. **English language; Scandinavian languages; Native American languages**; etc.; disciplines, classes of persons, types of newspapers, and names of individual persons, corporate bodies, and literary works entered under title with the subdivison *Language*, e.g. **Technology—Language; Children—Language**; etc.; and names countries, cities, etc., with the subdivison *Languages*, for materials on the several languages spoken in a place, e.g. **United States—Languages** [to be added as needed]

  BT **Anthropology**
      Communication
      Ethnology
  NT **Arabic language**
      Bengali language
      Bilingualism
      Children—Language
      Chinese language
      Conversation
      Danish language
      English language
      French language
      German language
      Grammar
      Greek language
      Hebrew language
      Hindi language
      Icelandic language
      Indian languages
      Japanese language
      Language and culture
      Latin language
      Linguistics
      Modern Greek language
      Modern languages
      Multilingualism
      Native American languages
      Norwegian language
      Old Norse language
      Phonetics
      Programming languages
      Rhetoric
      Romance languages
      Russian language
      Sanskrit language
      Scandinavian languages
      Semantics
      Sign language
      Sociolinguistics
      Spanish language
      Spelling bees
      Swedish language
      Translating and interpreting
      Universal language
      Verbal learning
      Vocabulary
      Voice
      Writing
      Yiddish language
  RT **Speech**

Language and languages—Business language
    USE   names of languages with unique language subdivisions, e.g. **English language—Business English; Japanese language—Business Japanese**; etc. [to be added as needed]
Language and languages—Comparative philology
    USE **Linguistics**
Language and languages—Etymology 412
    UF Etymology
         Word histories
    SA names of languages with the subdivision *Etymology*, e.g. **English language—Etymology** [to be added as needed]
Language and languages—Government policy (May subdiv. geog.) **306.449**
    UF Language policy
         National languages
         Official languages
Language and languages—Political aspects 400
    Use for general materials on the political aspects of languages.
    SA names of countries, cities, etc., with the subdivision *Languages*, e.g. **United States—Languages**; or with the two subdivisions *Languages—Political aspects*; and names of individual languages and groups of languages with the subdivision *Political aspects* [to be added as needed]
Language and society
    USE **Sociolinguistics**
Language arts 372.6; 400
    Use for materials on language and literature considered comprehensively as a school subject at the elementary level.
    UF Communication arts
    BT **Communication**
    NT **Creative writing**
         Literature
         Reading
         Speech
         Whole language

Writing
Language arts (Holistic)
    USE **Whole language**
Language arts—Patterning 372.6
    UF Patterns (Language arts)
         Reading—Patterning
         Writing—Patterning
Language disorders 616.85
    Use for materials on disorders of the central neurological functions affecting the reception, processing, or expression of language. Materials on disorders of the physiological mechanisms required for speech are entered under **Speech disorders**.
    UF Dysphasia
    BT **Communicative disorders**
    NT **Aphasia**
Language experience approach in education
    USE **Whole language**
Language games
    USE **Literary recreations**
Language, International
    USE **Universal language**
Language laboratories 407
    UF Foreign language laboratories
    RT **Modern languages—Study and teaching**
Language of flowers 302.2; 398.24
    UF Flower language
    BT **Plants—Folklore**
Language policy
    USE **Language and languages—Government policy**
Language, Universal
    USE **Universal language**
Languages
    USE **Language and languages** and countries, cities, etc., with the subdivision *Languages,* for materials on the several languages spoken in a place, e.g. **United States—Languages**; etc. [to be added as needed]
Languages, Modern
    USE **Modern languages**
Languages—Vocabulary
    USE **Vocabulary**
LANs (Computer networks)
    USE **Local area networks**
Lantern slides
    USE **Slides (Photography)**
Laptop computers
    USE **Portable computers**

Larceny
USE **Theft**
Large and small
USE **Size**
Large print books   028
UF   Books for sight saving
Books—Large print
Large type books
Sight saving books
BT   **Blind—Books and reading**
RT   **Big books**
Large type books
USE   **Large print books**
Laser-beam recording
USE   **Laser recording**
Laser photography
USE   **Holography**
Laser recording   621.36; 621.38
UF   Laser-beam recording
Recording, Laser
BT   **Optical data processing**
NT   **Holography**
RT   **Lasers**
Optical storage devices
Lasers (May subdiv. geog.)   **621.36**
SA   lasers in particular subjects or
fields of endeavor, e.g. **La-
sers in aeronautics** [to be
added as needed]
BT   **Light**
NT   **Lasers in aeronautics**
RT   **Laser recording**
Lasers in aeronautics   629.13
BT   **Aeronautics**
Lasers
Last judgment
USE   **Judgment Day**
Last rites (Sacraments)
USE   **Anointing of the sick**
Last sacraments
USE   **Anointing of the sick**
Last Supper   232.9
Use for materials on the final meal of Jesus
with his apostles, where the sacrament of the
Eucharist was instituted.
Last things (Theology)
USE   **Eschatology**
Latchkey children   306.874; 362.7; 640
BT   **Children of working parents**
Lateness
USE   **Punctuality**

Lathe work
USE   **Lathes**
Turning
Lathes   621.9
UF   Lathe work
BT   **Woodworking machinery**
RT   **Turning**
Latin America   980
Use for materials that discuss collectively
several or all of the countries of the Western
Hemisphere south of the United States in
which Spanish, Portuguese, or French is the
principal language.
UF   Spanish America
SA   names of individual Latin Amer-
ican countries [to be added as
needed]
BT   **America**
NT   **Pan-Americanism**
**Latin America—Politics and government
980**
BT   **Politics**
Latin American literature   860
Use for materials on the French, Portu-
guese, or Spanish literature of several Latin
American countries. May use same subdivi-
sions and names of literary forms as for **En-
glish literature**.
UF   South American literature
Spanish American literature
SA   names of individual Latin Amer-
ican literatures [to be added
as needed]
BT   **Literature**
NT   **Brazilian literature**
Mexican literature
Latin Americans (May subdiv. geog.)
920; 980
Use for materials on citizens of Latin
American countries. Materials on United
States citizens of Latin American descent are
entered under **Hispanic Americans**.
Latin language   470
May be subdivided like **English language**.
UF   Classical languages
BT   **Language and languages**
RT   **Romance languages**
Latin literature   870
May use same subdivisions and names of
literary forms as for **English literature**.
UF   Roman literature
BT   **Literature**
RT   **Classical literature**
Early Christian literature

Latinos (U.S.)
USE **Hispanic Americans**
Latitude   526; 527
UF   Degrees of latitude and longi-
tude
BT   **Earth**
Geodesy
Nautical astronomy
Latter-day Saints
USE   **Church of Jesus Christ of Lat-
ter-day Saints**
Latvia   947.96
Laughter   152.4
BT   **Emotions**
Launching of satellites
USE   **Artificial satellites—Launching**
Laundry   648
UF   Ironing
Washing
BT   **Cleaning**
Home economics
Household sanitation
Law (May subdiv. geog.)   **340**
UF   Jurisprudence
Laws
Statutes
SA   names of particular legal sys-
tems, e.g. **Islamic law**; spe-
cial branches of law, e.g.
Criminal law; subjects with
the subdivision *Law and leg-
islation*, e.g. **Automobiles—
Law and legislation**; and eth-
nic groups and classes of per-
sons with the subdivision *Le-
gal status, laws, etc.*, e.g.
**Handicapped—Legal status,
laws, etc.** [to be added as
needed]
BT   **Political science**
NT   **Abortion—Law and legislation**
Administration of justice
Administrative law
**Automobiles—Law and legisla-
tion**
**Chemical industry—Law and
legislation**
Commercial law
Common law
Constitutional law
Constitutions

Corporation law
Courts
Criminal law
Ecclesiastical law
Environmental law
Food—Law and legislation
Gun control
**Handicapped—Legal status,
laws, etc.**
Industrial laws and legislation
Internal revenue law
International law
Islamic law
Justice
Law reform
Lawyers
Libraries—Law and legislation
Litigation
Maritime law
Martial law
Medicine—Law and legislation
Military law
Natural law
Power of attorney
Safety regulations
Space law
Water rights
RT   **Legislation**
Law and legislation
USE   subjects with the subdivision
Law and legislation, e.g. **Au-
tomobiles—Law and legisla-
tion** [to be added as needed]
Law, Election
USE   **Election law**
Law enforcement (May subdiv. geog.)
363.2
BT   **Administration of criminal jus-
tice**
NT   **Criminal investigation**
Police
Law—Fiction
USE   **Legal stories**
Law of nations
USE   **International law**
Law of nature
USE   **Natural law**
Law of supply and demand
USE   **Supply and demand**
Law of the sea
USE   **Maritime law**

Law reform (May subdiv. geog.) **340**
    UF   Legal reform
    BT   **Law**
Law schools (May subdiv. geog.)
    340.071
    BT   **Colleges and universities**
Law suits
    USE **Litigation**
Law—United States   **349.73**
    UF   United States—Law
Law—Vocational guidance   **340.023**
    BT   **Professions**
          Vocational guidance
Lawmakers
    USE **Legislators**
Lawn tennis
    USE **Tennis**
Lawns (May subdiv. geog.)   **635.9; 712**
    BT   **Landscape gardening**
    RT   **Grasses**
Laws
    USE **Law**
          Legislation
Lawsuits
    USE **Litigation**
Lawyers (May subdiv. geog.)   **340.092; 920**
    UF   Attorneys
          Bar
          Barristers
          Jurists
          Legal profession
          Solicitors
    BT   **Law**
    NT   **Judges**
    RT   **Legal ethics**
Lawyers—Fiction
    USE **Legal stories**
Lawyers—Salaries, wages, etc. (May subdiv. geog.)   **331.2**
    BT   **Salaries, wages, etc.**
Lay ministry (May subdiv. geog.)   **253**
    UF   Volunteers in church work
    BT   **Church work**
    RT   **Laity**
Laymen
    USE **Laity**
Laziness   **179**
    UF   Indolence
          Sloth
    BT   **Personality**

Lead poisoning (May subdiv. geog.)
    615.9
    UF   Lead—Toxicology
    BT   **Occupational diseases**
          Poisons and poisoning
Lead—Toxicology
    USE **Lead poisoning**
Leadership   **158; 303.3**
    BT   **Ability**
          Executive ability
          Social groups
          Success
    NT   **Elite (Social sciences)**
League of Nations   **341.22**
    BT   **International arbitration**
          International cooperation
          International organization
          World War, 1914-1918—Peace
Learned institutions and societies
    USE **Learning and scholarship**
Learned societies
    USE **Societies**
Learning and scholarship (May subdiv. geog.)   **001.2**
    UF   Erudition
          Learned institutions and societies
          Scholarship
    BT   **Civilization**
          Intellectual life
    NT   **Humanities**
          Professional education
    RT   **Culture**
          Education
          Humanism
          Research
Learning center approach to teaching
    USE **Open plan schools**
Learning disabilities   **153.1; 371.9; 616.85**
    SA   types of learning disabilities [to be added as needed]
    BT   **Psychology of learning**
          Slow learning children
    NT   **Reading disability**
Learning, Psychology of
    USE **Psychology of learning**
Learning resource centers
    USE **Instructional materials centers**
Learning, Verbal
    USE **Verbal learning**

Lease and rental services (May subdiv. geog.)   **333.5**

 UF Lease services

  Rental services

 BT **Service industries**

Lease services

 USE **Lease and rental services**

Leather (May subdiv. geog.)   **675**

 BT **Animal products**

 RT **Hides and skins**

  Leather industry

  Tanning

Leather clothing

 USE **Leather garments**

Leather garments (May subdiv. geog.)   **391; 685**

 UF Leather clothing

 BT **Clothing and dress**

  Leather work

Leather industry (May subdiv. geog.)   **338.4**

 UF Leather industry and trade

 BT **Industries**

 NT **Shoe industry**

 RT **Leather**

Leather industry and trade

 USE **Leather industry**

Leather work (May subdiv. geog.)   **745.53**

 BT **Decoration and ornament**

  Decorative arts

  Handicraft

 NT **Leather garments**

Leave for parenting

 USE **Parental leave**

Leave of absence (May subdiv. geog.)   **331.25**

 BT **Hours of labor**

 NT **Parental leave**

Leaves   **575.5; 581.4**

 UF Foliage

 BT **Plants**

Lebanon   **956.92**

 May be subdivided like United States except for History.

Lebanon—History   **956.92**

Lebanon—History—1975-1976, Civil War   **956.9204**

Lectures and lecturing (May subdiv. geog.)   **808.5**

 Use for general materials on lectures and the art of delivering speeches on academic subjects. Collections of speeches on several subjects and materials about non-academic speeches are entered under **Speeches**. Collections of lectures on a single subject are entered under that subject.

 UF Addresses

  Speaking

 BT **Public speaking**

  Rhetoric

  Teaching

 NT **Radio addresses, debates, etc.**

 RT **Speeches**

Left and right

 USE **Left and right (Direction)**

  Right and left (Political science)

Left and right (Direction)   **152.1**

 Use for children's materials on left and right as indications of location or direction. Materials on political views or attitudes are entered under **Right and left (Political science)**. Materials on the physical characteristics of favoring one hand or the other are entered under **Left- and right-handedness**.

 UF Left and right

  Right and left

 BT **Direction sense**

Left- and right-handedness   **152.3**

 UF Handedness

  Right- and left-handedness

 BT **Psychophysiology**

Left (Political science)

 USE **Liberalism**

  Right and left (Political science)

Legacies

 USE **Inheritance and succession**

  Wills

Legal aid (May subdiv. geog.)   **362.5**

 Use for materials on legal services to the poor, usually provided under the sponsorship of local bar associations or governmental units.

 UF Legal assistance to the poor

  Legal representation of the poor

  Legal services for the poor

 BT **Public welfare**

Legal assistance to the poor

 USE **Legal aid**

Legal drama (Films)   **791.43**

 Use for individual works, collections, or materials about motion pictures dealing with trials or litigations.

 UF Courtroom drama

 BT **Motion pictures**

Legal drama (Radio programs)   791.44

Use for individual works, collections, or materials about radio programs dealing with trials or litigations.

UF   Courtroom drama

BT   **Radio programs**

Legal drama (Television programs) 791.45

Use for individual works, collections, or materials about television programs dealing with trials or litigations.

UF   Courtroom drama

BT   **Television programs**

Legal ethics (May subdiv. geog.)   **174; 340**

BT   **Ethics**

   Professional ethics

RT   **Lawyers**

Legal fiction (Literature)

USE   **Legal stories**

Legal holidays

USE   **Holidays**

Legal medicine

USE   **Medical jurisprudence**

Legal novels

USE   **Legal stories**

Legal profession

USE   **Lawyers**

Legal reform

USE   **Law reform**

Legal representation of the poor

USE   **Legal aid**

Legal responsibility

USE   **Liability (Law)**

Legal services for the poor

USE   **Legal aid**

Legal status, laws, etc.

USE   ethnic groups and classes of persons with the subdivision *Legal status, laws, etc.*, e.g. **Handicapped—Legal status, laws, etc.** [to be added as needed]

Legal stories   808.3; 808.83

Use for individual works, collections, or materials about fiction dealing with trials or litigations.

UF   Law—Fiction

   Lawyers—Fiction

   Legal fiction (Literature)

   Legal novels

   Trials—Fiction

BT   **Fiction**

Legal tender

USE   **Money**

Legations

USE   **Diplomatic and consular service**

Legendary characters   398.22

SA   names of individual legendary characters, e.g. **Bunyan, Paul (Legendary character)** [to be added as needed]

BT   **Legends**

   Mythology

NT   **Anansi (Legendary character)**

   Argonauts (Legendary characters)

   Cassandra (Legendary character)

   Cuchulain (Legendary character)

   Guinevere (Legendary character)

   Helen of Troy (Legendary character)

   Hercules (Legendary character)

   Jason (Legendary character)

   Lancelot (Legendary character)

   Medea (Greek mythology)

   Merlin (Legendary character)

   Morgan Le Fay (Legendary character)

   Oedipus (Legendary character)

   Pegasus (Greek mythology)

   Scheherazade (Legendary character)

Legends (May subdiv. geog.)   **398.2**

Use for individual works, collections, or materials about tales coming down from the past, especially those relating to actual events or persons. Collections of tales written between the eleventh and fourteenth centuries and dealing with the age of chivalry or the supernatural are entered under **Romances**.

UF   Folk tales

   Stories

   Tales

   Traditions

SA   relgious topics and names of individual persons or sacred works with the subdivision *Legends*; e.g. **Grail—Legends**; legends of particular ethnic or religious groups, e.g.

Legends—*Continued*
> **Jewish legends**; and names of individual legendary characters, e.g. **Bunyan, Paul (Legendary character)** [to be added as needed]

    BT   **Fiction**
          Literature
    NT   **Celtic legends**
          Christian legends
          Jewish legends
          Legendary characters
          Norse legends
          Tall tales
    RT   **Fables**
          Folklore
          Mythology
          Romances

Legends, Jewish
    USE **Jewish legends**

Legends—United States   398.20973; 973

Legerdemain
    USE **Juggling**
         Magic tricks

Legibility of handwriting
    USE **Handwriting**

Legislation (May subdiv. geog.)   328
> Use for materials on the theory of lawmaking and descriptions of the preparation and enactment of laws.

    UF   Laws
    SA   subjects with the subdivision *Law and legislation* [to be added as needed]
    BT   **Political science**
    NT   **Abortion—Law and legislation**
          Automobiles—Law and legislation
          Chemical industry—Law and legislation
          Food—Law and legislation
          Gun control
          Industrial laws and legislation
          Legislative bodies
          Libraries—Law and legislation
          Medicine—Law and legislation
          Parliamentary practice
    RT   **Law**

Legislation, Direct
    USE **Referendum**

Legislative bodies (May subdiv. geog.)   328.3
> Use for materials on various law making bodies considered collectively.

    UF   Legislatures
         Parliaments
    SA   names of individual legislative bodies, e.g. **United States. Congress** [to be added as needed]
    BT   **Constitutional law**
          Legislation
          Representative government and representation
    NT   **Parliamentary practice**
          Term limits (Public office)
          United States. Congress
          War and emergency powers

Legislative investigations
    USE **Governmental investigations**

Legislative reapportionment
    USE **Apportionment (Election law)**

Legislators (May subdiv. geog.)   328
    UF   Lawmakers
         Members of Parliament
    BT   **Statesmen**

Legislatures
    USE **Legislative bodies**

Legitimacy (Law)
    USE **Illegitimacy**

Leisure (May subdiv. geog.)   790.01
    UF   Free time (Leisure)
         Leisure time
    NT   **Hobbies**
         Retirement
    RT   **Recreation**

Leisure time
    USE **Leisure**

Lemon
    USE **Lemons**

Lemons   634; 641.3
    UF   Lemon
    BT   **Citrus fruits**

Lending
    USE **Loans**

Lending institutions
    USE **Financial institutions**

Lending of library materials
    USE **Library circulation**

Lenses   535

Lenses—*Continued*

    SA   types of lenses, e.g. **Contact lenses** [to be added as needed]

    BT   **Optical instruments**

    NT   **Contact lenses**

Lensless photography

    USE   **Holography**

Lent   263

    BT   **Church year**

    NT   **Good Friday**

            Holy Week

            Lenten sermons

    RT   **Easter**

Lent—Meditations   242

    BT   **Meditations**

Lenten sermons   252

Use for collections of sermons on any subject preached during the season of Lent.

    BT   **Lent**

            Sermons

Lepidoptera

    USE   **Butterflies**

            Moths

Leprosy (May subdiv. geog.)   **616.9**

    UF   Hansen's disease

    BT   **Diseases**

Lesbian marriage

    USE   **Same-sex marriage**

Lesbian rights

    USE   **Gay rights**

Lesbianism (May subdiv. geog.)   **306.76**

    BT   **Homosexuality**

    RT   **Lesbians**

Lesbians (May subdiv. geog.)   **306.76**

    UF   Gay women

            Gays, Female

            Homosexuals, Female

    BT   **Women**

    NT   **Gay parents**

            Gays and lesbians in the military

    RT   **Homosexuality**

            Lesbianism

            Lesbians' writings

Lesbians and gays in the military

    USE   **Gays and lesbians in the military**

Lesbians—Civil rights

    USE   **Gay rights**

Lesbians in the military

    USE   **Gays and lesbians in the military**

Lesbians—Ordination

    USE   **Ordination of gays and lesbians**

Lesbians' writings   **808.8**

Use for collections of lesbians' writings by more than one author and for materials about such writings.

    UF   Gay women's writings

            Writings of lesbians

    BT   **Literature**

    RT   **Lesbians**

Less developed countries

    USE   **Developing countries**

Letter-sound association

    USE   **Reading—Phonetic method**

Letter writing (May subdiv. geog.)   **383; 808.6**

Use for materials on composition, forms, and etiquette of correspondence. Materials limited to business correspondence are entered under **Business letters**. Collections of literary letters are entered under **Letters**.

    UF   Correspondence

    BT   **Etiquette**

            Literary style

            Rhetoric

    NT   **Business letters**

Lettering   745.6

    UF   Ornamental alphabets

    BT   **Decoration and ornament**

            Industrial painting

            Mechanical drawing

    NT   **Monograms**

    RT   **Alphabets**

            Initials

            Sign painting

Letters   808.86

Use for collections of literary letters. Materials on the composition, forms, and etiquette of correspondence are entered under **Letter writing**. Materials limited to business correspondence are entered under **Business letters**.

    UF   Correspondence

    SA   ethnic groups, classes of persons, and names of individual persons and families with the subdivision *Correspondence*, e.g. **Authors—Correspondence** [to be added as needed]

Letters—*Continued*
    NT   **American letters**
            Authors—Correspondence
            English letters
Letters of credit
    USE   **Credit**
            Negotiable instruments
Letters of marque
    USE   **Privateering**
Letters of recommendation
    USE   **Applications for positions**
Letters of the alphabet
    USE   **Alphabet**
Leukemia   616.99
    BT   **Blood—Diseases**
            Cancer
Levant
    USE   **Middle East**
Leveraged buyouts (May subdiv. geog.)
    338.8; 658.1
    UF   Buyouts, Leveraged
            Management buyouts
    BT   **Corporate mergers and acquisitions**
Levers   621.8
    BT   **Simple machines**
Lewis and Clark Expedition (1804-1806)
    973.4
    BT   **United States—Exploring expeditions**
            United States—History—1783-1815
Lexington (Mass.), Battle of, 1775
    973.3
    BT   **Battles**
            United States—History—1775-1783, Revolution—Campaigns
Liability for environmental damages
    (May subdiv. geog.)   **344**
    UF   Environmental damages, Liability for
    BT   **Environmental law**
            Liability (Law)
Liability (Law) (May subdiv. geog.)
    346.02
    UF   Accountability
            Legal responsibility
            Responsibility, Legal
    BT   **Contracts**
    NT   **Liability for environmental damages**

        Malpractice
Liability, Professional
    USE   **Malpractice**
Libel and slander (May subdiv. geog.)
    346.03
    UF   Character assassination
            Defamation
            Slander (Law)
    BT   **Journalism**
    NT   **Gossip**
    RT   **Freedom of speech**
            Freedom of the press
Liberalism (May subdiv. geog.)   **148; 320.5**
    UF   Left (Political science)
    BT   **Political science**
            Social sciences
    RT   **Right and left (Political science)**
Liberation movements, National
    USE   **National liberation movements**
Liberation theology (May subdiv. geog.)
    261.8
    UF   Theology of liberation
    BT   **Christianity—Doctrines**
            Church and social problems
            Theology
Liberty
    USE   **Freedom**
Liberty of conscience
    USE   **Freedom of conscience**
Liberty of speech
    USE   **Freedom of speech**
Liberty of the press
    USE   **Freedom of the press**
Liberty of the will
    USE   **Free will and determinism**
Librarians (May subdiv. geog.)   **020.92; 920**
    NT   **African American librarians**
            Black librarians
            Library technicians
    RT   **Libraries**
Librarians—Collective bargaining
    USE   **Collective bargaining—Librarians**
Librarians—Education
    USE   **Library education**
Librarians—Ethics   174
    UF   Librarians—Professional ethics
    BT   **Professional ethics**

Librarians—In-service training   020.71
   BT **Library education**
Librarians—Professional ethics
   USE **Librarians—Ethics**
Librarians—Rating (May subdiv. geog.)
   023
Librarians—Recruiting (May subdiv.
   geog.) **023**
   BT **Recruiting of employees**
Librarians—Training
   USE **Library education**
Librarians' unions (May subdiv. geog.)
   331.88
   UF Library unions
   BT **Labor unions**
Librarianship
   USE **Library science**
Libraries (May subdiv. geog.) **027**
   SA types of libraries, e.g. **Academic
      libraries**; names of individual
      libraries, e.g. **Library of
      Congress**; libraries and partic-
      ular groups of people, e.g. **Li-
      braries and African Ameri-
      cans**; and libraries and other
      subjects, e.g. **Libraries and
      community** [to be added as
      needed]
   BT **Documentation**
   NT **Academic libraries**
      Children's libraries
      Church libraries
      Digital libraries
      Hospital libraries
      Instructional materials centers
      Libraries and community
      Libraries and schools
      Library architecture
      Library catalogs
      Library cooperation
      Library of Congress
      Library resources
      Library services
      Library technical processes
      Public libraries
      School libraries
      Special libraries
      Young adults' libraries
   RT **Archives**
      Information services
      Librarians

Libraries—Acquisitions   025.2
   UF Acquisitions (Libraries)
      Book buying (Libraries)
      Libraries—Order department
      Library acquisitions
   BT **Libraries—Collection develop-
      ment**
      Library technical processes
   NT **Book selection**
Libraries—Administration   025.1
   UF Library administration
      Library policies
   NT **Library finance**
      Library trustees
Libraries and African Americans   027.6
   UF African Americans and libraries
      Afro-Americans and libraries
      Library services to African
      Americans
   BT **African Americans**
      Library services
Libraries and children
   USE **Children's libraries**
Libraries and community (May subdiv.
   geog.) **021.2**
   UF Community and libraries
   BT **Libraries**
   NT **Libraries—Public relations**
Libraries and readers
   USE **Library services**
Libraries and schools (May subdiv. geog.)
   021
   UF Schools and libraries
   BT **Libraries**
      Schools
   NT **Students—Library services**
   RT **Children's libraries**
      School libraries
Libraries and state
   USE **Libraries—Government policy**
Libraries and students
   USE **Students—Library services**
Libraries and the elderly
   USE **Elderly—Library services**
Libraries—Automation (May subdiv.
   geog.) **025.04**
   UF Library automation
   SA names of projects, formats, and
      systems, e.g. **MARC formats**
      [to be added as needed]
   BT **Automation**

Libraries—Automation—*Continued*
   NT   **Machine readable bibliographic data**
   RT   **Information systems**
        Online catalogs
Libraries—Boards of trustees
   USE **Library trustees**
Libraries, Business
   USE **Business libraries**
Libraries—Cataloging
   USE **Cataloging**
Libraries—Catalogs
   USE **Library catalogs**
Libraries—Censorship (May subdiv. geog.) **025.2**
   BT   **Censorship**
Libraries—Centralization (May subdiv. geog.) **021.6**
   UF   Library systems
Libraries—Circulation, loans
   USE **Library circulation**
Libraries—Collection development 025.2
   UF   Collection development (Libraries)
   BT   **Library technical processes**
   NT   **Book selection**
        Libraries—Acquisitions
Libraries—Collective bargaining
   USE **Collective bargaining—Librarians**
Libraries—Cooperation
   USE **Library cooperation**
Libraries, Corporate
   USE **Corporate libraries**
Libraries—Equipment and supplies 022
   UF   Library equipment and supplies
        Library supplies
   BT   **Furniture**
Libraries—Federal aid
   USE **Federal aid to libraries**
Libraries—Finance
   USE **Library finance**
Libraries—Government aid
   USE **Government aid to libraries**
Libraries—Government policy (May subdiv. geog.) **021.8**
   UF   Libraries and state
   BT   **Social policy**
   NT   **Federal aid to libraries**
        Government aid to libraries

Libraries, Governmental
   USE **Government libraries**
Libraries, Hospital
   USE **Hospital libraries**
Libraries—Law and legislation (May subdiv. geog.) **344**
   UF   Library laws
        Library legislation
   BT   **Law**
        Legislation
Libraries—Lighting 022
   BT   **Lighting**
Libraries, Music
   USE **Music libraries**
Libraries, National
   USE **National libraries**
Libraries—Order department
   USE **Libraries—Acquisitions**
Libraries, Presidential
   USE **Presidents—United States—Archives**
Libraries—Public relations (May subdiv. geog.) **021.7**
   UF   Public relations—Libraries
   BT   **Libraries and community**
   NT   **Book talks**
Libraries, Regional
   USE **Regional libraries**
Libraries—Special collections 026
     May be subdivided by subject or form, e.g. **Libraries—Special collections—Science fiction; Libraries—Special collections—Videotapes**; etc.
   UF   Special collections in libraries
Libraries—State aid
   USE **Government aid to libraries**
Libraries—Statistics 020
   BT   **Statistics**
Libraries—Technical services
   USE **Library technical processes**
Libraries—Trustees
   USE **Library trustees**
Libraries—United States 027.073
Library acquisitions
   USE **Libraries—Acquisitions**
Library administration
   USE **Libraries—Administration**
Library architecture (May subdiv. geog.) **727**
     Use for materials on the design of library buildings.
   BT   **Architecture**
        Libraries

Library assistants
USE **Library technicians**
Library automation
USE **Libraries—Automation**
Library boards
USE **Library trustees**
Library book fairs
USE **Books—Exhibitions**
Library cataloging
USE **Cataloging**
Library catalogs   017; 025.3
UF   Catalogs
Catalogs, Library
Libraries—Catalogs
SA   types of library catalogs, e.g.
Online catalogs [to be added
as needed]
BT   **Libraries**
NT   **Card catalogs**
Classified catalogs
Online catalogs
Subject catalogs
RT   **Cataloging**
Library circulation   025.6
UF   Book lending
Circulation of library materials
Lending of library materials
Libraries—Circulation, loans
BT   **Library services**
NT   **Interlibrary loans**
Library classification   025.4
May be further subdivided by a type of lit-
erature or by the subject of the materials clas-
sified.
UF   Books—Classification
Classification—Books
BT   **Cataloging**
Classification
Library technical processes
NT   **Dewey Decimal Classification**
RT   **Classified catalogs**
Library clerks
USE **Library technicians**
Library consortia
USE **Library cooperation**
Library cooperation (May subdiv. geog.)
021.6
UF   Consortia, Library
Libraries—Cooperation
Library consortia
BT   **Libraries**

NT   **Interlibrary loans**
Library information networks
Library education (May subdiv. geog.)
020.71
Use for materials on the education of librar-
ians. Materials on the instruction of readers in
library use are entered under **Bibliographic
instruction**.
UF   Education for librarianship
Librarians—Education
Librarians—Training
Library science—Study and
teaching
BT   **Education**
Professional education
NT   **Librarians—In-service training**
Library schools
Library education—Audiovisual aids
020.71
BT   **Audiovisual education**
Audiovisual materials
Library education—Curricula   020.71
BT   **Education—Curricula**
Library equipment and supplies
USE **Libraries—Equipment and
supplies**
Library extension (May subdiv. geog.)
021.6
BT   **Library services**
NT   **Bookmobiles**
Library finance (May subdiv. geog.)
025.1
UF   Libraries—Finance
BT   **Finance**
Libraries—Administration
NT   **Government aid to libraries**
RT   **Federal aid to libraries**
Library information networks (May
subdiv. geog.)   **021.6**
Use for materials on networks that facilitate
the sharing of information resources among
several libraries.
UF   Library networks
Library systems
BT   **Information networks**
Library cooperation
Library instruction
USE **Bibliographic instruction**
Library laws
USE **Libraries—Law and legislation**
Library legislation
USE **Libraries—Law and legislation**

Library materials
USE **Library resources**
Library networks
USE **Library information networks**
Library of Congress   027.573
UF   United States. Library of Congress
BT   **Libraries**
Library orientation
USE   **Bibliographic instruction**
Library policies
USE   **Libraries—Administration**
Library processing
USE   **Library technical processes**
Library reference services
USE   **Reference services (Libraries)**
Library resources (May subdiv. geog.)
025

Use for materials on the resources and collections available in libraries for research not limited to a single subject or discipline.

UF   Library materials
SA   subjects, ethnic groups, classes of persons, corporate bodies, individual persons, literary authors, and names of countries, cities, etc., with the subdivision *Library resources*, e.g. **United States—History—Library resources** [to be added as needed]
BT   **Libraries**
NT   **Government publications**
Library resources—Conservation and restoration   025.8
UF   Books—Preservation
Library resources—Preservation
Preservation of library resources
Library resources—Preservation
USE   **Library resources—Conservation and restoration**
Library schools (May subdiv. geog.)
020.71
BT   **Library education**
Library science (May subdiv. geog.)
020

Use for general materials on the knowledge and skill necessary for the organization and administration of libraries. Materials on services offered by libraries to patrons are entered under **Library services**.

UF   Librarianship

BT   **Documentation**
       Information science
NT   **Cataloging**
       Library surveys
       Library technical processes
RT   **Bibliography**
       Library services
Library science—Study and teaching
USE   **Library education**
Library services (May subdiv. geog.)
025.5

Use for materials on services offered by libraries to patrons. General materials on the knowledge and skill necessary for the organization and administration of libraries are entered under **Library science**.

UF   Libraries and readers
       Library services to readers
       Reader services (Libraries)
       Readers and libraries
SA   libraries and specific types of users or specific activities for which services are provided, e.g. **Elderly—Library services** [to be added as needed]
BT   **Libraries**
NT   **Bibliographic instruction**
       Elderly—Library services
       Libraries and African Americans
       Library circulation
       Library extension
       Reference services (Libraries)
       Students—Library services
RT   **Library science**
Library services to African Americans
USE   **Libraries and African Americans**
Library services to children
USE   **Children's libraries**
Library services to readers
USE   **Library services**
Library services to teenagers
USE   **Young adults' libraries**
Library services to the elderly
USE   **Elderly—Library services**
Library services to young adults
USE   **Young adults' libraries**
Library skills
USE   **Bibliographic instruction**
Library supplies
USE   **Libraries—Equipment and supplies**

Library surveys (May subdiv. geog.)
020
BT **Library science**
Surveys
Library systems
USE **Libraries—Centralization**
Library information networks
Library technical processes 025
Use for materials on the activities and processes concerned with the acquisition, organization, and preparation of library materials for use.
UF Centralized processing (Libraries)
Libraries—Technical services
Library processing
Processing (Libraries)
Technical services (Libraries)
BT **Libraries**
Library science
NT **Cataloging**
Libraries—Acquisitions
Libraries—Collection development
Library classification
Library technicians (May subdiv. geog.)
020.92
UF Library assistants
Library clerks
Paraprofessional librarians
BT **Librarians**
Paraprofessionals
Library trustees 021.8
UF Libraries—Boards of trustees
Libraries—Trustees
Library boards
BT **Libraries—Administration**
Trusts and trustees
Library unions
USE **Librarians' unions**
Library user orientation
USE **Bibliographic instruction**
Librettos 780; 780.26
Use for collections of miscellaneous librettos and for materials on the history and criticism of librettos and on writing librettos. Individual librettos and collections of librettos of a specific type are entered under the specific type of libretto.
SA types of librettos, e.g. **Opera librettos** [to be added as needed]
BT **Books**
NT **Opera librettos**

Libya 961.2
May be subdivided like United States except for History.
Licenses (May subdiv. geog.) 352.8
Use for general works on legal permissions to engage in business or perform other work or activities.
SA occupational groups, types of industries, and types of vehicles with the subdivision *Licenses*, e.g. **Physicians—Licenses**; which may be further subdivided geographically [to be added as needed]
BT **Commercial law**
Public administration
Lie detectors and detection 363.2
UF Polygraph
BT **Criminal investigation**
Medical jurisprudence
Truthfulness and falsehood
Life 128
Use for materials on philosophical or religious considerations of life. Materials on life from a scientific point of view are entered under **Life (Biology)**.
NT **Death**
Life expectancy
RT **Life (Biology)**
Life after death
USE **Future life**
Immortality
Life (Biology) 570.1
Use for materials on life from a scientific point of view. Materials on philosophical or religious considerations of life are entered under **Life**.
BT **Biology**
NT **Biosphere**
Gaia hypothesis
Genetics
Life cycles (Biology)
Middle age
Protoplasm
Reproduction
RT **Life**
Life care communities (May subdiv. geog.) 362.61; 363.5
Use for materials on retirement communities that guarantee services and medical care for the rest of a person's life.
UF Continuing care communities
Continuing care retirement communities
BT **Retirement communities**

454

Life cycles
    USE **Life cycles (Biology)**
         and types of plants or animals
         with the subdivision *Life cycles* [to be added as needed]

Life cycles (Biology)   **571.8**
    UF Life cycles
    SA types of plants or animals with the subdivision *Life cycles* [to be added as needed]
    BT **Biology**
         Cycles
         Life (Biology)

Life expectancy (May subdiv. geog.)
    304.6
    UF Expectancy of life
         Expectation of life
    BT **Age**
         Life
         Vital statistics
    NT **Longevity**

Life, Future
    USE **Future life**

Life histories
    USE **Biography**

Life insurance (May subdiv. geog.)
    368.32
    UF Insurance, Life
    BT **Insurance**
    NT **Group insurance**
    RT **Annuities**

Life on other planets   **576.8**
    Use for materials on the possibility of indigenous life in outer space. Materials on the biology of humans or other earth creatures while in outer space are entered under **Space biology**.
    UF Astrobiology
         Extraterrestrial life
    BT **Astronomy**
         Planets
         Universe
    NT **Extraterrestrial beings**
         Interstellar communication
    RT **Human-alien encounters**

Life—Origin   **113**
    UF Germ theory
         Origin of life
    BT **Evolution**

Life quality
    USE **Quality of life**

Life saving
    USE **Lifesaving**

Life sciences (May subdiv. geog.)   **570**
    UF Biosciences
    BT **Science**
    NT **Agriculture**
         Biology
         Medicine

Life sciences ethics
    USE **Bioethics**

Life skills (May subdiv. geog.)   **158; 640**
    Use for materials on skills needed by an individual to exist in modern society, including skills related to education, employment, finance, etc.
    UF Basic life skills
         Coping skills
         Functional competencies
         Fundamental life skills
         Life skills guides
         Living skills
         Personal life skills
    SA groups and classes of persons with the subdivision *Life skills guides*, e.g. **Elderly—Life skills guides** [to be added as needed]
    BT **Interpersonal relations**
         Success
    NT **Conduct of life**
         Elderly—Life skills guides
         Self-help techniques
         Self-improvement
         Social skills
         Study skills
         Survival skills
    RT **Human behavior**

Life skills guides
    USE **Life skills**
         and groups and classes of persons with the subdivision *Life skills guides*, e.g. **Elderly—Life skills guides** [to be added as needed]

Life span prolongation
    USE **Longevity**

Life styles
    USE **Lifestyles**

Life support systems (Medical environment)   **362.1**
    BT **Hospitals**
         Terminal care

Life support systems (Space environment)   **629.47**

Life support systems (Space environment)—*Continued*
- BT **Human engineering**
- **Space medicine**
- NT **Apollo project**
- **Lunar bases**
- **Space suits**

Life support systems (Submarine environment) 627
- BT **Human engineering**

Lifeguards (May subdiv. geog.) **797.21**
- BT **Water safety**

Lifelong education
- USE **Adult education**
- **Continuing education**

Lifesaving (May subdiv. geog.) **363.1**
- UF Life saving
- BT **Rescue work**
- RT **First aid**

Lifestyles (May subdiv. geog.) **306**
- UF Life styles
- SA types of lifestyles [to be added as needed]
- BT **Human behavior**
- **Manners and customs**
- NT **Alternative lifestyles**
- **Counter culture**
- **Unmarried couples**

Lifts
- USE **Elevators**
- **Hoisting machinery**

Light   535
- BT **Electromagnetic waves**
- **Physics**
- NT **Color**
- **Lasers**
- **Lighting**
- **Luminescence**
- **Refraction**
- RT **Optics**
- **Photometry**
- **Radiation**
- **Spectrum analysis**

Light and shade
- USE **Shades and shadows**

Light, Electric
- USE **Electric lighting**

Light production in animals
- USE **Bioluminescence**

Light ships
- USE **Lightships**

Light—Therapeutic use
- USE **Phototherapy**

Light verse
- USE **Humorous poetry**

Lighthouses (May subdiv. geog.) **387.1; 623.89; 627**
- BT **Navigation**
- NT **Lightships**

Lighting (May subdiv. geog.) **621.32**
- UF Illumination
- SA types of lighting and types of buildings, structures, rooms, installations, etc., with the subdivision *Lighting*, e.g. **Libraries—Lighting** [to be added as needed]
- BT **Interior design**
- **Light**
- NT **Candles**
- **Electric lighting**
- **Lamps**
- **Libraries—Lighting**
- **Photography—Lighting**
- **Stage lighting**
- **Streets—Lighting**

Lightning (May subdiv. geog.) **551.56**
- BT **Electricity**
- **Meteorology**
- **Thunderstorms**

Lightships (May subdiv. geog.) **623.89; 627**
- UF Light ships
- BT **Lighthouses**
- **Ships**

Limbs, Artificial
- USE **Artificial limbs**

Lime   631.8; 666
- UF Lime (Mineral)
- BT **Fertilizers**
- **Minerals**

Lime (Fruit)
- USE **Limes**

Lime (Mineral)
- USE **Lime**

Limericks   808.1; 808.81

Use for collections of limericks by one or several authors or for materials about limericks.
- UF Rhymes
- BT **Humorous poetry**
- RT **Nonsense verses**

Limes   634

Limes—*Continued*
- UF   Lime (Fruit)
- BT   **Citrus fruits**

Limitation of armament
- USE   **Arms control**

Limited access highways
- USE   **Express highways**

Limited companies
- USE   **Limited liability companies**

Limited liability companies (May subdiv. geog.)   **338.7**
- UF   Limited companies
  - LLCs (Limited liability companies)
  - Private companies
  - Private limited companies
- BT   **Corporation law**
  - **Corporations**

Lincoln, Abraham, 1809-1865   92; B
- BT   **Presidents—United States**

Lincoln Day
- USE   **Lincoln's Birthday**

Lincoln family   920; 929

Lincoln's Birthday   394.261
- UF   Lincoln Day
- BT   **Holidays**

Line engraving
- USE   **Engraving**

Linear algebra   512
- BT   **Algebra**
  - **Mathematical analysis**
- RT   **Topology**

Linear system theory
- USE   **System analysis**

Linen (May subdiv. geog.)   **677**
- BT   **Fabrics**
  - **Fibers**
- RT   **Flax**

Linguistic science
- USE   **Linguistics**

Linguistics (May subdiv. geog.)   **410**

Use for materials on the scientific study of speech and for comparative studies of languages. General materials on the history, philosophy, origin, etc., of languages are entered under **Language and languages**.
- UF   Comparative linguistics
  - Comparative philology
  - Language and languages—Comparative philology
  - Linguistic science
  - Philology
  - Philology, Comparative
- BT   **Language and languages**
- NT   **Grammar**
  - **Semantics**
  - **Sociolinguistics**
  - **Universal language**

Linoleum block printing   761
- UF   Block printing
- BT   **Printing**
  - **Prints**

Linotype   686.2
- BT   **Printing**
  - **Type and type-founding**
  - **Typesetting**

Lip-reading
- USE   **Lipreading**

Lipreading   418
- UF   Lip-reading
- BT   **Deaf—Means of communication**

Liquefaction of coal
- USE   **Coal liquefaction**

Liqueurs
- USE   **Liquors**

Liquid fuel
- USE   **Petroleum as fuel**

Liquids   532
- BT   **Fluid mechanics**
  - **Physics**
- NT   **Hydraulics**
  - **Hydrodynamics**
  - **Hydrostatics**

Liquor industry (May subdiv. geog.)   **338.4**
- BT   **Beverage industry**
- NT   **Bars**
- RT   **Liquors**

Liquor problem
- USE   **Alcoholism**
  - **Drinking of alcoholic beverages**

Liquors (May subdiv. geog.)   **641.2; 663**
- UF   Cordials (Liquor)
  - Drinks
  - Intoxicants
  - Liqueurs
  - Liquors and liqueurs
- SA   types of liquors and liqueurs [to be added as needed]
- BT   **Alcoholic beverages**
  - **Beverages**
- RT   **Brewing**
  - **Distillation**

Liquors—*Continued*
> Liquor industry

Liquors and liqueurs
> USE **Liquors**

List books
> USE **Books of lists**

Listening   153.6; 153.7
> BT **Attention**
> **Educational psychology**
> RT **Hearing**

Listening devices
> USE **Eavesdropping**

Lists
> USE **Books of lists**
> and topics with the subdivision
> *Lists,* e.g. **Sports—Lists** [to
> be added as needed]

Literacy (May subdiv. geog.)   302.2;
379.2
> UF Illiteracy
> BT **Education**
> NT **Computer literacy**
> **Functional literacy**
> **Information literacy**
> **Media literacy**
> **Technological literacy**
> **Visual literacy**

Literacy, Visual
> USE **Visual literacy**

Literary awards
> USE **Literary prizes**

Literary characters
> USE **Characters and characteristics**
> **in literature**

Literary collections
> USE **Anthologies**
> **Literature—Collections**
> and form headings for minor
> literary forms that represent
> collections of works of sever-
> al authors, e.g. **Essays;**
> **American essays; Parodies;**
> **Short stories;** etc.; major lit-
> erary forms and national liter-
> atures with the subdivision
> *Collections,* e.g. **Poetry—Col-**
> **lections; English literature—**
> **Collections;** etc.; and subjects
> with the subdivision *Literary*
> *collections,* for collections fo-
> cused on a single subject by

two or more authors involving
two or more literary forms,
e.g. **Cats—Literary collec-**
tions [to be added as needed]

Literary criticism
> USE **Criticism**
> **Literature—History and criti-**
> **cism**

Literary forgeries (May subdiv. geog.)
098
> UF Frauds, Literary
> BT **Counterfeits and counterfeiting**
> **Forgery**

Literary landmarks (May subdiv. geog.)
809
> UF Authors—Homes and haunts
> Landmarks, Literary
> BT **Historic buildings**
> **Literature—History and criti-**
> **cism**
> NT **English authors—Homes**

Literary landmarks—United States
810.9

Literary prizes (May subdiv. geog.)
807.9
> UF Book awards
> Book prizes
> Literary awards
> Literature—Prizes
> SA names of awards, e.g. **Caldecott**
> **Medal** [to be added as need-
> ed]
> BT **Awards**
> NT **Caldecott Medal**
> **Coretta Scott King Award**
> **Edgar Allan Poe Awards**
> **Hugo Award**
> **Literature—Competitions**
> **Nebula Award**
> **Newbery Medal**

Literary property
> USE **Copyright**
> **Intellectual property**

Literary recreations   793.73
> UF Language games
> Recreations, Literary
> BT **Amusements**
> NT **Charades**
> **Palindromes**
> **Plot-your-own stories**
> **Rebuses**

Literary recreations—*Continued*
      Riddles
      Word games
Literary style   808
  UF Style, Literary
  BT **Literature**
  NT **Letter writing**
  RT **Criticism**
      Rhetoric
Literary themes
  USE **Literature—Themes**
Literature   800

> Literatures are described by countries or geographic regions. In countries or regions with more than one major language the literature may be further qualified by the language in parentheses, e.g. **Canadian literature (French)**. There is no distinction made in subject headings between literary works in their original languages and in translations.

  UF Belles lettres
      Modern literature
  SA literatures of countries or of regions larger than a single country, e.g. **English literature**; **French literature**; **Scandinavian literature**; etc.; national or regional literatures qualified if needed by the language in which the literature was originally written or subdivided by a sub-set of authors within the literature, e.g. **African literature (English)**; **American literature—African American authors**; etc.; literatures of particular religions, e.g. **Christian literature**; literatures of languages not identified with a particular country, e.g. **Latin literature**; and subjects, themes, and stylistic features in literature, e.g. **Bible in literature**; **Children in literature**; **Characters and characteristics in literature**; **Symbolism in literature**; etc. [to be added as needed]
  BT **Humanities**
      Language arts
  NT **African literature**
      African literature (English)
      American literature
      Arabic literature

Authorship
Ballads
Bible in literature
Biography as a literary form
Black humor (Literature)
Brazilian literature
Campaign literature
Canadian literature
Catholic literature
Chapbooks
Characters and characteristics in literature
Children's literature
Chinese literature
Classical literature
Classicism
Communism and literature
Comparative literature
Criticism
Danish literature
Diaries
Drama
Early Christian literature
English literature
Epic literature
Erotic literature
Essay
Fables
Fiction
Folk literature
French literature
Gay men's writings
German literature
Gothic revival (Literature)
Greek literature
Hebrew literature
Humanism
Icelandic literature
Indian literature
Indian literature (English)
Irish literature
Jewish literature
Journalism
Latin American literature
Latin literature
Legends
Lesbians' writings
Literary style
Medieval literature
Mexican literature
Mock-heroic literature

Literature—*Continued*
  Modern Greek literature
  Modernism in literature
  Multicultural literature
  Music and literature
  Native American literature
  Norwegian literature
  Old Norse literature
  Parody
  Picaresque literature
  Poetry
  Portuguese literature
  Realism in literature
  Religion in literature
  Religious literature
  Romance literature
  Romances
  Russian literature
  Sagas
  Satire
  Scandinavian literature
  Short story
  Spanish literature
  Speeches
  Stories, plots, etc.
  Swedish literature
  Symbolism in literature
  Teenagers' writings
  West Indian literature
    (French)
  Wit and humor
  World War, 1939-1945—Literature and the war
  Young adult literature
 RT **Books**
Literature and communism
 USE **Communism and literature**
Literature and music
 USE **Music and literature**
Literature and the war
 USE names of wars with the subdivision *Literature and the war,* e.g. **World War, 1939-1945—Literature and the war** [to be added as needed]
Literature—Bio-bibliography   809
 RT **Authors**
Literature—Collections   808.8
  Use for collections of literary works by several authors not limited to a single literature or literary form or focused on a single subject.

 UF Collected works
  Collections of literature
  Literary collections
  Literature—Selections
 SA form headings for minor literary forms that represent collections of works of several authors, e.g. **Essays**; **American essays**; **Parodies**; **Short stories**; etc.; major literary forms and national literatures with the subdivision *Collections,* e.g. **Poetry—Collections**; **English literature—Collections**; etc.; and subjects with the subdivision *Literary collections,* for collections focused on a single subject by two or more authors involving two or more literary forms, e.g. **Cats—Literary collections** [to be added as needed]
Literature, Comparative
 USE **Comparative literature**
Literature—Competitions   807.9
 BT **Contests**
  Literary prizes
Literature—Criticism
 USE **Literature—History and criticism**
Literature—Dictionaries   803
 BT **Encyclopedias and dictionaries**
 NT **English literature—Dictionaries**
Literature, Erotic
 USE **Erotic literature**
Literature—Evaluation
 USE **Best books**
  Book reviewing
  Books and reading
  Criticism
  Literature—History and criticism
Literature—Film and video adaptations
 USE **Film adaptations**
  Television adaptations
Literature—History and criticism   809
  Use for materials that are themselves histories or criticisms of literature in general. Materials on the history, principles, methods, etc., of literary criticism are entered under **Criticism**.
 UF Appraisal of books
  Books—Appraisal

Literature—History and criticism—*Continued*

       Evaluation of literature
       Literary criticism
       Literature—Criticism
       Literature—Evaluation
  NT **Literary landmarks**
Literature—Indexes 016.8
Literature, Medieval
  USE **Medieval literature**
Literature—Outlines, syllabi, etc. 802
  NT **English literature—Outlines, syllabi, etc.**
Literature—Prizes
  USE **Literary prizes**
Literature—Selections
  USE **Literature—Collections**
Literature—Stories, plots, etc.
  USE **Stories, plots, etc.—Collections**
Literature—Themes 809
  UF Literary themes
      Themes in literature
  SA subjects, racial and ethnic groups, and classes of persons in literature, e.g. **Dogs in literature**; **Women in literature**; etc., and names of persons, families, and corporate bodies with the subdivision *In literature*, e.g. **Napoleon I, Emperor of the French, 1769-1821—In literature**, [to be added as needed]
  NT **African Americans in literature**
      Animals in literature
      Blacks in literature
      Children in literature
      Dogs in literature
      Minorities in literature
      Napoleon I, 1769-1821—In literature
      Nature in literature
      Travel in literature
      Women in literature
  RT **Characters and characteristics in literature**
Lithographers (May subdiv. geog.) **763.092; 920**
  BT **Artists**
Lithography (May subdiv. geog.) **686.2; 763; 764**

  UF Lithoprinting
  BT **Color printing**
      Printing
      Prints
  NT **Offset printing**
Lithoprinting
  USE **Lithography**
      Offset printing
Lithuania 947.93
Litigation (May subdiv. geog.) **347**
  UF Actions and defenses
      Civil law suits
      Defense (Law)
      Law suits
      Lawsuits
      Personal actions (Law)
      Suing (Law)
      Suits (Law)
  BT **Law**
  NT **Class actions (Civil procedure)**
      Witnesses
  RT **Arbitration and award**
      Civil procedure
Littering
  USE **Refuse and refuse disposal**
Little League baseball (May subdiv. geog.) **796.357**
  BT **Baseball**
Little magazines (May subdiv. geog.) **050**
  BT **Periodicals**
Little theater movement (May subdiv. geog.) **792**
  UF Community theater
  BT **Theater**
  RT **Amateur theater**
Liturgical year
  USE **Church year**
Liturgics
  USE **Liturgies**
Liturgies 203; 264
  Use for general materials on the forms of prayers, rituals, and ceremonies used in public worship, including the theological and historical study of liturgies, and for texts of liturgies from more than one religion.
  UF Church service books
      Liturgics
      Liturgy
      Ritual
      Service books (Liturgy)

Liturgies—*Continued*

SA   names of individual religions and denominations with the subdivision *Liturgy* or *Liturgy—Texts*; e.g. **Catholic Church—Liturgy; Catholic Church—Liturgy—Texts** etc. [to be added as needed]

BT   **Public worship**
      Rites and ceremonies

NT   **Catholic Church—Liturgy**
      Eucharist
      Hymns
      Judaism—Liturgy
      Mass (Liturgy)

RT   **Church music**
      Worship programs

Liturgy
USE   **Liturgies**
      and names of individual religions and denominations with the subdivision *Liturgy* e.g. **Judaism—Liturgy; Catholic Church—Liturgy;** etc. [to be added as needed]

Live poliovirus vaccine
USE   **Poliomyelitis vaccine**

Livestock
USE   **Domestic animals**
      Livestock industry

Livestock breeding (May subdiv. geog.) **636.08**
UF   Livestock—Breeding
BT   **Breeding**
      Livestock industry

Livestock—Breeding
USE   **Livestock breeding**

Livestock industry (May subdiv. geog.) **636**

Use for materials on stock raising as an industry. General materials on farm and other domestic animals are entered under **Domestic animals**.

UF   Animal husbandry
      Animal industry
      Livestock
      Stock raising
BT   **Agriculture**
      Economic zoology
NT   **Dairying**
      Livestock breeding
      Livestock judging

RT   **Domestic animals**

Livestock judging (May subdiv. geog.) **636**
UF   Stock judging
BT   **Livestock industry**

Living earth theory
USE   **Gaia hypothesis**

Living skills
USE   **Life skills**

Living together
USE   **Unmarried couples**

Living trusts (May subdiv. geog.) **346.05**
BT   **Trusts and trustees**

Living wills   344
BT   **Wills**
RT   **Right to die**
      Terminal care

Livres à clef
USE   **Romans à clef**

Lizards (May subdiv. geog.)   **597.95**
BT   **Reptiles**

LLCs (Limited liability companies)
USE   **Limited liability companies**

Loan associations
USE   **Savings and loan associations**

Loan funds, Student
USE   **Student loan funds**

Loans (May subdiv. geog.)   **332.7**
UF   Borrowing
      Lending
BT   **Finance**
NT   **Capital market**
      Government lending
      Home equity loans
      Interest (Economics)
      Microfinance
      Mortgages
      Personal loans
      Public debts
      Savings and loan associations
      Student aid
RT   **Credit**
      Investments

Loans, Personal
USE   **Personal loans**

Lobbying (May subdiv. geog.)   **328.3**

Use for materials on groups that promote their own interests with public officials. Materials on special interest groups that support sympathetic candidates for public office through campaign contributions are entered under **Political action committees**.

Lobbying—*Continued*
>UF Interest groups
>>Lobbying and lobbyists
>>Lobbyists
>>Pressure groups
>SA names of specific lobbying and
>>pressure groups [to be added
>>as needed]
>BT **Politics**
>>**Propaganda**
>RT **Political action committees**

Lobbying and lobbyists
>USE **Lobbying**

Lobbyists
>USE **Lobbying**

Lobsters (May subdiv. geog.)   **595.3**
>BT **Crustacea**
>>**Shellfish**

Local area networks (May subdiv. geog.)
>**004.6**
>UF LANs (Computer networks)
>BT **Computer networks**

Local government (May subdiv. geog.)
>**320.8; 352.14**

Use for materials on the government of districts, counties, townships, etc. Materials limited to county government only are entered under **County government**. Materials limited to the government of cities and towns are entered under **Municipal government**.

>UF Government, Local
>>Town meeting
>>Township government
>BT **Administrative law**
>>**Community organization**
>>**Political science**
>NT **County government**
>>**Metropolitan government**
>>**Municipal government**
>>**Public administration**
>>**State-local relations**

Local history   **907**

Use for materials on the writing and compiling of local histories. Collective histories of several localities are entered under the country, state, etc., with the subdivision *Local history*. Individual local histories are entered under the city, county, or other locality with the subdivision *History*.

>UF Community history
>>Regional history
>SA names of countries, states, etc.,
>>with the subdivision *Local
>>history*, e.g. **United States—**
>>**Local history**; **Ohio—Local
>>history**; etc.; and names of
>>cities, counties, or other localities with the subdivision *History*, e.g. **Chicago (Ill.)—History** [to be added as needed]
>BT **Historiography**
>>**History**
>NT **Ohio—Local history**
>>**United States—Local history**

Local-state relations
>USE **State-local relations**

Local traffic
>USE **City traffic**

Local transit (May subdiv. geog.)   **388.4**

Use for materials on the various modes of local public transportation.

>UF City transit
>>Mass transit
>>Municipal transit
>>Public transit
>>Rapid transit
>>Transit systems
>>Urban transportation
>BT **Traffic engineering**
>>**Transportation**
>NT **Buses**
>>**Street railroads**
>>**Subways**
>>**Taxicabs**

Localism
>USE **Regionalism**

Localisms
>USE names of languages with the
>>subdivision *Provincialisms,*
>>e.g. **English language—Provincialisms** [to be added as needed]

Loch Ness monster   **001.944**
>UF Nessie (Monster)
>BT **Monsters**

Lockouts
>USE **Strikes**

Locks and keys (May subdiv. geog.)
>**683**
>UF Keys
>BT **Burglary protection**

Locomotion   **152.3; 388**
>NT **Aeronautics**
>>**Animal locomotion**
>>**Flight**
>>**Horsemanship**

Locomotion—*Continued*
>> **Human locomotion**
>> **Navigation**
>> **Transportation**

Locomotives (May subdiv. geog.)   **625.26**
> BT   **Railroads**
> NT   **Steam locomotives**

Locomotives—Models   625.1
> UF   Model trains
> BT   **Models and modelmaking**

Locusts   595.7; 632
> BT   **Insect pests**
>> **Insects**

Log cabins and houses (May subdiv. geog.)   **728**
> UF   Cabins
> BT   **House construction**
>> **Houses**

Logarithms   513.2
> BT   **Algebra**
>> **Mathematics—Tables**
>> **Trigonometry—Tables**
> NT   **Slide rule**

Logging (May subdiv. geog.)   **634.9**
> Use for materials on the felling of trees and the transportation of logs to sawmills. Materials on lumber and the preparation of lumber are entered under **Lumber and lumbering**.
> UF   Timber—Harvesting
> BT   **Forests and forestry**

Logic   160
> UF   Argumentation
>> Deduction (Logic)
>> Dialectics
>> Fallacies
>> Induction (Logic)
> BT   **Intellect**
>> **Philosophy**
>> **Science—Methodology**
> NT   **Certainty**
>> **Critical thinking**
>> **Probabilities**
>> **Symbolic logic**
>> **Theory of knowledge**
> RT   **Reasoning**
>> **Thought and thinking**

Logic, Symbolic and mathematical
> USE   **Symbolic logic**

Lone Ranger films   791.43
> Use for individual works, collections, or materials about Lone Ranger films.
> BT   **Western films**

Loneliness   155.9; 158

> UF   Social isolation
> BT   **Emotions**
> RT   **Solitude**

Long distance running
> USE   **Marathon running**

Long distance swimming
> USE   **Marathon swimming**

Long distance telephone service (May subdiv. geog.)   **384.6**
> UF   Telephone—Long distance
> BT   **Telephone**

Long life
> USE   **Longevity**

Long-term care facilities (May subdiv. geog.)   **362.16**
> UF   Extended care facilities
> BT   **Hospitals**
>> **Medical care**
> NT   **Nursing homes**
>> **Sanatoriums**

Longevity (May subdiv. geog.)   **612.6; 613**
> UF   Life span prolongation
>> Long life
> BT   **Age**
>> **Life expectancy**
> NT   **Aging**
> RT   **Middle age**
>> **Old age**

Longitude   526; 527
> UF   Degrees of latitude and longitude
> BT   **Earth**
>> **Geodesy**
>> **Nautical astronomy**

Looking glasses
> USE   **Mirrors**

Looms   677; 746.1
> RT   **Weaving**

Loran   621.384
> BT   **Navigation**

Lord's Day
> USE   **Sabbath**

Lord's prayer   226.9; 242

Lord's Supper
> USE   **Eucharist**

Losing things
> USE   **Lost and found possessions**

Loss (Psychology)   155.9
> BT   **Psychology**

Lost and found possessions   330.1

Lost and found possessions—*Continued*
UF   Finding things
        Losing things
        Lost possessions
        Lost things
BT   **Property**
Lost architectural heritage
USE   **Lost architecture**
Lost architecture (May subdiv. geog.)
   720
   Use for materials on buildings and structures that have been destroyed or demolished.
UF   Lost architectural heritage
        Lost buildings
BT   **Architecture**
Lost buildings
USE   **Lost architecture**
Lost children
USE   **Missing children**
Lost continents   001.94; 398.23; 551.94
BT   **Continents**
        Geographical myths
NT   **Atlantis (Legendary place)**
Lost possessions
USE   **Lost and found possessions**
Lost things
USE   **Lost and found possessions**
Lost tribes of Israel   909
UF   Israel, Ten lost tribes of
        Jews—Lost tribes
        Ten lost tribes of Israel
BT   **Jews**
Lotteries (May subdiv. geog.)   **336.1**
BT   **Gambling**
Louisiana Purchase   973.4; 976.3
BT   **United States—History—1783-1815**
Love   152.4; 177; 306.7
UF   Affection
BT   **Emotions**
        Human behavior
NT   **Courtship**
        Crushes
        Intimacy (Psychology)
RT   **Friendship**
Love Canal Chemical Waste Landfill (Niagara Falls, N.Y.)   **363.72**
BT   **Hazardous waste sites**
        Landfills
Love poetry   808.1; 808.81
   Use for individual works, collections, or materials about love poetry.

BT   **Poetry**
RT   **Erotic poetry**
Love—Religious aspects   202; 231
UF   Love (Theology)
RT   **Charity**
Love stories   808.3; 808.83
   Use for individual works, collections, or materials about love stories.
UF   Romance novels
        Romances (Love stories)
        Romantic fiction
        Romantic stories
BT   **Fiction**
RT   **Erotic fiction**
        Gothic novels
        Romantic suspense novels
Love stories—Technique   808.3
BT   **Authorship**
Love (Theology)
USE   **Love—Religious aspects**
Low-calorie diet   613.2
SA   b
BT   **Diet**
RT   **Weight loss**
Low-carbohydrate diet   613.2
BT   **Diet**
RT   **Carbohydrates**
Low-cholesterol diet   613.2
BT   **Diet**
RT   **Cholesterol**
Low-fat diet   613.2
BT   **Diet**
RT   **Oils and fats**
Low income housing
USE   **Public housing**
Low-sodium diet
USE   **Salt-free diet**
Low temperature biology
USE   **Cryobiology**
Low temperatures   536; 621.5
UF   Cryogenics
BT   **Temperature**
NT   **Cryobiology**
RT   **Cold**
        Refrigeration
Loyalists, American
USE   **American Loyalists**
Loyalty   172
UF   Faithfulness
BT   **Ethics**
        Virtue
NT   **Patriotism**

Loyalty oaths
    USE   **Internal security**

LSD (Drug)   615
    UF   Acid (Drug)
          Lysergic acid diethylamide
    BT   **Hallucinogens**

Lubrication and lubricants   621.8
    UF   Grease
    BT   **Machinery**
    RT   **Bearings (Machinery)**
          Oils and fats

Lucumi (Religion)
    USE   **Santeria**

Luggage   685
    UF   Baggage
    BT   **Containers**

Lullabies (May subdiv. geog.)   **782.42**
    UF   Cradle songs
    BT   **Bedtime**
          Children's poetry
          Children's songs
          Songs

Lumber and lumbering (May subdiv. geog.)   **634.9; 674**

Use for general materials on lumber and the preparation of lumber. Materials on the felling of trees and the transportation of logs to sawmills are entered under **Logging**.

    UF   Timber
          Woods
    BT   **Forest products**
          Forests and forestry
          Trees
          Wood

Luminescence   535
    BT   **Light**
          Radiation
    NT   **Bioluminescence**
          Phosphorescence

Luminescent books
    USE   **Glow-in-the-dark books**

Luminous books
    USE   **Glow-in-the-dark books**

Lunar bases   629.45
    UF   Moon bases
    BT   **Civil engineering**
          Life support systems (Space environment)

Lunar eclipses   523.3
    UF   Eclipses, Lunar
          Moon—Eclipses
    BT   **Astronomy**

Lunar expeditions
    USE   **Space flight to the moon**

Lunar exploration
    USE   **Moon—Exploration**

Lunar geology   559.9
    UF   Geology, Lunar
          Geology—Moon
          Moon—Geology
    BT   **Astrogeology**
    NT   **Lunar soil**
          Moon rocks

Lunar petrology
    USE   **Moon rocks**

Lunar probes   629.43
    UF   Moon probes
    SA   names of specific lunar probe projects [to be added as needed]
    BT   **Space probes**
    NT   **Project Ranger**

Lunar rocks
    USE   **Moon rocks**

Lunar soil   523.3; 552.0999; 631.4
    UF   Moon soil
          Soils, Lunar
    BT   **Lunar geology**
    RT   **Moon—Surface**

Lunar surface
    USE   **Moon—Surface**

Lunar surface radio communication
    USE   **Radio in astronautics**

Luncheons   642
    BT   **Cooking**
          Menus
    RT   **Entertaining**

Lunchrooms
    USE   **Restaurants**

Lung cancer   616.99
    UF   Lungs—Cancer
    BT   **Cancer**
          Lungs—Diseases

Lungs   611; 612.2
    BT   **Respiratory system**

Lungs—Cancer
    USE   **Lung cancer**

Lungs—Diseases   616.2
    SA   types of lung diseases [to be added as needed]
    BT   **Diseases**
    NT   **Asthma**
          Lung cancer

Lungs—Diseases—*Continued*
       Pneumonia
       Tuberculosis
Lupus erythematosus   616.7
    BT   **Autoimmune diseases**
Lying
    USE **Truthfulness and falsehood**
Lyme disease (May subdiv. geog.)   616.9
    BT   **Diseases**
Lymphatic system   573.1; 612.4; 616.4
    BT   **Physiology**
Lynching (May subdiv. geog.)   364.1
    BT   **Crime**
    RT   **Vigilantes**
Lyricists (May subdiv. geog.)   **782.0092; 920**
    UF   Songwriters
    BT   **Poets**
Lyrics
    USE **Popular song lyrics**
Lysergic acid diethylamide
    USE **LSD (Drug)**
Machine design (May subdiv. geog.)   **621.8**
    UF   Machinery—Construction
         Machinery—Design and construction
    SA   types of machines, equipment, etc., with the subdivision *Design and construction*, e.g. **Airplanes—Design and construction** [to be added as needed]
    BT   **Design**
         Machinery
    NT   **Machinery—Models**
Machine intelligence
    USE **Artificial intelligence**
Machine language
    USE **Programming languages**
Machine readable bibliographic data   **025.3**
    UF   Bibliographic data in machine readable form
         Cataloging data in machine readable form
    SA   names of projects, formats, and systems, e.g. **MARC formats** [to be added as needed]
    BT   **Cataloging**
         Information services
         Information systems

Libraries—Automation
    NT   **MARC formats**
Machine readable catalog system
    USE **MARC formats**
Machine readable dictionaries   **413**
    UF   Dictionaries, Machine readable
    BT   **Encyclopedias and dictionaries**
Machine shop practice   **670.42**
    UF   Shop practice
    NT   **Drilling and boring (Metal, wood, etc.)**
         Grinding and polishing
    RT   **Machine shops**
Machine shops (May subdiv. geog.)   **670.42**
    RT   **Machine shop practice**
Machine tools (May subdiv. geog.)   **621.9**
    SA   types of machine tools [to be added as needed]
    BT   **Machinery**
         Tools
    NT   **Planing machines**
    RT   **Drilling and boring (Metal, wood, etc.)**
         Grinding and polishing
         Manufacturing processes
Machinery   **621.8**
    UF   Machines
    BT   **Manufactures**
         Mechanical engineering
         Power (Mechanics)
         Technology
         Tools
    NT   **Agricultural machinery**
         Bearings (Machinery)
         Belts and belting
         Construction equipment
         Conveying machinery
         Electric machinery
         Engines
         Gearing
         Hoisting machinery
         Hydraulic machinery
         Industrial equipment
         Lubrication and lubricants
         Machine design
         Machine tools
         Mechanical drawing
         Metalworking machinery
         Robots

Machinery—*Continued*
>> **Simple machines**
>> **Woodworking machinery**
> RT **Mechanics**
>> **Mills**
>> **Power transmission**

Machinery—Construction
> USE **Machine design**

Machinery—Design and construction
> USE **Machine design**

Machinery—Drawing
> USE **Mechanical drawing**

Machinery in industry
> USE **Industrial equipment**
>> **Machinery in the workplace**

Machinery in the workplace (May subdiv. geog.) **338**

Use for materials on the social and economic aspects of mechanization in the area of work.
> UF Machinery in industry
>> Technology in the workplace
> BT **Work environment**
> NT **Automation**

Machinery—Models 621.8
> UF Mechanical models
>> Models, Mechanical
> BT **Machine design**
>> **Models and modelmaking**

Machines
> USE **Machinery**

Machines, Simple
> USE **Simple machines**

Machu Picchu (Peru) 985
> BT **Sacred sites**

Macintosh (Computer) 004.165
> UF Apple Macintosh (Computer)
> BT **Computers**

Macroeconomics 339
> BT **Economics**

Madagascar 969.1

Made-for-TV movies
> USE **Television movies**

Madonna
> USE **Mary**

Magazine editing
> USE **Journalism—Editing**

Magazines
> USE **Periodicals**

Maghreb
> USE **North Africa**

Magic (May subdiv. geog.) **133.4**

Use for materials on charms, spells, etc., believed to have supernatural power. Materials on types of entertainment involving illusionistic tricks are entered under **Magic tricks**.
> UF Black art (Magic)
>> Black magic (Witchcraft)
>> Necromancy
>> Sorcery
>> Spells
> BT **Occultism**
> RT **Hallucinations and illusions**
>> **Magic tricks**
>> **Witchcraft**

Magic lanterns
> USE **Projectors**

Magic tricks 793.8
> UF Conjuring
>> Legerdemain
>> Prestidigitation
>> Sleight of hand
> BT **Amusements**
>> **Tricks**
> NT **Card tricks**
> RT **Hallucinations and illusions**
>> **Magic**

Magna Carta 342; 942.03
> BT **Charters**
>> **Great Britain—History—1154-1399, Plantagenets**

Magnet schools (May subdiv. geog.) **373.24**

Use for materials on schools offering special courses not available in the regular school curriculum and designed to attract students without reference to the usual attendance zone rules, often as an aid to voluntary school desegregation.
> BT **Public schools**
>> **School integration**
>> **Schools**

Magnet winding
> USE **Electromagnets**

Magnetic needle
> USE **Compass**

Magnetic recorders and recording 621.382

Use for general materials on audio, computer, and video recording on a magnetizable medium.
> UF Cassette recorders and recording
>> Tape recorders
> BT **Electronic apparatus and appliances**

Magnetic resonance accelerator
USE **Cyclotrons**
Magnetic resonance imaging   616.07
UF   Imaging, Magnetic resonance
MRI (Magnetic resonance imaging)
Nuclear magnetic resonance imaging
BT   **Diagnosis**
Magnetism   538
BT   **Physics**
NT   **Compass**
Electromagnetism
Electromagnets
Geomagnetism
Magnets
RT   **Electricity**
Magnets   538; 621.34
BT   **Magnetism**
NT   **Electromagnets**
Mahābhārata   891.4
BT   **Indian epic poetry**
Maiasaura   567.914
BT   **Dinosaurs**
Mail-order business (May subdiv. geog.)
658.8; 659.13
UF   Mail order catalogs
BT   **Business**
Direct selling
Selling
NT   **Direct marketing**
Mail order catalogs
USE   **Commercial catalogs**
Mail-order business
Mail service
USE   **Postal service**
Mainstreaming in education (May subdiv.
geog.)   371.9
BT   **Education**
Exceptional children
Handicapped children
RT   **Special education**
Maintenance and repair
USE   **Repairing**
and types of things that require
maintenance with the subdivision *Maintenance and repair,*
e.g. **Automobiles—Maintenance and repair; Buildings—Maintenance and repair;** etc.; and types of things

that require no maintenance
with the subdivision *Repairing,* e.g. **Radio—Repairing**
[to be added as needed]
Maintenance of biodiversity
USE   **Biodiversity conservation**
Maize
USE   **Corn**
Make-believe playmates
USE   **Imaginary playmates**
Makeup (Cosmetics)
USE   **Cosmetics**
Makeup, Theatrical
USE   **Theatrical makeup**
Making-choices stories
USE   **Plot-your-own stories**
Maladjusted children
USE   **Emotionally disturbed children**
Maladjustment (Psychology)
USE   **Adjustment (Psychology)**
Malaria (May subdiv. geog.)   616.9
BT   **Diseases**
Male actors (May subdiv. geog.)   791.4;
792; 920
Use for materials on several male actors that emphasize their identity as men. General materials on persons of the acting profession, whether male or female, are entered under **Actors**.
UF   Men actors
BT   **Actors**
Male change of life
USE   **Male climacteric**
Male circumcision
USE   **Circumcision**
Male climacteric   612.6
UF   Change of life in men
Climacteric, Male
Male change of life
Male menopause
Menopause, Male
BT   **Aging**
Male-female relationship
USE   **Man-woman relationship**
Male impersonators (May subdiv. geog.)
791.4
Use for materials on women who impersonate men for purposes of entertainment or comic effect. Materials on persons, especially men, who assume the dress of the opposite sex for psychological gratification are entered under **Transvestites**.
BT   **Impostors and imposture**

Male menopause
USE **Male climacteric**
Male role
USE **Sex role**
Malfeasance in office
USE **Misconduct in office**
Malformations, Congenital
USE **Birth defects**
Malignant tumors
USE **Cancer**
Malls, Shopping
USE **Shopping centers and malls**
Malnutrition (May subdiv. geog.)   **362.1;**
        616.3
  BT **Nutrition**
  RT **Starvation**
Malpractice (May subdiv. geog.)   **346.03**
  UF Liability, Professional
       Professional liability
       Professions—Tort liability
       Tort liability of professions
  SA types of professional personnel
       with the subdivision *Malprac-
       tice* [to be added as needed]
  BT **Liability (Law)**
  NT **Medical personnel—Malprac-
       tice**
       Physicians—Malpractice
Malpractice insurance (May subdiv.
     geog.)   **368.5**
  UF Insurance, Malpractice
       Insurance, Professional liability
       Professional liability insurance
  BT **Insurance**
Mammals (May subdiv. geog.)   **599**
  SA types of mammals, e.g. **Marine
       mammals**; **Primates**; **Bats**;
       etc. [to be added as needed]
  BT **Animals**
  NT **Badgers**
       Bats
       Bears
       Beavers
       Bison
       Camels
       Cats
       Cattle
       Chipmunks
       Deer
       Dogs
       Elephants

Fossil mammals
Horses
Marine mammals
Marsupials
Mice
Pigs
Primates
Rabbits
Reindeer
Seals (Animals)
Sheep
Squirrels
Whales
Wild cats
Mammals, Fossil
  USE **Fossil mammals**
Mammoths   **569**
  BT **Fossil mammals**
Man
  USE **Human beings**
Man—Antiquity
  USE **Human origins**
Man in space
  USE **Space flight**
Man—Influence of environment
  USE **Environmental influence on
       humans**
Man—Influence on nature
  USE **Human influence on nature**
Man—Origin
  USE **Human origins**
Man power
  USE **Manpower**
Man, Prehistoric
  USE **Fossil hominids**
       Prehistoric peoples
Man, Primitive
  USE **Primitive societies**
Man (Theology)
  USE **Human beings (Theology)**
Man-woman relationship (May subdiv.
     geog.)   **306.7**
  UF Female-male relationship
       Male-female relationship
       Men—Relations with women
       Men-women relationship
       Relationships, Man-woman
       Woman-man relationship
       Women-men relationship
       Women—Relations with men
  BT **Interpersonal relations**

Man-woman relationship—*Continued*
  RT **Dating (Social customs)**
Management (May subdiv. geog.)   **658**
  Use for materials on the theory of management and on the application of management principles to business and industry.
  UF   Administration
        Business administration
        Business management
        Industrial management
        Industrial organization
        Management science
        Organization and management
        Scientific management
  SA   types of management, e.g. **Office management**; types of businesses and industries, types of industrial plants and processes, and names of individual corporate bodies, with the subdivision *Management*, e.g. **Information systems—Management**; and types of institutions in the spheres of health, education, and social services, and names of individual institutions with the subdivision *Administration*, e.g. **Libraries—Administration**; **Schools—Administration**; etc. [to be added as needed]
  BT   **Business**
        Industries
  NT   **Conflict management**
        Crisis management
        Factory management
        Farm management
        Industrial efficiency
        Industrial relations
        Industrial welfare
        Information systems—Management
        Inventory control
        Job analysis
        Knowledge management
        Marketing
        Materials handling
        Natural resources—Management
        Occupational health and safety
        Office management

  Organizational behavior
  Organizational change
  Personnel management
  Planning
  Production standards
  Purchasing
  Sales management
  Time management
  RT   **Operations research**
Management buyouts
  USE   **Leveraged buyouts**
Management consultants
  USE   **Business consultants**
Management—Employee participation
  USE   **Participative management**
Management information systems (May subdiv. geog.)   **658.4**
  UF   Computer-based information systems
  BT   **Information systems**
Management of conflict
  USE   **Conflict management**
Management of knowledge assets
  USE   **Knowledge management**
Management science
  USE   **Management**
Managers
  USE   **Supervisors**
Mandates (May subdiv. geog.)   **321**
  BT   **International law**
        International organization
        International relations
Manga   **741.5**
  Use for individual works, collections, or materials about manga.
  BT   **Graphic novels**
  NT   **Gundam (Fictional character)**
        Josei
        Kodomo
        Mecha
        Neon Genesis Evangelion (Fictional robot)
        Seinen
        Shojo-ai
        Shojo manga
        Shonen-ai
        Shonen manga
Mania
  USE   **Manic-depressive illness**
Manic depression
  USE   **Manic-depressive illness**
Manic-depressive illness   **616.89**

Manic-depressive illness—_Continued_
- UF   Bipolar depression
  Bipolar disorder
  Mania
  Manic depression
  Manic-depressive psychoses
  Manic-depressive psychosis
  Melancholia
- BT   **Affective disorders**
  Mental illness
- RT   **Depression (Psychology)**

Manic-depressive psychoses
- USE   **Manic-depressive illness**

Manic-depressive psychosis
- USE   **Manic-depressive illness**

Manifest destiny (United States)
- USE   **United States—Territorial expansion**

Manikins (Fashion models)
- USE   **Fashion models**

Manipulative materials
- USE   **Manipulatives**

Manipulatives   371.33

Use for works on educational materials designed to be handled or touched by students in learning mathematical concepts.
- UF   Manipulative materials
  Manipulatives (Education)
- BT   **Audiovisual materials**
  Mathematics—Study and teaching
  Teaching—Aids and devices

Manipulatives (Education)
- USE   **Manipulatives**

Manned space flight
- USE   **Space flight**

Manned undersea research stations
- USE   **Undersea research stations**

Mannequins (Fashion models)
- USE   **Fashion models**

Manners
- USE   **Courtesy**
  Etiquette

Manners and customs   390
- UF   Ceremonies
  Customs, Social
  Folkways
  Social customs
  Social life and customs
  Traditions

- SA   ethnic groups and names of countries, cities, etc., with the subdivision _Social life and customs_ [to be added as needed]
- BT   **Civilization**
  Ethnology
- NT   **African Americans—Social life and customs**
  Anniversaries
  Blacks—Social life and customs
  Bohemianism
  Caste
  Chicago (Ill.)—Social life and customs
  Chivalry
  Clothing and dress
  Costume
  Country life
  Courts and courtiers
  Dating (Social customs)
  Dueling
  Excuses
  Fads
  Family traditions
  Festivals
  Folklore
  Funeral rites and ceremonies
  Gifts
  Holidays
  Hugging
  Jews—Social life and customs
  Lifestyles
  Marriage customs and rites
  Native Americans—Social life and customs
  Ohio—Social life and customs
  Seafaring life
  Taboo
  Tattooing
  Travel
  United States—Social life and customs
- RT   **Etiquette**
  Rites and ceremonies

Manpower (May subdiv. geog.)   **331.11**

Use for materials on the strength of a country in terms of available personnel, both military and industrial. Materials on personnel in specific fields are entered under kinds of workers, e.g. **Agricultural laborers; Nurses;**

Manpower—*Continued*
etc. Materials on investments of capital in training and educating employees to improve their productivity are entered under **Human capital**.

UF   Human resources
      Man power
SA   names of wars with the subdivision *Manpower*; e.g. **World War, 1939-1945—Manpower** [to be added as needed]
RT   **Labor supply**
      Military readiness

Manpower policy
USE **Labor policy**

Manslaughter
USE **Homicide**

Manual training
USE **Industrial arts education**

Manual workers
USE **Labor**
      Working class

Manufactures (May subdiv. geog.) **338.4; 670**
SA   types of manufacturing industries, e.g. **Textile industry**, and types of manufactures, e.g. **Glass manufacture** [to be added as needed]
BT   **Commercial products**
      Industries
NT   **Brand name products**
      Consumer goods
      Generic products
      Machinery
      Mills
      Papermaking
      Patents
      Prices
      Trademarks
      Waste products
RT   **Manufacturing industries**

Manufactures—Chicago (Ill.) **338.4**
UF   Chicago (Ill.)—Manufactures

Manufactures—Defects
USE **Product recall**

Manufactures—Ohio **338.4**
UF   Ohio—Manufactures

Manufactures recall
USE **Product recall**

Manufactures—United States **338.4**
UF   United States—Manufactures

Manufacturing in space
USE **Space industrialization**

Manufacturing industries (May subdiv. geog.) **338.4**
SA   types of manufacturing industries, e.g. **Textile industry**, and types of manufactures, e.g. **Glass manufacture** [to be added as needed]
BT   **Industries**
RT   **Manufactures**

Manufacturing processes (May subdiv. geog.) **658.5; 670**
UF   Industrial processing
      Production processes
SA   types of manufacturing industries, e.g. **Textile industry**, and types of manufactures, e.g. **Glass manufacture** [to be added as needed]
BT   **Industrial arts**
NT   **Forging**
      Founding
      Turning
      Welding
RT   **Machine tools**
      Materials

Manures
USE **Fertilizers**

Manuscripts (May subdiv. geog.) **091**
SA   subjects, literatures, groups of authors, individual literary authors, literary works entered under title, and sacred works with the subdivision *Manuscripts* [to be added as needed]
BT   **Archives**
      Bibliography
      Books
NT   **Illumination of books and manuscripts**
RT   **Autographs**
      Charters

Manuscripts, Illuminated
USE **Illumination of books and manuscripts**

Maoris (May subdiv. geog.) **305.89**
BT   **Indigenous peoples**

Map drawing **526**

Map drawing—*Continued*

UF   Cartography

       Plans

BT   **Drawing**

RT   **Topographical drawing**

Maple sugar (May subdiv. geog.)   **641.3; 664**

BT   **Sugar**

Maps   912

Use for general materials about maps and their history. Materials on the methods of map making and the mapping of areas are entered under **Map drawing**. Geographical atlases of world coverage are entered under **Atlases**.

UF   Cartography

       Chartography

       Plans

SA   types of maps, e.g. **Road maps**; subjects with the subdivision *Maps*, e.g. **Geology—Maps**; and names of countries, cities, etc., and names of wars with the subdivision *Maps* [to be added as needed]

BT   **Geography**

NT   **Atlases**

       Automobile travel—Guidebooks

       Chicago (Ill.)—Maps

       Geology—Maps

       Globes

       Moon—Maps

       Nautical charts

       Ohio—Maps

       Road maps

       United States—Maps

       World War, 1939-1945—Maps

RT   **Charts, diagrams, etc.**

Maps, Historical

USE   **Historical atlases**

Maps, Military

USE   **Military geography**

Marathon running (May subdiv. geog.)   **796.42**

UF   Long distance running

BT   **Running**

Marathon swimming (May subdiv. geog.)   **797.2**

UF   Long distance swimming

BT   **Swimming**

Marble (May subdiv. geog.)   **552; 553.5**

BT   **Rocks**

       Stone

MARC formats   025.3

UF   Machine readable catalog system

       MARC system

BT   **Bibliographic control**

       Machine readable bibliographic data

MARC system

USE   **MARC formats**

Marches (Demonstrations)

USE   **Demonstrations**

Marches (Exercises)

USE   **Marching drills**

Marches for civil rights

USE   **Civil rights demonstrations**

Marches (Music)   783.18

BT   **Military music**

Marching

USE   **Marching drills**

Marching drills (May subdiv. geog.)   **613.7**

UF   Drill (Nonmilitary)

       Drills, Marching

       Marches (Exercises)

       Marching

BT   **Physical education**

Mardi Gras

USE   **Carnival**

Mariculture

USE   **Aquaculture**

Marihuana

USE   **Marijuana**

Marijuana (May subdiv. geog.)   **362.29; 613.8; 615; 633.7**

UF   Cannabis

       Grass (Drug)

       Hashish

       Marihuana

       Pot (Drug)

BT   **Narcotics**

Marinas (May subdiv. geog.)   **387.1**

UF   Yacht basins

BT   **Boats and boating**

       Harbors

       Yachts and yachting

NT   **Docks**

Marine animals (May subdiv. geog.)   **591.77**

UF   Marine fauna

       Sea animals

BT   **Aquatic animals**

NT   **Corals**

       Marine mammals

Marine animals—*Continued*
  RT   **Marine biology**
Marine aquaculture
  USE **Aquaculture**
Marine aquariums (May subdiv. geog.)
      597.073; 639.34
  UF Salt water aquariums
      Sea water aquariums
  SA names of specific marine aquari-
      ums [to be added as needed]
  BT **Aquariums**
  NT **Marineland (Fla.)**
Marine architecture
  USE **Naval architecture**
Marine biology **578.77**
  UF Ocean life
      Sea life
  BT **Biology**
      Oceanography
  NT **Marine ecology**
      Marine plants
      Marine resources
  RT **Marine animals**
Marine disasters
  USE **Shipwrecks**
Marine drilling platforms
  USE **Drilling platforms**
Marine ecology (May subdiv. geog.)
      578.77
  BT **Ecology**
      Marine biology
  NT **Reef ecology**
Marine engineering (May subdiv. geog.)
      623.8
    Use for materials on engineering as applied
    to ships and their machinery.
  UF Naval engineering
  BT **Civil engineering**
      Engineering
      Mechanical engineering
      Naval architecture
      Naval art and science
      Steam navigation
Marine engines **623.87**
  BT **Engines**
      Shipbuilding
      Steam engines
Marine fauna
  USE **Marine animals**
Marine flora
  USE **Marine plants**

Marine geology
  USE **Submarine geology**
Marine insurance (May subdiv. geog.)
      368.2
  UF Insurance, Marine
  BT **Commerce**
      Insurance
      Maritime law
      Merchant marine
      Shipping
Marine law
  USE **Maritime law**
Marine mammals (May subdiv. geog.)
      599.5
  SA types of marine mammals [to be
      added as needed]
  BT **Mammals**
      Marine animals
  NT **Dolphins**
      Seals (Animals)
      Whales
Marine mineral resources (May subdiv.
  geog.) **333.8; 553**
  UF Mineral resources, Marine
      Ocean mineral resources
  BT **Marine resources**
      Mines and mineral resources
      Ocean bottom
      Ocean engineering
  NT **Ocean mining**
  RT **Ocean energy resources**
Marine painting (May subdiv. geog.)
      758
  UF Sea in art
      Seascapes
      Ships in art
  BT **Painting**
Marine plants (May subdiv. geog.) **579**
  UF Aquatic plants
      Marine flora
      Water plants
  BT **Marine biology**
      Plants
  NT **Algae**
  RT **Freshwater plants**
Marine pollution (May subdiv. geog.)
      363.739
  UF Ocean pollution
      Offshore water pollution
      Sea pollution

Marine pollution—*Continued*
  BT   **Oceanography**
        Water pollution
  RT   **Oil pollution of water**
Marine resources (May subdiv. geog.)
        333.91; 591.77
  UF Ocean—Economic aspects
        Ocean resources
        Resources, Marine
        Sea resources
  BT   **Commercial products**
        Marine biology
        Natural resources
        Oceanography
  NT   **Aquaculture**
        Marine mineral resources
        Ocean energy resources
        Ocean engineering
        Seafood
Marine salvage (May subdiv. geog.)
        387.5; 627
  UF Ship salvage
  BT   **International law**
        Maritime law
        Salvage
  RT   **Shipwrecks**
Marine transportation
  USE **Shipping**
Marineland (Fla.)   **597.073; 639.34**
  BT   **Marine aquariums**
Mariners
  USE **Sailors**
Mariner's compass
  USE **Compass**
Marionettes
  USE **Puppets and puppet plays**
Marital communication
  USE **Communication in marriage**
Marital counseling
  USE **Marriage counseling**
Marital infidelity
  USE **Adultery**
Marital separation
  USE **Separation (Law)**
Maritime discoveries
  USE **Exploration**
Maritime law (May subdiv. geog.)
        341.4; 343.09
  UF Law of the sea
        Marine law
        Merchant marine—Law and leg-
          islation

        Naval law
        Navigation—Law and legislation
        Sea laws
  BT   **International law**
        Law
        Shipping
  NT   **Freight**
        Marine insurance
        Marine salvage
        Merchant marine
        Pirates
        Ships—Safety regulations
  RT   **Commercial law**
        Territorial waters
Market gardening
  USE **Truck farming**
Market surveys (May subdiv. geog.)
        658.8
  BT   **Advertising**
        Surveys
  RT   **Public opinion polls**
Marketing (May subdiv. geog.)   **381;**
        658.8
    Use for materials on the principles and
  methods involved in the transfer of merchan-
  dise from producer to consumer. Materials on
  food buying are entered under **Grocery shop-**
  ping.
  UF Distribution (Economics)
        Merchandising
  SA   subjects with the subdivision
        Marketing, e.g. **Farm pro-**
        duce—Marketing [to be add-
        ed as needed]
  BT   **Business**
        Management
  NT   **Direct marketing**
        Direct selling
        Farm produce—Marketing
        Internet marketing
        New products
        Sales management
        Telemarketing
  RT   **Advertising**
        Selling
Marketing (Home economics)
  USE **Grocery shopping**
        Shopping
Marketing of farm produce
  USE **Farm produce—Marketing**
Markets (May subdiv. geog.)   **381; 658.8**
    Use for materials on places where many
  buyers and sellers are brought into contract

Markets—*Continued*
with one another in order to exhange goods and services.
- BT **Business**
  Cities and towns
  Commerce
- NT **Flea markets**
  Stock exchanges
- RT **Fairs**

Marking and grading (Education)
- USE **Grading and marking (Education)**

Marks
- USE **Hallmarks**
  and types of things with identifying marks, other than plate, with the subdivision *Marks,* e.g. **Pottery—Marks** [to be added as needed]

Marks on plate
- USE **Hallmarks**

Marriage (May subdiv. geog.) **306.81; 346.01**
- UF Married life
  Matrimony
- BT **Family**
  Sacraments
- NT **Betrothal**
  Communication in marriage
  Husbands
  Intermarriage
  Marriage contracts
  Marriage counseling
  Marriage customs and rites
  Married people
  Polygamy
  Remarriage
  Same-sex marriage
  Separation (Law)
  Teenage marriage
  Weddings
  Wives
- RT **Courtship**
  Domestic relations

Marriage—Annulment (May subdiv. geog.) **262.9; 346.01**
- UF Annulment of marriage

Marriage contracts (May subdiv. geog.) **306.81; 346.01**
- UF Antenuptial contracts
  Premarital contracts
  Prenuptial agreements
  Prenuptial contracts
- BT **Contracts**
  Marriage

Marriage counseling (May subdiv. geog.) **362.82**
- UF Marital counseling
  Premarital counseling
- BT **Counseling**
  Family life education
  Marriage
- RT **Divorce mediation**

Marriage—Cross-cultural studies 306.81

Marriage customs and rites (May subdiv. geog.) **392.5**
- UF Bridal customs
- BT **Manners and customs**
  Marriage
  Rites and ceremonies
  Weddings

Marriage, Interracial
- USE **Interracial marriage**

Marriage registers
- USE **Registers of births, etc.**

Marriage statistics
- USE **Vital statistics**

Married life
- USE **Marriage**

Married men
- USE **Husbands**

Married people (May subdiv. geog.) **306.872**
- UF Married persons
- BT **Family**
  Marriage
- NT **Husbands**
  Military spouses
  Wives

Married persons
- USE **Married people**

Married women
- USE **Wives**

Mars (Planet) 523.43
- BT **Planets**
- NT **Mars probes**

Mars (Planet)—Exploration 629.43
- BT **Planets—Exploration**

Mars (Planet)—Geology 559.9
- BT **Astrogeology**

Mars (Planet)—Pictorial works 523.43; 778.3

Mars (Planet)—Pictorial works—*Continued*
  BT   **Space photography**
Mars (Planet)—Satellites   523.9
  UF   Satellites—Mars
  BT   **Satellites**
Mars probes   629.43
  UF   Martian probes
  BT   **Mars (Planet)**
       Space probes
Marsh ecology (May subdiv. geog.)   577.68
  BT   **Ecology**
Marshall Plan
  USE **Reconstruction (1939-1951)**
Marshes (May subdiv. geog.)   551.41
  BT   **Wetlands**
Marsupials (May subdiv. geog.)   599.2
  BT   **Mammals**
Martial arts (May subdiv. geog.)   796.8
  BT   **Athletics**
  NT   **Archery**
       Dueling
       Jiu-jitsu
       Judo
       Karate
       Kung fu
       Tae kwon do
       Tai chi
  RT   **Self-defense**
       Self-defense for women
Martial law (May subdiv. geog.)   342
  BT   **Law**
  NT   **Habeas corpus**
  RT   **Military law**
Martian probes
  USE **Mars probes**
Martin Luther King Day   394.261
  BT   **Holidays**
Martyrs (May subdiv. geog.)   200.92; 272.092
  BT   **Church history**
       Heroes and heroines
  RT   **Persecution**
       Saints
Marxian theory
  USE **Marxism**
Marxism (May subdiv. geog.)   335.4
  UF   Marxian theory
       Marxist theory
  BT   **Economics**
       Philosophy
       Political science
       Sociology
  RT   **Class consciousness**
       Communism
       Dialectical materialism
       Socialism
Marxist theory
  USE **Marxism**
Mary   232.91
  UF   Blessed Virgin Mary
       Madonna
       Virgin Mary
  BT   **Saints**
Mary—Art   704.9
  BT   **Christian art**
Mary—Prayers   242
  BT   **Prayers**
Masai (African people) (May subdiv. geog.)   305.896
  BT   **Africans**
       Indigenous peoples
Mascots (May subdiv. geog.)   302.2223
  UF   School mascots
       Sports mascots
Masculine psychology
  USE **Men—Psychology**
Masculinity (May subdiv. geog.)   155.3
  UF   Masculinity (Psychology)
  BT   **Sex—Psychological aspects**
  RT   **Men**
Masculinity (Psychology)
  USE **Masculinity**
Masers   621.381
  BT   **Amplifiers (Electronics)**
       Electromagnetism
       Microwaves
Masks (Facial)   391.4
  BT   **Costume**
Masks (Plays)   808.2; 808.82
    Use for individual works, collections, or materials about masks.
  UF   Masques (Plays)
  BT   **Drama**
       Pageants
       Theater
Masks (Sculpture) (May subdiv. geog.)   731
  UF   Death masks
  BT   **Sculpture**
Masonic orders
  USE **Freemasons**
Masonry (May subdiv. geog.)   693

Masonry—*Continued*
  BT **Building**
       Stone
  NT **Cement**
       Concrete
       Plaster and plastering
       Stonecutting
  RT **Bricklaying**
Masons (Secret order)
  USE **Freemasons**
Masques (Plays)
  USE **Masks (Plays)**
Mass
  USE **Mass (Liturgy)**
Mass communication
  USE **Communication**
       Mass media
       Telecommunication
Mass culture
  USE **Popular culture**
Mass feeding
  USE **Food service**
Mass (Liturgy) 264
  UF Mass
  BT **Liturgies**
  RT **Eucharist**
Mass media (May subdiv. geog.) 302.23
  UF Mass communication
       Media
  SA topics with the subdivision *Press coverage*, e.g. **Food contamination—Press coverage** [to be added as needed]
  BT **Communication**
  NT **Motion pictures**
       Newspapers
       Periodicals
       Radio broadcasting
       Sex in mass media
       Television broadcasting
       Violence in mass media
  RT **Popular culture**
Mass media literacy
  USE **Media literacy**
Mass political behavior
  USE **Political participation**
       Political psychology
Mass psychology
  USE **Social psychology**
Mass spectra
  USE **Mass spectrometry**
Mass spectrometry 543; 547

  UF Mass spectra
       Mass spectrum analysis
  BT **Spectrum analysis**
Mass spectrum analysis
  USE **Mass spectrometry**
Mass transit
  USE **Local transit**
Massacres (May subdiv. geog.) 179.7; 904
  SA names of individual massacres, e.g. **Saint Bartholomew's Day, Massacre of, 1572** [to be added as needed]
  BT **Atrocities**
       History
       Persecution
  NT **Saint Bartholomew's Day, Massacre of, 1572**
Massage 613.7; 615.8
  BT **Physical therapy**
  NT **Acupressure**
       Chiropractic
       Electrotherapeutics
  RT **Osteopathic medicine**
Mastodon 569
  BT **Extinct animals**
       Fossil mammals
Mate selection in animals
  USE **Animal courtship**
Materia medica (May subdiv. geog.) 615
  UF Herbals
       Pharmacopoeias
  SA types of drugs [to be added as needed]
  BT **Medicine**
       Therapeutics
  NT **Anesthetics**
       Narcotics
  RT **Drugs**
       Pharmacology
       Pharmacy
Material culture (May subdiv. geog.) 306; 930.1
  Use for materials on the folk artifacts of a people produced by traditional methods.
  SA ethnic groups with the subdivision *Material culture*, e.g., **Native Americans—Material culture** [to be added as needed]
  BT **Culture**

Material culture—*Continued*
RT Folklore
Technology
Materialism (May subdiv. geog.) **146**
BT Philosophy
Positivism
RT Idealism
Realism
Materials 620.1

Use for comprehensive works on the basic processed materials used in engineering and industry. Works on unprocessed minerals and unprocessed animal and vegetable products are entered under **Raw materials**.

UF Engineering materials
Industrial materials
Strategic materials
SA types of materials, e.g. **Building materials**; **Hazardous substances**; etc.; and scientific and technical disciplines and types of equipment and construction with the subdivision *Materials* [to be added as needed]
NT **Adhesives**
Airplanes—Materials
Artists' materials
Building materials
Ceramics
Finishes and finishing
Hazardous substances
RT **Engineering**
Manufacturing processes
Materials handling (May subdiv. geog.)
388; 658.7
UF Handling of materials
Mechanical handling
BT **Management**
NT **Conveying machinery**
Freight
RT **Trucks**
Maternity
USE **Mothers**
Maternity leave (May subdiv. geog.)
331.44
BT **Parental leave**
Mathematical ability 153.9
UF Arithmetical ability
Number ability
BT **Ability**
Mathematical analysis 515
UF Analysis (Mathematics)

BT **Mathematics**
NT **Algebra**
Calculus
Functions
Graph theory
Linear algebra
Numerical analysis
Mathematical drawing
USE **Geometrical drawing**
Mechanical drawing
Mathematical logic
USE **Symbolic logic**
Mathematical models 511
UF Models
Models, Mathematical
SA subjects with the subdivision *Mathematical models*, e.g. **Pollution—Mathematical models** [to be added as needed]
BT **Mathematics**
NT **Computer simulation**
Fractals
Game theory
Pollution—Mathematical models
System analysis
Mathematical notation 510

Use for materials on the system of graphic symbols used in mathematics as well as for materials on the process or method of setting these down.

UF Mathematical symbols
Mathematics—Notation
Mathematics—Symbols
Notation, Mathematical
Symbols, Mathematical
RT **Mathematics**
Mathematical readiness 372.7
UF Arithmetical readiness
Mathematics readiness
Number readiness
Readiness for mathematics
BT **Arithmetic—Study and teaching**
Mathematics—Study and teaching
Mathematical recreations 793.74
UF Recreations, Mathematical
BT **Amusements**
Puzzles
Scientific recreations

Mathematical recreations—*Continued*
  NT **Number games**
Mathematical sequences
  USE **Sequences (Mathematics)**
Mathematical sets
  USE **Set theory**
Mathematical symbols
  USE **Mathematical notation**
Mathematicians (May subdiv. geog.)
    510.92; 920
  BT **Scientists**
  RT **Mathematics**
Mathematics (May subdiv. geog.)   **510**
  SA subjects with the subdivision
      Mathematics, e.g. **Astrono-**
      my—Mathematics [to be
      added as needed]
  BT **Science**
  NT **Algebra**
      Arithmetic
      Astronomy—Mathematics
      Binary system (Mathematics)
      Biomathematics
      Business mathematics
      Calculus
      Dynamics
      Fourth dimension
      Fractions
      Functions
      Game theory
      Geometry
      Group theory
      Mathematical analysis
      Mathematical models
      Measurement
      Metric system
      Number theory
      Patterns (Mathematics)
      Probabilities
      Sequences (Mathematics)
      Set theory
      Symbolic logic
      Trigonometry
      Word problems (Mathematics)
  RT **Mathematical notation**
      Mathematicians
Mathematics—Computer-assisted instruc-
  tion **372.7; 510.78**
  BT **Computer-assisted instruction**
Mathematics—Notation
  USE **Mathematical notation**

Mathematics readiness
  USE **Mathematical readiness**
Mathematics—Study and teaching (May
  subdiv. geog.) **372.7; 510.7**
  NT **Manipulatives**
      Mathematical readiness
Mathematics—Symbols
  USE **Mathematical notation**
Mathematics—Tables **510**
  UF Ready reckoners
  NT **Logarithms**
      Trigonometry—Tables
Mating behavior
  USE **Animal courtship**
      Sexual behavior in animals
Matrimony
  USE **Marriage**
Matter **117; 530**
  BT **Dynamics**
      Physics
  NT **Dark matter (Astronomy)**
Mausoleums
  USE **Tombs**
Maxims
  USE **Proverbs**
Mayas (May subdiv. geog.) **972.004**
  BT **Native Americans—Central**
      America
      Native Americans—Mexico
Maze gardens (May subdiv. geog.) **717**
  UF Labyrinth gardens
      Mazes
  BT **Gardens**
Maze puzzles **793.73**
  UF Mazes
  BT **Puzzles**
Mazes
  USE **Maze gardens**
      Maze puzzles
Meal planning
  USE **Menus**
      Nutrition
Meals
  USE types of meals, e.g. **Breakfasts**;
      Dinners; etc. [to be added as
      needed]
Meals for school children
  USE **School children—Food**
Meals on wheels programs (May subdiv.
  geog.) **362**
    Use for materials on programs that deliver
  meals to the homebound.

Meals on wheels programs—*Continued*
- UF Home delivered meals programs
- BT **Food relief**

Meanness
- USE **Bad behavior**

Measurement   389; 530.8
- UF Metrology
- SA subjects with the subdivision *Measurement*, e.g. **Air pollution—Measurement** [to be added as needed]
- BT **Mathematics**
- NT **Air pollution—Measurement**
  Geodesy
  Measuring instruments
  Photometry
  Surveying
  Volume (Cubic content)
- RT **Weights and measures**

Measurements, Electric
- USE **Electric measurements**

Measures
- USE **Weights and measures**

Measuring instruments   389; 681
- UF Instruments, Measuring
- BT **Measurement**
  Weights and measures

Meat (May subdiv. geog.)   **641.3; 664**
- SA types of meat [to be added as needed]
- BT **Food**
- NT **Beef**
  Carving (Meat, etc.)
  Cooking—Meat

Meat-eating animals
- USE **Carnivorous animals**

Meat industry (May subdiv. geog.) **338.1**
- UF Meat industry and trade
  Meat packing industry
  Packing industry
- BT **Food industry**
- NT **Meat inspection**
  Stockyards

Meat industry and trade
- USE **Meat industry**

Meat inspection (May subdiv. geog.) **363.19**
- UF Inspection of meat
- BT **Food adulteration and inspection**
  Meat industry
  Public health

Meat packing industry
- USE **Meat industry**

Mecha   741.5
Use for individual works, collections, or materials about mecha.
- UF Robot manga
- BT **Manga**
- NT **Fictional robots**
  Gundam (Fictional character)
  Neon Genesis Evangelion (Fictional robot)

Mechanic arts
- USE **Industrial arts**

Mechanical brains
- USE **Cybernetics**

Mechanical drawing   604.2
- UF Drafting, Mechanical
  Engineering drawing
  Industrial drawing
  Machinery—Drawing
  Mathematical drawing
  Plans
  Structural drafting
- BT **Drawing**
  Engineering
  Machinery
  Patternmaking
- NT **Blueprints**
  Graphic methods
  Lettering
- RT **Geometrical drawing**

Mechanical engineering (May subdiv. geog.)   **621**
Use for materials on the application of the principles of mechanics to the design, construction, and operation of machinery. Materials on the application of the principles of mechanics to engineering structures other than machinery are entered under **Applied mechanics**.
- BT **Civil engineering**
- NT **Electrical engineering**
  Machinery
  Marine engineering
  Mechanical movements
  Power (Mechanics)
  Power transmission
- RT **Steam engineering**

Mechanical handling
- USE **Materials handling**

Mechanical models
- USE **Machinery—Models**

Mechanical movements   531

Mechanical movements—*Continued*
  UF Mechanisms (Machinery)
  BT **Kinematics**
      Mechanical engineering
      Mechanics
      Motion
  NT **Robots**
      Simple machines
  RT **Gearing**
Mechanical musical instruments 786.6
  UF Musical instruments, Mechanical
  SA types of instruments, e.g. **Music
      boxes** [to be added as need-
      ed]
  BT **Musical instruments**
  NT **Music boxes**
Mechanical properties testing
  USE **Testing**
Mechanical speech recognition
  USE **Automatic speech recognition**
Mechanics 530; 531
  BT **Physics**
  NT **Applied mechanics**
      Dynamics
      Fluid mechanics
      Hydraulics
      Hydrodynamics
      Hydrostatics
      Mechanical movements
      Power (Mechanics)
      Simple machines
      Soil mechanics
      Statics
      Strains and stresses
      Strength of materials
      Vibration
      Viscosity
      Wave mechanics
  RT **Force and energy**
      Kinematics
      Machinery
      Motion
Mechanics, Applied
  USE **Applied mechanics**
Mechanics (Persons) (May subdiv. geog.)
    920
Mechanisms (Machinery)
  USE **Mechanical movements**
Medallions
  USE **Medals**
Medals (May subdiv. geog.) **355.1; 737**

  UF Badges of honor
      Medallions
  SA names of military services and
      other appropriate subjects with
      the subdivision *Medals,
      badges, decorations, etc.* [to
      be added as needed]
  NT **United States. Army—Medals,
      badges, decorations, etc.
      United States. Navy—Medals,
      badges, decorations, etc.**
  RT **Decorations of honor
      Insignia
      Numismatics**
Medals, badges, decorations, etc.
  USE types of armed forces with the
      subdivision *Medals, badges,
      decorations, etc.,* e.g. **United
      States. Army—Medals,
      badges, decorations, etc.** [to
      be added as needed]
Medea (Greek mythology) 398.22
  BT **Legendary characters**
Media
  USE **Mass media**
Media centers (Education)
  USE **Instructional materials centers**
Media coverage
  USE topics with the subdivision *Press
      coverage,* e.g. **Food contami-
      nation—Press coverage** [to
      be added as needed]
Media literacy (May subdiv. geog.)
    302.23
    Use for materials on a person's knowledge
    of and ability to use, interpret, and evaluate
    the mass media.
  UF Mass media literacy
  BT **Literacy**
Mediation
  USE **Arbitration and award**
Mediation, Divorce
  USE **Divorce mediation**
Mediation, Industrial
  USE **Industrial arbitration**
Mediation, International
  USE **International arbitration**
Medicaid (May subdiv. geog.)
    362.10973; 368.4
  UF Medical care for the poor
  BT **National health insurance
      Poor—Medical care**

Medicaid—*Continued*

      State medicine

RT   **Medicare**

Medical appointments and schedules

   USE   **Medical practice**

Medical botany   **581.6**

   UF   Botany, Medical

        Drug plants

        Herbal medicine

        Medicinal herbs

        Medicinal plants

        Plants, Medicinal

   BT   **Botany**

        Medicine

        Pharmacy

Medical care (May subdiv. geog.)   **362.1**

   Use for materials on the organization of services and facilities for medical care. Materials on the technical and scientific aspects of medical care are entered under **Medicine**.

   UF   Delivery of health care

        Delivery of medical care

        Health care

        Health care delivery

        Medical services

        Personal health services

   SA   ethnic groups, classes of persons, and names of wars with the subdivision *Medical care*, e.g. **Native Americans—Medical care**; **Elderly—Medical care**; etc. [to be added as needed]

   BT   **Public health**

   NT   **Access to health care**

        Armies—Medical care

        Dental care

        Elderly—Medical care

        Health facilities

        Health self-care

        Home care services

        Long-term care facilities

        Medical charities

        Mental health services

        Native Americans—Medical care

        Occupational health services

        Poor—Medical care

        Sports medicine

        Terminal care

        United States—History—1861-1865, Civil War—Medical care

        World War, 1939-1945—Medical care

   RT   **Health care reform**

        Medicine

Medical care—Access

   USE   **Access to health care**

Medical care—Costs (May subdiv. geog.)   **362.1**

   UF   Cost of medical care

        Medical service, Cost of

        Medicine—Cost of medical care

   BT   **Medical economics**

Medical care—Ethical aspects

   USE   **Medical ethics**

Medical care facilities

   USE   **Health facilities**

Medical care for the elderly

   USE   **Elderly—Medical care**

        Medicare

Medical care for the poor

   USE   **Medicaid**

        Poor—Medical care

Medical care—Government policy

   USE   **Medical policy**

Medical care reform

   USE   **Health care reform**

Medical care, Right to

   USE   **Right to health care**

Medical care—Social aspects

   USE   **Social medicine**

Medical centers (May subdiv. geog.)   **362.11**

   RT   **Hospitals**

Medical charities (May subdiv. geog.)   **362.1**

   UF   Charities, Medical

   BT   **Charities**

        Medical care

        Public health

   NT   **Institutional care**

   RT   **Hospitals**

Medical chemistry

   USE   **Clinical chemistry**

Medical colleges (May subdiv. geog.)   **610.71**

   UF   Medical schools

   BT   **Colleges and universities**

   RT   **Medicine—Study and teaching**

Medical consultation
USE **Medical practice**
Medical diagnosis
USE **Diagnosis**
Medical diagnostic imaging
USE **Diagnostic imaging**
Medical drama (Films)   791.43
Use for individual works, collections, or materials about medical films.
UF   Doctor films
BT   **Motion pictures**
**Medical drama (Radio programs)
791.44**
Use for individual works, collections, or materials about medical radio programs.
UF   Doctor radio programs
BT   **Radio programs**
**Medical drama (Television programs)
791.45**
Use for individual works, collections, or materials about medical television programs.
UF   Doctor television programs
BT   **Television programs**
Medical economics (May subdiv. geog.)
338.4
Use for comprehensive materials on the economic aspects of medical service from the point of view of both the practitioner and the public.
SA   types of medical services with the subdivision *Costs* [to be added as needed]
BT   **Economics**
NT   **Medical care—Costs**
Medical education
USE   **Medicine—Study and teaching**
Medical electricity
USE   **Electrotherapeutics**
Medical errors
USE   **Errors**
Medical personnel—Malpractice
Physicians—Malpractice
Medical ethics (May subdiv. geog.)
174.2
UF   Medical care—Ethical aspects
Medicine—Ethical aspects
SA   types of medical practices and procedures with the subdivision *Ethical aspects*, e.g.
Transplantation of organs, tissues, etc.—Ethical aspects
[to be added as needed]

BT   **Bioethics**
Ethics
Professional ethics
NT   **Euthanasia**
Human experimentation in medicine
Right to die
RT   **Social medicine**
Medical examinations
USE   **Periodic health examinations**
and subjects, classes of persons, ethnic groups, and military services with the subdivision *Medical examinations*, e.g.
Children—Medical examinations [to be added as needed]
Medical experimentation on humans
USE   **Human experimentation in medicine**
Medical fiction
USE   **Medical novels**
Medical folklore
USE   **Traditional medicine**
Medical genetics (May subdiv. geog.)
616
UF   Clinical genetics
Congenital diseases
Hereditary diseases
Heredity of diseases
SA   names of diseases with the subdivision *Genetic aspects* [to be added as needed]
BT   **Genetics**
Pathology
NT   **Birth defects**
Cancer—Genetic aspects
Genetic counseling
Medical inspection in schools
USE   **Children—Medical examinations**
Medical insurance
USE   **Health insurance**
Medical insurance, National
USE   **National health insurance**
Medical jurisprudence (May subdiv. geog.)   **614**
Use for materials on the application of medical knowledge to questions of law. Materials on the law as it affects medicine and the medical profession are entered under **Medicine—Law and legislation**.
UF   Forensic medicine
Jurisprudence, Medical

Medical jurisprudence—*Continued*
      Legal medicine
  BT **Forensic sciences**
  NT **DNA fingerprinting**
      Lie detectors and detection
      Poisons and poisoning
      Suicide
  RT **Medicine—Law and legislation**
Medical laws and legislation
  USE **Medicine—Law and legislation**
Medical malpractice
  USE **Medical personnel—Malpractice**
Medical missions (May subdiv. geog.)
      362.1
  UF Missions, Medical
  BT **Medicine**
Medical novels   **808.3**
  Use for individual works, collections, or materials about novels with a medical setting.
  UF Doctor novels
      Medical fiction
      Medicine—Fiction
  BT **Fiction**
Medical offices
  USE **Medical practice**
Medical partnership
  USE **Medical practice**
Medical personnel (May subdiv. geog.)
      610.69
  UF Health care personnel
      Health personnel
      Health professions
      Health sciences personnel
      Health services personnel
      Medical profession
  BT **Employees**
  NT **Nurses**
      Physicians
      Women in medicine
  RT **Medicine**
Medical personnel—Malpractice (May subdiv. geog.) **346.03**
  UF Medical errors
      Medical malpractice
  SA classes of persons in the medical field with the subdivision *Malpractice*; e.g. **Physicians—Malpractice** [to be added as needed]
  BT **Malpractice**
      Medicine—Law and legislation

Medical photography   **621.36; 778.3**
  BT **Photography**
      Photography—Scientific applications
Medical policy (May subdiv. geog.)
      362.1
  UF Government policy
      Health care policy
      Health policy
      Medical care—Government policy
      Medicine and state
      Public health—Government policy
  BT **Social policy**
Medical practice (May subdiv. geog.)
      610.6
  Use for materials on the organization and management of medicine as a profession. Scientific materials on the practice of medicine are entered under **Medicine**.
  UF Clinics
      Group medical practice
      Medical appointments and schedules
      Medical consultation
      Medical offices
      Medical partnership
      Medical profession
      Medicine—Practice
  SA types of medicine with the subdivision *Practice*, e.g. **Nuclear medicine—Practice** [to be added as needed]
  BT **Medicine**
  NT **Health maintenance organizations**
      Nuclear medicine—Practice
Medical profession
  USE **Medical personnel**
      Medical practice
      Medicine
Medical records (May subdiv. geog.)
      651.5
  UF Clinical records
      Health records
      Hospital care records
      Patient care records
Medical research
  USE **Medicine—Research**
Medical schools
  USE **Medical colleges**

Medical sciences
USE **Medicine**
Medical self-care
USE **Health self-care**
Medical service, Cost of
USE **Medical care—Costs**
Medical services
USE **Medical care**
Medical sociology
USE **Social medicine**
Medical technologists (May subdiv. geog.)
610.69
BT **Allied health personnel**
Medical technology (May subdiv. geog.)
610.28
BT **Medicine**
NT **Stem cell research**
Medical transplantation
USE **Transplantation of organs, tissues, etc.**
Medical waste disposal
USE **Medical wastes**
Medical wastes (May subdiv. geog.)
363.72
UF Disposal of medical waste
Hospital wastes
Infectious wastes
Medical waste disposal
Wastes, Medical
BT **Refuse and refuse disposal**
RT **Hazardous wastes**
Medicare (May subdiv. geog.) **368.4**
UF Medical care for the elderly
BT **Elderly—Medical care**
National health insurance
State medicine
RT **Medicaid**
Medication abuse 362.29; 613.8; 616.86
Use for materials on the abuse or misuse of therapeutic or medicinal drugs, either prescription or non-prescription.
UF Abuse of medications
Abuse of medicines
Pharmaceutical abuse
Prescription drug abuse
BT **Drug abuse**
Substance abuse
Medicinal chemistry
USE **Pharmaceutical chemistry**
Medicinal herbs
USE **Herbs—Therapeutic use**
Medical botany

Medicinal plants
USE **Medical botany**
Medicine (May subdiv. geog.) **610**
Use for materials on the technical and scientific aspects of medical care. Materials on the organization of services and facilities for medical care are entered under **Medical care**. Materials on the organization and management of medicine as a profession are entered under **Medical practice**.
UF Medical profession
Medical sciences
SA types of medicine, e.g. **Sports medicine**; and names of diseases and groups of diseases, e.g. **AIDS (Disease)**; **Fever**; **Nervous system—Diseases**; etc., and traditional medicine of particular ethnic groups, e.g. **Native American medicine** [to be added as needed]
BT **Life sciences**
Therapeutics
NT **Alternative medicine**
Anatomy
Aviation medicine
Biochemistry
Chinese medicine
Dentistry
Diagnosis
Emergency medicine
Endocrinology
Family medicine
First aid
Health
Holistic medicine
Hygiene
Immunology
Materia medica
Medical botany
Medical missions
Medical practice
Medical technology
Military medicine
Mind and body
Native American medicine
Nuclear medicine
Nursing
Orthopedics
Osteopathic medicine
Pathology
Periodic health examinations
Pharmacology

Medicine—*Continued*
>> Pharmacy
>> Physiology
>> Podiatry
>> Popular medicine
>> Preventive medicine
>> Psychiatry
>> Psychosomatic medicine
>> Quacks and quackery
>> Social medicine
>> Space medicine
>> Sports medicine
>> State medicine
>> Submarine medicine
>> Surgery
>> Therapeutics
>> Toxicology
>> Traditional medicine
>> Tropical medicine
>> Veterinary medicine
> RT **Diseases**
>> **Medical care**
>> **Medical personnel**
>> **Physicians**

Medicine and religion
> USE **Medicine—Religious aspects**

Medicine and state
> USE **Medical policy**

Medicine—Biography 610.92; 920
> BT **Biography**

Medicine—Cost of medical care
> USE **Medical care—Costs**

Medicine—Ethical aspects
> USE **Medical ethics**

Medicine—Fiction
> USE **Medical novels**

Medicine—Law and legislation (May subdiv. geog.) **344**

Use for materials on the law as it affects medicine and the medical profession. Materials on the application of medical knowledge to questions of law are entered under **Medical jurisprudence**.

> UF Medical laws and legislation
> BT **Law**
>> **Legislation**
> NT **Medical personnel—Malpractice**
>> **Physicians—Licenses**
>> **Physicians—Malpractice**
>> **Right to die**
> RT **Medical jurisprudence**

Medicine men
> USE **Shamans**

Medicine, Military
> USE **Military medicine**

Medicine—Miscellanea 610.2
> BT **Curiosities and wonders**

Medicine, Pediatric
> USE **Children—Diseases**

Medicine—Physiological effect
> USE **Pharmacology**

Medicine, Popular
> USE **Popular medicine**

Medicine—Practice
> USE **Medical practice**

Medicine, Preventive
> USE **Preventive medicine**

Medicine, Psychosomatic
> USE **Psychosomatic medicine**

Medicine—Religious aspects (May subdiv. geog.) **201; 261.5; 615.8**
> UF Medicine and religion
>> Religion and medicine
> NT **Spiritual healing**

Medicine—Research (May subdiv. geog.) **610.7**
> UF Medical research
> BT **Research**
> NT **Experimental medicine**
>> **Human experimentation in medicine**
>> **Stem cell research**

Medicine—Social aspects
> USE **Social medicine**

Medicine, State
> USE **State medicine**

Medicine—Study and teaching (May subdiv. geog.) **610.7**
> UF Medical education
> RT **Medical colleges**

Medicine—United States 610.973

Medieval architecture (May subdiv. geog.) **723**
> UF Architecture, Medieval
> BT **Architecture**
>> **Medieval civilization**
> NT **Byzantine architecture**
>> **Gothic architecture**
>> **Romanesque architecture**
> RT **Castles**
>> **Cathedrals**

Medieval art (May subdiv. geog.)
709.02
UF Art, Medieval
BT **Art**
Medieval civilization
NT **Byzantine art**
Gothic art
Illumination of books and manuscripts
Romanesque art
Medieval church history
USE **Church history—600-1500, Middle Ages**
Medieval civilization 909.07
Use for materials on cultural and intellectual developments in the Middle Ages not limited to a single country or region.
UF Civilization, Medieval
BT **Civilization**
NT **Feudalism**
Medieval architecture
Medieval art
Medieval literature
Medieval philosophy
Medieval tournaments
RT **Chivalry**
Middle Ages
Medieval Greece
USE **Greece—History—323-1453**
Medieval literature 809
May use same subdivisions as for Literature.
UF Literature, Medieval
BT **Literature**
Medieval civilization
NT **Early Christian literature**
Old Norse literature
Medieval philosophy 189
UF Philosophy, Medieval
BT **Medieval civilization**
Philosophy
Medieval tournaments (May subdiv. geog.) **394**
Use for materials on medieval contests in which mounted and armored contestants fought for a prize with blunted weapons and in accordance with certain rules, and for materials on modern re-enactments of such events.
UF Tournaments
BT **Chivalry**
Medieval civilization
Pageants

Meditation 158; 204; 248.3; 296.7
Use for materials on spiritual contemplation or mental prayer. Collections of personal reflections or thoughts for use in meditation are entered under **Meditations**.
BT **Devotional exercises**
Spiritual life
NT **Transcendental meditation**
RT **Meditations**
Meditations 204; 242
Use for collections of personal reflections or thoughts for use in meditation. Materials on spiritual contemplation or mental prayer are entered under **Meditation**.
SA religious topics, names of individual persons, and titles of sacred works with the subdivision *Meditations*, e.g. **Lent—Meditations** [to be added as needed]
BT **Devotional literature**
Prayers
NT **Lent—Meditations**
RT **Meditation**
Mediterranean Sea 551.462
BT **Seas**
Meetings, Public
USE **Public meetings**
Megalithic monuments (May subdiv. geog.) **930.1**
BT **Antiquities**
Archeology
Monuments
Melancholia
USE **Depression (Psychology)**
Manic-depressive illness
Melancholy 616.89
BT **Emotions**
Mood (Psychology)
Melodrama 808.82
Use for individual works, collections, or materials about melodrama.
BT **Drama**
Members of Parliament
USE **Legislators**
Memoirs
USE **Autobiographies**
Autobiography
Biography
Memorabilia
USE **Collectibles**
Memorial Day 394.262
UF Decoration Day
BT **Holidays**

Memorizing
  USE   subjects, types of literature, and
        titles of sacred works with
        the subdivision *Memorizing,*
        e.g. **Poetry—Memorizing** [to
        be added as needed]
Memory   153.1
  SA   subjects, types of literature, and
       titles of sacred works with
       the subdivision *Memorizing,*
       e.g. **Poetry—Memorizing** [to
       be added as needed]
  BT   **Brain**
       Educational psychology
       Intellect
       Psychology
       Psychophysiology
       Thought and thinking
  NT   **Amnesia**
       Attention
       False memory syndrome
       Forgetfulness
       Psychology of learning
       Recovered memory
  RT   **Mnemonics**
Memory devices (Computers)
  USE   **Computer storage devices**
Men (May subdiv. geog.)   **305.31**
  SA   men of particular racial, reli-
       gious or ethnic groups, e.g.
       African American men; **Jew-
       ish men**; and men in various
       occupations and professions,
       e.g. **Male actors** [to be added
       as needed]
  NT   **African American men**
       Brothers
       Fathers
       Gay men
       Husbands
       Jewish men
       Single men
       Sons
       Widowers
       Young men
  RT   **Masculinity**
Men actors
  USE   **Male actors**
Men—Biography   920
  BT   **Biography**

Men—Clothing
  USE   **Men's clothing**
Men—Diseases (May subdiv. geog.)
       616.0081
  BT   **Diseases**
Men—Education (May subdiv. geog.)
       370.81
  UF   Education of men
  BT   **Education**
  RT   **Coeducation**
Men—Employment (May subdiv. geog.)
       331.11
  BT   **Employment**
Men in business
  USE   **Businessmen**
Men—Psychology   155.3
  UF   Masculine psychology
  BT   **Psychology**
Men—Relations with women
  USE   **Man-woman relationship**
Men—Social conditions (May subdiv.
       geog.)   **305.32**
  BT   **Social conditions**
  NT   **Men's movement**
Men—Societies (May subdiv. geog.)   **367**
  UF   Men's clubs
       Men's organizations
  BT   **Clubs**
       Societies
Men-women relationship
  USE   **Man-woman relationship**
Mendel's law   576.5
  BT   **Breeding**
       Variation (Biology)
  NT   **Genetics**
  RT   **Heredity**
Mendicancy
  USE   **Begging**
Mendicant orders
  USE   **Franciscans**
Mending
  USE   **Clothing and dress—Repairing**
       Repairing
Mennonites (May subdiv. geog.)   **289.7**
  BT   **Christian sects**
  NT   **Amish**
Menopause   612.6; 618.1
  UF   Change of life in women
       Climacteric, Female
       Female climacteric
  BT   **Aging**

Menopause, Male
USE **Male climacteric**
Men's clothing (May subdiv. geog.)
646; 687
UF Men—Clothing
BT **Clothing and dress**
Men's clubs
USE **Men—Societies**
Men's liberation movement
USE **Men's movement**
Men's movement (May subdiv. geog.)
305.32
UF Men's liberation movement
BT **Men—Social conditions**
Men's organizations
USE **Men—Societies**
Menstruation 612.6
BT **Reproduction**
NT **Premenstrual syndrome**
Mental arithmetic 513
UF Mental calculation
BT **Arithmetic**
Mental calculation
USE **Mental arithmetic**
Mental deficiency
USE **Mental retardation**
Mental depression
USE **Depression (Psychology)**
Mental diseases
USE **Abnormal psychology**
Mental illness
Mental healing (May subdiv. geog.)
615.8
Use for materials on psychic or psychological means to treat illness. Materials on the use of faith, prayer, or religious means to treat illness are entered under **Spiritual healing**.
UF Healing, Mental
Mind cure
Psychic healing
BT **Alternative medicine**
NT **Hypnotism**
RT **Mental suggestion**
Mind and body
Psychotherapy
Spiritual healing
Subconsciousness
Suggestive therapeutics
Mental health (May subdiv. geog.)
362.2
UF Mental hygiene

SA ethnic groups, classes of persons, and names of individual persons with the subdivision *Mental health*, e.g. **Women—Mental health** [to be added as needed]
BT **Happiness**
Health
NT **Burn out (Psychology)**
Occupational therapy
Stress (Psychology)
Women—Mental health
RT **Abnormal psychology**
Mental illness
Mind and body
Psychiatry
Psychology
Mental health care
USE **Mental health services**
Mental health services (May subdiv. geog.) **362.2; 616.89**
UF Mental health care
Psychiatric care
Psychiatric services
SA ethnic groups, classes of persons, and names of individual educational institutions with the subdivision *Mental health services* [to be added as needed]
BT **Medical care**
NT **Crisis intervention (Mental health services)**
Mental hospitals
USE **Psychiatric hospitals**
Mental hygiene
USE **Mental health**
Mental illness (May subdiv. geog.) **362.2; 616.89**
Use for popular materials and materials on regional or social aspects of mental disorders. Materials on clinical aspects of mental disorders, including therapy, are entered under **Psychiatry**. Systematic descriptions of mental disorders are entered under **Abnormal psychology**.
UF Mental diseases
Psychoses
SA names of specific illnesses, e.g. **Manic-depressive illness** [to be added as needed]
BT **Abnormal psychology**
Diseases

Mental illness—*Continued*
    NT   **Manic-depressive illness**
         Multiple personality
         Neurasthenia
         Schizophrenia
    RT   **Mental health**
         Mentally ill
         Personality disorders
         Psychiatry
Mental illness—Drug therapy   616.89
    BT   **Drug therapy**
Mental illness—Jurisprudence
    USE   **Insanity defense**
Mental illness—Physiological aspects
    616.89
    BT   **Physiology**
Mental institutions
    USE   **Mentally ill—Institutional care**
Mental patients
    USE   **Mentally ill**
Mental retardation (May subdiv. geog.)
    362.3; 616.85
    UF   Mental deficiency
    BT   **Abnormal psychology**
    NT   **Down syndrome**
    RT   **Mentally handicapped**
Mental stereotype
    USE   **Stereotype (Social psychology)**
Mental stress
    USE   **Stress (Psychology)**
Mental suggestion   131; 154.7; 615.8
    UF   Autosuggestion
         Suggestion, Mental
    BT   **Mind and body**
         Parapsychology
         Subconsciousness
    NT   **Brainwashing**
    RT   **Hypnotism**
         Mental healing
         Suggestive therapeutics
Mental telepathy
    USE   **Telepathy**
Mental tests
    USE   **Intelligence tests**
         Psychological tests
Mental types
    USE   **Typology (Psychology)**
Mentally depressed
    USE   **Depression (Psychology)**
Mentally deranged
    USE   **Mentally ill**

Mentally handicapped (May subdiv.
    geog.)   305.9; 362.2; 362.3
    UF   Mentally retarded
    BT   **Handicapped**
    NT   **Mentally handicapped children**
    RT   **Mental retardation**
Mentally handicapped children (May
    subdiv. geog.)   155.45; 362.2;
    362.3
    UF   Children, Retarded
         Mentally retarded children
         Retarded children
    BT   **Child psychiatry**
         Handicapped children
         Mentally handicapped
    RT   **Slow learning children**
**Mentally handicapped children—Educa-
    tion** (May subdiv. geog.)   371.92
    BT   **Education**
         Special education
Mentally ill (May subdiv. geog.)   362.2;
    616.89
    UF   Insane
         Mental patients
         Mentally deranged
         Psychotics
    BT   **Sick**
    NT   **Emotionally disturbed children**
    RT   **Mental illness**
Mentally ill children
    USE   **Emotionally disturbed children**
Mentally ill—Institutional care (May
    subdiv. geog.)   362.2
    UF   Mental institutions
    BT   **Institutional care**
    RT   **Psychiatric hospitals**
Mentally retarded
    USE   **Mentally handicapped**
Mentally retarded children
    USE   **Mentally handicapped children**
Mentoring (May subdiv. geog.)   361;
    371.102; 658.3
    BT   **Counseling**
Menus   642
    UF   Bills of fare
         Meal planning
    BT   **Cooking**
         Diet
    NT   **Breakfasts**
         Dinners
         Luncheons

Menus—*Continued*
    RT   **Catering**
Mercantile buildings
    USE   **Commercial buildings**
Mercantile law
    USE   **Commercial law**
Mercenary soldiers (May subdiv. geog.)
    355.3
    UF   Mercenary troops
          Soldiers of fortune
    BT   **Military personnel**
          Soldiers
Mercenary troops
    USE   **Mercenary soldiers**
Merchandise
    USE   **Commercial products**
          Consumer goods
Merchandising
    USE   **Marketing**
          Retail trade
Merchant marine (May subdiv. geog.)
    387.5
    BT   **Maritime law**
          Sailors
          Ships
          Transportation
    NT   **Harbors**
          Marine insurance
    RT   **Shipping**
Merchant marine—Law and legislation
    USE   **Maritime law**
Merchant marine—Safety regulations
    USE   **Ships—Safety regulations**
Merchant marine—United States
    387.50973
Merchants (May subdiv. geog.)
    380.1092; 920
    BT   **Businesspeople**
Mercury   **546; 669**
    UF   Quicksilver
    BT   **Chemical elements**
          Metals
Mercury (Planet)   **523.41**
    BT   **Planets**
Mercy killing
    USE   **Euthanasia**
Mergers
    USE   **Corporate mergers and acqui-**
          sitions
          and types of institutions and
            types of industries and busi-

nesses with the subdivision
Mergers, e.g. **Railroads—**
Mergers [to be added as
needed]
Merlin (Legendary character)   **398.22**
    BT   **Legendary characters**
Mermaids and mermen   **398.21**
    BT   **Mythical animals**
Mesmerism
    USE   **Hypnotism**
Messages
    USE   types of public officials and
            names of individual public of-
            ficials with the subdivision
            Messages, e.g. **Presidents—**
            United States—Messages [to
            be added as needed]
Messages to Congress
    USE   **Presidents—United States—**
          Messages
Messiness   **648**
    UF   Disorderliness
          Sloppiness
    BT   **Human behavior**
Metabolism   **572**
    BT   **Biochemistry**
    NT   **Growth disorders**
          Minerals in the body
Metal finishing
    USE   **Metals—Finishing**
Metal work
    USE   **Metalwork**
Metallography   **669**
    Use for materials on the science of metal
    structures and alloys, especially the study of
    such structures with the microscope. Materials
    on the process of extracting metals from their
    ores, refining them, and preparing them for
    use, are entered under **Metallurgy.**
    UF   Metallurgical analysis
          Microscopic analysis
    BT   **Metals**
Metallurgical analysis
    USE   **Metallography**
Metallurgy (May subdiv. geog.)   **669**
    Use for materials on the process of extract-
    ing metals from their ores, refining them, and
    preparing them for use. Materials on the sci-
    ence of metal structures and alloys, especially
    the study of such structures with the micro-
    scope, are entered under **Metallography.**
    NT   **Electrometallurgy**
    RT   **Alloys**
          Chemical engineering

Metallurgy—*Continued*
> Industrial chemistry
> Metals
> Ores
> Smelting

Metals **669**
> SA types of metals [to be added as needed]
> BT Inorganic chemistry
>   Ores
> NT Alloys
>   Aluminum
>   Brass
>   Iron
>   Mercury
>   Metallography
>   Pewter
>   Precious metals
>   Soldering
>   Tin
>   Zinc
> RT Metallurgy
>   Metalwork

Metals—Finishing **671.7**
> UF Metal finishing
> BT Finishes and finishing
>   Metalwork

Metalwork (May subdiv. geog.) **671; 739**
> UF Metal work
> BT Decoration and ornament
> NT Architectural metalwork
>   Art metalwork
>   Bronzes
>   Copperwork
>   Dies (Metalworking)
>   Electroplating
>   Forging
>   Founding
>   Goldwork
>   Ironwork
>   Metals—Finishing
>   Plate metalwork
>   Sheet metalwork
>   Silverwork
>   Soldering
>   Steel
>   Tinwork
>   Welding
>   Wire craft
> RT Metals
>   Metalworking machinery

Metalworking machinery (May subdiv. geog.) **621.9**
> BT Machinery
> RT Metalwork

Metamorphosis **571.876**
> SA individual animals and groups of animals with the subdivision *Metamorphosis*, e.g. **Insects—Metamorphosis** [to be added as needed]
> BT Change

Metamorphosis—Folklore (May subdiv. geog.) **398.2**
> UF Metamorphosis (in religion, folklore, etc.)

Metamorphosis (in religion, folklore, etc.)
> USE Metamorphosis—Folklore
>   Metamorphosis—Religious aspects

Metamorphosis—Religious aspects **291**
> UF Metamorphosis (in religion, folklore, etc.)

Metaphysics **110**
> BT Philosophy
> NT Causation
>   Change
>   Existentialism
>   Space and time
>   Theory of knowledge
> RT God

Meteorites **523.5**
> BT Astronomy
>   Meteors

Meteorological instruments **551.5028**
> UF Instruments, Meteorological
> SA types of meteorological instruments [to be added as needed]
> BT Scientific apparatus and instruments
> NT Barometers
>   Thermometers

Meteorological observatories (May subdiv. geog.) **551.5028**
> UF Meteorology—Observatories
>   Observatories, Meteorological
>   Weather stations
> RT Meteorology

Meteorological satellites **551.63**
> UF Weather satellites

Meteorological satellites—*Continued*
    SA   names of satellites, e.g. **TIROS**
           satellites [to be added as
           needed]
    BT   **Artificial satellites**
    NT   **TIROS satellites**

Meteorology (May subdiv. geog.)   **551.5**
    Use for scientific materials on the atmosphere, especially weather factors. Materials on climate as it relates to humans and to plant and animal life, including the effects of changes of climate, are entered under **Climate**. Materials on the state of the atmosphere at a given time and place with respect to heat or cold, wetness or dryness, calm or storm, are entered under **Weather**.
    BT   **Earth sciences**
    NT   **Air**
          Auroras
          Clouds
          Cyclones
          Droughts
          Floods
          Fog
          Frost
          Humidity
          Lightning
          Meteorology in aeronautics
          Monsoons
          Precipitation (Meteorology)
          Rainbow
          Seasons
          Solar radiation
          Storms
          Sunspots
          Thunderstorms
          Tornadoes
          Weather control
          Weather—Folklore
          Weather forecasting
          Winds
    RT   **Atmosphere**
          Climate
          Meteorological observatories
          Weather

Meteorology in aeronautics   **629.132**
    BT   **Aeronautics**
          Meteorology

Meteorology—Observatories
    USE **Meteorological observatories**

Meteorology—Tables   **551.5**

Meteors   **523.5**
    UF   Falling stars
          Shooting stars

    BT   **Astronomy**
          Solar system
    NT   **Meteorites**

Meter
    USE **Musical meter and rhythm**
          Versification

Meters, Electric
    USE **Electric meters**

Meth (Drug)
    USE **Methamphetamine**

Methamphetamine   **362.29; 615**
    UF   Meth (Drug)
          Speed (Drug)
    BT   **Amphetamines**
    NT   **Crystal meth (Drug)**

Methodology
    USE subjects with the subdivision
          Methodology, e.g. **Science—**
          Methodology [to be added as
          needed]

Metric system   **389; 530.8**
    BT   **Arithmetic**
          Mathematics
    RT   **Decimal system**
          Weights and measures

Metrical romances
    USE **Romances**

Metrology
    USE **Measurement**
          Weights and measures

Metropolitan areas (May subdiv. geog.)
          307.76
    UF   Urban areas
    SA   names of metropolitan areas, e.g.
          **Chicago Metropolitan Area
          (Ill.)** [to be added as needed]
    BT   **Cities and towns—Growth**
    NT   **Suburbs**
          Urban renewal

Metropolitan finance   **336**
    Use for general materials on the public finance of metropolitan areas. Materials on the finance of a particular metropolitan area are entered under **Public finance** with the appropriate geographic subdivision.
    BT   **Municipal finance**
          Public finance

Metropolitan government   **320.8; 352.16**
    SA   names of metropolitan areas
          with the subdivision *Politics
          and government* [to be added
          as needed]
    BT   **Local government**

Metropolitan government—*Continued*

  NT   **Chicago Metropolitan Area (Ill.)—Politics and government**

  RT   **Municipal government**

Metropolitan planning

  USE **Regional planning**

Mexican American authors 810.9; 920

  SA   genres of American literature with the subdivision *Mexican American authors* [to be added as needed]

  BT   **Hispanic American authors**

Mexican American literature (English)

  USE **American literature—Mexican American authors**

Mexican American women (May subdiv. geog.) 305.868

  UF   Chicanas

  BT   **Mexican Americans**
         Women

Mexican Americans (May subdiv. geog.) 305.868; 973

Use for materials on American citizens of Mexican descent. Materials on noncitizens from Mexico are entered under **Mexicans—United States**. Use these same patterns for other ethnic groups in the U.S. and other countries.

  UF   Chicanos

  BT   **Ethnic groups**
         Hispanic Americans
         Immigrants—United States
         Minorities

  NT   **Mexican American women**

  RT   **Mexicans—United States**

Mexican Americans—Ethnic identity 305.868

Mexican literature 860; M860

May use same subdivisions and names of literary forms as for **English literature**.

  BT   **Latin American literature**
         Literature

Mexican War, 1846-1848 973.6

  UF   United States—History—1845-1848, War with Mexico

  BT   **United States—History—1815-1861**

Mexicans (May subdiv. geog.) 305.868; 920; 972

Mexicans—United States 305.868

Use for materials on noncitizens from Mexico. Materials on American citizens of Mexican descent are entered under **Mexican Americans**. Use these same patterns for other ethnic groups in the U.S. and other countries.

  BT   **Aliens—United States**
         Minorities

  RT   **Mexican Americans**

Mexico 972

May be subdivided like **United States** except for *History*.

Mexico—Presidents

  USE **Presidents—Mexico**

Mezzotint engraving 766

  BT   **Engraving**

MIAs

  USE **Missing in action**

Mice 599.35; 636.088

  UF   Mouse

  BT   **Mammals**

Microbes

  USE **Bacteria**
       Germ theory of disease
       Microorganisms
       Viruses

Microbial drug resistance

  USE **Drug resistance in microorganisms**

Microbial energy conversion

  USE **Biomass energy**

Microbiology 579

  SA   subjects with the subdivision *Microbiology* [to be added as needed]

  BT   **Biology**

  NT   **Air—Microbiology**
         Bacteriology
         Biotechnology
         Cheese—Microbiology
         Fermentation
         Food—Microbiology
         Soil microbiology

  RT   **Microorganisms**

Microbreweries (May subdiv. geog.) 663

  UF   Boutique breweries

  BT   **Breweries**

Microchemistry 540

  BT   **Chemistry**

Microcomputers

  USE **Personal computers**

Microcredit

  USE **Microfinance**

Microeconomics 338.5

  UF   Price theory

Microeconomics—*Continued*
    BT   **Economics**
Microelectronics   621.381
    UF   Microminiature electronic equipment
          Microminiaturization (Electronics)
    BT   **Electronics**
          Semiconductors
Microfilming
    USE **Microphotography**
Microfilms   302.23; 686.4
    BT   **Microforms**
Microfinance (May subdiv. geog.)   **332**
    UF   Microcredit
          Microloans
    BT   **Loans**
Microforms   302.23; 686.4
    UF   Micropublications
    SA   types of microforms [to be added as needed]
    NT   **Microfilms**
    RT   **Microphotography**
Microloans
    USE **Microfinance**
Microminiature electronic equipment
    USE **Microelectronics**
Microminiaturization (Electronics)
    USE **Microelectronics**
Microorganisms   579
    UF   Germs
          Microbes
          Microscopic organisms
    NT   **Bacteria**
          Drug resistance in microorganisms
          Probiotics
          Protozoa
          Viruses
    RT   **Microbiology**
Microphotography   686.4
    Use for materials on the photographing of objects of any size to produce minute images. Materials on the photographing of minute objects through a microscope are entered under **Photomicrography**.
    UF   Microfilming
    BT   **Photography**
    RT   **Microforms**
Microprocessors   004.16
    Use for materials on the silicon chip that contains the central processing units of a microcomputer or other electronic device.

    BT   **Computers**
Micropublications
    USE **Microforms**
Microscope and microscopy
    USE **Microscopes**
Microscopes   502.8
    UF   Microscope and microscopy
          Microscopic analysis
    BT   **Optical instruments**
    NT   **Electron microscopes**
    RT   **Photomicrography**
Microscopic analysis
    USE **Metallography**
          Microscopes
Microscopic organisms
    USE **Microorganisms**
Microsoft Word (Computer software) 005.5
    UF   Word (Computer software)
    BT   **Computer software**
Microwave communication systems 621.381
    BT   **Intercommunication systems**
          Shortwave radio
          Telecommunication
    NT   **Closed-circuit television**
Microwave cookery
    USE **Microwave cooking**
Microwave cooking   641.5
    UF   Microwave cookery
    BT   **Cooking**
Microwaves   537.5
    BT   **Electric waves**
          Electromagnetic waves
          Shortwave radio
    NT   **Masers**
Mid-career changes
    USE **Career changes**
Mid-life crisis
    USE **Midlife crisis**
Middle age   305.24
    BT   **Age**
          Life (Biology)
    NT   **Aging**
          Midlife crisis
    RT   **Longevity**
          Middle aged persons
Middle aged men (May subdiv. geog.) **305.244**
    BT   **Middle aged persons**

Middle aged persons (May subdiv. geog.)
305.24

BT **Age**

NT **Middle aged men**

Middle aged women

RT **Middle age**

Middle aged women (May subdiv. geog.)
305.244

BT **Middle aged persons**

Middle Ages 909.07

Use for materials on the history of the medieval world not limited to a single country or region.

UF Dark Ages

Middle Ages—History

BT **World history**

NT **Church history—600-1500, Middle Ages**

Knights and knighthood

World history—12th century

World history—13th century

World history—14th century

World history—15th century

RT **Europe—History—476-1492**

Medieval civilization

Middle Ages—History

USE **Middle Ages**

Middle Atlantic States

USE **Atlantic States**

Middle child

USE **Birth order**

Middle class (May subdiv. geog.) 305.5

UF Bourgeoisie

BT **Social classes**

Middle East 956

Use for materials on the region consisting of northeastern Africa and Asia west of Afghanistan. Materials on several Arabic-speaking countries are entered under **Arab countries**.

UF Levant

Near East

Orient

BT **Asia**

NT **Arab countries**

Israel

Middle East—Strategic aspects 956

BT **Military geography**

Strategy

Middle East War, 1991

USE **Persian Gulf War, 1991**

Middle English language

USE **English language—Middle English period**

Middle English literature

USE **English literature—Middle English period**

Middle schools (May subdiv. geog.)
373.236

UF Intermediate schools

BT **Schools**

RT **Elementary schools**

Junior high schools

Middle West 977

UF Central States

Midwest

North Central States

BT **Mississippi River Valley**

United States

RT **Old Northwest**

Midget cars

USE **Karts and karting**

Midlife crisis 305.244

UF Mid-life crisis

BT **Middle age**

Midwest

USE **Middle West**

Midwifery

USE **Midwives**

Midwives (May subdiv. geog.) 618.2

UF Birth attendants

Midwifery

Nurse midwives

BT **Childbirth**

Natural childbirth

Nurses

Migraine 616.8

BT **Headache**

Migrant labor (May subdiv. geog.)
331.5; 362.85

Use for materials on casual or seasonal workers who move from place to place in search of employment. Materials on the movement of population within a country for permanent settlement are entered under **Internal migration**.

UF Migratory workers

BT **Employees**

Labor

RT **Agricultural laborers**

Alien labor

Internal migration

Migration
    USE **Animals—Migration**
          Immigration and emigration
          and types of animals with the
          subdivision *Migration,* e.g.
          Birds—Migration [to be add-
          ed as needed]
Migration, Internal
    USE **Internal migration**
Migration of birds
    USE **Birds—Migration**
Migratory workers
    USE **Migrant labor**
Military aeronautics (May subdiv. geog.)
    358.4
    UF Aeronautics, Military
          Air warfare
          Naval aeronautics
    SA names of wars with the subdivi-
          sion *Aerial operations,* e.g.
          **World War, 1939-1945—Ae-
          rial operations** [to be added
          as needed]
    BT **Aeronautics**
          Military art and science
          War
    NT **Aerial reconnaissance**
          Air bases
          Air defenses
          Air power
          Aircraft carriers
          Military airplanes
          Parachute troops
          **World War, 1939-1945—Aerial
          operations**
Military aid
    USE **Military assistance**
Military air bases
    USE **Air bases**
Military airplanes (May subdiv. geog.)
    623.74
    UF Air warfare
          Airplanes, Military
          Naval airplanes
    SA types of military airplanes [to be
          added as needed]
    BT **Airplanes**
          Military aeronautics
    NT **Bombers**
Military art and science (May subdiv.
    geog.) **355**

    UF Army
          Fighting
          Military power
          Military science
    NT **Armed forces**
          Armor
          Artillery
          Battles
          Biological warfare
          Camouflage (Military science)
          Chemical warfare
          Civil defense
          Fortification
          Friendly fire (Military science)
          Guerrilla warfare
          Industrial mobilization
          Military aeronautics
          Military camps
          Military transportation
          Ordnance
          Psychological warfare
          Signals and signaling
          Strategy
          Tactics
          Veterans
          War games
    RT **Armies**
          Drill and minor tactics
          Military personnel
          Naval art and science
          War
          Weapons
Military art and science—Study and teach-
    ing
    USE **Military education**
Military assistance 355
    UF Arms sales
          Foreign aid program
          Military aid
          Military sales
          Mutual defense assistance pro-
          gram
    SA military assistance from particu-
          lar countries, e.g. **American
          military assistance** [to be
          added as needed]
    BT **Military policy**
    NT **American military assistance**
    RT **Arms transfers**
Military assistance, American
    USE **American military assistance**

Military atrocities
  USE **Atrocities**
        War crimes
Military bases (May subdiv. geog.)
    355.7
  UF Army bases
        Army posts
        Military facilities
        Military installations
        Military posts
Military biography
  USE names of armies and navies with
        the subdivision *Biography*,
        e.g. **United States. Army—**
        Biography; **United States.**
        Navy—Biography; etc. [to be
        added as needed]
Military camps (May subdiv. geog.)
    355.7
  UF Camps (Military)
  BT **Military art and science**
  NT **Concentration camps**
Military conscription
  USE **Draft**
Military courts
  USE **Courts martial and courts of**
        inquiry
Military crimes
  USE **Military offenses**
Military desertion (May subdiv. geog.)
    343; 355.1
  UF Army desertion
        Desertion
        Desertion, Military
  SA names of wars with the subdivi-
        sion *Desertions* [to be added
        as needed]
  BT **Military offenses**
  NT **World War, 1939-1945—Deser-**
        tions
  RT **Draft resisters**
Military desertion—United States   **343**
Military draft
  USE **Draft**
Military drill
  USE **Drill and minor tactics**
Military education (May subdiv. geog.)
    355.007; 355.5
  UF Army schools
        Military art and science—Study
        and teaching

Military schools
    Military training
    Schools, Military
  SA names of military schools, e.g.
        United States Military Acad-
        emy [to be added as needed]
  BT **Education**
  NT **Military training camps**
Military engineering (May subdiv. geog.)
    623
  SA names of wars with the subdivi-
        sion *Engineering and con-*
        struction [to be added as
        needed]
  BT **Civil engineering**
        Engineering
  NT **World War, 1939-1945—Engi-**
        neering and construction
  RT **Fortification**
Military facilities
  USE **Military bases**
Military forces
  USE **Armed forces**
Military geography   **355.4**
  UF Maps, Military
        Military maps
  SA areas of the world with the sub-
        division *Strategic aspects* [to
        be added as needed]
  BT **Geography**
  NT **Middle East—Strategic aspects**
Military government   **341.6; 355.4**
  Use for general materials on governments
  under military regimes, not limited to a single
  country.
  UF Government, Military
  SA names of countries with the sub-
        division *Politics and govern-*
        ment, or *History*, with appro-
        priate dates as needed, for
        materials on governments of
        particular countries under mil-
        itary rule; and names of
        countries occupied by foreign
        military governments with the
        appropriate subdivision under
        History, e.g., **Netherlands—**
        History—1940-1945, German
        occupation; **Japan—Histo-**
        ry—1945-1952, Allied occu-
        pation; etc. [to be added as
        needed]

Military government—*Continued*
  BT **Public administration**
  RT **Military occupation**
Military health
  USE **Military personnel—Health and hygiene**
Military history   355.009
  UF History, Military
      Wars
  SA names of countries with the subhead *Army* or the subdivision *Military history*, e.g. **United States. Army**; **United States—Military history**; and names of wars, battles, sieges, etc. [to be added as needed]
  BT **History**
  NT **Battles**
      Military policy
      United States. Army
      United States—Military history
  RT **Naval history**
Military hospitals (May subdiv. geog.)
      355.7
  UF Field hospitals
      Veterans—Hospitals
  SA names of wars with the subdivision *Medical care*, e.g. **World War, 1939-1945—Medical care** [to be added as needed]
  BT **Hospitals**
      Military medicine
  RT **Veterans**
Military installations
  USE **Military bases**
Military intelligence (May subdiv. geog.)
      355.3
  SA names of wars with the subdivision *Military intelligence*, e.g. **World War, 1939-1945—Military intelligence** [to be added as needed]
  BT **Intelligence service**
  NT **World War, 1939-1945—Military intelligence**
Military intervention
  USE **Intervention (International law)**
Military law (May subdiv. geog.)   343
  UF Articles of war
      War, Articles of
  BT **International law**
      Law

  NT **Draft**
      Military offenses
      Veterans—Legal status, laws, etc.
  RT **Courts martial and courts of inquiry**
      Martial law
      War
Military life
  USE **Military personnel**
      and names of countries with the subdivision *Armed forces* or the subheads *Army* or *Navy*; etc., with the subdivision *Military life*, e.g. **United States—Armed forces—Military life**; **United States. Army—Military life**; etc. [to be added as needed]
Military maneuvers (May subdiv. geog.)
      355.4
  BT **Tactics**
  NT **War games**
Military maps
  USE **Military geography**
Military medicine (May subdiv. geog.)
      616.9
  UF Field hospitals
      Medicine, Military
  SA names of wars with the subdivision *Medical care*, e.g. **World War, 1939-1945—Medical care** [to be added as needed]
  BT **Medicine**
  NT **Armies—Medical care**
      Military hospitals
  RT **Military personnel—Health and hygiene**
Military music (May subdiv. geog.)
      781.5
  SA names of wars with the subdivision *Songs* [to be added as needed]
  BT **Music**
  NT **Band music**
      Marches (Music)
      World War, 1939-1945—Songs
Military occupation   341.6; 355.4
  UF Occupation, Military
      Occupied territory

Military occupation—*Continued*
>SA names of occupied countries
>>with the appropriate subdivi-
>>sion under *History*, e.g.,
>>**Netherlands—History—1940-
>>1945, German occupation**;
>>**Japan—History—1945-1952,
>>Allied occupation**; etc. [to be
>>added as needed]
>BT **War**
>NT **World War, 1939-1945—Occu-
>>pied territories**
>RT **Military government**

Military offenses (May subdiv. geog.)
>**343; 355.1**
>UF Crimes, Military
>>Military crimes
>>Naval offenses
>>Offenses, Military
>SA types of military offenses, e.g.
>>**Military desertion** [to be
>>added as needed]
>BT **Criminal law**
>>**Military law**
>NT **Military desertion**

**Military offenses—United States   343;
355.1**
>UF United States—Military offenses

Military pensions (May subdiv. geog.)
>**331.25**
>UF Naval pensions
>>Pensions, Naval
>>War pensions
>BT **Pensions**
>RT **Veterans**

Military personnel (May subdiv. geog.)
>**355.3**
>UF Military life
>>Servicemen
>>Servicewomen
>SA names of countries with the sub-
>>division *Armed forces* or the
>>subheads *Army* or *Navy*, etc.,
>>with the subdivision *Military
>>life* or *Officers*, e.g. **United
>>States—Armed forces—Mili-
>>tary life**; **United States.
>>Army—Officers**; etc. [to be
>>added as needed]
>BT **Armed forces**
>>**War**

>NT **Admirals**
>>**Armies**
>>**Gays and lesbians in the mili-
>>tary**
>>**Generals**
>>**Mercenary soldiers**
>>**Navies**
>>**Recruiting and enlistment**
>>**Sailors**
>>**Soldiers**
>>**United States. Army—Military
>>life**
>>**United States. Army—Officers**
>>**United States. Navy—Officers**
>>**United States—Armed forces—
>>Military life**
>>**Women in the military**
>RT **Military art and science**
>>**Veterans**

Military personnel—Health and hygiene
>**613.6**
>UF Hygiene, Military
>>Military health
>>Soldiers—Hygiene
>SA names of wars with the subdivi-
>>sion *Health aspects* or *Medi-
>>cal care*, e.g. **World War,
>>1939-1945—Health aspects**;
>>**World War, 1939-1945—
>>Medical care**; etc. [to be
>>added as needed]
>BT **Hygiene**
>RT **Armies—Medical care**
>>**Military medicine**

Military personnel missing in action
>USE **Missing in action**

Military personnel—United States
>**355.30973**
>UF United States—Military person-
>>nel

Military policy (May subdiv. geog.)   **355**
>UF Defense policy
>>Government policy
>BT **Military history**
>NT **Military assistance**
>>**Military readiness**
>RT **National security**

Military policy—United States   355
>UF United States—Military policy
>NT **Strategic Defense Initiative**

Military posts
  USE **Military bases**
Military power
  USE **Armies**
       Military art and science
       Navies
       Sea power
Military preparedness
  USE **Military readiness**
Military readiness **355**

  Use for materials on military strength, including military personnel, munitions, natural resources, and industrial war potential. Materials on the implements of war are entered under **Ordnance** or **Military weapons**. Materials on the industries producing them are entered under **Defense industry**.

  UF Armaments
      Defense readiness
      Military preparedness
      National defenses
  SA names of countries with the sub-
      division *Defenses*, e.g. **United**
      States—Defenses [to be add-
      ed as needed]
  BT **Military policy**
  NT **United States—Defenses**
  RT **Armed forces**
      Arms control
      Arms race
      Defense industry
      Industrial mobilization
      Manpower
Military research (May subdiv. geog.)
      355
  UF Defense research
  BT **Research**
Military sales
  USE **Arms transfers**
       Defense industry
       Military assistance
Military schools
  USE **Military education**
Military science
  USE **Military art and science**
Military service, Compulsory
  USE **Draft**
Military service, Voluntary
  USE **Voluntary military service**
Military signaling
  USE **Signals and signaling**
Military spouses (May subdiv. geog.)
      306.872

  BT **Husbands**
      Married people
      Wives
Military strategy
  USE **Strategy**
Military supplies industry
  USE **Defense industry**
Military tactics
  USE **Tactics**
Military tanks (May subdiv. geog.) **358;**
      623.7
  UF Armored cars (Tanks)
      Tanks (Military science)
  BT **Military vehicles**
  RT **Tank warfare**
Military training
  USE **Military education**
Military training camps (May subdiv.
      geog.) **355.7**
  UF Students' military training camps
      Training camps, Military
  BT **Military education**
Military training, Universal
  USE **Draft**
Military transportation (May subdiv.
      geog.) **358**
  UF Transportation, Military
  SA names of wars with the subdivi-
      sion *Transportation*, e.g.
      World War, 1939-1945—
      Transportation [to be added
      as needed]
  BT **Military art and science**
      Transportation
  NT **Military vehicles**
Military uniforms (May subdiv. geog.)
      355.1
  UF Naval uniforms
      Uniforms, Military
      Uniforms, Naval
  SA names of military services with
      the subdivision *Uniforms*, e.g.
      United States. Army—Uni-
      forms [to be added as need-
      ed]
  BT **Uniforms**
Military vehicles (May subdiv. geog.)
      355.8
  UF Army vehicles
      Vehicles, Military

Military vehicles—*Continued*
 BT **Military transportation**
  Vehicles
 NT **Military tanks**
Military weapons (May subdiv. geog.)
  355.8; 623.4
 UF Armaments
  Arms sales
  Munitions
 SA names of wars with the subdivi-
  sion *Equipment and supplies*
  [to be added as needed]
 BT **Ordnance**
  Weapons
 NT **Nuclear weapons**
  Space weapons
  World War, 1939-1945—
   Equipment and supplies
 RT **Arms race**
  Defense industry
Militia
 USE names of countries and states
  with the subdivision *Militia,*
  e.g. **United States—Militia**
  [to be added as needed]
Militia movements (May subdiv. geog.)
  303.48
 Use for materials on anti-government
 paramilitary social movements.
 UF Militias
  Paramilitary militia movements
 BT **Radicalism**
  Social movements
Militias
 USE **Militia movements**
Milk (May subdiv. geog.) **637; 641.3**
 BT **Dairy products**
  Dairying
  Food
 NT **Dried milk**
Milk—Analysis 637; 641.3
Milk supply (May subdiv. geog.) **338.1**
 BT **Food adulteration and inspec-**
  tion
  Public health
Milky Way 523.1
 BT **Galaxies**
Mill and factory buildings
 USE **Factories**
Millenarianism
 USE **Millennium**

Millennialism
 USE **Millennium**
Millennium 236
 UF Millenarianism
  Millennialism
 BT **Eschatology**
 RT **Second Advent**
Millikan rays
 USE **Cosmic rays**
Millinery
 USE **Hats**
Milling (Flour)
 USE **Flour mills**
Millionaires (May subdiv. geog.) **920**
 BT **Rich**
Mills (May subdiv. geog.) **670.42**
 UF Mills and millwork
 SA types of mills [to be added as
  needed]
 BT **Manufactures**
  Technology
 NT **Flour mills**
 RT **Factories**
  Machinery
Mills and millwork
 USE **Mills**
Mime 792.3
 BT **Acting**
 RT **Pantomimes**
Mind
 USE **Intellect**
  Psychology
Mind and body 128; 150
 UF Body and mind
 BT **Brain**
  Medicine
  Parapsychology
  Philosophy
 NT **Abnormal psychology**
  Biofeedback training
  Body image
  Consciousness
  Mental suggestion
  Psychosomatic medicine
  Sleep
  Temperament
 RT **Holistic medicine**
  Human body
  Hypnotism
  Mental healing
  Mental health

Mind and body—*Continued*
   Phrenology
   Psychoanalysis
   Psychophysiology
   Spiritual healing
   Subconsciousness
Mind control
 USE **Brainwashing**
Mind cure
 USE **Mental healing**
Mind reading
 USE **Telepathy**
Mine surveying (May subdiv. geog.)
  622.028
 BT **Mining engineering**
   Prospecting
   Surveying
Mineral lands
 USE **Mines and mineral resources**
Mineral resources
 USE **Mines and mineral resources**
Mineral resources, Marine
 USE **Marine mineral resources**
Mineralogy
 USE **Minerals**
   Natural history
Minerals (May subdiv. geog.) **549**
 Use for materials on the chemical and geological aspects of natural compounds extracted from the earth. Materials on mines and mining and the potential economic value of minerals are entered under **Mines and mineral resources**.
 UF Mineralogy
 SA names of minerals, e.g. **Quartz**
   [to be added as needed]
 BT **Geology**
 NT **Asbestos**
   Gems
   Gypsum
   Lime
   Minerals in human nutrition
   Minerals in the body
   Ores
   Precious stones
   Quartz
 RT **Crystals**
   Mines and mineral resources
   Natural history
   Petrology
Minerals in human nutrition **612.3; 613.3**

BT **Food**
  Minerals
  Nutrition
Minerals in the body **612.3; 613.2**
 SA individual minerals in the body, e.g. **Iron in the body** [to be added as needed]
 BT **Metabolism**
   Minerals
   Minerals in the body
 NT **Iron in the body**
   Minerals in the body
Miners (May subdiv. geog.) **622.092; 920**
 SA types of miners [to be added as needed]
 BT **Labor**
 NT **Coal miners**
Miners—Diseases (May subdiv. geog.) **616.9**
 UF Miners' diseases
 BT **Occupational diseases**
Miners' diseases
 USE **Miners—Diseases**
Mines and mineral resources (May subdiv. geog.) **333.8; 338.2**
 Use for materials on mines and mining and the potential economic value of minerals. Materials on the chemical or geological aspects of natural compounds extracted from the earth are entered under **Minerals**.
 UF Mineral lands
   Mineral resources
   Mining
 SA types of mines and mining, e.g. **Coal mines and mining** [to be added as needed]
 BT **Economic geology**
   Natural resources
   Raw materials
 NT **Coal mines and mining**
   Gold mines and mining
   Marine mineral resources
   Mining engineering
   Precious metals
   Prospecting
   Silver mines and mining
 RT **Minerals**
Mines and mineral resources—United States **333.8; 338.2**
Miniature gardens **635.9**
 UF Gardens, Miniature
   Tray gardens

Miniature gardens—*Continued*
 BT **Gardens**
   Miniature objects
 RT **Container gardening**
   Indoor gardening
   Terrariums
Miniature objects   688; 745.592
 UF Miniatures
   Tiny objects
 SA types of objects with the subdivision *Models* [to be added as needed]
 BT **Art objects**
 NT **Doll furniture**
   Dollhouses
   Miniature gardens
   Miniature painting
   Models and modelmaking
 RT **Toys**
Miniature painting   751.7; 757
 UF Miniatures (Portraits)
   Portrait miniatures
 BT **Miniature objects**
   Painting
 RT **Portrait painting**
Miniatures
 USE **Miniature objects**
Miniatures (Illumination of books and manuscripts)
 USE **Illumination of books and manuscripts**
Miniatures (Portraits)
 USE **Miniature painting**
Minibikes   629.227
 BT **Bicycles**
   Motorcycles
Minimum drinking age
 USE **Drinking age**
Minimum wage (May subdiv. geog.) **331.2**
 BT **Salaries, wages, etc.**
Mining
 USE **Mines and mineral resources**
   Mining engineering
Mining, Electric
 USE **Electricity in mining**
Mining engineering (May subdiv. geog.) **622**
 UF Mining
 BT **Civil engineering**
   Coal mines and mining
   Engineering

Mines and mineral resources
 NT **Drilling and boring (Earth and rocks)**
   Mine surveying
   Ocean mining
 RT **Electricity in mining**
Mining, Ocean
 USE **Ocean mining**
Ministers (Diplomatic agents)
 USE **Diplomats**
Ministers of state
 USE **Cabinet officers**
Ministers of the gospel
 USE **Clergy**
Ministry   206; 253
 UF Clergy—Office
 SA ministries of particular religions, e.g. **Christian ministry** [to be added as needed]
 BT **Church work**
   Pastoral theology
 NT **Christian ministry**
 RT **Clergy**
Minor arts
 USE **Decorative arts**
Minor planets
 USE **Asteroids**
Minor tactics
 USE **Drill and minor tactics**
Minorites
 USE **Franciscans**
Minorities (May subdiv. geog.)   **305.8; 323.1**
 UF Foreign population
   Minority groups
 SA names of particular cthnic and racial minorities and of national groups in a foreign country, e.g. **African Americans**; **Mexican Americans**; **Mexicans—United States**; etc.; names of places with the subdivision *Race relations*, e.g. **United States—Race relations**; names of places with the subdivision *Ethnic relations*, e.g. **United States—Ethnic relations**; and headings for minorities in various industries and fields of endeavor, e.g., **Minorities in**

Minorities—*Continued*
    broadcasting [to be added as needed]
- NT **Aliens**
  Immigrants
  Mexican Americans
  Mexicans—United States
  Minorities in broadcasting
  Minorities in television broadcasting
  Minorities on television
  Minority business enterprises
  Minority women
  Minority youth
- RT **Discrimination**
  Ethnic relations
  Race relations
  Segregation

Minorities in broadcasting (May subdiv. geog.) **384.5; 791.4**

Use for materials on minority involvement in the broadcasting industry.
- UF Minority groups in broadcasting
- SA names of particular minority groups in broadcasting or in particular broadcast media, e.g. **African Americans in television broadcasting** [to be added as needed]
- BT **Broadcasting**
  Minorities
- NT **Minorities in television broadcasting**

Minorities in engineering **620**
- UF Minority groups in engineering
- BT **Engineering**

Minorities in literature **809**

Use for materials on the theme of minorities in works of literature.
- BT **Literature—Themes**

Minorities in motion pictures **791.43**

Use for materials on the depiction of minorities in motion pictures. Materials discussing all aspects of minorities' involvement in motion pictures are entered under Minorities in the motion picture industry.
- SA names of particular minority groups in motion pictures, e.g. African Americans in motion pictures [to be added as needed]
- BT **Motion pictures**

- NT **African Americans in motion pictures**
  Blacks in motion pictures

Minorities in television
- USE **Minorities on television**

Minorities in television broadcasting **791.45**

Use for materials on all aspects of minority involvement in television. Materials on the portrayal of minorities in television programs are entered under **Minorities on television**.
- UF Minorities in the television industry
- SA names of particular minority groups in television broadcasting, e.g. **African Americans in television broadcasting** [to be added as needed]
- BT **Minorities**
  Minorities in broadcasting
  Television broadcasting

Minorities in the motion picture industry (May subdiv. geog.) **791.43092**

Use for materials on all aspects of minority involvement in the motion picture industry. Materials on the portrayal of minorities in motion pictures are entered under Minorities in motion pictures.
- SA names of particular minority groups in the motion picture industry, e.g. African Americans in the motion picture industry [to be added as needed]
- BT **Motion picture industry**
- NT **African Americans in the motion picture industry**
  Blacks in the motion picture industry

Minorities in the television industry
- USE **Minorities in television broadcasting**

Minorities on television **791.45**

Use for materials on the portrayal of minorities in television programs. Materials on all aspects of minority involvement in television are entered under **Minorities in television broadcasting**.
- UF Minorities in television
- SA names of particular minority groups in television, e.g. **African Americans on television** [to be added as needed]
- BT **Minorities**
  Television

Minority business enterprises (May subdiv. geog.) **338.6**
    UF   Minority businesses
           Minority-owned business enterprises
    BT   **Business enterprises**
           Minorities
Minority business enterprises—Federal aid
    USE   **Federal aid to minority business enterprises**
Minority businesses
    USE   **Minority business enterprises**
Minority groups
    USE   **Minorities**
Minority groups in broadcasting
    USE   **Minorities in broadcasting**
Minority groups in engineering
    USE   **Minorities in engineering**
Minority-owned business enterprises
    USE   **Minority business enterprises**
Minority women **305.48**
    BT   **Minorities**
           Women
Minority youth **305.235**
    BT   **Minorities**
           Youth
Minstrels (May subdiv. geog.) **791.092; 920**
    BT   **Poets**
    NT   **Troubadours**
Mints (May subdiv. geog.) **332.4**
    BT   **Money**
    RT   **Coinage**
Miracle plays
    USE   **Mysteries and miracle plays**
Miracles (May subdiv. geog.) **202; 212; 231.7**

Use for materials on miracles in any or all religious traditions.
    RT   **Spiritual healing**
           Supernatural
Mirrors (May subdiv. geog.) **748.8**
    UF   Looking glasses
    BT   **Furniture**
Miscarriage **618.3**
    UF   Fetal death
    BT   **Pregnancy**
Miscellanea
    USE   **Books of lists**
           Curiosities and wonders

and subjects with the subdivision *Miscellanea*, e.g. **Medicine—Miscellanea** [to be added as needed]
Miscellaneous facts
    USE   **Books of lists**
           Curiosities and wonders
Misconduct in office (May subdiv. geog.) **353.4**
    UF   Malfeasance in office
           Official misconduct
    SA   names of specific incidents and offenses [to be added as needed]
    BT   **Conflict of interests**
           Criminal law
    NT   **Police corruption**
    RT   **Political corruption**
Misdemeanors (Law)
    USE   **Criminal law**
Misleading advertising
    USE   **Deceptive advertising**
Misrepresentation in advertising
    USE   **Deceptive advertising**
Missiles, Ballistic
    USE   **Ballistic missiles**
Missiles, Guided
    USE   **Guided missiles**
Missing children (May subdiv. geog.) **362.82; 363.2**
    UF   Lost children
    BT   **Children**
           Missing persons
    NT   **Runaway children**
Missing in action **341.6; 355.7**
    UF   MIAs
           Military personnel missing in action
    SA   names of wars with the subdivision *Missing in action* [to be added as needed]
    BT   **Prisoners of war**
           Soldiers
    NT   **World War, 1939-1945—Missing in action**
Missing persons (May subdiv. geog.) **363.2**
    BT   **Criminal investigation**
    NT   **Missing children**
           Runaway adults
           Runaway teenagers

Missionaries, Christian
USE **Christian missionaries**
Missions
USE names of Christian churches, de-
nominations, religious orders,
etc., with the subdivision *Mis-
sions,* e.g. **Catholic Church—
Missions;** and names of peo-
ples evangelized with the sub-
division *Christian missions,*
e.g. **Native Americans—
Christian missions** [to be
added as needed]
Missions, Christian
USE **Christian missions**
Missions, Medical
USE **Medical missions**
Mississippi River Valley   977
UF Mississippi Valley
BT **United States**
NT **Middle West**
Mississippi River Valley—History   977
UF New France—History
Mississippi Valley
USE **Mississippi River Valley**
Mistakes
USE **Errors**
Mixed marriage
USE **Interfaith marriage**
Intermarriage
Mixed media painting   751.4
BT **Painting**
Mixed race people
USE **Racially mixed people**
Mixology
USE **Bartending**
Mnemonics   153.1
SA subjects, types of literature, and
titles of sacred works with
the subdivision *Memorizing,*
e.g. **Poetry—Memorizing** [to
be added as needed]
NT **Poetry—Memorizing**
RT **Memory**
Mobile home living (May subdiv. geog.)
643; 728.7
BT **Home economics**
Mobile homes
NT **Trailer parks**
Mobile home parks
USE **Trailer parks**

Mobile homes (May subdiv. geog.)   **643;
728.7**
Use for materials on stationary transportable
structures designed for year-round living. Ma-
terials on structures mounted upon a truck or
towed by a truck or automobile for the pur-
pose of temporary dwelling or cargo hauling
are entered under **Travel trailers and camp-
ers**.
UF House trailers
Trailers
BT **Housing**
NT **Mobile home living**
RT **Travel trailers and campers**
Mobiles (Sculpture)   731
BT **Kinetic sculpture**
Sculpture
Mobilization, Industrial
USE **Industrial mobilization**
Mobs
USE **Crowds**
Riots
Mock epic literature
USE **Mock-heroic literature**
Mock-heroic literature   800
Use for individual works, collections, or
materials about mock-heroic literature.
UF Comic epic literature
Mock epic literature
BT **Literature**
Wit and humor
RT **Epic literature**
Humorous fiction
Model airplanes
USE **Airplanes—Models**
Model cars
USE **Automobiles—Models**
Model making
USE **Models and modelmaking**
Model ships
USE **Ships—Models**
Model trains
USE **Locomotives—Models**
Railroads—Models
Modeling   731.4; 738.1
UF Clay modeling
BT **Clay**
Sculpture
NT **Soap sculpture**
RT **Sculpture—Technique**
Modelmaking
USE **Models and modelmaking**

Models
   USE **Artists' models**
        Fashion models
        Mathematical models
        Models and modelmaking
        and types of objects with the subdivision *Models,* e.g. **Airplanes—Models** [to be added as needed]

Models and model making
   USE **Models and modelmaking**

Models and modelmaking   688
   UF Model making
       Modelmaking
       Models
       Models and model making
   SA types of objects with the subdivision *Models*, e.g. **Airplanes—Models** [to be added as needed]
   BT **Handicraft**
       Miniature objects
   NT **Airplanes—Models**
       Automobiles—Models
       Locomotives—Models
       Machinery—Models
       Motorboats—Models
       Patternmaking
       Railroads—Models
       Ships—Models

Models, Artists'
   USE **Artists' models**

Models, Mathematical
   USE **Mathematical models**

Models, Mechanical
   USE **Machinery—Models**

Models (Persons)
   USE **Artists' models**
        Fashion models

Modern architecture
   USE **Modernism in architecture**

Modern architecture—1600-1799 (17th and 18th centuries)
   USE **Architecture—17th and 18th centuries**

Modern architecture—1800-1899 (19th century)
   USE **Architecture—19th century**

Modern architecture—1900-1999 (20th century)
   USE **Architecture—20th century**

Modern architecture—2000-2099 (21st century)
   USE **Architecture—21st century**

Modern art
   USE **Modernism in art**

Modern art—1800-1899 (19th century)
   USE **Art—19th century**

Modern art—1900-1999 (20th century)
   USE **Art—20th century**

Modern art—2000-2099 (21st century)
   USE **Art—21st century**

Modern church history
   USE **Church history—1500-, Modern period**

Modern civilization   306.09; 909
   Use for materials on cultural and intellectual developments since 1453 not limited to a single country or region.
   UF Civilization, Modern
   BT **Civilization**
   NT **Enlightenment**

Modern civilization—1950-   306.09; 909.82
   Use for materials on cultural and intellectual developments since 1950 not limited to a single country or region.

Modern dance (May subdiv. geog.)
      792.8
   UF Interpretive dance
   BT **Dance**

Modern Greek language   489
   May be subdivided like **English language**.
   UF Greek language, Modern
       Romaic language
   BT **Language and languages**
   RT **Greek language**

Modern Greek literature   889
   May use same subdivisions and names of literary forms as for **English literature**.
   UF Greek literature, Modern
       Neo-Greek literature
       Romaic literature
   BT **Literature**

Modern history   909.08
   Use for materials covering the period after 1453.
   UF History, Modern
   BT **World history**

Modern history—1800-1899 (19th century)
   USE **World history—19th century**

Modern history—1900-1999 (20th century)
   USE **World history—20th century**

Modern history—1945-
USE **World history—1945-**
Modern history—Study and teaching
907
NT **Current events**
Modern languages   410

May be subdivided like **English language.**
Use for materials dealing collectively with living literary languages.

UF Languages, Modern
BT **Language and languages**
Modern languages—Conversation and
phrase books   418

Use for instructional materials or for books
of convenient conversations and phrases for
travelers.

UF Conversation and phrase books
Conversation in foreign languages
Conversations and phrases
Foreign language phrases
SA names of languages with the
subdivision *Conversation and*
phrase books, e.g. **French**
language—Conversation and
phrase books [to be added as
needed]

Modern languages—Study and teaching
418
RT **Language laboratories**
Modern literature
USE **Literature**
Modernism in literature
Modern painting—1800-1899 (19th centu-
ry)
USE **Painting—19th century**
Modern painting—1900-1999 (20th centu-
ry)
USE **Painting—20th century**
Modern painting—2000-2099 (21st century)
USE **Painting—21st century**
Modern philosophy   190

Use for materials on developments in Western philosophy since the Middle Ages.

UF Philosophy, Modern
BT **Philosophy**
NT **Enlightenment**
Existentialism
Phenomenology
Modern sculpture
USE **Modernism in sculpture**

Modern sculpture—1900-1999 (20th centu-
ry)
USE **Sculpture—20th century**
Modernism
USE **Modernism (Aesthetics)**
Modernism (Theology)
Modernism (Aesthetics)   700.1

Use for materials on the philosophy and
practice of the arts since the nineteenth century characterized by a self-conscious break
with the past and a search for new forms of
expression.

UF Modernism
Modernism (Arts)
BT **Aesthetics**
NT **Avant-garde (Aesthetics)**
Modernism in architecture
Modernism in art
Modernism in literature
Modernism in sculpture
RT **Postmodernism**
Modernism (Art)
USE **Modernism in art**
Modernism (Arts)
USE **Modernism (Aesthetics)**
Modernism in architecture   724

Use for materials on the theory and practice
of modernism in the architecture.

UF Architecture, Modern
Modern architecture
BT **Architecture**
Modernism (Aesthetics)
Modernism in art   709.04

Use for materials on the theory and practice
of modernism in the visual arts.

UF Modern art
Modernism (Art)
BT **Art**
Modernism (Aesthetics)
Modernism in literature   801
UF Modern literature
Modernism (Literature)
BT **Literature**
Modernism (Aesthetics)
Modernism in sculpture   735
UF Modern sculpture
Modernism (Sculpture)
Sculpture, Modern
BT **Modernism (Aesthetics)**
Sculpture
Modernism (Literature)
USE **Modernism in literature**

Modernism (Sculpture)
USE **Modernism in sculpture**
Modernism (Theology)   230; 273

    Use for materials on the movement in the Christian churches that applies modern critical methods to biblical study and the history of dogma, and emphasizes the spiritual and ethical side of religion over historic dogmas and creeds.

    UF   Modernism

          Modernist-fundamentalist controversy

    BT   **Christianity—Doctrines**

    RT   **Christian fundamentalism**

Modernist-fundamentalist controversy
USE   **Christian fundamentalism**

          Modernism (Theology)

Modernization
USE   **Modernization (Sociology)**
Modernization (Sociology) (May subdiv. geog.)   303.44

    Use for materials on the process by which traditional societies achieve the political, cultural, economic, and social characteristics of modernity.

    UF   Development

          Modernization

    BT   **Social change**

    RT   **Industrialization**

Mold (Fungi)
USE   **Molds (Fungi)**

Molding (Metal)
USE   **Founding**

Moldova   947.6

Molds (Botany)
USE   **Molds (Fungi)**

Molds (Fungi)   579.5

    UF   Mold (Fungi)

          Molds (Botany)

    BT   **Fungi**

Molecular biochemistry
USE   **Molecular biology**

Molecular biology   591.6

    UF   Biology, Molecular

          Molecular biochemistry

          Molecular biophysics

    BT   **Biochemistry**

          Biophysics

    NT   **Genetic code**

Molecular biophysics
USE   **Molecular biology**

Molecular cloning   572.8

    UF   DNA cloning

    BT   **Cloning**

          Genetic engineering

Molecular technology
USE   **Nanotechnology**

Molecules   539; 541.2

    BT   **Physical chemistry**

Molesting of children
USE   **Child sexual abuse**

Mollusks   594

    Use for materials on mollusks and for systematic and comprehensive materials on shells. Popular materials on shells and shell collecting are entered under **Shells**.

    BT   **Shellfish**

    RT   **Shells**

Monarchs
USE   **Kings and rulers**

Monarchy (May subdiv. geog.)   321; 321.8

    UF   Royal houses

          Royalty

          Sovereigns

    BT   **Constitutional history**

          Constitutional law

          Executive power

          Political science

    NT   **Empresses**

          Queens

    RT   **Kings and rulers**

Monasteries (May subdiv. geog.)   255; 271; 726

    UF   Cloisters

    BT   **Church architecture**

          Church history

    NT   **Abbeys**

          Convents

    RT   **Monasticism and religious orders**

Monastic orders
USE   **Monasticism and religious orders**

Monasticism
USE   **Monasticism and religious orders**

Monasticism and religious orders (May subdiv. geog.)   255; 271

    Use for materials on the institution of monasticism and for general materials on religious orders not limited to orders for a single sex. This heading may be subdivided by religion or denomination as needed.

    UF   Monastic orders

          Monasticism

          Orders, Monastic

Monasticism and religious orders—*Continued*

> Religious orders
> SA names of monastic and religious orders, e.g. **Franciscans** [to be added as needed]
> NT **Franciscans**
> **Monasticism and religious orders for men**
> **Monasticism and religious orders for women**
> RT **Hermits**
> **Religious life**

Monasticism and religious orders for men (May subdiv. geog.) **255; 271**

> This heading may be subdivided by religion or denomination as needed.
> UF Religious orders for men
> BT **Monasticism and religious orders**
> RT **Monks**

Monasticism and religious orders for women (May subdiv. geog.) **255; 271**

> This heading may be subdivided by religion or denomination as needed.
> UF Religious orders for women
> Sisterhoods
> BT **Convents**
> **Monasticism and religious orders**
> RT **Nuns**

Monetary policy (May subdiv. geog.) **332.4**

> UF Currency devaluation
> Devaluation of currency
> Free coinage
> Government policy
> BT **Economic policy**
> RT **Finance**
> **Fiscal policy**
> **Inflation (Finance)**
> **Money**

Monetary policy—United States **332.4**

> UF United States—Monetary policy

Monetary unions (May subdiv. geog.) **332.4**

> UF Common currencies
> BT **Money**

Money (May subdiv. geog.) **332.4**

> Use for materials on currency as a medium of exchange or measure of value and for general materials on various types of money.
> UF Currency
> Legal tender
> Standard of value
> BT **Economics**
> **Exchange**
> **Finance**
> NT **Barter**
> **Children's allowances**
> **Coinage**
> **Coins**
> **Counterfeits and counterfeiting**
> **Credit**
> **Euro**
> **Foreign exchange**
> **Mints**
> **Monetary unions**
> **Paper money**
> RT **Banks and banking**
> **Gold**
> **Monetary policy**
> **Silver**
> **Wealth**

Money-making projects for children **332.024; 650.1**

> UF Children's moneymaking projects
> Moneymaking projects for children
> BT **Business enterprises**
> RT **Children's allowances**

Money raising
> USE **Fund raising**

Moneymaking projects for children
> USE **Money-making projects for children**

Monkeys (May subdiv. geog.) **599.8**

> BT **Primates**

Monkeys—Behavior **599.8**

> UF Monkeys—Habits and behavior
> BT **Animal behavior**

Monkeys—Habits and behavior
> USE **Monkeys—Behavior**

Monks (May subdiv. geog.) **255; 271**

> RT **Monasticism and religious orders for men**

Monograms **745.6**

> UF Ciphers (Lettering)
> BT **Alphabets**
> **Decoration and ornament**

Monograms—*Continued*

    Lettering

RT **Initials**

Monologues 808.85

Use for individual works, collections, or materials about monologues. Monologues with incidental musical background and musical works in which spoken language is an integral part are entered under **Monologues with music**.

UF Declamations

      Narrations

BT **Recitations**

RT **Monologues with music**

Monologues with music 808.85; 782.2

Use for musical scores and for materials about monologues with incidental musical background and musical works in which spoken language is an integral part. Individual monologues without music, collections, and materials about monologues without music are entered under **Monologues**.

UF Musical declamation

      Narration with music

      Recitations with music

BT **Recitations**

RT **Monologues**

Monopolies (May subdiv. geog.) 338.8

BT **Commerce**

      Economics

RT **Competition**

      Corporation law

      Industrial trusts

      Restraint of trade

Monorail railroads (May subdiv. geog.) 385.5; 625.1

UF Railroads, Single rail

      Single rail railroads

BT **Railroads**

Monotheism (May subdiv. geog.) 211

BT **Religion**

      Theism

RT **God**

Monroe Doctrine 327.73

BT **International relations**

      Intervention (International law)

      United States—Foreign relations

Monsoons 551.51

BT **Meteorology**

Monster films

USE **Horror films**

Monsters 001.9; 398.2

Use for materials on legendary animals combining features of human and animal form or having the forms of various animals in combination. Materials on human abnormalities are entered under either **Birth defects** or **Growth disorders**.

BT **Animals—Folklore**

      Curiosities and wonders

      Folklore

      Mythology

NT **Dragons**

      Giants

      Loch Ness monster

      Sasquatch

      Yeti

Montessori method of education (May subdiv. geog.) 371.39

BT **Elementary education**

      Kindergarten

      Teaching

Months 529

SA names of the months [to be added as needed]

BT **Calendars**

      Chronology

NT **Special months**

Monumental brasses

USE **Brasses**

Monuments (May subdiv. geog.) 725

UF Statues

SA ethnic groups, classes of persons, individual persons, families, and wars with the subdivision *Monuments*, e.g. **World War, 1939-1945—Monuments** [to be added as needed]

BT **Architecture**

      Sculpture

NT **Historic buildings**

      Megalithic monuments

      National monuments

      Natural monuments

      Obelisks

      Pyramids

      Tombs

      World War, 1939-1945—Monuments

Mood disorders

USE **Affective disorders**

Mood (Psychology) 155.2

BT **Psychology**

NT **Melancholy**

Moon 523.3

Moon—*Continued*
  BT **Astronomy**
      Solar system
Moon bases
  USE **Lunar bases**
Moon—Eclipses
  USE **Lunar eclipses**
Moon—Exploration 629.45
  UF Lunar exploration
  BT **Space flight to the moon**
Moon—Folklore (May subdiv. geog.)
      398.26
Moon—Geology
  USE **Lunar geology**
Moon—Maps 523.3022
  BT **Maps**
Moon—Photographs
  USE **Moon—Pictorial works**
Moon—Pictorial works 523.3; 778.3
  UF Moon—Photographs
  BT **Space photography**
Moon probes
  USE **Lunar probes**
Moon—Religious aspects (May subdiv.
      geog.) **299.9**
Moon rocks 552.0999
  UF Lunar petrology
      Lunar rocks
  BT **Lunar geology**
      Petrology
Moon soil
  USE **Lunar soil**
Moon—Surface 523.3
  UF Lunar surface
  RT **Lunar soil**
Moon, Voyages to
  USE **Space flight to the moon**
Moon worship (May subdiv. geog.) **202**
  BT **Religion**
Moonlighting
  USE **Supplementary employment**
Moons
  USE **Satellites**
Moorish architecture
  USE **Islamic architecture**
Moors
  USE **Muslims**
Moral and philosophic stories
  USE **Didactic fiction**
      Fables
      Parables
Moral conditions 301; 306; 900

  UF Morals
  SA names of countries, cities, etc.,
      with the subdivision *Moral
      conditions* [to be added as
      needed]
  BT **Social conditions**
  NT **Chicago (Ill.)—Moral condi-
      tions**
      Ohio—Moral conditions
      **United States—Moral condi-
      tions**
Moral development 155.2; 155.4
  UF Ethical development
  BT **Child psychology**
      Moral education
Moral education (May subdiv. geog.)
      370.11
  UF Character education
      Ethical education
  BT **Education**
      Ethics
  NT **Moral development**
  RT **Religious education**
Moral philosophy
  USE **Ethics**
Moral theology, Christian
  USE **Christian ethics**
Morale 152.4
  SA types of morale, e.g. **Employee
      morale** [to be added as need-
      ed]
  BT **Courage**
  NT **Employee morale**
      Psychological warfare
Moralities
  USE **Morality plays**
Morality
  USE **Ethics**
Morality plays 792.1; 808.82
    Use for individual works, collections, or
  materials about plays in which the chief char-
  acters are personifications of abstract qualities.
  UF Moralities
  BT **Drama**
      English drama
      Religious drama
      Theater
  RT **Mysteries and miracle plays**
Morality stories
  USE **Didactic fiction**
Morality tales
  USE **Parables**

Morals
    USE   **Conduct of life**
            Ethics
            Human behavior
            Moral conditions
Moravians (May subdiv. geog.)   **284**
    UF   United Brethren
    BT   **Christian sects**
Morgan Le Fay (Legendary character)
    398.22
    BT   **Legendary characters**
Mormon Church
    USE   **Church of Jesus Christ of Lat-**
            ter-day Saints
Mormons (May subdiv. geog.)   **289.3092**
    RT   **Church of Jesus Christ of Lat-**
            ter-day Saints
Morocco   964
      May be subdivided like United States ex-
    cept for History.
Morphine   362.29; 615
    BT   **Narcotics**
    NT   **Heroin**
    RT   **Opium**
Morphology   571.3
    UF   Biological form
           Biological structure
           Comparative morphology
           Form in biology
           Structure in biology
    SA   animals, languages, plants, and
           crops with the subdivision
           Morphology [to be added as
           needed]
    BT   **Comparative anatomy**
Morse code
    USE   **Cipher and telegraph codes**
Mortality (May subdiv. geog.)   **304.6**
    UF   Burial statistics
           Death rate
           Mortuary statistics
    SA   ethnic groups, classes of per-
           sons, diseases, and animals
           with the subdivision *Mortality*,
           for works on the number of
           deaths during a given time
           among a particular groups or
           due to a particular cause, e.g.
           Infants—Mortality; **Tubercu-**
           losis—Mortality; etc. [to be
           added as needed]

    BT   **Population**
            Vital statistics
    NT   **Children—Mortality**
            Infants—Mortality
    RT   **Death**
Mortar   666; 691
    BT   **Adhesives**
            Plaster and plastering
Mortgage loans
    USE   **Mortgages**
Mortgages (May subdiv. geog.)   **332.63;**
    332.7
    UF   Home loans
           Mortgage loans
    BT   **Loans**
            Securities
Morticians
    USE   **Undertakers and undertaking**
Mortuary customs
    USE   **Cremation**
            Funeral rites and ceremonies
Mortuary statistics
    USE   **Mortality**
            Vital statistics
Mosaics (May subdiv. geog.)   **729;**
    738.5; 748.5
    BT   **Decoration and ornament**
            Decorative arts
    RT   **Mural painting and decoration**
Moslems
    USE   **Muslims**
Mosques (May subdiv. geog.)   **726**
    BT   **Islamic architecture**
            Religious institutions
            Temples
Mosquitoes   595.77
    BT   **Insects**
Mosquitoes—Control   363.7
    BT   **Pest control**
Mosses (May subdiv. geog.)   **588**
    BT   **Plants**
Motels
    USE   **Hotels and motels**
Mother and child
    USE   **Mother-child relationship**
Mother-child relationship   306.874
    UF   Child and mother
           Mother and child
    BT   **Children**
            Mothers
            Parent-child relationship

Mother-child relationship—*Continued*
  NT   **Mother-daughter relationship**
         Mother-son relationship
Mother-daughter relationship   305.4;
         306.874
  UF   Daughters and mothers
         Mothers and daughters
  BT   **Daughters**
         Mother-child relationship
         Mothers
Mother Goddess religion
  USE   **Goddess religion**
Mother-son relationship   306.874
  UF   Mothers and sons
         Sons and mothers
  BT   **Mother-child relationship**
         Mothers
         Sons
Motherhood   306.874
  BT   **Parenthood**
  RT   **Mothers**
Mothers (May subdiv. geog.)   **306.874**
  UF   Maternity
  BT   **Family**
         Women
  NT   **Divorced mothers**
         Mother-child relationship
         Mother-daughter relationship
         Mother-son relationship
         Stepmothers
         Surrogate mothers
         Teenage mothers
         Unmarried mothers
  RT   **Motherhood**
Mothers and daughters
  USE   **Mother-daughter relationship**
Mothers and sons
  USE   **Mother-son relationship**
Mother's Day   394.2628
  BT   **Holidays**
Mothers' pensions
  USE   **Child welfare**
Moths (May subdiv. geog.)   **595.78**
  UF   Cocoons
         Lepidoptera
  BT   **Insects**
  NT   **Caterpillars**
         Silkworms
  RT   **Butterflies**
Motion   531
  UF   Kinetics
  BT   **Dynamics**

  NT   **Mechanical movements**
         Speed
  RT   **Force and energy**
         Kinematics
         Mechanics
Motion picture actors and actresses
  USE   **Actors**
Motion picture adaptations
  USE   **Film adaptations**
Motion picture cameras   778.5
  UF   Movie cameras
  BT   **Cameras**
         Cinematography
  RT   **Amateur films**
Motion picture cartoons
  USE   **Animated films**
Motion picture direction
  USE   **Motion pictures—Production**
         and direction
Motion picture directors
  USE   **Motion picture producers and**
         directors
Motion picture festivals
  USE   **Film festivals**
Motion picture industry (May subdiv.
  geog.)   **384; 791.43**
  UF   Film industry (Motion pictures)
  BT   **Industries**
  NT   **African Americans in the mo-**
         tion picture industry
         Blacks in the motion picture
         industry
         Minorities in the motion pic-
         ture industry
         Motion picture producers and
         directors
         Motion pictures—Production
         and direction
         Women in the motion picture
         industry
  RT   **Motion pictures**
Motion picture musicals
  USE   **Musical films**
Motion picture photography
  USE   **Cinematography**
Motion picture plays
  USE   **Screenplays**
Motion picture plays—Technique   808.2
  UF   Motion pictures—Play writing
         Play writing
         Playwriting

Motion picture plays—Technique—*Continued*
- BT **Drama—Technique**

Motion picture posters
- USE **Film posters**

Motion picture producers
- USE **Motion picture producers and directors**

Motion picture producers and directors
(May subdiv. geog.) **791.43; 920**
- UF Film directors
  - Film producers
  - Motion picture directors
  - Motion picture producers
- BT **Motion picture industry**
- RT **Motion pictures—Production and direction**

Motion picture production
- USE **Motion pictures—Production and direction**

Motion picture projectors
- USE **Projectors**

Motion picture scripts
- USE **Screenplays**

Motion picture serials 791.43
Use for individual works, collections, or materials about motion picture serials.
- BT **Motion pictures**

Motion picture theaters (May subdiv. geog.) **725**
- UF Cinemas
  - Movie theaters
- BT **Theaters**

Motion pictures (May subdiv. geog.) **384; 791.43**
Use for general materials on motion pictures, including motion pictures as an art form. Materials on the technical aspects of making motion pictures and their projection onto a screen are entered under **Cinematography**. For materials on motion pictures produced by the motion picture industry of an individual country or on the motion pictures shown in a country, subdivide geographically, e.g. **Motion pictures—United States**.
- UF Cinema
  - Films
  - Movies
- SA types of motion pictures, e.g. **Documentary films; Horror films**; motion pictures and particular groups of persons, e.g., **Motion pictures and children**; motion pictures as used in various industries or fields of endeavor, e.g. **Motion pictures in education**; subjects and groups of persons portrayed in motion pictures, e.g. **Animals in motion pictures; Women in motion pictures**; groups of persons in the motion picture industry, e.g. **Women in the motion picture industry**; and names of individual motion pictures [to be added as needed]
- BT **Audiovisual materials**
  - **Mass media**
  - **Performing arts**
- NT **Academy Awards (Motion pictures)**
  - **Adventure films**
  - **African Americans in motion pictures**
  - **Amateur films**
  - **Animals in motion pictures**
  - **Animated films**
  - **Apocalyptic films**
  - **Bible films**
  - **Biographical films**
  - **Blacks in motion pictures**
  - **Comedy films**
  - **Documentary films**
  - **Epic films**
  - **Erotic films**
  - **Experimental films**
  - **Fantasy films**
  - **Film adaptations**
  - **Film noir**
  - **Gangster films**
  - **Horror films**
  - **Independent films**
  - **Legal drama (Films)**
  - **Medical drama (Films)**
  - **Minorities in motion pictures**
  - **Motion picture serials**
  - **Motion pictures and children**
  - **Motion pictures in education**
  - **Musical films**
  - **Mystery films**
  - **Science fiction films**
  - **Sherlock Holmes films**
  - **Short films**
  - **Silent films**

Motion pictures—*Continued*

  Sports drama (Films)
  Spy films
  Star Wars films
  Television movies
  Three Stooges films
  Vampire films
  War films
  Western films
  Women in motion pictures
  World War, 1939-1945—Motion pictures and the war

 RT Motion picture industry

Motion pictures, American

 USE Motion pictures—United States

Motion pictures and children (May subdiv. geog.) 305.23; 649; 791.43

Use for materials on the effect of motion pictures on children and youth.

 UF Children and motion pictures

 BT Children
   Motion pictures

Motion pictures and the war

 USE names of wars with the subdivision *Motion pictures and the war,* e.g. World War, 1939-1945—Motion pictures and the war [to be added as needed]

Motion pictures—Biography 791.43092; 920

 BT Biography

Motion pictures—Catalogs 016.79143

 UF Catalogs, Film
   Film catalogs
   Filmography

 SA types of motion pictures with the subdivision *Catalogs,* e.g. Science fiction films—Catalogs; and subjects, classes of persons, corporate entities, and names of individual persons with the subdivision *Filmography,* e.g. Animals—Filmography; Shakespeare, William, 1564-1616—Filmography; etc. [to be added as needed]

Motion pictures—Censorship (May subdiv. geog.) 791.43

 BT Censorship

Motion pictures—Ethical aspects 791.43

 UF Motion pictures—Moral and religious aspects

 BT Ethics

Motion pictures in education 371.33

 UF Educational films

 BT Audiovisual education
   Motion pictures
   Teaching—Aids and devices

Motion pictures—Moral and religious aspects

 USE Motion pictures—Ethical aspects
   Motion pictures—Religious aspects

Motion pictures—Play writing

 USE Motion picture plays—Technique

Motion pictures—Posters

 USE Film posters

Motion pictures—Production and direction (May subdiv. geog.) 384; 791.4302

 UF Film direction
   Film production
   Filmmaking
   Motion picture direction
   Motion picture production

 BT Motion picture industry

 RT Motion picture producers and directors

Motion pictures—Religious aspects (May subdiv. geog.) 204; 248.4; 791.43

 UF Motion pictures—Moral and religious aspects

Motion pictures—Reviews 791.43

Motion pictures—Television adaptations

 USE Television adaptations

Motion pictures—United States 791.430973

Use for materials on motion pictures produced by the motion picture industry of the United States or on motion pictures shown in the United States.

 UF American films
   American motion pictures
   Motion pictures, American

Motion study 658.5

 BT Factory management
   Industrial efficiency
   Job analysis

Motion study—*Continued*
>> Personnel management
>> Production standards
> RT Time study

Motivation (Psychology)   153.8
> UF Incentive (Psychology)
> BT Psychology
> NT Achievement motivation
>> Burn out (Psychology)
>> Competition (Psychology)
>> Wishes

Motor boats
> USE Motorboats

Motor buses
> USE Buses

Motor cars
> USE Automobiles

Motor coordination
> USE Movement education

Motor cycles
> USE Motorcycles

Motor trucks
> USE Trucks

Motor vehicle industry
> USE Automobile industry

Motor vehicles (May subdiv. geog.)
>> 388.3
> NT Alternative fuel vehicles
>> Automobiles
>> Buses
>> Trucks

Motor vehicles—Drivers' licenses
> USE Drivers' licenses

Motorboats (May subdiv. geog.)   623.82
> UF Motor boats
>> Power boats
> BT Boats and boating

Motorboats—Models   623.82
> BT Models and modelmaking

Motorcycles (May subdiv. geog.)
>> 629.227
> UF Motor cycles
> SA specific makes and models of
>> motorcycles [to be added as
>> needed]
> BT Bicycles
> NT Antique and vintage motorcy-
>> cles
>> Minibikes
> RT Motorcycling

Motorcycling (May subdiv. geog.)   796.7
> BT Cycling

> RT Motorcycles

Motoring
> USE Automobile travel

Motors
> USE Electric motors
>> Engines
>> and types of engines and mo-
>> tors, e.g. Steam engines;
>> Electric motors; etc., and
>> types of vehicles and makes
>> and models of vehicles with
>> the subdivision *Motors,* e.g.
>> Automobiles—Motors [to be
>> added as needed]

Motorways
> USE Express highways

Mottoes   808.88; 929.8
> Use for collections of mottoes and for ma-
> terials about mottoes.
> UF Emblems
> BT Heraldry
> RT National emblems

Moulding (Metal)
> USE Founding

Mound-builders
> USE Mounds and mound builders

Mounds and mound builders (May
>> subdiv. geog.)   930.1; 970.004
> UF Barrows
>> Graves
>> Mound-builders
> BT Archeology
>> Burial
>> Tombs
> RT Excavations (Archeology)

Mount Everest (China and Nepal)
> USE Everest, Mount (China and
>> Nepal)

Mount Rainier (Wash.)   979.7
> BT Mountains

Mountain animals (May subdiv. geog.)
>> 591.75
> UF Alpine animals
>> Alpine fauna
>> Mountain fauna
> BT Animals

Mountain bicycles
> USE Mountain bikes

Mountain bikes   629.227
> UF All terrain bicycles
>> Mountain bicycles

Mountain bikes—*Continued*
   BT **All terrain vehicles**
       Bicycles
Mountain biking (May subdiv. geog.)
      796.63
   UF All terrain cycling
   BT **Cycling**
Mountain climbing
   USE **Mountaineering**
Mountain ecology (May subdiv. geog.)
      577.5
   BT **Ecology**
Mountain fauna
   USE **Mountain animals**
Mountain flora
   USE **Mountain plants**
Mountain life (May subdiv. geog.)
      307.72
   BT **Country life**
Mountain people (May subdiv. geog.)
      307.7
   BT **Ethnology**
Mountain plants (May subdiv. geog.)
      581.7; 635.9
   UF Alpine flora
       Alpine plants
       Mountain flora
   BT **Plant ecology**
       Plants
Mountaineering (May subdiv. geog.)
      796.522
   UF Mountain climbing
       Rock climbing
   BT **Outdoor life**
   RT **Trails**
Mountains (May subdiv. geog.)   **551.43**
   SA names of mountain ranges and
       of individual mountains [to be
       added as needed]
   BT **Landforms**
       Physical geography
   NT **Everest, Mount (China and
       Nepal)**
       Mount Rainier (Wash.)
       Rocky Mountains
       Volcanoes
Mourning
   USE **Bereavement**
Mourning customs
   USE **Funeral rites and ceremonies**
Mouse
   USE **Mice**

Mouth   **591.4; 612.3**
   BT **Face**
       Head
Mouth—Diseases   **617.5**
   BT **Diseases**
   NT **Bad breath**
Movable books
   USE **Toy and movable books**
Movement disorders   **616.8**
   UF Diskinesia
   BT **Disabilities**
       Nervous system—Diseases
Movement education   **152.3; 153.7;
      372.86**
   UF Creative movement
       Motor coordination
   BT **Physical education**
Movement, Freedom of
   USE **Freedom of movement**
Movements of animals
   USE **Animal locomotion**
Movie cameras
   USE **Motion picture cameras**
Movie festivals
   USE **Film festivals**
Movie novelizations
   USE **Movie novels**
Movie novels   **808.3**
     Use for individual works, collections, or
  materials about novels based on movies.
   UF Movie novelizations
       Movie tie-ins
   BT **Fiction**
   RT **Radio and television novels**
Movie posters
   USE **Film posters**
Movie scripts
   USE **Screenplays**
Movie theaters
   USE **Motion picture theaters**
Movie tie-ins
   USE **Movie novels**
Movies
   USE **Motion pictures**
Moving   **648**
     Use for materials on changing the location
  of possessions, household, office, etc.
   UF Household moving
       Moving, household
   BT **Home economics**
Moving, household
   USE **Moving**

MP3 players   006.5; 621.389

> BT **Computer sound processing**
>
> **Sound—Recording and repro-**
>
> **ducing**

MRI (Magnetic resonance imaging)

> USE **Magnetic resonance imaging**

Mulattoes

> USE **Racially mixed people**

Multi-age grouping

> USE **Nongraded schools**

Multicultural diversity in the workplace

> USE **Diversity in the workplace**

Multicultural education (May subdiv.

> geog.)   **370.117**

Use for materials on the attempt to eradi-
cate racial and religious prejudices through the
study of various races, creeds, and immigrant
cultures.

> UF Intercultural education
>
> BT **Acculturation**
>
> **Education**
>
> **Multiculturalism**
>
> NT **Bilingual education**
>
> RT **International education**
>
> **Multicultural literature**

Multicultural literature   808.8

Use for collections that bring together literatures of various cultures for the purpose of
illustrating racial, religious, or ethnic diversity.

> BT **Literature**
>
> **Multiculturalism**
>
> RT **Multicultural education**

Multiculturalism (May subdiv. geog.)

> **305.8; 306.44**

Use for materials on policies or programs
that foster the preservation of various cultures
or cultural identities within a unified society.
Materials on the coexistence of several distinct ethnic, religious, or cultural groups within one society are entered under **Pluralism
(Social sciences)**. Materials on the presence of
two distinct cultures within a single country
or region are entered under **Biculturalism**.

> UF Diversity movement
>
> BT **Culture**
>
> **Social policy**
>
> NT **Diversity in the workplace**
>
> **Multicultural education**
>
> **Multicultural literature**
>
> RT **Biculturalism**
>
> **Ethnic relations**
>
> **Ethnicity**
>
> **Pluralism (Social sciences)**
>
> **Race relations**

Multilingual dictionaries

> USE **Polyglot dictionaries**

Multilingual glossaries, phrase books, etc.

> USE **Polyglot dictionaries**

Multilingualism (May subdiv. geog.)

> **306.44**

> BT **Language and languages**

Multimedia   006.7

Use for materials on computer systems,
software, or data items that allow users to ma-
nipulate diverse integrated media, such as text,
graphics, sound, etc.

> UF Computer-based multimedia in-
> formation systems
>
> Interactive media
>
> Interactive multimedia
>
> Multimedia computing
>
> Multimedia information systems
>
> Multimedia knowledge systems
>
> Multimedia systems
>
> SA subjects with the subdivision *In-
> teractive multimedia*, e.g. **Ge-
> ology—Interactive multime-
> dia** [to be added as needed]
>
> BT **Computer software**
>
> **Information systems**
>
> NT **Hyperlinks**
>
> **Podcasting**

Multimedia centers

> USE **Instructional materials centers**

Multimedia computing

> USE **Multimedia**

Multimedia information systems

> USE **Multimedia**

Multimedia knowledge systems

> USE **Multimedia**

Multimedia materials

> USE **Audiovisual materials**

Multimedia systems

> USE **Multimedia**

Multinational corporations (May subdiv.

> geog.)   **338.8; 658**

> UF Business—International aspects
>
> Corporations, Multinational
>
> International business enterprises
>
> BT **Business enterprises**
>
> **Commerce**
>
> **Corporations**
>
> **International economic rela-
> tions**
>
> NT **Foreign investments**

Multiple birth   618.2

Multiple birth—*Continued*
- UF Birth, Multiple
- SA types of multiple births, e.g.
  Twins [to be added as needed]
- BT **Childbirth**
- NT **Triplets**
  Twins
- RT **Multiple pregnancy**

Multiple personalities
- USE **Multiple personality**

Multiple personality 616.85
- UF Double consciousness
  Multiple personalities
  Personality, Multiple
  Split personality
- BT **Abnormal psychology**
  Mental illness
  Personality disorders
  Psychology

Multiple plot stories
- USE **Plot-your-own stories**

Multiple pregnancy 618.25
- UF Plural pregnancy
- BT **Pregnancy**
- RT **Multiple birth**

Multiplication 513.2
- BT **Arithmetic**

Multiracial people
- USE **Racially mixed people**

Mummies (May subdiv. geog.) 393
- BT **Archeology**
  Burial

Municipal administration
- USE **Municipal government**

Municipal art (May subdiv. geog.) 711
- UF Art, Municipal
  Civic art
  Municipal improvements
- BT **Art**
  Cities and towns
- RT **City planning**

Municipal civil service
- USE **Municipal officials and employees**

Municipal employees
- USE **Municipal officials and employees**

Municipal engineering (May subdiv. geog.) 628
- BT **Engineering**
  Public works

- NT **Drainage**
  Refuse and refuse disposal
  Sewerage
  Street cleaning
- RT **Sanitary engineering**

Municipal-federal relations
- USE **Federal-city relations**

Municipal finance (May subdiv. geog.) 336

Use for general materials on city finance and, when subdivided by country, state, or region, for general considerations of municipal finance in those places. Materials on the finance of individual cities, towns, or metropolitan areas are entered under **Public finance** with the appropriate geographic subdivision.
- UF Cities and towns—Finance
  Finance, Municipal
- BT **Municipal government**
  Public finance
- NT **Metropolitan finance**

Municipal government (May subdiv. geog.) 320.8; 352.16

Use for materials on the government of cities in general and, when subdivided by country, state, or region, for general consideration of municipal government in those places. Materials on the government of individual cities, towns, or metropolitan areas are entered under the name of the city, town, or area with the subdivision *Politics and government*.
- UF Cities and towns—Government
  City government
  Government, Municipal
  Municipal administration
  Municipalities
- SA names of cities, towns, and metropolitan areas with the subdivision *Politics and government* [to be added as needed]
- BT **Local government**
  Political science
- NT **Chicago (Ill.)—Politics and government**
  Federal-city relations
  Municipal finance
  Municipal government by city manager
  Municipal government by commission
  Public administration
  State-local relations
- RT **Metropolitan government**
  Municipal officials and employees

Municipal government by city manager
 320.8; 352.16
    UF   City manager
          Commission government with
            city manager
    BT   **Municipal government**
Municipal government by commission
    (May subdiv. geog.)   **320.8;**
    352.16
    UF   Commission government
          Government by commission
    BT   **Municipal government**
Municipal government—United States
    320.8; 352.160973
    UF   United States—Municipal gov-
          ernment
Municipal improvements
    USE **Cities and towns—Civic im-**
          provement
          Municipal art
Municipal officers
    USE **Municipal officials and em-**
          ployees
Municipal officials and employees
    352.16
    UF   Municipal civil service
          Municipal employees
          Municipal officers
          Town officers
    SA   names of cities with the subdivi-
          sion *Officials and employees*,
          e.g. **Chicago (Ill.)—Officials**
          and employees [to be added
          as needed]
    BT   **Civil service**
    RT   **Municipal government**
Municipal ownership   338.9; 352.5
    UF   Public ownership
    BT   **Corporations**
          Economic policy
          Government ownership
Municipal planning
    USE **City planning**
Municipal transit
    USE **Local transit**
Municipalities
    USE **Cities and towns**
          Municipal government
Munitions
    USE **Defense industry**
          Military weapons

Mural painting and decoration (May
    subdiv. geog.)   **729; 751.7**
    UF   Fresco painting
          Wall decoration
          Wall painting
    BT   **Decoration and ornament**
          Interior design
          Painting
    RT   **Mosaics**
Murder
    USE **Homicide**
Murder mysteries
    USE **Mystery and detective plays**
          Mystery fiction
          Mystery films
          Mystery radio programs
          Mystery television programs
Murder trials
    USE **Trials (Homicide)**
Muscles   611; 612.7
    BT   **Musculoskeletal system**
Muscular system
    USE **Musculoskeletal system**
Musculoskeletal system   611; 612.7
    UF   Muscular system
    BT   **Anatomy**
          Physiology
    NT   **Bones**
          Muscles
          Skeleton
    RT   **Human locomotion**
Museums (May subdiv. geog.)   **069; 708**
    SA   appropriate subjects and names
          of wars and of corporate
          bodies with the subdivision
          Museums, e.g. **World War,**
          1939-1945—Museums; and
          names of individual galleries
          and museums [to be added as
          needed]
    NT   **Art museums**
          Museums and schools
          World War, 1939-1945—Muse-
          ums
Museums and schools (May subdiv.
    geog.)   **069**
    UF   Schools and museums
    BT   **Museums**
          Schools
Museums—Ohio   708.171
Museums—United States   708.13

Mushrooms 579.6; 635
  UF Toadstools
  BT **Plants**
  RT **Fungi**
Music 780
  UF Classical music
  SA music of particular countries or ethnic groups, e.g. **American music**; **Native American music**; etc.; types of music, e.g. **Vocal music**; and subjects, classes of persons, and names of individual persons, corporate bodies, places, or wars, with the subdivision *Songs* for collections of songs or materials about songs pertaining to the topic or entity named, e.g. **Cowhands—Songs**; **Surfing—Songs**; **United States Military Academy—Songs** [to be added as needed]
  BT **Humanities**
  NT **African American music**
        African music
        American music
        Black music
        Bluegrass music
        Cajun music
        Chamber music
        Church music
        Composition (Music)
        Computer music
        Concerts
        Conducting
        Cowhands—Songs
        Dance music
        Electronic music
        Ensembles (Music)
        Folk music
        Harmony
        Instrumental music
        Instrumentation and orchestration
        Islamic music
        Jazz music
        Military music
        Music and literature
        Musical notation
        Musicians
        Native American music

        Orchestral music
        Organ music
        Piano music
        Popular music
        Radio and music
        Rock music
        Singing
        Violin music
        Vocal music
Music—Acoustics and physics 781.2
  UF Acoustics
  BT **Music—Theory**
        Physics
  RT **Sound**
Music, American
  USE **American music**
Music—Analysis, appreciation
  USE **Music appreciation**
        Music—History and criticism
Music and literature 780
  UF Literature and music
        Music and poetry
        Poetry and music
  BT **Literature**
        Music
Music and poetry
  USE **Music and literature**
Music and radio
  USE **Radio and music**
Music—Anecdotes 780
  UF Music—Anecdotes, facetiae, satire, etc.
  BT **Anecdotes**
Music—Anecdotes, facetiae, satire, etc.
  USE **Music—Anecdotes**
        Music—Humor
Music appreciation 781.1
  UF Appreciation of music
        Music—Analysis, appreciation
        Musical appreciation
  BT **Music—Study and teaching**
  RT **Music—History and criticism**
Music box
  USE **Music boxes**
Music boxes 786.6
  UF Music box
  BT **Mechanical musical instruments**
Music—Cataloging
  USE **Cataloging of music**

Music, Choral
    USE **Choral music**
Music—Composition
    USE **Composition (Music)**
Music conductors
    USE **Conductors (Music)**
Music—Criticism
    USE **Music—History and criticism**
Music—Discography   016.78
Music education
    USE **Music—Study and teaching**
Music—Examinations   780.76
    UF Music—Examinations, questions, etc.
    BT **Examinations**
Music—Examinations, questions, etc.
    USE **Music—Examinations**
Music festivals (May subdiv. geog.)
      780.79
    BT **Festivals**
    RT **Concerts**
Music, Gospel
    USE **Gospel music**
Music-halls
    USE **Concert halls**
Music—History and criticism   780.9
    UF Music—Analysis, appreciation
        Music—Criticism
        Musical criticism
    RT **Music appreciation**
Music—Humor   780
    UF Music—Anecdotes, facetiae, satire, etc.
    BT **Wit and humor**
Music—Instruction and study
    USE **Music—Study and teaching**
Music libraries (May subdiv. geog.)   026
    UF Libraries, Music
    BT **Special libraries**
Music—Notation
    USE **Musical notation**
Music—Psychological aspects   781
    UF Psychology of music
    BT **Psychology**
Music—Publishing (May subdiv. geog.)
      070.5
    BT **Publishers and publishing**
Music—Study and teaching (May subdiv. geog.)   780.7
    UF Music education
        Music—Instruction and study

        Musical education
        Musical instruction
        School music
    NT **Music appreciation**
Music—Theory   781
    NT **Composition (Music)**
        Counterpoint
        Harmony
        Music—Acoustics and physics
        Musical form
        Musical meter and rhythm
Music—Therapeutic use
    USE **Music therapy**
Music therapy   615.8; 616.89
    UF Music—Therapeutic use
        Musical therapy
    BT **Therapeutics**
Music videos   384.55; 778.59
    Use for individual works, collections, or materials about music videos.
    UF Videos, Music
    BT **Video recordings**
Musical ability   780.7
    UF Musical talent
    BT **Ability**
Musical accompaniment   781.47
    UF Accompaniment, Musical
    BT **Composition (Music)**
Musical appreciation
    USE **Music appreciation**
Musical comedies
    USE **Musicals**
Musical composition
    USE **Composition (Music)**
Musical criticism
    USE **Music—History and criticism**
Musical declamation
    USE **Monologues with music**
Musical education
    USE **Music—Study and teaching**
Musical ensembles
    USE **Ensembles (Music)**
Musical films   791.43
    Use for individual works, collections, or materials about musical films.
    UF Motion picture musicals
        Musicals (Motion pictures)
    BT **Motion pictures**
    RT **Musicals**
Musical form   784.18

Musical form—*Continued*

SA   names of musical forms expressed in the singular, to be used both for musical scores and for materials about the musical form, e.g. **Concerto** [to be added as needed]

BT   **Composition (Music)**
       Music—Theory

NT   **Concerto**
       Ensembles (Music)
       Fugue
       Opera
       Operetta
       Oratorio
       Sonata
       Suite (Music)
       Symphony

Musical instruction
USE   **Music—Study and teaching**

Musical instruments (May subdiv. geog.) **784.19**

UF   Instruments, Musical

SA   types of instruments, e.g. **Percussion instruments** [to be added as needed]

NT   **Bells**
       Drums
       Electronic musical instruments
       Mechanical musical instruments
       Organs (Musical instruments)
       Percussion instruments
       Stringed instruments
       Wind instruments

RT   **Instrumental music**
       Instrumentation and orchestration
       Orchestra
       Tuning

Musical instruments, Electronic
USE   **Electronic musical instruments**

Musical instruments, Mechanical
USE   **Mechanical musical instruments**

Musical meter and rhythm **781.2**
UF   Meter
BT   **Music—Theory**
       Rhythm

Musical notation (May subdiv. geog.) **780.1**
UF   Music—Notation

BT   **Music**

Musical revues, comedies, etc.
USE   **Musicals**

Musical talent
USE   **Musical ability**

Musical therapy
USE   **Music therapy**

Musicals (May subdiv. geog.) **782.1; 792.6**

Use for scores and for materials about musical comedies and revues.

UF   Dramatic music
       Musical comedies
       Musical revues, comedies, etc.

BT   **Theater**
RT   **Musical films**
       Operetta

Musicals (Motion pictures)
USE   **Musical films**

Musicians (May subdiv. geog.) **780.92; 920**

SA   types of musicians and names of individual musicians [to be added as needed]

BT   **Music**

NT   **African American musicians**
       Black musicians
       Composers
       Conductors (Music)
       Disc jockeys
       Ensembles (Music)
       Instrumentalists
       Singers

Musicians—Biography **780.92; 920**
BT   **Biography**

Musicians, Black
USE   **Black musicians**

Musicians—Portraits **780.92**

Musicians—United States **780.92; 920**
UF   American musicians

Muslim architecture
USE   **Islamic architecture**

Muslim art
USE   **Islamic art**

Muslim civilization
USE   **Islamic civilization**

Muslim countries
USE   **Islamic countries**

Muslim holy war
USE   **Jihad**

Muslim law
USE   **Islamic law**

Muslim literature
USE **Islamic literature**
Muslim sermons
USE **Islamic sermons**
Muslim women (May subdiv. geog.)
305.48
UF Islamic women
BT **Muslims**
Women
Muslims (May subdiv. geog.) **297.092**
UF Moors
Moslems
NT **Muslim women**
RT **Islam**
Muslims—United States **297.092**
NT **Black Muslims**
Mutation (Biology)
USE **Evolution**
Variation (Biology)
Mutilation, Female genital
USE **Female circumcision**
Mutual defense assistance program
USE **Military assistance**
Mutual funds (May subdiv. geog.)
332.63
UF Investment companies
Investment trusts
BT **Investments**
Mutual support groups
USE **Self-help groups**
Mutualism (Biology)
USE **Symbiosis**
Myanmar **959.1**
May be subdivided like United States except for History.
UF Burma
Mycenae (Extinct city) **949.5**
BT **Extinct cities—Greece**
Mycology
USE **Fungi**
Myocardial infarction
USE **Heart attack**
Myotherapy
USE **Acupressure**
MySpace (Web site) **004.69; 384.3**
BT **Social networking**
Web sites
Mysteries
USE **Mysteries and miracle plays**
Mystery and detective plays
Mystery fiction
Mystery films

Mystery radio programs
Mystery television programs
Mysteries and miracle plays **792.1;**
808.82
Use for individual plays, collections, or materials about medieval plays depicting the life of Jesus or legends of the saints.
UF Miracle plays
Mysteries
Mystery plays
BT **Bible plays**
English drama
Pageants
Religious drama
Theater
NT **Passion plays**
RT **Morality plays**
Mystery and detective comics
USE **Mystery comic books, strips,**
etc.
Mystery and detective films
USE **Mystery films**
Mystery and detective plays **808.82**
Use for individual works, collections, or materials about mystery and detective dramas.
UF Crime plays
Detective and mystery plays
Murder mysteries
Mysteries
Mystery plays
Private eye stories
Whodunits
BT **Drama**
Mystery and detective radio programs
USE **Mystery radio programs**
Mystery and detective stories
USE **Mystery fiction**
Mystery and detective television programs
USE **Mystery television programs**
Mystery comic books, strips, etc. **741.5**
Use for individual works, collections, or materials about mystery and detective comics.
UF Crime comics
Detective and mystery comic
books, strips, etc.
Detective comics
Mystery and detective comics
BT **Comic books, strips, etc.**
Mystery fiction **808.3; 808.83**
Use for individual works, collections, or materials about mystery fiction.
UF Crime stories
Detective and mystery stories

Mystery fiction—*Continued*

    Detective fiction

    Detective stories

    Murder mysteries

    Mysteries

    Mystery and detective stories

    Mystery stories

    Private eye stories

    Suspense novels

    Whodunits

BT   **Fiction**

NT   **Edgar Allan Poe Awards**

RT   **Ghost stories**

    Horror fiction

    Romantic suspense novels

    Spy stories

Mystery films   791.43

   Use for individual works, collections, or materials about mystery and detective films.

UF   Crime films

    Detective and mystery films

    Murder mysteries

    Mysteries

    Mystery and detective films

    Private eye stories

    Suspense films

    Whodunits

SA   particular kinds of detective and mystery films, e.g. **Sherlock Holmes films** [to be added as needed]

BT   **Motion pictures**

NT   **Sherlock Holmes films**

RT   **Film noir**

    Gangster films

    Spy films

Mystery graphic novels   741.5

   Use for individual works, collections, or materials about mystery graphic novels.

BT   **Graphic novels**

Mystery plays

USE   **Mysteries and miracle plays**

    Mystery and detective plays

Mystery radio programs   791.44

   Use for individual works, collections, or materials about mystery and detective radio programs.

UF   Crime programs

    Detective and mystery radio programs

    Murder mysteries

    Mysteries

    Mystery and detective radio programs

    Private eye stories

    Suspense programs

    Whodunits

BT   **Radio programs**

Mystery stories

USE   **Mystery fiction**

Mystery television programs   791.45

   Use for individual works, collections, or materials about mystery and detective television programs.

UF   Crime programs

    Detective and mystery television programs

    Murder mysteries

    Mysteries

    Mystery and detective television programs

    Private eye stories

    Suspense programs

    Whodunits

BT   **Television programs**

RT   **Spy television programs**

Mystical theology

USE   **Mysticism**

Mysticism (May subdiv. geog.)   204; 248.2

   May be subdivided by religion or sect.

UF   Dark night of the soul

    Mystical theology

BT   **Spiritual life**

NT   **Cabala**

    Theosophy

Mysticism—Comparative studies   204; 248.2

Mysticism—Islam (May subdiv. geog.) 297.4

UF   Islamic mysticism

BT   **Islam**

NT   **Sufism**

Mythical animals   398.24

UF   Animal lore

    Animals, Mythical

    Imaginary animals

    Imaginary creatures

SA   types of mythical animals [to be added as needed]

BT   **Mythology**

NT   **Dragons**

    Griffins

    Mermaids and mermen

Mythical animals—*Continued*
        Phoenix (Mythical bird)
        Sasquatch
        Unicorns
        Yeti
  RT   **Animals—Folklore**
Mythology   201; 398.2
  UF   Myths
  SA   mythology of ancient peoples,
        e.g. **Celtic mythology**; themes
        in mythology, e.g. **Fire in**
        mythology; and names of in-
        dividual gods and goddesses,
        e.g. **Vesta (Roman deity)** [to
        be added as needed]
  NT   **African mythology**
        Art and mythology
        Celtic mythology
        Chinese mythology
        Classical mythology
        Egyptian mythology
        Fire in mythology
        Geographical myths
        Legendary characters
        Monsters
        Mythical animals
        Norse mythology
        Symbolism
        Totems and totemism
  RT   **Folklore**
        Gods and goddesses
        Heroes and heroines
        Legends
        Religion
Mythology, Celtic
  USE **Celtic mythology**
Mythology, Classical
  USE **Classical mythology**
Mythology, Greek
  USE **Greek mythology**
Mythology in art
  USE **Art and mythology**
Mythology, Roman
  USE **Roman mythology**
Myths
  USE **Mythology**
Naive art
  USE **Outsider art**
Name
  USE names of countries, cities, etc.,
         individual persons, dieties,
         corporate bodies, ethnic

groups, wars, etc., with the subdivision *Name,* for materials on the name's origin, history, validity, etc. [to be added as needed]

Names (May subdiv. geog.)   **929.4**
  UF   Epithets
        Proper names
  SA   types of names, e.g. **Geographic**
        names; types of objects, do-
        mestic animals, events, orga-
        nization, and institutions with
        the subdivision *Names*, for
        materials on the naming of
        those items, e.g. **Pets—**
        Names; and names of coun-
        tries, cities, etc., individual
        persons, dieties, corporate
        bodies, ethnic groups, wars,
        etc., with the subdivision
        Name, for materials on the
        name's origin, history, validi-
        ty, etc. [to be added as need-
        ed]
  NT   **Code names**
        Geographic names
        Native American names
        Personal names
        Pseudonyms
        Terms and phrases
Names, Geographical
  USE **Geographic names**
Names, Personal
  USE **Personal names**
Names—Pronunciation   421
Nannies (May subdiv. geog.)   **649**
  UF   Nursemaids
  BT   **Child care**
Nanotechnology (May subdiv. geog.)
        620
  UF   Molecular technology
  BT   **Technology**
Napkin folding   642
  UF   Folding of napkins
  BT   **Table setting and decoration**
Napoleon I, 1769-1821—Drama   808.82
      Use for collections of plays about Napoleon. Materials on Napoleon as a character in drama are entered under **Napoleon I, Emperor of the French, 1769-1821—In literature**.

Napoleon I, 1769-1821—Fiction   808.83

Use for collections of fiction about Napoleon. Materials on Napoleon as a character in fiction are entered under **Napoleon I, Emperor of the French, 1769-1821—In literature**.

Napoleon I, 1769-1821—In art   704.9

Use for materials about the depiction of Napoleon in works of art.

UF   Napoleon in art

BT   **Art—Themes**

Napoleon I, 1769-1821—In literature 809

Use for materials about Napoleon as a character or as he is portrayed in works of fiction, drama, or poetry. Collections in which Napoleon is a character are entered under **Napoleon I, Emperor of the French, 1769-1821—Fiction**; **Napoleon I, Emperor of the French, 1769-1821—Drama**; or **Napoleon I, Emperor of the French, 1769-1821—Poetry**; as appropriate.

UF   Napoleon in fiction, drama, poetry, etc.

BT   **Literature—Themes**

Napoleon I, 1769-1821—Poetry   808.81

Use for collections of poetry about Napoleon. Materials on Napoleon as portrayed in poetry are entered under **Napoleon I, Emperor of the French, 1769-1821—In literature**.

Napoleon in art

USE   **Napoleon I, 1769-1821—In art**

Napoleon in fiction, drama, poetry, etc.

USE   **Napoleon I, 1769-1821—In literature**

Napoleonic Wars, 1800-1815   940.2

BT   **Europe—History—1789-1815**

France—History—1799-1815

Narcissism   616.85

BT   **Neuroses**

Personality disorders

Narcotic abuse

USE   **Drug abuse**

Narcotic addiction

USE   **Drug abuse**

Narcotic addiction counseling

USE   **Drug abuse counseling**

Narcotic addicts

USE   **Drug addicts**

Narcotic habit

USE   **Drug abuse**

Narcotic traffic

USE   **Drug traffic**

Narcotics (May subdiv. geog.)   **178; 394.1; 615**

Use for materials limited to those drugs that induce sleep or lethargy or deaden pain.

UF   Opiates

Soporifics

SA   types of narcotics [to be added as needed]

BT   **Drugs**

Materia medica

Psychotropic drugs

NT   **Cocaine**

Heroin

Marijuana

Morphine

Opium

Narcotics and crime

USE   **Drugs and crime**

Narcotics and criminals

USE   **Criminals—Drug use**

Narcotics and teenagers

USE   **Teenagers—Drug use**

Narcotics and youth

USE   **Youth—Drug use**

Narnia (Imaginary place)   809

BT   **Imaginary places**

Narration with music

USE   **Monologues with music**

Narrations

USE   **Monologues**

Recitations

Narrative poetry   808.1; 808.81

Use for individual works, collections, or materials about narrative poetry. Rhyming stories for very young children are entered under the form heading **Stories in rhyme**.

BT   **Poetry**

NT   **Epic poetry**

Historical poetry

Stories in rhyme

Nation of Islam

USE   **Black Muslims**

National anthems

USE   **National songs**

National Book Week   021.7

UF   Book Week, National

BT   **Books and reading**

National characteristics   305.8

UF   National images

National psychology

SA   national characteristics of particular countries, e.g. **American national characteristics** [to be added as needed]

BT   **Anthropology**

Nationalism

National characteristics—*Continued*
> **Social psychology**
> NT   **American national characteristics**
> RT   **Ethnopsychology**

National characteristics, American
> USE   **American national characteristics**

National community service
> USE   **National service**

National consciousness
> USE   **Nationalism**

National dances
> USE   **Folk dancing**

National debts
> USE   **Public debts**

National defenses
> USE   **Industrial mobilization**
>   **Military readiness**

National emblems (May subdiv. geog.) **929.9**
> UF   Emblems
>   National symbols
> SA   types of national emblems and national symbols, e.g. **Flags** [to be added as needed]
> BT   **Signs and symbols**
> RT   **Flags**
>   **Heraldry**
>   **Insignia**
>   **Mottoes**
>   **Seals (Numismatics)**
>   **State emblems**

National forests
> USE   **Forest reserves**

National Guard (U.S.)
> USE   **United States. National Guard**

National health insurance (May subdiv. geog.) **368.4**
> UF   Government health insurance
>   Medical insurance, National
>   National health service
>   Socialized medicine
> BT   **Health insurance**
> NT   **Medicaid**
>   **Medicare**
> RT   **State medicine**

National health service
> USE   **National health insurance**
>   **State medicine**

National heritage
> USE   **Cultural property**

National holidays
> USE   **Holidays**

National hymns
> USE   **National songs**

National images
> USE   **National characteristics**

National interest
> USE   **Public interest**

National landmarks
> USE   **National monuments**

National languages
> USE   **Language and languages—Government policy**

National liberation movements (May subdiv. geog.) **320.5**
> Use for materials on minority or other groups in armed rebellion against a colonial government or against a national government charged with corruption or foreign domination, usually in the period since World War II.
> UF   Liberation movements, National
> SA   names of individual liberation movements [to be added as needed]
> BT   **Nationalism**
>   **Revolutions**
> NT   **Guerrillas**

National libraries (May subdiv. geog.) **027.5**
> Use for materials on libraries maintained by government funds that serve a country as a whole, particularly in collecting and preserving that country's publications.
> UF   Libraries, National
> SA   names of individual national libraries [to be added as needed]
> BT   **Government libraries**

National monuments (May subdiv. geog.) **917.3**
> Use for materials on monuments, such as historic sites or geographic areas, that are owned and maintained in the public interest by a country's government.
> UF   Landmarks, Preservation of
>   National landmarks
> SA   names of individual national monuments [to be added as needed]
> BT   **Monuments**
>   **National parks and reserves**
> RT   **Historic sites**
>   **Natural monuments**

National parks and reserves (May subdiv. geog.)   **338.78; 363.6; 719**
- SA   names of individual national parks, e.g. **Yosemite National Park (Calif.)** [to be added as needed]
- BT   **Parks**
      Public lands
- NT   **National monuments**
- RT   **Conservation of natural resources**
      Forest reserves
      Natural monuments
      Wilderness areas

National parks and reserves—United States   719; 917.3
- UF   United States—National parks and reserves
- NT   **Yosemite National Park (Calif.)**

National patrimony
- USE   **Cultural property**

National planning
- USE   **Economic policy**
      Social policy

National product, Gross
- USE   **Gross national product**

National psychology
- USE   **Ethnopsychology**
      National characteristics

National resources
- USE   **Economic conditions**
      Natural resources
      United States—Economic conditions

National security (May subdiv. geog.)   **355**
- RT   **Economic policy**
      International relations
      Military policy

National security—United States   355
- UF   United States—National security

National self-determination (May subdiv. geog.)   **320.1; 341.26**
- UF   Self-determination, National
- BT   **Nationalism**
- RT   **Sovereignty**

National service (May subdiv. geog.)   **361.2**
- UF   Alternative military service
      National community service
- BT   **Public welfare**

- RT   **Volunteer work**

National socialism (May subdiv. geog.)   **320.5; 335.6**

   Use for materials limited to fascism in Germany during the Nazi regime.
- UF   Nazism
- BT   **Fascism**
      World War, 1939-1945—Causes
- RT   **Neo-Nazis**
      Socialism

National songs (May subdiv. geog.)   **782.42**
- UF   National anthems
      National hymns
      Patriotic songs
- BT   **Songs**
- NT   **War songs**
- RT   **Folk songs**
      Patriotic poetry

National songs—United States   782.42
- UF   American national songs
      United States—National songs
- BT   **American songs**

National symbols
- USE   **National emblems**

National treasure
- USE   **Cultural property**

Nationalism (May subdiv. geog.)   **320.5**
- UF   National consciousness
- BT   **International relations**
      Political science
- NT   **Ethnocentrism**
      National characteristics
      National liberation movements
      National self-determination
- RT   **Patriotism**
      Regionalism

Nationalism, Black
- USE   **Black nationalism**

Nationalism—United States   320.5

Nationalist China
- USE   **Taiwan**

Nationality (Citizenship)
- USE   **Citizenship**

Nationalization
- USE   **Government ownership**

Nationalization of railroads
- USE   **Railroads—Government policy**

Nationalized companies
- USE   **Government business enterprises**

Nations   900

  UF   Countries

  BT   **Political science**

Native American architecture (May subdiv. geog.)   **720.97; 970.004**

  UF   Indians of North America—Architecture

  BT   **Architecture**

  RT   **Native Americans—Dwellings**

Native American art (May subdiv. geog.)   **704; 709.01**

  UF   Indians of North America—Art

  BT   **Art**

Native American authors (May subdiv. geog.)   **810.9; 920**

  UF   American Indian authors

  BT   **Authors**

Native American children (May subdiv. geog.)   **305.23; 970.004**

  UF   Indians of North America—Children

        Native Americans—Children

  SA   children of specific Native American groups, e.g. **Navajo children** [to be added as needed]

  BT   **Children**

  NT   **Navajo children**

Native American costume (May subdiv. geog.)   **970.004**

  UF   Indians of North America—Costume

  BT   **Costume**

Native American dance (May subdiv. geog.)   **793.3; 970.004**

  UF   Indians of North America—Dances

  BT   **Folk dancing**

Native American games (May subdiv. geog.)   **790.1; 970.004**

  UF   Indians of North America—Games

  BT   **Games**

        Native Americans—Social life and customs

Native American languages (May subdiv. geog.)   **497**

Use for materials on the several languages of Native Americans.

  UF   Indian languages (North American)

Indians of North America—Languages

  SA   names of individual languages, e.g. **Navajo language** [to be added as needed]

  BT   **Language and languages**

  NT   **Navajo language**

Native American legends

  USE   **Native Americans—Folklore**

Native American literature (May subdiv. geog.)   **897**

Use for collections or materials about literature written in Native American languages by several Native American authors. Collections or materials about literature written in English by several Native American authors are entered under **American literature—Native American authors**.

  UF   Indians of North America—Literature

  BT   **Literature**

Native American medicine (May subdiv. geog.)   **615.8; 610**

  UF   Indians of North America—Medicine

  BT   **Medicine**

Native American music (May subdiv. geog.)   **780.89**

Use for musical transcriptions or for materials about the music of the Native Americans.

  UF   Indians of North America—Music

  BT   **Music**

Native American mythology

  USE   **Native Americans—Folklore**

          Native Americans—Religion

Native American names (May subdiv. geog.)   **929.4**

  UF   Indians of North America—Names

  BT   **Names**

Native American sign language   419

  UF   Indians of North America—Sign language

  BT   **Sign language**

Native American silverwork   739.2

  UF   Indians of North America—Silverwork

  BT   **Silverwork**

Native American women (May subdiv. geog.)   **305.4; 970.004**

  UF   Indians of North America—Women

        Native Americans—Women

Native American women—*Continued*
- SA women of specific Native American groups, e.g. **Navajo women** [to be added as needed]
- BT **Women**
- NT **Navajo women**

Native Americans (May subdiv. geog.)
  970.004

Use for general materials on the native peoples of the Western Hemisphere. Libraries that prefer not to subdivide by *United States* may also use this heading for materials limited to the native peoples of the United States. Phrase headings derived from this term may be similarly established for other ethnic groups and for specific Native American peoples and linguistic families. Topical subdivisions provided under this heading may also be used under other ethnic groups and under specific Native American peoples and linguistic families.

- UF American Indians
  - Indians of North America
  - Indigenous peoples—America
  - Pre-Columbian Americans
- SA names of particular Native American peoples and linguistic families, e.g. **Aztecs**; **Navajo Indians** etc. [to be added as needed]
- BT **Indigenous peoples**

Native Americans—Agriculture (May subdiv. geog.) **338.1; 630**
- UF Indians of North America—Agriculture
- BT **Agriculture**

Native Americans—Amusements
- USE **Native Americans—Social life and customs**

Native Americans—Antiquities (May subdiv. geog.) **970.004**
- UF Indians of North America—Antiquities
- BT **Antiquities**

Native Americans—Canada   971.004
- UF Canadian Indians
  - First nations
  - Indians of Canada
  - Indians of North America—Canada

Native Americans—Captivities (May subdiv. geog.) **970.004**

Use for materials on captivities by Native Americans

- UF Indians of North America—Captivities
- BT **Frontier and pioneer life**

Native Americans—Central America   972.8004
- UF Indians of Central America
- NT **Mayas**

Native Americans—Children
- USE **Native American children**

Native Americans—Christian missions (May subdiv. geog.) **266**
- UF Indian missions
  - Indians of North America—Christian missions
- BT **Christian missions**

Native Americans—Chronology
- USE **Native Americans—History—Chronology**

Native Americans—Claims (May subdiv. geog.) **323.1197; 970.004**
- UF Indians of North America—Claims
  - Native Americans—Land claims

Native Americans—Customs
- USE **Native Americans—Social life and customs**

Native Americans—Dwellings (May subdiv. geog.) **728; 970.004**
- UF Indians of North America—Dwellings
- NT **Tepees**
- RT **Native American architecture**

Native Americans—Economic conditions (May subdiv. geog.) **970.004**
- UF Indians of North America—Economic conditions
- BT **Economic conditions**

Native Americans—Education (May subdiv. geog.) **371.829; 970.004**
- UF Indians of North America—Education
  - Indians of North America—Schools
- BT **Education**

Native Americans—Ethnobiology (May subdiv. geog.) **578.6**
- BT **Ethnobiology**

Native Americans—Ethnobotany   581.6
- BT **Ethnobotany**

Native Americans—Ethnozoology   591.6
- BT **Ethnozoology**

Native Americans—First contact with Europeans (May subdiv. geog.)
   970.004
   UF   Indians of North America—First contact with Europeans
   BT   **Native Americans—History**
   RT   **Native Americans—Relations with early settlers**
Native Americans—Folklore (May subdiv. geog.)   **398**
   Use for collections of Native American legends, myths, tales, etc., and for materials about the folklore and mythology of Native Americans.
   UF   Indians of North America—Folklore
        Native American legends
        Native American mythology
   BT   **Folklore**
Native Americans—Forced removal
   USE   **Native Americans—Relocation**
Native Americans—Government policy
   USE   **Native Americans—Government relations**
Native Americans—Government relations (May subdiv. geog.)   **323.1197; 970.004**
   Use for materials on the Indian policy of the United States government and on relations between North American governments and the Native Americans.
   UF   Federal-Indian relations
        Indians of North America—Government relations
        Native Americans—Government policy
   RT   **Native Americans—Relations with early settlers**
Native Americans—Guatemala 972.81004
   UF   Indians of Central America—Guatemala
Native Americans—History   970.004
   UF   Indians of North America—History
   NT   **Native Americans—First contact with Europeans**
        Native Americans—Relations with early settlers
        Native Americans—Wars

Native Americans—History—Chronology 970.004
   Use for materials that list events and dates in the history of the Native Americans in the order of their occurrence.
   UF   Indians of North America—History—Chronology
        Native Americans—Chronology
Native Americans—Housing (May subdiv. geog.)   **307.3; 363.5**
   BT   **Housing**
Native Americans—Hunting (May subdiv. geog.)   **970.004**
   BT   **Hunting**
Native Americans—Industries (May subdiv. geog.)   **338.4; 680; 970.004**
   UF   Indians of North America—Industries
   BT   **Industries**
Native Americans—Land claims
   USE   **Native Americans—Claims**
Native Americans—Material culture (May subdiv. geog.)   **970.004**
Native Americans—Medical care (May subdiv. geog.)   **362.1**
   BT   **Medical care**
Native Americans—Mexico   972.004
   UF   Indians of Mexico
   NT   **Aztecs**
        Mayas
Native Americans—North America 970.004
   UF   Indians of North America
   SA   names of particular Native American peoples and linguistic families, e.g. **Navajo Indians** [to be added as needed]
Native Americans—Origin   970.004
   UF   Indians of North America—Origin
Native Americans—Peru   985
   UF   Indians of South America—Peru
Native Americans—Politics and government (May subdiv. geog.)   **970.004**
   UF   Indians of North America—Politics and government
        Native Americans—Tribal government
   BT   **Politics**
Native Americans—Psychology   155.8

Native Americans—Psychology—*Continued*

UF   Indians of North America—Psychology

BT   **Ethnopsychology**

Native Americans—Relations with early settlers (May subdiv. geog.)
970.004

UF   Indians of North America—Relations with early settlers

BT   **Native Americans—History**

RT   **Native Americans—First contact with Europeans**
      Native Americans—Government relations

Native Americans—Religion (May subdiv. geog.)   **270.089; 299.7; 299.8**

UF   Indians of North America—Religion
      Native American mythology

BT   **Religion**

Native Americans—Relocation (May subdiv. geog.)   **970.004**

UF   Forced removal of Indians
      Indian removal
      Native Americans—Forced removal
      Native Americans—Removal
      Removal of Indians

Native Americans—Removal

USE   **Native Americans—Relocation**

Native Americans—Reservations (May subdiv. geog.)   **333.1; 970.004**

UF   Indian reservations
      Indians of North America—Reservations

SA   names of native peoples, tribes, etc., with the subdivision *Reservations* [to be added as needed]

Native Americans—Rites and ceremonies
970.004

UF   Indians of North America—Rites and ceremonies

BT   **Rites and ceremonies**

NT   **Powwows**

Native Americans—Social conditions
(May subdiv. geog.)   **970.004**

UF   Indians of North America—Social conditions

BT   **Social conditions**

Native Americans—Social life and customs (May subdiv. geog.)
970.004

UF   Indians of North America—Social life and customs
      Native Americans—Amusements
      Native Americans—Customs

BT   **Manners and customs**

NT   **Native American games**
      Powwows

Native Americans—South America   980

UF   Indians of South America

NT   **Incas**

Native Americans—Southwestern States
979

NT   **Cliff dwellers and cliff dwellings**
      Navajo Indians

Native Americans—Tribal government

USE   **Native Americans—Politics and government**

Native Americans—United States
973.04

UF   Indians of North America

Native Americans—Wars (May subdiv. geog.)   **970.004**

UF   Indians of North America—Wars

BT   **Native Americans—History**

NT   **Black Hawk War, 1832**
      King Philip's War, 1675-1676
      Pontiac's Conspiracy, 1763-1765
      United States—History—1689-1697, King William's War
      United States—History—1755-1763, French and Indian War

Native Americans—West Indies
972.9004

UF   Indians of the West Indies

Native Americans—Women

USE   **Native American women**

Native peoples

USE   **Indigenous peoples**

Native plants (May subdiv. geog.)   **581.6**

UF   Indigenous plants

BT   **Plants**

Natives

USE   **Indigenous peoples**

Nativity of Jesus Christ

USE   **Jesus Christ—Nativity**

NATO
USE **North Atlantic Treaty Organization**

Natural beauty conservation
USE **Landscape protection**

Natural childbirth (May subdiv. geog.)
618.4
UF Lamaze method of childbirth
BT **Childbirth**
NT **Midwives**

Natural cycles
USE **Cycles**

Natural disasters (May subdiv. geog.)
904
SA types of natural disasters [to be added as needed]
BT **Disasters**
NT **Earthquakes**
Environmental degradation
Floods
Landslides
Storms
Tsunamis

Natural disasters—United States 973

Natural food cooking
USE **Cooking—Natural foods**

Natural foods (May subdiv. geog.)
641.3
UF Health foods
Organically grown foods
BT **Food**
RT **Cooking—Natural foods**

Natural gardening
USE **Organic gardening**

Natural gas (May subdiv. geog.) 553.2; 665.7
BT **Fuel**
Gases

Natural gas companies
USE **Gas companies**

Natural gas utilities
USE **Gas companies**

Natural history (May subdiv. geog.)
508
Use for materials on the unsystematic study of zoology, botany, mineralogy, etc., the collecting of specimens, and, with a geographic subdivision, the description of nature in a particular place. Materials on the study of animals and plants as an elementary school subject are entered under **Nature study**. General and theoretical materials on the natural world are entered under **Nature**.

UF Animal lore
Mineralogy
BT **Science**
NT **Aquariums**
Bible—Natural history
Bird watching
Fossils
Nature photography
RT **Biogeography**
Botany
Minerals
Nature
Zoology

Natural history—United States 508.73
UF Nature study—United States

Natural law 340
UF Law of nature
Natural rights
BT **Ethics**
Law
RT **International law**

Natural monuments (May subdiv. geog.)
719
Use for general materials on natural objects of historic or scientific interest such as caves, cliffs, and natural bridges.
UF Landmarks, Preservation of
Preservation of natural scenery
Protection of natural scenery
Scenery
SA names of individual natural monuments [to be added as needed]
BT **Landscape protection**
Monuments
Nature conservation
RT **National monuments**
National parks and reserves

Natural monuments—United States
719; 917.3

Natural parents
USE **Birthparents**

Natural pesticides 668
BT **Pesticides**

Natural religion
USE **Natural theology**

Natural resources (May subdiv. geog.)
333.7
UF National resources
SA types of natural resources [to be added as needed]
BT **Economic conditions**

538

Natural resources—*Continued*
NT Conservation of natural re-
sources
Energy resources
Forests and forestry
Marine resources
Mines and mineral resources
Water resources development
Water supply
RT Public lands
Natural resources—Management (May
subdiv. geog.) 333.7
BT Management
Natural resources—United States 333.7
Natural rights
USE Natural law
Natural satellites
USE Satellites
Natural selection 576.8
UF Survival of the fittest
BT Genetics
Variation (Biology)
RT Evolution
Heredity
Natural steam energy
USE Geothermal resources
Natural theology 210
Use for materials on the knowledge of
God's existence obtained by observing the
visible processes of nature.
UF Natural religion
BT Apologetics
Theology
NT Creation
RT Religion and science
Natural therapy
USE Naturopathy
Naturalism in art
USE Realism in art
Naturalism in literature
USE Realism in literature
Naturalists (May subdiv. geog.)
508.092; 920
SA types of naturalists, e.g. **Bota-
nists** [to be added as needed]
BT Scientists
NT Biologists
Botanists
Naturalization 323.6
BT Immigration and emigration
International law
Suffrage

RT Aliens
Americanization
Citizenship
Nature 508
Use for general and theoretical materials on
the natural world. Materials on the study of
animals and plants as an elementary school
subject are entered under **Nature study**. Ma-
terials on the unsystematic study of zoology,
botany, mineralogy, etc., the collecting of
specimens, and the description of nature in a
particular place are entered under **Natural
history**.
RT Natural history
Nature study
Nature and nurture (May subdiv. geog.)
155.2
UF Genetics and environment
Heredity and environment
Nurture and nature
BT Genetics
Heredity
Nature conservation (May subdiv. geog.)
333.72
UF Conservation of nature
Nature protection
Preservation of natural scenery
Protection of natural scenery
BT Conservation of natural re-
sources
NT Endangered species
Landscape protection
Natural monuments
Plant conservation
Wildlife conservation
Nature craft 745.5
Use for materials on crafts using objects
found in nature, such as leaves, shells, etc.
UF Naturecraft
BT Handicraft
NT Potpourri
Sand sculpture
Nature—Effect of human beings on
USE Human influence on nature
Nature in literature 809
BT Literature—Themes
Nature in the bible
USE Bible—Natural history
Nature photography (May subdiv. geog.)
778.9
UF Photography of nature

Nature photography—*Continued*
  SA photography of particular sub-
        jects in nature, e.g. **Photogra-**
        phy of birds [to be added as
        needed]
  BT **Natural history**
        Photography
  NT **Photography of animals**
        Photography of birds
        Photography of fishes
        Photography of plants
        Wildlife photography
  RT **Outdoor photography**
Nature poetry   808.1; 808.81
  Use for individual works or collections of
  poetry about nature.
  UF Nature—Poetry
  BT **Poetry**
Nature—Poetry
  USE **Nature poetry**
Nature prints   761
  BT **Printing**
        Prints
Nature protection
  USE **Nature conservation**
Nature study   372.35; 508.07
  Use for materials on the study of animals
  and plants as an elementary school subject.
  Materials on the unsystematic study of zoolo-
  gy, botany, mineralogy, etc., the collecting of
  specimens, and the description of nature in a
  particular place are entered under **Natural**
  history. General and theoretical materials on
  the natural world are entered under **Nature**.
  BT **Education**
        Science—Study and teaching
  RT **Nature**
        Outdoor education
        Outdoor life
Nature study—United States
  USE **Natural history—United States**
Nature television programs   791.45
  BT **Television programs**
Nature tourism
  USE **Ecotourism**
Nature trails (May subdiv. geog.)   **508**
  BT **Trails**
Naturecraft
  USE **Nature craft**
Naturopathy   615.5
  UF Natural therapy
  BT **Alternative medicine**
        Therapeutics
  RT **Chiropractic**

Nautical almanacs (May subdiv. geog.)
        528
  BT **Almanacs**
        Navigation
Nautical astronomy   527
  BT **Astronomy**
  NT **Latitude**
        Longitude
  RT **Navigation**
        Time
Nautical charts   623.89
  UF Charts, Nautical
        Navigation charts
        Navigation maps
        Pilot charts
  BT **Maps**
        Navigation
Navaho Indians
  USE **Navajo Indians**
Navaho language
  USE **Navajo language**
Navajo children (May subdiv. geog.)
        973.04
  UF Navajo Indians—Children
  BT **Native American children**
        Navajo Indians
Navajo Indians (May subdiv. geog.)
        973.04
  UF Navaho Indians
  BT **Native Americans—Southwest-**
        ern States
  NT **Navajo children**
        Navajo women
Navajo Indians—Children
  USE **Navajo children**
Navajo Indians—Women
  USE **Navajo women**
Navajo language   497
  UF Navaho language
  BT **Native American languages**
Navajo women (May subdiv. geog.)
        973.04
  UF Navajo Indians—Women
  BT **Native American women**
        Navajo Indians
Naval administration
  USE **Naval art and science**
        and names of countries with the
        subhead *Navy*, e.g. **United**
        States. Navy [to be added as
        needed]

Naval aeronautics
   USE **Military aeronautics**
Naval air bases
   USE **Air bases**
Naval airplanes
   USE **Military airplanes**
Naval architecture (May subdiv. geog.)
   623.8
   UF Marine architecture
   BT **Architecture**
   NT **Boatbuilding**
       Marine engineering
       Shipbuilding
       Steamboats
       Warships
Naval art and science (May subdiv.
   geog.) **359**
   UF Fighting
       Naval administration
       Naval science
       Naval warfare
       Navy
   SA names of wars with the subdivi-
       sion *Naval operations*, e.g.
       **World War, 1939-1945—Na-
       val operations** [to be added
       as needed]
   NT **Camouflage (Military science)**
       Marine engineering
       Navy yards and naval stations
       Privateering
       Sailors
       Sea power
       Signals and signaling
       Strategy
       Submarine warfare
       Torpedoes
       Warships
   RT **Military art and science**
       Navies
       Navigation
       War
Naval art and science—Study and teaching
   USE **Naval education**
Naval bases
   USE **Navy yards and naval stations**
Naval battles **359.4; 904**
   UF Naval warfare
   SA names of countries with the sub-
       division *Naval history*; names
       of wars with the subdivision

Naval operations, e.g. **World
   War, 1939-1945—Naval op-
   erations**; and names of spe-
   cific naval battles [to be add-
   ed as needed]
   BT **Battles**
   RT **Naval history**
Naval biography
   USE names of navies with the subdi-
       vision *Biography*, e.g. **United
       States. Navy—Biography** [to
       be added as needed]
Naval education (May subdiv. geog.)
   359.007
   UF Naval art and science—Study
       and teaching
       Naval schools
   BT **Education**
Naval engineering
   USE **Marine engineering**
Naval history **359.009**
   UF Wars
   SA names of countries with the sub-
       head *Navy* or the subdivision
       Naval history [to be added as
       needed]
   BT **History**
   NT **Pirates**
       Privateering
       United States—Naval history
   RT **Military history**
       Naval battles
       Sea power
Naval law
   USE **Maritime law**
Naval offenses
   USE **Military offenses**
Naval operations
   USE names of wars with the subdivi-
       sion *Naval operations*, e.g.
       **World War, 1939-1945—Na-
       val operations** [to be added
       as needed]
Naval pensions
   USE **Military pensions**
Naval personnel
   USE **Sailors**
Naval power
   USE **Sea power**
Naval schools
   USE **Naval education**

Naval science
  USE **Naval art and science**
Naval shipyards
  USE **Navy yards and naval stations**
Naval signaling
  USE **Signals and signaling**
Naval strategy
  USE **Strategy**
Naval uniforms
  USE **Military uniforms**
Naval warfare
  USE **Naval art and science**
      Naval battles
      Submarine warfare
Navies   359.3
  UF   Military power
       Navy
       Sea life
  SA   names of countries with the sub-
       head *Navy*, e.g. **United**
       States. Navy [to be added as
       needed]
  BT   **Armed forces**
       Military personnel
  NT   **Admirals**
       Sailors
       United States. Navy
  RT   **Naval art and science**
       Sea power
       Warships
Navigation (May subdiv. geog.)   **623.89;**
  629.04
  UF   Pilots and pilotage
       Seamanship
  BT   **Locomotion**
  NT   **Compass**
       Global Positioning System
       Harbors
       Inland navigation
       Knots and splices
       Lighthouses
       Loran
       Nautical almanacs
       Nautical charts
       Ocean currents
       Pilot guides
       Radar
       Shipwrecks
       Signals and signaling
       Steam navigation
       Winds

  RT   **Direction sense**
       Nautical astronomy
       Naval art and science
       Sailing
       Ship pilots
Navigation (Aeronautics)   629.132
  UF   Aerial navigation
       Aeronautics—Navigation
       Air navigation
  BT   **Aeronautics**
  NT   **Airplanes—Piloting**
       Radio in aeronautics
Navigation (Astronautics)   629.45
  UF   Astronavigation
       Space navigation
  BT   **Astrodynamics**
       Astronautics
  NT   **Astronautical instruments**
       Radio in astronautics
       Space vehicles—Piloting
  RT   **Space flight**
Navigation charts
  USE **Nautical charts**
Navigation—Law and legislation
  USE **Maritime law**
Navigation maps
  USE **Nautical charts**
Navigators
  USE **Explorers**
       Sailors
Navy
  USE **Naval art and science**
       Navies
       Sea power
       and names of countries with the
       subhead *Navy*, e.g. **United**
       States. Navy [to be added as
       needed]
Navy Sealab project
  USE **Sealab project**
Navy yards and naval stations (May
  subdiv. geog.)   **359.7**
  UF   Naval bases
       Naval shipyards
  BT   **Naval art and science**
Nazi persecution
  USE   religious groups and classes of
       persons with the subdivision
       Nazi persecution, e.g. **Handi-**
       capped—Nazi persecution [to
       be added as needed]

Nazi persecution of the handicapped
USE **Handicapped—Nazi persecution**
Nazism
USE **National socialism**
Neanderthals (May subdiv. geog.)
569.986
BT **Fossil hominids**
Near-death experiences   133.9; 155.9
Use for materials on the paranormal experiences of those who have survived near death or apparent death.
BT **Death**
RT **Parapsychology**
Near East
USE **Middle East**
Neatness
USE **Cleanliness**
Orderliness
Nebula Award   808.3
BT **Literary prizes**
Science fiction
Nebulae, Extragalactic
USE **Galaxies**
Necrologies
USE **Obituaries**
Necromancy
USE **Divination**
Magic
Needlepoint   746.44
UF Canvas embroidery
BT **Embroidery**
Needlework
Needlework (May subdiv. geog.)   **746.4**
SA types of needlework [to be added as needed]
BT **Decoration and ornament**
Decorative arts
NT **Appliqué**
Crocheting
Drawn work
Embroidery
Hardanger needlework
Knitting
Lace and lace making
Needlepoint
Patchwork
Quilting
Samplers
Smocking
Tapestry
RT **Dressmaking**
Sewing

Negotiable instruments (May subdiv. geog.)   **332.7**
UF Bills and notes
Bills of credit
Commercial paper
Instruments, Negotiable
Letters of credit
BT **Banks and banking**
Commercial law
Contracts
Credit
NT **Bonds**
Negotiation (May subdiv. geog.)   **158; 302.3**
UF Bargaining
Discussion
BT **Applied psychology**
NT **Collective bargaining**
Conflict management
Hostage negotiation
Industrial arbitration
Negritude
USE **Blacks—Race identity**
Negro leagues   796.357
BT **Baseball**
Negroes
USE **African Americans**
Blacks
Neighborhood (May subdiv. geog.)   **307.3**
UF Neighborhoods
BT **Community life**
Social groups
Neighborhood centers
USE **Community centers**
Social settlements
Neighborhood development
USE **Community development**
Neighborhood gardens
USE **Community gardens**
Neighborhoods
USE **Neighborhood**
Neo-fascism
USE **Fascism**
Neo-Nazis
Neo-Greek literature
USE **Modern Greek literature**
Neo-impressionism (Art)
USE **Impressionism (Art)**
Neo-Latin languages
USE **Romance languages**

Neo-Nazis (May subdiv. geog.)   **320.5**

Use for materials on political groups whose social beliefs or political agendas are reminiscent of those of Hitler's Nazis.

UF   Neo-fascism

Neo-nazism

BT   **Fascism**

RT   **National socialism**

Neo-nazism

USE   **Neo-Nazis**

Neolithic period

USE   **Stone Age**

Neon Genesis Evangelion (Fictional robot)   **741.5**

BT   **Fictional robots**

Manga

Mecha

Neon tubes   **621.32**

BT   **Electric signs**

Neopaganism (May subdiv. geog.)   **299**

BT   **Religions**

Neptune (Planet)   **523.48**

BT   **Planets**

Nero, 37-68   **92; B**

BT   **Emperors—Rome**

Nerves   **611; 612.8**

BT   **Nervous system**

Nerves—Diseases

USE   **Nervous system—Diseases**

Nervous breakdown

USE   **Neurasthenia**

Nervous exhaustion

USE   **Neurasthenia**

Nervous prostration

USE   **Neurasthenia**

Nervous system   **611; 612.8**

UF   Neurology

BT   **Anatomy**

Physiology

NT   **Abnormal psychology**

Brain

Nerves

Psychophysiology

Nervous system—Diseases   **616.8**

UF   Nerves—Diseases

Neuropathology

BT   **Diseases**

NT   **Communicative disorders**

Epilepsy

Movement disorders

Paralysis

Senile dementia

Nessie (Monster)

USE   **Loch Ness monster**

Nest building   **591.56**

UF   Building nests

Nesting (Animal behavior)

Nesting behavior

SA   types of animals and individual species on animals with the subdivision *Nests,* e.g. **Birds—Nests** [to be added as needed]

BT   **Animal behavior**

Animals—Habitations

Nesting (Animal behavior)

USE   **Nest building**

Nesting behavior

USE   **Nest building**

Nests

USE   types of animals and individual species of animals with the subdivision *Nests,* e.g. **Birds—Nests** [to be added as needed]

Netherlands   **949.2**

May be subdivided like United States except for History.

UF   Holland

Netherlands—History   **949.2**

Netherlands—History—1940-1945, German occupation   **949.207**

UF   German occupation of Netherlands, 1940-1945

Network theory

USE   **System analysis**

Networks (Associations, institutions, etc.)

USE   **Associations**

Networks, Computer

USE   **Computer networks**

Networks, Information

USE   **Information networks**

Neurasthenia   **616.85**

UF   Nervous breakdown

Nervous exhaustion

Nervous prostration

BT   **Mental illness**

Neurology

USE   **Nervous system**

Neuropathology

USE   **Nervous system—Diseases**

Neuroses   **616.85**

BT   **Abnormal psychology**

Neuroses—*Continued*
    NT   **Anxiety**
          Depression (Psychology)
          Narcissism
          Obsessive-compulsive disorder
          Panic disorders
          Phobias
          Post-traumatic stress disorder
Neurotic children
    USE **Emotionally disturbed children**
Neutrality (May subdiv. geog.)   **327.1;**
      341.6
    UF Nonalignment
    BT **International law**
          International relations
          International security
    RT **Intervention (International law)**
          Isolationism
Neutrality—United States   **327.73**
    UF United States—Neutrality
    RT **United States—Foreign rela-**
          tions
Neutron bomb (May subdiv. geog.)
      623.4
    UF Neutron bombs
    BT **Bombs**
          Neutron weapons
Neutron bombs
    USE **Neutron bomb**
Neutron weapons (May subdiv. geog.)
      623.4
    UF Enhanced radiation weapons
    BT **Nuclear weapons**
    NT **Neutron bomb**
Neutrons   **539.7**
    BT **Atoms**
          Particles (Nuclear physics)
New Age movement (May subdiv. geog.)
      130; 131; 299
    Use for materials on any of various post-1970 cults and organizations that incorporate Eastern or Native American religions, occult beliefs and practices, mysticism, or meditation techniques in an attempt to enhance consciousness and develop human potential.
    UF Aquarian Age movement
    BT **Cults**
          Occultism
          Social movements
New birth (Theology)
    USE **Regeneration (Christianity)**
New business enterprises (May subdiv.
    geog.)   **338.7**

    UF How to start a business
          Starting a business
    BT **Business enterprises**
New communities
    USE **Planned communities**
New countries
    USE **New states**
New Deal, 1933-1939   **973.917**
    BT **United States—History—1933-**
          1945
New England   **974**
    BT **United States**
New France—History
    USE **Canada—History—0-1763 (New**
          France)
          Mississippi River Valley—His-
          tory
New nations
    USE **New states**
New Negro Movement
    USE **Harlem Renaissance**
New product development
    USE **New products**
New products (May subdiv. geog.)
      658.5
    UF New product development
          Product development
    BT **Commercial products**
          Industrial research
          Marketing
New states   **321**
    UF New countries
          New nations
          States, New
    BT **Developing countries**
New Testament
    USE **Bible. N.T.**
New words   **417**
    UF Coinage of words
          Words, New
    BT **Vocabulary**
New Year   **394.2614**
    BT **Holidays**
New York Knicks (Basketball team)
      796.323
    UF Knicks (Basketball team)
    BT **Basketball teams**
New York (N.Y.)—Streets
    USE **Streets—New York (N.Y.)**
New Zealand   **993**
    May be subdivided like United States except for History.

Newbery Award
　　USE　**Newbery Medal**
Newbery Medal　028.5
　　UF　Newbery Award
　　　　Newbery Prize books
　　BT　**Children's literature**
　　　　Literary prizes
Newbery Prize books
　　USE　**Newbery Medal**
News agencies (May subdiv. geog.)
　　　　070.4
　　UF　News services
　　　　Wire services
　　BT　**Press**
News editing
　　USE　**Journalism—Editing**
News photography
　　USE　**Photojournalism**
News services
　　USE　**News agencies**
Newsletters　070.1
　　BT　**Journalism**
　　　　Newspapers
Newspaper advertising (May subdiv.
　　geog.)　**659.13**

　　Use for materials on advertising in newspapers. Materials on the advertising of newspapers are entered under **Advertising—Newspapers**.

　　UF　Advertising, Newspaper
　　BT　**Advertising**
　　　　Newspapers
Newspaper clippings
　　USE　**Clippings (Books, newspapers,**
　　　　etc.)
Newspaper work
　　USE　**Reporters and reporting**
Newspapers (May subdiv. geog.)　**070**

　　Use for materials limited to the history, organization, and management of newspapers. Materials on writing for the periodical press, on the editing of such writing, and on journalism as an occupation, are entered under **Journalism**.

　　SA　names of individual newspapers
　　　　[to be added as needed]
　　BT　**Mass media**
　　　　Serial publications
　　NT　**Clippings (Books, newspapers,**
　　　　etc.)
　　　　Newsletters
　　　　Newspaper advertising
　　　　Reporters and reporting

　　RT　**Journalism**
　　　　Periodicals
　　　　Press
Newspapers—Advertising
　　USE　**Advertising—Newspapers**
Newspapers—Editing
　　USE　**Journalism—Editing**
Newspapers—Great Britain　072
　　UF　English newspapers
Newspapers—Indexes　070.1
Newspapers—Sections, columns, etc.
　　　　070.4
　　SA　types of newspaper columns, e.g.
　　　　Advice columns [to be added
　　　　as needed]
　　NT　**Advice columns**
Newspapers—United States　071
　　UF　American newspapers
Nicene Creed　238
　　BT　**Creeds**
Nicknames (May subdiv. geog.)　**929.4**
　　UF　Epithets
　　　　Sobriquets
　　BT　**Personal names**
Nicotine habit
　　USE　**Tobacco habit**
Nigeria　966.9

　　May be subdivided like United States except for History.

Night　529
　　BT　**Chronology**
　　　　Time
　　NT　**Bedtime**
　　RT　**Day**
Night clubs, cabarets, etc. (May subdiv.
　　geog.)　**725**
　　UF　Cabarets
　　BT　**Theaters**
Night schools
　　USE　**Evening and continuation**
　　　　schools
Nike rocket　623.4
　　BT　**Guided missiles**
Nile River valley　962
　　UF　Nile Valley
　　BT　**Egypt**
　　　　Sudan
Nile Valley
　　USE　**Nile River valley**
Nineteen eighties (May subdiv. geog.)
　　　　909.82
　　UF　1980s

Nineteen eighties—*Continued*

    BT   **World history—20th century**

Nineteen fifties (May subdiv. geog.)
      909.82

    UF   1950s

    BT   **World history—20th century**

Nineteen forties (May subdiv. geog.)
      909.82

    UF   1940s

    BT   **World history—20th century**

Nineteen nineties (May subdiv. geog.)
      909.82

    UF   1990s

    BT   **World history—20th century**

Nineteen seventies (May subdiv. geog.)
      909.82

    UF   1970s

    BT   **World history—20th century**

Nineteen sixties (May subdiv. geog.)
      909.82

    UF   1960s

    BT   **World history—20th century**

Nineteen thirties (May subdiv. geog.)
      909.82

    UF   1930s

    BT   **World history—20th century**

Nineteen twenties (May subdiv. geog.)
      909.82

    UF   1920s

    BT   **World history—20th century**

Nineteenth century

    USE **World history—19th century**

Ninja (May subdiv. geog.)   **952**

    BT   **Japan—History—0-1868**

Nisei

    USE **Japanese Americans**

Nitrates   **553.6**

    BT   **Chemicals**

        Fertilizers

Nitrogen   **546; 665**

    BT   **Gases**

Noah's ark   **222; 398.22**

Nobel Prizes   **001.4; 807.9**

    BT   **Awards**

Nobility (May subdiv. geog.)   **305.5;**
      929.7

    UF   Peerage

    BT   **Upper class**

    NT   **Knights and knighthood**

    RT   **Aristocracy**

        Heraldry

Noise (May subdiv. geog.)   **363.74**

    SA   subjects with the subdivision
        Noise [to be added as needed]

    BT   **Public health**

        Sound

    NT   **Airplanes—Noise**

Noise pollution (May subdiv. geog.)
      363.74

    SA   subjects with the subdivision
        Noise [to be added as needed]

    BT   **Pollution**

    NT   **Airplanes—Noise**

Nomadic peoples

    USE **Nomads**

Nomads (May subdiv. geog.)   **305.9**

    UF   Nomadic peoples

        Pastoral peoples

    BT   **Primitive societies**

Nomenclature

    USE types of scientific and technical
        disciplines and types of sub-
        stances, plants, and animals
        with the subdivision *Nomen-*
        clature, for systematically de-
        rived lists of names or desig-
        nations that have been formal-
        ly adopted or sanctioned, and
        for discussions of the princi-
        ples involved in the creation
        and application of such
        names, e.g. **Botany—Nomen-**
        clature; scientific and techni-
        cal disciplines and types of
        animals, plants, and crops
        with the subdivision *Nomen-*
        clature (Popular), for lists or
        materials about popular, non-
        technical names or designa-
        tions of substances, species,
        etc., e.g. **Trees—Nomencla-**
        ture (Popular); and subjects,
        classes of persons, sacred
        works, and religious sects
        with the subdivision *Terminol-*
        ogy, for lists or discussions of
        words and expressions found
        in those works or used in
        those fields, e.g. **Botany—**
        Terminology [to be added as
        needed]

Nomenclature (Popular)
USE types of scientific and technical
disciplines and types of animals, plants, and crops with
the subdivision *Nomenclature
(Popular),* for lists of popular
or non-technical names or
designations of substances,
species, etc., e.g. **Trees—Nomenclature (Popular);** and
scientific and technical disciplines and types of sub-
stances, plants, and animals
with the subdivision *Nomenclature,* for systematically derived lists of names or designations that have been formally adopted or sactioned, and
for discussions of the principles involved in the creation
and application of such
names, e.g. **Botany—Nomenclature** [to be added as need-
ed]
Nomination
USE types of public officials and
names of individual public officials with the subdivision
Nomination, e.g. **Presidents—
United States—Nomination**
[to be added as needed]
Nomination of presidents
USE **Presidents—United States—
Nomination**
Non-institutional churches (May subdiv.
geog.) **289.9**
UF Avant-garde churches
Churches, Non-institutional
Noninstitutional churches
BT **Christian sects**
Non-professional theater
USE **Amateur theater**
Non-proliferation of nuclear weapons
USE **Arms control**
Non-promotion (School)
USE **Promotion (School)**
Non-victim crimes
USE **Crimes without victims**
Non-wage payments
USE **Employee benefits**

Nonalignment
USE **Neutrality**
Nonbook materials
USE **Audiovisual materials**
Noncitizens
USE **Aliens**
Nonconformity
USE **Conformity
Counter culture
Dissent**
Nondenominational churches
USE **Community churches**
Nonfiction films
USE **Documentary films**
Nonformal schools
USE **Experimental schools**
Nonfossil fuels
USE **Synthetic fuels**
Nongraded schools (May subdiv. geog.)
371.2
UF Multi-age grouping
Ungraded schools
BT **Ability grouping in education
Education—Experimental
methods
Schools**
Noninstitutional churches
USE **Non-institutional churches**
Nonlinguistic communication
USE **Nonverbal communication**
Nonnationals
USE **Aliens**
Nonnutritive sweeteners
USE **Sugar substitutes**
Nonobjective art
USE **Abstract art**
Nonprescription drugs 615
UF Drugs, Nonprescription
Over-the-counter drugs
Patent medicines
BT **Drugs**
Nonprint materials
USE **Audiovisual materials**
Nonprofit corporations
USE **Nonprofit organizations**
Nonprofit organizations (May subdiv.
geog.) **346; 658**
UF Corporations, Nonprofit
Nonprofit corporations
Nonprofit sector
Nonprofits

Nonprofit organizations—*Continued*
Not-for-profit organizations
Organizations, Nonprofit
BT **Associations**
Nonprofit sector
USE **Nonprofit organizations**
Nonprofitable drugs
USE **Orphan drugs**
Nonprofits
USE **Nonprofit organizations**
Nonpublic schools
USE **Church schools**
Private schools
Nonsense verses   808.1; 808.81
Use for individual works, collections, or materials about nonsense verse.
UF Rhymes
BT **Children's poetry**
Humorous poetry
Wit and humor
NT **Tongue twisters**
RT **Limericks**
Nonsupport
USE **Desertion and nonsupport**
Nonverbal communication   153.6; 302.2
UF Nonlinguistic communication
BT **Communication**
NT **Body language**
Hugging
Personal space
RT **Deaf—Means of communication**
Nonvictim crimes
USE **Crimes without victims**
Nonviolence (May subdiv. geog.)   179; 303.6
NT **Hunger strikes**
RT **Pacifism**
Passive resistance
Nonviolent noncooperation
USE **Passive resistance**
Nonwage payments
USE **Employee benefits**
Nonword stories
USE **Stories without words**
Nordic peoples
USE **Teutonic peoples**
Normal schools
USE **Teachers colleges**
Normandy (France), Attack on, 1944
940.54
UF D Day

BT **World War, 1939-1945—Campaigns**
Normans (May subdiv. geog.)   **941.02**
BT **Great Britain—History—1066-1154, Norman period**
RT **Vikings**
Norse languages
USE **Old Norse language**
Scandinavian languages
Norse legends   398.20893
BT **Legends**
Norse literature
USE **Old Norse literature**
Scandinavian literature
Norse mythology   293
UF Scandinavian mythology
BT **Mythology**
Norsemen
USE **Vikings**
North Africa   961
Use for materials dealing collectively with the region of Africa that includes Morocco, Algeria, Tunisia, and Libya.
UF Africa, North
Barbary States
Maghreb
BT **Africa**
North America   970
BT **America**
NT **Central America**
Northwest Coast of North America
Pacific Northwest
North Atlantic Treaty Organization
341.7
UF NATO
BT **International organization**
North Central States
USE **Middle West**
North Korea
USE **Korea (North)**
North Pole   910.9163; 998
BT **Polar regions**
RT **Arctic regions**
Northeast Africa   960
Use for materials dealing collectively with the region of Africa that includes Sudan, Ethiopia, Eritrea, Somalia, and Djibouti.
UF Africa, Northeast
BT **Africa**
Northeast Passage   998
BT **Arctic regions**
Exploration

Northeast Passage—*Continued*
    Voyages and travels
Northern lights
    USE   **Auroras**
Northmen
    USE   **Vikings**
Northwest Africa   964
    Use for materials dealing collectively with the region of Africa that includes Morocco, Western Sahara, Mauritania, Algeria, Mali, Tunisia, Libya, Niger, and Chad.
    UF   Africa, Northwest
    BT   **Africa**
**Northwest Coast of North America
    979.5**
    UF   Northwest, Pacific coast
          Pacific Northwest coast
    BT   **North America**
Northwest, Old
    USE   **Old Northwest**
Northwest, Pacific
    USE   **Pacific Northwest**
Northwest, Pacific coast
    USE   **Northwest Coast of North
          America**
Northwest Passage   971.9
    BT   **America—Exploration
          Arctic regions**
Northwest Territory
    USE   **Old Northwest**
Norway   948.1
    May be subdivided like United States except for History.
Norwegian drawn work
    USE   **Hardanger needlework**
Norwegian language   439.8
    May be subdivided like **English language**.
    BT   **Language and languages
          Scandinavian languages**
    NT   **Danish language**
Norwegian language—0-1350
    USE   **Old Norse language**
Norwegian literature   839.82
    May use same subdivisions and names of literary forms as for **English literature**.
    BT   **Literature
          Scandinavian literature**
Nose   611; 612.2
    BT   **Face
          Head**
    RT   **Smell**
Not-for-profit organizations
    USE   **Nonprofit organizations**

Notation, Mathematical
    USE   **Mathematical notation**
Novelists   809.3; 920
    SA   novelists of particular countries, e.g. **American novelists**; and names of individual novelists [to be added as needed]
    BT   **Authors**
    NT   **American novelists
          English novelists**
Novelists, American
    USE   **American novelists**
Novels
    USE   **Fiction**
Novels in letters
    USE   **Epistolary fiction**
Nuclear bomb shelters
    USE   **Air raid shelters**
Nuclear energy (May subdiv. geog.)
    333.792; 539.7
    UF   Atomic energy
          Atomic power
          Nuclear power
    BT   **Nuclear physics**
    NT   **Nuclear engineering
          Nuclear propulsion
          Nuclear reactors**
    RT   **Nuclear industry
          Nuclear power plants**
Nuclear engineering (May subdiv. geog.)
    621.48
    BT   **Engineering
          Nuclear energy
          Nuclear physics**
    NT   **Nuclear reactors
          Radioactive waste disposal
          Radioisotopes**
Nuclear freeze movement
    USE   **Antinuclear movement**
Nuclear fusion   539.7
    BT   **Nuclear physics**
Nuclear industry (May subdiv. geog.)
    333.792
    UF   Atomic industry
    BT   **Industries**
    RT   **Nuclear energy**
Nuclear magnetic resonance imaging
    USE   **Magnetic resonance imaging**
Nuclear medicine (May subdiv. geog.)
    616.07
    UF   Atomic medicine

Nuclear medicine—*Continued*
  BT   **Medicine**
  RT   **Radiation—Physiological effect**
Nuclear medicine—Practice (May subdiv.
    geog.) **616.07**
  BT   **Medical practice**
Nuclear non-proliferation
  USE **Arms control**
Nuclear particles
  USE **Particles (Nuclear physics)**
Nuclear physics **539.7**
  UF   Atomic nuclei
  BT   **Physics**
  NT   **Cosmic rays**
       Cyclotrons
       Nuclear energy
       Nuclear engineering
       Nuclear fusion
       Nuclear reactors
       Particles (Nuclear physics)
       Radiobiology
       Transmutation (Chemistry)
  RT   **Physical chemistry**
       Radioactivity
Nuclear pollution
  USE **Radioactive pollution**
Nuclear power
  USE **Nuclear energy**
Nuclear power plants (May subdiv. geog.)
    621.48
  UF   Atomic power plants
       Power plants, Nuclear
  BT   **Electric power plants**
  RT   **Nuclear energy**
Nuclear power plants—Accidents (May
    subdiv. geog.) **363.17**
Nuclear power plants—Environmental
    aspects (May subdiv. geog.)
    333.792; 621.48
  BT   **Environment**
       Environmental health
  NT   **Radioactive waste disposal**
  RT   **Antinuclear movement**
Nuclear power plants—Fires and fire
    prevention (May subdiv. geog.)
    363.37; 628.9
  BT   **Fire prevention**
       Fires
Nuclear power plants—Security mea-
    sures (May subdiv. geog.) **621.48**
Nuclear propulsion **621.48**
  UF   Atomic-powered vehicles

  SA   specific applications of nuclear
       propulsion, e.g. **Nuclear sub-**
       marines [to be added as
       needed]
  BT   **Nuclear energy**
  NT   **Nuclear submarines**
  RT   **Nuclear reactors**
Nuclear reactors (May subdiv. geog.)
    621.48
  UF   Reactors (Nuclear physics)
  BT   **Nuclear energy**
       Nuclear engineering
       Nuclear physics
  RT   **Nuclear propulsion**
Nuclear submarines (May subdiv. geog.)
    623.825
  UF   Atomic submarines
  BT   **Nuclear propulsion**
       Submarines
Nuclear test ban
  USE **Arms control**
Nuclear warfare (May subdiv. geog.)
    355.02
  UF   Atomic warfare
  BT   **War**
  RT   **Nuclear weapons**
Nuclear waste disposal
  USE **Radioactive waste disposal**
Nuclear weapons (May subdiv. geog.)
    355.8; 623.4
  UF   Atomic weapons
       Weapons, Atomic
       Weapons, Nuclear
  SA   types of nuclear weapons, e.g.
       Atomic bomb [to be added
       as needed]
  BT   **Military weapons**
  NT   **Antinuclear movement**
       Atomic bomb
       Ballistic missiles
       Hydrogen bomb
       Neutron weapons
  RT   **Nuclear warfare**
Nucleic acids **547; 572.8**
  UF   Polynucleotides
  BT   **Biochemistry**
  NT   **DNA**
       RNA
Nucleons
  USE **Particles (Nuclear physics)**
Nude in art **704.9; 743.4**

Nude in art—*Continued*

UF   Human anatomy in art

       Human figure in art

BT   **Art—Themes**

NT   **Artistic anatomy**

Number ability

USE   **Mathematical ability**

Number concept   119; 155.4; 372.7

Use for materials on the apperception and conceptualization of numbers. Materials on numbers, numbering, and systems of numeration are entered under **Numbers**. Materials on counting, including counting books, are entered under **Counting**.

BT   **Apperception**

       Psychology

RT   **Numbers**

Number games   793.74

BT   **Arithmetic—Study and teaching**

       Counting

       Mathematical recreations

Number patterns

USE   **Patterns (Mathematics)**

Number readiness

USE   **Mathematical readiness**

Number symbolism

USE   **Numerology**

       Symbolism of numbers

Number systems

USE   **Numbers**

Number theory   512.7

Use for materials on that branch of mathematics that involves the study of integers and their relation to one another.

UF   Theory of numbers

BT   **Algebra**

       Mathematics

       Set theory

NT   **Group theory**

RT   **Numbers**

Numbers   119; 513

Use for materials on numbers, numbering, and systems of numeration. Materials on the conceptualization of numbers are entered under **Number concept**. Materials on counting, including counting books, are entered under **Counting**. Materials on the graphic representation of numbers are entered under **Numerals**.

UF   Number systems

       Numeration

SA   names of individual numbers,

       e.g. **Three (The number)**;

       and systems of numeration,

       e.g. **Decimal system** [to be added as needed]

NT   **Binary system (Mathematics)**

       Decimal system

       Three (The number)

RT   **Arithmetic**

       Counting

       Number concept

       Number theory

       Numerals

       Symbolism of numbers

Numeral formation

USE   **Writing of numerals**

Numeral writing

USE   **Writing of numerals**

Numerals   513

Use for materials on the graphic representation of numbers.

SA   types of numerals, e.g. **Roman numerals** [to be added as needed]

NT   **Roman numerals**

       Writing of numerals

RT   **Numbers**

Numerals, Writing of

USE   **Writing of numerals**

Numeration

USE   **Numbers**

Numerical analysis   518

BT   **Mathematical analysis**

NT   **Approximate computation**

Numerical sequences

USE   **Sequences (Mathematics)**

Numerology   133.3

Use for materials on the occult significance of numbers. General materials on the symbolism of numbers, as in philosophy, religion, or literature, are entered under **Symbolism of numbers**.

UF   Number symbolism

       Sacred numbers

       Symbolic numbers

BT   **Occultism**

       Symbolism of numbers

Numismatics (May subdiv. geog.)   737

Use for materials on coins, paper money, medals, and tokens considered as works of art, as historical specimens, or as aids to the study of history, archeology, etc.

BT   **Ancient history**

       Archeology

       History

NT   **Seals (Numismatics)**

Numismatics—*Continued*
- RT **Coins—Collectors and collecting**
- **Medals**

Nunneries
- USE **Convents**

Nuns (May subdiv. geog.) **271; 255**
- UF Sisters (Religious)
- BT **Women**
- NT **Ex-nuns**
- RT **Monasticism and religious orders for women**

Nurse clinicians
- USE **Nurse practitioners**

Nurse midwives
- USE **Midwives**

Nurse practitioners (May subdiv. geog.) **610.73092; 920**
- UF Nurse clinicians
- BT **Allied health personnel**
- **Nurses**

Nursemaids
- USE **Nannies**

Nurseries, Day
- USE **Day care centers**

Nurseries (Horticulture) (May subdiv. geog.) **631.5; 635**
- BT **Fruit culture**
- **Gardening**
- NT **Plant propagation**

Nursery rhymes **398.8**

Use for collections of nursery rhymes or for materials about nursery rhymes.
- UF Poetry for children
- Rhymes
- BT **Children's poetry**
- **Children's songs**
- **Folklore**

Nursery schools (May subdiv. geog.) **372.21**
- BT **Elementary education**
- **Schools**
- RT **Day care centers**
- **Kindergarten**
- **Preschool education**

Nurses (May subdiv. geog.) **610.73092; 920**
- SA types of nurses [to be added as needed]
- BT **Medical personnel**
- NT **Midwives**
- **Nurse practitioners**

Practical nurses
School nurses
- RT **Nursing**

Nursing (May subdiv. geog.) **610.73; 649.8**
- SA types of nursing, e.g. **Home nursing**; and diseases and medical procedures with the subdivision *Nursing* [to be added as needed]
- BT **Medicine**
- **Therapeutics**
- NT **Cancer—Nursing**
- **Cooking for the sick**
- **First aid**
- **Heart—Surgery—Nursing**
- **Home nursing**
- **Practical nursing**
- RT **Nurses**
- **Sick**

Nursing homes (May subdiv. geog.) **362.1**
- BT **Hospitals**
- **Institutional care**
- **Long-term care facilities**

Nursing (Infant feeding)
- USE **Breast feeding**

Nurture and nature
- USE **Nature and nurture**

Nutrition (May subdiv. geog.) **613.2**
- UF Meal planning
- SA animals, plants and crops, ethnic groups, and classes of persons with the subdivision *Nutrition*, e.g. **Children—Nutrition**; names of diseases with the subdivision *Diet therapy*, e.g. **Cancer—Diet therapy**; and types of foods with the subdivision *Therapeutic use*; e.g. **Herbs—Therapeutic use** [to be added as needed]
- BT **Health**
- **Physiology**
- **Therapeutics**
- NT **Astronauts—Nutrition**
- **Carbohydrates**
- **Children—Nutrition**
- **Dietary supplements**
- **Eating customs**
- **Infants—Nutrition**

Nutrition—*Continued*

    Malnutrition

    Minerals in human nutrition

    Plants—Nutrition

    Proteins

    Vitamins

  RT **Diet**

    Digestion

    Food

Nutritional supplements

  USE **Dietary supplements**

Nuts (May subdiv. geog.) **581.4; 634**

    Names of specific kinds of nuts may be used for materials on the nut or the tree.

  SA types of nuts, e.g. **Pecans** [to be added as needed]

  BT **Food**

    Seeds

  NT **Pecans**

Nylon **677**

  BT **Synthetic fabrics**

Oak **583**

  UF Oaks

  BT **Trees**

    Wood

Oaks

  USE **Oak**

Oats **633.1**

  BT **Feeds**

Obedience **179**

  UF Disobedience

  BT **Virtue**

Obelisks (May subdiv. geog.) **721**

  BT **Archeology**

    Architecture

    Monuments

Obesity (May subdiv. geog.) **613.2; 616.3**

  UF Corpulence

    Fatness

    Overweight

  BT **Body weight**

Obituaries (May subdiv. geog.) **920**

  UF Death notices

    Necrologies

  SA ethnic groups and classes of persons with the subdivision *Obituaries* [to be added as needed]

  BT **Biography**

  NT **Dead**

Objets d'art

  USE **Art objects**

Obligation

  USE **Responsibility**

Obscene materials

  USE **Obscenity (Law)**

    Pornography

Obscenity (Law) (May subdiv. geog.) **345**

  UF Obscene materials

  BT **Criminal law**

  RT **Erotica**

    Pornography

Observatories, Astronomical

  USE **Astronomical observatories**

Observatories, Meteorological

  USE **Meteorological observatories**

Obsession (Psychology)

  USE **Obsessive-compulsive disorder**

Obsessive-compulsive disorder **616.85**

  UF Fixed ideas

    Obsession (Psychology)

    Obsessive-compulsive neuroses

  BT **Neuroses**

  RT **Compulsive behavior**

Obsessive-compulsive neuroses

  USE **Obsessive-compulsive disorder**

Obstetrics

  USE **Childbirth**

Obstinacy

  USE **Stubbornness**

Occidental civilization

  USE **Western civilization**

Occult fiction **808.3; 808.83**

    Use for individual works, collections, or materials about fiction dealing with supernatural powers.

  BT **Fiction**

  NT **Ghost stories**

    Gothic novels

  RT **Fantasy fiction**

Occult sciences

  USE **Occultism**

Occultism (May subdiv. geog.) **130**

  UF Hermetic art and philosophy

    Occult sciences

    Sorcery

  BT **Religions**

    Supernatural

  NT **Alchemy**

    Astrology

    Cabala

Occultism—*Continued*
>> Clairvoyance
>> Demonology
>> Divination
>> Magic
>> New Age movement
>> Numerology
>> Oracles
>> Palmistry
>> Prophecies
>> Spiritualism
>> Witchcraft
> RT **Parapsychology**

Occupation, Military
> USE **Military occupation**

Occupational accidents
> USE **Industrial accidents**

Occupational crimes
> USE **White collar crimes**

Occupational diseases (May subdiv. geog.) **616.9**
> UF Industrial diseases
>> Occupations—Diseases
> SA occupational groups with the subdivision *Diseases*, e.g. **Miners—Diseases**; types of industries with the subdivisions *Employees—Diseases*; e.g. **Chemical industry—Employees—Diseases**; and names of occupational diseases [to be added as needed]
> BT **Diseases**
> NT **Chemical industry—Employees—Diseases**
>> **Lead poisoning**
>> **Miners—Diseases**
> RT **Hazardous occupations**
>> **Occupational health and safety**

Occupational forecasting
> USE **Employment forecasting**

Occupational guidance
> USE **Vocational guidance**

Occupational health and safety (May subdiv. geog.) **363.11; 658.3**
> UF Health, Industrial
>> Industrial health
>> Industrial safety
>> Safety, Industrial
> BT **Environmental health**
>> **Management**
>> **Public health**

> NT **Burn out (Psychology)**
> RT **Hazardous occupations**
>> **Occupational diseases**
>> **Occupational health services**

Occupational health services (May subdiv. geog.) **331.25**
> Use for materials on health services for employees, usually provided at the place of work.
> UF Employee health services
> BT **Medical care**
> RT **Occupational health and safety**

Occupational injuries
> USE **Industrial accidents**

Occupational literacy
> USE **Functional literacy**

Occupational retraining (May subdiv. geog.) **331.25**
> UF Job retraining
>> Retraining, Occupational
> BT **Employees—Training**
>> **Labor supply**
>> **Occupational training**
>> **Technical education**
>> **Unemployed**
>> **Vocational education**

Occupational stress
> USE **Job stress**

Occupational therapy **615.8**
> BT **Mental health**
>> **Physical therapy**
>> **Physically handicapped—Rehabilitation**
>> **Therapeutics**
> RT **Handicraft**

Occupational training (May subdiv. geog.) **331.25; 374**
> Use for materials on teaching people a skill after formal education. Materials on teaching a skill during the educational process are entered under **Vocational education**. Materials discussing on-the-job training are entered under **Employees—Training**. Materials on retraining are entered under **Occupational retraining**.
> UF Job training
>> Training, Occupational
>> Training, Vocational
>> Vocational training
> BT **Technical education**
>> **Vocational education**
> NT **Employees—Training**
>> **Occupational retraining**

Occupations (May subdiv. geog.)
    331.702
    Use for descriptions and lists of occupations.
    UF   Careers
           Jobs
           Trades
           Vocations
    SA   fields of knowledge, professions, industries, and trades with the subdivision *Vocational guidance*, and ethnic groups and classes of persons with the subdivision *Employment*, e.g. **Women—Employment** [to be added as needed]
    NT   **Hazardous occupations**
           Job analysis
           Paraprofessionals
           Professions
           Vocation
    RT   **Employment**
           Vocational guidance
           Work

Occupations—Chicago (Ill.)   **331.702**
    UF   Chicago (Ill.)—Occupations

Occupations—Diseases
    USE **Occupational diseases**

Occupations—Ohio   **331.702**
    UF   Ohio—Occupations

Occupations—United States   **331.702**
    UF   United States—Occupations

Occupied territories
    USE names of wars with the subdivision *Occupied territories,* e.g. **World War, 1939-1945—Occupied territories** [to be added as needed]

Occupied territory
    USE **Military occupation**

Ocean   **551.46**
    UF   Oceans
    BT   **Earth**
           Physical geography
           Water
    NT   **Atlantic Ocean**
           Icebergs
           Indian Ocean
           Ocean bottom
           Ocean currents
           Ocean waves
           Pacific Ocean

           Tides
    RT   **Oceanography**
           Seashore

Ocean bottom   **551.46**
    UF   Ocean floor
           Sea bed
    BT   **Ocean**
           Submarine geology
    NT   **Marine mineral resources**

Ocean cables
    USE **Submarine cables**

Ocean currents   **551.46**
    UF   Currents, Ocean
    BT   **Navigation**
           Ocean
    NT   **El Niño Current**

Ocean drilling platforms
    USE **Drilling platforms**

Ocean—Economic aspects
    USE **Marine resources**
         Shipping

Ocean energy resources   **333.91**
    BT   **Energy resources**
           Marine resources
           Ocean engineering
    NT   **Geothermal resources**
    RT   **Marine mineral resources**

Ocean engineering (May subdiv. geog.)
    627
    Use for materials on engineering beneath the surface of the ocean.
    UF   Deep sea engineering
           Submarine engineering
           Undersea engineering
    BT   **Engineering**
           Marine resources
           Oceanography
    NT   **Drilling platforms**
           Marine mineral resources
           Ocean energy resources
           Ocean mining
           Offshore oil well drilling

Ocean farming
    USE **Aquaculture**

Ocean fishing
    USE **Saltwater fishing**

Ocean floor
    USE **Ocean bottom**

Ocean life
    USE **Marine biology**

Ocean liners   **387.2**
    BT   **Ships**

Ocean mineral resources
   USE   **Marine mineral resources**
Ocean mining (May subdiv. geog.)   **622**
   UF   Deep sea mining
         Mining, Ocean
   BT   **Marine mineral resources**
         Mining engineering
         Ocean engineering
Ocean pollution
   USE   **Marine pollution**
Ocean resources
   USE   **Marine resources**
Ocean routes
   USE   **Trade routes**
Ocean transportation
   USE   **Shipping**
Ocean travel   **910.4**
   UF   Cruises
         Sea travel
   BT   **Transportation**
         Travel
         Voyages and travels
   NT   **Steamboats**
         Yachts and yachting
Ocean waves   **551.46**
   UF   Breakers
         Sea waves
         Surf
         Swell
   BT   **Ocean**
         Waves
   NT   **Tsunamis**
Oceania   **995**
   Use for comprehensive materials on the lands and area of the central and southern Pacific Ocean, including Micronesia, Melanesia, and Polynesia. Comprehensive works on all the islands of the Pacific Ocean are entered under **Islands of the Pacific**.
   UF   South Pacific region
         South Sea Islands
         South Seas
         Southwest Pacific region
   BT   **Islands of the Pacific**
Oceanographic research
   USE   **Oceanography—Research**
Oceanography (May subdiv. geog.)
         551.46
   UF   Oceanology
   BT   **Earth sciences**
   NT   **Marine biology**
         Marine pollution
         Marine resources

         Ocean engineering
         Submarine geology
         Underwater exploration
   RT   **Ocean**
Oceanography—Atlantic Ocean   **551.46**
Oceanography—Computer software
         551.46
   BT   **Computer software**
Oceanography—Research (May subdiv. geog.)   **551.46**
   UF   Oceanographic research
   BT   **Research**
   NT   **Bathyscaphe**
         Undersea research stations
Oceanology
   USE   **Oceanography**
Oceans
   USE   **Ocean**
Oddities
   USE   **Curiosities and wonders**
Oedipus (Legendary character)   **398.22**
   BT   **Legendary characters**
Offenses against property (May subdiv. geog.)   **364.16**
   UF   Crimes against property
         Property, Crimes against
   SA   types of offenses, e.g. **Vandalism** [to be added as needed]
   BT   **Crime**
         Criminal law
   NT   **Arson**
         Extortion
         Fraud
         Plagiarism
         Theft
         Vandalism
Offenses against public safety (May subdiv. geog.)   **364.1**
   UF   Crimes against public safety
         Public safety, Crimes against
   SA   types of offenses, e.g. **Hijacking of airplanes** [to be added as needed]
   BT   **Crime**
         Criminal law
   NT   **Bombings**
         Hijacking of airplanes
         Riots
         Sabotage
Offenses against the person (May subdiv. geog.)   **364.15**

Offenses against the person—*Continued*
  UF Abuse of persons
      Assault, Criminal
      Crimes against the person
      Criminal assault
  SA types of offenses, e.g. **Kidnapping** [to be added as needed]
  BT **Crime**
      Criminal law
  NT **Homicide**
      Identity theft
      Kidnapping
      Rape
      Stalking
Offenses, Military
  USE **Military offenses**
Office buildings (May subdiv. geog.)
      725
  UF Buildings, Office
  BT **Buildings**
Office employees
  USE **Office workers**
Office equipment and supplies   651
  UF Business machines
      Office machines
      Office supplies
  SA types of office equipment and supplies [to be added as needed]
  BT **Bookkeeping**
      Office management
  NT **Calculators**
      Copying machines
      Keyboards (Electronics)
      Typewriters
Office etiquette
  USE **Business etiquette**
Office machines
  USE **Office equipment and supplies**
Office management   651.3
  UF Office procedures
  BT **Business**
      Factory management
      Industrial efficiency
      Management
  NT **Files and filing**
      Office equipment and supplies
      Office practice
      Secretaries
      Word processing
  RT **Personnel management**
Office practice   651.3

  UF Secretarial practice
  BT **Office management**
  NT **Keyboarding (Electronics)**
      Shorthand
      Typewriting
      Word processing
  RT **Office workers**
Office procedures
  USE **Office management**
Office romance
  USE **Sex in the workplace**
Office supplies
  USE **Office equipment and supplies**
Office work—Training
  USE **Business education**
Office workers (May subdiv. geog.)
      331.7; 651.3
  UF Clerical employees
      Clerical personnel
      Clerks
      Commercial employees
      Office employees
  BT **Employees**
  RT **Office practice**
Office workers—Salaries, wages, etc.
      (May subdiv. geog.)   **331.2**
  BT **Salaries, wages, etc.**
Officers
  USE names of armed forces with the subdivision *Officers,* e.g.
      United States. Army—Officers [to be added as needed]
Official languages
  USE **Language and languages—Government policy**
Official misconduct
  USE **Misconduct in office**
Official publications
  USE **Government publications**
Officials and employees
  USE **Civil service**
      Public officers
      and names of countries, states, cities, etc., and corporate bodies with the subdivision *Officials and employees,* e.g. **United States—Officials and employees; Ohio—Officials and employees; Chicago (Ill.)—Officials and employees; United Nations—Offi-**

Officials and employees—*Continued*
cials and employees; etc. [to
be added as needed]
Offset printing 686.2
    UF   Lithoprinting
    BT   **Lithography**
          Printing
Offshore oil industry (May subdiv. geog.)
    338.2
    UF   Oil industry, Offshore
    BT   **Petroleum industry**
    NT   **Offshore oil well drilling**
Offshore oil well drilling (May subdiv.
    geog.) **622**
    UF   Deep sea drilling (Petroleum)
          Oil well drilling, Offshore
          Oil well drilling, Submarine
          Submarine oil well drilling
          Underwater drilling (Petroleum)
    BT   **Ocean engineering**
          Offshore oil industry
          Oil well drilling
    NT   **Drilling platforms**
Offshore water pollution
    USE **Marine pollution**
Ohio 977.1
    The subdivisions under **Ohio** may be used
under the name of any state of the United
States or province of Canada. The subdivi-
sions under **United States** may be further
consulted as a guide for formulating other
headings as needed.
Ohio—Antiquities 977.1
    BT   **Antiquities**
Ohio—Bibliography 015.771; 016.9771
Ohio—Bio-bibliography 012
Ohio—Biography 920.0771
    BT   **Biography**
Ohio—Biography—Dictionaries
    920.0771
Ohio—Biography—Portraits 920.0771
Ohio—Boundaries 977.1
    BT   **Boundaries**
Ohio—Census 317.71
    BT   **Census**
Ohio—Church history 277.71
    UF   Church history—Ohio
          Ohio—Religious history
    BT   **Church history**
    RT   **Ohio—Religion**
Ohio—Civilization 977.1
    BT   **Civilization**
Ohio—Climate 551.69771

    BT   **Climate**
Ohio—Commerce 381
    BT   **Commerce**
Ohio—Constitution
    USE **Constitutions—Ohio**
Ohio—Constitutional history
    USE **Constitutional history—Ohio**
Ohio—Constitutional law
    USE **Constitutional law—Ohio**
Ohio—Description
    USE **Ohio—Description and travel**
Ohio—Description and travel 917.71
    UF   Ohio—Description
          Ohio—Travel
Ohio—Description and travel—Guidebooks
    USE **Ohio—Guidebooks**
Ohio—Description and travel—Views
    USE **Ohio—Pictorial works**
Ohio—Directories 917.710025
    Use for lists of names and addresses. Lists
of names without addresses are entered under
Ohio—Registers.
    BT   **Directories**
    RT   **Ohio—Registers**
Ohio—Economic conditions 330.9771
    BT   **Economic conditions**
Ohio—Economic policy
    USE **Economic policy—Ohio**
Ohio—Employees
    USE **Ohio—Officials and employees**
Ohio—Executive departments
    USE **Executive departments—Ohio**
Ohio—Executive departments—Reorganiza-
    tion
    USE **Administrative agencies—Reor-**
          ganization—Ohio
Ohio—Fiction 808.83; 813
    Use for collections of stories about Ohio.
Ohio—Gazetteers 917.71
    BT   **Gazetteers**
Ohio—Government employees
    USE **Ohio—Officials and employees**
Ohio—Government publications
    USE **Government publications—**
          Ohio
Ohio—Guidebooks 917.7104
    UF   Ohio—Description and travel—
          Guidebooks
Ohio—Historic buildings
    USE **Historic buildings—Ohio**
Ohio—History 977.1
    NT   **Constitutional history—Ohio**

Ohio—History—Societies   977.106
  BT   History—Societies
Ohio—History—Sources   977.1
Ohio—Industries
  USE   Industries—Ohio
Ohio—Intellectual life   977.1
  BT   Intellectual life
Ohio—Local history   977.1
  BT   Local history
Ohio—Manufactures
  USE   Manufactures—Ohio
Ohio—Maps   912.771
  BT   Maps
Ohio—Militia   355.3
  BT   Armed forces
Ohio—Moral conditions   977.1
  BT   Moral conditions
Ohio—Occupations
  USE   Occupations—Ohio
Ohio—Officials and employees   351.771
  UF   Ohio—Employees
        Ohio—Government employees
Ohio—Officials and employees—Salaries,
    wages, etc.   331.2
  BT   Salaries, wages, etc.
Ohio—Pictorial works   917.710022
  UF   Ohio—Description and travel—
        Views
Ohio—Politics and government   977.1
Ohio—Population   304.609771
  BT   Population
Ohio—Public buildings
  USE   Public buildings—Ohio
Ohio—Public lands
  USE   Public lands—Ohio
Ohio—Public works
  USE   Public works—Ohio
Ohio—Race relations   305.8009771
  BT   Race relations
Ohio—Registers   917.710025
    Use for lists of names without addresses.
    Lists of names that include addresses are en-
    tered under Ohio—Directories.
  RT   Ohio—Directories
Ohio—Religion   277.71
  BT   Religion
  RT   Ohio—Church history
Ohio—Religious history
  USE   Ohio—Church history
Ohio—Rural conditions   307.7209771
  BT   Rural sociology
Ohio—Social conditions   977.1

  BT   Social conditions
Ohio—Social life and customs   977.1
  BT   Manners and customs
Ohio—Social policy
  USE   Social policy—Ohio
Ohio—Statistics   317.71
  BT   Statistics
Ohio—Travel
  USE   Ohio—Description and travel
Oil
  USE   Oils and fats
        Petroleum
Oil burners   697
  BT   Heating
        Petroleum as fuel
Oil drilling platforms
  USE   Drilling platforms
Oil engines
  USE   Internal combustion engines
Oil fuel
  USE   Petroleum as fuel
Oil industry
  USE   Petroleum industry
Oil industry, Offshore
  USE   Offshore oil industry
Oil painting   751.45
    Use for materials on the technique of oil
    painting. For materials on oil paintings as
    works of art use Painting.
  BT   Painting
Oil pollution of rivers, harbors, etc.
  USE   Oil pollution of water
Oil pollution of water (May subdiv.
    geog.)   363.739; 628.1
  UF   Oil pollution of rivers, harbors,
        etc.
        Petroleum pollution of water
        Water—Oil pollution
  BT   Water pollution
  NT   Oil spills
  RT   Marine pollution
Oil spills (May subdiv. geog.)   363.738
  BT   Oil pollution of water
Oil well drilling (May subdiv. geog.)
    622
  UF   Drilling, Oil well
        Petroleum—Well boring
        Well drilling, Oil
  BT   Drilling and boring (Earth and
        rocks)
        Petroleum industry

Oil well drilling—*Continued*
  NT   **Offshore oil well drilling**
       Oil wells—Blowouts
  RT   **Oil wells**
Oil well drilling, Offshore
  USE **Offshore oil well drilling**
Oil well drilling, Submarine
  USE **Offshore oil well drilling**
Oil wells (May subdiv. geog.) **622**
  BT   **Petroleum industry**
  RT   **Oil well drilling**
Oil wells—Blowouts (May subdiv. geog.)
     622
  UF   Blowouts, Oil well
  BT   **Oil well drilling**
Oils and fats **665**
  UF   Animal oils
       Fats
       Grease
       Oil
       Vegetable oils
  NT   **Essences and essential oils**
       Petroleum
  RT   **Low-fat diet**
       Lubrication and lubricants
Old age (May subdiv. geog.) **305.26**
  BT   **Age**
  NT   **Aging**
       Retirement
  RT   **Elderly**
       Gerontology
       Longevity
Old age homes
  USE **Elderly—Institutional care**
Old age pensions (May subdiv. geog.)
     331.25; 368.3
  UF   Aged—Pensions
       Employees—Pensions
  BT   **Pensions**
       Retirement income
Old English language
  USE **English language—Old English**
       period
Old English literature
  USE **English literature—Old English**
       period
Old Icelandic language
  USE **Old Norse language**
Old Norse language **439**
  UF   Icelandic language—0-1500
       Norse languages
       Norwegian language—0-1350

       Old Icelandic language
       Old Norwegian language
  BT   **Language and languages**
       Scandinavian languages
Old Norse literature **839**
  UF   Norse literature
  BT   **Literature**
       Medieval literature
  NT   **Eddas**
       Sagas
  RT   **Icelandic literature**
       Scandinavian literature
Old Northwest **977**
    Use for materials on the region between the Ohio and Mississippi rivers and the Great Lakes.
  UF   Northwest, Old
       Northwest Territory
  BT   **United States**
  RT   **Middle West**
Old Norwegian language
  USE **Old Norse language**
Old Southwest **976**
    Use for materials on that section of the United States that comprised the southwestern part before the cessions of land from Mexico following the Mexican War. It included Louisiana, Texas, Arkansas, Tennessee, Kentucky and Missouri.
  UF   Southwest, Old
  BT   **United States**
Old Testament
  USE **Bible. O.T.**
Older persons
  USE **Elderly**
Oldest child
  USE **Birth order**
Olympic games **796.48; 796.98**
  UF   Olympics
  SA   topical headings for Olympic
       events of a particular year,
       e.g. **Olympic games, 1996**
       (Atlanta, Ga.) [to be added
       as needed]
  BT   **Athletics**
       Contests
       Games
       Sports
  NT   **Olympic games, 1996 (Atlanta,**
       Ga.)
       Special Olympics
Olympic games, 1996 (Atlanta, Ga.)
     796.48
  BT   **Olympic games**

Olympics
USE **Olympic games**
Ombudsman (May subdiv. geog.) **328.3;
342; 352.8**
UF Citizen's defender
Grievance procedures (Public ad-
ministration)
BT **Administrative law**
Public interest
One act plays 808.82
Use for individual works, collections, or
materials about one-act plays.
UF Plays
Short plays
BT **Amateur theater**
Drama
One parent family
USE **Single-parent families**
Online auctions
USE **Internet auctions**
Online books
USE **Electronic books**
Online catalogs (May subdiv. geog.)
025.3
UF Catalogs, Online
Online public access catalogs
OPACs (Online public access
catalogs)
BT **Library catalogs**
RT **Libraries—Automation**
Online chat groups 004.69
Use for materials on services that allow us-
ers to engage in conversations in real time.
Materials on services, commonly called elec-
tronic mailing lists, that allow subscribers to
post messages that are then distributed to oth-
er subscribers are entered under **Electronic
discussion groups**. Materials on services that
allow users to post messages and retrieve
messages from others who have some com-
mon interest are entered under **Computer
bulletin boards**.
UF Chat groups, Online
Chat rooms, Online
Internet chat groups
Online chat rooms
BT **Conversation**
RT **Computer bulletin boards**
Electronic discussion groups
Online chat rooms
USE **Online chat groups**
Online commerce
USE **Electronic commerce**
Online discussion groups
USE **Electronic discussion groups**

Online gambling
USE **Internet gambling**
Online journalism (May subdiv. geog.)
070.4
UF Electronic journalism
Internet journalism
BT **Journalism**
NT **Weblogs**
Online marketing
USE **Internet marketing**
Online public access catalogs
USE **Online catalogs**
Online publishing
USE **Electronic publishing**
Online reference services
USE **Electronic reference services
(Libraries)**
Online selling
USE **Internet marketing**
Online sex
USE **Computer sex**
Online shopping
USE **Internet shopping**
Online social networking
USE **Social networking**
Only child 155.44; 306.874
UF Single child
BT **Children**
Family size
OPACs (Online public access catalogs)
USE **Online catalogs**
Opaque projectors
USE **Projectors**
Open access publishing (May subdiv.
geog.) **070.5**
BT **Electronic publishing**
Open and closed shop (May subdiv.
geog.) **331.88**
UF Closed shop
Right to work
Union shop
BT **Labor**
Labor contract
Labor unions
Open classroom approach to teaching
USE **Open plan schools**
Open code software
USE **Open source software**
Open education
USE **Open plan schools**

Open heart surgery
    USE **Heart—Surgery**
Open housing
    USE **Discrimination in housing**
Open plan schools (May subdiv. geog.)
    371.2
> Use for materials on schools without interi-
> or walls.

    UF   Interest centers approach to
            teaching
         Learning center approach to
            teaching
         Open classroom approach to
            teaching
         Open education
    BT   **Education—Experimental
            methods**
    RT   **Experimental schools
         Individualized instruction**
Open source software   005.3
    UF   Open code software
    BT   **Computer software**
Open universities
    USE **Free universities**
Opera (May subdiv. geog.)   **782.1; 792.5**
> Use for musical scores and for materials
> about the opera.

    UF   Comic opera
         Dramatic music
         Operas
    BT   **Drama
         Musical form
         Performing arts
         Vocal music**
    NT   **Operetta**
Opera librettos   782.1026
> Use for individual opera librettos and for
> collections of opera librettos.

    UF   Operas—Librettos
    BT   **Librettos**
    RT   **Opera—Stories, plots, etc.**
Opera plots
    USE **Opera—Stories, plots, etc.**
Opera—Sound recordings   782.1
    BT   **Sound recordings**
Opera—Stories, plots, etc.   782.1026
    UF   Opera plots
    RT   **Opera librettos**
Operas
    USE **Opera**
Operas—Librettos
    USE **Opera librettos**

Operating systems (Computers)
    USE **Computer operating systems**
Operation Desert Storm
    USE **Persian Gulf War, 1991**
Operational analysis
    USE **Operations research**
Operational research
    USE **Operations research**
Operations research (May subdiv. geog.)
    658.5
    UF   Operational analysis
         Operational research
    BT   **Research
         System theory**
    RT   **Management
         Systems engineering**
Operations, Surgical
    USE **Surgery**
Operetta (May subdiv. geog.)   **782.1;
         792.5**
> Use for musical scores and for materials on
> the operetta as a musical form.

    UF   Comic opera
         Dramatic music
         Operettas
    BT   **Musical form
         Opera
         Vocal music**
    RT   **Musicals**
Operettas
    USE **Operetta**
Opiates
    USE **Narcotics**
Opinion polls
    USE **Public opinion polls**
Opinion, Public
    USE **Public opinion**
Opium (May subdiv. geog.)   **615**
    BT   **Narcotics**
    RT   **Morphine**
Opium—Physiological effect   615
    BT   **Drugs—Physiological effect**
Opposites   153.2
    UF   Antonyms
         Polarity
    BT   **Concepts**
    RT   **English language—Synonyms
            and antonyms**
**Optical data processing   006.4; 621.36;
         621.39**
    BT   **Data processing**
    NT   **Laser recording**

Optical discs
USE **Optical storage devices**
Optical illusions **152.14**
UF Illusions
BT **Hallucinations and illusions**
Psychophysiology
Vision
Optical instruments (May subdiv. geog.)
681
UF Instruments, Optical
BT **Scientific apparatus and in-**
struments
NT **Lenses**
Microscopes
Telescopes
RT **Optics**
Space optics
Optical scanners **006.4; 621.39**
BT **Computer peripherals**
Optical storage devices **004.5; 621.39**
Use for materials on data storage devices in
which audio, video, or other data are optically
encoded.
UF Optical discs
BT **Computer storage devices**
NT **CD-I technology**
CD-ROMs
Compact discs
DVDs
RT **Laser recording**
Optics **535; 621.36**
BT **Physics**
NT **Color**
Fiber optics
Perspective
Radiation
Refraction
Space optics
Spectrum analysis
Vision
RT **Light**
Optical instruments
Photometry
Optometry **617.7**
RT **Eye**
Oracles (May subdiv. geog.) **133.3**
BT **Occultism**
RT **Divination**
Prophecies
Oral history **907**
Use for materials on recording oral recollec-
tions of places, events, etc., from persons

drawing on their own life experiences. Oral
histories that focus on a particular topic or
place are entered under that topic or place.
BT **History**
Oral interpretation
USE **Recitations**
Orange (Fruit)
USE **Oranges**
Oranges (May subdiv. geog.) **634; 641.3**
UF Orange (Fruit)
BT **Citrus fruits**
Orations
USE **Speeches**
Oratorio **782.23**
Use for musical scores and for materials on
the oratorio as a musical form.
UF Oratorios
BT **Church music**
Musical form
Vocal music
Oratorios
USE **Oratorio**
Oratory
USE **Public speaking**
Orbital laboratories
USE **Space stations**
Orbital rendezvous (Space flight)
629.45
UF Rendezvous in space
Space orbital rendezvous
SA names of projects, e.g. **Apollo**
project; **Gemini project**; etc.;
and names of specific space
ships [to be added as needed]
BT **Space flight**
Space stations
Space vehicles
NT **Apollo project**
Gemini project
Orbiting vehicles
USE **Artificial satellites**
Space stations
Orchards
USE **Fruit culture**
Orchestra **784.2**
SA types of orchestras [to be added
as needed[
NT **Conductors (Music)**
Instrumentation and orchestra-
tion
Orchestral music
RT **Bands (Music)**
Conducting

Orchestra—*Continued*
> **Ensembles (Music)**
> **Musical instruments**

Orchestral music (May subdiv. geog.) **784.2**
> SA types of orchestral music, e.g. **Symphony** [to be added as needed]
> BT **Instrumental music**
> **Music**
> **Orchestra**
> NT **Concerto**
> **String orchestra music**
> **Suite (Music)**
> **Symphonic poems**
> **Symphony**

Orchestration
> USE **Instrumentation and orchestration**

Order 117
> NT **Orderliness**

Orderliness 640; 648
> UF Neatness
> Tidiness
> BT **Order**

Orders, Monastic
> USE **Monasticism and religious orders**

Ordination (May subdiv. geog.) **262; 265**
> BT **Rites and ceremonies**
> **Sacraments**
> NT **Ordination of gays and lesbians**
> **Ordination of women**
> RT **Clergy**

Ordination of gays and lesbians (May subdiv. geog.) **206**
> UF Gay men—Ordination
> Lesbians—Ordination
> BT **Ordination**

Ordination of women (May subdiv. geog.) **262**
> UF Women—Ordination
> BT **Ordination**
> RT **Women clergy**

Ordnance 355.8; 623.4
> Use for materials on military supplies including weapons, ammunition, and vehicles, and the task of procuring, testing, storing, and issuing such supplies.

> UF Cannon
> Guns
> SA types of military ordnance, e.g. **Bombs**; names of armies with the subdivision *Ordnance*, e.g. **United States. Army—Ordnance**; and names of wars with the subdivision *Equipment and supplies*, e.g. **World War, 1939-1945—Equipment and supplies** [to be added as needed]
> BT **Military art and science**
> NT **Ammunition**
> **Bombs**
> **Land mines**
> **Military weapons**
> **United States. Army—Ordnance**
> RT **Artillery**
> **Defense industry**
> **Projectiles**

Ore deposits (May subdiv. geog.) **553**
> SA types of ores, e.g. **Iron ores** [to be added as needed]
> BT **Geology**
> RT **Ores**

Ore dressing 622
> UF Dressing of ores
> BT **Smelting**

Oregon country
> USE **Pacific Northwest**

Oregon Trail 978
> BT **Overland journeys to the Pacific**
> **United States**

Ores (May subdiv. geog.) **553**
> SA types of ores, e.g. **Iron ores** [to be added as needed]
> BT **Minerals**
> NT **Iron ores**
> **Metals**
> RT **Metallurgy**
> **Ore deposits**

Organ
> USE **Organs (Musical instruments)**

Organ donation
> USE **Donation of organs, tissues, etc.**

Organ music 786.5

Organ music—*Continued*
    BT   **Church music**
           Instrumental music
           Music
Organ preservation (Anatomy)
    USE **Preservation of organs, tissues,**
           etc.
Organ transplants
    USE **Transplantation of organs, tis-**
           sues, etc.
Organic agriculture
    USE **Organic farming**
Organic chemicals
    USE **Organic compounds**
Organic chemistry   547
    UF   Chemistry, Organic
    BT   **Chemistry**
    NT   **Organic compounds**
Organic chemistry—Synthesis
    USE **Organic compounds—Synthesis**
Organic compounds   547
    UF   Organic chemicals
    SA   types of organic compounds and
           individual organic substances
           [to be added as needed]
    BT   **Chemicals**
           Organic chemistry
Organic compounds—Synthesis   547
    UF   Chemistry, Synthetic
           Organic chemistry—Synthesis
           Synthetic chemistry
    NT   **Polymers**
    RT   **Synthetic products**
Organic farming (May subdiv. geog.)
    631.5
    UF   Farming, Organic
           Organic agriculture
           Organiculture
    BT   **Agriculture**
Organic gardening (May subdiv. geog.)
    635
    UF   Natural gardening
           Organiculture
    BT   **Gardening**
           Horticulture
    RT   **Compost**
Organic waste as fuel
    USE **Waste products as fuel**
Organically grown foods
    USE **Natural foods**

Organiculture
    USE **Organic farming**
           Organic gardening
Organists (May subdiv. geog.)   **786.5092;**
    920
    BT   **Instrumentalists**
Organization and management
    USE **Management**
Organization development
    USE **Organizational change**
Organization (Sociology)
    USE **Organizational sociology**
Organization theory
    USE **Organizational sociology**
Organizational behavior (May subdiv.
    geog.)   **158.2; 302.3; 658**
    UF   Behavior in organizations
    BT   **Applied psychology**
           Management
           Social psychology
Organizational change (May subdiv.
    geog.)   **338.7; 658.4**
    UF   Change, Organizational
           Organization development
           Organizational development
           Organizational innovation
    BT   **Management**
    NT   **Downsizing of organizations**
Organizational culture
    USE **Corporate culture**
Organizational development
    USE **Organizational change**
Organizational downsizing
    USE **Downsizing of organizations**
Organizational innovation
    USE **Organizational change**
Organizational retrenchment
    USE **Downsizing of organizations**
Organizational sociology   302.3
    UF   Organization (Sociology)
           Organization theory
           Sociology of organizations
    BT   **Sociology**
    RT   **Bureaucracy**
Organizational stress
    USE **Job stress**
Organizations
    USE **Associations**
Organizations, Nonprofit
    USE **Nonprofit organizations**

Organized crime (May subdiv. geog.)
364.106
- UF Crime syndicates
- SA types of organized crime, e.g.
  Racketeering [to be added as needed]
- BT **Crime**
- NT **Gangs**
  Racketeering

Organized labor
- USE **Labor unions**

Organs (Anatomy)—Preservation
- USE **Preservation of organs, tissues, etc.**

Organs, Artificial
- USE **Artificial organs**

Organs (Musical instruments) (May subdiv. geog.) **786.5**
- UF Organ
  Pipe organs
- BT **Musical instruments**
- NT **Keyboards (Musical instruments)**

Orient
- USE **Asia**
  East Asia
  Middle East

Oriental architecture
- USE **Asian architecture**

Oriental art
- USE **Asian art**

Oriental civilization
- USE **Asia—Civilization**

Oriental rugs (May subdiv. geog.) **746.7**
- SA types of Oriental rugs [to be added as needed]
- BT **Rugs and carpets**

Orientalism (May subdiv. geog.) **303; 950**

Use for materials on the depiction or adoption of characteristics of Asian and Middle Eastern cultures by Westerners.
- BT **East and West**

Orientation
- USE **Direction sense**

Orienteering (May subdiv. geog.) **796.58**
- BT **Hiking**
  Racing
  Running
  Sports
- RT **Direction sense**
  Navigation

Origami **736**
- UF Japanese paper folding
  Paper folding
- BT **Paper crafts**

Origin
- USE subjects, ethnic groups, classes of persons, animals, plants, crops, and religions with the subdivision *Origin,* e.g.
  Life—Origin; Native Americans—Origin; etc. [to be added as needed]

Origin of life
- USE **Life—Origin**

Origin of man
- USE **Human origins**

Origin of species
- USE **Evolution**

Orlando (Legendary character)
- USE **Roland (Legendary character)**

Ornament
- USE **Decoration and ornament**

Ornamental alphabets
- USE **Alphabets**
  Illumination of books and manuscripts
  Lettering

Ornamental plants (May subdiv. geog.) **635.9; 715**
- UF Plants, Ornamental
- BT **Cultivated plants**
  Flower gardening
  Landscape gardening
- RT **Shrubs**

Orphan drugs **615**

Use for materials on drugs that appear to be useful for the treatment of rare disorders but owing to their limited commercial value have difficulty in finding funding for research and marketing.
- UF Nonprofitable drugs
- BT **Drugs**

Orphanages (May subdiv. geog.) **362.73**
- UF Charitable institutions
  Homes (Institutions)
- BT **Charities**
  Children—Institutional care
- RT **Child welfare**

Orphans (May subdiv. geog.) **305.23086; 362.73**
- UF Foundlings
- BT **Children**

Orphans—*Continued*
  RT **Abandoned children**
      Adopted children
Orthodox Eastern Church (May subdiv. geog.) **281.9**
  BT **Christian sects**
      Eastern churches
  NT **Greek Orthodox Church**
      Russian Orthodox Church
Orthography
  USE names of languages with the subdivision *Spelling*, e.g. **English language—Spelling** [to be added as needed]
Orthopedic apparatus 617
  UF Orthotic devices
  BT **Orthopedics**
  NT **Wheelchairs**
Orthopedic surgery
  USE **Orthopedics**
Orthopedics 616.7; 617.4
  UF Orthopedic surgery
  BT **Medicine**
      Surgery
  NT **Artificial limbs**
      Orthopedic apparatus
  RT **Physically handicapped**
Orthotic devices
  USE **Orthopedic apparatus**
Oscars (Motion pictures)
  USE **Academy Awards (Motion pictures)**
Osteopathic medicine (May subdiv. geog.) **610; 615.5**
    Use for materials on the therapeutic system based on the theory that disease is caused by loss of a structural integrity that can be restored by manipulation of the bones and muscles.
  UF Osteopathy
  BT **Medicine**
  RT **Chiropractic**
      Massage
Osteopathy
  USE **Osteopathic medicine**
Osteoporosis 616.7
  BT **Bones—Diseases**
Ostrogoths
  USE **Goths**
Out-of-body experiences
  USE **Astral projection**
Out-of-doors education
  USE **Outdoor education**

Out-of-work people
  USE **Unemployed**
Outdoor cooking 641.5
  UF Camp cooking
  BT **Camping**
      Cooking
  NT **Barbecue cooking**
Outdoor education (May subdiv. geog.) **371.3**
  UF Out-of-doors education
  BT **Education**
  RT **Nature study**
      Outdoor life
Outdoor life (May subdiv. geog.) **796.5**
  UF Rural life
  SA types of outdoor life, education, or activities [to be added as needed]
  NT **Hiking**
      Mountaineering
      Wilderness survival
  RT **Camping**
      Country life
      Nature study
      Outdoor education
      Sports
Outdoor photography 778.7
  UF Field photography
  BT **Photography**
  RT **Nature photography**
Outdoor recreation (May subdiv. geog.) **796**
  SA types of outdoor recreation, e.g. **Camping** [to be added as needed]
  BT **Recreation**
  NT **Camping**
      Cycling
      Recreational vehicles
      Roller skating
      Safaris
Outdoor survival
  USE **Wilderness survival**
Outer space 523.1
  UF Space, Outer
  BT **Astronautics**
      Astronomy
      Space sciences
  NT **Space environment**
      Space warfare

Outer space and civilization
USE **Astronautics and civilization**
Outer space—Colonies
USE **Space colonies**
Outer space—Communication
USE **Interstellar communication**
Outer space—Exploration 629.4
UF Exploration of space
Space exploration (Astronautics)
Space research
BT **Exploration**
Interplanetary voyages
Space flight
NT **Planets—Exploration**
Space probes
Outlaws
USE **Criminals**
Thieves
Outlines, syllabi, etc.
USE subjects with the subdivision
Outlines, syllabi, etc., e.g.
English literature—Outlines, syllabi, etc. [to be added as needed]
Output equipment (Computers)
USE **Computer peripherals**
Output standards
USE **Production standards**
Outsider art (May subdiv. geog.) **704**
UF Naive art
BT **Art**
Outsourcing (May subdiv. geog.)
658.723
UF Contracting for services
Contracting out
BT **Contracts**
Over-the-counter drugs
USE **Nonprescription drugs**
Overland journeys to the Pacific 978
Use for materials on the pioneers' crossing of the American continent toward the Pacific by foot, horseback, wagon, etc.
UF Transcontinental journeys (American continent)
BT **Frontier and pioneer life**
Voyages and travels
NT **Oregon Trail**
RT **West (U.S.)—Exploration**
Overpopulation (May subdiv. geog.)
363.9; 304.6
UF Population explosion

SA names of countries, cities, etc. with the subdivision *Population*, e.g. **United States—Population** [to be added as needed]
BT **Population**
Overseas study
USE **Foreign study**
Oversize books
USE **Big books**
Oversized books for shared reading
USE **Big books**
Overtime
USE **Hours of labor**
Overweight
USE **Obesity**
Ownership
USE **Property**
Oxyacetylene welding
USE **Welding**
Oxygen 546; 547; 665.8
BT **Chemical elements**
Gases
NT **Ozone**
Ozone 665.8
BT **Oxygen**
Ozone layer 363.738; 551.51
UF Ozonosphere
Stratospheric ozone
BT **Stratosphere**
Ozonosphere
USE **Ozone layer**
Pachycephalosaurus 567.914
BT **Dinosaurs**
Pacific Islands
USE **Islands of the Pacific**
Pacific Northwest 979.5
Use for materials on the old Oregon country, comprising the present states of Oregon, Washington, and Idaho, parts of Montana and Wyoming, and the province of British Columbia.
UF Northwest, Pacific
Oregon country
BT **North America**
United States
West (U.S.)
Pacific Northwest coast
USE **Northwest Coast of North America**
Pacific Ocean 551.465
BT **Ocean**

Pacific Ocean Islands
USE **Islands of the Pacific**
Pacific rim   330.99; 990
Use for materials on the periphery of the Pacific Ocean, especially as a region of inter-dependent economies.
RT **East Asia**
Islands of the Pacific
Pacific States   979
BT **West (U.S.)**
Pacifism (May subdiv. geog.)   **174; 303.6**
Use for materials on the renunciation of of-fensive or defensive military actions on moral grounds. Materials on social movements advocating peace are entered under **Peace movements**.
BT **War—Religious aspects**
RT **Conscientious objectors**
Nonviolence
Peace
Peace movements
Pack transportation
USE **Backpacking**
Packaging   658.5
SA types of packaging and packag-ing materials, and subjects with the subdivision *Packag-ing*, e.g. **Food—Packaging** [to be added as needed]
BT **Advertising**
Retail trade
NT **Aluminum foil**
Food—Packaging
Gift wrapping
RT **Containers**
Packing industry
USE **Meat industry**
PACs (Political action committees)
USE **Political action committees**
Paganism (May subdiv. geog.)   **292**
BT **Christianity and other religions**
Religions
NT **Goddess religion**
Wicca
Pageants (May subdiv. geog.)   **394; 791.6**
BT **Acting**
NT **Masks (Plays)**
Medieval tournaments
Mysteries and miracle plays
Parades
RT **Festivals**
Pain   152.1; 612.8

BT **Diagnosis**
Emotions
Psychophysiology
Senses and sensation
NT **Chronic pain**
Headache
RT **Anesthetics**
Pleasure
Suffering
Paint   645; 667
BT **Finishes and finishing**
RT **Corrosion and anticorrosives**
Pigments
Paint sniffing
USE **Solvent abuse**
Painted glass
USE **Glass painting and staining**
Painters (May subdiv. geog.)   **759; 920**
BT **Artists**
Painters' materials
USE **Artists' materials**
Painters—United States   759.13; 920
UF American painters
Painting   750
UF Paintings
SA painting of particular countries, e.g. **American painting**; types of painting, e.g. **Landscape painting**; and topics with the subdivision *Painting*; e.g. **Au-tomobiles—Painting** [to be added as needed]
BT **Art**
Graphic arts
NT **Acrylic painting**
American painting
Animal painting and illustra-tion
China painting
Color
Figure painting
Finger painting
Genre painting
Glass painting and staining
Indian painting
Landscape painting
Marine painting
Miniature painting
Mixed media painting
Mural painting and decoration
Oil painting

Painting—*Continued*
> **Perspective**
> **Portrait painting**
> **Scene painting**
> **Stencil work**
> **Still-life painting**
> **Textile painting**
> **Watercolor painting**
> RT **Composition (Art)**
> **Decoration and ornament**
> **Drawing**
> **Pictures**

Painting—15th and 16th centuries
> **709.02; 709.03**
> UF Painting, Renaissance
> Renaissance painting

Painting—17th and 18th centuries
> **759.04**
> UF Painting, Modern—17th-18th centuries

Painting—19th century   759.05
> UF Modern painting—1800-1899 (19th century)
> Painting, Modern—19th century

Painting—20th century   759.06
> UF Modern painting—1900-1999 (20th century)
> Painting, Modern—20th century
> SA types of twentieth-century painting, e.g. **Cubism** [to be added as needed]

Painting—21st century   759.07
> UF Modern painting—2000-2099 (21st century)
> Painting, Modern—21st century

Painting, American
> USE **American painting**

Painting books
> USE **Coloring books**

Painting—Color reproductions
> USE **Color prints**

Painting—Conservation and restoration
> **751.6**

Painting, Decorative
> USE **Decoration and ornament**

Painting, Finger
> USE **Finger painting**

Painting, Modern—17th-18th centuries
> USE **Painting—17th and 18th centuries**

Painting, Modern—19th century
> USE **Painting—19th century**

Painting, Modern—20th century
> USE **Painting—20th century**

Painting, Modern—21st century
> USE **Painting—21st century**

Painting, Renaissance
> USE **Painting—15th and 16th centuries**

Painting, Romanesque
> USE **Romanesque painting**

Painting—Technique   751.4

Paintings
> USE **Painting**

Pair system
> USE **Binary system (Mathematics)**

Pakistan   954.91
> May be subdivided like United States except for History.

Palaces (May subdiv. geog.)   **728.8**
> BT **Buildings**

Paleobotany
> USE **Fossil plants**

Paleolithic period
> USE **Stone Age**

Paleontology (May subdiv. geog.)   **560**
> UF Paleozoology
> BT **Historical geology**
> **Zoology**
> RT **Fossils**

Paleozoology
> USE **Paleontology**

Palestine   956.94
> Use for materials on the region on the eastern coast of the Mediterranean Sea that in ancient times was called the Land of Canaan, later the kingdoms of Israel and Judah, and in modern times comprises the entire state of Israel, as well as the various disputed territories.
> UF Holy Land
> Palestinian territories
> NT **West Bank**

Palestinian Arabs (May subdiv. geog.)
> **305.892; 956.94**
> UF Arabs—Palestine
> Palestinians
> BT **Arabs**
> RT **Jewish-Arab relations**

Palestinian-Israeli conflict, 1987-1992
> USE **Intifada, 1987-1992**

Palestinian-Israeli conflict, 2000-
> USE **Intifada, 2000-**

Palestinian territories
> USE **Palestine**

Palestinian uprising, 1987-1992
  USE **Intifada, 1987-1992**
Palestinian uprising, 2000-
  USE **Intifada, 2000-**
Palestinians
  USE **Palestinian Arabs**
Palindromes 793.734
  BT **Literary recreations**
      Word games
Palmistry 133.6
  BT **Divination**
      Fortune telling
      Occultism
Palsy
  USE **Parkinson's disease**
Pamphlets (May subdiv. geog.) 025.17
  UF Street literature
  BT **Press**
  NT **Chapbooks**
      Tracts
Pamphlets—Design 686.2
  BT **Design**
Pan-Africanism 320.5; 327
    Use for materials on the advocacy of either
    political alliance or close economic, cultural,
    and military cooperation among the countries
    of Africa.
  UF African relations
  BT **Africa—Politics and govern-
      ment**
Pan-Americanism 320.5; 327
    Use for materials on the advocacy of either
    political alliance or close economic, cultural,
    and military cooperation among the countries
    of North and South America.
  UF Inter-American relations
  BT **America—Politics and govern-
      ment**
      Latin America
Pan-Arabism 320.5
    Use for materials on the advocacy of either
    political alliance or close economic, cultural,
    and military cooperation among the Arab
    countries.
  UF Panarabism
  BT **Arab countries—Politics and
      government**
Panama Canal 972.87
  BT **Canals**
Panarabism
  USE **Pan-Arabism**
Panel discussions
  USE **Discussion groups**

Panel heating
  USE **Radiant heating**
Panhandling
  USE **Begging**
Panic disorders 362.2; 616.85
  BT **Abnormal psychology**
      Neuroses
Panics (Finance)
  USE **Financial crises**
Pantheism (May subdiv. geog.) 211.2;
      147
  BT **Philosophy**
      Religion
Pantomimes 792.3
  BT **Acting**
      Amateur theater
      Drama
      Theater
  NT **Shadow pantomimes and plays**
  RT **Ballet**
      Mime
Papacy 262
  UF Holy See
  BT **Catholic Church**
      Church history
  RT **Popes**
Papal encyclicals 262.9
  UF Encyclicals, Papal
  BT **Christian literature**
Papal visits (May subdiv. geog.) 262
  UF Popes—Travel
      Popes—Voyages and travels
  BT **Voyages and travels**
Paper (May subdiv. geog.) 676
  BT **Fibers**
  NT **Papermaking**
  RT **Paper industry**
Paper airplanes
  USE **Airplanes—Models**
Paper bound books
  USE **Paperback books**
Paper crafts 745.54
  UF Paper folding
      Paper sculpture
      Paper work
      Papier-mâché
  SA types of paper crafts [to be add-
      ed as needed]
  BT **Handicraft**
  NT **Decoupage**
      Gift wrapping

Paper crafts—*Continued*
    Origami
  RT **Papermaking**
Paper folding
  USE **Origami**
        Paper crafts
Paper hanging
  USE **Paperhanging**
Paper industry (May subdiv. geog.)
    338.4

    Use for materials on the business of making and selling paper. Materials on the technology and craft of making paper are entered under **Papermaking**.

  UF Papermaking industry
  BT **Industries**
  RT **Paper**
Paper making
  USE **Papermaking**
Paper manufacture
  USE **Papermaking**
Paper money (May subdiv. geog.) **332.4**
  BT **Money**
  RT **Inflation (Finance)**
Paper sculpture
  USE **Paper crafts**
Paper work
  USE **Paper crafts**
Paperback books **070.5**
  UF Paper bound books
  BT **Books**
        Editions
Paperhanging **698**
  UF Paper hanging
  BT **Interior design**
  RT **Wallpaper**
Papermaking (May subdiv. geog.) **676**

    Use for materials on the technology and craft of making paper. Materials on the business of making and selling paper are entered under **Paper industry**.

  UF Paper making
        Paper manufacture
  BT **Manufactures**
        Paper
  RT **Paper crafts**
Papermaking industry
  USE **Paper industry**
Papier-mâché
  USE **Paper crafts**
Parables **808**

    Use for individual works, collections, or materials about parables.

  UF Cautionary tales and verses
        Moral and philosophic stories
        Morality tales
  SA individual parables, e.g. **Prodigal son (Parable)** [to be added as needed]
  NT **Bible—Parables**
        Jesus Christ—Parables
        Prodigal son (Parable)
  RT **Allegories**
        Didactic fiction
        Didactic poetry
        Fables
Parachute troops **356**
  UF Paratroops
  SA names of armies with the subdivision *Parachute troops*, e.g. **United States. Army—Parachute troops** [to be added as needed]
  BT **Military aeronautics**
        Parachutes
  NT **United States. Army—Parachute troops**
Parachutes **629.134**
  BT **Aeronautics**
  NT **Parachute troops**
Parade floats
  USE **Parades**
Parades (May subdiv. geog.) **791.6**
  UF Floats (Parades)
        Parade floats
        Pomp
        Processions
  BT **Festivals**
        Pageants
Paradise **202; 236**

    Use for materials on the earthly paradise or on a blessed intermediate state in the afterlife.

  UF Earthly paradise
        Eden
        Garden of Eden
  BT **Future life**
  RT **Heaven**
        Utopias
Parallel economy
  USE **Underground economy**
Paralysis **616.8**
  SA individual organs and regions of the body with the subdivision *Paralysis* e.g. **Foot—Paralysis** [to be added as needed]

Paralysis—*Continued*
> BT Nervous system—Diseases
> NT Foot—Paralysis

Paralysis, Cerebral
> USE Cerebral palsy

Paramedical personnel
> USE Allied health personnel
> Emergency medical technicians

Paramedics, Emergency
> USE Emergency medical technicians

Paramilitary militia movements
> USE Militia movements

Paranormal phenomena
> USE Parapsychology

Paraprofessional librarians
> USE Library technicians

Paraprofessionals 331.7
> UF Paraprofessions and
> paraprofessionals
> SA types of paraprofessional person-
> nel, e.g. **Library technicians**;
> and fields of knowledge, pro-
> fessions, industries, and trades
> with the subdivision *Vocation-
> al guidance* [to be added as
> needed]
> BT Occupations
> Professions
> NT Library technicians

Paraprofessions and paraprofessionals
> USE Paraprofessionals

Parapsychology (May subdiv. geog.)
> 130

Use for materials on investigations of phenomena that appear to be contrary to physical
laws and beyond the normal sense percep-
tions.
> UF Paranormal phenomena
> Psi (Parapsychology)
> Psychic phenomena
> Psychical research
> BT Psychology
> Research
> Supernatural
> NT Apparitions
> Astral projection
> Extrasensory perception
> Hallucinations and illusions
> Mental suggestion
> Mind and body
> Psychics
> Psychokinesis

> Subconsciousness
> Visions
> RT Ghosts
> Occultism
> Spiritualism

Parasaurolophus 567.914
> BT Dinosaurs

Parasites 577.8; 578.6
> UF Animal parasites
> Diseases and pests
> Entozoa
> Epizoa
> SA types of animals and parts of
> the body with the subdivision
> *Parasites* [to be added as
> needed]
> BT Pests
> NT Bacteria
> RT Insect pests
> Symbiosis

Parasols
> USE Umbrellas and parasols

Paratroops
> USE Parachute troops

Parcel post
> USE Postal service

Pardon (May subdiv. geog.) 364.6
> BT Administration of criminal jus-
> tice
> Executive power
> RT Amnesty
> Clemency
> Forgiveness

Parent abuse
> USE Elderly abuse

Parent and child
> USE Parent-child relationship

Parent-child relationship 306.874

Use for materials on the psychological and
social interaction between parents and their
minor children. Materials on the skills, attri-
butes, and attitudes needed for parenthood are
entered under **Parenting**. Materials on the
principles and techniques of rearing children
are entered under **Child rearing**. Materials restricted to the legal right of parents to visit
their children in situations of separation, divorce, etc., are entered under **Visitation
rights (Domestic relations)**.
> UF Child and parent
> Parent and child
> BT Child-adult relationship
> Children
> Family

Parent-child relationship—*Continued*
> **Parents**
> NT **Adoption**
> **Child abuse**
> **Child custody**
> **Child rearing**
> **Children of divorced parents**
> **Children of working parents**
> **Conflict of generations**
> **Father-child relationship**
> **Mother-child relationship**
> **Parenting**
> **Stepchildren**

Parent participation in children's education
> USE **Education—Parent participation**

Parent-teacher associations (May subdiv. geog.) **371.19**
> UF Parents' and teachers' associations
> PTAs
> BT **Community and school**
> **Education—Societies**
> **Parent-teacher relationship**
> **Societies**
> RT **Home and school**

Parent-teacher conferences **371.103**
> UF Conferences, Parent-teacher
> Interviews, Parent-teacher
> Teacher-parent conferences
> BT **Parent-teacher relationship**

Parent-teacher relationship **371.19**
> UF Parent-teacher relationships
> Parents and teachers
> Teacher-parent relationship
> Teachers and parents
> NT **Parent-teacher associations**
> **Parent-teacher conferences**
> RT **Home and school**

Parent-teacher relationships
> USE **Parent-teacher relationship**

Parental behavior
> USE **Parenting**

Parental custody
> USE **Child custody**

Parental involvement in children's education
> USE **Education—Parent participation**

Parental kidnapping (May subdiv. geog.) **362.82**
> UF Child snatching by parents
> Custody kidnapping
> Kidnapping, Parental
> BT **Child custody**

Parental leave (May subdiv. geog.) **331.25**
> UF Family leave
> Infant care leave
> Leave for parenting
> BT **Leave of absence**
> NT **Maternity leave**

Parenthood **306.874; 649**
> BT **Family**
> NT **Fatherhood**
> **Motherhood**

Parenting (May subdiv. geog.) **306.874; 649**

> Use for materials on the skills, attributes, and attitudes needed for parenthood. Materials on the psychological and social interaction between parents and their minor children are entered under **Parent-child relationship**. Materials on the principles and techniques of rearing children are entered under **Child rearing**.

> UF Parental behavior
> BT **Parent-child relationship**
> NT **Grandparenting**
> **Grandparents as parents**
> **Part-time parenting**
> RT **Child rearing**

Parenting by grandparents
> USE **Grandparents as parents**

Parenting, Part-time
> USE **Part-time parenting**

Parents (May subdiv. gcog.) **306.874**
> SA parents of particular kinds of children, e.g. **Parents of handicapped children** [to be added as needed]
> BT **Family**
> **Parents**
> NT **Aging parents**
> **Birthparents**
> **Divorced parents**
> **Gay parents**
> **Parent-child relationship**
> **Parents**
> **Single parents**
> **Stepparents**
> **Teenage parents**

Parents and teachers
> USE **Parent-teacher relationship**

Parents' and teachers' associations
USE **Parent-teacher associations**
Parents, Biological
USE **Birthparents**
Parents' choice of school
USE **School choice**
Parents of handicapped children (May subdiv. geog.) **306.874**
BT **Handicapped children**
Parents, Unmarried
USE **Unmarried fathers**
Unmarried mothers
Parish libraries
USE **Church libraries**
Parish registers
USE **Registers of births, etc.**
Parkinson's disease **616.8**
UF Palsy
BT **Brain—Diseases**
Parks (May subdiv. geog.) **363.6; 712**
BT **Cities and towns**
Landscape architecture
NT **Amusement parks**
Botanical gardens
National parks and reserves
Zoos
RT **Playgrounds**
Parks—United States **363.6; 712; 917.3**
Parkways
USE **Express highways**
Parliamentary government
USE **Representative government and representation**
Parliamentary practice (May subdiv. geog.) **060.4**
UF Rules of order
BT **Debates and debating**
Legislation
Legislative bodies
Public meetings
Parliaments
USE **Legislative bodies**
Parochial schools
USE **Church schools**
Parodies **808.87**
Use for collections of parodies. Materials on the literary form of parody, that is, satirical or humorous imitation of a serious piece of literature, are entered under **Parody**.
SA types of literature, individual literary works entered under title, and names of prominent

authors with the subdivision *Parodies, imitations, etc.*, e.g. **Shakespeare, William, 1564-1616—Parodies, imitations, etc.** [to be added as needed]
NT **Fractured fairy tales**
Parodies, imitations, etc.
USE types of literature, individual literary works entered under title, and names of prominent authors with the subdivision *Parodies, imitations, etc.*, e.g. **Shakespeare, William, 1564-1616—Parodies, imitations, etc.** [to be added as needed]
Parody **808.7**
Use for materials about the literary form of parody, that is, satirical or humorous imitation of a serious piece of literature. Collections of parodies are entered under **Parodies**.
UF Comic literature
Travesty
BT **Literature**
Satire
Wit and humor
NT **Burlesque (Literature)**
Parole (May subdiv. geog.) **364.6**
BT **Administration of criminal justice**
Corrections
Punishment
Social case work
RT **Probation**
Part-time employment (May subdiv. geog.) **331.25**
UF Alternative work schedules
BT **Employment**
Hours of labor
Labor
NT **Job sharing**
Supplementary employment
Part-time parenting **306.874; 649**
Use for materials on parenting skills for separated, divorced, or surrogate parents who live apart from their children and spend less than full time with them.
UF Co-parenting
Joint custody of children
Parenting, Part-time
Shared parenting
BT **Parenting**
RT **Children of divorced parents**

Partial hearing
USE **Hearing impaired**
Partially hearing
USE **Hearing impaired**
**Participative management   331.89;
658.3**
  UF Consultative management
       Employees' representation in
         management
       Industrial councils
       Labor participation in manage-
         ment
       Management—Employee partici-
         pation
       Workers' participation in man-
         agement
       Workshop councils
  BT **Factory management**
       Industrial relations
       Personnel management
  RT **Collective bargaining**
Particles (Nuclear physics)   539.7
  UF Elementary particles (Physics)
       Nuclear particles
       Nucleons
  SA names of particles [to be added
        as needed]
  BT **Nuclear physics**
  NT **Electrons**
       Neutrons
       Protons
       Quarks
       String theory
Parties (May subdiv. geog.)   **793.2**
  SA types of parties [to be added as
        needed]
  BT **Entertaining**
  NT **Children's parties**
       Showers (Parties)
Parties, Political
USE **Political parties**
Partisans
  USE **Guerrillas**
Partita
  USE **Suite (Music)**
Partnership   338.7
  UF Companies
       Partnership—Law and legislation
  BT **Business enterprises**
  NT **Joint ventures**

Partnership—Law and legislation
  USE **Partnership**
Parts of speech
  USE names of languages with the
        subdivision *Parts of speech,*
        e.g. **English language—Parts
        of speech** [to be added as
        needed]
Passion of Christ
  USE **Jesus Christ—Passion**
Passion plays   792.1; 808.82
> Use for individual plays, collections, or ma-
> terials about medieval plays depicting the Pas-
> sion of Christ.

  BT **Bible plays**
       Mysteries and miracle plays
       Religious drama
       Theater
Passions
  USE **Emotions**
Passive resistance (May subdiv. geog.)
    303.6; 322.4
  UF Nonviolent noncooperation
  BT **Resistance to government**
  NT **Boycotts**
       Hunger strikes
  RT **Nonviolence**
Passover (May subdiv. geog.)   **296.4;
394.267**
  UF Pesach
  BT **Jewish holidays**
  NT **Seder**
Pastel drawing   741.2
  BT **Drawing**
  RT **Crayon drawing**
Pastimes
  USE **Amusements**
       Games
       Recreation
Pastoral drama   808.82
> Use for individual works, collections, or
> materials about pastoral drama.

  UF Rural comedies
  BT **Drama**
Pastoral fiction   808.3; 808.83
> Use for individual works, collections, or
> materials about novels or short stories with a
> rural setting and a tone of romantic nostalgia.

  UF Pastoral romances
       Rural comedies
  BT **Fiction**
Pastoral peoples
  USE **Nomads**

Pastoral poetry   808.1; 808.81

Use for individual works, collections, or materials about pastoral poetry.

UF   Bucolic poetry
Eclogues
Idyllic poetry
Rural poetry

BT   **Poetry**

Pastoral psychiatry
USE   **Pastoral psychology**

Pastoral psychology (May subdiv. geog.)
206; 253.5

Use for materials on the application of psychology and psychiatry by the clergy to the spiritual problems of individuals.

UF   Clerical psychology
Pastoral psychiatry
Psychology, Pastoral
Psychology, Religious
Religious psychology

BT   **Applied psychology**
Church work
Psychology of religion

RT   **Pastoral theology**

Pastoral romances
USE   **Pastoral fiction**

Pastoral theology (May subdiv. geog.)
206; 253

May be subdivided by sect or denomination.

UF   Pastoral work

BT   **Theology**

NT   **Ministry**
Preaching

RT   **Church work**
Clergy
Pastoral psychology

Pastoral work
USE   **Pastoral theology**

Pastors
USE   **Clergy**
Priests

Pastry (May subdiv. geog.)   641.8

BT   **Baking**
Cooking

RT   **Cake**

Pastures (May subdiv. geog.)   333.74

BT   **Agriculture**
Land use

Patchwork   746.46

BT   **Needlework**

Patchwork quilts
USE   **Quilts**

Patent medicines
USE   **Nonprescription drugs**

Patents (May subdiv. geog.)   608

BT   **Manufactures**

RT   **Intellectual property**
Inventions
Trademarks

Pathological psychology
USE   **Abnormal psychology**

Pathology   616.07

UF   Disease (Pathology)

BT   **Medicine**

NT   **Birth defects**
Diagnostic imaging
Fever
Medical genetics
Therapeutics

RT   **Diseases**
Preventive medicine

Patience   179

BT   **Human behavior**
Virtue

Patience (Game)
USE   **Solitaire (Game)**

Patient care records
USE   **Medical records**

Patients   362.1

SA   diseases with the subdivision *Patients*, e.g. **Cancer—Patients**; and organs or regions of the body with the subdivisions *Surgery—Patients*, or *Transplantation—Patients* [to be added as needed]

NT   **Cancer—Patients**

RT   **Sick**

Patios   643

UF   Decks (Domestic architecture)

BT   **Landscape architecture**

Patriotic poetry   808.1; 808.81

Use for individual works, collections, or materials about patriotic poetry.

BT   **Poetry**

RT   **National songs**

Patriotic songs
USE   **National songs**

Patriotism (May subdiv. geog.)   172

BT   **Citizenship**
Human behavior
Loyalty

RT   **Nationalism**

Patristic philosophy
   USE   **Fathers of the church**

Patristics
   USE   **Fathers of the church**

Patronage of the arts
   USE   **Art patronage**

Pattern making
   USE   **Patternmaking**

Pattern perception   152.14
   UF   Design perception
        Pattern recognition
   BT   **Perception**

Pattern recognition
   USE   **Pattern perception**

Patternmaking   671.2
   UF   Pattern making
   BT   **Models and modelmaking**
   NT   **Mechanical drawing**
   RT   **Design**
        Founding

Patterns
   USE   types of handicrafts and manu-
        factures with the subdivision
        Patterns, e.g. **Dressmaking—
        Patterns** [to be added as
        needed]

Patterns (Language arts)
   USE   **Language arts—Patterning**

Patterns (Mathematics)   372.7
   UF   Geometric patterns
        Number patterns
   BT   **Mathematics**

Paul Bunyan
   USE   **Bunyan, Paul (Legendary char-
        acter)**

Pauperism
   USE   **Poverty**

Pavements (May subdiv. geog.)   625.8
   RT   **Roads**
        Streets

Pay equity
   USE   **Equal pay for equal work**

Pay-per-view television
   USE   **Subscription television**

Pay television
   USE   **Subscription television**

Payroll taxes
   USE   **Unemployment insurance**

PC computers
   USE   **Personal computers**

PCs
   USE   **Personal computers**

Peace   172; 327.1; 341.7
   SA   names of wars with the subdivi-
        sion *Peace* e.g. **World War,
        1939-1945—Peace** [to be add-
        ed as needed]
   BT   **International relations**
   NT   **World War, 1914-1918—Peace**
   RT   **Arms control**
        International arbitration
        International security
        Pacifism
        Peace movements
        War

Peace keeping forces
   USE   **United Nations—Armed forces**

Peace movements (May subdiv. geog.)
        327.1

Use for materials on social movements advocating peace. Materials on the renunciation
of offensive or defensive military actions on
moral grounds are entered under **Pacifism**.

   UF   Antiwar movements
        War protest movements
   SA   names of wars with the subdivi-
        sion *Protest movements,* e.g.
        **World War, 1939-1945—
        Protest movements** [to be
        added as needed]
   BT   **Social movements**
   RT   **Demonstrations**
        Peace

Peaceful coexistence
   USE   **International relations**

Peacocks   598.6
   UF   Peafowl
        Peahens
   BT   **Birds**

Peafowl
   USE   **Peacocks**

Peahens
   USE   **Peacocks**

Pearl fisheries (May subdiv. geog.)
        338.3; 639
   UF   Pearlfisheries
   BT   **Commercial fishing**

**Pearl Harbor (Oahu, Hawaii), Attack on,
   1941**   940.54
   BT   **World War, 1939-1945—Cam-
        paigns**

Pearlfisheries
USE **Pearl fisheries**
Peasant art
USE **Folk art**
Peasantry (May subdiv. geog.) **305.5;
307.72**
BT **Feudalism
Labor**
RT **Agricultural laborers
Land tenure
Rural sociology**
Pecan
USE **Pecans**
Pecans 583; 634
UF Pecan
BT **Nuts**
Pedagogy
USE **Education
Education—Study and teaching
Teaching**
Peddlers and peddling (May subdiv.
geog.) **658.8**
UF Door to door selling
BT **Direct selling
Sales personnel**
Pediatric psychiatry
USE **Child psychiatry**
Pediatric surgery
USE **Children—Surgery**
Pediatrics
USE **Children—Diseases
Children—Health and hygiene
Infants—Diseases
Infants—Health and hygiene**
Pedigrees
USE **Genealogy
Heraldry**
Peer counseling (May subdiv. geog.)
158; 361.3
UF Peer counseling in rehabilitation
Peer counseling of students
Peer group counseling
Rehabilitation peer counseling
Student to student counseling
BT **Counseling**
Peer counseling in rehabilitation
USE **Peer counseling**
Peer counseling of students
USE **Peer counseling**
Peer group counseling
USE **Peer counseling**

Peer group influence
USE **Peer pressure**
Peer pressure (May subdiv. geog.)
303.3; 364.2
UF Peer group influence
BT **Socialization**
NT **Peer pressure in adolescence**
Peer pressure in adolescence (May
subdiv. geog.) **303.3**
BT **Peer pressure**
Peerage
USE **Nobility**
Pegasus (Greek mythology) 398.22
BT **Legendary characters**
Pelts
USE **Hides and skins**
Pen drawing 741.2
UF Ink drawing
BT **Drawing**
Pen names
USE **Pseudonyms**
Penal codes
USE **Criminal law**
Penal colonies (May subdiv. geog.) **365**
UF Expulsion
Transportation of criminals
BT **Colonies
Correctional institutions**
Penal institutions
USE **Correctional institutions
Prisons
Reformatories**
Penal law
USE **Criminal law**
Penal reform
USE **Prison reform**
Penance (May subdiv. geog.) **265**
UF Contrition
Reconciliation, Sacrament of
Sacrament of Reconciliation
BT **Sacraments**
RT **Confession
Forgiveness of sin
Repentance**
Pencil drawing 741.2
BT **Drawing**
Penguins (May subdiv. geog.) **598.47**
BT **Birds**
Penicillin 615
BT **Antibiotics**
Peninsulas (May subdiv. geog.) **551.41**

Peninsulas—*Continued*

    SA   names of peninsulas [to be added as needed]

    NT   **Arabian Peninsula**

Penitence

    USE   **Repentance**

Penitentiaries

    USE   **Prisons**

Penmanship

    USE   **Handwriting**

Pennsylvania Dutch (May subdiv. geog.)
    974.8

    UF   Pennsylvania Germans

Pennsylvania Germans

    USE   **Pennsylvania Dutch**

Penology

    USE   **Corrections**

           Punishment

Pensions (May subdiv. geog.)   **331.25;**
    353.5; 658.3

    UF   Compensation

    SA   ethnic groups, classes of persons, and employees in particular industries with the subdivision *Pensions*, e.g. **Teachers—Pensions; Chemical industry—Employees—Pensions**; etc. [to be added as needed]

    BT   **Annuities**

           Retirement income

    NT   **Individual retirement accounts**

           Military pensions

           Old age pensions

           Social security

Pensions, Naval

    USE   **Military pensions**

Pentagon (Va.) terrorist attack, 2001

    USE   **September 11 terrorist attacks, 2001**

Pentecostal churches (May subdiv. geog.)
    289.9

    Use for general materials on Christian denominations of the Pentecostal type. Materials on Christian movements that stress the personal experience of the Holy Spirit in daily life, with emphasis on personal holiness and spiritual gifts, especially the gift of tongues, are entered under **Pentecostalism**.

    BT   **Christian sects**

           Protestantism

    RT   **Pentecostalism**

Pentecostal movement

    USE   **Pentecostalism**

Pentecostalism (May subdiv. geog.)
    270.8

    Use for materials on Christian movements that stress the personal experience of the Holy Spirit in daily life, with emphasis on personal holiness and spiritual gifts, especially the gift of tongues. General materials on Christian denominations of the Pentecostal type are entered under **Pentecostal churches**.

    UF   Charismatic movement

           Charismatic renewal movement

           Pentecostal movement

    BT   **Christianity**

    RT   **Catholic charismatic movement**

           Glossolalia

           Pentecostal churches

           Spiritual gifts

Peonage (May subdiv. geog.)   **306.3; 331.5**

    UF   Servitude

    BT   **Forced labor**

    RT   **Contract labor**

           Slavery

People

    USE   **Ethnic groups**

           Indigenous peoples

           Persons

           and racial and ethnic groups and native peoples, e.g. **African Americans; Mexican Americans; Yoruba (African people)**; etc., and classes of persons, e.g. **Elderly; Handicapped; Explorers; Drug addicts**; etc. [to be added as needed]

People in space

    USE   **Space flight**

People's banks

    USE   **Cooperative banks**

People's Republic of China

    USE   **China**

Pep pills

    USE   **Amphetamines**

Percentage   **513.2**

    BT   **Arithmetic**

Perception   **152.1; 153.7**

    UF   Feeling

    SA   types of concepts and images, e.g. **Size; Shape**; etc. [to be added as needed]

Perception—*Continued*
  BT Intellect
      Psychology
      Senses and sensation
      Theory of knowledge
      Thought and thinking
  NT Concepts
      Consciousness
      Gestalt psychology
      Pattern perception
      Shape
      Size
  RT Apperception
      Intuition
Percussion instruments (May subdiv. geog.) **786.8**
  SA types of percussion instruments, e.g. **Drums** [to be added as needed]
  BT **Musical instruments**
  NT **Drums**
      Pianos
Perennials (May subdiv. geog.) **635.9**
  BT **Cultivated plants**
      Flower gardening
      Flowers
Perfectionism (Personality trait) **155.2**
  UF Self-expectations, Perfectionist
  BT **Personality**
Performance **155.2; 658.4**
  UF Competence
  BT **Work**
  NT **Achievement motivation**
      Performance standards
Performance art (May subdiv. geog.) **700**
  Use for materials on live performances by artists, drawing on literature, theater, music, film, etc., and combining elements of the various arts in untraditional ways.
  UF Happening (Art)
  BT **Art**
      Performing arts
Performance motivation
  USE **Achievement motivation**
Performance standards **658.5**
  UF Job performance standards
      Rating
      Work performance standards
  SA subjects and classes of persons with the subdivision *Rating*, e.g. **Bonds—Rating; Employ-**

ees**—Rating**; etc. [to be added as needed]
  BT **Performance**
Performing arts (May subdiv. geog.) **790.2**
  UF Show business
  SA specific art forms performed on stage or screen [to be added as needed]
  BT **Arts**
  NT **Ballet**
      Centers for the performing arts
      Dance
      Motion pictures
      Opera
      Performance art
      Theater
Performing arts audiences
  USE **Performing arts—Audiences**
Performing arts—Audiences (May subdiv. geog.) **791**
  UF Performing arts audiences
  BT **Audiences**
Perfumes (May subdiv. geog.) **391.6; 668**
  BT **Cosmetics**
      Essences and essential oils
  NT **Potpourri**
Periodic health examinations **616.07**
  UF Health examinations
      Medical examinations
      Physical examinations (Medicine)
  SA subjects, classes of persons, ethnic groups, and military services with the subdivision *Medical examinations*, e.g. **Children—Medical examinations** [to be added as needed]
  BT **Medicine**
Periodic law **546.8**
  BT **Physical chemistry**
  RT **Chemical elements**
Periodicals (May subdiv. geog.) **050**
  UF Annuals
      Journals
      Magazines
  SA subjects with the subdivision *Periodicals*, e.g. **Engineering—Periodicals**; and names of in-

Periodicals—*Continued*
        dividual periodicals [to be
        added as needed]
  BT **Mass media**
        Serial publications
  NT **Chapbooks**
        English periodicals
        Fanzines
        Little magazines
  RT **Journalism**
        Newspapers
        Press
Periodicals—Editing
  USE **Journalism—Editing**
Periodicals—Indexes   050
Periodicals—United States   051
  UF American periodicals
Periodicity
  USE **Cycles**
Permanent education
  USE **Continuing education**
Persecution (May subdiv. geog.)   **201;**
    909
  UF Persecutions
        Religious persecution
  SA religious groups with the subdi-
        vision *Persecutions*, e.g.
        Christians—Persecutions;
        Jews—Persecutions; etc.; and
        religious groups and classes
        of persons with the subdivi-
        sion *Nazi persecution*, e.g.
        **Handicapped—Nazi persecu-
        tion** [to be added as needed]
  BT **Atrocities**
  NT **Christians—Persecutions**
        Handicapped—Nazi persecution
        Jews—Persecutions
        Massacres
  RT **Freedom of religion**
        Martyrs
Persecutions
  USE **Persecution**
        and religious groups with the
        subdivision *Persecutions*, e.g.
        Christians—Persecutions;
        Jews—Persecutions; etc.; and
        religious groups and classes
        of persons with the subdivi-
        sion *Nazi persecution*, e.g.
        **Handicapped—Nazi persecu-
        tion** [to be added as needed]

Persephone (Greek deity)   202
  BT **Gods and goddesses**
Perseverance   179
  BT **Ethics**
Persia
  USE **Iran**
Persian Gulf War, 1991   956.7044
  UF Gulf War, 1991
        Middle East War, 1991
        Operation Desert Storm
  BT **United States—History—1989-**
Persistence   158
  BT **Personality**
Persistent pain
  USE **Chronic pain**
Personal actions (Law)
  USE **Litigation**
Personal appearance   391.6
  UF Appearance, Personal
        Beauty, Personal
        Physical appearance
        Self image
  NT **Body piercing**
        Personal grooming
        Tattooing
  RT **Clothing and dress**
Personal cleanliness
  USE **Hygiene**
Personal computers   004.16; 621.39
    Use for materials on small, usually desktop-
    sized computers that have a self-contained
    central processing unit.
  UF Desktop computers
        Home computers
        Microcomputers
        PC computers
        PCs
  BT **Computers**
Personal conduct
  USE **Conduct of life**
Personal development
  USE **Personality**
        Self-improvement
        Success
Personal films
  USE **Amateur films**
        Experimental films
Personal finance (May subdiv. geog.)
    332.024
  UF Budgets, Personal
        Domestic finance
        Family finance

Personal finance—*Continued*
    Finance, Personal
    Financial planning, Personal
    SA   ethnic groups, classes of persons, and names of individual persons with the subdivision *Personal finance*, e.g. **Retirees—Personal finance** [to be added as needed]
    BT   **Finance**
    NT   **Children's allowances**
          Consumer credit
          Estate planning
          Household budgets
          Insurance
          Saving and investment
          Tax planning
Personal freedom
    USE   **Freedom**
Personal grooming (May subdiv. geog.)
    391.6; 646.7
    UF   Beauty, Personal
          Good grooming
          Grooming, Personal
    BT   **Hygiene**
          Personal appearance
    NT   **Cosmetics**
          Hair
          Toiletries
    RT   **Clothing and dress**
Personal growth
    USE   **Self-improvement**
Personal health
    USE   **Health**
Personal health services
    USE   **Medical care**
Personal hygiene
    USE   **Hygiene**
Personal income tax
    USE   **Income tax**
Personal life skills
    USE   **Life skills**
Personal loans (May subdiv. geog.)
    332.7
    Use for materials on loans to individuals for personal rather than business uses.
    UF   Consumer loans
          Loans, Personal
          Small loans
    BT   **Consumer credit**
          Loans

    NT   **Cooperative banks**
          Savings and loan associations
Personal names (May subdiv. geog.)
    929.4
    UF   Baby names
          Christian names
          Family names
          First names
          Names, Personal
          Surnames
    SA   personal names of particular national or ethnic origins regardless of the place where they are found, e.g. **Scottish personal names** [to be added as needed]
    BT   **Names**
    NT   **Nicknames**
          Pseudonyms
          Scottish personal names
Personal names—United States
    929.40973
    UF   American personal names
Personal narratives
    USE   **Autobiographies**
           Biography
    and subjects with the subdivision *Biography* or *Correspondence;* and names of diseases, events, and wars with the subdivision *Personal narratives,* e.g. **World War, 1939-1945—Personal narratives** [to be added as needed]
Personal space   153.6; 302.2
    Use for materials on the sense of physical space required for psychological comfort.
    UF   Space, Personal
    BT   **Interpersonal relations**
          Nonverbal communication
          Space and time
Personal time management
    USE   **Time management**
Personality   155.2
    UF   Identity
          Personal development
    BT   **Consciousness**
          Psychology
    NT   **Body image**
          Bossiness
          Character
          Eccentrics and eccentricities

Personality—*Continued*
>> Ego (Psychology)
>> Forgetfulness
>> Identity (Psychology)
>> Laziness
>> Perfectionism (Personality trait)
>> Persistence
>> Self
>> Selfishness
>> Stubbornness
>> Typology (Psychology)
> RT Individuality
>> Persons

Personality disorders 616.85
> BT Abnormal psychology
> NT Multiple personality
>> Narcissism
> RT Hallucinations and illusions
>> Mental illness

Personality, Multiple
> USE Multiple personality

Personnel administration
> USE Personnel management

Personnel classification
> USE Job analysis

Personnel management (May subdiv. geog.) 658.3
> UF Career development
>> Employment management
>> Human resource management
>> Personnel administration
>> Supervision of employees
> SA names of corporate bodies and military services and types of industries, services, and organizations with the subdivision *Personnel management*, e.g. **Hospitals—Personnel management** [to be added as needed]
> BT Industrial relations
>> Management
> NT Absenteeism (Labor)
>> Affirmative action programs
>> Applications for positions
>> Counseling
>> Diversity in the workplace
>> Employee assistance programs
>> Employee morale
>> Employees—Dismissal
>> Employees—Training
>> Employment agencies
>> Hospitals—Personnel management
>> Job analysis
>> Job satisfaction
>> Job security
>> Labor turnover
>> Motion study
>> Participative management
>> Recruiting of employees
>> Supervisors
>> Time study
> RT Employees
>> Factory management
>> Office management

Personnel service in education
> USE Educational counseling

Persons 128
> Use for materials on human beings as individuals. Materials on the human species from the point of view of biology or anthropology are entered under **Human beings**.
> UF Categorics of persons
>> Classes of persons
>> Groups of persons
>> People
> SA classes of persons, e.g. **Elderly**; **Handicapped**; **Explorers**; **Drug addicts**; etc. [to be added as nceded]
> BT Human beings
> NT Celebrities
>> Exiles
>> Intellectuals
>> Psychics
>> Transvestites
> RT Individualism
>> Personality

Perspective 701
> UF Architectural perspective
> BT Descriptive geometry
>> Geometrical drawing
>> Optics
>> Painting
> RT Drawing

Persuasion (Psychology) 153.8
> UF Psychology, Applied
> BT Communication
>> Conformity
> RT Propaganda

Persuasion (Rhetoric)
    USE **Public speaking**
           Rhetoric
Peru   985
Perversion, Sexual
    USE **Sexual deviation**
Pesach
    USE **Passover**
Pest control (May subdiv. geog.)   **363.7;
    628.9; 632**
    UF   Extermination of pests
           Pest extermination
           Pests—Biological control
           Pests—Control
           Pests—Extermination
    SA   types of pests with the subdivi-
           sion *Control*, e.g. **Mosqui-
           toes—Control** [to be added
           as needed]
    BT   **Agricultural pests**
           Economic zoology
           Pests
    NT   **Mosquitoes—Control**
           Pesticides
Pest extermination
    USE **Pest control**
Pesticide pollution
    USE **Pesticides—Environmental as-
           pects**
Pesticides (May subdiv. geog.)   **632; 668**
    BT   **Agricultural chemicals**
           Pest control
           Poisons and poisoning
    NT   **Fungicides**
           Herbicides
           Insecticides
           Natural pesticides
Pesticides and wildlife   590
    UF   Wildlife and pesticides
    BT   **Pesticides—Environmental as-
           pects**
           Wildlife conservation
Pesticides—Environmental aspects (May
    subdiv. geog.)   **363.7; 632**
    UF   Environment and pesticides
           Pesticide pollution
    BT   **Environment**
           Pollution
    NT   **Pesticides and wildlife**
Pestilences
    USE **Epidemics**

Pests (May subdiv. geog.)   **591.6; 632**
    Use for materials on detrimental or annoy-
    ing animals or organisms.
    UF   Vermin
    SA   types of pests, e.g. **Agricultural
           pests**; **Flies**; etc.; and names
           of crops, trees, etc., with the
           subdivision *Diseases and
           pests*, e.g. **Fruit—Diseases
           and pests** [to be added as
           needed]
    BT   **Economic zoology**
    NT   **Agricultural pests**
           Flies
           Fruit—Diseases and pests
           Fungi
           Household pests
           Insect pests
           Parasites
           Pest control
Pests—Biological control
    USE **Pest control**
Pests—Control
    USE **Pest control**
Pests—Extermination
    USE **Pest control**
Pet-facilitated psychotherapy
    USE **Pet therapy**
Pet therapy   615.8
    UF   Animal-facilitated therapy
           Companion-animal partnership
           Pet-facilitated psychotherapy
    BT   **Animals and the handicapped**
           Therapeutics
Petrochemicals   661
    UF   Petroleum chemicals
    BT   **Chemicals**
Petroglyphs
    USE **Rock drawings, paintings, and
           engravings**
Petroleum (May subdiv. geog.)   **553.2;
    665.5**
    UF   Coal oil
           Crude oil
           Oil
    BT   **Oils and fats**
    NT   **Coal tar products**
           Gasoline
    RT   **Petroleum geology**
           Petroleum industry
Petroleum as fuel   338.4; 665.5

Petroleum as fuel—*Continued*

UF Fuel oil

      Liquid fuel

      Oil fuel

BT **Fuel**

NT **Oil burners**

Petroleum chemicals

USE **Petrochemicals**

Petroleum engines

USE **Internal combustion engines**

Petroleum geology (May subdiv. geog.) **553.2**

UF Geology, Petroleum

BT **Economic geology**

      Prospecting

RT **Petroleum**

Petroleum industry (May subdiv. geog.) **338.2**

UF Oil industry

      Petroleum industry and trade

BT **Industries**

NT **Offshore oil industry**

      Oil well drilling

      Oil wells

      Service stations

RT **Petroleum**

Petroleum industry and trade

USE **Petroleum industry**

Petroleum industry—Deregulation (May subdiv. geog.) **338.2**

Petroleum pipelines (May subdiv. geog.) **338.2; 665.5**

BT **Pipelines**

Petroleum pollution of water

USE **Oil pollution of water**

Petroleum—United States **553.2; 665.5**

Petroleum—Well boring

USE **Oil well drilling**

Petrology (May subdiv. geog.) **552**

SA types of rocks, e.g. **Granite** [to be added as needed]

BT **Science**

NT **Geochemistry**

      Moon rocks

RT **Geology**

      Minerals

      Rocks

      Stone

Pets (May subdiv. geog.) **636.088**

SA types of common pets, e.g. **Dogs**; and types of animals not ordinarily kept as pets,

e.g. **Snakes as pets** [to be added as needed]

BT **Animals**

NT **Snakes as pets**

RT **Domestic animals**

Pets and the handicapped

USE **Animals and the handicapped**

Pets—Housing (May subdiv. geog.) **690**

BT **Animal housing**

NT **Kennels**

Pets—Names **636.088**

Petting zoos **590.73**

BT **Zoos**

Pewter **673; 739.5**

BT **Alloys**

      Art metalwork

      Metals

Phantoms

USE **Apparitions**

      Ghosts

Pharmaceutical abuse

USE **Medication abuse**

Pharmaceutical chemistry **615**

UF Drugs—Chemistry

      Medicinal chemistry

BT **Chemistry**

NT **Disinfection and disinfectants**

RT **Pharmacy**

      Therapeutics

Pharmaceuticals

USE **Drugs**

Pharmacies

USE **Drugstores**

Pharmacodynamics

USE **Pharmacology**

Pharmacology **615**

Use for materials on the action and properties of drugs in general. Materials limited to the effect of drugs on the functions of living organisms are entered under **Drugs—Physiological effect**. Materials on the art or practice of preparing, preserving, and dispensing drugs are entered under **Pharmacy**.

UF Drugs—Adulteration and analysis

      Medicine—Physiological effect

      Pharmacodynamics

BT **Medicine**

NT **Drugs—Physiological effect**

      Drugs—Testing

      Toxicology

RT **Drug therapy**

      Drugs

      Materia medica

Pharmacology—*Continued*
  Pharmacy
Pharmacopoeias
  USE **Materia medica**
Pharmacotherapy
  USE **Drug therapy**
Pharmacy 615
  Use for materials on the art or practice of preparing, preserving, and dispensing drugs. Materials on the action and properties of drugs are entered under **Pharmacology**. Materials on business establishments that sell drugs are entered under **Drugstores**.
  BT **Chemistry**
      Medicine
  NT **Drugs**
      Homeopathy
      Medical botany
  RT **Materia medica**
      Pharmaceutical chemistry
      Pharmacology
Pheasants 598.6; 636.5
  BT **Birds**
      Game and game birds
Phenomenology 142
  BT **Modern philosophy**
  NT **Existentialism**
Philanthropists (May subdiv. geog.)
      361.7092; 920
  UF Altruists
      Humanitarians
  RT **Philanthropy**
Philanthropy (May subdiv. geog.) **177; 361.7**
  RT **Charitable organizations**
      Charities
      Endowments
      Philanthropists
Philately
  USE **Stamp collecting**
Philippines 959.9
  May be subdivided like United States except for History.
Philology
  USE **Language and languages**
      Linguistics
Philology, Comparative
  USE **Linguistics**
Philosophers (May subdiv. geog.) **180; 190; 920**
  RT **Philosophy**
Philosophers, American
  USE **Philosophers—United States**

Philosophers' stone
  USE **Alchemy**
Philosophers—United States 191; 920
  UF American philosophers
      Philosophers, American
Philosophy 100
  SA movements in philosophy, e.g. **Positivism**; philosophy of particular countries, e.g. **American philosophy**; philosophy associated with particular religions, e.g. **Christian philosophy**; and subjects with the subdivision *Philosophy*, e.g. **History—Philosophy** [to be added as needed]
  BT **Humanities**
  NT **Aesthetics**
      American philosophy
      Ancient philosophy
      Belief and doubt
      Causation
      Christian philosophy
      Comparative philosophy
      Empiricism
      Ethics
      Evolution
      Fate and fatalism
      Free will and determinism
      Gnosticism
      Good and evil
      Hindu philosophy
      History—Philosophy
      Humanism
      Idealism
      Ideology
      Indian philosophy
      Intuition
      Logic
      Marxism
      Materialism
      Medieval philosophy
      Metaphysics
      Mind and body
      Modern philosophy
      Pantheism
      Philosophy and religion
      Positivism
      Pragmatism
      Psychology
      Rationalism

Philosophy—*Continued*
>>> **Realism**
>>> **Reality**
>>> **Skepticism**
>>> **Soul**
>>> **Tao**
>>> **Theism**
>>> **Theory of knowledge**
>>> **Transcendentalism**
>>> **Truth**
> RT **Philosophers**

Philosophy, American
> USE **American philosophy**

Philosophy, Ancient
> USE **Ancient philosophy**

Philosophy and religion   210

Use for materials on the reciprocal relationship and influence between philosophy and religion. Materials on the nature, origin, or validity of religion from a philosophical point of view are entered under **Religion—Philosophy**.

> UF Religion and philosophy
> BT **Philosophy**
>>> **Religion**
> RT **Religion—Philosophy**

Philosophy—Encyclopedias   103
> BT **Encyclopedias and dictionaries**

Philosophy, Hindu
> USE **Hindu philosophy**

Philosophy—Historiography   109
> BT **Historiography**

Philosophy, Medieval
> USE **Medieval philosophy**

Philosophy, Modern
> USE **Modern philosophy**

Philosophy of history
> USE **History—Philosophy**

Philosophy of religion
> USE **Religion—Philosophy**

Phobias   616.85
> SA types of phobias, e.g. **Agoraphobia** [to be added as needed]
> BT **Fear**
>>> **Neuroses**
> NT **Agoraphobia**
>>> **Social phobia**

Phoenicians (May subdiv. geog.)   **939**
> BT **Ancient history**

Phoenix (Mythical bird)   398.2454
> BT **Mythical animals**

Phonetic spelling   411
> BT **Spelling reform**

Phonetics   414
> UF Phonics
>>> Phonology
> SA names of languages with the subdivision *Pronunciation* [to be added as needed]
> BT **Language and languages**
>>> **Sound**
> NT **English language—Pronunciation**
> RT **Reading—Phonetic method**
>>> **Speech**
>>> **Voice**

Phonics
> USE **Phonetics**
>>> **Reading—Phonetic method**

Phonograph   621.389
> UF Gramophone
>>> Record players
> NT **Compact disc players**
> RT **Sound—Recording and reproducing**

Phonograph records
> USE **Sound recordings**

Phonology
> USE **Phonetics**
>>> and names of languages with the subdivision *Pronunciation*, e.g. **English language—Pronunciation** [to be added as needed]

Phosphates   546; 553.6; 631.8
> BT **Fertilizers**

Phosphorescence   535
> BT **Luminescence**
>>> **Radioactivity**

Photo journalism
> USE **Photojournalism**

Photocopying   686.4
> UF Photocopying processes
>>> Photoduplication
>>> Photographic reproduction
>>> Xerography
> BT **Copying processes**
> RT **Copy art**

Photocopying machines
> USE **Copying machines**

Photocopying processes
> USE **Photocopying**

Photoduplication
> USE **Photocopying**

Photoelectric cells   537.5; 621.3815
  UF Electric eye
Photoengraving (May subdiv. geog.)
    686.2
  UF Halftone process
  BT **Engraving**
  RT **Photomechanical processes**
Photographers (May subdiv. geog.)
    770.92
  BT **Artists**
Photographic chemistry   771
    Use for materials on the chemical processes employed in photography.
  BT **Chemistry**
  NT **Photography—Processing**
  RT **Photography**
Photographic film
  USE **Photography—Film**
Photographic reproduction
  USE **Photocopying**
Photographic slides
  USE **Slides (Photography)**
Photographic supplies
  USE **Photography—Equipment and supplies**
Photographs   770
    Use for materials that discuss photographs as objects, including their classification, cataloging, copying, coloring, mounting, etc.
  UF Photos
      Snapshots
  SA subjects, classes of persons, names of wars, and names of cities, states, countries, and named entities, such as individual parks, structures, etc., with the subdivision *Pictorial works*, e.g. **Animals—Pictorial works; United States—History—1861-1865, Civil War—Pictorial works**; etc.; and names of persons or groups of persons with the subdivision *Pictorial works*, or *Portraits* [to be added as needed]
  BT **Pictures**
  RT **Photography**
Photographs—Conservation and restoration   771
  UF Conservation of photographs
      Preservation of photographs

      Restoration of photographs
Photographs from space
  USE **Space photography**
Photography (May subdiv. geog.)   770
  SA kinds of photography, e.g. **Portrait photography**; photography of particular subjects, e.g. **Photography of birds**; and subjects, classes of persons, names of wars, and names of cities, states, countries, and named entities, such as individual parks, structures, etc., with the subdivision *Pictorial works* [to be added as needed]
  BT **Graphic arts**
  NT **Aerial photography**
      Artistic photography
      Astronomical photography
      Cameras
      Cinematography
      Color photography
      Commercial photography
      Digital photography
      Filmstrips
      Holography
      Medical photography
      Microphotography
      Nature photography
      Outdoor photography
      Photojournalism
      Photomechanical processes
      Photomicrography
      Portrait photography
      Slides (Photography)
      Space photography
      Telephotography
      Three dimensional photography
      Underwater photography
      War photography
      Wildlife photography
  RT **Photographic chemistry**
      Photographs
Photography—Aesthetics
  USE **Artistic photography**
Photography, Artistic
  USE **Artistic photography**
Photography, Color
  USE **Color photography**

Photography, Combat
USE **War photography**
Photography—Darkroom technique
USE **Photography—Processing**
**Photography—Developing and developers
771**
BT **Photography—Processing**
Photography—Digital techniques
USE **Digital photography**
Photography—Enlarging 771
UF Enlarging (Photography)
**Photography—Equipment and supplies
771**
UF Photographic supplies
NT **Cameras**
Photography—Film 771
UF Photographic film
**Photography—Handbooks, manuals, etc.
770.2**
Photography in astronautics
USE **Space photography**
Photography—Lighting 771; 778.7
BT **Lighting**
Photography—Motion pictures
USE **Cinematography**
Photography of animals 778.9
Use for materials on the technique of photographing animals. Materials consisting of photographs and pictures of animals are entered under **Animals—Pictorial works**.
UF Animal photography
Animals—Photography
BT **Nature photography**
RT **Animal painting and illustration**
Animals—Pictorial works
Photography of birds 778.9
UF Bird photography
Birds—Photography
BT **Nature photography**
Photography of fishes 778.9
UF Fishes—Photography
BT **Nature photography**
Photography of nature
USE **Nature photography**
Photography of plants 778.9
UF Plants—Photography
BT **Nature photography**
Photography—Printing processes 771
BT **Photography—Processing**
Photography—Processing 771

UF Darkroom technique in photography
Photography—Darkroom technique
SA types of photographic processing techniques, e.g. **Photography—Developing and developers**; **Photography—Printing processes**; etc. [to be added as needed]
BT **Photographic chemistry**
NT **Photography—Developing and developers**
Photography—Printing processes
Photography—Retouching 771
UF Retouching (Photography)
**Photography—Scientific applications
778.3**
SA specific applications, e.g. **Medical photography** [to be added as needed]
NT **Medical photography**
Space photography
Photography, Stereoscopic
USE **Three dimensional photography**
Photography, War
USE **War photography**
Photojournalism (May subdiv. geog.)
070.4; 779
UF Journalistic photography
News photography
Photo journalism
BT **Commercial photography**
Journalism
Photography
NT **War photography**
Photomechanical processes 686.2
SA types of photomechanical processes, e.g. **Photoengraving** [to be added as needed]
BT **Illustration of books**
Photography
RT **Photoengraving**
Photometry 535
UF Electric light
BT **Measurement**
NT **Color**
RT **Light**
Optics

Photomicrography   778.3

Use for materials on the photographing of minute objects through a miscroscope. Materials on the photographing of objects of any size to produce minute images are entered under **Microphotography**.

BT   **Photography**
RT   **Microscopes**

Photos
USE   **Photographs**

Photosynthesis   572
BT   **Botany**

Phototherapy   615.8
UF   Electric light
Light—Therapeutic use
BT   **Physical therapy**
Therapeutics
RT   **Radiotherapy**
Ultraviolet rays

Photovoltaic power generation   621.31
UF   Solar cells
BT   **Solar energy**
NT   **Solar batteries**

Phrenology (May subdiv. geog.)   **139**
BT   **Brain**
Head
Psychology
RT   **Mind and body**
Physiognomy

Physical anthropology (May subdiv. geog.)   **599.9**
UF   Biological anthropology
BT   **Anthropology**
Ethnology
NT   **Human origins**

Physical appearance
USE   **Personal appearance**

Physical chemistry   541
UF   Chemistry, Physical and theoretical
Theoretical chemistry
BT   **Chemistry**
Physics
NT   **Atmospheric chemistry**
Atomic theory
Atoms
Catalysis
Colloids
Crystals
Electrochemistry
Molecules
Periodic law
Polymers

Radiochemistry
Solids
Thermodynamics
RT   **Nuclear physics**
Quantum theory

Physical culture
USE   **Physical education**

Physical disabilities
USE   **Disabilities**

Physical education (May subdiv. geog.)   **613.7; 796.07**
UF   Calisthenics
Physical culture
Physical education and training
Physical training
SA   types of sports activities with the subdivision *Training*, e.g. **Soccer—Training**; and names of sports and types of physical exercise [to be added as needed]
BT   **Education**
NT   **Coaching (Athletics)**
Games
Marching drills
Movement education
Physical fitness
Soccer—Training
RT   **Athletics**
Exercise
Gymnastics
Sports

Physical education and training
USE   **Physical education**

Physical education—Medical aspects
USE   **Sports medicine**

Physical examinations (Medicine)
USE   **Periodic health examinations**

Physical fitness (May subdiv. geog.)   **613.7**
UF   Endurance, Physical
Fitness
Physical stamina
Stamina, Physical
SA   classes of persons with the subdivision *Physical fitness*, e.g., **Women—Physical fitness** [to be added as needed]
BT   **Exercise**
Health
Health self-care

Physical fitness—*Continued*

    Physical education

  NT **Bodybuilding**

      Children—Physical fitness

      Kinesiology

      Physical fitness centers

      Posture

      Women—Physical fitness

Physical fitness centers (May subdiv. geog.) **613.7**

  UF Health clubs

      Health spas

      Recreation centers

      Spas

  BT **Physical fitness**

Physical geography (May subdiv. geog.) **910**

  Use for materials on the physical features of the earth's surface and its atmosphere. General materials, frequently school materials, describing the surface of the earth and its interrelationship with various peoples, animals, natural products, and industries are entered under **Geography**.

  BT **Geography**

      Geology

  NT **Deserts**

      Earthquakes

      Geysers

      Glaciers

      Ice

      Icebergs

      Lakes

      Mountains

      Ocean

      Rivers

      Seas

      Volcanoes

      Winds

  RT **Earth**

Physical geography—United States **917.3**

Physical sciences **500.2**

  BT **Science**

  NT **Astronomy**

      Chemistry

      Earth sciences

      Physics

Physical stamina

  USE **Physical fitness**

Physical therapy **615.8**

  UF Physiotherapy

  SA types of physical therapy, e.g. **Hydrotherapy**; and types of disabilities, injuries, or diseases with the subdivision *Physical therapy*, e.g. **Arthritis—Physical therapy** [to be added as needed]

  BT **Therapeutics**

  NT **Baths**

      Electrotherapeutics

      Hydrotherapy

      Massage

      Occupational therapy

      Phototherapy

      Radiotherapy

Physical training

  USE **Physical education**

Physically handicapped (May subdiv. geog.) **362.4**

  UF Crippled people

  SA types of physically handicapped persons, e.g. **Blind**; **Deaf**; etc. [to be added as needed]

  BT **Handicapped**

  NT **Blind**

      Deaf

      Hearing impaired

      Physically handicapped children

  RT **Orthopedics**

Physically handicapped children (May subdiv. geog.) **155.45; 362.4**

  UF Children, Crippled

      Crippled children

  BT **Handicapped children**

      Physically handicapped

Physically handicapped—Housing (May subdiv. geog.) **362.4**

  UF Housing for the physically handicapped

  BT **Housing**

Physically handicapped—Rehabilitation (May subdiv. geog.) **362.4**

  NT **Occupational therapy**

Physicians (May subdiv. geog.) **610.69; 920**

  UF Doctors

  SA types of medical specialists [to be added as needed]

  BT **Medical personnel**

Physicians—*Continued*
  NT **Radiologists**
      Surgeons
      Women physicians
  RT **Medicine**
Physicians—Directories **610.69**
  BT **Directories**
Physicians—Drug use (May subdiv. geog.)
      362.29; 610.69
  UF Drug abusing physicians
      Drug addicted physicians
Physicians—Licenses (May subdiv. geog.)
      344
  BT **Medicine—Law and legislation**
Physicians—Malpractice (May subdiv.
      geog.) **346.03**
  UF Medical errors
  BT **Malpractice**
      Medicine—Law and legislation
Physicists (May subdiv. geog.) **530.092;**
      920
  BT **Scientists**
Physics **530**
  BT **Physical sciences**
      Science
  NT **Astrophysics**
      Biophysics
      Electricity
      Electronics
      Gases
      Geophysics
      Gravitation
      Hydraulics
      Hydrostatics
      Light
      Liquids
      Magnetism
      Matter
      Mechanics
      Music—Acoustics and physics
      Nuclear physics
      Optics
      Physical chemistry
      Pneumatics
      Quantum theory
      Radiation
      Radioactivity
      Relativity (Physics)
      Solids
      Sound
      Statics
      Thermodynamics

      Weight
      Weights and measures
  RT **Dynamics**
Physics—Conferences (May subdiv. geog.)
      530
  UF Physics—Congresses
Physics—Congresses
  USE **Physics—Conferences**
Physics, Terrestrial
  USE **Geophysics**
Physiognomy **138**
  BT **Psychology**
  RT **Face**
      Phrenology
Physiological aspects
  USE types of activities and mental
       conditions with the subdivi-
       sion *Physiological aspects,*
       e.g. **Mental illness—Physio-**
       logical aspects {to be added
       as needed}
Physiological chemistry
  USE **Biochemistry**
Physiological effect
  USE types of drugs, chemicals, or en-
       vironmental phenomena or
       conditions with the subdivi
       sion *Physiological effect,* e.g.
       Alcohol—Physiological effect;
       Radiation—Physiological ef-
       fect; etc. [to be added as
       needed]
Physiological psychology
  USE **Psychophysiology**
Physiological stress
  USE **Stress (Physiology)**
Physiology **571; 612**
    Use for general materials on physiology and
    for materials on human physiology. Materials
    on the physiology of other animals or of
    plants are entered under the appropriate head-
    ing with the subdivision *Physiology.*
  UF Human physiology
  SA names of organs and regions of
       the body, types of plants and
       animals, and classes of per-
       sons with the subdivision
       Physiology, e.g. **Heart—Phys-**
       iology; Reptiles—Physiology;
       etc.; activities and mental
       conditions with the subdivi-
       sion *Physiological aspects,*

Physiology—*Continued*

e.g. **Mental illness—Physiological aspects**; and drugs, chemicals, and environmental phenomena or conditions with the subdivision *Physiological effect*, e.g. **Alcohol—Physiological effect**; **Radiation—Physiological effect**; etc. [to be added as needed]

BT **Biology**
    Medicine
    Science
NT **Blood**
    Body temperature
    Cardiovascular system
    Cells
    Comparative physiology
    Digestion
    Fatigue
    Glands
    Growth
    Health
    Heart—Physiology
    Human locomotion
    Immune system
    Lymphatic system
    Mental illness—Physiological aspects
    Musculoskeletal system
    Nervous system
    Nutrition
    Psychophysiology
    Reproduction
    Reproductive system
    Reptiles—Physiology
    Respiration
    Respiratory system
    Senses and sensation
    Skin
    Stress (Physiology)
RT **Anatomy**
    Human body

Physiology, Comparative
USE **Comparative physiology**

Physiology of plants
USE **Plant physiology**

Physiotherapy
USE **Physical therapy**

Physique
USE **Bodybuilding**

Phytogeography
USE **Plants—Geographical distribution**

Pi   **516.22**
BT **Plane geometry**

Pianists (May subdiv. geog.)   **786.2092; 920**
BT **Instrumentalists**

Piano
USE **Pianos**

Piano music   **786.2**
BT **Instrumental music**
    Music

Pianos (May subdiv. geog.)   **786.2**
UF **Piano**
BT **Percussion instruments**
NT **Keyboards (Musical instruments)**

Pianos—Tuning   **786.2**
BT **Tuning**

Picaresque literature   **800**

Use for individual works, collections, or materials about episodic accounts of the adventures of an engagingly roguish hero.

UF **Picaresque novels**
    Rogues and vagabonds—Fiction
BT **Fiction**
    Literature

Picaresque novels
USE **Picaresque literature**

Picketing
USE **Strikes**

Pickling
USE **Canning and preserving**

Pickup campers
USE **Travel trailers and campers**

Pictographs
USE **Picture writing**

Pictorial works
USE **Pictures**

and subjects, classes of persons, names of wars, and names of cities, states, countries, and named entities, such as individual parks, structures, etc., with the subdivision *Pictorial works*, e.g. **Animals—Pictorial works**; **United States—History—1861-1865, Civil War—Pictorial works**; **Chicago (Ill.)—Pictorial works**;

Pictorial works—*Continued*
>
> **Yosemite National Park (Calif.)—Pictorial works;**
>
> etc.; and names of persons or groups of persons with the subdivisions *Cartoons and caricatures; Pictorial works;* or *Portraits* [to be added as needed]

Picture books
>
> USE **Pictures**

Picture books for children
>
> Use for individual works, collections, or materials about picture books for children.
>
> BT **Children's literature**
> NT **Board books for children**
> **Coloring books**
> **Glow-in-the-dark books**
> **Stories without words**
> **Toy and movable books**
> RT **Illustration of books**

Picture books for children, Wordless
>
> USE **Stories without words**

Picture dictionaries 413
>
> Use for individual works, collections, or materials about picture dictionaries.
>
> UF Dictionaries, Picture
> Word books
> BT **Encyclopedias and dictionaries**

Picture frames and framing 684; 749
>
> UF Framing of pictures
> BT **Decoration and ornament**
> **Handicraft**

Picture galleries
>
> USE **Art museums**
> **Commercial art galleries**

Picture postcards
>
> USE **Postcards**

Picture puzzles 793.73
>
> BT **Puzzles**

Picture telephone
>
> USE **Video telephone**

Picture writing (May subdiv. geog.) 411
>
> Use for materials on the recording of events or the expression of messages by pictures representing actions or facts.
>
> UF Pictographs
> BT **Writing**
> RT **Hieroglyphics**

Pictures 025.17; 760
>
> Use for general materials on the study and use of pictures and for miscellaneous collections of pictures.

> UF Pictorial works
> Picture books
> SA subjects, classes of persons, names of wars, and names of cities, states, countries, and named entities, such as individual parks, structures, etc., with the subdivision *Pictorial works*, e.g. **Animals—Pictorial works; United States—History—1861-1865, Civil War—Pictorial works; Chicago (Ill.)—Pictorial works; Yosemite National Park (Calif.)—Pictorial works;** etc.; and names of persons or groups of persons with the subdivisions *Cartoons and caricatures*; *Pictorial works*; or *Portraits* [to be added as needed]
> BT **Art**
> NT **Cartoons and caricatures**
> **Engraving**
> **Etching**
> **Photographs**
> **Portraits**
> **Views**
> RT **Painting**

Pies 641.8652
>
> BT **Baking**
> **Cooking**

Pigments 547; 667; 751.2
>
> NT **Dyes and dyeing**
> RT **Color**
> **Paint**

Pigs (May subdiv. geog.) 599.63; 636.4
>
> UF Hogs
> Swine
> BT **Domestic animals**
> **Mammals**

Pilates method 613.7
>
> BT **Exercise**

Pilgrims and pilgrimages (May subdiv. geog.) 203; 263
>
> BT **Voyages and travels**
> RT **Shrines**

Pilgrims (New England colonists) 974.4
>
> BT **Puritans**
> **United States—History—1600-1775, Colonial period**

Pilot charts
USE **Nautical charts**
Pilot guides   623.89
UF   Coast pilot guides
BT   **Navigation**
Piloting
USE   types of aircraft with the subdivision *Piloting,* e.g. **Airplanes—Piloting** [to be added as needed]
Piloting (Astronautics)
USE   **Space vehicles—Piloting**
Pilots
USE   **Air pilots**
         Ship pilots
Pilots and pilotage
USE   **Navigation**
         Ship pilots
Piltdown forgery   569.9
UF   Piltdown man
BT   **Forgery**
         Fossil hominids
Piltdown man
USE   **Piltdown forgery**
Pimples (Acne)
USE   **Acne**
Ping-pong
USE   **Table tennis**
Pioneer life
USE   **Frontier and pioneer life**
Pipe fitting   696
RT   **Plumbing**
Pipe lines
USE   **Pipelines**
Pipe organs
USE   **Organs (Musical instruments)**
Pipelines (May subdiv. geog.)   **388.5; 621.8**
UF   Pipe lines
SA   types of pipelines [to be added as needed]
BT   **Hydraulic structures**
         Transportation
NT   **Petroleum pipelines**
Pipes, Tobacco
USE   **Tobacco pipes**
Piracy
USE   **Pirates**
Pirates (May subdiv. geog.)   **364.16; 910.4**

UF   Buccaneers
         Corsairs
         Piracy
BT   **Criminals**
         International law
         Maritime law
         Naval history
NT   **Privateering**
Pistols
USE   **Handguns**
Pity
USE   **Sympathy**
Place names
USE   **Geographic names**
Places of retirement
USE   **Retirement communities**
Places of work
USE   **Work environment**
Plagiarism   364.16
BT   **Authorship**
         Offenses against property
Plague (May subdiv. geog.)   **616.9**
UF   Black death
         Bubonic plague
BT   **Communicable diseases**
         Epidemics
Plain chant
USE   **Chants (Plain, Gregorian, etc.)**
Plainsong
USE   **Chants (Plain, Gregorian, etc.)**
Plane crashes
USE   **Aircraft accidents**
Plane geometry   516.22
UF   Geometry, Plane
BT   **Geometry**
NT   **Pi**
Plane trigonometry
USE   **Trigonometry**
Planetariums (May subdiv. geog.)   **520.74**
BT   **Astronomy**
Planetary satellites
USE   **Satellites**
Planetoids
USE   **Asteroids**
Planets   523.4
BT   **Astronomy**
         Solar system
NT   **Earth**
         Extrasolar planets
         Jupiter (Planet)

Planets—*Continued*

    Life on other planets

    Mars (Planet)

    Mercury (Planet)

    Neptune (Planet)

    Pluto (Dwarf planet)

    Saturn (Planet)

    Uranus (Planet)

    Venus (Planet)

  RT **Asteroids**

Planets—Exploration 523.4

  SA names of planets with the subdivision *Exploration* [to be added as needed]

  BT **Outer space—Exploration**

  NT **Mars (Planet)—Exploration**

Planets—Satellites

  USE **Satellites**

Planing machines 621.9

  BT **Machine tools**

Planned communities (May subdiv. geog.) **307.76**

  UF Housing estates

      New communities

      Residential developments

  BT **City planning**

Planned parenthood

  USE **Birth control**

Planning (May subdiv. geog.) **338.9; 658.4**

  SA types of planning, e.g. **Curriculum planning**; and types of activities, facilities, industries, services, and undertakings with the subdivision *Planning*, e.g. **Transportation—Planning** [to be added as needed]

  BT **Creation (Literary, artistic, etc.)**

      Executive ability

      Management

  NT **City planning**

      Curriculum planning

      Economic policy

      Estate planning

      Regional planning

      Social policy

      Strategic planning

      Tax planning

      Transportation—Planning

Plans

  USE **Geometrical drawing**

      Map drawing

      Maps

      Mechanical drawing

Plant anatomy

  USE **Plants—Anatomy**

Plant breeding 631.5

  Use for materials on attempts to produce new or improved varieties of plants through controlled reproduction. Materials on the continuance or multiplication of plants by successive production are entered under **Plant propagation**.

  UF Hybridization

  BT **Agriculture**

      Breeding

      Horticulture

  RT **Plant propagation**

Plant chemistry

  USE **Botanical chemistry**

      Plants—Analysis

Plant classification

  USE **Botany—Classification**

Plant closings

  USE **Plant shutdowns**

Plant conservation (May subdiv. geog.) **333.95; 639.9**

  UF Conservation of plants

      Plants—Conservation

      Protection of plants

      Wild flowers—Conservation

  BT **Conservation of natural resources**

      Economic botany

      Endangered species

      Nature conservation

  NT **Scarecrows**

  RT **Rare plants**

Plant defenses 581.4

  UF Defense mechanisms of plants

      Self-defense in plants

      Self-protection in plants

  BT **Plant ecology**

  RT **Poisonous plants**

Plant diseases (May subdiv. geog.) **571.9; 632**

  UF Botany—Pathology

      Diseases and pests

      Diseases of plants

      Garden pests

      Plant pathology

      Plants—Diseases

Plant diseases—*Continued*

    SA   types of crops, plants, trees, etc., with the subdivision *Diseases and pests* [to be added as needed]

    BT   **Agricultural pests**

          Diseases

          Fungi

    NT   **Fruit—Diseases and pests**

Plant distribution

    USE   **Plants—Geographical distribution**

Plant-eating animals

    USE   **Herbivores**

Plant ecology (May subdiv. geog.)   **581.7**

    UF   Botany—Ecology

          Plants—Ecology

    SA   types of plants and crops with the subdivision *Ecology* [to be added as needed]

    BT   **Ecology**

    NT   **Desert plants**

          Forest plants

          Mountain plants

          Plant defenses

    RT   **Forest influences**

          Symbiosis

Plant introduction (May subdiv. geog.)   **581.6; 631.5**

    BT   **Economic botany**

Plant lore

    USE   **Plants—Folklore**

Plant nutrition

    USE   **Plants—Nutrition**

Plant pathology

    USE   **Plant diseases**

Plant physiology   **571.2**

    UF   Botany—Physiology

          Physiology of plants

    BT   **Botany**

    NT   **Fertilization of plants**

          Germination

          Plants—Growth

          Plants—Nutrition

Plant propagation   **631.5**

    Use for materials on the continuance or multiplication of plants by successive production. Materials on attempts to produce new or improved varieties of plants through controlled reproduction are entered under **Plant breeding**.

    UF   Plants—Propagation

          Propagation of plants

    BT   **Fruit culture**

          Gardening

          Nurseries (Horticulture)

    NT   **Grafting**

          Seeds

    RT   **Plant breeding**

Plant shutdowns (May subdiv. geog.)   **338.6**

    UF   Closing of factories

          Plant closings

    BT   **Factories**

          Unemployment

Plant taxonomy

    USE   **Botany—Classification**

Plantation life (May subdiv. geog.)   **307.72**

    BT   **Country life**

Plantations (May subdiv. geog.)   **307.72**

    BT   **Farms**

Planting

    USE   **Agriculture**

          Gardening

          Landscape gardening

          Tree planting

Plants (May subdiv. geog.)   **580**

    Use for nonscientific materials. Materials on the science of plants are entered under **Botany**. Subdivisions used under this heading may be used under the names of orders, classes, or individual species of plants.

    UF   Flora

          Vegetable kingdom

    SA   types of plants characterized by their physical characteristics, environment, or use, e.g. **Climbing plants; Desert plants; Forage plants**; etc.; and names of botanical categories of plants, e.g. **Ferns** [to be added as needed]

    NT   **Aromatic plants**

          Bulbs

          Carnivorous plants

          Climbing plants

          Cultivated plants

          Desert plants

          Edible plants

          Ferns

          Fertilization of plants

          Flowers

          Forage plants

          Forest plants

          Fossil plants

Plants—*Continued*
>> Freshwater plants
>> Fruit
>> Fungi
>> Grasses
>> Herbs
>> Horticulture
>> House plants
>> Leaves
>> Marine plants
>> Mosses
>> Mountain plants
>> Mushrooms
>> Native plants
>> Poisonous plants
>> Popular plant names
>> Rare plants
>> Seeds
>> Shrubs
>> Tobacco
>> Trees
>> Vegetables
>> Weeds
> RT **Botany**
>> **Gardening**
>> **Herbicides**

Plants—Analysis   572
> UF   Plant chemistry
>> Plants—Chemical analysis
> BT   **Botanical chemistry**

Plants—Anatomy   571.3
> UF   Anatomy of plants
>> Botany—Anatomy
>> Botany—Structure
>> Plant anatomy
> BT   **Anatomy**
>> **Botany**

Plants—Chemical analysis
> USE   **Plants—Analysis**

Plants—Classification
> USE   **Botany—Classification**

Plants—Collection and preservation (May subdiv. geog.)   **580.75**
> UF   Botanical specimens—Collection and preservation
>> Collections of natural specimens
>> Herbaria
>> Preservation of botanical specimens
>> Specimens, Preservation of
> BT   **Collectors and collecting**
> NT   **Flowers—Drying**

Plants—Conservation
> USE   **Plant conservation**

Plants, Cultivated
> USE   **Cultivated plants**

Plants—Diseases
> USE   **Plant diseases**

Plants—Ecology
> USE   **Plant ecology**

Plants, Edible
> USE   **Edible plants**

Plants, Extinct
> USE   **Fossil plants**

Plants—Fertilization
> USE   **Fertilization of plants**

Plants—Folklore (May subdiv. geog.)
>> **398.24**
> UF   Plant lore
> BT   **Folklore**
> NT   **Ethnobotany**
>> **Language of flowers**

Plants, Fossil
> USE   **Fossil plants**

Plants—Geographical distribution   581.9
> UF   Geographical distribution of plants
>> Phytogeography
>> Plant distribution
> SA   types of plants with the subdivision *Geographical distribution* [to be added as needed]
> BT   **Biogeography**

Plants—Growth   571.8
> BT   **Plant physiology**

Plants in art   704.9
> SA   types of plants in art, e.g. **Flowers in art** [to be added as needed]
> BT   **Art—Themes**
> RT   **Botanical illustration**

Plants, Industrial
> USE   **Factories**

Plants, Medicinal
> USE   **Medical botany**

Plants—Names
> USE   **Botany—Nomenclature**
>> **Popular plant names**

Plants—Nomenclature
> USE   **Botany—Nomenclature**
>> **Popular plant names**

Plants—Nutrition   575.7; 631.5
> UF   Plant nutrition

Plants—Nutrition—_Continued_
    BT   **Nutrition**
          Plant physiology
Plants, Ornamental
    USE **Ornamental plants**
Plants—Photography
    USE **Photography of plants**
Plants—Propagation
    USE **Plant propagation**
Plants—Soilless culture
    USE **Hydroponics**
Plants—United States   581.973
    UF   Botany—United States
Plaster and plastering   693
    UF   Plastering
    BT   **Masonry**
    NT   **Cement**
          Concrete
          Mortar
          Stucco
Plaster casts   731.4
    UF   Casting
          Casts, Plaster
    BT   **Sculpture**
Plastering
    USE **Plaster and plastering**
Plastic industries
    USE **Plastics industry**
Plastic materials
    USE **Plastics**
Plastic surgery (May subdiv. geog.)
          617.9
    UF   Cosmetic surgery
          Reconstructive surgery
          Surgery, Plastic
    BT   **Surgery**
Plastics (May subdiv. geog.)   **668.4**
    UF   Plastic materials
    SA   names of specific plastics [to be
          added as needed]
    BT   **Polymers**
          Synthetic products
    NT   **Gums and resins**
          Synthetic rubber
    RT   **Plastics industry**
Plastics craft   745.57
    BT   **Handicraft**
Plastics industry (May subdiv. geog.)
          338.4; 668.4
    UF   Plastic industries
    BT   **Chemical industry**
    RT   **Plastics**

Plate   739.2
    UF   Gold plate
          Silver plate
    BT   **Goldwork**
          Silverwork
    NT   **Hallmarks**
          Sheffield plate
Plate metalwork   671.8
    BT   **Metalwork**
          Sheet metalwork
Plate tectonics   551.1
    BT   **Earth—Crust**
          Geophysics
    RT   **Continental drift**
          Submarine geology
Platforms, Drilling
    USE **Drilling platforms**
Play   790
    BT   **Recreation**
    NT   **Finger play**
          Imaginary playmates
          Sports
    RT   **Amusements**
          Games
Play centers
    USE **Community centers**
          Playgrounds
Play direction (Theater)
    USE **Theater—Production and di-
          rection**
Play production
    USE **Amateur theater**
          **Theater—Production and di-
          rection**
Play—Therapeutic use
    USE **Play therapy**
Play therapy   616.89; 618.9
    UF   Play—Therapeutic use
    BT   **Therapeutics**
Play writing
    USE **Drama—Technique**
          **Motion picture plays—Tech-
          nique**
          Radio plays—Technique
          Television plays—Technique
Playbills
    USE **Film posters**
Playgrounds (May subdiv. geog.)   **796.06**
    UF   Play centers
          Public playgrounds
          School playgrounds

Playgrounds—*Continued*
    BT   **Recreation**
           Sports facilities
    RT   **Community centers**
           Parks
Playhouses
    USE **Theaters**
Playing cards (May subdiv. geog.)   **795.4**
    UF   Cards, Playing
    NT   **Tarot**
    RT   **Card games**
Plays
    USE **Drama—Collections**
          One act plays
Plays for children
    USE **Children's plays**
Playwrights
    USE **Dramatists**
Playwriting
    USE **Drama—Technique**
          Motion picture plays—Technique
          Radio plays—Technique
          Television plays—Technique
Pleasure   **152.4**
    BT   **Emotions**
           Joy and sorrow
           Senses and sensation
    RT   **Happiness**
           Pain
Plot-your-own stories   **808.3**
    Use for individual works, collections, or materials about plot-your-own stories.
    UF   Choose-your-own story plots
          Making-choices stories
          Multiple plot stories
          Which-way stories
    BT   **Children's literature**
           Fiction
           Literary recreations
Plots (Drama, fiction, etc.)
    USE **Stories, plots, etc.**
Plows   **631.3**
    BT   **Agricultural machinery**
Plumbing   **696**
    BT   **Building**
    NT   **Sewerage**
    RT   **House drainage**
           Household sanitation
           Pipe fitting
Plural pregnancy
    USE **Multiple pregnancy**

Pluralism (Social sciences) (May subdiv. geog.)   **305.8**
    Use for materials on the coexistence of several distinct ethnic, religious, or cultural groups within one society. Materials on the presence of two distinct cultures within a single country or region are entered under **Biculturalism**. Materials on policies or programs that foster the preservation of various cultures or cultural identities within a unified society are entered under **Multiculturalism**.
    UF   Ethnic diversity
    BT   **Culture**
    NT   **Biculturalism**
    RT   **Ethnic relations**
           Ethnicity
           Multiculturalism
           Race relations
Pluto (Dwarf planet)   **523.48**
    BT   **Planets**
Plywood   **674**
    BT   **Wood**
PMS (Gynecology)
    USE **Premenstrual syndrome**
Pneumatic transmission
    USE **Compressed air**
Pneumatics   **533; 621.5**
    BT   **Physics**
    NT   **Aerodynamics**
           Compressed air
           Sound
    RT   **Gases**
Pneumonia   **616.2**
    BT   **Lungs—Diseases**
Pocket billiards
    USE **Pool (Game)**
Pocket calculators
    USE **Calculators**
Podcasting   **006.7**
    BT   **Multimedia**
           Video recordings
Podiatry   **617.5**
    UF   Chiropody
    BT   **Medicine**
    NT   **Foot—Care**
    RT   **Foot—Wounds and injuries**
Poetics   **808.1**
    Use for materials on the art and technique of poetry. General materials on the appreciation, philosophy, etc., of poetry are entered under **Poetry**.
    UF   Poetry—Technique
    BT   **Poetry**
    NT   **Rhyme**
           Rhythm

Poetics—*Continued*

Versification

Poetry 809.1

Use for general materials on poetry, not for individual works. Materials on the history and criticism of poetry from more than one literature are entered under **Poetry—History and criticism**. Materials on the art and technique of poetry are entered under **Poetics**. Collections of poetry are entered under **Poetry—Collections**; **English poetry—Collections**; etc.

UF   Poetry—Philosophy

SA   types of poetry, e.g. **Haiku**; and subjects, historical events, names of places, ethnic groups, classes of persons, and names of individual persons with the subdivision *Poetry*, to express the theme or subject content of collections of poetry, e.g. **Animals—Poetry**; **World War, 1939-1945—Poetry**; **Napoleon I, Emperor of the French, 1769-1821—Poetry**; etc. [to be added as needed]

BT   **Literature**

NT   **American poetry**

      Ballads

      Children's poetry

      Chinese poetry

      Didactic poetry

      Eddas

      Elegiac poetry

      English poetry

      Epistolary poetry

      Erotic poetry

      Fantasy poetry

      Free verse

      French poetry

      Haiku

      Humorous poetry

      Indian poetry

      Indian poetry (English)

      Islamic poetry

      Love poetry

      Narrative poetry

      Nature poetry

      Pastoral poetry

      Patriotic poetry

      Poetics

      Religious poetry

      Science fiction poetry

      Sea poetry

      Songs

      Sonnets

      War poetry

Poetry and music

USE   **Music and literature**

Poetry—Collections 808.81

UF   Poetry—Selections

      Rhymes

Poetry—Editing 070.5

BT   **Editing**

Poetry for children

USE   **Children's poetry**

      Nursery rhymes

Poetry, Historical

USE   **Historical poetry**

Poetry—History and criticism 809.1

Poetry—Memorizing 153.1

BT   **Mnemonics**

Poetry—Philosophy

USE   **Poetry**

Poetry—Selections

USE   **Poetry—Collections**

Poetry—Technique

USE   **Poetics**

Poets 809.1; 920

Use for materials on the lives of several poets, not limited to a single national literature.

SA   poets of particular countries, e.g. **American poets** [to be added as needed]

BT   **Authors**

NT   **American poets**

      English poets

      Lyricists

      Minstrels

      Troubadours

Poets, American

USE   **American poets**

Poison ivy 583

BT   **Poisonous plants**

Poisonous animals (May subdiv. geog.) **591.6**

SA   types of poisonous animals, e.g. **Rattlesnakes** [to be added as needed]

BT   **Animals**

      Dangerous animals

      Economic zoology

      Poisons and poisoning

NT   **Rattlesnakes**

Poisonous gases 363.17

Poisonous gases—*Continued*
- UF   Asphyxiating gases
  - Gases, Asphyxiating and poisonous
- BT   **Gases**
  - **Poisons and poisoning**
- NT   **Radon**

Poisonous gases—War use
- USE   **Chemical warfare**

Poisonous plants (May subdiv. geog.) **581.6**
- UF   Toxic plants
- SA   types of poisonous plants, e.g. **Poison ivy** [to be added as needed]
- BT   **Economic botany**
  - **Plants**
  - **Poisons and poisoning**
- NT   **Poison ivy**
- RT   **Plant defenses**

Poisonous substances
- USE   **Poisons and poisoning**

Poisons and poisoning   **363.17; 615.9**

Use for materials on poisonous substances and their use. Materials on the science that treats of poisons and their antidotes are entered under **Toxicology**.
- UF   Poisonous substances
  - Toxic substances
- SA   types of poisons or poisoning, e.g. **Lead poisoning**; and types of poisonous substances with the subdivision *Toxicology*, for materials on the influence of particular substances on humans and animals, e.g. **Insecticides—Toxicology** [to be added as needed]
- BT   **Accidents**
  - **Hazardous substances**
  - **Homicide**
  - **Medical jurisprudence**
- NT   **Food poisoning**
  - **Insecticides—Toxicology**
  - **Lead poisoning**
  - **Pesticides**
  - **Poisonous animals**
  - **Poisonous gases**
  - **Poisonous plants**
- RT   **Toxicology**

Poker   **795.412**
- BT   **Card games**

Poland   **943.8**

May be subdivided like United States except for History.

Polar expeditions
- USE   **Antarctica—Exploration**
  - **Arctic regions—Exploration**
  - **Scientific expeditions**

Polar lights
- USE   **Auroras**

Polar regions   **998**

Use for materials on both the Antarctic and Arctic regions.
- NT   **Antarctica**
  - **Arctic regions**
  - **North Pole**
  - **South Pole**

Polarity
- USE   **Opposites**

Police (May subdiv. geog.)   **363.2**
- UF   Police officers
  - Policemen
- BT   **Administration of criminal justice**
  - **Law enforcement**
- NT   **Animals in police work**
  - **Border patrols**
  - **Detectives**
  - **Police brutality**
  - **Police corruption**
  - **Policewomen**
  - **Secret service**
  - **State police**
- RT   **Crime**
  - **Criminal investigation**

Police brutality (May subdiv. geog.) **363.2**
- UF   Police—Complaints against
  - Police cruelty
  - Police repression
  - Police violence
- BT   **Police**

Police—Complaints against
- USE   **Police brutality**
  - **Police corruption**

Police—Corrupt practices
- USE   **Police corruption**

Police corruption (May subdiv. geog.) **363.2**
- UF   Corruption, Police
  - Police—Complaints against
  - Police—Corrupt practices

Police corruption—*Continued*
  BT **Misconduct in office**
      Police
Police cruelty
  USE **Police brutality**
Police, International
  USE **International police**
Police officers
  USE **Police**
Police repression
  USE **Police brutality**
Police, State
  USE **State police**
Police—United States   363.20973
  UF United States—Police
Police violence
  USE **Police brutality**
Policemen
  USE **Police**
Policewomen (May subdiv. geog.)   363.2
  UF Women police officers
  BT **Police**
      Women
Polio
  USE **Poliomyelitis**
Poliomyelitis (May subdiv. geog.)   616.8
  UF Infantile paralysis
      Polio
  BT **Diseases**
Poliomyelitis vaccine   614.4; 615
  UF Live poliovirus vaccine
      Sabin vaccine
      Salk vaccine
  BT **Vaccination**
Polishing
  USE **Grinding and polishing**
Politeness
  USE **Courtesy**
      Etiquette
Political action committees (May subdiv.
    geog.)   322.4; 324
  Use for materials on special interest groups
  that support sympathetic candidates for public
  office through campaign contributions. Materi-
  als on groups that promote their own interests
  with public officials are entered under **Lobby-
  ing**.
  UF Interest groups
      PACs (Political action commit-
        tees)
      Pressure groups
  BT **Political participation**
  RT **Lobbying**

Political activists (May subdiv. geog.)
    323
  BT **Political participation**
Political activity
  USE **Political participation**
      and classes of persons, types of
      industries, military services,
      and religious denominations,
      and names of corporate
      bodies and families with the
      subdivision *Political activity,*
      e.g. **Women—Political activi-
      ty** [to be added as needed]
Political aspects
  USE subjects with the subdivision *Po-
      litical aspects,* e.g. **Ethnic re-
      lations—Political aspects** [to
      be added as needed]
Political asylum
  USE **Asylum**
Political behavior
  USE **Political participation**
      Political psychology
Political boundaries
  USE **Boundaries**
Political campaign literature
  USE **Campaign literature**
Political campaigns
  USE **Politics**
Political conventions (May subdiv. geog.)
    324.5
  UF Conventions, Political
  BT **Conferences**
  NT **Primaries**
  RT **Political parties**
Political correctness   306
  BT **Ideology**
Political corruption (May subdiv. geog.)
    324; 353.4
  UF Boss rule
      Corruption in politics
      Graft in politics
      Political scandals
      Politics—Corrupt practices
      Spoils system
  BT **Conflict of interests**
      Political crimes and offenses
      Political ethics
      Politics
  NT **Whistle blowing**
  RT **Misconduct in office**

Political crimes and offenses (May subdiv. geog.) **364.1**
- UF   Crimes, Political
-       Sedition
- BT   **Criminal law**
-       **Political ethics**
-       **Subversive activities**
- NT   **Anarchism and anarchists**
-       **Assassination**
-       **Bombings**
-       **Concentration camps**
-       **Conspiracies**
-       **Political corruption**
-       **Political prisoners**
-       **Terrorism**
-       **Treason**

Political defectors
- USE   **Defectors**

Political economy
- USE   **Economics**

Political ethics (May subdiv. geog.)   **172**
- BT   **Ethics**
-       **Political science**
-       **Politics**
-       **Social ethics**
- NT   **Citizenship**
-       **Conflict of interests**
-       **Political corruption**
-       **Political crimes and offenses**
-       **Resistance to government**

Political extremism
- USE   **Radicalism**

Political geography
- USE   **Boundaries**
-       **Geopolitics**

Political participation (May subdiv. geog.) **323**
- UF   Citizen participation
-       Civic involvement
-       Community action
-       Mass political behavior
-       Political activity
-       Political behavior
- SA   subjects designating government activity with the subdivision *Citizen participation*, e.g. **Crime prevention—Citizen participation**; and corporate bodies, families, classes of persons, industries, military services, and religious denom-inations with the subdivision *Political activity*, e.g. **Women-en—Political activity** [to be added as needed]
- BT   **Politics**
- NT   **African Americans—Political activity**
-       **Blacks—Political activity**
-       **City planning—Citizen participation**
-       **Clergy—Political activity**
-       **College students—Political activity**
-       **Crime prevention—Citizen participation**
-       **Jews—Political activity**
-       **Political action committees**
-       **Political activists**
-       **Students—Political activity**
-       **Women—Political activity**
- RT   **Social action**

Political parties (May subdiv. geog.) **324.2**
- UF   Parties, Political
- SA   names of parties [to be added as needed]
- BT   **Political science**
-       **Politics**
- NT   **Democratic Party (U.S.)**
-       **Politics**
-       **Republican Party (U.S.)**
-       **Right and left (Political science)**
-       **Third parties (United States politics)**
- RT   **Political conventions**

Political parties—Finance
- USE   **Campaign funds**

Political prisoners (May subdiv. geog.) **365**
- UF   Prisoners of conscience
- BT   **Political crimes and offenses**
-       **Prisoners**

Political psychology (May subdiv. geog.) **302**
- UF   Mass political behavior
-       Political behavior
-       Politics—Psychological aspects
- BT   **Political science**
-       **Psychology**
-       **Social psychology**

Political psychology—*Continued*
- NT **Propaganda**
  Public opinion

Political refugees (May subdiv. geog.)
  325
- UF Displaced persons
  Refugees, Political
- SA refugees of particular countries, geographic regions, or ethnic groups, e.g. **Vietnamese refugees**; **Arab refugees**; etc., and names of wars with the subdivision *Refugees*, e.g. **World War, 1939-1945—Refugees** [to be added as needed]
- BT **Asylum**
  International law
  International relations
  Refugees
- NT **Defectors**
  Exiles
  World War, 1939-1945—Refugees

Political satire (May subdiv. geog.)
  808.7; 808.87
- BT **Satire**

Political scandals
- USE **Political corruption**

Political science (May subdiv. geog.)
  320

Use for materials on the science of politics. Materials on the various aspects of practical politics, such as electioneering, political machines, etc., are entered under **Politics**. Materials on the political processes of particular regions, countries, cities, etc., are entered under the place with the subdivision *Politics and government*.

- UF Civics
  Civil government
  Commonwealth, The
  Government
  Political theory
- SA movements in political philosophy, e.g. **Marxism**; topics with the subdivision *Political aspects*, e.g. **Ethnic relations—Political aspects**; and names of continents, areas, countries, cities, etc., and native peoples with the subdivision *Politics and government*, e.g. **United States—Politics and government**; **Native Americans—Politics and government** [to be added as needed]
- BT **Social sciences**
- NT **Anarchism and anarchists**
  Aristocracy
  Authority
  Bureaucracy
  Citizenship
  Civil rights
  Civil service
  Collectivism
  Communism
  Comparative government
  Conservatism
  Democracy
  Equality
  Executive power
  Federal government
  Freedom
  Geopolitics
  Ideology
  Imperialism
  Individualism
  Islam and politics
  Law
  Legislation
  Liberalism
  Local government
  Marxism
  Monarchy
  Municipal government
  Nationalism
  Nations
  Political ethics
  Political parties
  Political psychology
  Postcolonialism
  Power (Social sciences)
  Progressivism (United States politics)
  Public administration
  Public opinion
  Radicalism
  Representative government and representation
  Republics
  Resistance to government
  Revolutions

Political science—*Continued*
>> **Right and left (Political science)**
>> **Separation of powers**
>> **Social contract**
>> **Socialism**
>> **Sovereignty**
>> **State governments**
>> **States' rights**
>> **Suffrage**
>> **Taxation**
>> **Theocracy**
>> **Totalitarianism**
>> **Tribal government**
>> **United States—Politics and government**
>> **Utopias**
>> **World politics**
> RT **Politics**
>> **State, The**

Political science—Early works to 1800
> (May subdiv. geog.)   320

Political science—Religious aspects
> USE **Religion and politics**

Political theory
> USE **Political science**

Political violence
> USE **Sabotage**
>> **Terrorism**

Politicians (May subdiv. geog.)
> 324.2092; 920
> BT **Statesmen**
> NT **Women politicians**

Politicians—United States   324.2092; 920
> UF American politicians
>> United States—Politicians

Politics   324.7
> Use for materials on the various aspects of practical politics, such as electioneering, political machines, etc. Materials on the science of politics are entered under **Political science**.
> UF Campaigns, Political
>> Electioneering
>> Political campaigns
>> Politics, Practical
>> Practical politics
> SA subjects with the subdivision *Political aspects*, e.g. **Ethnic relations—Political aspects**; names of continents, areas, countries, cities, etc., and na-

tive peoples, with the subdivision *Politics and government*; and ethnic groups and classes of persons with the subdivision *Political activity*, e.g. **College students—Political activity** [to be added as needed]
> BT **Political parties**
> NT **Arab countries—Politics and government**
>> **Asia—Politics and government**
>> **Business and politics**
>> **Campaign funds**
>> **Campaign literature**
>> **Chicago (Ill.)—Politics and government**
>> **Elections**
>> **Latin America—Politics and government**
>> **Lobbying**
>> **Native Americans—Politics and government**
>> **Political corruption**
>> **Political ethics**
>> **Political participation**
>> **Political parties**
>> **Primaries**
>> **Regionalism**
>> **Religion and politics**
>> **Television and politics**
>> **United States—Politics and government**
> RT **Political science**

Politics and business
> USE **Business and politics**

Politics and Christianity
> USE **Christianity and politics**

Politics and government
> USE names of continents, areas, countries, cities, etc., and native peoples with the subdivision *Politics and government,* e.g. **United States—Politics and government; Arab countries—Politics and government; Native Americans—Politics and government;** etc. [to be added as needed]

Politics and Islam
USE **Islam and politics**
Politics and religion
USE **Religion and politics**
Politics and students
USE **Students—Political activity**
Politics and television
USE **Television and politics**
Politics—Corrupt practices
USE **Political corruption**
Politics, Practical
USE **Politics**
Politics—Psychological aspects
USE **Political psychology**
Politics—Religious aspects
USE **Religion and politics**
Polity, Ecclesiastical
USE **Church polity**
Pollen as food 641.3
BT **Food**
Pollination
USE **Fertilization of plants**
Polls
USE **Elections**
Public opinion polls
Pollution (May subdiv. geog.) 304.2; 363.73
UF Chemical pollution
Contamination of environment
Environmental pollution
SA types of pollution, e.g. **Air pollution** [to be added as needed]
BT **Environmental health**
Human influence on nature
Public health
Sanitary engineering
Sanitation
NT **Air pollution**
Noise pollution
Pesticides—Environmental aspects
Radioactive pollution
Space debris
Water pollution
RT **Environmental protection**
Hazardous wastes
Industrial waste
Pollution control industry
Refuse and refuse disposal

Pollution control
USE **Pollution control industry**
Pollution control devices (Motor vehicles)
USE **Automobiles—Pollution control devices**
Pollution control industry (May subdiv. geog.) 338.4; 363.73
UF Pollution control
Pollution—Prevention
BT **Industries**
NT **Automobiles—Pollution control devices**
Recycling
Refuse and refuse disposal
RT **Pollution**
Pollution—Mathematical models 304.2; 363.73
BT **Mathematical models**
Pollution of air
USE **Air pollution**
Pollution of water
USE **Water pollution**
Pollution—Prevention
USE **Pollution control industry**
Pollution, Radioactive
USE **Radioactive pollution**
Poltergeists
USE **Ghosts**
Polygamy (May subdiv. geog.) 306.84
BT **Marriage**
Polyglot dictionaries 413
Use for individual works, collections, or materials about polyglot dictionaries.
UF Dictionaries, Multilingual
Dictionaries, Polyglot
Multilingual dictionaries
Multilingual glossaries, phrase books, etc.
Polyglot glossaries, phrase books, etc.
BT **Encyclopedias and dictionaries**
Polyglot glossaries, phrase books, etc.
USE **Polyglot dictionaries**
Polygraph
USE **Lie detectors and detection**
Polymer clay craft 731.2; 738.1; 745.57
BT **Handicraft**
Polymerization
USE **Polymers**
Polymers 541; 547; 668.9
UF Polymerization

Polymers—*Continued*
    SA   types of polymers, e.g. **Plastics**
            [to be added as needed]
    BT   **Organic compounds—Synthesis**
            Physical chemistry
    NT   **Plastics**
Polynucleotides
    USE   **Nucleic acids**
Polytheism (May subdiv. geog.)   **211**
    BT   **Religion**
            Theism
    RT   **God**
            Gods and goddesses
Pomp
    USE   **Parades**
Pompeii (Extinct city)   **937**
    BT   **Extinct cities—Italy**
            Italy—Antiquities
Pond ecology (May subdiv. geog.)
            577.63
    BT   **Ecology**
Ponds (May subdiv. geog.)   **551.48**
    BT   **Water**
Ponies (May subdiv. geog.)   **636.1**
    UF   Foals
    BT   **Horses**
Pontiac's Conspiracy, 1763-1765   **973.2**
    BT   **Native Americans—Wars**
            United States—History—1600-
            1775, Colonial period
Pony express (May subdiv. geog.)   **383**
    BT   **Express service**
            Postal service
Pool (Game) (May subdiv. geog.)
            794.73
    UF   Pocket billiards
    BT   **Billiards**
Pools
    USE   **Swimming pools**
Poor (May subdiv. geog.)   **305.5; 362.5**
    UF   Poor people
            Poor persons
    BT   **Poverty**
            Public welfare
    NT   **Begging**
            Homeless persons
            Tramps
            Unemployed
Poor—Medical care (May subdiv. geog.)
            362.1
    UF   Medical care for the poor
    BT   **Medical care**

    NT   **Medicaid**
Poor people
    USE   **Poor**
Poor persons
    USE   **Poor**
Poor relief
    USE   **Charities**
            Domestic economic assistance
            Public welfare
Pop art   **709.04**
    BT   **Art**
Pop culture
    USE   **Popular culture**
Pop-up books
    USE   **Toy and movable books**
Popes   **262; 920**
    UF   Holy See
    BT   **Church history**
    RT   **Papacy**
Popes—Infallibility   **262**
    UF   Infallibility of the Pope
Popes—Temporal power   **262**
    UF   Temporal power of the Pope
    BT   **Church history**
Popes—Travel
    USE   **Papal visits**
Popes—Voyages and travels
    USE   **Papal visits**
Popular arts
    USE   **Popular culture**
Popular culture (May subdiv. geog.)
            306.4

    Use for materials on literature, art, music, motion pictures, etc., produced for a mass audience. General materials on learning and scholarship, literature, the arts, etc., are entered under **Intellectual life**.

    UF   Mass culture
            Pop culture
            Popular arts
    BT   **Communication**
            Culture
            Intellectual life
            Recreation
    NT   **Fads**
            Sex in popular culture
            Violence in popular culture
    RT   **Mass media**
Popular culture—Chicago (Ill.)   **977.3**
    UF   Chicago (Ill.)—Popular culture
Popular culture—United States   **973**
    UF   United States—Popular culture

Popular culture—United States—*Continued*
- NT **Americana**
- **Hip-hop culture**

Popular government
- USE **Democracy**

Popular medicine (May subdiv. geog.)
616.02

Use for medical books written for the layman.
- UF Medicine, Popular
- BT **Medicine**
- NT **Traditional medicine**
- RT **Health self-care**

Popular music (May subdiv. geog.)
781.64; 782.42164
- UF Popular songs
- SA types of popular music [to be added as needed]
- BT **Music**
- **Songs**
- NT **Blues music**
- **Country music**
- **Gospel music**
- **Rap music**
- **Reggae music**
- **Rock music**

Popular music—Texts
- USE **Popular song lyrics**

Popular music—Writing and publishing
070.5; 781.3
- UF Song writing
- Songwriting
- BT **Composition (Music)**

Popular plant names   580.1

Use for materials on the common or vernacular names of plants. Systematically derived lists of names or designations of plants and materials about such names are entered under **Botany—Nomenclature**.
- UF Plants—Names
- Plants—Nomenclature
- SA types of plants with the subdivision *Nomenclature (Popular)*, e.g. **Trees—Nomenclature (Popular)** [to be added as needed]
- BT **Plants**
- NT **Trees—Nomenclature (Popular)**
- RT **Botany—Nomenclature**

Popular song lyrics   782.42164
- UF Lyrics
- Popular music—Texts

Popular songs—Texts
Song lyrics

Popular songs
- USE **Popular music**

Popular songs—Texts
- USE **Popular song lyrics**

Popularity   158
- BT **Social psychology**

Population   304.6; 363.9
- UF Demography
- Foreign population
- SA ethnic groups and names of countries, cities, etc., with the subdivision *Population*, e.g. **United States—Population** [to be added as needed]
- BT **Economics**
- **Human ecology**
- **Sociology**
- **Vital statistics**
- NT **Baby boom generation**
- **Birth control**
- **Census**
- **Chicago (Ill.)—Population**
- **Cities and towns—Growth**
- **Eugenics**
- **Human fertility**
- **Human settlements**
- **Immigration and emigration**
- **Internal migration**
- **Mortality**
- **Ohio—Population**
- **Overpopulation**
- **United States—Population**
- RT **Birth rate**

Population explosion
- USE **Overpopulation**

Porcelain (May subdiv. geog.)   **738.2**

Use for materials on chinaware and porcelain for the table or decorative use. Materials on the technology of fired earthen products or on clay products intended for industrial use are entered under **Ceramics**.
- UF China (Porcelain)
- Chinaware
- Dishes
- SA types of porcelain [to be added as needed]
- BT **Decorative arts**
- **Pottery**
- **Tableware**
- NT **China painting**

Porcelain enamels
USE **Enamel and enameling**
Porcelain painting
USE **China painting**
Pornography (May subdiv. geog.) **176; 363.4; 364.1**
UF Obscene materials
NT **Child pornography**
RT **Erotica**
Obscenity (Law)
Portable computers 004.16
UF Handheld computers
Laptop computers
BT **Computers**
Portrait miniatures
USE **Miniature painting**
Portrait painting 757
UF Portraiture
BT **Painting**
Portraits
RT **Figure painting**
Miniature painting
Portrait photography (May subdiv. geog.) **778.9; 779**
UF Portraiture
BT **Photography**
Portraits
Portraits (May subdiv. geog.) **704.9; 757**
SA headings for collective and individual biography, classes of persons, and names of individuals with the subdivision *Portraits*, e.g. **United States—Biography—Portraits**; **Musicians—Portraits**; **Shakespeare, William, 1564-1616—Portraits**; etc. [to be added as needed]
BT **Art**
Biography
Pictures
NT **Cartoons and caricatures**
Portrait painting
Portrait photography
Portraiture
USE **Portrait painting**
Portrait photography
Ports
USE **Harbors**

Portugal 946.9
May be subdivided like United States except for History.
Portuguese literature 869
BT **Literature**
Romance literature
Position analysis
USE **Topology**
Positivism 146
BT **Philosophy**
Rationalism
NT **Materialism**
Pragmatism
RT **Agnosticism**
Deism
Realism
Post cards
USE **Postcards**
Post-colonialism
USE **Postcolonialism**
Post-impressionism
USE **Postimpressionism (Art)**
Post-modernism
USE **Postmodernism**
Post office
USE **Postal service**
Post-traumatic stress disorder (May subdiv. geog.) **616.85**
UF Posttraumatic stress disorder
Traumatic stress syndrome
BT **Anxiety**
Neuroses
Stress (Psychology)
Postage stamp collecting
USE **Stamp collecting**
Postage stamps (May subdiv. geog.) **383; 769.56**
UF Stamps, Postage
BT **Postal service**
RT **Stamp collecting**
Postage stamps—Collectors and collecting
USE **Stamp collecting**
Postal cards
USE **Postcards**
Postal delivery code
USE **Zip code**
Postal service (May subdiv. geog.) **354.75; 383**
UF Mail service
Parcel post
Post office

Postal service—*Continued*
BT **Communication**
Transportation
NT **Air mail service**
Pony express
Postage stamps
Zip code
Postal service—United States 354.75;
383
UF United States—Mail
United States—Postal service
Postcards (May subdiv. geog.) 383;
741.6
UF Picture postcards
Post cards
Postal cards
Postcards—Collectors and collecting
(May subdiv. geog.) 790.1
Postcolonial theory
USE **Postcolonialism**
Postcolonialism (May subdiv. geog.) 325
UF Post-colonialism
Postcolonial theory
BT **Political science**
Posters (May subdiv. geog.) 741.6
SA types of posters, e.g. **Film post-
ers**; and subjects, ethnic
groups, classes of persons, in-
dividual persons, corporate
bodies, and names of wars
with the subdivision *Posters*
[to be added as needed]
BT **Advertising**
Commercial art
NT **Film posters**
RT **Signs and signboards**
Postimpressionism (Art) (May subdiv.
geog.) 709.03
UF Post-impressionism
BT **Art**
Postmodernism (May subdiv. geog.)
190; 700.1
UF Post-modernism
BT **Aesthetics**
RT **Modernism (Aesthetics)**
Postpartum depression 618.7
BT **Depression (Psychology)**
Posttraumatic stress disorder
USE **Post-traumatic stress disorder**
Posture 613.7
BT **Physical fitness**

Pot (Drug)
USE **Marijuana**
Potable water
USE **Drinking water**
Potash 631.8; 668
BT **Fertilizers**
Potatoes (May subdiv. geog.) 635; 641.3
BT **Vegetables**
Potpourri 668; 745.92
BT **Herbs**
Nature craft
Perfumes
Potter, Harry (Fictional character) 823
UF Harry Potter (Fictional character)
BT **Fictional characters**
Potters (May subdiv. geog.) 738.092;
920
BT **Artists**
Potters' marks
USE **Pottery—Marks**
Pottery 666; 738
Use for materials on pottery for the table or
for decorative use. Materials on the technolo-
gy of fired earthen products or on clay prod-
ucts intended for industrial use are entered un-
der **Ceramics**.
UF Crockery
Dishes
Earthenware
Faience
Stoneware
SA types of pottery and pottery of
particular countries, e.g.
American pottery [to be add-
ed as needed]
BT **Ceramics**
Clay industry
Decoration and ornament
Decorative arts
Tableware
NT **American pottery**
Art pottery
Glazes
Porcelain
Terra cotta
RT **Vases**
Pottery, American
USE **American pottery**
Pottery—Marks 738
UF Potters' marks
Poultry (May subdiv. geog.) 598.6;
636.5

613

Poultry—*Continued*
- SA types of domesticated birds, e.g.
  Ducks [to be added as needed]
- BT **Birds**
  Domestic animals
- NT **Chickens**
  Cooking—Poultry
  Ducks
  Geese
  Turkeys

Poverty (May subdiv. geog.) **305.5; 362.5**
- UF Destitution
  Pauperism
- SA names of countries with the subdivisions *Economic conditions* and *Social conditions* [to be added as needed]
- BT **Economic conditions**
  Social problems
- NT **Homelessness**
  Poor
- RT **Basic needs**
  Domestic economic assistance
  Public welfare
  Subsistence economy

Powder, Smokeless
- USE **Gunpowder**

Powdered milk
- USE **Dried milk**

Power blackouts
- USE **Electric power failures**

Power boats
- USE **Motorboats**

Power failures
- USE **Electric power failures**

Power (Mechanics) **531; 621**

Use for materials on the physics and engineering aspects of power. Materials on the available sources of mechanical power in general are entered under **Energy resources**.
- UF Energy technology
- BT **Mechanical engineering**
  Mechanics
- NT **Compressed air**
  Electric power
  Energy resources
  Force and energy
  Machinery
  Power transmission
  Steam

Water power
Wind power

Power of attorney (May subdiv. geog.) **346.02**
- UF Durable power of attorney
- BT **Law**

Power plants
- USE **Electric power plants**

Power plants, Hydroelectric
- USE **Hydroelectric power plants**

Power plants, Nuclear
- USE **Nuclear power plants**

Power politics
- USE **Balance of power**
  Cold war

Power resources
- USE **Energy resources**

Power resources conservation
- USE **Energy conservation**

Power resources development
- USE **Energy development**

Power (Social sciences) (May subdiv. geog.) **303.3**
- BT **Political science**
- NT **Elite (Social sciences)**

Power stations
- USE **Electric power plants**

Power supply
- USE **Energy resources**

Power tools **621.9**
- BT **Tools**

Power transmission (May subdiv. geog.) **621.8**
- UF Transmission of power
- BT **Mechanical engineering**
  Power (Mechanics)
- NT **Cables**
  Electric power distribution
  Gearing
- RT **Belts and belting**
  Machinery

Power transmission, Electric
- USE **Electric lines**
  Electric power distribution

Powers, Separation of
- USE **Separation of powers**

POWs
- USE **Prisoners of war**

Powwows (May subdiv. geog.) **394.2; 970.004**

Powwows—*Continued*

    BT   **Festivals**

            Native Americans—Rites and ceremonies

            Native Americans—Social life and customs

Practical jokes   793

    UF   Pranks

    BT   **Jokes**

            Wit and humor

Practical nurses (May subdiv. geog.)   **610.73; 920**

    BT   **Nurses**

Practical nursing   610.73; 649.8

    BT   **Nursing**

Practical politics

    USE   **Politics**

Practical psychology

    USE   **Applied psychology**

Practice

    USE   types of professions with the subdivision *Practice,* e.g. **Nuclear medicine—Practice** [to be added as needed]

Practice teaching

    USE   **Student teaching**

Pragmatism   144

    BT   **Philosophy**

            Positivism

            Realism

            Theory of knowledge

    RT   **Empiricism**

            Reality

            Truth

            Utilitarianism

Prairie ecology (May subdiv. geog.)   **577.4**

    BT   **Ecology**

            Grassland ecology

Prairies (May subdiv. geog.)   **577.4; 578.74**

    BT   **Grasslands**

Praise of God   248.3

    UF   God—Praise

    BT   **Worship**

Pranks

    USE   **Practical jokes**

Prayer   204; 248.3

    May be subdivided by religion or sect. Use for materials about prayer. Collections of prayers are entered under **Prayers**.

    UF   Devotion

            Devotional theology

    BT   **Worship**

    RT   **Devotional exercises**

            Prayers

Prayer-books

    USE   **Prayers**

Prayer-books and devotions

    USE   **Prayers**

Prayer in the public schools (May subdiv. geog.)   **379.2**

    Use for materials on the inclusion of prayers or a period for silent prayer or meditation in the daily schedule of public schools. Materials on the teaching of religion in the public schools or on the religious freedom of students and school employees are entered under **Religion in the public schools**.

    UF   Prayers in the public schools

            School prayer

    BT   **Religion in the public schools**

Prayers   204; 242; 264

    Use for collections of prayers. Materials about prayer are entered under **Prayer**.

    UF   Collects

            Prayer-books

            Prayer-books and devotions

    SA   names of religions, denominations, religious orders, classes of persons for whose use the prayers are intended, and names of saints and deities to whom the prayers are directed with the subdivision *Prayers,* e.g. **Buddhism—Prayers; Sick—Prayers; Mary, Blessed Virgin, Saint—Prayers**; etc. [to be added as needed]

    BT   **Devotional literature**

    NT   **Buddhism—Prayers**

            Mary—Prayers

            Meditations

            Sick—Prayers

    RT   **Prayer**

Prayers in the public schools

    USE   **Prayer in the public schools**

Pre-Columbian Americans

    USE   **Native Americans**

Pre-Lenten festivities

    USE   **Carnival**

Preachers

    USE   **Clergy**

Preaching (May subdiv. geog.)   **206; 251**

    Use for materials on the art of writing and delivering sermons. Collections of sermons not limited to a single topic, occasion, or Christian denomination are entered under **Sermons**.

  UF   Speaking
  BT   **Pastoral theology**
        Public speaking
        Rhetoric
  RT   **Sermons**

Precious metals (May subdiv. geog.)
      553.4; 669

  UF   Bullion
  BT   **Metals**
        Mines and mineral resources
  NT   **Gold**
        Silver

Precious stones (May subdiv. geog.)
      553.8

    Use for mineralogical or technological materials on gem stones. Materials on cut and polished precious stones treated from the point of view of art or antiquity are entered under **Gems**. Materials on gems in which the emphasis is on the setting are entered under **Jewelry**.

  UF   Gemstones
        Jewels
  SA   names of precious stones [to be added as needed]
  BT   **Minerals**
  NT   **Diamonds**
  RT   **Gems**

Precipitation forecasting
  USE **Weather forecasting**

Precipitation (Meteorology) (May subdiv. geog.)   **551.57**

  BT   **Meteorology**
        Water
        Weather
  NT   **Rain**
        Snow

Precocious children
  USE **Gifted children**

Predators
  USE **Predatory animals**

Predatory animals (May subdiv. geog.)
      591.5

  UF   Predators
  SA   types of predatory animals [to be added as needed]
  BT   **Animals**
  NT   **Birds of prey**

Predestination   **202; 234**

  UF   Election (Theology)
        Foreordination
  BT   **Theology**
  RT   **Fate and fatalism**
        Free will and determinism

Predictions
  USE **Forecasting**
        Prophecies

Prefabricated buildings (May subdiv. geog.)   **693**

  UF   Buildings, Prefabricated
  BT   **Buildings**
  NT   **Prefabricated houses**

Prefabricated houses (May subdiv. geog.)
      693; 728

  BT   **Domestic architecture**
        House construction
        Houses
        Prefabricated buildings

Pregnancy   **599; 612.6; 618.2**

  BT   **Reproduction**
  NT   **Miscarriage**
        Multiple pregnancy
        Prenatal care
        Teenage pregnancy
  RT   **Childbirth**

Prehistoric animals   **560**

  UF   Animals, Prehistoric
  BT   **Animals**
        Fossils
  NT   **Dinosaurs**
  RT   **Extinct animals**

Prehistoric art (May subdiv. geog.)
      709.01

  UF   Art, Prehistoric
  BT   **Art**
  NT   **Rock drawings, paintings, and engravings**

Prehistoric man
  USE **Fossil hominids**
        Prehistoric peoples

Prehistoric peoples (May subdiv. geog.)
      930.1

  UF   Man, Prehistoric
        Prehistoric man
        Prehistory
  SA   names of prehistoric peoples, e.g. **Cro-Magnons**; etc.; and names of countries, cities, etc., with the subdivision *An-*

Prehistoric peoples—*Continued*
           tiquities, e.g. **United States— Antiquities** [to be added as needed]
  BT **Antiquities**
       Archeology
       Human beings
  NT **Cave dwellers**
       Cro-Magnons
  RT **Human origins**
Prehistory
  USE **Archeology**
       Fossil hominids
       Prehistoric peoples
Prejudice
  USE **Prejudices**
Prejudice in testing
  USE **Test bias**
Prejudice-motivated crimes
  USE **Hate crimes**
Prejudices (May subdiv. geog.) **152.4; 177; 303.3**
  UF Bias (Psychology)
       Bigotry
       Prejudice
  SA types of prejudice [to be added as needed]
  BT **Attitude (Psychology)**
       Emotions
       Interpersonal relations
  NT **Antisemitism**
       Discrimination
       Ethnocentrism
       Racism
       Sexism
Prejudicial publicity
  USE **Freedom of the press and fair trial**
Prelude and fugue
  USE **Fugue**
Preludes and fugues
  USE **Fugue**
Premarital contracts
  USE **Marriage contracts**
Premarital counseling
  USE **Marriage counseling**
Premature burial (May subdiv. geog.) **306.9**
  UF Burial, Premature
  BT **Burial**
Premenstrual syndrome **618.1**

  UF PMS (Gynecology)
       Premenstrual tension
  BT **Menstruation**
Premenstrual tension
  USE **Premenstrual syndrome**
Premiers
  USE **Prime ministers**
Prenatal care (May subdiv. geog.) **618.2**
  BT **Pregnancy**
Prenatal diagnosis **618.3**
  BT **Diagnosis**
  NT **Amniocentesis**
       Genetic counseling
Prenuptial agreements
  USE **Marriage contracts**
Prenuptial contracts
  USE **Marriage contracts**
Prepaid group medical practice
  USE **Health maintenance organizations**
Preparation guides for examinations
  USE **Examinations—Study guides**
Prepared cereals **641.3; 664**
  UF Breakfast cereals
       Cereals, Prepared
  BT **Breakfasts**
       Food
Preprimers
  USE **Easy reading materials**
Presbyterian Church (May subdiv. geog.) **285**
  BT **Christian sects**
Presbyterian Church—Sermons **252**
  BT **Sermons**
Preschool children
  USE **Children**
Preschool education (May subdiv. geog.) **372.21**
  UF Children—Education
       Education, Preschool
       Infants—Education
  BT **Education**
  NT **Readiness for school**
  RT **Kindergarten**
       Nursery schools
Preschool reading materials
  USE **Easy reading materials**
Prescription drug abuse
  USE **Medication abuse**
Preselection of sex
  USE **Sex preselection**

Presents
USE **Gifts**
Preservation
USE types of foods and other things
preserved with the subdivision
Preservation, e.g. **Fruit—
Preservation; Wood—Preservation;** etc.; antiquities and
types of natural objects, including animal specimens and
plant specimens, with the subdivision *Collection and preservation,* e.g. **Birds—Collection and preservation;** and
types of art objects, library
materials, architecture, and
land vehicles with the subdi-
vision *Conservation and res-
toration,* e.g. **Automobiles—
Conservation and restoration**
[to be added as needed]
Preservation of antiquities
USE **Antiquities—Collection and
preservation**
Preservation of biodiversity
USE **Biodiversity conservation**
Preservation of botanical specimens
USE **Plants—Collection and preser-
vation**
Preservation of buildings
USE **Architecture—Conservation
and restoration**
Preservation of food
USE **Food—Preservation**
Preservation of forests
USE **Forest conservation**
Preservation of historical records
USE **Archives**
Preservation of library resources
USE **Library resources—Conserva-
tion and restoration**
Preservation of natural resources
USE **Conservation of natural re-
sources**
Preservation of natural scenery
USE **Landscape protection
Natural monuments
Nature conservation**
**Preservation of organs, tissues, etc.
617.9**

UF Organ preservation (Anatomy)
Organs (Anatomy)—Preservation
RT **Transplantation of organs, tis-
sues, etc.**
Preservation of photographs
USE **Photographs—Conservation
and restoration**
Preservation of specimens
USE **Taxidermy**
Preservation of wildlife
USE **Wildlife conservation**
Preservation of wood
USE **Wood—Preservation**
Preservation of works of art
USE subjects with the subdivision
Conservation and restoration,
e.g. **Painting—Conservation
and restoration** [to be added
as needed]
Preservation of zoological specimens
USE **Zoological specimens—Collec-
tion and preservation**
Preservationism (Historic preservation)
USE **Historic preservation**
Preserving
USE **Canning and preserving**
Presidential aides
USE **Presidents—United States—
Staff**
Presidential campaigns—United States
USE **Presidents—United States—
Election**
Presidential libraries
USE **Presidents—United States—Ar-
chives**
Presidents (May subdiv. geog.) **352.23;
920**
SA names of presidents [to be add-
ed as needed]
BT **IIeads of state**
NT **Vice-presidents**
RT **Executive power**
Presidents—Mexico 920; 972
UF Mexico—Presidents
Presidents—Powers
USE **Executive power**
Presidents' spouses—United States 920
UF First ladies—United States
Presidents—United States—
Spouses
Presidents' wives—United States

Presents' spouses—United States—*Continued*

> Wives of presidents—United States

Presidents—United States   352.230973; 920

> When applicable, the subdivisions under this heading may be used under names of presidents, prime ministers, and other rulers.

UF   United States—Presidents

SA   names of presidents [to be added as needed]

NT   **Lincoln, Abraham, 1809-1865**

Presidents—United States—Appointment 352.23

Presidents—United States—Archives 026

UF   Libraries, Presidential

Presidential libraries

Presidents—United States—Libraries

SA   names of individual libraries [to be added as needed]

BT   **Archives**

NT   **Harry S. Truman Library (Independence, Mo.)**

Presidents—United States—Assassination 364.15; 973

BT   **Assassination**

Presidents—United States—Burial

USE   **Presidents—United States—Death and burial**

Presidents—United States—Children 920

Presidents—United States—Death and burial   393; 973

UF   Presidents—United States—Burial

Presidents—United States—Funeral and memorial services

Presidents—United States—Memorial services

Presidents—United States—Election 324.973

> May further subdivide by date.

UF   Campaigns, Presidential—United States

Electoral college

Presidential campaigns—United States

BT   **Elections**

Presidents—United States—Family   920

Presidents—United States—Fathers   920

Presidents—United States—Funeral and memorial services

USE   **Presidents—United States—Death and burial**

Presidents—United States—Health 352.23; 920

UF   Presidents—United States—Illness

Presidents—United States—Homes   728

Presidents—United States—Illness

USE   **Presidents—United States—Health**

Presidents—United States—Impeachment 342

Presidents—United States—Inability to serve

USE   **Presidents—United States—Succession**

Presidents—United States—Inaugural addresses   352.23

BT   **Speeches**

Presidents—United States—Inauguration 352.23

Presidents—United States—Libraries

USE   **Presidents—United States—Archives**

Presidents—United States—Medals 352.23

Presidents—United States—Memorial services

USE   **Presidents—United States—Death and burial**

Presidents—United States—Messages 352.23

UF   Messages to Congress

Presidents—United States—State of the Union message

State of the Union messages

Presidents—United States—Mothers 920

Presidents—United States—Nomination 324.50973

UF   Nomination of presidents

Presidents—United States—Portraits 973

Presidents—United States—Power

USE   **Executive power—United States**

Presidents—United States—Press relations   070.4; 352.230973

Presidents—United States—Protection
352.23
Presidents—United States—Quotations
818
   BT   **Quotations**
Presidents—United States—Relations
   with Congress   328.73; 352.23
Presidents—United States—Religion
920
Presidents—United States—Resignation
352.23
Presidents—United States—Sports   920
Presidents—United States—Spouses
   USE   **Presidents' spouses—United**
         States
Presidents—United States—Staff   352.23
   UF   Presidential aides
   BT   **Executive departments—United**
         States
Presidents—United States—State of the
   Union message
   USE   **Presidents—United States—**
         Messages
Presidents—United States—Succession
342; 352.23
   UF   Presidents—United States—In-
         ability to serve
Presidents—United States—Tombs
917.3
Presidents—United States—Travel
352.23
   UF   Presidents—United States—Voy-
         ages and travels
Presidents—United States—Voyages and
   travels
   USE   **Presidents—United States—**
         Travel
Presidents' wives—United States
   USE   **Presidents' spouses—United**
         States
Press (May subdiv. geog.)   070
   SA   topics with the subdivision *Press*
         coverage, e.g. **Food contami-**
         nation—Press coverage [to
         be added as needed]
   BT   **Journalism**
         Propaganda
         Publicity
   NT   **Alternative press**
         Broadcast journalism
         Freedom of the press

         Freedom of the press and fair
         trial
         News agencies
         Pamphlets
   RT   **Newspapers**
         Periodicals
         Public opinion
Press and government
   USE   **Press—Government policy**
Press censorship
   USE   **Freedom of the press**
Press clippings
   USE   **Clippings (Books, newspapers,**
         etc.)
Press coverage
   USE   topics with the subdivision *Press*
         coverage, e.g. **Food contami-**
         nation—Press coverage [to
         be added as needed]
Press—Government policy (May subdiv.
   geog.)   **323.44**
   UF   Government and the press
         Press and government
   BT   **Freedom of information**
Press relations
   USE   types of public officials and
         names of individual public of-
         ficials with the subdivision
         Press relations, e.g. **Presi-**
         dents—United States—Press
         relations [to be added as
         needed]
Press working of metal
   USE   **Sheet metalwork**
Pressure groups
   USE   **Lobbying**
         Political action committees
Prestidigitation
   USE   **Magic tricks**
Pretenders
   USE   **Impostors and imposture**
Prevention
   USE   types of diseases, medical condi-
         tions, and situations to be
         avoided with the subdivision
         Prevention, e.g. **AIDS (Dis-**
         ease)—Prevention; Acci-
         dents—Prevention; etc. [to
         be added as needed]
Prevention of accidents
   USE   **Accidents—Prevention**

Prevention of crime
USE **Crime prevention**
Prevention of cruelty to animals
USE **Animal welfare**
Prevention of disease
USE **Preventive medicine**
Prevention of fire
USE **Fire prevention**
Prevention of smoke
USE **Smoke prevention**
Preventive medicine (May subdiv. geog.)
613
UF Diseases—Prevention
Medicine, Preventive
Prevention of disease
SA names of diseases with the sub-
division *Prevention*, e.g.
AIDS (Disease)—Prevention
[to be added as needed]
BT **Medicine**
NT **Communicable diseases—Pre-
vention**
Health
Heart diseases—Prevention
Hygiene
Vaccination
RT **Pathology**
Price controls
USE **Wage-price policy**
Price indexes, Consumer
USE **Consumer price indexes**
Price theory
USE **Microeconomics**
Price-wage policy
USE **Wage-price policy**
Prices (May subdiv. geog.) **338.5**
SA subjects with the subdivision
Prices, e.g. **Art—Prices** [to
be added as needed]
BT **Commerce**
Consumption (Economics)
Economics
Finance
Manufactures
NT **Art—Prices**
Books—Prices
Consumer price indexes
Farm produce—Marketing
Stock price indexes
Wage-price policy

RT **Cost and standard of living**
Salaries, wages, etc.
Supply and demand
Pride and vanity **179**
UF Vanity
BT **Conduct of life**
Sin
RT **Snobs and snobbishness**
Priests (May subdiv. geog.) **200.92;**
270.092
UF Pastors
SA names of church denominations
with the subdivision *Clergy*,
e.g. **Catholic Church—Cler-
gy** [to be added as needed]
BT **Clergy**
NT **Catholic Church—Clergy**
Ex-priests
Primaries (May subdiv. geog.) **324.5**
UF Direct primaries
BT **Elections**
Political conventions
Politics
Primary education
USE **Elementary education**
Primates (May subdiv. geog.) **599.8**
SA types of primates, e.g. **Monkeys**
[to be added as needed]
BT **Mammals**
NT **Apes**
Human beings
Monkeys
Primates—Behavior (May subdiv. geog.)
599.8
UF Primates—Habits and behavior
BT **Animal behavior**
Primates—Habits and behavior
USE **Primates—Behavior**
Prime ministers (May subdiv. geog.)
352.23; 920
May use same subdivisions, following geo-
graphic subdivision, as for **Presidents—Unit-
ed States**.
UF Premiers
BT **Cabinet officers**
Executive power
Prime ministers—Great Britain
352.230941; 920
UF Great Britain—Prime ministers
Primers
USE **Easy reading materials**

Primitive Christianity
    USE   **Church history—30-600, Early
                church**
Primitive man
    USE   **Primitive societies**
Primitive societies (May subdiv. geog.)
            305.8; 306
        Use for materials on nonliterate,
    nonindustrialized peoples.
    UF   Man, Primitive
            Primitive man
            Primitive society
            Society, Primitive
    BT   **Civilization
            Ethnology**
    NT   **Nomads**
Primitive society
    USE   **Primitive societies**
Princes (May subdiv. geog.)   **920**
    UF   Princes and princesses
            Royalty
    BT   **Courts and courtiers**
Princes and princesses
    USE   **Princes
            Princesses**
Princesses (May subdiv. geog.)   **920**
    UF   Princes and princesses
            Royalty
    BT   **Courts and courtiers**
Printing (May subdiv. geog.)   **686.2**
    SA   types of printing processes [to
            be added as needed]
    BT   **Bibliography
            Book industry
            Graphic arts
            Industrial arts
            Publishers and publishing**
    NT   **Advertising layout and typog-
            raphy
            Color printing
            Electrotyping
            Linoleum block printing
            Linotype
            Lithography
            Nature prints
            Offset printing
            Proofreading
            Textile printing
            Type and type-founding
            Typesetting
            Typography**

    RT   **Books
            Prints**
Printing—Exhibitions (May subdiv. geog.)
            686.2074
    BT   **Exhibitions**
Printing—Specimens   686.2
    UF   Type specimens
    BT   **Advertising
            Initials**
    RT   **Type and type-founding**
Printing—Style manuals   686.02
    UF   Style manuals
    RT   **Authorship—Handbooks, man-
            uals, etc.**
Prints   769
    SA   prints of particular countries, e.g.
            American prints [to be add-
            ed as needed]
    BT   **Graphic arts**
    NT   **American prints
            Bookplates
            Color prints
            Linoleum block printing
            Lithography
            Nature prints
            Woodcuts**
    RT   **Printing**
Prints, American
    USE   **American prints**
Prison escapes
    USE   **Escapes**
Prison labor
    USE   **Convict labor**
Prison reform (May subdiv. geog.)   **365**
    UF   Penal reform
    BT   **Social problems**
Prison schools
    USE   **Prisoners—Education**
Prisoners (May subdiv. geog.)   **365**
    UF   Convicts
            Prisoners and prisons
    BT   **Criminals**
    NT   **Convict labor
            Political prisoners**
    RT   **Prisoners of war
            Prisons**
Prisoners and prisons
    USE   **Prisoners
            Prisoners of war
            Prisons**

Prisoners and prisons—*Continued*
> and names of wars with the subdivision *Prisoners and prisons,* e.g. **World War, 1939-1945—Prisoners and prisons** [to be added as needed]

Prisoners—Education (May subdiv. geog.) 365
> UF   Education of criminals
> Education of prisoners
> Prison schools
> BT   **Adult education**
> **Prisons**

Prisoners of conscience
> USE   **Political prisoners**

Prisoners of war (May subdiv. geog.) 341.6; 355.7
> UF   Exchange of prisoners of war
> POWs
> Prisoners and prisons
> SA   names of wars with the subdivision *Prisoners and prisons,* e.g. **World War, 1939-1945—Prisoners and prisons** [to be added as needed]
> BT   **War**
> NT   **Missing in action**
> **United States—History—1861-1865, Civil War—Prisoners and prisons**
> **World War, 1939-1945—Prisoners and prisons**
> RT   **Concentration camps**
> **Prisoners**
> **Prisons**

Prisons (May subdiv. geog.) 365
> UF   Imprisonment
> Jails
> Penal institutions
> Penitentiaries
> Prisoners and prisons
> SA   types of prisons, names of individual prisons, and names of wars with the subdivision *Prisoners and prisons,* e.g. **World War, 1939-1945—Prisoners and prisons** [to be added as needed]
> BT   **Administration of criminal justice**
> **Correctional institutions**
> **Punishment**
> NT   **Escapes**
> **Prisoners—Education**
> **Probation**
> **Reformatories**
> **United States—History—1861-1865, Civil War—Prisoners and prisons**
> **World War, 1939-1945—Prisoners and prisons**
> RT   **Prisoners**
> **Prisoners of war**

Prisons—United States 365
> UF   United States—Prisons

Privacy (May subdiv. geog.) 323.44
> BT   **Social psychology**
> RT   **Secrecy**
> **Solitude**

Privacy, Right of
> USE   **Right of privacy**

Private art collections
> USE   **Art collections**

Private companies
> USE   **Limited liability companies**

Private enterprise
> USE   **Free enterprise**

Private eye stories
> USE   **Mystery and detective plays**
> **Mystery fiction**
> **Mystery films**
> **Mystery radio programs**
> **Mystery television programs**

Private funding of the arts
> USE   **Art patronage**

Private limited companies
> USE   **Limited liability companies**

Private property, Right of
> USE   **Right of property**

Private schools (May subdiv. geog.) 371.02; 373.2
> UF   Boarding schools
> Independent schools
> Nonpublic schools
> BT   **Schools**
> NT   **Church schools**
> **English public schools**

Private theater
> USE   **Amateur theater**

Privateering (May subdiv. geog.) 359.4
> UF   Letters of marque

Privateering—*Continued*
    BT   **International law**
          Naval art and science
          Naval history
          Pirates
Privatization (May subdiv. geog.)   **338.9**
    Use for materials on the transfer of public assets and service functions to the private sector.
    UF   Denationalization
    BT   **Economic policy**
          Industrial policy
    RT   **Government ownership**
Prize fighting
    USE **Boxing**
Prizes (Rewards)
    USE **Awards**
Pro-abortion movement
    USE **Pro-choice movement**
Pro-choice movement (May subdiv. geog.)
     179.7; 363.46
    UF   Abortion rights movement
          Freedom of choice movement
          Pro-abortion movement
          Right to choose movement
    BT   **Social movements**
    RT   **Abortion—Ethical aspects**
          Abortion—Religious aspects
          Women's rights
Pro-life movement (May subdiv. geog.)
     179.7; 363.46
    UF   Anti-abortion movement
          Antiabortion movement
          Right-to-life movement (Anti-abortion movement)
    BT   **Social movements**
    RT   **Abortion—Ethical aspects**
          Abortion—Religious aspects
          Women's rights
Probabilities   **519.2**
    UF   Fortune
          Statistical inference
    BT   **Algebra**
          Logic
          Mathematics
          Statistics
    NT   **Average**
          Game theory
          Reliability (Engineering)
          Sampling (Statistics)
    RT   **Risk**

Probate law and practice (May subdiv. geog.)   **346.05**
    BT   **Civil procedure**
          Inheritance and succession
Probation (May subdiv. geog.)   **364.6**
    UF   Reform of criminals
          Suspended sentence
    BT   **Corrections**
          Criminal law
          Prisons
          Punishment
          Reformatories
          Social case work
    RT   **Juvenile courts**
          Parole
Probiotics   **613.2; 615.1**
    BT   **Dietary supplements**
          Microorganisms
Problem children
    USE **Emotionally disturbed children**
Problem drinking
    USE **Alcoholism**
Problem families—Counseling of
    USE **Family therapy**
Problem solving   **153.4; 510.76**
    BT   **Psychology**
    NT   **Conflict management**
          Crisis management
          Critical thinking
          Group problem solving
    RT   **Decision making**
Problems, exercises, etc.
    USE subjects with the subdivision *Problems, exercises, etc.,* for compilations of practice problems or exercises for use in the study of a topic, e.g. **Chemistry—Problems, exercises, etc.** [to be added as needed]
Procedural due process
    USE **Due process of law**
Processing (Libraries)
    USE **Library technical processes**
Processions
    USE **Parades**
Procurement, Government
    USE **Government purchasing**
Prodigal son (Parable)   **226.8**
    BT   **Parables**

Producers
    USE   types of producers and directors
             in specific media, e.g. **Motion
             picture producers and direc-
             tors**; **Theatrical producers
             and directors**; etc. [to be
             added as needed]

Product development
    USE **New products**

Product recall (May subdiv. geog.)
    658.5
    UF   Commercial products recall
           Manufactures—Defects
           Manufactures recall
           Recall of products
    BT   **Consumer protection**

Product safety (May subdiv. geog.)
    363.19; 658.5
    UF   Unsafe products
    BT   **Consumer protection**

Production
    USE **Economics**
           Industries

Production engineering
    USE **Factory management**

Production processes
    USE **Manufacturing processes**

Production standards   **658.5**
    Use for materials on the unit time value for
    the accomplishment of a work task as deter-
    mined by work measurement techniques.
    UF   Output standards
           Standards of output
           Time production standards
           Work standards
    SA   types of industries and processes
            with the subdivision *Produc-
            tion standards*, e.g. **Automo-
            bile industry—Production
            standards** [to be added as
            needed]
    BT   **Labor productivity
           Management**
    NT   **Automobile industry—Produc-
           tion standards
           Motion study
           Time study**

Productivity of labor
    USE **Labor productivity**

Products, Agricultural
    USE **Farm produce**

Products, Animal
    USE **Animal products**

Products, Commercial
    USE **Commercial products**

Products, Dairy
    USE **Dairy products**

Products, Generic
    USE **Generic products**

Professional associations
    USE **Trade and professional associa-
           tions**

Professional education (May subdiv.
    geog.)   **378**
    SA   types of professions with the
            subdivision *Study and teach-
            ing*, e.g. **Medicine—Study
            and teaching** [to be added as
            needed]
    BT   **Education
           Higher education
           Learning and scholarship**
    NT   **Colleges and universities
           Library education**
    RT   **Technical education
           Vocational education**

Professional ethics (May subdiv. geog.)
    174
    SA   types of professional ethics, e.g.
            Medical ethics; professions
            and types of professional per-
            sonnel with the subdivision
            Ethics, e.g. **Librarians—Eth-
            ics**; and subjects with the
            subdivision *Ethical aspects* [to
            be added as needed]
    BT   **Ethics**
    NT   **Business ethics
           Journalistic ethics
           Legal ethics
           Librarians—Ethics
           Medical ethics**

Professional liability
    USE **Malpractice**

Professional liability insurance
    USE **Malpractice insurance**

Professional sports (May subdiv. geog.)
    796
    SA   types of sports [to be added as
            needed]
    BT   **Sports**

Professions (May subdiv. geog.)   **331.702**

Professions—*Continued*
    UF   Careers
           Jobs
           Vocations
    SA   types of professions with the
           subdivision *Vocational guid-*
           ance, e.g. **Law—Vocational**
           guidance [to be added as
           needed]
    BT   **Occupations**
           Self-employed
    NT   **College graduates**
           Law—Vocational guidance
           Paraprofessionals
    RT   **Vocational guidance**
Professions—Tort liability
    USE **Malpractice**
Professors
    USE **Educators**
           Teachers
Profit   338.5; 658.15
    BT   **Business**
           Capital
           Economics
           Wealth
    NT   **Capitalism**
    RT   **Income**
           Risk
Profit sharing (May subdiv. geog.)
           331.2; 658.3
    BT   **Commerce**
           Salaries, wages, etc.
    RT   **Cooperation**
Program evaluation in education
    USE **Educational evaluation**
Programmed instruction   371.39
    UF   Programmed textbooks
    SA   subjects with the subdivision
           Programmed instruction [to
           be added as needed]
    BT   **Teaching—Aids and devices**
    NT   **Computer-assisted instruction**
           English language—Pro-
           grammed instruction
           Teaching machines
Programmed textbooks
    USE **Programmed instruction**
Programming (Computers)
    USE **Computer programming**
Programming languages   005.13
    UF   Computer languages
           Computer program languages

           Machine language
           Programming languages (Com-
           puters)
           Programming languages (Elec-
           tronic computers)
    SA   names of specific languages, e.g.
           FORTRAN (Computer lan-
           guage) [to be added as need-
           ed]
    BT   **Computer software**
           Language and languages
    NT   **FORTRAN (Computer lan-**
           guage)
           HTML (Document markup
           language)
    RT   **Computer programming**
Programming languages (Computers)
    USE **Programming languages**
Programming languages (Electronic com-
           puters)
    USE **Programming languages**
Programs, Computer
    USE **Computer software**
Programs, Radio
    USE **Radio programs**
Programs, Television
    USE **Television programs**
Programs, Twelve-step
    USE **Twelve-step programs**
Progress   303.44
    UF   Social progress
    BT   **Civilization**
    NT   **Science and civilization**
Progressive education
    USE **Education—Experimental**
           methods
Progressivism (United States politics)
           320.973
    BT   **Political science**
Prohibited books
    USE **Books—Censorship**
Prohibition (May subdiv. geog.)   **344**
    Use for materials on the legal prohibition of
    liquor traffic and liquor manufacture.
    BT   **Criminal law**
    RT   **Temperance**
Project Apollo
    USE **Apollo project**
Project Gemini
    USE **Gemini project**
Project method in teaching   371.3
    BT   **Teaching**

Project Ranger   629.43
    UF   Ranger project
    BT   **Lunar probes**
Project schools
    USE   **Experimental schools**
Project Sealab
    USE   **Sealab project**
Project Telstar
    USE   **Telstar project**
Project Voyager   629.43
    UF   Voyager project
    BT   **Astronautics—United States**
Projectiles (May subdiv. geog.)   **623.4**
    UF   Shells (Projectiles)
    NT   **Ammunition**
          Bombs
          Guided missiles
          Rockets (Aeronautics)
    RT   **Ordnance**
Projective geometry   516
    UF   Geometry, Projective
    BT   **Geometry**
Projectors   778.2
    UF   Film projectors
          Magic lanterns
          Motion picture projectors
          Opaque projectors
          Slide projectors
          Stereopticon
Proletariat (May subdiv. geog.)   **305.5**
    BT   **Labor**
          Socialism
          Working class
Proliferation of arms
    USE   **Arms race**
Promises   170
    BT   **Ethics**
Promotion in school
    USE   **Promotion (School)**
Promotion (School)   371.2
    UF   Grade repetition
          Grade retention
          Non-promotion (School)
          Promotion in school
          Retention, Grade
          School grade retention
          School promotion
          Student promotion
    BT   **Grading and marking (Education)**

Promptness
    USE   **Punctuality**
Pronunciation
    USE   names of languages with the subdivision *Pronunciation,* e.g. **English language—Pronunciation** [to be added as needed]
Proofreading   070.5; 686.2
    BT   **Printing**
Propaganda   303.3; 327.1
    SA   propaganda of particular countries, e.g. **American propaganda**; and names of wars with the subdivision *Propaganda,* e.g. **World War, 1939-1945—Propaganda** [to be added as needed]
    BT   **Political psychology**
          Public opinion
    NT   **American propaganda**
          Lobbying
          Press
          Psychological warfare
          World War, 1939-1945—Propaganda
    RT   **Advertising**
          Persuasion (Psychology)
          Publicity
Propaganda, American
    USE   **American propaganda**
Propagation of plants
    USE   **Plant propagation**
Propellers, Aerial
    USE   **Aerial propellers**
Proper names
    USE   **Names**
Property (May subdiv. geog.)   **330.1**
    UF   Ownership
    BT   **Economics**
    NT   **Airspace law**
          Cultural property
          Eminent domain
          Income
          Intellectual property
          Lost and found possessions
          Real estate
          Right of property
          Surplus government property
          Timesharing (Real estate)
    RT   **Wealth**

Property, Crimes against
    USE   **Offenses against property**
Property, Right of
    USE   **Right of property**
Property rights
    USE   **Right of property**
Property tax—Assessment
    USE   **Tax assessment**
Prophecies   133.3; 202
    UF   Predictions
         Prophecies (Occult sciences)
         Prophecies (Occultism)
         Prophecy
    SA   subjects, titles of sacred works,
         and names of persons with
         the subdivision *Prophecies*,
         e.g. **Bible—Prophecies** [to be
         added as needed]
    BT   **Occultism**
         Supernatural
    RT   **Divination**
         Oracles
Prophecies (Bible)
    USE   **Bible—Prophecies**
Prophecies (Occult sciences)
    USE   **Prophecies**
Prophecies (Occultism)
    USE   **Prophecies**
Prophecy
    USE   **Prophecies**
Prophets (May subdiv. geog.)   200.92
    BT   **Religious biography**
Proportion (Architecture)
    USE   **Architecture—Composition,**
         proportion, etc.
Proportional representation (May subdiv.
    geog.)   328.3
    UF   Representation, Proportional
    BT   **Constitutional law**
         Representative government and
         representation
    RT   **Elections**
Proprietary rights
    USE   **Intellectual property**
Prose literature, American
    USE   **American prose literature**
Prose literature, English
    USE   **English prose literature**
Prosody
    USE   **Versification**
Prospecting (May subdiv. geog.)   622

    BT   **Gold mines and mining**
         Mines and mineral resources
         Silver mines and mining
    NT   **Mine surveying**
         Petroleum geology
Prosthesis
    USE   **Artificial limbs**
         Artificial organs
Prostitution (May subdiv. geog.)   176;
    306.74; 363.4; 364.1
    BT   **Sexual ethics**
         Social problems
         Women—Social conditions
    NT   **Juvenile prostitution**
Protection
    USE   subjects with the subdivision
         Protection, e.g. **Birds—Pro-**
         tection [to be added as need-
         ed]
Protection against burglary
    USE   **Burglary protection**
Protection of animals
    USE   **Animal welfare**
Protection of birds
    USE   **Birds—Protection**
Protection of children
    USE   **Child welfare**
Protection of environment
    USE   **Environmental protection**
Protection of game
    USE   **Game protection**
Protection of natural scenery
    USE   **Landscape protection**
         Natural monuments
         Nature conservation
Protection of plants
    USE   **Plant conservation**
Protection of wildlife
    USE   **Wildlife conservation**
Protectionism (May subdiv. geog.)   382
    UF   Free trade and protection
    BT   **Commercial policy**
    RT   **Free trade**
         Tariff
Proteins   547; 572
    BT   **Biochemistry**
         Nutrition
    NT   **Enzymes**
Protest
    USE   **Dissent**

Protest marches and rallies
USE **Demonstrations**
Protest movements (May subdiv. geog.)
303.48
SA names of wars and other objects
of protest with the subdivision
Protest movements, e.g.
**World War, 1939-1945—
Protest movements** [to be
added as needed]
BT **Social movements**
NT **World War, 1939-1945—Pro-
test movements**
RT **Demonstrations**
Protestant churches (May subdiv. geog.)
280
Use for materials on Protestant denomina-
tions treated collectively. Works on Protestant
church buildings are entered under **Church
buildings**.
UF Denominations, Protestant
Protestant denominations
SA names of Protestant churches,
e.g. **Presbyterian Church** [to
be added as needed]
BT **Christian sects**
Church history
Protestantism
Protestant denominations
USE **Protestant churches**
Protestant Episcopal Church in the U.S.A.
USE **Episcopal Church**
Protestant Reformation
USE **Reformation**
Protestant work ethic
USE **Work ethic**
Protestantism (May subdiv. geog.) **280**
BT **Christianity**
Church history
NT **Evangelicalism**
Pentecostal churches
Protestant churches
RT **Reformation**
Protests, demonstrations, etc.
USE **Demonstrations**
Protons **539.7**
UF Hydrogen nucleus
BT **Atoms**
Particles (Nuclear physics)
Protoplasm **571.6**
BT **Biology**
Life (Biology)

RT **Cells**
Embryology
Protozoa **579.4**
BT **Microorganisms**
Proverbs (May subdiv. geog.) **398.9**
UF Adages
Maxims
Sayings
BT **Folklore**
Quotations
RT **Epigrams**
Providence and government of God
202; 214; 231
UF God—Providence and govern-
ment
God—Sovereignty
BT **God**
Provincialism
USE **Regionalism**
Provincialisms
USE names of languages with the
subdivision *Provincialisms,*
e.g. **English language—Pro-
vincialisms** [to be added as
needed]
Pruning **631.5**
BT **Forests and forestry**
Fruit culture
Gardening
Trees
Pseudonyms **929.4**
UF Anonyms
Fictitious names
Pen names
BT **Names**
Personal names
Psi (Parapsychology)
USE **Parapsychology**
Psyche (Greek deity) **202**
BT **Gods and goddesses**
Psychiatric care
USE **Mental health services**
Psychiatric hospitals (May subdiv. geog.)
362.2
UF Mental hospitals
BT **Hospitals**
RT **Mentally ill—Institutional care**
Psychiatric services
USE **Mental health services**
Psychiatrists (May subdiv. geog.) **920;**
926

Psychiatrists—*Continued*
    UF   Psychopathologists
    BT   **Psychologists**
Psychiatry (May subdiv. geog.)   **616.89**
    Use for materials on clinical aspects of mental disorders, including therapy. Popular materials and materials on regional or social aspects of mental disorders are entered under **Mental illness**. Systematic descriptions of mental disorders are entered under **Abnormal psychology**.
    BT   **Medicine**
    NT   **Adolescent psychiatry**
          Child psychiatry
          Psychotherapy
    RT   **Abnormal psychology**
          Mental health
          Mental illness
Psychic healing
    USE   **Mental healing**
Psychic phenomena
    USE   **Parapsychology**
Psychical research
    USE   **Parapsychology**
Psychics (May subdiv. geog.)   **133.8092**
    UF   Clairvoyants
    BT   **Parapsychology**
          Persons
Psychoactive drugs
    USE   **Psychotropic drugs**
Psychoanalysis (May subdiv. geog.)
          150.19; 616.89
    BT   **Psychology**
    NT   **Ego (Psychology)**
          Psychosomatic medicine
    RT   **Abnormal psychology**
          Hypnotism
          Mind and body
          Subconsciousness
Psychogenetics
    USE   **Behavior genetics**
Psychokinesis   **133.8**
    UF   Telekinesis
    BT   **Parapsychology**
          Spiritualism
Psychological aspects
    USE   subjects with the subdivision
          Psychological aspects, e.g.
          Drugs—Psychological aspects; World War, 1939-1945—Psychological aspects;
          etc. [to be added as needed]

Psychological stress
    USE   **Stress (Psychology)**
Psychological tests (May subdiv. geog.)
          150.28
    UF   Mental tests
    BT   **Psychology**
    NT   **Ability—Testing**
    RT   **Educational tests and measurements**
Psychological types
    USE   **Typology (Psychology)**
Psychological warfare   **355.3**
    Use for materials on methods used to undermine the morale of the civilian population and the military forces of an enemy country.
    UF   War of nerves
    SA   names of wars with the subdivision *Psychological aspects* [to be added as needed]
    BT   **Applied psychology**
          Military art and science
          Morale
          Propaganda
          War
    NT   **Brainwashing**
          World War, 1939-1945—Psychological aspects
Psychologists (May subdiv. geog.)
          150.92; 920
    NT   **Psychiatrists**
          School psychologists
    RT   **Psychology**
Psychology (May subdiv. geog.)   **150**
    UF   Mind
    SA   religions, theological topics, titles of individual sacred works, types of animals, classes of persons, ethnic groups, and names of individual persons, including individual literary authors, with the subdivision *Psychology,* e.g. **Christianity—Psychology; Women—Psychology; Native Americans—Psychology;** etc.; and subjects with the subdivision *Psychological aspects* for materials on the relationship of particular situations, conditions, activities, environments, or objects to the mental con-

dition or personality of the individual, e.g. **Color—Psychological aspects** [to be added as needed]

BT **Brain**
Philosophy
Soul

NT **Adjustment (Psychology)**
Adolescent psychology
Aggressiveness (Psychology)
Apperception
Applied psychology
Assertiveness (Psychology)
Attention
Attitude (Psychology)
Autonomy (Psychology)
Behavior genetics
Behaviorism
Bible—Psychology
Change (Psychology)
Child psychology
Choice (Psychology)
Color—Psychological aspects
Competition (Psychology)
Consciousness
Criminal psychology
Developmental psychology
Dogs—Psychology
Educational psychology
Ego (Psychology)
Emotions
Ethnopsychology
Genius
Gestalt psychology
Habit
Human behavior
Identity (Psychology)
Ideology
Imagination
Individuality
Instinct
Intellect
Intimacy (Psychology)
Intuition
Loss (Psychology)
Memory
Men—Psychology
Mood (Psychology)
Motivation (Psychology)
Multiple personality
Music—Psychological aspects
Number concept
Parapsychology
Perception
Personality
Phrenology
Physiognomy
Political psychology
Problem solving
Psychoanalysis
Psychological tests
Psychology of religion
Psychophysiology
Reasoning
Rejection (Psychology)
Risk-taking (Psychology)
Security (Psychology)
Self-acceptance
Self-consciousness
Self-control
Self-destructive behavior
Self-esteem
Self-perception
Self-realization
Senses and sensation
Sex—Psychological aspects
Social psychology
Stress (Psychology)
Subconsciousness
Temperament
Thought and thinking
Typology (Psychology)
Values
Women—Psychology

RT **Mental health**
Psychologists

Psychology and religion
USE **Psychology of religion**

Psychology, Applied
USE **Applied psychology**
Persuasion (Psychology)

Psychology, Comparative
USE **Comparative psychology**

Psychology—Computer simulation   150
BT **Computer simulation**

Psychology of color
USE **Color—Psychological aspects**

Psychology of learning   153.1
UF Learning, Psychology of
BT **Animal intelligence**
Child psychology
Education

Psychology of learning—*Continued*
     Educational psychology
     Memory
   NT **Behavior modification**
       Biofeedback training
       Brainwashing
       Concept learning
       Feedback (Psychology)
       Learning disabilities
       Reading comprehension
       Verbal learning
Psychology of music
   USE **Music—Psychological aspects**
Psychology of religion   200.1
   UF Psychology and religion
       Psychology, Religious
       Religion and psychology
       Religion—Psychological aspects
       Religious psychology
   SA religious topics, titles of individ-
       ual sacred works, and names
       of religions with the subdivi-
       sion *Psychology* [to be added
       as needed]
   BT **Psychology**
       Religion
   NT **Christianity—Psychology**
       Faith—Psychology
       Pastoral psychology
Psychology, Pastoral
   USE **Pastoral psychology**
Psychology, Pathological
   USE **Abnormal psychology**
Psychology, Religious
   USE **Pastoral psychology**
       Psychology of religion
Psychology, Structural
   USE **Gestalt psychology**
Psychopathologists
   USE **Psychiatrists**
Psychopathology
   USE **Abnormal psychology**
Psychopathy
   USE **Abnormal psychology**
Psychopharmaceuticals
   USE **Psychotropic drugs**
Psychophysics
   USE **Psychophysiology**
Psychophysiology   152
   Use for materials on the relationship be-
   tween psychological and physiological pro-
   cesses.

   UF Behavioral psychology
       Physiological psychology
       Psychophysics
   BT **Nervous system**
       Physiology
       Psychology
   NT **Behaviorism**
       Color sense
       Emotions
       Human engineering
       Hypnotism
       Left- and right-handedness
       Memory
       Optical illusions
       Pain
       Senses and sensation
       Sleep
       Temperament
   RT **Mind and body**
Psychoses
   USE **Mental illness**
Psychosomatic medicine (May subdiv.
   geog.)   **616.08**
   UF Medicine, Psychosomatic
   BT **Abnormal psychology**
       Medicine
       Mind and body
       Psychoanalysis
Psychotherapy (May subdiv. geog.)
   616.89
   UF Therapy, Psychological
   BT **Psychiatry**
       Therapeutics
   NT **Biofeedback training**
       Family therapy
       Sex therapy
       Transactional analysis
   RT **Mental healing**
       Suggestive therapeutics
Psychotic children
   USE **Emotionally disturbed children**
Psychotics
   USE **Mentally ill**
Psychotropic drugs   615
   Use for general materials on the group of
   drugs that act on the central nervous system
   to affect behavior, mental activity, or percep-
   tion, including the antipsychotic drugs,
   antidepressants, hallucinogenic agents, and
   tranquilizers.

   UF Psychoactive drugs
       Psychopharmaceuticals

Psychotropic drugs—*Continued*

    SA   types of drugs and names of individual drugs [to be added as needed]

    BT   **Drugs**

    NT   **Antidepressants**

          Hallucinogens

          Narcotics

          Stimulants

PTAs

    USE   **Parent-teacher associations**

Pteranodon   567.918

    BT   **Dinosaurs**

          Pterosaurs

Pterodactyls   567.918

    BT   **Dinosaurs**

Pterosaurs   567.918

    BT   **Dinosaurs**

    NT   **Pteranodon**

Puberty   612.6

    BT   **Sex—Physiological aspects**

    RT   **Adolescence**

Public accommodations, Discrimination in

    USE   **Discrimination in public accommodations**

Public administration   351

    Use for general materials on the conduct of public business not limited to a specific place.

    UF   Administration

    SA   names of countries, states, cities, etc., with the subdivision *Politics and government*, e.g. **United States—Politics and government** [to be added as needed]

    BT   **Local government**

          Municipal government

          Political science

    NT   **Administrative agencies**

          Bureaucracy

          Civil service

          Intelligence service

          Licenses

          Military government

          United States—Politics and government

    RT   **Administrative law**

          Public officers

Public assistance

    USE   **Public welfare**

Public buildings (May subdiv. geog.)   **352.5; 725**

    Use for materials on buildings owned by the public and maintained at public expense, such as government office buildings, public libraries, public schools, etc. Materials on buildings that are privately owned and maintained and are open to the public for business or entertainment are entered under **Buildings** or under the specific type of building.

    UF   Government buildings

    SA   names of individual public buildings [to be added as needed]

    BT   **Buildings**

          Public works

    NT   **Capitols**

Public buildings, American

    USE   **Public buildings—United States**

Public buildings—Chicago (Ill.)   **725.09773**

    UF   Chicago (Ill.)—Public buildings

Public buildings—Ohio   **725.09771**

    UF   Ohio—Public buildings

Public buildings—United States   **352.5; 725.0973**

    Use for materials on U.S. federal government buildings located in or outside of the United States, including materials on U.S embassy or consulate buildings abroad.

    UF   Public buildings, American

          United States—Government buildings

          United States—Public buildings

Public debts (May subdiv. geog.)   **336.3**

    Use for materials on government debts.

    UF   Debts, Public

          Federal debt

          Government debts

          National debts

    SA   names of wars with the subdivision *Finance*, e.g. **World War, 1939-1945—Finance** [to be added as needed]

    BT   **Debt**

          Loans

          Public finance

    RT   **Bonds**

          Deficit financing

Public debts—United States   **336.3**

    UF   United States—Public debts

Public demonstrations

    USE   **Demonstrations**

Public documents
USE **Government publications**
Public domain
USE **Public lands**
Public domain software
USE **Free computer software**
Public enterprises
USE **Government business enter-
prises**
Public figures
USE **Celebrities**
Public finance (May subdiv. geog.) **336**
Use for general materials on the raising and
expenditure of funds in the public sector, and,
with a geographic subdivision, for materials
on the public finance of countries, states, lo-
calities, cities, etc.
UF Finance, Public
BT **Finance**
NT **Budget**
Deficit financing
Federal aid
Fiscal policy
Government aid
Government lending
Grants-in-aid
Metropolitan finance
Municipal finance
Public debts
Tariff
Taxation
Public health (May subdiv. geog.)
362.1; 614
UF Hygiene, Social
Public hygiene
Social hygiene
BT **Health**
Human services
Social problems
State medicine
NT **Burial**
Cemeteries
Communicable diseases
Community health services
Cremation
Disinfection and disinfectants
Environmental health
Epidemics
**Food adulteration and inspec-
tion**
Health boards
Health facilities
Hospitals

Immunization
Meat inspection
Medical care
Medical charities
Milk supply
Noise
Occupational health and safety
Pollution
Refuse and refuse disposal
School hygiene
Sewage disposal
Social medicine
Street cleaning
Vaccination
Water pollution
RT **Sanitation**
Public health boards
USE **Health boards**
Public health—Evaluation (May subdiv.
geog.) **362.1**
UF Health program evaluation
Public health—Government policy
USE **Medical policy**
Public health—United States
362.10973; 614
UF United States—Public health
Public housing (May subdiv. geog.)
363.5
UF Government housing
Housing projects, Government
Low income housing
BT **Housing**
Public hygiene
USE **Public health**
Public interest (May subdiv. geog.) **172;
320.01; 344**
UF National interest
BT **State, The**
NT **Ombudsman**
Whistle blowing
Public lands (May subdiv. geog.) **333.1**
UF Crown lands
Public domain
BT **Colonization**
Land use
NT **Forest reserves**
Land grants
National parks and reserves
RT **Natural resources**
Public lands—Ohio 333.109771
UF Ohio—Public lands

Public lands—United States   333.10973
    UF   United States—Public lands
Public libraries (May subdiv. geog.)
    027.4
    UF   County libraries
    BT   **Libraries**
    NT   **Regional libraries**
Public meetings (May subdiv. geog.)
    302.3
    UF   Meetings, Public
    BT   **Freedom of assembly**
    NT   **Demonstrations**
          Parliamentary practice
Public officers   320
    Use for general materials on elected government officials not limited to a particular jurisdiction.
    UF   Elected officials
          Government officials
          Officials and employees
          Public officials
    SA   names of countries, states, cities, etc., with the subdivision *Officials and employees* [to be added as needed]
    NT   **Term limits (Public office)**
    RT   **Civil service**
          Public administration
Public officials
    USE **Public officers**
Public opinion (May subdiv. geog.)
    303.3
    UF   Opinion, Public
    SA   subjects with the subdivision *Public opinion*, e.g. **World War, 1939-1945—Public opinion**; and names of countries with the subdivision *Foreign opinion* for materials dealing with foreign public opinion about the country, e.g. **United States—Foreign opinion** [to be added as needed]
    BT   **Freedom of conscience**
          Political psychology
          Political science
          Social psychology
    NT   **Propaganda**
          Public opinion polls
          Publicity
          United States—Foreign opinion

World War, 1939-1945—Public opinion
    RT   **Attitude (Psychology)**
          Press
          Public relations
Public opinion polls (May subdiv. geog.)
    303.3
    Use for general materials and for materials on the technique of polling public opinion. Materials on polls on a specific topic are entered under the appropriate heading for the topic with the subdivision *Public opinion*. Materials on polls taken in a specific place are entered **Public opinion** subdivided geographically. Materials on polls limited to a specific class of persons are entered under the appropriate heading for the class of persons with the subdivision *Attitudes*.
    UF   Opinion polls
          Polls
          Straw votes
    BT   **Public opinion**
    RT   **Market surveys**
Public ownership
    USE **Government ownership**
           Municipal ownership
Public playgrounds
    USE **Playgrounds**
Public procurement
    USE **Government purchasing**
Public purchasing
    USE **Government purchasing**
Public records—Preservation
    USE **Archives**
Public relations (May subdiv. geog.)
    659.2
    SA   topics with the subdivision *Public relations*, e.g. **Libraries—Public relations** [to be added as needed]
    NT   **Business entertaining**
          Customer relations
    RT   **Advertising**
          Public opinion
          Publicity
Public relations—Libraries
    USE **Libraries—Public relations**
Public safety, Crimes against
    USE **Offenses against public safety**
Public schools (May subdiv. geog.)
    371.01
    Use for materials on preschool, elementary, and secondary schools supported by state and local government. Materials on British en-

Public schools—*Continued*
dowed secondary schools that are open to public admission but are not financed or administered by any government body are entered under **English public schools**.
  BT **Schools**
  NT **Evening and continuation schools**
      High schools
      Junior high schools
      Magnet schools
      Religion in the public schools
      Rural schools
      Summer schools
Public schools and religion
  USE **Religion in the public schools**
Public schools, Endowed (Great Britain)
  USE **English public schools**
Public schools, English
  USE **English public schools**
Public schools—United States
      371.010973
  UF United States—Public schools
Public service commissions (May subdiv. geog.) **354.72**
  Use for materials on bodies appointed to regulate or control public utilities.
  UF Public utility commissions
  BT **Corporation law**
      Corporations
      Industrial policy
Public service corporations
  USE **Public utilities**
Public shelters
  USE **Air raid shelters**
Public speaking 808.5
  Use for materials on the art of delivering speeches. Collections of speeches on several subjects and materials about speeches that have already been delivered are entered under **Speeches**. Materials limited to scholarly lectures are entered under **Lectures and lecturing**.
  UF Elocution
      Oratory
      Persuasion (Rhetoric)
      Speaking
  BT **Communication**
  NT **Acting**
      Book talks
      Chalk talks
      Debates and debating
      Lectures and lecturing
      Preaching
      Voice culture

  RT **Speeches**
      Voice
Public television (May subdiv. geog.) **384.55**
  UF Educational television
  BT **Television broadcasting**
Public transit
  USE **Local transit**
Public utilities (May subdiv. geog.) **343.09; 354.72; 363.6**
  UF Public service corporations
      Utilities, Public
  NT **Electric utilities**
      Gas companies
      Telegraph
      Telephone
      Water supply
Public utility commissions
  USE **Public service commissions**
Public welfare (May subdiv. geog.) **361.6**
  Use for materials on tax-supported welfare activities. Materials on privately supported welfare activities are entered under **Charities**. Materials on the methods employed in welfare work, public or private, are entered under **Social work**. General materials on the various policies, programs, services, and facilities to meet basic human needs, such as health, education, and welfare, are entered under **Human services**.
  UF Poor relief
      Public assistance
      Relief, Public
      Social welfare
      Welfare, Public
      Welfare reform
  BT **Human services**
      Social work
  NT **Child care services**
      Child welfare
      Disaster relief
      Food relief
      Institutional care
      Legal aid
      National service
      Poor
      Social medicine
      Volunteer work
      Welfare state
  RT **Charities**
      Poverty
Public works (May subdiv. geog.) **352.7; 363**

Public works—*Continued*
- BT **Civil engineering**
  Domestic economic assistance
- NT **Infrastructure (Economics)**
  Municipal engineering
  Public buildings
- RT **City planning**

Public works—Chicago (Ill.)   363.09773
- UF Chicago (Ill.)—Public works

Public works—Ohio   352.7; 363.09771
- UF Ohio—Public works

Public works—United States   352.7; 363.0973
- UF United States—Public works

Public worship (May subdiv. geog.)
  203; 264
  May be subdivided by religion or sect.
- UF Church attendance
- BT **Worship**
- NT **Liturgies**
  Worship programs

Publicity (May subdiv. geog.)   **659**
- BT **Public opinion**
- NT **Press**
- RT **Advertising**
  Propaganda
  Public relations

Publishers and authors
- USE **Authors and publishers**

Publishers and publishing (May subdiv.
  geog.)   **070.5**
- UF Book trade
  Publishing
- SA types of literature, types of pub-
  lished materials, and names of
  individual corporate bodies
  and religious denominations
  with the subdivision *Publish-
  ing,* e.g. **Music—Publishing**
  [to be added as needed]
- NT **Authors and publishers**
  Editing
  Electronic publishing
  Music—Publishing
  Printing
  Publishers' catalogs
  **Publishers' standard book
  numbers**
  Serial publications
- RT **Book industry**
  Books
  Booksellers and bookselling

Publishers and publishing—Exhibitions
- USE **Books—Exhibitions**

Publishers' catalogs   015
  Use for catalogs produced by publishers and
  for materials about such catalogs. Retail book
  catalogs and book auction catalogs and mate-
  rials about such catalogs are entered under
  Booksellers' catalogs.
- UF Books—Catalogs
  Catalogs
  Catalogs, Publishers'
- BT **Publishers and publishing**

**Publishers' standard book numbers
  070.5**
- UF Book numbers, Publishers' stan-
  dard
  Standard book numbers
- BT **Publishers and publishing**
- NT **International Standard Book
  Numbers**

Publishing
- USE **Publishers and publishing**
  and types of literature, types of
  published materials, and
  names of individual corporate
  bodies and religious denominations with the subdivision
  Publishing, e.g. **Music—Publishing** [to be added as need-
  ed]

Pubs
- USE **Bars**

Puffins (May subdiv. geog.)   **598.4**
- BT **Birds**

Pugilism
- USE **Boxing**

Pulleys   621.8
- BT **Simple machines**

Pulmonary resuscitation
- USE **Artificial respiration**

Pulsars   523.8
- UF Pulsating radio sources
- BT **Astronomy**

Pulsating radio sources
- USE **Pulsars**

Pumping machinery   621.6
- UF Pumps
- SA types of pumping machinery,
  e.g. **Heat pumps** [to be add-
  ed as needed]
- BT **Engines**
  Hydraulic engineering
- NT **Heat pumps**

Pumps
USE **Pumping machinery**
Punctuality   640
UF   Lateness
Promptness
Tardiness
BT   **Time**
Virtue
Punctuation   411; 421
UF   English language—Punctuation
BT   **Rhetoric**
Punishment (May subdiv. geog.)   **364.6**
UF   Discipline
Penology
BT   **Administration of criminal justice**
Corrections
NT   **Capital punishment**
Correctional institutions
Parole
Prisons
Probation
Reformatories
Torture
RT   **Crime**
Criminal law
Punishment in schools
USE   **School discipline**
Puns   808.88
Use for collections of puns or for materials about puns.
UF   Puns and punning
BT   **Wit and humor**
Puns and punning
USE   **Puns**
Puppets and puppet plays   791.5
Use for individual works, collections, or materials about puppets and puppet plays.
UF   Marionettes
SA   types of puppets or puppet plays [to be added as needed]
BT   **Drama**
Folk drama
Theater
NT   **Shadow pantomimes and plays**
Puppies
USE   **Dogs**
Purchasing (May subdiv. geog.)   **658.7**
Use for general materials on buying and materials on buying by commercial enterprises. Materials on consumer buying are entered under **Shopping**.
UF   Buying

SA   types of products and services with the subdivision *Purchasing*, e.g. **Automobiles—Purchasing** [to be added as needed]
BT   **Management**
NT   **Government purchasing**
Installment plan
Shopping
Pure food
USE   **Food adulteration and inspection**
Purgatory   202; 236
BT   **Eschatology**
Purification of water
USE   **Water purification**
Puritans (May subdiv. geog.)   **285**
BT   **Christian sects**
NT   **Pilgrims (New England colonists)**
RT   **Calvinism**
Church of England—United States
Congregationalism
Puzzles   793.73
Use for individual works, collections, or materials about puzzles.
SA   types of puzzles, e.g. **Crossword puzzles** [to be added as needed]
BT   **Amusements**
NT   **Bible games and puzzles**
Crossword puzzles
Jigsaw puzzles
KenKen
Mathematical recreations
Maze puzzles
Picture puzzles
Rebuses
Sudoku
RT   **Riddles**
Pyramids (May subdiv. geog.)   **722; 909**
BT   **Ancient architecture**
Archeology
Monuments
Pyrography (May subdiv. geog.)   **745.51**
UF   Fire etching
Wood-burning
BT   **Etching**
Woodwork
Quacks and quackery (May subdiv. geog.)   **615.8**

Quacks and quackery—*Continued*
- BT **Impostors and imposture**
  Medicine
  Swindlers and swindling

Quakers
- USE **Society of Friends**

Qualitative analysis
- USE **Analytical chemistry**

Quality control   519.8; 658.5
- SA industries, processes, and materials with the subdivision *Quality control* [to be added as needed]
- BT **Reliability (Engineering)**
  Sampling (Statistics)
- NT **Steel industry—Quality control**

Quality of life (May subdiv. geog.)
303.3
Use for materials on the objective standards and subjective attitudes by which individuals and groups assess their life situations.
- UF Life quality
- BT **Economic conditions**
  Social conditions
- NT **Cost and standard of living**
- RT **Basic needs**

Quantitative analysis
- USE **Analytical chemistry**

Quantity cookery
- USE **Quantity cooking**

Quantity cooking   641.5
Use for materials limited to the preparation and cooking of food in large quantities. Materials on the preparation, delivery, and serving of ready-to-eat foods in large quantities outside of the home are entered under **Food service**.
- UF Cooking for large numbers
  Quantity cookery
- BT **Cooking**
- RT **Food service**

Quantum mechanics
- USE **Quantum theory**

Quantum theory   530.12
- UF Quantum mechanics
- BT **Dynamics**
  Physics
- NT **Wave mechanics**
- RT **Atomic theory**
  Force and energy
  Physical chemistry
  Radiation
  Relativity (Physics)
  Thermodynamics

Quarantine
- USE **Communicable diseases**

Quarks   539.7
- BT **Particles (Nuclear physics)**

Quarries and quarrying (May subdiv. geog.)   **622**
- UF Stone quarries
- BT **Economic geology**
- RT **Stone**

Quartz (May subdiv. geog.)   **549**
- UF Rock crystal
- BT **Crystals**
  Minerals

Quasars   523.1
- UF Quasi-stellar radio sources
- BT **Astronomy**
  Radio astronomy

Quasi-stellar radio sources
- USE **Quasars**

Québec (Province)   971.4

Québec (Province)—History   971.4

Québec (Province)—History—Autonomy and independence movements   **971.4**
- UF Québec (Province)—Separatist movement
  Separatist movement in Québec (Province)
- BT **Separatist movements**

Québec (Province)—Separatist movement
- USE **Québec (Province)—History—Autonomy and independence movements**

Queens (May subdiv. geog.)   **920; 929.7**
Use for materials on women monarchs as well as on wives or consorts of monarchs.
- UF Royalty
  Rulers
  Sovereigns
- SA names of queens, e.g. **Elizabeth II, Queen of Great Britain, 1926-** ; ethnic groups with the subdivision *Queens*, and countries, cities, etc., with the subdivision *Kings and rulers* [to be added as needed]
- BT **Monarchy**
- NT **Elizabeth II, 1926-**
- RT **Courts and courtiers**
  Empresses
  Kings and rulers

Queens—Great Britain   920; 941

Queens—Great Britain—*Continued*
  UF   Great Britain—Queens
  SA   names of British queens [to be
       added as needed]
Queries
  USE   **Questions and answers**
Questions and answers   793.73

  Use for collections of informal quizzes on
various subjects. Informal quizzes on a particular subject are entered under the subject with
the subdivision *Miscellanea*. Materials on formal examinations are entered under **Examinations**. Examination questions on a particular
subject are entered under the subject with the
subdivision *Examinations*, e.g. **Music—Examinations**. Compilations of practice problems
or exercises for use in the study of a topic are
entered under the topic with the subdivision
Problems, exercises, etc., e.g. **Chemistry—
Problems, exercises, etc.**

  UF   Answers to questions
       Queries
       Quizzes
       Trivia
  SA   subjects with the subdivision
       Miscellanea, e.g. **Medicine—
       Miscellanea** [to be added as
       needed]
  NT   **Examinations**
Quick and easy cookery
  USE   **Quick and easy cooking**
Quick and easy cooking   641.5

  Use for materials containing recipes or
cooking techniques emphasizing economy of
preparation time and the use of readily available ingredients.

  UF   Convenience cooking
       Easy and quick cooking
       Quick and easy cookery
       Quick-meal cooking
       Time saving cooking
  BT   **Cooking**
Quick-meal cooking
  USE   **Quick and easy cooking**
Quicksilver
  USE   **Mercury**
Quilt designing
  USE   **Quilts—Design**
Quilting (May subdiv. geog.)   746.46
  BT   **Needlework**
       Sewing
  RT   **Quilts**
Quilts (May subdiv. geog.)   746.46
  UF   Coverlets
       Patchwork quilts
  BT   **Interior design**

  RT   **Quilting**
Quilts—Design   746.46
  UF   Quilt designing
  BT   **Design**
Quintets   785
  BT   **Chamber music**
Quislings
  USE   **World War, 1939-1945—Col-
        laborationists**
Quit-smoking programs
  USE   **Smoking cessation programs**
Quizzes
  USE   **Questions and answers**
Qumran texts
  USE   **Dead Sea scrolls**
Quotations   080; 808.88
  UF   Sayings
  SA   subjects, classes of persons, eth-
       nic groups, and names of in-
       dividuals with the subdivision
       Quotations [to be added as
       needed]
  BT   **Epigrams**
  NT   **Presidents—United States—
       Quotations**
       Proverbs
Qur'an
  USE   **Koran**
Rabbis (May subdiv. geog.)   296.6; 920
  BT   **Clergy**
       Judaism
Rabbits (May subdiv. geog.)   599.32;
       636
  UF   Bunnies
       Bunny rabbits
       Hares
  BT   **Mammals**
Rabies   616.9; 636.089
  UF   Hydrophobia
  BT   **Communicable diseases**
Race   599.97
  BT   **Ethnology**
  NT   **Ethnocentrism**
Race awareness (May subdiv. geog.)
       305.8
  UF   Race identity
       Racial identity
  SA   names of racial groups with the
       subdivision *Race identity* [to
       be added as needed]
  BT   **Race relations**

Race awareness—*Continued*
  NT **African Americans—Race iden-
        tity**
      Blacks—Race identity
      Racism
Race discrimination (May subdiv. geog.)
      305.8
  Use for materials on the restriction or deni-
  al of rights, privileges, or choice because of
  race. Materials on prejudicial attitudes about
  particular groups because of their race are en-
  tered under **Racism**.
  UF Racial discrimination
  SA types of discrimination, e.g. **Dis-
        crimination in education** [to
        be added as needed]
  BT **Discrimination**
      Race relations
      Racism
      Social problems
Race identity
  USE **Race awareness**
        and names of racial groups
        with the subdivision *Race
        identity,* e.g. **Blacks—Race
        identity; African Ameri-
        cans—Race identity;** etc. [to
        be added as needed]
Race prejudice
  USE **Racism**
Race problems
  USE **Race relations**
Race psychology
  USE **Ethnopsychology**
Race relations 305.8
  UF Integration, Racial
      Interracial relations
      Race problems
      Racial integration
  SA names of countries, cities, etc.,
        with the subdivision *Race re-
        lations,* e.g. **United States—
        Race relations** [to be added
        as needed]
  BT **Acculturation**
      Ethnology
      Sociology
  NT **Chicago (Ill.)—Race relations**
      Culture conflict
      Discrimination
      Interracial adoption
      Ohio—Race relations
      Race awareness

      Race discrimination
      Racism
      School integration
      Segregation
      South Africa—Race relations
      United States—Race relations
      White supremacy movements
  RT **Ethnic relations**
      Minorities
      Multiculturalism
      Pluralism (Social sciences)
Race relations and the church
  USE **Church and race relations**
Races of people
  USE **Ethnology**
Racial balance in schools
  USE **School integration**
      Segregation in education
Racial bias
  USE **Racism**
Racial discrimination
  USE **Race discrimination**
Racial identity
  USE **Race awareness**
Racial integration
  USE **Race relations**
Racial intermarriage
  USE **Interracial marriage**
Racially mixed people (May subdiv.
      geog.) **305.8**
  UF Bi-racial people
      Mixed race people
      Mulattoes
      Multiracial people
  BT **Ethnic groups**
Racing (May subdiv. geog.) **796**
  SA types of racing and names of
        races, e.g. **Indianapolis 500**
        [to be added as needed]
  BT **Sports**
  NT **Airplane racing**
      Automobile racing
      Bicycle racing
      Boat racing
      Horse racing
      Orienteering
      Soap box derbies
  RT **Running**
Racism (May subdiv. geog.) **305.8;**
      320.5
  Use for materials on prejudicial attitudes
  about particular groups because of their race.

Racism—*Continued*

Materials on the restriction or denial of rights, privileges, or choice because of race are entered under **Race discrimination**.

 UF Race prejudice

   Racial bias

 BT **Attitude (Psychology)**

   Prejudices

   Race awareness

   Race relations

 NT **Race discrimination**

   White supremacy movements

Racketeering (May subdiv. geog.)
  364.106

 UF Crime syndicates

 BT **Crime**

   Organized crime

 NT **Extortion**

Racquetball (May subdiv. geog.)
  796.343

 BT **Ball games**

   Sports

Radar **621.3848**

 BT **Navigation**

   Radio

   Remote sensing

Radar defense networks (May subdiv. geog.) **623**

 UF Defenses, Radar

 BT **Air defenses**

Radiant heating **697**

 UF Panel heating

 BT **Heating**

Radiation **539.2**

 BT **Optics**

   Physics

   Waves

 NT **Cosmic rays**

   Electromagnetic waves

   Gamma rays

   Infrared radiation

   Luminescence

   Radioactivity

   Radium

   Sound

   Spectrum analysis

   Ultraviolet rays

   X-rays

 RT **Light**

   Quantum theory

Radiation biology

 USE **Radiobiology**

Radiation—Physiological effect **612**

 RT **Atomic bomb—Physiological effect**

   Nuclear medicine

Radiation—Safety measures **363.1; 612**

 BT **Accidents—Prevention**

Radiation, Solar

 USE **Solar radiation**

Radiation therapy

 USE **Radiotherapy**

Radicalism (May subdiv. geog.) **320.5**

 Use for materials on extremist social and political movements of either the right or the left.

 UF Extremism (Political science)

   Political extremism

   Radicals and radicalism

 BT **Political science**

   Revolutions

   Right and left (Political science)

 NT **Militia movements**

 RT **Counter culture**

Radicals and radicalism

 USE **Radicalism**

Radio (May subdiv. geog.) **621.384**

 UF Wireless

 SA radio and other subjects, e.g. **Radio and music**; and radio in various industries or fields of endeavor, e.g. **Radio in aeronautics** [to be added as needed]

 BT **Telecommunication**

 NT **Radar**

   Radio and music

   Radio frequency modulation

   Radio in aeronautics

   Radio in astronautics

   Radio in education

   Shortwave radio

Radio addresses, debates, etc. (May subdiv. geog.) **384.54; 808.5; 808.85**

 UF Radio lectures

 BT **Debates and debating**

   Lectures and lecturing

   Radio broadcasting

   Radio scripts

Radio advertising (May subdiv. geog.) **659.14**

Radio advertising—*Continued*
UF   Commercials, Radio
     Radio commercials
BT   **Advertising**
     Radio broadcasting
Radio and music   780; 781.5
UF   Music and radio
BT   **Music**
     Radio
NT   **Disc jockeys**
Radio and television novels   808.3
Use for individual works, collections, or materials about novels based on radio or television programs.
UF   Radio novels
     Television novels
BT   **Fiction**
RT   **Movie novels**
Radio astronomy (May subdiv. geog.)
     522
SA   names of celestial radio sources, e.g. **Quasars** [to be added as needed]
BT   **Astronomy**
     Interstellar communication
NT   **Quasars**
Radio authorship   808
UF   Radio script writing
     Radio writing
BT   **Authorship**
     Radio broadcasting
NT   **Radio plays—Technique**
RT   **Radio scripts**
Radio broadcasting (May subdiv. geog.)
     384.54
UF   Radio industry
SA   radio broadcasting of particular kinds of programs, e.g. **Radio broadcasting of sports** [to be added as needed]
BT   **Broadcasting**
     Mass media
NT   **Radio addresses, debates, etc.**
     Radio advertising
     Radio authorship
     Radio broadcasting of sports
     Radio programs
     Radio stations
Radio broadcasting of sports (May subdiv. geog.)   **070.4**
UF   Sports broadcasting
     Sports in radio

BT   **Broadcast journalism**
     Radio broadcasting
Radio chemistry
USE   **Radiochemistry**
Radio comedies
USE   **Comedy radio programs**
Radio comedy programs
USE   **Comedy radio programs**
Radio commercials
USE   **Radio advertising**
Radio drama
USE   **Radio plays**
Radio—Equipment and supplies
     621.384028
NT   **Radio—Receivers and reception**
RT   **Radio supplies industry**
Radio equipment industry
USE   **Radio supplies industry**
Radio frequency modulation   621.384
UF   FM radio
     Frequency modulation, Radio
BT   **Radio**
NT   **Shortwave radio**
Radio in aeronautics   629.135
BT   **Aeronautics**
     Navigation (Aeronautics)
     Radio
Radio in astronautics   629.4
UF   Lunar surface radio communication
BT   **Astronautics—Communication systems**
     Navigation (Astronautics)
     Radio
Radio in education   371.33
UF   Education and radio
BT   **Audiovisual education**
     Radio
     Teaching—Aids and devices
Radio industry
USE   **Radio broadcasting**
     Radio supplies industry
Radio journalism
USE   **Broadcast journalism**
Radio lectures
USE   **Radio addresses, debates, etc.**
Radio novels
USE   **Radio and television novels**
Radio operators (May subdiv. geog.)
     621.3841

Radio plays   808.2; 808.82

Use for individual works, collections, or materials about radio plays.

UF   Radio drama

Scenarios

BT   **Drama**

Radio programs

NT   **Soap operas**

RT   **Radio scripts**

Radio plays—Technique   808.2

UF   Play writing

Playwriting

BT   **Drama—Technique**

Radio authorship

RT   **Television plays—Technique**

Radio programs (May subdiv. geog.)
384.54

Use for individual works, collections, or materials about radio programs.

UF   Programs, Radio

SA   types of programs and names of specific programs [to be added as needed]

BT   **Radio broadcasting**

NT   **Adventure radio programs**

Biographical radio programs

Comedy radio programs

Fantasy radio programs

Horror radio programs

Legal drama (Radio programs)

Medical drama (Radio programs)

Mystery radio programs

Radio plays

Radio serials

Science fiction radio programs

Sports drama (Radio programs)

Spy radio programs

Talk shows

Variety shows (Radio programs)

War radio programs

Westerns (Radio programs)

RT   **Radio scripts**

**Radio—Receivers and reception
621.384**

UF   Radio reception

Radios

BT   **Radio—Equipment and supplies**

Radio reception

USE   **Radio—Receivers and reception**

Radio—Repairing   621.384

UF   Radio repairs

Radio servicing

Radio repairs

USE   **Radio—Repairing**

Radio script writing

USE   **Radio authorship**

Radio scripts   791.44; 808.88

Use for individual works, collections, or materials about radio scripts.

NT   **Radio addresses, debates, etc.**

RT   **Radio authorship**

Radio plays

Radio programs

Radio serials   791.44

Use for individual works, collections, or materials about radio serials.

BT   **Radio programs**

RT   **Soap operas**

Radio servicing

USE   **Radio—Repairing**

Radio stations (May subdiv. geog.)
384.54

SA   names of specific radio stations [to be added as needed]

BT   **Radio broadcasting**

NT   **Amateur radio stations**

Radio supplies industry (May subdiv. geog.)   **338.4**

UF   Radio equipment industry

Radio industry

BT   **Industries**

RT   **Radio—Equipment and supplies**

Radio waves

USE   **Electric waves**

Radio writing

USE   **Radio authorship**

Radioactive fallout (May subdiv. geog.)
539.7

UF   Dust, Radioactive

Fallout, Radioactive

BT   **Atomic bomb**

Hydrogen bomb

Radioactive pollution

Radioactive isotopes

USE   **Radioisotopes**

Radioactive pollution (May subdiv. geog.)
363.17; 363.73; 621.48

Radioactive pollution—*Continued*
 UF Environmental radioactivity
 Nuclear pollution
 Pollution, Radioactive
 BT **Pollution**
 Radioactivity
 NT **Radioactive fallout**
 RT **Radioactive waste disposal**
Radioactive substances
 USE **Radioactivity**
Radioactive waste disposal (May subdiv.
 geog.) **363.72; 621.48**
 UF Nuclear waste disposal
 BT **Nuclear engineering**
 Nuclear power plants—Envi-
 ronmental aspects
 Radioactivity
 Refuse and refuse disposal
 RT **Radioactive pollution**
Radioactivity **539.7**
 UF Radioactive substances
 BT **Physics**
 Radiation
 NT **Cosmic rays**
 Phosphorescence
 Radioactive pollution
 Radioactive waste disposal
 Radiobiology
 Radiochemistry
 Radiotherapy
 Transmutation (Chemistry)
 RT **Nuclear physics**
 Radium
 Radon
 Uranium
Radiobiology **571.4**
 UF Radiation biology
 BT **Biology**
 Biophysics
 Nuclear physics
 Radioactivity
Radiocarbon dating **539.7**
 UF Carbon 14 dating
 Dating, Radiocarbon
 BT **Archeology**
Radiochemistry **541**
 UF Radio chemistry
 BT **Physical chemistry**
 Radioactivity
Radiography
 USE **X-rays**
Radioisotopes **621.48**

 UF Radioactive isotopes
 BT **Isotopes**
 Nuclear engineering
Radiologists (May subdiv. geog.) **920**
 BT **Physicians**
 RT **Radiotherapy**
Radios
 USE **Radio—Receivers and recep-**
 tion
Radiotherapy **615.8**
 UF Radiation therapy
 BT **Electrotherapeutics**
 Physical therapy
 Radioactivity
 Therapeutics
 RT **Phototherapy**
 Radiologists
 Radium
 Ultraviolet rays
 X-rays
Radium **546; 661; 669**
 BT **Chemical elements**
 Radiation
 RT **Radioactivity**
 Radiotherapy
Radium emanation
 USE **Radon**
Radon **363.738; 546**
 UF Radium emanation
 BT **Poisonous gases**
 RT **Radioactivity**
Rage
 USE **Anger**
Railroad accidents (May subdiv. geog.)
 363.12
 UF Collisions, Railroad
 Derailments
 Railroads—Accidents
 Train wrecks
 BT **Accidents**
 Disasters
Railroad construction
 USE **Railroad engineering**
Railroad engineering (May subdiv. geog.)
 625.1
 UF Railroad construction
 BT **Civil engineering**
 Engineering
 Railroads
Railroad fares
 USE **Railroads—Rates**

Railroad mergers
USE **Railroads—Mergers**
Railroad rates
USE **Railroads—Rates**
Railroad workers
USE **Railroads—Employees**
Railroads (May subdiv. geog.) **385;**
625.1
UF Railways
Trains
SA names of individual railroads [to
be added as needed]
BT **Transportation**
NT **Cable railroads**
Electric railroads
Express service
Freight
Locomotives
Monorail railroads
Railroad engineering
Street railroads
Subways
Railroads—Accidents
USE **Railroad accidents**
Railroads and state
USE **Railroads—Government policy**
Railroads, Cable
USE **Cable railroads**
Railroads—Consolidation
USE **Railroads—Mergers**
Railroads—Employees (May subdiv.
geog.) **331.7**
UF Railroad workers
BT **Employees**
Railroads—Fares
USE **Railroads—Rates**
Railroads—Finance (May subdiv. geog.)
385
BT **Finance**
NT **Railroads—Rates**
Railroads—Government ownership
USE **Railroads—Government policy**
Railroads—Government policy (May
subdiv. geog.) **354.6; 385**
UF Government ownership of rail-
roads
Government regulation of rail-
roads
Nationalization of railroads
Railroads and state

Railroads—Government owner-
ship
Railroads, Nationalization of
State and railroads
State ownership of railroads
BT **Government ownership**
Industrial policy
NT **Railroads—Rates**
Railroads—Mergers (May subdiv. geog.)
338.8
UF Railroad mergers
Railroads—Consolidation
BT **Corporate mergers and acqui-**
sitions
Railroads—Models 625.1
UF Model trains
BT **Models and modelmaking**
Railroads, Nationalization of
USE **Railroads—Government policy**
Railroads—Rates (May subdiv. geog.)
385
UF Railroad fares
Railroad rates
Railroads—Fares
BT **Railroads—Finance**
Railroads—Government policy
RT **Freight**
Railroads—Safety appliances
USE **Railroads—Safety devices**
Railroads—Safety devices 625.10028
UF Railroads—Safety appliances
BT **Accidents—Prevention**
Safety devices
NT **Railroads—Signaling**
Railroads—Signaling 625.1
UF Block signal systems
Interlocking signals
BT **Railroads—Safety devices**
Signals and signaling
Railroads, Single rail
USE **Monorail railroads**
Railroads—Statistics 385
BT **Statistics**
Railways
USE **Railroads**
Rain (May subdiv. geog.) **551.57**
UF Rain and rainfall
Rainfall
BT **Precipitation (Meteorology)**
NT **Acid rain**
Floods

Rain—*Continued*
    RT   **Droughts**
           Forest influences
           Storms
Rain and rainfall
    USE **Rain**
Rain forest ecology (May subdiv. geog.)
     577.34
    BT   **Ecology**
Rain forests (May subdiv. geog.)
     577.34; 634.9

Use for materials on forests of broad-leaved, mainly evergreen trees found in moist climates in the tropics, subtropics, and some parts of the temperate zones. Materials on impenetrable thickets of second-growth vegetation replacing tropical rain forests that have been disturbed or degraded are entered under **Jungles**.

    UF Rainforests
          Tropical rain forests
    BT   **Forests and forestry**
    RT   **Jungles**
Rain making
    USE **Weather control**
Rainbow   **551.56**
    BT   **Meteorology**
    RT   **Refraction**
Rainfall
    USE **Rain**
Rainfall and forests
    USE **Forest influences**
Rainforests
    USE **Rain forests**
Rallies (Protest)
    USE **Demonstrations**
Ramadan (May subdiv. geog.)   **297.3**
    BT   **Islamic holidays**
Rāmāyaṇa   **891.4**
    BT   **Indian epic poetry**
Ranch life (May subdiv. geog.)   **307.72; 636**
    BT   **Farm life**
           Frontier and pioneer life
    NT   **Cowhands**
Random sampling
    USE **Sampling (Statistics)**
Ranger project
    USE **Project Ranger**
Rank
    USE **Social classes**
Rap music (May subdiv. geog.)
     782.421649

    UF Rap songs
          Rapping (Music)
    BT   **African American music**
           Popular music
Rap songs
    USE **Rap music**
Rape (May subdiv. geog.)   **362.883; 364.15**
    UF Assault, Sexual
          Sexual assault
    BT   **Offenses against the person**
           Sex crimes
    NT   **Date rape**
Rapid reading
    USE **Speed reading**
Rapid transit
    USE **Local transit**
Rapping (Music)
    USE **Rap music**
Raptorex   **567.912**
    BT   **Dinosaurs**
Rare animals (May subdiv. geog.)
     591.68
    SA   names of specific animals, e.g.
          Bison [to be added as needed]
    BT   **Animals**
    RT   **Endangered species**
           Extinct animals
           Wildlife conservation
Rare books (May subdiv. geog.)   **090**
    UF Antiquarian books
          Bibliography—Rare books
          Book rarities
    BT   **Books**
Rare plants (May subdiv. geog.)   **581.68**
    BT   **Plants**
    RT   **Endangered species**
           Plant conservation
Rates
    USE types of services, utilities, transportation systems, etc., with the subdivision *Rates*, e.g. **Railroads—Rates** [to be added as needed]
Rating
    USE **Performance standards**
          and subjects and classes of persons with the subdivision *Rating,* e.g. **Bonds—Rating;**

Rating—*Continued*

   Employees—Rating; etc. [to be added as needed]

Ratio and proportion **513.2**
 BT **Arithmetic**
   Geometry

Rationalism **149; 211**
 BT **Philosophy**
   Religion
   Secularism
   Theory of knowledge
 NT **Empiricism**
   Enlightenment
   Intuition
   Positivism
   Reason
   Skepticism
 RT **Agnosticism**
   Atheism
   Belief and doubt
   Deism
   Free thought
   Realism

Rattlesnakes (May subdiv. geog.) **597.96**
 BT **Poisonous animals**
   Snakes

Raw materials (May subdiv. geog.)
 333.7

Use for works on unprocessed minerals and unprocessed animal and vegetable products. Comprehensive works on the basic processed materials used in engineering and industry are entered under **Materials**.
 BT **Commercial products**
 NT **Farm produce**
   Forest products
   Mines and mineral resources

Rayon **677**
 BT **Synthetic fabrics**

Rays, Ultra-violet
 USE **Ultraviolet rays**

Re-enlistment
 USE **Recruiting and enlistment**

Reaction (Political science)
 USE **Conservatism**

Reactions, Chemical
 USE **Chemical reactions**

Reactors (Nuclear physics)
 USE **Nuclear reactors**

Reader services (Libraries)
 USE **Library services**

Readers
 USE **Reading materials**

Readers and libraries
 USE **Library services**

Readers' theater (May subdiv. geog.)
 792

Use for materials on the dramatic reading of plays before an audience.
 BT **Theater**

Readiness for mathematics
 USE **Mathematical readiness**

Readiness for reading
 USE **Reading readiness**

Readiness for school **372.21**
 UF School readiness
 BT **Elementary education**
   Preschool education

Reading **372.4; 418**

Use for materials on methods of teaching reading and for general materials on the art of reading. Materials on teaching slow readers are entered under **Reading—Remedial teaching**. Materials on the cultural or informational aspects of reading and general discussions of books are entered under **Books and reading**.
 UF Children's reading
   Reading—Study and teaching
 BT **Language arts**
 NT **Books and reading**
   Reading comprehension
   Reading disability
   Reading—Phonetic method
   Reading readiness
   Speed reading
   Word recognition
   Word skills

Reading clinics
 USE **Reading—Remedial teaching**

Reading comprehension **372.48**
 BT **Psychology of learning**
   Reading
   Verbal learning

Reading disability **371.91**
 SA types of reading disabilities, e.g.
   Dyslexia [to be added as needed]
 BT **Learning disabilities**
   Reading
 NT **Dyslexia**

Reading interests
 USE **Books and reading**

Reading interests of children
 USE **Children—Books and reading**

Reading interests of teenagers
 USE **Teenagers—Books and reading**

Reading interests of young adults
 USE **Teenagers—Books and reading**
Reading materials   372.41; 418
  Use for materials in English intended to be used in teaching reading or language skills. Such materials in other languages are entered under the language with the subdivision *Reading materials.*
 UF English language—Reading materials
   Readers
 SA names of languages other than English with the subdivision *Reading materials,* e.g. **French language—Reading materials** [to be added as needed]
 BT **Children's literature**
 NT **Basal readers**
   Big books
   Easy reading materials
   Hornbooks
   Recitations
 RT **Books and reading**
Reading—Patterning
 USE **Language arts—Patterning**
Reading—Phonetic method   372.46
 UF Letter-sound association
   Phonics
 BT **English language—Pronunciation**
   Reading
 RT **Phonetics**
Reading readiness   372.41
 UF Readiness for reading
 BT **Reading**
Reading—Remedial teaching   372.43
 UF Reading clinics
   Remedial reading
Reading—Study and teaching
 USE **Reading**
Readings and recitations
 USE **Recitations**
Readings (Anthologies)
 USE **Anthologies**
Ready reckoners
 USE **Mathematics—Tables**
Real estate (May subdiv. geog.)   **333.3**
  Use for materials on land and buildings considered as property. Materials on the buying and selling of real property are entered under **Real estate business**. General materials on land apart from the aspect of ownership are entered under **Land use**.

 UF Real property
   Realty
 BT **Land use**
   Property
 NT **Farms**
   Landlord and tenant
   Real estate business
   Real estate investment
 RT **Land tenure**
Real estate business (May subdiv. geog.)   **333.33; 346.04**
  Use for materials limited to the buying and selling of real property. General materials on land and buildings considered as property are entered under **Real estate**.
 BT **Business**
   Real estate
 NT **Houses—Buying and selling**
   Timesharing (Real estate)
Real estate investment (May subdiv. geog.)   **332.63**
 UF Investment in real estate
   Real property investment
 BT **Investments**
   Real estate
   Speculation
Real estate investment—Taxation (May subdiv. geog.)   **343.05**
 BT **Taxation**
Real estate timesharing
 USE **Timesharing (Real estate)**
Real property
 USE **Real estate**
Real property investment
 USE **Real estate investment**
Real property tax—Assessment
 USE **Tax assessment**
Realism   149
 BT **Philosophy**
 NT **Pragmatism**
 RT **Idealism**
   Materialism
   Positivism
   Rationalism
Realism in art   709.03
 UF Naturalism in art
 BT **Art**
Realism in literature   809
 UF Naturalism in literature
 BT **Literature**
Reality   111

Reality—*Continued*
　BT　**Philosophy**
　　　Truth
　RT　**Pragmatism**
　　　Theory of knowledge
Reality shows (Television)
　USE　**Reality television programs**
Reality television programs (May subdiv.
　　geog.)　**791.45**
　　Use for individual works, collections, or
　materials about reality television programs.
　UF　Reality shows (Television)
　BT　**Television programs**
Realty
　USE　**Real estate**
Reapers
　USE　**Harvesting machinery**
Reapportionment (Election law)
　USE　**Apportionment (Election law)**
Reason　128; 160
　BT　**Intellect**
　　　Rationalism
　NT　**Reasoning**
Reasoning　153.4; 160
　BT　**Psychology**
　　　Reason
　　　Thought and thinking
　NT　**Critical thinking**
　RT　**Intellect**
　　　Logic
Rebellions
　USE　**Insurgency**
　　　Revolutions
Rebels (Social psychology)
　USE　**Alienation (Social psychology)**
Rebirth
　USE　**Reincarnation**
Rebuses　793.73
　BT　**Literary recreations**
　　　Puzzles
　　　Riddles
Recall of products
　USE　**Product recall**
Recall (Political science) (May subdiv.
　　geog.)　**324.6**
　BT　**Impeachments**
　　　**Representative government and
　　　representation**
Recessions (May subdiv. geog.)　**338.5**
　UF　Business recessions
　　　Economic recessions

　SA　names of countries, states, cities,
　　　etc., with the subdivision *Eco-
　　　nomic conditions* [to be added
　　　as needed]
　BT　**Business cycles**
Recipes
　USE　**Cooking**
Reciprocity
　USE　**Commercial policy**
Recitation of the Koran
　USE　**Koran—Recitation**
Recitations　808.85
　　Use for collections of material written or
　selected for oral presentation and for materials
　about recitation.
　UF　Declamations
　　　Narrations
　　　Oral interpretation
　　　Readings and recitations
　BT　**Reading materials**
　　　School assembly programs
　NT　**Choral speaking**
　　　Koran—Recitation
　　　Monologues
　　　Monologues with music
Recitations with music
　USE　**Monologues with music**
Reclamation of land (May subdiv. geog.)
　　627; 631.6
　　Use for general materials on reclamation,
　including drainage and irrigation.
　UF　Clearing of land
　　　Land, Reclamation of
　BT　**Agriculture**
　　　Civil engineering
　　　Hydraulic engineering
　　　Land use
　NT　**Drainage**
　RT　**Irrigation**
Recluses
　USE　**Hermits**
Recombinant DNA　572.8
　BT　**DNA**
　　　Genetic engineering
　　　Genetic recombination
Recombination, Genetic
　USE　**Genetic recombination**
Recommendations for positions
　USE　**Applications for positions**
Reconciliation, Sacrament of
　USE　**Penance**

Reconnaissance, Aerial
   USE   **Aerial reconnaissance**
Reconstruction (1865-1876) (May subdiv.
   geog.)   **973.8**
   UF   Carpetbag rule
         United States—History—1861-
         1865, Civil War—Reconstruc-
         tion
   BT   **United States—History—1865-
         1898**
Reconstruction (1914-1939) (May subdiv.
   geog.)   **940.3**
   UF   World War, 1914-1918— Recon-
         struction
   RT   **Foreign aid
         International cooperation
         World War, 1914-1918—Eco-
         nomic aspects**
Reconstruction (1939-1951) (May subdiv.
   geog. except U.S.)   **940.53**
   UF   Marshall Plan
         World War, 1939-1945—Recon-
         struction
   NT   **World War, 1939-1945—Civil-
         ian relief
         World War, 1939-1945—Repa-
         rations**
   RT   **Foreign aid
         International cooperation
         World War, 1939-1945—Eco-
         nomic aspects**
Reconstructive surgery
   USE   **Plastic surgery**
Record players
   USE   **Phonograph**
Recorded books
   USE   **Audiobooks**
Recording, Laser
   USE   **Laser recording**
Recordings, Sound
   USE   **Sound recordings**
Records of achievement
   USE   **World records**
Records of births, etc.
   USE   **Registers of births, etc.
         Vital statistics**
Records, Phonograph
   USE   **Sound recordings**
Records—Preservation
   USE   **Archives**

Records, Sports
   USE   **Sports records**
Records, World
   USE   **World records**
Recovered memories
   USE   **Recovered memory**
Recovered memory   **616.85**
   UF   Delayed memory
         Recovered memories
         Repressed memory
   BT   **Memory**
   RT   **False memory syndrome**
Recovering addicts   **362.29; 616.86**
   BT   **Drug addicts**
   RT   **Recovering alcoholics**
Recovering alcoholics   **362.292; 616.86**
   BT   **Alcoholics**
   RT   **Recovering addicts**
Recovery of space vehicles
   USE   **Space vehicles—Recovery**
Recreation (May subdiv. geog.)   **790**
   UF   Pastimes
         Relaxation
   SA   classes of persons with the sub-
         division *Recreation*, e.g. **El-
         derly—Recreation** [to be
         added as needed]
   NT   **Camps
         Community centers
         Elderly—Recreation
         Games
         Hobbies
         Outdoor recreation
         Play
         Playgrounds
         Popular culture
         Resorts
         Sports
         Vacations**
   RT   **Amusements
         Leisure
         Sports facilities**
Recreation centers
   USE   **Community centers
         Physical fitness centers**
Recreational vehicles (May subdiv. geog.)
         629.226
   UF   RVs

Recreational vehicles—*Continued*
　　SA　types of recreational vehicles,
　　　　　e.g. **Travel trailers and**
　　　　　campers [to be added as
　　　　　needed]
　　BT　**Outdoor recreation**
　　　　　Vehicles
　　NT　**Travel trailers and campers**
Recreations, Literary
　　USE　**Literary recreations**
Recreations, Mathematical
　　USE　**Mathematical recreations**
Recreations, Scientific
　　USE　**Scientific recreations**
Recruiting
　　USE　**Recruiting and enlistment**
　　　　　Recruiting of employees
　　　　　and types of employees and
　　　　　professions with the subdivi-
　　　　　sion *Recruiting,* e.g. **Librari-**
　　　　　ans—Recruiting; and names
　　　　　of armed forces and of armies
　　　　　and navies with the subdivi-
　　　　　sion *Recruiting and enlistment*
　　　　　[to be added as needed]
Recruiting and enlistment　355.2
　　UF　Armed forces—Recruiting, enlist-
　　　　　ment, etc.
　　　　　Enlistment
　　　　　Re-enlistment
　　　　　Recruiting
　　　　　Recruiting, enlistment, etc.
　　SA　names of armed forces and of
　　　　　armies and navies with the
　　　　　subdivision *Recruiting and en-*
　　　　　listment, e.g. **United States—**
　　　　　Armed Forces—Recruiting
　　　　　and enlistment; United
　　　　　States. Army—Recruiting
　　　　　and enlistment; etc. [to be
　　　　　added as needed]
　　BT　**Armed forces**
　　　　　Military personnel
　　NT　**Draft**
　　　　　United States. Army—Recruit-
　　　　　ing and enlistment
　　　　　United States. Navy—Recruit-
　　　　　ing and enlistment
　　　　　United States—Armed
　　　　　Forces—Recruiting and en-
　　　　　listment
　　　　　Voluntary military service

Recruiting, enlistment, etc.
　　USE　**Recruiting and enlistment**
　　　　　and names of armed forces and
　　　　　of armies and navies with the
　　　　　subdivision *Recruiting and en-*
　　　　　listment, e.g. **United States—**
　　　　　Armed Forces—Recruiting and
　　　　　enlistment; United States.
　　　　　Army—Recruiting and enlist-
　　　　　ment; etc. [to be added as
　　　　　needed]
Recruiting of employees (May subdiv.
　　geog.)　**658.3**
　　UF　Recruiting
　　SA　types of employees and profes-
　　　　　sions with the subdivision *Re-*
　　　　　cruiting, e.g. **Librarians—Re-**
　　　　　cruiting [to be added as
　　　　　needed]
　　BT　**Personnel management**
　　NT　**Employment agencies**
　　　　　Librarians—Recruiting
Rectors
　　USE　**Clergy**
Recurrent education
　　USE　**Continuing education**
Recycling (May subdiv. geog.)　**628.4**
　　UF　Conversion of waste products
　　　　　Recycling (Waste, etc.)
　　SA　subjects with the subdivision
　　　　　Recycling, e.g. **Aluminum—**
　　　　　Recycling [to be added as
　　　　　needed]
　　BT　**Energy conservation**
　　　　　Pollution control industry
　　　　　Salvage
　　NT　**Aluminum—Recycling**
　　RT　**Refuse and refuse disposal**
　　　　　Waste products
Recycling (Waste, etc.)
　　USE　**Recycling**
Red　535.6; 752
　　BT　**Color**
Redemption
　　USE　**Salvation**
Reducing
　　USE　**Weight loss**
Reef ecology (May subdiv. geog.)　**577.7**
　　BT　**Ecology**
　　　　　Marine ecology

Reenactment of historical events
USE **Historical reenactments**
Reference books (May subdiv. geog.)
028.7

Use for materials about reference books. Reference books themselves are entered under **Encyclopedias and dictionaries**; or under the appropriate subjects with the subdivisions *Dictionaries*; *Bibliography*; etc., as needed.

BT **Bibliography**
Books
Books and reading
NT **Encyclopedias and dictionaries**
Reference books—Reviews 028.1
Reference services (Libraries) (May subdiv. geog.) **025.5**

Use for materials on activities designed to make information available to library users, including direct personal assistance.

UF Library reference services
Reference work (Libraries)
BT **Information services**
Library services
NT **Electronic reference services (Libraries)**
Reference work (Libraries)
USE **Reference services (Libraries)**
Referendum (May subdiv. geog.) **328.2**
UF Direct legislation
Initiative and referendum
Legislation, Direct
BT **Constitutional law**
Democracy
Elections
Refinishing furniture
USE **Furniture finishing**
Reflexology (May subdiv. geog.) **615.8**
BT **Alternative medicine**
Reforestation (May subdiv. geog.)
333.75; 634.9
BT **Forests and forestry**
RT **Tree planting**
Reform, Agrarian
USE **Land reform**
Reform of criminals
USE **Corrections**
Probation
Reformatories
Reform of health care delivery
USE **Health care reform**
Reform of medical care delivery
USE **Health care reform**

Reform schools
USE **Reformatories**
Reform, Social
USE **Social problems**
Reformation (May subdiv. geog.) **270.6**
UF Protestant Reformation
SA names of religious sects, e.g.
Huguenots [to be added as needed]
BT **Christianity**
Church history—1500-, Modern period
NT **Calvinism**
Huguenots
RT **Counter-Reformation**
Protestantism
Reformatories (May subdiv. geog.) **365**
UF Penal institutions
Reform of criminals
Reform schools
BT **Children—Institutional care**
Correctional institutions
Prisons
Punishment
NT **Probation**
RT **Juvenile delinquency**
Reformers (May subdiv. geog.) **920**

Use for materials about political, social, or religious reformers.

NT **Abolitionists**
Suffragists
Refraction **535**
UF Dioptrics
BT **Light**
Optics
RT **Rainbow**
Refrigeration (May subdiv. geog.) **621.5**
UF Cooling appliances
Freezing
Refrigeration and refrigerating machinery
Refrigerators
BT **Frost**
RT **Air conditioning**
Cold storage
Low temperatures
Refrigeration and refrigerating machinery
USE **Refrigeration**
Refrigerators
USE **Refrigeration**
Refugees (May subdiv. geog.) **305.9; 341.4; 362.87**

Refugees—*Continued*
UF Displaced persons
SA refugees of particular countries, geographic regions, or ethnic groups, e.g. **Vietnamese refugees**; **Arab refugees**; etc., and names of wars with the subdivision *Refugees*, e.g. **World War, 1939-1945—Refugees** [to be added as needed]
BT **Aliens**
    Homeless persons
    Immigration and emigration
NT **Arab refugees**
    Political refugees
    Vietnamese refugees
RT **Sanctuary movement**
Refugees, Arab
USE **Arab refugees**
Refugees, Political
USE **Political refugees**
Refuse and refuse disposal (May subdiv. geog.) **363.72; 628.4**
UF Disposal of refuse
    Garbage
    Garbage disposal
    Incineration
    Littering
    Solid waste disposal
    Waste disposal
SA types of refuse, e.g. **Industrial waste**; types of waste disposal, e.g. **Radioactive waste disposal**; **Sewage disposal**; etc.; and types of industries, plants, and facilities with the subdivision *Waste disposal*, e.g. **Chemical industry—Waste disposal** [to be added as needed]
BT **Municipal engineering**
    Pollution control industry
    Public health
    Sanitary engineering
    Sanitation
NT **Chemical industry—Waste disposal**
    Hazardous wastes
    Industrial waste
    Medical wastes
    Radioactive waste disposal

Sewage disposal
RT **Pollution**
    Recycling
    Salvage
    Street cleaning
    Waste products
Regattas
USE **Boat racing**
Regency novels **808.3**
Use for individual works, collections, or materials about historical novels set during or around the period when the future George IV of England acted as Regent for George III (1811-1820).
BT **Historical fiction**
Regeneration (Christianity) **234; 248.2**
UF Born again Christianity
    New birth (Theology)
    Regeneration (Theology)
BT **Christianity—Doctrines**
    Salvation
RT **Conversion**
Regeneration (Theology)
USE **Regeneration (Christianity)**
Reggae music (May subdiv. geog.) **781.646**
BT **Popular music**
Regimental histories
USE names of wars with the subdivision *Regimental histories,* e.g. **World War, 1939-1945—Regimental histories** [to be added as needed]
Regional development
USE **Community development**
    Regional planning
Regional history
USE **Local history**
Regional libraries (May subdiv. geog.) **027.4**
Use for materials on public libraries serving several communities, counties, or other regions.
UF County libraries
    District libraries
    Libraries, Regional
BT **Public libraries**
Regional planning (May subdiv. geog.) **307.1; 711**
UF County planning
    Metropolitan planning
    Regional development
    State planning

Regional planning—*Continued*
  BT **Land use**
      Planning
  NT **Coastal zone management**
      Rural development
  RT **City planning**
      Landscape protection
Regionalism (May subdiv. geog.) **320.4;**
      330.9
  Use for materials on the political or economic power or interests of geographic areas within nations or beyond national boundaries.
  UF Localism
      Provincialism
      Sectionalism
  BT **Geography**
      Politics
  RT **Nationalism**
Regionalism—United States **917.3; 973**
  UF Sectionalism (United States)
Registers
  USE **Registers of births, etc.**
      and subjects, ethnic groups, classes of persons, names of countries, cities, etc., and names of families and of corporate bodies, such as colleges and universities, with the subdivision *Registers,* for lists of persons or organizations without addresses or other identifying data, e.g. **United States—Registers; United States Military Academy—Registers;** etc. [to be added as needed]
Registers of births, etc. (May subdiv. geog.) **929**
  UF Birth records
      Births, Registers of
      Burial statistics
      Deaths, Registers of
      Marriage registers
      Parish registers
      Records of births, etc.
      Registers
      Vital records
  BT **Genealogy**
  NT **Wills**
  RT **Vital statistics**
Registration of voters
  USE **Voter registration**

Regulatory agencies
  USE **Administrative agencies**
Rehabilitation
  USE classes of persons with the subdivision *Rehabilitation,* e.g. **Drug addicts—Rehabilitation; Physically handicapped—Rehabilitation;** etc. [to be added as needed]
Rehabilitation peer counseling
  USE **Peer counseling**
Reign of Terror
  USE **France—History—1789-1799, Revolution**
Reincarnation **129**
  UF Rebirth
  BT **Theosophy**
  RT **Soul**
Reindeer (May subdiv. geog.) **599.65; 636.2**
  BT **Deer**
      Domestic animals
      Mammals
Reinforced concrete **691**
  BT **Building materials**
      Concrete
Rejection (Psychology) **155.9**
  BT **Psychology**
Relations among ethnic groups
  USE **Ethnic relations**
Relations with Congress
  USE names of presidents with the subdivision *Relations with Congress* [to be added as needed]
Relationships, Man-woman
  USE **Man-woman relationship**
Relative humidity
  USE **Humidity**
Relativity (Physics) **530.11**
  BT **Physics**
  RT **Gravitation**
      Quantum theory
      Space and time
Relaxation
  USE **Recreation**
      Rest
Reliability (Engineering) **620**
  UF Reliability of equipment
      Systems reliability

Reliability (Engineering)—*Continued*
  BT **Engineering**
       Probabilities
       Systems engineering
  NT **Quality control**
       Structural failures
       Testing
Reliability of equipment
  USE **Reliability (Engineering)**
Relics (May subdiv. geog.)   **203**
  UF Relics and reliquaries
Relics and reliquaries
  USE **Relics**
Relief, Public
  USE **Public welfare**
Religion   **200**
  SA names of peoples, ethnic groups, countries, states, etc., and individual persons with the subdivision *Religion*, e.g. **Native Americans—Religion**; **African Americans—Religion**; **United States—Religion**; **Shakespeare, William, 1564-1616—Religion**; etc.; religious subjects subdivided by religion or sect, e.g. **Laity—Catholic Church**; and other subjects with the subdivision *Religious aspects*, e.g. **Ethnic relations—Religious aspects**; **Love—Religious aspects**; etc., which may be further subdivided by religion or sect [to be added as needed]
  NT **African Americans—Religion**
       Agnosticism
       Ancestor worship
       Animism
       Art and religion
       Atheism
       Blacks—Religion
       Communism and religion
       Deism
       Faith
       Heresy
       Monotheism
       Moon worship
       Native Americans—Religion
       Ohio—Religion
       Pantheism
       Philosophy and religion

       Polytheism
       Psychology of religion
       Rationalism
       Religion and politics
       Religion and science
       Religion and sociology
       Religion in literature
       Religious awakening
       Religious education
       Religious fundamentalism
       Religious institutions
       Religious life
       Santeria
       Sun worship
       Supernatural
       Theism
       United States—Religion
       Visions
       War—Religious aspects
       Worship
  RT **God**
       Mythology
       Religions
       Theology
Religion and art
  USE **Art and religion**
Religion and communism
  USE **Communism and religion**
Religion and education
  USE **Church and education**
Religion and literature
  USE **Religion in literature**
       Religious literature
Religion and medicine
  USE **Medicine—Religious aspects**
Religion and philosophy
  USE **Philosophy and religion**
Religion and politics (May subdiv. geog.)
       201; 261.7; 322
  UF Political science—Religious aspects
       Politics and religion
       Politics—Religious aspects
       Religion—Political aspects
       Religions—Political aspects
  BT **Politics**
       Religion
  NT **Christianity and politics**
Religion and psychology
  USE **Psychology of religion**

Religion and science (May subdiv. geog.)
    215
  UF   Science and religion
        Science—Religious aspects
  BT   **Religion**
        Science
  NT   **Bible and science**
  RT   **Creationism**
        Evolution
        Natural theology
Religion and social problems
  USE **Church and social problems**
Religion and society
  USE **Religion and sociology**
Religion and sociology (May subdiv.
    geog.)   **306.6**
  Use for materials on religious sociology in general. Materials on the sociology of Christian denominations and on social theory from a Christian point of view are entered under **Christian sociology**. Materials on the practical treatment of social problems from the point of view of the church are entered under **Church and social problems**.
  UF   Religion and society
        Religion—Social aspects
        Religious sociology
        Society and religion
        Society—Religious aspects
        Sociology and religion
        Sociology of religion
  SA   sociology associated with particular religions, e.g. **Christian sociology** [to be added as needed]
  BT   **Religion**
        Sociology
  NT   **Christian sociology**
Religion and state
  USE **Church and state**
Religion and war
  USE **War—Religious aspects**
Religion—Government policy
  USE **Church and state**
Religion in literature   **809**
  UF   Religion and literature
  BT   **Literature**
        Religion
  RT   **Bible in literature**
Religion in the public schools (May
    subdiv. geog.)   **379.2**
  Use for materials on the teaching of religion in the public schools or on the religious freedom of students and school employees. Materials on the inclusion of prayers or a period for silent prayer or meditation in the daily schedule of public schools are entered under **Prayer in the public schools**.
  UF   Bible in the schools
        Fundamentalism and education
        Public schools and religion
  BT   **Church and education**
        Church and state
        Public schools
        Religious education
  NT   **Prayer in the public schools**
Religion—Philosophy   **210**
  Use for materials on the nature, origin, or validity of religion from a philosophical point of view. Materials on the reciprocal relationship and influence between philosophy and religion are entered under **Philosophy and religion**.
  UF   Philosophy of religion
  RT   **Philosophy and religion**
Religion—Political aspects
  USE **Religion and politics**
Religion—Psychological aspects
  USE **Psychology of religion**
Religion—Social aspects
  USE **Religion and sociology**
Religion—Study and teaching
  USE **Theology—Study and teaching**
Religions (May subdiv. geog.)   **200**
  Use for materials on the major world religions. Materials on independent religious groups whose teachings or practices fall within the normative bounds of the major world religions are entered under **Sects**. Materials on groups or movements whose beliefs or practices differ significantly from the traditional religions, often focused upon a charismatic leader, are entered under **Cults**.
  UF   Comparative religion
  SA   names of religions and of sects within the major world religions [to be added as needed]
  BT   **Civilization**
  NT   **Bahai Faith**
        Brahmanism
        Buddhism
        Christianity
        Christianity and other religions
        Confucianism
        Cults
        Druids and Druidism
        Gnosticism
        Hinduism
        Islam
        Jainism

Religions—*Continued*
    Judaism
    Neopaganism
    Occultism
    Paganism
    Sects
    Shamanism
    Shinto
    Sikhism
    Taoism
    Theosophy
    Voodooism
    Zoroastrianism
  RT Gods and goddesses
    Religion
Religions—Biography
  USE Religious biography
Religions—Political aspects
  USE Religion and politics
Religious and ecclesiastical institutions
  USE Religious institutions
Religious art (May subdiv. geog.)   203;
    704.9
  UF Religious art and symbolism
    Religious painting
    Religious sculpture
    Sacred art
  BT Art
  NT Christian art
  RT Art and religion
Religious art and symbolism
  USE Religious art
Religious aspects
  USE subjects with the subdivision *Re-
    ligious aspects,* e.g. **Ethnic
    relations—Religious aspects;
    Love—Religious aspects;** etc.,
    which may be further subdi-
    vided by the names of reli-
    gions or sects [to be added as
    needed]
Religious awakening (May subdiv. geog.)
    204; 269
  Use for materials on a renewal of interest in
  religion.
  UF Awakening, Religious
    Revival (Religion)
  BT Religion
Religious belief
  USE Faith
Religious biography   200.92; 920
  UF Religions—Biography

  SA biography of particular religions,
    e.g. **Christian biography** [to
    be added as needed]
  BT Biography
  NT Christian biography
    Prophets
    Saints
Religious ceremonies
  USE Rites and ceremonies
Religious covenants
  USE Covenants
Religious cults
  USE Cults
Religious denominations
  USE Sects
Religious drama   792.1; 808.82
  Use for collections or materials about reli-
  gious drama, not for individual works.
  BT Drama
    Religious literature
  NT Bible plays
    Easter—Drama
    Jesus Christ—Drama
    Morality plays
    Mysteries and miracle plays
    Passion plays
Religious education (May subdiv. geog.)
    207
  Use for materials on the instruction of reli-
  gion in schools and private life. Materials lim-
  ited to the instruction of Christian religion in
  schools and private life are entered under
  Christian education. Materials on the relation
  of the church to education and on the history
  of the part that the church has taken in secular
  education are entered under **Church and education**. Materials on church supported and
  controlled elementary and secondary schools
  are entered under **Church schools**.
  UF Theological education
  BT Education
    Religion
  NT Christian education
    Religion in the public schools
    Sunday schools
  RT Moral education
    Theology—Study and teaching
Religious festivals
  USE Religious holidays
Religious fiction   808.3; 808.83
  Use for individual works, collections, or
  materials about fiction that promotes religious
  teachings or exemplifies a religious way of
  life.

Religious fiction—*Continued*
SA fiction associated with particular religions, e.g. **Christian fiction** [to be added as needed]
BT **Fiction**
NT **Christian fiction**
   Jewish religious fiction
Religious freedom
USE **Freedom of religion**
Religious fundamentalism (May subdiv. geog.) **200**
Use for religious groups opposed to modernity and secularism and seeking a revival of orthodox or conservative beliefs and practices.
UF Fundamentalism
   Fundamentalist movements
SA fundamentalism of various religions, e.g. **Islamic fundamentalism** [to be added as needed]
BT **Religion**
NT **Christian fundamentalism**
   Islamic fundamentalism
Religious graphic novels   741.5
Use for individual works, collections, or materials about religious graphic novels.
BT **Graphic novels**
Religious history
USE **Church history**
Religious holidays (May subdiv. geog.) **263; 394.265**
Use for materials on religious holidays in general. Materials on secular holidays are entered under **Holidays**. Materials on secular festivals other than holidays are entered under **Festivals**.
UF Church festivals
   Ecclesiastical fasts and feasts
   Fasts and feasts
   Feast days
   Holy days
   Religious festivals
SA holidays of particular religions, e.g. **Jewish holidays**; and names of specific religious holidays and observances, e.g. **Christmas**; **Lent**; etc. [to be added as needed]
BT **Holidays**
   Rites and ceremonies
NT **Advent**
   Christian holidays
   Church year
   Islamic holidays

   Jewish holidays
RT **Fasting**
   Festivals
Religious institutions (May subdiv. geog.) **206; 260**
UF Churches
   Congregations
   Ecclesiastical institutions
   Institutions, Ecclesiastical
   Institutions, Religious
   Religious and ecclesiastical institutions
   Religious organizations
BT **Associations**
   Religion
NT **Mosques**
   Synagogues
   Temples
Religious liberty
USE **Freedom of religion**
Religious life (May subdiv. geog.) **204; 248.4**
Use for materials that describe or promote personal or community religious and devotional life.
SA groups and classes of persons with the subdivision *Religious life* [to be added as needed]
BT **Religion**
NT **Asceticism**
   Celibacy
   Christian life
   Family—Religious life
   Spiritual life
   Teenagers—Religious life
   Women—Religious life
   Youth—Religious life
RT **Monasticism and religious orders**
Religious life (Christian)
USE **Christian life**
Religious literature   800
UF Religion and literature
SA literatures of particular religions or denominations, e.g. **Catholic literature** [to be added as needed]
BT **Literature**
NT **Christian literature**
   Devotional literature
   Islamic literature
   Jewish literature

Religious literature—*Continued*
  Religious drama
  Religious poetry
  Sacred books
  RT **Bible as literature**
Religious music
  USE **Church music**
Religious orders
  USE **Monasticism and religious orders**
Religious orders for men
  USE **Monasticism and religious orders for men**
Religious orders for women
  USE **Monasticism and religious orders for women**
Religious organizations
  USE **Religious institutions**
Religious painting
  USE **Religious art**
Religious pamphlets
  USE **Tracts**
Religious persecution
  USE **Persecution**
Religious poetry 808.1; 808.81
  Use for collections or materials about religious poetry, not for individual works.
  BT **Poetry**
    Religious literature
  RT **Hymns**
Religious psychology
  USE **Pastoral psychology**
    Psychology of religion
Religious sculpture
  USE **Religious art**
Religious sociology
  USE **Religion and sociology**
Religious summer schools (May subdiv. geog.) **207; 268**
  UF Bible classes
    Vacation church schools
    Vacation schools, Religious
  BT **Schools**
    Summer schools
Religious tolerance (May subdiv. geog.) **261.7**
  Use for general materials on religous tolerance. Materials on a particular religion's or denomination's position on religious tolerance are entered under this heading subdivided by the name of the religion or denomination.
  BT **Toleration**

Relocation
  USE ethnic groups and classes of persons with the subdivision *Relocation,* e.g. **Native Americans—Relocation;** which may be further subdivided geographically [to be added as needed]
Relocation of Japanese Americans, 1942-1945
  USE **Japanese Americans—Evacuation and relocation, 1942-1945**
Remarriage (May subdiv. geog.) **306.84**
  BT **Marriage**
Remedial reading
  USE **Reading—Remedial teaching**
Remedial teaching
  USE school subjects with the subdivision *Remedial teaching*, e.g. **Reading—Remedial teaching** [to be added as needed]
Remodeling
  USE types of buildings and parts of buildings with the subdivision *Remodeling,* e.g. **Houses—Remodeling; Kitchens—Remodeling;** etc. [to be added as needed]
Remodeling (Architecture)
  USE **Houses—Remodeling**
Remodeling of houses
  USE **Houses—Remodeling**
Remodeling of kitchens
  USE **Kitchens—Remodeling**
Remote sensing (May subdiv. geog.) **621.36**
  UF Sensing, Remote
    Terrain sensing, Remote
  BT **Aerial photography**
  NT **Aerial reconnaissance**
    Electronic surveillance
    Radar
  RT **Space optics**
Removal of Indians
  USE **Native Americans—Relocation**
Renaissance (May subdiv. geog.) **940.2**
  Use for materials on cultural and intellectual developments in the fifteenth and sixteenth centuries not limited to a single country or region.
  BT **Civilization**

Renaissance—*Continued*
   RT **Humanism**
Renaissance architecture
   USE **Architecture—15th and 16th centuries**
Renaissance art
   USE **Art—15th and 16th centuries**
Renaissance decoration and ornament
   USE **Decoration and ornament— 15th and 16th centuries**
Renaissance English literature
   USE **English literature—16th and 17th centuries**
Renaissance painting
   USE **Painting—15th and 16th centuries**
Rendezvous in space
   USE **Orbital rendezvous (Space flight)**
Renewable energy resources (May subdiv. geog.) **333.79**
   UF Alternate energy resources
       Alternative energy resources
   SA types of renewable resources [to be added as needed]
   BT **Energy resources**
   NT **Geothermal resources**
       Solar energy
       Water power
       Wind power
Renown
   USE **Fame**
Rental services
   USE **Lease and rental services**
Reorganization of administrative agencies
   USE **Administrative agencies—Reorganization**
Repairing 620
   UF Fixing
       Maintenance and repair
       Mending
       Repairs
   SA types of things that require maintenance with the subdivision *Maintenance and repair,* e.g. **Automobiles—Maintenance and repair**; **Buildings—Maintenance and repair**; etc.; and types of things that require no maintenance with the subdivision *Repair-*

ing, e.g. **Radio—Repairing** [to be added as needed]
Repairs
   USE **Repairing**
Reparations
   USE names of wars with the subdivision *Reparations,* e.g. **World War, 1939-1945—Reparations** [to be added as needed]
Reparations for historical injustices (May subdiv. geog.) **305.8; 341.6**
   UF Restitution for historical injustices
Repentance 234
   UF Contrition
       Penitence
   RT **Penance**
Report writing 808
   UF Reports—Preparation
       Research paper writing
       Term paper writing
   BT **Authorship**
   NT **School reports**
Reporters and reporting (May subdiv. geog.) **070.4**
   UF Newspaper work
   BT **Journalism**
       Newspapers
Reports—Preparation
   USE **Report writing**
Reports, Teachers'
   USE **School reports**
Representation
   USE **Representative government and representation**
Representation, Proportional
   USE **Proportional representation**
Representative government and representation (May subdiv. geog.) **321.8**
   UF Parliamentary government
       Representation
       Self-government
   BT **Constitutional history**
       Constitutional law
       Political science
   NT **Apportionment (Election law)**
       Legislative bodies
       Proportional representation
       Recall (Political science)
   RT **Democracy**
       Elections

Representative government and represen-
tation—*Continued*
       Republics
       Suffrage
Representatives, House of (U.S.)
   USE **United States. Congress. House**
Repressed memory
   USE **Recovered memory**
Reprint editions
   USE **Reprints (Publications)**
Reprints (Publications)   016
   UF Bibliography—Reprint editions
       Reprint editions
   BT **Books**
       Editions
Reproduction   573.6; 612.6
   BT **Biology**
       Life (Biology)
       Physiology
   NT **Animal reproduction**
       Artificial insemination
       Breeding
       Cells
       Fertility
       Fertilization in vitro
       Fetus
       Genetics
       Human artificial insemination
       Infertility
       Menstruation
       Pregnancy
       Sex preselection
   RT **Embryology**
       Reproductive system
       Sex—Physiological aspects
Reproduction processes
   USE **Copying processes**
Reproduction—Technological innovations
   USE **Reproductive technology**
Reproductive behavior
   USE **Sexual behavior in animals**
Reproductive organs
   USE **Reproductive system**
Reproductive system   573.6; 611; 612.6
   UF Generative organs
       Genitalia
       Reproductive organs
       Sex organs
   BT **Anatomy**
       Physiology
       Sex—Physiological aspects
   RT **Reproduction**

Reproductive technology (May subdiv.
   geog.)   **612.6**
   UF Assisted reproduction
       Reproduction—Technological in-
         novations
   BT **Biotechnology**
Reprographic art
   USE **Copy art**
Reprography
   USE **Copying processes**
Reptiles (May subdiv. geog.)   **597.9**
   SA types of reptiles [to be added as
         needed]
   BT **Animals**
   NT **Alligators**
       Crocodiles
       Fossil reptiles
       Lizards
       Snakes
       Turtles
Reptiles, Fossil
   USE **Fossil reptiles**
Reptiles—Physiology   **597.9**
   BT **Physiology**
Republic of China, 1949-
   USE **Taiwan**
Republic of South Africa
   USE **South Africa**
Republic of the Congo
   USE **Congo (Republic)**
Republican Party (U.S.)   **324.2734**
   BT **Political parties**
Republics   **321.8**
   UF Commonwealth, The
   BT **Constitutional history**
       Constitutional law
       Political science
   NT **Federal government**
   RT **Democracy**
       Representative government and
         representation
Rescue dogs (May subdiv. geog.)   **636.73**
   BT **Rescue work**
       Working dogs
Rescue of Jews, 1939-1945
   USE **World War, 1939-1945—**
         Jews—Rescue
Rescue operations, Space
   USE **Space rescue operations**
Rescue work (May subdiv. geog.)   **363.3**
   UF Search and rescue operations

Rescue work—*Continued*
    BT   **Civil defense**
    NT   **First aid**
          Lifesaving
          Rescue dogs
          Space rescue operations
    RT   **Survival after airplane accidents, shipwrecks, etc.**
Research (May subdiv. geog.)   **001.4**
    UF   Research and development
    SA   subjects with the subdivision *Research* [to be added as needed]
    NT   **Agriculture—Research**
          Animal experimentation
          Discoveries in science
          Dissertations
          Industrial research
          Intelligence service
          Medicine—Research
          Military research
          Oceanography—Research
          Operations research
          Parapsychology
          Surveys
    RT   **Information services**
          Learning and scholarship
Research and development
    USE **Research**
Research buildings
    USE **Laboratories**
Research paper writing
    USE **Report writing**
Reservations
    USE names of native peoples, tribes, etc., with the subdivision *Reservations*, e.g. **Native Americans—Reservations** [to be added as needed]
Reservoirs (May subdiv. geog.)   **627; 628.1**
    BT   **Hydraulic structures**
Resettlement
    USE **Land settlement**
Residences
    USE **Domestic architecture**
           Houses
Residential developments
    USE **Planned communities**
Residential security
    USE **Burglary protection**

Residential treatment centers
    USE **Group homes**
Resignation
    USE classes of persons and names of individual persons with the subdivision *Resignation,* e.g. **Presidents—United States—Resignation** [to be added as needed]
Resins
    USE **Gums and resins**
Resistance of materials
    USE **Strength of materials**
Resistance to drugs in microorganisms
    USE **Drug resistance in microorganisms**
Resistance to government (May subdiv. geog.)   **322.4**
    UF   Government, Resistance to
    BT   **Political ethics**
          Political science
    NT   **Civil disobedience**
          Hunger strikes
          Passive resistance
    RT   **Insurgency**
          Revolutions
Resistance welding
    USE **Electric welding**
Resorts (May subdiv. geog.)   **790**
    BT   **Recreation**
    NT   **Health resorts**
          Summer resorts
          Winter resorts
Resource management
    USE **Conservation of natural resources**
Resources, Marine
    USE **Marine resources**
Respiration   **573.2; 612.2**
    UF   Breathing
    BT   **Physiology**
    RT   **Respiratory system**
Respiration, Artificial
    USE **Artificial respiration**
Respiratory organs
    USE **Respiratory system**
Respiratory system   **573.2; 611; 612.2**
    UF   Respiratory organs
    BT   **Anatomy**
          Physiology
    NT   **Lungs**

Respiratory system—*Continued*
RT **Respiration**
Respite care
USE **Home care services**
Responsibility 170
UF Accountability
Obligation
BT **Ethics**
Responsibility, Legal
USE **Liability (Law)**
Rest 613.7
UF Relaxation
BT **Health**
Hygiene
NT **Sleep**
RT **Fatigue**
Restaurants (May subdiv. geog.) 647.95
UF Cafes
Coffee shops
Lunchrooms
Restaurants, bars, etc.
SA types of restaurants [to be added
as needed]
BT **Food service**
NT **Coffeehouses**
Fast food restaurants
Tearooms
RT **Bars**
Restaurants, bars, etc.
USE **Bars**
Restaurants
Restitution for historical injustices
USE **Reparations for historical in-
justices**
Restoration of automobiles
USE **Automobiles—Conservation
and restoration**
Restoration of buildings
USE **Architecture—Conservation
and restoration**
Restoration of furniture
USE **Furniture finishing
Furniture—Repairing**
Restoration of photographs
USE **Photographs—Conservation
and restoration**
Restoration of works of art
USE subjects with the subdivision
Conservation and restoration,
e.g. **Painting—Conservation
and restoration** [to be added
as needed]

Restraint of trade (May subdiv. geog.)
338.6
UF Restrictive trade practices
Trade, Restraint of
BT **Commerce**
Commercial law
RT **Boycotts**
Corporation law
Industrial trusts
Monopolies
Unfair competition
Restrictive trade practices
USE **Restraint of trade**
Résumés (Employment) 650.14
UF Job résumés
BT **Applications for positions**
Job hunting
Resurrection
USE **Future life**
Resurrection of Jesus Christ
USE **Jesus Christ—Resurrection**
Resuscitation, Heart
USE **Cardiac resuscitation**
Resuscitation, Pulmonary
USE **Artificial respiration**
Retail franchises
USE **Franchises (Retail trade)**
Retail stores
USE **Stores**
Retail trade (May subdiv. geog.) 381;
658.8
UF Merchandising
BT **Commerce**
NT **Advertising**
Chain stores
Department stores
Direct selling
Discount stores
Drugstores
Franchises (Retail trade)
General stores
Inventory control
Packaging
Sales personnel
Selling
Shopping centers and malls
Stores
Supermarkets
Retarded children
USE **Mentally handicapped children**

Retention, Grade
　USE **Promotion (School)**
Retired people
　USE **Retirees**
Retired persons
　USE **Retirees**
Retirees (May subdiv. geog.)　**155.67;**
　　305.9
　UF　Retired people
　　　Retired persons
　RT　**Elderly**
　　　Retirement
Retirees—Personal finance　332.024
Retirement (May subdiv. geog.)　**305.26;**
　　306.3
　BT　**Leisure**
　　　Old age
　NT　**Retirement income**
　RT　**Elderly—Life skills guides**
　　　Retirees
Retirement communities (May subdiv.
　geog.)　**307.7; 363.5**
　UF　Places of retirement
　BT　**Elderly—Housing**
　NT　**Life care communities**
Retirement income (May subdiv. geog.)
　　331.25; 353.5
　BT　**Income**
　　　Retirement
　NT　**Annuities**
　　　Individual retirement accounts
　　　Old age pensions
　　　Pensions
Retouching (Photography)
　USE　**Photography—Retouching**
Retraining, Occupational
　USE　**Occupational retraining**
Retreats (May subdiv. geog.)　**269**
　　Use for materials on periods of withdrawal
　from daily routine for the purpose of prayer,
　meditation, and study.
　BT　**Spiritual life**
Retrenchment of organizations
　USE　**Downsizing of organizations**
Retrieval of information
　USE　**Information retrieval**
Return migration (May subdiv. geog.)
　　304.8
　　Use for materials on the return of emigrants
　to their country of origin.
　BT　**Immigration and emigration**

Reunions, Family
　USE　**Family reunions**
Revelation　202; 231.7
　BT　**God**
　　　Supernatural
　　　Theology
Revenge
　UF　Vengence
　RT　**Vendetta**
Revenue
　USE　**Tariff**
　　　Taxation
Revenue sharing (May subdiv. geog.)
　　336.1
　　Use for materials on the practice of return-
　ing a percentage of federal tax money to state
　and local governments for locally directed and
　controlled public service programs.
　UF　Federal revenue sharing
　　　Tax sharing
　BT　**Intergovernmental tax relations**
Reviewing (Books)
　USE　**Book reviewing**
Reviews
　USE　topics and types of books with
　　　the subdivision *Reviews,* e.g.
　　　Motion picture—Reviews;
　　　Reference books—Reviews;
　　　etc.; and topics, types of liter-
　　　ature, ethnic groups, classes
　　　of persons, and names of
　　　places with the subdivision
　　　Book reviews; e.g. **Sociolo-**
　　　gy—Book reviews; Chil-
　　　dren's literature—Book re-
　　　views; etc., for collections of
　　　reviews [to be added as need-
　　　ed]
Revival (Religion)
　USE　**Evangelistic work**
　　　Religious awakening
　　　Revivals
Revivals (May subdiv. geog.)　**204; 269**
　UF　Revival (Religion)
　BT　**Evangelistic work**
Revivals—Music
　USE　**Gospel music**
Revolution, American
　USE　**United States—History—1775-**
　　　1783, Revolution

Revolution, French
　USE　**France—History—1789-1799,
　　　　Revolution**
Revolutions (May subdiv. geog.)　**303.6**
　UF　Coups d'état
　　　Rebellions
　　　Sedition
　SA　names of countries with the ap-
　　　propriate subdivision under
　　　History, e.g. **France—Histo-
　　　ry—1789-1799, Revolution**
　　　[to be added as needed]
　BT　**Political science**
　NT　**France—History—1789-1799,
　　　Revolution**
　　　**Hungary—History—1956, Rev-
　　　olution**
　　　Insurgency
　　　National liberation movements
　　　Radicalism
　　　**Russia—History—1917-1921,
　　　Revolution**
　　　Slave revolts
　　　**United States—History—1775-
　　　1783, Revolution**
　RT　**Resistance to government**
Revolvers
　USE　**Handguns**
Rewards (Prizes, etc.)
　USE　**Awards**
Rh factor
　USE　**Blood groups**
Rhetoric　**808**
　UF　Composition (Rhetoric)
　　　English language—Rhetoric
　　　Persuasion (Rhetoric)
　　　Speaking
　SA　names of languages with the
　　　subdivision *Composition and
　　　exercises*, e.g. **English lan-
　　　guage—Composition and ex-
　　　ercises** [to be added as need-
　　　ed]
　BT　**Language and languages**
　NT　**Criticism**
　　　Debates and debating
　　　Figures of speech
　　　Lectures and lecturing
　　　Letter writing
　　　Preaching
　　　Punctuation

　　　Satire
　RT　**English language—Composition
　　　and exercises**
　　　Literary style
Rheumatism　**616.7**
　BT　**Diseases**
　NT　**Gout**
Rhyme　**808.1**
　SA　names of languages with the
　　　subdivision *Rhyme* [to be add-
　　　ed as needed]
　BT　**Poetics**
　　　Versification
　NT　**English language—Rhyme**
　　　Stories in rhyme
Rhymes
　USE　**Limericks**
　　　Nonsense verses
　　　Nursery rhymes
　　　Poetry—Collections
Rhythm　**808.1**
　BT　**Aesthetics**
　　　Poetics
　NT　**Musical meter and rhythm**
　　　Versification
　RT　**Cycles**
Ribbon work　**746**
　BT　**Handicraft**
Ribonucleic acid
　USE　**RNA**
Ribose nucleic acid
　USE　**RNA**
Ribozymes
　USE　**Catalytic RNA**
Rich (May subdiv. geog.)　**305.5; 920**
　UF　Affluent people
　　　High income people
　　　Rich people
　　　Rich persons
　　　Wealthy people
　BT　**Social classes**
　NT　**Millionaires**
Rich people
　USE　**Rich**
Rich persons
　USE　**Rich**
Riches
　USE　**Wealth**
Riddles　**398.6; 793.735; 808.88**
　Use for collections of riddles considered as
folklore, as games, or as literary exercises, by

Riddles—*Continued*
one or several authors, and for materials about riddles.

    UF   Conundrums

           Enigmas

    BT   **Amusements**

           Literary recreations

    NT   **Charades**

           Rebuses

    RT   **Puzzles**

Ride sharing

    USE **Car pools**

Riding

    USE **Horsemanship**

Rifles (May subdiv. geog.)   **683.4**

    UF   Carbines

           Guns

    BT   **Firearms**

Right and left

    USE **Left and right (Direction)**

          Right and left (Political science)

Right- and left-handedness

    USE **Left- and right-handedness**

Right and left (Political science)   **320.5**

Use for general materials on political views or attitudes, i.e. conservative, traditional, liberal, radical, etc. Materials on the physical characteristics of favoring one hand or the other are entered under **Left- and right-handedness**. Materials on left and right as indications of location or direction are entered under **Left and right (Direction)**.

    UF   Left and right

           Left (Political science)

           Right and left

           Right (Political science)

    BT   **Political parties**

           Political science

    NT   **Radicalism**

    RT   **Conservatism**

           Liberalism

Right of assembly

    USE **Freedom of assembly**

Right of association

    USE **Freedom of association**

Right of asylum

    USE **Asylum**

Right of privacy (May subdiv. geog.)   **323.44**

    UF   Invasion of privacy

           Privacy, Right of

    BT   **Civil rights**

    NT   **Eavesdropping**

           Trade secrets

           Wiretapping

Right of property (May subdiv. geog.)   **323.4**

    UF   Private property, Right of

           Property, Right of

           Property rights

    BT   **Civil rights**

           Property

Right (Political science)

    USE **Conservatism**

          Right and left (Political science)

Right to a fair trial

    USE **Fair trial**

Right to bear arms

    USE **Gun control**

Right to choose movement

    USE **Pro-choice movement**

Right to counsel (May subdiv. geog.)   **323.4**

    BT   **Civil rights**

Right to die (May subdiv. geog.)   **179.7**

    BT   **Death**

           Medical ethics

           Medicine—Law and legislation

    RT   **Euthanasia**

           Living wills

           Suicide

Right to health care (May subdiv. geog.)   **362.1**

    UF   Health care, Right to

           Medical care, Right to

           Right to medical care

    BT   **Human rights**

Right to know

    USE **Freedom of information**

Right-to-life movement (Anti-abortion movement)

    USE **Pro-life movement**

Right to medical care

    USE **Right to health care**

Right to work

    USE **Open and closed shop**

Righteous Gentiles in the Holocaust (May subdiv. geog.)   **940.53**

    BT   **Holocaust, 1939-1945**

           World War, 1939-1945— Jews—Rescue

Rights, Human
    USE   **Human rights**
Rights of animals
    USE   **Animal rights**
Rights of employees
    USE   **Employee rights**
Rights of gays
    USE   **Gay rights**
Rights of lesbians
    USE   **Gay rights**
Rights of man
    USE   **Human rights**
Rights of women
    USE   **Women's rights**
Rights, Proprietary
    USE   **Intellectual property**
Riot control (May subdiv. geog.)   **303.6**
    UF   Riots—Control
    BT   **Crowds**
          Riots
Riots (May subdiv. geog.)   **303.6**
    UF   Civil disorders
          Mobs
    SA   names of institutions with the
          subdivision *Riots*; and names
          of specific riots [to be added
          as needed]
    BT   **Crime**
          Freedom of assembly
          Offenses against public safety
    NT   **Riot control**
    RT   **Crowds**
          Demonstrations
Riots—Control
    USE   **Riot control**
Ripoffs
    USE   **Fraud**
Risk   **338.5; 368**
    BT   **Economics**
    RT   **Probabilities**
          Profit
Risk-taking (Psychology)   **155.2**
    BT   **Psychology**
Rites and ceremonies (May subdiv. geog.)
    390
    UF   Ceremonies
          Ecclesiastical rites and ceremo-
          nies
          Religious ceremonies
          Ritual
          Traditions

    SA   classes of persons and ethnic
          groups with the subdivision
          Rites and ceremonies, e.g.
          **Native Americans—Rites
          and ceremonies**; and names
          of individual religions and de-
          nominations with the subdivi-
          sion *Liturgy* or *Customs and
          practices*, e.g. **Catholic
          Church—Liturgy**; **Judaism—
          Customs and practices**; etc.
          [to be added as needed]
    NT   **Canonization**
          Catholic Church—Liturgy
          Funeral rites and ceremonies
          Initiation rites
          **Judaism—Customs and prac-
          tices**
          Liturgies
          Marriage customs and rites
          **Native Americans—Rites and
          ceremonies**
          Ordination
          Religious holidays
          Sacraments
          Secret societies
    RT   **Manners and customs**
Ritual
    USE   **Liturgies**
          Rites and ceremonies
River animals
    USE   **Stream animals**
River ecology (May subdiv. geog.)   **577.6**
    BT   **Ecology**
River pollution
    USE   **Water pollution**
Rivers (May subdiv. geog.)   **551.48**
    SA   names of rivers [to be added as
          needed]
    BT   **Physical geography**
          Water
          Waterways
    NT   **Stream animals**
          Water power
    RT   **Floods**
          Hydraulic engineering
          Inland navigation
RNA   **572.8**
    UF   Ribonucleic acid
          Ribose nucleic acid
    BT   **Nucleic acids**

RNA—*Continued*
  NT **Catalytic RNA**
Roaches (Insects)
  USE **Cockroaches**
Road construction
  USE **Roads**
Road engineering
  USE **Highway engineering**
Road machinery (May subdiv. geog.)
    625.7
  BT **Construction equipment**
Road maps   912
  UF Roads—Maps
  SA names of countries, areas, states,
      cities, etc., with the subdivi-
      sion *Maps* [to be added as
      needed]
  BT **Maps**
  RT **Automobile travel—Guidebooks**
Road safety
  USE **Traffic safety**
Road signs
  USE **Signs and signboards**
Roads (May subdiv. geog.)   **388.1; 625.7**
  UF Construction of roads
      Highway construction
      Highways
      Road construction
      Thoroughfares
  BT **Civil engineering**
      Transportation
  NT **Alaska Highway (Alaska and**
      Canada)
      Express highways
      Roadside improvement
      Scenic byways
      Street cleaning
      Trails
  RT **Highway engineering**
      Pavements
      Soil mechanics
      Streets
Roads—Maps
  USE **Road maps**
Roadside improvement (May subdiv.
    geog.)   **713**
  UF Highway beautification
  BT **Grounds maintenance**
      Landscape architecture
      Roads
Robbers
  USE **Thieves**

Robins (May subdiv. geog.)   **598.8**
  BT **Birds**
Robinsonades   808.3; 808.83
    Use for individual works, collections, or
    materials about fictional works describing a
    character's survival without the aid of civiliza-
    tion, as on a desert island.
  BT **Adventure fiction**
      Imaginary voyages
Robot manga
  USE **Mecha**
Robotics
  USE **Robots**
Robots (May subdiv. geog.)   **629.8**
    Use for general materials on robots and
    robotics. Materials limited to robots in indus-
    try are entered under **Industrial robots**.
  UF Automata
      Automatons
      Robotics
  BT **Machinery**
      Mechanical movements
  NT **Industrial robots**
Robots, Industrial
  USE **Industrial robots**
Rock and roll music
  USE **Rock music**
Rock climbing
  USE **Mountaineering**
Rock crystal
  USE **Quartz**
Rock drawings
  USE **Rock drawings, paintings, and**
      engravings
Rock drawings, paintings, and engrav-
    ings (May subdiv. geog.)   **759.01**
  UF Petroglyphs
      Rock drawings
      Rock engravings
      Rock paintings
  BT **Archeology**
      Prehistoric art
  NT **Cave drawings and paintings**
Rock engravings
  USE **Rock drawings, paintings, and**
      engravings
Rock gardens (May subdiv. geog.)
    635.9
  BT **Gardens**
Rock music (May subdiv. geog.)   **781.66;**
    782.42166
  UF Rock and roll music

669

Rock music—*Continued*
  BT **Music**
      Popular music
Rock paintings
  USE **Rock drawings, paintings, and engravings**
Rock tombs
  USE **Tombs**
Rocket airplanes
  USE **Rocket planes**
Rocket flight
  USE **Space flight**
Rocket planes (May subdiv. geog.) **629.133**
  UF Airplanes, Rocket propelled
      Rocket airplanes
  SA names of rocket planes, e.g.
      X-15 (Rocket aircraft) [to be added as needed]
  BT **High speed aeronautics**
      Space vehicles
  NT **X-15 (Rocket aircraft)**
Rocketry (May subdiv. geog.) **621.43**
  BT **Aeronautics**
      Astronautics
  NT **Guided missiles**
      Rockets (Aeronautics)
      Space vehicles
Rockets (Aeronautics) (May subdiv. geog.) **629.133**
  UF Aerial rockets
  SA types of rockets and missiles and names of specific rockets and missiles [to be added as needed]
  BT **Aeronautics**
      High speed aeronautics
      Projectiles
      Rocketry
  NT **Artificial satellites—Launching**
      Ballistic missiles
      Guided missiles
  RT **Interplanetary voyages**
      Jet propulsion
Rocks (May subdiv. geog.) **552**
    Use for general materials on naturally occurring solid minerals. Materials on stone as a building material are entered under **Stone**.
  SA varieties of rock, e.g. **Granite** [to be added as needed]
  NT **Granite**
      Marble

  RT **Geology**
      Petrology
      Stone
Rocky Mountains **978**
  BT **Mountains**
Rodeos (May subdiv. geog.) **791.8**
  BT **Sports**
  RT **Cowhands**
      Horsemanship
Roentgen rays
  USE **X-rays**
Rogues and vagabonds—Fiction
  USE **Picaresque literature**
Roland (Legendary character) **398.22**
  UF Orlando (Legendary character)
  BT **Folklore**
Roland (Legendary character)—Romances **821**
Role conflict **302.5**
    Use for materials on the conflict within one person who is being called upon to fulfill two or more competing roles.
  BT **Social conflict**
      Social role
Role playing **302**
  BT **Social role**
  NT **Fantasy games**
Role playing games
  USE **Fantasy games**
Role, Social
  USE **Social role**
Roller coasters (May subdiv. geog.) **791.06**
  BT **Amusements**
Roller skating (May subdiv. geog.) **796.2**
  UF Skating
  BT **Outdoor recreation**
  NT **Rollerblading**
      Skateboarding
Rollerblading **796.2**
  UF In-line skating [*Former heading*]
  BT **Roller skating**
Romaic language
  USE **Modern Greek language**
Romaic literature
  USE **Modern Greek literature**
Roman antiquities
  USE **Classical antiquities**
      Rome—Antiquities
      Rome (Italy)—Antiquities

Roman architecture (May subdiv. geog.)
722
UF Architecture, Roman
BT **Ancient architecture**
Architecture
Roman art (May subdiv. geog.) **709.37**
UF Art, Roman
Classical art
BT **Ancient art**
Art
Classical antiquities
Roman Catholic Church
USE **Catholic Church**
Roman civilization
USE **Rome—Civilization**
Roman emperors
USE **Emperors—Rome**
Roman Empire
USE **Rome**
Roman literature
USE **Latin literature**
Roman mythology 292.1
UF Mythology, Roman
BT **Classical mythology**
Roman numerals 513
BT **Numerals**
Roman philosophy
USE **Ancient philosophy**
Romance graphic novels 741.5
Use for individual works, collections, or materials about romance graphic novels.
BT **Graphic novels**
Romance languages 440
UF Neo-Latin languages
SA names of languages belonging to the Romance group, e.g.
French language [to be added as needed]
BT **Language and languages**
NT **French language**
Spanish language
RT **Latin language**
Romance literature 840
SA names of literatures belonging to the Romance group, e.g.
French literature [to be added as needed]
BT **Literature**
NT **French literature**
Portuguese literature
Spanish literature

Romance novels
USE **Love stories**
Romances 808.8
Use for individual works, collections, or materials about medieval tales dealing with the age of chivalry or the supernatural. They may be either in verse or in prose and may or may not have a basis in fact. Contemporary romance novels are entered under **Love stories** or **Romantic suspense novels**.
UF Chivalry—Romances
Metrical romances
Stories
SA names of historic persons and legendary characters with the subdivision *Romances*, e.g.
Roland (Legendary character)—Romances [to be added as needed]
BT **Fiction**
Literature
NT **Arthurian romances**
RT **Chivalry**
Epic poetry
Fables
Legends
Romances (Love stories)
USE **Love stories**
Romanesque architecture (May subdiv. geog.) **723**
UF Architecture, Romanesque
BT **Architecture**
Medieval architecture
Romanesque art (May subdiv. geog.) **709.02**
UF Art, Romanesque
BT **Medieval art**
NT **Romanesque painting**
Romanesque painting (May subdiv. geog.) **759.02**
UF Painting, Romanesque
BT **Romanesque art**
Romanies
USE **Gypsies**
Romans à clef 808.3
Use for individual works, collections, or materials about novels in which fictional characters and events can be readily identified with real persons and events.
UF Livres à clef
BT **Fiction**
Romantic crushes
USE **Crushes**

Romantic fiction

    USE **Love stories**

Romantic stories

    USE **Love stories**

Romantic suspense novels 808.3

    Use for individual works, collections, or materials about modern romantic suspense novels. Medieval tales are entered under **Romances**.

    UF   Suspense novels

    BT   **Adventure fiction**

    RT   **Gothic novels**

          Love stories

          Mystery fiction

          Spy stories

Romanticism (May subdiv. geog.) 141; 709.03; 809

    BT   **Aesthetics**

Romanticism in art 709.03

    BT   **Art**

Rome 937

    Use for materials about the city of Rome in antiquity or about the Roman Empire. Materials on the modern city of Rome are entered under **Rome (Italy)**. Materials on the ruins and remains of ancient Rome, the city and its environs, are entered under **Rome (Italy)—Antiquities**. Materials on Roman antiquities in several countries are entered under **Rome—Antiquities**. Materials on Roman antiquities limited to one modern country, city, etc., are entered under the place with the subdivision *Antiquities*.

    UF   Roman Empire

Rome—Antiquities 937

    Use for materials on Roman antiquities in several countries. Materials on Roman antiquities limited to one modern country, city, etc., are entered under the place with the subdivision *Antiquities*. Materials on the ruins and remains of ancient Rome, the city and its environs, are entered under **Rome (Italy)—Antiquities**.

    UF   Roman antiquities

    BT   **Classical antiquities**

Rome—Biography 920.037

    UF   Classical biography

    BT   **Biography**

Rome—Civilization 937

    Use for materials on the civilization of ancient Rome. Materials on both ancient Greek and Roman civilizations are entered under **Classical civilization**.

    UF   Roman civilization

    BT   **Classical civilization**

Rome—Description

    USE   **Rome—Description and travel**

Rome—Description and travel 913.7; 937

    Use for descriptive materials on the Roman Empire including accounts by travelers of ancient times.

    UF   Rome—Description

Rome—Geography 913.7

    Use for geographic materials on ancient Rome.

    UF   Classical geography

    BT   **Ancient geography**

          Historical geography

Rome—History 937

Rome (Italy) 945

    Use for materials on the modern city of Rome. Materials about the city of Rome in antiquity or about the Roman Empire are entered under **Rome**.

Rome (Italy)—Antiquities 937

    Use for materials on the ruins and remains of ancient Rome, the city and its environs. Materials on Roman antiquities in several countries are entered under **Rome—Antiquities**. Materials on Roman antiquities limited to one modern country, city, etc., are entered under the place with the subdivision *Antiquities*.

    UF   Roman antiquities

    BT   **Classical antiquities**

Rome (Italy)—Description and travel 914.5

Rome (Italy)—History 945

Roofs (May subdiv. geog.) 690; 695; 721

    BT   **Architecture—Details**

          Buildings

Rookwood pottery 738

    BT   **Art pottery**

Rooming houses

    USE   **Hotels and motels**

Roommates 643

    RT   **Shared housing**

Rooms (May subdiv. geog.) 643; 645

    SA   types of rooms [to be added as needed]

    BT   **Buildings**

          Houses

    NT   **Bathrooms**

          Garden rooms

          Kitchens

    RT   **Interior design**

Root crops (May subdiv. geog.) 633; 635

    BT   **Vegetables**

    RT   **Feeds**

Rope 677

Rope—*Continued*
    NT   **Cables**
          Knots and splices
    RT   **Hemp**
Roses (May subdiv. geog.)   **583; 635.9**
    BT   **Flowers**
Rosetta stone   **493**
    BT   **Hieroglyphics**
Rosin
    USE   **Gums and resins**
Rotation of crops
    USE   **Crop rotation**
Roughage
    USE   **Food—Fiber content**
Round stage
    USE   **Arena theater**
Routes of trade
    USE   **Trade routes**
Rowing (May subdiv. geog.)   **797.12**
    UF   Crew (Rowing)
          Sculling
    BT   **Athletics**
          Boats and boating
          Exercise
          Sports
          Water sports
Royal houses
    USE   **Kings and rulers**
          Monarchy
Royalty
    USE   **Kings and rulers**
          Monarchy
          Princes
          Princesses
          Queens
Rubber   **678**
    BT   **Forest products**
Rubber, Artificial
    USE   **Synthetic rubber**
Rubber, Synthetic
    USE   **Synthetic rubber**
Rubber tires
    USE   **Tires**
Rudeness
    USE   **Bad behavior**
Rug cleaning
    USE   **Rugs and carpets—Cleaning**
Rugs
    USE   **Rugs and carpets**
Rugs and carpets (May subdiv. geog.)
        645; 677; 746.7

    UF   Carpets
          Rugs
    BT   **Decorative arts**
          Interior design
    NT   **Hooked rugs**
          Oriental rugs
Rugs and carpets—Cleaning   **677**
    UF   Carpet cleaning
          Rug cleaning
Ruins
    USE   **Antiquities**
          Excavations (Archeology)
          Extinct cities
Rule, Golden
    USE   **Golden rule**
Rule of equal time (Broadcasting)
    USE   **Equal time rule (Broadcasting)**
Rulers
    USE   **Emperors**
          Heads of state
          Kings and rulers
          Queens
Rules of order
    USE   **Parliamentary practice**
Rummage sales (May subdiv. geog.)
        381.195
    UF   Jumble sales
    BT   **Secondhand trade**
          Selling
Runaway adults (May subdiv. geog.)
        173; 306.88
    UF   Husbands, Runaway
          Runaway husbands
          Runaway wives
          Wives, Runaway
    BT   **Desertion and nonsupport**
          Missing persons
Runaway children (May subdiv. geog.)
        305.23086; 362.74
    BT   **Children**
          Homeless persons
          Missing children
Runaway husbands
    USE   **Runaway adults**
Runaway slaves
    USE   **Fugitive slaves**
Runaway teenagers (May subdiv. geog.)
        362.74
    BT   **Homeless persons**
          Missing persons
          Teenagers

Runaway wives
USE **Runaway adults**
Running (May subdiv. geog.)   **796.42**
BT **Track athletics**
NT **Jogging**
Marathon running
Orienteering
RT **Racing**
Rural architecture
USE **Farm buildings**
Rural churches (May subdiv. geog.)
254
UF Churches, Country
Churches, Rural
Country churches
BT **Church work**
Rural comedies
USE **Pastoral drama**
Pastoral fiction
Rural community development
USE **Rural development**
Rural conditions
USE names of countries, states, etc.,
with the subdivision *Rural
conditions,* e.g. **United
States—Rural conditions;
Ohio—Rural conditions;** etc.
[to be added as needed]
Rural credit
USE **Agricultural credit**
Rural development (May subdiv. geog.)
307.1
UF Rural community development
BT **Agriculture—Government poli-
cy**
Community development
Economic development
Regional planning
Rural education
USE **Rural schools**
Rural electrification (May subdiv. geog.)
621.319
BT **Electrification**
RT **Electricity in agriculture**
Rural families
USE **Farm family**
Rural high schools
USE **Rural schools**
Rural life
USE **Country life**
Farm life

Outdoor life
Rural poetry
USE **Pastoral poetry**
Rural schools (May subdiv. geog.)   **371**
UF Country schools
District schools
High schools, Rural
Rural education
Rural high schools
BT **Public schools**
Schools
Rural sociology   307.72
Use for materials on the discipline of rural
sociology and the theory of social organiza-
tion in rural areas. Materials on the rural con-
ditions of particular regions, countries, cities,
etc., are entered under the place with the sub-
division *Rural conditions.* Descriptive, popu-
lar, and literary materials on living in the
country are entered under **Country life**.
UF Sociology, Rural
SA names of countries, states, etc.,
with the subdivision *Rural
conditions* [to be added as
needed]
BT **Sociology**
NT **Ohio—Rural conditions**
**United States—Rural condi-
tions**
Urbanization
RT **Country life**
Farm family
Farm life
Peasantry
Rural-urban migration
USE **Internal migration**
Russia   947
Use for materials on Russia from its origins
to the present, including the Russian Empire
and the Soviet Union. Subject headings for
the various republics, nationalities, and ethnic
groups of the former Soviet Union are to be
added as needed. The non-Russian republics
of the former Soviet Union are: Armenia (Re-
public); Azerbaijan; Belarus; Estonia; Georgia
(Republic); Kazakhstan; Kyrgyzstan; Latvia;
Lithuania; Moldova; Tajikistan; Turkmenistan;
Ukraine; and Uzbekistan.
UF Russia (Federation) [*Former
heading*]
NT **Russians**
Russia—Communism
USE **Communism—Russia**
Russia (Federation)
USE **Russia**

Russia (Federation)—History—1991-
    USE   **Russia—History—1991-**

Russia—History   947

Russia—History—0-1801   947

Russia—History—0-1917   947

Russia—History—19th century   947

Russia—History—20th century   947

Russia—History—1900-1917   947

Russia—History—1905, Revolution
    947.08

Russia—History—1917-1921, Revolution
    947.084

    UF   Russian revolution
        Soviet Union—History—1917-
        1921, Revolution [*Former*
        heading]

    BT   **Revolutions**

Russia—History—1917-1925   947.084

    UF   Soviet Union—History—1917-
        1925 [*Former heading*]

Russia—History—1917-1991, Soviet
    Union   947.084

    UF   Soviet Union [*Former heading*]
        Soviet Union—History [*Former*
        heading]
        Union of Soviet Socialist Repub-
        lics
        USSR

Russia—History—1925-1953   947.084

    UF   Soviet Union—History—1925-
        1953 [*Former heading*]

Russia—History—1953-1991   947.085

    UF   Soviet Union—History—1953-
        1991 [*Former heading*]

Russia—History—1985-1991   947.085

Russia—History—1991-   947.086

    UF   Russia (Federation)—History—
        1991- [*Former heading*]

Russian Church
    USE   **Russian Orthodox Church**

Russian communism
    USE   **Communism—Russia**

Russian language   491.7

    May be subdivided like English language.

    BT   **Language and languages**

Russian literature   891.7

    May use same subdivisions and names of
    literary forms as for English literature.

    UF   Soviet literature [*Former head-
        ing*]

    BT   **Literature**

Russian Orthodox Church (May subdiv.
    geog.)   **281.9**

    UF   Russian Church

    BT   **Christian sects**
        Orthodox Eastern Church

Russian revolution
    USE   **Russia—History—1917-1921,**
        Revolution

Russians (May subdiv. geog.)   **920; 947**

    BT   **Russia**

Russo-Finnish War, 1939-1940
    948.9703

    UF   Finno-Russian War, 1939-1940
        Soviet Union—History—1939-
        1940, War with Finland

    BT   **Europe—History—1918-1945**

Russo-Turkish War, 1853-1856
    USE   **Crimean War, 1853-1856**

Rust
    USE   **Corrosion and anticorrosives**

Rustless coatings
    USE   **Corrosion and anticorrosives**

RVs
    USE   **Recreational vehicles**

Sabbath   263; 296.4

    UF   Lord's Day

    BT   **Judaism**

Sabin vaccine
    USE   **Poliomyelitis vaccine**

Sabotage (May subdiv. geog.)   **331.89;**
    364.16

    UF   Political violence

    BT   **Offenses against public safety**
        Strikes
        Subversive activities
        Terrorism

Sacrament of Reconciliation
    USE   **Penance**

Sacraments   234; 265

    BT   **Church**
        Grace (Theology)
        Rites and ceremonies

    NT   **Anointing of the sick**
        Baptism
        Confirmation
        Eucharist
        Marriage
        Ordination
        Penance

Sacred art
    USE   **Religious art**

Sacred books (May subdiv. geog.)   **208**
   SA   names of sacred books [to be
          added as needed]
   BT   **Religious literature**
   NT   **Bible**
          Koran
          Vedas
Sacred music
   USE   **Church music**
Sacred numbers
   USE   **Numerology**
          Symbolism of numbers
Sacred sites (May subdiv. geog.)   **203**
   NT   **Machu Picchu (Peru)**
          Shrines
Sacrifice   **203**
   UF   Burnt offering
   BT   **Worship**
   NT   **Atonement—Christianity**
Safaris (May subdiv. geog.)   **796.5;**
          910.2
   BT   **Adventure and adventurers**
          Outdoor recreation
          Scientific expeditions
          Travel
   RT   **Hunting**
Safe sex
   USE   **Safe sex in AIDS prevention**
          Sexually transmitted diseases—
          Prevention
Safe sex in AIDS prevention   **613.9;**
          616.97
   Use for materials limited to safe sexual
practices in the prevention of AIDS. Materials
on AIDS prevention in general not limited to
safe sexual practices are entered under **AIDS
(Disease)—Prevention**.
   UF   Safe sex
   BT   **AIDS (Disease)—Prevention**
          Sexual hygiene
Safety appliances
   USE   **Safety devices**
Safety devices   **363.19; 620.8**
   UF   Safety appliances
          Safety equipment
   SA   subjects with the subdivision
          Safety devices, e.g. **Rail-
          roads—Safety devices** [to be
          added as needed]
   NT   **Railroads—Safety devices**
   RT   **Accidents—Prevention**
Safety education (May subdiv. geog.)
          363.1; 371.7

   BT   **Accidents—Prevention**
Safety equipment
   USE   **Safety devices**
Safety, Industrial
   USE   **Occupational health and safety**
Safety measures
   USE   **Accidents—Prevention**
          and   subjects with the subdivi-
          sion *Safety measures*, e.g.
          **Aeronautics—Safety mea-
          sures** [to be added as needed]
Safety regulations (May subdiv. geog.)
          343; 363.1
   Use for collections or materials about rules
regarding safety that have the force of law.
   SA   subjects with the subdivision
          Law and legislation or *Safety
          regulations*, e.g. **Food—Law
          and legislation**; **Ships—Safe-
          ty regulations**; etc. [to be
          added as needed]
   BT   **Accidents—Prevention**
          Law
   NT   **Drivers' licenses**
          Ships—Safety regulations
          Traffic regulations
Sagas (May subdiv. geog.)   **398.22; 839**
   BT   **Folklore**
          Literature
          Old Norse literature
          Scandinavian literature
Sailboarding
   USE   **Windsurfing**
Sailing (May subdiv. geog.)   **623.88;**
          797.124
   BT   **Ships**
          Water sports
   NT   **Windsurfing**
   RT   **Boats and boating**
          Navigation
          Yachts and yachting
Sailors (May subdiv. geog.)   **387.5092;**
          623.88092; 920
   UF   Mariners
          Naval personnel
          Navigators
          Sailors' life
          Sea life
          Seamen
   SA   names of navies, e.g. **United
          States. Navy** [to be added as
          needed]

Sailors—*Continued*
- BT **Military personnel**
  Naval art and science
  Navies
- NT **Merchant marine**
  Ship pilots
- RT **Seafaring life**

Sailors—Fiction
- USE **Sea stories**

Sailors' handbooks
- USE **United States. Navy—Handbooks, manuals, etc.**

Sailors' life
- USE **Sailors**
  Seafaring life

Sailors' song
- USE **Sea songs**

Sailplanes (Aeronautics)
- USE **Gliders (Aeronautics)**

Saint Bartholomew's Day, Massacre of, 1572   944
- UF St. Bartholomew's Day, Massacre of, 1572
- BT **France—History—1328-1589, House of Valois**
  Huguenots
  Massacres

Saint Francis, Order of
- USE **Franciscans**

Saint Valentine's Day
- USE **Valentine's Day**

Saints (May subdiv. geog.)   **200.92; 920**
- SA saints of particular religions, e.g. **Christian saints**; and names of individual saints [to be added as needed]
- BT **Religious biography**
- NT **Christian saints**
  Mary
- RT **Martyrs**

Salads   641.8
- BT **Cooking**
- RT **Cooking—Vegetables**

Salamanders (May subdiv. geog.)   **597.6**
- BT **Amphibians**

Salaries
- USE **Salaries, wages, etc.**

Salaries, wages, etc. (May subdiv. geog.)   **331.2; 658.3**

Use for materials on all forms of compensation for work performed or services rendered, including salaries, wages, fees, commissions, fringe benefits, and pensions.
- UF Compensation
  Employees—Salaries, wages, etc.
  Fees
  Salaries
  Wages
- SA types of professional personnel, types of workers, and classes of persons with the subdivision *Salaries, wages, etc.,* e.g. **Lawyers—Salaries, wages, etc.; Office workers—Salaries, wages, etc.; Handicapped—Salaries, wages, etc.;** industries and types of institutions with the subdivisions *Employees—Salaries, wages, etc.,* e.g. **Chemical industry—Employees—Salaries, wages, etc.; Colleges and universities—Employees—Salaries, wages, etc.;** and countries, states, cities, etc., with the subdivisions *Officials and employees—Salaries, wages, etc.,* e.g. **Ohio—Officials and employees—Salaries, wages, etc.** [to be added as needed]
- BT **Income**
- NT **Chemical industry—Employees—Salaries, wages, etc.**
  Colleges and universities—Employees—Salaries, wages, etc.
  Employee benefits
  Equal pay for equal work
  Handicapped—Salaries, wages, etc.
  Job analysis
  Lawyers—Salaries, wages, etc.
  Minimum wage
  Office workers—Salaries, wages, etc.
  Ohio—Officials and employees—Salaries, wages, etc.
  Profit sharing
  Wage-price policy
- RT **Cost and standard of living**
  Prices

Sale of infants
- USE **Adoption—Corrupt practices**

Sales agents
USE **Sales personnel**
Sales, Auction
USE **Auctions**
Sales management (May subdiv. geog.)
658.8
BT **Management**
Marketing
Selling
Sales personnel (May subdiv. geog.)
381.092; 658.85
UF Clerks (Retail trade)
Sales agents
Salesmen
Saleswomen
Traveling sales personnel
BT **Retail trade**
NT **Peddlers and peddling**
Sales tax (May subdiv. geog.) **336.2**
BT **Taxation**
Salesmanship
USE **Selling**
Salesmen
USE **Sales personnel**
Saleswomen
USE **Sales personnel**
Saline water
USE **Sea water**
Saline water conversion
USE **Sea water conversion**
Salk vaccine
USE **Poliomyelitis vaccine**
Salmon (May subdiv. geog.) **597.5**
BT **Fishes**
Saloons
USE **Bars**
Salt free diet
USE **Salt-free diet**
Salt-free diet **613.2**
UF Low-sodium diet
Salt free diet
BT **Cooking**
Diet
Salt water
USE **Sea water**
Salt water aquariums
USE **Marine aquariums**
Saltwater fishing (May subdiv. geog.)
799.16
UF Ocean fishing
Sea fishing

BT **Fishing**
Salutations
USE **Etiquette**
Salvage (May subdiv. geog.) **627; 628.4**
Use for materials on the recovery of equipment, parts, cargo, merchandise, structures, or waste, not limited to ships or shipwrecks.
UF Salvage (Waste, etc.)
Utilization of waste
Waste reclamation
NT **Marine salvage**
Recycling
Waste products as fuel
RT **Refuse and refuse disposal**
Salvage (Waste, etc.)
USE **Salvage**
Salvation **202; 234**
UF Redemption
BT **Doctrinal theology**
NT **Atonement—Christianity**
Conversion
Faith
Grace (Theology)
Regeneration (Christianity)
Sanctification
Salvation Army **287.9**
BT **Christian missions**
Christian sects
Salvation—Biblical teaching **234**
Salvation history
USE **Salvation—History of doctrines**
Salvation—History of doctrines **202;**
234
UF Salvation history
BT **Doctrinal theology**
Same-sex marriage (May subdiv. geog.)
306.81; 346.01
UF Gay marriage
Homosexual marriage
Lesbian marriage
BT **Marriage**
Samplers (May subdiv. geog.) **746.3**
BT **Embroidery**
Needlework
Sampling (Statistics) **519.5**
UF Random sampling
BT **Probabilities**
Statistics
NT **Quality control**
Samurai (May subdiv. geog.) **952**
BT **Japan—History—0-1868**
Sanatoriums (May subdiv. geog.) **362.16**

Sanatoriums—*Continued*
UF   Sanitariums
BT   **Long-term care facilities**
RT   **Hospitals**
Sanctification   202; 234
BT   **Salvation**
**Sanctions (International law)   327.1;
341.5**
UF   Economic sanctions
BT   **Economic policy**
**International economic rela-
tions**
International law
Sanctuary (Law)
USE   **Asylum**
Sanctuary movement (May subdiv. geog.)
261.8
Use for materials on any network of reli-
gious congregations or churches that shelter
refugees or illegal aliens.
BT   **Asylum**
Church and social problems
Social movements
RT   **Illegal aliens**
Refugees
Sand dunes (May subdiv. geog.)   **551.3**
UF   Dunes
BT   **Seashore**
Sand sculpture (May subdiv. geog.)   **736**
BT   **Nature craft**
Sculpture
Sandwiches (May subdiv. geog.)   **641.8**
BT   **Cooking**
Sanitariums
USE   **Sanatoriums**
Sanitary affairs
USE   **Sanitary engineering**
Sanitation
Sanitary engineering (May subdiv. geog.)
628
UF   Environmental health engineering
Sanitary affairs
BT   **Engineering**
NT   **Drainage**
Pollution
Refuse and refuse disposal
Sewerage
Soil microbiology
Street cleaning
RT   **Municipal engineering**
Sanitation

Sanitary landfills
USE   **Landfills**
Sanitation (May subdiv. geog.)   **363.72;
648**
UF   Sanitary affairs
SA   subjects, types of industries, and
names of individual corporate
bodies with the subdivision
Sanitation, e.g. **Hospitals—
Sanitation** [to be added as
needed]
NT   **Cemeteries**
Cleaning
Cleanliness
Cremation
Disinfection and disinfectants
Hospitals—Sanitation
Household sanitation
Pollution
Refuse and refuse disposal
School hygiene
Smoke prevention
Ventilation
Water purification
RT   **Hygiene**
Public health
Sanitary engineering
Sanitation, Household
USE   **Household sanitation**
Sanskrit language   491
BT   **Indian languages**
Language and languages
Santa Claus   394.2663
BT   **Christmas**
Santeria (May subdiv. geog.)   **299.6**
UF   Lucumi (Religion)
BT   **Religion**
Sarcosuchus imperator   567.9
BT   **Dinosaurs**
Sasquatch   001.9
UF   Big foot
Bigfoot
BT   **Monsters**
Mythical animals
SAT
USE   **Scholastic Assessment Test**
Satan
USE   **Devil**
Satellite communication systems
USE   **Artificial satellites in telecom-
munication**

Satellites   523.9
   UF   Moons
          Natural satellites
          Planetary satellites
          Planets—Satellites
   SA   names of planets with the subdivision *Satellites*, e.g. **Mars (Planet)—Satellites** [to be added as needed]
   BT   **Solar system**
   NT   **Mars (Planet)—Satellites**
Satellites, Artificial
   USE   **Artificial satellites**
Satellites—Mars
   USE   **Mars (Planet)—Satellites**
Satire   808.7; 808.87
   UF   Comic literature
   SA   satire of particular countries, e.g. **American satire** [to be added as needed]
   BT   **Literature**
          Rhetoric
          Wit and humor
   NT   **American satire**
          Burlesque (Literature)
          English satire
          Invective
          Parody
          Political satire
Satire, American
   USE   **American satire**
Satire, English
   USE   **English satire**
Saturn (Planet)   523.46
   BT   **Planets**
Saucers, Flying
   USE   **Unidentified flying objects**
Sauces   641.8
   BT   **Cooking**
Saudi Arabia   953.8
   May be subdivided like United States except for History.
Saving and investment (May subdiv. geog.)   **332.024**
   UF   Capital accumulation
          Capital formation
          Economy
          Investment and saving
          Saving and thrift
          Thrift
   BT   **Capital**
          Economics

          Personal finance
          Wealth
   NT   **Savings and loan associations**
   RT   **Investments**
Saving and thrift
   USE   **Saving and investment**
Savings and loan associations (May subdiv. geog.)   **332.3**
   UF   Building and loan associations
          Loan associations
   BT   **Banks and banking**
          Cooperation
          Cooperative societies
          Investments
          Loans
          Personal loans
          Saving and investment
   RT   **Cooperative banks**
Savings banks
   USE   **Banks and banking**
Saws   621.9
   BT   **Carpentry tools**
          Tools
Sayings
   USE   **Epigrams**
          Proverbs
          Quotations
Scandals (May subdiv. geog.)   **302.2**
   BT   **History**
Scandinavian languages   439
   UF   Norse languages
   BT   **Language and languages**
   NT   **Danish language**
          Icelandic language
          Norwegian language
          Old Norse language
          Swedish language
Scandinavian literature   839
   UF   Norse literature
   BT   **Literature**
   NT   **Danish literature**
          Eddas
          Icelandic literature
          Norwegian literature
          Sagas
          Swedish literature
   RT   **Old Norse literature**
Scandinavian mythology
   USE   **Norse mythology**

Scandinavians (May subdiv. geog.)   **920; 948**

Use for materials on the people of Scandinavia since the tenth century. Materials on earlier Scandinavians are entered under **Vikings**.

NT   **Vikings**

Scarecrows   632

BT   **Plant conservation**

Scenarios

USE   **Radio plays**

Stories, plots, etc.

Television plays

Scene painting   792.02

BT   **Painting**

Theaters—Stage setting and scenery

Scenery

USE   **Landscape protection**

Natural monuments

Views

Wilderness areas

Scenery (Stage)

USE   **Theaters—Stage setting and scenery**

Scenic byways (May subdiv. geog.)   **910.2**

UF   Scenic highways

Scenic roads

BT   **Roads**

Scenic highways

USE   **Scenic byways**

Scenic roads

USE   **Scenic byways**

Scented gardens

USE   **Fragrant gardens**

Scepticism

USE   **Skepticism**

Scheherazade (Legendary character)   398.22

BT   **Legendary characters**

Schizophrenia   616.89

BT   **Mental illness**

Scholarship

USE   **Learning and scholarship**

Scholarship funds

USE   **Scholarships**

Scholarships (May subdiv. geog.)   **371.2; 378.3**

UF   Bursaries

Fellowships

Scholarship funds

Scholarships, fellowships, etc.

SA   fields of study, ethnic groups, and classes of persons with the subdivision *Scholarships*, [to be added as needed]

BT   **Education**

Endowments

Student aid

Scholarships, fellowships, etc.

USE   **Scholarships**

Scholastic achievement

USE   **Academic achievement**

Scholastic achievement tests

USE   **Achievement tests**

Scholastic Aptitude Test

USE   **Scholastic Assessment Test**

Scholastic Assessment Test   378.1

UF   SAT

Scholastic Aptitude Test

BT   **Colleges and universities—Entrance examinations**

Examinations

School achievement tests

USE   **Achievement tests**

School administration and organization

USE   **Schools—Administration**

School-age fathers

USE   **Teenage fathers**

School-age mothers

USE   **Teenage mothers**

School and community

USE   **Community and school**

School and home

USE   **Home and school**

School architecture

USE   **School buildings**

School assembly programs   371.8

UF   Assembly programs, School

School entertainments

Schools—Exercises and recreations

Schools—Opening exercises

BT   **Student activities**

NT   **Commencements**

Recitations

RT   **Drama in education**

School athletics

USE   **School sports**

School attendance (May subdiv. geog.)   **371.2**

School attendance—*Continued*
- UF   Absence from school
  - Absenteeism (Schools)
  - Attendance, School
  - Compulsory school attendance
- BT   **Schools—Administration**
- RT   **Compulsory education**
  - **Dropouts**

School boards (May subdiv. geog.)
353.8
- UF   Boards of education
- BT   **Schools—Administration**

School books
- USE   **Textbooks**

School buildings (May subdiv. geog.)
371.6; 727
- UF   Buildings, School
  - School architecture
  - School houses
  - Schoolhouses
- BT   **Buildings**
  - **Schools**

School busing
- USE   **Busing (School integration)**
  - **School children—Transportation**

School children (May subdiv. geog.)
155.42; 305.234
- BT   **Children**
  - **Students**

School children—Food   371.7; 642
- UF   Food for school children
  - Meals for school children
  - School lunches
- BT   **Children—Nutrition**
  - **Diet**
  - **Food**

School children—Medical examinations
- USE   **Children—Medical examinations**

School children—Transportation   371.8
- UF   School busing
- BT   **Transportation**
- NT   **Busing (School integration)**

School choice (May subdiv. geog.)   **379.1**
   Use for materials on choosing a school and on the right of parents to choose their children's school.
- UF   Choice of school
  - Parents' choice of school
  - Schools—Selection
- BT   **Education**

- NT   **College choice**

School clubs
- USE   **Students—Societies**

School counseling (May subdiv. geog.)
371.4
   Use for materials on the assistance given to students by schools, colleges, or universities in understanding and coping with adjustment problems. Materials on the assistance given to students in the selection of a program of studies are entered under **Educational counseling**.
- UF   Guidance counseling, School
- BT   **Counseling**
- RT   **Educational counseling**
  - **School psychologists**

School desegregation
- USE   **School integration**

School discipline   371.5
- UF   Discipline of children
  - Punishment in schools
- BT   **Schools—Administration**
  - **Teaching**
- NT   **Classroom management**
  - **Student government**

School dropouts
- USE   **Dropouts**

School entertainments
- USE   **School assembly programs**

School excursions
- USE   **Field trips**

School fiction
- USE   **School stories**

School finance
- USE   **Education—Finance**

School furniture
- USE   **Schools—Equipment and supplies**

School grade retention
- USE   **Promotion (School)**

School houses
- USE   **School buildings**

School hygiene   371.7
- BT   **Children—Health and hygiene**
  - **Health education**
  - **Hygiene**
  - **Public health**
  - **Sanitation**
- RT   **School nurses**

School inspection
- USE   **School supervision**
  - **Schools—Administration**

School integration (May subdiv. geog.)
379.2
UF Desegregated schools
      Desegregation in education
      Education—Integration
      Integrated schools
      Integration in education
      Racial balance in schools
      School desegregation
BT **Race relations**
NT **Busing (School integration)**
      Magnet schools
RT **Segregation in education**

School journalism
USE **College and school journalism**

School libraries (May subdiv. geog.)
027.8
BT **Instructional materials centers**
      Libraries
NT **Elementary school libraries**
      High school libraries
      Students—Library services
RT **Libraries and schools**

School life
USE **Students**

School lunches
USE **School children—Food**

School management and organization
USE **Schools—Administration**

School mascots
USE **Mascots**

School media centers
USE **Instructional materials centers**

School music
USE **Music—Study and teaching**
      School songbooks
      Singing

School newspapers
USE **College and school journalism**

School nurses (May subdiv. geog.)
371.7
BT **Nurses**
RT **Health education**
      School hygiene

School organization
USE **Schools—Administration**

School playgrounds
USE **Playgrounds**

School plays
USE **Children's plays**
      College and school drama

School prayer
USE **Prayer in the public schools**

School principals
USE **School superintendents and**
      principals

School promotion
USE **Promotion (School)**

School prose
USE **Children's writings**

School psychologists (May subdiv. geog.)
371.7
BT **Psychologists**
RT **School counseling**

School readiness
USE **Readiness for school**

School reports 371.2
UF Educational reports
      Reports, Teachers'
      Teachers' reports
BT **Report writing**
RT **Grading and marking (Education)**

School shootings (May subdiv. geog.)
371.7
UF Shootings in schools
BT **Crime**
      School violence

School shops 373.2
UF Industrial arts shops
BT **Technical education**

School songbooks 782.42
UF School music
BT **Songbooks**
      Songs
NT **Children's songs**

School sports (May subdiv. geog.) **371.8**
UF Interscholastic sports
      School athletics
BT **Sports**
      Student activities
RT **College sports**

School stories 808.83
Use for individual works, collections, or materials about school stories.
UF School fiction
      Schools—Fiction
BT **Fiction**

School superintendents and principals
(May subdiv. geog.) **371.2**
UF School principals
      Superintendents of schools
BT **Schools—Administration**

School superintendents and principals—
Continued
  RT **School supervision**
School supervision **371.2**
  Use for materials on the supervision of instruction. Materials on the management and organization of schools and on the administrative duties of educators are entered under **Schools—Administration**.
  UF Inspection of schools
        Instructional supervision
        School inspection
        Supervision of schools
  BT **Schools—Administration**
        Teaching
  RT **School superintendents and**
        principals
School surveys
  USE **Educational surveys**
School taxes
  USE **Education—Finance**
School teaching
  USE **Teaching**
School trips
  USE **Field trips**
School verse
  USE **Children's writings**
School violence (May subdiv. geog.)
        371.7
  UF Student violence
        Violence in schools
  BT **Juvenile delinquency**
        Violence
  NT **School shootings**
School vouchers
  USE **Educational vouchers**
School yearbooks **371.8**
  UF Annuals
        College yearbooks
        High school yearbooks
        Student yearbooks
  BT **Serial publications**
        Yearbooks
Schoolhouses
  USE **School buildings**
Schools (May subdiv. geog.) **371**
  SA types of schools, e.g. **Church**
        schools; **Rural schools**; etc.;
        names of individual schools;
        and subjects with the subdivision *Study and teaching*, e.g.
        Science—Study and teaching
        [to be added as needed]

  NT **Business schools**
        Charter schools
        Church schools
        Colleges and universities
        Correspondence schools and
          courses
        Elementary schools
        Evening and continuation
          schools
        Experimental schools
        High schools
        Junior high schools
        Kindergarten
        Libraries and schools
        Magnet schools
        Middle schools
        Museums and schools
        Nongraded schools
        Nursery schools
        Private schools
        Public schools
        Religious summer schools
        Rural schools
        School buildings
        Single-sex schools
        Summer schools
        Urban schools
  RT **Education**
Schools—Accreditation (May subdiv.
        geog.) **379.1**
  UF Accreditation (Education)
        Educational accreditation
  SA types of educational institutions
        and names of individual institutions with the subdivision
        Accreditation, e.g. **Colleges**
        and universities—Accreditation; and subjects with the
        subdivision *Study and teaching*, for accreditation of programs of study in those subjects, e.g. **Mathematics—**
        Study and teaching [to be
        added as needed]
Schools—Administration (May subdiv.
        geog.) **371.2**
  Use for materials on the management and organization of schools and on the administrative duties of educators. Materials on the supervision of instruction are entered under **School supervision**.
  UF Educational administration
        Inspection of schools

684

Schools—Administration—*Continued*
  School administration and organization
  School inspection
  School management and organization
  School organization
  Schools—Management and organization
 NT **Articulation (Education)**
    School attendance
    School boards
    School discipline
    School superintendents and principals
    School supervision
    Schools—Centralization
    Schools—Decentralization
    Student government
Schools and libraries
 USE **Libraries and schools**
Schools and museums
 USE **Museums and schools**
Schools—Centralization (May subdiv. geog.) **379.1**
 UF Centralization of schools
    Consolidation of schools
 BT **Schools—Administration**
Schools—Curricula
 USE **Education—Curricula**
Schools—Decentralization (May subdiv. geog.) **379.1**
 UF Decentralization of schools
 BT **Schools—Administration**
Schools—Equipment and supplies **371.6**
 UF School furniture
 BT **Furniture**
Schools—Exercises and recreations
 USE **School assembly programs**
Schools—Fiction
 USE **School stories**
Schools—Management and organization
 USE **Schools—Administration**
Schools, Military
 USE **Military education**
Schools, Nonformal
 USE **Experimental schools**
Schools—Opening exercises
 USE **School assembly programs**
Schools—Selection
 USE **School choice**
Schools—United States **371.00973**

 UF American schools
Science (May subdiv. geog.) **500**
 NT **Astronomy**
    Bible and science
    Biology
    Botany
    Chaos (Science)
    Chemistry
    Computer science
    Discoveries in science
    Earth sciences
    Environmental sciences
    Forensic sciences
    Fossils
    Fraud in science
    Geology
    Life sciences
    Mathematics
    Natural history
    Petrology
    Physical sciences
    Physics
    Physiology
    Religion and science
    Science and civilization
    Science and the humanities
    Space sciences
    System theory
    Zoology
 RT **Laboratories**
    Scientific apparatus and instruments
    Scientists
Science and civilization (May subdiv. geog.) **306.4**
 UF Civilization and science
    Science and society
 BT **Civilization**
    Progress
    Science
Science and religion
 USE **Religion and science**
Science and society
 USE **Science and civilization**
Science and space
 USE **Space sciences**
Science and state
 USE **Science—Government policy**
Science and the Bible
 USE **Bible and science**
Science and the humanities **001.3**

685

Science and the humanities—*Continued*
UF Humanities and science
BT **Humanities**
      Science
Science—Exhibitions   507.4
UF Science fairs
BT **Exhibitions**
NT **Science projects**
Science experiments
USE **Science—Experiments**
Science—Experiments   507
UF Experiments, Scientific
      Science experiments
      Scientific experiments
SA branches of science with the
      subdivision *Experiments*, e.g.
      Chemistry—Experiments to
      be added as needed]
RT **Science projects**
Science fair projects
USE **Science projects**
Science fairs
USE **Science—Exhibitions**
Science fiction   808.3; 808.83
Use for individual works, collections, or materials about fiction based on imagined developments in science and technology.
UF Space flight (Fiction)
BT **Adventure fiction**
      Fiction
NT **Dystopias**
      Hugo Award
      Imaginary voyages
      Nebula Award
      Utopian fiction
RT **Fantasy fiction**
      Interplanetary voyages
**Science fiction comic books, strips, etc.
   741.5**
Use for individual works, collections, or materials about science fiction comics.
BT **Comic books, strips, etc.**
Science fiction films (May subdiv. geog.)
   791.43
Use for individual works, collections, or materials about science fiction films.
SA types of science fiction films,
      e.g. **Star Wars films** [to be
      added as needed]
BT **Motion pictures**
NT **Star Wars films**
RT **Fantasy films**

Science fiction films—Catalogs
   016.79143
Science fiction graphic novels   741.5
Use for individual works, collections, or materials about science fiction graphic novels.
BT **Graphic novels**
Science fiction plays   808.82
Use for individual works, collections, or materials about science fiction plays.
BT **Drama**
Science fiction poetry   808.1; 808.81
Use for individual works, collections, or materials about science fiction poetry.
BT **Poetry**
Science fiction radio programs   791.44
Use for individual works, collections, or materials about science fiction radio programs.
BT **Radio programs**
**Science fiction television programs
   791.45**
Use for individual works, collections, or materials about science fiction television programs.
BT **Television programs**
RT **Fantasy television programs**
Science—Government policy (May subdiv.
   geog.)   **353.7; 500**
UF Science and state
      Science policy
Science—Islamic countries   508.53
UF Arab science
      Islamic science
Science journalism
USE **Scientific journalism**
Science laboratories
USE **Laboratories**
Science—Methodology   501
UF Scientific method
NT **Logic**
Science policy
USE **Science—Government policy**
Science projects   507.8
UF Science fair projects
BT **Science—Exhibitions**
RT **Science—Experiments**
Science—Religious aspects
USE **Religion and science**
Science—Societies (May subdiv. geog.)
   506
UF Scientific societies
BT **Societies**
Science—Study and teaching (May
   subdiv. geog.)   **507**

Science—Study and teaching—*Continued*
UF Scientific education
NT **Nature study**
Science—Study and teaching—Audiovisu-
al aids **507.8**
Science—Study and teaching—Evaluation
(May subdiv. geog.) **507.6**
Science—United States **509.73**
Scientific apparatus and instruments
502.8
UF Apparatus, Scientific
Instruments, Scientific
Scientific instruments
SA types of instruments, e.g. **Aero-**
nautical instruments; and
names of specific instruments
[to be added as needed]
NT **Aeronautical instruments**
Astronomical instruments
Chemical apparatus
Electric apparatus and appli-
ances
Electronic apparatus and ap-
pliances
Engineering instruments
Meteorological instruments
Optical instruments
RT **Science**
Scientific breakthroughs
USE **Discoveries in science**
Scientific creationism
USE **Creationism**
Scientific discoveries
USE **Discoveries in science**
Scientific education
USE **Science—Study and teaching**
Scientific errors
USE **Errors**
Scientific expeditions **508**
UF Expeditions, Scientific
Polar expeditions
SA names of regions explored with
the subdivision *Exploration*
for materials on scientific ex-
peditions to regions that are
unsettled or sparsely settled
and largely unknown to the
world at large, e.g. **Antarcti-**
ca—Exploration; names of
countries, states, etc., with the
subdivision *Exploring expedi-*

tions for materials on explora-
tions sponsored by those gov-
ernments; and names of expe-
ditions [to be added as need-
ed]
BT **Voyages and travels**
NT **Antarctica—Exploration**
Arctic regions—Exploration
Safaris
RT **Exploration**
Scientific experiments
USE **Science—Experiments**
Scientific fraud
USE **Fraud in science**
Scientific instruments
USE **Scientific apparatus and in-**
struments
Scientific journalism (May subdiv. geog.)
070.4
UF Journalism, Scientific
Science journalism
BT **Journalism**
Scientific laboratories
USE **Laboratories**
Scientific management
USE **Management**
Scientific method
USE **Science—Methodology**
Scientific names of plants
USE **Botany—Nomenclature**
Scientific plant names
USE **Botany—Nomenclature**
Scientific recreations **793.8**
UF Recreations, Scientific
BT **Amusements**
NT **Mathematical recreations**
Scientific societies
USE **Science—Societies**
Scientific writing
USE **Technical writing**
Scientists (May subdiv. geog.) **920;**
509.2
SA types of scientists and names of
individual scientists [to be
added as needed]
NT **Astronomers**
Biologists
Chemists
Geologists
Mathematicians
Naturalists

Scientists—*Continued*
Physicists
RT **Science**
Scipionyx 567.912
BT **Dinosaurs**
Scottish clans
USE **Clans—Scotland**
Scottish personal names (May subdiv.
geog.) 929.4
BT **Personal names**
Scottish tartans
USE **Tartans**
Scouts and scouting (May subdiv. geog.)
369.4
BT **Clubs**
Community life
NT **Boy Scouts**
Girl Scouts
Scrapbook journaling
USE **Scrapbooking**
Scrapbooking 745.593
UF Scrapbook journaling
BT **Handicraft**
Screen printing
USE **Silk screen printing**
Screening for drug abuse
USE **Drug testing**
Screenplays 808.2; 808.82
Use for individual works, collections, or
materials about motion picture plays.
UF Film scripts
Motion picture plays
Motion picture scripts
Movie scripts
BT **Drama**
Screws 621.8
BT **Simple machines**
Scriptures, Holy
USE **Bible**
Scuba diving (May subdiv. geog.) 797.2
Use for materials on free diving with the
aid of a self-contained underwater breathing
apparatus. Materials on free diving with mask,
fins, and snorkel are entered under **Skin div-
ing**. Materials on diving from a board or plat-
form are entered under **Diving**. Materials on
underwater diving with equipment are entered
under **Deep diving**.
UF Free diving
BT **Deep diving**
Water sports
Sculling
USE **Rowing**

Sculptors (May subdiv. geog.) 730.92;
920
BT **Artists**
Sculptors—United States 730.92; 920
UF American sculptors
Sculpture 730
UF Statues
SA sculpture of particular countries,
e.g. **Greek sculpture**; and
specific types of sculpture [to
be added as needed]
BT **Art**
Decoration and ornament
NT **American sculpture**
Brasses
Bronzes
Greek sculpture
Indian sculpture
Kinetic sculpture
Masks (Sculpture)
Mobiles (Sculpture)
Modeling
Modernism in sculpture
Monuments
Plaster casts
Sand sculpture
Soap sculpture
RT **Carving (Decorative arts)**
Sculpture—20th century 735
UF Modern sculpture—1900-1999
(20th century)
Sculpture, Modern—20th century
Sculpture—21st century 735
Sculpture, Greek
USE **Greek sculpture**
Sculpture in motion
USE **Kinetic sculpture**
Sculpture, Modern
USE **Modernism in sculpture**
Sculpture, Modern—20th century
USE **Sculpture—20th century**
Sculpture—Technique 731.4
RT **Modeling**
SDI (Ballistic missile defense system)
USE **Strategic Defense Initiative**
Sea animals
USE **Marine animals**
Sea bed
USE **Ocean bottom**
Sea farming
USE **Aquaculture**

Sea fisheries
USE **Commercial fishing**
Sea fishing
USE **Saltwater fishing**
Sea food
USE **Seafood**
Sea in art
USE **Marine painting**
Sea laboratories
USE **Undersea research stations**
Sea laws
USE **Maritime law**
Sea life
USE **Marine biology**
Navies
Sailors
Seafaring life
Sea mosses
USE **Algae**
Sea poetry 808.1; 808.81
Use for individual works, collections, or materials about poetry about the sea.
BT **Poetry**
NT **Sea songs**
Sea pollution
USE **Marine pollution**
Sea power 359
UF Dominion of the sea
Military power
Naval power
Navy
SA names of countries with the subhead *Navy* or the subdivision *Naval history*, e.g. **United States. Navy; United States—Naval history**; etc. [to be added as needed]
BT **Naval art and science**
NT **Warships**
RT **Naval history**
Navies
Sea resources
USE **Marine resources**
Sea routes
USE **Trade routes**
Sea shells
USE **Shells**
Sea-shore
USE **Seashore**
Sea songs 782.42
UF Chanties
Sailors' song

BT **Sea poetry**
Songs
Sea stories 808.3; 808.83
Use for individual works, collections, or materials about sea stories.
UF Sailors—Fiction
BT **Adventure and adventurers**
Adventure fiction
Fiction
Sea transportation
USE **Shipping**
Sea travel
USE **Ocean travel**
Sea water 551.46
UF Saline water
Salt water
BT **Water**
Sea water aquariums
USE **Marine aquariums**
Sea water conversion (May subdiv. geog.)
628.1
UF Conversion of saline water
Desalination of water
Desalting of water
Saline water conversion
BT **Water purification**
Sea waves
USE **Ocean waves**
Seafaring life 910.4
UF Sailors' life
Sea life
SA names of countries with the subhead *Navy*, e.g. **United States. Navy** [to be added as needed]
BT **Adventure and adventurers**
Manners and customs
Voyages and travels
RT **Sailors**
Seafood (May subdiv. geog.) **641.3**
UF Sea food
SA names of marine fish, shellfish, etc., used as food [to be added as needed]
BT **Food**
Marine resources
NT **Cooking—Seafood**
RT **Fish as food**
Sealab project 551.46
UF Navy Sealab project
Project Sealab
BT **Undersea research stations**

Seals (Animals) (May subdiv. geog.)
    599.79
    BT **Mammals**
         Marine mammals
Seals (Numismatics) (May subdiv. geog.)
    737; 929.8
    UF Emblems
         Signets
    BT **Heraldry**
         History
         Inscriptions
         Numismatics
    RT **National emblems**
Seamanship
    USE **Navigation**
Seamen
    USE **Sailors**
Search and rescue operations
    USE **Rescue work**
Search dogs (May subdiv. geog.)   **636.73**
    BT **Working dogs**
Search engines
    USE **Web search engines**
Searching the Internet
    USE **Internet searching**
Seas (May subdiv. geog.)   **551.46**
    SA names of seas, e.g. **Mediterra-**
         nean Sea [to be added as
         needed]
    BT **Earth**
         Physical geography
         Water
    NT **Mediterranean Sea**
Seascapes
    USE **Marine painting**
Seashore (May subdiv. geog.)   **551.45**
    UF Sea-shore
    BT **Landforms**
    NT **Beaches**
         Sand dunes
    RT **Coasts**
         Ocean
Seashore ecology (May subdiv. geog.)
    577.69
    BT **Ecology**
Seasons (May subdiv. geog.)   **508.2; 525**
    BT **Astronomy**
         Climate
         Meteorology
    NT **Autumn**
         Spring

         Summer
         Winter
Seaweeds
    USE **Algae**
Secession (May subdiv. geog.)   **973.713**
    BT **Sovereignty**
    RT **Separatist movements**
Secession—Southern States   **973.713**
    BT **United States—History—1861-**
         1865, Civil War
    NT **United States—History—1861-**
         1865, Civil War—Causes
Secessionist movements
    USE **Separatist movements**
Seclusion
    USE **Solitude**
Second Advent   **236**
    UF Second coming of Christ
    BT **Eschatology**
    NT **Judgment Day**
    RT **Millennium**
Second coming of Christ
    USE **Second Advent**
Second economy
    USE **Underground economy**
Second hand trade
    USE **Secondhand trade**
Second job
    USE **Supplementary employment**
Second World War
    USE **World War, 1939-1945**
Secondary education (May subdiv. geog.)
    373
    UF Education, Secondary
         High school education
         Secondary schools
    BT **Education**
    NT **Adult education**
         Evening and continuation
         schools
    RT **High schools**
         Junior high schools
Secondary employment
    USE **Supplementary employment**
Secondary school libraries
    USE **High school libraries**
Secondary schools
    USE **High schools**
         Junior high schools
         Secondary education

Secondhand trade (May subdiv. geog.)
381
- UF   Second hand trade
  Used merchandise
- SA   types of secondhand trade, e.g.
  Garage sales [to be added as needed]
- BT   **Selling**
- NT   **Flea markets**
  Garage sales
  Rummage sales
  Thrift shops

Secrecy   **158.2; 302.5**
- UF   Concealment
- NT   **Children's secrets**
- RT   **Privacy**

Secret service (May subdiv. geog.)
363.28
Use for materials on governmental service of a secret nature.
- SA   names of wars with the subdivision *Secret service* [to be added as needed]
- BT   **Police**
- NT   **Espionage**
  World War, 1939-1945—Secret service
- RT   **Detectives**
  Intelligence service
  Spies

Secret service—United States   363.28
- UF   United States—Secret service

Secret societies (May subdiv. geog.)
366; 371.8
- SA   names of secret societies, e.g.
  Freemasons [to be added as needed]
- BT   **Rites and ceremonies**
  Societies
- NT   **Freemasons**
  Ku Klux Klan
- RT   **Fraternities and sororities**

Secret writing
- USE   **Cryptography**

Secretarial practice
- USE   **Office practice**

Secretaries (May subdiv. geog.)   **651.3**
- BT   **Office management**

Secrets, Trade
- USE   **Trade secrets**

Sectionalism
- USE   **Regionalism**

Sectionalism (United States)
- USE   **Regionalism—United States**

Sects (May subdiv. geog.)   **209; 280**
Use for materials on independent religious groups whose teachings or practices fall within the normative bounds of the major world religions. Materials on the major world religions are entered under **Religions**. Materials on groups or movements whose beliefs or practices differ significantly from the traditional religions, often focused upon a charismatic leader, are entered under **Cults**.
- UF   Church denominations
  Denominations, Religious
  Religious denominations
- SA   names of churches and sects within the major world religions, e.g. **Presbyterian Church**; **Hasidim**; etc. [to be added as needed]
- BT   **Church history**
  Religions
- NT   **Christian sects**
  Islamic sects
- RT   **Cults**

Secular humanism
- USE   **Secularism**

Secularism (May subdiv. geog.)   **171; 211**
Use for materials on any intellectual or philosophical movement or set of beliefs that promotes human values as separate and distinct from religious doctrines.
- UF   Humanism, Secular
  Secular humanism
- BT   **Ethics**
  Utilitarianism
- NT   **Atheism**
  Rationalism
- RT   **Humanism**

Securities (May subdiv. geog.)   **332.63**
- UF   Capitalization (Finance)
  Dividends
- SA   types of securities [to be added as needed]
- BT   **Finance**
  Investments
  Stock exchanges
- NT   **Bonds**
  Capital market
  Day trading (Securities)
  Futures
  Insider trading
  Mortgages
  Stocks

Securities exchange
USE **Stock exchanges**
Securities fraud (May subdiv. geog.)
345; 364.1
UF Stock fraud
Stock market fraud
BT **Fraud**
Securities trading, Insider
USE **Insider trading**
Security, Internal
USE **Internal security**
Security, International
USE **International security**
Security measures
USE subjects with the subdivision *Security measures*, e.g. **Nuclear power plants—Security measures** [to be added as needed]
Security (Psychology)   152.4; 155.2
BT **Emotions**
Psychology
Security traders
USE **Stockbrokers**
Seder   296.4
BT **Judaism—Customs and practices**
Passover
Sedition
USE **Political crimes and offenses**
Revolutions
Seed capital
USE **Venture capital**
Seeds   581.4
BT **Plant propagation**
Plants
NT **Nuts**
Seeds—Germination
USE **Germination**
Seeing eye dogs
USE **Guide dogs**
Seeking attention
USE **Showing off**
Segregation (May subdiv. geog.)   **305.8**
UF Desegregation
SA segregation in particular areas, e.g. **Segregation in education**; and racial and ethnic groups and classes of persons with the subdivision *Segregation*, e.g. **African Ameri-**

cans**—Segregation** [to be added as needed]
BT **Race relations**
NT **African Americans—Segregation**
Apartheid
Blacks—Segregation
Segregation in education
RT **Discrimination**
Minorities
Segregation in education (May subdiv. geog.)   **379.2**
UF Education—Integration
Education—Segregation
Integration in education
Racial balance in schools
BT **Segregation**
RT **Discrimination in education**
School integration
Segregation in housing
USE **Discrimination in housing**
Segregation in public accommodations
USE **Discrimination in public accommodations**
Seinen   741.5
Use for individual works, collections, or materials about manga for men ages 18-30.
BT **Manga**
Seismic sea waves
USE **Tsunamis**
Seismography
USE **Earthquakes**
Seismology
USE **Earthquakes**
Selection, Artificial
USE **Breeding**
Selective service
USE **Draft**
Self   126; 155.2
BT **Consciousness**
Individuality
Personality
NT **Ego (Psychology)**
Human body
Identity (Psychology)
Self-acceptance   155.2
UF Self-love (Psychology)
BT **Psychology**
RT **Self-confidence**
Self-esteem
Self-perception

Self-actualization
    USE **Self-realization**
Self-assurance
    USE **Self-confidence**
           Self-reliance
Self-awareness
    USE **Self-perception**
Self-care, Health
    USE **Health self-care**
Self-care, Medical
    USE **Health self-care**
Self-change techniques
    USE **Self-help techniques**
Self-concept
    USE **Self-perception**
Self-confidence 155.2
    UF   Self-assurance
    BT   **Emotions**
    RT   **Assertiveness (Psychology)**
          Self-acceptance
          Self-consciousness
          Self-esteem
          Self-reliance
Self-consciousness 155.2
    UF   Embarrassment
    BT   **Psychology**
    RT   **Self-confidence**
          Self-esteem
          Self-perception
Self-control 153.8
    UF   Self-discipline
          Self-mastery
          Will power
          Willpower
    BT   **Psychology**
Self-culture
    USE **Self-improvement**
           Self-instruction
Self-defense 613.6; 796.8
    UF   Fighting
    NT   **Boxing**
          Jiu-jitsu
          Judo
          Karate
          Self-defense for children
          Self-defense for women
          Tae kwon do
    RT   **Martial arts**
Self-defense for children 613.6; 796.8
    UF   Children—Defense
          Children—Self-defense

    BT   **Self-defense**
Self-defense for women 613.6; 796.8
    UF   Fighting
          Women—Self-defense
          Women's self-defense
    BT   **Self-defense**
    RT   **Martial arts**
Self-defense in animals
    USE **Animal defenses**
Self-defense in plants
    USE **Plant defenses**
Self-destructive behavior 155.2
    BT   **Psychology**
Self-determination, National
    USE **National self-determination**
Self-determination (Psychology)
    USE **Autonomy (Psychology)**
Self-development
    USE **Self-improvement**
           Self-instruction
Self-directed change
    USE **Self-help techniques**
Self-direction (Psychology)
    USE **Autonomy (Psychology)**
Self-discipline
    USE **Self-control**
Self-education
    USE **Self-instruction**
Self-employed (May subdiv. geog.)
          331.12
    UF   Freelancers
    BT   **Businesspeople**
    NT   **Entrepreneurs**
          Home-based business
          Professions
Self-employed women (May subdiv. geog.)
          331.4
    UF   Women, Self-employed
    BT   **Women—Employment**
Self-esteem 155.2
    UF   Self-love (Psychology)
          Self-respect
    BT   **Psychology**
    RT   **Self-acceptance**
          Self-confidence
          Self-consciousness
          Self-perception
Self-evaluation in education
    USE **Educational evaluation**
Self-examination, Medical
    USE **Health self-care**

Self-expectations, Perfectionist
   USE **Perfectionism (Personality trait)**
Self-fulfillment
   USE **Self-realization**
Self-government
   USE **Democracy**
         Representative government and representation
Self-government (in education)
   USE **Student government**
Self health care
   USE **Health self-care**
Self-help groups   361.4; 616.85
   UF Mutual support groups
         Support groups
   BT **Counseling**
Self-help medical care
   USE **Health self-care**
Self-help techniques   155.2; 158.1
   UF Self-change techniques
         Self-directed change
   BT **Applied psychology**
         Life skills
   NT **Affirmations**
Self image
   USE **Personal appearance**
Self-improvement   158
   UF Personal development
         Personal growth
         Self-culture
         Self-development
   BT **Life skills**
   RT **Self-instruction**
Self-instruction   371.39
   UF Home education
         Home study courses
         Self-culture
         Self-development
         Self-education
         Teach yourself courses
   SA subjects with the subdivision
         Programmed instruction, e.g.
         English language—Programmed instruction [to be added as needed]
   BT **Education**
         Study skills
   RT **Correspondence schools and courses**
         Self-improvement

Self-love (Psychology)
   USE **Self-acceptance**
         Self-esteem
Self-mastery
   USE **Self-control**
Self-medication
   USE **Health self-care**
Self-mutilation (May subdiv. geog.)   **616.85**
   BT **Abnormal psychology**
Self-perception   155.2
   UF Self-awareness
         Self-concept
   BT **Psychology**
   NT **Body image**
   RT **Self-acceptance**
         Self-consciousness
         Self-esteem
Self-protection in animals
   USE **Animal defenses**
Self-protection in plants
   USE **Plant defenses**
Self-realization   155.2; 158
   UF Fulfillment, Self
         Self-actualization
         Self-fulfillment
   BT **Psychology**
   RT **Success**
Self-reliance   179
   UF Self-assurance
   RT **Self-confidence**
         Survival skills
Self-respect
   USE **Self-esteem**
Selfishness   179
   BT **Personality**
Selling (May subdiv. geog.)   **381; 658.8**
   UF Salesmanship
   BT **Business**
         Retail trade
   NT **Auctions**
         Direct selling
         Mail-order business
         Rummage sales
         Sales management
         Secondhand trade
   RT **Advertising**
         Marketing
Selling of infants
   USE **Adoption—Corrupt practices**
Semantics   121; 302.2; 401

Semantics—*Continued*
- BT **Language and languages**
  Linguistics
- NT **Semiotics**

Semiarid regions
- USE **Arid regions**

Semiconductors 621.3815
- BT **Electric conductors**
  Electronics
- NT **Microelectronics**
  Transistors

Semiotics 302.2; 401

> Use for materials on the relationship be-
> tween signs and symbols and whatever it is
> they stand for.

- BT **Semantics**
- NT **Visual literacy**
- RT **Signs and symbols**

Semitic peoples (May subdiv. geog.)
  305.892
- BT **Ethnology**

Senate (U.S.)
- USE **United States. Congress. Senate**

Senescence
- USE **Aging**

Senile dementia 616.8
- BT **Nervous system—Diseases**

Senior centers (May subdiv. geog.)
  362.6
- UF Centers for older people
  Centers for the elderly
  Elderly centers
- BT **Community centers**

Senior citizens
- USE **Elderly**

Sense of direction
- USE **Direction sense**

Senses and sensation 152.1; 612.8
- BT **Intellect**
  Physiology
  Psychology
  Psychophysiology
  Theory of knowledge
- NT **Color sense**
  Gestalt psychology
  Hearing
  Pain
  Perception
  Pleasure
  **Senses and sensation in ani-
  mals**
  Smell

Taste
Touch
Vision

Senses and sensation in animals 573.8
- UF Animal senses
  Animals—Senses and sensation
- SA particular senses in animals, e.g.
  Hearing in animals [to be
  added as needed]
- BT **Senses and sensation**
- NT **Hearing in animals**
  Vision in animals

Sensing, Remote
- USE **Remote sensing**

Sensitivity training
- USE **Group relations training**

Separate development (Race relations)
- USE **Apartheid**

Separation anxiety in children 155.4
- BT **Anxiety**
  Child psychology

Separation (Law) (May subdiv. geog.)
  306.89
- UF Marital separation
- BT **Divorce**
  Marriage

Separation of church and state
- USE **Church and state**

Separation of powers (May subdiv. geog.)
  320.4; 342
- UF Division of powers
  Powers, Separation of
- BT **Constitutional law**
  Executive power
  Political science

**Separation of powers—United States
  320.473**
- UF United States—Separation of
  powers

Separatism, Black
- USE **Black nationalism**

Separatist movement in Québec (Province)
- USE **Québec (Province)—History—
  Autonomy and independence
  movements**

Separatist movements (May subdiv.
  geog.) **320.54**
- UF Secessionist movements
- SA names of regions, countries, etc.
  with the subdivision *Autonomy and independence move-*

Separatist movements—*Continued*

        ments [to be added as needed]

  BT **Social movements**

  NT **Québec (Province)—History—Autonomy and independence movements**

  RT **Secession**

September 11 terrorist attacks, 2001   **973.931**

  UF Pentagon (Va.) terrorist attack, 2001

        Terrorist attacks, September 11, 2001

        World Trade Center (New York, N.Y.) terrorist attack, 2001

  BT **Terrorism—United States**

Sepulchers

  USE **Tombs**

Sepulchral brasses

  USE **Brasses**

Sequences (Mathematics)   **510**

  UF Mathematical sequences

        Numerical sequences

  BT **Algebra**

        Mathematics

Serial killers (May subdiv. geog.)   **364.15**

  UF Serial murderers

  BT **Criminals**

        Homicide

  NT **Jack the Ripper murders, London, England, 1888**

Serial murderers

  USE **Serial killers**

Serial publications (May subdiv. geog.)   **050**

  Use for general materials on publications in any medium issued in successive parts bearing numerical or chronological designations and intended to be continued indefinitely.

  BT **Bibliography**

        Publishers and publishing

  NT **Almanacs**

        Newspapers

        Periodicals

        School yearbooks

        Yearbooks

  RT **International Standard Serial Numbers**

Serigraphy

  USE **Silk screen printing**

Sermon on the mount   **226.9**

Sermons (May subdiv. geog.)   **204; 252**

  Use for collections of sermons of several religions and for collections of Christian sermons not limited to a single topic, occasion, or Christian denomination. Materials on the art of writing and delivering sermons are entered under **Preaching**.

  SA sermons of particular countries, languages, or religions, e.g. **English sermons; Islamic sermons**; etc.; sermons preached at particular times of year or on particular occasions, e.g. **Lenten sermons**; and topics and Christian denominations with the subdivision *Sermons*, e.g. **Christian life—Sermons; Presbyterian Church—Sermons**; etc. [to be added as needed]

  BT **Christian literature**

  NT **American sermons**

        Christian life—Sermons

        English sermons

        Islamic sermons

        Lenten sermons

        Presbyterian Church—Sermons

  RT **Preaching**

Serpents

  USE **Snakes**

Servants

  USE **Household employees**

Service books (Liturgy)

  USE **Liturgies**

Service, Customer

  USE **Customer services**

Service dogs (May subdiv. geog.)   **636.73**

  BT **Working dogs**

Service (in industry)

  USE **Customer services**

Service industries (May subdiv. geog.)   **338.4**

  SA types of service industries [to be added as needed]

  BT **Industries**

  NT **Food service**

        Hospitality industry

        Hotels and motels

        Lease and rental services

        Undertakers and undertaking

Service stations (May subdiv. geog.)   **629.28**

Service stations—*Continued*
    UF   Filling stations
          Gas stations
    BT   **Automobile industry**
          Petroleum industry
Servicemen
    USE   **Military personnel**
Services, Customer
    USE   **Customer services**
Services for
    USE   classes of persons, ethnic
          groups, animals, and types of
          schools with the subdivision
          Services for, e.g. **Handi-**
          capped—Services for [to be
          added as needed]
Services for the handicapped
    USE   **Handicapped—Services for**
Services of worship
    USE   **Worship programs**
Servicewomen
    USE   **Military personnel**
Servitude
    USE   **Peonage**
          Slavery
Servomechanisms   **629.8**
    UF   Automatic control
    BT   **Automation**
          Feedback control systems
Set theory   **511.3**
    UF   Aggregates
          Classes (Mathematics)
          Ensembles (Mathematics)
          Mathematical sets
          Sets (Mathematics)
    BT   **Mathematics**
    NT   **Arithmetic**
          Boolean algebra
          Fractals
          Functions
          Number theory
          Topology
    RT   **Symbolic logic**
Sets, Fractal
    USE   **Fractals**
Sets (Mathematics)
    USE   **Set theory**
Sets of fractional dimension
    USE   **Fractals**
Settlement of land
    USE   **Land settlement**

Settlements, Social
    USE   **Social settlements**
Seven Wonders of the World   **930**
    BT   **Ancient architecture**
          Ancient art
Seven Years' War, 1756-1763   **940.2**
    BT   **Europe—History—1492-1789**
    NT   **United States—History—1755-**
          1763, French and Indian
          War
Seventeenth century
    USE   **World history—17th century**
Seville (Spain). World's Fair, 1992
    USE   **Expo 92 (Seville, Spain)**
Sewage disposal (May subdiv. geog.)
          628.3
    BT   **Public health**
          Refuse and refuse disposal
    RT   **Water pollution**
Sewerage (May subdiv. geog.)   **628**
    UF   Sewers
    BT   **House drainage**
          Municipal engineering
          Plumbing
          Sanitary engineering
    RT   **Drainage**
Sewers
    USE   **Sewerage**
Sewing   **646.2**
    BT   **Home economics**
    NT   **Embroidery**
          Quilting
          Soft toy making
    RT   **Dressmaking**
          Needlework
          Sewing machines
Sewing machines   **646.2044**
    RT   **Sewing**
Sex   **306.7**
    Use for materials on the social and behavioral aspects of sexuality. Materials on the physiological traits that distinguish the male and female of a species and on the physiological aspects of sexuality are entered under Sex/Physiological aspects. Materials on the psychology of sexuality are entered under Sex/Psychological aspects.
    UF   Human beings—Sexual behavior
          Human sexuality
          Sexual behavior
          Sexual practices
          Sexuality

Sex—*Continued*

    SA   social groups and classes of persons with the subdivision *Sexual behavior*, e.g. **College students—Sexual behavior** [to be added as needed]

    BT   **Human behavior**

    NT   **Bisexuality**

           College students—Sexual behavior

           Computer sex

           Homosexuality

           Sex crimes

           Sex in the workplace

           Sex role

           Sexual abstinence

           Sexual deviation

           Sexual harassment

    RT   **Sexual disorders**

           Sexual ethics

Sex bias

    USE   **Sexism**

Sex (Biology)

    USE   **Sex—Physiological aspects**

Sex change

    USE   **Transsexualism**

Sex crimes (May subdiv. geog.)   **364.15**

    UF   Sexual abuse

           Sexual crimes

           Sexual offenses

    SA   types of sex crimes [to be added as needed]

    BT   **Crime**

           Sex

    NT   **Child sexual abuse**

           Incest

           Rape

Sex differences (Psychology)   **155.3**

    BT   **Sex—Psychological aspects**

    NT   **Androgyny**

           Sex role

Sex discrimination (May subdiv. geog.) **305.3**

Use for materials on the restriction or denial of rights, privileges, or choice because of one's sex. Materials on prejudicial attitudes toward people because of their sex are entered under **Sexism**.

    BT   **Discrimination**

           Sexism

    NT   **Equal rights amendments**

           Women's rights

Sex disorders

    USE   **Sexual disorders**

Sex education (May subdiv. geog.)   **372.37; 613.9071; 649**

    UF   Sex instruction

    BT   **Family life education**

    RT   **Sexual hygiene**

Sex in art

    USE   **Erotic art**

Sex in mass media (May subdiv. geog.)   **302.23**

    BT   **Mass media**

Sex in popular culture (May subdiv. geog.)   **306.7**

    BT   **Popular culture**

Sex in the office

    USE   **Sex in the workplace**

Sex in the workplace (May subdiv. geog.)   **306.7; 658**

    UF   Office romance

           Sex in the office

    BT   **Sex**

    RT   **Sexual harassment**

Sex instruction

    USE   **Sex education**

Sex organs

    USE   **Reproductive system**

Sex—Physiological aspects   **571.8; 612.6**

Use for materials on the physical traits that distinguish the male and female of a species and on the physiological aspects of sexuality. Materials on the social and behavioral aspects of sexuality are entered under Sex. Materials on the psychology of sexuality are entered under Sex/Psychological aspects.

    UF   Sex (Biology) [*Former heading*]

           Sexuality

    BT   **Biology**

    NT   **Puberty**

           Reproductive system

           Sexual behavior in animals

           Sexual disorders

    RT   **Reproduction**

Sex predetermination

    USE   **Sex preselection**

Sex preselection   **612.6**

    UF   Choice of sex of offspring

           Preselection of sex

           Sex predetermination

           Sex selection

    BT   **Reproduction**

Sex—Psychological aspects 155.3

Use for materials on the psychology of sexuality. Materials on the social and behavioral aspects of sexuality are entered under Sex. Materials on the physiological traits that distinguish the male and female of a species and on the physiological aspects of sexuality are entered under Sex/Physiological aspects.

UF   Sex (Psychology) [*Former heading*]

Sexual behavior, Psychology of

Sexual psychology

Sexuality

BT   **Psychology**

NT   **Femininity**

Masculinity

Sex differences (Psychology)

Sex (Psychology)

USE   **Sex—Psychological aspects**

Sex role 305.3

Use for materials on the patterns of attitudes and behavior that are regarded as appropriate to one sex rather than the other.

UF   Female role

Gender identity

Male role

Sexual identity

BT   **Sex**

Sex differences (Psychology)

Social role

NT   **Androgyny**

Transsexualism

RT   **Sexism**

Sex selection

USE   **Sex preselection**

Sex therapy 616.6; 616.85

BT   **Psychotherapy**

RT   **Sexual disorders**

Sexism (May subdiv. geog.) **305.3**

Use for materials on prejudicial attitudes toward people because of their sex. Materials on the restriction or denial of rights, privileges, or choice because of one's sex are entered under **Sex discrimination**.

UF   Sex bias

BT   **Attitude (Psychology)**

Prejudices

NT   **Sex discrimination**

RT   **Sex role**

Sexual abstinence 176; 306.73

Use for materials on abstinence from sexual activity. Materials on the virtue that moderates and regulates the sexual appetite in human beings are entered under **Chastity**. Materials on the renunciation of marriage for religious reasons are entered under **Celibacy**.

UF   Abstinence, Sexual

BT   **Asceticism**

Sex

RT   **Birth control**

Celibacy

Chastity

Sexual abuse

USE   **Child sexual abuse**

Sex crimes

Sexual harassment

Sexual assault

USE   **Rape**

Sexual behavior

USE   **Sex**

Sexual behavior in animals 591.56

UF   Animal sexual behavior

Animals—Sexual behavior

Breeding behavior

Mating behavior

Reproductive behavior

BT   **Animal behavior**

Sex—Physiological aspects

NT   **Animal courtship**

Sexual behavior, Psychology of

USE   **Sex—Psychological aspects**

Sexual crimes

USE   **Sex crimes**

Sexual deviation (May subdiv. geog.) **306.7; 616.85**

UF   Deviation, Sexual

Perversion, Sexual

Sexual perversion

BT   **Sex**

Sexual disorders

Sexual disorders 616.6; 616.85

UF   Sex disorders

BT   **Sex—Physiological aspects**

NT   **Sexual deviation**

RT   **Sex**

Sex therapy

Sexual ethics (May subdiv. geog.) **176**

BT   **Ethics**

NT   **Adultery**

Chastity

Free love

Prostitution

Sexual harassment

RT   **Sex**

Sexual harassment (May subdiv. geog.) **331.13; 344**

Sexual harassment—*Continued*
    UF   Harassment, Sexual
           Sexual abuse
    BT   **Sex**
           Sexual ethics
    RT   **Sex in the workplace**
Sexual hygiene   613.9
    UF   Hygiene, Sexual
           Social hygiene
    BT   **Hygiene**
    NT   **Birth control**
           Safe sex in AIDS prevention
           Sexually transmitted diseases—Prevention
    RT   **Sex education**
           Sexually transmitted diseases
Sexual identity
    USE **Sex role**
Sexual offenses
    USE **Sex crimes**
Sexual perversion
    USE **Sexual deviation**
Sexual practices
    USE **Sex**
Sexual psychology
    USE **Sex—Psychological aspects**
Sexuality
    USE **Sex**
          Sex—Physiological aspects
          Sex—Psychological aspects
Sexually abused children
    USE **Child sexual abuse**
Sexually transmitted diseases (May subdiv. geog.)   **616.95**
    UF   VD
           Venereal diseases
    SA   types of sexually transmitted diseases [to be added as needed]
    BT   **Communicable diseases**
    NT   **Syphilis**
    RT   **Sexual hygiene**
Sexually transmitted diseases—Prevention   **616.95**
    UF   Safe sex
    BT   **Sexual hygiene**
Shade gardens
    USE **Gardening in the shade**
Shades and shadows   741.2
    UF   Light and shade
           Shadows
    BT   **Drawing**

Shadow economy
    USE **Underground economy**
Shadow pantomimes and plays (May subdiv. geog.)   **791.5**
    BT   **Amateur theater**
           Pantomimes
           Puppets and puppet plays
           Shadow pictures
           Theater
Shadow pictures   793
    UF   Hand shadows
           Shadowplay
    BT   **Amusements**
    NT   **Shadow pantomimes and plays**
Shadowpact (Fictional characters)   **741.5**
    BT   **Fictional characters**
           Superheroes
Shadowplay
    USE **Shadow pictures**
Shadows
    USE **Shades and shadows**
Shady gardens
    USE **Gardening in the shade**
Shaft sinking
    USE **Drilling and boring (Earth and rocks)**
Shakers (May subdiv. geog.)   **289**
    BT   **Christian sects**
Shakespeare, William, 1564-1616   **822.3**
    When applicable, the subdivisions provided with this heading may be used for other voluminous authors, e.g. Dante; Goethe; etc. These headings are to be used for materials about Shakespeare and about his writings. The texts of his plays, etc., are not given subject headings.
Shakespeare, William, 1564-1616—Adaptations   **822.3**
    May be used for individual works, collections, or materials about literary, cinematic, video, or television adaptations of Shakespeare's works.
    UF   Shakespeare, William, 1564-1616—Paraphrases
Shakespeare, William, 1564-1616—Allusions   **822.3**
Shakespeare, William, 1564-1616—Anniversaries   **822.3**
Shakespeare, William, 1564-1616—Authorship   **822.3**
    UF   Bacon-Shakespeare controversy
Shakespeare, William, 1564-1616—Bibliography   **016.8223**

Shakespeare, William, 1564-1616—Biography—Psychology

USE **Shakespeare, William, 1564-1616—Psychology**

Shakespeare, William, 1564-1616—Characters   822.3

Shakespeare, William, 1564-1616—Comedies   822.3

Use for materials about the comedies, not for the texts of the plays.

Shakespeare, William, 1564-1616—Concordances   822.303

UF   Shakespeare, William, 1564-1616—Indexes

Shakespeare, William, 1564-1616—Criticism   822.3

Use for materials discussing the criticism of Shakespeare's works, including historical materials. Criticism of Shakespeare's works in general is entered under **Shakespeare, William, 1564-1616**. Criticism of the comedies is entered under **Shakespeare, William, 1564-1616—Comedies**; criticism of the sonnets under **Shakespeare, William, 1564-1616—Sonnets**; etc. Criticism of an individual play is entered under **Shakespeare, William, 1564-1616**, followed by the title of the play.

UF   Shakespeare, William, 1564-1616—Criticism, interpretation, etc.

Shakespeare, William, 1564-1616—Psychological studies

Shakespeare, William, 1564-1616—Criticism, interpretation, etc.

USE   **Shakespeare, William, 1564-1616—Criticism**

Shakespeare, William, 1564-1616—Dictionaries   822.303

BT   **Encyclopedias and dictionaries**

Shakespeare, William, 1564-1616—Discography   016.8223

Shakespeare, William, 1564-1616—Dramatic production   822.3

UF   Shakespeare, William, 1564-1616—Stage setting and scenery

Shakespeare, William, 1564-1616—Ethics   822.3

UF   Shakespeare, William, 1564-1616—Moral ideas

Shakespeare, William, 1564-1616—Religion and ethics

Shakespeare, William, 1564-1616—Filmography   016.8223

Shakespeare, William, 1564-1616—Histories   822.3

Use for materials about the histories, not for the texts of the plays.

Shakespeare, William, 1564-1616—Indexes

USE   **Shakespeare, William, 1564-1616—Concordances**

Shakespeare, William, 1564-1616—Influence   822.3

Use for materials on Shakespeare's influence on national literatures, literary movements, or specific persons.

Shakespeare, William, 1564-1616—Knowledge   822.3

Use for materials on Shakespeare's knowledge or treatment of specific subjects. May be subdivided by subject, e.g. **Shakespeare, William, 1564-1616—Knowledge—Animals**; etc.

Shakespeare, William, 1564-1616—Moral ideas

USE   **Shakespeare, William, 1564-1616—Ethics**

Shakespeare, William, 1564-1616—Paraphrases

USE   **Shakespeare, William, 1564-1616—Adaptations**

Shakespeare, William, 1564-1616—Parodies, imitations, etc.   822.3

UF   Shakespeare, William, 1564-1616—Parodies, travesties, etc.

Shakespeare, William, 1564-1616—Parodies, travesties, etc.

USE   **Shakespeare, William, 1564-1616—Parodies, imitations, etc.**

Shakespeare, William, 1564-1616—Poetic works   822.3

Use for materials about the poetic works, not for the poetic texts themselves.

Shakespeare, William, 1564-1616—Portraits   822.3022

Shakespeare, William, 1564-1616—Psychological studies

USE   **Shakespeare, William, 1564-1616—Criticism**

Shakespeare, William, 1564-1616—Psychology

Shakespeare, William, 1564-1616—Psychology   822.3

UF   Shakespeare, William, 1564-1616—Biography—Psychology

Shakespeare, William, 1564-1616—Psychological studies

Shakespeare, William, 1564-1616—Quotations 822.3

Shakespeare, William, 1564-1616—Religion 822.3

UF   Shakespeare, William, 1564-1616—Religion and ethics

Shakespeare, William, 1564-1616—Religion and ethics

USE   **Shakespeare, William, 1564-1616—Ethics**

       Shakespeare, William, 1564-1616—Religion

Shakespeare, William, 1564-1616—Sonnets 822.3

Use for materials about the sonnets, not for the texts of the sonnets.

Shakespeare, William, 1564-1616—Stage history 792; 822.3

BT   **Theater**

Shakespeare, William, 1564-1616—Stage setting and scenery

USE   **Shakespeare, William, 1564-1616—Dramatic production**

Shakespeare, William, 1564-1616—Style

USE   **Shakespeare, William, 1564-1616—Technique**

Shakespeare, William, 1564-1616—Technique 822.3

UF   Shakespeare, William, 1564-1616—Style

Shakespeare, William, 1564-1616—Tragedies 822.3

Use for materials about the tragedies, not for the texts of the plays.

Shamanism (May subdiv. geog.) 291.144; 291.66

BT   **Religions**

RT   **Shamans**

Shamans (May subdiv. geog.) 200.92

UF   Medicine men

RT   **Shamanism**

Shame 152.4

BT   **Emotions**

RT   **Guilt**

Shape 516

UF   Shapes

       Size and shape

SA   types of geometric shapes, e.g. **Square** [to be added as needed]

BT   **Concepts**

       Geometry

       Perception

NT   **Circle**

       Square

       Triangle

Shapes

USE   **Shape**

Sharecropping (May subdiv. geog.) 333.33

BT   **Farm tenancy**

Shared custody

USE   **Child custody**

Shared housing (May subdiv. geog.) 363.5; 643

Use for materials on two or more single, unrelated adults who live together.

UF   Home sharing

       House sharing

BT   **Housing**

NT   **Unmarried couples**

RT   **Roommates**

Shared parenting

USE   **Part-time parenting**

Shared reading books

USE   **Big books**

Shares of stock

USE   **Stocks**

Shareware (Computer software) 005.3

Use for materials on computer software offered to consumers on a trial basis with the provision that they pay a voluntary fee if they want to use it.

UF   Software for sharing

BT   **Computer software**

Sharing of jobs

USE   **Job sharing**

Sheep (May subdiv. geog.) 599.649; 636.3

UF   Lambs

BT   **Domestic animals**

       Mammals

Sheet metalwork 671.8

UF   Press working of metal

BT   **Metalwork**

NT   **Plate metalwork**

Sheffield plate 739.2

BT   **Plate**

Shellfish (May subdiv. geog.) 594; 641.3

BT   **Aquatic animals**

NT   **Crabs**

       Crustacea

       Lobsters

       Mollusks

Shells (May subdiv. geog.) **591.47; 594.147**

Use for popular materials on seashells and shell collecting. Systematic and comprehensive materials on shells are entered under **Mollusks**.

UF   Sea shells
RT   **Mollusks**

Shells (Projectiles)
USE   **Projectiles**

Shelterbelts
USE   **Windbreaks**

Shelters, Air raid
USE   **Air raid shelters**

Sherlock Holmes (Fictitious character)
USE   **Holmes, Sherlock (Fictional character)**

Sherlock Holmes films   **791.43**

Use for individual works, collections, or materials about Sherlock Holmes films.

BT   **Motion pictures**
    Mystery films

Shia
USE   **Shiites**

Shiism
USE   **Shiites**

Shiites (May subdiv. geog.)   **297.82**

UF   Shia
    Shiism
BT   **Islamic sects**

Shinto (May subdiv. geog.)   **299.5**

BT   **Religions**

Ship building
USE   **Shipbuilding**

Ship models
USE   **Ships—Models**

Ship pilots (May subdiv. geog.)   **623.89**

UF   Pilots
    Pilots and pilotage
BT   **Sailors**
RT   **Navigation**

Ship safety
USE   **Ships—Safety regulations**

Ship salvage
USE   **Marine salvage**

Shipbuilding (May subdiv. geog.)   **623.8**

UF   Ship building
    Ships—Construction
BT   **Naval architecture**
NT   **Marine engines**
    Steamboats
RT   **Boatbuilding**
    Ships

Shipping (May subdiv. geog.)   **387.5**

UF   Marine transportation
    Ocean—Economic aspects
    Ocean transportation
    Sea transportation
    Water transportation
BT   **Transportation**
NT   **Harbors**
    Inland navigation
    Marine insurance
    Maritime law
    Territorial waters
RT   **Merchant marine**

Shipping—United States   **387.00973**

Ships (May subdiv. geog.)   **387.2; 623.82**

UF   Vessels (Ships)
SA   types of ships and vessels and names of individual ships [to be added as needed]
NT   **Clipper ships**
    Hospital ships
    Lightships
    Merchant marine
    Ocean liners
    Sailing
    Steamboats
    Submarines
    Warships
    Yachts and yachting
RT   **Boats and boating**
    Shipbuilding

Ships—Construction
USE   **Shipbuilding**

Ships in art
USE   **Marine painting**

Ships—Models   **623.82**

UF   Model ships
    Ship models
BT   **Models and modelmaking**

Ships—Safety regulations (May subdiv. geog.)   **341.7; 343**

UF   Merchant marine—Safety regulations
    Ship safety
BT   **Maritime law**
    Safety regulations

Shipwrecks   **363.12; 910.4**

UF   Marine disasters
SA   names of wrecked ships [to be added as needed]

Shipwrecks—*Continued*
  BT **Accidents**
      Adventure and adventurers
      Disasters
      Navigation
      Voyages and travels
  RT **Marine salvage**
      **Survival after airplane acci-
        dents, shipwrecks, etc.**
Shoe industry (May subdiv. geog.)
      338.4; 685
  BT **Clothing industry**
      Leather industry
  RT **Shoes**
Shoes (May subdiv. geog.) 391.4; 646;
      685
  UF Boots
      Footwear
  BT **Clothing and dress**
  RT **Shoe industry**
Shojo-ai 741.5
    Use for individual works, collections, or
    materials about shojo-ai.
  UF Girl-love manga
      Yuri
  BT **Manga**
Shojo manga 741.5
    Use for individual works, collections, or
    materials about manga for girls ages 12-18.
  BT **Manga**
Shonen-ai 741.5
    Use for individual works, collections, or
    materials about shonen-ai.
  UF Boy-love manga
      Yaoi
  BT **Manga**
Shonen manga 741.5
    Use for individual works, collections, or
    materials about manga for boys ages 12-18.
  BT **Manga**
Shooting (May subdiv. geog.) 799.3
    Use for materials on the use of firearms.
    Materials on shooting game are entered under
    Hunting.
  NT **Archery**
      Decoys (Hunting)
  RT **Firearms**
      Hunting
Shooting stars
  USE **Meteors**
Shootings in schools
  USE **School shootings**

Shop management
  USE **Factory management**
Shop practice
  USE **Machine shop practice**
Shop windows
  USE **Show windows**
Shoplifting (May subdiv. geog.) 364.16
  BT **Theft**
Shoppers' guides
  USE **Consumer education**
      Shopping
Shopping (May subdiv. geog.) 381; 640
    Use for materials on consumer buying.
    General materials on buying and materials on
    buying by commercial enterprises are entered
    under **Purchasing**.
  UF Buyers' guides
      Marketing (Home economics)
      Shoppers' guides
  SA types of products and services
        with the subdivision *Purchas-
        ing*, e.g. **Automobiles—Pur-
        chasing** [to be added as need-
        ed]
  BT **Home economics**
      Purchasing
  NT **Grocery shopping**
      Internet shopping
  RT **Consumer education**
Shopping centers and malls (May subdiv.
      geog.) 381; 658.8
  UF Malls, Shopping
      Shopping malls
  BT **Commercial buildings**
      Retail trade
  RT **Stores**
Shopping—Computer network resources
  USE **Internet shopping**
Shopping—Internet resources
  USE **Internet shopping**
Shopping malls
  USE **Shopping centers and malls**
Shops
  USE **Stores**
Short films 791.43
    Use for individual works, collections, or
    materials about short films.
  BT **Motion pictures**
Short plays
  USE **One act plays**
Short stories 808.83
    Use for collections of short stories by one
    author or by several authors. Materials on the

Short stories—*Continued*
short story as a literary form and on the technique of writing short stories are entered under **Short story**.
- UF Stories
- BT **Fiction**

Short stories—Indexes   016.80883

Short story   808.3
Use for materials on the short story as a literary form and on the technique of writing short stories. Collections of stories are entered under **Short stories**.
- BT **Authorship**
  Fiction
  Literature
- RT **Storytelling**

Shorthand   653
- UF Stenography
- BT **Business education**
  Office practice
  Writing
- RT **Abbreviations**

Shortwave radio (May subdiv. geog.)   621.3841
- UF High-frequency radio
  UHF radio
  Ultrahigh frequency radio
  Very high frequency radio
  VHF radio
- BT **Radio**
  Radio frequency modulation
- NT **Amateur radio stations**
  Citizens band radio
  Microwave communication systems
  Microwaves

Shotguns   683.4
- UF Guns
- BT **Firearms**

Show business
- USE **Performing arts**

Show windows (May subdiv. geog.)   659.1
- UF Shop windows
  Window dressing
- BT **Advertising**
  Decoration and ornament
  Windows

Showers (Parties)   793.2
- UF Baby showers
  Bridal showers
  Wedding showers
- BT **Parties**

Showing off   302.5
- UF Attention-seeking
  Seeking attention
- BT **Human behavior**

Shrines (May subdiv. geog.)   203; 263; 726
- BT **Sacred sites**
- NT **Tombs**
- RT **Pilgrims and pilgrimages**

Shroud, Holy
- USE **Holy Shroud**

Shroud of Turin
- USE **Holy Shroud**

Shrubs (May subdiv. geog.)   582.1; 635.9
- BT **Plants**
  Trees
- NT **Evergreens**
- RT **Landscape gardening**
  Ornamental plants

Shyness   155.2
- UF Bashfulness
- BT **Emotions**

Sibling rivalry   306.875
- BT **Child psychology**
  Siblings

Sibling sequence
- USE **Birth order**

Siblings   155.44; 306.875
- UF Brothers and sisters
  Sisters and brothers
- BT **Family**
- NT **Brothers**
  Sibling rivalry
  Sisters
  Triplets
  Twins

Sick (May subdiv. geog.)   305.9; 362.1
- BT **Handicapped**
- NT **Church work with the sick**
  Cooking for the sick
  First aid
  Invalids
  Mentally ill
  Terminally ill
- RT **Diseases**
  Home nursing
  Nursing
  Patients

Sick—Prayers   204; 242
- BT **Prayers**

Sickness
    USE   **Diseases**
SIDS (Disease)
    USE   **Sudden infant death syndrome**
Sieges
    USE   **Battles**
Sight
    USE   **Vision**
Sight saving books
    USE   **Large print books**
Sign language   419
    UF   Deaf—Sign language
    BT   **Language and languages**
    NT   **Native American sign language**
    RT   **Deaf—Means of communication**
           Signs and symbols
Sign painting   667
    BT   **Advertising**
           Industrial painting
    NT   **Alphabets**
    RT   **Lettering**
           Signs and signboards
Signaling
    USE   types of transportation and communication with the subdivision *Signaling*, e.g. **Railroads—Signaling** [to be added as needed]
Signals and signaling (May subdiv. geog.)
           388; 621.382
    UF   Coastal signals
           Fog signals
           Military signaling
           Naval signaling
    SA   types of transportation and communication with the subdivision *Signaling*, e.g. **Railroads—Signaling** [to be added as needed]
    BT   **Communication**
           Military art and science
           Naval art and science
           Navigation
           Signs and symbols
    NT   **Railroads—Signaling**
           Sonar
    RT   **Flags**
Signboards
    USE   **Signs and signboards**

Signed editions
    USE   **Autographed editions**
Signets
    USE   **Seals (Numismatics)**
Signs (Advertising)
    USE   **Signs and signboards**
Signs and signboards (May subdiv. geog.)
           659.13
    UF   Billboards
           Road signs
           Signboards
           Signs (Advertising)
    BT   **Advertising**
    NT   **Electric signs**
    RT   **Posters**
           Sign painting
Signs and symbols (May subdiv. geog.)
           302.2; 419
    UF   Emblems
           Symbols
    BT   **Communication**
    NT   **Ciphers**
           Cryptography
           Heraldry
           National emblems
           Signals and signaling
           State emblems
    RT   **Abbreviations**
           Semiotics
           Sign language
           Symbolism
Signs and symbols in literature
    USE   **Symbolism in literature**
Sikhism (May subdiv. geog.)   **294.6**
    BT   **Religions**
Silage and silos   633.2
    UF   Silos
    BT   **Feeds**
           Forage plants
Silence   534
    BT   **Sound**
Silent films (May subdiv. geog.)   **791.43**
       Use for individual works, collections, or materials about films made before the development of films with sound.
    UF   Silent motion pictures
    BT   **Motion pictures**
Silent motion pictures
    USE   **Silent films**
Silk (May subdiv. geog.)   **677**
    BT   **Fabrics**
           Fibers

Silk—*Continued*
    RT   **Silkworms**
Silk screen printing (May subdiv. geog.)
      764
    UF   Screen printing
          Serigraphy
    BT   **Color printing**
          Stencil work
    RT   **Textile printing**
Silkworms (May subdiv. geog.)   **595.78;**
      638
    UF   Cocoons
    BT   **Beneficial insects**
          Insects
          Moths
    RT   **Silk**
Silos
    USE **Silage and silos**
Silver (May subdiv. geog.)   **332.4; 669**
    BT   **Chemical elements**
          Precious metals
    NT   **Silverwork**
    RT   **Coinage**
          Money
Silver articles
    USE **Silverwork**
Silver mines and mining (May subdiv.
      geog.) **622**
    BT   **Mines and mineral resources**
    NT   **Prospecting**
Silver plate
    USE **Plate**
          Silverware
Silver work
    USE **Silverwork**
Silversmithing
    USE **Silverwork**
Silverware (May subdiv. geog.)   **642;**
      739.2
    UF   Flatware, Silver
          Silver plate
    BT   **Decorative arts**
          Silverwork
          Tableware
Silverwork (May subdiv. geog.)   **739.2**
    UF   Silver articles
          Silver work
          Silversmithing
    BT   **Art metalwork**
          Metalwork
          Silver

    NT   **Native American silverwork**
          Plate
          Silverware
Simple machines   **621.8**
    UF   Machines, Simple
    SA   types of simple machines, e.g.
          Wheels [to be added as need-
          ed]
    BT   **Machinery**
          Mechanical movements
          Mechanics
    NT   **Inclined planes**
          Levers
          Pulleys
          Screws
          Wedges
          Wheels
Simplicity   **179; 646.7**
    BT   **Conduct of life**
Simulation, Computer
    USE **Computer simulation**
Simulation games   **003**
    UF   Gaming simulations
    BT   **Game theory**
    NT   **War games**
Simulation games in education   **371.39**
    UF   Educational gaming
          Educational simulation games
          Gaming, Educational
    BT   **Education**
          Educational games
          Game theory
Sin   **205; 241**
    BT   **Ethics**
          Good and evil
          Theology
    NT   **Avarice**
          Guilt
          Pride and vanity
    RT   **Forgiveness of sin**
Sin, Forgiveness of
    USE **Forgiveness of sin**
Sinai Campaign, 1956   **956.04**
    UF   Anglo-French intervention in
          Egypt, 1956
          Arab-Israel War, 1956
          Israel-Arab War, 1956
    BT   **Egypt—History**
          Israel-Arab conflicts
Singers (May subdiv. geog.)   **782.0092;**
      920

Singers—*Continued*
    BT **Musicians**
    NT **African American singers**
Singing (May subdiv. geog.)   **782; 783**
    UF School music
    BT **Music**
    NT **Songbooks**
        Voice culture
    RT **Choirs (Music)**
        Vocal music
        Voice
Singing games (May subdiv. geog.)
        796.1
    BT **Games**
Singing societies
    USE **Choral societies**
Single child
    USE **Only child**
Single men (May subdiv. geog.)   **155.6;**
        306.81
    UF Bachelors
        Unmarried men
    BT **Men**
        Single people
    NT **Divorced men**
Single-parent families (May subdiv. geog.)
        306.85
    Use for materials on households in which a
    parent living without a partner is rearing chil-
    dren. Materials on parents who were not mar-
    ried at the time of the birth of their children
    are entered under **Unmarried fathers** or **Un-
    married mothers.**
    UF One parent family
        Single parent family
    BT **Family**
    RT **Single parents**
Single parent family
    USE **Single-parent families**
Single parents (May subdiv. geog.)
        306.85
    BT **Parents**
        Unmarried couples
    NT **Children of single parents**
        Unmarried fathers
        Unmarried mothers
    RT **Single-parent families**
Single parents' children
    USE **Children of single parents**
Single people (May subdiv. geog.)
        155.6; 306.81
    UF Unmarried people

    NT **Divorced people**
        Single men
        Single women
Single rail railroads
    USE **Monorail railroads**
Single-sex education
    USE **Single-sex schools**
Single-sex schools (May subdiv. geog.)
        370
    UF Single-sex education
    BT **Schools**
Single women (May subdiv. geog.)
        155.6; 306.81
    UF Unmarried women
    BT **Single people**
        Women
    NT **Divorced women**
Sirius   **523.8**
    BT **Stars**
Sisterhoods
    USE **Monasticism and religious or-
         ders for women**
Sisters   **306.875**
    BT **Siblings**
        Women
Sisters and brothers
    USE **Siblings**
Sisters (Religious)
    USE **Nuns**
Sit-down strikes
    USE **Strikes**
Sit-ins for civil rights
    USE **Civil rights demonstrations**
Sitcoms
    USE **Comedy television programs**
Site oriented art
    USE **Earthworks (Art)**
Sitters (Babysitters)
    USE **Babysitters**
Situation comedies
    USE **Comedy television programs**
Six Day War, 1967
    USE **Israel-Arab War, 1967**
Sixteenth century
    USE **World history—16th century**
Size   **530.8**
    UF Large and small
        Size and shape
        Small and large
    BT **Concepts**
        Perception

Size and shape
    USE   **Shape**
           Size

Skateboarding (May subdiv. geog.)
    796.22
    BT   **Roller skating**

Skating
    USE   **Ice skating**
           Roller skating

Skeletal remains
    USE   **Anthropometry**

Skeleton   **573.7; 611**

    Use for materials limited to the morphology or mechanics of the skeleton, human or animal. Comprehensive and systematic materials on the anatomy of bones are entered under **Bones**.

    BT   **Musculoskeletal system**
    RT   **Bones**

Skepticism   **149; 186; 211**
    UF   Scepticism
           Unbelief
    BT   **Free thought**
           Philosophy
           Rationalism
    RT   **Agnosticism**
           Belief and doubt
           Truth

Sketching
    USE   **Drawing**

Ski resorts (May subdiv. geog.)   **796.93**
    BT   **Winter resorts**

Skidoos
    USE   **Snowmobiles**

Skiing (May subdiv. geog.)   **796.93**
    UF   Skis and skiing
           Snow skiing
    BT   **Winter sports**

Skill
    USE   **Ability**

Skilled labor (May subdiv. geog.)   **331.7**
    BT   **Labor**

Skills
    USE   **Ability**

Skin   **611; 612.7**
    BT   **Anatomy**
           Physiology

Skin—Care   **616.5; 646.7**
    UF   Skin care
           Skin—Care and hygiene

Skin care
    USE   **Skin—Care**

Skin—Care and hygiene
    USE   **Skin—Care**

Skin—Diseases   **616.5**
    UF   Dermatitis
    SA   types of skin diseases [to be added as needed]
    BT   **Diseases**
    NT   **Acne**

Skin diving (May subdiv. geog.)   **797.2**

    Use for materials on free diving with mask, fins, and snorkel. Materials on free diving with the aid of a self-contained underwater breathing apparatus are entered under **Scuba diving**. Materials on diving from a board or platform are entered under **Diving**. Materials on underwater diving with equipment are entered under **Deep diving**.

    UF   Free diving
           Snorkeling
           Underwater swimming
    BT   **Deep diving**
           Water sports

Skinheads
    USE   **White supremacy movements**

Skins
    USE   **Hides and skins**

Skis and skiing
    USE   **Skiing**

Skits (May subdiv. geog.)   **791**
    BT   **Amusements**
           Theater

Sky   **520; 551.5**
    BT   **Astronomy**
           Atmosphere
    NT   **Constellations**

Sky diving
    USE   **Skydiving**

Skydiving (May subdiv. geog.)   **797.5**
    UF   Sky diving
    BT   **Aeronautical sports**

Skyscrapers (May subdiv. geog.)   **690; 720**
    UF   High rise buildings
    BT   **Buildings**

Skyscrapers—Earthquake effects (May subdiv. geog.)   **690; 725**
    BT   **Buildings—Earthquake effects**
           Earthquakes

Slander (Law)
    USE   **Libel and slander**

Slang
    USE   names of languages with the
            subdivision *Slang,* e.g. **En-
            glish language—Slang** [to be
            added as needed]
Slanted journalism
    USE   **Journalism—Objectivity**
Slapstick comedies
    USE   **Comedies**
           Comedy films
           Comedy television programs
Slave insurrections
    USE   **Slave revolts**
Slave narratives   **306.3**
    BT   **Autobiography**
          Slavery
Slave revolts (May subdiv. geog.)   **326;
    909**
    UF   Slave insurrections
    BT   **Revolutions**
    RT   **Slavery**
Slave trade (May subdiv. geog.)   **306.3;
    381**
    BT   **International law**
          Slavery
Slavery (May subdiv. geog.)   **177; 306.3;
    326; 342**
    UF   Abolition of slavery
          Antislavery
          Servitude
    BT   **Crimes against humanity**
    NT   **Slave narratives**
          Slave trade
          Slaves
    RT   **Abolitionists**
          Forced labor
          Peonage
          Slave revolts
          Slaves—Emancipation
Slavery—Emancipation
    USE   **Slaves—Emancipation**
Slavery—United States   **306.3; 326.0973**
    RT   **Southern States—History**
          Underground railroad
Slavery—United States—Fiction   **808.83;
    813**
    Use for collections of stories dealing with
  slavery in the United States.
Slaves (May subdiv. geog.)   **306.3**
    BT   **Slavery**
    NT   **Fugitive slaves**

Slaves—Emancipation (May subdiv.
    geog.)   **306.3**
    UF   Abolition of slavery
          Antislavery
          Emancipation of slaves
          Slavery—Emancipation
    BT   **Freedom**
    RT   **Abolitionists**
          Slavery
Sled dog racing (May subdiv. geog.)
    798.8
    UF   Dog sled racing
    BT   **Winter sports**
Sledding (May subdiv. geog.)   **796.9**
    BT   **Winter sports**
    RT   **Sleds**
Sledges
    USE   **Sleds**
Sleds   **688.7**
    UF   Sledges
          Sleighs and sledges
    BT   **Vehicles**
    RT   **Sledding**
Sleep   **154.6; 616.8**
    BT   **Health**
          Hygiene
          Mind and body
          Psychophysiology
          Rest
          Subconsciousness
    NT   **Bedtime**
          Insomnia
          Sleep apnea
    RT   **Dreams**
Sleep apnea   **616.8**
    BT   **Sleep**
Sleeplessness
    USE   **Insomnia**
Sleighs and sledges
    USE   **Sleds**
Sleight of hand
    USE   **Juggling**
          Magic tricks
Slide projectors
    USE   **Projectors**
Slide rule   **510.28**
    BT   **Calculators**
          Logarithms
Slides (Photography)   **778.2**
    UF   Color slides
          Lantern slides

Slides (Photography)—*Continued*
    Photographic slides
  BT **Photography**
  RT **Filmstrips**
Sloppiness
  USE **Messiness**
Sloth
  USE **Laziness**
Slovakia 943.73
    May be subdivided like United States except for History.
  RT **Czechoslovakia**
Slow food movement (May subdiv. geog.)
    641.01
  BT **Gastronomy**
      Social movements
Slow learning children (May subdiv.
    geog.) **155.4; 371.92**
    Use for materials on children with less than average intelligence and slow social development who can nonetheless be educated and lead a normal life.
  BT **Exceptional children**
  NT **Learning disabilities**
  RT **Mentally handicapped children**
Slum clearance
  USE **Urban renewal**
Small and large
  USE **Size**
Small arms
  USE **Firearms**
Small business (May subdiv. geog.)
    338.6; 658.02
    Use for materials on small independent business enterprises.
  BT **Business**
  NT **Entrepreneurship**
      Home-based business
      Underground economy
Small cars
  USE **Compact cars**
Small claims courts (May subdiv. geog.)
    347
  BT **Civil procedure**
      Courts
Small loans
  USE **Personal loans**
Smell 152.1
  BT **Senses and sensation**
  RT **Nose**
Smelting (May subdiv. geog.) **669**
  BT **Furnaces**

  NT **Blast furnaces**
      Electrometallurgy
      Ore dressing
  RT **Metallurgy**
Smocking 746.44
  BT **Needlework**
Smoke-ending programs
  USE **Smoking cessation programs**
Smoke prevention (May subdiv. geog.)
    363.738; 628.5
  UF Prevention of smoke
  BT **Sanitation**
Smoke stacks
  USE **Chimneys**
Smokeless powder
  USE **Gunpowder**
Smoking (May subdiv. geog.) **178;**
    613.85
  NT **Cigarettes**
      Cigars
      Tobacco habit
      Tobacco pipes
  RT **Tobacco**
Smoking cessation programs (May
    subdiv. geog.) **613.85**
  UF How-to-stop-smoking programs
      Quit-smoking programs
      Smoke-ending programs
  BT **Tobacco habit**
Smuggling (May subdiv. geog.) **364.1**
  UF Contraband trade
  BT **Crime**
      Tariff
Smuggling of drugs
  USE **Drug traffic**
Snack foods (May subdiv. geog.) **641.5;**
    642
  UF Snacks
  BT **Food**
Snacks
  USE **Snack foods**
Snakes (May subdiv. geog.) **597.96**
  UF Serpents
      Vipers
  SA types of snakes, e.g. **Rattlesnakes** [to be added as needed]
  BT **Reptiles**
  NT **Rattlesnakes**
      Snakes as pets
Snakes as pets 636.088

Snakes as pets—*Continued*
    BT   **Pets**
          Snakes
Snapshots
    USE **Photographs**
Snobbery
    USE **Snobs and snobbishness**
Snobbishness
    USE **Snobs and snobbishness**
Snobbism
    USE **Snobs and snobbishness**
Snobs and snobbishness (May subdiv.
    geog.)   **303.3**
    UF   Snobbery
          Snobbishness
          Snobbism
    RT   **Pride and vanity**
Snorkeling
    USE **Skin diving**
Snow (May subdiv. geog.)   **551.57**
    BT   **Precipitation (Meteorology)**
    NT   **Avalanches**
    RT   **Blizzards**
          Storms
Snow boarding
    USE **Snowboarding**
Snow skiing
    USE **Skiing**
Snowboarding (May subdiv. geog.)
    796.939
    UF   Snow boarding
    BT   **Winter sports**
Snowmobiles (May subdiv. geog.)
    629.22; 796.94
    UF   Skidoos
    BT   **All terrain vehicles**
Soap (May subdiv. geog.)   **668**
    BT   **Cleaning compounds**
    RT   **Detergents**
Soap box derbies (May subdiv. geog.)
    796.6
    BT   **Racing**
Soap carving
    USE **Soap sculpture**
Soap operas (May subdiv. geog.)
    791.44; 791.45
    Use for individual works, collections, or
    materials about soap operas.
    BT   **Radio plays**
          Television plays
    RT   **Radio serials**
          Television serials

Soap sculpture   **736**
    UF   Soap carving
    BT   **Modeling**
          Sculpture
Soaring flight
    USE **Gliding and soaring**
Sobriquets
    USE **Nicknames**
Soccer (May subdiv. geog.)   **796.334**
    BT   **Ball games**
          Football
          Sports
Soccer—Training   **796.334**
    BT   **Physical education**
Social ability
    USE **Social skills**
Social action (May subdiv. geog.)   **361.2**
    UF   Social activism
    SA   subjects with the subdivision
          Citizen participation, e.g. **City
          planning—Citizen participa-
          tion** [to be added as needed]
    BT   **Social policy**
    NT   **City planning—Citizen partici-
          pation**
          Humanitarian intervention
    RT   **Political participation**
          Social problems
          Social work
Social activism
    USE **Social action**
Social adjustment   **158; 303.3**
    UF   Adjustment, Social
    BT   **Human behavior**
          Interpersonal relations
          Social psychology
    NT   **Socially handicapped**
    RT   **Deviant behavior**
Social alienation
    USE **Alienation (Social psychology)**
Social anthropology
    USE **Ethnology**
Social aspects
    USE subjects with the subdivision *So-
          cial aspects,* e.g. **Genetic en-
          gineering—Social aspects** [to
          be added as needed]
Social behavior
    USE **Human behavior**
Social case work (May subdiv. geog.)
    361.3

Social case work—*Continued*
- UF   Case work, Social
  - Family social work
- BT   **Social work**
- NT   **Parole**
  - **Probation**
- RT   **Counseling**

Social change (May subdiv. geog.)
    303.4; 909
- UF   Change, Social
  - Cultural change
  - Social evolution
- BT   **Anthropology**
  - **Social sciences**
  - **Sociology**
- NT   **Community development**
  - **Modernization (Sociology)**
  - **Urbanization**

Social classes (May subdiv. geog.)
    305.5; 323.3
- UF   Class distinction
  - Rank
  - Social distinctions
- BT   **Caste**
  - **Sociology**
- NT   **Class consciousness**
  - **Elite (Social sciences)**
  - **Intellectuals**
  - **Middle class**
  - **Rich**
  - **Upper class**
  - **Working class**

Social competence
- USE   **Social skills**

Social conditions   **306.09; 909**

Use for materials on the social aspects of several of the following topics: labor, poverty, education, health, housing, recreation, moral conditions.
- UF   Social history
- SA   racial and ethnic groups, classes of persons, and names of countries, cities, etc., with the subdivision *Social conditions* [to be added as needed]
- BT   **Sociology**
- NT   **African Americans—Social conditions**
  - **Blacks—Social conditions**
  - **Chicago (Ill.)—Social conditions**
  - **Cost and standard of living**
  - **Counter culture**
  - **Economic conditions**
  - **Jews—Social conditions**
  - **Labor**
  - **Men—Social conditions**
  - **Moral conditions**
  - **Native Americans—Social conditions**
  - **Ohio—Social conditions**
  - **Quality of life**
  - **Social movements**
  - **Social policy**
  - **Social problems**
  - **United States—Social conditions**
  - **Urbanization**
  - **Women—Social conditions**

Social conflict (May subdiv. geog.)
    303.6
- UF   Class conflict
  - Class struggle
  - Conflict, Social
- BT   **Social psychology**
  - **Sociology**
- NT   **Conflict management**
  - **Conflict of generations**
  - **Role conflict**

Social conformity
- USE   **Conformity**

Social contract   **320.01; 320.1**
- BT   **Political science**
  - **Sociology**

Social customs
- USE   **Manners and customs**

Social democracy
- USE   **Socialism**

Social deviance
- USE   **Deviant behavior**

Social distinctions
- USE   **Social classes**

Social drinking
- USE   **Drinking of alcoholic beverages**

Social ecology
- USE   **Human ecology**

Social equality
- USE   **Equality**

Social ethics (May subdiv. geog.)   **170**
- BT   **Ethics**
  - **Sociology**
- NT   **Political ethics**
- RT   **Social problems**

Social evolution
USE **Social change**
Social geography
USE **Human geography**
Social group work (May subdiv. geog.)
361.4; 362
UF Group social work
Group work, Social
Social work with groups
BT **Counseling**
Social work
Social groups (May subdiv. geog.)
302.3; 305
UF Group dynamics
Groups, Social
BT **Sociology**
NT **Elite (Social sciences)**
Leadership
Neighborhood
Social psychology
Teams in the workplace
Social history
USE **Social conditions**
Social hygiene
USE **Public health**
Sexual hygiene
Social identity
USE **Group identity**
Social insurance
USE **Social security**
Social isolation
USE **Loneliness**
Social justice (May subdiv. geog.) **303.3**
BT **Equality**
Justice
Social learning
USE **Socialization**
Social life and customs
USE **Manners and customs**
and names of ethnic groups, countries, cities, etc., with the subdivision *Social life and customs,* e.g. **Native Americans—Social life and customs; Jews—Social life and customs; United States—Social life and customs;** etc. [to be added as needed]
Social medicine (May subdiv. geog.)
306.4; 362.1
Use for materials on the study of social, genetic, and environmental influences on human

disease and disability, as well as the promotion of health measures to protect both the individual and the community.
UF Medical care—Social aspects
Medical sociology
Medicine—Social aspects
BT **Medicine**
Public health
Public welfare
Sociology
NT **Hospices**
RT **Medical ethics**
Social movements (May subdiv. geog.)
303.48
SA types of social movements, e.g. **Environmental movement** [to be added as needed]
BT **Social conditions**
Social psychology
NT **Animal rights movement**
Anti-apartheid movement
Antinuclear movement
Environmental movement
Labor movement
Militia movements
New Age movement
Peace movements
Pro-choice movement
Pro-life movement
Protest movements
Sanctuary movement
Separatist movements
Slow food movement
Survivalism
White supremacy movements
Youth movement
Social networking (May subdiv. geog.)
303.48
Use for materials on a variety of Internet applications designed to help connect friends, business associates, or other individuals with common interests.
UF Online social networking
Social networks
SA Names of social networking sites, e.g. MySpace (Web site) [to be added as needed]
BT **Communication**
NT **Facebook (Web site)**
MySpace (Web site)
Twitter (Web site)
Social networks
USE **Social networking**

Social phobia   158.2
   BT **Phobias**
Social planning
   USE **Social policy**
Social policy (May subdiv. geog.)   **361.6**
    Use for materials on the ways a society reg-
    ulates the relationships among individuals,
    groups, communities, and institutions, and on
    systematic procedures for achieving social
    goals and managing available resources to at-
    tain social change.
   UF Government policy
      National planning
      Social planning
      State planning
   SA ethnic groups, classes of per-
      sons, and topics with the sub-
      division *Government policy*,
      e.g. **Homeless persons—Gov-**
      ernment policy; and types of
      activities, facilities, industries,
      services, and undertakings
      with the subdivision *Planning*,
      e.g. **Transportation—Plan-**
      ning [to be added as needed]
   BT **Planning**
      Social conditions
   NT **Arts—Government policy**
      Education—Government policy
      Homeless persons—Govern-
      ment policy
      Land reform
      Libraries—Government policy
      Medical policy
      Multiculturalism
      Social action
      Urban policy
      Welfare state
   RT **Economic policy**
Social policy—Chicago (Ill.)   361.6;
      977.3
   UF Chicago (Ill.)—Social policy
Social policy—Ohio   361.6; 977.1
   UF Ohio—Social policy
Social policy—United States   361.6; 973
   UF United States—Social policy
Social problems (May subdiv. geog.)
      361.1
   UF Reform, Social
      Social reform
      Social welfare
   BT **Social conditions**
      Sociology

   NT **Alcoholism**
      Child labor
      Church and social problems
      Crime
      Discrimination
      Drug abuse
      Fetal alcohol syndrome
      Homelessness
      Juvenile delinquency
      Poverty
      Prison reform
      Prostitution
      Public health
      Race discrimination
      Solvent abuse
      Substance abuse
      Suicide
      Unemployment
   RT **Social action**
      Social ethics
Social problems and the church
   USE **Church and social problems**
Social problems in education
   USE **Educational sociology**
Social progress
   USE **Progress**
Social psychology (May subdiv. geog.)
      302
   UF Mass psychology
   BT **Human ecology**
      Psychology
      Social groups
      Sociology
   NT **Alienation (Social psychology)**
      Ambition
      Audiences
      Class consciousness
      Cooperativeness
      Discrimination
      Empathy
      Interpersonal relations
      Interviewing
      National characteristics
      Organizational behavior
      Political psychology
      Popularity
      Privacy
      Public opinion
      Social adjustment
      Social conflict
      Social movements

Social psychology—*Continued*
>> Social role
>> Social status
>> Stereotype (Social psychology)
>> Violence
> RT Applied psychology
>> Crowds
>> Ethnopsychology

Social reform
> USE Social problems

Social responsibility of business (May subdiv. geog.)   174; 658.4
> UF Business—Social responsibility
>> Corporate accountability
>> Corporate responsibility
>> Corporations—Social responsibility
>> Industries—Social responsibility
> BT Business
>> Business ethics

Social role   302
> UF Role, Social
> BT Social psychology
> NT Role conflict
>> Role playing
>> Sex role

Social sciences (May subdiv. geog.)   300
> Use for general and comprehensive materials on the various branches of knowledge dealing with human society, such as sociology, political science, economics, etc.
> UF Social studies
> BT Civilization
> NT Anthropology
>> Conservatism
>> Cross-cultural studies
>> Economics
>> Gerontology
>> History
>> Human behavior
>> Liberalism
>> Political science
>> Social change
>> Social surveys
>> Sociology

Social security (May subdiv. geog.)   362; 368.4
> UF Insurance, Social
>> Social insurance
> BT Pensions
> NT Workers' compensation

Social service
> USE Social work

Social settlements (May subdiv. geog.)   361.7; 362.5
> UF Church settlements
>> Neighborhood centers
>> Settlements, Social
> SA names of settlements, e.g. **Hull House (Chicago, Ill.)** [to be added as needed]
> BT Charities
>> Industrial welfare
>> Social work
> NT Community centers
>> Hull House (Chicago, Ill.)

Social skills (May subdiv. geog.)   302; 646.7
> UF Interpersonal competence
>> Social ability
>> Social competence
> BT Interpersonal relations
>> Life skills

Social standing
> USE Social status

Social status (May subdiv. geog.)   302
> UF Social standing
>> Socio-economic status
>> Status, Social
> BT Social psychology

Social studies
> USE Geography
>> History
>> Social sciences

Social surveys (May subdiv. geog.)   300.7
> Use for materials on the methods employed in conducting surveys of social and economic conditions.
> UF Community surveys
> SA names of regions, countries, cities, etc., with the subdivision *Social conditions* [to be added as needed]
> BT Social sciences
>> Surveys

Social surveys—United States   301

Social systems (May subdiv. geog.)   301
> BT Sociology
>> System theory

Social values (May subdiv. geog.)   303.3
> UF Group values
> BT Values

Social welfare
 USE **Charities**
  Public welfare
  Social problems
  Social work
Social work (May subdiv. geog.) **361.3**
 Use for materials on the methods employed in welfare work, public or private. Materials on privately supported welfare activities are entered under **Charities**. Materials on tax-supported welfare activities are entered under **Public welfare**. General materials on the various policies, programs, services, and facilities to meet basic human needs, such as health, education, and welfare, are entered under **Human services**.
 UF Social service
  Social welfare
  Welfare work
 SA social work with particular groups of people, e.g. **Social work with the elderly**; and classes of persons and ethnic groups with the subdivision *Services for*, e.g. **Handicapped—Services for** [to be added as needed]
 BT **Human services**
 NT **Charities**
  Child care services
  Child welfare
  Community organization
  Community services
  Crisis centers
  Group homes
  Handicapped—Services for
  Hotlines (Telephone counseling)
  Industrial welfare
  Public welfare
  Social case work
  Social group work
  Social settlements
  Social work with the elderly
 RT **Social action**
Social work with groups
 USE **Social group work**
Social work with the elderly (May subdiv. geog.) **362.6**
 BT **Elderly**
  Social work
Socialism (May subdiv. geog.) **320.5; 335**
 UF Social democracy

 BT **Collectivism**
  Economics
  Political science
 NT **Collective settlements**
  Dialectical materialism
  Government ownership
  Proletariat
  Utopias
 RT **Communism**
  Marxism
  National socialism
Socialism—United States 320.5; 335.00973
Socialization (May subdiv. geog.) **303.3**
 Use for materials on the process by which individuals acquire group values and learn to function effectively in society.
 UF Children—Socialization
  Social learning
 BT **Acculturation**
  Child rearing
  Education
  Sociology
 NT **Americanization**
  Peer pressure
Socialization of industry
 USE **Government ownership**
Socialized medicine
 USE **National health insurance**
  State medicine
Socially handicapped (May subdiv. geog.) **362**
 UF Culturally deprived
  Culturally handicapped
  Disadvantaged
  Underprivileged
 BT **Handicapped**
  Social adjustment
 NT **Socially handicapped children**
Socially handicapped children (May subdiv. geog.) **362.74**
 UF Culturally deprived children
  Culturally handicapped children
  Disadvantaged children
  Underprivileged children
 BT **Handicapped children**
  Socially handicapped
 RT **At risk students**
Socials
 USE **Church entertainments**
Societies (May subdiv. geog.) **060**
 UF Learned societies

Societies—*Continued*

    SA   types of societies, e.g. **Choral societies**; subjects, ethnic groups, classes of persons, corporate bodies, individual persons, and sacred works with the subdivision *Societies*, e.g. **Agriculture—Societies**; **Women—Societies**; etc.; and names of individual societies [to be added as needed]

    BT   **Associations**

    NT   **Agriculture—Societies**
          Boys' clubs
          Chemistry—Societies
          Choral societies
          Cooperative societies
          Education—Societies
          Elderly—Societies
          Girls' clubs
          History—Societies
          Labor unions
          Men—Societies
          Parent-teacher associations
          Science—Societies
          Secret societies
          Students—Societies
          Women—Societies

    RT   **Clubs**

Society and art
    USE **Art and society**

Society and language
    USE **Sociolinguistics**

Society and religion
    USE **Religion and sociology**

Society of Friends (May subdiv. geog.) **289.6**

    UF   Friends, Society of
          Quakers

    BT   **Christian sects**

Society, Primitive
    USE **Primitive societies**

Society—Religious aspects
    USE **Religion and sociology**

Socio-economic status
    USE **Social status**

Sociobiology   **304.5; 577.8; 591.56**

    Use for materials on the biological basis of social behavior, especially as transmitted genetically.

    UF   Biology—Social aspects

    BT   **Comparative psychology**
          Sociology

Sociolinguistics (May subdiv. geog.) **306.44**

    Use for materials on the study of the social aspects of language, particularly linguistic behavior, as determined by sociocultural factors.

    UF   Language and society
          Society and language
          Sociology of language

    BT   **Language and languages**
          Linguistics
          Sociology

Sociology (May subdiv. geog.)   **301**

    SA   sociology of particular religions, e.g. **Christian sociology**; and racial and ethnic groups, classes of persons, and names of countries, cities, etc., with the subdivision *Social conditions*, e.g. **United States—Social conditions** [to be added as needed]

    BT   **Social sciences**

    NT   **Christian sociology**
          Cities and towns
          Communication
          Educational sociology
          Equality
          Ethnic relations
          Ethnopsychology
          Family
          Human ecology
          Human settlements
          Individualism
          Information society
          Labor
          Marxism
          Organizational sociology
          Population
          Race relations
          Religion and sociology
          Rural sociology
          Social change
          Social classes
          Social conditions
          Social conflict
          Social contract
          Social ethics
          Social groups
          Social medicine
          Social problems

Sociology—*Continued*
       Social psychology
       Social systems
       Socialization
       Sociobiology
       Sociolinguistics
       Urban sociology
  RT **Civilization**
       Culture
Sociology and art
  USE **Art and society**
Sociology and religion
  USE **Religion and sociology**
Sociology—Book reviews   301
Sociology, Christian
  USE **Christian sociology**
Sociology of language
  USE **Sociolinguistics**
Sociology of organizations
  USE **Organizational sociology**
Sociology of religion
  USE **Religion and sociology**
Sociology, Rural
  USE **Rural sociology**
Sociology, Urban
  USE **Urban sociology**
Sodium content of food
  USE **Food—Sodium content**
Soft toy making   745.592
  UF Stuffed toy making
  BT **Sewing**
      Toy making
Softball (May subdiv. geog.)   **796.357**
  BT **Ball games**
      Baseball
      Sports
Software, Computer
  USE **Computer software**
Software for sharing
  USE **Shareware (Computer soft-**
      ware)
Software viruses
  USE **Computer viruses**
Soil conservation (May subdiv. geog.)
     631.4
  UF Conservation of the soil
  BT **Conservation of natural re-**
      sources
      Environmental protection
  RT **Erosion**
      Soil erosion
Soil ecology (May subdiv. geog.)   **577.5**

  UF Edaphology
  BT **Ecology**
      Soils
Soil engineering
  USE **Soil mechanics**
Soil erosion (May subdiv. geog.)   **631.4**
  UF Top soil loss
  BT **Erosion**
  RT **Soil conservation**
Soil fertility
  USE **Soils**
Soil mechanics   620.1
  UF Soil engineering
      Soils (Engineering)
  BT **Mechanics**
      Structural engineering
  RT **Foundations**
      Roads
      Soils
Soil microbiology   631.4
  UF Soils—Bacteriology
  BT **Microbiology**
      Sanitary engineering
  RT **Agricultural bacteriology**
Soilless agriculture
  USE **Hydroponics**
Soils (May subdiv. geog.)   **631.4**
  UF Soil fertility
  BT **Agriculture**
      Economic geology
  NT **Clay**
      Compost
      Fertilizers
      Soil ecology
  RT **Agricultural chemistry**
      Soil mechanics
Soils—Bacteriology
  USE **Soil microbiology**
Soils (Engineering)
  USE **Soil mechanics**
Soils, Lunar
  USE **Lunar soil**
Solace
  USE **Consolation**
Solar batteries   621.31
  UF Batteries, Solar
      Solar cells
      Sun powered batteries
  BT **Electric batteries**
      Photovoltaic power generation
      Solar radiation

Solar cells
   USE **Photovoltaic power generation**
         Solar batteries
Solar eclipses   523.7
   UF Eclipses, Solar
        Sun—Eclipses
   BT **Astronomy**
Solar energy (May subdiv. geog.)
        333.792; 621.47
   UF Solar power
   BT **Energy resources**
        Renewable energy resources
        Solar radiation
        Sun
   NT **Photovoltaic power generation**
        Solar engines
        Solar heating
Solar engines   621.47
   BT **Engines**
        Solar energy
Solar heating (May subdiv. geog.)
        621.47; 697
   SA types of solar heating applica-
        tions, e.g. **Solar homes** [to be
        added as needed]
   BT **Heating**
        Solar energy
   NT **Solar homes**
Solar homes (May subdiv. geog.)   **697;
        728**
   BT **Domestic architecture**
        Houses
        Solar heating
Solar physics
   USE **Sun**
Solar power
   USE **Solar energy**
Solar radiation   523.7; 621.47
   UF Radiation, Solar
        Sun—Radiation
   BT **Meteorology**
        Space environment
   NT **Global warming**
        Solar batteries
        Solar energy
        Sunspots
Solar system   523.2
   BT **Astronomy**
        Stars
   NT **Asteroids**
        Comets

        Earth
        Meteors
        Moon
        Planets
        Satellites
        Sun
Solder and soldering
   USE **Soldering**
Soldering   671.5
   UF Solder and soldering
   BT **Metals**
        Metalwork
   RT **Welding**
Soldiers (May subdiv. geog.)   **355.0092;
        920**
   UF Army life
        Soldiers' life
   SA names of countries with the sub-
        head *Army* and the subdivi-
        sion *Military life*, e.g. **United
        States. Army—Military life**
        [to be added as needed]
   BT **Armies**
        Military personnel
   NT **Mercenary soldiers**
        Missing in action
        **United States. Army—Military
        life**
        United States. Army—Officers
   RT **Veterans**
Soldiers' handbooks
   USE **United States. Army—Hand-
        books, manuals, etc.**
Soldiers—Hygiene
   USE **Military personnel—Health
        and hygiene**
Soldiers' life
   USE **Soldiers**
        and namcs of countris with the
        subhead *Army* and the subdi-
        vision *Military life*, e.g. **Unit-
        ed States. Army—Military
        life** [to be added as needed]
Soldiers of fortune
   USE **Mercenary soldiers**
Soldiers' songs
   USE **War songs**
Soldiers—United States   355.0092; 920
   UF GIs
        United States—Soldiers

Solicitors

    USE   **Lawyers**

Solid geometry   516.23

    UF   Geometry, Solid

    BT   **Geometry**

Solid waste disposal

    USE   **Refuse and refuse disposal**

Solids   530.4; 531; 541

    BT   **Physical chemistry**

          Physics

    NT   **Crystals**

Solitaire (Game)   795.4

    UF   Patience (Game)

    BT   **Card games**

Solitude   155.9

    UF   Seclusion

    RT   **Loneliness**

          Privacy

Solvent abuse (May subdiv. geog.)
    362.29

    UF   Aerosol sniffing

          Glue sniffing

          Inhalant abuse

          Inhalation abuse of solvents

          Paint sniffing

    BT   **Social problems**

          Substance abuse

    RT   **Drug abuse**

Somalia   967.73

    May be subdivided like United States except for History.

Sonar   621.389

    UF   Sound navigation

    BT   **Signals and signaling**

Sonata   784.18

    Use for musical scores and for materials on the sonata as a musical form.

    UF   Sonatas

    BT   **Musical form**

Sonatas

    USE   **Sonata**

Song books

    USE   **Songbooks**

Song lyrics

    USE   **Popular song lyrics**

Song writing

    USE   **Composition (Music)**

          **Popular music—Writing and
            publishing**

Songbooks (May subdiv. geog.)   782.42

    Use for general collections of songs that contain both words and music. Similar collec-

tions limited to sacred songs are entered under **Hymnals**. Materials about songs are entered under **Songs**. Collections of songs on a single subject are entered under the subject with the subdivision *Songs*.

    UF   Song books

    BT   **Singing**

          Songs

    NT   **Hymnals**

          School songbooks

Songs   782.42

    Use for materials about songs. General collections of songs that contain both words and music are entered under **Songbooks**. Collections of songs that contain the words but not the music are entered under **Poetry—Collections** for classical songs and under **Popular song lyrics** for popular songs.

    SA   types of songs, e.g. **Children's songs**; songs of particular countries, e.g. **American songs**; subjects, classes of persons, and names of persons, corporate bodies, places, or wars, with the subdivision *Songs*, for collections or individual songs about the topic or associated with the entity named, e.g. **Cowhands—Songs**; **Surfing—Songs**; **United States Military Academy—Songs**; **World War, 1939-1945—Songs**; etc.; and names of individual songs [to be added as needed]

    BT   **Poetry**

          Vocal music

    NT   **African songs**

          American songs

          Ballads

          Carols

          Children's songs

          Cowhands—Songs

          Folk songs

          Hymns

          Lullabies

          National songs

          Popular music

          School songbooks

          Sea songs

          Songbooks

          State songs

          Students' songs

          Surfing—Songs

          United States. Army—Songs

Songs—*Continued*
>**War songs**

Songs, African
>USE **African songs**

Songs, African American
>USE **African American music**

Songs and music
>USE music of particular countries or ethnic groups, e.g. **American music; Native American music;** etc.; types of music, e.g. **Vocal music;** and subjects, classes of persons, and names of individual persons, corporate bodies, places, or wars, with the subdivision *Songs* for collections of songs or materials about songs pertaining to the topic or entity named, e.g. **Cowhands—Songs; Surfing—Songs; United States Military Academy—Songs** [to be added as needed]

Songs for children
>USE **Children's songs**

Songwriters
>USE **Composers**
>
>**Lyricists**

Songwriting
>USE **Composition (Music)**
>
>**Popular music—Writing and publishing**

Sonnets   808.1
>Use for collections of or materials about sonnets.
>
>BT **Poetry**

Sons   306.874
>BT **Family**
>
>**Men**
>
>NT **Father-son relationship**
>
>**Mother-son relationship**

Sons and fathers
>USE **Father-son relationship**

Sons and mothers
>USE **Mother-son relationship**

Soothsaying
>USE **Divination**

Soporifics
>USE **Narcotics**

Sorcery
>USE **Magic**
>
>**Occultism**
>
>**Witchcraft**

Sororities
>USE **Fraternities and sororities**

Sorrow
>USE **Bereavement**
>
>**Grief**
>
>**Joy and sorrow**

Soul   128; 233
>UF Spirit
>
>BT **Future life**
>
>**Human beings (Theology)**
>
>**Philosophy**
>
>NT **Immortality**
>
>**Psychology**
>
>RT **Reincarnation**

Sound   534; 620.2
>UF Acoustics
>
>BT **Physics**
>
>**Pneumatics**
>
>**Radiation**
>
>NT **Architectural acoustics**
>
>**Computer sound processing**
>
>**Hearing**
>
>**Noise**
>
>**Phonetics**
>
>**Silence**
>
>**Sound effects**
>
>**Soundproofing**
>
>**Sounds**
>
>**Ultrasonics**
>
>**Vibration**
>
>RT **Music—Acoustics and physics**

Sound effects   534; 620.2
>BT **Sound**

Sound insulation
>USE **Soundproofing**

Sound navigation
>USE **Sonar**

Sound processing, Computer
>USE **Computer sound processing**

Sound recording
>USE **Sound—Recording and reproducing**

Sound—Recording and reproducing   621.389
>Use for materials on the equipment or the process by which sound is recorded. Materials on sound recordings that emphasize the content of the recording rather than the equipment, process, or format are entered under **Sound recordings**. Materials about the format are entered under the format, e.g. **Compact discs**.

Sound—Recording and reproducing—
Continued
- UF High-fidelity sound systems
  [*Former heading*]
  Sound recording
  Stereophonic sound systems
  [*Former heading*]
- SA methods of recording, e.g. **Magnetic recorders and recording** [to be added as needed]
- NT **Compact disc players**
  MP3 players
- RT **Phonograph**
  Sound recordings

Sound recordings (May subdiv. geog.)
384; 621.389; 780.26

Use for general materials and for materials on sound recordings that emphasize the content of the recording rather than the format. Materials about the format are entered under the format, e.g. **Compact discs**. Materials about the equipment or the process by which sound is recorded are entered under **Sound—Recording and reproducing**.

- UF Audio cassettes
  Audiotapes
  Cassette tapes, Audio
  Discography
  Phonograph records
  Recordings, Sound
  Records, Phonograph
  Tape recordings, Audio
- SA types of sound recordings, e.g. **Compact discs** and types of music with the subdivision *Sound recordings*, e.g. **Opera—Sound recordings** [to be added as needed]
- BT **Audiovisual materials**
- NT **Audiobooks**
  Compact discs
  Grammy Awards
  Opera—Sound recordings
- RT **Sound—Recording and reproducing**

Sound recordings—Copyright
- USE **Copyright—Sound recordings**

Sound waves 534; 620.2
- BT **Vibration**
  Waves
- NT **Ultrasonic waves**

Soundproofing 620.2; 693.8
- UF Insulation (Sound)
  Sound insulation

- BT **Architectural acoustics**
  Sound

Sounds 534; 620.2
- BT **Sound**

Soups (May subdiv. geog.) **641.8**
- BT **Cooking**

Sources
- USE historical subjects, periods of history, individual literary and sacred works, and names of wars with the subdivision *Sources,* e.g. **World War, 1939-1945—Sources;** and subjects, ethnic groups, classes of persons, coporate bodies, and names of countries, states, etc., with the subdivisions *History—Sources;* e.g. **United States—History—Sources** [to be added as needed]

South Africa 968

Use for materials on the Republic of South Africa.
- UF Republic of South Africa
  Union of South Africa
- BT **Africa**
  Southern Africa

South Africa—History 968

South Africa—Race relations 305.800968; 968
- BT **Race relations**
- NT **Anti-apartheid movement**
  Apartheid

South African Dutch
- USE **Afrikaners**

South Africans, Afrikaans-speaking
- USE **Afrikaners**

South America 980
- BT **America**

South American literature
- USE **Latin American literature**

South Atlantic States
- USE **Atlantic States**

South Korea
- USE **Korea (South)**

South Pacific region
- USE **Oceania**

South Pole 998
- BT **Polar regions**
- RT **Antarctica**

South Sea Islands
USE **Oceania**
South Seas
USE **Oceania**
South (U.S.)
USE **Southern States**
Southeast Asia   959
Use for materials dealing collectively with the region of Asia that includes Burma, Thailand, Malaysia, Singapore, Indonesia, Vietnam, Cambodia, Laos, and the Philippines.
UF   Asia, Southeastern
BT   **Asia**
NT   **Indochina**
Southern Africa   968
Use for materials dealing collectively with the area south of the countries of Zaire and Tanzania. Southern Africa includes the political entities of Angola, Botswana, Comoros, Lesotho, Madagascar, Malawi, Mozambique, Namibia, South Africa, Swaziland, Zambia, and Zimbabwe. Materials on the Republic of South Africa are entered under **South Africa**.
UF   Africa, Southern
BT   **Africa**
NT   **South Africa**
Southern cooking   641.5975
BT   **Cooking**
Southern lights
USE   **Auroras**
Southern literature
USE   **American literature—Southern States**
Southern States   975
UF   South (U.S.)
BT   **United States**
Southern States—African Americans
USE   **African Americans—Southern States**
Southern States—History   975
BT   **United States—History**
RT   **Slavery—United States**
Southwest, New
USE   **Southwestern States**
Southwest, Old
USE   **Old Southwest**
Southwest Pacific region
USE   **Oceania**
Southwestern States   979
Use for materials on that part of the United States that corresponds roughly with the old Spanish province of New Mexico, including the present Arizona, New Mexico, southern Colorado, Utah, Nevada, and California.
UF   Southwest, New
BT   **United States**

Sovereigns
USE   **Emperors**
Kings and rulers
Monarchy
Queens
Sovereignty (May subdiv. geog.)   320.1
BT   **International law**
Political science
NT   **Secession**
RT   **National self-determination**
Soviet communism
USE   **Communism—Russia**
Soviet literature
USE   **Russian literature**
Soviet Union
USE   **Russia—History—1917-1991, Soviet Union**
Soviet Union—Communism
USE   **Communism—Russia**
Soviet Union—History
USE   **Russia—History—1917-1991, Soviet Union**
Soviet Union—History—1917-1921, Revolution
USE   **Russia—History—1917-1921, Revolution**
Soviet Union—History—1917-1925
USE   **Russia—History—1917-1925**
Soviet Union—History—1925-1953
USE   **Russia—History—1925-1953**
Soviet Union—History—1939-1940, War with Finland
USE   **Russo-Finnish War, 1939-1940**
Soviet Union—History—1953-1991
USE   **Russia—History—1953-1991**
Soybean (May subdiv. geog.)   633.3
BT   **Forage plants**
Space age
USE   **Astronautics and civilization**
Space and time   115
UF   Time and space
BT   **Fourth dimension**
Metaphysics
Space sciences
Time
NT   **Cyberspace**
Personal space
Time travel
RT   **Relativity (Physics)**
Space-based weapons
USE   **Space weapons**

Space biology   571.0919; 612

Use for materials on the biology of humans or other earth creatures while in outer space. Materials on the possibility of indigenous life in outer space are entered under **Life on other planets**.

UF   Astrobiology

Cosmobiology

BT   **Biology**

Space sciences

NT   **Space medicine**

Space chemistry   523

UF   Astrochemistry

Cosmochemistry

BT   **Chemistry**

Space colonies   629.44; 999

Use for materials on communities established in space or on natural extraterrestrial bodies. Materials on bases established on natural extraterrestrial bodies for specific functions other than colonization are entered under **Extraterrestrial bases**. Materials on manned installations orbiting in space for specific functions, such as servicing space ships, are entered under **Space stations**.

UF   Colonies, Space

Communities, Space

Outer space—Colonies

BT   **Astronautics and civilization**

RT   **Extraterrestrial bases**

Space commercialization

USE   **Space industrialization**

Space communication

USE   **Astronautics—Communication**
systems

Interstellar communication

Space debris   629.4

UF   Debris in space

Junk in space

Space pollution

BT   **Pollution**

Space environment

Space environment   629.4

UF   Environment, Space

Extraterrestrial environment

Space weather

BT   **Astronomy**

Outer space

NT   **Cosmic rays**

Solar radiation

Space debris

Space exploration (Astronautics)

USE   **Outer space—Exploration**

Space flight   629.4

Use for materials on the physics and technical details of flight beyond the earth's atmosphere. General materials and imaginary accounts of travel to other planets are entered under **Interplanetary voyages**.

UF   Humans in space

Man in space

Manned space flight

People in space

Rocket flight

Space travel

SA   names of projects, e.g. **Gemini**
project; and space flight to particular places, e.g. **Space**
flight to the moon [to be added as needed]

BT   **Aeronautics—Flights**

Astronautics

NT   **Astronauts**

Extravehicular activity (Space
flight)

Gemini project

Orbital rendezvous (Space
flight)

Outer space—Exploration

Space flight to the moon

RT   **Astrodynamics**

Interplanetary voyages

Navigation (Astronautics)

Space medicine

Space vehicles

Space flight (Fiction)

USE   **Imaginary voyages**

Science fiction

Space flight—Law and legislation

USE   **Space law**

Space flight—Rescue work

USE   **Space rescue operations**

Space flight to the moon   629.45

UF   Flight to the moon

Lunar expeditions

Moon, Voyages to

Voyages to the moon

BT   **Astronautics**

Space flight

NT   **Apollo project**

Moon—Exploration

Space heaters   644; 697

BT   **Heating**

NT   **Fireplaces**

Stoves

Space industrial processing
USE **Space industrialization**
Space industrialization (May subdiv.
geog.) **629.44**
UF Commercial endeavors in space
Industrial uses of space
Manufacturing in space
Space commercialization
Space industrial processing
Space manufacturing
Space stations—Industrial appli-
cations
BT **Industrialization**
Space laboratories
USE **Space stations**
Space law (May subdiv. geog.) **341.4**
UF Aerospace law
Artificial satellites—Law and
legislation
Astronautics—Law and legisla-
tion
Space flight—Law and legisla-
tion
Space stations—Law and legisla-
tion
BT **Astronautics and civilization**
International law
Law
Space manufacturing
USE **Space industrialization**
Space medicine **616.9**
UF Aerospace medicine
Bioastronautics
BT **Medicine**
Space biology
Space sciences
NT **Life support systems (Space
environment)**
Weightlessness
RT **Aviation medicine**
Space flight
Space navigation
USE **Navigation (Astronautics)**
Space nutrition
USE **Astronauts—Nutrition**
Space optics **535**
BT **Optics**
Space sciences
NT **Astronautical instruments**
Astronomical instruments

RT **Optical instruments**
Remote sensing
Space orbital rendezvous
USE **Orbital rendezvous (Space
flight)**
Space, Outer
USE **Outer space**
Space, Personal
USE **Personal space**
Space photography **778.3**
UF Photographs from space
Photography in astronautics
SA celestial bodies or objects in
space with the subdivision
Pictorial works [to be added
as needed]
BT **Photography**
**Photography—Scientific appli-
cations**
NT **Mars (Planet)—Pictorial works**
Moon—Pictorial works
Space platforms
USE **Space stations**
Space pollution
USE **Space debris**
Space power
USE **Astronautics and civilization**
Space probes **629.43**
Use for materials on space exploration by
remote control from earth.
SA types of probes, e.g. **Lunar
probes**; **Mars probes**; etc.;
and names of space vehicles
and space projects, e.g. **Proj-
ect Voyager** [to be added as
needed]
BT **Outer space—Exploration**
Space vehicles
NT **Lunar probes**
Mars probes
Space rescue operations **629.45**
UF Rescue operations, Space
Space flight—Rescue work
Space vehicles—Rescue work
BT **Rescue work**
Space research
USE **Outer space—Exploration**
Space sciences
Space rockets
USE **Space vehicles**

Space sciences (May subdiv. geog.)
 500.5

Use for general materials and for scientific results of space exploration and scientific applications of space flight.

UF Science and space

Space research

BT **Science**

NT **Outer space**

Space and time

Space biology

Space medicine

Space optics

RT **Astronautics**

Astronomy

Space sciences—International cooperation
 500.5

BT **International cooperation**

Space ships

USE **Space vehicles**

Space shuttles 629.44

SA names of individual space shuttles [to be added as needed]

BT **Space vehicles**

Space stations 629.44

Use for materials on manned installations orbiting in space for specific functions, such as servicing space ships. Materials on bases established on natural extraterrestrial bodies for specific functions other than colonization are entered under **Extraterrestrial bases**. Materials on communities established in space or on natural extraterrestrial bodies are entered under **Space colonies**.

UF Orbital laboratories

Orbiting vehicles

Space laboratories

Space platforms

BT **Artificial satellites**

Astronautics

Space vehicles

NT **Orbital rendezvous (Space flight)**

Space stations—Industrial applications

USE **Space industrialization**

Space stations—Law and legislation

USE **Space law**

Space suits 629.47

UF Astronauts—Clothing

BT **Life support systems (Space environment)**

Space telecommunication

USE **Interstellar communication**

Space travel

USE **Interplanetary voyages**

Space flight

Space vehicle accidents 363.12; 629.4

UF Astronautical accidents

Astronautics—Accidents

Space vehicles—Accidents

BT **Accidents**

Space vehicles 629.47

UF Space rockets

Space ships

Spacecraft

BT **Rocketry**

NT **Orbital rendezvous (Space flight)**

Rocket planes

Space probes

Space shuttles

Space stations

RT **Artificial satellites**

Astronautics

Space flight

Space vehicles—Accidents

USE **Space vehicle accidents**

Space vehicles—Extravehicular activity

USE **Extravehicular activity (Space flight)**

Space vehicles—Guidance systems
 629.47

Space vehicles—Instruments

USE **Astronautical instruments**

Space vehicles—Piloting 629.45

UF Piloting (Astronautics)

BT **Astronauts**

Navigation (Astronautics)

Space vehicles—Propulsion systems
 629.47

Space vehicles—Recovery 629.4

UF Recovery of space vehicles

Space vehicles—Rescue work

USE **Space rescue operations**

Space vehicles—Thermodynamics
 629.47

BT **Thermodynamics**

Space vehicles—Tracking 629.4

UF Tracking of satellites

Space walk

USE **Extravehicular activity (Space flight)**

Space warfare (May subdiv. geog.) **358**

> Use for materials on interplanetary warfare, attacks on earth from outer space, and warfare among the nations of earth in outer space.

   UF   Interplanetary warfare

         Interstellar warfare

         Space wars

   BT   **Outer space**

         War

   NT   **Space weapons**

         Strategic Defense Initiative

Space wars

   USE   **Space warfare**

Space weapons   **358**

   UF   Space-based weapons

         Star Wars weapons

         Weapons, Space

   BT   **Military weapons**

         Space warfare

   RT   **Strategic Defense Initiative**

Space weather

   USE   **Space environment**

Spacecraft

   USE   **Space vehicles**

Spain   **946**

> May be subdivided like United States except for History.

Spain—History   **946**

   NT   **Spanish-American War, 1898**

         Spanish Armada, 1588

Spain—History—1898, War of 1898

   USE   **Spanish-American War, 1898**

Spain—History—1936-1939, Civil War 946.081

Spain—History—1939-1975   **946.082**

Spain—History—1975-   **946.083**

Spanish America

   USE   **Latin America**

Spanish American literature

   USE   **American literature (Spanish)**

         Latin American literature

Spanish-American War, 1898 (May subdiv. geog.)   **973.8**

   UF   American-Spanish War, 1898

         Spain—History—1898, War of 1898

         United States—History—1898, War of 1898

   BT   **Spain—History**

         United States—History—1865-1898

         United States—History—1898-1919

Spanish Armada, 1588   **942.05; 946**

   UF   Armada, 1588

         Invincible Armada

   BT   **Great Britain—History—1485-1603, Tudors**

         Spain—History

Spanish language   **460**

> May be subdivided like **English language**.

   BT   **Language and languages**

         Romance languages

Spanish literature   **860**

> May use same subdivisions and names of literary forms as for **English literature**.

   BT   **Literature**

         Romance literature

Sparring

   USE   **Boxing**

Spas

   USE   **Health resorts**

         Physical fitness centers

Speaking

   USE   **Debates and debating**

         Lectures and lecturing

         Preaching

         Public speaking

         Rhetoric

         Speech

         Voice

Speaking choirs

   USE   **Choral speaking**

Speaking in tongues

   USE   **Glossolalia**

Speaking with tongues

   USE   **Glossolalia**

Spear fishing (May subdiv. geog.)   **799.1**

   BT   **Fishing**

Special collections in libraries

   USE   **Libraries—Special collections**

Special education (May subdiv. geog.)   **371.9**

   SA   classes of exceptional children with the subdivision *Education* [to be added as needed]

   BT   **Education**

   NT   **Mentally handicapped children—Education**

   RT   **Mainstreaming in education**

Special libraries (May subdiv. geog.)
026; 027.6

Use for materials on libraries covering specialized subjects, containing special format materials, or serving a specialized clientele.

SA   types of special libraries, e.g.
Business libraries [to be added as needed]

BT   **Libraries**

NT   **Business libraries**
Corporate libraries
Government libraries
Music libraries

Special months (May subdiv. geog.)
394.26

SA   names of particular months of celebration or commemoration, e.g. **Black History Month** [to be added as needed]

BT   **Months**

NT   **Black History Month**

Special Olympics (May subdiv. geog.)
796.087

BT   **Olympic games**
Sports for the handicapped

Special weeks (May subdiv. geog.)
394.26

SA   names of particular weeks of celebration or commemoration, e.g. **Holy Week** [to be added as needed]

BT   **Week**

NT   **Holy Week**

Specialists exchange programs
USE   **Exchange of persons programs**

Specie
USE   **Coins**

Specifications
USE   types of engineering, construction, industries, products, and merchandise with the subdivision *Specifications,* for works on the particular qualities prescribed for a product to meet specific requirements [to be added as needed]

Specimens, Preservation of
USE   **Plants—Collection and preservation**
Taxidermy
Zoological specimens—Collection and preservation

and types of natural specimens with the subdivision *Collection and preservation,* e.g.
Birds—Collection and preservation [to be added as needed]

Spectacles
USE   **Eyeglasses**

Specters
USE   **Apparitions**
Ghosts

Spectra
USE   **Spectrum analysis**

Spectrochemical analysis
USE   **Spectrum analysis**

Spectrochemistry
USE   **Spectrum analysis**

Spectroscopy
USE   **Spectrum analysis**

Spectrum analysis   **535.8**

UF   Spectra
Spectrochemical analysis
Spectrochemistry
Spectroscopy

BT   **Astronomy**
Astrophysics
Chemistry
Optics
Radiation

NT   **Mass spectrometry**

RT   **Light**

Speculation (May subdiv. geog.)   **332.64**

BT   **Finance**

NT   **Real estate investment**

RT   **Investments**
Stock exchanges

Speech   **302.2; 372.62; 410; 612.7**

UF   Speaking

BT   **Language arts**

NT   **Speech disorders**
Speech processing systems
Speech therapy
Voice culture

RT   **Language and languages**
Phonetics
Voice

Speech correction
USE   **Speech therapy**

Speech disorders   **616.85**

Use for materials on disorders of the physiological mechanisms required for speech. Ma-

Speech disorders—*Continued*

terials on disorders of the central neurological functions affecting the reception, processing, or expression of language are entered under **Language disorders**.

UF   Defective speech

Speech pathology

Stammering

Stuttering

BT   **Communicative disorders**

Speech

NT   **Aphasia**

Speech, Freedom of

USE   **Freedom of speech**

Speech pathology

USE   **Speech disorders**

Speech problems

USE   **Aphasia**

Speech processing systems   006.5

UF   Computer speech processing systems

Electronic speech processing systems

Speech scramblers

BT   **Speech**

NT   **Automatic speech recognition**

Speech synthesis

RT   **Computer sound processing**

Speech recognition, Automatic

USE   **Automatic speech recognition**

Speech scramblers

USE   **Speech processing systems**

Speech synthesis   006.5

BT   **Speech processing systems**

Speech therapy   616.85

UF   Speech correction

BT   **Speech**

Speeches   808.85

Use for collections of speeches on several subjects and materials about speeches that have already been delivered. Materials on the art of delivering speeches are entered under **Public speaking** or under **Lectures and lecturing**. Collections of speeches on a single subject are entered under that subject.

UF   Addresses

Orations

Speeches, addresses, etc.

SA   speeches of particular countries, e.g. **American speeches** [to be added as needed]

BT   **Literature**

NT   **After dinner speeches**

American speeches

English speeches

Presidents—United States—Inaugural addresses

Toasts

RT   **Lectures and lecturing**

Public speaking

Speeches, addresses, etc.

USE   **Speeches**

Speeches, addresses, etc., American

USE   **American speeches**

Speeches, addresses, etc., English

USE   **English speeches**

Speed   531

UF   Velocity

BT   **Motion**

Speed (Drug)

USE   **Methamphetamine**

Speed reading   372.45

UF   Accelerated reading

Faster reading

Rapid reading

BT   **Reading**

Speed, Supersonic

USE   **Supersonic aerodynamics**

Speleology

USE   **Caves**

Spellers   418

BT   **English language—Spelling**

Spelling   411

NT   **English language—Spelling**

Spelling reform

Spelling bees (May subdiv. geog.)   **418**

BT   **Language and languages**

Spelling reform   418

UF   English language—Spelling reform

BT   **Spelling**

NT   **Phonetic spelling**

Spells

USE   **Charms**

Magic

Spherical trigonometry

USE   **Trigonometry**

Spices   641.3

SA   types of spices [to be added as needed]

BT   **Food**

Spider-Man (Fictional character)   741.5

UF   Spider Man (Fictional character) [*Former heading*]

Spider-Man (Fictional character)—*Continued*

   BT   **Fictional characters**

         Superheroes

Spider Man (Fictional character)

   USE   **Spider-Man (Fictional character)**

Spiders (May subdiv. geog.)   **595.4**

   BT   **Arachnids**

Spies (May subdiv. geog.)   **327.12; 353.1; 355.3**

   UF   Intelligence agents

         Spying

   BT   **Espionage**

         Subversive activities

   RT   **Secret service**

Spinning (May subdiv. geog.)   **677; 746.1**

   BT   **Textile industry**

   RT   **Yarn**

Spinosaurus   **567.912**

   BT   **Dinosaurs**

Spiral gearing

   USE   **Gearing**

Spires (May subdiv. geog.)   **721**

   UF   Steeples

   BT   **Architecture**

         Church architecture

Spirit

   USE   **Soul**

Spiritism

   USE   **Spiritualism**

Spirits   **133.9**

   UF   Invisible world

   BT   **Supernatural**

   NT   **Angels**

         Apparitions

         Ghosts

   RT   **Demonology**

         Spiritualism

Spiritual gifts   **234**

   Use for materials on extraordinary phenomena, such as glossolalia, visions, prophecies and interpretations, healings, discernment of spirits, etc. Materials dealing collectively with ordinary spiritual phenomena, such as faith, hope, love, patience, temperance, etc., are entered under **Virtue**.

   UF   Charismata

         Gifts of grace

         Gifts of the Holy Spirit

         Gifts, Spiritual

   BT   **Grace (Theology)**

   NT   **Glossolalia**

         Spiritual healing

         Visions

   RT   **Catholic charismatic movement**

         Holy Spirit

         Pentecostalism

Spiritual healing (May subdiv. geog.)   **203; 234; 615.8**

   Use for materials on the use of faith, prayer, or other religious means to treat illness. Materials on psychic or psychological means to treat illness are entered under **Mental healing**.

   UF   Divine healing

         Evangelistic healing

         Faith cure

         Faith healing

         Healing, Spiritual

   BT   **Medicine—Religious aspects**

         Spiritual gifts

   RT   **Christian Science**

         Mental healing

         Mind and body

         Miracles

         Subconsciousness

         Suggestive therapeutics

Spiritual life (May subdiv. geog.)   **204; 248**

   Use for materials on spiritual practices and on the relationship that individuals may attain with the sacred. May be subdivided by religion or sect.

   BT   **Religious life**

   NT   **Conversion**

         Faith

         Hope

         Meditation

         Mysticism

         Retreats

Spiritualism (May subdiv. geog.)   **133.9**

   Use for materials on extraordinary spiritual phenomena, especially contact with the spirits of the dead.

   UF   Spiritism

   BT   **Occultism**

         Supernatural

   NT   **Psychokinesis**

   RT   **Apparitions**

         Parapsychology

         Spirits

Spirituals (Songs) (May subdiv. geog.)   **782.25**

   BT   **Folk songs—United States**

         Hymns

Spirituals (Songs)—*Continued*
    RT   **African American music**
           Gospel music
Splicing
    USE   **Knots and splices**
Splicing of genes
    USE   **Genetic engineering**
Split personality
    USE   **Multiple personality**
Spoils system
    USE   **Political corruption**
Sponges (May subdiv. geog.)   **593.4**
    BT   **Aquatic animals**
Sport utility vehicles (May subdiv. geog.)
        629.22
    UF   SUVs (Vehicles)
    BT   **Vehicles**
Sporting equipment
    USE   **Sporting goods**
Sporting goods (May subdiv. geog.)
        796.028
    UF   Sporting equipment
           Sports—Equipment and supplies
    RT   **Sports**
Sports (May subdiv. geog.)   **796**
    SA   types of sports and names of
           sports competitions [to be
           added as needed]
    BT   **Play**
           Recreation
    NT   **Aeronautical sports**
           Baseball
           Basketball
           Bullfights
           Coaching (Athletics)
           College sports
           Cycling
           Extreme sports
           Field hockey
           Fishing
           Football
           Golf
           Gymnastics
           Lacrosse
           Olympic games
           Orienteering
           Professional sports
           Racing
           Racquetball
           Rodeos
           Rowing
           School sports

           Soccer
           Softball
           Sports cards
           Sports for women
           Sports records
           Sports teams
           Sports tournaments
           Sportsmanship
           Tennis
           Track athletics
           Triathlon
           Violence in sports
           Volleyball
           Water sports
           Winter sports
    RT   **Amusements**
           Athletes
           Athletics
           Games
           Outdoor life
           Physical education
           Sporting goods
           Sports facilities
Sports and drugs
    USE   **Athletes—Drug use**
Sports—Audiences
    USE   **Sports spectators**
Sports betting (May subdiv. geog.)   **796**
    UF   Sports handicapping
    BT   **Gambling**
Sports broadcasting
    USE   **Radio broadcasting of sports**
           Television broadcasting of
           sports
Sports cards (May subdiv. geog.)   **769**
    UF   Cards, Sports
    SA   types of cards for specific
           sports, e.g. **Baseball cards** [to
           be added as needed]
    BT   **Sports**
    NT   **Baseball cards**
Sports cars (May subdiv. geog.)   **629.222**
    SA   names of specific sports cars [to
           be added as needed]
    BT   **Automobiles**
Sports coaching
    USE   **Coaching (Athletics)**
Sports—Corrupt practices (May subdiv.
    geog.)   **796**
    UF   Cheating in sports
           Corruption in sports

Sports—Corrupt practices—*Continued*
Sports scandals
BT **Criminal law**
Sports drama (Films)   791.43
Use for individual works, collections, or materials about sports drama on film.
BT **Motion pictures**
Sports drama (Radio programs)   791.44
Use for individual works, collections, or materials about sports drama on the radio.
BT **Radio programs**
Sports drama (Television programs) 791.45
Use for individual works, collections, or materials about sports drama on television.
BT **Television programs**
Sports—Equipment and supplies
USE **Sporting goods**
Sports events
USE names of specific sports events, e.g. **Super Bowl (Game)** [to be added as needed]
Sports facilities (May subdiv. geog.) **796.06**
SA types of sports facilities [to be added as needed]
NT **Golf courses**
    Playgrounds
    Stadiums
    Swimming pools
RT **Recreation**
    Sports
Sports fans
USE **Sports spectators**
Sports—Fiction   808.83
Use for collections of sports stories.
UF Sports stories
SA types of sports with the subdivision *Fiction*, e.g. **Baseball—Fiction** [to be added as needed]
Sports for the handicapped (May subdiv. geog.) **796.01**
BT **Handicapped**
NT **Special Olympics**
    Wheelchair sports
Sports for women (May subdiv. geog.) **796**
UF Women—Sports
SA types of sports for women, e.g., **Basketball for women** [to be added as needed]
BT **Sports**

NT **Basketball for women**
Sports—Graphic novels   741.5
BT **Graphic novels**
Sports handicapping
USE **Sports betting**
Sports in radio
USE **Radio broadcasting of sports**
Sports in television
USE **Television broadcasting of sports**
Sports—Lists   796
Sports mascots
USE **Mascots**
Sports—Medical aspects
USE **Sports medicine**
Sports medicine (May subdiv. geog.) **613.7; 617.1**
UF Athletic medicine
    Physical education—Medical aspects
    Sports—Medical aspects
BT **Medical care**
    Medicine
Sports records (May subdiv. geog.)   **796**
Use for materials on top performances or achievements.
UF Records, Sports
BT **Sports**
RT **Sports—Statistics**
    World records
Sports scandals
USE **Sports—Corrupt practices**
Sports spectators (May subdiv. geog.) **306.4; 796**
UF Sports—Audiences
    Sports fans
BT **Audiences**
Sports—Statistics   796
SA types of sports with the subdivision *Statistics* [to be added as needed]
BT **Statistics**
RT **Sports records**
Sports stories
USE **Sports—Fiction**
Sports teams (May subdiv. geog.) **796.06**
SA types of sports teams, e.g. **Baseball teams**, and names of individual teams, e.g. **New York Knicks (Basketball**

Sports teams—*Continued*

team) [to be added as needed]
- BT **Sports**
- NT **Baseball teams**
  Basketball teams

Sports tournaments (May subdiv. geog.)
796
- UF Tournaments
- SA types of sports with the subdivision *Tournaments*, e.g. **Tennis—Tournaments**; names of sports tournaments, e.g. **Super Bowl** [to be added as needed]
- BT **Contests**
  Sports
- NT **Super Bowl (Game)**
  Tennis—Tournaments

Sports violence
- USE **Violence in sports**

Sportsmanship (May subdiv. geog.)   175
- UF Bad sportsmanship
- BT **Human behavior**
  Sports

Spot welding
- USE **Electric welding**

Spouses
- USE **Husbands**
  Wives

Spraying and dusting (May subdiv. geog.)
632
- UF Dusting and spraying
- BT **Agricultural pests**
  Fruit—Diseases and pests
- NT **Aeronautics in agriculture**
- RT **Fungicides**
  Herbicides
  Insecticides

Spreadsheet software   005.54
- UF Electronic spreadsheets
- BT **Computer software**

Spring   508.2; 578.43
- BT **Seasons**

Spun glass
- USE **Glass fibers**

Spy films   791.43
Use for individual works, collections, or materials about spy films.
- UF Espionage films
  Suspense films
- BT **Motion pictures**
- RT **Mystery films**

Spy novels
- USE **Spy stories**

Spy radio programs   791.44
Use for individual works, collections, or materials about spy radio programs.
- UF Suspense programs
- BT **Radio programs**

Spy stories   808.3; 808.83
Use for individual works, collections, or materials about spy stories.
- UF Espionage stories
  Spy novels
- BT **Adventure fiction**
- RT **Mystery fiction**
  Romantic suspense novels

Spy television programs   791.45
Use for individual works, collection, or materials about spy television programs.
- UF Espionage television programs
  Suspense programs
- BT **Television programs**
- RT **Mystery television programs**

Spying
- USE **Espionage**
  Spies

Square   516
- BT **Geometry**
  Shape

Square dancing (May subdiv. geog.)
793.3
- BT **Folk dancing**

Square root   513.2
- BT **Arithmetic**

Squirrels   599.36
- BT **Mammals**
- NT **Chipmunks**

Sri Lanka   954.93
May be subdivided like United States except for History.
- UF Ceylon

SST (Supersonic transport)
- USE **Supersonic transport planes**

St. Bartholomew's Day, Massacre of, 1572
- USE **Saint Bartholomew's Day, Massacre of, 1572**

St. Francis, Order of
- USE **Franciscans**

St. Valentine's Day
- USE **Valentine's Day**

Stabilization in industry
- USE **Business cycles**

Stadia
- USE **Stadiums**

Stadiums (May subdiv. geog.)   **796.06**
- UF   Ballparks
-       Stadia
- BT   **Sports facilities**

Staff
- USE   types of institutions, types of public officials, and names of individual public officials with the subdivision *Staff,* e.g. **Presidents—United States—Staff** [to be added as needed]

Stage
- USE   **Acting**
-       **Drama**
-       **Theater**

Stage history
- USE   names of dramatists with the subdivision *Stage history,* e.g. **Shakespeare, William, 1564-1616—Stage history** [to be added as needed]

Stage lighting   **792.02**
- UF   Television—Stage lighting
-       Theaters—Stage lighting
- BT   **Lighting**

Stage scenery
- USE   **Theaters—Stage setting and scenery**

Stage setting
- USE   **Theaters—Stage setting and scenery**

Stagecoaches
- USE   **Carriages and carts**

Stained glass
- USE   **Glass painting and staining**

Stalking (May subdiv. geog.)   **364.1**
- UF   Antistalking laws
-       Stalking—Law and legislation
- BT   **Offenses against the person**

Stalking—Law and legislation
- USE   **Stalking**

Stamina, Physical
- USE   **Physical fitness**

Stammering
- USE   **Speech disorders**

Stamp collecting (May subdiv. geog.)   **769.56**

Use for materials on the collecting, buying, and selling of postage stamps.
- UF   Philately
-       Postage stamp collecting

      Postage stamps—Collectors and collecting

      Stamps—Collectors and collecting
- BT   **Collectors and collecting**
- RT   **Postage stamps**

Stamps—Collectors and collecting
- USE   **Stamp collecting**

Stamps, Postage
- USE   **Postage stamps**

Standard book numbers
- USE   **Publishers' standard book numbers**

Standard of living
- USE   **Cost and standard of living**

Standard of value
- USE   **Money**

Standard time
- USE   **Time**

Standards
- USE   subjects, types of school and institutions, and types of industries with the subdivision *Standards,* e.g. **Environmental protection—Standards;** which may be further subdivided geographically [to be added as needed]

Standards of output
- USE   **Production standards**

Star Wars (Ballistic missile defense system)
- USE   **Strategic Defense Initiative**

Star Wars films   **791.43**

Use for individual works, collections, or materials about Star Wars films.
- BT   **Motion pictures**
-       **Science fiction films**

Star Wars weapons
- USE   **Space weapons**

Stars   **523.8**
- SA   names of constellations and of individual stars, e.g. **Sirius** [to be added as needed]
- NT   **Black holes (Astronomy)**
-       **Galaxies**
-       **Sirius**
-       **Solar system**
-       **Supernovas**
- RT   **Astronomy**
-       **Constellations**

Stars—Atlases   **523.8022**

Stars—Atlases—_Continued_
UF   Astronomy—Atlases
        Atlases, Astronomical
BT   **Atlases**
Starting a business
USE   **New business enterprises**
Starvation (May subdiv. geog.)   **363.8**
NT   **Famines**
RT   **Fasting**
      Hunger
      Malnutrition
State aid to education
USE   **Government aid to education**
State aid to libraries
USE   **Government aid to libraries**
State and agriculture
USE   **Agriculture—Government policy**
State and environment
USE   **Environmental policy**
State and railroads
USE   **Railroads—Government policy**
State and the arts
USE   **Federal aid to the arts**
State birds   **598**
BT   **Birds**
      State emblems
State constitutions
USE   **Constitutions**
        Constitutions—United States
State emblems (May subdiv. geog.)
      929.9
UF   Emblems, State
      State symbols
SA   types of state emblems and state
      symbols, e.g. **State birds**;
      State flowers [to be added as
      needed]
BT   **Signs and symbols**
NT   **State birds**
      State flowers
RT   **National emblems**
State encouragement of science, literature,
    and art
USE   **Cultural policy**
State encouragement of the arts
USE   **Arts—Government policy**
        Federal aid to the arts
State-federal relations
USE   **Federal-state relations**
State flowers   **582.13**

BT   **Flowers**
      State emblems
State governments   **352.13**
Use for general materials on state govern-
ment not limited to a single state.
UF   United States—State govern-
      ments
SA   names of states with the subdi-
      vision _Politics and govern-_
      ment, e.g. **Ohio—Politics and**
      government [to be added as
      needed]
BT   **Political science**
NT   **Federal-state relations**
      Governors
      State-local relations
RT   **Federal government**
State, Heads of
USE   **Heads of state**
State libraries (May subdiv. geog.)
      027.5
Use for materials on government libraries,
maintained by state funds, that preserve state
records and publications.
BT   **Government libraries**
State-local relations (May subdiv. geog.)
      320.4; 320.8; 352.13
UF   City-state relations
      Local-state relations
BT   **Local government**
      Municipal government
      State governments
State-local tax relations
USE   **Intergovernmental tax relations**
State medicine (May subdiv. geog.)
      362.1; 368.4; 614
Use for general materials on the relations of
the state to medicine, public health, medical
legislation, examinations of physicians by
state boards, etc.
UF   Medicine, State
      National health service
      Socialized medicine
BT   **Medicine**
NT   **Medicaid**
      Medicare
      Public health
RT   **National health insurance**
State ministries
USE   **Executive departments**
State of the Union messages
USE   **Presidents—United States—**
        Messages

State ownership
  USE **Government ownership**
State ownership of railroads
  USE **Railroads—Government policy**
State planning
  USE **Economic policy**
       Regional planning
       Social policy
State police (May subdiv. geog.) **363.2**
  UF Police, State
  BT **Police**
State regulation of industry
  USE **Industrial policy**
State rights
  USE **States' rights**
State songs 782.42
  BT **Songs**
State symbols
  USE **State emblems**
State, The 320.1
  UF Commonwealth, The
  NT **Church and state**
      Public interest
      Welfare state
  RT **Political science**
States, New
  USE **New states**
States' rights 321.02; 342
  UF State rights [*Former heading*]
  BT **Political science**
Statesmen (May subdiv. geog.) **920**
  NT **Diplomats**
      Heads of state
      Legislators
      Politicians
Statesmen—United States 973
  NT **Founding Fathers of the Unit-**
      ed States
Statics 531
  BT **Mechanics**
      Physics
  NT **Hydrostatics**
      Strains and stresses
  RT **Dynamics**
Statistical diagrams
  USE **Statistics—Graphic methods**
Statistical inference
  USE **Probabilities**
Statistics 001.4; 310
  Use for materials on the theory and meth-
  ods of statistics.

  SA subjects and names of countries,
      cities, etc., with the subdivi-
      sion *Statistics* [to be added as
      needed]
  BT **Economics**
  NT **Agriculture—Statistics**
      Average
      Census
      Chicago (Ill.)—Statistics
      Education—Statistics
      Gross national product
      Libraries—Statistics
      Ohio—Statistics
      Probabilities
      Railroads—Statistics
      Sampling (Statistics)
      Sports—Statistics
      United States—Statistics
      Vital statistics
Statistics—Graphic methods 001.4
  UF Statistical diagrams
  BT **Graphic methods**
Statues
  USE **Monuments**
       Sculpture
Status, Social
  USE **Social status**
Statutes
  USE **Law**
Stealing
  USE **Theft**
Steam 536; 621.1
  BT **Heat**
      Power (Mechanics)
      Water
  RT **Steam engineering**
Steam engineering (May subdiv. geog.)
      621.1
  BT **Engineering**
  NT **Steam engines**
      Steam navigation
      Steam power plants
  RT **Mechanical engineering**
      Steam
Steam engines 621.1
  BT **Engines**
      Steam engineering
  NT **Condensers (Steam)**
      Marine engines
      Steam turbines
Steam heating (May subdiv. geog.) **697**

Steam heating—*Continued*
  BT Heating
Steam locomotives (May subdiv. geog.)
    625.26
  BT Locomotives
Steam navigation (May subdiv. geog.)
    387; 623.89
  BT Navigation
      Steam engineering
      Transportation
  NT Marine engineering
      Steam turbines
  RT Steamboats
Steam power plants (May subdiv. geog.)
    621.1
  BT Electric power plants
      Steam engineering
Steam turbines (May subdiv. geog.)
    621.1
  BT Steam engines
      Steam navigation
      Turbines
Steamboats (May subdiv. geog.) 387.2;
    623.82
  UF Steamships
  BT Boats and boating
      Naval architecture
      Ocean travel
      Shipbuilding
      Ships
  RT Steam navigation
Steamships
  USE Steamboats
Steel 669; 672
  BT Iron
      Metalwork
  NT Structural steel
Steel construction (May subdiv. geog.)
    693
  UF Building, Iron and steel
      Iron and steel building
  BT Building
      Structural engineering
  RT Structural steel
Steel engraving
  USE Engraving
Steel industry (May subdiv. geog.)
    338.4; 672
  UF Steel industry and trade
  BT Industries
  RT Iron industry

Steel industry and trade
  USE Steel industry
Steel industry—Labor productivity (May
    subdiv. geog.) 338.4
  BT Labor productivity
Steel industry—Quality control (May
    subdiv. geog.) 338.4; 672
  BT Quality control
Steel industry—Technological innovations
    338.4
  BT Technological innovations
Steel, Structural
  USE Structural steel
Steeples
  USE Spires
Steers
  USE Beef cattle
Stegosaurus 567.915
  BT Dinosaurs
Stem cell research (May subdiv. geog.)
    616.007
  BT Medical technology
      Medicine—Research
Stencil work (May subdiv. geog.) 686.2;
    745.7
  BT Decoration and ornament
      Painting
  NT Silk screen printing
Stenography
  USE Shorthand
Step dancing (May subdiv. geog.)
    793.31
  BT Dance
Step-parents
  USE Stepparents
Stepchildren 306.874
  BT Children
      Parent-child relationship
Stepfamilies 306.874
  UF Stepfamily
  BT Family
Stepfamily
  USE Stepfamilies
Stepfathers 306.874
  BT Fathers
      Stepparents
Stepmothers 306.874
  BT Mothers
      Stepparents
Stepparents 306.874
  UF Step-parents

Stepparents—*Continued*
- BT **Parents**
- NT **Stepfathers**
  Stepmothers

Stereo photography
- USE **Three dimensional photography**

Stereophonic sound systems
- USE **Sound—Recording and reproducing**

Stereophotography
- USE **Three dimensional photography**

Stereopticon
- USE **Projectors**

Stereoscopic photography
- USE **Three dimensional photography**

Stereotype (Social psychology) (May subdiv. geog.)   **303.3**
- UF Mental stereotype
  Stereotyped behavior
- BT **Attitude (Psychology)**
  Social psychology
  Thought and thinking

Stereotyped behavior
- USE **Stereotype (Social psychology)**

Sterility in animals
- USE **Infertility**

Sterility in humans
- USE **Infertility**

Sterilization (Birth control) (May subdiv. geog.)   **363.9; 613.9**
- BT **Birth control**
- NT **Vasectomy**

Steroids   572; 612
- UF Anabolic steroids
- BT **Biochemistry**
  Drugs
- RT **Athletes—Drug use**
  Hormones

Stewardesses, Airline
- USE **Flight attendants**

Stewards, Airline
- USE **Flight attendants**

Still-life painting   758
- BT **Painting**

Stills
- USE **Distillation**

Stimulants   613.8; 615

- SA types of stimulants, e.g. **Amphetamines**; and names of individual stimulants [to be added as needed]
- BT **Drugs**
  Psychotropic drugs
- NT **Amphetamines**
  Hallucinogens

Stock averages
- USE **Stock price indexes**

Stock brokerage firms
- USE **Stockbrokers**

Stock brokers
- USE **Stockbrokers**

Stock car racing (May subdiv. geog.)   **796.72**
- BT **Automobile racing**

Stock control
- USE **Inventory control**

Stock exchange
- USE **Stock exchanges**

Stock exchange crashes
- USE **Financial crises**

Stock exchanges (May subdiv. geog.)   **332.64**
- UF Securities exchange
  Stock exchange
  Stock market
- BT **Finance**
  Markets
- NT **Bonds**
  Insider trading
  Securities
  Wall Street (New York, N.Y.)
- RT **Investments**
  Speculation
  Stocks

Stock fraud
- USE **Securities fraud**

Stock indexes
- USE **Stock price indexes**

Stock judging
- USE **Livestock judging**

Stock market
- USE **Stock exchanges**

Stock market fraud
- USE **Securities fraud**

Stock market panics
- USE **Financial crises**

Stock price indexes (May subdiv. geog.)   **332.63**

Stock price indexes—*Continued*
UF   Stock averages
        Stock indexes
BT   **Prices**
Stock raising
USE   **Livestock industry**
Stock yards
USE   **Stockyards**
Stockbrokers (May subdiv. geog.)
      332.62
UF   Brokers (Stocks)
        Investment brokers
        Security traders
        Stock brokerage firms
        Stock brokers
BT   **Brokers**
Stockings
USE   **Hosiery**
Stocks (May subdiv. geog.)   **332.63**
UF   Dividends
        Shares of stock
BT   **Commerce**
      Securities
RT   **Bonds**
      Corporations
      Investments
      Stock exchanges
Stocks—Insider trading
USE   **Insider trading**
Stockyards (May subdiv. geog.)   **338.4**
UF   Stock yards
BT   **Meat industry**
Stoics   **188**
BT   **Ancient philosophy**
      Ethics
Stomach   **612.3**
BT   **Anatomy**
RT   **Digestion**
Stomach exercises
USE   **Abdominal exercises**
Stone (May subdiv. geog.)   **553.5; 693**

    Use for materials on stone as a building
material. General materials on naturally occur-
ring solid minerals are entered under **Rocks**.

SA   types of stone, e.g. **Marble** [to
        be added as needed]
BT   **Building materials**
      Economic geology
NT   **Granite**
      Marble
      Masonry
      Stonecutting

RT   **Petrology**
      Quarries and quarrying
      Rocks
Stone Age (May subdiv. geog.)   **930.1**
UF   Eolithic period
        Neolithic period
        Paleolithic period
BT   **Civilization**
RT   **Stone implements**
Stone-cutting
USE   **Stonecutting**
Stone implements (May subdiv. geog.)
      930.1
UF   Flint implements
BT   **Implements, utensils, etc.**
RT   **Stone Age**
Stone quarries
USE   **Quarries and quarrying**
Stonecutting (May subdiv. geog.)   **693**
UF   Stone-cutting
BT   **Masonry**
      Stone
Stonehenge (England)   **936.2**
BT   **Great Britain—Antiquities**
Stoneware
USE   **Pottery**
Storage
USE   types of commodities, foods,
        materials, industrial products,
        etc., with the subdivision
        Storage, e.g. **Grain—Storage**
        [to be added as needed]
Storage batteries   **621.31**
UF   Batteries, Electric
BT   **Electric apparatus and appli-
      ances**
RT   **Electric batteries**
Storage devices, Computer
USE   **Computer storage devices**
Storage in the home   **648**
UF   Home storage
BT   **Home economics**
Store buildings
USE   **Commercial buildings**
Stores (May subdiv. geog.)   **381**
UF   Retail stores
        Shops
SA   types of stores, e.g. **Drugstores**
        [to be added as needed]
BT   **Commercial buildings**
      Retail trade

Stores—*Continued*

NT   **Chain stores**

      Department stores

      Discount stores

      Drugstores

      General stores

      Supermarkets

      Thrift shops

RT   **Shopping centers and malls**

Stories

USE   **Anecdotes**

      Bible stories

      Fairy tales

      Fiction

      Legends

      Romances

      Short stories

      Stories in rhyme

      Stories without words

      Storytelling

      and national literatures and literary or musical forms with the subdivision *Stories, plots, etc.,* e.g. **Ballet—Stories, plots, etc.; Opera—Stories, plots, etc.;** etc. [to be added as needed]

Stories for children

USE   **Children's stories**

Stories in rhyme   **808.1; 808.81**

Use as a form heading for narrative poems for very young children. Narrative poetry and materials about narrative poetry for older children and for adults are entered under **Narrative poetry**.

UF   Stories

BT   **Narrative poetry**

      Rhyme

Stories, plots, etc.   **808**

Use for materials that analyze plots or discuss the technique of constructing plots. Collections of plots of a specific literary or musical form are entered under that form with the subdivision *Stories, plots, etc.* General collections of literary plots are entered under **Stories, plots, etc.—Collections**.

UF   Dramatic plots

      Fictional plots

      Plots (Drama, fiction, etc.)

      Scenarios

SA   national literatures and literary or musical forms with the subdivision *Stories, plots, etc.,* e.g. **Ballet—Stories, plots,**

etc.; **Opera—Stories, plots, etc.** [to be added as needed]

BT   **Literature**

Stories, plots, etc.—Collections   **802**

Use for collections of literary plots. Materials that analyze plots or discuss the technique of constructing plots are entered under **Stories, plots, etc.**

UF   Literature—Stories, plots, etc.

SA   national literatures and specific genres of literature with the subdivision *Stories, plots, etc.* [to be added as needed]

Stories without words

Use as a form heading for stories for children told only through a sequence of pictures.

UF   Nonword stories

      Picture books for children, Wordless

      Stories

      Wordless stories

BT   **Picture books for children**

Storms (May subdiv. geog.)   **551.55**

SA   types of storms [to be added as needed]

BT   **Meteorology**

      Natural disasters

      Weather

NT   **Blizzards**

      Cyclones

      Dust storms

      Hurricanes

      Thunderstorms

      Tornadoes

      Typhoons

RT   **Rain**

      Snow

      Winds

Storytelling (May subdiv. geog.)   **027.62; 372.67**

UF   Stories

BT   **Children's literature**

RT   **Folklore**

      Short story

Storytelling—Collections   **808.85**

Use for collections of stories compiled primarily for oral presentation.

UF   Collected works

      Collections of literature

Stoves (May subdiv. geog.)   **697**

BT   **Heating**

      Space heaters

Strain (Psychology)
USE **Stress (Psychology)**
Strains and stresses   531; 620.1; 624.1
UF Stresses
BT **Mechanics**
Statics
**Structural analysis (Engineer-
ing)**
RT **Strength of materials**
Strangers and children
USE **Children and strangers**
Strategic aspects
USE areas of the world with the sub-
division *Strategic aspects*, e.g.
**Middle East—Strategic as-
pects** [to be added as needed]
Strategic Defense Initiative   358.1
UF SDI (Ballistic missile defense
system)
Star Wars (Ballistic missile de-
fense system)
BT **Military policy—United States**
Space warfare
United States—Defenses
RT **Space weapons**
Strategic management
USE **Strategic planning**
Strategic materials
USE **Materials**
Strategic planning (May subdiv. geog.)
352.3; 658.4
UF Strategic management
BT **Planning**
Strategy   355.4
UF Military strategy
Naval strategy
SA countries and areas of the world
with the subdivision *Strategic
aspects*, e.g. **Middle East—
Strategic aspects** [to be add-
ed as needed]
BT **Military art and science**
Naval art and science
NT **Middle East—Strategic aspects**
Tactics
Stratigraphic geology (May subdiv. geog.)
551.7
May be subdivided by geological period.
UF Geology, Stratigraphic
BT **Geology**
NT **Fossils**

Stratosphere   551.5
BT **Upper atmosphere**
NT **Ozone layer**
Stratospheric ozone
USE **Ozone layer**
Straw votes
USE **Public opinion polls**
Strawberries   634
BT **Berries**
Stream animals (May subdiv. geog.)
578.76
UF River animals
Stream fauna
BT **Animals**
Rivers
Stream ecology (May subdiv. geog.)
577.6
BT **Ecology**
Freshwater ecology
Stream fauna
USE **Stream animals**
Streamlining
USE **Aerodynamics**
Street cars
USE **Street railroads**
Street cleaning (May subdiv. geog.)
363.72; 628.4
BT **Cleaning**
Municipal engineering
Public health
Roads
Sanitary engineering
Streets
RT **Refuse and refuse disposal**
Street gangs
USE **Gangs**
Street life (May subdiv. geog.)   **307.76**
UF Urban street life
BT **City and town life**
Street lighting
USE **Streets—Lighting**
Street literature
USE **Pamphlets**
Street people
USE **Homeless persons**
Street railroads (May subdiv. geog.)
388.4; 625.6
UF Interurban railroads
Street cars
Trams
Trolley cars

Street railroads—*Continued*
    BT   **Local transit**
          Railroads
    RT   **Cable railroads**
          Electric railroads
Street traffic
    USE **City traffic**
           Traffic engineering
Streets (May subdiv. geog.)   **388.4; 625.7**
    UF   Alleys
          Avenues
          Boulevards
          Thoroughfares
    BT   **Cities and towns**
          Civil engineering
          Transportation
    NT   **City traffic**
          Street cleaning
    RT   **Pavements**
          Roads
Streets—Chicago (Ill.)   **977.3**
    UF   Chicago (Ill.)—Streets
Streets—Lighting (May subdiv. geog.)
    628.9
    UF   Cities and towns—Lighting
          Street lighting
    BT   **Lighting**
Streets—New York (N.Y.)   **974.7**
    UF   New York (N.Y.)—Streets
    RT   **Wall Street (New York, N.Y.)**
Strength of materials   **620.1**
    UF   Resistance of materials
    SA   types of materials with the sub-
          division *Testing*, e.g. **Con-**
          crete—Testing [to be added
          as needed]
    BT   **Mechanics**
          Structural analysis (Engineer-
          ing)
    NT   **Concrete—Testing**
    RT   **Building materials**
          Strains and stresses
          Testing
Strength training
    USE **Weight lifting**
Stress management   **155.9**
    BT   **Health**
Stress (Physiology)   **612; 616.8**
    UF   Physiological stress
          Tension (Physiology)
    BT   **Adaptation (Biology)**
          Physiology

    NT   **Job stress**
Stress (Psychology)   **155.9; 616.89**
    UF   Emotional stress
          Mental stress
          Psychological stress
          Strain (Psychology)
          Tension (Psychology)
    BT   **Mental health**
          Psychology
    NT   **Anxiety**
          Burn out (Psychology)
          Job stress
          Post-traumatic stress disorder
Stresses
    USE **Strains and stresses**
Stretching exercises   **613.7**
    BT   **Exercise**
Strikes (May subdiv. geog.)   **331.892**
    This heading may also be subdivided by in-
    dustry or occupation and then geographically,
    e.g. **Strikes—Automobile industry—United**
    States.
    UF   Lockouts
          Picketing
          Sit-down strikes
          Strikes and lockouts
          Work stoppages
    BT   **Industrial relations**
          Labor disputes
    NT   **Sabotage**
    RT   **Collective bargaining**
          Industrial arbitration
          Injunctions
          Labor unions
Strikes and lockouts
    USE **Strikes**
Strikes—Automobile industry—United
    States   **331.892**
Strikes—United States   **331.892**
String figures (May subdiv. geog.)
    793.9
    UF   Cat's cradle
          String games
    BT   **Amusements**
String games
    USE **String figures**
String models
    USE **String theory**
String orchestra music   **784.7**
    BT   **Orchestral music**
String theory   **530.14; 539.7**
    UF   String models

String theory—*Continued*

    BT   **Particles (Nuclear physics)**

Stringed instruments (May subdiv. geog.)
      787

    UF   Bowed instruments

    SA   types of stringed instruments [to
          be added as needed]

    BT   **Musical instruments**

    NT   **Guitars**
          Violins
          Violoncellos

Stroke   **616.8**

    UF   Apoplexy
          Cerebrovascular disease

    BT   **Brain—Diseases**

Structural analysis (Engineering)   **624**

    UF   Architectural engineering
          Theory of structures

    BT   **Structural engineering**

    NT   **Strains and stresses**
          Strength of materials

Structural drafting

    USE   **Mechanical drawing**

Structural engineering (May subdiv.
    geog.)   **624.1**

    UF   Architectural engineering

    BT   **Civil engineering**
          Engineering

    NT   **Building**
          Foundations
          Hydraulic structures
          Soil mechanics
          Steel construction
          **Structural analysis (Engineer-
          ing)**

Structural failures (May subdiv. geog.)
      624.1

    UF   Collapse of structures
          Failures, Structural

    SA   types of structural failures, e.g.
          Building failures [to be add-
          ed as needed]

    BT   **Reliability (Engineering)**

    NT   **Building failures**

Structural materials

    USE   **Building materials**

Structural psychology

    USE   **Gestalt psychology**

Structural steel   **691**

    UF   Steel, Structural

    BT   **Building materials**
          Civil engineering

        Steel

    RT   **Steel construction**

Structural zoology

    USE   **Animals—Anatomy**

Structure in biology

    USE   **Morphology**

Structures

    USE   **Buildings**

Structures, Garden

    USE   **Garden structures**

Stubbornness   **155.2; 179**

    UF   Obstinacy

    BT   **Personality**

Stucco   **693**

    BT   **Building materials**
          Decoration and ornament
          Plaster and plastering

Student achievement

    USE   **Academic achievement**

Student activities (May subdiv. geog.)
      371.8

    UF   Extracurricular activities

    BT   **Students**

    NT   **After school programs**
          Cheerleading
          College and school drama
          College and school journalism
          College sports
          Field trips
          School assembly programs
          School sports

Student aid (May subdiv. geog.)   **371.2;
      378.3**

    UF   Financial aid to students
          Student financial aid

    BT   **College costs**
          Loans

    NT   **Scholarships**
          Student loan funds

Student busing

    USE   **Busing (School integration)**

Student cheating

    USE   **Cheating (Education)**

Student clubs

    USE   **Students—Societies**

Student councils

    USE   **Student government**

Student dishonesty

    USE   **Cheating (Education)**

Student dropouts

    USE   **Dropouts**

Student evaluation of teachers   371.14
    UF   Student rating of teachers
           Teachers, Student rating of
    BT   **Teacher-student relationship**
Student exchange programs (May subdiv. geog.)   **370.116**
    UF   Exchange of students
           Exchange programs, Student
           International exchange of students
    BT   **Exchange of persons programs**
           International education
Student financial aid
    USE **Student aid**
Student government (May subdiv. geog.)   **371.5**
    UF   Self-government (in education)
           Student councils
           Student self-government
    BT   **School discipline**
           Schools—Administration
Student guidance
    USE **Educational counseling**
Student life
    USE **College students**
           Students
Student loan funds (May subdiv. geog.)   **371.2; 378.3**
    UF   Loan funds, Student
    BT   **College costs**
           Student aid
Student movement
    USE **Youth movement**
Student promotion
    USE **Promotion (School)**
Student protests, demonstrations, etc.
    USE **Students—Political activity**
           Youth movement
Student rating of teachers
    USE **Student evaluation of teachers**
Student revolt
    USE **Students—Political activity**
           Youth movement
Student self-government
    USE **Student government**
Student societies
    USE **Students—Societies**
Student songs
    USE **Students' songs**
Student-teacher relationships
    USE **Teacher-student relationship**

Student teaching   370.71
    UF   Practice teaching
           Teachers—Practice teaching
    BT   **Teachers—Training**
           Teaching
Student to student counseling
    USE **Peer counseling**
Student violence
    USE **School violence**
Student yearbooks
    USE **School yearbooks**
Students (May subdiv. geog.)   **371.8**
    UF   School life
           Student life
    SA   types of students, e.g. **College students** [to be added as needed]
    NT   **At risk students**
           College students
           Dropouts
           Foreign students
           High school students
           School children
           Student activities
           Underachievers
Students and libraries
    USE **Students—Library services**
Students—Counseling
    USE **Educational counseling**
Students, Foreign
    USE **Foreign students**
Students—Grading and marking
    USE **Grading and marking (Education)**
Students—Library services (May subdiv. geog.)   **027.62**
    UF   Libraries and students
           Students and libraries
    BT   **Libraries and schools**
           Library services
           School libraries
Students' military training camps
    USE **Military training camps**
Students—Political activity (May subdiv. geog.)   **324; 371.8**
    UF   Politics and students
           Student protests, demonstrations, etc.
           Student revolt
    BT   **Political participation**
           Youth movement

Students—Societies (May subdiv. geog.)
    371.8
    UF   School clubs
          Student clubs
          Student societies
    BT   **Societies**
    NT   **Fraternities and sororities**
Students' songs   **782.42**
    UF   College songs
          Student songs
    BT   **Songs**
    NT   **United States Military Academy—Songs**
Students—United States   **371.80973**
Students with problems
    USE   **At risk students**
Studio pottery
    USE   **Art pottery**
Study abroad
    USE   **Foreign study**
Study and teaching
    USE   **Education**
          and subjects with the subdivision *Study and teaching,* e.g.
          Science—Study and teaching [to be added as needed]
Study, Foreign
    USE   **Foreign study**
Study guides
    USE   named examinations with the subdivision *Study guides,* e.g. **Graduate Record Examination—Study guides;** and subjects, educational levels, and names of educational institutions with the subdivisions *Examinations—Study guides,* e.g. **English language—Examinations—Study guides** [to be added as needed]
Study guides for examinations
    USE   **Examinations—Study guides**
Study methods
    USE   **Study skills**
Study overseas
    USE   **Foreign study**
Study skills   **371.3028**
    UF   How to study
          Study methods

    SA   subjects with the subdivision *Study and teaching,* e.g. **Art—Study and teaching** [to be added as needed]
    BT   **Education**
          Life skills
          Teaching
    NT   **Examinations—Study guides**
          Homework
          Independent study
          Self-instruction
Study-work plan
    USE   **Cooperative education**
Stuffed bears (Toys)
    USE   **Teddy bears**
Stuffed toy making
    USE   **Soft toy making**
Stunt flying (May subdiv. geog.)   **797.5**
    UF   Aerobatics
    BT   **Airplanes—Piloting**
Stunt men
    USE   **Stunt performers**
Stunt performers (May subdiv. geog.)
    791.4
    UF   Stunt men
    BT   **Actors**
Stuttering
    USE   **Speech disorders**
Style in dress
    USE   **Clothing and dress**
          Costume
          Fashion
Style, Literary
    USE   **Literary style**
Style manikins
    USE   **Fashion models**
Style manuals
    USE   **Printing—Style manuals**
Sub-Saharan Africa   **960**
    UF   Africa, Sub-Saharan
          Black Africa
    BT   **Africa**
Subconsciousness   **127; 154.2**
    BT   **Parapsychology**
          Psychology
    NT   **Hallucinations and illusions**
          Mental suggestion
          Sleep
    RT   **Consciousness**
          Dreams
          Hypnotism

Subconsciousness—*Continued*
> **Mental healing**
> **Mind and body**
> **Psychoanalysis**
> **Spiritual healing**

Subculture
> USE **Counter culture**

Subgravity state
> USE **Weightlessness**

Subject catalogs   016; 017
> UF   Catalogs, Subject
> BT   **Library catalogs**
> NT   **Subject headings**

Subject dictionaries
> USE **Encyclopedias and dictionaries**

Subject headings   025.4
> UF   Thesauri
> BT   **Cataloging**
>   **Indexes**
>   **Subject catalogs**

Submarine boats
> USE **Submarines**

Submarine cables   384.1; 384.6
> UF   Cables, Submarine
>   Ocean cables
> BT   **Telecommunication**
>   **Telegraph**

Submarine diving
> USE **Deep diving**

Submarine engineering
> USE **Ocean engineering**

Submarine exploration
> USE **Underwater exploration**

Submarine geology (May subdiv. geog.)   551.46
> UF   Marine geology
>   Underwater geology
> BT   **Geology**
>   **Oceanography**
> NT   **Ocean bottom**
> RT   **Plate tectonics**

Submarine medicine   616.9
> UF   Underwater medicine
>   Underwater physiology
> BT   **Medicine**

Submarine oil well drilling
> USE **Offshore oil well drilling**

Submarine photography
> USE **Underwater photography**

Submarine research stations
> USE **Undersea research stations**

Submarine vehicles
> USE **Submersibles**

Submarine warfare (May subdiv. geog.)   359.9
> UF   Naval warfare
>   Warfare, Submarine
> BT   **Naval art and science**
>   **War**
> NT   **Submarines**
>   **Torpedoes**
>   **World War, 1939-1945—Naval operations—Submarine**

Submarines (May subdiv. geog.)   359.9; 623.82

> Use for materials on submarines only. Materials on other underwater craft are entered under **Submersibles**.

> UF   Submarine boats
> BT   **Ships**
>   **Submarine warfare**
>   **Submersibles**
>   **Warships**
> NT   **Nuclear submarines**

Submersibles   623.82
> UF   Submarine vehicles
>   Undersea vehicles
> SA   types of submersibles [to be added as needed]
> BT   **Vehicles**
> NT   **Bathyscaphe**
>   **Submarines**

Subscription television (May subdiv. geog.)   384.55
> UF   Pay-per-view television
>   Pay television
>   Television, Subscription
> BT   **Television broadcasting**

Subsidies (May subdiv. geog.)   338.9

> Use for materials on financial or other aid given, without equivalent recompense, by governments or governmental agencies to private enterprises.

> UF   Corporate welfare
>   Government subsidies
>   Grants
>   Subventions
> SA   types of subsidies, e.g. **Agricultural subsidies**; and federal aid to specific endeavors, e.g. **Federal aid to minority business enterprises** [to be added as needed]

Subsidies—*Continued*
- BT **Domestic economic assistance**
  Economic policy
- NT **Agricultural subsidies**
  Federal aid to minority business enterprises
  Transfer payments

Subsistence economy (May subdiv. geog.)
330.9
- BT **Cost and standard of living**
- NT **Barter**
- RT **Poverty**

Substance abuse (May subdiv. geog.)
362.29
- UF Abuse of substances
  Chemical dependency
- BT **Social problems**
- NT **Drug abuse**
  Medication abuse
  Solvent abuse

Substantive due process
- USE **Due process of law**

Substitute products 338
- SA types of substitute products, e.g.
  Sugar substitutes [to be added as needed]
- BT **Commercial products**
- NT **Sugar substitutes**
- RT **Synthetic products**

Subterfuge
- USE **Deception**

Subterranean water
- USE **Groundwater**

Subtraction 513.2
- BT **Arithmetic**

Suburban areas
- USE **Suburbs**

Suburban life (May subdiv. geog.)
307.74
- BT **Suburbs**

Suburbs (May subdiv. geog.) 307.76
- UF Suburban areas
  Suburbs and environs
- SA names of suburban areas, e.g.
  Chicago Suburban Area (Ill.) [to be added as needed]
- BT **Cities and towns—Growth**
  City planning
  Metropolitan areas
- NT **Suburban life**

Suburbs and environs
- USE **Suburbs**

Subventions
- USE **Subsidies**

Subversive activities (May subdiv. geog.)
322.4; 327.12

Use for materials on any attempt to subvert, overthrow, or cause the destruction of any established or legally constituted government. Materials on the offense of acting to overthrow one's own government or to harm or kill its sovereign are entered under **Treason**.
- UF Fifth column
- BT **Insurgency**
- NT **Espionage**
  Political crimes and offenses
  Sabotage
  Spies
  Terrorism
  Treason
- RT **Internal security**

Subways (May subdiv. geog.) 388.4; 625.4
- UF Underground railroads
- BT **Local transit**
  Railroads

Success 158; 650.1
- UF Fortune
  Personal development
- BT **Business ethics**
  Wealth
- NT **Academic achievement**
  Leadership
  Life skills
- RT **Ability**
  Self-realization

Succession
- USE presidents, prime ministers, and other rulers with the subdivision *Succession,* e.g. **Presidents—United States—Succession** [to be added as needed]

Sudan 962.4

May be subdivided like United States except for History.
- NT **Nile River valley**

Sudden death in infants
- USE **Sudden infant death syndrome**

Sudden infant death syndrome 618.92
- UF Cot death
  Crib death
  Infant sudden death
  SIDS (Disease)
  Sudden death in infants

Sudden infant death syndrome—*Continued*
　　BT　**Infants—Death**
Sudoku　793.73
　　BT　**Puzzles**
Suffering　128; 152.1; 214
　　UF　Affliction
　　RT　**Joy and sorrow**
　　　　Pain
Suffrage (May subdiv. geog.)　324.6
　　UF　Franchise
　　　　Voting
　　SA　ethnic groups and classes of persons with the subdivision *Suffrage* [to be added as needed]
　　BT　**Citizenship**
　　　　Constitutional law
　　　　Democracy
　　　　Elections
　　　　Political science
　　NT　**African Americans—Suffrage**
　　　　Blacks—Suffrage
　　　　Naturalization
　　　　Voter registration
　　　　Women—Suffrage
　　RT　**Representative government and representation**
Suffragettes
　　USE　**Suffragists**
Suffragists (May subdiv. geog.)　324.6; 920
　　UF　Suffragettes
　　BT　**Reformers**
　　RT　**Feminism**
　　　　Women—Suffrage
Sufism (May subdiv. geog.)　297.4
　　BT　**Mysticism—Islam**
　　RT　**Dervishes**
Sugar　641.3; 664
　　SA　types of sugar [to be added as needed]
　　BT　**Food**
　　NT　**Maple sugar**
　　　　Syrups
Sugar substitutes　641.3; 664
　　UF　Artificial sweeteners
　　　　Nonnutritive sweeteners
　　BT　**Substitute products**
Suggestion, Mental
　　USE　**Mental suggestion**
Suggestive therapeutics　615.8
　　UF　Therapeutics, Suggestive

　　BT　**Therapeutics**
　　RT　**Hypnotism**
　　　　Mental healing
　　　　Mental suggestion
　　　　Psychotherapy
　　　　Spiritual healing
Suicidal behavior
　　USE　**Suicide—Psychological aspects**
Suicide (May subdiv. geog.)　179.7; 362.28
　　UF　Attempted suicide
　　　　Suicide attempts
　　SA　classes of persons and ethnic groups with the subdivision *Suicide*, e.g. **Teenagers—Suicide** [to be added as needed]
　　BT　**Medical jurisprudence**
　　　　Social problems
　　NT　**Teenagers—Suicide**
　　RT　**Homicide**
　　　　Right to die
Suicide attempts
　　USE　**Suicide**
Suicide bombers (May subdiv. geog.)　303.6
　　BT　**Terrorism**
Suicide—Psychological aspects　616.85
　　UF　Suicidal behavior
　　BT　**Human behavior**
Suing (Law)
　　USE　**Litigation**
Suite (Music)　784.18
　　Use for musical scores and for materials on the suite as a musical form.
　　UF　Partita
　　　　Suites
　　BT　**Musical form**
　　　　Orchestral music
Suites
　　USE　**Suite (Music)**
Suits (Law)
　　USE　**Litigation**
Suits of armor
　　USE　**Armor**
Sulfa drugs
　　USE　**Sulfonamides**
Sulfonamides　615
　　UF　Sulfa drugs
　　BT　**Drugs**
Sulfur
　　USE　**Sulphur**
Sulphur　546; 553.6; 661

Sulphur—*Continued*
  UF Sulfur
  BT **Chemical elements**
Summer 508.2; 578.43
  BT **Seasons**
Summer camps
  USE **Camps**
Summer cottages
  USE **Vacation homes**
Summer employment (May subdiv. geog.)
    331.1
  BT **Employment**
  RT **Teenagers—Employment**
      Youth—Employment
Summer homes
  USE **Vacation homes**
Summer resorts (May subdiv. geog.)
    790
  BT **Resorts**
Summer schools (May subdiv. geog.)
    371.2
  UF Vacation schools
  BT **Public schools**
      Schools
  NT **Religious summer schools**
Summer theater (May subdiv. geog.)
    792.0224
  BT **Theater**
Sun 523.7
  UF Solar physics
  BT **Astronomy**
      Solar system
  NT **Solar energy**
      Sunspots
Sun-dials
  USE **Sundials**
Sun—Eclipses
  USE **Solar eclipses**
Sun—Folklore (May subdiv. geog.)
    398.26
Sun powered batteries
  USE **Solar batteries**
Sun—Radiation
  USE **Solar radiation**
Sun—Religious aspects (May subdiv.
    geog.) **299.9**
Sun-spots
  USE **Sunspots**
Sun worship (May subdiv. geog.) **202**
  BT **Religion**
Sunday schools (May subdiv. geog.) **268**
  UF Bible classes

  BT **Church work**
      Religious education
  NT **Bible—Study and teaching**
Sundials (May subdiv. geog.) **681.1**
  UF Horology
      Sun-dials
  BT **Clocks and watches**
      **Garden ornaments and furni-
      ture**
      Time
Sunken cities
  USE **Extinct cities**
Sunken treasure
  USE **Buried treasure**
Sunnis (May subdiv. geog.) **297.82**
  UF Sunnites
  BT **Islamic sects**
Sunnites
  USE **Sunnis**
Sunspots 523.7
  UF Sun-spots
  BT **Meteorology**
      Solar radiation
      Sun
Super Bowl (Game) 796.332
  BT **Football**
      Sports tournaments
Super markets
  USE **Supermarkets**
Supercomputers (May subdiv. geog.)
    004.1
    Use for materials on extraordinarily power-
  ful computers.
  BT **Computers**
Superconducting materials
  USE **Superconductors**
Superconductive devices
  USE **Superconductors**
Superconductivity
  USE **Superconductors**
Superconductors 537.6; 621.3
  UF Superconducting materials
      Superconductive devices
      Superconductivity
  BT **Electric conductors**
      Electronics
**Superhero comic books, strips, etc.
    741.5**
    Use for individual works, collections, or
  materials about superhero comics.
  BT **Comic books, strips, etc.**

Superhero films   791.43

Use for individual works, collections, or materials about superhero films.

SA   films with particular superheroes, e.g. **Superman films** [to be added as needed]

BT   **Adventure films**

NT   **Superman films**

Superhero graphic novels   741.5

Use for individual works, collections, or materials about superhero graphic novels.

SA   names of individual superheroes, e.g. **Superman (Fictional character)** [to be added as needed]

BT   **Graphic novels**

Superhero radio programs   791.44

Use for individual works, collections, or materials about superhero radio programs.

BT   **Adventure radio programs**

Superhero television programs   791.45

Use for individual works, collections, or materials about superhero television programs.

BT   **Adventure television programs**

Superheroes   808.3

SA   names of superheroes, e.g. **Superman (Fictional character)** or groups of superheroes, e.g. **Justice League (Fictional characters)** [to be added as needed]

NT   **Justice League (Fictional characters)**

Shadowpact (Fictional characters)

Spider-Man (Fictional character)

Superman (Fictional character)

Wonder Woman (Fictional character)

Superhighways

USE   **Express highways**

Superintendents of schools

USE   **School superintendents and principals**

Superman (Fictional character)   741.5

BT   **Fictional characters**

Superheroes

Superman films   791.43

Use for individual works, collections, or materials about Superman films.

BT   **Superhero films**

Supermarket shopping

USE   **Grocery shopping**

Supermarkets (May subdiv. geog.)   **658.8**

UF   Super markets

BT   **Grocery trade**

Retail trade

Stores

Supernatural   133; 202; 398.2

BT   **Religion**

NT   **Exorcism**

Occultism

Parapsychology

Prophecies

Revelation

Spirits

Spiritualism

RT   **Miracles**

Supernatural graphic novels   741.5

Use for individual works, collections, or materials about supernatural graphic novels.

BT   **Graphic novels**

Supernovae

USE   **Supernovas**

Supernovas   523.8

UF   Supernovae

BT   **Stars**

Supersonic aerodynamics   629.132

UF   Aerodynamics, Supersonic

High speed aerodynamics

Speed, Supersonic

BT   **Aerodynamics**

High speed aeronautics

NT   **Aerothermodynamics**

Supersonic airliners

USE   **Supersonic transport planes**

Supersonic transport planes   629.133

UF   SST (Supersonic transport)

Supersonic airliners

BT   **Jet planes**

Supersonic waves

USE   **Ultrasonic waves**

Supersonics

USE   **Ultrasonics**

Superstition (May subdiv. geog.)   **001.9; 398**

UF   Folk beliefs

Traditions

BT   **Folklore**

NT   **Charms**

RT   **Errors**

Supervision of employees
USE **Personnel management**
Supervision of schools
USE **School supervision**
Supervisors (May subdiv. geog.) **331.7;
658.3**
UF Foremen
Managers
BT **Factory management**
Personnel management
Supplementary employment (May subdiv.
geog.) **331.1**
UF Employment, Supplementary
Moonlighting
Second job
Secondary employment
BT **Labor**
Part-time employment
Supply and demand 332; 338.5; 658.8
UF Law of supply and demand
SA occupational groups and types of
employees with the subdivi-
sion *Supply and demand*, e.g.
**Unskilled labor—Supply and
demand**; **Chemical indus-
try—Employees—Supply and
demand** [to be added as
needed]
BT **Economics**
NT **Chemical industry—Employ-
ees—Supply and demand**
**Unskilled labor—Supply and
demand**
RT **Competition**
Exchange
Prices
Support groups
USE **Self-help groups**
Support of children
USE **Child support**
Supreme Court—United States
USE **United States. Supreme Court**
Surf
USE **Ocean waves**
Surf riding
USE **Surfing**
Surface of the earth
USE **Earth—Surface**
Surfboarding
USE **Surfing**
Surfing (May subdiv. geog.) **797.3**

UF Body surfing
Surf riding
Surfboarding
BT **Water sports**
Surfing—Songs 782.42
UF Surfing—Songs and music
BT **Songs**
Surfing—Songs and music
USE **Surfing—Songs**
Surgeons (May subdiv. geog.) **617.092;
920**
BT **Physicians**
Surgery (May subdiv. geog.) **617**
UF Operations, Surgical
SA classes of persons, names of dis-
eases, and names of organs
and regions of the body with
the subdivision *Surgery* [to be
added as needed]
BT **Medicine**
NT **Artificial organs**
Cancer—Surgery
Children—Surgery
Cryosurgery
Heart—Surgery
Orthopedics
Plastic surgery
**Transplantation of organs, tis-
sues, etc.**
Vivisection
RT **Anesthetics**
Antiseptics
Surgery, Plastic
USE **Plastic surgery**
Surgical transplantation
USE **Transplantation of organs, tis-
sues, etc.**
Surnames
USE **Personal names**
Surplus government property (May
subdiv. geog.) **352.5**
UF Excess government property
Government property, Surplus
BT **Property**
Surrealism (May subdiv. geog.) **709.04;
759.06; 809**
Use for the movement or style of surrealism
in literature or in the visual arts.
BT **Arts**
**Surrogate mothers 176; 306.874;
346.01**
BT **Mothers**

Surveillance, Electronic
  USE **Electronic surveillance**
Surveying (May subdiv. geog.)   **526.9**
  UF Land surveying
      Land surveys
  SA names of countries, cities, etc.,
      with the subdivision *Surveys*,
      for works containing the re-
      sults of land surveys in those
      places, e.g. **United States—
      Surveys** [to be added as
      needed]
  BT **Civil engineering**
      Geography
      Measurement
  NT **Mine surveying**
      Topographical drawing
  RT **Geodesy**
Surveys   **001.4**
  UF Government surveys
  SA types of surveys, e.g. **Market
      surveys**; and names of coun-
      tries, cities, etc., with the sub-
      division *Surveys*, for works
      containing the results of land
      surveys in those places, e.g.
      United States—Surveys [to
      be added as needed]
  BT **Research**
  NT **Educational surveys**
      Library surveys
      Market surveys
      Social surveys
**Survival after airplane accidents, ship-
  wrecks, etc.** (May subdiv. geog.)
  613.6
  UF Castaways
  RT **Aircraft accidents**
      Rescue work
      Shipwrecks
      Wilderness survival
Survival of the fittest
  USE **Natural selection**
Survival skills   **613.6**
  Use for materials on skills needed to sur-
  vive in a hazardous environment, usually
  stressing self-reliance and economic self-
  sufficiency.
  UF Emergency survival
      Human survival skills

  SA types of survival, e.g. **Wilder-
      ness survival** [to be added as
      needed]
  BT **Civil defense**
      **Environmental influence on
      humans**
      Human ecology
      Life skills
  NT **Wilderness survival**
  RT **Self-reliance**
Survivalism (May subdiv. geog.)   **320.5;
      613.6**
  UF Survivalist movements
  BT **Social movements**
Survivalist movements
  USE **Survivalism**
Suspended sentence
  USE **Probation**
Suspense films
  USE **Adventure films**
      Mystery films
      Spy films
Suspense novels
  USE **Adventure fiction**
      Mystery fiction
      Romantic suspense novels
Suspense programs
  USE **Mystery radio programs**
      Mystery television programs
      Spy radio programs
      Spy television programs
Sustainable agriculture (May subdiv.
  geog.)   **338.1**
  UF Sustainable farming
  BT **Agriculture**
Sustainable architecture (May subdiv.
  geog.)   **720**
  UF Environmentally friendly archi-
      tecture
  BT **Architecture**
Sustainable development (May subdiv.
  geog.)   **333.71; 338.9**
  Use for materials on economic development
  that satisfies the needs of the present generation without depleting natural resources for
  the future or having adverse environmental effects. General materials on the environmental
  impact of economic development are entered
  under **Economic development—Environmental aspects**.
  UF Economic sustainability
      Sustainable economic develop-
      ment

Sustainable development—*Continued*

    BT   **Economic development**

Sustainable economic development

    USE   **Sustainable development**

Sustainable farming

    USE   **Sustainable agriculture**

SUVs (Vehicles)

    USE   **Sport utility vehicles**

Swamp animals (May subdiv. geog.)
    578.768

    UF   Swamp fauna

    BT   **Animals**

Swamp ecology (May subdiv. geog.)
    577.68

    BT   **Ecology**

          Wetland ecology

Swamp fauna

    USE   **Swamp animals**

Swamps (May subdiv. geog.)   **551.41**

    BT   **Wetlands**

Swashbucklers

    USE   **Adventure fiction**

          Adventure films

Sweden   **948.5**

    May be subdivided like United States except for History.

Swedish language   **439.7**

    May be subdivided like **English language**.

    BT   **Language and languages**

          Scandinavian languages

Swedish literature   **839.7**

    May use same subdivisions and names of literary forms as for **English literature**.

    BT   **Literature**

          Scandinavian literature

Sweets

    USE   **Candy**

          Confectionery

Swell

    USE   **Ocean waves**

Swimming (May subdiv. geog.)   **797.2**

    BT   **Water sports**

    NT   **Diving**

          Marathon swimming

          Synchronized swimming

Swimming pools (May subdiv. geog.)
    690; 725; 797.2

    UF   Pools

    BT   **Sports facilities**

Swindlers and swindling (May subdiv.
    geog.)   **364.16**

    UF   Con artists

          Con game

          Confidence game

    BT   **Crime**

          Criminals

    NT   **Counterfeits and counterfeiting**

          Credit card fraud

          Quacks and quackery

    RT   **Fraud**

          Impostors and imposture

Swine

    USE   **Pigs**

Switchboard hotlines

    USE   **Hotlines (Telephone counseling)**

Switzerland   **949.4**

    May be subdivided like United States except for History.

Swords (May subdiv. geog.)   **623.441;
    739.722**

    BT   **Weapons**

Symbiosis   **577.8**

    UF   Mutualism (Biology)

    BT   **Biology**

          Ecology

    RT   **Parasites**

          Plant ecology

Symbolic logic   **511.3**

    UF   Logic, Symbolic and mathematical

          Mathematical logic

    BT   **Logic**

          Mathematics

    NT   **Boolean algebra**

    RT   **Set theory**

Symbolic numbers

    USE   **Numerology**

          Symbolism of numbers

Symbolism (May subdiv. geog.)   **203;
    302.2; 700**

    SA   symbolism of particular religions, e.g. **Christian symbolism**; and symbolism in particular subjects, e.g. **Symbolism in literature** [to be added as needed]

    BT   **Art**

          Mythology

    NT   **Christian symbolism**

          Figures of speech

          Heraldry

          Symbolism in literature

          Symbolism of numbers

Symbolism—*Continued*
    RT **Signs and symbols**
Symbolism in literature   809
    UF Signs and symbols in literature
    BT **Literature**
         Symbolism
    RT **Allegory**
Symbolism of numbers (May subdiv.
    geog.)   **203; 246; 809**

Use for general materials on the symbolism of numbers, as in philosophy, religion, or literature. Materials on the occult significance of numbers are entered under **Numerology**.

    UF Number symbolism
         Sacred numbers
         Symbolic numbers
    BT **Symbolism**
    NT **Numerology**
    RT **Cabala**
         Numbers
Symbols
    USE **Signs and symbols**
Symbols, Mathematical
    USE **Mathematical notation**
Sympathy   177
    UF Pity
    BT **Conduct of life**
         Emotions
Symphonic poems   784.2
    BT **Orchestral music**
Symphonies
    USE **Symphony**
Symphony   784.18; 784.2

Use for musical scores and for materials on the symphony as a musical form.

    UF Symphonies
    BT **Musical form**
         Orchestral music
Symptoms
    USE **Diagnosis**
Synagogues (May subdiv. geog.)   **296.6;
    726**
    BT **Buildings**
         Religious institutions
         Temples
    RT **Judaism**
Synchronized swimming   797.2
    UF Water ballet
    BT **Swimming**
Synods
    USE **Councils and synods**

Synonyms and antonyms
    USE names of languages with the subdivision *Synonyms and antonyms*, e.g. **English language—Synonyms and antonyms** [to be added as needed]
Synthesizer music
    USE **Electronic music**
Synthesizer (Musical instrument)
    USE **Synthesizers (Musical instruments)**
Synthesizers (Musical instruments)
    786.7
    UF Synthesizer (Musical instrument)
    BT **Electronic musical instruments**
Synthetic chemistry
    USE **Organic compounds—Synthesis**
Synthetic detergents
    USE **Detergents**
Synthetic drugs of abuse
    USE **Designer drugs**
Synthetic fabrics   677
    SA types of synthetic fabrics [to be added as needed]
    BT **Fabrics**
         Synthetic products
    NT **Nylon**
         Rayon
Synthetic foods
    USE **Artificial foods**
Synthetic fuels   662
    UF Artificial fuels
         Nonfossil fuels
    BT **Fuel**
         Synthetic products
Synthetic products (May subdiv. geog.)
    670
    SA types of synthetic products and names of specific products [to be added as needed]
    BT **Industrial chemistry**
    NT **Artificial foods**
         Plastics
         Synthetic fabrics
         Synthetic fuels
         Synthetic rubber
    RT **Organic compounds—Synthesis**
         Substitute products
Synthetic rubber   678

Synthetic rubber—*Continued*
  UF Rubber, Artificial
      Rubber, Synthetic
  BT **Plastics**
      Synthetic products
Syphilis (May subdiv. geog.) **616.95**
  BT **Sexually transmitted diseases**
Syria 956.91
    May be subdivided like United States ex-
    cept for History.
Syrups 641.3
  BT **Sugar**
System analysis 003; 004.2; 658.4
  UF Flow charts
      Flowcharting
      Linear system theory
      Network theory
      Systems analysis
  BT **Cybernetics**
      Mathematical models
      System theory
  NT **Fuzzy systems**
      System design
      Systems engineering
System design 003; 004.2; 621.39
  UF Systems design
  BT **System analysis**
  NT **Database design**
System engineering
  USE **Systems engineering**
System theory 003
  UF Systems, Theory of
      Theory of systems
  BT **Science**
  NT **Chaos (Science)**
      Cybernetics
      Operations research
      Social systems
      System analysis
      Systems engineering
Systematic botany
  USE **Botany—Classification**
Systematic theology
  USE **Doctrinal theology**
Systems analysis
  USE **System analysis**
Systems, Database management
  USE **Database management**
Systems design
  USE **System design**
Systems engineering 620
  UF System engineering

  BT **Automation**
      Cybernetics
      Engineering
      Industrial design
      System analysis
      System theory
  NT **Bionics**
      Reliability (Engineering)
  RT **Operations research**
Systems, Fuzzy
  USE **Fuzzy systems**
Systems reliability
  USE **Reliability (Engineering)**
Systems, Theory of
  USE **System theory**
T groups
  USE **Group relations training**
T-shirts 391; 687
  UF Tee shirts
  BT **Clothing and dress**
Table decoration
  USE **Table setting and decoration**
Table etiquette (May subdiv. geog.)
        395.5
  BT **Eating customs**
      Etiquette
  RT **Dining**
Table setting and decoration 642
  UF Table decoration
  BT **Decoration and ornament**
  NT **Flower arrangement**
      Napkin folding
      Tableware
Table talk
  USE **Conversation**
Table tennis (May subdiv. geog.) **796.34**
  UF Ping-pong
  BT **Ball games**
Tables (May subdiv. geog.) **645; 749**
  BT **Furniture**
Tables (Systematic lists)
  USE subjects with the subdivision *Ta-*
        bles, e.g. **Meteorology—Ta-**
        bles; Trigonometry—Tables
        etc. [to be added as needed]
Tableware (May subdiv. geog.) **642**
  UF Dishes
  BT **Table setting and decoration**
  NT **Glassware**
      Porcelain
      Pottery

Tableware—*Continued*
    Silverware
Taboo (May subdiv. geog.)   **390**
    BT   **Manners and customs**
Tactics   **355.4**
    UF   Military tactics
    BT   **Military art and science**
         Strategy
    NT   **Biological warfare**
         Drill and minor tactics
         Guerrilla warfare
         Military maneuvers
         War games
Tadpoles
    USE **Frogs**
Tae kwon do (May subdiv. geog.)   **796.815**
    BT   **Karate**
         Martial arts
         Self-defense
Tai chi (May subdiv. geog.)   **613.7; 796.815**
    UF   Tai ji quan
         Taichi
    BT   **Exercise**
         Martial arts
Tai ji quan
    USE **Tai chi**
Taichi
    USE **Tai chi**
Tailoring (May subdiv. geog.)   **646.4; 687**
    UF   Garment making
    BT   **Clothing and dress**
         Clothing industry
    RT   **Dressmaking**
Taiwan   **951.24**

Use for materials dealing with the island of Taiwan, regardless of time period, or with the post-1948 Republic of China. Materials dealing with mainland China, regardless of time period, or with the People's Republic of China and comprehensive materials on China including Taiwan are entered under **China**. May be subdivided like **United States** except for *History*.

    UF   China (Republic)
         Formosa
         Nationalist China
         Republic of China, 1949-
Tajikistan   **958.6**
Takeovers, Corporate
    USE **Corporate mergers and acquisitions**

Talebearing
    USE **Tattling**
Talent
    USE **Ability**
         Genius
Talents
    USE **Ability**
Tales
    USE **Fables**
         Fairy tales
         Folklore
         Legends
Talismans
    USE **Charms**
Talk shows (May subdiv. geog.)   **791.44; 791.45**

Use for individual works, collections, or materials about talk shows.

    BT   **Interviewing**
         Radio programs
         Television programs
Talking
    USE **Conversation**
Talking books
    USE **Audiobooks**
Tall tales   **398.2; 808.83**

Use for individual works, collections, or materials about tall tales.

    BT   **Folklore**
         Legends
         Wit and humor
Talmud   **296.1**
    BT   **Hebrew literature**
         Jewish literature
         Judaism
Tank tactics
    USE **Tank warfare**
Tank warfare (May subdiv. geog.)   **358**
    UF   Antitank warfare
         Tank tactics
    SA   names of individual wars with the subdivision *Tank warfare* e.g. **World War, 1939-1945—Tank warfare** [to be added as needed]
    BT   **War**
    NT   **World War, 1939-1945—Tank warfare**
    RT   **Military tanks**
Tanks (Military science)
    USE **Military tanks**
Tanning   **675**

Tanning—*Continued*
>BT **Industrial chemistry**
>RT **Hides and skins**
>**Leather**

Tantrums, Temper
>USE **Temper tantrums**

Tao 181
>UF Dao
>Way (Chinese philosophy)
>BT **Philosophy**
>RT **Taoism**

Taoism (May subdiv. geog.) 299.5
>BT **Religions**
>RT **Tao**

Tap dancing 792.7
>BT **Dance**

Tap water
>USE **Drinking water**

Tape recorders
>USE **Magnetic recorders and re-cording**

Tape recordings, Audio
>USE **Sound recordings**

Tape recordings, Video
>USE **Videotapes**

Tapestry (May subdiv. geog.) 677; 746.3
>BT **Decoration and ornament**
>**Decorative arts**
>**Interior design**
>**Needlework**

Tardiness
>USE **Punctuality**

Tariff (May subdiv. geog.) 336.2; 382
>UF Custom duties
>Customs (Tariff)
>Duties
>Revenue
>BT **Commercial policy**
>**Economic policy**
>**Public finance**
>NT **Smuggling**
>RT **Free trade**
>**Protectionism**

Tariff—United States 382; 336.2
>UF United States—Tariff

Tarot (May subdiv. geog.) 133.3; 795.4
>Use for materials on the cards and the game.
>UF Tarot (Game)
>BT **Card games**
>**Fortune telling**
>**Playing cards**

Tarot (Game)
>USE **Tarot**

Tartans 391; 929.6
>UF Highland costume
>Scottish tartans
>BT **Clans—Scotland**

Taste 152.1
>BT **Senses and sensation**

Taste (Aesthetics)
>USE **Aesthetics**

Tatting 746.43
>BT **Lace and lace making**

Tattling 177; 302.3
>UF Talebearing
>BT **Gossip**

Tattooing (May subdiv. geog.) 391.6
>UF Tattoos (Body markings)
>BT **Manners and customs**
>**Personal appearance**

Tattoos (Body markings)
>USE **Tattooing**

Taverns
>USE **Bars**

Tax assessment (May subdiv. geog.) 336.2
>Use for general materials on the valuation of property for determining tax liability. Materials on the assessment of property for tax purposes in a particular place are entered under **Taxation** followed by the appropriate geographical subdivision.
>UF Appraisal
>Assessment
>Assessment, Tax
>Property tax—Assessment
>Real property tax—Assessment
>BT **Taxation**
>**Valuation**
>NT **Tax exemption**

Tax avoidance
>USE **Tax evasion**
>**Tax planning**

Tax credits (May subdiv. geog.) 336.2
>BT **Income tax**

Tax evasion (May subdiv. geog.) 345
>UF Tax avoidance
>Tax fraud
>BT **Criminal law**
>**White collar crimes**

Tax exempt status
>USE **Tax exemption**

Tax exemption (May subdiv. geog.)
    336.2
    UF Exemption from taxation
        Tax exempt status
    BT **Tax assessment**
Tax fraud
    USE **Tax evasion**
Tax planning (May subdiv. geog.)
    343.04
    UF Tax avoidance
        Tax saving
    BT **Personal finance**
        Planning
        Taxation
    RT **Estate planning**
Tax relations, Intergovernmental
    USE **Intergovernmental tax relations**
Tax saving
    USE **Tax planning**
Tax sharing
    USE **Intergovernmental tax relations**
        Revenue sharing
Taxation (May subdiv. geog.)   **336.2**
    UF Direct taxation
        Duties
        Revenue
        Taxes
    SA subjects with the subdivision
        Taxation, e.g. **Real estate in-**
        vestment—Taxation [to be
        added as needed]
    BT **Political science**
        Public finance
    NT **Income tax**
        Inheritance and transfer tax
        Intergovernmental tax relations
        Internal revenue
        Real estate investment—Taxa-
        tion
        Sales tax
        Tax assessment
        Tax planning
        Tithes
Taxation of legacies
    USE **Inheritance and transfer tax**
Taxation—United States   **336.200973**
    UF United States—Taxation
Taxes
    USE **Taxation**
Taxicabs (May subdiv. geog.)   **338.34232**

    UF Cabs
        Taxis (Vehicles)
    BT **Local transit**
        Vehicles
Taxidermy (May subdiv. geog.)   **590.75**
    UF Preservation of specimens
        Specimens, Preservation of
    SA types of specimens with the sub-
        division *Collection and pres-*
        ervation, e.g. **Birds—Collec-**
        tion and preservation [to be
        added as needed]
    RT **Zoological specimens—Collec-**
        tion and preservation
Taxis (Vehicles)
    USE **Taxicabs**
Taxonomy (Botany)
    USE **Botany—Classification**
Tea (May subdiv. geog.)   **633.7; 641.8**
    Use for materials on the plant or on the
    beverage. Materials on the meal are entered
    under **Afternoon teas.**
    BT **Beverages**
    RT **Afternoon teas**
        Tea industry
Tea houses
    USE **Tearooms**
Tea industry (May subdiv. geog.)   **338.1;**
    338.4
    UF Tea trade
    BT **Beverage industry**
    NT **Tearooms**
    RT **Tea**
Tea rooms
    USE **Tearooms**
Tea shops
    USE **Tearooms**
Tea trade
    USE **Tea industry**
Teach yourself courses
    USE **Self-instruction**
Teacher exchange programs (May subdiv.
    geog.)   **370.116**
    UF Exchange of teachers
    BT **Exchange of persons programs**
        International education
Teacher-parent conferences
    USE **Parent-teacher conferences**
Teacher-parent relationship
    USE **Parent-teacher relationship**
Teacher-student relationship   **371.1;**
    378.1

Teacher-student relationship—*Continued*
- UF   Student-teacher relationships
-       Teacher-student relationships
- BT   **Child-adult relationship**
-       **Interpersonal relations**
-       **Teaching**
- NT   **Student evaluation of teachers**

Teacher-student relationships
- USE **Teacher-student relationship**

Teacher training
- USE **Teachers—Training**

Teachers (May subdiv. geog.)   **371.1; 920**

Use for materials on educators engaged in classroom or other instruction. Materials on people engaged professionally in the field of education in general are entered under **Educators**.
- UF   College teachers
-       Faculty (Education)
-       Professors
- BT   **Educators**
- NT   **Colleges and universities—Faculty**
- RT   **Teaching**

Teachers and parents
- USE **Parent-teacher relationship**

Teachers colleges (May subdiv. geog.)   **378.1**

Use for general and historical materials about teachers colleges. Materials on their educational functions are entered under **Teachers—Training**.
- UF   Normal schools
-       Training colleges for teachers
- SA   names of teachers colleges [to be added as needed]
- BT   **Colleges and universities**
-       **Education—Study and teaching**
- RT   **Teachers—Training**

Teachers' institutes
- USE **Teachers' workshops**

Teachers—Pensions (May subdiv. geog.)   **331.25**
- SA   types of educational institutions and names of individual educational insititutions with the subdivisions *Faculty—Pensions*, e.g. **Colleges and universities—Faculty—Pensions** [to be added as needed]

Teachers—Practice teaching
- USE **Student teaching**

Teachers' reports
- USE **School reports**

Teachers, Student rating of
- USE **Student evaluation of teachers**

Teachers—Training (May subdiv. geog.)   **370.71**

Use for materials on the history and methods of training teachers, including the educational functions of teachers colleges. Materials on the study of education as a discipline are entered under **Education—Study and teaching**. Materials on the art of teaching and methods of teaching are entered under **Teaching**.
- UF   Teacher training
-       Teachers—Training of
- BT   **Education—Study and teaching**
-       **Teaching**
- NT   **Student teaching**
-       **Teachers' workshops**
- RT   **Teachers colleges**

Teachers—Training of
- USE **Teachers—Training**

Teachers' workshops (May subdiv. geog.)   **371.1**
- UF   Teachers' institutes
-       Workshops, Teachers'
- BT   **Teachers—Training**

Teaching (May subdiv. geog.)   **371.102**

Use for materials on the art of teaching and methods of teaching. Materials on the study of education as a discipline are entered under **Education—Study and teaching**. Materials on the history and methods of training teachers, including the educational functions of teachers colleges, are entered under **Teachers—Training**.
- UF   Instruction
-       Pedagogy
-       School teaching
- SA   subjects with the subdivision *Study and teaching*, e.g. **Science—Study and teaching** [to be added as needed]
- BT   **Education**
- NT   **Classroom management**
-       **Cooperative learning**
-       **Educational psychology**
-       **Examinations**
-       **Lectures and lecturing**
-       **Montessori method of education**
-       **Project method in teaching**
-       **School discipline**
-       **School supervision**

Teaching—*Continued*
  Student teaching
  Study skills
  Teacher-student relationship
  Teachers—Training
  Teaching teams
  Tutors and tutoring
 RT **Teachers**
Teaching—Aids and devices   371.33
 UF Educational media
  Instructional materials
  Teaching materials
 NT **Audiovisual materials**
  Bulletin boards
  Flannel boards
  Manipulatives
  Motion pictures in education
  Programmed instruction
  Radio in education
  Teaching machines
  Television in education
 RT **Educational technology**
Teaching—Data processing
 USE **Computer-assisted instruction**
Teaching—Experimental methods
 USE **Education—Experimental methods**
Teaching, Freedom of
 USE **Academic freedom**
Teaching machines   371.33
 BT **Programmed instruction**
  Teaching—Aids and devices
Teaching materials
 USE **Teaching—Aids and devices**
Teaching teams   371.14
 UF Team teaching
 BT **Teaching**
Teachings of Jesus Christ
 USE **Jesus Christ—Teachings**
Teahouses
 USE **Tearooms**
Team problem solving
 USE **Group problem solving**
Team teaching
 USE **Teaching teams**
Team work in the workplace
 USE **Teams in the workplace**
Teams in the workplace (May subdiv. geog.) **658.4**
 UF Team work in the workplace
  Teamwork in the workplace
  Work groups

  Work teams
 BT **Social groups**
  Work environment
Teamwork in the workplace
 USE **Teams in the workplace**
Tearooms (May subdiv. geog.) **647.95**
  Use for materials on public establishments devoted primarily to serving tea.
 UF Tea houses
  Tea rooms
  Tea shops
  Teahouses
  Teashops
 BT **Restaurants**
  Tea industry
Teas
 USE **Afternoon teas**
Teashops
 USE **Tearooms**
Teasing   158.2; 302.3
 BT **Aggressiveness (Psychology)**
  Interpersonal relations
Technical assistance (May subdiv. geog.) **338.91; 361.6**
  Use for materials on foreign aid in the form of technical expertise. Materials on the transfer of innovations in technology from one country to another are entered under **Technology transfer**.
 UF Aid to developing areas
  Assistance to developing areas
  Foreign aid program
 SA technical assistance from particular countries, e.g. **American technical assistance** [to be added as needed]
 BT **Foreign aid**
  International economic relations
 NT **American technical assistance**
 RT **Community development**
  Technology transfer
Technical assistance, American
 USE **American technical assistance**
Technical chemistry
 USE **Industrial chemistry**
Technical education (May subdiv. geog.) **370.11; 373.246; 374**
 UF Industrial education
  Industrial schools
  Technical schools
  Trade schools

Technical education—*Continued*
- SA technical subjects with the sub-division *Study and teaching,* e.g. **Engineering—Study and teaching** [to be added as needed]
- BT **Education**
  Higher education
  Technology
- NT **Apprentices**
  Correspondence schools and courses
  Engineering—Study and teaching
  Evening and continuation schools
  Occupational retraining
  Occupational training
  School shops
- RT **Employees—Training**
  Industrial arts education
  Professional education
  Vocational education

Technical schools
- USE **Technical education**

Technical service
- USE **Customer services**

Technical services (Libraries)
- USE **Library technical processes**

Technical terms
- USE **Technology—Dictionaries**

Technical writing   808
- UF Scientific writing
- BT **Authorship**
  Technology—Language

Technique
- USE subjects and names of authors and artists with the subdivision *Technique,* e.g. **Fiction—Technique; Painting—Technique; Shakespeare, William, 1564-1616—Technique;** etc. [to be added as needed]

Technological change
- USE **Technological innovations**

Technological innovations (May subdiv. geog.) **338**

Use for materials on technological improvements in materials, production methods, processes, organization, or management. Works on original devices or processes are entered under **Inventions**.

- UF Innovations, Technological
  Technological change
- SA subjects with the subdivision *Technological innovations,* e.g. **Automobiles—Technological innovations; Steel industry—Technological innovations** [to be added as needed]
- BT **Inventions**
  Technology
- NT **Agricultural innovations**
  Automobiles—Technological innovations
  Steel industry—Technological innovations
- RT **Industrial research**

Technological literacy (May subdiv. geog.) **302.2**

Use for materials on a person's comprehension of technological innovation and the ability to use particular innovations appropriately.

- BT **Literacy**

Technological transfer
- USE **Technology transfer**

Technology (May subdiv. geog.)   **600**
- UF Applied science
  High tech
  High technology
- SA technology and other subjects, e.g. **Technology and civilization** [to be added as needed]
- NT **Distillation**
  Electronics
  Engineering
  Green technology
  Industrial chemistry
  Information technology
  Inventions
  Machinery
  Mills
  Nanotechnology
  Technical education
  Technological innovations
  Technology and civilization
  Technology transfer
- RT **Industrial arts**
  Material culture

Technology and civilization (May subdiv. geog.) **303.4**
- UF Civilization and technology
- BT **Civilization**
  Technology

Technology and civilization—*Continued*
  NT **Computers and civilization**
  RT **Industrial revolution**
Technology—Dictionaries 603
  UF Technical terms
  BT **Encyclopedias and dictionaries**
Technology in the workplace
  USE **Machinery in the workplace**
Technology—Language 601; 603
  NT **Technical writing**
Technology transfer (May subdiv. geog.)
    338.9

Use for materials on the transfer of innovations in technology from one country to another. Materials on foreign aid in the form of technical expertise are entered under **Technical assistance**. May be subdivided by the region or country receiving the technology. Where applicable, make an additional entry under this heading subdivided by the region or country transferring the technology.

  UF Technological transfer
       Transfer of technology
  BT **Inventions**
       Technology
  RT **International cooperation**
       International relations
       Technical assistance
Teddy bears (May subdiv. geog.) 790.1
  UF Stuffed bears (Toys)
  BT **Toys**
Tee shirts
  USE **T-shirts**
Teen age
  USE **Adolescence**
Teen suicide
  USE **Teenagers—Suicide**
Teenage behavior
  USE **Adolescent psychology**
       Etiquette for children and
         teenagers
       Teenagers—Conduct of life
Teenage consumers
  USE **Young consumers**
Teenage drinking
  USE **Teenagers—Alcohol use**
Teenage dropouts
  USE **Dropouts**
Teenage fathers (May subdiv. geog.)
    306.874; 362.7

Use for materials focusing on fathers who are teenagers. Materials on fathers who at the time of a child's birth were not married to the child's mother are entered under **Unmarried**

fathers. Materials focusing on fathers rearing children without a partner in the household are entered under **Single-parent families**.

  UF Adolescent fathers
       School-age fathers
  BT **Fathers**
       Teenage parents
Teenage gangs
  USE **Gangs**
Teenage literature
  USE **Young adult literature**
Teenage marriage (May subdiv. geog.)
    306.81
  BT **Marriage**
Teenage mothers (May subdiv. geog.)
    306.874; 362.7; 362.83

Use for materials focusing on mothers who are teenagers. Materials on mothers who at the time of giving birth were not married to the child's father are entered under **Unmarried mothers**. Materials focusing on mothers rearing children without a partner in the household are entered under **Single-parent families**.

  UF Adolescent mothers
       School-age mothers
  BT **Mothers**
       Teenage parents
  RT **Teenage pregnancy**
Teenage parents (May subdiv. geog.)
    306.874; 362.7
  BT **Parents**
       Teenagers
  NT **Teenage fathers**
       Teenage mothers
Teenage pregnancy (May subdiv. geog.)
    362.7; 618.2
  UF Adolescent pregnancy
  BT **Pregnancy**
  RT **Teenage mothers**
Teenage prostitution
  USE **Juvenile prostitution**
Teenage suicide
  USE **Teenagers—Suicide**
Teenagers (May subdiv. geog.) 305.235

Use for materials about teen youth. Materials on the time of life extending from thirteen to twenty-five years, as well as on people in that general age range, are entered under **Youth**. Materials limited to people in the general age range of eighteen through twenty-five years of age are entered under **Young men** or **Young women**. Materials on the process or state of growing up are entered under **Adolescence**.

  UF Adolescents
       Teens

Teenagers—*Continued*
  Young adults
  Young people
  Young persons
  BT **Age**
      Youth
  NT **Gay teenagers**
      Runaway teenagers
      Teenage parents
  RT **Boys**
      Girls
Teenagers—Alcohol use (May subdiv.
    geog.)   **362.292; 613.81; 616.86**
  UF Alcohol and teenagers
      Drinking and teenagers
      Teenage drinking
      Teenagers and alcohol
  NT **Drinking age**
Teenagers and alcohol
  USE **Teenagers—Alcohol use**
Teenagers and drugs
  USE **Teenagers—Drug use**
Teenagers and narcotics
  USE **Teenagers—Drug use**
Teenagers—Attitudes (May subdiv. geog.)
    155.5; 305.235
  BT **Attitude (Psychology)**
**Teenagers—Books and reading   011.62;
    028.5**

  Use for materials on the reading interests of
  teenagers and for lists of books for teenagers.
  Collections or materials about literature published for teenagers are entered under **Young
  adult literature**.

  UF Books and reading for teenagers
      Books and reading for young
        adults
      Reading interests of teenagers
      Reading interests of young
        adults
      Young adults—Books and read-
        ing
  BT **Books and reading**
Teenagers—Conduct of life   173
  UF Behavior of teenagers
      Teenage behavior
  BT **Conduct of life**
  NT **Etiquette for children and
      teenagers**
Teenagers—Development
  USE **Adolescence**
Teenagers—Drug use (May subdiv. geog.)
    362.29; 613.8; 616.86

  UF Drugs and teenagers
      Narcotics and teenagers
      Teenagers and drugs
      Teenagers and narcotics
  BT **Youth—Drug use**
  RT **Juvenile delinquency**
Teenagers—Employment (May subdiv.
    geog.)   **331.3**
  BT **Age and employment**
      Employment
      Youth—Employment
  RT **Summer employment**
Teenagers—Etiquette
  USE **Etiquette for children and
      teenagers**
Teenagers—Literature
  USE **Young adult literature**
Teenagers—Psychiatry
  USE **Adolescent psychiatry**
Teenagers—Psychology
  USE **Adolescent psychology**
Teenagers—Religious life (May subdiv.
    geog.)   **204; 248.4**
  BT **Religious life**
      Youth—Religious life
Teenagers—Suicide (May subdiv. geog.)
    362.28; 616.85
  UF Teen suicide
      Teenage suicide
  BT **Suicide**
Teenagers—United States   305.2350973
  UF American teenagers
  BT **Youth—United States**
Teenagers' writings   818.8
  UF Writings of teenagers
  BT **Literature**
Teens
  USE **Teenagers**
Teepees
  USE **Tepees**
Teeth   611; 612.3; 617.6
  BT **Head**
  RT **Dentistry**
Teeth—Diseases   617.6
  BT **Diseases**
Telecommunication (May subdiv. geog.)
    384; 621.382
  UF Mass communication
  SA subjects with the subdivision
      Communication systems, e.g.
      Astronautics—Communica-

Telecommunication—*Continued*

> **tion systems** [to be added as needed]

- BT **Communication**
- NT **Artificial satellites in telecommunication**
  - **Astronautics—Communication systems**
  - **Broadcasting**
  - **Computer networks**
  - **Data transmission systems**
  - **Electronic mail systems**
  - **Fax transmission**
  - **Intercommunication systems**
  - **Interstellar communication**
  - **Microwave communication systems**
  - **Radio**
  - **Submarine cables**
  - **Telecommuting**
  - **Telegraph**
  - **Telephone**
  - **Television**
  - **Wireless communication systems**

Telecommuting (May subdiv. geog.) **331.25; 658.3**

> Use for materials on employment at home with computers, word processors, etc., connected to a central work site, permitting employees to substitute telecommunications for transportation.

- UF Alternate work sites
  - Work at home
  - Working at home
- BT **Automation**
  - **Telecommunication**

Teleconferencing **384; 658.4**

- UF Conference calls (Teleconferencing)
  - Telephone—Conference calls
- BT **Telephone**

Telegraph (May subdiv. geog.) **384.1; 621.383**

- BT **Public utilities**
  - **Telecommunication**
- NT **Cipher and telegraph codes**
  - **Submarine cables**

Telegraph codes
- USE **Cipher and telegraph codes**

Telekinesis
- USE **Psychokinesis**

Telemarketing (May subdiv. geog.) **381; 658.8**

> Use for materials on the use of electronic media as a form of marketing that bypasses retail outlets in the advertising and selling of goods.

- UF Electronic marketing
- BT **Direct selling**
  - **Marketing**

Telepathy **133.8**

- UF Mental telepathy
  - Mind reading
- BT **Extrasensory perception**
- RT **Clairvoyance**

Telephone (May subdiv. geog.) **384.6; 621.385**

- BT **Public utilities**
  - **Telecommunication**
- NT **Cellular telephones**
  - **Long distance telephone service**
  - **Teleconferencing**
  - **Video telephone**

Telephone—Conference calls
- USE **Teleconferencing**

Telephone counseling
- USE **Hotlines (Telephone counseling)**

Telephone directories
- USE names of countries, cities, etc., corporate bodies, classes of persons, ethnic groups, and types of organizations and industries with the subdivision *Telephone directories,* e.g. **Chicago (Ill.)—Telephone directories** [to be added as needed]

Telephone—Long distance
- USE **Long distance telephone service**

Telephotography **778.3**

- BT **Photography**

Telescope
- USE **Telescopes**

Telescopes (May subdiv. geog.) **522; 681**

- UF Telescope
- BT **Astronomical instruments**
  - **Optical instruments**
- NT **Hubble Space Telescope**

Televangelists (May subdiv. geog.) **269.2092**

Televangelists—*Continued*

UF Television evangelists

BT **Clergy**

Television personalities

Television (May subdiv. geog.) **302.23; 384.55; 621.388**

Use for materials on the technology of television. Materials on what is seen on television are entered under **Television programs**.

UF TV

SA television and particular groups of people, e.g. **Television and children**; and television in various industries or fields of endeavor, e.g. **Television in education** [to be added as needed]

BT **Telecommunication**

NT **African Americans on television**

Closed caption television

Closed-circuit television

Color television

High definition television

Home video systems

Minorities on television

Television and children

Television and politics

Television and youth

Television broadcasting

Television in education

Video art

Video telephone

Violence on television

Women on television

Television actors

USE **Actors**

Television adaptations **791.45**

Use for individual works, collections, or materials about television adaptations of material from other media.

UF Adaptations

Literature—Film and video adaptations

Motion pictures—Television adaptations

SA names of authors, titles of anonymous literary works, types of literature, and types of musical compositions with the subdivision *Adaptations*, for individual works, collections,

or criticism and interpretation of literary, cinematic, video, or television adaptations, e.g., **Shakespeare, William, 1564-1616—Adaptations; Beowulf—Adaptations; Arthurian romances—Adaptations**; etc. [to be added as needed]

BT **Television plays**

Television programs

Television scripts

Television advertising (May subdiv. geog.) **659.14**

UF Commercials, Television

Television commercials

BT **Advertising**

Television broadcasting

Television and children (May subdiv. geog.) **305.23; 384.55; 791.45**

Use for materials on the effect of television on children.

UF Children and television

BT **Children**

Television

Television and infrared observation satellite

USE **TIROS satellites**

Television and politics (May subdiv. geog.) **324**

UF Politics and television

Television in politics

BT **Politics**

Television

NT **Equal time rule (Broadcasting)**

Fairness doctrine (Broadcasting)

Television and youth (May subdiv. geog.) **305.235; 384.55; 791.45**

UF Youth and television

BT **Television**

Youth

Television—Audiences

USE **Television viewers**

Television authorship (May subdiv. geog.) **808**

UF Television writing

BT **Authorship**

NT **Television plays—Technique**

Television broadcasting (May subdiv. geog.) **384.55**

UF Television industry

Television broadcasting—*Continued*
- SA   television broadcasting of particular kinds of programs, e.g. **Television broadcasting of sports** [to be added as needed]
- BT   **Broadcasting**
    Mass media
    Television
- NT   **African Americans in television broadcasting**
    Cable television
    Emmy Awards
    Minorities in television broadcasting
    Public television
    Subscription television
    Television advertising
    Television broadcasting of news
    Television broadcasting of sports
    Television—Production and direction
    Television programs
    Television scripts
    Television stations
    Women in television broadcasting

Television broadcasting of news (May subdiv. geog.)   **070.4**
- UF   Television coverage of news
    Television journalism
    Television news
- BT   **Broadcast journalism**
    Television broadcasting

Television broadcasting of sports (May subdiv. geog.)   **070.4**
- UF   Sports broadcasting
    Sports in television
    Television sports
- BT   **Broadcast journalism**
    Television broadcasting

Television broadcasting—Vocational guidance   384.55
- BT   **Vocational guidance**

Television cartoons
- USE   **Animated television programs**

Television—Censorship (May subdiv. geog.)   **384.55**
- BT   **Censorship**
- NT   **V-chips**

Television, Closed-circuit
- USE   **Closed-circuit television**

Television comedies
- USE   **Comedy television programs**

Television comedy programs
- USE   **Comedy television programs**

Television commercials
- USE   **Television advertising**

Television coverage of news
- USE   **Television broadcasting of news**

Television drama
- USE   **Television plays**

Television—Equipment and supplies   621.388
- NT   **Television—Receivers and reception**
    Videodisc players
- RT   **Television supplies industry**
    Video recording

Television equipment industry
- USE   **Television supplies industry**

Television evangelists
- USE   **Televangelists**

Television fans
- USE   **Television viewers**

Television films
- USE   **Television movies**

Television games
- USE   **Video games**

Television in education (May subdiv. geog.)   **371.33**
- UF   Education and television
    Educational television
- BT   **Audiovisual education**
    Teaching—Aids and devices
    Television

Television in politics
- USE   **Television and politics**

Television industry
- USE   **Television broadcasting**
    Television supplies industry

Television journalism
- USE   **Broadcast journalism**
    Television broadcasting of news

Television movies   791.45

Use for individual works, collections, or materials about television movies.
- UF   Made-for-TV movies
    Television films

Television movies—*Continued*
>BT **Motion pictures**
>**Television programs**

Television news
>USE **Television broadcasting of news**

Television novels
>USE **Radio and television novels**

Television personalities (May subdiv. geog.) **791.45**
>UF TV personalities
>BT **Celebrities**
>NT **Televangelists**

Television plays **808.2; 808.82**
>Use for individual works, collections, or materials about television plays.
>UF Scenarios
>Television drama
>BT **Drama**
>**Television programs**
>NT **Soap operas**
>**Television adaptations**
>RT **Television scripts**

Television plays—Technique **808.2**
>UF Play writing
>Playwriting
>BT **Drama—Technique**
>**Television authorship**
>RT **Radio plays—Technique**

Television—Production and direction (May subdiv. geog.) **384.55; 791.4502**
>BT **Television broadcasting**

Television programs (May subdiv. geog.) **791.45**
>Use for materials on what is seen on television. Materials on the technology of television are entered under **Television**.
>UF Programs, Television
>SA types of television programs and names of specific programs [to be added as needed]
>BT **Television broadcasting**
>NT **Adventure television programs**
>**Animated television programs**
>**Biographical television programs**
>**Comedy television programs**
>**Documentary television programs**
>**Fantasy television programs**
>**Horror television programs**
>**Legal drama (Television programs)**
>**Medical drama (Television programs)**
>**Mystery television programs**
>**Nature television programs**
>**Reality television programs**
>**Science fiction television programs**
>**Sports drama (Television programs)**
>**Spy television programs**
>**Talk shows**
>**Television adaptations**
>**Television movies**
>**Television plays**
>**Television serials**
>**Variety shows (Television programs)**
>**Violence on television**
>**War television programs**
>**Westerns (Television programs)**
>RT **Television scripts**

Television—Receivers and reception **621.388**
>UF Television reception
>Television sets
>BT **Television—Equipment and supplies**
>NT **V-chips**

Television reception
>USE **Television—Receivers and reception**

Television—Repairing **621.388**

Television scripts **791.45; 808.88**
>Use for individual works, collections, or materials about television scripts.
>BT **Television broadcasting**
>NT **Television adaptations**
>RT **Television plays**
>**Television programs**

Television serials **791.45**
>Use for individual works, collections, or materials about television serials.
>BT **Television programs**
>RT **Soap operas**

Television sets
>USE **Television—Receivers and reception**

Television sports
>USE **Television broadcasting of sports**

Television—Stage lighting
USE **Stage lighting**
Television stations (May subdiv. geog.)
384.55
BT **Television broadcasting**
Television, Subscription
USE **Subscription television**
Television supplies industry (May subdiv.
geog.) **338.4; 384.55**
UF Television equipment industry
Television industry
RT **Television—Equipment and
supplies**
Television viewers (May subdiv. geog.)
302.23; 791.4
UF Television—Audiences
Television fans
Television watchers
BT **Audiences**
Television watchers
USE **Television viewers**
Television writing
USE **Television authorship**
Telstar project 621.382
UF Bell System Telstar satellite
Project Telstar
BT **Artificial satellites in telecom-
munication**
Temper tantrums 152.4
UF Tantrums, Temper
BT **Emotions
Human behavior**
Temperament 155.2
BT **Mind and body
Psychology
Psychophysiology**
NT **Typology (Psychology)**
RT **Character**
Temperance 178; 241; 613.81
Use for materials on the virtue of temper-
ance or on the temperance movement.
UF Abstinence
Drunkenness
Intemperance
Intoxication
Total abstinence
BT **Virtue**
RT **Alcoholism
Drinking of alcoholic beverages
Prohibition**
Temperature 536
NT **Low temperatures**

RT **Cold
Heat
Thermometers**
Temperature, Animal and human
USE **Body temperature**
Temperature, Body
USE **Body temperature**
Temples (May subdiv. geog.) **203; 726**
BT **Buildings
Religious institutions**
NT **Mosques
Synagogues**
Temporal power of the Pope
USE **Popes—Temporal power**
Temporary employment (May subdiv.
geog.) **331.25**
UF Employment, Temporary
BT **Employment**
Ten commandments 222
UF Decalogue
Ten lost tribes of Israel
USE **Lost tribes of Israel**
Tenant and landlord
USE **Landlord and tenant**
Tenant farming
USE **Farm tenancy**
Tenement houses (May subdiv. geog.)
647
UF Tenements (Apartment houses)
BT **Apartment houses**
Tenements (Apartment houses)
USE **Tenement houses**
Tennis (May subdiv. geog.) **796.342**
UF Lawn tennis
BT **Sports**
Tennis—Tournaments (May subdiv.
geog.) **796.342**
BT **Sports tournaments**
Tenpins
USE **Bowling**
Tension (Physiology)
USE **Stress (Physiology)**
Tension (Psychology)
USE **Stress (Psychology)**
Tents (May subdiv. geog.) **796.54**
BT **Camping**
Tenure of land
USE **Land tenure**
Tenure of office
USE **Civil service**
Tepees 728; 970.004

Tepees—*Continued*
    UF   Teepees
           Wigwams
    BT   **Native Americans—Dwellings**
Terezin (Czechoslovakia: Concentration camp)   **365; 943.7**
    BT   **Concentration camps**
Term limitations (Public office)
    USE **Term limits (Public office)**
Term limits (Public office) (May subdiv. geog.)   **328**
    UF   Term limitations (Public office)
    BT   **Legislative bodies**
          Public officers
Term limits (Public office)—United States   **328.73**
    UF   United States—Term limits (Public office)
Term paper writing
    USE **Report writing**
Terminal care (May subdiv. geog.)   **362.17; 616; 649.8**
    UF   Care of the dying
    BT   **Medical care**
    NT   **Hospices**
          Life support systems (Medical environment)
    RT   **Death**
          Living wills
          Terminally ill
Terminally ill (May subdiv. geog.)   **362.17; 649.8**
    UF   Dying patients
           Fatally ill patients
    BT   **Sick**
    NT   **Terminally ill children**
    RT   **Death**
          Terminal care
Terminally ill children (May subdiv. geog.)   **362.17; 649.8**
    UF   Dying children
           Fatally ill children
    BT   **Terminally ill**
    RT   **Children—Death**
Terminals, Computer
    USE **Computer terminals**
Termination of pregnancy
    USE **Abortion**
Terminology
    USE **Terms and phrases**
          and subjects, classes of persons, sacred works, and religious

sects with the subdivision *Terminology,* for lists or discussions of words and expressions found in those works or used in those fields, e.g. **Botany—Terminology;** names of languages with the subdivision *Terms and phrases,* e.g. **English language—Terms and phrases;** scientific and technical disciplines and types of substances, plants, and animals with the subdivision *Nomenclature,* for systematically derived lists of names or designations that have been formally adopted or sanctioned, and for discussions of the principles involved in the creation and application of such names, e.g. **Botany—Nomenclature;** and scientific and technical disciplines and types of animals, plants, and crops with the subdivision *Nomenclature (Popular),* for lists or materials about popular, nontechnical names or designations of substances, species, etc., **Trees—Nomenclature (Popular)** [to be added as needed]
Terms and phrases   **030**
    UF   Commonplaces
           Terminology
    SA   names of languages with the subdivision *Terms and phrases*, e.g. **English language—Terms and phrases;** subjects, classes of persons, sacred works, and religious sects with the subdivision *Terminology*, for lists or discussions of words and expressions found in those works or used in those fields, e.g. **Botany—Terminology**; scientific and technical disciplines and types of substances, plants, and animals with the subdivision *Nomenclature*, for sys-

Terms and phrases—*Continued*
tematically derived lists of names or designations that have been formally adopted or sanctioned, and for discussions of the principles involved in the creation and application of such names, e.g. **Botany—Nomenclature**; and scientific and technical disciplines and types of animals, plants, and crops with the subdivision *Nomenclature (Popular)*, for lists or materials about popular, non-technical names or designations of substances, species, etc., **Trees—Nomenclature (Popular)** [to be added as needed]
  BT **Names**
  RT **Allusions**
Terns (May subdiv. geog.) **598.3**
  BT **Birds**
      Water birds
Terra cotta (May subdiv. geog.) **620.1; 691**
  BT **Building materials**
      Decoration and ornament
      Pottery
Terrain sensing, Remote
  USE **Remote sensing**
Terrapins
  USE **Turtles**
Terrariums (May subdiv. geog.) **635.9**
  BT **Indoor gardening**
  RT **Miniature gardens**
Terrestrial physics
  USE **Geophysics**
Territorial expansion
  USE names of countries, regions, etc., with the subdivision *Territorial expansion*, e.g. **United States—Territorial expansion** [to be added as needed]
Territorial questions
  USE names of wars with the subdivision *Territorial questions*, e.g. **World War, 1939-1945—Territorial questions**; which may be further subdivided

geographically [to be added as needed]
Territorial waters (May subdiv. geog.) **341.4; 342**
  UF Economic zones (Maritime law)
      Three-mile limit
  BT **Shipping**
  RT **Continental shelf**
      Maritime law
Territorial waters—United States **341.4; 342**
  UF United States—Territorial waters
Territories and possessions
  USE names of countries with the subdivision *Territories and possessions,* or *Colonies,* e.g. **United States—Territories and possessions; Great Britain—Colonies;** etc. [to be added as needed]
Terror, Reign of
  USE **France—History—1789-1799, Revolution**
Terror tales
  USE **Ghost stories**
      Horror fiction
Terrorism (May subdiv. geog.) **303.6**
  UF Political violence
      Terrorist acts
  BT **Insurgency**
      Political crimes and offenses
      Subversive activities
  NT **Bioterrorism**
      Bombings
      Domestic terrorism
      Ecoterrorism
      Hostages
      Sabotage
      Suicide bombers
  RT **Anarchism and anarchists**
Terrorism—Prevention (May subdiv. geog.) **363.32**
  UF Anti-terrorism
      Counter-terrorism
      War on terrorism
Terrorism—United States **303.6; 322.4**
  NT **September 11 terrorist attacks, 2001**
Terrorist acts
  USE **Terrorism**

Terrorist attacks, September 11, 2001
    USE   **September 11 terrorist attacks, 2001**

Terrorist bombings
    USE   **Bombings**

Test bias   **371.2601**
    UF   Bias in testing
           Prejudice in testing
    BT   **Discrimination in education**
           Educational tests and measurements

Test pilots
    USE   **Air pilots**
           Airplanes—Testing

Test preparation guides
    USE   **Examinations—Study guides**

Test tube babies
    USE   **Fertilization in vitro**

Test tube fertilization
    USE   **Fertilization in vitro**

Testing   **620**
    UF   Mechanical properties testing
    SA   things tested with the subdivision *Testing*, e.g. **Ability—Testing**; **Airplanes—Testing**; **Concrete—Testing**; etc [to be added as needed]
    BT   **Reliability (Engineering)**
    NT   **Electric testing**
    RT   **Strength of materials**

Testing for drug abuse
    USE   **Drug testing**

Tests
    USE   **Educational tests and measurements**
           Examinations

Teutonic peoples (May subdiv. geog.)
       305.83
    UF   Nordic peoples
           Teutonic race
    SA   names of particular Teutonic peoples, e.g. **Goths** [to be added as needed]
    NT   **Anglo-Saxons**
           Goths

Teutonic race
    USE   **Teutonic peoples**

Textbooks (May subdiv. geog.)   **371.3**
    UF   School books

    SA   branches of study with the subdivision *Textbooks*, e.g. **Arithmetic—Textbooks** [to be added as needed]
    BT   **Books**

Textile chemistry   **677**
    UF   Chemistry, Textile
    BT   **Industrial chemistry**
           Textile industry
    NT   **Dyes and dyeing**

Textile design (May subdiv. geog.)   **746**
    UF   Fabric design
    BT   **Commercial art**
           Decoration and ornament
           Design
    NT   **Textile painting**
    RT   **Textile printing**

Textile fibers
    USE   **Fibers**

Textile industry (May subdiv. geog.)
       338.4; 677
    SA   types of articles manufactured, e.g **Rugs and carpets**; **Hosiery**; etc. [to be added as needed]
    BT   **Industries**
    NT   **Bleaching**
           Cotton manufacture
           Dyes and dyeing
           Hosiery
           Spinning
           Textile chemistry
           Textile printing
           Weaving

Textile painting (May subdiv. geog.)
       746.6
    BT   **Painting**
           Textile design

Textile printing (May subdiv. geog.)
       746.6
    UF   Block printing
    BT   **Printing**
           Textile industry
    RT   **Silk screen printing**
           Textile design

Textiles
    USE   **Fabrics**

Texts
    USE   types of lesser-known languages, dialects, early periods of languages, liturgies, and types of

Theaters—Stage setting and scenery—
Continued
   Theatrical scenery
  NT **Scene painting**
Theatrical costume
  USE **Costume**
Theatrical direction
  USE **Theater—Production and di-
    rection**
Theatrical directors
  USE **Theatrical producers and di-
    rectors**
Theatrical makeup 791.43; 791.45; 792
  UF Makeup, Theatrical
  BT **Cosmetics**
    Costume
Theatrical producers
  USE **Theatrical producers and di-
    rectors**
Theatrical producers and directors (May
  subdiv. geog.) **792; 920**
  UF Theatrical directors
    Theatrical producers
  RT **Theater—Production and di-
    rection**
Theatrical production
  USE **Theater—Production and di-
    rection**
Theatrical scenery
  USE **Theaters—Stage setting and
    scenery**
Theft (May subdiv. geog.) **364.16**
  UF Larceny
    Stealing
  BT **Crime**
    Offenses against property
  NT **Art thefts**
    Bank robberies
    Identity theft
    Shoplifting
  RT **Thieves**
Theism (May subdiv. geog.) **211**
  BT **Philosophy**
    Religion
    Theology
  NT **Monotheism**
    Polytheism
  RT **Atheism**
    Deism
    God
Theme parks
  USE **Amusement parks**

Themes in art
  USE **Art—Themes**
Themes in literature
  USE **Literature—Themes**
Theocracy (May subdiv. geog.) **321**
  BT **Church and state**
    Political science
Theological education
  USE **Religious education**
    Theology—Study and teaching
Theology (May subdiv. geog.) **202; 230**
  NT **Apologetics**
    Atheism
    Church
    Covenants
    Deism
    Doctrinal theology
    Eschatology
    Faith
    Feminist theology
    Good and evil
    Immortality
    Liberation theology
    Natural theology
    Pastoral theology
    Predestination
    Revelation
    Sin
    Theism
    Worship
  RT **God**
    Religion
Theology, Doctrinal
  USE **Doctrinal theology**
Theology of liberation
  USE **Liberation theology**
Theology—Study and teaching (May
  subdiv. geog.) **202; 230.07**
  UF Education, Theological
    Religion—Study and teaching
    Theological education
  NT **Catechisms**
  RT **Religious education**
Theoretical chemistry
  USE **Physical chemistry**
Theory of games
  USE **Game theory**
Theory of graphs
  USE **Graph theory**
Theory of knowledge 001.01; 121
  Use for materials on the origin, nature,
  methods, and limits of human knowledge.

Theory of knowledge—*Continued*
    UF   Cognition
         Epistemology
         Knowledge, Theory of
         Understanding
    BT   **Consciousness**
         Logic
         Metaphysics
         Philosophy
    NT   **Belief and doubt**
         Certainty
         Cognitive styles
         Empiricism
         Gestalt psychology
         Ideology
         Intuition
         Perception
         Pragmatism
         Rationalism
         Senses and sensation
    RT   **Apperception**
         Intellect
         Reality
         Truth
Theory of numbers
    USE **Number theory**
Theory of structures
    USE **Structural analysis (Engineer-ing)**
Theory of systems
    USE **System theory**
Theosophy (May subdiv. geog.) **299**
    BT   **Mysticism**
         Religions
    NT   **Reincarnation**
         Vedanta
         Yoga
Therapeutic systems
    USE **Alternative medicine**
Therapeutic use
    USE subjects with the subdivision *Therapeutic use,* e.g. **Cold—Therapeutic use; Herbs—Therapeutic use** etc. [to be added as needed]
Therapeutics 615.5
    UF   Diseases—Treatment
         Therapy
         Treatment
         Treatment of diseases

    SA   types of therapies, e.g. **Hydro-therapy**; diseases with the subdivision *Treatment*, e.g. **AIDS (Disease)—Treatment**; subjects with the subdivision *Therapeutic use*, e.g. **Cold—Therapeutic use; Herbs—Therapeutic use**; etc.; diseases with the subdivision *Diet therapy*, e.g. **Cancer—Diet therapy**; and types of drugs and names of specific drugs [to be added as needed]
    BT   **Medicine**
         Pathology
    NT   **AIDS (Disease)—Treatment**
         Antiseptics
         Aromatherapy
         Art therapy
         Cold—Therapeutic use
         Diet in disease
         Diet therapy
         Drug abuse—Treatment
         Drug therapy
         Drugs
         Electrotherapeutics
         Gene therapy
         Healing
         Herbs—Therapeutic use
         Hydrotherapy
         Materia medica
         Medicine
         Music therapy
         Naturopathy
         Nursing
         Nutrition
         Occupational therapy
         Pet therapy
         Phototherapy
         Physical therapy
         Play therapy
         Psychotherapy
         Radiotherapy
         Suggestive therapeutics
    RT   **Pharmaceutical chemistry**
Therapeutics, Suggestive
    USE **Suggestive therapeutics**
Therapy
    USE **Therapeutics**
Therapy, Gene
    USE **Gene therapy**

Therapy, Psychological
    USE   **Psychotherapy**
Thermal insulation
    USE   **Insulation (Heat)**
Thermal waters
    USE   **Geothermal resources**
           Geysers
Thermoaerodynamics
    USE   **Aerothermodynamics**
Thermodynamics   536
    SA   subjects with the subdivision
           Thermodynamics, e.g. **Space**
           vehicles—Thermodynamics
           [to be added as needed]
    BT   **Dynamics**
           Physical chemistry
           Physics
    NT   **Aerothermodynamics**
           Entropy
           Heat engines
           Heat pumps
           Space vehicles—Thermodynam-
           ics
    RT   **Heat**
           Heat engines
           Quantum theory
Thermometers   536
    UF   Thermometry
    BT   **Heat**
           Meteorological instruments
    RT   **Temperature**
Thermometry
    USE   **Thermometers**
Thesauri
    USE   **Subject headings**
           and names of languages with
           the subdivision *Synonyms and*
           antonyms, e.g. **English lan-**
           guage—Synonyms and ant-
           onyms [to be added as need-
           ed]
Theses
    USE   **Dissertations**
Thieves (May subdiv. geog.)   **364.3**
    UF   Bandits
           Brigands
           Burglars
           Highwaymen
           Outlaws
           Robbers
    BT   **Criminals**

    RT   **Theft**
Think tanks
    USE   **Group problem solving**
Thinking
    USE   **Thought and thinking**
Third parties (United States politics)
           324.273
    BT   **Political parties**
           United States—Politics and
           government
Third World
    USE   **Developing countries**
Third World War
    USE   **World War III**
Thirteenth century
    USE   **World history—13th century**
Thirty Years' War, 1618-1648 (May
           subdiv. geog.)   **909.08; 940.2**
    BT   **Europe—History—1492-1789**
           Germany—History—1517-1740
Thor (Norse deity)   202
    BT   **Gods and goddesses**
Thoroughfares
    USE   **Roads**
           Streets
Thought and thinking   153.4
    UF   Thinking
    BT   **Educational psychology**
           Psychology
    NT   **Attention**
           Critical thinking
           Ideology
           Memory
           Perception
           Reasoning
           Stereotype (Social psychology)
    RT   **Intellect**
           Logic
Thought control
    USE   **Brainwashing**
Threatened species
    USE   **Endangered species**
Three dimensional photography   778.4
    UF   3-D photography
           Photography, Stereoscopic
           Stereo photography
           Stereophotography
           Stereoscopic photography
    BT   **Photography**
    RT   **Holography**

Three-mile limit
USE **Territorial waters**
Three Stooges films   791.43
Use for individual works, collections, or materials about Three Stooges films.
BT **Comedy films**
Motion pictures
Three (The number)   513
BT **Numbers**
Thrift
USE **Saving and investment**
Thrift shops (May subdiv. geog.)   **381.19**
UF Charity shops
BT **Secondhand trade**
Stores
Thrillers
USE **Adventure fiction**
Adventure films
Throat   611; 612; 617.5
BT **Anatomy**
NT **Voice**
Thunderstorms (May subdiv. geog.)
551.55
BT **Meteorology**
Storms
NT **Lightning**
Tiananmen Square Incident, Beijing
(China), 1989   951.05
UF Beijing Massacre, 1989
China—History—1989,
Tiananmen Square Incident
Ticks   595.4
BT **Arachnids**
Tidal waves
USE **Tsunamis**
Tide pool ecology (May subdiv. geog.)
577.69
BT **Ecology**
Tides (May subdiv. geog.)   **551.46**
BT **Ocean**
Tidiness
USE **Orderliness**
Tie dyeing   746.6
BT **Dyes and dyeing**
Tiles (May subdiv. geog.)   **666; 693;**
738.6
UF Ceramic tiles
BT **Building materials**
Ceramics
Timber
USE **Forests and forestry**
Lumber and lumbering

Trees
Wood
Timber—Harvesting
USE **Logging**
Time   529
UF Horology
Standard time
NT **Calendars**
Chronology
Clocks and watches
Day
Night
Punctuality
Space and time
Sundials
Time management
RT **Cycles**
Nautical astronomy
Time and space
USE **Space and time**
Time management   640; 650.1
UF Allocation of time
Personal time management
BT **Management**
Time
Time production standards
USE **Production standards**
Time saving cooking
USE **Quick and easy cooking**
Time sharing (Real estate)
USE **Timesharing (Real estate)**
Time study   658.5
BT **Factory management**
Industrial efficiency
Job analysis
Personnel management
Production standards
RT **Motion study**
Time travel   115
BT **Fourth dimension**
Space and time
Timesharing (Real estate) (May subdiv.
geog.)   **333.3; 333.5; 643**
UF Condominium timesharing
Real estate timesharing
Time sharing (Real estate)
Vacation home timesharing
BT **Condominiums**
Housing
Property
Real estate business

Tin 669
- BT **Chemical elements**
- **Metals**

Tinsmithing
- USE **Tinwork**

Tinwork (May subdiv. geog.) 673
- UF Tinsmithing
- BT **Metalwork**

Tiny objects
- USE **Miniature objects**

Tires (May subdiv. geog.) 678
- UF Rubber tires
- BT **Wheels**

Tiros (Meteorological satellite)
- USE **TIROS satellites**

TIROS satellites 551.5
- UF Television and infrared observation satellite
- Tiros (Meteorological satellite)
- BT **Meteorological satellites**

Tissue donation
- USE **Donation of organs, tissues, etc.**

Tissues—Transplantation
- USE **Transplantation of organs, tissues, etc.**

Tithes (May subdiv. geog.) 248; 254
- BT **Church finance**
- **Ecclesiastical law**
- **Taxation**

Toadstools
- USE **Mushrooms**

Toasts 808.5; 808.85
- UF Healths, Drinking of
- BT **Epigrams**
- **Speeches**
- RT **After dinner speeches**

Tobacco (May subdiv. geog.) 633.7
- BT **Plants**
- NT **Cigarettes**
- **Cigars**
- RT **Smoking**

Tobacco habit (May subdiv. geog.) 178; 613.85; 616.86
- UF Addiction to nicotine
- Addiction to tobacco
- Nicotine habit
- BT **Habit**
- **Smoking**
- NT **Smoking cessation programs**

Tobacco industry (May subdiv. geog.) 338.17371
- BT **Industries**

Tobacco pipes 688
- UF Pipes, Tobacco
- BT **Smoking**

Toilet preparations
- USE **Toiletries**

Toilet training 649
- BT **Child rearing**

Toiletries 646.7
- UF Toilet preparations
- BT **Personal grooming**
- RT **Cosmetics**

Tolerance
- USE **Toleration**

Toleration (May subdiv. geog.) 179; 323
- UF Bigotry
- Intolerance
- Tolerance
- BT **Interpersonal relations**
- NT **Academic freedom**
- **Freedom of conscience**
- **Freedom of religion**
- **Religious tolerance**
- RT **Discrimination**

Toll roads
- USE **Express highways**

Tombs (May subdiv. geog.) 726
- UF Graves
- Mausoleums
- Rock tombs
- Sepulchers
- Vaults (Sepulchral)
- SA classes of persons, and names of families, royal houses, dynasties, etc., with the subdivision *Tombs*, e.g. **Presidents—United States—Tombs** [to be added as needed]
- BT **Archeology**
- **Architecture**
- **Burial**
- **Monuments**
- **Shrines**
- NT **Brasses**
- **Catacombs**
- **Epitaphs**
- **Mounds and mound builders**

Tombs—*Continued*
    RT   **Cemeteries**
Tomography   616.07; 621.36
    UF   CAT scan
            Computerized tomography
    BT   **X-rays**
Tongue twisters   398.8
    BT   **Children's poetry**
            Folklore
            Nonsense verses
Tools (May subdiv. geog.)   **621.9**
    SA   types of tools [to be added as needed]
    BT   **Implements, utensils, etc.**
    NT   **Agricultural machinery**
            Carpentry tools
            Machine tools
            Machinery
            Power tools
            Saws
            Weapons
Top soil loss
    USE   **Soil erosion**
Topographical drawing   526
    BT   **Drawing**
            Surveying
    RT   **Map drawing**
Topology   514
    UF   Position analysis
    BT   **Geometry**
            Set theory
    NT   **Fractals**
            Graph theory
    RT   **Linear algebra**
Tories, American
    USE   **American Loyalists**
Tornadoes (May subdiv. geog.)   **551.55**
    UF   Twisters (Tornadoes)
    BT   **Meteorology**
            Storms
            Winds
Torpedoes (May subdiv. geog.)   **623.4**
    BT   **Explosives**
            Naval art and science
            Submarine warfare
Tort liability of professions
    USE   **Malpractice**
Tortoises
    USE   **Turtles**
Torture (May subdiv. geog.)   **365**
    BT   **Criminal procedure**
            Cruelty

            Punishment
Total abstinence
    USE   **Temperance**
Totalitarianism (May subdiv. geog.)   **321.9**
    UF   Authoritarianism
    BT   **Political science**
    NT   **Communism**
            Dictators
            Fascism
Totem poles (May subdiv. geog.)   **299.7; 704.9; 731**
    BT   **Totems and totemism**
Totems and totemism (May subdiv. geog.)   **202**
    BT   **Ethnology**
            Mythology
    NT   **Totem poles**
Touch   152.1; 612
    UF   Feeling
    BT   **Senses and sensation**
    NT   **Hugging**
Touring, Bicycle
    USE   **Bicycle touring**
Tourism
    USE   **Tourist trade**
            Travel
Tourist accommodations
    USE   **Hotels and motels**
            Youth hostels
Tourist industry
    USE   **Tourist trade**
Tourist trade (May subdiv. geog.)   **338.4**
    UF   Tourism
            Tourist industry
            Tourists
            Travel industry
    BT   **Commerce**
    NT   **Cultural tourism**
            Ecotourism
    RT   **Travel**
Tourists
    USE   **Tourist trade**
            Travelers
Tournaments
    USE   **Medieval tournaments**
            Sports tournaments
            and types of sports and games with the subdivision *Tournaments,* e.g. **Tennis—Tourna-**

Tournaments—*Continued*
>   ments [to be added as needed]

Town life
>   USE   **City and town life**

Town meeting
>   USE   **Local government**

Town officers
>   USE   **Municipal officials and employees**

Town planning
>   USE   **City planning**

Towns
>   USE   **Cities and towns**

Towns, Abandoned
>   USE   **Ghost towns**

Township government
>   USE   **Local government**

Toxic dumps
>   USE   **Hazardous waste sites**

Toxic plants
>   USE   **Poisonous plants**

Toxic substances
>   USE   **Hazardous substances**
>   **Poisons and poisoning**

Toxic wastes
>   USE   **Hazardous wastes**

Toxicology   571.9; 615.9

Use for materials on the science that treats of poisons and their antidotes. Materials on poisonous substance and their use are entered under **Poisons and poisoning**.

>   UF   Chemicals—Toxicology
>   SA   types of poisons or poisoning, e.g. **Lead poisoning**; and types of poisonous substances with the subdivision *Toxicology*, for materials on the influence of particular substances on humans and animals, e.g. **Insecticides—Toxicology** [to be added as needed]
>   BT   **Medicine**
>   **Pharmacology**
>   RT   **Poisons and poisoning**

Toy and movable books

Use for individual works, collections, or materials about toy and movable books.

>   UF   Movable books
>   Pop-up books
>   BT   **Picture books for children**
>   NT   **Glow-in-the-dark books**

Toy making (May subdiv. geog.)
>   **745.592**
>   BT   **Handicraft**
>   NT   **Soft toy making**
>   **Wooden toy making**
>   RT   **Toys**

Toys (May subdiv. geog.)   **688.7; 790.1**
>   SA   types of toys [to be added as needed]
>   BT   **Amusements**
>   NT   **Doll furniture**
>   **Dollhouses**
>   **Dolls**
>   **Electric toys**
>   **Electronic toys**
>   **Teddy bears**
>   RT   **Miniature objects**
>   **Toy making**

Track and field
>   USE   **Track athletics**

Track athletics (May subdiv. geog.)
>   **796.42**
>   UF   Field athletics
>   Track and field
>   SA   types of track sports [to be added as needed]
>   BT   **Athletics**
>   **Sports**
>   NT   **Running**

Tracking and trailing (May subdiv. geog.)   **799.2**
>   UF   Trailing
>   BT   **Hunting**
>   NT   **Animal tracks**
>   RT   **Animal behavior**

Tracking of satellites
>   USE   **Artificial satellites—Tracking**
>   **Space vehicles—Tracking**

Tracks of animals
>   USE   **Animal tracks**

Traction engines
>   USE   **Tractors**

Tractors (May subdiv. geog.)   **629.225; 631.3**
>   UF   Traction engines
>   BT   **Agricultural machinery**

Tracts   243

Use for collections, individual works or materials about religious pamphlets.

>   UF   Religious pamphlets
>   BT   **Chapbooks**
>   **Pamphlets**

Trade
    USE   **Business**
              Commerce
Trade agreements (Labor)
    USE   **Industrial arbitration**
              Labor contract
Trade and professional associations (May subdiv. geog.)   **381; 650**
    UF   Professional associations
            Trade associations
    BT   **Associations**
Trade associations
    USE   **Trade and professional associations**
Trade, Balance of
    USE   **Balance of trade**
Trade barriers
    USE   **Commercial policy**
Trade, Boards of
    USE   **Chambers of commerce**
Trade catalogs
    USE   **Commercial catalogs**
Trade deficits
    USE   **Balance of trade**
Trade expositions
    USE   **Trade shows**
Trade fairs
    USE   **Trade shows**
Trade, International
    USE   **International trade**
Trade marks
    USE   **Trademarks**
Trade, Restraint of
    USE   **Restraint of trade**
Trade routes (May subdiv. geog.)   **387**
    UF   Ocean routes
            Routes of trade
            Sea routes
    BT   **Commerce**
            Commercial geography
            Transportation
Trade schools
    USE   **Technical education**
Trade secrets (May subdiv. geog.)   **346.04; 658.4**
    UF   Business secrets
            Commercial secrets
            Industrial secrets
            Secrets, Trade
    BT   **Right of privacy**
            Unfair competition

Trade shows (May subdiv. geog.)   **659.1**
    UF   Industrial exhibitions
            Trade expositions
            Trade fairs
    BT   **Exhibitions**
            Fairs
Trade surpluses
    USE   **Balance of trade**
Trade-unions
    USE   **Labor unions**
Trade waste
    USE   **Industrial waste**
            Waste products
Trademarks (May subdiv. geog.)   **346.04; 929.9**
    UF   Company symbols
            Corporate symbols
            Trade marks
    SA   types of industries and products with the subdivision *Trademarks*, for materials on the words, letters, or symbols used by the manufacturers or dealers of those goods to distinguish them from the goods of others, e.g. **Glassware—Trademarks** [to be added as needed]
    BT   **Commerce**
            Manufactures
    NT   **Glassware—Trademarks**
    RT   **Brand name products**
            Patents
Trades
    USE   **Industrial arts**
            Occupations
Trading card games
    USE   **Collectible card games**
Trading cards (May subdiv. geog.)   **741.6**
    BT   **Collectibles**
Traditional medicine (May subdiv. geog.)   **615.8**
    UF   Folk medicine
            Folklore, Medical
            Medical folklore
    SA   traditional medicine of particular ethnic groups, e.g. **Native American medicine** [to be added as needed]

Traditional medicine—*Continued*
  BT   **Medicine**
       Popular medicine
Traditions
  USE **Folklore**
       Legends
       Manners and customs
       Rites and ceremonies
       Superstition
Traffic accidents (May subdiv. geog.)
    363.12
  UF Automobile accidents
       Automobiles—Accidents
       Car accidents
       Car wrecks
       Highway accidents
  BT   **Accidents**
Traffic, City
  USE **City traffic**
Traffic control
  USE **Traffic engineering**
       Traffic regulations
Traffic engineering (May subdiv. geog.)
    388.4
  Use for materials on the planning of the flow of traffic and related topics, largely as they concern street transportation in cities and metropolitan areas.
  UF Street traffic
       Traffic control
  BT   **Engineering**
       Highway engineering
       Transportation
  NT **Car pools**
       City traffic
       Express highways
       Local transit
       Traffic safety
  RT **Traffic regulations**
Traffic regulations (May subdiv. geog.)
    388.4
  UF Traffic control
  BT   **Safety regulations**
  RT **Automobiles—Law and legisla-tion**
       Traffic engineering
Traffic safety (May subdiv. geog.)
    363.12
  UF Highway safety
       Road safety
  BT   **Highway transportation**
       Traffic engineering

Trafficking in drugs
  USE **Drug traffic**
Trafficking in narcotics
  USE **Drug traffic**
Tragedies 808.82
  Use for individual works or for collections. Materials about tragedy as a literary form are entered under **Tragedy**.
  BT   **Drama**
Tragedy 792.1; 809.2
  Use for materials on tragedy as a literary form. Individual works and collections of tragedies are entered under **Tragedies**.
  BT   **Drama**
  RT **Tragicomedy**
Tragicomedy 809.2
  BT   **Drama**
  RT **Comedy**
       Tragedy
Trail riding (May subdiv. geog.) **798.2**
  BT   **Horsemanship**
Trailer camps
  USE **Trailer parks**
Trailer parks (May subdiv. geog.) **647; 796.54**
  UF Mobile home parks
       Trailer camps
  BT   **Campgrounds**
       Mobile home living
Trailers
  USE **Mobile homes**
       Travel trailers and campers
Trailing
  USE **Tracking and trailing**
Trails (May subdiv. geog.) **796.51**
  BT   **Roads**
  NT **Appalachian Trail**
       Nature trails
  RT **Hiking**
       Mountaineering
Train wrecks
  USE **Railroad accidents**
Training
  USE types of sports activities, plants and crops, animals, and classes of persons with the subdivision *Training*, e.g. **Soccer—Training; Horses—Training; Teachers—Training;** etc. [to be added as needed]
Training camps, Military
  USE **Military training camps**

Training colleges for teachers
USE **Teachers colleges**
Training, Occupational
USE **Occupational training**
Training of animals
USE **Animals—Training**
Training of children
USE **Child rearing**
Training of employees
USE **Employees—Training**
Training, Vocational
USE **Occupational training**
Trains
USE **Railroads**
Traitors (May subdiv. geog.) **364.1**
NT **Collaborationists**
RT **Treason**
Tramps (May subdiv. geog.) **305.5**
Use for materials on homeless persons who travel about from place to place and work in occasional jobs.
UF Hoboes
Vagabonds
Vagrants
BT **Homeless persons**
Poor
RT **Begging**
Unemployed
Trams
USE **Street railroads**
Transactional analysis **158**
BT **Psychotherapy**
Transatlantic flights
USE **Aeronautics—Flights**
Transcendental meditation **158**
BT **Meditation**
Transcendentalism (May subdiv. geog.) **141**
BT **Philosophy**
RT **Idealism**
Transcontinental journeys (American continent)
USE **Overland journeys to the Pacific**
Transcultural studies
USE **Cross-cultural studies**
Transfer of technology
USE **Technology transfer**
Transfer payments (May subdiv. geog.) **339.5**
UF Government transfer payments

BT **Domestic economic assistance**
Economic policy
Subsidies
Transfer tax
USE **Inheritance and transfer tax**
Transformation (Genetics)
USE **Genetic transformation**
Transformers, Electric
USE **Electric transformers**
Transgenics
USE **Genetic engineering**
Transistor amplifiers **621.3815**
UF Amplifiers, Transistor
Audio amplifiers, Transistor
Transistor audio amplifiers
BT **Amplifiers (Electronics)**
Transistors
Transistor audio amplifiers
USE **Transistor amplifiers**
Transistors **621.3815**
BT **Electronics**
Semiconductors
NT **Transistor amplifiers**
Transit systems
USE **Local transit**
Translating and interpreting (May subdiv. geog.) **418**
UF Interpreting and translating
BT **Language and languages**
Transmission of data
USE **Data transmission systems**
Transmission of power
USE **Electric lines**
Electric power distribution
Power transmission
Transmissions, Automobile
USE **Automobiles—Transmission devices**
Transmutation (Chemistry) **539.7**
Use for materials on the transmutation of metals in nuclear physics. Materials on medieval attempts to change base metals into gold are entered under **Alchemy.**
UF Transmutation of metals
BT **Atoms**
Nuclear physics
Radioactivity
NT **Cyclotrons**
RT **Alchemy**
Transmutation of metals
USE **Alchemy**
Transmutation (Chemistry)

Transplantation
    USE   **Transplantation of organs, tissues, etc.**

        and organs of the body with the subdivision *Transplantation,* e.g. **Heart—Transplantation** [to be added as needed]

Transplantation of organs, tissues, etc. (May subdiv. geog.)   **617.9**
    UF   Medical transplantation
        Organ transplants
        Surgical transplantation
        Tissues—Transplantation
        Transplantation
    SA   organs of the body with the subdivision *Transplantation,* e.g. **Heart—Transplantation** to be added as needed]
    BT   **Surgery**
    NT   **Heart—Transplantation**
    RT   **Donation of organs, tissues, etc.**
        Preservation of organs, tissues, etc.

Transplantation of organs, tissues, etc.—Ethical aspects   **174**
    UF   Transplantation of organs, tissues, etc.—Moral and religious aspects
    BT   **Bioethics**

Transplantation of organs, tissues, etc.—Moral and religious aspects
    USE   **Transplantation of organs, tissues, etc.—Ethical aspects**
        Transplantation of organs, tissues, etc.—Religious aspects

Transplantation of organs, tissues, etc.—Religious aspects   **201; 241**
    UF   Transplantation of organs, tissues, etc.—Moral and religious aspects

Transportation (May subdiv. geog.)   **388**
    SA   subjects, classes of person, and names of wars with the subdivision *Transportation,* e.g. **Hazardous substances—Transportation; School children—Transportation; World War, 1939-1945—Transportation;** etc. [to be added as needed]
    BT   **Locomotion**
    NT   **Air travel**
        Automobile travel
        Bridges
        Canals
        Car pools
        Commercial aeronautics
        Express service
        Freight
        Harbors
        Hazardous substances—Transportation
        Highway transportation
        Inland navigation
        Local transit
        Merchant marine
        Military transportation
        Ocean travel
        Pipelines
        Postal service
        Railroads
        Roads
        School children—Transportation
        Shipping
        Steam navigation
        Streets
        Trade routes
        Traffic engineering
        Trucking
        Vehicles
        Waterways
        World War, 1939-1945—Transportation
    RT   **Commerce**

Transportation, Highway
    USE   **Highway transportation**

Transportation, Military
    USE   **Military transportation**

Transportation of criminals
    USE   **Penal colonies**

Transportation—Planning (May subdiv. geog.)   **338**
    BT   **Planning**

Transsexualism (May subdiv. geog.)   **305.3; 616.85**
    UF   Change of sex
        Sex change
        Transsexuality

Transsexualism—*Continued*

  BT **Sex role**

Transsexuality

  USE **Transsexualism**

Transvestites (May subdiv. geog.)

    306.77

  Use for materials on persons, especially men, who assume the dress of the opposite sex for psychological gratification. Materials on men who impersonate women for purposes of entertainment or comic effect are entered under **Female impersonators**. Materials on women who impersonate men for purposes of entertainment or comic effect are entered under **Male impersonators**.

  UF Crossdressers

  BT **Persons**

Trapping (May subdiv. geog.) **639**

  NT **Fur trade**

  RT **Game and game birds**

    Hunting

Traumatic stress syndrome

  USE **Post-traumatic stress disorder**

Travel **910**

  Use for materials on the art and enjoyment of travel and advice for travelers. Descriptions of actual voyages are entered under **Voyages and travels** or under the name of a place with the subdivision *Description and travel*. An account of an extinct city or town by a traveler in ancient times is entered under the name of the extinct city or town, without further subdivision, e.g. **Delphi (Extinct city)**.

  UF Group travel

    Journeys

    Tourism

  SA names of cities (except extinct cities), countries, states, etc., with the subdivision *Description and travel*, e.g. **United States—Description and travel**; and ethnic groups, classes of persons, and names of individuals with the subdivision *Travel*, e.g. **Handicapped—Travel** [to be added as needed]

  BT **Manners and customs**

  NT **Adventure travel**

    Air travel

    Automobile travel

    Bicycle touring

    Handicapped—Travel

    Ocean travel

    Safaris

    Travel in literature

Voyages around the world

  RT **Tourist trade**

    Voyages and travels

Travel—Authorship

  USE **Travel writing**

Travel books

  USE **Voyages and travels**

    Voyages around the world

Travel guides

  USE **Automobile travel—Guidebooks** and names of cities (except ancient cities), countries, states, etc., with the subdivision *Guidebooks*, e.g. **Chicago (Ill.)—Guidebooks; United States—Guidebooks;** etc. [to be added as needed]

Travel in literature **809**

  Use for materials about the theme of travel in literature. Materials about non-fiction travel writing, collections of travel writings, and accounts of voyages and travels not limited to a single place are entered under **Voyages and travels**. Accounts of voyages and travels limited to a single place are entered under the name of the place with the subdivision *Description and travel*.

  UF Voyages and travels in literature

  BT **Literature—Themes**

    Travel

  RT **Voyages and travels**

Travel industry

  USE **Tourist trade**

Travel trailers and campers (May subdiv. geog.) **629.226; 796.7**

  Use for materials on structures mounted upon a truck or towed by a truck or automobile for the purpose of temporary dwelling or cargo hauling. Materials on stationary transportable structures designed for year-round living are entered under **Mobile homes**.

  UF Automobiles—Trailers

    Campers and trailers

    House trailers

    Pickup campers

    Trailers

  BT **Camping**

    Recreational vehicles

  NT **Vans**

  RT **Mobile homes**

Travel writing (May subdiv. geog.) **808**

  Use for materials about the art of travel writing. Materials about a particular place are entered under the name of the place with the subdivision *Description and travel*, e.g. **Chicago (Ill.)—Description and travel**.

Travel writing—*Continued*
- UF Travel—Authorship
- BT **Authorship**

Travelers (May subdiv. geog.) 910.92; 920
- UF Tourists
  - Voyagers
- SA travelers from particular countries, e.g. **American travelers**; and ethnic groups, classes of person, and names of individuals with the subdivision *Travel*, e.g. **Presidents—United States—Travel** [to be added as needed]
- BT **Voyages and travels**
- NT **American travelers**
- RT **Explorers**

Traveling sales personnel
- USE **Sales personnel**

Travels
- USE **Voyages and travels**

Travesty
- USE **Burlesque (Theater)**
  - **Parody**

Tray gardens
- USE **Miniature gardens**

Treason (May subdiv. geog.) 364.1

Use for materials on the offense of acting to overthrow one's own government or to harm or kill its sovereign. Materials on any attempt to subvert, overthrow, or cause the destruction of any established or legally constituted government are entered under **Subversive activities**.
- UF High treason
- BT **Crime**
  - **Political crimes and offenses**
  - **Subversive activities**
- RT **Traitors**

Treasure trove
- USE **Buried treasure**

Treaties 341; 341.3
- SA names of countries with the subdivision *Foreign relations—Treaties*, and names of wars with the subdivision *Treaties* [to be added as needed]
- BT **Diplomacy**
  - **International law**
  - **International relations**

- NT **International arbitration**
  - **United States—Foreign relations—Treaties**
  - **World War, 1939-1945—Treaties**

Treatment
- USE **Therapeutics**
  - and types of diseases with the subdivision *Treatment,* e.g. **AIDS (Disease)—Treatment** [to be added as needed]

Treatment of diseases
- USE **Therapeutics**

Tree houses (May subdiv. geog.) 690
- BT **Buildings**

Tree planting (May subdiv. geog.) 635.9
- UF Planting
- BT **Forests and forestry**
- NT **Windbreaks**
- RT **Reforestation**
  - **Trees**

Trees (May subdiv. geog.) 582.16; 635.9

Names of nuts and tree fruits may be used for either the nut or fruit or the tree.
- UF Arboriculture
  - Timber
- SA types of trees, e.g. **Oak** [to be added as needed], in the singular form
- BT **Plants**
- NT **Christmas trees**
  - **Dwarf trees**
  - **Evergreens**
  - **Fruit culture**
  - **Lumber and lumbering**
  - **Oak**
  - **Pruning**
  - **Shrubs**
  - **Wood**
- RT **Forests and forestry**
  - **Landscape gardening**
  - **Tree planting**

Trees—Nomenclature (Popular) 582.16
- BT **Popular plant names**

Trees—United States 582.160973

Trent Affair, 1861 973.7
- BT **United States—History—1861-1865, Civil War**

Trial by jury
- USE **Jury**

Trial by publicity
    USE   **Freedom of the press and fair trial**
Trial marriage
    USE   **Unmarried couples**
Trials (May subdiv. geog.)   **345; 347**
    May be qualified by topic, e.g. **Trials (Homicide)**.
    BT   **Criminal law**
    NT   **Courts martial and courts of inquiry**
           Trials (Homicide)
           War crime trials
           Witnesses
    RT   **Crime**
Trials—Fiction
    USE   **Legal stories**
Trials (Homicide) (May subdiv. geog.)   **345**
    UF   Homicide trials
           Murder trials
           Trials (Murder)
    BT   **Homicide**
           Trials
Trials (Murder)
    USE   **Trials (Homicide)**
Triangle   **516.15**
    BT   **Geometry**
           Shape
Triathlon   **796.42**
    BT   **Sports**
Tribal government (May subdiv. geog.)   **306.2**
    BT   **Political science**
           Tribes
Tribes (May subdiv. geog.)   **305.8**
    UF   Tribes and tribal system
    BT   **Clans**
           Family
    NT   **Tribal government**
Tribes and tribal system
    USE   **Tribes**
Triceratops   **567.915**
    BT   **Dinosaurs**
Tricks   **793.5**
    SA   types of tricks [to be added as needed]
    BT   **Amusements**
    NT   **Card tricks**
           Juggling
           Magic tricks
Tricycles   **629.227; 796.6**

    UF   Trikes
    BT   **Vehicles**
    RT   **Cycling**
Trigonometry   **516.24**
    UF   Plane trigonometry
           Spherical trigonometry
    BT   **Geometry**
           Mathematics
Trigonometry—Tables   **516.24**
    BT   **Mathematics—Tables**
    NT   **Logarithms**
Trikes
    USE   **Tricycles**
Trinity   **231**
    BT   **Christianity—Doctrines**
           God—Christianity
    NT   **Holy Spirit**
Triplets   **155.44; 306.875**
    BT   **Multiple birth**
           Siblings
Tripoline War, 1801-1805
    USE   **United States—History—1801-1805, Tripolitan War**
Tripolitan War, 1801-1805
    USE   **United States—History—1801-1805, Tripolitan War**
Trivia
    USE   **Curiosities and wonders**
           Questions and answers
Trojan War   **292.1**
    BT   **Greek mythology**
           Troy (Extinct city)
Trolley cars
    USE   **Street railroads**
Troodon   **567.912**
    BT   **Dinosaurs**
Tropes
    USE   **Figures of speech**
Tropical conditions
    USE   subjects with the subdivision *Tropical conditions*, e.g. **Building—Tropical conditions** or the subdivision *Tropics*, e.g. **Agriculture—Tropics** [to be added as needed]
Tropical diseases
    USE   **Tropical medicine**
Tropical fish (May subdiv. geog.)   **597.17**
    BT   **Fishes**

Tropical hygiene
  USE **Tropical medicine**
Tropical jungles
  USE **Jungles**
Tropical medicine (May subdiv. geog.)
      614
  UF Diseases, Tropical
      Tropical diseases
      Tropical hygiene
  SA types of tropical diseases, e.g.
      Yellow fever [to be added as
      needed]
  BT **Medicine**
  NT **Yellow fever**
Tropical rain forests
  USE **Rain forests**
Tropics **910.913**
  SA subjects with the subdivision
      Tropics, e.g. **Agriculture—
      Tropics** or *Tropical condi-
      tions*, e.g. **Building—Tropical
      conditions** [to be added as
      needed]
  BT **Earth**
  NT **Agriculture—Tropics**
Troubadours (May subdiv. geog.) **849.1;
      920**
  BT **French poetry**
      Minstrels
      Poets
Trout fishing (May subdiv. geog.) **799.1**
  BT **Fishing**
Troy (Extinct city) **939**
  UF Ilium (Extinct city)
  BT **Extinct cities—Turkey**
      Turkey—Antiquities
  NT **Trojan War**
Truck crops
  USE **Truck farming**
Truck farming (May subdiv. geog.) **635**
  UF Garden farming
      Market gardening
      Truck crops
      Truck gardening
  BT **Agriculture**
      Gardening
      Horticulture
  RT **Vegetable gardening**
Truck freight
  USE **Trucking**

Truck gardening
  USE **Truck farming**
Trucking (May subdiv. geog.) **388.3**
  UF Truck freight
  BT **Freight**
      Transportation
Trucks (May subdiv. geog.) **629.224**
  UF Motor trucks
  SA types of trucks and names of
      specific makes and models [to
      be added as needed]
  BT **Automobiles**
      Highway transportation
      Motor vehicles
  RT **Materials handling**
Trucks—Weight **629.224**
Trust **158.2**
  BT **Attitude (Psychology)**
      Emotions
Trust companies (May subdiv. geog.)
      332.2
  BT **Business**
      Corporations
  RT **Banks and banking**
      Trusts and trustees
Trust funds
  USE **Trusts and trustees**
Trustees
  USE **Trusts and trustees**
Trusts and trustees (May subdiv. geog.)
      346.05
  UF Boards of trustees
      Fiduciaries
      Trust funds
      Trustees
  SA types of trustees, e.g. **Library
      trustees** [to be added as
      needed]
  BT **Contracts**
  NT **Library trustees**
      Living trusts
  RT **Estate planning**
      Executors and administrators
      Inheritance and succession
      Trust companies
Trusts, Industrial
  USE **Industrial trusts**
Truth **121**
  BT **Belief and doubt**
      Philosophy

Truth—*Continued*
> NT **Reality**
> **Truthfulness and falsehood**
> RT **Certainty**
> **Pragmatism**
> **Skepticism**
> **Theory of knowledge**

Truth in advertising
> USE **Deceptive advertising**

Truthfulness and falsehood   177
> UF Credibility
> Falsehood
> Lying
> Untruth
> BT **Human behavior**
> **Truth**
> NT **Deception**
> **Lie detectors and detection**
> RT **Honesty**

Tsunamis (May subdiv. geog.)   **551.46**
> UF Earthquake sea waves
> Seismic sea waves
> Tidal waves
> BT **Natural disasters**
> **Ocean waves**

Tuberculosis (May subdiv. geog.)   **616.9**
> BT **Lungs—Diseases**

Tuberculosis—Mortality (May subdiv. geog.)   **616.9**

Tuberculosis—Vaccination (May subdiv. geog.)   **614.4**
> BT **Vaccination**

Tugboats (May subdiv. geog.)   **623.82**
> BT **Boats and boating**

Tuition
> USE **College costs**
> **Colleges and universities—Finance**
> **Education—Finance**

Tumbling   796.47
> BT **Acrobats and acrobatics**

Tumors   616.99
> NT **Cancer**

Tundra ecology (May subdiv. geog.)   **577.5**
> BT **Ecology**

Tuning   784.192
> SA types of instruments with the subdivision *Tuning* [to be added as needed]
> NT **Pianos—Tuning**
> RT **Musical instruments**

Tunnels (May subdiv. geog.)   **388; 624.1**
> BT **Civil engineering**
> NT **Excavation**
> RT **Drilling and boring (Earth and rocks)**

Turbines   621.406
> BT **Engines**
> **Hydraulic machinery**
> NT **Gas turbines**
> **Steam turbines**

Turin Shroud
> USE **Holy Shroud**

Turkey   956.1
> May be subdivided like United States except for History.

Turkey—Antiquities   956.1
> BT **Antiquities**
> NT **Troy (Extinct city)**

Turkeys (May subdiv. geog.)   **598.6; 636.5**
> BT **Birds**
> **Poultry**

Turkmenistan   958.5

Turncoats
> USE **Defectors**

Turning   621.9
> UF Lathe work
> Wood turning
> BT **Carpentry**
> **Manufacturing processes**
> RT **Lathes**
> **Woodwork**

Turnpikes (Modern)
> USE **Express highways**

Turtles (May subdiv. geog.)   **597.92**
> UF Terrapins
> Tortoises
> BT **Reptiles**

Tutoring
> USE **Tutors and tutoring**

Tutors
> USE **Tutors and tutoring**

Tutors and tutoring (May subdiv. geog.)   **371.39**
> Use for general materials on one on-one instruction. Materials on the adaptation of instruction to meet individual needs within a group are entered under **Individualized instruction**.
> UF Tutoring
> Tutors
> BT **Teaching**

Tutors and tutoring—*Continued*
  NT **Independent study**
      Individualized instruction
Tutsi (African people) (May subdiv.
      geog.) **305.896**
  BT **Africans**
      Indigenous peoples
TV
  USE **Television**
TV personalities
  USE **Television personalities**
Twelfth century
  USE **World history—12th century**
Twelve-step programs 362.29
  UF Programs, Twelve-step
      Twelve steps (Self-help)
  SA names of specific twelve-step
      programs [to be added as
      needed]
  BT **Behavior modification**
  RT **Alcoholism**
      Compulsive behavior
      Drug abuse
Twelve steps (Self-help)
  USE **Twelve-step programs**
Twentieth century
  USE **World history—20th century**
Twenty-first century
  USE **World history—21st century**
Twins 155.44; 306.875
  BT **Multiple birth**
      Siblings
Twisters (Tornadoes)
  USE **Tornadoes**
Twitter (Web site) 004.69; 384.3
  BT **Social networking**
      Web sites
Two-career couples
  USE **Dual-career families**
Two-career families
  USE **Dual-career families**
Two-career family
  USE **Dual-career families**
Two-income families
  USE **Dual-career families**
Two-year colleges
  USE **Junior colleges**
Type and type-founding (May subdiv.
      geog.) **686.2**
  UF Type and type founding
  BT **Founding**
      Printing

  NT **Computer fonts**
      Linotype
  RT **Initials**
      Printing—Specimens
      Typesetting
      Typography
Type and type founding
  USE **Type and type-founding**
Type design
  USE **Typography**
Type-setting
  USE **Typesetting**
Type specimens
  USE **Printing—Specimens**
Typefaces
  USE **Typography**
Types, Psychological
  USE **Typology (Psychology)**
Typesetting 686.2
  UF Composition (Printing)
      Type-setting
  BT **Printing**
  NT **Linotype**
  RT **Type and type-founding**
Typewriters 652.3; 681
  BT **Office equipment and supplies**
Typewriting 652.3
  UF Typing
  BT **Business education**
      Office practice
      Writing
  RT **Keyboarding (Electronics)**
Typhoid fever (May subdiv. geog.)
      616.9
  UF Enteric fever
  BT **Diseases**
Typhoons (May subdiv. geog.) **551.55**
      Use for cyclonic storms originating in the
    region of the China Seas and the Philippines.
  BT **Cyclones**
      Storms
      Winds
  RT **Hurricanes**
Typing
  USE **Typewriting**
Typography 686.2
  UF Type design
      Typefaces
  BT **Graphic arts**
      Printing
  NT **Advertising layout and typog-
      raphy**

Typography—*Continued*
    RT   **Type and type-founding**
Typology (Psychology)   **155.2**
    UF   Mental types
          Psychological types
          Types, Psychological
    BT   **Personality**
          Psychology
          Temperament
    NT   **Enneagram**
Tyrannosaurus Rex   **567.912**
    BT   **Dinosaurs**
UFO abduction
    USE **Alien abduction**
UFOs
    USE **Unidentified flying objects**
UHF radio
    USE **Shortwave radio**
Ukraine   **947.7**
Ultrahigh frequency radio
    USE **Shortwave radio**
Ultrasonic waves   **534.5**
    UF   Supersonic waves
          Waves, Ultrasonic
    BT   **Sound waves**
          Ultrasonics
Ultrasonic waves—Industrial applications
    (May subdiv. geog.)   **620.2**
Ultrasonics   **534.5**
    UF   Inaudible sound
          Supersonics
    BT   **Sound**
    NT   **Ultrasonic waves**
Ultraviolet rays   **535.01; 621.36**
    UF   Rays, Ultra-violet
    BT   **Electromagnetic waves**
          Radiation
    RT   **Phototherapy**
          Radiotherapy
Umbrellas and parasols   **391.4; 685**
    UF   Parasols
    BT   **Clothing and dress**
UN
    USE **United Nations**
Unbelief
    USE **Skepticism**
Unborn child
    USE **Fetus**
Uncles (May subdiv. geog.)   **306.87**
    BT   **Family**
Unconventional warfare
    USE **Guerrilla warfare**

Undenominational churches
    USE **Community churches**
Underachievers (May subdiv. geog.)
    371.28
    BT   **Students**
Underdeveloped areas
    USE **Developing countries**
Undergraduates
    USE **College students**
Underground architecture (May subdiv.
    geog.)   **624.1; 690; 720**
    UF   Underground design
    BT   **Architecture**
    NT   **Basements**
          Earth sheltered houses
Underground design
    USE **Underground architecture**
Underground economy (May subdiv.
    geog.)   **381**
    Use for materials on goods and services that are produced and sold legally but not reported or taxed. Materials on illegal trade aimed at avoiding government regulations, such as fixed prices or rationing, are entered under **Black market**.
    UF   Economy, Underground
          Hidden economy
          Informal sector (Economics)
          Parallel economy
          Second economy
          Shadow economy
          Untaxed income
    BT   **Economics**
          Small business
    NT   **Barter**
          Illegal aliens
    RT   **Black market**
Underground films
    USE **Experimental films**
Underground houses
    USE **Earth sheltered houses**
Underground literature
    USE **Alternative press**
Underground movements
    USE names of wars with the subdivision *Underground movements,* e.g. **World War, 1939-1945—Underground movements** [to be added as needed]
Underground press
    USE **Alternative press**

Underground railroad (May subdiv. geog.) **326**
  RT **Slavery—United States**
Underground railroads
  USE **Subways**
Underground water
  USE **Groundwater**
Underprivileged
  USE **Socially handicapped**
Underprivileged children
  USE **Socially handicapped children**
Underprivileged students
  USE **At risk students**
Undersea engineering
  USE **Ocean engineering**
Undersea exploration
  USE **Underwater exploration**
Undersea research stations **551.46**
  UF Manned undersea research stations
      Sea laboratories
      Submarine research stations
      Underwater research stations
  SA names of special research projects and stations, e.g. **Sealab project** [to be added as needed]
  BT **Oceanography—Research**
      Underwater exploration
  NT **Sealab project**
Undersea vehicles
  USE **Submersibles**
Understanding
  USE **Intellect**
      Theory of knowledge
Undertakers and undertaking (May subdiv. geog.) **363.7; 393**
  UF Funeral directors
      Morticians
  BT **Service industries**
Underwater diving
  USE **Deep diving**
Underwater drilling (Petroleum)
  USE **Offshore oil well drilling**
Underwater exercises
  USE **Aquatic exercises**
Underwater exploration (May subdiv. geog.) **551.46; 627**
  UF Submarine exploration
      Undersea exploration

  BT **Exploration**
      Oceanography
  NT **Buried treasure**
      Deep diving
      Undersea research stations
Underwater geology
  USE **Submarine geology**
Underwater medicine
  USE **Submarine medicine**
Underwater photography **778.7**
  UF Deep-sea photography
      Submarine photography
  BT **Photography**
Underwater physiology
  USE **Submarine medicine**
Underwater research stations
  USE **Undersea research stations**
Underwater swimming
  USE **Skin diving**
Undocumented aliens
  USE **Illegal aliens**
Unemployed (May subdiv. geog.) **331.13**
  UF Jobless people
      Out-of-work people
  BT **Labor supply**
      Poor
      Unemployment
  NT **Food relief**
      Occupational retraining
  RT **Domestic economic assistance**
      Tramps
Unemployment (May subdiv. geog.) **331.13**
  UF Joblessness
  BT **Employment**
      Labor supply
      Social problems
  NT **Employment agencies**
      Plant shutdowns
      Unemployed
Unemployment insurance (May subdiv. geog.) **368.4**
  UF Insurance, Unemployment
      Labor—Insurance
      Payroll taxes
  BT **Insurance**
Unfair competition (May subdiv. geog.) **338.6**
  UF Competition, Unfair
      Fair trade
      Unfair trade practices

Unfair competition—*Continued*
    BT   **Commercial law**
    NT   **Trade secrets**
    RT   **Restraint of trade**
Unfair trade practices
    USE **Unfair competition**
Ungraded schools
    USE **Nongraded schools**
Unicorns   398.2454
    BT   **Mythical animals**
Unidentified flying objects   001.9
    UF   Flying saucers
          Saucers, Flying
          UFOs
    BT   **Aeronautics**
          Astronautics
    RT   **Human-alien encounters**
Uniforms (May subdiv. geog.)   **391**
    SA   classes of persons and names of
          individual corporate bodies
          and military services with the
          subdivision *Uniforms*, e.g.
          United States. Army—Uni-
          forms [to be added as need-
          ed]
    BT   **Clothing and dress**
          Costume
    NT   **Military uniforms**
Uniforms, Military
    USE **Military uniforms**
Uniforms, Naval
    USE **Military uniforms**
Union churches
    USE **Community churches**
Union of South Africa
    USE **South Africa**
Union of Soviet Socialist Republics
    USE **Russia—History—1917-1991,**
          Soviet Union
Union shop
    USE **Open and closed shop**
Unions, Labor
    USE **Labor unions**
Unison speaking
    USE **Choral speaking**
Unitarianism (May subdiv. geog.)   **289.1**
    BT   **Christian sects**
          Congregationalism
United Brethren
    USE **Moravians**
United Nations   341.23
    UF   UN

    BT   **International arbitration**
          International cooperation
          International organization
United Nations—Armed forces   341.23;
    355.3
    UF   Peace keeping forces
    BT   **Armed forces**
United Nations—Employees
    USE **United Nations—Officials and**
          employees
United Nations—Finance   336.09;
    341.23
    BT   **Finance**
United Nations—Information services
    341.23
    BT   **Information services**
United Nations—Officials and employees
    341.23
    UF   United Nations—Employees
United States   973
    The subdivisions under **United States**, with
    the exception of the period divisions of histo-
    ry, may be used under the name of any coun-
    try or region. The subdivisions under **Ohio**
    may be used under names of states, and those
    under **Chicago (Ill.)** under cities. Corporate
    name headings for corporate entities within
    the United States government, such as govern-
    ment agencies and departments, which are
    used either as authors or as subjects, have a
    period rather than a dash between the parts,
    e.g. **United States. Army**; and may be added
    as needed.
    UF   US
          USA
    SA   regions of the United States and
          groups of states, e.g. **New**
          England; Southern States;
          etc. [to be added as needed]
    NT   **Appalachian Region**
          Atlantic States
          Gulf States (U.S.)
          Middle West
          Mississippi River Valley
          New England
          Old Northwest
          Old Southwest
          Oregon Trail
          Pacific Northwest
          Southern States
          Southwestern States
          West (U.S.)
    RT   **Americans**

United States. Army 355

Subdivisions used under this heading may be used under armies of other countries as appropriate.

BT **Armies**
   Military history
   United States—Armed forces

United States. Army—Appointments and retirements 355.1

UF United States. Army—Retirements

United States. Army—Biography 920

BT **Biography**

United States. Army—Chaplains 355.3; 920

BT **Chaplains**

United States. Army—Demobilization 355.2

United States. Army—Enlistment

USE **United States. Army—Recruiting and enlistment**

United States. Army—Examinations 355.1

UF Army tests
BT **Examinations**

United States. Army—Handbooks, manuals, etc. 355

UF Soldiers' handbooks
   United States. Army—Officers' handbooks
   United States. Army—Soldiers' handbooks

United States. Army—Insignia 355.1

BT **Insignia**

United States. Army—Medals, badges, decorations, etc. 355.1

BT **Insignia**
   Medals

United States. Army—Military life 355.1

BT **Military personnel**
   Soldiers

United States. Army—Music

USE **United States. Army—Songs**

United States. Army—Officers 355.3

BT **Military personnel**
   Soldiers

United States. Army—Officers' handbooks

USE **United States. Army—Handbooks, manuals, etc.**

United States. Army—Ordnance 355.8

UF United States. Army—Ordnance and ordnance stores
BT **Ordnance**

United States. Army—Ordnance and ordnance stores

USE **United States. Army—Ordnance**

United States. Army—Parachute troops 356

UF United States—Parachute troops
BT **Parachute troops**

United States. Army—Recruiting and enlistment 355.2

UF United States. Army—Enlistment
BT **Recruiting and enlistment**

United States. Army—Retirements

USE **United States. Army—Appointments and retirements**

United States. Army—Soldiers' handbooks

USE **United States. Army—Handbooks, manuals, etc.**

United States. Army—Songs 782.42

UF United States. Army—Music
   United States. Army—Songs and music
BT **Songs**

United States. Army—Songs and music

USE **United States. Army—Songs**

United States. Army—Uniforms 355.1

United States. Congress 328.73

UF Congress (U.S.)
BT **Legislative bodies**

United States. Congress. House 328.73

UF House of Representatives (U.S.)
   Representatives, House of (U.S.)

United States. Congress. Senate 328.73

UF Senate (U.S.)

United States. Constitution 342.73

Use for the text of the United States Constitution and for materials about that document.

UF American constitution
   Constitution (U.S.)

United States. Constitution. 1st-10th amendments 342.73

Use for the text of the United States Bill of rights and for materials about that document.

UF American Bill of rights
   Bill of rights (U.S.)
   United States—Bill of rights

United States. Library of Congress

USE **Library of Congress**

United States. National Guard 355.3

United States. National Guard—*Continued*
  UF   National Guard (U.S.)
  BT   **United States—Militia**
United States. Navy   359
  Subdivisions used under **United States. Army** may be used under this heading and under navies of other countries as appropriate.
  BT   **Navies**
       United States—Armed forces
United States. Navy—Biography   920
  BT   **Biography**
United States. Navy—Enlistment
  USE   **United States. Navy—Recruiting and enlistment**
United States. Navy—Handbooks, manuals, etc.   359
  UF   Sailors' handbooks
       United States. Navy—Officers' handbooks
       United States. Navy—Sailors' handbooks
United States. Navy—Insignia   359.1
  BT   **Insignia**
United States. Navy—Medals, badges, decorations, etc.   359.1
  BT   **Insignia**
       Medals
United States. Navy—Officers   359.3
  BT   **Military personnel**
United States. Navy—Officers' handbooks
  USE   **United States. Navy—Handbooks, manuals, etc.**
United States. Navy—Recruiting and enlistment   359.2
  UF   United States. Navy—Enlistment
  BT   **Recruiting and enlistment**
United States. Navy—Sailors' handbooks
  USE   **United States. Navy—Handbooks, manuals, etc.**
United States. Supreme Court   347.73
  UF   Supreme Court—United States
  BT   **Courts**
United States. Supreme Court—Biography   920
  BT   **Biography**
United States—Annexations
  USE   **United States—Territorial expansion**
United States—Antiquities   973
  BT   **Antiquities**
United States—Appropriations and expenditures   352.4

  UF   Federal spending policy
       Government spending policy
  BT   **Budget—United States**
United States—Archives
  USE   **Archives—United States**
United States—Armed forces   355.00973
  SA   official names and branches of the armed forces, e.g. **United States. Army**; **United States. Navy**; etc. [to be added as needed]
  BT   **Armed forces**
  NT   **United States. Army**
       United States. Navy
United States—Armed forces—Gays
  USE   **Gays and lesbians in the military**
United States—Armed forces—Military life   355.10973
  BT   **Military personnel**
United States—Armed Forces—Recruiting and enlistment   355.2
  BT   **Recruiting and enlistment**
United States—Atlases
  USE   **United States—Maps**
United States—Bibliography   015.73; 016.973
United States—Bicentennial celebrations
  USE   **American Revolution Bicentennial, 1776-1976**
United States—Bill of rights
  USE   **United States. Constitution. 1st-10th amendments**
United States—Bio-bibliography   012
United States—Biography   920.073
  BT   **Biography**
United States—Biography—Dictionaries   920.073
United States—Biography—Portraits   920.073
  UF   United States—History—Portraits
United States—Boundaries   973
  BT   **Boundaries**
United States—Budget
  USE   **Budget—United States**
United States—Campaign funds
  USE   **Campaign funds—United States**
United States—Census   317.3; 352.7
  BT   **Census**

United States—Centennial celebrations, etc.   973

    NT   American Revolution Bicentennial, 1776-1976

United States—Church and state

    USE   Church and state—United States

United States—Church history   277.3

    UF   Church history—United States

        United States—Religious history

    BT   Church history

    RT   United States—Religion

United States—Cities and towns

    USE   Cities and towns—United States

United States—Civil defense

    USE   Civil defense—United States

United States—Civil service

    USE   Civil service—United States

United States—Civilization   973

    BT   Civilization

    NT   Americana

United States—Civilization—1960-1970   973.92

United States—Civilization—1970-   973.92

United States—Civilization—Foreign influences   973

United States—Climate   551.6973

    BT   Climate

United States—Commerce   381; 382.0973

    BT   Commerce

United States—Commerce—Japan   382

United States—Commercial policy

    USE   Commercial policy—United States

United States—Constitutional history

    USE   Constitutional history—United States

United States—Constitutional law

    USE   Constitutional law—United States

United States—Constitutions

    USE   Constitutions—United States

United States—Courts

    USE   Courts—United States

United States—Cultural policy

    USE   Cultural policy—United States

United States—Declaration of independence   973.3

    UF   Declaration of independence (U.S.)

United States—Defenses   355.4

    BT   Military readiness

    NT   Strategic Defense Initiative

United States—Description

    USE   United States—Description and travel

United States—Description and travel   917.3

    UF   United States—Description

        United States—Travel

    BT   Geography

United States—Description and travel—Guidebooks

    USE   United States—Guidebooks

United States—Description and travel—Views

    USE   United States—Pictorial works

United States—Diplomatic and consular service

    USE   American diplomatic and consular service

United States—Directories   917.30025

    Use for lists of names and addresses. Lists of names without addresses are entered under United States—Registers.

    BT   Directories

    RT   United States—Registers

United States—Economic conditions   330.973

    UF   National resources

    BT   Economic conditions

United States—Economic policy

    USE   Economic policy—United States

United States—Elections

    USE   Elections—United States

United States—Emigration and immigration

    USE   United States—Immigration and emigration

United States—Employees

    USE   United States—Officials and employees

United States—Environmental policy

    USE   Environmental policy—United States

United States—Ethnic relations   305.8

United States—Ethnology

    USE   Ethnology—United States

United States—Executive departments

    USE   Executive departments—United States

United States—Executive departments—Reorganization

> USE **Administrative agencies—Reor-
> ganization—United States**

United States—Executive power

> USE **Executive power—United
> States**

United States—Exploration   973

> UF   Exploration—United States
>
> BT   **America—Exploration**
>
> **Exploration**
>
> NT   **West (U.S.)—Exploration**

**United States—Exploring expeditions
910.973; 973**

Use for materials on exploring expeditions
sponsored by the United States. Materials on
early exploration of a particular place are entered under the name of the place with the
subdivision *Exploration.*

> UF   American exploring expeditions
>
> SA   names of expeditions, e.g. **Lewis
> and Clark Expedition (1804-
> 1806)** [to be added as need-
> ed]
>
> BT   **Explorers**
>
> NT   **Lewis and Clark Expedition
> (1804-1806)**

United States—Fiscal policy

> USE   **Fiscal policy—United States**

United States—Flags

> USE   **Flags—United States**

**United States—Foreign economic rela-
tions   337.73**

> UF   Foreign economic relations—
> United States
>
> BT   **International economic rela-
> tions**

United States—Foreign opinion (May
subdiv. geog.)   **303.3; 973**

Use for materials on foreign public opinion
about the United States. May be further subdivided by the country holding the opinion, e.g.
United States—Foreign opinion—France.

> UF   Anti-Americanism
>
> Antiamericanism
>
> United States—Foreign public
> opinion
>
> BT   **Public opinion**

**United States—Foreign opinion—France
303.3; 973**

Use for materials on French public opinion
about the United States.

United States—Foreign policy

> USE   **United States—Foreign rela-
> tions**

United States—Foreign population

> USE   **Aliens—United States**
>
> **Immigrants—United States**

United States—Foreign public opinion

> USE   **United States—Foreign opinion**

United States—Foreign relations (May
subdiv. geog.)   **327.73**

When further subdividing geographically,
provide an additional subject entry with the
two places in reversed positions, i.e. **United
States—Foreign relations—Iran** and also
Iran—Foreign relations—United States.

> UF   United States—Foreign policy
>
> BT   **Diplomacy**
>
> **International relations**
>
> **World politics**
>
> NT   **Monroe Doctrine**
>
> RT   **Neutrality—United States**

**United States—Foreign relations—Iran
327.73055**

> NT   **Iran hostage crisis, 1979-1981**

**United States—Foreign relations—Trea-
ties   327.73; 341.3**

> UF   United States—Treaties
>
> BT   **Treaties**

United States—Gazetteers   917.3003

> BT   **Gazetteers**

United States—Geographic names

> USE   **Geographic names—United
> States**

United States—Geography   917.3

> BT   **Geography**

United States—Government

> USE   **United States—Politics and
> government**

United States—Government buildings

> USE   **Public buildings—United States**

United States—Government employees

> USE   **United States—Officials and
> employees**

United States—Government publications

> USE   **Government publications—
> United States**

United States—Governmental investigations

> USE   **Governmental investigations—
> United States**

United States—Guidebooks   917.304

> UF   United States—Description and
> travel—Guidebooks

United States—Historic buildings
　USE　**Historic buildings—United States**
United States—Historical geography
　　911
　BT　**Historical geography**
United States—Historical geography— Maps　911
　BT　**United States—Maps**
United States—Historiography　973.07
　UF　United States—History—Historiography
　BT　**Historiography**
United States—History　973
　UF　American history
　NT　**Americana**
　　　Constitutional history—United States
　　　Southern States—History
　　　West (U.S.)—History
United States—History—1600-1775, Colonial period　973.2
　　Use for materials on American history from the earliest permanent English settlements on the Atlantic coast up to the American Revolution. Materials on the period of discovery are entered under **United States—Exploration**.
　UF　American colonies
　　　Colonial history (U.S.)
　NT　**Bacon's Rebellion, 1676**
　　　King Philip's War, 1675-1676
　　　Pilgrims (New England colonists)
　　　Pontiac's Conspiracy, 1763-1765
　　　United States—History—1689-1697, King William's War
　　　United States—History—1755-1763, French and Indian War
United States—History—1675-1676, King Philip's War
　USE　**King Philip's War, 1675-1676**
United States—History—1689-1697, King William's War　973.2
　UF　King William's War, 1689-1697
　BT　**Native Americans—Wars**
　　　United States—History—1600-1775, Colonial period
United States—History—1755-1763, French and Indian War　973.2
　UF　French and Indian War

　BT　**Native Americans—Wars**
　　　Seven Years' War, 1756-1763
　　　United States—History—1600-1775, Colonial period
United States—History—1775-1783, Revolution　973.3
　　May be subdivided like **United States—History—1861-1865, Civil War**.
　UF　American Revolution
　　　Revolution, American
　　　War of the American Revolution
　BT　**Revolutions**
　NT　**American Loyalists**
　　　Boston Tea Party, 1773
　　　Canadian Invasion, 1775-1776
　　　Fourth of July
United States—History—1775-1783, Revolution—Campaigns　973.3
　NT　**Bunker Hill (Boston, Mass.), Battle of, 1775**
　　　Concord (Mass.), Battle of, 1775
　　　Lexington (Mass.), Battle of, 1775
United States—History—1775-1783, Revolution—Centennial celebrations, etc.
　USE　**American Revolution Bicentennial, 1776-1976**
United States—History—1783-1809
　USE　**United States—History—1783-1815**
United States—History—1783-1815　973.3; 973.4
　UF　Confederation of American colonies
　　　United States—History—1783-1809
　NT　**Lewis and Clark Expedition (1804-1806)**
　　　Louisiana Purchase
　　　War of 1812
United States—History—1783-1865　973
United States—History—19th century　973.5
United States—History—1801-1805, Tripolitan War　973.4
　UF　Tripoline War, 1801-1805
　　　Tripolitan War, 1801-1805
United States—History—1812-1815, War of 1812
　USE　**War of 1812**

798

United States—History—1815-1861
  973.5; 973.6
  NT Black Hawk War, 1832
      Mexican War, 1846-1848
United States—History—1845-1848, War
  with Mexico
  USE Mexican War, 1846-1848
United States—History—1861-1865, Civil
  War 973.7
  UF American Civil War
      Civil War—United States
  NT Confederate States of America
      Secession—Southern States
      Trent Affair, 1861
United States—History—1861-1865, Civil
  War—Biography 920; 973.7092
  BT Biography
United States—History—1861-1865, Civil
  War—Campaigns (May subdiv.
  geog.) 973.7
  SA names of battles, e.g. Gettys-
      burg (Pa.), Battle of, 1863
      [to be added as needed]
  NT Antietam (Md.), Battle of, 1862
      Appomattox Campaign, 1865
      Gettysburg (Pa.), Battle of,
      1863
United States—History—1861-1865, Civil
  War—Causes 973.7
  BT Secession—Southern States
United States—History—1861-1865, Civil
  War—Centennial celebrations, etc.
  973.7
United States—History—1861-1865, Civil
  War—Drama 808.82; 812
  Use for collections of plays dealing with
  the Civil War.
  BT Historical drama
United States—History—1861-1865, Civil
  War—Fiction 808.83; 813
  Use for collections of stories dealing with
  the Civil War.
United States—History—1861-1865, Civil
  War—Health aspects (May subdiv.
  geog.) 973.7
United States—History—1861-1865, Civil
  War—Historiography 973.7
  BT Historiography
United States—History—1861-1865, Civil
  War—Medical care 973.7
  BT Medical care

United States—History—1861-1865, Civil
  War—Naval operations 973.7
United States—History—1861-1865, Civil
  War—Personal narratives 973.7
  Use for collective or individual eyewitness
  reports or autobiographical accounts of the
  war in general. Accounts limited to a specific
  topic are entered under that topic.
  BT Autobiographies
      Biography
United States—History—1861-1865, Civil
  War—Pictorial works 973.7022
United States—History—1861-1865, Civil
  War—Prisoners and prisons
  973.7
  BT Prisoners of war
      Prisons
United States—History—1861-1865, Civil
  War—Reconstruction
  USE Reconstruction (1865-1876)
United States—History—1861-1865, Civil
  War—Sources 973.7
United States—History—1865-1898
  973.8
  NT Reconstruction (1865-1876)
      Spanish-American War, 1898
United States—History—1898-1919
  973.9; 973.91
  NT Spanish-American War, 1898
United States—History—1898, War of
  1898
  USE Spanish-American War, 1898
United States—History—20th century
  973.9
United States—History—1914-1918, World
  War
  USE World War, 1914-1918—United
      States
United States—History—1919-1933
  973.91
United States—History—1933-1945
  973.917
  NT New Deal, 1933-1939
United States—History—1939-1945, World
  War
  USE World War, 1939-1945—United
      States
United States—History—1945- 973.92
United States—History—1945-1953
  973.918
United States—History—1953-1961
  973.921

United States—History—1961-1974
973.92

   NT   Vietnam War, 1961-1975
       Watergate Affair, 1972-1974

United States—History—1974-1989
973.92

United States—History—1989-   973.928

   NT   Persian Gulf War, 1991

United States—History—21st century
973.93

United States—History—Bibliography
016.973

United States—History—Chronology
973

United States—History—Dictionaries
973.03

   BT   History—Dictionaries

United States—History—Drama   808.82;
812

Use for collections of plays dealing with American history.

   BT   Historical drama

United States—History—Examinations
973.076

   UF   United States—History—Examinations, questions, etc.

   BT   United States—History—Study and teaching

United States—History—Examinations, questions, etc.

   USE   United States—History—Examinations

United States—History—Fiction   808.83;
813

Use for collections of stories dealing with American history.

United States—History—Historiography

   USE   United States—Historiography

United States—History—Library resources   973.07

United States—History—Outlines, syllabi, etc.   973.02

   BT   United States—History—Study and teaching

United States—History—Periodicals
973.05

United States—History—Poetry   808.81;
811

Use for collections of poetry dealing with American history.

   BT   Historical poetry

United States—History—Portraits

   USE   United States—Biography—Portraits

United States—History—Societies
973.06

   BT   History—Societies

United States—History—Sources   973

United States—History—Study and teaching   973.07

   NT   United States—History—Examinations

       United States—History—Outlines, syllabi, etc.

United States—Immigration and emigration   325; 325.73

   UF   United States—Emigration and immigration

   SA   names of immigrant groups, e.g. Mexican Americans; Mexicans—United States [to be added as needed]

   BT   Americanization
       Immigration and emigration

   RT   Aliens—United States
       Immigrants—United States

United States—Industrial policy

   USE   Industrial policy—United States

United States—Industries

   USE   Industries—United States

United States—Insular possessions

   USE   United States—Territories and possessions

United States—Intellectual life   973

   BT   Intellectual life

United States—Intelligence service

   USE   Intelligence service—United States

United States—Internal security

   USE   Internal security—United States

United States—Land settlement

   USE   Land settlement—United States

United States—Land surveys

   USE   United States—Surveys

United States—Languages   306.44

Use for materials on the several languages spoken in the United States.

United States—Law

   USE   Law—United States

United States—Local history   973

   BT   Local history

United States—Mail
USE **Postal service—United States**
United States—Manufactures
USE **Manufactures—United States**
United States—Maps   912.73
UF   United States—Atlases
BT   **Atlases**
       Maps
NT   **United States—Historical geography—Maps**
United States Military Academy
    355.0071
UF   USMA
       West Point (Military academy)
BT   **Colleges and universities**
United States Military Academy—Registers   355.0071
United States Military Academy—Songs
    782.42
UF   United States Military Academy—Songs and music
BT   **Students' songs**
United States Military Academy—Songs
    and music
USE   **United States Military Academy—Songs**
United States—Military history
    355.00973; 973
BT   **Military history**
United States—Military offenses
USE   **Military offenses—United States**
United States—Military personnel
USE   **Military personnel—United States**
United States—Military policy
USE   **Military policy—United States**
United States—Militia   355.3
BT   **Armed forces**
NT   **United States. National Guard**
United States—Monetary policy
USE   **Monetary policy—United States**
United States—Moral conditions   973
BT   **Moral conditions**
United States—Municipal government
USE   **Municipal government—United States**
United States—National characteristics
USE   **American national characteristics**

United States—National parks and reserves
USE   **National parks and reserves—United States**
United States—National security
USE   **National security—United States**
United States—National songs
USE   **National songs—United States**
United States—Naval history   359.00973
BT   **Naval history**
United States—Neutrality
USE   **Neutrality—United States**
United States—Occupations
USE   **Occupations—United States**
United States—Officials and employees
    351.73
UF   United States—Employees
       United States—Government employees
RT   **Civil service—United States**
United States—Parachute troops
USE   **United States. Army—Parachute troops**
United States—Peoples
USE   **Ethnology—United States**
United States—Pictorial works
    917.30022
UF   United States—Description and travel—Views
United States—Police
USE   **Police—United States**
United States—Politicians
USE   **Politicians—United States**
United States—Politics
USE   **United States—Politics and government**
United States—Politics and government
    973
UF   American government
       American politics
       United States—Government
       United States—Politics
BT   **Political science**
       Politics
       Public administration
NT   **Third parties (United States politics)**
United States—Popular culture
USE   **Popular culture—United States**
United States—Population   304.60973
BT   **Population**

United States—Postal service
USE **Postal service—United States**
United States—Presidents
USE **Presidents—United States**
United States—Prisons
USE **Prisons—United States**
United States—Public buildings
USE **Public buildings—United States**
United States—Public debts
USE **Public debts—United States**
United States—Public health
USE **Public health—United States**
United States—Public lands
USE **Public lands—United States**
United States—Public schools
USE **Public schools—United States**
United States—Public works
USE **Public works—United States**
United States—Race relations
305.800973
BT **Race relations**
United States—Registers   917.30025
Use for lists of names without addresses. Lists of names that include addresses are entered under **United States—Directories**.
RT **United States—Directories**
United States—Religion   200.973; 277.3
BT **Religion**
RT **United States—Church history**
United States—Religious history
USE **United States—Church history**
United States—Rural conditions
307.720973
BT **Rural sociology**
United States—Secret service
USE **Secret service—United States**
United States—Separation of powers
USE **Separation of powers—United States**
United States—Social conditions   973
BT **Social conditions**
United States—Social life and customs
973
BT **Manners and customs**
United States—Social policy
USE **Social policy—United States**
United States—Soldiers
USE **Soldiers—United States**
United States—State governments
USE **State governments**
United States—Statistics   317.3
BT **Statistics**

United States—Surveys   972
Use for materials containing the results of land surveys of the United States.
UF   United States—Land surveys
United States—Tariff
USE **Tariff—United States**
United States—Taxation
USE **Taxation—United States**
United States—Term limits (Public office)
USE **Term limits (Public office)—United States**
United States—Territorial expansion
973
UF   Expansion (United States politics)
Manifest destiny (United States)
United States—Annexations
Westward movement
United States—Territorial waters
USE **Territorial waters—United States**
United States—Territories and possessions   325; 973
UF   United States—Insular possessions
United States—Travel
USE **United States—Description and travel**
United States—Treaties
USE **United States—Foreign relations—Treaties**
United States—Vice-presidents
USE **Vice-presidents—United States**
United States—World War, 1914-1918
USE **World War, 1914-1918—United States**
United States—World War, 1939-1945
USE **World War, 1939-1945—United States**
United States—World War, 1939-1945—Casualties
USE **World War, 1939-1945—Casualties—United States**
United States—World War, 1939-1945—Casualties—Statistics
USE **World War, 1939-1945—Casualties—United States—Statistics**
United Steelworkers of America   331.88
BT **Labor unions**
Universal bibliographic control
USE **Bibliographic control**

Universal history
    USE   **World history**
Universal language   401
    UF   International language
            Language, International
            Language, Universal
            World language
    BT   **Language and languages**
            Linguistics
    NT   **Esperanto**
Universal military training
    USE   **Draft**
Universe   113; 523.1

    Use for materials limited to the physical description of the universe. General and theoretical materials on the science or philosophy of the universe are entered under **Cosmology**.

    UF   Cosmogony
            Cosmography
    NT   **Astronomy**
            Cosmology
            Life on other planets
    RT   **Creation**
Universities
    USE   **Colleges and universities**
Universities and colleges
    USE   **Colleges and universities**
University degrees
    USE   **Academic degrees**
University extension (May subdiv. geog.)
        378.1
    BT   **Colleges and universities**
            Distance education
            Higher education
    NT   **Adult education**
            Correspondence schools and courses
University graduates
    USE   **College graduates**
University libraries
    USE   **Academic libraries**
University students
    USE   **College students**
Unmarried couples (May subdiv. geog.)
        306.84
    UF   Cohabitation
            Common law marriage
            Living together
            Trial marriage
            Unmarried people
    BT   **Lifestyles**
            Shared housing

    NT   **Single parents**
Unmarried fathers (May subdiv. geog.)
        306.874; 362.82

    Use for materials on fathers who at the time of childbirth were not married to the child's mother. Materials on fathers rearing children without a partner in the household are entered under **Single-parent families**. Materials on fathers who are teenagers are entered under **Teenage fathers**.

    UF   Parents, Unmarried
            Unmarried parents
            Unwed fathers
    BT   **Fathers**
            Single parents
    RT   **Illegitimacy**
Unmarried men
    USE   **Single men**
Unmarried mothers (May subdiv. gcog.)
        306.874; 362.83

    Use for materials on mothers who at the time of giving birth were not married to the child's father. Materials on mothers rearing children without a partner in the household are entered under **Single-parent families**. Materials on mothers who are teenagers are entered under **Teenage mothers**.

    UF   Parents, Unmarried
            Unmarried parents
            Unwed mothers
    BT   **Mothers**
            Single parents
    RT   **Illegitimacy**
Unmarried parents
    USE   **Unmarried fathers**
            Unmarried mothers
Unmarried people
    USE   **Single people**
            Unmarried couples
Unmarried women
    USE   **Single women**
Unsafe products
    USE   **Product safety**
Unselfishness
    USE   **Altruism**
Unskilled labor (May subdiv. geog.)
        331.7
    UF   Unskilled workers
    BT   **Labor**
Unskilled labor—Supply and demand
        331.12
    BT   **Supply and demand**
Unskilled workers
    USE   **Unskilled labor**

Untaxed income
USE **Underground economy**
Untruth
USE **Truthfulness and falsehood**
Unwed fathers
USE **Unmarried fathers**
Unwed mothers
USE **Unmarried mothers**
Upholstery   684.1; 747
BT **Interior design**
NT **Draperies**
RT **Furniture**
Upper atmosphere   551.5
UF Atmosphere, Upper
BT **Atmosphere**
NT **Stratosphere**
Upper class (May subdiv. geog.)   **305.5**
UF Fashionable society
High society
Upper classes
BT **Social classes**
NT **Aristocracy**
Nobility
Upper classes
USE **Upper class**
Uranium (May subdiv. geog.)   **669**
BT **Chemical elements**
RT **Radioactivity**
Uranus (Planet)   523.47
BT **Planets**
Urban agriculture (May subdiv. geog.)
338.1
UF Urban farming
BT **Agriculture**
Urban areas
USE **Cities and towns**
Metropolitan areas
Urban development
USE **Cities and towns—Growth**
City planning
Urbanization
Urban ecology (May subdiv. geog.)
577.5
UF Urban environment
BT **Cities and towns**
Ecology
Urban education
USE **Urban schools**
Urban environment
USE **Urban ecology**

Urban farming
USE **Urban agriculture**
Urban-federal relations
USE **Federal-city relations**
Urban fiction   808.83
Use for individual works, collections or materials about fiction dealing with the harsh, often violent, side of contemporary city life.
UF Hip-hop fiction
BT **Fiction**
Urban folklore (May subdiv. geog.)
398.2
UF Urban legends
BT **Folklore**
Urban forestry (May subdiv. geog.)
577.3; 634.9
UF City forestry
Urban forests
BT **Forests and forestry**
Urban forests
USE **Urban forestry**
Urban homesteading (May subdiv. geog.)
363.5
BT **Houses—Buying and selling**
Housing
Urban renewal
Urban housing
USE **Housing**
Urban legends
USE **Urban folklore**
Urban life
USE **City and town life**
Urban planning
USE **City planning**
Urban policy (May subdiv. geog.)
307.76; 320.8
UF Urban problems
BT **City and town life**
Economic policy
Social policy
Urban sociology
RT **City planning**
Urban renewal
Urban problems
USE **Urban policy**
Urban renewal (May subdiv. geog.)
307.3
Use for materials on the economic, sociological, and political aspects of urban redevelopment. Materials on the architectural and engineering aspects are entered under **City planning**.
UF Slum clearance

Urban renewal—*Continued*
   BT **Metropolitan areas**
       Urban sociology
   NT **Community development**
       Urban homesteading
   RT **City planning**
       Community organization
       Urban policy
Urban renewal—Chicago (Ill.)   307.3
   UF Chicago (Ill.)—Urban renewal
Urban renewal—United States   307.3
Urban-rural migration
   USE **Internal migration**
Urban schools (May subdiv. geog.)   371
   UF City schools
       Inner city schools
       Urban education
   BT **Schools**
Urban sociology (May subdiv. geog.)
     307.76
   UF Sociology, Urban
   BT **Sociology**
   NT **City and town life**
       Urban policy
       Urban renewal
       Urbanization
   RT **Cities and towns**
Urban street life
   USE **Street life**
Urban traffic
   USE **City traffic**
Urban transportation
   USE **Local transit**
Urbanization (May subdiv. geog.)
     307.76
   Use for materials on the process by which town and communities acquire urban characteristics.
   UF Cities and towns, Movement to
       Urban development
   BT **Cities and towns**
       Rural sociology
       Social change
       Social conditions
       Urban sociology
   RT **Cities and towns—Growth**
US
   USE **United States**
USA
   USE **United States**

Usage
   USE names of languages and groups of languages with the subdivision *Usage,* e.g. **English language—Usage** [to be added as needed]
Used merchandise
   USE **Secondhand trade**
Useful insects
   USE **Beneficial insects**
USMA
   USE **United States Military Academy**
USSR
   USE **Russia—History—1917-1991, Soviet Union**
Utensils
   USE **Implements, utensils, etc.**
Utensils, Kitchen
   USE **Kitchen utensils**
Utilitarianism   144
   BT **Ethics**
   NT **Secularism**
   RT **Pragmatism**
Utilities (Computer programs)
   USE **Utilities (Computer software)**
Utilities (Computer software)   005.4
   Use for materials on software used to perform standard computer system operations such as sorting data, searching for viruses, copying data from one file to another, etc.
   UF Computer utility programs
       Computers—Utility programs
       Utilities (Computer programs)
       Utility programs (Computer software)
   BT **Computer software**
Utilities, Public
   USE **Public utilities**
Utility programs (Computer software)
   USE **Utilities (Computer software)**
Utilization of waste
   USE **Salvage**
Utopian fiction   808.3; 808.83
   Use for individual works, collections, or materials about imaginative accounts of ideal societies. Theoretical materials about ideal societies and accounts of practical attempts to create such societies are entered under **Utopias.**
   UF Ideal states
       Utopian literature
   BT **Fantasy fiction**
       Science fiction

Utopian fiction—*Continued*

RT **Dystopias**
Utopias

Utopian literature

USE **Utopian fiction**
Utopias

Utopias   321; 335

Use for theoretical materials on ideal societies and for accounts of practical attempts to create such societies. Imaginative accounts of ideal societies are entered under **Utopian fiction**.

UF   Ideal states
Utopian literature

BT   **Political science**
Socialism

RT   **Collective settlements**
Paradise
Utopian fiction

Uzbekistan   958.7

V-chips   363.3

UF   Violence chips

BT   **Television—Censorship**
Television—Receivers and reception

Vacation church schools

USE   **Religious summer schools**

Vacation home timesharing

USE   **Timesharing (Real estate)**

Vacation homes (May subdiv. geog.) **643.2; 728.72**

UF   Summer cottages
Summer homes
Vacation houses

BT   **Houses**

Vacation houses

USE   **Vacation homes**

Vacation schools

USE   **Summer schools**

Vacation schools, Religious

USE   **Religious summer schools**

Vacations (May subdiv. geog.)   **331.25; 658.3**

BT   **Recreation**

RT   **Holidays**

Vaccination (May subdiv. geog.)   **614.4**

Use for materials on active immunization with a vaccine. Materials on any process, active or passive, that leads to increased immunity are entered under **Immunization**.

UF   Inoculation

SA   types of animals and types of diseases with the subdivision *Vaccination*, e.g. **Cattle—**

Vaccination; **Tuberculosis—Vaccination** [to be added as needed]

BT   **Immunization**
Preventive medicine
Public health

NT   **Cattle—Vaccination**
Poliomyelitis vaccine
Tuberculosis—Vaccination

Vacuum tubes   537.5; 621.3815

UF   Electron tubes

BT   **Electronic apparatus and appliances**

NT   **Cathode ray tubes**

RT   **X-rays**

Vagabonds

USE   **Tramps**

Vagrants

USE   **Tramps**

Valentine's Day   394.2618

UF   Saint Valentine's Day
St. Valentine's Day

BT   **Holidays**

Valuation   338.5

Use for general materials on the appraisal of property. Materials on valuation of particular types of property are entered under the type of property, e.g. **Real estate**. Materials on valuation for taxing purposes are entered under **Tax assessment**.

UF   Appraisal
Capitalization (Finance)

NT   **Tax assessment**

Values   121; 170; 303.3

Use for materials on moral and aesthetic values.

UF   Axiology
Human values
Worth

BT   **Aesthetics**
Ethics
Psychology

NT   **Social values**

Vampire films   791.43

Use for individual works, collections, or materials about vampire films.

UF   Vampires in motion pictures

BT   **Horror films**
Motion pictures

Vampires (May subdiv. geog.)   **398.21**

BT   **Folklore**

Vampires in motion pictures

USE   **Vampire films**

Van pools
USE **Car pools**
Vandalism (May subdiv. geog.) **364.16**
UF Destruction of property
BT **Offenses against property**
NT **Graffiti**
Vanishing species
USE **Endangered species**
Vanity
USE **Pride and vanity**
Vans (May subdiv. geog.) **728.7**
BT **Travel trailers and campers**
Variation (Biology) **576.5**
UF Mutation (Biology)
BT **Biology**
Genetics
Heredity
NT **Adaptation (Biology)**
Mendel's law
Natural selection
RT **Evolution**
Variety shows (Radio programs)
791.44
Use for individual works, collections, or
materials about variety shows on the radio.
BT **Radio programs**
Variety shows (Television programs)
791.45
Use for individual works, collections, or
materials about variety shows on television.
BT **Television programs**
Varnish and varnishing **667; 698**
BT **Finishes and finishing**
Varsity sports
USE **College sports**
Vascular system
USE **Cardiovascular system**
Vasectomy **613.9**
BT **Sterilization (Birth control)**
Vases (May subdiv. geog.) **731; 738**
RT **Glassware**
Pottery
Vassals
USE **Feudalism**
Vatican City **945.6**
Use for geographical and descriptive materi-
als on the independent papal state in Rome.
Materials on the central administration of the
Roman Catholic Church are entered under
Catholic Church.
Vatican City—Foreign relations
USE **Catholic Church—Foreign rela-
tions**

Vatican Council (2nd: 1962-1965) **262**
BT **Councils and synods**
Vaudeville (May subdiv. geog.) **792.7**
BT **Amusements**
Theater
Vaults (Sepulchral)
USE **Tombs**
VCRs
USE **Video recording**
VD
USE **Sexually transmitted diseases**
Vedanta (May subdiv. geog.) **294.5**
BT **Hinduism**
Theosophy
Vedas **294.5**
BT **Hinduism**
Sacred books
Vegetable gardening (May subdiv. geog.)
635
UF Kitchen gardens
BT **Gardening**
Horticulture
RT **Truck farming**
Vegetables
Vegetable kingdom
USE **Botany**
Plants
Vegetable oils
USE **Essences and essential oils**
Oils and fats
Vegetables (May subdiv. geog.) **635;
641.3**
SA types of vegetables [to be added
as needed]
BT **Food**
Plants
NT **Celery**
Cooking—Vegetables
Potatoes
Root crops
RT **Vegetable gardening**
Vegetables—Canning
USE **Vegetables—Preservation**
Vegetables—Preservation (May subdiv.
geog.) **641.4**
UF Vegetables—Canning
BT **Canning and preserving**
Vegetarian cookery
USE **Vegetarian cooking**
Vegetarian cooking (May subdiv. geog.)
641.5

Vegetarian cooking—*Continued*
   UF   Vegetarian cookery
   BT   **Cooking**
   RT   **Cooking—Vegetables**
Vegetarianism (May subdiv. geog.)
       613.2
   BT   **Diet**
Vehicles (May subdiv. geog.) **388; 629.2**
   SA   types of vehicles and names of
         specific makes and models of
         vehicles [to be added as
         needed]
   BT   **Transportation**
   NT   **Air-cushion vehicles**
        All terrain vehicles
        Automobiles
        Bicycles
        Carriages and carts
        Military vehicles
        Recreational vehicles
        Sleds
        Sport utility vehicles
        Submersibles
        Taxicabs
        Tricycles
Vehicles, Military
   USE   **Military vehicles**
Velociraptors **567.912**
   BT   **Dinosaurs**
Velocity
   USE   **Speed**
Vendetta (May subdiv. geog.) **364.256**
   UF   Blood feuds
        Feuds
   RT   **Revenge**
Veneers and veneering **674; 698**
   BT   **Cabinetwork**
        Furniture
Venereal diseases
   USE   **Sexually transmitted diseases**
Venezuela **987**
   May be subdivided like United States ex-
   cept for History.
Vengence
   USE   **Revenge**
Ventilation **697.9**
   SA   types of buildings with the sub-
         division *Heating and ventila-*
         tion, e.g. **Houses—Heating**
         and ventilation [to be added
         as needed]

   BT   **Air**
        Home economics
        Household sanitation
        Hygiene
        Sanitation
   RT   **Air conditioning**
        Heating
Ventriloquism **793.8**
   BT   **Amusements**
        Voice
Venture capital **332**
   UF   Seed capital
   BT   **Capital**
Venus (Planet) **523.42**
   BT   **Planets**
Verbal abuse
   USE   **Invective**
Verbal learning **153.1; 370.15**
   Use for materials on the process of learning
   and understanding written or spoken language,
   ranging from learning to associate two non-
   sense syllables to solving problems presented
   in verbal terms.
   UF   Learning, Verbal
   BT   **Language and languages**
        Psychology of learning
   NT   **Reading comprehension**
Vermin
   USE   **Household pests**
        Pests
Vers libre
   USE   **Free verse**
Verse epistles
   USE   **Epistolary poetry**
Versification **808.1**
   UF   English language—Versification
        Meter
        Prosody
   BT   **Authorship**
        Poetics
        Rhythm
   NT   **Rhyme**
Vertebrates (May subdiv. geog.) **596**
   BT   **Animals**
Very high frequency radio
   USE   **Shortwave radio**
Vessels (Ships)
   USE   **Ships**
Vesta (Roman deity) **292.2**
   BT   **Gods and goddesses**
Veterans (May subdiv. geog.) **305.9;
       920**
   UF   War veterans

Veterans—*Continued*

SA   names of wars with the subdivision *Veterans*, e.g. **World War, 1939-1945—Veterans** [to be added as needed]

BT   **Military art and science**
Veterans

NT   **Veterans**
World War, 1939-1945—Veterans

RT   **Military hospitals**
Military pensions
Military personnel
Soldiers

Veterans Day   **394.264**

UF   Armistice Day

BT   **Holidays**

Veterans—Education (May subdiv. geog.) **362.86**

UF   Education of veterans

BT   **Education**

Veterans—Employment (May subdiv. geog.) **331.5**

BT   **Employment**

Veterans—Hospitals

USE   **Military hospitals**

Veterans—Legal status, laws, etc. (May subdiv. geog.) **343**

BT   **Military law**

Veterans—United States   **305.9; 353.5380973; 920**

Veterinary medicine (May subdiv. geog.) **636.089**

SA   types of animals with the subdivision *Diseases*, e.g. **Horses—Diseases**; or with the subdivision *Wounds and injuries*, e.g. **Horses—Wounds and injuries** [to be added as needed]

BT   **Medicine**

RT   **Animals—Diseases**

VHF radio

USE   **Shortwave radio**

Viaducts

USE   **Bridges**

Vibration   **531; 620.3**

BT   **Mechanics**
Sound

NT   **Sound waves**
Waves

Vicarious atonement

USE   **Atonement—Christianity**

Vice   **170**

UF   Vices

SA   types of vices [to be added as needed]

BT   **Conduct of life**
Ethics
Human behavior

RT   **Crime**

Vice-presidents (May subdiv. geog.) **352.23; 920**

BT   **Presidents**

Vice-presidents—United States   **352.23; 920**

UF   United States—Vice-presidents

Vices

USE   **Vice**

Victimless crimes

USE   **Crimes without victims**

Victims of atomic bombings

USE   **Atomic bomb victims**

Victims of crime

USE   **Victims of crimes**

Victims of crimes (May subdiv. geog.) **362.88**

UF   Crime victims
Victims of crime

BT   **Crime**

NT   **Abused women**
Adult child abuse victims

Victorian architecture (May subdiv. geog.) **724**

BT   **Architecture—19th century**
Gothic revival (Architecture)

Victorian literature

USE   **English literature—19th century**

Victoriana (May subdiv. geog.) **745.1; 747.0942**

BT   **Antiques**
Collectibles

Video art (May subdiv. geog.) **700; 791.45**

Use for materials on works of art created with the use of television and video recording technology.

UF   Electronic art

BT   **Art**
Television
Video recording

Video cameras, Home

USE   **Camcorders**

Video cassette recorders and recording
USE **Video recording**
Video cassettes
USE **Videotapes**
Video disc players
USE **Videodisc players**
Video display terminals
USE **Computer monitors**
Video games   688.7; 794.8
UF   Electronic games
Television games
SA   types of video games and names
of individual games [to be
added as needed]
BT   **Electronic toys**
Games
Video recording   384.55; 621.388;
778.59
Use for materials on either the equipment
or the process by which video or video and
audio materials are recorded.
UF   VCRs
Video cassette recorders and re-
cording
Videorecorders
Videotape recorders and record-
ing
NT   **Camcorders**
Video art
Videotapes
RT   **Home video systems**
Television—Equipment and
supplies
Video recordings   384.55; 621.388
Use for materials about video recordings
and for individual video recordings, regardless
of format.
UF   Videorecordings
Videos
BT   **Audiovisual materials**
NT   **Closed caption video record-**
ings
Music videos
Podcasting
Videotapes
Video recordings, Closed caption
USE   **Closed caption video record-**
ings
Video recordings for the hearing impaired
USE   **Closed caption video record-**
ings
Video tapes
USE   **Videotapes**

Video telephone   384.6; 621.386
UF   Picture telephone
Videophone
BT   **Data transmission systems**
Telephone
Television
Videocassettes
USE   **Videotapes**
Videodisc players   384.55; 621.388
UF   Video disc players
BT   **Television—Equipment and**
supplies
Videodiscs
USE   **DVDs**
Videophone
USE   **Video telephone**
Videorecorders
USE   **Video recording**
Videorecordings
USE   **Video recordings**
Videos
USE   **Video recordings**
Videos, Music
USE   **Music videos**
Videotape recorders and recording
USE   **Video recording**
Videotapes   384.55; 778.59
Use for materials on the tape format for
video recordings. Materials about video re-
cordings that emphasize the content of the re-
cording rather than the format are entered un-
der **Video recording**.
UF   Tape recordings, Video
Video cassettes
Video tapes
Videocassettes
BT   **Audiovisual materials**
Home video systems
Video recording
Video recordings
Vietnam   959.7
May be subdivided like United States ex-
cept for History.
Vietnam War, 1961-1975   959.704
May use appropriate subdivisions under
World War, 1939-1945.
UF   Vietnamese Conflict, 1961-1975
Vietnamese War, 1961-1975
BT   **United States—History—1961-**
1974
Vietnamese Conflict, 1961-1975
USE   **Vietnam War, 1961-1975**

Vietnamese refugees (May subdiv. geog.)
    305.9
  BT **Refugees**
Vietnamese War, 1961-1975
  USE **Vietnam War, 1961-1975**
Views **910.22**
    Use for collections of pictures of many places.
  UF Scenery
  SA countries, states, cities, etc., and named entities, such as individual parks, structures, etc., with the subdivision *Pictorial works*, e.g. **Chicago (Ill.)—Pictorial works**; **United States—Pictorial works**; **Yosemite National Park (Calif.)—Pictorial works**; etc. [to be added as needed]
  BT **Pictures**
Vigilance committees
  USE **Vigilantes**
Vigilantes (May subdiv. geog.) **364.1; 364.4**
  UF Vigilance committees
  BT **Crime**
      Criminal law
  RT **Lynching**
Vikings (May subdiv. geog.) **948**
    Use for materials on early Scandinavian people. Materials on the people since the tenth century are entered under **Scandinavians**.
  UF Norsemen
      Northmen
  BT **Scandinavians**
  RT **Normans**
Villages (May subdiv. geog.) **307.76**
  BT **Cities and towns**
Vines
  USE **Climbing plants**
Vineyards (May subdiv. geog.) **634.8**
  UF Viticulture
  BT **Farms**
  RT **Grapes**
      Wine and wine making
Vintage automobiles
  USE **Antique and classic cars**
Vintage cars
  USE **Antique and classic cars**
Vintage motorcycles
  USE **Antique and vintage motorcycles**

Violence (May subdiv. geog.) **303.6**
  SA types of violence [to be added as needed]
  BT **Aggressiveness (Psychology)**
      Social psychology
  NT **Domestic violence**
      Hate crimes
      School violence
      Violence in mass media
      Violence in popular culture
      Violence in sports
      Violence in the workplace
      Violence on television
Violence chips
  USE **V-chips**
Violence in mass media (May subdiv. geog.) **302.23**
  BT **Mass media**
      Violence
Violence in popular culture (May subdiv. geog.) **306.4**
  BT **Popular culture**
      Violence
Violence in schools
  USE **School violence**
Violence in sports (May subdiv. geog.) **796**
  UF Sports violence
  BT **Sports**
      Violence
Violence in television
  USE **Violence on television**
Violence in the workplace (May subdiv. geog.) **658.4**
  UF Workplace violence
  BT **Violence**
      Work environment
Violence on television **302.23; 791.45**
  UF Violence in television
  BT **Television**
      Television programs
      Violence
Violin
  USE **Violins**
Violin music **787.2**
  BT **Music**
Violin players
  USE **Violinists**
Violinists (May subdiv. geog.) **787.2092; 920**
  UF Violin players

Violinists—*Continued*
>BT **Instrumentalists**

Violins (May subdiv. geog.) **787.2**
>UF Fiddle
>
>Violin
>
>BT **Stringed instruments**

Violoncellists (May subdiv. geog.)
787.4092
>UF Cellists
>
>Cello players
>
>Violoncello players
>
>BT **Instrumentalists**

Violoncello
>USE **Violoncellos**

Violoncello players
>USE **Violoncellists**

Violoncellos **787.4**
>UF Cello
>
>Violoncello
>
>BT **Stringed instruments**

Vipers
>USE **Snakes**

Virgin Mary
>USE **Mary**

Virtual libraries
>USE **Digital libraries**

Virtual reality **006.8**
>UF Artificial reality
>
>BT **Computer simulation**
>
>RT **Computer graphics**

Virtue **170**
>UF Virtues
>
>SA types of virtues [to be added as needed]
>
>BT **Conduct of life**
>
>**Ethics**
>
>**Human behavior**
>
>NT **Charity**
>
>**Chastity**
>
>**Courage**
>
>**Courtesy**
>
>**Faith**
>
>**Forgiveness**
>
>**Gratitude**
>
>**Hope**
>
>**Justice**
>
>**Loyalty**
>
>**Obedience**
>
>**Patience**
>
>**Punctuality**
>
>**Temperance**

Virtues
>USE **Virtue**

Viruses **579.2**
>UF Microbes
>
>BT **Microorganisms**
>
>NT **Chickenpox**

Viruses, Computer
>USE **Computer viruses**

Visceral learning
>USE **Biofeedback training**

Viscosity **532; 620.1**
>BT **Hydrodynamics**
>
>**Mechanics**

Vision **152.14; 573.8; 612.8; 617.7**
>UF Sight
>
>BT **Optics**
>
>**Senses and sensation**
>
>NT **Color sense**
>
>**Optical illusions**
>
>**Vision disorders**
>
>RT **Eye**

Vision disorders **362.4; 617.7**
>UF Defective vision
>
>Impaired vision
>
>Visual handicaps
>
>Visual impairments
>
>BT **Vision**
>
>NT **Blindness**
>
>**Color blindness**

Vision in animals **573.8**
>UF Animals—Vision
>
>BT **Senses and sensation in animals**

Visions **133.8; 204; 248.2**
>BT **Parapsychology**
>
>**Religion**
>
>**Spiritual gifts**
>
>NT **Dreams**
>
>**Hallucinations and illusions**
>
>RT **Apparitions**

Visitation rights (Domestic relations)
(May subdiv. geog.) **306.8**
>BT **Domestic relations**
>
>RT **Child custody**

Visitors' exchange programs
>USE **Exchange of persons programs**

Visual handicaps
>USE **Vision disorders**

Visual impairments
>USE **Vision disorders**

Visual instruction

USE **Audiovisual education**

Visual literacy (May subdiv. geog.) **153; 707**

Use for materials on the ability to interpret and evaluate visual objects and symbols, such as television, motion pictures, art works, etc.

UF Literacy, Visual

BT **Arts**

Literacy

Semiotics

Vital records

USE **Registers of births, etc.**

Vital statistics **304.6; 310**

UF Burial statistics

Death rate

Marriage statistics

Mortuary statistics

Records of births, etc.

SA names of countries, cities, etc., and names of ethnic groups with the subdivision *Vital statistics*, for compilations of birth, marriage, and death statistics; and names of wars with the subdivision *Casualities—Statistics*, e.g. **World War, 1939-1945—Casualties—Statistics**; **World War, 1939-1945—Casualties—United States—Statistics**; etc. [to be added as needed]

BT **Statistics**

NT **Birth rate**

Census

Life expectancy

Mortality

Population

RT **Registers of births, etc.**

Vitamins **572; 613.2; 615**

BT **Food**

Nutrition

NT **Dietary supplements**

Viticulture

USE **Grapes**

Vineyards

Wine and wine making

Vivisection **179**

BT **Animal experimentation**

Surgery

Vocabulary **418**

UF English language—Vocabulary

Languages—Vocabulary

Words

BT **Language and languages**

NT **New words**

Word recognition

Vocal culture

USE **Voice culture**

Vocal ensembles

USE **Ensembles (Music)**

Vocal music (May subdiv. geog.) **782**

BT **Music**

NT **Cantatas**

Carols

Choral music

Folk songs

Hymns

Opera

Operetta

Oratorio

Songs

RT **Singing**

Vocation **158.6; 253**

BT **Duty**

Ethics

Occupations

Work

Vocation, Choice of

USE **Vocational guidance**

Vocational education (May subdiv. geog.) **370.113; 373.246; 374**

Use for materials on teaching a skill during the educational process. Materials on teaching people a skill after formal education are entered under **Occupational training**. Materials discussing on-the-job training are entered under **Employees—Training**. Materials on retraining are entered under **Occupational retraining**.

UF Career education

SA types of industries, professions, etc., with the subdivision *Study and teaching*, e.g. **Agriculture—Study and teaching** [to be added as needed]

BT **Education**

NT **Agriculture—Study and teaching**

Cooperative education

Employees—Training

Industrial arts education

Occupational retraining

Occupational training

Vocational education—*Continued*
    Vocational guidance
  RT **Professional education**
    Technical education
Vocational guidance (May subdiv. geog.)
    331.702; 371.4

Use for materials on the activities and programs designed to help people plan, choose, and succeed in their careers. Materials on the assistance given to students by schools, colleges, or universities in the selection of a program of studies suited to their abilities, interests, future plans, and general circumstances are entered under **Educational counseling**.

  UF Career counseling
      Career development
      Career guidance
      Careers
      Choice of profession, occupation, vocation, etc.
      Employment guidance
      Guidance, Vocational
      Job placement guidance
      Occupational guidance
      Vocation, Choice of
  SA vocational guidance for particular classes of persons, e.g. **Vocational guidance for the handicapped**; and fields of knowledge, corporate bodies, military services, professions, and industries and trades with the subdivision *Vocational guidance* [to be added as needed]
  BT **Counseling**
    Vocational education
  NT **Career changes**
    Job hunting
    Law—Vocational guidance
    Television broadcasting—Vocational guidance
    Vocational guidance for the handicapped
  RT **Educational counseling**
    Employment
    Occupations
    Professions
Vocational guidance for the handicapped (May subdiv. geog.) **371.4**
  BT **Handicapped**
    Vocational guidance
Vocational training
  USE **Occupational training**

Vocations
  USE **Occupations**
    Professions
Vodun
  USE **Voodooism**
Voice **783**
  UF Speaking
  BT **Language and languages**
    Throat
  NT **Automatic speech recognition**
    Ventriloquism
  RT **Phonetics**
    Public speaking
    Singing
    Speech
Voice culture **808.5**
  UF Vocal culture
      Voice training
  BT **Public speaking**
    Singing
    Speech
Voice training
  USE **Voice culture**
Volatile oils
  USE **Essences and essential oils**
Volcanoes (May subdiv. geog.) **551.21**
  SA names of volcanoes [to be added as needed]
  BT **Geology**
    Mountains
    Physical geography
Volleyball (May subdiv. geog.) **796.325**
  BT **Ball games**
    Sports
Volume (Cubic content) **389; 530.8**
  UF Cubic measurement
  BT **Geometry**
    Measurement
    Weights and measures
Volume feeding
  USE **Food service**
Voluntarism
  USE **Volunteer work**
Voluntary associations
  USE **Associations**
Voluntary military service (May subdiv. geog.) **355.2**
  UF Military service, Voluntary
      Volunteer military service
  BT **Armed forces**
    Recruiting and enlistment

Voluntary organizations
    USE **Associations**
Volunteer military service
    USE **Voluntary military service**
Volunteer work (May subdiv. geog.)
        361.3
    UF Voluntarism
          Volunteering
          Volunteerism
          Volunteers
    SA types of volunteer work and
          names of volunteer programs,
          e.g. **Meals on wheels pro-**
          grams [to be added as need-
          ed]
    BT **Public welfare**
    NT **Caregivers**
          Foster grandparents
    RT **Charities**
          National service
Volunteering
    USE **Volunteer work**
Volunteerism
    USE **Volunteer work**
Volunteers
    USE **Volunteer work**
Volunteers in church work
    USE **Lay ministry**
Voodoo
    USE **Voodooism**
Voodooism (May subdiv. geog.)   **299.6**
    UF Vodun
          Voodoo
          Voudou
          Voudouism
    BT **Religions**
Voter registration (May subdiv. geog.)
        324.6
    UF Registration of voters
    BT **Elections**
          Suffrage
Voting
    USE **Elections**
          Suffrage
Vouchers, Educational
    USE **Educational vouchers**
Voudou
    USE **Voodooism**
Voudouism
    USE **Voodooism**

Voyager project
    USE **Project Voyager**
Voyagers
    USE **Explorers**
          Travelers
Voyages and travels   **910.4**
    Use for materials about non-fiction travel
  writing, for collections of travel writings, and
  for accounts of voyages and travels not limited to a single place. Materials about the
  theme of travel in literature are entered under
  Travel in literature. Materials on the art and
  enjoyment of travel and advice for travelers
  are entered under **Travel**.
    UF Journeys
          Travel books
          Travels
    SA names of cities (except extinct
          cities), states, countries, conti-
          nents, etc., with the subdivi-
          sion *Description and travel*;
          e.g. **United States—Descrip-**
          tion and travel; names of ex-
          tinct cities or towns, without
          further subdivision, for ac-
          counts of those places by
          travelers in ancient times, e.g.
          Delphi (Extinct city); names
          of individual ships; names of
          regions, e.g. **Arctic regions**;
          ethnic groups, classes of per-
          sons, and names of individu-
          als with the subidivision
          Travel, e.g. **Handicapped—**
          Travel; names of countries
          sponsoring exploring expedi-
          tions with the subdivision *Ex-*
          ploring expeditions; e.g. **Unit-**
          ed States—Exploring expedi-
          tions; and names of places
          that were unsettled or sparsely
          settled and largely unknown
          to the world at large at the
          time of exploration, with the
          subdivision *Exploration*, e.g.
          America—Exploration [to be
          added as needed]
    BT **Geography**
    NT **Adventure travel**
          Aeronautics—Flights
          Air travel
          Automobile travel
          Northeast Passage

Voyages and travels—*Continued*

> Ocean travel
>
> Overland journeys to the Pacific
>
> Papal visits
>
> Pilgrims and pilgrimages
>
> Scientific expeditions
>
> Seafaring life
>
> Shipwrecks
>
> Travelers
>
> Voyages around the world
>
> Whaling
>
> Yachts and yachting

  RT **Adventure and adventurers**

  Exploration

  Explorers

  Travel

  Travel in literature

Voyages and travels in literature

  USE **Travel in literature**

Voyages around the world   910.4

  UF Circumnavigation

  Travel books

  BT **Travel**

  Voyages and travels

Voyages to the moon

  USE **Imaginary voyages**

  Space flight to the moon

Wage-price controls

  USE **Wage-price policy**

Wage-price policy (May subdiv. geog.)
331.2

  UF Government policy

  Price controls

  Price-wage policy

  Wage-price controls

  BT **Inflation (Finance)**

  Prices

  Salaries, wages, etc.

Wages

  USE **Salaries, wages, etc.**

Wagons

  USE **Carriages and carts**

Waiters and waitresses (May subdiv.
geog.) **642**

  UF Waitresses

  BT **Food service**

Waitresses

  USE **Waiters and waitresses**

Wakefulness

  USE **Insomnia**

Walking (May subdiv. geog.)   **796.51**

  BT **Aerobics**

  Athletics

  Human locomotion

  RT **Hiking**

Walking in space

  USE **Extravehicular activity (Space
flight)**

Wall decoration

  USE **Mural painting and decoration**

Wall painting

  USE **Mural painting and decoration**

Wall Street (New York, N.Y.)   332.6

> Use for materials on the activities of Wall
> Street as a financial district. Historical and de-
> scriptive materials on Wall Street as a street
> are entered under **Streets—New York (N.Y.)**.

  BT **Stock exchanges**

  RT **Streets—New York (N.Y.)**

Wallpaper (May subdiv. geog.)   **676;
747**

  BT **Interior design**

  RT **Paperhanging**

Walls   690; 721

  BT **Buildings**

  Civil engineering

Walt Disney World (Fla.)   791.06

  UF Disney World (Fla.)

  BT **Amusement parks**

War   172; 303.6; 355.02

  UF Fighting

  Wars

  SA names of wars, battles, etc., e.g.
**United States—History—
1861-1865, Civil War; Gettysburg (Pa.), Battle of,
1863**; and war and other subjects, e.g. **War and civilization** [to be added as needed]

  NT **Arms control**

  Battles

  Chemical warfare

  Children and war

  Guerrilla warfare

  Intervention (International law)

  Military aeronautics

  Military occupation

  Military personnel

  Nuclear warfare

  Prisoners of war

  Psychological warfare

  Space warfare

  Submarine warfare

War—*Continued*
      Tank warfare
      War and civilization
      War and emergency powers
      War casualties
      War crimes
      War—Religious aspects
      World War III
  RT **Armed forces**
      International law
      Military art and science
      Military law
      Naval art and science
      Peace
War and children
  USE **Children and war**
War and civilization (May subdiv. geog.)
    172; 303.4
  UF Civilization and war
  BT **Civilization**
      War
War and emergency powers (May subdiv.
  geog.) **342**
  UF Emergency powers
      War powers
  BT **Constitutional law**
      Executive power
      Legislative bodies
      War
War and industry
  USE **War—Economic aspects**
War and religion
  USE **War—Religious aspects**
War, Articles of
  USE **Military law**
War—Casualties
  USE **War casualties**
War casualties (May subdiv. geog.)
    363.3498
  UF War—Casualties
  SA names of wars with the subdivi-
      sion *Casualties*, e.g. **World
      War, 1939-1945—Casualties**
      [to be added as needed]
  BT **War**
  NT **World War, 1939-1945—Casu-
      alties**
War crime trials (May subdiv. geog.)
    341.6; 345
  BT **Trials**
War crimes (May subdiv. geog.) **341.6;
    345; 364.1**

  UF Military atrocities
  SA names of wars with the subdivi-
      sion *Atrocities*, e.g. **World
      War, 1939-1945—Atrocities;**
      and names of specific atroci-
      ties [to be added as needed]
  BT **Crimes against humanity**
      International law
      War
War—Economic aspects (May subdiv.
  geog.) **303.6**
  Use for materials discussing the economic
  causes of war and the effect of war on indus-
  try and trade.
  UF Economics of war
      Industry and war
      War and industry
  SA names of wars with the subdivi-
      sion *Economic aspects* [to be
      added as needed]
  NT **Industrial mobilization**
      **World War, 1939-1945—Eco-
      nomic aspects**
  RT **International competition**
War films **791.43**
  Use for individual works, collections, or
  materials about war films in general, not lim-
  ited to a particular war.
  UF Anti-war films
  SA names of wars with the subdivi-
      sion *Motion pictures and the
      war*; e.g. **World War, 1939-
      1945—Motion pictures and
      the war** [to be added as
      needed]
  BT **Historical drama**
      Motion pictures
  NT **World War, 1939-1945—Mo-
      tion pictures and the war**
War games (May subdiv. geog.) **355.48;
    793.92**
  UF War—Simulation games
      Wargames
  BT **Military art and science**
      Military maneuvers
      Simulation games
      Tactics
War of 1812 **940.2; 973.5**
  UF United States—History—1812-
      1815, War of 1812
  BT **Great Britain—History—1714-
      1837**

War of 1812—*Continued*
>> United States—History—1783-
>> 1815

War of nerves
>> USE **Psychological warfare**

War of the American Revolution
>> USE **United States—History—1775-
>> 1783, Revolution**

War on terrorism
>> USE **Terrorism—Prevention**

War pensions
>> USE **Military pensions**

War photography 070.4; 779
>> UF Combat photography
>> Photography, Combat
>> Photography, War
>> BT **Photography**
>> **Photojournalism**

War poetry 808.1; 808.81
>> Use for individual works or collections of war poetry, or for materials about war poetry in general, not confined to a particular war.
>> UF Anti-war poetry
>> SA names of wars with the subdivision *Poetry* [to be added as needed]
>> BT **Poetry**
>> NT **World War, 1939-1945—Poetry**
>> RT **War songs**

War powers
>> USE **War and emergency powers**

War protest movements
>> USE **Peace movements**

War radio programs 791.44
>> Use for individual works, collections, or materials about war radio programs.
>> BT **Radio programs**

War—Religious aspects 201; 261.8
>> May be subdivided by religion or sect.
>> UF Religion and war
>> War and religion
>> SA names of wars with the subdivision *Religious aspects*, e.g. **World War, 1939-1945—Religious aspects** [to be added as needed]
>> BT **Religion**
>> **War**
>> NT **Conscientious objectors**
>> **Pacifism**

War reparations (May subdiv. geog.)
>> 364.15; 364.16

>> SA individual wars with the subdivision *Reparations*, e.g. **World War, 1939-1945—Reparations** [to be added as needed]
>> BT **War reparations**
>> NT **War reparations**

War ships
>> USE **Warships**

War—Simulation games
>> USE **War games**

War songs (May subdiv. geog.) 782.42
>> UF Battle songs
>> Soldiers' songs
>> BT **National songs**
>> **Songs**
>> NT **World War, 1939-1945—Songs**
>> RT **War poetry**

War stories 808.3; 808.83
>> Use for individual works, collections, or materials about war stories.
>> UF Anti-war stories
>> SA names of wars and battles with the subdivision *Fiction*, e.g. **World War, 1939-1945—Fiction** [to be added as needed]
>> BT **Fiction**
>> **Historical fiction**

War television programs 791.45
>> Use for individual works, collections, or materials about war television programs.
>> BT **Television programs**

War use
>> USE subjects with the subdivision *War use*, e.g. **Dogs—War use** [to be added as needed]

War use of animals
>> USE **Animals—War use**

War use of dogs
>> USE **Dogs—War use**

War veterans
>> USE **Veterans**

War work
>> USE names of wars with the subdivision *War work*, e.g. **World War, 1939-1945—War work** [to be added as needed]

Warfare, Submarine
>> USE **Submarine warfare**

Wargames
>> USE **War games**

Warm air heating
>> USE **Hot air heating**

Wars
    USE   **Military history**
          Naval history
          War
          and ethnic groups with the sub-
          division *Wars,* e.g. **Native**
          Americans—Wars [to be
          added as needed]
Wars of the Roses, 1455-1485
    USE   **Great Britain—History—1455-**
          1485, Wars of the Roses
Warships (May subdiv. geog.)   **359.8;**
          623.825
    UF   Battle ships
          Battleships
          War ships
    SA   names of countries with the sub-
          head *Navy,* e.g. **United**
          States. Navy; and names of
          individual warships [to be
          added as needed]
    BT   **Naval architecture**
          Naval art and science
          Sea power
          Ships
    NT   **Aircraft carriers**
          Submarines
    RT   **Navies**
Washing
    USE   **Laundry**
Wasps   **595.79**
    BT   **Insects**
Waste as fuel
    USE   **Waste products as fuel**
Waste disposal
    USE   **Refuse and refuse disposal**
          and types of waste disposal,
          e.g. **Radioactive waste dis-**
          posal; Sewage disposal; etc.;
          and types of industries, plants,
          and facilities with the subdivi-
          sion *Waste disposal,* e.g.
          Chemical industry—Waste
          disposal [to be added as
          needed]
Waste (Economics)   **339.4**
    BT   **Economics**
Waste products (May subdiv. geog.)
          628.4
    UF   By-products
          Junk

          Trade waste
    BT   **Industrial chemistry**
          Manufactures
    NT   **Industrial waste**
    RT   **Recycling**
          Refuse and refuse disposal
Waste products as fuel (May subdiv.
      geog.)   **333.793; 662**
    UF   Energy conversion from waste
          Organic waste as fuel
          Waste as fuel
    BT   **Salvage**
    RT   **Biomass energy**
Waste reclamation
    USE   **Salvage**
Wastes, Hazardous
    USE   **Hazardous wastes**
Wastes, Medical
    USE   **Medical wastes**
Watches
    USE   **Clocks and watches**
Water (May subdiv. geog.)   **551.4; 553.7**
    UF   Hydrology
    BT   **Earth sciences**
          Hydraulics
    NT   **Drinking water**
          Floods
          Frost
          Geysers
          Groundwater
          Hydrotherapy
          Ice
          Lakes
          Ocean
          Ponds
          Precipitation (Meteorology)
          Rivers
          Sea water
          Seas
          Steam
    RT   **Hydraulic engineering**
          Water rights
Water—Analysis   **546; 628.1**
    BT   **Analytical chemistry**
    RT   **Water pollution**
Water animals
    USE   **Aquatic animals**
Water ballet
    USE   **Synchronized swimming**
Water birds (May subdiv. geog.)
          598.176

Water birds—*Continued*
 UF Aquatic birds
 Water fowl
 Wild fowl
 SA types of water birds [to be added as needed]
 BT **Birds**
 NT **Terns**
Water conduits
 USE **Aqueducts**
Water conservation (May subdiv. geog.)
 333.91
 UF Conservation of water
 BT **Conservation of natural resources**
 NT **Xeriscaping**
 RT **Water supply**
Water cure
 USE **Hydrotherapy**
Water exercises
 USE **Aquatic exercises**
Water farming
 USE **Hydroponics**
Water flow
 USE **Hydraulics**
Water fluoridation (May subdiv. geog.)
 628.1
 UF Fluoridation of water
 Water—Fluoridation
 BT **Water supply**
Water—Fluoridation
 USE **Water fluoridation**
Water fowl
 USE **Water birds**
Water gardens (May subdiv. geog.)
 635.9; 712
 UF Aquatic gardens
 Garden ponds
 Garden pools
 BT **Gardens**
 Landscape architecture
Water—Oil pollution
 USE **Oil pollution of water**
Water plants
 USE **Freshwater plants**
 Marine plants
Water pollution (May subdiv. geog.)
 363.739; 628.1
 UF Detergent pollution of rivers, lakes, etc.
 Pollution of water
 River pollution

 SA types of pollution, e.g. **Oil pollution of water** [to be added as needed]
 BT **Environmental health**
 Pollution
 Public health
 NT **Acid rain**
 Marine pollution
 Oil pollution of water
 RT **Industrial waste**
 Sewage disposal
 Water—Analysis
Water power (May subdiv. geog.)
 333.9; 621.2
 UF Hydroelectric power
 Water-power
 BT **Energy resources**
 Hydraulics
 Power (Mechanics)
 Renewable energy resources
 Rivers
 Water resources development
 NT **Hydraulic engineering**
 Hydraulic machinery
 Hydroelectric power plants
Water-power
 USE **Water power**
Water—Purification
 USE **Water purification**
Water purification (May subdiv. geog.)
 628.1
 UF Purification of water
 Water—Purification
 BT **Sanitation**
 Water supply
 NT **Sea water conversion**
Water resources development (May subdiv. geog.) **333.91**
 BT **Energy development**
 Natural resources
 NT **Irrigation**
 Water power
 RT **Water supply**
Water rights (May subdiv. geog.)
 333.91; 346.04
 BT **Law**
 RT **Water**
Water safety **363.14; 797.028**
 UF Aquatic sports—Safety measures
 Drowning prevention
 Water sports—Safety measures

Water safety—*Continued*
  BT   Accidents—Prevention
  NT   Lifeguards
Water skiing (May subdiv. geog.)   797.3
  BT   Water sports
Water sports (May subdiv. geog.)   797
  UF   Aquatic sports
  SA   types of water sports [to be add-
       ed as needed]
  BT   Sports
  NT   Boats and boating
       Canoes and canoeing
       Deep diving
       Diving
       Rowing
       Sailing
       Scuba diving
       Skin diving
       Surfing
       Swimming
       Water skiing
       Yachts and yachting
Water sports—Safety measures
  USE   Water safety
Water supply (May subdiv. geog.)
       363.6; 628.1
  UF   Waterworks
  BT   Natural resources
       Public utilities
  NT   Aqueducts
       Dams
       Drinking water
       Forest influences
       Irrigation
       Water fluoridation
       Water purification
  RT   Water conservation
       Water resources development
       Wells
Water supply engineering (May subdiv.
       geog.)   628.1
  BT   Civil engineering
       Engineering
  NT   Drilling and boring (Earth and
       rocks)
  RT   Hydraulic engineering
Water transportation
  USE   Shipping
Watercolor painting (May subdiv. geog.)
       751.42
  UF   Watercolors
  BT   Painting

Watercolors
  USE   Watercolor painting
Watergate Affair, 1972-1974   973.924
  BT   United States—History—1961-
       1974
Watering places
  USE   Health resorts
Waterways (May subdiv. geog.)   386
       Use for materials on rivers, lakes, and ca-
       nals used for transportation.
  BT   Transportation
  NT   Canals
       Lakes
       Rivers
  RT   Inland navigation
Waterwise gardening
  USE   Xeriscaping
Waterworks
  USE   Water supply
Wave mechanics   530.12; 531
  BT   Mechanics
       Quantum theory
       Waves
Waves   531
  BT   Hydrodynamics
       Vibration
  NT   Electric waves
       Ocean waves
       Radiation
       Sound waves
       Wave mechanics
Waves, Electromagnetic
  USE   Electromagnetic waves
Waves, Ultrasonic
  USE   Ultrasonic waves
Way (Chinese philosophy)
  USE   Tao
Wealth (May subdiv. geog.)   330.1
  UF   Distribution of wealth
       Fortunes
       Riches
  BT   Economics
       Finance
  NT   Cost and standard of living
       Economic conditions
       Gross national product
       Income
       Inheritance and succession
       Profit
       Saving and investment
       Success

Wealth—*Continued*
   RT   **Capital**
         Money
         Property
Wealthy people
   USE **Rich**
Weaponry
   USE **Weapons**
Weapons (May subdiv. geog.)   **355.8;**
        623.4
   UF Arms and armor
         Weaponry
   SA types of weapons, e.g. **Swords**
         [to be added as needed]
   BT **Tools**
         Weapons
   NT **Bow and arrow**
         Firearms
         Knives
         Military weapons
         Swords
         Weapons
   RT **Armor**
         Military art and science
Weapons, Atomic
   USE **Nuclear weapons**
Weapons industry
   USE **Defense industry**
          Firearms industry
Weapons, Nuclear
   USE **Nuclear weapons**
Weapons, Space
   USE **Space weapons**
Weariness
   USE **Fatigue**
Weather (May subdiv. geog.)   **551.6**
    Use for materials on the state of the atmosphere at a given time and place with respect to heat or cold, wetness or dryness, calm or storm. Scientific materials on the atmosphere, especially weather factors, are entered under **Meteorology**. Materials on climate as it relates to humans and to plant and animal life, including the effects of changes of climate, are entered under **Climate**.
   SA names of countries, cities, etc.,
         with the subdivision *Climate*,
         e.g. **United States—Climate**
         [to be added as needed]
   NT **Humidity**
         Precipitation (Meteorology)
         Storms
         Weather control
         Weather forecasting

         Winds
   RT **Climate**
         Meteorology
Weather control   **551.68**
   UF Artificial weather control
         Cloud seeding
         Rain making
         Weather modification
   BT **Meteorology**
         Weather
Weather—Folklore (May subdiv. geog.)
        398.26
   UF Weather lore
   BT **Folklore**
         Meteorology
         Weather forecasting
Weather forecasting (May subdiv. geog.)
        551.63
   UF Precipitation forecasting
   BT **Forecasting**
         Meteorology
         Weather
   NT **Weather—Folklore**
Weather lore
   USE **Weather—Folklore**
Weather modification
   USE **Weather control**
Weather satellites
   USE **Meteorological satellites**
Weather stations
   USE **Meteorological observatories**
Weaving (May subdiv. geog.)   **677;**
        746.1; 746.41
   UF Hand weaving
   SA types of woven articles, e.g.
         Rugs and carpets [to be added as needed]
   BT **Handicraft**
         Textile industry
   NT **Basket making**
         Lace and lace making
   RT **Fabrics**
         Looms
Web databases   **005.75; 025.04**
   BT **Databases**
Web logs
   USE **Weblogs**
Web pages
   USE **Web sites**
Web publishing
   USE **Electronic publishing**

Web search engines   025.04252
    UF   Search engines
         Web searching
         World Wide Web searching
    SA   names of individual Web search
         engines, e.g. **Google** [to be
         added as needed]
    BT   **Internet searching**
         World Wide Web
    NT   **Google**
Web searching
    USE **Internet searching**
         Web search engines
Web servers   004.67
    UF   World Wide Web servers
    BT   **World Wide Web**
Web sites   025.0422
    UF   Web pages
         Websites
         World Wide Web pages
         World Wide Web sites
    SA   names of individual web sites,
         e.g. **Google**; and topics, geo-
         graphic names, categories of
         persons, ethnic groups, etc.,
         with the subdivision *Internet*
         resources [to be added as
         needed]
    BT   **Internet resources**
         World Wide Web
    NT   **Facebook (Web site)**
         Google
         MySpace (Web site)
         Twitter (Web site)
         Wikis (Computer science)
Web sites—Design   005.7
    BT   **Design**
Weblogs   006.7
    UF   Blogs
         Web logs
    BT   **Diaries**
         Online journalism
Websites
    USE **Web sites**
Wedding showers
    USE **Showers (Parties)**
Weddings (May subdiv. geog.)   **392.5;
    395.2**
    BT   **Marriage**
    NT   **Marriage customs and rites**
Wedges   621.8

    BT   **Simple machines**
Weed killers
    USE **Herbicides**
Weeds (May subdiv. geog.)   **632**
    BT   **Agricultural pests**
         Economic botany
         Gardening
         Plants
Week   **529**
    BT   **Calendars**
         Chronology
    NT   **Special weeks**
    RT   **Days**
Weight   **530.8**
    UF   Weight (Physics)
    SA   types of objects and substances
         with the subdivision *Weight*,
         e.g. **Trucks—Weight** [to be
         added as needed]
    BT   **Physics**
    NT   **Body weight**
    RT   **Weights and measures**
Weight control
    USE **Weight loss**
Weight gain   **613.2**
    UF   Gaining weight
    BT   **Body weight**
    RT   **Diet**
Weight lifting (May subdiv. geog.)
         796.41; 613.7
    UF   Strength training
         Weight training
         Weightlifting
    BT   **Athletics**
         Exercise
    RT   **Bodybuilding**
Weight loss   **613.2**
    UF   Dieting
         Diets, Reducing
         Reducing
         Weight control
    BT   **Body weight**
    RT   **Diet**
         Exercise
         Low-calorie diet
Weight (Physics)
    USE **Weight**
Weight training
    USE **Weight lifting**
Weightlessness   **531**

Weightlessness—*Continued*
UF   Free fall
      Gravity free state
      Subgravity state
      Zero gravity
BT   **Environmental influence on humans**
      Space medicine

Weightlifting
USE   **Weight lifting**

Weights and measures (May subdiv. geog.)   **389; 530.8**
UF   Measures
      Metrology
SA   types of objects and substances with the subdivision *Weight*, e.g. **Trucks—Weight** [to be added as needed]
BT   **Physics**
NT   **Electric measurements**
      Measuring instruments
      Volume (Cubic content)
RT   **Measurement**
      Metric system
      Weight

Welding   **671.5**
UF   Oxyacetylene welding
BT   **Blacksmithing**
      Forging
      Ironwork
      Manufacturing processes
      Metalwork
NT   **Electric welding**
RT   **Soldering**

Welding, Electric
USE   **Electric welding**

Welfare agencies
USE   **Charities**

Welfare, Public
USE   **Public welfare**

Welfare reform
USE   **Public welfare**

Welfare state (May subdiv. geog.)   **330.12; 361.6**
BT   **Economic policy**
      Public welfare
      Social policy
      State, The

Welfare work
USE   **Charities**
      Social work

Welfare work in industry
USE   **Industrial welfare**

Well boring
USE   **Drilling and boring (Earth and rocks)**

Well drilling, Oil
USE   **Oil well drilling**

Wells (May subdiv. geog.)   **551.49; 628.1**
BT   **Hydraulic engineering**
RT   **Drilling and boring (Earth and rocks)**
      Water supply

Werewolves   **398.21**
BT   **Folklore**

West Africa   **966**
   Use for materials dealing collectively with the southern half of the western bulge of the African continent, bounded on the north by the Sahara and on the south and west by the Atlantic Ocean. The term usually includes Benin, Burkina Faso, Cameroon, Gambia, Ghana, Guinea, Guinea-Bissau, Ivory Coast, Liberia, Nigeria, Senegal, Sierra Leone, and Togo, and sometimes Mali, Mauritania, and Niger as well.
UF   Africa, West
BT   **Africa**
NT   **French-speaking West Africa**

West Bank   **956.95**
UF   Judea and Samaria
      West Bank of the Jordan River
BT   **Palestine**

West Bank of the Jordan River
USE   **West Bank**

West Germany
USE   **Germany (West)**

West Indian literature (French)   **840**
   Use for collections and for materials on West Indian literature written originally in French.
BT   **Literature**

West Indies Region
USE   **Caribbean Region**

West Point (Military academy)
USE   **United States Military Academy**

West (U.S.)   **978**
   Use for the region west of the Mississippi River.
UF   Western States
SA   names of individual states in this region [to be added as needed]
BT   **United States**

West (U.S.)—*Continued*
  NT **Pacific Northwest**
      Pacific States
West (U.S.)—Exploration 978
  BT **United States—Exploration**
  RT **Overland journeys to the Pacific**
West (U.S.)—History 978
  UF Westward movement
  BT **United States—History**
Western civilization 306.09; 909
  Use for materials on the culture and society stemming from the Greco-Roman traditions of the occident rather than those of Islam, India, or the Far East.
  UF Civilization, Western
      Occidental civilization
  BT **Civilization**
      East and West
Western comic books, strips, etc. 741.5
  Use for individual works, collections, or materials about Western comics.
  BT **Comic books, strips, etc.**
Western Europe
  USE **Europe**
Western films 791.43
  Use for individual works, collections, or materials about Western films.
  UF Westerns
  SA types of Western films, e.g.
      Lone Ranger films [to be added as needed]
  BT **Adventure films**
      Historical drama
      Motion pictures
  NT **Lone Ranger films**
Western Hemisphere
  USE **America**
Western States
  USE **West (U.S.)**
Western stories 808.3; 808.83
  Use for individual works, collections, or materials about post-19th-century fiction set in the 19th-century American West.
  UF Westerns
  BT **Adventure fiction**
      Fiction
      Historical fiction
Westerns
  USE **Western films**
      Western stories
      Westerns (Radio programs)
      Westerns (Television programs)

Westerns (Radio programs) 791.44
  Use for individual works, collections, or materials about Westerns on the radio.
  UF Westerns
  BT **Radio programs**
Westerns (Television programs) 791.45
  Use for individual works, collections, or materials about Westerns on television.
  UF Westerns
  BT **Television programs**
Westminster Abbey 726.5
  BT **Abbeys**
      Church buildings
Westward movement
  USE **Land settlement—United States**
      United States—Territorial expansion
      West (U.S.)—History
Wetland ecology (May subdiv. geog.) 577.68
  BT **Ecology**
  NT **Swamp ecology**
Wetlands (May subdiv. geog.) 551.41
  SA types of wetlands, e.g. **Marshes** [to be added as needed]
  BT **Landforms**
  NT **Bogs**
      Marshes
      Swamps
Whales (May subdiv. geog.) 599.5
  BT **Mammals**
      Marine mammals
Whaling (May subdiv. geog.) 639.2
  BT **Commercial fishing**
      Hunting
      Voyages and travels
Wheat (May subdiv. geog.) 633.1
  BT **Grain**
Wheel chairs
  USE **Wheelchairs**
Wheelchair basketball (May subdiv. geog.) 796.32
  BT **Basketball**
      Wheelchair sports
Wheelchair sports (May subdiv. geog.) 796.04
  BT **Sports for the handicapped**
  NT **Wheelchair basketball**
Wheelchairs 617
  UF Wheel chairs
  BT **Chairs**
      Orthopedic apparatus

Wheels   621.8; 629.2
    UF   Car wheels
    BT   **Simple machines**
    NT   **Gearing**
          Tires
Which-way stories
    USE **Plot-your-own stories**
Whistle blowing (May subdiv. geog.)
      174; 342; 353.4

    Use for materials on the practice of calling public attention to corruption, mismanagement, or waste in government, business, the military, etc.

    UF   Blowing the whistle
          Whistleblowing
    BT   **Political corruption**
          Public interest
Whistleblowing
    USE **Whistle blowing**
White collar crimes (May subdiv. geog.)
      364.16
    UF   Occupational crimes
    BT   **Crime**
    NT   **Fraud**
          Tax evasion
White supremacist movements
    USE **White supremacy movements**
White supremacy movements (May subdiv. geog.)   **320.5**
    UF   Skinheads
          White supremacist movements
    BT   **Race relations**
          Racism
          Social movements
Whitechapel murders, 1888
    USE **Jack the Ripper murders, London, England, 1888**
Whittling
    USE **Wood carving**
Whodunits
    USE **Mystery and detective plays**
          Mystery fiction
          Mystery films
          Mystery radio programs
          Mystery television programs
Whole language   372.62

    Use for materials on the integration of listening, speaking, writing, and reading skills in meaningful situations in which children participate actively.

    UF   Integrated language arts (Holistic)
          Language arts (Holistic)
          Language experience approach in education
    BT   **Education—Experimental methods**
          Language arts
Wholistic medicine
    USE **Holistic medicine**
Wica
    USE **Wicca**
Wicca (May subdiv. geog.)   **133.4**
    UF   Wica
    BT   **Paganism**
    RT   **Goddess religion**
          Witchcraft
Wickedness
    USE **Good and evil**
Widowers (May subdiv. geog.)   **306.88**
    BT   **Men**
Widows (May subdiv. geog.)   **306.88**
    BT   **Women**
Wife abuse (May subdiv. geog.)   **362.82**
    UF   Abuse of wives
          Abused wives
          Battering of wives
          Wife battering
          Wife beating
    BT   **Domestic violence**
    RT   **Abused women**
Wife battering
    USE **Wife abuse**
Wife beating
    USE **Wife abuse**
Wigs (May subdiv. geog.)   **391.5**
    BT   **Clothing and dress**
          Costume
          Hair
Wigwams
    USE **Tepees**
Wikis (Computer science)   004.693
    BT   **Web sites**
Wild animal dwellings
    USE **Animals—Habitations**
Wild animals
    USE **Animals**
          Wildlife
Wild cats (May subdiv. geog.)   **599.75; 636.8**

    Use for materials on non-domesticated species of cats or domestic cats living in a wild state. Materials on domestic cats are entered under Cats.

Wild cats—*Continued*

UF   Felidae

      Feral cats

      Wildcats

SA   types of wild cats [to be added

      as needed]

BT   **Mammals**

RT   **Cats**

Wild children (May subdiv. geog.)

    155.45

Use for materials on children who have been raised by animals or have lived their formative years in the wild without contact with human society.

UF   Feral children

      Wolf children

BT   **Exceptional children**

Wild flowers (May subdiv. geog.)

    582.13

UF   Wildflowers

BT   **Flowers**

Wild flowers—Conservation

USE **Plant conservation**

Wild fowl

USE **Game and game birds**

       Water birds

Wildcats

USE **Wild cats**

Wilderness areas (May subdiv. geog.)

    333.78

UF   Scenery

BT   **Forest reserves**

RT   **Conservation of natural re-**

      sources

      National parks and reserves

Wilderness survival (May subdiv. geog.)

    613.6; 796.5

UF   Bush survival

      Outdoor survival

BT   **Camping**

      Outdoor life

      Survival skills

RT   **Survival after airplane acci-**

      dents, shipwrecks, etc.

Wildfires (May subdiv. geog.)   **363.37**

BT   **Fires**

Wildflowers

USE **Wild flowers**

Wildlife (May subdiv. geog.)   **333.95;**

    639

Use for materials on wild animals in their natural environment, especially mammals, birds, and fishes that are hunted for sport or food.

UF   Feral animals

      Wild animals

SA   types of wildlife, e.g. **Desert**

      animals [to be added as

      needed]

BT   **Animals**

NT   **Game and game birds**

RT   **Wildlife conservation**

Wildlife and pesticides

USE **Pesticides and wildlife**

Wildlife attracting   **639.9**

UF   Attracting wildlife

BT   **Animals**

NT   **Bird attracting**

Wildlife conservation (May subdiv. geog.)

    639.9

UF   Conservation of wildlife

      Preservation of wildlife

      Protection of wildlife

BT   **Conservation of natural re-**

      sources

      Economic zoology

      Endangered species

      Environmental protection

      Nature conservation

NT   **Birdbanding**

      Birds—Protection

      Game protection

      Game reserves

      Pesticides and wildlife

      Wildlife refuges

RT   **Rare animals**

      Wildlife

Wildlife photography   **778.9**

BT   **Nature photography**

      Photography

Wildlife refuges (May subdiv. geog.)

    639.9

UF   Wildlife sanctuaries

SA   names of specific refuges [to be

      added as needed]

BT   **Wildlife conservation**

Wildlife sanctuaries

USE **Wildlife refuges**

Will

USE **Brainwashing**

       Free will and determinism

Will power

USE **Self-control**

Willpower
   USE **Self-control**
Wills (May subdiv. geog.)   **346.05**
   UF Bequests
       Legacies
   BT **Genealogy**
       Registers of births, etc.
   NT **Living wills**
   RT **Executors and administrators**
       Inheritance and succession
Wind
   USE **Winds**
Wind instruments (May subdiv. geog.)
       788
   SA types of wind instruments [to be
       added as needed]
   BT **Musical instruments**
   NT **Brass instruments**
       Flutes
       Woodwind instruments
Wind power (May subdiv. geog.)   **333.9;**
       621.4
   BT **Energy resources**
       Power (Mechanics)
       Renewable energy resources
   RT **Windmills**
Windbreaks   **634.9**
   UF Shelterbelts
   BT **Tree planting**
Windmills (May subdiv. geog.)   **621.4**
   RT **Wind power**
Window dressing
   USE **Show windows**
Window gardening (May subdiv. geog.)
       635.9
   UF Windowbox gardening
       Windowsill gardening
   BT **Gardening**
       Indoor gardening
   NT **House plants**
   RT **Container gardening**
       Flower gardening
Windowbox gardening
   USE **Window gardening**
Windows (May subdiv. geog.)   **721**
   BT **Architecture—Details**
       Buildings
   NT **Show windows**
Windows, Stained glass
   USE **Glass painting and staining**

Windowsill gardening
   USE **Window gardening**
Winds   **551.51**
   UF Gales
       Wind
   BT **Meteorology**
       Navigation
       Physical geography
       Weather
   NT **Cyclones**
       Hurricanes
       Tornadoes
       Typhoons
   RT **Storms**
Windsurfing (May subdiv. geog.)   **797.3**
   UF Board sailing
       Sailboarding
   BT **Sailing**
Wine and wine making (May subdiv.
       geog.)   **641.2; 663**
   UF Viticulture
   BT **Alcoholic beverages**
   RT **Grapes**
       Vineyards
Wing chun
   USE **Kung fu**
Winter   **398.33; 578.43**
   BT **Seasons**
Winter gardening (May subdiv. geog.)
       635.9; 712
   Use for materials on the culture of decora-
   tive plants that bloom outdoors in winter.
   BT **Gardening**
Winter resorts (May subdiv. geog.)
       796.9
   BT **Resorts**
   NT **Ski resorts**
Winter sports (May subdiv. geog.)
       796.9
   UF Ice sports
   SA types of winter sports [to be
       added as needed]
   BT **Sports**
   NT **Hockey**
       Ice fishing
       Ice skating
       Skiing
       Sled dog racing
       Sledding
       Snowboarding
Wire craft   **745.5**

Wire craft—*Continued*
  BT **Handicraft**
      Metalwork
Wire services
  USE **News agencies**
Wireless
  USE **Radio**
Wireless communication systems (May
    subdiv. geog.) **384.5**
  UF Communication systems, Wire-
      less
      Wireless information networks
  BT **Telecommunication**
Wireless information networks
  USE **Wireless communication sys-
      tems**
Wiretapping (May subdiv. geog.) **363.25**
  BT **Criminal investigation**
      Right of privacy
  RT **Eavesdropping**
Wiring, Electric
  USE **Electric wiring**
Wishes **153.8**
  BT **Motivation (Psychology)**
Wit and humor **808.7; 808.87**
  Use for individual works, collections, or
  materials about wit and humor.
  UF Facetiae
      Humor
  SA wit and humor of particular
      countries or ethnic groups,
      e.g. **American wit and hu-
      mor**; **Jewish wit and humor**,
      etc., and subjects with the
      subdivision *Humor*, e.g. **Mu-
      sic—Humor** [to be added as
      needed]
  BT **Literature**
  NT **American wit and humor**
      Black humor (Literature)
      Cartooning
      Chapbooks
      Comedies
      Comedy
      Comic books, strips, etc.
      English wit and humor
      Epigrams
      Humorists
      Humorous fiction
      Humorous poetry
      Jewish wit and humor
      Jokes

      Mock-heroic literature
      Music—Humor
      Nonsense verses
      Parody
      Practical jokes
      Puns
      Satire
      Tall tales
      **World War, 1939-1945—Hu-
      mor**
  RT **Anecdotes**
Witchcraft (May subdiv. geog.) **133.4**
  UF Black art (Magic)
      Black magic (Witchcraft)
      Sorcery
  BT **Folklore**
      Occultism
  NT **Witches**
  RT **Magic**
      Wicca
Witches (May subdiv. geog.) **133.4**
  UF Covens
  BT **Witchcraft**
Witnesses (May subdiv. geog.) **345; 347**
  UF Cross-examination
  BT **Litigation**
      Trials
Wives (May subdiv. geog.) **306.872**
  UF Married women
      Spouses
  BT **Family**
      Marriage
      Married people
      Women
  NT **Military spouses**
Wives of presidents—United States
  USE **Presidents' spouses—United
      States**
Wives, Runaway
  USE **Runaway adults**
Wok cooking **641.7**
  BT **Cooking**
Wolf children
  USE **Wild children**
Woman
  USE **Women**
Woman-man relationship
  USE **Man-woman relationship**
Women (May subdiv. geog.) **305.4**
  UF Woman

Women—*Continued*

SA women of particular racial, religious or ethnic groups, e.g. **Mexican American women**; **Jewish women**; women in various occupations and professions, e.g. **Women artists**; **Policewomen**; **Women in the motion picture industry**; etc.; and names of wars and military services with the subdivision *Women*, e.g. **World War, 1939-1945—Women** [to be added as needed]

NT **Abused women**
African American women
Black women
Businesswomen
Daughters
Jewish women
Lesbians
Mexican American women
Minority women
Mothers
Muslim women
Native American women
Nuns
Policewomen
Single women
Sisters
Widows
Wives
Women air pilots
Women artists
Women astronauts
Women athletes
Women authors
Women clergy
Women in medicine
Women in the military
Women in the motion picture industry
Women judges
Women physicians
World War, 1939-1945—Women
Young women

RT **Femininity**

Women actors
USE **Actresses**

Women air pilots (May subdiv. geog.)
629.13092; 920

BT **Air pilots**
Women

Women artists (May subdiv. geog.)
709.2; 920

Use for materials on the attainments of several women in the area of art.

BT **Artists**
Women

Women astronauts (May subdiv. geog.)
629.450082

BT **Astronauts**
Women

Women athletes (May subdiv. geog.)
796.082

BT **Athletes**
Women

Women authors   809; 920

Use for collections and for materials on the attainments of several women authors not limited to a single national literature or literary form.

SA literary forms and national literatures with the subdivision *Women authors*, e.g. **American literature—Women authors** [to be added as needed]

BT **Authors**
Women

Women—Biography   920
BT **Biography**

Women—Biography—Dictionaries
920.72

Women, Black
USE **Black women**

Women—Civil rights
USE **Women's rights**

Women clergy (May subdiv. geog.)
200.92; 270.092

BT **Clergy**
Women

RT **Ordination of women**

Women—Clothing
USE **Women's clothing**

Women—Clubs
USE **Women—Societies**

Women—Diseases (May subdiv. geog.)
616.0082; 618.1

UF Diseases of women
Gynecology

BT **Diseases**

NT **Breast cancer**

RT **Women—Health and hygiene**

Women—Dress
USE **Women's clothing**
Women—Education (May subdiv. geog.)
371.822
UF Education of women
BT **Education**
RT **Coeducation**
Women—Emancipation
USE **Women's rights**
Women—Employment (May subdiv.
geog.) **331.4**
UF Girls—Employment
Working women
SA women in various occupations
and professions, e.g. **Women
artists**; **Policewomen**; **Wom-
en in the motion picture in-
dustry**; etc. [to be added as
needed]
BT **Employment**
NT **Equal pay for equal work
Self-employed women**
Women—Enfranchisement
USE **Women—Suffrage**
Women Equal rights
USE **Women's rights**
Women—Health and hygiene (May
subdiv. geog.) **613**
UF Gynecology
Women—Hygiene
BT **Health
Hygiene**
NT **Women—Mental health
Women—Physical fitness**
RT **Women—Diseases**
Women—History 305.409
Use for comprehensive materials on the his-
tory of women, their socio-economic, politi-
cal, and legal position, their participation in
historical events, and their contributions to so-
ciety. Materials dealing specifically with
women's social condition and status, including
historical discussions of the same, are entered
under **Women—Social conditions**.
BT **Feminism
History**
Women—Hygiene
USE **Women—Health and hygiene**
Women—Identity 305.4
UF Female identity
Feminine identity
BT **Identity (Psychology)**

Women in art 704.9
Use for materials on women depicted in
works of art. Materials on the attainments of
several women in the area of art are entered
under **Women artists**.
BT **Art—Themes**
Women in business
USE **Businesswomen**
Women in literature 809
Use for materials on the theme of women
in works of literature. Collections and materials on several women authors not limited to a
single national literature or literary form are
entered under **Women authors**.
BT **Literature—Themes**
Women in medicine (May subdiv. geog.)
610.82
BT **Medical personnel
Women**
Women in motion pictures (May subdiv.
geog.) **791.43**
Use for materials discussing the portrayal of
women in motion pictures. Materials discussing all aspects of women's involvement in
motion pictures are entered under **Women in
the motion picture industry**.
BT **Motion pictures**
Women in television
USE **Women on television**
Women in television broadcasting (May
subdiv. geog.) **384.55; 791.45**
Use for materials on all aspects of women's
involvement in the television industry. Materi-
als on the portrayal of women in television
programs are entered under **Women on televi-
sion**.
UF Women in the television indus-
try
BT **Television broadcasting**
Women in the armed forces
USE **Women in the military**
Women in the Bible 220.8
UF Bible—Women
Women in the military (May subdiv.
geog.) **355.0082**
UF Armed forces—Women
Women in the armed forces
BT **Military personnel
Women**
Women in the motion picture industry
(May subdiv. geog.) **791.43**
Use for materials discussing all aspects of
women's involvement in motion pictures. Ma-
terials discussing the portrayal of women in
motion pictures are entered under **Women in
motion pictures**.

Women in the motion picture industry—
Continued
    BT   **Motion picture industry**
         Women
Women in the television industry
    USE   **Women in television broadcasting**
Women judges (May subdiv. geog.) **347; 920**
    BT   **Judges**
         Women
Women-men relationship
    USE   **Man-woman relationship**
Women—Mental health (May subdiv. geog.) **362.2**
    BT   **Mental health**
         Women—Health and hygiene
    RT   **Women—Psychology**
Women on television **791.45**
Use for materials on the portrayal of women in television programs. Materials on all aspects of women's involvement in the television industry are entered under **Women in television broadcasting**.
    UF   Women in television
    BT   **Television**
Women—Ordination
    USE   **Ordination of women**
Women—Physical fitness (May subdiv. geog.) **613.7**
    BT   **Physical fitness**
         Women—Health and hygiene
Women physicians (May subdiv. geog.) **610.69; 920**
    BT   **Physicians**
         Women
Women police officers
    USE   **Policewomen**
Women—Political activity (May subdiv. geog.) **324**
    BT   **Political participation**
    NT   **Women politicians**
Women politicians (May subdiv. geog.) **324.2092; 920**
    BT   **Politicians**
         Women—Political activity
Women—Psychology **155.3**
    UF   Feminine psychology
    BT   **Psychology**
    RT   **Women—Mental health**
Women—Relations with men
    USE   **Man-woman relationship**

Women—Religious life (May subdiv. geog.) **204; 248.4**
    BT   **Religious life**
Women—Self-defense
    USE   **Self-defense for women**
Women, Self-employed
    USE   **Self-employed women**
Women—Social conditions (May subdiv. geog.) **305.42**
Use for materials dealing specifically with women's social condition and status, including historical discussions of the same. Comprehensive materials on the history of women are entered under **Women—History**.
    BT   **Social conditions**
    NT   **Prostitution**
         Women's movement
Women—Societies (May subdiv. geog.) **367**
    UF   Women—Clubs
         Women's clubs
         Women's organizations
    BT   **Clubs**
         Societies
Women—Sports
    USE   **Sports for women**
Women—Suffrage (May subdiv. geog.) **324.6**
    UF   Women—Enfranchisement
         Women's suffrage
    BT   **Suffrage**
         Women's rights
    RT   **Suffragists**
Women—United States **305.40973**
Women's clothing (May subdiv. geog.) **646**
    UF   Women—Clothing
         Women—Dress
    BT   **Clothing and dress**
Women's clubs
    USE   **Women—Societies**
Women's friendship
    USE   **Female friendship**
Women's liberation movement
    USE   **Women's movement**
Women's movement (May subdiv. geog.) **305.42; 323.3**
Use for materials on activities aimed at obtaining equal rights and opportunities for women. Materials on the theory of the political and social equality of the sexes and women's perspectives on various subjects are entered under **Feminism**.
    UF   Women's liberation movement

Women's movement—*Continued*
>BT **Women—Social conditions**
>>**Women's rights**
>
>RT **Feminism**

Women's organizations
>USE **Women—Societies**

Women's rights (May subdiv. geog.)
323.3; 342
>UF Emancipation of women
>>Rights of women
>>Women—Civil rights
>>Women—Emancipation
>>Women—Equal rights
>
>BT **Civil rights**
>>**Sex discrimination**
>
>NT **Women—Suffrage**
>>**Women's movement**
>
>RT **Feminism**
>>**Pro-choice movement**
>>**Pro-life movement**

Women's self-defense
>USE **Self-defense for women**

Women's suffrage
>USE **Women—Suffrage**

Wonder Woman (Fictional character)
741.5
>BT **Fictional characters**
>>**Superheroes**

Wonders
>USE **Curiosities and wonders**

Wood (May subdiv. geog.)   **620.1; 674**
>UF Timber
>>Woods
>
>SA types of wood, e.g. **Oak** [to be
>>added as needed]
>
>BT **Building materials**
>>**Forest products**
>>**Fuel**
>>**Trees**
>
>NT **Lumber and lumbering**
>>**Oak**
>>**Plywood**
>>**Woodwork**
>
>RT **Forests and forestry**

Wood block printing
>USE **Wood engraving**
>>**Woodcuts**

Wood-burning
>USE **Pyrography**

Wood carving   731.4; 736
>UF Carving, Wood
>>Whittling

>BT **Carving (Decorative arts)**
>>**Decoration and ornament**
>>**Woodwork**

Wood engraving   761
>UF Block printing
>>Wood block printing
>
>BT **Engraving**

Wood finishing   698
>BT **Finishes and finishing**
>NT **Furniture finishing**

Wood—Preservation   674
>UF Preservation of wood

Wood toy making
>USE **Wooden toy making**

Wood turning
>USE **Turning**

Woodcuts   761
>UF Block printing
>>Wood block printing
>
>BT **Prints**

Wooden toy making   745.592
>UF Wood toy making
>BT **Toy making**
>>**Woodwork**

Woods
>USE **Forests and forestry**
>>**Lumber and lumbering**
>>**Wood**

Woodwind instruments   877.2
>BT **Wind instruments**

Woodwork (May subdiv. geog.)   **684**
>BT **Architecture—Details**
>>**Decorative arts**
>>**Wood**
>
>NT **Furniture making**
>>**Pyrography**
>>**Wood carving**
>>**Wooden toy making**
>
>RT **Cabinetwork**
>>**Carpentry**
>>**Turning**

Woodworking machinery   621.9; 684
>SA types of woodworking machines
>>[to be added as needed]
>
>BT **Machinery**
>NT **Lathes**

Wool (May subdiv. geog.)   **677**
>BT **Animal products**
>>**Fabrics**
>>**Fibers**

Word books
USE **Picture dictionaries**
Word building
USE **Word skills**
Word (Computer software)
USE **Microsoft Word (Computer software)**
Word games 793.734
SA types of word games, e.g.
Crossword puzzles [to be added as needed]
BT **Games**
Literary recreations
NT **Crossword puzzles**
Palindromes
Word histories
USE **Language and languages—Etymology**
Word problems (Mathematics) 510
BT **Mathematics**
Word processing 005.52
BT **Office management**
Office practice
RT **Desktop publishing**
Word processing software
Word processing software 005.52
BT **Computer software**
RT **Word processing**
Word processor keyboarding
USE **Keyboarding (Electronics)**
Word recognition 372.46
BT **Reading**
Vocabulary
Word skills 372.4; 418
Use for educational materials on consonants, blends, vowels, prefixes and suffixes, digraphs, syllables, root words, rhyming, and alphabet, etc.
UF Word building
Words
BT **Reading**
RT **English language—Spelling**
Wordless stories
USE **Stories without words**
Words
USE **Vocabulary**
Word skills
Words, New
USE **New words**
Work 158.7; 306.3
Use for materials on the physical or mental exertion of individuals to produce or accomplish something. Materials on the collective human activities involved in the production and distribution of goods and services in an economy, as well as materials on the group of workers who render these services for wages, are entered under **Labor**.
NT **Job satisfaction**
Performance
Vocation
Work and family
Work environment
Work ethic
RT **Labor**
Occupations
Work addiction
USE **Workaholism**
Work and family (May subdiv. geog.) 306.3; 306.87; 646.7
Use for materials on the conflict or balance in people's lives between the demands of work and family.
UF Family and work
BT **Family**
Work
RT **Dual-career families**
Work at home
USE **Home-based business**
Telecommuting
Work-based learning
USE **Cooperative education**
Work environment (May subdiv. geog.) 331.25; 620.8
UF Places of work
Work places
Working environment
Workplace environment
Worksite environment
BT **Environment**
Work
NT **Machinery in the workplace**
Teams in the workplace
Violence in the workplace
Work ethic (May subdiv. geog.) 174
UF Protestant work ethic
BT **Ethics**
Work
Work groups
USE **Teams in the workplace**
Work—Law and legislation
USE **Labor laws and legislation**
Work performance standards
USE **Performance standards**
Work places
USE **Work environment**

Work satisfaction
    USE   **Job satisfaction**
Work standards
    USE   **Production standards**
Work stoppages
    USE   **Strikes**
Work stress
    USE   **Job stress**
Work teams
    USE   **Teams in the workplace**
Workaholic syndrome
    USE   **Workaholism**
Workaholism   155.2; 616.85
    UF   Addiction to work
           Compulsive working
           Work addiction
           Workaholic syndrome
    BT   **Compulsive behavior**
Workers
    USE   **Employees**
           Labor
           Working class
Workers' compensation (May subdiv.
    geog.) **368.4**
    UF   Compensation
           Employers' liability
           Insurance, Workers' compensa-
              tion
           Workmen's compensation
    BT   **Accident insurance**
           Health insurance
           Social security
Workers' participation in management
    USE   **Participative management**
Workforce diversity
    USE   **Diversity in the workplace**
Working animals (May subdiv. geog.)
    636.088
    SA   animals in specific working situ-
              ations [to be added as need-
              ed]
    BT   **Animals**
           Domestic animals
           Economic zoology
    NT   **Animals in police work**
           Animals—War use
           Working dogs
Working at home
    USE   **Home-based business**
           Telecommuting

Working children
    USE   **Child labor**
Working class (May subdiv. geog.)
    305.5

    Use for materials on the social class com-
    posed of persons who work for wages, usually
    in manual labor.

    UF   Blue collar workers
           Factory workers
           Industrial workers
           Labor and laboring classes
           Laborers
           Laboring class
           Laboring classes
           Manual workers
           Workers
           Working classes
    BT   **Social classes**
    NT   **Proletariat**
    RT   **Labor**
Working classes
    USE   **Working class**
Working couples
    USE   **Dual-career families**
Working day
    USE   **Hours of labor**
Working dogs (May subdiv. geog.)
    362.4; 636.73
    BT   **Dogs**
           Working animals
    NT   **Guide dogs**
           Hearing ear dogs
           Rescue dogs
           Search dogs
           Service dogs
Working environment
    USE   **Work environment**
Working hours
    USE   **Hours of labor**
Working parents' children
    USE   **Children of working parents**
Working robots
    USE   **Industrial robots**
Working women
    USE   **Women—Employment**
Workmen's compensation
    USE   **Workers' compensation**
Workplace environment
    USE   **Work environment**
Workplace violence
    USE   **Violence in the workplace**

Workshop councils
USE **Participative management**
Workshops, Teachers'
USE **Teachers' workshops**
Worksite environment
USE **Work environment**
World
USE **Earth**
World economics
USE **Commercial geography**
Commercial policy
Economic conditions
International competition
World government
USE **International organization**
World history   909
UF   Universal history
BT   **History**
NT   **Ancient history**
Geography
Middle Ages
Modern history
World history—12th century   909
UF   Twelfth century
SA   names of regions, countries, cit-
ies, etc., with the subdivision
History—12th century [to be
added as needed]
BT   **Middle Ages**
World history—13th century   909
UF   Thirteenth century
SA   names of regions, countries, cit-
ies, etc., with the subdivision
History—13th century [to be
added as needed]
BT   **Middle Ages**
World history—14th century   909
UF   Fourteenth century
SA   names of regions, countries, cit-
ies, etc., with the subdivision
History—14th century [to be
added as needed]
BT   **Middle Ages**
World history—15th century   909
UF   Fifteenth century
SA   names of regions, countries, cit-
ies, etc., with the subdivision
History—15th century [to be
added as needed]
BT   **Middle Ages**
World history—16th century   909

UF   History, Modern—16th century
Sixteenth century
SA   names of regions, countries, cit-
ies, etc., with the subdivision
History—16th century [to be
added as needed]
World history—17th century   909
UF   History, Modern—17th century
Seventeenth century
SA   names of regions, countries, cit-
ies, etc., with the subdivision
History—17th century [to be
added as needed]
World history—18th century   909.7
UF   Eighteenth century
History, Modern—18th century
SA   names of regions, countries, cit-
ies, etc., with the subdivision
History—18th century [to be
added as needed]
World history—19th century   909.81
UF   History, Modern—19th century
Modern history—1800-1899
(19th century)
Nineteenth century
SA   names of regions, countries, cit-
ies, etc., with the subdivision
History—19th century [to be
added as needed]
World history—20th century   909.82
UF   History, Modern—20th century
Modern history—1900-1999
(20th century)
Twentieth century
SA   names of regions, countries, cit-
ies, etc., with the subdivision
History—20th century [to be
added as needed]
NT   **Nineteen eighties**
Nineteen fifties
Nineteen forties
Nineteen nineties
Nineteen seventies
Nineteen sixties
Nineteen thirties
Nineteen twenties
World War, 1914-1918
World War, 1939-1945
World history—1945-   909.82
UF   History, Modern—1945-
Modern history—1945-

World history—21st century 909.83

    UF   History, Modern—21st century

           Twenty-first century

    SA   names of regions, countries, cities, etc., with the subdivision *History—21st century* [to be added as needed]

World language

    USE **Universal language**

World music 781.62

    BT   **Folk music**

World order

    USE **International relations**

World organization

    USE **International organization**

World politics 909

    Use for historical accounts of international political affairs. Materials on the theory of international relations are entered under **International relations**.

    UF   International politics

    SA   names of countries with the subdivisions *Foreign relations* and *Politics and government* [to be added as needed]

    BT   **Political science**

    NT   **United States—Foreign relations**

           World War, 1914-1918

           World War, 1939-1945

           World War III

    RT   **Geopolitics**

           International organization

           International relations

World politics—1945- 909.82

World politics—1945-1965 909.82

World politics—1945-1991 909.82

    NT   **Cold war**

World politics—1965- 909.82

World politics—1991- 909.82

World records 030

    UF   Human records

           Records of achievement

           Records, World

           World's records

    BT   **Curiosities and wonders**

    RT   **Sports records**

World Trade Center (New York, N.Y.) terrorist attack, 2001

    USE **September 11 terrorist attacks, 2001**

World War I

    USE **World War, 1914-1918**

World War II

    USE **World War, 1939-1945**

World War, 1914-1918 (May subdiv. geog.) **940.3; 940.4**

    May be subdivided like World War, 1939-1945.

    UF   First World War

           World War I

    BT   **Europe—History—1871-1918**

           World history—20th century

           World politics

World War, 1914-1918—Chemical warfare (May subdiv. geog.) **940.4**

    UF   World War, 1914-1918—Gas warfare

    BT   **Chemical warfare**

World War, 1914-1918—Economic aspects (May subdiv. geog.) **940.3**

    RT   **Reconstruction (1914-1939)**

World War, 1914-1918—Gas warfare

    USE **World War, 1914-1918—Chemical warfare**

World War, 1914-1918—Peace 940.3

    BT   **Peace**

    NT   **League of Nations**

World War, 1914-1918—Reconstruction

    USE **Reconstruction (1914-1939)**

World War, 1914-1918—Territorial questions (May subdiv. geog.) **940.3**

    BT   **Boundaries**

World War, 1914-1918—United States 940.3; 940.4; 973.91

    UF   United States—History—1914-1918, World War

           United States—World War, 1914-1918

World War, 1939-1945 (May subdiv. geog.) **940.53; 940.54**

    Subdivisions used under this heading may be used under other wars.

    UF   Second World War

           World War II

    SA   names of battles, campaigns, sieges, etc., e.g. **Ardennes (France), Battle of the, 1944-1945**; **Pearl Harbor (Oahu, Hawaii), Attack on, 1941**; etc. [to be added as needed]

World War, 1939-1945—*Continued*
  BT Europe—History—1918-1945
      World history—20th century
      World politics
World War, 1939-1945—Aerial opera-
    tions (May subdiv. geog.) **940.54**
  UF World War, 1939-1945—Battles,
      sieges, etc.
  BT **Military aeronautics**
World War, 1939-1945—African Ameri-
    cans (May subdiv. geog.) **940.53;
    940.54**
  BT **African Americans**
World War, 1939-1945—Amphibious op-
    erations **940.54**
  BT **World War, 1939-1945—Naval
      operations**
World War, 1939-1945—Antiwar move-
    ments
  USE **World War, 1939-1945—Pro-
      test movements**
World War, 1939-1945—Armistices
    940.53
World War, 1939-1945—Arms
  USE **World War, 1939-1945—
      Equipment and supplies**
World War, 1939-1945—Art and the
    war (May subdiv. geog.) **940.53**
  UF World War, 1939-1945—Iconog-
      raphy
      World War, 1939-1945, in art
  BT **Art**
World War, 1939-1945—Atrocities (May
    subdiv. geog.) **940.54**
  SA names of specific atrocities and
      crimes [to be added as need-
      ed]
  BT **Atrocities**
  NT **Handicapped—Nazi persecution**
World War, 1939-1945—Battlefields
    (May subdiv. geog.) **940.54**
World War, 1939-1945—Battles, sieges,
    etc.
  USE **World War, 1939-1945—Aerial
      operations
      World War, 1939-1945—Cam-
      paigns
      World War, 1939-1945—Naval
      operations**
World War, 1939-1945—Biography **920**
  BT **Biography**

World War, 1939-1945—Blockades (May
    subdiv. geog.) **940.54**
World War, 1939-1945—Campaigns
    (May subdiv. geog.) **940.54**
  UF World War, 1939-1945—Battles,
      sieges, etc.
  SA names of battles, campaigns,
      sieges, etc., e.g. **Ardennes
      (France), Battle of the,
      1944-1945** [to be added as
      needed]
  NT **Ardennes (France), Battle of
      the, 1944-1945
      Britain, Battle of, 1940
      Normandy (France), Attack on,
      1944
      Pearl Harbor (Oahu, Hawaii),
      Attack on, 1941**
World War, 1939-1945—Cartoons and
    caricatures (May subdiv. geog.)
    940.53
  BT **Cartoons and caricatures**
World War, 1939-1945—Casualties (May
    subdiv. geog.) **940.54**
  BT **War casualties**
World War, 1939-1945—Casualties—Sta-
    tistics **940.54**
World War, 1939-1945—Casualties—
    United States **940.54**
  UF United States—World War,
      1939-1945—Casualties
World War, 1939-1945—Casualties—
    United States—Statistics **940.54**
  UF United States—World War,
      1939-1945—Casualties—Statis-
      tics
World War, 1939-1945—Causes **940.53**
  NT **National socialism**
World War, 1939-1945—Censorship
    (May subdiv. geog.) **940.54**
  BT **Censorship**
World War, 1939-1945—Charities
  USE **World War, 1939-1945—Civil-
      ian relief
      World War, 1939-1945—War
      work**
World War, 1939-1945—Chemical war-
    fare (May subdiv. geog.) **940.54**
  BT **Chemical warfare**
World War, 1939-1945—Children
    940.53

World War, 1939-1945—Children—*Continued*

BT **Children and war**

World War, 1939-1945—Civilian evacuation

USE **World War, 1939-1945—Evacuation of civilians**

World War, 1939-1945—Civilian relief (May subdiv. geog.) **940.54**

UF World War, 1939-1945—Charities

BT **Charities**
Food relief
Foreign aid
Reconstruction (1939-1951)
World War, 1939-1945—War work

RT **World War, 1939-1945—Refugees**

World War, 1939-1945—Collaborationists (May subdiv. geog.) **940.53**

UF Fifth column
Quislings

BT **Collaborationists**

World War, 1939-1945—Conferences (May subdiv. geog.) **940.53**

UF World War, 1939-1945—Congresses

BT **Conferences**

World War, 1939-1945—Congresses

USE **World War, 1939-1945—Conferences**

World War, 1939-1945—Conscientious objectors (May subdiv. geog.) **940.53**

BT **Conscientious objectors**

World War, 1939-1945—Correspondents

USE **World War, 1939-1945—Journalists**

World War, 1939-1945—Desertions (May subdiv. geog.) **940.54**

BT **Military desertion**

World War, 1939-1945—Destruction and pillage (May subdiv. geog.) **940.54**

World War, 1939-1945—Diplomatic history 940.53

NT **World War, 1939-1945—Governments in exile**

World War, 1939-1945—Displaced persons

USE **World War, 1939-1945—Refugees**

World War, 1939-1945—Draft resisters (May subdiv. geog.) **940.54**

BT **Draft resisters**

World War, 1939-1945—Economic aspects (May subdiv. geog.) **940.53**

Use for materials on the economic causes of the war and the effect of the war on commerce and industry.

BT **War—Economic aspects**

NT **World War, 1939-1945—Finance**
World War, 1939-1945—Manpower
World War, 1939-1945—Reparations

RT **Reconstruction (1939-1951)**

World War, 1939-1945—Education and the war (May subdiv. geog.) **940.53**

BT **Education**

World War, 1939-1945—Engineering and construction (May subdiv. geog.) **940.54**

BT **Military engineering**

World War, 1939-1945—Equipment and supplies (May subdiv. geog.) **940.54**

UF World War, 1939-1945—Arms
World War, 1939-1945—Military supplies
World War, 1939-1945—Military weapons
World War, 1939-1945—Ordnance
World War, 1939-1945—Supplies
World War, 1939-1945—Weapons

BT **Military weapons**

World War, 1939-1945—Ethical aspects 940.53

UF World War, 1939-1945—Moral and religious aspects

BT **Ethics**

World War, 1939-1945—Evacuation of civilians (May subdiv. geog.) **940.54**

UF Civilian evacuation
World War, 1939-1945—Civilian evacuation

World War, 1939-1945—Evacuation of civilians—*Continued*
> BT Civil defense
> World War, 1939-1945—Refugees
>
> NT Japanese Americans—Evacuation and relocation, 1942-1945

World War, 1939-1945—Fiction   808.83
> Use for collections of stories dealing with the Second World War. Materials about the depiction of the war in literature are entered under **World War, 1939-1945—Literature and the war**.

World War, 1939-1945—Finance (May subdiv. geog.)   **940.53**
> Use for materials on the cost and financing of the war, including war debts, and the effect of the war on financial systems, including inflation.
>
> BT **World War, 1939-1945—Economic aspects**

World War, 1939-1945—Food supply (May subdiv. geog.)   **940.53**
> BT **Food relief**

World War, 1939-1945—Forced repatriation (May subdiv. geog.)   **940.53**
> RT **World War, 1939-1945—Refugees**

World War, 1939-1945—Governments in exile   **940.53**
> BT **World War, 1939-1945—Diplomatic history**

World War, 1939-1945—Guerrillas
> USE **World War, 1939-1945—Underground movements**

World War, 1939-1945—Health aspects (May subdiv. geog.)   **940.54**

World War, 1939-1945—Hospitals
> USE **World War, 1939-1945—Medical care**

World War, 1939-1945—Human resources
> USE **World War, 1939-1945—Manpower**

World War, 1939-1945—Humor (May subdiv. geog.)   **940.53**
> BT **Wit and humor**

World War, 1939-1945—Iconography
> USE **World War, 1939-1945—Art and the war**

World War, 1939-1945, in art
> USE **World War, 1939-1945—Art and the war**

World War, 1939-1945, in literature
> USE **World War, 1939-1945—Literature and the war**

World War, 1939-1945, in motion pictures
> USE **World War, 1939-1945—Motion pictures and the war**

World War, 1939-1945—Influence (May subdiv. geog.)   **940.53**

World War, 1939-1945—Jews   **940.53**
> BT **Jews**
> RT **Holocaust, 1939-1945**

World War, 1939-1945—Jews—Rescue (May subdiv. geog.)   **940.54**
> UF Rescue of Jews, 1939-1945
> BT **Jews—Persecutions**
> NT **Righteous Gentiles in the Holocaust**

World War, 1939-1945—Journalists (May subdiv. geog.)   **940.54**
> UF World War, 1939-1945—Correspondents
> World War, 1939-1945—War correspondents
> BT **Journalists**

World War, 1939-1945—Literature and the war   809; 940.53
> Use for materials on the depiction of the war in literature. Collections of stories dealing with the Second World War are entered under **World War, 1939-1945—Fiction**.
>
> UF World War, 1939-1945, in literature
> BT **Literature**

World War, 1939-1945—Manpower (May subdiv. geog.)   **940.54**
> UF World War, 1939-1945—Human resources
> BT **World War, 1939-1945—Economic aspects**

World War, 1939-1945—Maps (May subdiv. geog.)   **940.53**
> BT **Maps**

World War, 1939-1945—Medical care (May subdiv. geog.)   **940.54**
> UF World War, 1939-1945—Hospitals
> BT **Medical care**

World War, 1939-1945—Military intelligence (May subdiv. geog.)   **940.54**
> BT **Military intelligence**

World War, 1939-1945—Military supplies
  USE   **World War, 1939-1945—**
        Equipment and supplies
World War, 1939-1945—Military weapons
  USE   **World War, 1939-1945—**
        Equipment and supplies
World War, 1939-1945—Missing in ac-
  tion (May subdiv. geog.)   **940.54**
  BT   **Missing in action**
       World War, 1939-1945—Pris-
       oners and prisons
World War, 1939-1945—Monuments
  (May subdiv. geog.)   **725**
  BT   **Monuments**
World War, 1939-1945—Moral and reli-
  gious aspects
  USE   **World War, 1939-1945—Ethi-**
        cal aspects
        World War, 1939-1945—Reli-
        gious aspects
World War, 1939-1945—Motion pictures
  and the war   **791.43; 940.53**
  Use for materials about films dealing with
  the Second World War or about the use of
  motion pictures in the war effort.
  UF   World War, 1939-1945, in mo-
       tion pictures
  BT   **Motion pictures**
       War films
World War, 1939-1945—Museums (May
  subdiv. geog.)   **940.53**
  BT   **Museums**
World War, 1939-1945—Naval opera-
  tions (May subdiv. geog.)   **940.54**
  UF   World War, 1939-1945—Battles,
       sieges, etc.
  NT   **World War, 1939-1945—Am-**
       phibious operations
World War, 1939-1945—Naval opera-
  tions—Submarine (May subdiv.
  geog.)   **940.54**
  UF   World War, 1939-1945—Subma-
       rine operations
  BT   **Submarine warfare**
World War, 1939-1945—Occupied terri-
  tories   **940.54**
  SA   names of occupied countries
       with the appropriate subdivi-
       sion under *History*, e.g.,
       Netherlands—History—1940-
       1945, German occupation;

Japan—History—1945-1952,
  Allied occupation; etc. [to be
  added as needed]
  BT   **Military occupation**
       World War, 1939-1945—Terri-
       torial questions
World War, 1939-1945—Ordnance
  USE   **World War, 1939-1945—**
        Equipment and supplies
World War, 1939-1945—Peace (May
  subdiv. geog.)   **940.53**
World War, 1939-1945—Personal narra-
  tives   **940.53; 940.54**
  Use for collective or individual eyewitness
  reports or autobiographical accounts of the
  war in general. Accounts limited to a specific
  topic are entered under that topic.
  BT   **Autobiographies**
       Biography
World War, 1939-1945—Pictorial works
  940.53022
World War, 1939-1945—Poetry   **808.81**
  Use for collections of poetry dealing with
  the Second World War.
  BT   **Historical poetry**
       War poetry
World War, 1939-1945—Prisoners and
  prisons (May subdiv. geog.)
  940.54
  BT   **Concentration camps**
       Prisoners of war
       Prisons
  NT   **World War, 1939-1945—Miss-**
       ing in action
World War, 1939-1945—Propaganda
  (May subdiv. geog.)   **940.54**
  BT   **Propaganda**
World War, 1939-1945—Protest move-
  ments (May subdiv. geog.)
  940.53
  UF   World War, 1939-1945—Antiwar
       movements
       World War, 1939-1945—Pro-
       tests, demonstrations, etc.
  BT   **Protest movements**
World War, 1939-1945—Protests, demon-
  strations, etc.
  USE   **World War, 1939-1945—Pro-**
        test movements
World War, 1939-1945—Psychological
  aspects (May subdiv. geog.)
  940.53
  BT   **Psychological warfare**

World War, 1939-1945—**Public opinion**
(May subdiv. geog.) **940.53**
BT **Public opinion**
World War, 1939-1945—Railroads
USE **World War, 1939-1945—Transportation**
World War, 1939-1945—Reconstruction
USE **Reconstruction (1939-1951)**
World War, 1939-1945—**Refugees** (May subdiv. geog.) **940.53**
UF World War, 1939-1945—Displaced persons
BT **Political refugees**
NT **World War, 1939-1945—Evacuation of civilians**
RT **World War, 1939-1945—Civilian relief**
World War, 1939-1945—Forced repatriation
World War, 1939-1945—**Regimental histories 940.54**
World War, 1939-1945—**Religious aspects** (May subdiv. geog.) **940.53**
UF World War, 1939-1945—Moral and religious aspects
World War, 1939-1945—**Reparations 940.53**
BT **Reconstruction (1939-1951)**
World War, 1939-1945—Economic aspects
World War, 1939-1945—Resistance movements
USE **World War, 1939-1945—Underground movements**
World War, 1939-1945—**Secret service** (May subdiv. geog.) **940.54**
BT **Secret service**
World War, 1939-1945—**Social aspects** (May subdiv. geog.) **940.53**
World War, 1939-1945—Social work
USE **World War, 1939-1945—War work**
World War, 1939-1945—**Songs 782.42**
UF World War, 1939-1945—Songs and music
BT **Military music**
War songs
World War, 1939-1945—Songs and music
USE **World War, 1939-1945—Songs**
World War, 1939-1945—**Sources 940.53**

World War, 1939-1945—Submarine operations
USE **World War, 1939-1945—Naval operations—Submarine**
World War, 1939-1945—Supplies
USE **World War, 1939-1945—Equipment and supplies**
World War, 1939-1945—**Tank warfare** (May subdiv. geog.) **940.54**
BT **Tank warfare**
World War, 1939-1945—**Territorial questions** (May subdiv. geog.) **940.53**
BT **Boundaries**
NT **World War, 1939-1945—Occupied territories**
World War, 1939-1945—**Theater and the war** (May subdiv. geog.) **792; 940.53**
BT **Theater**
World War, 1939-1945—**Transportation** (May subdiv. geog.) **940.54**
UF World War, 1939-1945—Railroads
BT **Transportation**
World War, 1939-1945—**Treaties** (May subdiv. geog.) **940.53**
BT **Treaties**
World War, 1939-1945—**Underground movements** (May subdiv. geog.) **940.54**
UF Anti-fascist movements
Anti-Nazi movement
World War, 1939-1945—Guerrillas
World War, 1939-1945—Resistance movements
World War, 1939-1945—**United States 940.53; 940.54; 973.917**
UF United States—History—1939-1945, World War
United States—World War, 1939-1945
World War, 1939-1945—**Veterans** (May subdiv. geog.) **305.9**
BT **Veterans**
World War, 1939-1945—War correspondents
USE **World War, 1939-1945—Journalists**
World War, 1939-1945—**War work** (May subdiv. geog.) **940.53**

World War, 1939-1945—War work—*Continued*
  UF World War, 1939-1945—Charities
      World War, 1939-1945—Social work
  NT **World War, 1939-1945—Civilian relief**
World War, 1939-1945—Weapons
  USE **World War, 1939-1945—Equipment and supplies**
World War, 1939-1945—Women (May subdiv. geog.) **940.53; 940.54**
  BT **Women**
World War III 355
  UF Third World War
  BT **War**
      World politics
World Wide Web 025.042
  UF World Wide Web (Information retrieval system)
  BT **Internet**
  NT **Web search engines**
      Web servers
      Web sites
World Wide Web (Information retrieval system)
  USE **World Wide Web**
World Wide Web pages
  USE **Web sites**
World Wide Web searching
  USE **Internet searching**
       Web search engines
World Wide Web servers
  USE **Web servers**
World Wide Web sites
  USE **Web sites**
World's Fair (1992: Seville, Spain)
  USE **Expo 92 (Seville, Spain)**
World's fairs
  USE **Exhibitions**
       Fairs
World's records
  USE **World records**
Worms 592
  BT **Animals**
Worry 152.4
  BT **Emotions**
  RT **Anxiety**
Worship 203; 248.3; 264
  UF Devotion

  BT **Religion**
      Theology
  NT **Church year**
      Devotional exercises
      Interfaith worship
      Praise of God
      Prayer
      Public worship
      Sacrifice
Worship of the dead
  USE **Ancestor worship**
Worship programs 264
  Use for individual works or collections of services of any type for use in public worship other than authorized standard liturgies.
  UF Services of worship
      Worship services
  BT **Public worship**
  RT **Liturgies**
Worship services
  USE **Worship programs**
Worth
  USE **Values**
Wounded, First aid to
  USE **First aid**
Wounds and injuries 617.1
  UF Injuries
  SA classes of persons, animals, organs of the body, and plants and crops with the subdivision *Wounds and injuries*, e.g. **Horses—Wounds and injuries; Foot—Wounds and injuries;** etc. [to be added as needed]
  BT **Accidents**
  NT **Disabilities**
      Fractures
Wrapping of gifts
  USE **Gift wrapping**
Wrath
  USE **Anger**
Wrecks
  USE **Accidents**
Wrestling (May subdiv. geog.) **796.812**
  BT **Athletics**
Writers
  USE **Authors**
Writing 411
  Use for materials on the process or result of recording language in the form of conventionalized visible marks or signs on a surface.

Writing—*Continued*

Materials limited to writing with a pen or pencil and practical or prescriptive guides to penmanship or the art of writing are entered under **Handwriting**. Materials on handwriting as an expression of the writer's character are entered under **Graphology**. Materials on the alphabet or writing of a particular language are entered under the name of the language with the subdivisions *Alphabet* and *Writing*.

- BT **Communication**
  - **Language and languages**
  - **Language arts**
- NT **Abbreviations**
  - **Alphabet**
  - **Autographs**
  - **Braille**
  - **Calligraphy**
  - **Cryptography**
  - **Cuneiform inscriptions**
  - **Graphology**
  - **Handwriting**
  - **Hieroglyphics**
  - **Picture writing**
  - **Shorthand**
  - **Typewriting**
  - **Writing of numerals**
- RT **Ciphers**

Writing (Authorship)
- USE **Authorship**
  - **Creative writing**

Writing of numerals   513
- UF Numeral formation
  - Numeral writing
  - Numerals, Writing of
- BT **Handwriting**
  - **Numerals**
  - **Writing**

Writing—Patterning
- USE **Language arts—Patterning**

Writing—Study and teaching
- USE **Handwriting**

Writings of gay men
- USE **Gay men's writings**

Writings of lesbians
- USE **Lesbians' writings**

Writings of teenagers
- USE **Teenagers' writings**

Wrought iron work
- USE **Ironwork**

X-15 (Rocket aircraft) (May subdiv. geog.)   **629.133**
- BT **Rocket planes**

X-rays   **539.7**
- UF Radiography
  - Roentgen rays
  - X rays
- BT **Electromagnetic waves**
  - **Radiation**
- NT **Gamma rays**
  - **Tomography**
- RT **Radiotherapy**
  - **Vacuum tubes**

X rays
- USE **X-rays**

Xeriscaping (May subdiv. geog.)   **635.9**
- UF Waterwise gardening
- BT **Landscape gardening**
  - **Water conservation**

Xerographic art
- USE **Copy art**

Xerography
- USE **Photocopying**

YA literature
- USE **Young adult literature**

Yacht basins
- USE **Marinas**

Yachting
- USE **Yachts and yachting**

Yachts and yachting (May subdiv. geog.)   **797.1**
- UF Yachting
- BT **Boatbuilding**
  - **Boats and boating**
  - **Ocean travel**
  - **Ships**
  - **Voyages and travels**
  - **Water sports**
- NT **Marinas**
- RT **Sailing**

Yaoi
- USE **Shonen-ai**

Yard sales
- USE **Garage sales**

Yarn   **677**
- RT **Spinning**

Yearbooks   **050**
- UF Annuals
- SA subjects with the subdivision *Periodicals*, e.g. **Engineering—Periodicals** [to be added as needed]
- BT **Serial publications**
- NT **School yearbooks**
- RT **Almanacs**

Yeast 641.3
 BT Fungi
Yellow fever (May subdiv. geog.) 616.9
 BT Tropical medicine
Yeti 001.9
 UF Abominable snowman
 BT Monsters
  Mythical animals
Yiddish language 439
  May be subdivided like **English language**.
 UF Jewish language
  Jews—Language
 BT Language and languages
Yiddish literature 839
  May use same subdivisions and names of
  literary forms as for **English literature**.
 BT Jewish literature
Yoga 181; 613.7
 BT Hindu philosophy
  Hinduism
  Theosophy
 NT Chakras
  Hatha yoga
Yoga exercises
 USE Hatha yoga
Yoga, Hatha
 USE Hatha yoga
Yom Kippur 296.4
 UF Atonement, Day of
  Day of Atonement
 BT Jewish holidays
Yom Kippur War, 1973
 USE Israel-Arab War, 1973
Yoruba (African people) (May subdiv.
  geog.) 305.896
 BT Africans
  Indigenous peoples
Yosemite National Park (Calif.) 719;
  979.4
 BT National parks and reserves—
  United States
Yosemite National Park (Calif.)—Pictori-
  al works 979.4
Young adult literature (May subdiv.
  geog.) 808; 808.8; 809
  Use for collections or materials about litera-
  ture published for teenage readers. Materials
  on the reading interests of teenagers and lists
  of books for teenagers are entered under
  Teenagers—Books and reading.
 UF Books for teenagers
  Teenage literature
  Teenagers—Literature

  YA literature
  Young adults' literature
 BT Literature
Young adults
 USE Teenagers
  Youth
Young adults—Books and reading
 USE Teenagers—Books and reading
Young adults' libraries (May subdiv.
  geog.) 027.62
 UF Library services to teenagers
  Library services to young adults
  Young adults' library services
 BT Libraries
Young adults' library services
 USE Young adults' libraries
Young adults' literature
 USE Young adult literature
Young consumers (May subdiv. geog.)
  640.73; 658.8
 UF Children as consumers
  Teenage consumers
  Youth market
 BT Consumers
Young men (May subdiv. geog.) 305.31
  Use for materials on men in the general age
  range of eighteen through twenty-five years.
  Materials on the time of life between thirteen
  and twenty-five, as well as on people in that
  greater age range are entered under **Youth**.
 BT Men
  Youth
 RT Boys
Young people
 USE Teenagers
  Youth
Young persons
 USE Teenagers
  Youth
Young women (May subdiv. geog.)
  305.4
  Use for materials on women in the general
  age range of eighteen through twenty-five
  years. Materials on the time of life between
  thirteen and twenty-five, as well as on people
  in that greater age range are entered under
  Youth.
 BT Women
  Youth
 RT Girls
Youngest child
 USE Birth order

Youth (May subdiv. geog.)   **305.235**

Use for materials on the time of life between thirteen and twenty-five years, as well as on people in this general age range. Materials limited to teen youth are entered under **Teenagers**. Materials limited to people in the general age range of eighteen through twenty-five years of age are entered under **Young men** or **Young women**. Materials on the process or state of growing up are entered under **Adolescence**.

UF   Young adults
     Young people
     Young persons
SA   youth of particular racial or ethnic groups [to be added as needed]
BT   **Age**
NT   **African American youth**
     Church work with youth
     Dropouts
     Gay youth
     Minority youth
     Teenagers
     Television and youth
     Young men
     Young women

Youth—Alcohol use (May subdiv. geog.)   **616.86; 613.81**

UF   Alcohol and youth
     Drinking and youth
NT   **Drinking age**

Youth and drugs
USE   **Youth—Drug use**
Youth and narcotics
USE   **Youth—Drug use**
Youth and television
USE   **Television and youth**

Youth—Drug use (May subdiv. geog.)   **613.8; 616.86**

UF   Drugs and youth
     Narcotics and youth
     Youth and drugs
     Youth and narcotics
NT   **Teenagers—Drug use**
RT   **Juvenile delinquency**

Youth—Employment (May subdiv. geog.)   **331.3**

UF   Boys—Employment
     Girls—Employment
BT   **Age and employment**
     Employment
NT   **Teenagers—Employment**
RT   **Summer employment**

Youth hostels (May subdiv. geog.)   **910.46**

UF   Hostels, Youth
     Tourist accommodations
BT   **Community centers**
     Hotels and motels

Youth market
USE   **Young consumers**

Youth movement (May subdiv. geog.)   **322.4**

UF   Student movement
     Student protests, demonstrations, etc.
     Student revolt
BT   **Social movements**
NT   **Students—Political activity**

Youth—Religious life (May subdiv. geog.)   **204; 248.4**

BT   **Religious life**
NT   **Teenagers—Religious life**

Youth—United States   **305.230973**

UF   American youth
NT   **Teenagers—United States**

Yuri
USE   **Shojo-ai**

Zaire
USE   **Congo (Democratic Republic)**

Zen Buddhism (May subdiv. geog.)   **294.3**

BT   **Buddhism**

Zeppelins
USE   **Airships**

Zero gravity
USE   **Weightlessness**

Zeus (Greek deity)   **292.2**

BT   **Gods and goddesses**

Zinc   **669**

BT   **Chemical elements**
     Metals

Zines
USE   **Fanzines**

Zionism (May subdiv. geog.)   **320.5**

UF   Zionist movement
RT   **Jews—Restoration**

Zionist movement
USE   **Zionism**

Zip code (May subdiv. geog.)   **383**

UF   Postal delivery code
BT   **Postal service**

Zodiac   **133.5; 523**

Zodiac—*Continued*
   BT **Astrology**
        Astronomy
Zombies   398.21
   BT **Dead**
        Folklore
Zoning (May subdiv. geog.)   **346.04; 354.3**
   UF City planning—Zone system
        Districting (in city planning)
   BT **City planning**
Zoological gardens
   USE **Zoos**
Zoological specimens—Collection and preservation   **590.75**
   UF Collections of natural specimens
        Preservation of zoological specimens
        Specimens, Preservation of
   SA types of specimens with the subdivision *Collection and preservation*, e.g. **Birds—Collection and preservation** [to be added as needed]
   BT **Collectors and collecting**
   NT **Birds—Collection and preservation**
   RT **Taxidermy**
Zoology   590
   Use for materials on the science of animals. Nonscientific materials on animals are entered under **Animals**.
   UF Animal kingdom
        Animal physiology
        Fauna
   SA names of divisions, classes, etc., of the animal kingdom, e.g. **Invertebrates; Vertebrates;**

Birds; Mammals; etc.; and names of animals [to be added as needed]
   BT **Biology**
        Science
   NT **Animal behavior**
        Animals—Anatomy
        Comparative anatomy
        Comparative psychology
        Economic zoology
        Embryology
        Paleontology
   RT **Animals**
        Natural history
        Zoos
Zoology—Anatomy
   USE **Animals—Anatomy**
Zoology, Economic
   USE **Economic zoology**
Zoology of the Bible
   USE **Bible—Natural history**
Zoology—United States
   USE **Animals—United States**
Zoos (May subdiv. geog.)   **590.73**
   UF Zoological gardens
   SA names of individual zoos [to be added as needed]
   BT **Parks**
   NT **Petting zoos**
   RT **Animals**
        Zoology
Zoroastrianism (May subdiv. geog.)   **295**
   BT **Religions**
Zulu (African people) (May subdiv. geog.)   **305.896**
   BT **Africans**
        Indigenous peoples